DATE DUE

			PRINTED IN U.S.A.

Poetry Criticism

Guide to Gale Literary Criticism Series

For criticism on	Consult these Gale series
Authors now living or who died after December 31, 1959	*CONTEMPORARY LITERARY CRITICISM (CLC)*
Authors who died between 1900 and 1959	*TWENTIETH-CENTURY LITERARY CRITICISM (TCLC)*
Authors who died between 1800 and 1899	*NINETEENTH-CENTURY LITERATURE CRITICISM (NCLC)*
Authors who died between 1400 and 1799	*LITERATURE CRITICISM FROM 1400 TO 1800 (LC)* *SHAKESPEAREAN CRITICISM (SC)*
Authors who died before 1400	*CLASSICAL AND MEDIEVAL LITERATURE CRITICISM (CMLC)*
Authors of books for children and young adults	*CHILDREN'S LITERATURE REVIEW (CLR)*
Dramatists	*DRAMA CRITICISM (DC)*
Poets	*POETRY CRITICISM (PC)*
Short story writers	*SHORT STORY CRITICISM (SSC)*
Black writers of the past two hundred years	*BLACK LITERATURE CRITICISM (BLC)*
Hispanic writers of the late nineteenth and twentieth centuries	*HISPANIC LITERATURE CRITICISM (HLC)*
Native North American writers and orators of the eighteenth, nineteenth, and twentieth centuries	*NATIVE NORTH AMERICAN LITERATURE (NNAL)*
Major authors from the Renaissance to the present	*WORLD LITERATURE CRITICISM, 1500 TO THE PRESENT (WLC)*

ISSN 1052-4851

Poetry Criticism

Excerpts from Criticism of the Works of the Most Significant and Widely Studied Poets of World Literature

VOLUME 21

Carol T. Gaffke
Anna J. Sheets
Editors

GALE

DETROIT · LONDON

Library of Congress Catalog Card Number 91-118494
ISBN 0-7876-2012-2
ISSN 1052-4851

Printed in the United States of America

10   9   8   7   6   5   4   3   2   1

Contents

Preface vii

Acknowledgments xi

Preface

A Comprehensive Information Source on World Poetry

Poetry Criticism (PC) provides substantial critical excerpts and biographical information on poets throughout the world who are most frequently studied in high school and undergraduate college courses. Each *PC* entry is supplemented by biographical and bibliographical material to help guide the user to a fuller understanding of the genre and its creators. Although major poets and literary movements are covered in such Gale Literary Criticism Series as *Contemporary Literary Criticism (CLC)*, *Twentieth-Century Literary Criticism (TCLC)*, *Nineteenth-Century Literature Criticism (NCLC)*, *Literature Criticism from 1400 to 1800 (LC)*, and *Classical and Medieval Literature Criticism (CMLC)*, *PC* offers more focused attention on poetry than is possible in the broader, survey-oriented entries on writers in these Gale series. Students, teachers, librarians, and researchers will find that the generous excerpts and supplementary material provided by *PC* supply them with the vital information needed to write a term paper on poetic technique, to examine a poet's most prominent themes, or to lead a poetry discussion group.

Coverage

In order to reflect the influence of tradition as well as innovation, poets of various nationalities, eras, and movements are represented in every volume of *PC*. Each author entry presents a historical survey of the critical response to that author's work; the length of an entry reflects the amount of critical attention that the author has received from critics writing in English and from foreign critics in translation. Since many poets have inspired a prodigious amount of critical explication, *PC* is necessarily selective, and the editors have chosen the most significant published criticism to aid readers and students in their research. In order to provide these important critical pieces, the editors will sometimes reprint essays that have appeared in previous volumes of Gale's Literary Criticism Series. Such duplication, however, never exceeds fifteen percent of a *PC* volume.

Organization

Each *PC* author entry consists of the following components:

■ **Author Heading:** the name under which the author wrote appears at the beginning of the entry, followed by birth and death dates. If the author wrote consistently under a pseudonym, the pseudonym will be listed in the author heading and his or her legal name given in parentheses in the lines immediately preceding the Introduction. Uncertainty as to birth or death dates is indicated by question marks.

■ **Introduction:** a biographical and critical essay introduces readers to the author and the critical discussions surrounding his or her work.

■ **Author Portrait:** a photograph or illustration of the author is included when available.

■ **Principal Works:** the author's most important works are identified in a list ordered chronologically by first publication dates. The first section comprises poetry collections and book-length poems. The second section gives information on other major works by the author. For foreign authors, original foreign-language publication information is provided, as well as the best and most complete English-language editions of their works.

- **Criticism:** critical excerpts chronologically arranged in each author entry provide perspective on changes in critical evaluation over the years. All individual titles of poems and poetry collections by the author featured in the entry are printed in boldface type to enable a reader to ascertain without difficulty the works under discussion. For purposes of easy identification, the critic's name and the publication date of the essay are given at the beginning of each piece of criticism. Unsigned criticism is preceded by the title of the journal in which it originally appeared. Publication information (such as publisher names and book prices) and parenthetical numerical references (such as footnotes or page and line references to specific editions of a work) have been deleted at the editor's discretion to enable smoother reading of the text.

- **Explanatory Notes:** introductory comments preface each critical excerpt, providing several types of useful information, including: the reputation of a critic, the importance of a work of criticism, and the specific type of criticism (biographical, psychoanalytic, historical, etc.).

- **Author Commentary:** insightful comments from the authors themselves and excerpts from author interviews are included when available.

- **Bibliographical Citations:** information preceding each piece of criticism guides the interested reader to the original essay or book.

- **Further Reading:** bibliographic references accompanied by descriptive notes at the end of each entry suggest additional materials for study of the author. Boxed material following the Further Reading provides references to other biographical and critical series published by Gale.

Other Features

- **Cumulative Author Index:** comprises all authors who have appeared in Gale's Literary Criticism Series, along with cross-references to such Gale biographical series as *Contemporary Authors* and *Dictionary of Literary Biography*. This cumulated index enables the user to locate an author within the various series.

- **Cumulative Nationality Index:** includes all authors featured in *PC,* arranged alphabetically under their respective nationalities.

- **Cumulative Title Index:** lists in alphabetical order all individual poems, book-length poems, and collection titles contained in the *PC* series. Titles of poetry collections and separately published poems are printed in italics, while titles of individual poems are printed in roman type with quotation marks. Each title is followed by the author's name and the volume and page number corresponding to the location of commentary on specific works. English-language translations of original foreign-language titles are cross-referenced to the foreign titles so that all references to discussion of a work are combined in one listing.

Citing *Poetry Criticism*

When writing papers, students who quote directly from any volume in the Literary Criticism Series may use the following general formats to footnote reprinted criticism. The first example pertains to material drawn from periodicals, the second to material reprinted from books:

[1]David Daiches, "W. H. Auden: The Search for a Public," *Poetry* LIV (June 1939), 148-56; excerpted and reprinted in *Poetry Criticism*, Vol. 1, ed. Robyn V. Young (Detroit: Gale Research, 1990), pp. 7-9.

[2]Pamela J. Annas, *A Disturbance in Mirrors: The Poetry of Sylvia Plath* (Greenwood Press, 1988); excerpted and reprinted in *Poetry Criticism*, Vol. 1, ed. Robyn V. Young (Detroit: Gale Research, 1990), pp. 410-14.

Comments Are Welcome

Readers who wish to suggest authors to appear in future volumes, or who have other suggestions, are cordially invited to contact the editors.

Acknowledgments

The editors wish to thank the copyright holders of the excerpted criticism included in this volume and the permissions managers of many book and magazine publishing companies for assisting us in securing reproduction rights. We are also grateful to the staffs of the Detroit Public Library, the Library of Congress, the University of Detroit Mercy Library, Wayne State University Purdy/Kresge Library Complex, and the University of Michigan Libraries for making their resources available to us. Following is a list of the copyright holders who have granted us permission to reproduce material in this volume of *PC*. Every effort has been made to trace copyright, but if omissions have been made, please let us know.

COPYRIGHTED EXCERPTS IN *PC*, VOLUME 21, WERE REPRODUCED FROM THE FOLLOWING PERIODICALS:

COPYRIGHTED EXCERPTS IN *PC*, VOLUME 21, WERE REPRODUCED FROM THE FOLLOWING BOOKS:

PHOTOGRAPHS AND ILLUSTRATIONS APPEARING IN *PC*, VOLUME 21, WERE RECEIVED FROM THE FOLLOWING SOURCES:

Aleksandr (Aleksandrovich) Blok
1880-1921

Russian poet, dramatist, essayist, critic, and autobiographer.

INTRODUCTION

The leading figure of the Russian symbolist movement, Blok is considered the outstanding poet of the final years of Imperial Russia. While Blok's early poems reveal his efforts to find the true essence of reality in beauty, his later poetry is more concrete, frequently focusing on Russia, its history, and its future. Despite the shifting focus of his poetry, however, Blok retained the visionary outlook characteristic of the symbolists, and his ultimate source of inspiration remained constant as well. All of his poetry is infused with what he called the "spirit of music": an emotional and intellectual sense of exaltation and vivacity, and the fount of all creativity. Blok is today best remembered as the creator of the controversial *Dvenadsat'* (1918; *The Twelve*), praised as the greatest poetic celebration of the October Revolution.

Biographical Information

Born on the grounds of St. Petersburg University, Blok spent his childhood at Shakhmatovo, a small estate outside Moscow that belonged to his maternal grandfather. His parents, Alexandra Andreyevna and Alexander L'vovich, a brilliant lawyer, separated shortly before his birth, and Blok had slight contact with his father throughout his life. Raised in a cultured and literary atmosphere, first at Shakhmatovo and later in St. Petersburg, Blok was a mediocre student who much preferred the intellectual stimulation he found at home to his school work. At his father's insistence, he entered the School of Law at St. Petersburg University in 1898, the same year he fell in love with Lyubov Dmitrevna Mendeleeva, his future wife. Eventually changing his course of study from law to philology, Blok devoted much of his college years to composing poetry and studying the writings of the mystical philosopher and poet Vladimir Soloviev. For Blok, Lyubov was the incarnation of Soloviev's concept of the Eternal Feminine—Sophia, who represented eternal love and wisdom. Blok became the center of an admiring coterie of rising symbolist poets who worshipped his wife as the "Beautiful Lady," a figure Blok apotheosized in his poems of the early 1900s. However, by the time Blok's first collection of verse, *Stikhi o prekrasnoi dame* (1905), was published, his marriage had deteriorated. Lyubov had fallen in love with Andrey Biely—Blok's friend and a fellow symbolist. From this point on, the rarefied wonder of Blok's early verse gave way to earthbound pessimism: his poetry, as well as his dramas, revealed his self-destructive bitterness. During the last decade of his life, Blok gradually abandoned mortal women in his search for Sophia, and he began to turn to Russia itself as his new ideal. His verse increasingly evidenced his concern for his country's culture and destiny, most strikingly in *The Twelve*.

Major Works

Critics often divide Blok's poetic career into three periods. His earliest poems were inspired by Soloviev's writings on Sophia, as well as by his wife, in whom he found Sophia reborn. In these works, which were written primarily between 1898 and 1904, Blok addresses a "Beautiful Lady" who is the incarnation of the divine and the object of ideal love. The imagery of the poems—twilight skies, delicate rains, wispy clouds, and golden landscapes—reinforces the ethereal qualities Blok perceived in his beloved. By the time *Stikhi o prekrasnoi dame* was published, Blok was suffering from an emotional crisis that had a significant impact on the direction his poetry was to take. Disillusioned by his inability to reconcile his ideal visions with the coarse nature of reality, Blok sought an outlet for his frustrations in St. Petersburg night life. Drinking escapades with gypsies, womanizing, and reckless passion became the new subjects of his poetry. Like the poems of the first period, these verses reveal Blok's obsession with the feminine ideal. In these later works, however, Blok seeks out his beloved in the material rather than the spiritual world: in taverns, brothels, and city tenements. Again, the imagery of the poems—snowstorms, howling winds, and the darkness of night—reflects the poet's emotional state. In the most famous poem from this period, "Neznakomka" (1907; "The Unknown Lady," a title he also used for a later drama), Blok views his beloved through a wine-induced haze in a noisy suburban restaurant. Toward the end of the decade, Blok's poetry changed course once again. His love of Russia and concern for its future replaced the quest for the feminine ideal. Written shortly after the Bolshevik ascension, *The Twelve* describes an unruly group of twelve Red Guardsmen as they march through the streets of St. Petersburg, looting, shouting obscenities, and mocking the bourgeoisie. At the end of the poem, Christ appears as the invisible leader of the men, seemingly implying that the guardsmen are to be identified with the twelve apostles, and the October Revolution with Russia's salvation. *The Twelve* was soon followed by *Skify* (1918), a threatening call for Western support of the new regime, but Blok wrote little thereafter, telling his friends that due to the hunger, violence, and devastation caused by the Russian civil war he could no longer sense the "music" of his earlier life.

Critical Reception

The image of Christ in the conclusion of *The Twelve* has been a common point of departure for Blok's critics throughout the twentieth century. Upon its publication, *The Twelve* provoked heated controversy in Russian political circles. Blok's contemporaries, most of whom interpreted *The Twelve* as a religious justification for the Bolshevik Revolution, believed that the work represented a radical shift in Blok's social views. Praised by communists as a stirring affirmation of the new regime, it drew the scorn of Marxists and enraged the intelligentsia. Among later critics, *The Twelve* has elicited a variety of readings. Some scholars argue that the poem is not a glorification of communism because Blok, as a member of the intelligentsia, never fully grasped the meaning of the revolution. Others maintain that the poem betrays no political sympathies whatsoever; rather, Blok was simply responding to a creative inspiration over which he had no control, in this case "the music of the revolution," as Blok himself phrased it. *The Twelve* has also been studied in terms of topics that are pertinent to Blok's poetry as a whole, notably the dichotomy between the real and the ideal and Blok's conflicting loyalties to the intelligentsia and to the masses.

Overall, scholars have generally agreed that the importance of Blok's position within Russian literature and culture lies in his successful transversal of two eras. As Marc Slonim has stated, "His poetry proclaimed in prophetic lines the collapse of the world to which he belonged. He tried to transmit his message to the new world that was being born amid the chaos of an implacable upheaval, and he also attempted to discern and to welcome the future. Thus he stands at the crossroads of two epochs . . . the last poet of Imperial Russia is the first poet of its triumphant Revolution."

PRINCIPAL WORKS

Poetry

Stikhi o prekrasnoi dame [*Verses about the Beautiful Lady*] 1905
Nechayannaya radost 1907
Snezhnye maski [*The Snow Mask*] 1907
Zemlya v Snegu 1908
Nochniye chasy [*The Violet of the Night*] 1911
Solovyinny sad [*Of What the Wind Sings*] 1913
Stikhi o Rossii [*Garden of Nightingales*] 1916
*Dvenadsat' [*The Twelve*] 1918
*Skify [*The Scythians*] 1918
Vozmezdie [*Retaliation*] 1922
Selected Poems 1968

Other Major Works

Balaganchik [*The Puppet Show*] (drama) 1906

Korol na ploshchadi [*The King in the Square*] (drama) 1907
Pesnya sudby [*The Song of Fate*] (drama) 1909
Neznakomka [*The Stranger*] (drama) 1913
Rossiia i intelligentsiia (essays) 1918
Rosa i krest [*The Rose and the Cross*] (drama) 1920
Dnevik Al. Bloka. 1911-1913 (diaries) 1928
Dnevik Al. Bloka. 1917-1921 (diaries) 1928
Alexandr Blok: The Journey to Italy (essays, sketches, and poetry) 1973

*These works were published together in a single volume in 1918.

CRITICISM

Viktor Zhirmunskij (essay date 1921)

SOURCE: "The Passion of Aleksandr Blok," in *Twentieth-Century Russian Literary Criticism,* edited by Victor Erlich, Yale University Press, 1975, pp. 117-37.

[*In the following essay, which first appeared in Zhirmunskij's* The Poetry of Alexander Blok *(1921), Zhirmunskij traces the development of Blok's love poetry and his poetry about Russia, underscoring the spiritual basis of both sets of verse.*]

I

Blok's path is one of coming to know life through love. Its outer boundaries are marked by the religious lyrics **"Verses about the Beautiful Lady"** on the one hand, and by the gypsy motifs of the poet's last years on the other. Vladimir Solov'ëv appears as the poet's first teacher and Apollon Grigor'ev as his literary fellow-traveler and friend late in life. The changes in the symbolic imagery embodying the love object in Blok's poetry correspond to the successive stages of this inner experience.

Blok's early lyrical poetry is full of romantic presentiments of a first, as yet enigmatic, love. The predominant imagery is that of evening twilight, pale blue mists, transparent dawns, wisps of the azure sky glimpsed through spring clouds—and the first, indistinct summons of the infinite and the mysterious, which had penetrated the poet's soul along with the languor of spring and the expectation of the dawn (**"Ante Lucem"**):

Twilight, the twilight of spring,
Gelid the waves at my feet,
Hopes not of this world in my heart,
Waves that run up on the sands.

Echoes, a faraway song,
But I'm unable to make them out.
There, on the opposite shore,
Lonely, a soul breaks into tears . . .

The first vision of romantic love is the image of the un-worldly Beloved. The loved one appears to the poet in a celestial, mysterious radiance: she is the "Beautiful Lady," the "Tsarevna-Bride," the "Mysterious Maiden of the Sunset," the "Mistress of the Universe," the "Majestic Eternal Wife." The poet calls her (always with capital letters) "Radiant," "Luminous," "Golden-Haired," "Unattainable," "Holy." He is the knightly troubadour who is bent in submissive expectation before the image of the Madonna, guarding the "covenant of serving the Unattainable One":

> The fickle shades of day quicken away.
> The churchbell's call is sharp and clear.
> The churchsteps are illuminated bright,
> Their stone alive—awaiting your footfall.
>
> You'll pass through here, touch the cold stone
> Attired in the awful sacredness of ages,
> And, perhaps, you'll let fall a single spring flower
> Here, in these shadows, by the icons grave . . .

In his early verses Blok is the disciple of Vladimir Solov'ëv, the poet of the "eternal feminine," of the religious principle of love. The **"Verses about the Beautiful Lady"** are filled with esoteric expectation of the actual appearance of the eternal feminine, of the descent of divine love. The eschatological yearnings (for example, of Andrej Belyj, Merezhkovskij, and others) that at the turn of the century had spurred the resurgence of the mystical strain in Russian poetry take on here the aspect of some new and intensely personal revelation through love:

> All visions are so fleeting—
> Shall I believe in them?
> But perhaps I am loved,
> Though accidental, poor, mortal,
> By the Mistress of the Universe,
> By Beauty unutterable.

These mystical presentiments of the manifestation of the divine in love ("theophany") ally Blok's verse not only with the lyrical poetry of Vladimir Solov'ëv, but—through Solov'ëv and perhaps also directly—with "Hymns to the Night" of the German romantic poet Novalis and with Dante's *La Vita Nuova*. But this faith in the reality of the vision that has appeared to the poet is accompanied in Blok by a discordant note of doubt and fear. We find this expression of an all too human weakness, of powerlessness before a wondrous gift, in the opening poem of the first collection. The possibility of betraying the exalted Beloved, indeed, the entire further development of the poet is prefigured thus:

> I have forebodings of Thee. Time is going—
> I fear for all that in Thy face I see.
>
> The sky's aflame, intolerably glowing;
> Silent, I wait in love and agony.
>
> The sky's aflame, draws near Thy apparition,
> But it is strange. Thy look will change on Thee.

> And in me Thou dost wake a bold suspicion—
> Thy face will change from what it used to be.
>
> How I shall fall! how sorrowful and lowly,
> Unmastered all my mortal fantasy!
>
> The sky's aflame, draws near Thy splendor holy,
> But it is strange. Thy look will change on Thee.

"Unexpected Joy," the second collection of poems (which was later included in Blok's second volume), develops under the sign of this duality. The poet is at the "crossroads." The image of the Beloved recedes into the past and becomes shrouded in fog. The poet leaves the world of mysterious presentiments and visions and enters life on earth. Characteristically "modern" motifs begin to appear in his poems: the city at night, flooded with electric light, the noise of restaurants at night, and the faces of earthly women. He seeks in this life reflections of the celestial vision and catches vague glimpses of another, "more real" reality in it:

> In taverns, on corners, winding lanes,
> Trapped in an electrical daydream
> I sought the infinitely beautiful ones,
> Those forever in love with fame . . .

A woman encountered by chance in the city streets at night is transformed into the mysterious Stranger, in whose features the poet sees his only Beloved:

> And every evening, at the appointed hour,
> (Or do I only dream this?)
> A girlish figure, swathed in silks,
> Moves in the misty window.
>
> And slowly, passing amongst the drunkards,
> Always unaccompanied, alone,
> Breathing perfume and mists,
> She takes a seat by the window.
>
> And her resilient silks
> And her hat with funereal plumes
> And her narrow hand all covered in rings
> Are redolent of ancient legends . . .

At this stage in the development of the poet's romantic consciousness we encounter for the first time that dualistic perception of life that found its most complete expression in the lyrical drama *The Stranger*. Each of Blok's poems now unfolds on two different planes: the first is that of everyday, actual "reality"; the second is that of the "super-real," in which the only events important and of interest to the poet, spiritual events, occur. Thus, one of Blok's most memorable poems, **"In the Restaurant,"** tells of a chance and, on the surface, insignificant encounter. The poet sees a woman he does not know in a suburban restaurant, sends her a rose, meets her indignant look with a bold gaze, and so on. But then, suddenly, this insignificant event acquires a profound meaning on another plane, when behind the features of the unknown woman there appears to the poet a vision of his one and only Beloved, whom his soul once glimpsed in a dream, the image of the mysterious Stranger:

> You tore away like a frightened bird,
> You passed—light as my dream . . .
> And perfumes sighed, lashes slumbered,
> Anxiously silks began to whisper . . .

This is why the account of a "meeting in a restaurant" begins with agitated words that underscore emphatically its exceptional significance: "*Never shall I forget /* (Whether that evening was or not). . . ." It is also why the poet's courtship of the unknown lady is set off by a grand, dramatic gesture: "I sent you a single black rose in a goblet / of Aÿ, that was gold as the sky. . . ."

Blok was drawn to the gypsy song because he sensed in it an elemental sweep of passion, an untrammeled breadth of revelry and daring.

—Viktor Zhirmunskij

The romantic hovering between two worlds known to us from Hoffmann's *Kunstmärchen,* has its own artistic laws. From the heights of mystic inspiration earthly reality seems illusory, unreal; romantic irony distorts it into a hideous grotesque. That is what happens in the description of the summer resort in the environs of St. Petersburg, with which the ballad **"The Stranger"** opens, or in the description of the tavern and of the literary salon in the lyric drama of the same title:

> . . . Far off, above the dust of lanes,
> Above the boredom of cottages,
> The gilded sign of a bakery glimmers faintly,
> And the cry of a child rings out.
>
> . . . . .
>
> Above the lake, the rowlocks scrape,
> And a woman's screech rings out,
> While in the sky, inured to everything,
> The moon's disc senselessly grimaces.

On the other hand, from the viewpoint of common, everyday experience, the poet's mystical insight is subject to doubt, and his vision of the Stranger seems only a poetic illusion, a play of the imagination, or perhaps, a dream vision (compare such expressions, characteristic of the poet's precarious sense of reality: "Or do I only *dream* this?" "You passed, light as my *dream,*" "whether it was or not, that evening"). The poet himself half begins to regard his visions as having been induced by dreams or drunken delirium:

> Out of the crystal fog,
> Out of the unseen *dream,*

> Someone's image, someone strange . . .
> (*In the restaurant,* in a private room,
> *Over a bottle of wine*) . . .

In the ballad **"The Stranger"** and in the lyric drama of the same title the miraculous vision of the one and only Beloved is set in the ambience of a drinking house, and it is induced by the intoxication gradually overcoming the poet:

> And every evening my only friend
> Is mirrored in my wine glass
> And, like myself, is subdued and dazed
> By the tart and mysterious liquor . . .

As in the stories of Hoffmann and Edgar Allan Poe, the features of the celestial Beloved are seen through the midst of the poet's growing intoxication, which obliterates the usual boundaries of daily consciousness:

> . . . And the drooping ostrich plumes
> Wave in my brain,
> And blue fathomless eyes
> Flower on a distant shore . . .

But for the romantic poet intoxication has merely raised the curtain of consciousness, has merely set ajar the door leading from the world of illusions into the world of higher reality: "You are right, you drunken monster; / I know: truth lies in wine."

Beginning with the period to which the poems about the "Stranger" belong, one can note certain new facts in Blok's poetic development that the poet himself evaluates from some higher point of view, as a religious sin, a defection or betrayal of the adolescent ideal of eternal love. Yet it is at this time that Blok's work gradually outgrows its prayerlike immobility, its contemplative purity, and is enriched by the complex, contradictory, and chaotic content of earthly life with its sufferings and sins. It is the period of Blok's greatest poetic accomplishments. The basic theme of Blok's new verses (the collection **"The Earth in Snow,"** which was included in the second volume) is the poet's entrance into life, his merging with the creative, superabundant element of life through the medium of vivid and passionate love experience:

> O Spring without end, without limit—
> Endless and limitless dream!
> I accept and acknowledge you, Life!
> I salute you with the clang of my shield!
>
> . . . . .
>
> At the threshold I meet you—
> With wild wind in your serpent-coiled curls
> With the inscrutable name of a god
> On your cold and tightly closed lips . . .

The basic aspiration of the poet's soul has remained essentially unchanged: there is the same expectation of a miracle, the same quest of the infinite that we observed in the poems of his youth. Only the object of these romantic yearnings has changed; they are no longer directed toward the pure and chaste love for the celestial Beloved, but rather toward the caresses of an earthly lover—sinful and passionate. The image of the exalted Beloved now vanishes entirely only to yield to the Snow Maiden, Faina, Valentina, Carmen—figures marking the furthest stages in the history of romantic love:

> They were many. But by one
> Feature did I bring them all together,
> By beauty alone, by mad beauty,
> Whose name is passion and my life . . .

These figures have only one thing in common: in the glow of amorous passion, in the kisses and embraces of these worldly lovers, the poet seeks momentary ecstasy, self-forgetfulness, rapture. He reaches toward supreme emotional intensity as a way of transcending the boundaries of ordinary experience, of entering the world of inspiration and delirium, of mystical intoxication.

> Such joy to enfold in my arms your
> Cold shoulders, thus sheltered from wind:
> You think it is a tender caress,
> I know it is rebellious rapture!
>
> Like candles at night, your bright eyes
> Glimmer, and greedily I listen—
> A terrible tale begins rustling,
> The sidereal boundary heaves . . .

The entire "landscape of the soul" changes: instead of the transparent spring dawns and the golden-tinged azure that provided the backdrop for the celestial Beloved in Blok's early poems, we find a "ringing" blizzard, a "turbulent wind" that "singes" the face, "the conflagration of the white-winged snowstorm," a troika run amok, carrying the poet and his love away over the dark, open "abysses," into the "snowy night": "And the blue wind strolls above your sable furs."

The boundlessness of love ecstasy lends Blok's lyrics of this period (**"The Earth in Snow," "Night Hours"**) a boldness and irrationality of design never before encountered in Russian poetry. One almost feels the presence of the primeval chaos of creation, of cosmic forces unleashed, descending upon the poet from the "terrible" night world and inundating the circumscribed realm of daytime consciousness.

> In a light heart—passion and insouciance
> As if a signal had been given me from the sea.
> Over the bottomless gulf into eternity,
> Breathless, a charger speeds.
>
> The snowy wind, your breath,
> My drunken lips . . .
> Valentina, star, dream!
> How your nightingales sing! . . .
>
> Terrible world! Too narrow for the heart!
> Filled with the delirium of your kisses,

> The dark gloom of gypsy songs,
> The hurried flight of comets!

The love lyrics of Blok's last period represent a movement away from Vladimir Solov'ëv to Apollon Grigor'ev and the gypsy romance. Yet it should be clear from the foregoing that what is at work here is not simply a "canonization of the gypsy song," in other words of an inferior literary branch with its own distinctive themes, which had remained hitherto beyond the pale of "high" poetry. Rather, it is a complex mediation of these motifs, through the resources of romanticism and of a mystical vision of life. Blok was drawn to the gypsy song because he sensed in it an elemental sweep of passion, an untrammeled breadth of revelry and daring. But he was even more responsive to those notes of spiritual frenzy that Apollon Grigor'ev had first overheard in the gypsy choruses (see his poems "The Struggle," "Improvisations of a Wandering Romantic") and that had suggested to Dostoevsky the scene of Dmitrij's orgy with Grushen'ka at Mokroe in *The Brothers Karamazov*. The strange lure of dark passion, the mystical gusts and the flights of inspiration blend with a feeling of sin and suffering, of anguish and disarray. But in this very sin and suffering, in the very image of the sinful beloved there is something irresistibly appealing, a promise of yet unknown, impossible delights, of a reaching beyond the mundane, the everyday:

> Unfaithful one, o cunning one,
> Insidious, dance on!
> And be forever poison to
> My dissipated soul!
>
> I'll lose my mind, my mind I'll lose
> I'll madly rave, in love,
> That you're all night, that you're all gloom,
> That you're all drunken too . . .
>
> That you have torn from me my soul,
> You've poisoned it all through,
> That you I sing, I sing of you,
> And numberless my songs!

In his last poems, which were included in the second and third (posthumous) editions of the third volume, Blok is a poet of wild, drunken, gypsy love and of an increasingly oppressive hangover. The enraptured flights of his earlier passionate verses give way to the increasingly oppressive consciousness of spiritual disintegration and fall. Fall and sin are revealed to the poet in the fullness of their terrifying religious aspect as "satanic depth":

> I will not hide myself from you,
> Look closely at me:
> I stand among charred ruins,
> Scorched by tongues
> Of netherworldly flame . . .

The awareness of spiritual abasement, of sin and fall, saturate all Blok's last poems (see especially **"Humiliation," "Black Blood"**—in general, the sections "The Terrible World" and "Retribution"), but in this very fall there are mystically rapturous flights that lend the poet's intoxication a cosmic thrust:

> Your very name sounds despicable to me,
> But when you screw up your eyes,
> I hear—the foaming current howls,
> The storm approaches from the desert . . .

The image of the celestial Beloved recurs in retrospection ("Do you remember first love, and dawns, dawns, dawns?"), but now it chastizes the "apostate" and threatens imminent "retribution" or belated and useless "repentance" (**"The Steps of the Commander"**):

> What price your repellent freedom
> Now that you've known fear, Don Juan?
>
> . . . . .
>
> What are the sounds of bliss to a betrayer?
> Life's instances have been numbered . . .

From the depths of his fall the poet again raises a wail of lamentation to the childhood vision of pure and chaste love ("O, moments of kisses not for sale! / O, caresses of unbought maidens!"). The poet's penitential, autobiographical verses project the image of the one and only Beloved:

> The days flew by, whirling in a cursed swarm,
> Wine and passion tore my life asunder . . .
> And suddenly I recollected you standing by the
>   altar,
> I called to you, as if calling to my youth.
>
> I called to you, but you refused to turn your head,
> I wept real tears, but you refused to condescend.
> You sadly muffled yourself in a light blue cloak
> And went out from the house into the damp
>   night . . .

But these recollections remain too distant to be of any use in the present. The poet speaks more and more frequently about life as "empty," "needlessly lived to the end," "oppressive and insane," "insane and fathomless." "And it's become mercilessly clear— / Life has finished and gone."

Hopeless emptiness and ennui, like a dull hangover, replace the unrestrained raptures and sufferings of past years. The "gray morning" dawns, only to be followed by "Cruel day, day of iron."

> O, how rich I was once upon a time,
> And all of it—not worth a kopeck coin,
> Enmity, love, fame, and gold,
> And above all—mortal anguish . . .

Aversion to the past and despair of the future, and in the present the inescapable grief and ennui, the acedia, or spiritual sloth, well known to the ancient religious writers—or, to use more recent if less significant analogies, Weltschmerz or Baudelairean Spleen—gradually take possession of the poet. He suffers from a metaphysical sickness of the soul, "the ailment mysteriously and steadily consuming me" (see particularly **"Dances of Death," "The Life of My Friend,"** in the cycle "Terrible World"):

> Night, a street, a lamp, a druggist's shop,
> A meaningless and dullish light.
> Even if you live another quarter century—
> Everything will be like this. There's no way out.
>
> You'll die—and start again from the beginning,
> And everything will be repeated as of old:
> The night, the icy ripples on the channel,
> The druggist's shop, the street, the lamp.

Perhaps the most profound expression of this final phase in the development of the romantic poet is to be found in the poem **"To the Muse,"** which significantly opens volume 3 of Blok's verse. Here the Muse and the Beloved merge in one image, and the intimate and personal aspects of love experience expand into a suprapersonal perspective on the meaning of life sought through love. In the depth and power of his tragic sense of life Blok approaches here the most mature poems of Tjutchev, dedicated as they are to his tragic "last love":

> In your hidden melodies
> There are fatal tidings of doom.
> There is a curse of sacred covenants,
> A profanation of happiness.
>
> And such an alluring force
> That I am ready to reiterate the rumor
> That you have brought the angels down to earth,
> With the enticements of your beauty.
>
> . . . . .
>
> I do not know why, at daybreak,
> In the hour when no strength was left to me
> I did not perish, but observed your countenance
> And begged for your consolations.
>
> . . . . .
>
> And your terrible caresses
> Were more treacherous than the northern night
> And more intoxicating than golden Aÿ,
> And briefer than a gypsy's love . . .
>
> And there was a fatal joy
> In trampling on things held sacred,
> And this passion, bitter as wormwood,
> Was a frenzied delight for the heart.

What is the source of the tragic in this poem, of the most profound disillusionment and despair in the very moment of amorous passion? What one hears in these lines is not the simple, ordinary pangs of love, but a spiritual torment, a religious sickness of particular acuity. The "terrible caresses" of the Beloved (let us also recall: the "terrible tale," the "terrible world," "terrible embraces"), the "trampling on things held sacred," beauty not as joy, but as a curse ("the whole curse of your beauty")—all of this reveals to us a particular realm of experience, the nature of which has been most clearly stated in the works of Dostoevsky:

> Beauty—this is a terrible and awful thing! Terrible because it is indefinable, and it cannot be defined because God has posed only enigmas. Here all shores meet, here all contradictions live together. I, brother, am very uneducated, but I have thought much about this. There are fearfully many mysteries! Too many enigmas oppress man on earth. Solve them as you will, you will not emerge dry from the water. Beauty! Here I cannot bear the fact that a man, a man even with a lofty heart and with a lofty mind begins with the ideal of the Madonna, yet ends with the ideal of Sodom. What's even more awful is that the person who, though already with the ideal of Sodom in his soul, yet does not deny the ideal of the Madonna, and his heart glows with it, and truly glows as in his youthful, sinless years. No, man is broad, far too broad, I would narrow him. The devil only knows what it is all about! What to the mind is ignominious, is nothing but beauty to the heart. Is there beauty in Sodom? Rest assured that it is to be found in Sodom for the overwhelming majority of people—did you know this secret or not? What is awful is that beauty is not only terrible, but also a mysterious thing. Here the devil struggles with God, but the field of battle is the heart of men.
>
> [*The Brothers Karamazov*]

These words of Dostoevsky's contain the best interpretation of Alexander Blok's tragic poetry. What was it that led the poet of the Beautiful Lady down such paths, what brought him from "the ideal of the Madonna" to the "ideal of Sodom"? A mystical craving for the infinite, the quest of an unprecedented intensity of experience, of moments of ecstasy which, even if leading to sin and suffering, harbor or promise that *goût de l'Infini* without which everyday life becomes monotonous and vapid in its simple and modest joys and sufferings. Thus, as was already indicated, the chaste adolescent poet's yearning for the appearance of the "Tsarevna-Bride" can be seen to stem from the same aspiration that was to serve as the impetus for the amorous and sinful passion of his last years. "Is there beauty in Sodom?" In both his early and late poetry the romantic poet refuses to settle for anything less than infinite happiness.

> What is happiness? The evening cool,
> In the darkening garden, in remote corners of the
>   woods?
> Or the gloomy, wanton delights
> Of wine, passions, the soul's perdition?

This spiritual maximalism of the romantic individualist arises from the feeling of the infinity of man's soul, of its inability to be content with anything finite and limited. The soul, poisoned by limitless desires, seeks infinite experiences that alone are capable of satiating its mystical hunger. Limitless demands on life, the pursuit of the unprecedented and miraculous makes simple, commonplace actuality insipid. The sense of emptiness and futility, the

oppressive hangover inescapably follow the tormenting flights of passionate feeling.

Having immersed himself in the congenial turmoil of the popular rebellion, Blok overheard its rhythms and caught sight of its images. But in recreating them he did not conceal their tragic contradictions, just as in confronting his own fate he made no secret of alienation, confusion, or anguish.

—Viktor Zhirmunskij

This unsatiable spiritual hunger, these limitless demands on life, coupled with the inability to find a satisfactory outlet for an awakened religious consciousness, had been spawned by early nineteenth-century romanticism. Romantic "maximalism" had many variants ranging from the impiety, disillusionment, and religious despair of Byron to the religious humility and the morbid renunciation of personal will and happiness of those German romantics who turned for support to the mystical world view of the medieval church. In the love lyrics of Alfred de Musset or, in particular, of Clemens Brentano, who was in many respects closer to Blok than other of his contemporaries, we find the by now familiar forms of the romantic cleavage between the "ideal of the Madonna" and "the ideal of Sodom." It is Dostoevsky who confronts this problem most directly and thus foreshadows Blok's spiritual quest. In Dostoevsky's novels, as in the verses of the modern poet, the Russian folk element found its fullest expression—that total absence of measure in everything, that maximalism of the spirit for which all that is limited and contingent in *life* is only a barrier to the unconditional, anarchic urge toward creative freedom and self-affirmation. "No, man is broad, far too broad, I would narrow him. . . . Here the devil struggles with God, but the field of battle is the heart of men."

II

The cycle of poems Blok dedicated to his "native land" was composed in the years following the 1905 Revolution, at a time when it had become clear to many that the days which would decide the fate of Russia were drawing near. These "Verses about Russia" stand in the tradition of the religious trend in Russian social thought, the tradition of Khomjakov, Tjutchev, Dostoevsky, Solov'ëv. It is not the political fortunes of his native land that concern the poet, but the salvation of its living soul. The poet views his country's calling, its predestined path, and the victories and battles on that path, in the same way that he had regarded his own fate—as a religious tragedy, a struggle for the divine calling of the human personality. But Blok differs from his predecessors in that he approaches the fate of Russia not as a thinker, through an abstract idea, but as a poet, through intimate love. For him Russia is the Beloved, and as the features of the Beloved change in his poetry—from the image of the Beautiful Lady to that of the Muse in his last poems—so also his feelings for his native land finds its expression in the changing symbols of romantic love. At first, whether a betrothed, a wife, or a mother, she recalls the luminous features of the celestial Beloved:

> . . . With a tinkling of crystal
> She filled me with hope,
> Surrounded me with a luminous circle.

> . . . This is a light, paradisial image,
> This is your beloved . . .

In **"On the Field of Kulikovo"** (1908) the celestial Beloved guards the sleeping warriors:

> . . . In the middle of the plain at nightfall,
> by the sombre Don,
> I heard Your voice in my prophet's heart call
> with the cry of the swan . . .

> . . . And when, next morning, the horde moved on
> darkening the field,
> made by no human hands Your image shone
> permanent in my shield.

But the Beloved Russia had already taken on different features in Blok's poetry. He had glimpsed in her that turbulent, chaotic, ecstatically passionate, intoxicating aspect that he saw simultaneously in the features of Faina or Carmen. This motif appears as early as **"On the Field of Kulikovo"**:

> . . . Our road lies over the steppe and through
>   infinite
> anguish, your anguish, Russia:
> even the night beyond the frontier limit
> I do not fear . . .

> . . . The wild mare of the steppe sweeps on, on,
>   over the feather-grass . . .

> endlessly! Milestone and precipice flicker . . .
> draw rein! . . .

> . . . There is no rest. The wild mare galloping
> knows no sleep.

"New America" represents the poet's conscious renunciation of his youthful Slavophile dream of Russia as a bride chosen by God, a devout maiden ("Holy Russia"):

"New America"

> You'll pretend to be devout,
> You'll pretend to be an old woman,
> The prayerful voice, the churchbell's peal,
> Behind the crosses—more crosses and more . . .

> Yet at times your frankincense and benzoin
> Will be telling a different tale:

> No, the face beneath the colored kerchief
> Is neither senile nor pious!

> Through the bows to the earth, and the candles,
> Through litany after litany—
> I can hear quiet, whispered words,
> I can glimpse your burning cheeks . . .

A new image of the Beloved Russia now appears to the poet, that of "drunken Russia" ("they will hear the voice of drunken Russia / and rest beneath the tavern's roof"), of a "fatal native land," whose beauty is "robber-like":

> I cannot offer you my pity,
> I carry my cross as I can . . .
> Squander your wild beauty
> on every new magician!

> If they seduce you and deceive you,
> you'll not be broken or collapse;
> though suffering may overshadow
> the beauty of your face perhaps . . .

The Twelve, dedicated to the October Revolution, has its place in this sequence of images. At the time of this poem's appearance it was all too often treated as a political document that supposedly represented a radical shift in the poet's social views. Actually, *The Twelve* brings to their logical conclusion the most significant elements of Blok's work. Like the poet's entire work, it is completely removed from politics, programs, and the like; the problem it poses is not a political, but a religious and moral one, and its message is individual rather than social. However strange it might seem at first glance, the poem's fundamental theme is not that of a social system, but that of the soul's salvation—the souls of the Red Guard Petrushka, so unexpectedly placed at the poem's center, and of his eleven comrades, and more broadly, the collective soul of Russia in turmoil, her "unencompassable expanses," her "robber-like beauty."

Of course, the "old world" and its representatives—the "Comrade priest," the "writer-orator," the "lady in the astrakhan coat," and the "bourgeois, hungry as a dog"—hardly enjoy the author's artistic sympathy. Such sympathy would be incompatible with his spiritual maximalism, with that instinctive rejection of habit and routine in both private and public life, that thirst for the boundless and the absolute that has already been mentioned. Let us recall a poem of 1908 in which the poet directly addresses his readers:

> You're easily satisfied with a wife and a job,
> And with your piddling constitution,
> But the poet's reach is as wide as the world,
> And constitutions mean little to him!

> Even if I die by a fence like a dog,
> If life tramples me into the dirt—
> I'll know: it was the Lord who has bathed me in
>   snow,
> 'Twas the blizzard that held me in its arms!

To be sure, the poet had succeeded in overhearing in the Revolution the new rhythms of an as yet unwritten Marseillaise:

> The wind plays up: snow flutters down.
> Twelve men are marching through the town.
>
> Their rifle butts on black slings sway.
> Lights left, right, left, wink all the way . . .
>
> . . . Keep a Revolutionary Step!
> The Relentless Enemy Will Not Stop!

But Blok's affinity for the Revolution was hardly a commitment to a definite system of political and social ideas. On the contrary, it was the element of popular revolt—"with or against God"—in which Blok sensed a stance closely akin to his own spiritual maximalism, his religious rebellion, his "trampling on things held sacred":

> Grip your gun like a man, brother!
> Let's have a crack at Holy Russia,
> Mother
> Russia
> with her big, fat arse!
> Freedom, freedom! Down with the cross!

The essential fact about *The Twelve* is that this poem grows organically out of Blok's entire poetic experience, out of the artistic achievements and symbols in which the religious tragedy of his own life had been revealed to him. The poet had heard the sounds of the snowstorm, which acts as a backdrop to *The Twelve,* in his earlier poems about the blizzard, the "snow love," and the **"Snow Maiden"**; it had become the accustomed "landscape of his soul," a setting for the poet's mystical transports and downfalls. The further development of this artistic theme is found in **"Verses about Russia"**: "Where violently the blizzard piles up / snow to the roof of a frail dwelling"; "You stand in the wild blizzard, / my fatal native land." Significantly, these images coincide with the epigraph from Pushkin's "The Devils," which Dostoevsky used as an inscription in his novel of the same title. The story of the Red Guard Petruskha's love for the prostitute Katja, which suddenly assumes the dimensions of the central event of this "political" poem, had been told previously in Blok's "gypsy" poems. We confront here once again that spiritual maximalism in love that Dostoevsky had epitomized in Dmitrij Karamazov's words about Grushen'ka ("Grushen'ka, the witch, has such a single curve of a body . . .") and that permeates the love lyrics of Blok's third volume:

> Oh, brother, brother, brother,
> I loved that girl . . .
> such nights we had together,
> me and that girl . . .
> For the wicked come-hither
> her eyes would shoot at me,
> and for the crimson mole
> in the crook of her arm,
> I shot her in my fury—
> like the fool I am . . .

Finally these triumphal motifs of popular rebellion yield to a mood of inconsolable anguish, of life's emptiness and aimlessness, of a dull hangover, of spiritual torpor, already a religious despair, in the wake of an intoxicating religious rebellion:

> My God, what a life!
> I've had enough!
> I'm bored!
>
> I'll scratch my head
> and dream a dream . . .
>
> I'll chew my quod
> to pass the time . . .
>
> I'll swig enough
> to kill my drought . . .
>
> I'll get my knife
> and slit your throat!
>
> Fly away, mister, like a starling,
> before I drink your blue veins dry
> for the sake of my poor darling
> with her dark and roving eye . . .
> Blessed are the dead which die in the Lord . . .
> I'm bored!

Having immersed himself in the congenial turmoil of the popular rebellion, Blok overheard its rhythms and caught sight of its images. But in recreating them he did not conceal their tragic contradictions, just as in confronting his own fate he made no secret of alienation, confusion, or anguish. Therein lies his honesty with himself and his contemporaries. Therein lies his achievement as a poet of the Revolution (not a poet-Revolutionary). In this sense *The Scythians* is much farther removed from primary and genuine creative experience and more discursive and tendentious, as would be any abstract commentary that sought to encapsulate in neat, logical concepts the authenticity and intensity of the poet's vision.

Leon Trotsky (essay date 1924)

SOURCE: "Alexander Blok," in *Literature and Revolution,* Russell & Russell, 1957, pp. 116-25.

[*In the following essay, originally published in 1924, Trotsky discusses* The Twelve *and Blok's understanding of the Bolshevik Revolution.*]

Blok belonged entirely to pre-October literature. Blok's impulses—whether towards tempestuous mysticism, or towards revolution—arise not in empty space, but in the very thick atmosphere of the culture of old Russia, of its landlords and intelligentsia. Blok's symbolism was a reflection of this immediate and disgusting environment. A symbol is a generalized image of a reality. Blok's lyrics are romantic, symbolic, mystic, formless and unreal. But they presuppose a very real life with definite forms and relationships. Romantic symbolism is only a going away from life, in the sense of an abstraction from its concreteness, from individual traits, and from its proper names; at bottom, symbolism is a means of transforming and sublimating life. Blok's starry, stormy and formless lyrics reflect a definite environment and period, with its manner of living, its customs, its rhythms, but outside of this period, they hang like a cloud-patch. This lyric poetry will not outlive its time or its author.

Blok belonged to pre-October literature, but he overcame this, and entered into the sphere of October when he wrote *The Twelve.* That is why he will occupy a special place in the history of Russian literature.

One should not allow Blok to be obscured by those petty poetic and semi-poetic demons who whirl around his memory, and who to this very day, the pious idiots! cannot understand how Blok recognized Mayakovsky as a great talent, and yawned frankly over Gumilev. Blok, the "purest" of lyricists, did not speak of pure art, and did not place poetry above life. On the contrary, he recognized the fact that "art, life and politics were indivisible and inseparable." "I am accustomed," writes Blok in his preface to *Retaliation,* written in 1919, "to put together the facts accessible to my eye in a given time in every field of life, and I am sure that all together they always create one musical chord." This is much bigger and stronger and deeper than a self-sufficient æstheticism, than all the nonsense about art being independent of social life.

Blok knew the value of the intelligentsia: "I am none the less a blood-relation of the intelligentsia," he said, "but the intelligentsia has always been negative. If I did not go over to the Revolution, it is still less worth while to go over to the War." Blok did not "go over to the Revolution," but he took his spiritual course from it. Already the approach of the Revolution of 1905 opened up the factory to Blok, and for the first time raised his art above lyrical nebulousness. The first Revolution entered his soul and tore him away from individualistic self-contentment and mystic quietism. Blok felt the reaction between the two Revolutions to be an emptiness of spirit, and the aimlessness of the epoch he felt to be a circus, with cranberry sauce for blood. Blok wrote of "the true mystic twilight of the years which preceded the first Revolution" and of "the untrue mystic after-effect which immediately followed it." (*Retaliation.*) The second Revolution gave him a feeling of wakening, of movement, of purpose and of meaning. Blok was not the poet of the Revolution. Blok caught hold of the wheel of the Revolution as he lay perishing in the stupid *cul de sac* of pre-revolutionary life and art. The poem called *The Twelve,* Blok's most important work, and the only one which will live for ages, was the result of this contact.

As he himself said, Blok carried chaos within himself all his life. His manner of saying this was formless, just as his philosophy of life and his lyrics were on the whole formless. What he felt to be chaos was his incapacity to combine the subjective and the objective, his cautious

and watchful lack of will power, in an epoch which saw the preparation and afterwards the letting loose of the greatest events. Throughout all his changes, Blok remained a true decadent, if one were to take this word in a large historic sense, in the sense of the contrast between decadent individualism and the individualism of the rising bourgeoisie.

Blok's anxious state of chaos gravitated into two main directions, the mystic and the revolutionary. But in neither direction did it resolve itself to the end. His religion was unclear and infirm, not imperative like his lyrics. The Revolution which descended on the poet like a hail of facts, like a geologic avalanche of events, refuted or rather swept away the pre-revolutionary Blok, who was wasting himself in languor and presentiments. It drowned the tender, gnat-like note of individualism in the roaring and heaving music of destruction. And here one had to choose. Of course, the parlor poets could continue their chirping without choosing, and needed merely to add their complaints about the difficulties of life. But Blok, who was carried away by the period, and who translated it into his own inner language, had to choose, and he chose by writing *The Twelve.*

This poem is unquestionably Blok's highest achievement. At bottom it is a cry of despair for the dying past, and yet a cry of despair which rises in a hope for the future. The music of the terrible events inspired Blok. It seemed to say to him: "Everything which you have written up to now is not right. New people are coming. They bring new hearts. They do not need this. Their victory over the old world signifies a victory over you, over your lyrics, which voiced only the torment of the old world before its death." Blok heard this, and accepted it, and because it was hard to accept, and because he sought support for his lack of faith in his revolutionary faith, and because he wanted to fortify and convince himself, he expressed his acceptance of the Revolution in the most extreme images, that the bridges behind him might be burned. Blok does not make even a shadow of an attempt to sugar the revolutionary change. On the contrary, he takes it in its most uncouth forms and only in its uncouth forms—a strike of prostitutes, for instance, the murder of Katka by a Red guard, the pillage of a bourgeois home—and, he says, *I accept this,* and he sanctifies all this provocatively with the blessings of Christ, and perhaps tries even to save the artistic image of Christ by propping it up with the Revolution.

But none the less, *The Twelve* is not a poem of the Revolution. It is the swan song of the individualistic art that went over to the Revolution. And this poem will remain. The twilight lyrics of Blok are gone into the past, and will never return, for such times will not come again, but *The Twelve* will remain with its cruel wind, with its placard, with Katka lying on the snow, with the revolutionary step, and with the old world like a mangy cur.

The fact that Blok wrote *The Twelve* and that he became silent after *The Twelve,* that he stopped hearing music, is due as much to Blok's character as to the very extraordinary "music" which he grasped in 1918. The convulsive and pathetic break with the whole past became, for the poet, a fatal rupture. Aside from the destructive processes which were going on in his organism, Blok could have been kept going perhaps only by a continual development of revolutionary events, by a powerful spiral of shocks that would embrace the whole world. But the march of history is not adapted for the psychic needs of a romanticist who is struck by the Revolution. And to be able to maintain oneself on the temporary sand-banks, one has to have a different training, a different faith in the Revolution, an understanding of its sequential rhythms, and not only an understanding of the chaotic music of its tides. Blok did not and could not have all this. The leaders of the Revolution were all people whose psychology and behavior were strange to him. That is why he withdrew into himself, and became silent after *The Twelve.* And those with whom he had lived spiritually, the wise men and the poets, the same who are always "negative," turned away from him with malice and with hate. They could not forgive him his phrase, the mangy cur. They stopped shaking hands with Blok, as with a traitor, and only after his death did they "make peace with him," and tried to show that *The Twelve* contained nothing unexpected, and that it was not of October, but of the old Blok, and that all the elements of *The Twelve* had their roots in the past, and let not the Bolsheviks imagine that Blok was one of theirs. This contention is not hard to gather from Blok's various other works. There are rhythms, alliterations, strophes which find their full development in *The Twelve.* But one can find in the individualist Blok other rhythms and moods also; and it was this same Blok who, just in 1918, found in himself (certainly not on the pavement, but in himself) the broken music of *The Twelve.* The pavement of October was needed for this. Others escaped abroad from this pavement, or moved into interior islands. Here is the crux of the matter and this is what they do not forgive Blok for!

> Thus rave all the fed,
> Thus longs the satisfaction of important bellies,
> Their trough is overturned,
> And confusion is in their foul pen.
>   (A. Blok, **"The Fed"**)

But just the same, *The Twelve* is not a poem of the Revolution; because, after all, the meaning of the Revolution as an element (if one were to consider it as an element only) does not consist in releasing individualism that had been driven into a blind alley. The inner meaning of the Revolution remains somewhere outside the poem. The poem itself is eccentric, in the sense of the word as it is used in physics. That is why Blok crowns his poem with Christ. But Christ belongs in no way to the Revolution, only to Blok's past.

When Eichenvald, expressing the bourgeois attitude towards *The Twelve,* says openly and most maliciously, that the acts of Blok's heroes are characteristic of the "comrades," he fulfills the task he has set himself, namely, to slander the Revolution. A Red guard kills Katka, for jealousy. Is this possible, or is it impossible? It is entirely possible. But had such a Red guard been caught, he would have been sentenced to be shot by the Revolution-ary Tribunal. The Revolution which applies the frightful sword of Terrorism, guards it severely as a State right. Were Terror used for personal ends, the Revolution would be threatened by inevitable destruction. As early as the beginning of 1918, the Revolution put an end to anarchistic unruliness, and carried on a merciless and victorious struggle with the disintegrating methods of guerrilla warfare.

"Open up the cellars; the *sansculottes* are now having their holiday." And this happened. But what bloody collisions took place for this very reason between the Red guards and the hooligans! "Soberness" was written on the banner of the Revolution. The Revolution was ascetic, especially in this most intense period. Therefore Blok does not give a picture of the Revolution, and certainly not of the work of its vanguard, but of its accompanying phenomena which were called forth by it, but which were in essence contrary to it. The poet seems to want to say that he feels the Revolution in this also, that he feels its sweep, the terrible commotion in the heart, the awakening, the bravery, the risk, and that even in these disgusting, senseless and bloody manifestations is reflected the spirit of the Revolution which, to Blok, is the spirit of Christ rampant.

Of all the things which have been written about Blok and about *The Twelve,* perhaps the most impossible are the writings of Mr. Chukovsky. His booklet about Blok is not worse than his other books. They reveal an external vivacity combined with an inability to bring the least order into his thoughts, an unevenness of exposition, a provincial newspaper rhythm, as well as a meager pedantism and a tendency to generalize on the basis of external antitheses. And Chukovsky always discovers what no one else has ever seen. Has anyone ever considered *The Twelve* as the poem of the Revolution, that very Revolution which took place in October? Heaven forbid! Chukovsky will immediately explain all about it, and will reconcile Blok with "public opinion." *The Twelve* does not sing the Revolution, but Russia, in spite of the Revolution: "Here is an obstinate nationalism which, unembarrassed by anything, wants to see holiness even in ugliness, as long as this ugliness is Russia." (K. Chukovsky, *A Book About Alexander Blok.*) Blok then accepts Russia, in spite of the Revolution, or, to be more exact, in spite of the ugliness of the Revolution. This seems to be his reasoning; that much seems definite. At the same time, however, it turns out that Blok was always (!) the poet of the Revolution, "but not of the Revolution which is taking place now, but of another revolution, national and Russian. . . ." This is jumping from the frying pan into the fire. Thus Blok in *The Twelve* did not sing of Russia in spite of the Revolution, but sang of a revolution, not of the one which has taken place, but of another one, the exact address of which is fully known to Chukovsky. This is the way this talented fellow says it: "The Revolution he sang of was not the Revolution which was taking place around him, but another one, a true one, a flaming one." But we just heard that he sang of ugliness, and not of a burning flame, and he sang of this ugliness because it was a Russian one, and not because it was revolutionary. And now we discover that he did not make his peace with the ugliness of the true revolution at all, just because that ugliness was Russian, but that he sang exaltingly of a revolution, of another one, a true and flaming one, only because that revolution was directed against an existing ugliness.

Vanka kills Katka with the rifle which was given him by his class to defend the Revolution. We say that this is incidental to the Revolution, but not of the Revolution. Blok means his poem to say: I accept this also, because here, also, I hear the dynamics of events, and the music of the storm. Now comes his interpreter Chukovsky, and explains it. The murder of Katka by Vanka is the ugliness of the Revolution. Blok accepts Russia, even with this ugliness, because it is Russian. But at the same time when he sings of the murder of Katka by Vanka and of the pillaging of the houses, Blok sings of a revolution, but not of this ugly present-day real Russian Revolution, but of another, a truer, flaming one. The address of this true and flaming revolution Chukovsky will tell us soon, right away.

But if the Revolution to Blok is Russia herself, just as she is, then what is the meaning of the "orator," who looks upon the Revolution as treason? What is the meaning of the priest who walks by the side? What is the meaning of "the old world like a mangy cur"? What is the meaning of Denikin, Miliukov, Chernov and the émigrés? Russia has been split in half. That is the Revolution. Blok called one-half a mangy cur, and the other half he blessed with the blessings at his command, that is, with verses and with Christ. But Chukovsky declares all this to be a mere misunderstanding. What charlatanism of words, what an indecent slovenliness of thought, what a spiritual devastation, what a cheap and mean and shameful jabber of speech!

To be sure, Blok is not one of ours, but he reached towards us. And in doing so, he broke down. But the result of his impulse is the most significant work of our epoch. His poem, *The Twelve,* will remain forever.

C. M. Bowra (essay date 1932)

SOURCE: "The Position of Alexander Blok," in *The Criterion,* Vol. XI, No. XLIV, April, 1932, pp. 422-38.

[*In the following essay, Bowra assesses Blok's place among European poets, identifying and examining three phases in his poetic development.*]

Alexander Block died on August 7th, 1921. His funeral was conducted with all the honours due to a great poet who had died before his time at the early age of forty-one. In the ten years since his death his reputation has not suffered, and impartial judges place him in the select company of great Russian poets. But he has left no followers. The man who wrote the first and greatest poem of the Russian Revolution has become a figure of history, admired for his poetic achievement, studied with the sympathy and slight condescension that we keep for the past, but without followers and without influence on living writers. Modern Russia has made many experiments, in

Futurism and folk-song, in classicism and ballad, but it has never looked back to Blok. The truth is that Blok, despite the miracle of *The Twelve,* despite his enthusiastic advocacy of the October Revolution, belonged to a generation whose force was spent. The new world had nothing to learn from him, and because his chapter is closed, it is possible to consider his place in European literature, to assess his peculiar contribution and to see why in spite of his extraordinary talents he belongs to the past.

> **What Valéry has done in France and Mr. Yeats in Ireland, Blok did in Russia.**
>
> —*C. M. Bowra*

The special interest of Blok as a figure, not in Russian but European poetry, is that he is one of a group of poets who in different countries started from the Symbolist ideals of Mallarmé and developed them in directions which would have startled and perhaps horrified their creator. What Valéry has done in France and Mr. Yeats in Ireland, Blok did in Russia. He took the Symbolist theory and tried it, altering it as he found its limitations, gradually emancipating himself from its strictest tenets as he found it inadequate for the expression of his emotional experience. In this and in other respects his poetic development was curiously like that of Mr. Yeats. Both began with writing poetry withdrawn from common experience and based on dreams. Both revolted from this with something of horror and a sense of having been tricked. For both there followed a period of transition when they passed from the poetry of trance and vision to a harder outline and less 'dream-burdened' style, training themselves with poetical drama. Blok's last stage, the stage of his great lyrics and *The Twelve,* is singularly reminiscent of Mr. Yeats's poetry after 1910. It reveals the same passionate intensity, the same absorption in the emotions and finally the same prophetic insight and burning loyalty to his country. *The Twelve,* like "Easter, 1916," is the remarkable record of a seer brought into touch with an appalling reality and writing of it. Unfortunately, beyond this no comparison is possible because after 1919 Blok hardly wrote again.

This similarity of two destinies is instructive, as it shows how two men, quite uninfluenced one by another, both assailed the same problems in literature and found similar solutions. Yeats living in western Europe is still the great poet of his age, still maturing and developing his poetry in perfect accord with his times. Blok's work has been less fortunate because of the violent break which modern Russia has made with its traditional culture, and he is already with the past. But both poets are part of the same movement, had because of this, they have an interest additional to that found in their work. They are both the ripe products of French Symbolism as it was taught by Mallarmé, and they are of a special interest because their work is a commentary on its adequacy and their lives a measure of its power to stimulate poetic achievement.

The Russian Symbolist movement began about 1894, a time when Russian poetry had reached its lowest ebb. It was in its origin simply a revival of poetry under French influence, learning lessons from Baudelaire and Verlaine and concerned deeply with restoring the beauty and purity of verse. Its leaders, Constantine Balmont and Valeri Bryusov, were symbolists only in the broadest sense. They had absorbed none of the severer lessons of Mallarmé, but they wanted to rid poetry of its prose elements and to restore its lost element of music. From the French they had learned a courage in the treatment of new themes, a high sense of art and the importance of personal passion. From Baudelaire they had learned

> les parfums, les couleurs, et les sons se répondent

and their ideal was to produce an exquisite, allusive poetry free of any desire to preach or to impart information. The severer doctrine was better understood by Annensky, who in his sensitive and concise verse approached much nearer to the condition of music than either Balmont or Bryusov, but his work passed almost unnoticed and his influence was small.

Apart from Annensky, the first wave of the Russian Symbolists achieved little in words that would have satisfied Mallarmé, but though their art looked back to Baudelaire, their philosophy of life was profoundly original and was deduced from their theory of art. They accepted wholeheartedly the notion of the antithesis between poetry and science with its corollary that the stuff of the one is not the stuff of the other. Believing that when the poet creates, reality is revealed to him as it can never be through the reasoning intellect, they concentrated their attention on this, just as Mr. Yeats in his early poetry considered that the state of poetic creation was a state of trance, revealing a world that could only be found in this way, whose problems could only be solved in dreams. The Russian Symbolists, having separated poetry from science, thought that all that mattered was poetry and that its raw state was the only reality. This mystical idealism is to be found in Vyacheslav Ivanov and Theodor Sologub, but it reached its culmination in Blok.

Blok served hardly any apprenticeship as a poet. His early verse is astonishingly perfect, and to the onlooker it must have seemed that here was an exquisite and gifted poet who had done at twenty-three what he would probably spend his life in repeating. He soon became the inspired mouthpiece of the younger Symbolists and found his high priest in Andrey Bely. What they valued in him was the extraordinary life to which his verse gave expression. In 1901 and 1902 Blok was the subject of a remarkable mystical experience He lived a life of spiritual association with a 'Beautiful Lady,' a divine figure who has something in common with the Sophia of the mystic philosopher Soloviev. Beginning as an undefined 'She,' she becomes 'the Queen of purity,' 'the Beautiful Lady,' 'the Mysterious Virgin.' She is at once an incarnation of the divine and an object of ideal love. The poems to her are a triumph of emotional evocation. Put into prose they mean little, but as they stand in verse with their devotion to 'la musique avant toute chose,' they convey those mysterious and exquisite emotions which Blok felt towards her. There are no clear outlines, all is mist and solitude, but in this vague world the poet waits for her anxiously, hears at dawn or sunset her footsteps in the infinite sky, shuts his eyes for fear or cries to her, knowing that she will understand his cry.

More than any poetry of his contemporaries, more perhaps than almost any written in France by the leaders of the movement, this poetry is all but entirely symbolist. It calls up only frames of mind, and they are full of emotion. They could not be called up in prose at all, and if they could, one would be very like another. But by the mysterious quality of his verse, by its cadence and associations, Blok recreates in his readers just that indefinable series of emotions in which he knew the Beautiful Lady and wrote about her. He does precisely what Valéry claims as the task of the poet, when he says: 'Il ne s'agit point du tout en poésie de transmettre a quelqu'un ce qui se passe d'intelligible dans un autre. Il s'agit de créer dans le premier un état dont l'expression soit précisément et singulièrement celle qui le lvi communique.' By the pure doctrine of Symbolism he may be judged and found satisfactory.

The vision of the Beautiful Lady was for Blok and his friends much more than a poetic fantasy. It was an experience so real and so powerful that it became almost a cult and aroused unimaginable expectations. Bely records how the circle trusted in the vision as a direct manifestation of God, portending some overpowering revelation, and waited for it to come. It never came. While they were still waiting, the vision ceased. Blok had already begun to write poems telling his fear that She would desert him, and before the volume of poems *To the Beautiful Lady* had been published, he found himself emptied of his ecstatic experience and confronted by disciples who complained that they had been betrayed.

The end of this extraordinary marvel was a crisis in Blok's life and poetry. He had to start afresh with a gnawing conviction that he had been tricked, that he had failed in a task which had absorbed his whole being. The disillusionment was deeply embittering and made him a far less happy man; but out of the conflict in himself which it started, he began to make a new kind of poetry. The change was gradual. He was too deeply accustomed to his other world to bring his thoughts down to earth at once. In the poems of this period of transition, written between 1904 and 1908 and published by him in the second volume of his collected works, we see him finding his way to a new manner and to a new view of life.

It is hard to characterize this intermediate poetry of Blok's. It is experimental both in matter and manner and does not submit easily to generalization. Perhaps one clue is that Blok was trying to find some place midway between the world of dreams and the world of fact. At least he sometimes gives a reality to visions, sometimes sees reality in a haze of dream. To the second class belong those sketches of Petersburg and the Neva delta, marshy plains where buildings and human beings fade into mist and the division is imperceptible between life and dream. To the first class belong many poems where dreams are made to live with a sudden importance for him. He calls up the shadows of jesters, kings and knights in the poem **'Shadows on the Wall,'** and speaks to them of all they once meant to him, or he writes of mischievous spirits of woods and fields, called **'Earth's Bubbles'** after Macbeth's words. The climax of this style is the famous poem **'The Unknown Woman.'** In this Blok, under the influence of wine, sees a woman passing between the diners and drinkers at a restaurant. She is described realistically with her rings and feathered hat, though she is a creature of vision as much as The Beautiful Lady—but this one is seen only in wine. The bitterness of defeat is clothed in a lyrical poem of singularly exquisite style.

Blok was a creature of strong emotions, and they often carried him away from gloom. Lacking entirely irony and shyness, and being used, as Russians are, to following the vagaries of his powerful temperament, he was able to write a poetry that covered most of the passions known to humanity.

—*C. M. Bowra*

More interesting than these poems of dream, where words are still symbols of emotions and to some extent of ideas, are those poems where Blok is feeling his way to a more definite utterance and writing about more ordinary things. A beautiful example of a poem which is half symbolical is **'Son and Mother.'** In this the symbolism is of Christ and the Virgin, the story of His first wanderings and divine neglect of His mother because of His thoughts of God, but the inner meaning is of Blok who deserts his mother and comes back to her—to die. Simpler even than this is a purely descriptive poem of a woman growing old in her hut after her daughter has died, sitting and sewing with her needle and thread. In this, too, there is some elementary symbolism. The thread is associated with the thread of life, but such an association means little outside itself. The poet is beginning to find his way from symbols of a mystical reality to something more concrete. He is content now to convey some emotional passage of events through simple words. Gradually he is coming to see common things as full of significance, though he cannot say quite what they signify. They touch his pity or his affection, and for the time that is enough for him.

But the mood of underlying bitterness could not be placated in this way. Blok felt deeply that once his visions had duped him, and to the anger that this feeling aroused he returned. In his lyrical play, *The Unknown Woman,* he made satirical fun of his first ideal love, and when he came to his next volume in 1907 he combined a consummate style with a deep sense of a discord at the heart of things.

In the poems here collected lies Blok's chief claim to fame. His style has changed. Diffuseness and vagueness have given place to a hard outline, an economy of effects and a boldness of imagery that are unique in Russian literature. The varied rhythms of his middle period yield to more conventional forms used with easy mastery. Particularly he loves the four-lined stanza which he learned from Fet, with its octosyllabic lines and alternate female and male rhymes. He can now say in four verses what before took eight, and the concentration of thought leads to a great increase of power. There is now no place for rhetoric or sentimentality. This poetry is full of powerful emotion, expressed with a directness and clarity that are unique in our time.

The contents of these poems are extremely varied. The greater bulk deals with the poet's own life. Perhaps at the root of most lies his deep underlying gloom from which he tries to escape by different ways, only to find himself back where he started. In **'The Dance of Death'** he sees himself as a corpse brought back from the grave to mix with living men and women. The second part of this is characteristic of his pessimistic despair at his worst, and it shows the concentration of his art.

> Night, a street, a lamp, a chemist-shop,
> A meaningless and dull world.
> Live another quarter of a century—
> All will be the same. There is no way out.
>
> Die—you will begin afresh
> And all will be repeated as of old:
> Night, the canal's frozen ripple,
> The chemist-shop, the street, the lamp.

But no poetry, and no poet, can live for ever on despair. Blok was a creature of strong emotions, and they often carried him away from gloom. Lacking entirely irony and shyness, and being used, as Russians are, to following the vagaries of his powerful temperament, he was able to write a poetry that covered most of the passions known to humanity. This is itself a high claim in a time when the passions have been desiccated by analysis and education, but the measure of his power is more fully realized when we add that to this great material he gave a form that is without rival in directness and vividness of presentation. He has a gift of seeing only the passion that dominates him and avishing on it the powers of a most fertile imagination and a singularly rich speech. He is sparing of images, but when they come nothing can withstand them. The brilliant pictures lift the passions into the world of pure art, making them radiant and triumphant. Their use is essential to the poem, as they give absolutely the right emotional note. Without them the poem might be intelligible as prose, but only with them does it reveal its individuality and take its readers by storm into catching the exact intonation of the poet's meaning. This was a relic of the lessons Blok had learned in his symbolist youth, and this use of images exactly suited his intention. He places some compelling, concrete image as the keystone of a poem, whose lines it co-ordinates and whose weight it sustains. His method is not to accumulate image upon image, but to concentrate on a single picture, which contains in itself what is most important in the poem and subdues a set of details to a unity of design.

No less surprising than the power of presentation is the great range of subject, the endless variety of these poems. In his love poems alone Blok has struck more chords than any living writer. What Yeats has done in depth and intensity, Blok has done in variety and range. No doubt he was helped to this by his lack of irony or any false sense of shame, civilizing qualities so inimical to genius. If we allow him every advantage in his circumstances, remembering that he lived in a society singularly free and candid, his performance is still astonishing because it is seldom that men taste all the possibilities of passion without losing much of their personality in the process. In some ways Blok's performance recalls that of Verlaine, who equally had no sense of shame, but the resemblance is superficial. Whatever Blok touches, he treats it with seriousness and intensity, without any of Verlaine's happy air of indiscretion or love of being naughty. He can be purely lyrical, seeing his love as an angel shape coming with the smell of mint, or he can explore the dark places of lust, discord, and humiliation. The poem **'Humiliation'** is a study of venal love as searching and realistic as his poems of pure love are ethereal and mysterious. The depths he plumbs fill him at times with intolerable guilt and remorse, and he writes with heart-rending intimacy of his melancholy walks through the storm-ridden city waiting to be forgiven. When forgiveness comes, he bursts into a song of praise, or he stands apart from passion and mocks the memory of his past loves, seeing himself on a mountain from which he sends down an avalanche into the valleys where he once loved and kissed. He can make poetry even out of small disagreements which arise because he is glad when his wife is melancholy or because when he is ill he feels no more need of her tender caresses.

The same sincerity and power can be seen in all Blok's poems which deal with the emotions. He always lifts them to the level of music and rids them of that particular setting which might make them unbearably painful or compel us to intrude our moral judgments of the poet. At this level there is no place for condemnation, because the poem explains so perfectly what the poet feels that any desire to judge him is at once answered, and here indeed to know him is to forgive him. Nor in many cases is any moral judgment called for. Blok had a great store of pity which makes some of his poems tremble with emotion. In **'On a Child's Death'** or **'A Voice from the Chorus'** there is a note of pity which recalls the finest quality of Pushkin's verse. In the first the intolerable burden of death struggles with religious resignation, and tears are not defeated by the presence of Infinite Wisdom. In the second, perhaps the finest of all his personal poems, he warns his friends of their present lives and the dark future before them,

> We weep, how often, I and you,
> Over our lives' poor pitiful ways,
> But if, my friends, we only knew
> The cold and gloom of coming days!

> To-day a gentle hand you press,
> Play with it, sparkling, wild,
> And weep to find untruthfulness,
> Or in your hands a knife caress,
>   Poor child, poor child!

> There is no end to craft or lies,
> No sign of death appears;
> A blackening light will blind the eyes
> And planets madly sweep the skies
>   For years, for years.

> The last age shall be worst of all,
> Which you and I shall see.
> The sky will be wrapped in a guilty pall,
> On lips shall laughter freeze and fall,
> The waste of Not-to-be . . .

> You wait for spring, my child, but spring
> Will cheat your eyes.
> To heaven you summon up the sun—
> No sun will rise.
> You cry, but crying like a stone
> Sinks down and dies.

> Be happy with your lives and ways—
> Silent as water, low as grass!
> Oh, if we knew what comes to pass,
> The cold and gloom of coming days!

Pity and tenderness, pity for a generation doomed to disaster, tenderness for those who cannot defend themselves against the blows of chance, these are perhaps the outstanding features of Blok's lyrical poetry. Released from his visions he wrote from the rich treasures of his own nature, forgetting his own disillusionment in his sorrow for others. He saw himself with curiously dispassionate eyes and was completely devoid of self-pity or the other emotions which too often follow from a life which has no self-discipline. His poetry is the record of his emotional life, but it has come through an intelligence singularly candid and free from prepossession. He sees himself somehow as a spectacle and removes any suspicions that he is dramatizing himself in the cause of literature or adding for effect anything alien to the pure original emotion. Other poets, for instance, have written about their death-beds, and the results have seldom been fortunate. But Blok's poem **'Vsye eto bylo, bylo, bylo'** is a triumph. Each suggested death-bed is a perfect miniature sketched with the few right words, and the whole is pulled into shape by the last verse where the different prospects of death and life after death are absorbed into a confession of faith that what he has loved so passionately cannot pass beyond tracking, that he cannot forget all the trembling of this pitiful life and all this unintelligible passion.

In these straightforward, strong poems Blok's characteristic qualities have perhaps passed outside his time, and he writes, as great poets have written, of fundamental things in clear and masterful words. If he had always written like this, we could say that all he had learned from France was a high standard of workmanship and a belief in the importance of his own emotions. But he could have learned as much from his own countrymen, Pushkin and Lermontov, and it might seem absurd to say that he was ever a symbolist again after the publication of his first volume of verse. But though he had been brought to earth and though he made his style more concise and more exact every year, yet fundamentally, despite his early crisis and the despair which it induced in him, Blok kept to the end of his poetic activity something of his old visionary self. Unlike Mr. Yeats who after the poems of his early manhood seems to have lost the gift of ready and easy inspiration, Blok's experience of poetic creation remained something quite remarkable and in a sense outside himself. He does not seem to have written anything unless, as he thought, it was given to him almost in vision. In his poem **'Artist'** (written in 1913, when he was at the height of his powers), he tells the process by which he makes a poem. He begins by describing himself as waiting for something to happen. He hears a far-off ringing, which comes nearer. Then an extraordinary state overwhelms him, the state of poetic trance.

> A whirlwind from the sea? Are song-birds calling?
> From paradisal Trees? Does Time stand fast?
> Or are the apple-blooms of maytime falling
> In snowy showers? Has an angel passed?

The trance lasts, holding out a promise of some inconceivable destiny, but then comes the crisis. The reason enters, conquers the vision and kills it. All that is left is—the poem. This is like a captive bird in a cage.

> Here is my cage with heavy iron door,
> Burnished and golden in the sunset fire.
> And here my bird, who was so gay before,
> Swings on the hoop and sings behind the wire.
>
> Its wings are clipped, its songs are learned by
>   heart.
> You like to listen at the cage's door?
> The songs delight you, while my wounds still
>   smart.
> I wait for something and am bored once more.

All that is left of the fine frenzy is the poem, and what can that mean to the poet who has known whence it came? What interest can he take in this captive relic of that exalted experience?

As the creative vision still remained something sublime and external for Blok, he still attached a vast metaphysical importance to it and never acquiesced in a material philosophy. He still needed some power above himself which should be the focus of his emotions and give shape to the diverse phenomena of his imaginative life. He could only accept their significance if they were attached to some principle. The symbolism of the Church, which naturally played a large part in his imagery, was never a dominating influence. Its insistent ethical claims meant little to him, and its limited freedom was not sufficient for his vast emotional wants. He needed something transcendental to

keep his devotion, something with a promise of an unreckonable revelation. The habit he had formed as a young man of expecting something incalculable to happen had not really left him. He still was a reader of signs, and the signs were still given him in his poetic experience. Gradually a single object came to attract his powers and interest, something vague and yet sufficiently concrete, something which could be the object of devoted love and yet submit to his mordant irony and carping blame. In Russia he found the final object of his dreams. Here was the ideal entity, mysterious, cruel and lovable, ideal and yet perfectly real, known in the countryside which he loved, in the humble multitudes whom he championed, in the religion where he sought for symbols of suffering and sacrifice. Russia revived to some degree the feelings he had had for the Beautiful Lady, but it had more personality and stirred all his emotions from hatred and contempt to love and devoted service.

In the section of his third volume called **Native Land,** Blok collected his poems on Russia from 1907 to 1916. The thread that runs through them is the notion of suffering, purification and ultimate glory. Though she is now tyrannical, yet the time of revelation is coming. Just as in his youth, he had waited for an apocalypse, so now he waited for another; but he expected it to come through blood and destruction. When the war came, Blok felt that the time of testing was near. As the slaughter continued and nothing happened, he grew gloomy and distrustful, writing magnificently of the dumbness and emptiness everywhere in the world. He still felt that the Kingdom of God was at hand, and then he fell again into gloom, asking how long the vultures must wheel and the mothers go on weeping. He felt a wind battering at his house, and he was not sure what it portended. Was there a bride waiting, and had he the courage to open his door and go out to her?

When the first revolution came in March, 1917, Blok was delighted; but his nature was not satisfied till the second revolution in October. His aunt records his feelings at the time: 'It seemed to him that the old world was really destroyed and that in its place there must appear something new and beautiful. He went about young, cheerful, fresh, with shining eyes, listening for that revolutionary music in the noise of the old world's collapse which on his own testimony sounded unceasingly in his ears.'

The reflection of this mood can be seen in **The Twelve,** written in January, 1918. It was at once acclaimed as a masterpiece, recited before large crowds nightly and translated into most European languages. It is quite unlike any other poem of Blok's, and it is incontestably a masterpiece. Its method recalls in some ways *The Waste Land,* though it is less consistently symbolical and has a narrative structure. The rhythms vary from sharp octosyllabic couplets to free verse and verse formed on the songs of the streets and factories. The language is conversational, even slang. The rhymes are irregular and often dissonant, but the deliberate discords are well fitted to this crowded epic of a falling world. The real difficulty is what Blok meant by it. What is the significance of this story of twelve red guardsmen walking round in a snowstorm, shooting and bullying the bourgeoisie, quarrelling over a girl and shooting her by mistake, only to find in the end that Christ is leading them on?

Blok's incontestable fame lies in his personal lyrics. In these he achieved a body of poetry unequalled in our time for their power, style, and range.

—*C. M. Bowra*

Taken apart from Blok's other poetry the poem, magnificent and moving as it is, must remain a puzzle; but if we remember its antecedents, its meaning is clear enough. Christ stands for that salvation which Blok had for years dreamed to be impending for Russia. It comes through blood and slaughter, through men who do not know what they are doing. The theory that blood could purify had been stated by Blok as far back as 1910, when he wrote **'I dut chaoy, i dni, i gody.'** There he had seen the sword as the accompaniment of the cross. The same idea remained with him. The old world must be destroyed, and then would come the Earthly Paradise, the goal of all his visions for which he had waited these long years. To this purpose all the movements of **The Twelve** contribute. The bourgeois standing in the cold, the mangy dog that follows the soldiers, the blinding snowstorm and the red flag—the symbolism of these is simple enough. In a march like this there will be those who care nothing and those who are slow to follow. The whirling, spiral snowstorm is Blok's favourite image for passion, in which men do what they do not understand. The killing of the girl Katya is part of the plan. It represents the mad destruction of what men have once loved, but now hate because they think they have been betrayed. Her death makes them gloomy and repentant and the more ready to follow their leader, Christ, the symbol of spiritual self-sufficiency and exaltation produced by suffering and pain.

With **The Twelve** and **The Scythians,** a call to Europe not to desert Russia in her need written in the same month, Blok ended his poetical life. For three and a half years he lived on, protected by his great name and the kind offices of Maxim Gorky who got him a post under the new government. He worked hard, editing, translating, writing a history of the first revolution, but hardly any poetry. He started work again at his autobiographical poem **Retaliation,** but gave it up. Something had gone out of him. He was ill, he was extremely depressed. He seems to have lost faith in himself, in the revolution, in life. Gorky has left a terrible picture of him in his last days, bursting from his habitual silence into a denunciation of the intellect: 'The thing is that we have become too clever to believe in God and not strong enough to believe in ourselves. . . . The brain, the brain. . . . It is not an organ to be relied upon— it is monstrously developed. It is a swelling like a goitre.' He died in the hot summer of 1921, sitting upright on his chair, keeping the silence he had kept for many days. A vast procession filed through his sultry room as he lay unrecognizable on the bed where, because of his pain, he had not been able to lie for some weeks.

Blok's incontestable fame lies in his personal lyrics. In these he achieved a body of poetry unequalled in our time for their power, style, and range. But besides these there are those more intimate, more debatable poems where he expressed his philosophy of life, his mysticism and inspired hopes. These are harder to judge. They are certainly not suited to the temperament of modern Russia and there is a bitter irony in this prophet of the revolution preaching what he did. He believed that the time had come when the intellect would yield to the inspired stirrings of the heart and the scientific view of life to ecstatic exaltation. Over these poems there hangs the pathos of false prophecy, and the pathos is no less because Blok realized that he was wrong before he died. With the Revolution he thought that at last his visionary expectations were to be fulfilled, but the Christ who led the Twelve turned out to be the god of materialism and mechanization. Once again his visions had played him false, and if in the last resort, a poet must be judged only on the truth of what he writes, Blok must join the company of those who for all their eloquence lacked a real vision of reality. He must come down to posterity through the gate of lying dreams.

And yet this is not all the truth. Blok stood for a principle that is not yet dead, however difficult it may seem. He considered, and his life was a defence of his belief, that a poet must write out of his intuition, his emotional experience, ridding himself of the deceptive processes of logic and dialectic. To this doctrine he remained true to the last, and his words to Gorky were his dying defence of it. Nor, strictly speaking, is any other theory of poetry defensible or tenable. The processes of demonstration have their uses in prose, but they have few in poetry. What disturbs us in Blok, what makes him seem a strange enough figure even to Western Europe to-day, was that his instinct was too withdrawn in dreams always to note actual events with a clear eye. He was too full of hope and faith, too devoted to his belief in a coming Kingdom of God. To those who read poets for their practical judgment or for their political insight, he will seem unsatisfactory, though even they will do well to remember that he saw clearer than any other poet the coming agony of Russia, foretelling it again and again with an uncanny prescience. But for others who read poetry for the quality of the vision it records, Blok must have a special place. He was entirely true to his standards, and his poetry is always poetry, powerful to recreate in his hearers that almost audible music which he heard when inspiration descended on him and he lived outside time in a region of unspeakable joy.

Janko Lavrin (essay date 1935)

SOURCE: "Alexander Blok," in *Aspects of Modernism: From Wilde to Pirandello,* Books for Libraries Press, 1968, pp. 115-38.

[*In the following excerpt, originally published in 1935,
Lavrin investigates Blok's poetry in terms of romanticism
and Russian symbolism.*]

I

Although the poetic work of Alexander Blok is striking
and original enough to defy any labels, some of its aspects can best be understood if treated in connection with
the Russian symbolism. The latter came mainly out of that
"decadent" current whose devotees were anxious to raise
the formal standard of poetry, and also to free the literature of their country from various social and other purposes. Realizing the dangers of too narrow an "art for art's
sake" (combined with an equally narrow egotism, derived
from Nietzsche), a few members of that group began to
champion a deeper conception and a religious affirmation
of life. This effort had to pass through numerous literary
as well as philosophic ventures and adventures, before it
crystallized—during the first few years of the present century—into a definite movement, and reached its height in
such poets as Vyacheslav Ivanov, Andrey Biely, and
Alexander Blok.

One of the characteristics of that movement was a strong
impulse to go beyond mere art and literature, and to create
a new consciousness, a new man. Such an aim was bound
however to come into contact with the religious thought
of Russia: with that of Dostoevsky, and also of Vladimir
Solovyev—a remarkable thinker who had been working
(during the last quarter of the nineteenth century) towards
an harmonious union of art, philosophy, religion and life.
Utopian as he was, Solovyev dreamed of a universal regeneration through love, and through such an inner change
as would lead mankind to what he called the "integral
fullness of existence".

His literary work was a sincere endeavour to unify all
constructive aspects of modern mentality for the sake of
such fullness. Unfortunately, his philosophic training did
not entirely save him from the fallacies of those romantics
who, instead of unifying such elements as thought, emotion, science, religion, philosophy and art, only confused
them, that is, blurred the boundaries between them. Deeply versed in European and Eastern thought, in the teaching of the gnostics, as well as in Christian mysticism,
Solovyev recorded his spiritual strivings, not only in his
philosophic essays, but also in several poems, since his
involved theories did not kill the poet in him. With his
belief that "all transient things are but symbols"; with his
visionary power and his will to change the present-day
man, he may justly be called the first important representative of the Russian symbolism proper (as distinct from
the French symbolism, for example, which was concerned
chiefly with new methods of poetic expression). And
Solovyev's influence is conspicuous most of all in Alexander Blok—the towering figure of that school.

II

It sounds like a paradox that Alexander Blok, who is now
regarded as the greatest Russian modernist, had practically no idea of modern poetry until he was eighteen. The
favourite reading of his youth was the dreamy Zhukovsky,
and those German romantics with whom he felt a certain
affinity. Of decisive importance for his development was,
however, his acquaintance with Solovyev's works. These
were largely responsible for the trend, perhaps even for
the awakening, of his poetic genius. Like Solovyev, he
identified the "World-Soul", or the "Sophia", of the gnostics with the mystical Eternal Feminine from which he
began to expect a kind of salvation and a transfiguration
of life, with all his erotic ardour. His awakened sex turned
thus entirely within, to the phantoms conjured up by his
own poetic imagery. He not only thought—he actually felt
Love to be the key to the mystery of life and the universe.
And the result of his inspirations was one of the most
accomplished romantic books in modern literature: his
Verses about the Lady Fair.

These first poems of his, which appeared in 1905, blend
Solovyev's visionary yearning for the miraculous with the
erotic dreaminess of a Novalis, and the music of Shelley with the tenderness of Dante's *Vita Nuova*. They are
like the prayers of a troubadour singing the praise of the
Eternal Feminine. Unaware of the world around, he sings
like a man in a trance, or like a medium whose very passivity is one of the causes of his intoxication. His images
are vague as if enveloped in a haze; but they are suggestive by their vagueness, as well as by Blok's uncanny
sense for the "aura" of words and symbols. His language
may still be reminiscent at times of Solovyev, but the
melody is entirely his own. And it reveals already a treasury of new rhythms, of new musical and prosodic
devices.

It was above all Solovyev the mystic that hovered like a
guardian spirit over Blok's poetry of that period. Yet the
prayer-like serenity of those early poems (he wrote about
eight hundred of them before he was twenty-five) was
disturbed, more than once, by sudden flashes of the opposite depth: that of spiritual split and descent, of disappointment, of rebellion, indicated so far only in terms of
forebonding and of fear.

> I am afraid of my double-faced soul,
> And I carefully conceal
> My diabolic and wild face
> Underneath this sacred armour.

Aware of such a danger, he clung the more fervently to
his mystical Beatrice. But his premonitions that the inevitable was bound to happen are uttered in a number of
poems, and above all in these verses, addressed to her.

> I have foreknown Thee! Oh, I have foreknown
>   Thee.
>   Going,
> The years have shown me Thy premonitory face.
> Intolerably clear, the farthest sky is glowing.
> I wait in silence Thy withheld and worshipped
>   grace!
> The farthest sky is glowing: white for Thy
>   appearing.

Yet terror clings to me: Thy image will be strange.
And insolent suspicion will arouse upon Thy
    nearing.
The features long foreknown, beheld at last will
    change.
How shall I then be fallen!—low, with no defender:
Dead dreams will conquer me, the glory, glimpsed,
    will change.
The farthest sky is glowing! Nearer looms the
    splendour.
Yet terror clings to me. Thy image will be strange.

III

What happened was in fact a complete change of her image, resulting from the split between the actual life and Blok's inner vision of life. To follow this mutation means to penetrate into the tragedy of Blok the man and the poet, for as a true Russian he never made a distinction between the two.

In an essay written in 1910 (during the growing crisis of Russian symbolism) Blok gives a flowery and yet carefully veiled explanation of what had taken place. He deals in it with spiritual realities only; but as these are treated in their intersection with his poetic activities on the one hand, and with the actual life around on the other, Blok touches upon the problem of Art and Life in some of its acutest "personal" aspects. He realized soon enough that the phantom of his Beatrice had been turned into a vague myth which, instead of bridging, only widened the gap between the actual and the transcendental. The myth became, moreover, untenable as soon as Blok was compelled to descend into the region of concrete love and of the concrete everyday existence. The two worlds—the world of values and the world of facts—proved incompatible at once. There even was no guarantee that his glowing visions of old had not been mere subjective fancies, instead of intuitions with a higher reality behind them.

In this state of doubt and bewilderment, Blok was assailed by a swarm of "doubles" which had been dormant in him as an antithesis to the former dreamer. A further complication may have been due to his disappointment in his married life from which he had expected a miracle that never came. Be this as it may, he suddenly found himself cut off from the "streaming light" of those regions where his imagination had soared before. And on the plane of actual life his Lady Fair became an impossibility, a phantom. His visions now appeared as unreal to him as a puppet show.

"If I painted a picture of it", he confesses in his essay, "I would depict it in this manner: in the lilac dusk of an endless world there sways an enormous white catafalque, and on it lies a doll whose face is dimly reminiscent of the countenance which once had shone through the heavenly dawns. . . . And so all is finished: my miraculous world has turned into the arena of my personal acting—into a puppet-show in which I myself act in the company of my strange puppets. In other words, my own life has become

art. . . . I stand before it all without knowing what to do either with the show, or with my life turned into art; for in my immediate presence there lives my own phantom-creation: neither alive nor dead—a blue ghost. . . . It is here that arises the problem of the curse of art, of a return to life, of service to the community. . . ."

Blok is here confronted with the problem of art and life, not from the angle of "aestheticism", but from that of the life-values which he is unable to find on the plane of life itself. Having lost his romantic faith, he has still preserved all his romantic temperament and nostalgia which was now beginning to play a regular spiritual havoc with him. To the question as to what to do in such a situation, he answers that there might be "several horrid outlets", but such an answer is in itself an evasion. It is all the more interesting to study in this light the whole of Blok's subsequent poetry. For his work became henceforth a strange psychological and human document.

Blok's lyrical play, *The Puppet Show* (*Balaganchik*, 1905), was one of his first successful attempts to ridicule his former visionary phase by means of a buffoonery. In another little play, *The Unknown Lady* (*Neznakomka*), he lets his mystical Beatrice—symbolized as a star—fall down on to our earth where she becomes an ordinary prostitute. In a haunting poem under the same title (written a few years later) we find her in a suburban tavern near Petrograd. In black silk and in a hat with ostrich feathers, she sits there every night, and surrounded by drunkards, still emanates the mystery of another world:

And in my brain the soft slow flittering
Of ostrich feathers waves once more;
And fathomless the azure glittering
Where two eyes blossom on the shore.

But glimpses of the sort are accessible to the poet only through drunkenness, through wine. In wine alone he still recovers, now and then, his lost visions for which he yearns in the squalor of existence all the more strongly the less he believes in their reality. A general feature of Blok's love poems is that in all the women he sings, he still wishes to find a reflection of his vanished Beatrice, whereby he only widens the gap between the ideal and the real.

IV

Such moods on the part of Blok coincided with the general gloom and despondency after the abortive revolution of 1905. The atmosphere of emptiness, of nihilism, of a cynical *après nous le déluge,* grew in intensity near after year—until the great explosion of 1917 took place. And this background strengthened the poignancy of Blok's poetry which now became, more than ever, a diary of his intimate experiences.

The early phase of Blok's poetry was that of an ecstatic trance from which he had a rude awakening. But when deprived of the ecstasies of the height, and unable to continue his "puppet-show" as though his subjective phantoms were the real thing, he yet refused any compromise with reality. He plunged instead into the lower depths of the subconscious and began to drug himself with the emotional chaos of the "psychics". The ecstasy of despair he preferred to no ecstasy at all. Had he found a religious outlet, or else had he been shallow enough to adopt the gospel of the "æsthetes", he would have been spared that pessimism which henceforth clung to him for good. For the only intensity he knew from now on was the intensity of negation. But even in this mood and on this level Blok needed a substitute for his Beatrice. And he discovered it in a new beloved to whom he transferred all his disappointed yearning, as well as his passion for the unfathomable and the boundless. This new beloved of his was Russia. Not the "holy", but the irrational Russia of endless spaces, of winds and blizzards, of flying *troikas*, of maddening nostalgia, drunkenness, poverty and chaos.

> I will listen to the voice of drunken Russia,
> And I will rest under a tavern roof.

Snow-masks—such is the title of his first book of that period. And its main note is the one of intoxication. Intoxication with blizzards, with wine and with morbid passion. The delight of self-annihilation rings in the accents of his sensual **"Faina"**. In the more virile verses of another section, **"Enchantment through Fire"**, one feels a note of temporary acceptance of life. This is followed however by a still greater despondency and by a wish to forget himself in psychic drugs. But a time came when even these would help no longer. He was compelled to look at the world with a sobered mind and with more than sobered eyes.

V

The prevalent mood of that phase (roughly from 1908 to 1917) can best be defined as spiteful apathy. The drabness and vulgarity of existence overpowered him to such an extent as to make all effort seem futile. The title of a typical record of those years, *The Loathsome World,* is in itself significant. In *Iambi* he tried to stir up his crushed faith in life. In the romantic drama, *The Rose and the Cross* (1912), his smouldering devotion to the Lady Fair flared up once more; and in the cycle "Carmen" he rekindled his former passion. Yet the fire that was now burning came too much out of the ashes. Everything seemed drab and empty. Forebodings of a great universal catastrophe—on an apocalyptic scale—began to hover over some of his poems like ominous shadows. But the deeper he penetrated into the pain and futility of life he saw around, the more intense he became as a poet. His language was now laconic, terse and realistic. Having abandoned the method of vague and abstract symbols, he made his very realism intensely symbolic. An approximate idea of this can perhaps be gathered from the **"Danse Macabre"**, paraphrased by R. M. Hewitt.

> It's hard for a corpse in this world of men.
> Better remain apart, alone;
> You have to mix with them now and then

> Or you'll never succeed in your career.
> But oh! the fear that they might hear
>   The rattle of bone on bone.

> Live men still sleep when the dead man rises.
> His thoughts are black as the day is long,
> Plods to the office, bank, or assizes,
> Where quills whisper a welcome-song.

> Hour by hour must the dead man labour;
> At last he's free, and puts on his coat,
> Wags his haunches, grins at his neighbour
> And feeds him a bawdy anecdote.

> The rain has smeared with a nameless liquor
> Houses and churches and humans grimy;
> But the dead man drives where the mud is thicker,
> Knowing a place that is still more slimy.

> A gilded hall with mirrors about it.
> Imbecile hostess and husband fool
> Are glad to see him, who can doubt it?—
> His evening suit was made by Poole.

> Corpse, be brave now, raise thanksgiving:
> They can't hear the rattle against that band;
> No easy work to prove you are living,
> But go round briskly, shake their hand.

> Who is that by the distant column?
> His eyes light up, for she too is dead.
> Under their patter, with faces solemn,
> Words that are real words are said.

> "Weary friend, I am lost and strange here."
> "Weary friend, I've nothing to tell."
> "It's midnight now." "Oh, there's no danger—
> Dance with my niece, she likes you well."

> And over there with senses reeling,
> Waiting, alert, her blood on fire,
> The virgin stands, her eyes revealing
> The ecstasy of life's desire.

> With fluent malice more than human,
> He murmurs into her ear alone,
> Just as a live man woos a woman.
> "How clever he is, how kind and dear!"
> But somewhere near she can faintly hear
>   The rattle of bone on bone.

Another longer poem (or succession of poems), **"The Life of My Friend"**, is written in the same vein. In his beautiful **"Garden of Nightingales"** the disappointed dreamer emerged with all the magic of his art, whereas in several other verses his love of Russia came up again—with the old vehemence but a new accent. When everything had betrayed him; when he was tormented by forebodings about "the cold and gloom of days to come", his love for Russia still remained. He knew her vices, her wickedness, her squalor; still he loved her with a love a typical utterance of which are the following lines (1914):

To sin, unashamed, to lose, unthinking,
The count of careless nights and days,
And then, while the head aches with drinking,
Steal to God's house, with eyes that glaze;

Thrice to bow down to earth, and seven
Times cross oneself beside the door,
With the hot brow, in hope of heaven,
Touching the spittle-covered floor;

With brass farthing's gift dismissing
The offering, the holy Name
To mutter with loose lips, in kissing
The ancient, kiss-worn icon-frame.

And coming home, then, to be tricking
Some wretch out of the same small coin,
And with an angry hiccup, kicking
A lean cur in his trembling groin.

And where the icon's flame is quaking
Drink tea, and reckon loss and gain,
From the fat chest of drawers taking
The coupons wet with spittle-stain;

And sunk in feather-bed to smother
In slumber, such as bears may know,—
Dearer to me than every other
Are you, Russia, even so.

VI

Blok's mixture of spite with despair—a mixture so frequent in his poems of those years—was but inverted idealism of an incurable dreamer. For his visions still pursued him, tormented him even in the quagmire of that existence which he was doomed to witness and to share. His negation was thus only the other side of his suppressed craving for a change radical enough to cleanse the earth and make it worthy of a new mankind.

More than once he prophesied the approach of a universal upheaval. And when the upheaval came in the shape of the Russian revolution, he greeted it with an enthusiasm full of sudden hopes and expectations. In joining the most radical revolutionary group—the bolsheviks—he was ready to give all his art to the "service of community" and to work for a regeneration of man and life. He saw a symbolic meaning even in the apocalyptic horror of those years. It was the irrational volcanic character of the events that seemed to justify some of his hopes to see at last a really new and better earth to live in. Far from being perturbed by it all, he identified it with that elemental "spirit of music" which—according to him—is at the bottom of all creative revolutions. That spirit he contrasted with the rationalist civilization of Western Europe for which he saw no perspective in the future.

. . . . .

The old romantic in Blok thus came out, as strongly as ever, also in his attitude towards the revolution. More-over, his new hopes stirred up his poetic genius as well. It was in January, 1918, that is, during the cruellest civil war and havoc, that he wrote his last two important poems, *The Twelve* and *Scythians*.

VII

The first of them is the high watermark of Blok's creative power. Owing to its wealth of rhythms, phrases and musical dissonances, it defies all attempts at an adequate translation, whether in verse or in prose. But even those who can read it in the original will miss a great deal if they don't look upon it as a synthetic expression of Blok's muse. Here he succeeds in blending practically all the ingredients of his poetry. His love of the "mad" irrational Russia with her wind-swept spaces, his revel in chaos, his wish to destroy for the sake of regeneration, his tedium and his ardent visions—they all combine in this realistic and yet symbolic rhapsody of his. The very opening reminds one of Blok's winds and blizzards:

Black night.
White snow.
The wind, the wind!
It will not let you go.
The wind, the wind!
Through God's whole world it blows.
The wind is weaving the white snow.
Brother ice peeps from below.
Stumbling and tumbling,
Folk slip and fall.
God pity all!

The wind is a whirl, the snow is a dance.
In the night twelve men advance.
Black, narrow rifle straps,
Cigarettes, tilted caps.

The narrative incident itself is crude and could have been taken from any police chronicle. One of the twelve bolshevist guards, who control Petrograd at night, shoots, in a fit of jealousy, his sweetheart Katya—a lewd street-girl "whose stockings are stuffed with Kerensky coins". This motive is cunningly interwoven with the chaos of a bleak northern winter and with the orgy of revolution. The atmosphere is suggested by the very rhythm, tone and accent of each stanza. And as to Blok's own mood and temper, we can gather them from the way he derides the old "bourgeois" order:

A bourgeois, a lonely mourner,
His nose tucked in his ragged fur.
Stands lost and idle in the corner,
Tagged by a cringing, mangy cur.
The bourgeois, like the hungry mongrel—
A silent question—stands and begs;
The old world, like a kinless mongrel,
Stands there, its tail between its legs.

Nothing that belongs to the old world matters. Even the "holy Russia" of the good old days can be blasphemed, trampled underfoot for the sake of a new era, of a new world.

More daring, friends, take the lot!
At Holy Russia let's fire a shot!
At hutted Russia,
Fat rumped and solid.
Russia the stolid!
Ekh, ekh, unhallowed, unblessed.

The fury of destruction permeates the very air. But it is destruction not for its own sake. Its meaning is deeper. It is creative in its very essence, although the perpetrators themselves may not be aware of it. And so "the twelve" march. Through destruction, crime and chaos they march on, until they find themselves in rather unexpected company:

Forward as a haughty host they tread.
A hungry mongrel shambles in the rear.
Bearing forth the banner's windy red,
Where the vagrant snow-veils veer,
In dim hands no bullets sear,
On the tempest gently thrown,
Like a snow of diamonds blown,
In mist-white roses garlanded—
Christ marches on. And the twelve are led.

VIII

This poem, which is now world famous, vibrates with revolutionary pathos. Still, it remains elusive enough to be interpreted in various ways, particularly its end. Christ at the head of the twelve bolshevist guards may look to some readers like a *deus ex machina*. The more so because nothing in the poem makes one expect such a denouement. On the other hand, he stands here as a Messianic symbol of the revolution itself; as a promise of new life purified through suffering, through the Inferno of blood, crime and starvation. It is said that Blok himself was not quite sure as to the real meaning of the poem and that he attentively listened to his critics who seemed to be anxious to "explain" it. One thing however is beyond doubt: *The Twelve* marks a final attempt on his part to conquer faith in humanity, in life. And this attempt he expressed with a verbal power which raised even the revolutionary street-jargon and the modern factory song into high poetry.

Less elusive and almost programmatic is his other and weaker poem, *Scythians.* It is a platform counterpart to *The Twelve.* Blok challenges in it the lukewarm "bourgeois" West to join in the universal brotherhood inaugurated by Russia, or else—to tremble before a barbaric invasion to come. Conscious of being one of the builders of a new world, he addresses the Western nations both as a Russian and a revolutionary:

Yes, you have long since ceased to love
As our cold blood can love; the taste
You have forgotten of a love
That burns like fire and like fire lays waste.

Yes, Russia is a Sphinx. Exulting, grieving,
And sweating blood, she cannot sate

Her eyes that gaze and gaze and gaze
At you with stone-lipped love for you, and hate.

This "stone-lipped love" and hatred in one with regard to the European West suggest the Messianic Slavophil Dostoevsky. Blok's Utopia, too, is permeated with frank Messianism. But in his case it is turned towards a future inaugurated by the revolution. So he shouts to the sceptical and reluctant Western Europe:

Come unto us, from the black ways of war,
Come to our peaceful arms and rest.
Comrades, while it is not too late,
Sheathe the sword. May brotherhood be blessed.

And in case the Western peoples should refuse to join, he threatens them with the "Asiatic face" of Russia, as well as with Russia's indifference to their future fate:

We will not move when the ferocious Hun
Despoils the corpse and leaves it bare,
Burns towns, herds cattle in the church
And smell of white flesh roasting fills the air.

IX

"Life is only worth while when we make immense demands upon it," Blok wrote in an essay at the time of his two revolutionary rhapsodies. "All or nothing! A faith, not in what is not found upon earth, but in what ought to be there, although at the present time it does not exist and may not come for quite a while."

Looking upon the Revolution with such an attitude, he saw its true scope in nothing less than "to lay hold of the whole world—a true revolution cannot desire anything less, though whether this aim will be accomplished or not we cannot guess. It cherishes the hope of raising a universal cyclone which will carry to lands buried in snow the warm wind and the fragrance of orange groves, and will water the sun-scorched plains of the south with the refreshing rain from the north. *Peace and the brotherhood of nations* is the banner under which the Russian revolution goes on its way. This is the theme of its roaring flood. This is the music which he who has ears to hear should hear."

Such was the idea which Alexander Blok, who was a typical intellectual, had of the great proletarian revolution. He was as uncompromising as the most ruthless Marxians, but he differed from them in that he was too impatient to see the economic and political upheaval completed by an adequate inner revolution in man himself.

It must have been the discrepancy between the external and the inner revolution—a discrepancy which assumed most unpalatable aspects during the ravages of the civil war, the famine and the Cheka—that eventually damped Blok's hopes and enthusiasm. The fact is that when he saw the actual trend of events, he soon became tired and passive. Disappointment closed upon him once more, and he remained practically silent during the last two years of his life. He died in 1921, at the age of forty.

Blok's death coincided with a complete dissolution of the Russian school of symbolism, of which he was the acknowledged leader.

Marc Slonim (essay date 1953)

SOURCE: "Block and the Symbolists," in *Modern Russian Literature: From Chekhov to the Present,* Oxford University Press, 1953, pp. 184-210.

[In the following excerpt, Slonim studies the progression of Blok's poetry in relation to both his life and social and political conditions in Russia; identifies the major elements of Blok's style; and comments on Blok's views concerning the role of the artist in society.]

Russian Symbolism still awaits its historian: this rich and complex movement, with all its ramifications, is not as yet thoroughly explored. But one thing we know with certainty is that its whole course has been encompassed by and summarized in the work of Alexander Blok (1880-1921), the greatest Russian poet of the twentieth century. His name must be added to the list of five luminaries of Russian poetry: Pushkin, Lermontov, Nekrassov, Fet, and Tiutchev. As time goes by Blok grows in stature and acquires a prophetic significance. He was not simply a man who wrote beautiful verse; he was the embodiment of Russian culture. If Pushkin inaugurated an entire period of Russian civilization and indicated its further development, Blok—heir to the legacy of Pushkin—marked the last flowering and the end of that period. He expressed a world that came to completion and destruction during his lifetime—and he accepted its collapse in the name of the future. He tried—in his own words—to 'hearken to the music of the revolution,' which was drowning out the music of culture. This attempt compelled him to deny and reject what he cherished and to welcome a new era of strangers and Scythians. Therein lay his tragedy: he could not reconcile the two truths, could not accept one to the exclusion of the other—and he remained torn by his inner struggle, at the watershed of two eras, turning backward and looking forward, like double-faced Janus. This tragic duality caused the cleavage in his poetry as well as in his life.

Alexander Blok's father, a professor of law, an excellent scholar and musician, was moody and ironical, cruel and rebellious—Dostoevsky wanted to write a novel about him. He was incessantly quarreling with his wife, the idealistic and highly cultured daughter of the botanist Beketov, rector of the University of St. Petersburg. The parents separated when Alexander was three years old. The child was brought up for the most part at Shakhmatovo, the Moscow estate of his maternal grandparents. It was a typical gentlefolk's nest, an aristocratic manor enveloped in an atmosphere of artistic and intellectual refinement.

Blok began writing poems at the age of five, and the Russian and European classics were familiar to him from early childhood. Protected from material cares, sheltered from ugliness and coarseness, he grew up among flowers, books, and music, surrounded by men and women whose chief interests were literature, science, and art. His development was organic—what others had to study came to him as easily as breathing; he naturally belonged to the top group of Russian educated society.

At the age of eighteen this tall, athletic, handsome, gray-eyed youth of restrained manners conveyed the impression of strength, purity, and depth. In 1898 he met 15-year-old Liubov Mendeleyeva, daughter of the famous chemist, on whose large estate amateur theatricals were organized each summer. She played Ophelia, and he fell in love with her. This love coincided with another event—his acquaintance with the work of Solovyov—and Blok's feelings for the blue-eyed, ravishingly beautiful girl blended with those about Solovyov's mystical search for Eternal Womanhood.

Literary symbolism, religious aspirations, and youthful passion created in Blok a peculiar state of mind that lasted several years and resulted in two cycles of poems ('**Ante Lucem**' and '**Verses about the Lady Beautiful**'). All his friends (among whom were Andrei Bely and a few young men who later became minor Symbolists) were completely under the spell of Solovyov. They shared his mystical expectancy and his feeling of the imminent end of history (which they awaited in comfortable surroundings). Above all they accepted enthusiastically his concept of Sophia, the Eternal Wisdom, which was also Eternal Love. And was not Liubov Mendeleyeva the embodiment of this idea, and did not Blok's love for her bear all the signs of platonic and mystical passion? In their imagination she was the Belle Dame to whom poems were offered up like incense. Her gestures and words were watched and interpreted as mystical revelations. Blok's stanzas, translucent in their symbolic imagery, sang of the delicate tints of the dawn, the azure of the sky; in fragrant meadows the Lover awaited the descent of Light, which was the Glory of the World and the Beloved.

The mystical sweetness of these lyrics (which were slightly reminiscent of certain pieces of the Pre-Raphaelites) had, however, an emotional quality that Blok's friends failed to understand but that captivated the readers of the poems. Blok used all the Symbolistic terminology and imagery, of which he had an exceptional grasp, but his '**Verses about the Lady Beautiful**' were different from the erudite chants of Ivanov, the exuberant songs of Balmont, the gelid odes of Briussov, and the ambiguous lines of Hippius. They had a genuine emotional force, their spiritual flights were presented as spontaneous revelations of earthly love—and this bestowed upon them a unique tone. The poems in which his friends saw 'heavenly accents' and allusions to 'the illuminating essence of all things under the coarse bark of matter' had been inspired by incidents of real life. The seven hundred pieces of these chivalric ballads, which sounded like a litany and in which the poet's 'tireless ear was attuned to the distant call of another soul, the flutter of angelic wings,' were a lyrical diary, an intimate story of Blok's personal experience. The *Canzoniere* of Petrarch offer the closest literary parallel to this highly subjective and enchantingly musical poetry.

Blok and Liubov were married in 1903, and those who met them at that time always spoke of the harmonious light this couple irradiated: they seemed the embodiment of happiness, beauty, and triumphant youth. Blok himself said then that he had found 'the fixed fount,' 'a firm ground of mystical faith which spreads its blessings over life.'

In 1904, when *Verses about the Lady Beautiful* was published, Blok became a welcome guest in the salons of St. Petersburg literati. Merezhkovsky and his wife, Hippius, saw in him the prince of a religious revival; a veritable cult of admirers rallied round the minstrel of the Belle Dame. Most of them failed to perceive in the behavior of their idol the ominous signs of an approaching crisis. But for those who had more insight Blok's frigidity, the stony gaze of his gray eyes, his abrupt silences in response to outbursts at mystical eloquence, his cryptic and often caustic remarks appeared suspicious. He suffered from fits of depression, and often felt a satanic urge to be ironical and destructive.

His peace of mind had been disrupted by an unconscious restlessness. 'I am longing for something clear, calm, and white,' he wrote to his mother at the time. In vain did Merezhkovsky try to chain him to his logical formulas and to interest him in various religious theories. Blok, in whom the symptoms of an inner discord were growing daily, followed his own painful path. The Russian troubadour was through. The mystical mist that had beautified all contours and hidden reality under a haze of pink and gold was being swept away by the contact with the reality of life during the stormy pre-Revolutionary days. Blok was falling from his mystical heights into the vale of tears, peopled by prostitutes instead of the Lady Beautiful, and crowded with factories rather than fairy castles. It was a debacle and a new birth: he was reborn into the world of sin and pain. His faith in the supernatural was badly shaken, heaven became distant and chill, and his mystical beliefs were shattered when confronted with the ugliness of man's condition. A terrifying moral problem suddenly yawned before him like a chasm.

Together with his father's spirit of rebelliousness and irony he had inherited, on his maternal side, Beketov's realistic and analytical disposition. His critical sense was as keen as his aesthetic sensitivity. He could perceive, with pitiless precision, both his inner self and the external world. Every day he was shedding his youthful illusions about love, about his own wife, his friends—and about poetry and Russian life. These illusions melted away like the sugar-candy angel on top of a Christmas tree bright with many candles.

An emotional crisis, combined with a crisis of his conscience, upset his entire way of life. He still spent Sunday evenings at Sologub's, where the Modernists read their ophidian and demoniac works; he still attended Merezhkovsky's salon (transformed into a hothouse by a profusion of lilies and roses) and listened to Hippius as she discoursed on Christ, mystical bliss, and asceticism, smoking long, perfumed cigarettes the while; he still climbed up to The Tower, where Viacheslav Ivanov, master of ceremonies, made subtle comments on theurgical art, on Eros, Dionysus, and the religion of popular myth—but Blok's heart was with none of them: he had tired of their sterile sophistication. These intellectuals dwelt in an artificial world of their own making, and real life—the life of persecuted revolutionists, starving peasants, striking workers, and homeless tramps—had nothing to do with that world. In Blok's case the inevitable discrepancy between ideal vision and coarse reality, which leads to conflict, frustration, and rebellion—the three phases of romantic plight—had been made all the more bitter by the bankruptcy of the 1905 Revolution, which he resented as a terrible blow.

His new cycles of poems, **'Earth's Bubbles'** (1905) and **'The City'** (1906), dealt with grimacing hunchbacks and witches; 'nocturnal violets' blossomed but seldom in his landscapes of city tenements, factory walls, barracks, and street lamps blinking in the autumnal fog. Life appeared to him as a Punch-and-Judy show-booth, as a stupid children's play (*The Little Show-Booth*). He still longed for the Belle Dame—'be thy name blest'—but he knew that 'she had gone off to the fields, never more to return.' 'I understood everything—and I am going away. Blessed be the dream of the past, but the soul is incurable.' The universe, said Blok, is impelled by music, passion, love, preference, strength—whereas he found around him only din, disharmony, bloodless hearts, and vile bodies. His 'prophetic boredom' and melancholy were, like Lermontov's, the result of his hypersensitivity. Yet he was too strong and too passionate not to attempt to overcome despair and grief. Thus began that period of dissipation which horrified Bely and led to his break with Blok. The poet sought an outlet in demonism and a wild expenditure of energy. Love affairs substituted for love, the Belle Dame was replaced by pretty women. In **'The Stranger'** (1907), one of his most discussed poems, which critics such as Philosophov dubbed 'absolutely incomprehensible not only to laymen but to specialists,' the scene of his encounter with the Unknown Lady is laid not in meadows at dawn, but on a sultry evening, in a suburban restaurant, among roistering tosspots.

He did not separate from his wife, but they led independent lives. His next collections of poems, *The Masque of Snow* (1908) and *Faina* (1909), were dedicated to Natalia Volokhova, the actress, whose dark beauty held him captive for some time. The reading of these sensual, despairing, and melancholy stanzas at one of Ivanov's Wednesday nights provoked consternation and astonishment among those whom Blok styled 'professional mystics.'

Blok now entered a world of tempestuousness and madness. He compared himself to a winged demon, and found a grim satisfaction in frittering away his physical and spiritual powers on parties, feminine conquests, and drinking bouts with the gypsies. Sometimes he consoled himself by saying that all this excitement, all this turmoil conveyed to him a 'sense of the beyond,' that there was a kind of mystical experience in the intemperances of the flesh: wine, women, and song had always been the path to supersensual illuminations; the precipice of evil was closer to the heaven of purity than was sober triviality.

Blok's best and most popular stanzas compare Russia to women: to a wench whose eyes shine from under her shawl; to a treacherous mistress whose traits do not alter despite all her adventures; to a mother who cries over her children.

—Marc Slonim

The attraction of evil and of demonism was, however, of short duration. He could not help feeling the contradiction between his true longings and the trumpery he was playing with: taverns, sprees, cruel or frivolous toyings with women. 'It becomes more and more difficult to live,' he complains in a letter. 'It is so cold. I am wasting a lot of money senselessly—and there is such a complete void all around me: as if everybody had left me and ceased to love me; perhaps they never did. I am on an island, in the midst of an empty, icy sea. My anxiety is not pointless: I see too many things clearly, soberly.'

His double vision tormented him: he perceived two aspects of truth, and they were forever irreconcilable. Dreams did not help; they made life more unbearable: 'It is windy out in the streets; prostitutes are shivering on sidewalks, people are starving, are hanged; there is reaction all over the country; life in Russia is cold, difficult, disgusting.' He sneered at his mystical friends: 'If all these chatterboxes were to lose weight and become quite thin because of their search (which is useless except for certain *refined natures*), nothing would change in Russia.' This hostile attitude toward intellectuals was becoming constantly intensified. He reproached them with their separation from the people, their lack of real experience in life, and questioned their 'vertical culture,' which now seemed to him artificial and highly perishable.

There was a fundamental difference between Blok and other Symbolist leaders: the others looked for principles and abstractions that would provide them with illumination, while he tried to find truth through intensely lived emotional experiences—and his poetry mirrored this intimate and individual process. His approach to art also was undergoing a change. In *The Rose and the Cross* (1913), a bizarre drama in the style of the troubadours, he insisted on the unity of art and the moral ideal: their separation was fatal to the artist; it degraded his work, and betrayed his love. His own existence in the meantime was a constant flight from himself, and he responded to his failure to find consolation by writing despairingly gloomy and poignant verse. His most striking poems of this period are

contained in *Harps and Violins* (1912), *The Frightening World,* and *Retaliation* (1909-16).

Complete negation pervades these collections. 'The worlds are flying. The years are flying. The empty universe looks at us through the night of its eyes—and the tired, hollow soul still speaks of happiness. What is happiness? A brief and tense moment, oblivion, a suspension of cares—and the heart-breaking, mysterious flight is resumed again.' It is a flight through a 'terrifying world' of boredom, triviality, and annihilation. The poet's personal life is a failure. His heart is a 'rouged corpse.' 'O yes, I was rich once, but now nothing is worth a copper coin: neither hatred, nor love, nor gossip, nor gold—not even my moral grief.' There is nothing to adore and to hope for, everything is shattered, and he is lost upon paths of demonism and revelry, even as he had previously been lost on the Path of Light. Duality prevails: 'This world is too narrow for my heart.' He is weary of passion: 'The same caresses and entreaties, the boring quiver of eager lips, and of too familiar shoulders.' 'Well, kiss my dying lips, undo your woeful zone.' 'The soul did not escape the invisible decay.' 'He who has once tasted the air of freedom can no longer breathe here below.' As the poet Khodassevich put it, Blok suffered from insomnia of the heart.

After the deaths of his young child and his father in 1909, Blok went abroad, but his protracted travels did little to change his mood. He found in Europe the same feeling of instability, the same failure of the intellectuals, and the triumph of that very bourgeoisie and that same middle class which he hated with the double hatred of a romantic and a Russian radical. 'Men disgust me; life is horrible,' he wrote from France. 'European life is as revolting as that in Russia; in general, the life of all men the world over is a monstrous, dirty puddle.'

But paralleling these statements there is an effort to find a way of salvation and a growing interest in problems of culture, art, and Russian history. With the same emotional intensity that made him suffer because of the discrepancy between dreams and reality, Blok feels the dichotomy between his sense of justice and his search for truth, and the unjust social and political conditions in Russia. When, in 1908, he delivered a public lecture on the intelligentsia, his audience was shocked by the violence of his diatribe: he accused the intellectuals of not understanding their own country and of having lost all ties with the people. Scion of the culture created by aristocrats and intellectuals, he questioned that culture's validity and predicted its imminent collapse. Gogol, said Blok, talked of Russian taciturnity and slumber; they had come to an end, however, and the Gogolian troika—symbol of Russia—was rushing onward like the wind and the intellectuals ought to throw themselves under the hoofs of the steeds. Sacrifice and self-annihilation were the only things left to them: 'They are regarding us from the brink of the blue precipice of the future and are luring us thither.' Thenceforth the theme of Russia became the prevalent one in his poetry and determined its further development. He turned to his country with the passion and exasperation a lover feels toward a perfidious yet irresistible woman. In his allegoric drama, *The Song of Fate* (1909), Faina, an enigmatic, passionate, and dissolute woman who disappears in a blizzard, symbolizes Russia, while Herman, the lover whom she at first rejects, represents the intellectuals.

It was soon like a new infatuation: he fled 'into the fields, the endless plain, to the people, to Russia.' He tenderly devoted his lyrics to 'our roads and our fogs and the whispers of our oats.' The poverty and humility of the countryside moved him to tears: 'O my starving land, what are you telling my heart?—O my wife, why are you weeping so bitterly?' 'O Russia, beggarly Russia, your gray huts, your soughing songs are for me like the first tears of love.' His feelings for her are as dualistic as Lermontov's 'strange love'; Blok talks of his 'beloved fatal country.'

His best and most popular stanzas compare Russia to women: to a wench whose eyes shine from under her shawl; to a treacherous mistress whose traits do not alter despite all her adventures; to a mother who cries over her children. But gradually new notes steal into the music he hears amid Russian scenes. He calls the era of reaction the 'years of sloth'; he sees oppression hovering like a hawk over the villages, and finally raises the question of Russia's destiny. What is the meaning of her history, what is the significance of her fate? 'I do not see thy face behind the snow, the woods, the steppes, behind thy incomprehensible width and breadth.'

History provides him an answer. In his lyrics **'On the Battle of Kulikovo Field'** (where the Russians fought the Tartar invaders) he exclaims: 'Eternal combat! We dreamed only of calm and peace amid dust and blood! The mare of the steppes runs and crushes the grass!' 'Our road is the road of the steppe and of shoreless grief—thy grief O Russia!—yet I fear not the darkness beyond the border.' The road of struggle and suffering leads, despite oppression and misery, to wild freedom.

Blok has the premonition of an approaching catastrophe, but his hope in Russia's glorious future remains unshaken. Through fiery purification Russia will come to a new birth. 'Russia is not yet a genius,' he writes in his notes. 'The future is only fermenting within her. But she stands in the very center of events, on that narrow strip where the breath of the spirit is blowing.'

Resuming the tradition of Slavophile and messianic dreams, he now follows in the wake of the odes of Khomiakov and Tiutchev. 'There is art and death in Europe. Russia is life. I am neither with those who are for old Russia nor with the partisans of Europeanization (the Socialists, the Constitutional Democrats, Vengerov, to give examples), but for some new Russia—or for no Russia at all: either she will no longer exist or she will follow a road entirely different from that of Europe.' Yet instead of repeating the idyllic stuff of the old-fashioned nationalists, he foresees clearly the industrial development of the country. In 1913 he wrote **'The New America,'** an extraordinary poem in which he predicted the industrial transformation of Russia.

In 1912-14, in addition to his heightened interest in politics, he held a strong conviction of the doom of aristocratic culture; he was awaiting the cataclysm that was to destroy it: 'In our hearts the seismograph's arm has already moved.' The publication of **Retaliation,** an autobiographical narrative poem with realistic descriptions of social conditions and of the revolutionary movement, completed his break with Ivanov, whom he attacked for his 'inane wordiness.' At the same time Blok was writing splendid love lyrics dedicated to Liubov Delmas, the leading actress of the Musical Drama Theater, with whom he was then in love (**'Carmen'** and parts of *Harps and Violins*). He welcomed the Revolution of 1917 as the fulfilment of a dream, as the beautiful and tragic birth of a new world, and pleaded with the intellectuals to hearken to its music. 'I hate the bourgeois, the devil, and the liberals.' His enthusiasm was not affected by the events: 'Why is it so gloomy outside?' he asked—and answered: 'Because it is so bright within.' He was well aware of the destructive, fiery elements of the upheaval, but insisted that the task of the intelligentsia was to channel this fire, to transform the wild rebellion of the Razins and Pugachevs 'into a musical wave.'

His *Scythians* (1918) expressed the opinions of a considerable number of radicals, for the most part extreme Socialist Revolutionaries, whose spokesman was the critic Ivanov-Razumnik. Revolution was for them an expression of genuine national traits. 'Yes,' said Blok in this poem, 'we are Scythians; we are Asiatics with slanting and eager eyes. We have the strength of those who bent low the necks of wild horses and tamed rebellious women captives.' The Russians are capable of understanding and appreciating the West, which they had shielded from the Mongols in the past; they can understand the keen Gallic spirit and the somber Teutonic genius; they are ready to co-operate for the good of the world and humanity, but woe to the West if it refuses to respond to the Russian call and attend 'the feast of work and peace.' For then the hordes of Scythians and Asiatics would sweep together as one avalanche upon the doomed lands of Europe, and would devastate the old and dying world of Western civilization.

This ode, which reverted to Dostoevsky's concept of the scope and universality of the Russians, also deals with Solovyov's prediction of the 'yellow peril'; in Blok's vision, however, the union of Russia and Asia would occur only if Europe refused to collaborate with the Scythians.

An even greater stir was aroused by Blok's *The Twelve* (1918). The protagonists of this poem are Red soldiers who plunder and murder; they go marching through a St. Petersburg blizzard, bandits and dreamers inspired by the hatred of the bourgeois world and by a confused yearning for a better life. Christ himself appears at the end of the poem as their invisible leader. Thus the twelve bandits become the twelve apostles, and out of the blood and filth of Terror and Anarchy emerges the image of a new Gospel that justifies all the cruelty and destructiveness of Bolshevism.

The Twelve sounded like a dirge for the old Russia—and like an Easter Mass announcing the Resurrection; death and the hope for a new life were blended in it. There was a background of atonement to this panorama of ruin, bloodshed, and conflagration, as if these constituted the price Russians had to pay for all the sins they had committed. The realistically drawn figures of the poem were symbolic: the frightened bourgeois with the old cur shivering at his feet personified the past; the lady in furs cursing the Revolution and the long-haired writer whining over the end of Russia represented the intellectuals; the uncouth, ignorant soldiers were the people—blind in their violence yet marching toward a luminous goal. The image of Christ was not accidental: Populism and a religious interpretation of the Revolution were combined in this final vision of the Crucified.

The impression produced by *The Twelve* was overwhelming. The poem provoked endless discussions. Gorky saw it as a satire; Gumilev found Christ an 'artificial addition' to a dynamic piece of sharp realism; the descriptions of the capital, of the Red soldiers, of Katya, the mistress of one of them, were acclaimed as great poetic achievements even by those who rejected the idea of the poem. Blok wrote in his diary: 'Did I make a song of praise? I simply registered a fact: if you stare into the swirling blizzard on *this road* you will see Jesus Christ. But sometimes I myself deeply hate this feminine ghost . . . The Bolsheviks are right in being afraid of *The Twelve*.'

The majority of the intellectuals considered the poem a blasphemy, an offense against the humanistic tradition, and a blind acceptance of the Communist regime. The rumor spread that Blok had sold out to the Communists. Old friends refused to shake hands with him. More than thirty years after the publication of *The Twelve* Bunin attacked it in his memoirs and dubbed it ridiculous, naïve, and unpoetic.

Blok suffered from the hostility shown to him on all sides, but he admitted to a friend: 'I love *The Twelve*. I fought against what I wrote, yet I felt it as a supreme truth.' Were not the intellectuals again shying away from reality? Was it not their task to assume direction during the holocaust? Instead of helping the people they were afraid of the blood and horrors of the catastrophe; they were betraying their own country—and if Blok now hated all those who, like Merezhkovsky and Hippius, were setting the pack on him, his reasons were more ideological than personal. His tragedy lay in the fact that while he was accused of having betrayed the intellectuals and, in his turn, charging them with having betrayed the people, the Revolution had deceived and cheated him. In vain did he try to convince himself that it did not matter that the Revolution 'cruelly cheats and easily maims the worthy ones in its whirlpool, but brings the unworthy ones to the shore,' because 'this neither changes the direction of the stream nor its thunderous roar, which proclaims great things.'

Every month, confronting him with privations, executions, outbursts of hatred and violence, with terror, civil war, and failures, brought him new disappointments, made him sad and weary. The dream of revolution failed him as his other dreams had. The only thing he still continued to believe in was the presentiment of an enormous change. 'Don't you know,' he wrote Hippius, 'that there will be no Russia—in the same way that Rome ceased to exist not in the fifth century but in the first year of the first century? In the same way as there will be no Germany, England, France? That the world is already rebuilt? That the old world has already melted away?'

Blok's lines are immediately recognizable by the flow of his euphonic rhythms, by his antithetic metaphors, by his change of inflections, and by the emotional intensity, often poignancy, of his expressions.

—Marc Slonim

In 1919-20 he worked for Gorky's *International Literature,* made translations, wrote *Rameses,* a historical drama, delivered his lecture on the 'Crisis in Humanism,' in which he denounced the death of the old ideologies. From time to time he made brief appearances at public meetings: staring over the heads of the audience he would read his poems, stonily aloof to both catcalls and applause. He did not conceal his critical attitude toward the government and its policy, and was arrested as politically suspect, but was released almost immediately. In February 1921, at Pushkin's festival, Blok made a remarkably bold speech on 'secret freedom.' 'Calm and freedom are necessary for the release of harmony. Bureaucrats attempt to take them away and to force poetry into artificial channels . . . they are worse than philistines.'

In revolutionary Petrograd, city of starvation, typhus, and fear, where the relics of Imperial Russia looked like ghosts in a graveyard, Blok also seemed a ghost from a forlorn past. He was broken, dispirited, and ill. 'There are no sounds! All sounds have ceased,' he told Chukovsky. 'There is nothing to breathe with, either. It is impossible to write under such oppression.' He was too weak, too exhausted physically to leave the capital or to emigrate; his friends (including Gorky) tried to obtain a governmental permit for him to go abroad, but bureaucratic red tape delayed the issuance of a passport—and when things were cleared up, it was already too late. The last entries in his diary speak again of his 'love-hatred of Russia. At this moment, I have neither soul nor body; I am ill as I have never been before. Vile, rotten Mother Russia has devoured me, has gobbled me up as a sow gobbles one of its suckling pigs.'

This was written in May 1921. In June he was suffering from scurvy and asthmatic attacks, and lapsed into a state of severe mental depression; in July he broke down completely and went out of his mind; delirious and in excruciating pain, he died on 20 August (New Style) 1921.

. . . . .

'What is a poet? A man who writes verse? Of course not. A poet is the bringer of rhythm. And it is the waves of rhythm that direct the universe and the human spirit.' Blok argues against Faust, who believed that 'at the beginning there was the Deed.' 'At the beginning,' Blok contends, 'was Music. Music is the essence of the world. The world grows in resilient rhythms.' The poet is bound to clash with the multitude, the mob. Their clash is inevitable, and so is the destruction of the poet. He perishes—but this is only the breaking up of the instrument; the sounds continue to ring. In the history of mankind there are non-musical epochs, when the bark of matter is thick and heavy, and music is exiled to the nether regions. Then man is alienated, divorced from music. Revolutions, cataclysms change this situation and bring forth the spirit of music from prison and out into the open.

This philosophy determined the character of Blok's work. The precision of Pushkin's sensuous perception, the harmony between his eye and his ear explain in part the plastic quality of his imagery as well as the fullness and vitality of the older poet's work. Blok's hearing, however, was more perceptive than his sight. He was guided by sound and grasped its slightest nuances—and he renders in the changing tonalities of his lilting melodious verse a wide range of phenomena, from the forest's murmur to the storm's roaring. Most of his similes and symbols are of an auditory nature. It is also typical of him to speak of 'elemental' sounds: 'the wild howl of violins,' 'the tune of the wind,' 'the harps and strings of the blizzard.' The dynamic substance of the world is revealed to him in the polyphonic peals of thunder, in the surge of the surf.

Two other elements molded his style more specifically: the refined and highly literary tradition of the Symbolists, and the low trend of popular poetry. He borrowed from the Symbolists all the technical devices of musicality and often lapsed into that 'eloquence' which he at last came to reject and despise. His less successful poems are pale and wordy; they are no better than the verses of the average twentieth-century Symbolist poet. But when he abandons the nebulous eloquence of the Symbolists, the mellowness and passionate anxiety of his poems exhibit high individuality. Blok's lines are immediately recognizable by the flow of his euphonic rhythms, by his antithetic metaphors ('hot snowy sob,' 'resounding silence'), by his change of inflections, and by the emotional intensity, often poignancy, of his expressions. 'A poem is a canopy stretched on the sharp points of several words. Those words shine like stars,' he wrote, and this explains the parallel structure of his poems.

A poem by Blok is seldom a mere description, a narrative, or a statement: it is either an inner monologue or a conversational address, and this gives it its dramatic quality. Even in his odes, such as *The Scythians,* which reminds one of Pushkin's 'To the Calumniators of Russia,' Blok exhorts or threatens; the figure of speech and the exclamatory turn are everywhere. This strongly inflected and accented poetry (often with an uneven number of syllables in each line) incorporates not only the classic meters of which Blok was fond, but also the melody or the texture of the old drawing-room ballad, of folklore poetry, and of the gypsy song. His predecessors (whom he loved and sometimes imitated) were Fet, Polonsky, and Apollon Grigoriev. The lilting rhythms of the gypsy song, with its uneven beat and abrupt alternation of fire and melancholy, suited Blok perfectly; many of his best lyrics are a curious transposition of gypsy tunes into the moods, forms, and vocabularies of modern Symbolism.

The folklore ballad and the rollicking, racy quatrains of the streets, factories, and villages were also molded into refined lines, particularly in *The Twelve,* in which the popular and literary currents meet and merge into musical unity. This is not the urbanism of Briussov (whom, by the way, Blok imitated in a few pieces) but a deliberate attempt to achieve the reunion of two currents: that of the intelligentsia and that of the people—or, as Blok would say, of culture and of nation. This poet of the cleft spirit, who had passed from demonism to spirituality and had arrived through the squandering of his passions at the adoration of Beauty and the Motherland, is the personification and the culmination of Russian romanticism; in his sufferings, wanderings and contradictions he is a descendant of Lermontov. But like all Russian romantics—including Gogol and Dostoevsky—Blok was not satisfied with a truth that is above and beyond men. He looked for moral and social values he could assert in his life and in his poetry. Thus, in his own evolution, he repeated not only the development of Symbolism but of Russian literature in the nineteenth century.

His attempts to gain a firm ground failed completely, and the same fate he saw for poets as the bearers of the spirit of music befell him. Many of Russia's great poets met with tragic ends, as in the cases of Pushkin and Lermontov; tragic conflicts underly the lives of Nekrassov and Grigoriev, while not a few minor poets had fates as dire as that of Polezhaev, whose body was gnawed by rats. But Blok's whole life was tragic; he had resolved none of his contradictions—and had tasted defeat as a man, as a citizen, and as an artist. His personal life had been a tormented and checkered one, and he was constantly aware of the emotional schism within himself. Always a maximalist, he could never accept the middle way, the mean that mediocrity calls golden, and he oscillated between extremes: demonism and mystical purity, blissful reverie and the crushing burden of earthiness and the flesh. His internal striving for harmony always clashed with external reality, with a world that is prey to discord—and he found himself isolated and lonely.

In addition to this emotional rift there was also a tragic conflict in his conscience: he realized the discrepancy between the vertical culture of educated society and the condition of the lower classes. The feeling of guilt within him was as acute as it was in Nekrassov, the poet who is most akin to Blok in spirit; and, like Nekrassov, he found a way of partial atonement in his love of Russia, in the Populist religious cult of the Motherland, of which he talks in erotic terms. His dream of sacrifice for and devotion to the people was destroyed when the Revolution, which he had tried to accept despite its fury, deceived his passionate expectations. One could regard the two defeats of Blok—the personal and the socio-political—as one great emotional frustration of unrequited love: a Freudian interpretation could easily define the patriotism of this unhappy lover as substitution and sublimation.

And, finally, as a poet he aspired to something he could not wholly achieve, and this was his ultimate disappointment.

At one time he had been fascinated by the arts and had compared their hypnotic attraction to that exerted by a 'bottomless pit.' Then he had asked himself what endured in the world of art, and what would be left for a man who wanted to live by art alone, and gave the answer: 'Three strokes in a drawing by Michael Angelo, a line of Aeschylus—that is all—and a universal void, and a rope around one's neck.' He said he loved only art, death, and children, but he also stated that 'if the circle of existence is straight, that of art is even more so.'

It is amazing to what an extent this poet, whose work is a lyrical confession, was concerned with the civic duty of the artist. 'Let them say to thee "Poet, forget, return to clever coziness!" No, better to perish out in the fierce frost! There is neither coziness nor rest.' To the artist's customary preoccupation with form and content he added his own anxiety about the proper significance of poetry. In 1910 he defined himself as a 'social animal' who had a 'passion for service,' and this explains the apparent paradox: a lyricist, a lover of gypsy songs, a religious symbolist, and a highly subjective poet of passions and sorrow, Blok was at the same time a civic bard, a great national poet. Yet here again he could not attain a harmonious solution. He knew that the artist inevitably clashes with his environment, and he hesitated between the affirmation of the poet's supreme freedom and the imposition of the message he *ought* to bring to his contemporaries. In 1921, in his last poem, he turned to Pushkin and asked his help in the 'unequal struggle.' This was the struggle for the artist's freedom against the external pressure during the years of the all-absorbing Revolution, which demanded made-to-order ideas and images.

Blok's work expressed the aspirations of the old intelligentsia as well as the tragedy of his own generation. He gave clear utterance to that dim foreboding of the end which was diffused through Russian literature before World War I. The way he addressed his Muse was perfectly appropriate: 'Your mysterious refrains bear the tidings of fateful destruction.' His poetry proclaimed in prophetic lines the collapse of the world to which he belonged. He tried to transmit his message to the new world that was being born amid the chaos of an implacable upheaval, and he also attempted to discern and to welcome the future. Thus he stands at the crossroads of two epochs—and therein lies his exceptional importance for Russian literature and culture: the last poet of Imperial Russia is the first poet of its triumphant Revolution.

Blok's formal, emotional, and ideological influence was very great. His way of writing molded dozens of poets.

None of his contemporaries escaped his imprint, and long after his death the echo of his poems was still resounding not only in Soviet poetry but also in the works of Russian *émigrés* scattered the world over. Blok created an important school, and many minor streams were fed from the wellspring he revealed.

His fortunes in Soviet Russia were complex and contradictory. The official line recommended acceptance of him—but not without caution and many reservations. He was recognized as one of the greatest Russian poets, and the study of his work was included in high-school curriculums; textbooks referred to him as a great master and one of the outstanding figures in national letters. This point, however, has been questioned in the course of some literary discussions. Readers have often been warned by Communist critics not only against the 'religious deviations' of *The Twelve,* or the 'Populist flavor' of *The Scythians,* but also against the mystical and romantic trends of Blok's poetry. Anatol Lunacharsky called him the 'last poet of the nobility.' Gorbachev wrote in *Capitalism and Russian Literature*: 'Blok's work is reactionary, formally and ideologically; the proletarian literary tradition has no use for it.' During World War II Blok was hailed for his patriotic stanzas, particularly **'On the Battle of Kulikovo Field,'** but as soon as the war was over, and particularly between 1946 and 1950, Soviet criticism displayed a certain hostility toward 'Blok's formalistic tendency' and his 'too subjective lyrics.' On the other hand, his anti-European stand, his 'Scythian' national pride, and his prophetic **'The New America'** were quoted with definite approval. The fluctuations of the party line did not, however, affect Blok's popularity with readers: his collected works, as well as selections from his poems, find a large and ready sale.

There is no evidence that interest in Blok has ever dwindled. What Eugene Zamiatin said the day of Blok's death is as true today as it was in 1921: 'Blok will live as long as dreamers exist—and their tribe is immortal.'

Times Literary Supplement (essay date 1956)

SOURCE: "Romantic Poet of Russia," in *Times Literary Supplement,* No. 2841, August 10, 1956, p. 474.

[*In the following essay, the critic outlines the predominant characteristics of Blok's early and late poetry and also comments on the continuity of his work as a whole.*]

Alexander Blok was Russia's last great romantic, and one of her greatest poets by any standard. He was nurtured by symbolism, and its method admirably suited his aims, but he outgrew all the Russian symbolists in sheer power of vision and talent.

Born in 1880, Blok began his creative life at the turn of the century and it was imbued with that semi-mystical, semi-decadent atmosphere peculiar to Russia. Widespread interest in mysticism, and even occultism, accompanied—by mere chance—the sudden awakening in Russia of poetic imagination and aesthetic sensibility. This atmosphere was bound to influence the symbolist poets and colour their conception of art. Blok often mentioned in his letters the mystical atmosphere with which he was surrounded. Especially, he came under the influence of Vladimir Solovyov and the latter's mystical vision of Sophia, or Divine Wisdom. Solovyov's Sophia—the *Weltseele* of German Romanticism—becomes the undefined "She" of Blok's early poems, and "The Beautiful Lady," the heroine and inspiration of his poetry for many years to come.

Blok never lost his old transcendentalism. He shed mysticism, but he continued to see "a greater reality" behind everyday reality, hidden mysteries and inner meanings. In this respect he remained a pure symbolist.

—*Times Literary Supplement*

In spite of this mystical background, every poem in his ***Verses about the Beautiful Lady*** can be explained biographically. At the age of twenty, Blok met his future wife, Lyubov Mendeleyev, the daughter of the famous Russian scientist. The fact that her name meant "love" was regarded by Blok himself, and his friends—notably Andrey Bely—as symbolic, and his marriage as a kind of mystical union between the poet and the incarnation of his vision. Lyubov Mendeleyev was Blok's Beautiful Lady. Perceiving in her the divine Sophia, he wooed her with superhuman adoration. His relations with her are treated in a mystical spirit, and his vision of her is intermingled with his own eschatological expectations.

The resulting cycle of poems enriched Russian literature with its most immaterial, most spontaneous and most emotional love poems. Translated into prose, they do not mean much but they have the power of transferring to the reader the magic of a mood, a semi-somnolent state between dream and consciousness. There is nothing in Russian poetry comparable to this diffuse, rarefied music of words, so subjective and personal, which would have satisfied the most rigorous tenets of Mallarmé and Verlaine.

The most surprising fact about these poems is that they were addressed to a real person, and this of course was bound to bring the poet sooner or later down to earth. Soon after his marriage, Blok realized that the woman whom he had regarded as a metaphysical being asked to be regarded just as a woman, and this discovery deeply shocked him. His notebooks reflect the torment he felt at the fading of his spiritual vision. He was now unable to hear his "music of the spheres"; his inspiration, depending on Lyubov's image, meant everything to him, and it had deserted him. How far this was due to Andrey Bely's having fallen in love with Mme. Blok we shall not know until Bely's archives are published in full. Blok's letters included in the second volume of the present edition of his works—though some are published for the first time—do not shed new light on the affair. What seems certain, however, is that Andrey Bely, who at first shared Blok's belief that Lyubov was Sophia, soon ceased to behold her as a metaphysical ideal. It seems that Blok's wife reciprocated his feelings to some extent. Blok sensed the attraction between his "spiritual brother" and his "Beautiful Lady." Emptied of his inspiration, he fell into a deep gloom. His disillusionment greatly embittered him.

In the long introduction to the present edition, Mr. Vl. Orlov, the foremost living Blok scholar, declares that this first phase of the poet's work has been over-emphasized, thus obscuring his later achievements. The almost adulatory reverence paid to his early poetry has given rise to "the legend of Alexander Blok." This took root among the Russian symbolists, but it still lingers among Blok's critics. Mr. Orlov sets out to destroy this legend, to present Blok as a great Russian poet, and to show how ephemeral were his links with the decadent aesthetes. It is wrong, he says, to accept in Blok's poetry as important and fundamental all that was created by the influence of the period, the milieu, and literary fashion.

The first volume, however, contains poetry which, though covering a span of only five or six years, is extraordinarily mature and which determined Blok's entire creative output. To ignore it would be to ignore Blok. There is much more continuity between his early and later work than the Soviet critic would have us believe.

Blok never lost his old transcendentalism. He shed mysticism, but he continued to see "a greater reality" behind everyday reality, hidden mysteries and inner meanings. In this respect he remained a pure symbolist: the search for the unknown, the poets' "poursuite de l'inconnaissable," was a cornerstone of symbolist aesthetics. Playing with the idea that reality could not be absolute but was merely relative, the symbolists cultivated in themselves a feeling that beyond the appearances of this world there was a mysterious, perhaps essential, reality. All of them agreed that reality was "something more than *that*." And it was the task of the poet to unravel this mystery. Their poetic reality therefore was merely a reality perceived subjectively. The symbolists tried to go beyond the individual poetic fact, to attain a higher reality, and—as one French poet said—"une émotion poétique de sens universel." They tried to capture within their souls universal voices, an echo of divine realities. Blok's mystical temperament made these precepts not merely part of an aesthetic, but a dominant strain running throughout his work. The contrast between vision and reality determined most of his later poetry. He also remained first and foremost a lyricist. All his works are to a large extent mirrors of his inner, spiritual life, and they are wholly intuitive. The central theme of Blok's *Weltanschauung* was a musical perception of the world.

Blok was not concerned with music as art, but with the intuitive "voice of music singing from within," with music as the symbol of the universal soul, the symbol of "elemental force." To this conception of music as the essence of being Blok remained faithful all his life. He applied the initial criterion of music to all the problems he came across, whether philosophical, historical, social or artistic. For Blok "music creates the world," it is "the fluid thought of the world."

The predominance of the musical over the logical element can be seen throughout Blok's work. His early lyrics are almost pure music; they are as nebulous as dreams. It was Blok's vagueness, so compatible with music and "heavenly song," that enabled him to achieve his highest romantic effects. For Blok was the greatest romantic of Russia, with the exception, perhaps, of Lermontov. His later poetry (from 1905 onwards) is, like Heine's, the expression of one continuous dissonance between the Real and the Ideal. Moving between dream and reality he continued to use symbols for what was still visionary if not mystical verse. They conveyed his complex, often irrational, state of mind.

At no time does Blok become a realist and cease to be a pure lyricist. His later poetry is even more musical than his early lyrics, but it does become more solid, more material. Undoubtedly, it gains in power. By 1909 his new manner was complete. Diffuseness and vagueness had given place to a firmer outline, an economy of effect, and a boldness of imagery unique in Russian poetry. At the same time his serenity of vision had yielded to violent and uncontrollable emotions.

When he fell into the despondency caused by disillusionment with his ideal, Blok turned violently against mysticism. He ridiculed it in his dramatic trilogy, but did not succeed in making his spiritual experiences objective. *The Puppet Show, The King in the Market Place* and *The Stranger* remain the most expressive examples of lyrical symbolist drama in Russia. Blok created his own, deeply subjective kind of play, intensely poetical and yet full of irony. But he did not cease to seek the Eternal Feminine. Not having found her in Sophia—the terrestrial image of whom his wife had been—he turned to other women— incarnations of evil and dissolution: sensuality was substituted for the ethereal and prayer-like adoration of the Beautiful Lady. Blok's gypsy days gave him back the inspiration he had lost, and posterity gained some of the most beautiful and melodious romances in the Russian language.

Blok's stylistic experiments in his poems devoted to the city are perhaps the most important step towards the suppression of his own "musicolyrical" element. In **"Earth Bubbles"** and in **"Free Thoughts"** he achieves a more concrete manner which leads him to his third volume of poetry.

Though Blok had been brought to earth and though he was making his style more direct and more forcible every year, yet he always kept something of his old visionary self. His momentary social *élan* foundered in a disgust with men, with the crowd and vulgarity. Once again, Blok moved towards a new mystical world. Russia became to him everything that till then he had sought in women. Russia became the focus of his emotions. Love and anger were combined in Blok's feelings about his country, love of the ideal and anger with the real. His mature work is characterized by the rejection of the "terrible world" of Russian reality and the assertion of a romantic ideal. Thus Blok became the poet of a tragic theme—the tragedy of duality—love of life in its ideal image of the future, and aversion to life, taken historically. Blok considered that such a dual approach to life (love-hate) was proper to a tragic conception of the world. On the other hand, Blok loved this terrible world and saw no contradiction in his attitude. "Even a world in despair is wonderful," he wrote. "I love this terrible world and glimpse beyond it another world."

Between 1908 and 1917 Blok did not experience Russia on a terrestrial plane; he visualized a supra-terrestrial Russia, Another World. And perhaps it is true to say that Blok did not experience the Revolution: he heard the music of his revolution. When he found nothing in reality that corresponded to this inner music he ceased to write. He died in 1921 at the age of forty-one, tired, bewildered, and disillusioned. If Blok is linked at all with the realistic Russian poetry of the nineteenth century, it is merely by the isolated instances of a realistic tendency in his work. These appear in his third volume of verse. In **"Retribution,"** and in **"The Rose and the Cross,"** he outgrows lyricism, but not entirely; his *Scythians* is a monumental ode, remote from impressionist lyricism. But realism is not characteristic of his work as a whole. He retained to the last a romantic understanding of art, and his romanticism culminated in his greatest poem—*The Twelve.*

When the Revolution came it seemed to Blok that the old world was really wrecked, and that something new and beautiful must appear in its place. A contemporary wrote that at that time Blok "went about, young, cheerful, fresh, with shining eyes, listening to that revolutionary music in the noise of the old world's collapse which, on his own testimony, sounded unceasingly in his ears." Blok saw in the Revolution a new manifestation of the Spirit of Music. He believed that men were coming closer now to the elemental in nature—that they were growing more "musical."

He achieved in *The Twelve* a perfect fusion of the musical and realistic elements. There is a simple narrative, the setting is Petrograd in winter, in the early days of the Revolution. The characters are few: twelve Red Guards patrol the streets of the city in a bitter snowstorm. They are rather an anarchic mob than a vanguard of the working classes, tormented by lust and jealousy and guilt. The only incident is the killing of a girl of the streets, the faithless friend of one of them. The scene evoked is almost crudely real; the vocabulary belongs to the slang of the streets, terse and wonderfully simple. The short, fragmentary scenes are set against the background of the blizzard—a familiar motif to Blok—the rhythm of the wind and snow sounding an ominous note throughout the poem. Through the different rhythms—of folk-song, burial march, then of the drawing-room and the snowstorm and wind— two strains seem to predominate: the Marseillaise and the cheap waltz tune.

With a real setting and with apparently real people, Blok succeeds in suggesting that both scene and people are symbolical of something much greater outside themselves. The twelve soldiers do not know where they are going and what they are doing, but they follow, in spite of themselves, a divine leader. The unexpected appearance of Christ at the end of the poem has caused much speculation. It seems that Blok himself could not really explain why he had placed Christ at the head of his Red Army men: "When I finished [the poem] I was myself surprised: Why Christ? But the more I looked at it, the clearer did I see Christ." The effect of the poem, however, does not depend on any message. It is still open to conjecture whether Blok saw in Christ a symbol of redemption through suffering and blood. Blok's Christ is rather a symbol of the Spirit of Music, a symbol of rebellion and freedom, of the new life and strength which the poet felt in the air, of the spirit which bore in itself the promise of a transformation of the world.

There is something ironic in the fact that it was given to this remote lyricist to write the most significant poem of the Revolution. For, from the Soviet point of view, Blok's understanding of the Revolution was limited. He never succeeded in adopting entirely the revolutionary ideology in its materialistic form. The new transformed world which was to be born out of the ruins and ashes was of no concern to him. And he did not fit into this new world just as he did not quite fit into the old pre-revolutionary world. Blok belonged to a transitional period; he remains essentially the poet of the turning-point between two worlds. Imbued with the spirit of the period, he was truly one of those whom he himself called "the children of the terrible years of Russia."

F. D. Reeve (essay date 1960)

SOURCE: "Structure and Symbol in Blok's *The Twelve*," in *The American Slavic and East European Review,* Vol. XIX, No. 2, April, 1960, pp. 259-75.

[*In the following essay, Reeve offers a reading of* The Twelve *as an apolitical poem, in which the Christ figure symbolizes "apotheosis in suffering not through it" and "real freedom in actual restraint as distinguished from the idea of liberation."*]

One's usual sense of chronology and politics suggests that Russian poetry after 1917 was quite different from Russian poetry before 1917 and quite different from post-war European poetry. Perhaps the historians and politicians have again persuaded us into oversimplification, because Russian poetry did not change *that* way until the institutionalization of repression under industrial expansion in the late 1920's and early 1930's.

That Brjusov early became a Communist Party member was politically exiting to his friends, important for the Party, but not artistically significant. Like any "change," it followed not from the character of the new but from the failure of the old, in this instance, from Brjusov's creative attrition. Brjusov did not so much become a member of the Party as he stopped being a non-member, much in the sense that he stopped being a Symbolist when the social principles and patterns which tolerated the esthetic values associated with Symbolism altered and, in alteration, required fresh satisfaction and different values.

What may be considered to have been the two latent and commingled tendencies in Symbolism, particularly in the work of Blok, split openly under the disintegration of those values and that social cohesiveness, peculiar to Russia between 1900 and 1914—that liberalism—which had understood the world, whether well or badly, as a unity. Futurism and Acmeism are both continuations of aspects of Symbolism, necessary consequences of its discipline and practice in a world of fractured values and chaotic performance.

If Romanticism may, for a moment, be considered the attempt in art to get away from the things of this world, and Realism, the attempt to get to the things of this world, Futurism may, again for a moment and despite the urbanistic current in it, be labelled the continuation of the Romantic aspect of Symbolism, and Acmeism, despite its exotic current, of the Realistic aspect. Each movement celebrated half of what the Symbolists had celebrated, adjusting history and society to a fresh, vigorous but unendurably partial understanding. Together, both cited those French and other European writers whom the Symbolists had first praised in the name of the same rejuvenation which Symbolism had come in on, namely, a return to the original roots of poetry. The Acmeists emphasized craftsmanship and concreteness; the Futurists, the ebulliently personal, the general, and the transcendental. The Soviet government's approval of Futurism, particularly of the work of Mayakovsky, and its rejection of other literary programs and examples meant that what was personal, general, and intellectually conservative in Futurism was included as part of the understanding the government's program represented. What was transcendental was quickly limited to metaphoric exaggeration, a politically harmless indulgence.

As organizations, the groups of poets organized as Futurists, Acmeists, Imaginists, Cosmists or whatever, operated after the Symbolists had become passé. As poets, however, they were young contemporaries of the Symbolists and frequently promoted by them, as Blok promoted Kljuev or Esenin. Their success or failure depended not so much on political change (outside of political persecution) as on the maturation of their own talents and on public recognition, often tardy, as it was of Pasternak.

More importantly, the work of this period that used political change to promote itself is, regardless of author, without value now that the "change" is history. Neither Brjusov nor Mayakovsky's, neither Belyi nor Bednyi's political poetry is of more than topical interest. Bednyi's poetry is cliché. Belyi is remembered chiefly for his prose and for his propaedeutic critical writings, preludes to the more competent work of the Formalist critics. Mayakovsky is a monument of a certain kind of wonderful vitality and imaginativeness. Brjusov is associated with an esthetic movement at the end of the nineteenth century. The one frequently cited example of the successful marriage of art and politics is Blok's *The Twelve.* Its political associations are, however, not so much intentional as merely coincidental. Its design is apolitical. It is a poem about revelation.

The Twelve is in twelve sections. Some are short, some long; some divided into measured stanzas, some in a kind of movement that approximates "free" verse but nonetheless with a co-ordinating scheme of rhyme and rhythm. The poem was written in the ten-day interval January 8-18, 1918. It was begun a couple of days before Blok finished his article "Russia and the Intelligentsia" ("Rossija i intelligencija").

The opening section is a lyric description of atmosphere, an invocation of setting, in which man and nature are presented as inextricably bound together in a given historical moment. The seemingly insignificant details or desires of ordinary people in their ordinary lives are made to take on meaning by being isolated and frozen (very much in the manner of Dostoevsky) as symbols against an emotional intensity carried by a set of natural images, which themselves are symbols or verge on being symbols. The section is a series of deft, thumb-nail sketches of dramatic oppositions—of man to nature and of men to themselves—and suggested consequent losses. The end of the section turns to the rest of the poem as a dramatic analysis and resolution of the conflicts "pictured" in it.

> Black night.
> White snow.
> Wind, wind!
> A man can't stand up.
> Wind, wind—
> All over God's world!
>
> . . . . .
>
> The wind is cutting!
> And the cold's as bad!
> The bourgeois on the corner
> Has hid his nose in his collar.
> But who's this?—Long hair,
>
> And he says in an undertone:
> "Traitors!
> "Russia's lost!"
> Must be a writer—
> Some Cicero . . .
>
> . . . . .
>
> Bread!
> What's ahead?
> Go on!
>
> Black, black the sky.

> Spite, mournful spite
> Boils in the heart . . .
> Black spite, holy spite . . .
> Comrade! Look out
> Both eyes!
>
> *Chërnyi vecher.*
> *Belyi sneg.*
> *Veter, veter!*
> *Na nogakh ne stoit chelovek.*
> *Veter, veter—*
> *Na vsëm bozh'em svete!*
>
> . . . . .
>
> *Veter khlëstkij!*
> *Ne otstaët i moroz!*
> *I burzhui na perekrëstke*
> *V vorotnik upriatal nos.*
> *A eto kto?—Dlinnya volosy*
>
> *I govorit vpolgolosa:*
> *—Predateli!*
> *—Pogibla Rossija!*
> *Dolzhno byt', pisatel'—*
> *Vitija . . .*
>
> . . . . .
>
> *Khleba!*
> *Chto vperedi?*
> *Prokhodi!*
>
> *Chërnoe, chërnoe nebo.*
>
> *Zloba, grustnaja zloba*
> *Kipit v grudi . . .*
> *Chërnaja zloba, svjataja zloba . . .*
> *Tovarishch! Gliadi*
> *V oba!*

The second section introduces the twelve Red Guardsmen as if coming out of the violence of nature and of men. Van'ka, a friend of one of the twelve, is "occupied" with a prostitute, Kat'ka, as a few lines of dialogue among the twelve indicate. The third "stanza" of the section followed like the other two, by the burden "Eh, eh, without a cross!" is again a description of the emotional content of what the twelve men feel and of what we, as readers, are in this moment to perceive of the total process of change.

The third section, consisting of three four-line songs of which the second was a Russian soldier's song, is a lyric interlude. The fourth section is a description of Van'ka's seduction of Kat'ka from the point of view of and rather in the tone of one who has been there before, so to speak. The words move quickly and tightly until consummation of the vulgarity itself, as given sardonically in the last word of the section:

> Ah, you, Katia, my Katia,
> You fat little mug . . .

> *Akh, ty, Kat'ja, moja Kat'ja,*
> *Tolstomorden'kaja . . .*

In the fifth section, the tone of voice, of language is, again, that of colloquial talk, of slang, but it is not dialogue and the dominant point of view or attitude is that of an outsider, that of the poet. The section is a resumé of Katia's professional history. Three people seem to be speaking simultaneously: Katia to herself, remembering; someone, presumably among the twelve, who has known her and wants her; and the poet.

In the sixth section, the center and the climax of the poem, the Red Guardsman Petrukha shoots at Van'ka and Kat'ka. Van'ka escapes: Kat'ka is killed. Petrukha curses her, and he turns, as if with the author, to the revolution at hand, as indicated by the two lines that close the section, that are the middle couplet in the third stanza of the second section, and a variation of which are part of Petrukha's effort at assuaging his conscience in the tenth section:

> Keep in revolutionary step!
> The indefatigable enemy doesn't nap!
>
> *Revoliuc'onnyi derzhite shag!*
> *Neugomonnyi ne dremlet vrag!*

As the troop marches on, in the seventh section, Petrukha begins to feel remorse and guilt, remembering the ecstasy he had experienced with the girl and his commitment to her. His comrades tease him for his regret, and the group begins looting, in the excitement of which Petrukha's remorse is momentarily lost.

The remainder of the poem is a series of different sorts of lyric digressions or interruptions of Petrukha's dialogue between self and soul. The eighth section contains two folk-songs of lamentation, in wording much like part of the third section, and is the beginning of Petrukha's purgation.

The ninth section is a lyric interlude, quickly identifiable as such by the opening lines, which are from a nineteenth-century Russian romance adapted from a poem by F. N. Glinka:

> The city noise cannot be heard,
> Calm surrounds the Neva tower.
>
> *Ne slyshno shumu gorodskogo,*
> *Nad nevskoj bashnej tishina.*

The image of the bourgeois standing on the street-corner, his collar up around his ears, occurs as in the first section. It is this time coupled with the image of the mangy cur, with which the bourgeois is identified.

The tenth section is, after a short transition, a return to the debate in Petrukha's mind: what he has lost of himself by the violence of murder and openly sexual commitment and what he owes to himself and to others in terms of the new future the revolution promises.

The eleventh section, which ends with the same burden as the tenth (one word short):

> Forward, forward,
> Working class!
>
> *Vperëd, vperëd,*
> *Rabochij narod!*

is a kind of photograph by the poet of the twelve men's procession through the snowstorm, the red flag high and foremost. If the twelve men are, as the last two lines of the section suggest is possible, to be taken as the revolutionary movement and the people in revolt, they themselves are so oblivious of the essence of their work, of their reform, that we, as readers, cannot be expected to apply such an interpretation to the poem as a whole. Although it is true that Blok, in his critical articles, often referred to a parallel between the period of the rise of Christianity in Rome and the revolutionary period in Russia which he himself was living through, there is nothing in this poem, so far as I see, to support the idea that the twelve Red soldiers are parallels to the Apostles. Whatever consciousness of their mission they have is sharply limited and, I think Blok suggests, ultimately to be subverted, by violence and a passion for self-satisfaction.

The twelfth section repeats the vocabulary and images of the preceding parts of the poem and the three dominant points of view: the guardsmen's attitude to their adventure, Petrukha's "interior monologue," and the poet's observations and finally moral understanding. The marchers, the dog, the snowstorm, the bullet, the blood—all come together at the end with Christ:

> . . . So they march in solemn step—
> Behind—the hungry dog,
> Ahead—with the bloody flag,
> Unseen behind the snowstorm,
> Unhurt by the bullet,
> In gentle tread above the storm,
> Dusted with the pearly snow,
> In a white halo of roses—
> Ahead—goes Jesus.
>
> . . . *Tak idut derzhavnym shagom—*
> *Pozadi—golodnyi pës,*
> *Vperedi—s krovavym flagom,*
> *I za v'jugoj nevidim,*
> *I ot puli nevredim,*
> *Nezhnoj postup'ju nadv'juzhnoj,*
> *Snezhnoj rossyp'ju zhemchuzhnoj,*
> *V belom venchike is roz—*
> *Vperedi—Isus Khristos.*

The Twelve contradicts the usual political interpretation of art which asserts the artist's satisfaction with his elaboration of a political theme. *The Twelve* has no political theme. One may give the poem a political reading, of course, but such a reading shows that the poem is neither for nor against the revolution most people assert it apotheosizes and is against revolution in general, passively admitting the fact of violence and physical change.

The existence of a political theme would necessarily form the axis of the poem, as it does in Blok's short political lyrics or in *Skify* (*The Scythians*). There is no political axis in *The Twelve*. On the contrary, the structure of the poem confirms that, whatever it may yield to even contradictory, political readings, it is apolitical, using the violence of a political change for its own non-political and non-violent ends. Medvedev, who studied the manuscript, has succinctly stated Blok's composition of it:

> It seems that the chapters written on white paper, i.e., those written first, include all the chief moments of the dramatic plot of the poem. This includes the appearance, the "first sortie," of the twelve Red Guardsmen and—as exposition of dramatic action— the conversation between Van'ka and Kat'ka (ch. II), Kat'ka's murder—the climax of the poem (ch. VI)— Petrukha's suffering (ch. VII) and the resolution of his anguish—an original social catharsis: *to the grief of all the bourgeois we will fan the world conflagration* (ch. VIII and ch. XII to line 327). It is very significant that all of chapter XII to the lyric ending with Christ is given in the poem as a continuation of Petrukha's monologue begun in chapter VIII and interrupted by the lyric digression of the intervening chapters. . . .

The writing of the poem began with the central dramatic episode—the love tragedy of Kat'ka-Petrukha-Van'ka, an original modification of the old romantic plot several times before used by Blok—Columbine-Pierrot-Harlequin.

[*Dramy i poemy Al. Bloka,* 1928]

The Twelve is a series of lyric poems around a central dramatic plot. The dramatic plot, or axis, is interrupted by lyric intervals. The poem is a love story. It is a concatenation of scenes and interludes which in the writing were composed into a total drama. Each section was conceived as a separate poem with separate motifs, a different aspect of the central plot, a separate example of Blok's understanding. Medvedev points out that the poem was written in sections which were later reshuffled into their present order, and that the title itself, which many people have considered provocative of the poem or as a provocative theme, first occurs on the eleventh page of the manuscript, indicating that, like most titles, it was come upon during work on the poem it labels and that, like any good title, its function is to shed other light on, to be still another aspect of, the whole poem.

In short, we have no evidence either inside or outside the poem to contradict Blok's own comment that

> . . . who interprets *The Twelve* as a political poem is either blind to art or else up to his ears in political mud or possessed with great rancor—whether he be friend or enemy to my poem.

At the same time it would be incorrect to deny any connection between *The Twelve* and politics. The truth is that the poem was written in that exceptional, and always brief, period when a cyclone of revolution causes a storm on all the seas—of nature, life, and art. On the sea of human life there is also a backwater, like the Markizovaja Pond, which is called politics.

As puzzling to commentators as the politics of the poem is the use of the Christ-figure at the end. Gumilëv, in a public lecture in 1919, was one of the first to say that it disturbed him, that it was a superfluity tacked on for "purely literary effect." Blok himself said then, and wrote in his notebooks and diary, that he was not satisfied with the Christ-figure, but could not imagine an alternative. Why he could not, in terms of his understanding generally, is given in an entry in his diary of 1918:

> The Marxists are the most intelligent critics, and the Bolsheviks are correct in being chary of *The Twelve.* But the artist's "tragedy" remains a tragedy. Besides: *if* there existed in Russia a real clergy and not just a class of morally obtuse people called clergy, it would have long ago "mastered" the fact that "Christ is with the Red Guardsmen." It is hardly possible to dispute this truth so simple for those who have read the Gospel and thought about it. . . .

> "The Red Guard" is the "water" on the millwheel of the Christian church. . . . (As rich Jewry was the water on the millwheel of sovereignty, which not one "monarch" figured out in time).

> This is the terror (if they could understand this). This is the weakness of the Red Guard also: mere children in an iron age; an orphan, wooden church at a drunken and bawdy fair.

> Did I really "eulogize" [Christ]? (as Kamenev said). I only verified a fact: if you look into the eye of the snow-storm *on this road* you will see "Jesus Christ." But sometimes I myself deeply hate this feminine specter.

Two years later he still supported his poem; in fact, he called it

> . . . whatever it may be, the best I have written. Because then I lived contemporaneously.

It is not adequate to say that the theme of the poem and the poem itself follow from Blok's work on his article "The Intelligentsia and the Revolution" or are verified by the article on Gatiline, not merely because the political attitude in the articles is transformed in the poem, but because the political animus of the articles is only facultative in the poem. The fact that the poem is, basically, a love story not only co-ordinates it thematically with Blok's other work during his lifetime but also requires us to look more deeply into the poem for its sources and meaning.

The poem's immediate and unusual success seems to me to depend on its dramatic organization of powerful symbols. Whatever may be the poem's failures in terms of its possibilities, its impact is that of a violent confrontation among essential but disparate symbols that directly apply to actual life.

Psychologically speaking, a symbol is considered an archaic concept which is a direct consequence of human opposition to change and which is an attempt to restore, at least partially, what has been changed. The aim of the symbol is to repress the painful circumstances of change—that is, of the conditions which gave rise to the symbol—or, at least, to prevent their return. In these terms, all symbols have an historical content and an emotional significance. Although values, as predictions of probabilities of satisfaction, may shift from symbol to symbol, a symbol remains

> . . . a condensation of the genetic past . . . and of the future. . . . [of a] wish to experience a gratification which was denied in the setting that gave rise to the symbol.
>
> [S. G. Margolin, *Symbols and Values,* 1954]

Symbols have kernels of grief, of forgotten sadness or loss. They communicate change by naming it as an historical event; they express the anxiety of the disrupted equilibrium concomitant on change and the anxiety that follows awareness of the new experience.

In short, what is considered the psychological function of symbols is, in terms of the content taken up by this poem, very much the same as the ultimate esthetic function: the organization of the determinate negation of established reality—ultimate freedom—and its actualization. The symbols of the mind in its historic play and the images of art in their systematic elaboration here correspond. This is exactly what we find in the poem.

The symbol of the Christ-figure is excellent illustration both of the success of the correspondence and of the imperfection or inadequacy of the representation and its elaboration. Blok himself suggests this [in his diary]:

> Religion is junk (priests and so on). The terrible thought nowadays: not that the Red Guardsmen are "unworthy" of Christ, who now goes with them, but that it is precisely He who goes with them, when it ought to be Someone Else.

> Romanticism is junk. Everything that's *settled* into dogma, delicate dust, *fantasticality* has become junk. Only *élan* is left.

He says the same thing in his notebook. He says the same thing, sharply, in his letter to Mayakovsky [on December 30, 1918]:

> Your cry is still only a cry of pain and not of joy (Wagner). In destroying we are still the same slaves of the old world; destruction of tradition is the same tradition.

He says it tactfully in his letter [on August 12, 1918] to Annenkov, who illustrated an edition of *The Twelve*:

> About Christ: He's not at all like that: little, hunched over like a dog from behind, carries the flag precisely and *goes away.* "Christ with the flag"—it's—"like that and not like that." Do you know (I do, by all my life) that when a flag flies in the wind (when it rains or snows or *especially* in the dark of night) then *it* makes you think of some enormous person somehow related to it (he doesn't hold it, carry it, but somehow—I don't know how to put it). . . .

> Or again: . . . I again looked at the whole picture, looked, and suddenly remembered: Christ . . . by Dürer! (i.e., something completely different from this, an *extraneous* remembrance).

According to Medvedev, the manuscripts confirm the guess that the Christ-figure is, actually, a culminating figure, that it runs through all the variants and early versions of the poem and that it is not a sudden invention or addition but an intended functional persona.

In tone the poem is oddly, in moments heretically, religious: the eighth section is composed of two stanzas from an old Russian peasant song (the first and three-fourths of the seventh stanzas), four distichs based on imitation of an habitual concept of folk poetry but savagely, ironically directed against bourgeois standards and mores, a line from the Church Slavonic burial service asking mercy, and a last line—"It's boring!" The poem is dramatic, attacking the indifferent, forward movement of an insensate society through the vitality of its lowest and its highest common denominators.

The figure of Christ is both low and high, both immediate, in the sense of suffering, and eschatological, in terms of divinity. Furthermore, the corruption which Blok is moving against has been, as he sees it, largely impelled by a stupid and perverse imitation of Christ, that is, by the inanities and barbarities of standardized religious and intellectual practice and behavior at the expense of what we might call the essential in man and what Blok chooses to organize under the spirit of music.

The difficulty with the Christ-figure is its historical and, therefore, poetic limitation: it is, really, only half a symbol. It is adequate to the content of the poem but not to the poem's meaning. It carries everything except the notion of gratification, that is, except the notion of ultimate freedom. This is the basic failure of the poem and the cause of our dissatisfaction with it: that it sets out to delimit just such a notion, but, at the end, seems to subvert its own system. The actual Christ-figure is a sensational analogy to an aspect of the freedom the poem is about. Christ *is* the redeemer of both the living and the dead. In terms of meaning, however, neither Christian theory nor Christian practice is adequate to the dilemma dramatized by this poem. The Christ-figure is actual contrast to, or dramatization of the contrast between, the failures of men and the limitations imposed on them by their history of failures.

If one interprets the Christ-figure as a symbol of some principle of liberation or as the herald of a new world, or as manifestation of the concept of redemption through suffering, one restricts the poem to a political signification, and the whole poem does not tolerate this. The Christ-figure may indeed be taken as a messenger, but rather like the messenger in a Greek tragedy who announces both the pathos and the epiphany, apotheosis *in* suffering, not through it. This is the notion, carried as an image, of real freedom in actual restraint, as distinguished from the idea of liberation. Historical tradition and the processes of religious thought weight interpretation of the Christ-figure on the side of redemption, as opposed to the side of essential freedom. Although Blok uses the figure in this second, and what he would call musical, sense, he was aware that intellectual history imposed the first, and for his purposes unsuccessful, understanding. If we can see the Christ-figure not in terms of a church or a religious doctrine or even as historical agent but as incarnation of the experience of ignorance and loss and of the concept of ultimate, free reality, I do not think it presents any difficulties to us. The trouble is that, because the figure in the poem is not carefully defined—however mysterious it may be—and because the figure in our culture comes cluttered with other uses, it is not easy to see it this way.

Necessarily Blok himself, although holding to this notion of passive and essential freedom, described what he had in mind in terms of cycles of retribution and resurrection. Since the revenge—redemption cycle of the 1917 Revolution seemed actualization of his belief, he frequently described it in terms of that belief, thinking it apt description:

> A completely new world is upon us, a completely new
> life is coming.

I mean that such description should not be taken literally, although it is a prophetic assertion, any more than that line in the first stanza of **The Twelve** which reads literally, but asserts nothing—

> Wind, wind
> All over God's world!
>
> *Veter, veter*
> *Na vsëm bozh'em svete!*

should be construed as involving divinity. The Russian phrase is, rather, equivalent to something like "all over the lot." The word "God's" is used completely colloquially suggesting a particular kind of universality which is not involved in a religious context.

Blok uses Christian symbols in a non-Christian or even anti-doctrinaire understanding. In part, they elaborate tersely his notion, fully presented in "Catiline," for example, of the essential analogy between the historical moments of 1917 Russia and Rome after Christ's birth. Chiefly, however, they involve that metaphysic of absolute freedom toward which, he believes, meaningful life must move. In the first section, Blok ridicules the doctrine and the performance of institutionalized religion. Addressing "Comrade Priest," the poet asks:

> Remember how you used to go
> Belly foremost,
> And the belly with its cross
> Shone on the people?
>
> *Pomnish', kak byvalo*
> *Brjukhom shël vperëd,*
> *I krestom sijalo*
> *Brjukho na narod?*

In the second section, following introduction of the twelve soldiers, Blok picks up the cross again but in a sharply different sense:

> Freedom, freedom,
> Oh, oh, without a cross!
>
> *Svoboda, svoboda,*
> *Ekh, ekh, bez kresta!*

He means without the priest's badge of office, and he means that without the idea of purification and redemption the passion of protest becomes only self-indulgence and self-consummation (Kat'ka and Van'ka). He also means that the idea of freedom of which the cross may be taken as symbol and Christ as agent is really independent of either. Blok understands a dilemma which he cannot resolve and of which this poem is the expression.

The love story of Kat'ka-Petrukha-Van'ka merges into the love story in which Christ is the central figure:

> Oh, oh, go ahead and sin!
> It'll be easier for your soul!
>
> *Ekh, ekh, sogreshi!*
> *Budet legche dlja dushi!*

This is the movement toward freedom, which can be understood only as a contradiction and never actualized. Insofar as the poem seeks to preserve that integrity of this paradox—that the necessary quest for freedom destroys the capacity to be free—it is an anti-revolutionary poem. The hope for freedom is countered but not controverted by the experience of failure.

Our response to the poem is complicated by the colloquial elements woven into it. Some seem dramatically tied to the poem's movement; others seem affixed, the way children pin the tail on the donkey. Professor Stremooukhoff has suggested [in conversation] that the method was taken over from Richepin's *Chansons des Gueux*. That is to say that its provenience was literary and French.

Zhirmunskij refers to the correspondence between Vlas's vision in Dostoevsky's story "Vlas" and the appearance of the Christ-figure at the end of Blok's poem [*Poezija Aleksandra Bloka*, 1922]. Something of the theme and method of **The Twelve** is evident also in Blok's own early work—for example, in the 1904 poem **"Fraud"**—and in his later work as well—for example, the 1918 project for a play about Christ. It is also probable that Blok's affection for

Grigor'ev's work and the gypsy romance had made available to his consciousness, as it were, certain motifs and types of lyric used in *The Twelve.* Above all, however, the material seems to come from Blok's own sense of the character and vitality of the times: this, he suggests, is what people were occupied with; this is the way they talked; this is the expense. The second stanza in the third section was, Chukovskij has pointed out, a Russian soldiers' *chastushka* or epigrammatic lyric:

> Ah, you, bitter-misery,
> Sweet life!
> A torn greatcoat,
> An Austrian gun!

> *Ekh, ty, gore-gor'koe,*
> *Sladkoe zhit'ë!*
> *Rvanoe pal'tishko,*
> *Avstrijskoe ruzh'ë!*

In the eighth section, the first three lines, which are variants of the lines just quoted, and lines thirteen through fifteen, addressed by Petrukha to a real or imagined bourgeois, are from an old Russian folk-song:

> Oh, you, bitter-misery!
> Boring boredom,
> Deadly!

> . . . . .

> I'll drink your blood
> For my lady-love,
> My dark eyes . . .

> *Okh, ty, gore-gor'koe!*
> *Skuka skuchnaja,*
> *Smertnaja!*

> . . . . .

> *Vyp'ju krovushku*
> *Za zaznobushku,*
> *Chernobrovushku . . .*

Orlov among others has pointed out [in Blok, *Sochineija,* 1946] that the lines in the tenth and eleventh sections—

> Forward, forward, forward
> Working class!

are a variant of two lines from the revolutionary song "Varshavjanka" that had been very popular at the turn of the century.

The poem builds up its impact, in part, by use of then contemporary political slogans, fragments of street conversations, signs on political banners, dialectical expressions and word forms, slang phrases, revolutionary jargon, vulgarisms and obscenities. The language has an immediacy and force about it—much of it is presented as dialogue—that resemble those of the stage. Its closeness

to the reader is further emphasized by the contrasting use of phrases from the liturgy and imitations of the grand style, as in the almost "montage" technique of the last section, for example.

***The Twelve* is an example of Blok's life-long fascination with the theater and the possibilities of drama. He knew that the real suffering of real people was essential to tragedy, that the author must do more than extend his consciousness—he must re-enact it totally.**

—*F. D. Reeve*

The love story is tied to its time by what the lovers say, by the phrases of straight description of them, and, chiefly, by Blok's comments on it and by the series of parallels he sets up: for example, the twelve soldiers are walking, the lovers are walking, Kat'ka walks the streets for a living, the poor walk begging—and the dog-bourgeois walks behind them all. This sense of motion, this image of walking in all its ramifications, as given in the poem, is a symbol combining by a principle of dramatic apposition a series of highly charged, essentially lyric perceptions. Structurally, the poem is a concatenation of alternating scenes of exposition and action narrated as if by a chorus, an omniscient but present intermediary. In moments of lyric digression, the judgment of the author is obvious. In moments of dramatic narrative, phrases of the actors stand apart. A number of figures fitted to the play and independent of the author's biases are the objective equivalents of emotional responses, the impersonal symbols which, rubbed against each other, as it were, by coincidence and violence, generate and carry the poem's meaning. The poem is intensely abstract and directly passionate at the same time. Each aspect is both complementary and disturbing to the other. This is another way of saying that the Christ-figure is a necessary and unsatisfactory symbol of apotheosis—necessary, in that the emotional intensity leads to a culminating definition; unsatisfactory, in that apotheosis is a removal of, and from, actual passion.

From this point of view, *The Twelve* is an example of Blok's life-long fascination with the theater and the possibilities of drama. He knew that the real suffering of real people was essential to tragedy, that the author must do more than extend his consciousness—he must re-enact it totally. He was certain that public desire for mere entertainment would pass and, with it, an author's indifference to theatrical reality and his consequent reliance on a director. He envisioned a return to the immediacy of the Greek theater, characterized, as he had it, by the involvement of an educated and responsive audience and the anamnestic myth, analogous to Plato's, informing the life of the community.

Despite his theory, all his plays are clearly adaptations of the efforts of the late medieval actors' theater—the Harlequin-Pierrot-Columbine triangle and the improvisational, sad buffoonery of the commedia dell'arte tradition—to the essential effort at revelation of the medieval mystery or passion plays. Blok's "biggest" play, *The Rose and the Cross,* almost performed by the Moscow Art Theatre, is a good illustration, not only because of its development, in stages, from original idea as a ballet with the lady Chatelaine, a Troubadour, and a "Devil's Emissary" to an opera and, finally, after a period in which Blok read extensively in medieval French, Latin, and Italian literature, to a play, but also because of the setting—Languedoc and Brittany in the early twelfth century—and the use of castles and knights—Bertran is called the Knight of Woe—and the series of dove-tailed triangles of relationships. Each triangle, like each person, is emotionally or morally imperfect or corrupt. Out of this imperfection or corruption, the person moves in such a way as to violate another relationship and establish an imperfect triangle analogous to the one left behind, until, at the end, everyone is cut off from the central object of desire, the lady Izora, by death or by having gone away or by failing to understand where one is at all. The play is very much a lesson. In his instructions to the actors of the Moscow Art Theatre, Blok set out directly to contradict the obvious: his play is not an historical drama, specifically because upper-class life and morality "of whatever period or whatever nation never differ." History, he says, was merely a convenience he used to represent his plan. The words of the songs are, he says, irrelevant, but the rhythm of them, once met, will remain and will evoke further modulations. The images of sea and of snow, of motion and of dream, of joy and of suffering run throughout the play as throughout a poem. The allegorical figure Joy-Suffering taken, Blok says, from an old Cornwall dialect song in a collection of Breton folksongs, is a "poetic" symbol, not a dramatic symbol, an illustration of a point of moral view.

The play is about Bertran, who, Blok says, is "not the hero but the head and the heart of the play." From another point of view, however, it is not about *him* or about an aspect of Christianity at all. It is equally about mystery, about the character Gaetan, about whom Blok calls *xenos,* the stranger, the man who is here but does not belong. "This is the artist," and he is the real subject. Generalized, of course, he is Everyman alienated in the twentieth century. In a world in which the only significant communication can be, as Blok himself argued, communication by gesture, the hero as symbol has no real role. Really, history does not repeat itself, as Blok says in the "General Plan of the *Historical Scenes,*" and this play, like *The Twelve,* is an intense, brilliant, but not finally successful effort to cross from myth to theater, to animate myth into theater, to transform allegory into the substance of life and make both sing with meaning and beauty.

The movement of *The Twelve* is very much like that of the tragic rhythm of drama: a statement of a dilemma or impasse in terms of contrasting or opposing sides or principles; consequent suffering or intensely emotional activity that destroys simultaneously the integrity of both conflicting principles; apotheosis or epiphany in which the sense of loss is sublimated and the change defined by

an understanding. It is the movement of that essential music which Blok considered the moving principle of life and which Gogol had identified with God.

> What is a poet? A man who writes in verse? No, of course not. A poet is a carrier of rhythm.

The Twelve is further delimited in scope, however, by the absence of character development and by its predominant lyric tone. Although its success may follow directly from its lack of grandeur, the absence of a sense of greatness (which is not absent in **Retribution**) or merely of size contradicts the dramatic movement. The poem seems too small for what it says it is about. Its symbols like the Christ-figure seem to have escaped it.

It is Blok's most popular poem. It is his last important one. It is the final example of those principles of versification and esthetic understanding which he had long maintained and periodically refined. It is the central example—although I do not think it Blok's best poem—of the interplay between pictures and meaning in poetry, of the fusion of image and idea through the office of symbols. It is a rather successful attempt to bind politics, in the broadest sense, and art, to make each inform on the other, to present poetry as a significant description of what is going on.

In our Western tradition—and this includes Blok's Russia—the image of Christ is that of a hero, a god, and an idea, and at the same time—as Blok would have liked to have used it—of a real value which has never been, and never can be, actualized.

Boris Thomson (essay date 1978)

SOURCE: "The Necessity of Art: The Last Years of Aleksandr Blok," in *Lot's Wife and the Venus of Milo: Conflicting Attitudes to the Cultural Heritage in Modern Russia,* Cambridge University Press, 1978, pp. 29-52.

[In the following excerpt, Thomson examines the evolution of Blok's views on culture and the role of the artist in society in terms of the Russian struggle between the intelligentsia and the masses.]

> Those who look into the future have no regrets for
>   the past.
>
>   —Aleksandr Blok
>
> Who will shed tears for the wife in the Book?
> For isn't she one of the least of the dead?
> But I know that my heart will never forget
> That she gave up her life for a single look.
>   —Anna Akhmatova, 'Lot's Wife'

If the Symbolists often thought of themselves as intermediaries between different levels of existence, each of which had to be experienced to the full, then in their ceaseless shuttling between the extremes of human nature they ran the usual risk of all double agents, that of losing their sense of direction and identity, and finally of being 'turned'. Poison and devilry became such familiar attributes of art in their work that they gradually lost the ability to distinguish between the inspirations of divine beauty and goodness and the venomous exhalations of Hell, as did Blok for example, in his famous poem **'To the Muse'** (**'K Muze'**, 1908). But whereas for some of the Symbolists such paradoxes were little more than an intellectual game, for Blok they expressed in eschatological terms, the central dilemma behind all his work.

Like others before him Blok realized that the Western orientation of the Russian intelligentsia had alienated them from the vast majority of their fellow-countrymen; but he saw this not just as a regrettable fact of life, but as a moral challenge. The artist's primary duty, he believed, lay with his people, even if this meant opposing those very values of the intelligentsia which had made him what he was. . . .

How much of the art created by the alienated Westernized intelligentsia, to which Blok himself belonged, was meaningful to the vast masses of the people? How much, if any, would outlast its time?

Throughout Blok's writings on this subject there runs a deep feeling of guilt at the thought of living as an artist at the expense of the people who provided his inspiration. This parasitism could only lead to Nemesis, but the fearful welcome that he extended to this prospect is far removed from the paradox-mongering of Bryusov's 'The Coming Huns'. For central to all Blok's thinking is his conviction of the supreme value of art, or at least of artistic inspiration. The value did not lie in the actual 'message' or moral; the visible, paraphrasable content of a work of art provided only, as it were, the staves, over which hovered the 'music', mysterious, irresistible, and unanalysable ('Don't listen to the words of the song; listen only to the voice'). 'Music' remained for Blok a symbol of the source of inspiration, an elemental power, the rhythm of history, an image of divine creativity: 'In the beginning was music. Music is the essence of the world.' It followed from this that the artist was powerless in the grip of his inspiration; he could take no part in directing it and could bear no responsibility for the consequences. His justification consisted simply in blindly obeying the promptings of a higher power, working its will through him as merely one of many possible channels. It followed too that the efforts of the individual artist to do justice to the overwhelming power of his inspiration were pitifully inadequate:

> In the light of this knowledge the actual works of artists become secondary, since to date they are all imperfect creations, mere fragments of much greater conceptions, reservoirs of music that have managed to incorporate only a tiny part of what was glimpsed in the delirium of the creative consciousness.

Even the greatest artist was therefore doomed to fail the power that had chosen him.

Thus the conflict between Blok's view of art as a cosmic force of universal concern, and his simultaneous aware-

ness of the inadequacy and pretentiousness of much of the poetry that he and his fellow-Symbolists were composing led him to veer between hope and despair at ever achieving anything in so compromised a medium:

> But I am an intellectual, a writer, and my weapon is the word. I distrust words, but I have to pronounce them. Distrusting all 'literariness', I, nevertheless, look for a literary answer; all of us share a secret hope that the gulf between words and deeds may not last for ever, that there is a word, which can pass into action.

In the years 1908-16 Blok wrestled despairingly with these dilemmas. The changes in society that he had dreamed of seemed remoter than ever. The Great War had shown the essential barbarism of Western culture, and Russia was yet again following its lead. This sense of guilt and helplessness is reflected in Blok's own work; from 1914 onwards he wrote less and less poetry (thirty-seven poems in 1914, ten in 1915, six in 1916, one in 1917). For this reason the revolutions of 1917 brought him renewed hope. At first he co-operated willingly with the Provisional Government and worked on the commission charged with investigating the crimes of the former Tsarist ministers; but with time he came to be dissatisfied with the slowness of the legal procedures. He began to doubt whether anything had really changed, and to fear that he too, both as man and as artist, was still incurably contaminated by the old order. As in 1908 he began to look for another revolution which would transform the whole of life: 'We (the whole world) are trapped in our own lies. We need something totally new'.

On 14 April 1917, Blok summed up his dilemma: the Revolution had given him the freedom to return to art; but was his art required any longer?

> I must get on with *my own business,* establish my own inner freedom, make time and resources available for being an artist . . . I have no clear idea of what is going on, and yet by the will of fate I have been made a witness of a great epoch. By the will of fate (not my own *puny powers*) I am an artist, i.e. a witness. Does democracy need the artist?

In the summer of 1917 Blok's diaries demonstrate his total identification with the common people and his eagerness to anticipate and rebut the sneers and jibes of the bourgeoisie. The death of a tree prompted the following reflections:

> The tree in front of my window has withered. A bourgeois especially one with an aesthete's snout would simply say: the workers at work again. But first of all you need to know; well, perhaps something heavy had been dumped here, or perhaps there was no way of avoiding it, or perhaps it was simply a very clumsy worker (many of them have not yet acquired the art [*kul'tura*] of precise movements).

In 1908 Blok had contrasted the culture of the people with the culture of the intellectual élite, but now he was extolling even their lack of culture, their inability to perform simple tasks competently. On several occasions he compares the workers to children, ignorant but innocent. It was no longer a question of replacing a false culture by a true one, but increasingly of rejecting all culture as bourgeois.

Blok was acutely conscious of such 'bourgeois' impulses still latent within himself, for example, in his instinctive indignation at the decision of Finland and the Ukraine to secede from Russia. By a characteristic and revealing process of thought he passes from guilt at these reflexes to the thought that perhaps even the noblest ideals had been so compromised by their bourgeois origins that they too were endangered:

> Yesterday I had to tell Ol'denburg that, to be frank, nationalism and even cadetism run in my blood, and that it is shaming for me to love my own, and that a bourgeois is anyone who has accumulated valuables of whatever description, even spiritual ones (this is the psychology of *'la lanterne'* and of all extremist 'senseless' protests); Kuprianovich agreed with me, with the proviso that all this has an economic basis; but my feeling is that it happens of its own accord that intelligence, morality and especially art—become the object of hatred. This is one of the most terrible tongues of the fires of revolution, but it's a fact, and more characteristic of Russians than anyone else.

The revolution, then, had to tread a narrow path between the extremes of anarchy and stagnation, until it had brought Russia and the world safely to their new destination. But what was the role of art in all this? At times Blok felt that the established culture of Russia had a mission to control and direct the destructive power of the revolution and prevent it from totally annihilating the past:

> And this is the task of Russian culture—to direct the fire on to what needs to be burnt; to transform the energies of Razin and Pugachev into a conscious musical rhythm; to set up obstacles which will not weaken the force of the fire, but organize it, organize these chaotic impulses; the slow smouldering fire, in which there also lurks the possibility of a chaotic flare-up, must be steered into the Rasputin corners of the soul and be fanned into a pyre reaching to the sky to burn out every trace of our sly, servile, lazy lust. One of the means of organization is industrialization.

But on other occasions Blok would reject this view of the revolution as a potentially purifying force, which only needed to be directed by the right hands, as unacceptably paternalistic. History had its own logic, and its own morality. . . .

And at times his hatred for bourgeois Western-based culture was so intense that he was happy to contemplate the prospect of the revolution flooding Western Europe in an orgy of destruction. During the Tartar invasions Russia had borne the brunt of the attack; in so doing she had saved Western culture but at the cost of delaying and distorting the development of her own. Now it was Russia that was the vehicle of history, and there was no reason why she should protect European culture from annihilation:

> We are fed up, this is what Europe will never understand, because all this is so *simple,* and in their muddled brains it's so confused. But though they despise us more than ever, they are mortally afraid of us, I think; because, if it really came to it, we would happily let the yellow races through Russia and flood not just the cathedral at Rheims, but all their other holy department-stores. We are a dam, but there is a sluice in the dam, and from now on nothing can stop anyone from opening that sluice 'in full awareness of his revolutionary power'.

Indeed this kind of blanket destruction sometimes seemed to Blok to be the only way forward. In his best known formulation of the idea, the poem *The Scythians* (*Skify,* 1918), the phrase 'the savage Huns' is used to recall the imagery of Ivanov and Bryusov.

Throughout the summer and autumn of 1917 Blok's sympathies oscillated between the Bolsheviks and the other parties. At times he felt that history was working through the Bolsheviks:

> The Bolsheviks are just a group acting on the surface, and behind them there lurks something that has not yet manifested itself.

But in the elections of July 1917 he voted for the S.R.s. We do not know Blok's immediate reactions to the Bolshevik coup because he later destroyed his diaries and notebooks relating to this period, but the next surviving lines and above all the poem *The Twelve* (*Dvenadtsat',* 1918) reveal his total identification with the new revolution. He was not worried by the Bolsheviks' disregard for the legal and democratic niceties; such concerns seemed trivial by the side of the cosmic events that were unfolding. On 15 January he wrote in his notebook the phrase: 'The end of the historical process.'

The chaos and destruction of the first days of the revolution therefore seemed to him to be only temporary and insignificant side-effects of the colossal process of building a new culture. In his notes on a conversation with Yesenin at the beginning of 1918 he wrote:

> The destruction (of churches and the Kremlin which doesn't worry Yesenin) is only for the hell of it. I asked him if there weren't any who destroyed in the name of higher values. He said 'No' (are my thoughts ahead of their time?)

Despite Yesenin's categorical answer Blok remained confident that the destruction brought by the revolution was primarily creative (he had quoted Bakunin's words to this effect as long ago as 1906). In the article 'The Intelligentsia and the Revolution' (Intelligentsiya i revolyutsiva', January 1918) he wrote:

> Don't be afraid. Do you think that a single grain of what is truly valuable can be lost? Our love is too

small if we tremble for what we love. 'Perfect love casteth out fear'. Don't be afraid of the destruction of Kremlins, palaces, pictures, books. We must preserve them for the people; but if they are lost the people will not lose everything. A palace destroyed is no longer a palace. A Kremlin wiped off the face of the earth is no longer a Kremlin. A Tsar who has fallen off his throne is no longer a Tsar. The true Kremlins are within our hearts, the true Tsars within our heads. The eternal forms that have been revealed to us can be taken away only with our heads and our hearts. Did you think that the revolution would be an idyll? That creation need not destroy anything in its path?

Here again we meet the old paradoxes of placing a supreme valuation on culture. Just because it possesses eternal values that are not of this world, its temporal visible manifestations can be sacrificed almost without a qualm. But how long can such values survive without any material form? Surely hardly beyond the memories of the last generation to see them. Even more dangerously, Blok's ecstatic confidence in a new Golden Age to come made him feel that anyway a few lost works of art here and there would not be too serious. What was fit to survive into the new age would mostly survive. A rough sort of justice would be done, but it would still be justice. . . .

It must be remembered too that Blok did not spare himself from his indictment of the Russian bourgeoisie and intelligentsia. In his article 'Russian Dandies' ('Russkiye dendi', 1918) he wrote up a conversation he had had with a young intellectual, Stenich. Stenich had declared:

> We are all worthless, we are flesh of the flesh, bone of the bone of the bourgeoisie . . . I am intelligent enough to understand that it can't go on like this, and that the bourgeoisie will be destroyed. But if socialism does materialize, nothing remains for us but to die; we still have no conception of money; we are all well off and utterly incapable of earning anything by our labour. We are all on drugs and opium; our women are nymphomaniacs. We are a minority, but we are influential among the young; we pour scorn on those who are interested in socialism, work and the revolution. We live only for poetry; I have not missed a single collection in the last five years . . . Nothing interests us but poetry. We are empty, utterly empty.

This revelation of the bankruptcy of the aestheticism of the intelligentsia ends with the young man turning on Blok:

> You are to blame that we are like this. You and all you contemporary poets . . . We asked for bread and you gave us a stone.

Blok ends with the comment: 'I didn't know how to defend myself; and I didn't want to; and anyway I couldn't.'

The article raises the dilemma of the artist in its most agonizing form. Is art simply escapism and, in times of crisis, a dangerous luxury? Is the artist responsible for the interpretations of his work and the uses to which it is put? Is art quite inseparable from the society which has pro-

duced it, a class with leisure to read and cultivate its good taste, and the comfortable assurance that cultural superiority justifies a superiority in material terms as well? During 1917 and the early part of 1918 Blok was ready to answer 'yes' to all these questions, and one can only admire him for the courage with which he faced them.

They form the background to his great poem, *The Twelve.* The immediate inspiration came from the dispersal of the Constituent Assembly by the Bolsheviks on 6 January 1918, and, as Anatoliy Yakobson has pointed out, the murder of Shingarev and Kokoshkin in their hospital beds later the same night. The poem celebrates the destruction and desecration of the hopes and ideals of the Russian intelligentsia over the previous century, and, finally, on top of everything else, introduces the figure of Christ at the head of the Red Guards. In the last nine lines the violence and cacophony of all that has gone before suddenly yield to more conventionally 'beautiful' imagery and mellifluous rhymes and rhythms. The image seems to be alarmingly like that of 'Gentle Jesus, meek and mild', but the context is now the Day of Judgement.

In the reunion of these two seemingly contradictory images lies much of the power of the poem, but it also raises unanswerable questions. Who is this Christ? He is 'ahead' of the Red Guards, but how far is He identified with them here and now, and how far does He stand for the new age, as yet out of sight? Do the Red Guards recognize or accept Him as their leader?—after all they shoot at Him. Is He the old Christ or a new one?

The questions are unanswerable because Blok himself did not know the answers (the poem was written in a state bordering on ecstasy) and his own complex and changing attitudes to the poem would make a study in themselves.

In the usual interpretation of the poem the figure of Christ stands for the new culture that will spring out of the ruins of the old—indeed the suddenness of His appearance suggests that it has already arrived—as Christianity had emerged from the collapse of the Roman Empire (Blok himself seemed to sanction this interpretation in a group of articles beginning with 'Catiline', 'Katilina', 1918). But it is disturbing that the only image Blok can find for the new age is the central image of the culture that he saw and heard crashing in ruins around him.

Evidently there were times when Blok rebelled against this image as too weak and gentle an ideal to stand at the head of the revolution. As he wrote in his diary for 10 March 1918: 'I myself sometimes hate this effeminate apparition'. Perhaps, even in January 1918, Blok was afraid that the revolution had not gone far enough and was threatened by the few old values that it still seemed to retain. Yet, even as one argues this case, one is aware of the extraordinary blessing that Christ seems to confer on the Bolsheviks—the surface meaning of the poem is undeniable too. The two attitudes combined form the culmination of Blok's conflicting attitudes to the culture of the past. Many of Blok's own later writings are, directly, or indirectly, concerned with understanding his own poem.

These conflicting possibilities in the figure of Christ explain how it was that Blok could be both assured of the irresistible advance of a new historical era, and also alarmed by the dangers of the revolution being sucked back into the evils of the bourgeois past. In his note-book for 24 February 1918 he recorded without comment the prophecy of A. G. Gornfel'd: 'The Bolsheviks are creating a huge class of petty bourgeoisie, with all its typical tendency to rapacity etc.' The article "Fellow-citizens' ('Sograzhdane', April 1918), sums up his horror at the reappearance of bourgeois tastes. What was alarming was not just the reappearance of the old bourgeoisie, but the fact that the workers and the peasants were aping the same contemptible airs. The new age that seemed to have dawned in January 1918, no longer seemed so imminent. Without retracting a single word of *The Twelve,* Blok now began to look at it rather differently.

In his article 'Catiline', written in May 1918, Blok recounts the history of the famous Catiline conspiracy and then moves on to the theory that Catullus in his ode 'Attis' was somehow referring to this failure. The interrelation of poetic inspiration and social revolution deliberately recalls the creation of *The Twelve,* but the real significance of the article lies in Blok's reinterpretation of its central symbol. In *The Twelve* Christ had placed Himself at the head of the twelve Red soldiers, but the Catiline conspiracy is not directly linked to the coming of Christ; it is merely symptomatic of the greater revolution already imminent. Even though as a revolutionary Catiline might have failed, he had hammered the first nail into the coffin of

> the 'great culture' which had given birth to and was still to give birth to so many treasures, but which in a few decades was to hear a final and everlasting sentence in a different court, a court that was no respecter of persons, the court of Jesus Christ.

Thus the once short distance between the Red Guards and Christ has lengthened to an indeterminate number of years and even decades. This did not alter the significance of the revolution one whit: when Christ was born the final fall of the Roman Empire was still centuries away, but the crucial event by which the new era would date its calendar, had already occurred, hardly noticed or appreciated by the outside world. It meant simply that the Bolshevik revolution was not, after all, the last word; it was just the beginning of the end. The final outcome was as unforeseeable as the triumph of Christianity had been. . . .

Russia's role, then, as in the days of the Scythians and the Huns, was to revivify the world with a new, even if seemingly barbaric, culture. Just because she was so backward (as in the old Slavophil argument) and had been spared the corruption and decay of the West, she was closer to the elemental essence of culture, and so better placed to set the world straight again. . . .

Because the elements were now expressing themselves through the masses the old bourgeois intelligentsia was incapable of recognizing or protecting the new face of culture. It was no paradox then to call the barbarian masses its true guardians:

> If we are to talk of bringing the masses to culture then it is by no means certain who has the greater right to bring whom: the civilized—the barbarians, or *vice versa,* since the civilized are now exhausted, and have lost their cultural value; at such a time the unconscious guardians of culture are the young and fresh barbarian masses.

This culture is not to be mocked; it is alarming and possibly even fatal for those who have been nourished by the old world:

> This music is a wild chorus, a formless howl to the civilized ear. It is almost unbearable for many of us, and today it will not seem funny if I say that for many of us it will be fatal. It is ruinous for those achievements of civilization which had seemed unassailable; it is totally opposed to our familiar melodies of 'the true, the good and the beautiful'; it is utterly hostile to much that has been instilled in us by our upbringing and education in the Europe of the last century.

The Russian intelligentsia was therefore caught in a terrible dilemma: as humanists they could never accept this new culture; but if they could not accept it they would find themselves cut off from all culture, both of the past and the future. The clock could not be put back, and if Europe would not recognize these truths then she would have to be forced to recognize them.

In fact, by the time that Blok came to write 'The Collapse of Humanism' his thoughts had already begun to take a new turn. His earlier fascination with violence 'in the name of higher values' was wearing off in the face of the nihilism that he saw around him: 'Life is becoming monstrous, hideous, senseless, Robberies everywhere. The Mendeleyev flat with its *peredvizhnik* archive is in danger of being lost. The touchstone for judging the new order was still art, and he was coming increasingly to realize that his own poetry and inspiration were of no interest or use to it. He recorded laconically in his diary the verdict of a publisher's reader: 'My verse is of no use to the workers.'

On 6 January 1919 Ionov, the notoriously insensitive chief editor of the State Publishing House (Gosizdat) rang up Blok to discuss the possibility of bringing out a new edition of *The Twelve.* Blok asked him ironically if he didn't think the poem was a bit out-of-date by now. Ionov willingly agreed:

> Absolutely true. One comrade has already made this point, but we have decided to publish the best works of Russian literature, even if they have only a historical significance.

Reflecting on this barbarism from a cultural representative of the new government, Blok went on to raise profound moral (and indeed prophetic) questions about the future of art under such circumstances. Again the guilt that he felt as a privileged intellectual is in evidence, but it is no longer allowed to dictate a total rejection of culture. . . .

Of crucial importance in the evolution of Blok's outlook was his appointment to the Repertory Section of the Theatre Department of the Ministry for Enlightenment, and later to the directorship of the Grand Dramatic Theatre. Unable to write more than a handful of poems during these last years, he found his main purpose in life in recreating on stage the great dramatic masterpieces of the world.

It was not just a personal satisfaction that he drew from this work; he felt that he was playing a vital role in preparing the masses to create their own culture. . . .

But with the deepening of social chaos all around Blok began to lose his confidence in the unaided triumph of culture. He was appalled by the continuing illiteracy of new prose and poetry; there seemed to be no sign of the cultural rebirth of which he had dreamed: 'One begins to be terrified for culture—is it really irreparable, is it really buried under the ruins of civilization?' Everywhere he seemed to see not the creation of a culture, but its extinction. . . .

In the struggle to protect culture against the onslaught of barbarism Blok now felt that his theatre stood in the front line. He no longer argued that his role went no further than presenting plays for the proletariat to take its pick of; instead, he declared that his theatre should be a 'leader' (the Russian word *povodyr'* has the sense of a 'leader of the blind'). He was no longer so sure that the masses could be trusted to recognize true art, and so he began to adopt utilitarian arguments and to emphasize the 'relevance' of a particular play to the present. . . .

His earlier uncertainty (in 'The Collapse of Humanism') as to who had the greater right to bring whom to culture, the civilized the barbarians, or *vice versa,* was now resolved once and for all. It was clearly the educated classes who were able to give a lead, and the illiterates, who, for all their distrust of any kind of education imposed from above, would have to be brought to culture. . . .

This new position represents a complete break with the romantic assumptions that had governed Blok's thinking at least since 1908, and opens the way for his final rediscovery of classical values. The earlier Apocalyptic interpretation of the revolution as 'the end of the historical process' is abandoned once and for all. At first Blok tried to replace it with a cyclic conception of history, as in the prose foreword of July 1919 to **Retribution (Vozmezdiye)**, which 'arose under the pressure of my constantly growing hatred for the various theories of progress'. . . .

It was not easy for him to accept the idea of cyclicism; one of his most desperate poems, **'Night, a street, a lamp, a chemist's' (Noch', ulitsa, fonar', apteka')** had been devoted to a nightmarish vision of just such a universe. By temperament he was one of those who looked for a direc-

tion and purpose to history. So he tried to believe that a way out of this cycle would eventually appear: 'One day man will learn, and the crowd will learn too.' But until that happy day the example of classical art provided a lifeline; art was no longer for Blok a breath of the elemental powers of the cosmos but something quite opposed to them, even a talisman against them. Its medicinal qualities now outweighed its poisons.

> There is in the great works of the past, even the distant past, a characteristic, imperishable intoxication, a joy which is generously spilled over anyone who approaches them with an open heart; the ideas and the situations may be different from ours; but in every great work the main thing is something which has no name, which defies explanation or analysis . . . It was this creative spirit of Shakespeare and Schiller which helped us all in 1919 because we believed in its absolute and continuing vitality. But it is not easy to believe even in this in such times as ours when the lives of men are broken from top to bottom, when at times it seems that nothing has the right to survive from the old world. In order to believe in the creative spirit of great works one must be infected by this spirit and experience its timeless power on oneself.

Blok had turned his back on his earlier conception of the pitiful inadequacy of actual works of art beside the overwhelming experience of artistic inspiration; it was now the artists and their works who defined for him the nature and the mystery of art. . . .

It is . . . the individuality and caprice of a work of art that constitute its value. The grandiose claims for the social, revolutionary and cosmic significance of art have dropped away; the elements have disappeared; only art remains. The cult of the 'wild and formless howl' of the barbarians has been replaced by the classical virtues of restraint, balance and harmony. Fittingly enough Blok's last public speech was devoted to the one figure in Russian culture who embodies just these virtues, Pushkin. . . .

In his last poem **'To the Pushkin House' ('Pushkinskomu domu'**, February 1921), Blok himself managed to demonstrate just these virtues. It is a marvellous, apparently totally unBlokian poem, light and dancing with a wry but not ironic smile. It is the only one of Blok's poems which evokes the classical past (the rhythms pay homage to Pushkin's triumphant 'Feast of Peter the First', 'Pir Petra Pervogo'). It is the exemplification of his belated discovery of the culture of the past.

FURTHER READING

Abernathy, Robert. "A Vowel Fugue in Blok." *International Journal of Slavic Linguistics and Poetics* VII (1963): 88-107.

A close analysis of the occurrence of stressed-vowel patterns in the third part of Blok's poem "Na pole Kulikovom."

Bowlt, John E. "Aleksandr Blok: The Poem 'The Unknown Lady'." *Texas Studies in Literature and Language* XVII (1975): 349-56.
Studies how Blok first creates and then destroys tension between the material and spiritual worlds in his poem "The Unknown Lady."

Byrns, Richard H. "The Artistic Worlds of Vrubel and Blok." *Slavic and East European Journal* 23, No. 1 (Spring 1979): 38-50.
Points out affinities between Blok's poetry and the paintings of Mixail Vrubel, focusing on both artists' representation of the symbolic figures of the "Demon" and the "Feminine Idealized."

Cooper, Nancy L. "Images of Hope and Despair in the Last Part of Blok's 'Gorod'." *Slavic and East European Journal* 35, No. 4 (Winter 1991): 503-17.
Studies the imagery and symbolism of the poems comprising the third part of Blok's "Gorod" cycle.

Elagin, Ivan. "Poe in Blok's Literary Heritage." *The Russian Review* 32, No. 4 (October 1973): 403-12.
Notes the influence of Edgar Allan Poe's works and the symbolist aesthetic on Blok's poetry.

Hughes, Robert P. "Nothung, the Cassia Flower, and a 'Spirit of Music' in the Poetry of Aleksandr Blok." *California Slavic Studies* VI (1971): 49-60.
Explores the role of "actual music" in Blok's life and poetry, focusing on his interest in the operas of Richard Wagner and Georges Bizet.

Kaun, Alexander. "1917 and After." In *Soviet Poets and Poetry*, pp. 28-34. Berkeley: University of California Press, 1943.
Includes Blok in a discussion of the Russian intelligentsia's reaction to the Bolshevik Revolution, remarking of *The Twelve*, "With this one glorious exception, the revolution has not been adequately recorded as yet in a work of art."

Lednicki, Waclaw. "Blok's 'Polish Poem'." In *Russia, Poland and the West: Essays in Literary and Cultural History*, pp. 349-99. New York: Roy Publishers, 1954.
Discusses the Polish motifs in Blok's *Vozmezdie* and speculates on Blok's sources of inspiration and influences.

Masing-Deli, Irene. "Limitation and Pain in Brjusov's and Blok's Poetry." *Slavic and East European Journal* 19, No. 4 (Winter 1975): 388-402.
Compares Blok's treatment of the themes of limitation and pain with that of another Russian symbolist, Valery Brjusov, arguing that "Brjusov's system represent[s] an aesthetic and psychological preference for limitation, where pain functions as a stimulant, whereas Blok's system represents a metaphysical protest against limitation, with pain functioning as a (last) link with reality."

Maslenikov, Oleg A. "Andrey Biely and Alexander Blok." In *The Frenzied Poets: The Russian Symbolists*, pp. 146-96. Berkeley: University of California Press, 1952.
Chronicles the tumultuous friendship of Blok and Biely and its influence on the careers of both poets.

McCarey, Peter, and Mariarosario Cardines. "The Harrowing of Hell and Resurrection: Dante's *Inferno* and Blok's *Dvenadsat'*." *The Slavonic and East European Review* 63, No. 3 (July 1985): 337-48.
Explores the relationship between Dante's *Inferno* and *The Twelve*, with the primary aim of uncovering the meaning of Christ's appearance at the head of the Red Guardsmen in Blok's poem.

Schapiro, Leonard. "The Last Years of Alexander Blok." In *Russian Studies*, edited by Ellen Dahrendorf, pp. 359-75. London: Collins Harvill, 1986.
Seeks to determine the reasons for Blok's slight literary output after the publication of *The Twelve*, focusing on public reaction to the poem as well as Blok's own feelings toward the work.

Struve, Gleb. "The Transition from Russian to Soviet Literature." In *Literature and Revolution in Soviet Russia, 1917-62*, edited by Max Hayward and Leopold Labedz, pp. 1-27. London: Oxford University Press, 1963.
A historical discussion of the distinction between "Russian" and "Soviet" literature in which Struve briefly discusses *The Twelve* and Blok's changing attitudes toward the Bolshevik Revolution.

Vogel, Lucy E. "Blok in the Land of Dante." *The Russian Review* 26, No. 1 (January-October 1967): 251-63.
Examines some of the poems from Blok's cycle of "Italian Verses," relating how Blok viewed his 1909 trip to Italy as a spiritual descent into Dante's *Inferno*.

————. *Aleksandr Blok: The Journey to Italy, with English Translations of the Poems and Prose Sketches on Italy*. Ithaca, N. Y.: Cornell University Press, 1973, 275 p.
A detailed record of Blok's trip to Italy in 1909, the purpose of which, in Vogel's words, is "to study Blok's immediate impressions of the Italian scene in relation to his art, and to interpret the profound impact of this journey on his thought."

Vroon, Ronald. "Cycle and History: The Case of Aleksandr Blok's 'Rodina'." *Slavic and East European Journal* 28, No. 3 (Fall 1984): 340-57.
Examines the relationship between the theme of eternal return in "Rodina" and the structure of the poetic cycle.

Weidlé, Wladimir. "The Poison of Modernism." In *Russian Modernism: Culture and the Avant-Garde, 1900-1930*, edited by George Gibian and H. W. Tjalsma, pp. 18-30. Ithaca, N. Y.: Cornell University Press, 1976.

Traces Blok's disdain for Russian modernism to his aversion to the doctrine of "art for art's sake."

Woodward, James B. "Rhythmic Modulations in the *dol'nik* Trimeter of Blok." *The Slavic and East European Journal* XII, No. 3 (Fall 1968): 297-310.
  An analysis of the expressive function of meter and accent in Blok's poetry.

Additional coverage of Blok's life and career is contained in the following sources published by Gale Research: *Contemporary Authors,* **Vol. 104, and** *Twentieth-Century Literary Criticism,* **Vol. 5.**

Dante
1265-1321

(Full name Dante Alighieri) Italian poet, prose writer, and philosopher.

INTRODUCTION

Regarded as one of the finest poets that Italy has ever produced, Dante is also celebrated as a major influence in Western culture. His masterpiece, *La Divina Commedia (The Divine Comedy)* is universally known as one of the great poems of world literature. Divided into three sections—*Inferno, Purgatorio,* and *Paradiso*—*The Divine Comedy* presents an encyclopedic overview of the mores, attitudes, beliefs, philosophies, aspirations, and material aspects of the medieval world. More than a summa of medieval life, however, Dante's poem is a superb work of fiction with poignant dramatic episodes and unforgettable characters. Dante's verse collection entitled *Vita Nuova (The New Life),* though not of the stature of *The Divine Comedy,* is well known for its exaltation of Beatrice, an idealized figure who inspired love poetry imbued with a fervent religious undertone.

Biographical Information

Dante was born in Florence in 1265. Little is known about his early education, but scholars surmise that he received formal instruction in grammar, language, and philosophy at one of the Franciscan schools in the city. At the age of nine he purportedly glimpsed Beatrice, a girl eight years old, and that encounter was to affect his life dramatically. Struck by her beauty, he fell in love. Nine years later he saw her again, and when she greeted him, his love was confirmed. (Whether Beatrice really existed and whether her factual existence matters have been topics of some debate; she is generally identified as Beatrice Portinari.) During his teens, Dante demonstrated a keen interest in literature and undertook an apprenticeship with Brunetto Latini, a celebrated poet and prose writer of vernacular Italian, who expanded Dante's knowledge of literature and rhetoric. Associating with a circle of respected Florentine poets, Dante befriended Guido Cavalcanti, and the poet helped Dante refine his literary skills. In 1283 Dante inherited a modest family fortune from his parents, both of whom died during his childhood but took care to pre-arrange his marriage to Gemma Donati in 1285. In 1287 Dante enrolled in the University of Bologna, but by 1289 he enlisted in the Florentine army and took part in the Battle of Campaldino. The death of Beatrice Portinari in 1290 proved to be a turning point in Dante's life, ultimately inspiring his Christian devotion and poetry, most notably as the ideal lady who leads him to redemption in *The Divine Comedy.* Stricken with grief,

he committed himself to the study of philosophical works of Boethius, Cicero, and Aristotle, and earnestly wrote poetry, establishing his own poetic voice in innovative canzoni, or lyrical poems. Dante also became increasingly active in perilous Florentine politics, aligning himself with the White Guelfs. The Black Guelfs, supported by papal forces, staged a coup in 1301 and established themselves as absolute rulers. Prominent Whites, including Dante, were stripped of their possessions and banished from the city. Dante never returned, spending his remaining years in Verona and later in Ravenna, where he died in 1321.

Major Works

Written in commemoration of Beatrice's death, *The New Life* reflects Dante's first effort to depict her as an abstract model of love and beauty. In this collection of early canzoni, Dante uses a refreshing and innovative approach, or *stil nuovo,* in love poetry that equates the love experience with a divine and mystical spiritual revelation. *Il Convivo (The Banquet),* is another collection of canzoni, accompanied by extensive prose commentary, that further develops the poet's use of the *stil nuovo*. An unfinished Latin tract, *De Vulgari Eloquentia (Eloquence in the Vernacular Tongue)* is a theoretical discussion of the origin of Italian dialects and literary language and examines how they relate to the composition of vernacular poetry; and *De Monarchia (On Monarchy)*, a Latin treatise, presents the poet's Christian political philosophy. *The Divine Comedy* describes Dante's imagined journey through Hell and Purgatory to Paradise. The *Inferno,* the most popular and widely studied section of *The Divine Comedy,* recounts Dante's experiences in Hell with the Roman poet Vergil, his mentor and protector. Constructed as a huge funnel with nine descending circular ledges, Dante's Hell features a vast, meticulously organized torture chamber in which sinners, carefully classified according to the nature of their sins, suffer hideous punishment, often depicted with ghoulish attention to detail. Those who recognize and repudiate their sins are given the opportunity to attain Paradise through the arduous process of purification, which continues in the *Purgatorio.* A shift from human reason to divine revelation takes place in Purgatory, a place where penitents awaiting the final journey to Paradise continually reaffirm their faith and atone for the sins they committed on earth. A mood of brotherly love, modesty, and longing for God prevails in Purgatory. Although in Hell Vergil, a symbol of human reason, helps Dante understand sin, in Purgatory the poet needs a more powerful guide who represents faith: Beatrice. Finally, the *Paradiso* manifests the process of spiritual regeneration and purification required to meet God, who rewards the poet with perfect knowledge.

Critical Reception

Although Dante's *Divine Comedy* caused an immediate sensation during his life, his fame waned during the Italian Renaissance, only to be revived in the nineteenth and, especially, twentieth centuries. Many scholars have examined the structural unity of the poem, discussing the interrelationship between medieval symbolism and allegory within the different parts of the poem and exploring Dante's narrative strategy. Others have marvelled at the seemingly inexhaustible formal and semantic richness of Dante's poetic text. With its various enigmatic layers of philological and philosophical complexities, *The Divine Comedy* has received scrutiny by critics, literary theorists, linguists, and philosophers, who have cherished the immortal work precisely because it translates the harsh truth about the human condition into poetry of timeless beauty. *The New Life* has long basked in the reflected glory of *The Divine Comedy.* Criticism has almost invariably been positive, although an occasional scholar has taken exception to its sensibility, finding in it an overwrought imagination and sensitivity unbecoming a great poet. Many commentators have proposed that Beatrice is a symbol, although of what there is no consensus. The story of Dante's love for her is often taken as allegory, particularly by critics reading the book in the light of his later works.

PRINCIPAL WORKS

Poetry

Vita Nuova [*New Life*] c.1292
Convivio [*The Banquet*] (poetry with commentary) c.1304
Divina Commedia [*Divine Comedy*] c.1307-21

Other Major Works

De Vulgari Eloquentia [*Eloquence in the Vernacular Tongue*] (unfinished prose) c. 1304
De Monarchia [*On the Monarchy*] (prose) c.1309
Epistolae [*Letters*] (letters) c.1313

CRITICISM

Domenico Vittorini (essay date 1958)

SOURCE: "Dante's Concept of Love," in *High Points in the History of Italian Literature,* David McKay Company, Inc., 1958, pp. 53-67.

[*The following essay looks at love in its various forms in* Vita Nuova, Convivio, *and the* Divina Commedia.]

The aim of this essay is to study Dante's love concept as revealed in the *Vita Nuova* (*New Life*), the *Convivio* (*The Banquet*), and the *Divina Commedia* (*Divine Comedy*).

We shall be guided by what Dante tells us in each of his three works, and we shall not allow ourselves to be influenced by any preconceived conclusions concerning his love concept. It is a simple matter to reduce a man to a formula, but, actually, it is inhuman, abstract, and often useless to do so. It is preferable to see the poet's ideas as an integral part of his life, a solution, or an attempt at a solution, of particular moments of his existence. Nor do we wish to reduce Dante's love concept to that of the courtly tradition of his time. This can only be, as it was, a starting point, from which he moved on as does every great poet in the moment of his artistic creation. Therefore, we do not desire either to force Dante within a preconceived system of love or to steep him in the courtly tradition.

We are guided in our discussion by the difference that exists between culture and art. Culture is looked upon here as something a poet receives from the atmosphere in which he is born and lives; and art, which is original creation, as an activity that needs new attitudes and directions. Those who follow this distinction seek more diversity than uniformity in the works of a poet that reflect various moments of his existence.

The historical school, which deserves so much praise for a serious and documented study of Dante's works, often offers the drawback of wishing to reduce Dante the poet to the culture of his time by presupposing that the culture of an age constitutes a determined and homogeneous block rather than a whole of different tendencies. A critic, applying this absolute and unitarian concept of the culture of a given time, quotes from various authors in order to document what he wishes to see in a determined work of the poet, a dangerous procedure, unless it is accompanied by the certitude on the part of the critic that Dante actually knew a definite book.

The three pivotal points of these considerations will be, as we have stated, a careful study of the three major works of the great Italian poet: the *Vita Nuova,* the *Convivio,* and the *Commedia.* In a special way we shall dwell on the thirtieth and thirty-first cantos of the *Purgatorio* and the poetic figuration of Beatrice in the *Paradiso.*

Dante lived a "courtly" life previous to his exile in 1302, and he sought refuge in it after Florence drove him away from his Baptistery, his "bel San Giovanni." There is no doubt that he generally followed the Provençal concept of love, in spite of the harsh words with which he refers to the widow of Nino Visconti and the sonnets exchanged with Forese. This concept was a part of the poetic culture of his day, followed by the poets of the *Dolce Stil Nuovo* who were all members of the White Party. Either one wrote according to the popular manner whose realism, lack of form, and barbaric rhymes displeased Dante, or one belonged to the group of chosen minds for whom Love was a spiritual reaction expressed in "sweet rhymes." Content and form were intimately united in Dante's poetics.

Michele Barbi, in his introduction to the *Convivio,* attempts to remove every contradiction between the *Vita Nuova,* the *Convivio,* and the *Commedia,* reducing to an oversimplified form the genesis of the three works. Barbi does not take into consideration that logic can also be *a posteriori,* and then, in its absolutism, offends life that does not flow placidly and peacefully among meadows flowering with asphodels. Aristide Marigo, too, in his learned article *Amore intellettivo nell'evoluzione filosofica di Dante* (Intellective Love in the philosophical evolution of Dante), following Giulio Salvadori, concludes that in the *Vita Nuova* "the description of the reactions of the soul, traditional subject matter of erotic lyricism, is closely connected with the solution of the problem of knowledge." For Marigo, the *Dolce Stil Nuovo* began "at Bologna where studies of philosophy are fervidly pursued, and where ancient wisdom is less subjected to theological interpretations," thus giving a value of absolute certainty to a very contingent fact, and creating a critical determinism without any philosophical basis.

For us, the *Dolce Stil Nuovo* represents the development, original and personal in the various poets, of the theory of courtly love with close connections with the Provençal tradition. To bring into play the averroistic current in order to explain the poetry of Cavalcanti and the mystic currents to explain that of Dante is to look at the problem from an external vantage, leaving a great amount of liberty to the will of each critic.

There is perfect agreement among critics as to the brief plot of the *Vita Nuova*: the meeting with Beatrice at the age of nine and at eighteen years of age, her salutation to the poet, her ceasing to speak to him, the presentiment of the death of the young woman, her death, the brief obscuring of Dante's love for her because of the passion that suddenly flared within the heart of the poet for the *Donna Gentile.* These events are translated in the *Vita Nuova* through the Pythagorical numbers of three and nine, and through other ideas generally accepted by the poets of high style, such as the angelic woman, the unity of love, the justification of love as a force that leads man to God. On the whole, the short plot of Dante's book is woven with courtly love and a great deal of convention, but also with sudden outcries of true feeling that reveal the most personal aspects of the poet's character.

In his love concept, as presented in the *Vita Nuova,* Dante keeps himself closely tied to courtly tradition and presents to us a love circumscribed by virtue. Out of respect for this tradition, he writes concerning sensuality: "And since to dwell on passions and deeds of such an extreme youthfulness seems to be a type of literature worthy of the *fabula,* I shall leave them aside." He very urgently informs us that passion was totally absent from his love for Beatrice. He says so in the prose of the *Vita Nuova,* but the reader, in perusing his first sonnet written, if we believe the poet, when he was eighteen years of age in 1283, cannot help asking himself whether the poet does not insist so vigorously on the absolute spirituality of his love precisely because he wished to exclude from it his inevitably sensuous reaction to the beauty of Beatrice. And why, if it were not so, would he have imagined that Love appeared to him and

> *ne le braccia avea*
> *Madonna involta in un drappo dormendo?*
>
> in his arms he had
> Madonna enveloped in a cloth and asleep?

Even the prose, written in 1292, in which the sonnet is set, has kept the reflection of this sensuality: *"Ne le sue braccia mi parea vedere una persona dormire nuda, salvo che involta mi parea in un drappo sanguigno leggeramente"* (In his arms seemed to me to see asleep a naked person, except that she was lightly enveloped in a crimson cloth). The poet constantly makes Herculean efforts to force his love within the formula of courtliness, thus doing violence to the literal truth of the situation. We have already seen how Dante sacrifices to this ideal the women of the foil.

From courtly tradition Dante borrows his custom of rendering actual reality through a vague halo, reached by not mentioning by name the places or persons to which he refers. A clear example of this is in Chapter XXIII when he refers to his half-sister by the terms *"donna pietosa e di novella etate"* (compassionate Lady, very young in years). Likewise, in the last sonnet dedicated to the women of the foil, he refers to Florence by the term *"sopradetta cittade"* (above-mentioned city). Only here and there the character of conventionality is broken by a sincere and lacerating cry in which the reader realizes that the poetic expression has become fused with the torment of the heart of the poet. At other times Dante's genius draws away subconsciously from tradition, and then his art levels down toward a realism that surprises the reader, as when Beatrice is described to us when she laughs with her friends at the poet. However, it is useless to deny that the basic tone of the *Vita Nuova* is conventional, but it is equally true that the poetry that will live forever is that born by breaking the conventions that tradition offered the poet.

In his above-mentioned introduction, Michele Barbi presents the *Convivio* as a work of pure doctrine corresponding to the mature age of the poet. Barbi represents more fully than any other critic a reaction to Witte and to Vossler who wished to see in the *Convivio* an intellectual and even a religious crisis in Dante. We deny the existence in Dante of the rationalism of the type of the nineteenth century, but we believe and declare that the doctrine of love contained in the *Convivio* is of a different nature from that in the *Commedia,* and especially that in the *Paradiso,* where it is characterized by a contemplative element and by Platonism.

Although the existence of doctrine in the *Convivio* cannot be denied, nevertheless it is useless to try to remove the dissonances and downright clashes that exist between it and the *Vita Nuova* and between it and the *Commedia.* It is impossible to see on the same human and poetic plane the love for the Gentle Lady in the *Vita Nuova* that makes of it the first psychological novel in Italian literature, and its negation in the *Convivio,* where Dante tells us that it was not love for a woman, but love for philosophy. Dante is so definite in his likes and dislikes as to make it difficult for us to cavil when we discuss his attitudes. He is a poor witness for the defense lawyers. If we follow Barbi when he enjoins us to explain Dante with Dante, we find that the poet has not made the differentiation, inferred by Barbi, between the woman of the *Vita Nuova* and that of the *Convivio.* Dante explicitly declares that almost three years after Beatrice's death *"quella gentile donna, cui feci manzione ne la fine de la* Vita Nuova, *parve primamente, accompagnata d'Amore, a li occhi miei e prese luogo alcuno ne la mia mente"* (that Gentle Lady, whom I mentioned at the end of the *Vita Nuova,* accompanied by Love, appeared to my eyes at first and took some place in my mind), and later relates again his falling in love, adroitly and slowly changing the human and beautifully youthful countenance of the Gentle Lady into the dignified and august one of philosophy. He tells us the reason with blinding clarity: *"Dico che pensai da molti, diretro da me, forse sarei stato ripreso di levezza d'animo, udendo me essere dal*

primo amore mutato; perchè a torre via questa riprensione, nullo migliore argomento era che dire quale era quella donna che m'avea mutato" (I say that I thought that by many, behind my back, I should be perhaps accused of levity of mind upon hearing that I had changed from my first love; whereupon, to remove this accusation, there was no better argument than to say who was the woman who had changed me).

The *Convivio* most clearly shows this most human preoccupation, if one agrees with us, that Dante was struggling against his political detractors who were "cruel and pitiless" in a quite different manner from the ladies whom they courted in society. Here it was a question of defending one's reputation that, as Dante informs us, had fallen very low. There is no doubt for us that in the *Vita Nuova* Dante was referring to a woman with whom he was temporarily in love when he wrote about forgetting Beatrice for the time being. In fact, in commenting upon the sonnet *Gentil pensiero che parla di voi* (A gentle thought that speaks of you), Dante wrote: *"E dissi questo sonetto, lo quale comincia: 'Gentil pensiero,' e dico 'gentile' in quanto ragionava di gentile donna, chè per altro era vilissimo"* (and I said this sonnet, which begins "Gentle Thought," and I say "gentle" in that it spoke of a gentle lady, for, as to the rest, it was most vile). So that sad episode appeared to him later when the fire of passion was extinguished and he had returned to the love of Beatrice. The nature of this "most vile" love was forgotten when he wrote the *Convivio.*

On the *Convivio* is projected the shadow of his exile, and this is the truly living part in it, the part that urges Dante to write unforgettable pages in which he narrates his peregrinations and confesses to us his loneliness, and then breaks forth into the lament: *"Veramente io sono legno senza vela e senza governo, portato a diversi porti e foci e liti dal vento secco che vapora la dolorosa povertade"* (Truly have I been a ship without sails and without rudder, carried to diverse ports, mouths of rivers, and shores by the dry wind that dolorous poverty blows). His greatest enemy is the "infamy" that persecuted him so unjustly with the danger of robbing him of his livelihood. With a smile that curves his lips toward spurning this world, he lingers to describe with bitterness the nobility of fame that grows so easily with our friends and infamy that assumes monstrous proportions with our enemies.

I repeat that there is no doubt that the *Convivio* is a book of doctrine, but the primary reason why Dante wrote it was to put an end, as he himself says, "to the great infamy and danger" that pursued him in his exile. He was like Boethius who wrote his *De Consolatione Philosophiae* in order to excuse *"sotto pretesto di consolazione la perpetuale infamia del suo essilio"* (under the pretext of consolation the perpetual infamy of his exile). Even more clearly, Dante stated: *"Movemi timore d'infamia. . . . Temo la infamia di tanta passione avere seguita, quanta concepe chi legge le sopra nominate canzoni in me avere signoreggiata"* (I am moved by fear of infamy. . . . I fear to have followed the infamy of such a great passion as he who reads the above-mentioned *canzoni* believes to have mastered me). He struggles valiantly to remove this infamy, showing that *"non passione ma virtù sia stata la movente cagione"* (not passion but virtue was the moving cause).

In the **Vita Nuova** Dante rejected sensuality because of the noble aspirations of his soul and an aesthetic principle. Here, under the cold maxims, there is a struggle for life: *"ischiudere ogni falsa opinione da me, per la quale fosse sospicato lo mio amore essere per sensibile dilettazione"* (to cut off every false opinion of me, through which it could have been suspected that my love was for a sensuous delectation). It was but natural that Dante's love concept in such a situation remained *disumanato* (deprived of its human quality), and in a very different sense in which it was in the **Commedia.** The verse: *"Questi mi face una donna guardare"* (This makes me look at a woman) is commented upon thus by the poet: *"ove si vuole sapere che questa donna è la Filosofia; la quale veramente è donna piena di dolcezza, ornata d'onestade, mirabile di sapere, gloriosa di libertade, sì come nel terzo tratto, dove la sua nobiltade si tratterà, fia manifesto. E là dove dice: 'Chi veder vuol la salute, faccia che li occhi d'esta donna miri; li occhi di questa donna sono le sue dimostrazioni, le quali, dritte ne li occhi de lo 'ntelletto, innamorano l'anima, liberata da le contradizioni"* (where one must understand that this woman is Philosophy, who truly is a woman full of sweetness, ornamented by stateliness, admirable for knowledge, glorious for freedom, as will be manifest in the third treatise where her nobility will be discussed. And there where it says: *He who wishes to see his own salvation must look into the eyes of this woman*, the eyes of this woman are her demonstrations, which, straight into the eyes of the intellect, make the soul, freed of all contradictions, fall in love). He even reaches the point of placing the love of Philosophy before the love of Beatrice. And he does so in no uncertain terms, going so far as to state that he felt that the love of Philosophy occupied a larger place in his heart than did that of Beatrice.

No matter how hard one tries, one will never be able to take away from the **Convivio** many of the abstractions from the love concept of the poet. We do not blame him, of course. But we do blame his enemies who forced him to give a political answer to a political accusation that aimed at damaging the reputation of the great and impecunious man.

The "true" revelation of what actually happened in his life is found in the **Commedia,** the book of intimacy and the autobiography of his soul; the true answer, if one admits the principle that a later document wipes out and nullifies the previous utterances of what concerns the "objective" truth of the events. The most limpid mirror is found in Dante's confession at the summit of Purgatory and precisely in the Earthly Paradise where he, purified of the weight of the flesh through the vision of evil in both the Inferno and Purgatory, reacquires the original perfection of man and becomes worthy of gazing into the eyes of Beatrice.

The narrative of what actually happened after Beatrice's death is violently contrary to what Dante had written in the **Convivio**. Here we read that he used to go *"dov'ella [la Filosofia] si dimostrava veracemente, cioè ne le scuole de li religiosi e a le disputazioni de li filosofanti. Sì che in picciol tempo, forse di trenta mesi, cominciai tanto a sentire de la sua dolcezza, che lo suo amore cacciava e distruggeva ogni altro pensiero"* (where it [philosophy] showed itself most truly, that is to say in the schools of religious people and in the discussions of philosophers. So that in a very short time, perhaps in thirty months, I began to feel so much of its sweetness that its love drove out and destroyed every other thought). But Beatrice knows that the truth is quite different. And she "regal in her rebellious act" accuses Dante of having been unfaithful to her. It is of no use to quibble; the time to which the poet refers in the two works is the same, that after Beatrice's death:

> *Sì tosto come in su la soglia fui*
> *Di mia seconda etade e mutai vita,*
> *Questi si tolse a me, a diessi altrui.*
> *Quando di carne a spirto era salita,*
> *E bellezza e virtù cresciuta m'era,*
> *Fu'io a lui men cara e men gradita;*
> *E volse i passi suoi per via non vera,*
> *Imagini di ben seguendo false,*
> *Che nulla promission rendono intera.*

> As soon as I was on the threshold
> Of my second age, and I changed my life,
> This man relinquished me, and gave himself to others.
> When from my flesh I had become pure spirit,
> And my beauty and virtue had increased,
> I became to him less dear and less acceptable;
> And he turned his steps on the wrong path,
> Following false images of good,
> Which render no promise in its entirety.

What the nature of this betrayal was is said later on when Beatrice, woman even to the point of being moved by jealousy, shouts to Dante:

> *E quali agevolezze o quali avanzi*
> *Nella fronte degli altri si mostraro,*
> *Perchè dovessi lor passeggiare anzi?*

> And what greater promises and qualities
> Showed themselves on the forehead of others,
> That you should pay courtship to them?

We are far from singling out this contradiction in order to indict the poet. Indeed, we see in his confession not only that of the lover, which is addressed to Beatrice, but that of the poet and man, which is addressed to all of us. He wished to confess that when he was young he was too earthy and carnal to be able to love according to the norms of courtly love. And now, only when the passing of years has deepened in him the meaning of the values of life, has he become capable of perfect love.

Dante resumed in the *Commedia* the theme of love, clinging to the facts, as related in the *Vita Nuova.* These were for him a living reality under the poetic veil that enveloped them without minimizing or destroying them. In fact, in the *Commedia* he refers to Beatrice as being the same girl whom he saw, loved, and sang to in the *Vita Nuova.* She was the same girl whose love "m'avea gia trafitto, Prima ch'io fuor di puerizia fosse" (had transfixed me, Before I were out of my childhood). Beatrice is attired as she was in the *Vita Nuova* and produces on him the same effects that she exercised on him as she was wont to do in his youth: *"sicchè d'amor sentii la gran potenza"* (so that I felt the great power of love).

To identify so clearly the Beatrice whom the poet meets on the summit of Purgatory with the girl of whom he sang in the *Vita Nuova* is another proof of the absurdity of Barbi's thesis, which states categorically that Dante *"annetteva all'esser filosofo il dovere di comportarsi ad ogni età seconda che la ragione richiede; e come le rime d'amore, e le passioni che le ispirano, sono convenienti o giustificate nell'adolescenza, così ad età matura conviene 'pur virilmente' poetare"* (attached to being a philosopher the duty of behaving at every age according to the requirements of reason; and as love rhymes, and the passions that inspire them, are becoming to and justifiable in adolescence, so it is required to write poetry "more virile" at a later age). If this were true, one would find it difficult to explain why Dante returned to the love of a woman, be it spiritualized like that of Beatrice, in the last years of his life, and dedicated to it the last thoughts of his mind and the last throbbing of his heart. The progression established by Barbi does not exist in Dante. The *Convivio* was written with a polemic spirit. The *Commedia* remains a book of intimacy. Dante is still a "servant of Love" in the *Commedia,* but he undertook a journey that superficial poets of the courts had never been able to undertake. Beatrice is still his "Lady," but she is the Lady who loves him. There is in the *Commedia* the remembrance of the physical charm of Beatrice together with that of her friends whom Dante had invoked to do honor to her, and whose fresh beauty now adorns the slope of Purgatory and the Earthly Paradise.

The women of the foil have reacquired their physiognomy and they perform a function close to that which the poet gave them: to serve as intermediaries between himself and Beatrice. Had these maidens not appeared near Beatrice in the *Vita Nuova*? Had they not tried to console the grieving poet? Had he not confided to them his unrequited love? And here is Lucia, Lia, and Matelda, who reappear in the *Commedia* without any fear of offending the purest love of Dante for Beatrice. Her friends on earth have now become her maidens in the world of perfections, where love can be revealed without danger of being spotted by earthly considerations.

The *Commedia* represents another phase of the poet's life, a life more thoughtful and pensive than the one projected in the *Vita Nuova.* The *Commedia* is illumined by two lights, Virgil and Beatrice: Virgil, the symbol of the elevating power of poetry; Beatrice, the symbol of intellectual love. The *Commedia* was the book over which Beatrice presided, just as Aristotle, "the master of those who know," presided over the *Convivio.*

In the *Commedia* Dante develops and deepens the love concept of the poetry of his youth by giving to it a philosophical character. In the *Purgatorio* Love appears to him as an innate force that bends man toward the object by which he feels attracted. From it depends "ogni buono operare e il contrario" (every good deed and its contrary), and it is

> *sementa in voi d'ogni virtute*
> *E d'ogni operazion che merta pene.*

> a seed in you of every virtue
> And of every deed that deserves punishment.

In the second canticle Love assumes always new forms as the mind of the poet returns to meditate on this great force. Yet, he never dissociates his thinking from his human experience. Even before meeting Beatrice, as he climbs the slopes of Purgatory, Dante has a dream in which the impure thought of the *femmina balba* (the stammering old female), "who turned Ulysses away from his delectable path," disturbed his mind. The victory of the lady, "holy and swift," shows the victory of the poet's idealism over the seduction of the flesh that rises from the forbidding darkness of the night.

The *Purgatorio* reflects Dante's thoughts on Love considered as a cosmic force and as an individual experience.

—Domenico Vittorini

The search as to what Love really was, was so insistent that, after having discussed its nature in the seventeenth and eighteenth cantos of the *Purgatorio,* he returned to it in the twenty-fifth, exposing in it the generation of man in terms extremely scientific and realistic. Thus the *Purgatorio* reflects Dante's thoughts on Love considered as a cosmic force and as an individual experience. Without this assiduous and passionate work of Dante's thought on Love it is difficult to understand his confession to Beatrice, in the thirty-first canto, of the wanderings of the poet after her death. He unveils there his whole soul, proclaiming his love, perfect and pure, for the woman whom he knew in his youth. Only after his long journey through the horrors of the *Inferno* and the sufferings of the *Purgatorio* does Dante realize, in his thoughtful maturity, that Love, according to the ideal of the poets of Provence, has become a deep and living reality. It is there, at the summit of the mountain of Purgatory, that he offers to Beatrice the love that he has not been able to offer her on this earth.

The *Commedia* is radiant with love. It is, indeed, essentially a love poem in which Dante kept the promise made to Beatrice at the very end of the *Vita Nuova,* that he would say of her what had never been said of any other woman.

It must not be believed that Beatrice in the *Commedia* assumes the abstract form of a symbol, even if critics have seen in her theology or revelation. Her profile in the *Commedia* is much stronger and more concrete than in the *Vita Nuova* where the pearl-like color of her forehead passes lightly in the guise of the souls that the poet believed reflected in the transparency of the Heaven of the Moon. Beatrice is thoroughly humanized in the *Paradiso.* Her smile has virtually tried the ingenuity of the poet in his attempt to render it in numberless ways. It is a great blunder to imagine that Beatrice's body has left no trace in Dante's memory, nor, consequently, in his book.

Nor is it to be believed that the love concept, resumed in the *Commedia,* became a diaphanous or an anemic mysticism. It was the mysticism of a man who was very severely tried by experience and who matured in a life of grief that would have broken any other man.

The basic ideas of the *Vita Nuova* reappear in it, but transformed. Thus the Provençal principle, that Love leads man to God, reappears here, too, but lives again in the light of all that Beatrice, so frail a remembrance in terms of the human, had been in reality for him during the years of his exile. Beatrice becomes in the *Commedia* a synonym of truth or, at least, the one who leads Dante toward absolute truth, that is God:

> *Quel sol, che pria d'amor mi scaldò il petto,*
> *Di bella verità m'avea scoverto,*
> *Provando e riprovando, il dolce aspetto.*

> That sun, which first warmed my breast with love,
> Of beautiful truth had discovered to me,
> By proving over and over again, the sweet
>   countenance.

Love in the *Commedia* has gone beyond the human; it has become a flight above the earthly conditions of man, a conquest of the immutable values of truth, whose degrees of continuous ascent are symbolized by Dante and Beatrice rising through the sphere of Paradise. It may not be amiss to note that in the *Convivio* the seven spheres had been the symbol of the seven liberal arts, of the trivium and the quadrivium. The highest point of the ascent through Paradise is reached in the

last canto when the love of Beatrice, through the mystic St. Bernard, allows Dante to see the innermost nature of the universe:

> *Nel suo profondo vidi che s'interna,*
> *Legato con amore in un volume,*
> *Ciò che per l'universo si squaderna:*
> *Sustanza ed accidente, e lor costume,*
> *Quasi conflati insieme per tal modo,*
> *Che ciò ch'io dico è un semplice lume.*

> I saw that in its depths penetrate,
> Bound with love in one volume,
> What through the universe is unfolded
> In multiplicity of forms:
> Substances and accidents and their ways,
> Almost perfectly blended together, in such a manner
> That what I write gives but a feeble glimmer of its
>   actual reality.

The *Paradiso* is the kingdom of absolute faith reached through the love of Beatrice. It is Beatrice who keeps alive in him the faith that to live is to pass through "the large sea of being," and that the shadow of God is projected over the universe. In the *Vita Nuova* Dante had identified Love with Beatrice. In the *Paradiso* the theme of Love is resumed but in proportions that make it embrace cosmic Love. The last line of the *Commedia* reveals the unity between God and Love, between Love and universal life, and it gives us one of the first revelations of the hidden God of whom Pascal spoke.

Allen Tate (essay date 1959)

SOURCE: "The Symbolic Imagination: The Mirrors of Dante," in *Collected Essays,* Alan Swallow, 1959, pp. 408-31.

[In the excerpt that follows, Tate explores reflected light as an image in the Comedy.*]*

It is right even if it is not quite proper to observe at the beginning of a discourse on Dante, that no writer has held in mind at one time the whole of **The Divine Comedy**: not even Dante, perhaps least of all Dante himself. If Dante and his Dantisti have not been equal to the view of the whole, a view shorter than theirs must be expected of the amateur who, as a writer of verses, vainly seeks absolution from the mortal sin of using poets for what he can get out of them. I expect to look at a single image in the *Paradiso,* and to glance at some of its configurations with other images. I mean the imagery of light, but I mean chiefly its reflections. It was scarcely necessary for Dante to have read, though he did read, the *De Anima* to learn that sight is the king of the senses and that the human body, which like other organisms lives by *touch,* may be made actual in language only through the imitation of *sight.* And sight in language is imitated not by means of "description"— *ut pictura poesis*—but by doubling the image: our confidence in its spatial reality is won quite simply by casting the image upon a glass, or otherwise by the insinuation of space between.

I cannot undertake to examine here Dante's double imagery in all its detail, for his light alone could lead us into complexities as rich as life itself. I had almost said richer than life, if by life we mean (as we must mean) what we ourselves are able daily to see, or even what certain writers have seen, with the exception of Shakespeare, and possibly of Sophocles and Henry James. A secondary purpose that I shall have in view will be to consider the dramatic implications of the light imagery as they emerge at the resolution of the poem, in Canto XXXIII of the *Paradiso*. These implications suggest, to my mind, a radical change in the interpretation of *The Divine Comedy,* and impel me to ask again: What kind of poem is it? In asking this question I shall not be concerned with what we ordinarily consider to be literary criticism; I shall be only incidentally judging, for my main purpose is to describe.

In *Purgatorio* XXX Beatrice appears to Dante first as a voice (what she says need not detain us here), then as light; but not yet the purest light. She is the light of a pair of eyes in which is reflected the image of the gryphon, a symbol of the hypostatic union, of which she herself is a "type." But before Dante perceives this image in her eyes, he says: "A thousand desires hotter than flame held my eyes bound to the shining eyes. . . ." I see no reason to suppose that Dante does not mean what he says. *Mille disiri più che fiamma caldi* I take to be the desires, however interfused by this time with courtly and mystical associations, of a man for a woman: the desires that the boy Dante felt for the girl Beatrice in 1274 after he had passed her in a street of Florence. She is the same Beatrice, Dante the same Dante, with differences which do not reject but rather include their sameness. Three dancing girls appear: Dante's allegory, formidable as it is, intensifies rather than impoverishes the reality of the dancers as girls. Their dance is a real dance, their song, in which they make a charming request of Beatrice, is a real song. If Dante expected us to be interested in the dancers only as the Theological Virtues, I see no good reason why he made them girls at all. They are sufficiently convincing as the Three Graces, and I cannot feel in the pun a serious violation of Dante's confidence. The request of the girls is sufficiently remarkable: *Volgi, Beatrice, volgi gli occhi santi*—"Turn, Beatrice, turn those holy eyes." Let Dante see your holy eyes; look into his eyes. Is it extravagant to substitute for the image of the gryphon the image of Dante in Beatrice's eyes? I think not. *He is in her eyes*—as later, in *Paradiso* XXXIII, he will be "in" God. Then a startling second request by the dancers: "Of thy grace do us the favor that thou unveil thy mouth to him"—*disvele / a lui la bocca tua* . . . "that he may discern the second beauty which thou hidest"—*la seconda belleza che tu cele.* At this point we get one of the innumerable proofs of Dante's greatness as a poet. We are not shown *la*

seconda belleza, the smiling mouth; we are shown, instead, in the first four *terzine* of the next canto, the effect on Dante. For neither Dante nor Homer *describes* his heroine. As Beatrice's mouth is revealed, all Dante's senses but the sense of sight are *tutti spenti*; and sight itself is caught in *l'antica rete*—"the ancient net"—a variation of *l'antica fiamma*—"the ancient flame"—that he had felt again when he had first seen Beatrice in the Earthly Paradise.

What the net is doing here seems now to me plain, after some ten years of obtuseness about it. The general meaning is, as Charles Williams holds, that Dante, having chosen the Way of Affirmation through the physical image, feels here in the Earthly Paradise all that he had *felt* before, along with what he now *knows.* Why did he put the worldly emotion of his youthful life into the figure of the net? It is not demanded by the moment; we should not have the sense of missing something if it were not there. If it is a simple metaphor for the obfuscation of sensuality, it is not a powerful metaphor; we must remember that Dante uses very few linguistic metaphors, as distinguished from analogical or symbolic objects; when he uses them they are simple and powerful. The net, as I see it, is not simply a metaphor for the "catching" of Dante by Beatrice in 1274, though it is partly *that* ancient net; it is also a net of even more famous antiquity, that in which Venus caught Mars; and it is thus a symbolic object. Moreover, if Beatrice's eyes are univocally divine, why do the three Theological Dancers reproach him with gazing at her "too fixedly"—*troppo fiso*—as if he or anybody else could get too much of the divine light? He is, of course, not yet ready for the full Beatific Vision. But an astonishing feature of the great scene of the divine pageant is that, as a trope, a subjective effect, the smile of Beatrice simultaneously revives his human love (Eros) and directs his will to the anticipation of the Beatific Vision (Agapé): both equally, by means of the action indicated by the blinding effect of both; he is blinded by the net and by the light, not alternately but at one instant.

To bring together various meanings at a single moment of action is to exercise what I shall speak of here as the symbolic imagination; but the line of *action* must be unmistakable, we must never be in doubt about what is happening; for at a given stage of his progress the hero does one simple thing, and one only. The symbolic imagination conducts an action through analogy, of the human to the divine, of the natural to the supernatural, of the low to the high, of time to eternity. My literary generation was deeply impressed by Baudelaire's sonnet *Correspondances,* which restated the doctrines of medieval symbolism by way of Swedenborg; we were impressed because we had lost the historical perspective leading back to the original source. But the statement of a doctrine is very different from its possession as experience in poetry. Analogical symbolism need not move towards an act of imagination. It may see in active experience the qualities necessary for static symbolism; for example, the Grave of Jesus, which for the theologian may be a symbol to be expounded in the Illuminative Way, or for the mystic may be an object of contemplation in the Unitive Way. Despite the timeless orders of both rational discourse and intuitive contemplation, it is the business of the symbolic poet to return to the order of temporal sequence—to *action*. His purpose is to show men experiencing whatever they may be capable of, with as much meaning as he may be able to see in it; but the action comes first. Shall we call this the Poetic Way? It is at any rate the way of the poet, who has got to do his work with the body of this world, whatever that body may look like to him, in his time and place—the whirling atoms, the body of a beautiful woman, or a deformed body, or the body of Christ, or even the body of this death. If the poet is able to put into this moving body, or to find in it, a coherent chain of analogies, he will inform an intuitive act with symbolism; his will be in one degree or another the symbolic imagination. . . .

I . . . repeat that Dante was the great master of the symbolism, the meaning of which I have been trying to suggest. But the symbolic "problem" of **The Divine Comedy** we must not suppose Dante to have undertaken analytically; it is our problem, not his. Dr. Flanders Dunbar has stated it with great penetration:

> As with his progress he perceives more and more of ultimate reality through the symbol [Beatrice], at the same time the symbol occupies less and less of his attention, until ultimately it takes its place among all created things on a petal of the rose, while he gazes beyond it into the full glory of the sun.

The symbolic problem, then, is: How shall Dante move step by step (literally and allegorically) from the Dark Wood, the negation of light, to the "three circles, of three colors and one magnitude," God Himself, or pure light, where there are no sensible forms to reflect it? There can be no symbol for God, for that which has itself informed step by step the symbolic progress. Vision, giving us clear visual objects, through physical sight, moving steadily upward towards its anagogical transfiguration, is the first matrix of the vast analogical structure. As Dante sees more he sees less: as he sees more light the nearer he comes to its source, the less he sees of what it had previously lit up. In the Empyrean, at the climax of the Illuminative Way, Beatrice leaves Dante and takes her place in the Rose; St. Bernard now guides him into the Intuitive Way.

For the Illuminative Way is the way to knowledge through the senses, by means of aided reason, but here the "distance" between us and what we see is always the distance between a concept and its object, between the human situation in which the concept arises and the realization of its full meaning. Put otherwise, with the beginning of the **Vita Nuova** in mind, it is the distance between the knowledge of love, which resulted from the earthly love of Dante for Beatrice; and the distant "object," or God, that had made the love in the first place possible: the distance between Beatrice and the light which had made it possible for him to see her. The Kantian synthetic proposition of the entire poem, as we enter it through the symbolism of light, is: Light is Beatrice. Here the eye is still on the human image; it is still on it up to the moment when she takes her place with the other saints in the Rose, where she is only one of many who turn their eyes to the "eternal fountain." Light is Beatrice; light is her *smile;* her final smile, which Dante sees as she enters the Rose, is no longer the mere predicate of a sentence, for there is now no distance between the smile and what had lit it. Although, in so far as it is a smile at all, it is still the smile at the unveiling of the mouth, it is now the smile without the mouth, the smile of light. And thus we arrive at the converse of the proposition: Beatrice is light. Now Dante's eye is on the light itself, but he cannot see it because Beatrice, through whose image he had progressively seen more light, has disappeared; and he can see nothing. There is nothing to *see*. For that which enables sight is not an object of vision. What has been seen is, in what is surely one of the greatest passages of all poetry, "the shadowy prefaces of their truth." Illumination, or intellect guided by divine grace, powerful as it is, halts at the "prefaces." But the Unitive Way leads to the Presence, where both sight and discursive thought cease.

Whether Dante should have tried to give us an image of God, of that which is without image and invisible, is an unanswerable question. Is it possible that we have here a break in the symbolic structure, which up to the end of the poem has been committed to the visible? At the end we are with Love, whose unpredicated attribute is the entire universe. Has Dante given us, in the "three circles, of three colors and one magnitude," merely the trinitarian and doctrinal equivalent of the ultimate experience, instead of an objective symbol of the experience itself? In the terms of Dante's given structure, such a symbol was perhaps not possible; and strictly speaking it is never possible. If he was going to give us anything he doubtless had to give us just what he gave; he gave it in an act of great artistic heroism. For in the center of the circles he sees the image of man. This is the risk, magnified almost beyond conception, of St. Catherine: the return of the suprarational and suprasensible to the "common thing." It is the courage to see again, even in its ultimate cause, the Incarnation.

If we will look closely at the last four lines of the **Paradiso,** and double back on our tracks, I believe that we will see that there is no break in the *dramatic* structure—the structure of the action. For the poem is an action: a man is acting and going somewhere, and things are happening both to him and around him; otherwise the poem would be—what I may have given the impression of its being— a symbolic machine. In the space of an essay I cannot prepare properly the background of the suggestion that I am about to offer. For one thing, we should have to decide who "Dante" is, and where he is in the action that he has depicted—questions that nobody seems to know much about. For what it may be worth, I suggest that the poet has undertaken to involve a fictional character named Dante—at once the poet and not the poet of that name—in a certain action of the greatest possible magnitude, the issue of which is nothing less, perhaps something greater, than life or death. In this action the hero fails. He fails in the sense that he will have to start over again when he steps out of the "poem," as he surely must do if he is going to write it.

Thus I see *The Divine Comedy* as essentially dramatic and, in one of its modes, tragic. Are we to suppose that the hero actually attained to the Beatific Vision? No; for nobody who had would be so foolish as to write a poem about it, if in that spiritual perfection it could even occur to him to do so. The poem is a vast paradigm of the possibility of the Beatific Vision. No more than its possibility for the individual person, for "Dante" himself, is here entertained. What shall we make of his failure of memory, the slipping away of the final image, which he calls *tanto oltraggio*—"so great an outrage?" It would be a nice question to decide whether something had slipped away, or whether it had ever been fully there. The vision is imagined, it is *imaged;* its essence is not possessed. I confess that it is not an argument from the poem to say that had Dante claimed its possession, he would have lost that "good of the intellect" which we forfeit when we presume to angelic knowledge; and it was through the good of the intellect that he was able to write the poem. But it is an external argument that I believe cannot be entirely ignored.

The last *terzina* of the last canto tells us: *All' alta fantasia qui mancò possa*—"To the high fantasy here power failed." What power failed? The power to write the poem, or the power to possess as experience the divine essence? Is it a literary or a religious failure? It is obviously and honorably both. It makes no more sense to say Dante achieved his final vision as direct experience than to say that Sophocles married his mother and put out his own eyes; that the experience of the *Oedipus Rex* represents the personal experience of Sophocles. What Dante achieved is an *actual* insight into the great dilemma, eternal life or eternal death, but he has not hedged the dilemma like a bet to warrant himself a favorable issue. As the poem closes, he still faces it, like the rest of us. Like Oedipus, the fictional Dante learns in humility a certain discipline of the will: we may equate up to a point the dark-blindness of Oedipus and the final light-blindness of Dante; both men have succeeded through suffering in blinding themselves to knowledge-through-sense, in the submission of *hybris* to a higher will. The fictional Dante at the end steps out of the frame and becomes again the historical Dante; Oedipus steps out of his frame, his fictional plot is done, he is back in the world of unformed action, blind and, like Dante, an exile. Shall Oedipus be saved? Shall Dante? We do not know, but to ask the question is to point to a primary consideration in the interpretation of *The Divine Comedy,* particularly if we are disposed, as some commentators have been, to believe that Dante the man used his poem arrogantly to predict his own salvation.

If Dante does not wholly succeed in giving us in the "three circles, of three colors and one magnitude," an image of the Godhead, I think we are ready to see that it was not necessary; it was not a part of his purpose. Such an image is not the "final cause" of the poem. The poem is an action; it is an action to the end. For the image that Dante gives us of the Godhead is not an image to be received by the reader as essential knowledge in his own "angelic" intelligence, as an absolute apart from the action. It is a dramatic image; the image is of the action and the action is Dante's. To read Canto XXXIII in any other way would be perhaps to commit the blunder that M. Gilson warns us against: the blunder of thinking that Dante was writing a super-philosophical tract, or a pious embellishment of the doctrines of Thomas Aquinas, instead of a poem. The question, then, is not what is the right anagogical symbol for God; it is rather what symbol for God will serve tropologically (that is, morally and dramatically) for the tragic insight of the poet who knows, through the stages of the Three Ways, that the Beatific Vision is possible but uncertain of realization. Dante sees himself, Man, in the Triune Circles, and he is in the Seraphic Heaven of Love. But at the end desire and will are like a "wheel moving equally"; motion imparted to it at one point turns it as a whole, but it has to be moved, as the wheel of our own desire and will must be moved, by a force outside it. The wheel is Dante's last symbol of the great failure. Since it must be moved, it is not yet at one, not yet in unity, with the divine will; it obeys it, as those other wheels, the sun and stars, moved by love, obey.

I take it that the wheel is the final geometrical projection of the *visual* matrix of analogy; it is what the eye sees, the material form, and what in its anagoge it eventually aspires to become. We must remember that Beatrice's eyes are spheres, no less than the physical universe itself, which is composed of concentric spheres. The first circles that Dante shows us are in Canto III of the *Inferno,* Charon's—"for round his eyes were wheels of flame." The last, the Triune Circles, are the anagoge of the visual circle, and are without extension; they are pure light, the abstraction or sublimation of flame. Flame burning in a circle and light lighting up a circle, and what it encloses, are the prime sensible symbols of the poem. Only Satan, at the geometrical center of the world, occupies a point that cannot be located on any existing area of the cosmos. This is the spherical (or circular) expression of Satan's absolute privation of light-as-love which in the Empyrean turns the will-wheel of Dante with the cosmic spheres. These are the will of God as love; and if we ignore the dramatic structure, and fail to look closely at the symbolic, we shall conclude that Dante is at one with the purpose of the universe. But, as we have seen, the symbolic structure is complicated by the action, and in the end the action prevails. That is to say, Dante is *still moving.* Everything that moves, says Dante the Thomist in his letter to Can Grande, has some imperfection in it because it is, in the inverse degree of its rate of motion, removed from the Unmoved Mover, the

Triune Circles, God. By a twist of this argument, which, of course, as I shall presently indicate, is specious, Satan himself has no imperfection: he too lies immobile—except for the fanning wings that freeze the immobile damned in Giudecca—as the Still Point in the Triune Circles is immobile. If Dante's will is turning like a wheel, he is neither damned nor saved; he is morally active in the universal human predicament. His participation in the love imparted as motion to the universe draws him towards the Triune Circles and to the immobility of peace at the center, as it draws all creatures; but a defection of the will could plunge him into the other "center."

Now Dante is astonished when he sees in the Primum Mobile a reversal of the ratio of speed of the spheres as he had observed it on earth, through the senses. "But in the universe of sense," he says to Beatrice, "we may see the circlings more divine as from the center they are more removed." In the spiritual universe the circlings are more divine the nearer they are to the center. It is a matter of perspective; from the earth outward the revolutions of the spheres are increasingly rapid up to the ninth, the Primum Mobile, whose speed is just short of infinite; the Primum Mobile is trying to achieve with all points of its surface a simultaneous contact with the Still Point of the Empyrean. What he sees in the Primum Mobile is this perspective visually reversed; instead of being the outer "crust" of the universe, the Primum Mobile is actually next to the central Still Point, whirling with inconceivable speed. God, the Still Point, is a non-spatial entity which is *everywhere* and *nowhere*. The Ptolemaic cosmos, which had been Christianized by the imposition of the angelic hierarchy of Dionysius, has been, in a way not to be completely visualized, turned inside out. The spheres, which began their career as an astronomical hypothesis, are now no longer necessary; they are replaced in the ultimate reality by nine non-spatial gradations of angelic intelligence, in three triads, the last and ninth circle of "fire" being that of the simple angels, the "farthest" removed in the non-spatial continuum from the Divine Love.

Where then is the earth, with Satan at its exact center? I think we must answer: Where it has always been. But "where" that is we had better not try to say. At any rate neither Satan nor the earth is at the spiritual center. His immobility thus has no perfection. In the full spiritual reality, of which the center of the material universe becomes an outermost "rind," beyond space, Satan does not exist: he exists in the world of sense and in the human will. The darkness of hell, from the point of view of God (if I may be allowed the expression), is not an inner darkness, but an outer. So, in the progress from hell to the Empyrean, Dante has come from the inner darkness of man to the inner light of God; from the outer darkness of God to the outer light of man.

This anagogical conversion of symbol that I have been trying to follow in one of its threads is nowhere by Dante merely *asserted;* it is constantly moving, rendered moment by moment as *action.* Like most good poets, great or minor, Dante wrote better than he had meant to do; for if we took him at his word, in the letter to Can Grande, we should conclude that the **Paradiso** is a work of rhetoric calculated "to remove those living in this life from a state of misery and to guide them to a state of happiness." It seems probable that persons now enrolled among the Blessed got there without being compelled to see on the way all that Dante saw. Were we reading the poem for that kind of instruction, and knew not where else to find it, we might conclude that Dante's *luce intellectual,* with its transformations in the fourfold system of interpretation, is too great a price to pay even for salvation; or, at any rate, for most of us, the wrong price. It would perhaps be a mistake for a man to decide that he has become a Christian at the instance of Dante, unless he is prepared to see all that Dante saw—which is one thing, but always seen in at least two ways.

A clue to two of the ways is the mirror symbol. As we approach it, the kind of warning that Dante at intervals pauses to give us is not out of place. For if the way up to now has been rough, we may expect it from now on to be even rougher. The number of persons, objects, and places in **The Divine Comedy** that are reflections, replicas, or manifestations of things more remote is beyond calculation. The entire natural world is a replica *in reverse* of the supernatural world. That, I believe, we have seen so far only on the dubious authority of my own assertion. But if Dante is a poet (I agree with M. Gilson that he is) he will not be satisfied with assertion as such, even with the authority of the Church to support it. The single authority of poetry is a difficult criterion of actuality that must always remain beyond our reach. And in some sense of this actuality Dante has got to place his vast two-way analogy (heaven like the world, the world like heaven) on the scene of action, and make it move. Let us take the stance of Dante at the beginning of **Paradiso** XXVIII, and try to suggest some of the ways in which he moves it:

> as in the mirror a taper's flame, kindled behind a man, is seen by him before it be in his sight or thought,
>
> as he turns back to see whether the glass speak truth to him, and sees that it accords with it as song-words to the music;
>
> so my memory recalls that I did turn, gazing upon the lovely eyes whence love had made the noose to capture me;
>
> and when I turned, and my own eyes were struck by what appears in that orb whenever upon its circling the eye is well fixed,
>
> a point I saw which rayed forth light so keen that all the vision that it flames upon must close because of its sharp point.

(One observes in passing that even in the Primum Mobile Beatrice bears the net-noose dimension of meaning.) Beatrice's eyes are a mirror in which is reflected that "sharp point," to which Dante, still at a distance from it, now turns his direct gaze. As he looks at it he sees for the first time what its reflection in Beatrice's eyes could not convey: that it is the sensible world turned inside out. For the sensible world as well as her eyes is only a reflection of the light from the sharp point. Now he is looking at the thing-in-itself. *He has at last turned away from the mirror which is the world.* What happens when we turn away from a mirror to look directly at the object which we saw reflected? I must anticipate Beatrice's famous experiment with one of my own. If you will place upon a table a box open at one end, the open end towards a mirror, and then look into the mirror, you will see the open end. Turn from the mirror and look at the box itself. You still see the open end, and thus you see the object *reversed.* If the box were reproduced, in the sense of being continued or moved *into* the mirror, the actual box would present, when we turn to it, a closed end; for the box and its reflection would show their respectively corresponding sides in congruent projection. Quantitative visualization of the cosmic reversal is not completely possible. But through the mirror analogy Dante performs a stupendous feat of the imagination that in kind has probably not been rivalled by any other poet. And it is an analogy that has been firmly grounded in action.

In conclusion I shall try to point to its literal base; for we have seen it, in *Paradiso* XXVIII, only as a simile; and if we had not had it laid down earlier as a physical fact to which we must assent, a self-contained phenomenon of the natural order, it would no doubt lack at the end that fullness of actuality which we do not wholly understand, but which we require of poetry. The self-contained fact of the natural order is established in Canto II of the *Paradiso,* where Beatrice performs a physical experiment. Some scholars have been moved by it to admire Dante for this single ray of positivistic enlightenment feebly glowing in the mind of a medieval poet. So far as I know, our critics have not considered it necessary to be sufficiently unenlightened to see that Beatrice's experiment is merely poetry.

Before I reproduce it I shall exhibit a few more examples of the mirror symbol that appear at intervals in the five last cantos. In Canto XXIX, 25-27, form permeates matter "as in glass . . . a ray so glows that from its coming to its pervading all, there is no interval." Still in XXIX, 142-145, at the end: "See now the height and breadth of the eternal worth, since it has made itself so many mirrors in which it is reflected, remaining in itself one as before." At line 37 of Canto XXX we enter the Empyrean where Dante sees the great River of Light "issuing its living sparks"; it too is a mirror, for Beatrice explains: "The river and the topaz gems that enter and go forth, and the smiling grasses are prefaces of their truth" (i.e., of what they reflect). In Canto XXX, 85-87, Dante bends down to the waves "to make mirrors of my eyes"; and again in XXX he sees the Rose of Paradise, another mirror, in one of his great similes:

> And as a hillside reflects itself in water at its foot,
>   as if to look upon its own adornment, when it is
>   rich in grasses and in flowers,

> so, mounting in the light, around, around, casting
>   reflection in more than a thousand ranks I saw all
>   that of us have won return up yonder.

And finally the climactic reflection, the "telic principle" and the archetype of them all, in Canto XXX, 127-132:

> The circling that in thee [in the Triune God]
>   appeared to be conceived as a reflected light, by
>   my eyes scanned a little,
> in itself, of its own color, seemed to be painted
>   with our effigy, and thereat my sight was all
>   committed to it.

Where have these mirrors, which do their poetic work, the work of making the supra-sensible visible—one of the tasks of all poetry—where have they come from? The remote frame is doubtless the circular or spherical shape of the Ptolemaic cosmos; but if there is glass in the circular frame, it reflects nothing until Virgil has left Dante to Beatrice's guidance in the Earthly Paradise (*Purgatorio* XXXI); where we have already glanced at the unveiling of mouth and eyes. I suggest that Beatrice's eyes in *Purgatorio* XXXI are the first mirror. But the image is not, at this early stage of Beatrice, sufficiently developed to bear all the strain of analogical weight that Dante intends to put upon it. For that purpose the mirror must be established as a literal mirror, a plain mirror, a "common thing."

He not only begins with the common thing; he continues with it, until at the end we come by disarming stages to a scene that no man has ever looked upon before. Every detail of Paradise is a common thing; it is the cumulative combination and recombination of natural objects beyond their "natural" relations, which staggers the imagination. "Not," says Beatrice to Dante, "that such things are in themselves harsh; but on your side is the defect, in that your sight is not yet raised so high."

A mirror is an artifact of the practical intellect, and as such can be explained by natural law: but there is no natural law which explains man as a mirror reflecting the image of God. The great leap is made in the interval between Canto II and Canto XXXIII of the *Paradiso.*

Dante, in Canto II, is baffled by the spots on the moon, supposing them to be due to alternating density and rarity of matter. No, says Beatrice in effect, this would be monism, a materialistic explanation of the diffusion of the divine light. The true explanation is very different: all saved souls are equally saved, and all the heavenly spheres are equally in heaven; but the divine light reaches the remoter spheres and souls according to the spiritual gifts of which they were capable in the natural world. "This is the formal principle," Beatrice says, summing up, "which produces, in conformity to the excellence of the object, the turbid and the clear."

Meanwhile she has asked Dante to consider a physical experiment to illustrate the unequal reception of the divine substance. Take three mirrors, she says, and set two of them side by side, and a third in the middle but farther back. Place a candle behind you, and observe its image reflected in each of the three mirrors. The middle reflection will be smaller but not less bright than the two others: "smaller" stands quantitatively for unequal reception of a quality, spiritual insight; "not less bright" likewise for equality of salvation. But what concerns us is a certain value of the experiment that Dante, I surmise, with the cunning of a great poet, slyly refuses to consider: the dramatic value of the experiment.

There are *three* mirrors each reflecting the *one* light. In the heart of the Empyrean, as we have seen, Dante says:

> In the profound and shining being of the deep light
>   appeared to me *three* circles, of *three* colors and
>   one magnitude.

In the middle is the effigy of man. The physical image of Dante had necessarily been reflected in each of the three mirrors of Canto II; but he had not seen it. I suggest that he was not then ready to see it; his dramatic (i.e., tropological) development fell short of the final self-knowledge. Self-knowledge comes to him, as an Aristotelian Recognition and Reversal, when he turns the cosmos inside out by turning away from the "real" mirrors to the one light which has cast the three separate images. For the first time he sees the "one magnitude," the candle itself. And it is all done with the simple apparatus and in conditions laid down in Canto II; he achieves the final anagoge and the dramatic recognition by turning around, as if he were still in Canto II, and by looking at the candle that has been burning all the time behind his back.

I have described some motions of the symbolic imagination in Dante, and tried to develop a larger motion in one of its narrower aspects. What I have left out of this discussion is very nearly the entire poem. In the long run the light-imagery is not the body, it is what permits us to *see* the body, of the poem. The rash suggestion that **The Divine Comedy** has a tragic mode—among other modes—I shall no doubt be made to regret; I cannot defend it further here. Perhaps the symbolic imagination is tragic in sentiment, if not always in form, in the degree of its development. Its every gain beyond the simple realism of experience imposes so great a strain upon any actuality of form as to set the ultimate limit of the gain as a defeat. The high order of the poetic insight that the final insight must elude us, is dramatic in the sense that its fullest image is an action in the shapes of this world: it does not reject, it includes; it sees not only with but through the natural world, to what may lie beyond it. Its humility is witnessed by its modesty. It never begins at the top; it carries the bottom along with it, however high it may climb.

Renato Poggioli   (essay date 1965)

SOURCE: "Paolo and Francesca," in *Dante: A Collection of Critical Essays,* Prentice-Hall, Inc., 1965, pp. 61-77.

[*The following excerpt discusses the Paolo and Francesca episode in the* Inferno. *Poggioli's essay originally appeared in a longer form in the June 1957 issue of* PMLA.]

. . . Francesca tells her story as if she were reminiscing aloud. One day, Paolo and she were reading together, for their own entertainment, the romance of Lancelot du Lac, and particularly that section of the romance describing how the protagonist was overpowered by his passion for the fair Guinevere. Francesca alludes to all this very succinctly, through the single phrase: "how love seized him" (*come amor lo strinse*), where she uses a violent verb, *stringere*, "to grasp" or "to squeeze," to indicate the violence of the passion mastering the knight's soul. We imagine the two sitting beside each other: one listening, the other, probably Francesca, reading aloud. But the only thing we are told by Francesca is that they were alone, without the company of even the fear of their weakness, or the suspicion of their own selves. It would be impossible to state more concisely the perfidy of temptation, lying in wait to assail two unprepared and defenseless human hearts. The malice of sin threatens and ruins our souls when they yield to self-oblivion, when they abandon themselves, deceitfully, to their own innocence:

> *"Noi leggiavamo un giorno per diletto*
> *di Lancialotto come amor lo strinse:*
> *soli eravamo e sanza alcun sospetto."*

["We were reading one day for delight of Lancelot, how love seized him: We were alone and unsuspecting."]

Francesca's memory rehearses all the unforgettable instants of that fatal moment. They were looking down at the pages of their book, when the suggestive power of the story suddenly raised their gazes toward each other; or, as Francesca says, "that reading made us lift our eyes." This happened more than once: and Francesca seems to lengthen the duration of each of those instants by the dieresis on the word *fiate*, "times." At every turn, each recognized the same paleness on the other's face. Yet the reading would have perhaps failed to seduce them into sin; if the climax of the tale had not finally broken down all restraints and overcome their resistance:

> *"Per piú fiate li occhi ci sospinse*
> *quella lettura, e scolorocci il viso;*
> *ma solo un punto fu quel che ci vinse."*

["Several times our reading caused our eyes to meet and our faces to pale; But it was one point alone that overcame us."]

The crucial point, the passage by which they were vanquished, is that famous scene in the romance where the noble Gallehaut begs Guinevere to reward the gentle knight Lancelot for loving her so loyally and faithfully, and the Queen complies and kisses Lancelot on his lips. The scene, and the electric effect of its reading, are recalled by Francesca with some of the loveliest lines of the canto:

> *"Quando leggemmo il disïato riso*
> *esser baciato da cotanto amante,*
> *questi, che mai da me non fia diviso,*
>
> *la bocca mi baciò tutto tremante."*

> ["When we read how the longed-for smile was kissed by so great a lover, this one, who shall never be parted from me, kissed my mouth, all trembling."]

The transition from a vicarious to a genuine consummation, from the first kiss of Lancelot and Guinevere, which belongs to the realm of imagination, to the first kiss of Paolo and Francesca, which took place in the realm of experience, is beautifully conveyed not only by the change of rhythmical pace, but also by the sudden transformation of Francesca's mode of expression, by the metamorphosis of her language. The lips of Guinevere, the heroine of the romance, are at first marvellously metaphorized into a *disïato riso,* or "longed-for smile." These words are made even more insistently caressing by the dieresis lengthening the adjective and intensifying the radiance of the image. The select choice of words and sounds, as well as the trope itself, by which the curved lips of the loved and loving Queen lose all physical reality, becoming as light and incorporeal as their inviting and wordless smile, tend to give a spiritualized and idealized vision of that imaginary embrace. While the Queen's inviting gesture is re-experienced from the viewpoint of the knight, dazzled by the sight of her seductive smile, the kiss by which Lancelot seals her lips is instead re-evoked from the standpoint of Guinevere, as shown by the passive form of the verb "being kissed" (*esser baciato*), which suggests a feeling of feminine abandon, a gesture of self-offering. As for the complement agreeing with that passive form, "by so great a lover" (*da cotanto amante*), it reveals Francesca's awareness of the personal merits of her partner in passion and sin, and tends to equate his qualities with Lancelot's aristocratic and chivalric virtues. All this implies a process of self-identification: if Francesca sees in her lover the peer of such a worthy as Lancelot, she may also see in herself the equal of his Queen; and she may even think that she had a right to betray Gianciotto, if Guinevere betrayed King Arthur himself. But here the parallelism, and double impersonation, suddenly end. Up to now Francesca has evoked a vision of romantic love through both empathy and sympathy, through the alluring mirror of both sentiment and art. As soon as she deals, not with the fleshless kiss of two fictitious creatures, but with the real one of two living beings, she immediately realizes that she was no Guinevere, and that Paolo was no Lancelot. This realization is evident in the line where she alludes, simply and directly, to her lover. Now she

does not refer to him with the usual *costui,* "that one," but with *questi,* "this one," so as to indicate his physical and moral nearness to her. The relative clause following this pronoun (*questi, che mai da me non fia diviso,* "this one who will be never divided from me"), is a cry of possession, where pride mingles with despair. That pronoun and that cry presuppose either a fleeting turn of her eyes, or merely a blind gesture of her hand, as if to assure herself, as well as the two visitors, that her lover still is, and will forever remain, at her side. All this takes but a line, which separates, as a curtain or a barrier, the kiss she once read about from the kiss still alive in the memory of her flesh. Only after having raised such a barrier will she be able to re-evoke, in its loneliness and singularity, their own kiss: which she however catches only in Paolo's gesture. Paolo is described as she saw him at that moment, moving toward her full of trembling and fear. The vision reveals him to us as a weaker and more human vessel than even the timid Lancelot. And we, the readers, see Francesca receiving the kiss not on curved, but on closed and unsmiling lips, to which she refers by using a cruder, singular word. This is what we meant by the transformation of Francesca's language: and such a falling off from the spiritual to the physiological, from the "smile" (*riso*) of Guinevere to the "mouth" (*bocca*) of Francesca, is but the shift or descent from literature to life, from fiction to reality, from romanticism to realism; or more simply, from sentimental fancy to moral truth. Lust and adultery replace for a moment passion and love: a cry of nature breaks forever the mirror of illusion and the veil of self-deceit.

The proof of this is evident in the two statements by which Francesca concludes her tale, each being enclosed in a single line. The first is but an exclamation, ambiguous and significant at the same time. Its clear purport is the acknowledgment, on Francesca's part, of the role which the reading of that famous medieval romance played in their life, as well as the recognition that that role was identical with the one played by Gallehaut in the story they read not too wisely but too well. The ambiguity lies in the mixed tone of the phrase, conveying a double sense of regret for all the bliss and evil of which that hour was the seed: *"Galeotto fu il libro e chi lo scrisse"*—"Gallehaut was the book and he who wrote it."

By equating the effect of that reading with the action performed by Gallehaut, by identifying the unknown author of the romance with Gallehaut himself, who still preserves a graceful dignity despite the vileness of his services, Francesca treats the book and its author as if she would like to accuse and to absolve them at the same time. She cannot forget the beauty of the story and the glamor of the characters, since that beauty and that glamor still reflect a kind of redeeming light on the sin they committed at the example of Lancelot and Guinevere. While on one side Francesca tries to emphasize in her story all the aspects that may ennoble her experience, she has still too much sense of responsibility to lay more than part of their guilt on others than Paolo and herself. She knows that she has been more sinning than sinned against; hence she dares not call the romance and its writer by the ugly name of panderers. The reader feels nothing more need be added, yet Francesca has something more to say. Strangely enough, she feels it necessary to allude to what happened after the reading had aroused and bared to them their own "dubious desires." To be sure, the allusion is merely negative in character, and takes the form of another reference to the book which they forgot and discarded, as soon as it had led them to their first kiss: "'*Quel giorno piú non vi leggemmo avante.* [That day we read no more therein.]'"

At first sight, the final words of Francesca (since these are her final words) seem to be superfluous, and even to lack propriety: they may sound impudent, or at least too complacent, even more than merely unnecessary. What is Francesca's purpose in telling Dante that they did not read in that book any further? Why unveil so deviously, as well as so brutally, those intimate secrets which even a lost woman prefers to keep hidden? Only a harlot, devoid of the last shred not only of modesty, but even of self-respect, would go so far as to speak of her fall in such cynical terms. There is a difference between unchastity and impurity: a woman may be candid without being shameless. In all her behavior Francesca has consistently shown not only great delicacy of feeling, but also tactfulness and good taste. She has given proof of intellectual and moral courage by facing truth in all its nakedness, yet she has constantly avoided the pitfalls of vulgarity and coarseness. If such is the case, we are forced to conclude that her final words must mean something less plain and obvious than what they seem to suggest. I am unwilling to follow the example of some interpreters, who take those words at their face value. The clue we need is perhaps to be found in the very turn of the phrases by which Francesca opens and closes the story of her fall. The first and the last line of that story begin with almost identical words: "one day," "that day" (*un giorno, quel giorno*). In the second case the temporal reference appears to be hardly useful or necessary. It would have been sufficient to say, "and then we read no further." Yet Francesca feels the need to emphasize that they did not read any further "that day." These two small words cannot be explained away as a mere pleonasm, as syllables that are there solely to fill the line. They become pertinent and relevant, and as such, necessary, only if they are supposed to hint or imply that Paolo and Francesca took up again, on other occasions, the reading of the book which had been "the first root" of their sin. Why does Francesca wish to suggest these successive readings, after the one which was interrupted by their first kiss, on the first day of their love? Such a question may not be answered, yet it must be asked. The only thing we need to realize is that Francesca wants us to know that the two lovers returned on other days to the book which once for all has acted as their go-between. The reason for this, as for Francesca's indirect reference to such a fact, may be seen in a wish not so much to recapture the wild happiness of

the first, fatal moment, as to recover, if only for an instant, the idealizing and sublimating illusions which literature creates around the realities of sex and lust. It was the worship of passion, the ideology of love, its idolatry and cult, which had hidden from their consciences the danger of damnation and the ugliness of sin; it was the written word, both harmless and harmful, that had spelled their doom. Yet they tasted the intoxicating sweetness of that worship or cult not only before, but even after knowing the bitterness of sin.

Now that Francesca has ended her story, the canto goes rapidly toward its end. At this point, Dante has very little to tell us. He merely observes that while Francesca had been talking, Paolo had been unashamedly weeping, and implies that his tears did not stop even after she had ceased to speak. From Dante's manner of speaking, rather than from what he says, we realize that he must never have taken his eyes from Francesca's face all the while she had been talking to him: and this is perhaps the first time he has been able to look into the tearful countenance of her lover. The echoes of Francesca's words, which still fill and rend his heart, or perhaps, even more, the pitiful spectacle of Paolo's grief, are too much for Dante, who breaks down under the stress. The poet suddenly swoons, and falls down like a dead man:

> *Mentre che l' uno spirito questo disse,*
> *l'altro piangea, sí che di pietade*
> *io venni men cosí com'io morisse;*
> *e caddi come corpo morto cade.*

[While one spirit spoke thus the other wept so that out of pity I grew faint and fell as a dead body falls.]

Dante loses his senses out of compassion, while Paolo and Francesca lost their senses out of passion alone: yet, although caused by sentimental participation rather than by moral complicity, his fall parallels their fall. The almost perfect iambic beat of the line seems to reproduce the thud of his body, which for a while will lie on the earth as a lifeless object, as a soulless thing. . . .

The love story which Dante retells in his own way (which coincides, although only in part, with Francesca's way), is "romantic" in the old-fashioned meaning of that term: a meaning fully preserved in the French adjective *romanesque,* but partly surviving even in the epithet "romantic," to which modern usage has given such a broad semantic range. Medieval culture was full of trends which may be defined as "romantic" in the traditional sense; and it expressed those trends in literary forms which, being essentially anticlassical and new, took for their name the word from which both "romantic" and *romanesque* were to derive, that is, "romance." . . . But Dante dares probe the innermost secrets of both passion and lust: and this is why, instead of contemplating "romantic love" from without, he dares to reconstruct the sinful story of Paolo and Francesca from inside, within the framework of the "romance" itself. Yet, as we shall see later, that framework is used not to re-evoke romantic love, but to exorcise it. . . .

The most relevant document which Dante left imbedded in the canto itself [is] Francesca's manner of speaking, the language and diction she employs in telling her story of passion and death. The heroine makes abundant use of the medieval casuistry of love, and her discourse, far from being spontaneous, is rather deliberately constructed. Her words are, and are meant to be, highly conventional, even rhetorical, in character. This conventionalism is so intentional, and so intense, that we cannot certainly apply to her, and to her speech, the definition that Dante gives elsewhere (***Purgatorio***, xxiv. 52-54) of himself, and of his own poetry of love:

> io mi son un che quando
> amore spira noto, ed a quel modo,
> che ditta dentro vo significando.

[I am one who takes note when love inspires me and expresses it as it is written within me.]

By these words Dante means that when a genuine feeling of love truly inspires a poet's heart, it immediately determines the forms of expression best suited to itself. To do so, that feeling must have some purity and innocence, that love must be a matter of the soul, rather than of the senses. The feeling dictating Francesca's fashionable diction is of a very different sort; at any rate, the love of which she speaks in conventional terms is not necessarily identical with the love which bursts forth through the shell of that diction and often breaks it. When she is less self-conscious, Francesca's passion overflows beyond the barriers of convention, and even of convenance; but generally she tries to keep within the limits of a studied elegance, of a stylized modulation of both thought and speech. And this amounts to saying that one of the outstanding critical hypotheses, the one maintaining that Francesca speaks according to the tenets of the *dolce stil nuovo*, is completely wrong. The point may be proved in many ways: for instance, by arguing that no woman was ever a member of Dante's "circle," or that no feminine character ever speaks in the first person in any of the poems written by the poets of that school. It is true that Francesca's speech is full of literary mannerisms, but it is easier to find among them a few peculiar Provençal traits, than any characteristic features of "the sweet new style." The most typical Provençalism to be found in Francesca's speech is *piacer,* nearer, even linguistically, to the original *plazer,* than its equivalent *piacenza,* normally used before Dante's time by the Italian imitators of the Troubadours. As a matter of fact, Francesca uses the term *piacer* or *plazer* in a novel way, by applying it to masculine, rather than feminine, beauty; and this reference to the good looks of her lover contributes to the almost womanly, or at least, unmanly, impression that Paolo seems to produce.

Even so we must still recognize that the first line of Francesca's confession sounds not merely as a reminiscence, but as a repetition of the main belief of "the sweet new style" school, according to which there is an affinity, nay, an identity, between love and a noble heart. That line, which reads: *"Amor ch'al cor gentil ratto s'apprende,"* seems to be an echo, or rather a replica, of the opening words of the famous *canzone* by Guido Guinicelli: *"Al cor gentil ripara sempre amore,"* which the young Dante had paraphrased in the beginning of a famous sonnet of the ***Vita Nuova***: *"Amore e il cor gentil sono una cosa.* [Love is one with the gentle heart.]"

Yet, if my reading of the episode is right, I feel that despite their verbal identities Francesca's statement and the passages just quoted have different, even opposite, meanings. As used by Francesca, *amore* and *cor gentile* signify an experience and a reality that cannot be compared, except in contrast, with the ideals and values those two formulae designate in the language of Guinicelli and Dante. When these two poets connect those two concepts, they intend to say that the spiritual power of love finds its natural abode in a heart made noble by its own merits and virtues. But when Francesca makes the same connection, she means instead that passional love is the calling and destiny of every heart which is noble in this word's literal sense, that is, made such by the gentility of its blood. This is the way Francesca feels, as is proved by the manner in which she speaks about herself and of her own passion and person, or alludes to Paolo, whom she implicitly defines *cotanto amante,* "so great a lover," by so defining Lancelot. One must not forget that the notary Guinicelli, and that Dante, who was officially a member of the medical guild, were respectively citizens of Bologna and Florence, of two free communes, of two democratic commonwealths. Their very conception of love, despite its aristocratic origins, reflects already the cultural awareness of the new burghers' class. The "sweet new style" reacts against the feudal ideology of the Troubadours and their disciples, who believed literally in the doctrine of courtly love, and considered it a privilege of the highly placed and the well born. But Francesca was the member of a family that tried to reduce the city of Ravenna into its own fief, and the pride of her birth and station induces her to prefer the Provençal view. That view had survived the decline of Provençal poetry and culture, and had found new expression in the prose fiction of Northern France, where an equally refined, but less spiritual, sort of love was still considered as the exclusive privilege of knights and dames, of men and women of great breeding and lineage. For Dante and his group love will always remain a matter of election and grace, based on the reciprocal sympathy of two lofty souls; and the poet rephrases this doctrine in a famous passage in the ***Purgatorio*** (xxii. 10-12), through the following words attributed to Virgil:

> " . . . Amore,
> acceso di virtù, sempre altro accese,
> pur che la fiamma sua paresse fuore;"

[" . . . Love by virtue kindled always kindles another, provided only that it show its flame;"]

It has been suggested that these lines are meant as a kind of retractation of the principle embodied in the line where Francesca speaks of the fatality of love, of its refusal to absolve any person being loved from loving in return (*amor ch' a nullo amato amar perdona*); but the hypothesis seems to be groundless. Through the words just quoted Dante qualifies in a higher ethical sense the doctrine of his youth, his own belief in the reciprocity of spiritual love. As for Francesca's statement, no palinode was required, exactly because its equivocal meaning is clarified by the moral lesson contained in the entire episode. No correction was in this case necessary since, despite all appearances, even when using the same verbal expressions, she does not speak the language of Dante, or of all the poets who, as he said in another canto of the **Purgatorio** (xxvi. 99), *"rime d'amor usar dolci e leggiadre."*

Nor, despite the Provençal mannerisms of her speech, have we any right to deduce that Francesca's manner of speaking is an echo of the diction of the Troubadours. Only Dante himself may help us to find the literary models and the stylistic examples after which he patterned Francesca's discourse. He offers such a help in another part of the canto just mentioned, where he affirms that Arnaut Daniel was the best craftsman of the vernacular word (**Purgatorio,** xxvi. 117-119), and surpassed all his rivals in both *"versi d'amore e prose di romanzi."*

With this simple line, Dante sums up all the main forms of the literature in the vulgar tongue, as it had developed at that time in Tuscany and in Italy, as well as in Provence and France. He obviously considers only the forms endowed with formal dignity, addressed to a literate and nonpopular audience, dealing in different ways with the same great medieval theme, which, for the intellectual as well as for the social élite, was the theme of love. There is no doubt that Francesca's speech must be patterned on either one of these two main forms. It is true that Francesca's language is highly literary in character, and has very little to do with popular speech: its very sophistication and complexity stand out against the background of the simple style used by Dante in the narrative parts of the canto, and in the whole of his poem. Yet this does not mean that Francesca's manner of speaking is necessarily poetic, especially in the lyrical sense. We have already stated that that language differs from the style which Dante himself called both "sweet" and "new"; and one may add, not too paradoxically, that, although Dante shapes her words and thoughts into the rhythmical and metrical structure of the **Commedia,** she speaks not in verse but in prose. Thus, by making use of the line quoted above, one could say that her forms of expression derive not from the tradition of the poetry of love (*versi d'amore*), either in the *lingua del sí or the langue d'hoc*, but from the tradition of love fiction (*prose di romanzi*) in the *langue d'oïl*. After all, the name "Francesca" means nothing else but "French." Dante's heroine translates into her own terms the idiom she has learned from such French literary sources as the romance of Lancelot, hence the formal conventionality, the rhetorical stylization, of her speech. Almost dialectically, that conventionality and

that stylization transform themselves into their very opposites, becoming thus the aptest instrument, the most natural vehicle of which Francesca could avail herself not only to relate her story, but even to idealize and sublimate it.

This general imitation of the tone of the romantic narratives she used to admire so much does not mean that Francesca imitates in any special way the particular language of the romance of Lancelot, nor that, while re-evoking the effect provoked by the reading of that romance, the poet patterned the story of its two readers after the most important episode of the romance itself. Immoral literature may influence life, but not in such a way as to pattern life after itself. When she establishes an apparently perfect parallel between the two "first" kisses, the one exchanged between Lancelot and Guinevere, and the one exchanged between Paolo and herself, Francesca gives the impression of remembering the one as fully as the other: yet Dante knows that she is wrong. The parallelism she implies is partial or relative; and one could say that she unconsciously reshapes the literary kiss to make it better agree with the real one. In other terms, she recollects what she did experience far better than what she did read. Her words mislead the reader (if not the poet) into believing that Lancelot and Guinevere too were "alone and without any suspicion" (*soli e senza alcun sospetto*), while, in their meeting in the grove at night, they were not only accompanied by Gallehaut, but also attended by the Queen's ladies in waiting, who were lingering nearby. What is even more important is that in the book it is the woman, and not the man, who kisses first. As a matter of fact, while the romance fails to mention that the Knight returned the Queen's kiss, Francesca does the same in regard to her response to Paolo's embrace. The parallel is partly one also of contrast, and the implication of this is so obviously suggestive that we do not need to dwell upon it. These details may however point out that Dante cared more for the spirit than for the letter of his text; and this scorn for literalness must be certainly taken into account also in regard to what we have said about his decision to let Francesca speak according to the diction of the love romances.

The very fact that the poet does not adopt the same diction himself, and fails to use it fully in those passages where the character speaking in the first person is not Francesca, but the protagonist of his own poem, clearly shows that even Dante the character avoids involving his own views and values in the language employed by his heroine. The man writing this canto is no longer the young literary enthusiast who once liked so much the French romances so dear to all the Paolos and the Francescas as to define them *Arthuri regis ambages pulcherrimae,* as he did in a famous passage of *De Vulgari Eloquentia,* where however the word *ambages* is rather equivocal, and may mean "fancies," as well as "adventures." Here Dante uses the language of the romances almost critically, or rather, as a dramatic device, through which he projects the psychology of Francesca, and within which he encloses her personality as within a shell. Francesco de Sanctis recognized the magnificent total result of Dante's vision and perspective, while ignoring the process or the method by which that result was achieved. In other words, he paid attention to the natural effects, rather than to the artificial components, of Francesca's speech. It is perhaps for this reason that he was led to interpret the canto in tragic, rather than in *romanesque* terms. Yet this was at least in part a happy mistake, because it saved him from the far more serious error of reading Francesca's words in lyrical key. With his profound insight, the great critic felt that, despite all appearances, Francesca speaks not only outside the frame of reference of "the new sweet style," but in opposition to it. This is what he means when he says that Francesca, "this first-born daughter of Dante," is also "the first truly living woman to appear on the poetic horizon of the modern age." Although readily admitting that such a figure could be created only after "a long elaboration of the feminine ideal in the poetry of the Troubadours and in the very lyrics of Dante," he ends by saying that Francesca is the opposite of Beatrice. Within the poetic tradition from which the latter derives, "man fills the stage with himself; it is he who acts, and speaks, and dreams; while woman remains in the background, named and not represented, like Selvaggia and Mandetta; she stays there as man's shadow, as a thing he owns, as an object he has wrought, as the being issued from his rib, devoid of a separate personality of her own.". . .

The last clue is a negative one: Paolo's silence, and the significance of that silence. Paolo has no existence of his own. He speaks no word during the entire episode; and even when Francesca refers to her lover, the poet pays no attention to him. Dante seems to notice his presence only at the end, and does so only to remark that Paolo must have been weeping for a long time. It was natural for the poet to place Francesca in the foreground of the episode, and Paolo in its background; yet this fails to explain the poet's almost absolute indifference to the lesser of these two protagonists. Such an indifference is not casual, but deliberate. Dante's scorn is not directed toward Paolo as a separate person, but toward what he stands for; and as such it involves all men who, like him, are the slaves, rather than the masters, of love. The passionate man, hardly ever as interesting or suggestive as the passionate woman, is never called hero, while many a woman in love is a heroine. It is said that love exalts the lowly, and humbles the lofty ones; but this is true only in the sense that the first is the feminine, and the second the masculine alternative. Especially in love is "the female of the species more deadly than the male." For man, even more than for woman, love is almost always a *liaison dangereuse*. Either one of the two actors or victims of a love story will look pathetic to the eyes of mankind, but while pathos may enhance a woman's personality, it lessens man's stature. A pathetic hero is a contradiction in terms, since he is made to look not only unheroic, but even unmanly. This Dante understood well: so, while raising Francesca to prominence,

he reduced Paolo almost to nought. De Sanctis recognized this very well: "Who is Paolo? He is not the man, or the manly type, such as to form an antithesis, to establish a dualism. Francesca fills the stage wholly with herself. Paolo is the mute expression of Francesca; the string trembling at what she says, the gesture accompanying her voice. The one speaks while the other weeps; the tears of the one are the words of the other."

This statement, a perfect aesthetic justification of Dante's conception, implies that the main character of the episode absorbs the lesser one; that its protagonist is this couple of lovers, even more than Francesca herself that the two lovers form a single personality though such a personality is shaped by its feminine component, rather than by its masculine one. In this very conception Dante shows outstanding originality. No poet went as far as Dante in this reduction to a cipher of the masculine partner of a great passion. Considered alone, Paolo, a bleak pale creature whose only action is weeping, pales nearly to a vanishing point. Love changes man into woman's shadow, and this is true of Paolo not only as the ghost he now is, but as the man he once was. Francesca projects the memory of herself even before the time of her fatal affair, but evokes her lover only during the moment of their sin. And, unconsciously, she fixes him forever in a vision of passive pusillanimity. At least in appearance she describes him in the very moment he acted like a man: when he took the initiative, as he was supposed to do, and kissed her on her mouth. Yet Francesca finds it fit to remember that even in that instant of daring he was trembling in every fiber of his body, like a leaf. Commenting upon the simple and terrible words, *tutto tremante,* by which Francesca recalls the emotions of her lover in that moment of anguish and bliss, Francesco de Sanctis is led to observe that "certainly Paolo's flesh did not tremble out of fright." I am not so sure: I may even be ready to maintain exactly the opposite. Paolo perhaps trembled because he was afraid: of woman and love, or of death and of sin; or simply of the unknown, even of his own fear itself. In this passivity and pusillanimity Paolo strangely resembles the hero to whom Francesca and the poet liken him. In the second of the two romances of which he is the protagonist, *Le Chevalier de la Charrette,* Lancelot is described as willing to look like a coward, and even to risk infamy, merely to pursue his love object; while in *Lancelot du Lac* the Queen kisses him first, as soon as she realizes that he does not dare to do so himself; and, as the text states with comical naïveté, she gives herself the illusion of being the receiver rather than the giver, by taking the knight by his chin: "Et la roine voit bien que li chevaliers n'en ose plus fere; si le prent pour let menton et le base" (xxxi).

All this may suffice to prove not only that Francesca towers above Paolo, but that the poet towers above both. As I have frequently hinted, this cannot be said of Dante the character, whom the author, with great humility and charity, equates with the lesser part of his double creation. This happens at the very ending of the episode, when the reader witnesses at the same time, in two different men, almost the same heartbreak. It is at this point that we suddenly realize that Paolo had been unashamedly sobbing for the entire duration of Francesca's speech; and immediately after this, we learn that Dante has fainted as soon as Francesca has uttered her last word. For a while, at the close of the canto, Dante the character becomes thus the equal of Paolo, and even of Lancelot, who for a while seems to swoon himself, while talking with the Queen of his still unrewarded love. In this brief moment, Dante himself is but a creature of pathos, a victim of pity and self-pity, like Paolo and Lancelot. Dante the poet stops short of the ridiculous, but it is only the timely fall of the curtain which saves the final scene of the episode from an unexpected caricatural effect.

Dante was one of those few human beings equally able to understand [two] kinds of love; and he understood them both as a man and as a poet. He was able to understand the kind of love which stops at the "sweet sighs," and which is generally expressed in lyric form, as well as the kind that experiences the "dubious desires," and manifests itself in romantic fiction.

—*Renato Poggioli*

All this amounts to saying that love cannot ever be the tragic passion par excellence. Tolstoy acknowledged as much when he attributed the following words to Konstantin Levin, the masculine protagonist of *Anna Karenina:* "To my mind, love . . . both sorts of love, which you remember Plato defines in his *Banquet,* serve as the test of men. Some men only understand one sort, and some only the other. And those who only know the non-Platonic love have no need to talk of tragedy. . . . In Platonic love there can be no sort of tragedy . . . because in that love all is clear and pure because. . . . But perhaps you are right. Very likely . . . I don't know. I don't know."

Unlike Tolstoy and his hero, Dante was one of those few human beings equally able to understand both kinds of love; and he understood them both as a man and as a poet. He was able to understand the kind of love which stops at the "sweet sighs," and which is generally expressed in lyric form, as well as the kind that experiences the "dubious desires," and manifests itself in romantic fiction. In the same way he understood that neither kind can be tragic. Dante is a moral realist, always subordinating pathos to ethos. So it is improper to interpret the episode of Paolo and Francesca in the light of the romantic view of poetry and life, as de Sanctis did, or according to the decadent view as did Gabriele D'Annunzio in his *Francesca da*

Rimini. The latter is not a tragedy, but merely a "poem of blood and lust" (*poema di sangue e di lussuria*), as the author himself so aptly said. In the same way, while using continuously, and almost exclusively, the criterion of tragedy, Francesco de Sanctis gave us an interpretation of the Paolo and Francesca episode far more pathetic than tragic. "Sin is the highest pathos of tragedy, since this contradiction (between the sense of sin and the erotic impulse) is placed not without, but within the two lovers' souls," says the critic, thus reducing the situation to a psychological crisis, even more than to a moral conflict. It is in "the sweet thoughts," even more than in "the dubious desires," that de Sanctis sees "the tragic core of the story, the divine tragedy left unsaid on Francesca's lips, and which only Dante's reverie, so movingly imagined, calls forth and re-enacts," thus showing that he conceives the fall and the ruin of the two lovers in sentimental terms. De Sanctis concludes his analysis by affirming that "pity is the muse of this tragedy, which the poet unfolds only in its main lines, filling the rest with silence and mystery. . . ." But tragedy is made not only of pathos and pity, but also of ethos and terror. A full study of de Sanctis' essay reveals that the critic is reading their episode not in the light of tragedy, but in the light of romantic drama: as a story of love and death, stirring our emotions and feelings rather than our moral sense, as an effusion of sentiment, so pure as to need no catharsis. There is no doubt that this canto is based on an interplay of passion and compassion: yet neither one nor the other, not even their synthesis, can be taken at its face value.

I have already stated that Dante wrote the episode in the key of the love romances, but even this needs qualification, and cannot be taken for granted. In what he did, Dante went beyond not only the form he chose, but also beyond the sentiment which normally inspires or dictates that form. The love romance is primarily, but not exclusively, a medieval genre, so that it recurs even in modern literature, where it changes its style, replacing the convention of fancy with the conventions of realism, and taking the name and the shape of the novel, or of other types of fiction. Yet the new product will remain a love romance if it still expresses sentiment without judging it. This is certainly not the case with such a work as *Anna Karenina,* where the writer condemns his heroine at least by implication, by referring her judgment to the tribunal of God. Such is the sense of the scriptural epigraph that Tolstoy placed at the head of his novel: "Vengeance is mine; I will repay, saith the Lord" (Romans XII.19). Yet the same epigraph would be at least partly improper if placed at the head of this canto, since it would reflect solely the standpoint of Dante the character. In this episode, as in the entire ***Commedia,*** God has already taken his vengeance, and Dante is a witness of this. Paolo and Francesca have been condemned to everlasting death, to the damnation of their souls: when faced with such a revelation, the best man can do is silently to bow his head. Yet Dante is not to be satisfied with this, and gives to God's verdict the assent of his own conscience, even if he does so without words. Though verbally unstated, Dante's judgment is framed in literary terms;

his moral message is implicit in the situation and the structure of the story, so that no further intervention on the poet's part is required to make it meaningful to us.

Dante achieves this result by a dialectical treatment of the romance form—by what one might call a double mirror trick. There is no doubt that the poet derived the idea that the reading of the Lancelot romance had been "the first root" of the passion and ruin of the two lovers, not on the authority of any external tradition; but solely on the inner urgings of his own imagination. If the "how" and "why" of Francesca's fall is an invention of Dante's, then its supposed occasion becomes highly suggestive and significant. The real kiss of Paolo and Francesca follows the imaginary kiss of Lancelot and Guinevere, as an image reflecting its object in a perspective similar and different at the same time. In brief, the seduction scene fulfills within the entire episode the function of a play within a play: more properly, of a romance within a romance. This creates an effect of parody, or, if we prefer to use a less negative term, something akin to what in modern times has been called "romantic irony," which in this case operates in an antiromantic sense. This means that the two romances, one of which may be likened to a frame, and the other to the picture enclosed therein, react reciprocally in such a way as to annihilate each other. In his analysis of *Madame Bovary,* starting from the presupposition that the modern novel is but an offspring of the ancient romance, and that originally the former was but a love story like the latter (as proved by the fact that in French both are still called by the same name), Albert Thibaudet ends by saying that Flaubert's masterpiece is in reality a *contre-roman.* In the same way, the "romance" of Paolo and Francesca becomes in Dante's hands an "antiromance," or rather, both things at once. As such, it is able to express and to judge romantic love at the same time. While Dante the character manifests his sorrowful regret through the mute eloquence of his bewilderment, and later of his swoon, so Dante the poet expresses his judgment without uttering a word, without even a gesture or a sign of reproof or reproach. Dante does not preach or plead, nor does he need to superimpose an edifying sermon on the structure of his story. His ethical message may be easily read not in the spirit, but in the very letter of his tale. It is Francesca herself that he entrusts with the literary moral of his fable. This moral is very simple, and could be summed up in the statement that writing and reading romantic fiction is almost as bad as yielding to romantic love. This obvious and almost naïve truth is all contained in the famous line, "Galeotto fu il libro e chi lo scrisse," by which, as Francesco D'Ovidio says, the poet confesses his horrified feeling at the thought that he too "could become a Gallehaut to somebody else." But there is no reason for such a fear, since that line helps to destroy the very suggestion on which it is built. It is with traits like this that the poet created this masterpiece, based on the avoidance of tragedy, as well as on the moral sublimation of the romance form.

Thomas Goddard Bergin   (essay date 1969)

SOURCE: "Hell: Topography and Demography," in *Diversity of Dante,* Rutgers University Press, 1969, pp. 47-64.

[*In the following essay, the* Inferno *is esteemed—more so than the other two books of the* Commedia—*as an example of "sublime" storytelling and dramatic description of personality and scene.*]

Over the centuries scholars, experts, and merely humble readers of the **Comedy** have asked the question: why did Dante write his great work? To celebrate Beatrice and establish his reputation, as may be said of the **Vita nuova**? To give himself a standing among intellectuals, as is, in part at least, the avowed intent of the **Convivio**? To instruct the public on matters of general interest, somewhat neglected by others, as is the stated purpose of the *De vulgari eloquentia* and the *De monarchia*? For purposes of moral and political propaganda, evidence of which is not lacking in the **Comedy** itself? Or shall we see in the **Comedy,** as Flamini did, part III of the poet's autobiography, the **Vita nuova** and the **Convivio** being respectively parts I and II? Didactic, confessional, polemical—the poem is all this in intent. But in fact it is a poem and, as such, must have been conceived primarily as a work of art. Whatever his ultimate purpose, the poet's immediate urgency must have been the construction of a *navicella* fit to carry the burden of his message. Neither exhortation nor instruction would be of any avail if his public did not read the book. As the various apostrophes to the reader indicate, scattered as they are at discreetly arranged intervals, our poet always had his audience in mind.

Nor is there any doubt of his concern with narrative plan and tactics. "Neither the world, nor the theologians," confesses Dorothy Sayers, "nor even Charles Williams had told me the one great, obvious, glaring fact about Dante Alighieri of Florence—that he was simply the most incomparable story-teller who ever set pen to paper." It is time, perhaps, to tell the news to others or at least remind ourselves of it; if this were not the simple truth of the matter the world would not have taken him to its heart and even theologians might have found him less fascinating. It has always seemed to me that, like all good story-tellers, Dante puts forth a great and calculated effort in the first chapter of his tale in order to seize our interest and give us the initial impetus to carry through. From the story-telling point of view, the **Inferno** is the richest of the three great divisions in action, variety, characterization, and dramatic description. Here, in the words of Malagoli, "poetry finds its place suspended, as it were, between the savor of concrete things and a breath of the sublime." No doubt this is a commonplace, but like all sound commonplaces it bears repeating, especially in an age—as ours seems to be—when the "theologians" or at least the anagogical explicators are so busy with "figures," symbols, and the authenticity of Dante's Thomism.

I believe, too, that the aforementioned qualities, which characterize attractive and absorbing narration, can be brought out by consideration of the physical background of the story and the individuals who stand out against it; the shape and topography of the *doloroso regno* and its *gravi cittadin,* the "concrete things" of which Malagoli speaks. Most of the allegory of the *Inferno* is inherent in the tale and not embroidered over it (as is the case with the entrance to Purgatory, or the political vision at the end of that *cantica*); most of the instruction is likewise implicit (unlike the lectures on vows, moon spots, and angelic natures in the *Paradiso*). These are things of beauty and moral utility, but I doubt whether most readers would have reached them, were it not for the immediacy and the realism of the *Inferno*; "To possess poetry it was necessary to pass through man," says Salvatore Quasimodo of our poet, and the reader, too, I think, must prepare himself for the great illuminations of the later *cantiche* by submersion in the harsh and craggy world of the *Inferno,* vibrant with spectacular and diversified personalities, for in truth the characters of the *Inferno* are similar only if seen *sub specie theologiae;* intellectually, physically, and even morally they run through the entire human spectrum.

The configuration of Hell, in a sense, matches the design of the other two realms. It is a kind of mirror image of Purgatory; in the one case we have a series of descending ditches, in the other a like pattern of ascending terraces. It is suggestive, too, of the Rose of the Empyrean, in that, seen from the bottom, it could well have the aspect of a vast amphitheater. Ranged above Dante as he stands on the ice of Cocytus are the rows of sinners (though he cannot see them), even as the serried ranks of saints meet his eye ascending from the center of the Rose. These symbolic similarities have their purpose, but if we turn from symbolism to realism we shall soon see how vastly different the Infernal topography is from that of either of its sister realms. However we may admire the formalized beauty of Purgatory or the significant spaciousness of Heaven I think we shall have to concede that Hell is richer in the variety of its landscape. Indeed, this must necessarily be so even for the sake of the allegory; for there is but one way to salvation and there are many avenues of error. So the terraces of the way of redemption are similar, for one inspiration motivates all the penitent, and since the Blessed, as Dante tells us, really dwell in only one heaven, the symbolic appearances they make hardly call for differentiation save in their order. What matters to the penitent and the saved is what they have in common: the damned can be—indeed, must be—individualized and solitary, and hence different.

It follows that the compartments of Hell are very sharply divided, and passing from one to the other requires great effort and ingenuity on the part of Dante and Virgil; on occasion it is not made quite clear just how they do it. For the inmates, passage from one section to another is impossible (this law is clearly stated in *Inf,* XXIII, 55-57). In Purgatory all the terraces are connected by stairways, apparently open to all, and, once the true Purgatory has begun, relatively easy of

ascent; in the symbolic Heaven the law of spiritual gravity makes the ascent easy—indeed, inevitable—and the true Heaven has no subdivisions. Leaving aside the allegory of these distinctions, we may see at once that the Inferno is of necessity less homogeneous than its sister realms and has, on the score of topographical diversity, much to offer. There are—in defiance it would seem of the basic allegory, although Dante knows how to turn it to his purpose—even occasions when the poets go up instead of down. But at this point it might be useful to remind ourselves in detail of the pattern—which is in effect also to recall to our minds the general scheme of Hell.

Topographical Hell does not begin with Canto I of the poem. Whatever be their thematic or structural connections, the action of the first two cantos takes place on our earth. Nor do I think the sinister portal marks the limit of the true Hell; it is a signpost but not a boundary marker. This is made clear by the nature of the souls we find just beyond it, who may not claim Infernal citizenship. Since the first circle is clearly labeled as such by Dante we may, for topographical purposes, think of the entire kingdom as encircled by the Acheron, much as the mighty ocean (in myth as in fact) encircles our living world. Apparently the only way to reach the *città dolente* is by crossing this dread river; we may visualize it, I think, as somewhat high-banked. If it were not, the simile of the falling autumn leaves would lack something in accuracy. It must be tolerably wide and deep, else there were no need of a ferryman. Once across, a somewhat surprising landscape confronts the poets and the reader. Although Dante cannot see very clearly, it is evident that he is walking not upon a craggy, descending gradient but upon a plain, and light soon appears to illuminate the path to the illustrious souls of the past. Presently, the poets approach a noble castle, which has around it all the appurtenances of a pastoral scene from the chivalrous romances. It has a *bel fiumicello,* Hell's second and often forgotten river—is it connected with the more conventional Infernal system of waterworks, one wonders? Probably not. Whatever its source, its correspondences are evocative and honorable. For as Dante will have to cross Lethe to walk with Beatrice and touch his brow to the river of grace in order to have his supreme vision, so here he must cross this little stream in order to mingle with the *spiriti magni.* Is it allegorically eloquence, as Benvenuto says—or something better? Beyond it lies a meadow of fresh green, and rising from that, the pleasant little hill (open, luminous, and high) from which Dante can survey the great shades of antiquity. It is a foretaste of both the Garden of the princes and the Earthly Paradise itself, not elaborated, but adequately outlined; the princes, to be sure, have flowers of unearthly beauty and fragrance, but even the princes do not have the castle or the river. (Hell is extremely well irrigated, no small feature of its attraction.) This oasis of virtue, this subdued but authentic pastoral, may be for the scholar (and possibly the author) a *"locus amoenus topos,"* but for the reader, as for the pilgrim Dante, it is a genuine part of Hell's landscape.

Both the illumination and the spaciousness of Limbo are stressed by contrast to the circle of the lustful, where Dante takes note of the smaller scope (*men loco cinghia*) and the oppressive darkness. Of the landscape as such he says nothing; one has the impression of the sinners whipped around in a kind of void, with the poets standing on a ledge to watch them as one might watch the wheeling of birds from the brow of a cliff. If there is a plain of any extent either around them or beneath them they cannot see it; the ecstasy of lovers, however illicit, does not allow them to tread the earth. In the succeeding circle of the gluttonous, our feet are on recognizable ground again, though it is by no means firm ground, but the cold, soggy mud of a snow-swept bog. It does not seem to be a particularly extensive meadow—or swamp, for it has something of that nature—since the poets can get through it fairly rapidly, but it cannot be too small either, since, when Dante comes to (and just how he moved from the lustful to this category he does not tell us; did Virgil carry him in his swoon?) he beholds "new torments and new tormented ones" as far as his eye can see in the oppressive darkness. It is, we may say, a muddy arc of level ground leading to a downward path, which brings the travellers to the jousting place of the avaricious and prodigal.

The fourth circle gives us another plain; this time it is not sodden with rain but arid and rocky. By way of somber relief, the brooklet, "darker than perse," meets the poets as they leave the grim jousting and pours down to what Binyon calls a "fen," in which the various kinds of wrathful wallow and complain. One has the impression of a pond, choked with mud or perhaps weeds, yet sufficiently deep to require a boat for passage. It reminds us a little of the Acheron, boatman and all, and it, too, marks a frontier, setting the lower Hell off from the upper. But here we may simply note its aspect: part river, like the Acheron; part swamp, something like the mud of Ciacco's discontent, but more so, and put into sharp contrast with the dry (and sterile) setting for the avaricious. Further on comes yet another surprise—the walls of a city, beyond which Dante can discern the towers of sinister worship, even as the medieval traveller, when approaching the gates of a walled town, must have seen the spires of the churches and the public buildings looming large beyond them. There is, indeed, a good deal of contemporary detail in this passage. Describing the burial ground just inside the walls, Dante tells us that it could be compared to Aliscamps, *dove Rodano stagna,* just as, in fact, the muddy Styx lies sluggish and menacing behind them. We may note again that for all the overriding claustrophobia of Hell, which narrows as the poets descend, the perverse cemetery of the heretics is quite spacious, "a wide, desolate campagna," as L. O. Kuhns called it. It may be remarked here that the funnel shape of Hell suggests that each successive category of sinners is smaller in number, and broadly speaking, this is true. At the frontier the indifferent are countless—"I had not thought death had undone so many"—while the very center contains only one sinner, the arch-

fiend himself. Furthermore, it seems likely that there are more incontinent than violent, more violent than deceitful. But I am not sure this principle holds in every detail—Dante probably does not mean to imply that there are more simonists than thieves, for example—and, in the descriptions of landscape that chiefly concern us here, some of the lower *bolge,* circles, are made to appear relatively spacious.

Comes then the pause on the brink of lower Hell, followed by the slithering descent to the rings of the violent. This zone has a kind of unity in its variety which is appropriate to its quasi-autonomy as a subdivision; it is all on one level and reproduces the general motif of the upper Hell, having again an encircling river, a wood (it was a thicket of spirits in Limbo but a wood for all that) and, innermost, the burning sand, constantly rekindled by the flakes of flame. It is a microcosm in which topographical or meteorological elements previously encountered reappear in somewhat different combination. (This manipulation of the familiar is a constant weapon of Dante's art; we shall not enlarge on it here.) It is worth noting, I think, how in this area Dante makes a special effort to give his landscape some resemblance to our earth. The landslip by which the poets descend to the encounter with the centaurs is like the one near Trent; the wood is strange indeed but the Maremma comes to mind; the dikes by which the fiery desert is traversed are not unlike those lining the Brenta. This is a device to which Dante frequently resorts in the course of his poem; the examples here are especially notable because they are found in every one of the three violent circles. Here the effect is to make us feel at once familiar with the successive scenes and horrified at them, as of a well-known landscape seen through dark, distorting glasses. However familiar the dikes and the Maremma and the landslide, the blood-red rivers serve to indicate that we are no longer in our world. The province of the violent is half recognizable and half unnatural, a proper setting for the venerable Brunetto (wise and erudite but no longer free to move with the solemn gravity of the sage) and the misguided Piero, loyal to his master but "towards himself unjust."

Separation, isolation, contrast: such are the principles of Hell's scheme. The circles are set off from each other as we have noted, and the larger subdivisions even more dramatically so. Between the march of Violence and the double kingdom of Fraud there is an even deeper descent than that which separates the upper realm from the outer circle of the murderers and robbers. Only by persuading the genius of Fraud himself to bear them into his abyss can the poets descend in safety (and terror) to the Malebolge.

Malebolge too has its own integrity. It is hard to speak of landscape here for the *bolge* are, in the main, too narrow to allow much scope for scenery of any kind. Yet there is plenty of diversity. In the ditches of the seducers and panders, the soothsayers and the hypocrites, the impression of very restricted space is particularly strong and we focus but little on the environment. Narrow also is the unfragrant abode of the flatterers, almost, one would suspect, the narrowest of all. On the other hand, there is a suggestion that the ghastly plain occupied by the sowers of discord must be of some extent since the multitude of mutilated figures Dante meets there is greater than could have been found in all the battlefields of strife-torn Apulia. I have the feeling—perhaps because of the reference to the Libyan sands—that the thieves also have considerable space to maneuver in. But this is only one kind of variation; we may note how Dante again mixes the elements of his *mises en scène.* We have plains, a desert, and water (or at least liquid—as in the case of the *fiumicello* of Limbo, one must wonder a little bit about the source of the barrators' pitch—is it connected with the main rivers, and if not, how does it cross them, for surely it must be a complete circle?). In a more specialized area we have a privy, a hospital, and a two-lane city street. Another intriguing variant—not strictly topographical—appears in Dante's change of direction; no less than three times he reverses his usual Infernal descent to move upward. Virgil carries him up the bank of the simonists, and helps him out of the valley of the thieves, but Dante makes quite a point (and an incidental moral allegory) of his own laborious climb up from the sixth *bolgia.* One would think there would be also some slight ascent necessary to escape from the *Malebranche* even if the bridge is broken, but Dante mentions only the precipitous toboggan ride (Virgil being the vehicle) down the outer wall into the pouch of the hypocrites.

The one element so far lacking in the wide range of physical backgrounds is supplied by the last stage of all—the ice floor of the Inferno. So looking back now that we have seen it all we can see that we have truly had everything: plains, deserts, swamps, rivers, lakes, woods, even, in essence, mountains. We have tramped under rain, hail, snow, fire, and hurricane; to be sure there has been visible no sun nor moon nor sky but there have been plenty of fiery illumination and (in Limbo) a pleasant and soothing radiance that, if not quite sunshine, is the next best thing. All of these elements have combined and separated and recombined in new patterns, sometimes unobtrusive and sometimes forced upon our attention. It is no wonder that the reader cannot lay the book down, no wonder that Coleridge could say that "the topographic reality of Dante's journey through Hell" is "one of his great charms" and "gives a striking peculiarity to his poetic power."

Though perhaps it is not strictly within our province, we cannot omit a word on the second landscape of Hell: the landscape of reference. We have noted Dante's use of a scene familiar to his readers to reinforce the verisimilitude of various features of the Infernal world: the landslip near Trent, the dikes of the Brenta, to which we could add a number of others, the falls of San Benedetto, the towers of Bologna, the frozen Danube, and the like. But there is also a landscape of suggestion; the *Inferno* is punctuated with vignettes of our own earth, the effect of which is to relieve the oppressive atmosphere of Hell and incidentally to celebrate the transient but authentic beauty of our mortal habitat. I have in mind such passages as the opening of Canto XXIV, painting the first days of the "stripling year" or the evocation of summer twilight in Canto XXVI "when the fly gives way to the mosquito." Such nostalgic pictures of the world of the living are possible only in the *Inferno*; it is only Hell's "exiles of eternity" who may sigh for the "sweet light" and the "life serene." "Above in lovely Italy," Virgil may say, almost casually; in the *Purgatorio,* Sapia repudiates (as she must) her earthly citizenship, and in the *Paradiso* our world has become a mere "threshing floor." If the "brooklets" of the Casentino, which Master Adam yearns for, are not strictly speaking a part of Hell's topography, they yet serve to refresh his memory and illuminate his inner vision—and the reader's as well.

But it is time now to consider the population of these diversified zones and climates which make up the domain of the three-faced Emperor. Ernst Robert Curtius wrote some years ago that the personnel of the *Comedy* had never been adequately analyzed; we can hardly hope to approach adequacy in the scope of these pages, but we may bring together a few interesting facts with attendant implications. Let us begin with some census figures.

By my count, there are 164 definitely named or easily identified characters in the *Inferno*. (I count here only residents and not figures merely alluded to.) Of these, some eighty are from the classical world, four may be thought of as biblical, and the rest are largely from Dante's own contemporary society, though we must allow ourselves a little freedom in the definition of this area. The mingling of these various sects is not without its purpose. Putting together such figures as Judas on the one hand and Brutus and Cassius on the other is in line with our poet's deliberate and self-conscious historical syncretism, the principal cultural intention of the *Comedy,* which is sharpened here if we recall that Satan is the third element of the group: Old Testament, New Testament, and classical betrayers meet at the center of the universe. But I think that in the *Inferno* Dante is not so much concerned with the blending of the classical and the Judeo-Christian traditions as such (this is more marked in the *Purgatorio,* though since he cannot bring it out in the characters of the narrative it has to be emphasized in the embellishment and the collateral rhetoric) as with blending antiquity and the present into one homogeneous family of man. It has been frequently observed, in this connection, that Dante creates his own "exemplary figures"; characters such as Francesca and Ugolino have all the eternal mythopoeic virtue of any character from Homer or Sophocles. It is less commonly noted that his strategy has both fronts in mind: Ulysses, Jason, and Alexander mingle, not unobtrusively perhaps, but in a quite familiar fashion, with sly plotters from Romagna, Bolognese seducers, or petty Italian tyrants. Dante's own familiarity with Virgil has a unique immediacy and spontaneity. The poet uses his own person as a symbol of the present confronting the past, with reverence always but with no abdication of personality. So Myrrha and Gianni Schicchi are seen as two of a kind, Pier da Medicina introduces Curio with a kind of ferocious camaraderie, and Sinon and Maestro Adamo belabor each other with intimate invective, caricaturing at the same time that they stress the syncretistic intent of the poem. No wonder Dante listens with rapt attention! Only in the *Inferno* is such magnificent cosmopolitanism possible.

Among the nonclassical figures resident in Hell the preponderance is Italian. I count sixty-four Italians as against sixteen others in this general category (excluding the four biblical figures). Perhaps here it should be noted that in the large, anonymous, vaguely estimated groups, Italians also have a disproportionate representation; it would seem that numerous *Lucchesi* and Sardinians swim in the pitch of the barrators, and Caccianemico clearly implies that the Bolognese are well represented among the panders. Florence's name is, as we remember, "spread through Hell," by now comfortably stocked with Pisans and Genoese too, if we are to put faith in the poet's invectives. In any event, of the sixty-four Italians specifically named the majority (forty-one) are Tuscan, and of these, twenty-six are Florentines. (Our figures include the otherwise unidentified "ancient of St. Zita" of Canto XXI, and the anonymous but clearly Florentine suicide of Canto XIII.) Tuscans also have the widest spread of all Hell's delegations: we find two of them among the incontinent, three among the heretics, thirteen with the violent, no less than fourteen included in the impartially fraudulent (representing five of the ten Malebolge), and a respectable quota of nine authentic traitors. Not even the classical delegates, all taken together, have such a wide range, though they come close: of them I find five incontinent, one heretic (we know Epicurus is there although we do not actually see his tomb), six violent, twelve in the Malebolge (though representing six pouches), and two arch-traitors (or three, if we assume, as perhaps we should, that Antenor has come to rest in the ice-zone that bears his name). When it comes to speaking parts, the Tuscans have twenty-one out of the entire sixty-five (or sixty-six if Paolo speaks the vindictive line "Caina awaits"; some have thought so and it is an attractive notion). Of course, as Dante recurrently makes clear, it is natural that Tuscans should speak more readily than the rest; after all, their visitor and interlocutor is a compatriot. On the subject of Tuscans, and in a larger way Italians, it is interesting to note how many are related: there are three of the Cavalcanti tribe; two, possibly three, Pazzi; two of either the Abati or Donati, depending on the identity of Buoso of Canto XXV; two Ubaldini; and no less than four of the illustrious clan of the Conti Guidi. Some of them have kinsmen in the other realms too, the house of Swabia and (by now) the Donati are represented in all three kingdoms. But our pilgrim will meet only six more fellow-townsmen over the rest of his journey; Hell, the most generous of the realms in its admission policy, is also, in respect to Dante's contacts, the most homelike.

But let us go a little further with our quotas. From the region comprising Emilia, Romagna, and the *Marche,* which had for Dante a kind of social unity, we count twelve representatives, from Lombardy four, from what we might call the Veneto two. From Sardinia also we have two, and one each from Latium, Liguria, and Southern Italy. Cities with more than one representative, aside from Florence, are Bologna with four, and Lucca, Pisa, Pistoia, Padua, and Faenza two each. These figures are, I think, of some interest as signifying what Dante thought of or—more accurately—felt as Italy; they are diversified, but it is notable that some areas are not represented at all, and some very inadequately. Pier and his Emperor must stand for all of Italy south of the Garigliano River, and there are no Venetians to be found in spite of the vivid depiction of their *arsenà* in Canto XXI.

The foreign element requires some distinction in classification. I count among contemporaries or quasi-contemporaries of the poet only four foreigners: one German (if Frederick II may be so counted), two Englishmen, and a Navarrese—the only foreigner with a speaking part. Of course the scope of Infernal demography is not limited to Dante's contemporaries alone; the impression of cosmopolitanism that Hell gives derives from the large contribution made by various traditions of the past. Here the diversity is impressive. Classical figures are numerous; I count some fifty Greeks and twenty-seven Romans. Most of these are mere names in the Limbo catalogs (I include that of *Purgatorio* XXII as well as *Inferno* IV), which include thirty-three Greeks—thirty-four if we count Manto—and twenty-two Romans; it still leaves a substantial number to season Hell's population. Other figures from antiquity not strictly Graeco-Roman but adding their touch of the exotic are Semiramis, Dido, Cleopatra, and the Etruscan Aruns. Caiaphas, Annas, Potiphar's wife, and of course Judas are from Scripture; from the early Christian centuries we have Pope Anastasius (there, alas, by mistake) and Attila; the Romance tradition gives us four (one lover, two traitors, and the troubadour Bertran de Born), and I count five Arabs. The classical figures have only five "speaking parts" but they have no grounds for complaint since one of them is the eloquent Ulysses, and Virgil is a constant and articulate representative of antiquity. The other categories have only three speaking parts.

The sex census is not without interest. Hell is pretty solidly a man's world; of all the characters even so much as mentioned, only twenty-four are women and, of these, fifteen are Limbo dwellers and so merely names. Of the remaining nine, it is interesting to note that all but one (Manto) have some erotic significance: they include one prostitute and seven illicit lovers. The nature of the sins of Myrrha and Potiphar's wife puts them among the falsifiers for purposes of Dante's categories, but their motivation is lust. There are no women in all the circles of the violent, none in Cocytus; they seem also to have been innocent of gluttony, avarice, and seven out of ten of the lesser kinds of fraud.

Even in general categories Dante speaks of them only twice; there are *femmine* in the Limbo and sorry witches among the soothsayers. (Indeed Dante is probably showing his medievalism in this area.) In the *Inferno,* we may add, the only female resident with a speaking part is Francesca (for Beatrice is a transient and Thaïs is merely quoted). There are no children at all (there is nothing, happily, to make us think that Ugolino's sons are Hell dwellers) save for the anonymous *infanti* of Limbo, more tenderly referred to by Virgil as "innocent little ones" in the *Purgatorio,* balancing, as Dante's love for symmetry would require, the "childish voices" of the lower tiers of the celestial rose.

Hell is pretty much solidly a man's world; of all the characters even so much as mentioned [in *Inferno*], only twenty-four are women and, of these, fifteen are Limbo dwellers and so merely names. . . . There are no women in all the circles of the violent. . . ; they seem also to have been innocent of gluttony, avarice, and seven out of ten of the lesser kinds of fraud.

—Thomas Goddard Bergin

Finally, our census shows that Dante has been faithful to the prescription laid down by Cacciaguida, and in his Hell he has eyes only for the "best people." Even many of the anonymous hordes are made up of souls of distinction, "ladies and knights of old," "popes and cardinals," "scholars of great fame," and the like and, as for the citizens mentioned by name, I can find only one, Asdente, who might claim unconditionally to represent the proletariat. To be sure Vanni Fucci and Ciampolo are both bastards but the former's father was of the Pistoiese Lazzari and, according to Benvenuto, Ciampolo's mother was a noblewoman.

We must not omit, in our summary census of the lower world, the very special and flamboyant sector made up of the monsters, guardians, and officiating demons. These are numerous; "more than a thousand" of Heaven's outcasts line the walls of Dis, an unspecified number of demons lash the panders and seducers, and it seems safe to assume that not all of the *Malebranche* are introduced by name nor, of course, all of the Centaurs. Those specifically identified by my count run to thirty-four. Here too Dante's mixture of breeds and races is noteworthy; the classic tradition supplies the backbone of the corps, from Charon through to five of the six giants ringing the well of Cocytus, but Nimrod and Satan himself may claim a different origin, and Malacoda and his merry men might almost be called contemporary or at least medieval figures. Nor is the fair sex unrepresented in this important caste: the Furies are mentioned by name, and we may suppose that Medusa either actually appears or hovers just behind the wall as Virgil puts his protective hand over Dante's eyes; the Harpies, too, are feminine, as are the keen and savage bitches of the same wood. (Hell does not lack for its fauna.) A surprising number of monsters have speaking parts; all of the vivacious *Malebranche* get in their word, the Furies speak in unison, and seven other "officials" raise their voices in complaint or admonition—indeed two of them, Plutus and Nimrod, have the distinction of having languages of their own.

I do not know whether it has been remarked that Dante gives, demographically at least, to his somber province of eternity (or more correctly, St. Thomas would remind us, aeviternity) a dimension also in time. For Hell's community, as the traveller Dante knows it, has a past as well as a future. Those who have been in Hell and have moved on are numerous: all the patriarchs (the catalog of their names in the beginning of Canto IV balances that of the classical spirits mentioned at the end) and Cato and Trajan and Ripheus—as we learn from subsequent *cantiche.* There are those yet to come: Boniface, Clement, and of course Gianciotto; the usurers Vitaliano and Buiamonte; Carlino de' Pazzi; and, as we learn elsewhere, Forese Donati. (Six Italians, of whom we may note three are Florentines, to round out the census.) This gives to the season in Hell a kind of stereoscopic sharpness that is missing alike from Heaven, which is truly eternal, and from Purgatory, where all dwellers are transients. Incidentally, there are transients in Hell too, not only Dante Alighieri but Beatrice, who descends to speak with Virgil in Limbo, and the intervening angel who opens the gate of Dis.

Much of the fascination of the subterranean journey springs from Dante's adroit manipulation of the constants in his pattern. Here his formula of repetition with variation is well exemplified. To linger a little over one example: many critics have noticed the similarities of the stories of Francesca and Ugolino; in both cases we see a pair, eternally linked by passion, of which one weeps "and weeping speaks" and the other remains silent. But they do not stand alone; very similar is the pairing of Ulysses and Diomed, and other duos come readily to mind—Catalano and Loderingo, Sinon and Maestro Adamo, the two infuriated Alberti of Cocytus—each pair subtly distinguished by distribution of lines, attitudes, or characterizations. And there are other groupings too: there are many rugged individualists like Ciacco or Capaneus or Pier della Vigna or Brunetto; there are recurrent trios—the three Florentine sodomites, the three usurers (in both cases alluding to missing partners), the climactic trinity of treason in Satan's jaws. Larger groups are exemplified by the thieves, falsifiers, and traitors, in which the interplay of conversation is general (I distinguish between such articulate groups and the classical figures of Limbo or the blood-submerged murderers, for the latter are really only catalogs); the liveliest group scene of all is, of course, the *Malebranche* at play.

With infinite art and discretion Dante shifts his focus within the vast range at his disposal; we may note, since we have been speaking of the *Malebranche,* how this spirited portrayal of group action contrasts with the passive and mute parade of the *bolgia* that precedes it and the recurrent pair pattern of the canto immediately following. And as there are shifts of *personae* groupings, so there are shifts of tone and one may say of genre. The high tragedy of Canto V is succeeded by the sordid brutishness of Ciacco, and that in turn by the impersonal contempt of Canto VII, which needs the figure of Fortune to give it any touch of warmth. Again, and more subtly, we may note how the vertiginous and unwholesome metamorphosis of thief into serpent is succeeded by the solemn procession of the false counselors, self-contained in their fiery agony and still preserving their personalities and intellectual superiority—followed in their turn by the mangled yet still defiant figures of the schismatics.

Curtius comments on the cabalistic significance of the numbers in the various groups: there is a "decad" of the violent-against-neighbor category, a "heptad" of sodomites, and the number of illicit lovers specifically named adds up to the "highly symbolic" number nine. (He might have added that it is composed of three classical figures, three Orientals, and three Christians.) But a consideration of Dante's *philarithmia* would take us out of the area of the concrete; for our purposes, it is more to the point to note the variation of plastic groups, skillfully mixed with diversification of genres and even thematic substance. Let us look, for example, at the successive circles of the violent. The murderers and robbers are merely a mute catalog, the conversational charge in this canto (and there is no canto in the whole *Inferno* without conversation) is given the centaurs; no murderer speaks. This is followed immediately by the dramatic monologue of Pier della Vigna, and that circle closes on a note of vigorous action. Another monologue, that of Capaneus, follows, but it is aggressive, where Pier's had been apologetic or defensive; hard upon it comes Brunetto, the content of whose discourse brings us from the walls of Thebes back to the familiar Florentine motif, carried on in the next canto but now by a restless and agitated trio. A final threesome reinforces the theme of Florence the greedy; again one speaks, while two listen, and a fourth is mentioned.

We may use the same zone to illustrate how landscape is utilized to give each setting its particular character: the large numbers of murderers are bathed in blood, the uneasy throng of the lowest division prowls, sits, or lies on burning sand; two individual speakers raise their voices against the same background while another speaks from a contorted tree; one trio squats in suffering while another plays hide and seek in unholy shrubbery; landscape, kinetics, and plastic arrangements are incessantly varied. The whole scope of the *Inferno* would of course provide many more examples. The symbolism of the settings has been studied by all commentators and if we were to consider the reactions of Dante the pilgrim to the various zones and their inhabitants, we should add another element of diversification.

No other *cantica* has this kaleidoscopic richness of scene, action, and personalities, which combine to give its realism a fascinating diversity and its story line a compelling magnetism. It would be impossible to read the *Purgatorio* and ignore allegory; it is, as Eliot has said, impossible to read the *Paradiso* without at least some interest in the doctrine expounded. There is allegory as well as doctrine in the *Inferno,* but the reader can forget both as he follows the magnificent narrative—even though his be a *piccioletta barca.* The articulate and vigorous inhabitants of the dark world of sin have seen to that—and the setting against which they display their passion and their pain has its part in their triumph.

Joan M. Ferrante   (essay date 1975)

SOURCE: "Dante," in *Women as Image in Medieval Literature,* Columbia University Press, pp. 129-52.

[*In the following essay, Ferrante explains in detail Dante's evolving notion of woman, beginning with* Vita Nuova *and continuing through* Paradiso.]

Although he begins as a lyric poet within the same tradition, Dante moves beyond the *stilnovisti* in several significant ways. He turns outward beyond himself in order to understand the love he experiences, not just to acknowledge the beneficial effect of the woman, but to find a deeper significance in her existence and in his love for her. He is able to affirm secular love as the first stage of divine love: if a woman's beauty reflects heavenly beauty, if her powers to refine man come from God, then it is by seeking the source of her beauty, not by rejecting her, that man should reach God. Dante accepts the attraction he feels to physical beauty and ascribes it to the reflection of a higher beauty, so that he is able to preserve his love for a woman without letting it come into conflict with his love for God. In Paradise, he suggests that man can perceive the divine light only through the mediation of woman—until the end of his journey, Dante's eyes cannot bear the divine light except as it is reflected in Beatrice's eyes.

It is the beauty which appears in a wise woman, the spiritual beauty reflected in her physical appearance, which first awakens the love that lies dormant in the noble heart:

> *Amor e'l cor gentil son una cosa*
> . . . . .
> *Bieltate appare in saggia donna pui*
> *che piace a gli occhi sì, che dentro al core*
> *nasce un disio de la cosa piacente;*
> . . . . .
> *che fa svegliar lo spirito d'Amore*
> *E simil face in donna omo valente.*
>
> [*Vita Nuova,* XX]

Love and the noble heart are one

. . . . .

Beauty then appears in a wise woman
which pleases the eyes so much that within the heart
is born a desire for the pleasing object;

. . . . .

it awakens the spirit of Love.
And a worthy man has the same effect on a woman.

It is not insignificant that a worthy man can arouse the same response in a woman—the instinct to love what is pleasing and to desire what one loves is common to all human beings and, if properly guided by reason, will lead ultimately to God, who alone can fully satisfy human desires. Love is the spiritual uniting of the soul with the beloved object (*cosa amata*), of the lover with the beloved person (*persona amata*), Dante explains in the *Convivio*. From such a union both parties profit—each communicates his qualities to the other. What is unusual in Dante's view of love, particularly after the thirteenth century, is that human love between man and woman is not just a figure for the love of man and God, but a necessary step towards that love. One love does not cancel out the other; the one augments the other. In Purgatory, Virgil explains that love is not like the possession of material objects (the more one has, the less others can have); with love, the more one has, the more there is for all (canto XV).

Man reaches God through woman. Mary provides the way for all mankind, Beatrice for Dante. Together they enable Dante to see God: through Beatrice in the Earthly Paradise he will see the dual nature of Christ, the manifestation of God in time; through the Virgin he will see the trinity, outside time in the Empyrean. Women have both a symbolic and an active function in the salvation of man. At every stage of the upward journey they guide by love and prayer, by criticism and example. As reflections of God, as symbols of virtue and love, they draw out the good that is in man; as loving and compassionate beings, they bring the straying man back with their criticism, and help expiate his sins with their prayers. All women, not just the Virgin, can be intermediaries between God and man through love, moving man with their beauty and God with their prayers.

In the *Vita Nuova,* we see Dante guided by the understanding of women away from the selfish love of the early lyrics to the kind of love that will end in God. When Dante needs comfort and sympathy in his love, he instinctively turns to women. After Beatrice dies and he needs to talk about her, it is only to women that he can speak, because he spoke to them of her while she was alive (XXXI, **"Li occhi dolenti"**). His faith in their understanding is justified by their perception of his problem. They are always aware of his suffering and give him the opportunity to relieve it, but they also alert him to what is wrong in his love and so set him on the right path. Noticing his violent reaction to Beatrice, one of them asks to what end he loves his lady if he cannot bear her presence. He answers that he

used to seek her greeting, until she denied it to him, but now he is content to praise her. Dante does not, however, deceive the lady with this answer as he deceives himself. If your happiness lies in praising her, she continues, why do you write about your own condition? It is this comment that sets Dante thinking of love in a new way. He writes the canzone **"Donne che avete intelletto d'amore,"** addressed to ladies who understand love, in which God and the angels hint at Beatrice's purpose on earth (and even seem to anticipate the *Comedy*: "one who will say to the damned in Hell, I have seen the hope of the blessed," XIX). This lady's reproof, and Dante's shame, will be echoed with greater intensity in the Earthly Paradise, when Beatrice confronts Dante with his failures and compels him to face and to admit the truth.

In the *Vita Nuova*, we see Dante guided by the understanding of women away from the selfish love of the early lyrics to the kind of love that will end with God.

—*Joan M. Ferrante*

Women's understanding of love is not confined to sympathy for the poet. They feel compassion for him because they are capable of experiencing the same kind of love themselves. What a wise woman can do for a man—awaken the love that sleeps in the noble heart—a worthy man can do for a woman (see **"Amor e'l cor gentil"**). Indeed, Dante reverses the traditional roles so that a man can act as intermediary with God for a woman: he can move God with his prayers for her soul, as Pier Pettinaio does for Sapia (*Pg.* XIII), the first example of the effectiveness of prayer that occurs in Purgatory. The presentation of woman as a complete human being, an intelligent companion rather than simply the reflection of a higher good, distinguishes Dante from the other writers discussed in this study (with the exception of Marie de France). When Dante says, at the end of the *Vita Nuova, "io spero di dicer di lei quello che mai non fue detto d'alcuna"* (XLII: I hope to say of her what has never been said about any woman), he means the glorification of Beatrice as the reflection of God, but in fact he does something even more unusual for the dignity of women by presenting them as human beings.

Dante passes through several stages in his view of love and in his response to women, stages that can be traced through his works. He begins fairly conventionally in the lyrics with analyses of his emotions and his conflicts, looking inward and concentrating on his own suffering. His symptoms are typical: love causes him to tremble and faint in the presence of his lady; it sends his spirits scattering and makes him weep; it creates conflicts between his heart and soul. Sometimes the conventions of his tradition fail him: the poems he writes to another lady as a decoy to hide his love for Beatrice (in order to maintain the required secrecy), give rise to gossip which makes Beatrice withdraw her greeting from him. After Beatrice's death, even the poetic forms no longer serve: Dante begins poems which he cannot finish, or is dissatisfied with what he has done (see *VN*: XXVII, XXXIII, XXXIV, incomplete canzoni, false starts). He gives up writing about Beatrice at the end of the *Vita Nuova,* until he can find a new way to speak of her, a new mode, which the *Comedy* will provide.

Meanwhile, not yet understanding what love is, he looks to other women for the satisfaction he cannot have from Beatrice and yet must ultimately find only through her. The turning to other women not for comfort but for love is another convention of the lyric tradition which, as we have seen, reveals a conflict within the poet. Sometimes Dante dismisses the second woman: in **"Per quella via che la bellezza corre"** (*Dante's Lyric Poetry,* translated and edited by Foster and Boyde), a girl following the road by which beauty enters the mind to awaken love is stopped by a voice from the tower (Dante's mind); the voice tells her to go away, for another lady reigns there. Sometimes he tries to justify the existence of both women: in **"Due donne in cima de la mente mia,"** when two women argue about love in his mind, asking how one heart can be divided between two ladies with perfect love, he answers that one is beauty, whom he loves for the sake of delight, and the other is virtue, whom he loves for action. He pretends that he made another woman the subject of his poems as a shield to keep his love for Beatrice secret (*VN*, V). The most important of the other women, judging from the lengths Dante goes to to explain her away, is the *donna gentile,* the lady who offers sympathy after the death of Beatrice. Her compassion unleashes his tears, enabling him to wallow in his grief and return to the self-centered state of his early love. His attachment to her gives rise to a conflict between those elements which find an outlet in her company, his heart and desire, and those which are loyal to Beatrice, his soul and reason. (*Core* and *appetito* are masculine, *anima* and *ragione* are feminine, so it is the feminine side of Dante that remains true to the right love.) Although his soul and reason prevail, Dante is apparently not satisfied with the victory, for he feels obliged in the *Convivio* to deny the existence of the *donna gentile* altogether by turning her into an abstraction.

Dante's love for the *donna gentile* becomes a figure for his pursuit of wisdom, the studies he turned to after Beatrice died. The pursuit of wisdom is also a form of love: a "philosopher," Dante points out, is not a wise man but a lover of wisdom (*Conv.,* III, xi, 5), so philosophy is an amorous use of wisdom. Dante explains that he imagined Philosophy as a lady because he could not write of her otherwise in the vulgate (though he finds a way to do so in the long commentaries of the *Convivio*) and because his audience would not have believed in a love for philosophy as readily as in the

love for a woman. It is still difficult to believe in such a love when one reads the poems, which are so full of conventional love-lyric elements. Boethius, who provided the model of Philosophy as a woman, does not write love poems to her. If Dante's canzoni to the *donna gentile* are poetic fictions, as he claims, then the literal meaning cannot be true and an allegorical explanation must be found for every part. This puts a dreadful burden on the poems. It is hard to believe that passages about the fierce and disdainful lady refer to the poet's failing vision, impaired by excessive study, or that the look of the lady's eyes and the smile of her mouth are the demonstrations and persuasions of philosophy. Dante feels obliged to deny the *donna gentile* in the *Convivio* because he is still thinking in terms of one-to-one symbolic relations: if he loves Beatrice, he cannot love another woman; if Beatrice is love, the *donna gentile* must be wisdom.

In a sense, Dante is making the same sort of error, only at a higher level, in the commentaries of the *Convivio* that he made when he was first attracted to the *donna gentile* in the *Vita Nuova.* Not being fully aware of Beatrice's significance, he looked only for a superficial satisfaction from her, hence he needed a substitute in a second woman when he lost the first. He rejects the second lady in the *Convivio* by denying her real existence and making her an abstraction, a figure of Philosophy, but he will give up the personification in the *Comedy* to return to a real woman, Beatrice, who is at the same time a personification. In a sense he admits the existence of the *donna gentile* in the *Comedy* when Beatrice accuses him of forgetting her after she died and giving himself to another (*Pg.* XXX, 126: *"questi si tolse a me e diessi altrui"*). In fact, Beatrice absorbs the figure of Philosophy, for she is Wisdom in the highest sense, when it is indistinguishable from Love. Her explanations prepare Dante's mind, but it is her look and her smile, not her demonstrations and persuasions—her love, not her learning—which give him the power to ascend through the heavens. Dante says in the *Convivio* that the same disposition that enables a man to love enables him to follow wisdom, that those men who live by their senses can neither fall in love nor have an apprehension of Philosophy (III, xiii, 4). That is, he does not deny human love, simply his love for another woman. In a way, his identification of the *donna gentile* with Philosophy is a step towards his identification of Beatrice with Christ in the fullest sense, as the Logos, as Theology and Faith. Dante's problem with her was only that he did not go beyond the beauty and compassion of the woman he saw to the divine beauty she reflected; he did not, when he wrote the *Convivio,* see that all women finally lead back to God, when one is ready to see God.

But even in the commentary Dante wrote on his early poems, the *Vita Nuova,* one can see the direction he is moving in. The poems themselves are not very different from other stilnovist lyrics, but the explanations of their origin prepare us for the identification of Beatrice with Christ in the *Comedy.* The most obvious example is the vision he has of her death, with the portents in nature, and the angels singing Hosanna as they accompany her in her ascension (XXIII). After that vision, he sees Beatrice once more, preceded by Giovanna Primavera, as Christ was preceded by John the Baptist (he connects Primavera with *prima verrà,* he who will come first, XXIV). There are other hints: in her name, the one who beatifies; in her number, nine, whose root is based on the trinity; in the colors in which she first appears, red and white; and in the fact that her death gives him new life. But he begins to see her real significance and to follow her to God only when he can no longer see her (that is why he says that to speak of her death would be to praise himself, because she died to save him, XXVIII). In Purgatory (XXX, 121 ff), she describes how she sustained him while she was alive, but after her death, when she could not reach him through visions, she had to descend to Hell to summon Virgil; the coming in person, even to Hell, to save the sinner who refused to heed the divine message is another echo of Christ.

As he begins to associate Beatrice with God, Dante also begins to see Love, Amore, in a new light. His first impulse is to reject the Ovidian figure he has spoken of so often in his lyrics. Love is not a corporal substance, Dante suddenly declares (*VN,* XXV), but an accident in substance, a figure of speech with some truth behind it. In his visions of Amore, Dante had suggested something more than the traditional God of Love; his words were spoken in Latin for greater dignity, often with overtones of the Christian God: *Ego dominus tuus* (III), *Ego tamquam centrum circuli* (XII). It is as if God had appeared to Dante in a form he would recognize and heed, that of Amore, just as He appeared in a form that would attract him, that of Beatrice. Dante begins to associate Amore with Beatrice after the vision of her death, when Love tells him that anyone with subtle perception would call Beatrice Love because of the great resemblance she bears to him. Dante had often seen Amore in Beatrice's eyes, but he still treats the two of them as separate forces. It is only in the *Comedy,* when Dante has come to understand that God is Love and Beatrice is a reflection of God, that he can return to the figure of Amore without embarrassment. Then he uses the very conventional images of Amore drawing arms from Beatrice's eyes in order to strike him (*Pg.* XXXI, 116-17) and making a net of her eyes to catch him (*Par.* XXVIII, 11-12). In the same way, he can acknowledge the signs of the "antica fiamma" without guilt, because they are all part of the same impulse (XXX, 48).

In the *Comedy,* Dante's major figures are complex symbols and real people at the same time. Beatrice is Wisdom and Theology and Christ, but she is also the Florentine woman Dante loved on earth and the lady of the lyric tradition, whose appearance in the Earthly Paradise affects him as it did in life—he can hardly speak; he weeps, hangs his head at her reproofs, and finally faints (*Pg.* XXX-XXXI). She gives him his name, his identity, like the heroine of a courtly romance. Her

name has been the inspiration to move him through his journey: when he is tired, it makes him climb (*Pg.,* VI, 46), when he is afraid, it draws him through the fire of lust (*Pg.,* XXVII, 36). Twelve lines of persuasion from Virgil do nothing, but the simple words *"Tra Beatrice e te è questo muro"* do all. Only his love for her gives him the will and courage to move. But she also forces him to see himself as he is, and to accept responsibility for what he has done. She inspired him to good on earth while she was alive, now she moves his mind to follow her to God. She raises him to the height of his powers and beyond (*transumanar, Par.* I, 70), to the vision of God and eternity that he remembers but cannot retain; it is she who "imparadises" his mind (*Par.* XXVIII, 3: *"quella che imparadisa la mia mente"*). In her eyes he sees first the dual nature, God-man, in the changing aspect of the gryphon (*Pg.,* XXXI), and later the point of light with the nine circles around it on which all the visible universe depends (*Par.* XXVIII, 11-12). She is the continual source of his power, for it is through her eyes that he receives the reflected light of God which draws him upward.

In the *Comedy,* Dante's major figures are complex symbols and real people at the same time. Beatrice is wisdom and Theology and Christ, but she is also the Florentine woman Dante loved on earth and the lady of the lyric tradition.

—Joan M. Ferrante

Beatrice draws Dante towards God because she is Love, but she enables him to see because she is also Wisdom, Theology, and Contemplation. It is she who summons Virgil to show Dante the full extent of sin and virtue, appearing to Virgil like the lady of a stilnovist poem, her eyes shining more than stars, her speech angelic, so lovely he begs her to command him (*Inf.* II). Allegorically, the vision of the lady he loved appears in Dante's mind (represented by the figure of Virgil), and rouses it to look truthfully at itself. Virgil, insofar as he represents human reason and learning in Dante, can bring him only so far; he can teach only what logic can deduce. As he moves upwards through Purgatory he refers more and more to Beatrice, who must explain what he cannot. His wisdom is limited; hers is not, because she sees with God's light, that is, she understands through grace. Dante makes the figure that stands for his mind, for his reason and its limitations, masculine (he chooses Virgil, specifically, because he is *the* poet, and carries the full aura of classical learning). However, the figure who brings the light of true understanding, who introduces divine grace into his mind is a woman. In Beatrice's first and last appearances in the *Comedy,* she is seated beside Rachel, who represents Contemplation, the highest function of the human mind. That is the gift Beatrice bestows on Dante, the capacity to contemplate God directly.

As a figure of Wisdom and Theology, as well as the reflection of God in human form, Beatrice has similarities with Christ, which Dante intimated in the *Vita Nuova*. He carries this connection into the *Comedy*, particularly in the Earthly Paradise, where Beatrice appears after the figures who represent the books of the Bible, seated on the cart which is the church, and which she defends against its enemies. Her appearance is heralded by three shouts: *"Benedictus qui venis"* (*Pg.* XXX, 19), a clear reference to Christ, even retaining the masculine form; *"Veni, sponsa de Libano"* (XXX, 11), a reference to the bride of the Canticles, the church through which mankind is wed to Christ; and *"Manibus, oh, date lilia plenis"* (XXX, 21), a reference to the young Marcellus, who should have been Roman emperor. Thus Beatrice is associated with Christ in three ways: as the saviour, as the representative of all mankind, and as his regent on earth, the emperor. She tells her nymphs what Christ told his disciples, *"Modicum et non videbitis me"* (XXXIII, 10-12), and to save Dante, as Christ saved man, she descended to Hell: *"soffristi per la mia salute / in inferno lasciar le tue vestige,"* Dante says in his final praise (*Par.* XXXI, 79-81: "you were willing, for my salvation, to leave your traces in Hell").

Beatrice is the most important woman in the poem, the most directly concerned with Dante's salvation, but she works with and for the Virgin Mary. It is Mary who sends Beatrice to rouse Dante's mind, just as God sent Christ. The poem begins and ends with the Virgin, the mediatrix between man and God, the woman in whom all compassionate women are contained, the ultimate *"donna gentile,"* as Beatrice calls her (*Inf.* II, 94). Through her, Dante will see the trinity and within it Christ's human features, because Mary gave Christ those features. In Mary, one sees the closest human resemblance to Christ (*Par.* XXXII, 85-86); when Dante looks at her, he feels he has seen nothing so like God (l. 93). Up to this point, Dante has seen Christ only symbolically: in Beatrice herself, through Beatrice in the gryphon, and in the figures of the eagle and the cross. Mary has been present as a force throughout Purgatory: she is the first example of the remedial virtue on each level; in the Anti-Purgatory, the souls sing *Ave Maria* (Pg. III) and *Salve Regina* (VII), and Mary sends the angels to guard them from the serpent that tempts and threatens them. She is both the model to follow in virtue and the source of mercy in sin. And her presence dominates the end of Paradise as well: she is first seen in XXIII as a rose, the principal flower in the garden of the church triumphant, where angels and saints sing *Regina coeli,* and where she and Christ alone appear in their bodies (XXV, 127-28); and in the Empyrean, Dante sees all the souls of the blessed (the bride of Christ) as one rose, her symbol (XXX).

Mary is the power which moves and completes the action. She alone can dispose Dante to see Christ (*Par.*

XXXII, 87). "He who wants grace and does not come to you would have his desire fly without wings," Bernard says in his prayer to her (*Par.* XXXIII, 13-15), echoing the words of his own sermon (In vigil. nativ.). She is the queen of heaven, who can dispose things as she wishes: *"Regina che puoi / ciò che tu vuoli"* (*Par.* XXXIII, 34-35), Bernard says, making explicit what Virgil had often alluded to in Hell in order to open the way for Dante (cf. *Inf.* III, 95-96, *"vulosi così colà dove si puote / ciò che si vuole"*; also *Inf.* V, 23-24). Christ is called the *"alto filio di Dio e di Maria"* (*Par.* XXIII, 136-37), as if the emperor and queen ruled together. Mary is, in other words, the counterpart of God the father, but the female side of God, the mercy that can break harsh justice (*Inf.* II, 94-96). Mary, who is God in His power and mercy, forms a female trinity with Beatrice (Christ and Wisdom) and Lucy (the Holy Spirit and Love). Lucy is Dante's patron, a martyr described in the *Legenda Aurea* as the temple of the Holy Spirit. Like the Holy Spirit, she is a messenger, carrying Mary's request to Beatrice that she save Dante, and carrying Dante to the gate of Purgatory. She appears in his dream as a bird, a symbol of the Holy Spirit. The Holy Spirit is Love, and Lucy, who moves Beatrice, is Love: Bernard says of Lucy that "she moved your lady" (*Par.* XXXII, 137: *"mosse la tua donna"*); Beatrice tells Virgil, "Love moved me" (*Inf.* II, 72; *"Amor mi mosse"*). As the patron saint of eyesight, she also brings the grace that helps Dante to see, to understand, and to endure the vision.

There is good precedent for the glorification of the Virgin in the mystical writings of Bernard and Bonaventure, both of whom figure importantly in Dante's Paradise, and there is some precedent for a trinity that includes female figures (in interpretations of pagan goddesses, see Appendix). But there is nothing to compare with Dante's concept of a trinity of female figures who effect his salvation, all historical women—the mother of Christ, the third-century martyr, and the thirteenth-century Florentine woman. What Dante says with this trinity is that man learns to know God through a woman, that his desire to become one with her can lead him to union with God, and that it is the female side of God's nature that allows man to be saved. Beatrice speaks of God in female terms, as *"l'ultima salute,"* the ultimate salvation, in which Dante may "inher" himself (*t'inlei*) (*Par.* XXII, 124-27); cf. *Par.* VII, 142-44, *"la somma beninanza."* (In *Par.* XXXIII, 100 ff, Dante describes God in the final vision as *"quella luce"* and calls him *"lei."*) This goes far beyond the inspiration to good deeds and virtue that a woman can be in courtly poetry; indeed it solves the problem of secular limitations that such poetry raises by making human love an essential step towards divine love and by making the woman he loves a reflection of God. And it suggests that in His mercy and love—traits associated with women in the Bible and in secular literature—God has a female side.

It is not surprising, then, that Dante can also see female qualities in man as good. In the three realms of the **Comedy,** he uses a confusion of sexes to make a moral point, but not in the restricted way we have seen in biblical exegesis. For Dante, it depends on the context. In Hell, to be female is bad; it indicates weakness and insufficient moral strength. In Purgatory, it is a desirable counterbalance to bad male traits; and in Paradise, it indicates simply that there is no essential distinction of sex in eternity—man can be spoken of as female, woman as male, all are saved. What Dante is concerned with is the essence of humanity which, like the essence of divinity, is both male and female.

The confusion of sex is part of the price souls pay for their sins in Hell, because they have succumbed to their lower impulses and surrendered to their weaknesses. When Dante first sees Ciacco, the glutton, he describes him as a shade, an *"ombra,"* which is a feminine noun, and therefore he refers to him with feminine pronouns (*Inf.* VI, ll. 38-43: *ella, una, lei*). Ciacco corrects Dante, using a masculine adjective to describe himself (*"disfatto,"* undone), but then he too speaks of himself in the feminine, "io anima trista non son sola" (l. 55: I, unhappy soul, am not alone). It is true that Dante is dealing with *anime* and *ombre,* which are necessarily feminine grammatically, but he uses the feminine pronouns to introduce only certain souls, leaving the reader uncertain for some time as to the sex of the person involved. That Dante intends this confusion to redound to the soul's shame seems likely from the care he takes to identify as men the people he particularly admires before any doubt can be raised. He speaks of Brunetto Latini as male (XV, 23) before he knows who he is, though he has just been talking of *anime* (there is, of course, an irony in this reference, since Brunetto denied his sex in his sexual tastes). He has Farinata speak before the pilgrim even sees him, using a masculine adjective (X, 27). In this case, Dante makes an interesting contrast between Farinata's awesome dignity and Cavalcanti's plaintive distress for his son, which is modeled on the lamentations of a woman, as Auerbach points out. Dante speaks of Cavalcanti as *"un ombra . . . in ginocchie levata"* (53-54: a shade, risen on her knees).

When confusion of sex occurs in Purgatory, it serves a different purpose from the shame it carries in Hell. It is not a disgrace to be identified as or with women. Manfredi identifies himself by the good women in his family, his grandmother; Costanza, and his daughter. He is described with feminine pronouns and adjectives (III, 79 ff: *lei, ella, pudica, onesta*) as he approaches Dante at the head of a group of souls that move like sheep. The analogy with sheep, like the feminine references, emphasizes the humility and gentleness that contrast so sharply with the furious warrior he was in life (*"Orribil furon li peccati miei,"* l. 121: Horrible were my sins). His female side is good, and it is necessary to offset the violence of his life. Similarly, Sordello, who appears like Farinata, proud and disdainful, is described as an *"anima . . . sola soletta . . . altera e disdegnosa"* (VI, 58 ff). He is referred to in the feminine for eleven lines and Dante makes no effort to counter the effect. Guido Guinizelli is first referred to as *"colei"*

(*Pg.* XXVI, 74), and later compared to a mother whose sons discover her burning (93 ff), but Dante finally calls him "father." Dante himself, like Manfredi, is identified with women in Purgatory; he is one who goes by the grace of a lady (XXVI, 59-60) and the one who wrote *Donne ch'avete intelletto d'amore* (XXIV, 51).

In Paradise the confusion of sex contributes to the sense of mankind as one, of the union or fusion of male and female. Piccarda, a woman, is addressed by Dante as *"ben creato spirito,"* reversing the patterns of Hell and Purgatory; Cunizza is a *"beato spirito"* (*Par.* IX, 20). Boethius is described in female pronouns, like some of his companions in the sphere of the sun, though all of them were men; they are also compared to ladies in a dance (*Par.* X, 79). (Cf. John the Evangelist, *Par.* XXV, 103-4, who is likened to a "happy virgin" entering the dance.) In Paradise the sex of the soul depends on whether he or she is called *luce* (fem.) or *lume* (masc.), *anima* or *spirito,* apparently at random, indicating that sex matters little in this realm. Peter Damian, the contemplative (a state symbolically associated with women, e.g. Rachel, and Mary, the sister of Martha), is called *"vita beata"* and *"sacra lucerna,"* and addressed as female by Dante (XXI, 55-73). He even describes himself at first with feminine words (l. 67), and only towards the end of his speech makes it clear that he was a man (114-21). God, as we have noted, is *"l'ultima salute"* in whom Dante "inhers" himself. Dante says of himself in relation to Beatrice, *"quella reverenza che s'*indonna / *di tutto me"* (VII, 13-14). The word *indonna* means "takes control of, rules over" (from *dominare*), but the form, based on the word for "lady," is suggestive, particularly since Dante says later on, in XXVII (ll. 88-89), *"la mente innamorata, che* donnea / *con la mia donna sempre"* (*donneare* means "to behave like a lover"). They are odd verbs and Dante seems to suggest by his use of them that he feels himself becoming one with Beatrice.

The ambiguous use of pronouns is one of the most striking ways Dante shows the fusion of male and female elements. But he also adopts more traditional methods, as in the symbolic use of supernatural females, like harpies and sirens, and the identification of women with specific sins and virtues. The Harpies provide a rather interesting variation on the motif of the soul as woman, in that in them it is combined with the motif of the soul as bird.

The harpy-souls make their nests in the trees which are the bodies of the suicides (*Inf.* XIII), an unnatural joining of soul and body in those who unnaturally severed soul from body. The monster soul continually attacks the body it was supposed to save. The sirens are a conventional symbol of temptation, used as such by Dante in **Purgatory** XXXI, 45, but treated unconventionally in the *femina balba* and her echoes in the poem. The *femina balba* (*Pg.* XIX), who appears to Dante in a dream, ugly and deformed, represents the sins of self-indulgence, avarice, gluttony, and lust. As Dante stares at her, his look gives her life, speech, and finally beauty. That is, the man's will gives force to his desires—the siren can lead him astray only if he gives her power over him. Dante counters the attraction of the siren with Lia, who appears in the next dream and represents the real beauty of the active life. Her words and rhymes echo the siren's, as a subtle indication of the contrast. The siren sings *"Io son . . . io son dolce serena"* (XIX, 19), and uses *dismago, vago, appago,* as rhymes in her song (ll. 20-24); Lia sings *"io mi son Lia"* (XXVII, 101) and uses *smaga, vaga, appaga* (104-8). Beatrice, when she appears to Dante in the Earthly Paradise, not in a dream but in her real form, seems to echo the siren's repeated words in her *"Ben son, ben son, Beatrice,"* emphasizing that hers is the beauty he should have followed, always, not just while her body was before him on earth.

In the examples of specific sins and virtues, Dante is once again more conventional in Hell than in the other realms. There he associates women primarily with lust and deception (fraud), the sins traditionally connected with women in religious tradition. Lust is a sin that renders man effeminate, by encouraging him to indulge his desires at the cost of his duties. Dante shows this by presenting, in Canto V, a series of women who are also queens—Semiramide, Dido, Cleopatràs, Elena—all of whom abandoned their public responsibilities in order to satisfy their passions; the implication is that any man who gives himself to lust becomes a woman. When Francesca and Paolo appear, they too reverse the expected roles: he stands by, weeping, while she narrates the story of their affair to Dante. Within the story there is another reversal: she wants Dante to think that Paolo made love to her, so she changes the details of the literary work she claims as the inspiration for their love so that the man, Lancelot, becomes the aggressor. In fact, as Musa has pointed out, it was Guenevere who kissed him. Similarly, one must assume, Francesca was really the active force in her affair with Paolo.

The circle of fraud also has a female cast to it, particularly in the early sections, which have to do with satisfying the selfish and self-indulgent desires of others. The monster who represents fraud, Gerione, although it has the face of a just man, is spoken of only in female terms: as "a beast" (XVII, 1: *"la fier"*); "she who makes all the world stink" (XVII, 3: *"colei che tutto il mondo appuzza"*); "that filthy image of fraud" (7: *"quella sozza imagine di froda"*), etc., so that one must think of it as female. The first section of this circle is filled with pimps and seducers, men who exploit and abuse women for profit. But most of the women they betray had already betrayed others: Jason seduces and abandons Isifile, "the young girl who had first deceived all the others" (XVIII, 92-93), on an island where impious women had put all their men to death (89-90); he also betrays Medea who, although Dante does not mention it, had deceived her family in order to go off with her lover. In the same canto, but the next section, are the flatterers, a man and a woman. The woman is a literary figure, Taidè, portrayed as a

symbol of the horrors of flattery: she is described as a whore who scratches herself with her shitty nails, alternately squatting and standing, reminding us of the connection between prostitution and flattery in biblical exegesis.

The third section of fraud is simony, in which the bride of Christ, the church, is prostituted by the greed of popes (XIX, 2-4, 56-57, 108). In this case the woman is the victim and the sin is treated as a perversion of love which is the gift of the Holy Spirit. In the fourth section the false prophets are bisexual, the perverted use of their gifts making women of them: Tiresia changed all his members from male to female and then, by striking copulating serpents with his rod, returned to his manly feathers (XX, 45), a sarcastic reference to his beard and probably to other parts. Euripilo is said to have been an augur in Greece when Greece was void of males (1. 108), as if, by remaining there, he assumed a woman's role. The third classical prophet is Manto, herself a woman but seen here in a distorted female form, her hair covering her breasts on her twisted trunk (52-53).

With few exceptions, the rest of Hell is a male realm, whereas in Purgatory the female influence is felt strongly throughout, in itself an indication of Dante's unusual moral view. The light of Venus shines on the mountain of Purgatory in Canto I, and the power of love is felt thenceforth. Love is the basis of salvation in Purgatory, as distorted love is the basis on which the sins are divided (*Pg.* XVII). Love, for Dante, means woman, and thus women prevail here, furthering the salvation of men by example or by prayer. They are present in various ways: as the illustrations of the virtues and vices that enclose each level; as the relatives whose prayers are sought by the souls; as the three heavenly women who guide Dante's journey; or as the symbolic figures he meets in the Earthly Paradise, Matelda and the nymphs. Woman's love binds man not only through sexual ties but through family ties, and the family is also an important element in Purgatory. Men look to their wives or daughters for the prayers that will help pay the debt incurred by their sins. Family ties also connect the souls with earth and bind the three realms together: Manfredi, in Purgatory, has a father in Hell, Frederic II, and a grand-mother in heaven, as well as a loving daughter on earth; Forese, in Purgatory, has a brother who is destined to go to Hell (see *Pg.,* XXIV, 82 ff), a sister, Piccarda, who is in heaven, and a good wife on earth. (Note that in both cases the women are in heaven.) It is characteristic of the sense of balance in this *cantica* that there are such differences within families, that not all wives or daughters are good (Manfredi's daughter is good, Gherardo's is bad; Bonconte's wife has forgotten him, Forese's has shortened his time of penance with her prayers). Equality of sex is part of the balance, hence Dante has a woman helped by the prayers of a man, and men helped by the prayers of women. Contemporary women are as open to corruption as contemporary men, Forese points out, contrasting Florentine women of his day with his wife; but

Cacciaguida, in Paradise, will praise Florentine women of the past as simple and virtuous, like their men.

The examples of virtues and vices that are presented to the eye or ear in each section are drawn from still earlier times, classical antiquity, or the Bible. Here too, there is a balance of male and female both good and bad: Mary is given as an example of every virtue, and she is usually paired with men, seldom with other women; the vices are shown in numerous examples, male and female, with men predominating. But it is Mary's presence as an example of every virtue that creates the strongest impression of a female inspiration to good, which is born out in the Earthly Paradise by the seven nymphs who are the seven virtues. (They are not the same seven as the antidotes to the vices; the nymphs are the theological and cardinal virtues.) They have been seen all through Purgatory as stars (four in the day and three at night) but in the Earthly Paradise, where man is restored to a state of innocence, they appear as women. "Noi siam qui ninfe, e nel ciel siamo stelle," they tell Dante (*Pg.* XXXI, 106), a striking use of the lyric image of the lady as a star. In either form, they exert an influence over man for his good.

One cannot speak of the Earthly Paradise without thinking of Adam and Eve, who lost it for themselves and for mankind. Dante thinks of Eve several times as he reaches the top of the mountain. (Her existence has never been entirely forgotten in Purgatory: in VIII, 99, she is mentioned in connection with the serpent; in XII, 10, the souls of the proud are called sons of Eve.) Dante attacks her boldness, as the only one who rebelled where all obeyed (XXIX, 24-27), and laments all that she, the ancient mother, lost (XXX, 52, and XXXII, 32). The heavenly procession seems more inclined to accuse Adam (XXXII, 37), whose name they utter as they approach the tree; this suggests that Dante is making an error in blaming Eve, when he too should be blaming Adam, that is, himself, for losing paradise through sin. In any case, before he can rise to heaven, he must not only be purged of his sins, but reunited with Eve, with the other part of himself, woman. He meets a woman in the Earthly Paradise who will wash away his sins in the river of Lethe. She is, among other things, a restored Eve, now the only inhabitant of the Earthly Paradise—or the only one from Dante's point of view. It may well be that, like Beatrice, Matelda would be different for every man or woman who reached this point. It is Beatrice who names Matelda, almost at the end of her role in the poem. Matelda, whose identity is left vague, intentionally I think, is a composite of various historical women and female ideals: both Lia and Rachele, figures of the active and contemplative lives, whose appearance in Dante's dream foreshadows his meetings with Matelda; the countess Matelda who served as mediatrix between pope and emperor, a key function for Dante; perhaps the mystic Mateldas who wrote of their visions of God; and Eve, the rightful inhabitant of the Earthly Paradise—all these and perhaps more. It is not by accident that her name is not revealed for five cantos, so that we are free to make of her what we will; and, if she is a restored Eve, the more women she embodies, the better. Dante's meeting with her prepares him for his union with Beatrice. He feels a desire to be with Matelda, expressed in terms of Hero's desire for Leander, strong enough to make him swim the Hellespont (XXVIII, 70 ff). This seems a more violent image than the scene in the Earthly Paradise calls for but it is meant to emphasize the power of Dante's emotion, which is sexual yet free of sin, as sex was meant to be in paradise. When he sees Beatrice, two cantos later, Dante feels the old flame but his love for her is now pure. He can rise to heaven with her.

It is particularly significant that Dante's journey to paradise is made in the company of a woman—mankind achieves perfection by the reunion, in a state of restored innocence, of man and woman. This union of male and female is essential to the order of Paradise, both as a symbol of and a step towards the union of man with God. Union is the basis of harmony in heaven. Although many of the souls Dante meets here were committed to the celibate life, Dante finds ways to affirm human love. His love for Beatrice, and hers for him, dominates the journey, which is climaxed by Bernard's love for the Virgin Mary. The circle of Venus (love) is inhabited by men and women notorious for their earthly loves, like Raab, the biblical prostitute, and Cunizza, whose affair with the poet Sordello was a scandal of her day. Dante does not choose the famous repentant prostitutes so often mentioned in religious teaching, Mary Magdalene or Mary of Egypt, but women known for the force of their devotion. *"Mi vinse il lume d'esta stella,"* Cunizza says (IX, 33). She who had several affairs is saved, while Francesca, who had only one, is damned, because Francesca was dominated by her selfish desires, Cunizza by a great capacity for love. I do not, of course, deny the importance of repentance in the salvation of Raab or Cunizza (Folco, who appears in the same sphere, certainly changed his way of life from courtly poet to bishop). I simply want to emphasize that Dante is more concerned here with the force of love than with repentance. It is interesting, in light of this, that Cunizza and Raab are in a higher sphere than Piccarda and Costanza, two women who wished to remain virgins and who became nuns but were forcibly taken out of the cloister by their families and forced to marry. Their desires never wavered, we are told, but the force of their wills was lacking. This is why Dante thinks he sees reflections when he sees them—they lack substance—and it is why he places those who loved with great force of will, even if they loved men, above the would-be nuns.

What is important in all this is not that love is central to Dante's idea of Paradise—that goes without saying—but that earthly human love is a major part of love, a part which he does not deny even in heaven. In the circle of Venus Dante creates several new words to express the mystical union of separate beings: *"s'inluia"* (IX, 73), *"m'intuassi," "t'inmii"* (81), in this case to describe the union of Dante with the soul of Cunizza. That is, the force of love in this circle focuses Dante's desire on union, which is the final end of his journey. Dante uses the image of union between man and woman, namely marriage, to describe the ardor of two monastic saints and founders of orders, Francis and Dominic: Thomas Aquinas narrates at length and in passionate language Francis' love for Poverty, their marriage, and the fervor of his followers for his bride (XI); and Bonaventure describes Dominic's love for his bride, Faith (XII).

> The integration of self, the completion of man through union with woman, which was a secular ideal in twelfth-century literature and a religious ideal for a few theologians, is achieved by Dante [in *Paradiso*].
>
> —*Joan M. Ferrante*

Behind these images lies the marriage of Christ and his church, a figure Dante uses mainly in his attacks on the abuses of the popes and the curia, their prostitution of God's bride. But in the Empyrean, he describes the rose as the bride of Christ. The rose is the figure of all mankind united in love; and in the rose we see the perfect balance of human elements, of Jews and Christians, adults and children, men and women, in overlapping halves. Children who died before the age of reason occupy the lower half, adults the upper; Christians are on one side, Jews on the other. Men and women alternate at all levels. For the most part, they seem to sit in vertical rows; all the souls seated beneath Mary are women, those seated beneath John the Baptist are men, but this does not hold true throughout, since Beatrice sits two seats below Peter. I have not found a clear pattern for the male-female arrangement, but judging from the number of individuals Dante points out in the rose, he does seem to intend an equal number of each sex, which would be consonant with the balance of the other parts. In any case, the vision Dante offers of mankind saved and glorified is a vision of the perfect integration of the human race with God and with itself. And Dante, a man, achieves that vision through the inspiration and active help of three women: Mary, through whom Christ brought salvation to all men; Lucy, the patron saint who cares for those devoted to her; and Beatrice, the lady Dante loved in life.

The integration of self, the completion of man through union with woman, which was a secular ideal in twelfth century literature and a religious ideal for a few theologians, is achieved here by Dante. For him, the integration is possible only in heaven, or in a vision, and only after the woman who inspires it is dead. Nonetheless, he achieves it not by rejecting the love of woman, as so much of thirteenth-century literature did, but by

affirming and transforming it. (And, perhaps most startling of all in the context of this study, he offers the same possibility of perfection to woman.) Bernard and Bonaventure say it is only through Mary that man can reach God. Dante says it is through Mary and through human love for a real woman that he can achieve union with God. Beatrice may stand for many things, as the pilgrim Dante and his reader come slowly to see, but his first perception of her was as a living being, a beautiful woman, and it is because he saw *her,* that he came to see God.

Teodolinda Barolina (essay date 1979)

SOURCE: "Bertran de Born and Sordello: The Poetry of Politics in Dante's *Comedy,*" in *PMLA,* Vol. 94, No. 3, May 1979, pp. 395-404.

[*In the following essay, Dante's treatment of poets in his writings is perceived to serve his political themes.*]

The stature Dante grants Sordello in the ***Comedy*** has long puzzled critics, since it seems greater than warranted by the achievements of this Provençal poet. Not only does the meeting with Sordello, in the sixth canto of the ***Purgatorio,*** serve as the catalyst for the stirring invective against Italy that concludes the canto, but Sordello is assigned the important task of guiding Vergil and Dante to the valley of the princes and identifying for the two travelers its various royal inhabitants. This seems a large role for a poet who was—and is—best known as the author of a satirical lament with political overtones, the lament for Blacatz. Indeed, although there is a definite consonance between the tone of that lament and the hortatory tone of the character in the ***Comedy,*** Sordello's poetic oeuvre does not by itself convincingly account for his function in Dante's poem. In the absence of other explanations, however, critics have traditionally agreed that we must turn to Sordello's *planh* for an understanding of his position in the ***Comedy.***

In this so-called lament Sordello violently satirizes the princes of Europe, whom he criticizes for their cowardice; in fact, the work is more a *sirventes* than a *planh,* more a diatribe against the living than a lament for the dead. The poem begins conventionally enough, bewailing the death of Blacatz and complaining, in the usual manner, that all virtue and bravery have died with him; it soon becomes apparent, however, that this death is more a pretext than a theme. Consequently, Blacatz is not mentioned after the first verse:

> *Planher vuelh en Blacatz en aquest leugier so,*
> *ab cor trist e marrit; et ai en be razo,*
> *qu'en luy ai mescabat senhor et amic bo,*
> *e quar tug l'ayp valent en sa mort perdut so;*
> *tant es mortals lo dans qu'ieu non ai sospeisso*
> *que jamais si revenha, s'en aital guiza no;*
> *qu'om li traga lo cor e que n manio l baro*
> *que vivon descorat, pueys auran de cor pro.*

Premiers manje del cor, per so que grans ops l'es
l'emperaire de Roma, s'elh vol los Milanes
per forsa conquistar . . .

I want to lament Sir Blacatz in this light melody, with
a sad and afflicted heart; and I have good reason, for
in him I have lost a lord and a good friend, and because
all that is virtuous is lost in his death. This damage is
so fatal that I have no hope that it can ever be remedied,
if not in this way: let his heart be taken out and the
barons eat of it who live without heart—then will they
have heart.

Let the first to eat of the heart, because he has great
need of it, be the Emperor of Rome, if he wants to
conquer the Milanese by force . . .

Using throughout the poem the motif of Blacatz' heart
as a necessary source of courage for the cowardly kings,
Sordello pillories a different prince in each stanza. By
the end he has indicted the emperor, Frederick II, as
well as Louis IX of France, Henry III of England,
Ferdinand III of Castile and León, James I of Aragon,
Thibaut I of Navarre, Raymond VII of Toulouse, and
Raymond Bérenger IV of Provence—all for being too
weak and spineless to fight for their rightful territories.

The Sordello of **Purgatorio** VII is also given to judging the behavior of rulers; here, too, he rebukes the
princes for negligence and for failing to govern properly, much as he had done in his lament while on earth.
There has been a shift, however, from the simple feudal attitude of the *planh,* in which the loss of land is
considered a stain on the personal honor of the prince,
to the lofty Dantesque concept of the sovereign's moral obligation to his subjects. Once this inevitable transposition has been taken into account, the correspondences between the historical Sordello and the Sordello of the **Comedy** are clear enough—and yet somehow
inadequate, for the discrepancy between the poet's stature as a person and his stature as a character remains.
Neither Sordello's poetry nor his Lombard origins (which
permit him to greet Vergil with the famous verse "O
Mantoano, io son Sordello / de la tua terra!" 'O Mantuan, I am Sordello of your land!') satisfactorily justify his prominence in the **Comedy**—justify it, that is, in
a more than mechanical way.

It is this gap between the real and the fictional that has
made Sordello the subject of so much critical debate,
to the point of being labeled "l'enigma dantesco" by a
scholar who believed that the character would remain
a problem until biographical material was discovered
to explain Dante's esteem for him. In this paper, however, I propose a reading for Sordello that requires no
external data. I submit that there is an internal coherence to the Sordello episode, that there are internal
reasons both for his role and for his stature. A comparison between Sordello and another of the **Comedy**'s
poets, Bertran de Born, will, I believe, shed some light
on Dante's underlying logic and intentions.

The analogy between Sordello and Bertran de Born is
by no means self-evident. Indeed, Thomas Bergin sets
up a quite different pattern, claiming that there is a trio
of Provençal poets in the **Comedy,** composed of Bertran in the **Inferno,** Arnaut Daniel in the **Purgatorio,**
and Folquet de Marselha in the **Paradiso.** "Of all
Dante's triads," he writes, "the Provençal poets are most
obviously and architectonically disposed, one for each
cantica, each one clearly and prominently placed, varying only, I would say, in their degree of integration
with their milieu." But Bergin is then left with the
problem of a fourth poet who wrote in the *langue
d'oc*—Sordello—and is forced to conclude that Dante
did not intend Sordello "to 'count' as a Provençal figure. . . . Dante sees in Sordello not the Provençal poet
but the Italian-born patriot and judge of princes." This
interpretation violates one sense of the episode, for
Sordello's tribute to Vergil at the beginning of **Purgatorio** vii is clearly the tribute of one poet to another.

Without denying the validity of Bergin's Provençal trio,
I would comment that, although Dante is a poet of
symmetries, his symmetries are not necessarily straightforward or clear-cut. In fact, Dante tends to establish
contradictory or, rather, counterbalancing symmetrical
structures, such as the odd asymmetrical canticle of
thirty-four cantos, which then creates a new symmetry
by bringing the total number of cantos to one hundred.
Similarly, the neat symmetrical relationship between
the **Comedy**'s three Provençal poets is marred by the
presence of a fourth, Sordello, and again the solution
may be overlapping symmetries: the trio pointed to by
Bergin and the duo that I am suggesting, which, significantly, includes as its pivotal figure precisely the poet
excluded by the first arrangement. My claim that Sordello should be juxtaposed with Bertran de Born, as
Cacciaguida is with Brunetto, or Cunizza with Francesca, is based on one simple but, I believe, telling observation: of all the lyric poets in the **Comedy** only Bertran and Sordello are not love poets. In other words, if
we look, not at the restricted group of Provençal poets,
but at the larger group of all lyric poets in the **Comedy**—
Bertran de Born, Sordello, Bonagiunta da Lucca, Guido
Guinizzelli, Arnaut Daniel, and Folquet de Marselha (in
order of appearance)—the first two stand out as poets
whose major poetic concerns are different from those
of the others; indeed, Bertran and Sordello are revealed
as the **Comedy**'s two "political" poets. Surely this identifying bond between them is sufficient basis for comparison.

Before examining these two poets as they are presented in the **Comedy,** I should like to say a word about
the poetry of Bertran de Born. He, too, was celebrated
for laments; the two traditionally attributed to him are
both for Prince Henry, also called the Young King
(because he was crowned during his father's lifetime,
since Henry II of England hoped thus to ensure the
succession), a prince with whom Bertran was presumably on intimate terms. These poems are the famous
"Si tuit li dol e lh plor e lh marrimen" and the less well
known "Mon chan fenisc ab dol et ab maltraire." It is

worth noting that, unlike Sordello's *planh* for Blacatz, these are true laments. They follow the *planh*'s customary format of both praising the dead man and mourning his loss. The first stanza of "Si tuit li dol" is representative of the poem and of the genre:

> *Si tuit li dol e lh plor e lh marrimen*
> *E las dolors e lh dan e lh chaitivier*
> *Qu'om anc auzis en est segle dolen*
> *Fossen ensems, sembleran tot leugier*
> *Contra la mort del jove rei engles,*
> *Don rema pretz e jovens doloros*
> *E l mons oscurs e teintz e tenebros,*
> *Sems de tot joi, ples de tristor e d'ira.*

If all the sorrow, tears, anguish, pain, loss, and misery which man has heard of in this sorrowful life were heaped together, they would all seem light compared to the death of the young English king; for him worth and youth grieve, and the world is dark, covered over, and in shade, lacking all joy, full of sadness and spite. (*Die Lieder Betrans von Born*)

The grief of the poet is echoed formally in the repetition of "marrimen" and "ira" at the end of the first and last lines of each stanza. The Young King ("jove rei engles") is also mentioned in each stanza, indeed always in the same place, at the end of the fifth line, thus constituting with "marrimen" and "ira" the obsessive poles about which the poem moves.

Bertran was also the author of numerous *sirventes* celebrating war, poems that take delight in describing the carnage of the battlefield in vivid detail:

> *Ie us dic que tan no m'a sabor*
> *Manjar ni beure ni dormir*
> *Com a, quan auch cridar: "A lor!"*
> *D'ambas las partz et auch ennir*
> *   Chavals vochs per l'ombratge,*
> *Et auch cridar: "Aidatz! Aidatz!"*
> *E vei chazer per los fossatz*
> *   Paucs e grans per l'erbatge,*
> *E vei los mortz que pels costatz*
> *An los tronzos ab los cendatz.*

I tell you that there is no such savor for me in eating or drinking or sleeping, as when I hear men shouting "At them!" from both sides, and hear the horses neighing in the shadows; and hear men cry "Help! Help!" and see small and great fall in the ditches, on the grass; and when I see the dead, who through their sides have the stumps of lances with silken pennants. (*Die Lieder Bertrans von Born*)

In these poems, Bertran constantly urges the barons on to battle, as does Sordello in his lament for Blacatz. Sordello, however, recommends war as an antidote for cowardly behavior, which he finds reprehensible in princes, and as a means of securing lost territory, whereas Bertran's reasons for warmongering are unabashedly mercenary and self-serving, and his only concern is loot. Therefore, even when Bertran and Sordello share similar social themes and a similar polemical bent, Bertran's verse completely lacks the didactic element that distinguishes the poetry of Sordello. Sordello, in his lament for Blacatz, as in his "Ensenhamens d'onor," wants to instruct us in correct chivalric and princely conduct (this is explicit in the title of the longer work, "The Teachings of Honor"). It is this aspect of Sordello's poetry and personality that must have initially appealed to Dante and provided him with the starting point for the character of the **Comedy**.

The canto in which the travelers first meet Sordello, the sixth of the **Purgatorio**, is known as one of the three "political" cantos of the **Comedy**, forming a triad with the sixth cantos of the **Inferno** and the **Paradiso** (in the **Inferno** Dante focuses on Florence, in the **Purgatorio** on Italy, and in the **Paradiso** on the empire). Although the political aspect of **Purgatorio** vi comes to the fore most clearly in the invective beginning "Ahi serva Italia, di dolore ostello" (l. 76), it is signaled from the line in which Dante apostrophizes a soul, as yet unidentified, by referring to the part of Italy from which it came: "o anima lombarda. . . . " (l. 61). This soul turns out to be Sordello, whose Lombard origins immediately draw him to Vergil. The invective against Italy derives from the ironic contrast between Sordello's loving response to Vergil as a fellow Mantuan ("e l'un l'altro abbracciava" 'and one embraced the other' [**Purg.** vi.75]) and the discord characteristic of Italy, where fellow citizens "gnaw" rather than embrace each other ("e l'un l'altro si rode / di quei ch'un muro e una fossa serra" 'and one gnaws at the other, of those who are enclosed by one wall and one moat' [**Purg.** vi.83-84]). The appellation "anima lombarda" brings to mind another episode—also political—where an Italian place-name is used as a form of address; I refer to **Inferno** x, where Farinata degli Uberti calls out to Dante, "O Tosco che vii. In his re-creation of the historical Bertran, Dante has as a starting point the amorality of Bertran's verse, as well as its sanguinary and bloodthirsty qualities, which Dante reproduces in the carnage of the ninth *bolgia*. But Dante's elaboration of Bertran does not rest primarily on his poetry. The key to the Dantesque character lies in the reports about Bertran that circulated in the Provençal *vidas*. The *vidas*, or biographies, exaggerate Bertran's already inflated notion of himself as Prince Henry's counselor; hence, we learn from them that Bertran was Henry's chief adviser, personally responsible for fanning the hostilities between the prince and his father. Moreover, and more important, the *vidas* specify that Bertran did this with his poetry:

> *Et era seigner, totas vez qan se volia, del rei Henric*
> *d'Englaterra e del fill de lui; mas totz temps volia*
> *qu'ill aguesson gerra ensems, lo paire e l fills e ill*
> *fraire, l'uns ab l'autre, e totz temps volc qe l reis de*
> *Franssa e l reis d'Englaterra agessen gerra ensems;*

e s'il avian patz ni treva, ades se penava e is percassava ab sos sirventes *de desfar la patz e de mostrar cum chascuns era desonratz en la patz* [emphasis mine].

And he was lord, whenever he wished, of King Henry of England and of his son. But he always wanted them to wage war against each other, the father and the son and the brother, the one against the other, and he always wanted the King of France and the King of England to wage war. And if they had peace or a truce, he would put himself to great pains and strive *with his sirventes* to undo the peace and to show how each one was dishonored by peace.

The sinners of the ninth *bolgia* are the sowers of discord; the wounds they display on their bodies correspond to the wounds that they inflicted on the social fabric during their lifetimes. Hence Bertran arrives carrying his head before him like a lantern; it is severed from his body to indicate that he severed the son from the father. His account of his sin conforms closely to the *vida* (there are even similar turns of phrase; compare "lo paire e l fills e ill fraire, l'uns ab l'autre" with "il padre e 'l figlio in sé"):

> *"E perché tu di me novella porti,*
> *sappi ch'i' son Bertram dal Bornio, quelli*
> *che diedi al re giovane i ma' conforti.*
> *Io feci il padre e 'l figlio in sé ribelli;*
> *Achitofèl non fé più d'Absalone*
> *e di Davìd coi malvagi punzelli,*
> *Perch'io parti' così giunte persone,*
> *partito porto il mio cerebro, lasso!,*
> *dal suo principio ch'è in questo troncone,*
> *Così s'osserva in me lo contrapasso."*

"And so that you may carry news of me, know that I am Bertran de Born, the one who gave the evil counsels to the young king. I made the father and the son into rebels against each other; Ahithophel did no more for Absalom and David with his wicked incitements. Because I disjoined persons thus united, I carry my brain, alas! disjoined from its root in this trunk. So in me the *contrapasso* is observed." (*Inf.* xxviii.133-42)

The theme of *Inferno* xxviii, the sowing of discord, is fundamentally political. Bertran's sin was distinctly political; although the social unit he affected was technically the family, the family in question was a royal one, so that his actions necessarily had social and political consequences. In fact, not only Bertran's but all the sins of *Inferno* xxviii can be classified as social and political. Mohammed and Alì (and Fra Dolcino, who is mentioned by Mohammed) brought schism into the church; Pier da Medicina was a troublemaker in the courts of Romagna; Gaius Scribonius Curio indirectly started the civil wars by inciting Caesar to cross the Rubicon; Mosca de' Lamberti authorized the killing of Buondelmonte, thus giving rise to the Florentine factions and internecine fighting of Dante's day.

These souls are not developed as characters in any way; they are permitted only depersonalized existences un-

der the label of "seminator di scandalo e di scisma" (l. 35). They have no significance for Dante other than as exempla of a particular sin. This is especially obvious in the depiction of Bertran de Born, as such treatment is unexpected; the *De Vulgari Eloquentia* and the *Convivio* attest to Dante's previous interest in (and respect for) Bertran both as poet and as personality. Yet here Bertran, too, is kept at a distance. He expounds the nature of his sin and its exact repercussions in Hell with mathematical clarity and precision; he presents one by one, as though filling out a dossier, his name, the sin for which he is in this *bolgia,* a biblical comparison (should the visitors need elucidation), and the correspondences between sin and punishment. It is no accident that he, of all the sinners in the *Inferno,* should be the one to enunciate the law of the *contrapasso.* The cold, clinical quality of his words is heightened by the pathetic interpolations "Oh me!" and "lasso!" (ll. 123, 140), so at variance with the tone of the rest of his speech. In a canto where all the figures are exemplary, Bertran de Born is served up as the last and supreme exemplum: his sin is the worst, his punishment the most gruesome.

All Dante's efforts in *Inferno* xxviii, in terms of the characters he presents and the way in which he presents them, are directed toward making a statement about schism, that is, toward making a political statement. This intention is reflected not only in the sins represented but in other, more subtle ways as well. The tone of the canto is set from the beginning by the fifteen-line comparison describing five battles that encompass the political history of southern Italy from Roman times to the takeover by Charles of Anjou in 1266 (ll. 7-21). The reference by name to Livy, historian of Rome, is noteworthy (it is the only time in the *Comedy* that he is mentioned), as is the bewildering array of proper names, which has the effect of battering the reader with historical and political data. Furthermore, it is certainly significant that *Inferno* xxviii contains clear reminiscences of other cantos in the *Inferno* where Dante airs his political beliefs, namely, *Inferno* vi, where he discusses Florence with Ciacco, and *Inferno* x, where he meets the great Ghibelline leader, Farinata.

In *Inferno* vi Dante questions Ciacco about the whereabouts of five well-known Florentines; one of these men, Mosca de' Lamberti, turns up in Canto xxviii among the sowers of discord. There the dialogue between Dante and Mosca is reminiscent of the dialogue between Dante and Farinata in Canto x; in both passages Dante retorts acrimoniously, saying something that causes the sinner even greater suffering. A last link between these cantos is the prophesying that occurs in all of them (politics being in some respects the art of successfully foretelling the future). In *Inferno* vi Ciacco hints at Dante's exile by predicting the overthrow of his party, the Bianchi; Farinata, in *Inferno* x, also alludes to Dante's exile, and then goes on to explain the nature of foresight in Hell. Therefore, it hardly seems coincidental that in *Inferno* xxviii "l'antiveder" 'foresight' (l. 78) is once more practiced, this time by Mohammed and Pier da Medicina. These correspondences are signposts marking the similar thematic concerns that underlie all three cantos.

As a canto that deals with a political theme—specifically, the "unmaking of peace," to borrow a phrase from the Provençal *vida*—*Inferno* xxviii stands in opposition to that canto of unity and peacemaking, *Purgatorio* vi. Stylistic points of comparison between the two cantos support this conclusion. In his reading of *Purgatorio* vi, Aurelio Roncaglia has drawn attention to the recurrence of expressions denoting separation; these expressions, like "nave sanza nocchiere" 'ship without helmsman,' "sella vota" 'empty saddle,' and "vedova Roma" 'widowed Rome,' are concentrated in the invective against Italy. Roncaglia's conclusion is that "La frequenza di questa sigla avulsiva rappresenta la tormentosa fissità d'uno stato sentimentale di lacerazione" 'the frequency of this rending motif represents the tormenting fixity of a sentimenta state of laceration' ["Il canto vi del *Purgatorio*," *Rassegna della letteratura italiana*, 60 (1956)]. *Inferno* xxviii also displays a motif of laceration tied to a discourse on politics; as is typical of Hell, however, the laceration is expressed, not through mere metaphors of bereavement, but through physical wounds. Hence we find, to mention only two of the *bolgia*'s inhabitants, Alì "fesso nel volto dal mento al ciuffetto" 'with his face cleft from his chin to his forelock' (l. 33) and Pier da Medicina "che forata avea la gola / e tronco 'l naso infin sotto le ciglia, / e non avea mai ch'una orecchia sola" 'who had his throat pierced and his nose cut off up to his eyebrows and who had only one ear' (ll. 64-68). Another similarity is the massive use of proper names in both cantos, which serves to stress the historical, specific, and ephemeral nature of politics. For example, in *Inferno* xxviii, between lines 14 and 18, the following names occur: Ruberto Guiscardo, Ceperan, Pugliese, Tagliacozzo, and Alardo; in *Purgatorio* vi, in only two lines, we find Montecchi, Cappelletti, Monaldi, and Filippeschi.

Inferno xxviii, then, stands in opposition to *Purgatorio* vi, and in much the same way as did *Inferno* x. In the episodes of Farinata and Sordello the theme "division versus unity" is treated under the rubric, so to speak, of "love of one's native land." In the episodes of Bertran and Sordello, the same theme is treated under the rubric "poets who in their poetry fostered either divisiveness or unity." The Provençal *vida* specifically declares that Bertran strove to stir up trouble between father and son "ab sos sirventes" 'with his *sirventes*'; there is perhaps an allusion to this in Dante's verse "quelli / che diedi al re giovane i ma' conforti" 'the one who gave the evil counsels to the young king,' where the nature of they "conforti" is not specified but certainly implied. Bertran is Sordello's poetic counterpart; this is confirmed and thrown into relief by their being the only two lyric poets in the *Comedy* who are not love poets. Bertran's political poetry fostered disunity and schism by encouraging the Young King to disobey his father. Sordello's political poetry, by criticizing the princes in a way that prefigures Dante's own critical stance in *Purgatorio* vi and vii, served the final goal of political unity. Their poetry thus becomes emblematic of everything that each comes to stand for in the *Comedy*: one for separating, disjoining, undoing, taking apart what ought to be united; the other for crossing over, bringing together, reuniting what has been torn asunder. The relationship between the two political poets is one more strand in the web of overlapping political themes that converge in the sixth and seventh cantos of the *Purgatorio* and that could be diagramed as follows:

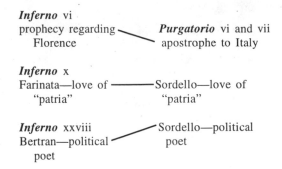

Inferno vi
prophecy regarding —— *Purgatorio* vi and vii
Florence   apostrophe to Italy

Inferno x
Farinata—love of ———— Sordello—love of
   "patria"   "patria"

Inferno xxviii   Sordello—political
Bertran—political   poet
   poet

In the *Comedy,* therefore, Dante uses Bertran and Sordello as exempla of the uses to which a poet can put his poetry in the service of the state. For Dante, a poet does not function in a vacuum; in fact, after the *stil novo* phase, in which he addressed himself to a small group of initiates, Dante kept on enlarging his audience until it included, in the *Comedy,* anyone capable of following him. One could almost say that the larger the audience, the greater the poet. Political poets by necessity address themselves to a larger audience than do love poets; hence theirs is a greater responsibility. As one would expect, the poet in Hell, Bertran, is the exemplum of the political poet who misused his position in life. By abetting disobedience and revolt, Bertran put his poetry to bad use, mishandling the responsibility that a poet has to his audience. Sordello, in Purgatory, is the counterexemplum: the political poet who behaved responsibly and put his poetry to good use.

We can now see why Sordello is treated far more sympathetically in the *Comedy* than his influence or position in life would lead us to expect. The historical Sordello has been absorbed by a Sordello whose function confers on him some signal honors and privileges not granted to any other lyric poet. For instance, only the epic poets are permitted to move in the *Comedy,* while the lyric poets remain fixed in their respective circles, terraces, or heavens. And yet Sordello moves. Although it is true that, since he cannot leave Ante-Purgatory, he cannot move "up" in the way that Vergil and Statius do, he is nonetheless the only lyric poet to move at all. (I do not refer to movement that is part of punishment or purgation, like Guinizzelli's motion through the flames.) Sordello's presence spans three cantos, from *Purgatorio* vi to viii (he is mentioned for the last time in *Purgatorio* ix.58: "Sordel rimase e l'altre genti forme" 'Sordello remained and the other noble souls'), thus holding the stage longer than any other lyric poet. He greets Vergil in a manner that foreshadows Statius' greeting of Vergil later on. Most important, he serves as a guide to the travelers, even saying "a guida mi t'accosto" 'I will take your side as guide' (*Purg.* vii.42), thus implicitly aligning himself with the other two poet-guides, Vergil and Statius. All in all, Sordello's pre-eminence among the lyric poets in the *Comedy* is quite out of keeping with his worldly fame; one could say that he enjoys quasi-epic status.

This status is underscored by the similarity between the valley of the princes and Limbo, the home of the classical poets; as Bergin points out, "The garden of the princes is the 'amoenus locus' corresponding to the Limbo of the *Inferno.*" Moreover, the word "onesto," etymologically related to the word "onore," which occurs eight times in various forms in *Inferno* iv and which is Limbo's verbal talisman, is twice used in connection with Sordello: "e nel mover de li occhi *onesta* e tarda" 'and in the movement of your eyes how dignified and slow' (*Purg.* vi.63); "Poscia che l'accoglienze *oneste* e liete" 'After the dignified and joyful greetings' (*Purg.* vii.1; my italics in both quotations). These efforts to link Sordello to the *Comedy*'s epic and classical poets also serve to separate and distinguish him from the *Comedy*'s lyric love poets.

By the time Dante came to write the *Comedy* he was incapable of an unalloyed aesthetic judgment; hence Sordello, owing to his role as a moral and political poet in the service of political unity, is given marks of distinction not accorded to other lyric poets, even though this group includes some whom we would consider poetically greater than he. For that matter, Bertran too is a greater poet than Sordello, objectively speaking, and we have seen how little this fact counts in the final judgment. Sordello's position depends entirely on the importance Dante attaches to political unity and peace as the basis, the sine qua non, of mankind's temporal well-being. Sordello's poetry does not have the educational value of epic poetry, nor does it speak to all humanity; Dante feels, however, that it comes closer to these ideals than does any other form of lyric poetry. Consequently, Dante deliberately links Sordello to the epic poets. He also takes care to make clear that, in this respect as well, Bertran is the exact opposite of Sordello. The description of Bertran in *Inferno* xxviii as one who carries his head like a lantern ("e 'l capo tronco tenea per le chiome, / pesol con mano a guisa di lanterna" 'and it was holding the truncated head by the hair, dangling in its hand like a lantern' [ll. 121-22]) and lights the way for himself by himself ("Di sé facea a sé stesso lucerna" 'Of itself it was making for itself a lamp' [l. 124]) cannot but call to mind Statius' tribute to Vergil in *Purgatorio* xxii: "Facesti come quei che va di notte, / che porta il lume dietro e sé non giova, / ma dopo sé fa le persone dotte" 'You did as one who goes by night, who carries the light behind him and helps not himself, but makes those who come after him wise' (ll. 67-69). Bertran is a gro-

tesque inversion of Vergil: in one there is total severance, a self-sufficiency that is not strength but meaninglessness, whereas in the other there is a sharing, a passing on, and an illumination of others even at the expense of oneself.

To end, I should like to return briefly to the world outside the *Comedy.* As we have seen, a comparison of the poetry of Bertran and Sordello reveals how different their attitudes are. It is interesting that Dante's treatment of these figures parallels the actual disparity; he sets them up for comparison in order to reveal them as polar opposites. In some ways, however, Dante reverses the real-life situation. Sordello, who wrote a biting and savage poem (which, had it been acted on, would have resulted in fighting in every corner of Europe), is reincarnated as an emblem of unity; whereas Bertran, whose poems in fact had little political impact, becomes an emblem of schism. The point is that both these decisions, although justifiable, are not without their arbitrary features. Dante was not interested in finding for each character in his poem a niche to correspond exactly to the merits of that person as a historical figure; he is interested in creating ideal categories that will illuminate the structure of reality as he sees it. Into these categories he fits his characters. Only in this way could his poem avoid being an inventory of dead souls and become what he wanted it to be and what it is—an insight into the nature of things so compelling that it directs the wills of the living and obliges them, through a recognition of reality, to be saved.

So it is for souls in general, and so it is for poets. If Dante has two political poets, they must perforce have more than gossip value; they must illustrate more than the fate that each found on dying. The ideal categories would naturally have to do with the use or misuse of their poetry, and Dante would look for figures whose biographies and poetic output worked well within these categories, even if not slavishly corresponding in all details. Accordingly, in his treatment of Bertran de Born and Sordello we have a clear example of Dante's deliberate revision of history for didactic purposes, to impart a moral lesson concerning the ways we use our gifts vis-à-vis society, and an instance of the truth of Irma Brandeis' precept that "Dante in his *Comedy* never *serves* history; he uses it . . ." [*The Ladder of Vision: A Study of Dante's "Comedy"*, 1960]. Dante's handling of the poets Bertran and Sordello thus permits us a fascinating glimpse into the workings of his own creative and poetic strategies; to put it another way, we can learn from these episodes not only something about the poetry of politics but a little about the politics of poetry as well.

Cecil Grayson (essay date 1980)

SOURCE: "Dante's Theory and Practice of Poetry," in *The World of Dante: Essays on Dante and His Time*, Clarendon Press, 1980, pp. 146-65.

[*In the following essay, Grayson contends that the Divina Commedia is a* summa *of poetic knowledge and technique.*]

When Dante, at the age of about forty, wrote his major work of poetic theory, entitled *De Vulgari Eloquentia*, he was in exile from Florence, where he had established over some twenty years a leading reputation as a poet. He had begun in early youth in the style of Guittone d'Arezzo, but he soon broke away, together with certain Florentine contemporaries and under the influence of the Bolognese Guinizelli, from the rhetorical mannerisms and dialectical contortions of Guittone, to concentrate his attention exclusively and in a particular way on the theme of love. Dante then created what he himself calls the *"dolce stil novo"* (sweet new style), of which he gives a much discussed definition in a conversation with the poet Buonagiunta da Lucca in **Purgatorio,** xxiv. 49-63:

> 'Ma dì s' i' veggio qui colui che fore
> trasse le nove rime, cominciando
> "Donne ch'avete intelletto d'amore".'
> E io a lui: 'I' mi son un che, quando
> Amor mi spira, noto, e a quel modo
> ch'e' ditta dentro vo significando'.
> 'O frate, issa vegg' io' diss' elli 'il nodo
> che 'l Notaro e Guittone e me ritenne
> di qua dal dolce stil novo ch'i' odo.
> Io veggio ben come le vostre penne
> di retro al dittator sen vanno strette,
> che de le nostre certo non avvenne;
> e qual più a gradire oltre si mette,
> non vede più da l'uno a l'altro stilo';
> e, quasi contentato, si tacette.

A full consideration of this passage is not possible here, but certain points may be underlined: first, that Dante distinguished himself, not from contemporaries, but from earlier generations of poets, Giacomo da Lentini (*il Notaro*), Guittone, and Buonagiunta; second, that this distinction lies in strict adherence to the inspiration of love; third, that his new style began with a particular *canzone* which figures in his **Vita Nuova.** Indeed the entire conversation takes us back specifically to this early work, and it is there we must look for a more precise interpretation of its meaning and especially of the apparently Romantic canon of inspiration expressed by Dante in his reply to Buonagiunta. The **Vita Nuova,** composed about 1292, consists of a prose account in forty-two chapters of the story of his love for Beatrice from the age of nine until some time after her death, set around a selection of his poems, thirty-one in all between *canzoni*, sonnets, and *ballate*. Besides being a kind of amorous autobiography the **Vita Nuova** is also a poetic autobiography, binding in strict relation the progress of his Muse with that of his love. In this sense it represents Dante's view of his own poetic evolution from the sonnet that brought him the friendship of Guido Cavalcanti, through lyrics still savouring of Provençal and Guittonian style and attitudes, and marked by preoccupation with the tragic

nature and vicissitudes of love, to a serene and simpler celebration of love that ennobles the mind and transcends even death itself. The turning-point in his outlook on love and poetry is described in chapter xviii, which is the prelude to the *canzone* **"Donne ch'avete intelletto d'amore"**. Suddenly, it would seem, love ceased to exist outside Dante in material manifestations like the salutation Beatrice had denied him, and became instead part of himself, no longer uncertain of its object but identified with a new poetry of praise. It is this assurance and this identity which determine the "sweet new style". Dante then tells us how he came to write his famous *canzone*:

> *Avvenne poi che passando per uno cammino lungo lo quale sen gia uno rivo chiaro molto, a me giunse tanta volontade di dire, che io cominciai a pensare lo modo ch'io tenesse; e pensai che parlare di lei non si convenia che io facesse, se io non parlasse a donne in seconda persona, e non ad ogni donna, ma solamente a coloro che sono gentili e che non sono pure femmine. Allora dico che la mia lingua parlò quasi come per se stessa mossa, e disse:* Donne ch'avete intelletto d'amore. *Queste parole io ripuosi ne la mente con grande letizia, pensando di prenderle per mio cominciamento; onde poi, ritornato a la sopradetta cittade, pensando alquanti die, cominciai una canzone con questo cominciamento . . .* (**VN** xix).

Dante's *canzone* celebrates Beatrice as a creature of divine origin, whose mission on earth is to purify and ennoble through love those who look upon her (and especially the poet himself), and whose return is desired by heaven. What in Guinizelli's *canzone* "Al cor gentil ripara sempre amore" had been an elaborate apology to God (he had mistaken his lady for a divine messenger), here is transformed into the central substance of a new love poetry. The process of its creation as described by Dante is not, however, such as to support any Romantic interpretation of the inspiration of love mentioned by Dante in his reply to Buonagiunta. The inspiration he writes of in **Vita Nuova** moves from a generic impulse to write something on this theme of praise, through reflection on how he shall do so, to the spontaneous formulation of an opening line of address; and only after several days and further thought does he compose the poem. The dictates of love referred to by Buonagiunta are emotional, but they are also intellectual, and as Dante then came to realize, they were the only ones justifiable for vernacular poetry. Chapter xxv of **Vita Nuova** makes this major point abundantly clear: it is historically wrong to write vernacular poetry except about love. In the sonnet of the preceding chapter Dante had represented Love as a being, speaking and smiling. He now digresses in order to explain this personification and to make his first important programmatic declaration of poetic theory:

> *A cotale cosa dichiarare, secondo che è buono a presente, prima è da intendere che anticamente non erano dicitori d'amore in lingua volgare, anzi erano dicitori d'amore certi poete in lingua latina . . . E non è molto numero d'anni passati, che apparìro prima*

questi poete volgari; ché dire per rima in volgare tanto è quanto dire per versi in latino, secondo alcuna proporzione. E segno che sia picciolo tempo, è che se volemo cercare in lingua d'oco e in quella di sì, noi non troviamo cose dette anzi lo presente tempo per cento e cinquanta anni. E la cagione per che alquanti grossi ebbero fama di sapere dire, è che quasi fuoro li primi che dissero in lingua di sì. E lo primo che cominciò a dire sì come poeta volgare, si mosse pero che volle fare intendere le sue parole a donna, a la quale era malagevole d'intendere li versi latini. E questo è contra coloro che rimano sopra altra matera che amorosa, con ciò sia cosa che cotale modo di parlare fosse dal principio trovato per dire d'amore. Onde, con ciò sia cosa che a li poete sia conceduta maggiore licenza di parlare che a li prosaici dittatori, e questi dicitori per rima non siano altro che poete volgari, degno e ragionevole è che a loro sia maggiore licenza largita di parlare che a li altri parlatori volgari: onde, se alcuna figura o colore rettorico è conceduto a li poete, conceduto è a li rimatori (VN xxv).

Dante goes on to exemplify the use of personification by Virgil, Lucan, Horace, and Ovid, who used this figure with proper justification, unlike some vernacular poets he knows. Apart from this polemical aside, it is notable that Dante here looks back over the tradition of Romance vernacular poetry and sees it as the continuator, if in a restricted field, of Latin verse. Indeed, he goes further and claims the identity of poetic activity whether it be in Latin or vernacular: the modern "dicitori" are specifically called "poete volgari." Love poetry in vernacular has for Dante a practical, historical origin, but its function and its means of expression are not different: it is on a par with, and may take its measure from ancient Latin poetry. These are the first seeds of a poetic theory of imitation of Latin poetry which Dante will elaborate later in his *De Vulgari Eloquentia.* Yet at this stage there are no very evident traces of such imitation in the *Vita Nuova* poems themselves beyond the parallel of personification already mentioned. It is therefore impossible to speak in any usual sense of "classicism" in this work, which in its poetry is firmly set in the Romance tradition, while owing something in its prose to Cicero, Boethius and medieval hagiography. We shall understand more clearly what kind of imitation Dante had in mind in his early writings when we come to examine his *Convivio* and *De Vulgari Eloquentia.*

The composition of *Vita Nuova,* however, marked the climax, not the beginning of the kind of poetry referred to as the 'dolce stil novo'. Very soon after it was completed, he left the narrow confines of its poetic theory and practice—several years in fact before the imagined conversation with Buonagiunta of 1300 in Purgatory, which looks back to a particular moment of his poetic career already past. To that same moment there refers also the encounter, again in Purgatory, with Guido Guinizelli, whom he reveres as

> . . . . *padre*
> *mio e de li altri miei miglior che mai*
> *rime d'amore usar dolci e leggiadre;*

the Guinizelli whose pregnant equation of love and the gentle heart Dante had resolved into his own poetry of praise in *Vita Nuova.* Yet Guinizelli modestly diverts Dante's eulogy of his fame to another figure in the same circle of Purgatory, that of the Provençal poet Arnaut Daniel, who stands for another, slightly later moment of Dante's poetic development quite different from the poems for Beatrice. Nor is this the only diversion from the "dolce stil novo" in the years after her death. The final chapter of *Vita Nuova* clearly promised some work in further, fuller praise of Beatrice after a "mirabile visione", something the like of which had never been said of any woman; and for this purpose Dante professed to be studying with all his might. The promise was not kept until fifteen or more years later and in a very different form in the *Comedy.* It is inconceivable that when recording that promise he could have had anything in mind resembling that later fulfilment, which was impossible without the intervening expansion of his own conception and experience of poetry. To this experience we now turn.

Whatever his intention in 1292, and whether or not this promise was the motive, Dante devoted himself for a period to philosophical studies, and wrote certain love poems which he later interpreted in his *Convivio* allegorically. If these were still outwardly love poems, however interpreted, and in a similar style to the *canzoni* of *Vita Nuova,* they were not for Beatrice. Nor were the so-called "rime petrose" (stone poems) of 1296, which in their linguistic and metrical brilliance imitated from Arnaut Daniel, and in their violent protests of unrequited love, are the reverse of the earlier "sweet new style". The limits of his poetic experience widen still further with the exchange, also in these years, of crude, realistic, slanging sonnets with his relative by marriage Forese Donati. This is for Dante a period not only of much technical experiment in verse but of evident violence and involvement in affairs, which soon lead him away from philosophy and into the arena of the growing political conflict within and outside Florence. In the years 1292 to about 1298 Beatrice seems to be eclipsed from his poetry: contemporary issues and problems of a philosophical, moral, and personal nature find expression in verse that is merely in part, and even then in appearance only, based on the poetic theory of *Vita Nuova.* Outside such theory, for instance, fall the so-called doctrinal *canzoni* (on topics such as nobility, courtesy, avarice), which are usually ascribed to the decade before Dante's exile.

It is not surprising that Dante's muse is virtually silent between 1298 and 1302, or that this silence should be broken with the great canzone **"Tre donne intorno al cor mi son venute"**, lamenting the decay of justice. As soon as the profound upheaval of his life permitted, we find him striving to repair the damages of his experience, and to draw together in a new theoretical formulation the scattered elements of his past, to sum up, as it were, and also to explain to himself as well as to others what he had tried to do, and where he stood poetically. Simultaneously or in rapid succession he began and subsequently left unfinished two important works, **Convivio** and *De vulgari eloquentia,* written between 1304 and 1307. **Convivio** is explicitly a work of self-justification and rehabilitation with Florence and with his critics. By a prose commentary in Italian on fourteen *canzoni* he intends to elucidate their true meaning and so spread a banquet of learning before a wide audience; for, although literally they appear to be love poems, they in effect express love of philosophy, whom Dante says he meant by the compassionate 'donna gentile' who comforted him for a short time after Beatrice's death in **Vita Nuova.** I do not propose to discuss the credibility of this identification. One thing is absolutely clear: **Convivio** is a justification of his having embraced philosophy to the detriment of Beatrice, and a defence of a very different conception of poetry from that practised and to some extent explained in Beatrice's book, **Vita Nuova.** Although, as we have seen, Dante there discussed the use of personification and referred to other rhetorical devices, he made no mention of allegory or of a possible different interpretation of the poems included in the work. There are some explanations in the prose of **Vita Nuova** of the structure and intention of the lyrics, but they are simple, often superfluous, and have nothing to do with allegory. The literal sense of **Vita Nuova** is by no means easy for the modern reader to grasp and appreciate, yet there is nothing in it to suggest that the work is intended to convey a different message. Hence the difficulty in accepting Dante's later statement about the role of the *"donna gentile".*

The theory behind the *canzoni* of **Convivio,** on the other hand, explicitly postulates a poetry which exists on at least two levels: the literal, whereby they appear superficially to be love poems (of *"passione"*), and the allegorical, whereby they are shown in fact to be poems about philosophy (of *"vertù"*) needing and being the occasion for displaying considerable knowledge. Poetry, says Dante, is *"una bella menzogna"* (a beautiful lie) which conceals *"una veritade ascosa"* (a hidden truth). He possibly got this formula from Horace, but he could have found it in a long traditional dispute from Augustine to Thomas about the truth or falsehood of poetry. Yet there are no explicit allusions in **Convivio** to that past controversy, which was soon to flare up again around Albertino Mussato, and to provoke the defence of poetry by Petrarch and Boccaccio. Dante's love poetry included in **Vita Nuova** had needed no other defence than the historical and rhetorical tradition he outlined in chapter XXV. Sufficient defence of this new poetry is that, like that of antiquity, its outward beauty is an attractive fiction that conveys to those who can understand an inner *"sentenza"* or truth. Its beauty is one thing, its goodness another. The only echo in **Convivio** of the ancient controversy lies in the reference, which he does not develop, to the difference between poets' and theologians' allegory; that is, that whereas poets start from a literal truth that is invented or imagined (and its opponents belittled this as a falsehood, and so of little account or even positively dangerous), theologians move from the scriptural text which

is historically true in itself. Even though Dante might appear to imply by his exposition of the four possible senses that the moral and analogical, applicable to the scriptures, also apply to his poetry, he does not pursue them in the remainder of his commentary; only the first two senses, the literal and allegorical, are explained, while the other two seem to be the inert remains of a traditional exegetical framework. At the time of writing **Convivio** Dante evidently saw no problems in using such a scheme. Yet these same four senses recur in a very similar form in the letter to Can Grande della Scala, commonly attributed to Dante, concerning the interpretation of the **Comedy,** which we shall consider later, since it is probable that there they were intended to have different weight and more far-reaching implications.

The allegorical conception of poetry in **Convivio,** however, needs qualification. Firstly, we do not know for certain that when Dante wrote these *canzoni* originally, he intended them to have such a double sense. Most scholars attribute them to the early 1290s, ten years before the **Convivio** commentary was written. Whether or not he did so conceive them, they become in this work like so many pegs on which to hang a demonstration of wide moral and philosophical knowledge in Italian prose, and it is this, far more than the poetry, which seems to occupy his attention. Indeed, in Book IV, the *canzone* **"Le dolci rime d'amor ch'io solia"** is in no sense an allegorical canzone, but a disquisition in verse on nobility, which is then amplified at considerable length in the last and longest book of the unfinished work. Whenever he wrote this *canzone* (my own view is that it belongs to his early exile and not before), it in no way fits the initial pattern of **Convivio,** which promised to open up the true sense of certain love poems and show them to be expressions of love of philosophy. This seems to indicate clearly that it is the moral, scientific and political content that urges him to write, together with the explicit conviction that this Italian prose will permit him to show far more clearly than in poetry the beauty and powers of the vernacular. In this context poetic considerations, and with them the allegorical virtues of poetry theorized about at the beginning of Book II, recede into the background, and the suspicion arises that these were in some way a mere excuse and a point of departure for quite unpoetic goals. **Vita Nuova** had been written at the climax of a particular poetic experience which he there summed up to pass almost at once to others quite different and even totally opposite; and yet prose and verse in **Vita Nuova** were intimately bound up together in a unity of style and content. By contrast **Convivio** looks like an afterthought, a deliberate superimposition on a poetic experience long past, of more urgent considerations which he had not yet found the means to express in poetry. There is something artificial and forced about this marriage of poetry and prose, and consequently about the entire concept of poetry as allegory which is its ostensible basis.

In the second place, something should be said of the nature of the allegory Dante expounds. The form and content of the poems are similar in general to those of his earlier love *canzoni* and sonnets: the beauty of the lady, her eyes, her effects on him, and so on, are described in the verse and then interpreted in the prose in terms of the virtues of philosophy and Dante's own experience and difficulties in pursuing its study. Yet a great part of the explanation is taken up, not with strictly allegorical interpretation of the poems, but with erudite commentary and digression about topics arising from this, as, for example, the long explanation of the heavens equated with the parts of the trivium and quadrivium arising from the mention of the heaven of Venus in the first line of the first *canzone*. All this adds still further to the impression of a late superstructure standing on a very narrow base not designed originally to carry it. The object of these observations is to clarify the nature and extent of Dante's allegorical conception of poetry at that time, and to show that it was relatively undeveloped and of limited importance except as a means to an end. We do not know why he abandoned the *Convivio* unfinished (before completing the fourth of the projected fourteen books), but the work seems to contain the seeds of its own disintegration, especially in Book IV. To leave the *"dolci rime"* for plain statement in verse was to recognize what is abundantly evident from the prose, that the bounds of amorous poetry, however allegorically interpreted, were impossibly narrow and indeed a failure for any other purpose than that for which he had originally used it. If he wanted to say more in poetry as opposed to prose, he would have to find another more capacious form, not in itself necessarily allegorical.

There is reason to suppose that *De Vulgari Eloquentia* was begun after *Convivio* and possibly abandoned not long after that work had also been left unfinished. It reflects Dante's confidence in his poetic achievement and in his ability to teach others how to select and handle the "vulgare illustre" of Italy. For this supreme instrument he believes only the supreme form of the *canzone* and the most excellent style are appropriate. By way of illustration Dante quotes himself as *the* poet of "vertù", that is of the *canzoni* of *Convivio*, and his friend Cino da Pistoia as *the* poet of love. This does not exclude the citation also of Dante's love poetry, nor does it imply any superiority of or necessity for allegory, which is at no point mentioned or discussed. His definition of poetry as "fictio rhetorica musicaque poita" might suggest that he is reformulating the idea of the "beautiful lie", but recent examination of the history of the term "fictio" has shown it might but did not inevitably mean for Dante a false or at least different device for concealing another truth. Besides, such a restricted interpretation of "fictio" simply would not fit the range of poetry quoted by him in *De Vulgari Eloquentia*. The term is therefore most probably used by Dante merely to indicate in the most general way the imaginative substance of the poet's creation to which he gives material expression through the medium of rhetoric and music, that is through established artistic elaboration of language and numerical, rhythmical disposition into verse. "Fictio" is simply what the poet

makes within him as opposed to what is created or exists outside him. Dante says little of the process involved, but it is clear that he had a high conception of the poetic activity, at least at the superior level of what he calls the "tragic style", and that he equated, as he had already done in *Vita Nuova,* the vernacular and classical poets. The definition of poetry already quoted applies to both. The difference between them is that the great poets have composed in a language and with an art controlled by rules, whilst the moderns have written and still write "casu magis quam arte", that is, as it were, by rule of thumb. The whole object of *De Vulgari Eloquentia* is to remedy this situation; and Dante's fundamental originality lies in recognizing the possibility of a regularized vernacular literary language and an organized art of vernacular expression for all purposes.

Dante goes on to declare that the closer we imitate the classical writers, the more correctly will we write vernacular poetry, not only by studying their theoretical works such as the *Ars Poetica* of Horace (frequently referred to in *De Vulgari Eloquentia*), but by learning from their example the most noble constructions and expressions. Yet Dante was not intending the kind of imitation later preached and practised by humanists. When he meets Virgil at the beginning of *Inferno,* he greets him with the words:

> *Tu se' lo mio maestro e 'l mio autore,*
> *tu se' solo colui da cu' io tolsi*
> *lo bello stilo che m'ha fatto onore.*

This 'bello stilo' cannot be other than that of his *canzoni* of *Convivio*. We have the clear confirmation in *De Vulgari Eloquentia* in the passage where Dante classifies tragedy as the highest style, comedy as the lower, elegy as the most humble. These were not for him specific genres; still less, in the case of the first two, dramatic forms. They were distinct qualities of subject and appropriate expression. So he writes: "Si tragice canende videntur, tunc assumendum est vulgare illustre, et per consequens cantionem oportet ligare. Si vero comice, tunc quandoque mediocre, quandoque humile vulgare sumatur; et huius discretionem in quarto huius reservamus ostendere. Si autem elegiace, solum humile oportet nos sumere" (II. iv. 6). Dante never got as far as Book IV. Yet when we further recall that he makes Virgil refer in *Inferno* XX, 113, to "l'alta mia tragedìa", meaning his *Aeneid,* we begin to see more clearly how Dante can have claimed to imitate Virgil's style in his own *canzoni,* and to appreciate how and why Dante came to call his own great poem a comedy. He inherited from medieval rhetorical tradition the distinction of the three styles, high, medium, and low, and their identification with tragedy, comedy, and elegy. These long-established associations are highly significant for understanding Dante's view of classical poetry and of its relation as a model to vernacular poets. In *De Vulgari Eloquentia* we learn this specifically only with regard to the tragic style, which we use "quando cum gravitate sententie tam superbia carminum quam constructionis elatio et excellentia vocab-ulorum concordat" (II. iv. 7). The remainder of the unfinished Book II deals in detail with these attributes of vernacular poetry. Little is said of inspiration, much of the need for hard work, sound doctrine and what he calls "discretio", good taste and discernment. No room for Romantic spontaneity here either. The poet drinks from Helicon: from then on "hoc opus et labor est", it needs vigorous intelligence and long apprenticeship to art and learning. But poets who have all these quali-ties, he writes, "hii sunt quos poeta Eneidorum sexto dei dilectos et ab ardente virtute sublimatos ad ethera deorumque filios vocat, quanquam figurate loquatur" (II. iv. 10). Echoing Virgil Dante is conscious of being one of these select few, of resembling the ancient po-ets, not because there is close material similarity be-tween his *canzoni* and their epics, but in the pursuit of a high artistic ideal of poetic expression, a perfect marriage between grave content and noble form, as in the "bello stilo" of his lyric and doctrinal verse that had brought him fame.

> **Dante . . . [declares] that the closer we imitate the classical writers, the more correctly we write vernacular poetry, not only by studying their theoretical works . . . , but by learning from their example the most noble constructions and expressions.**
>
> **—Cecil Grayson**

Like **Vita Nuova** and **Convivio**, *De Vulgari Eloquentia* looks back on and sums up poetic experience already past, this time extracting not a sentimental or philo-sophical lesson, but the essence of an aristocratic ideal of language and art, the technique of word selection, verse construction, and composition suited to the three noblest subjects: *Salus, Venus, Virtus* (Arms, Love, Virtue). Although in its basic principles this work may be said to be prophetic for Italian language and liter-ature, for Dante it had no future. As with **Vita Nuova** and **Convivio**, reflection and theory follow after prac-tice, they do not dictate it. We are here at the extreme end of a conventional traditional love poetry from Provence down to Dante, from which almost every-thing possible has been extracted. Only the intensely personal note of Petrarch, who is the true heir to the linguistic and artistic aristocracy of *De Vulgari Elo-quentia*, remains to complete the process. As with **Vita Nuova** and **Convivio**, so with *De Vulgari Eloquentia* fresh practice supervenes to absorb, transcend and even contradict the theory formulated or in the very process of formulation. We do not know exactly when Dante began the poem he calls his "commedìa" in contrast to Virgil's "tragedìa". It certainly follows, possibly inter-rupts *De Vulgari Eloquentia*, and it certainly precedes, in its beginning, 1313. But, whenever within the limits of 1307-13 he began, this vast narrative personal poem far exceeds the boundaries of Dante's previous prac-tice and poetics as we know them. Admittedly he never wrote the part of *De Vulgari Eloquentia* about come-dy, but it is highly improbable that so wide a mixture of styles and language could there have occurred to him. The general statement we have noted belies this. There the comic style would mingle the medium and the humble, whereas it can be maintained that in his major poem there is also the sublime, in those passag-es which we might describe in Dante's own terminolo-gy as 'tragic'. In effect the **Comedy** cuts vertically through the essentially horizontal stylistic-linguistic stratification of *De Vulgari Eloquentia*, and contravenes by its mixture in one composition of grave, grotesque, and sordid, the classical Horatian principle of deco-rum. It is true that we may find here and there in Dante's past, seeds of the vigour and realism, crudeness and sublimity that go into his poem: the particular experi-ences of the pre-exile decade, the exchange of sonnets with Forese, the "rime petrose", the doctrinal and alle-gorical *canzoni*, even perhaps the controversial sonnet sequence based on the *Roman de la rose*, known as the *Fiore* (though I am not wholly convinced by the argu-ments advanced for the attribution to Dante). In any event these are brief and isolated moments, stylistical-ly coherent and compact in themselves. They foreshad-ow neither the extent nor the amalgam of the **Comedy**, only perhaps some of its elements. From having at different times played on different strings of the poetic lyre, with preference for that of the "bello stilo", Dante now sounds them all at once, accommodating his style to the vastness and variety of his subject, exploring and wilfully expanding that vernacular which he had striven not long before to contract and refine as the most sublime poetic instrument of Italy. The classical ideals of *De Vulgari Eloquentia* seem to have been thrown to the winds. In their place is a new view and a new use of the ancient poets. In his 'tragic' *canzoni* Dante had imitated Virgil in a particular way, learning from him a general lesson of grave and harmonious balance in poetic expression. As Dante enters Hell, this 'bello stilo' is behind him; before him lies a journey like that of Aeneas, through a realm full of Virgilian reminiscences, though scarcely less rich in Ovidian echoes. This sort of classicism in the **Comedy**—bor-rowing, imitating freely, vying with the classical poets, using their mythology, invocations, similes, and com-parisons—is obviously quite different from the kind of imitation he had in mind in *De Vulgari Eloquentia* or had ever practised before in his own verse. If the result proves to us the power of Dante's genius to bring to-gether in one vast poetic synthesis the pagan and Chris-tian worlds, assimilating ancient art and learning to medieval philosophy and theology, while infinitely extending the capacities of a medium he had once believed inferior to Latin and appropriate only to po-etry of love, it created for subsequent generations se-rious problems of aesthetic appreciation which lie at the basis of a long tradition of fragmentation of the poetry of the *Comedy* from the fifteenth century down to Croce. The very variety and range of vision and style of the poem, which we regard as its strength, was for centuries an obstacle to its acceptance and recognition, being the very antithesis of what Dante himself and earlier striven for, and the opposite of the classical tendencies which dominated European literature down to the eighteenth century.

We do not know, and may never know precisely what profound experience inspired the *Comedy* and determined this fundamental change in direction of his poetic art from an aristocratic ideal to a democratic necessity to communicate to all men a personal vision of a universal significance. From the impersonal, esoteric, allegorical love poet in the tragic style he becomes the poet-prophet of the *Comedy,* intensely personal, omniscient, masterful, and confident that his is a creation to which both heaven and earth have lent their hand. He has the enthusiasm and spiritual vitality of the biblical prophets, sharing their reforming zeal and their pregnant, enigmatic, and figurative language. His medium is a powerful narrative, dense with realistic pictorial detail, for which medieval vision literature offers only pale precedents. Dante's journey through Hell, Purgatory, and Paradise is not a vision like many of those imaginary voyages of the Middle Ages. It is not a fiction constructed to convey something else; not a this for that; not a 'beautiful lie' concealing a "hidden truth"; not, like his allegorical *canzoni,* a poetic invention in one set of terms which hides a different meaning. In a sense it is a true fiction, an account of something which Dante would persuade us to believe actually happened to him, and it is in itself totally and literally true and meaningful. It is evident that we are faced here with a quite different concept of poetry from that of *Convivio.* There, when explaining the four senses, Dante had observed on the distinction between poets' and theologians' allegory; and he was right not to try to make them all apply to his *canzoni,* as they are properly applicable only to the Scriptures, whose literal sense, being the word of God, is true and not an invention like that of poets. The scriptures can bear such different senses because God alone has the power to confer eternal significance on the words and things of this world. Dante did not presume so much in *Convivio.* His poetics there follow a traditional concept of poetic invention sustained and justified by hidden truth, and within this tradition he is at pains to uphold the right of his amorous canzoni to the respect of the learned because of their underlying moral and scientific content. In the *Comedy* on the other hand, the need for that kind of justification disappears because poetry as fable, as a 'lie', has given place to the idea of poetry as the direct expression of the truth.

How then should we take the letter to Can Grande della Scala, which is accepted by the majority of scholars as an authentic work of Dante? In the letter the poem is said to have several senses, and specifically the four we have already encountered. The example cited by way of illustration is the same as in *Convivio,* the bib-

lical "Israel ex Aegypto", but there is no mention here of the distinction between theologians' and poets' allegory—a silence which might be taken to imply the author's belief in the truth of his poem on a par with the Scriptures. Yet the letter clarifies only two of the four senses, the literal and allegorical, which are said respectively to be: 'status animarum post mortem simpliciter sumptus' ("the state of souls after death, pure and simple"), and "homo prout merendo et demerendo per arbitrii libertatem iustitie premiandi et puniendi obnoxius est" ("man according as by his merits or demerits in the exercise of his free will, he is deserving of reward or punishment by justice"). These statements raise some difficulties. In the first place the definition of the subject of the poem seems far too simple, and the allegorical sense is hardly distinguishable from the literal. Furthermore a fundamental problem arises when we try to compare the poem with the biblical example cited, for it is difficult to parallel a historical event in this world which prefigures the next, with the description of a voyage in the next world itself. The *Comedy* already represents the other world, and would therefore seem to embrace all within its literal sense. In short it is not easy to discover another, other-worldly interpretation in something which of its nature already appears to contain the whole truth. For this reason, whatever past and present commentators and interpreters may say, it is a hopeless task to attempt to distinguish, throughout the whole poem, clear-cut different levels of meaning on the basis of the four senses. This is not to deny that there is allegory in the *Comedy,* but it is sporadic rather than fundamental and consistent. On occasions Dante calls our attention to the meaning hidden behind his verse (cf. *Purg.* viii. 20), and there are certainly episodes and descriptions with obvious allegorical significance (e.g. the procession in the Earthly Paradise). But the meaning and power of the poem lie in the open and direct nature of its vast and complex narrative, in the vigour and drama of the representation of men and things.

If we are left with a sense of dissatisfaction by the letter to Can Grande, must we conclude that it cannot be by Dante? I do not think so. Indeed the history of his poetic career, as I have tried to show, leads us to suppose that poetic creation would for Dante automatically be followed by critical reflection upon it. As we saw with *Vita Nuova, Convivio,* and *De Vulgari Eloquentia,* Dante paused at various stages in his career to look back on his production and formulate his poetics on preceding experience. There could be nothing more natural, therefore, in such a series than some attempt at self-commentary also for the *Comedy.* Nor should we necessarily be surprised at what may appear the inadequacy of such an attempt, if it is in fact represented by the letter to Can Grande, as Dante made use of the only critical-exegetical method available to him, the traditional "accessus ad auctores" and the scheme of the four senses. If this instrument turns out to be incapable of explaining the poem critically to our satisfaction, so much the worse for that traditional type of exegesis. We should also beware of falling into the trap of believing that Dante composed his poem starting from the poetics enunciated in the letter. Such a manner of proceding would be entirely contrary to the whole of his experience, throughout which the moment of critical reflection always comes after the poetry, and never precedes and dictates it. If we look at the letter in this light, it should acquire the purely relative importance it deserves, and cease to be the strait jacket some scholars have wished to make of it.

Any reader of the *Comedy* must be aware, and take due account, of Dante's often repeated conviction that he is fulfilling a divine mission, having been chosen like Aeneas and St. Paul to reveal to men a special vision of God's justice. In the letter to Can Grande the expression of the ineffable in *Paradiso* is compared with the language of Ezekiel and Daniel and with that of the mystics Richard of St. Victor and Bernard, and Plato is cited to illustrate the use of metaphorical language to express things perceived by the intellect which normal speech cannot formulate. In other words the author of the letter seems to claim for poetry, as Dante himself also does in his poem, the power to express, on a par with theology and philosophy, the eternal truths the intellect perceives. Such a concept of poetry and its role is very different from that which informs *Convivio*: put into effect in the *Comedy* it produces a poetry far more varied than the limited range and functions of his allegorical *canzoni*. Already in *Convivio* Dante glimpsed the possibility of poetry achieving, albeit indirectly, the expression of philosophical truth. In the *Comedy,* however, he faces directly and without intermediary fictions the expression in poetry of the deepest intellectual and spiritual experiences. Here beauty and goodness ("bellezza" and "bontà") are one in the splendour of the poetry of the literal sense.

Beneath this literal meaning readers will continue to find deeper layers of truth, for the *Comedy* has in common with few other great works of art the quality of an inexhaustible fount of wisdom and inspiration. It is in no sense my intention to undervalue this quality. My purpose has been rather to concentrate attention on the poetic innovation of the *Comedy* in relation to Dante's earlier theory and practice; to which I now return in conclusion. It has often been said that the poem draws together all Dante's knowledge and experience in a final autobiographical and at the same time universally valid statement, for which *Vita Nuova* and *Convivio* were the essential prelude and preparation; and that, in a wider context, the *Comedy* represents a kind of medieval *summa*—the last great encyclopedia of the Middle Ages. On the plane of his poetic evolution this ultimate achievement is neither a logical nor a predictable development; although, as he formulated in *De Vulgari Eloquentia* the ideal of a refined, aristocratic poetry within narrowly prescribed limits, he was already reaching out in the prose of *Convivio* to extend its bounds and spread its message to a wider audience. The eclectic solution of the style of the *Comedy* contradicts and at the same time absorbs that theory and practice. Allegorical love poetry and doc-

trinal *canzoni* are then abandoned for a wider, all-embracing concept of poetry capable of expressing directly within the same composition philosophy and theology, science, invective, prophecy, emotional and spiritual experience from the lowest depths of squalor to the vision of God Himself. To Renaissance critics Dante not only thereby transgressed stylistic and linguistic decorum, he tried incorrectly and unjustifiably to be more than a poet. Although classical prejudices of form have largely disappeared, and more modern times have accepted and appreciate the multiformity of language and style as the necessary clothing of the *Comedy,* the extension of the range of poetry into the realms of thought and science, the expression through poetry of aesthetically speaking non-lyrical subjects has seemed to many a major problem of Dante scholarship, involving fundamentally the poetic unity of the *Comedy.* We cannot, however, expect Dante to have anticipated Croce's aesthetic, nor his work to conform to ideas of poetry outside his own age and experience. Nonetheless, even in relation to his own age and experience, his *Comedy* is a remarkable departure. Dante called it his 'commedìa', but he would not have demurred, as we certainly do not, at the addition by a sixteenth-century editor of the epithet 'divina'; for before Dante had finished, he referred to the *Comedy* as his 'poema sacro', not merely because its subject concerned divine things, but because he felt himself a poet endowed with sacred inspiration. It was this powerful conviction and his all-embracing vision of heaven and earth, of man and eternity, that broke down all his earlier theories of poetry, and dictated in practice a kind of artistic freedom which no rules and prescriptions could then contain, nor have ever since succeeded in classifying.

John Freccero (essay date 1983)

SOURCE: "The Significance of Terza Rima," in *Dante, Petrarch, Boccaccio,* Medieval and Renaissance Texts and Studies, 1983, pp. 3-16.

[*In the following essay, Dante's* terza rima *is seen as a model for the "synthesis of time and meaning into history."*]

The perennial problem in literary interpretation is the problem of the relationship of form to content, or of poetics to thematics. In recent years, there can be little doubt that formalism has occupied our attention, both in linguistics and in criticism, with Russian formalism, American New Criticism and the formalism of the French Structuralists. The proper concern of poetics, according to Roman Jakobson, for example, is metalinguistic: not with the message itself, but rather with the message's awareness of itself as message. The most creative and interesting critical developments of the past few decades have been characterized by a concern for poetics, in Jakobson's sense, at least in the study of modern literature.

The single exception I can think of to this dominance of formal studies is in the field of medieval literature. Here the most significant contributions have involved taking content, particularly theology, very seriously. Perhaps Leo Spitzer was the precursor of this tendency, with his insistence on the importance of historical semantics for examining the coherence of the works he studied. In our own day, literary students, particularly in English, have found in the Bible and in the exegetical tradition a repository of semantic values and symbolic associations that seem essential for the coherence and meaning of medieval works. They have shown convincingly that it is impossible any longer to treat those works in the same way that we treat contemporary secular texts, written in our own cultural context.

In the field of Dante studies, it is the unique and permanent contribution of Charles Singleton to have brought poetics and thematics together in the interpretation of the poem. By refusing to accept the traditional dichotomy of poetry and belief, an older version of the opposition I have been describing, he demonstrated the relevance of theology not only to the literary archeologist, but also to the literary critic. His formal criticism represents a dramatic departure from the tradition of the *lectura dantis,* for it deals with the unity and coherence of the entire poem, rather than with single cantos or lyric passages. At the same time, that view of the whole necessarily involves accepting theology as part of that coherence. In this essay, I should like to extend his assertion of the relationship of theology to poetry in Dante's poem by offering one example where they are, quite literally, indistinguishable. I have deliberately chosen a title that brings together both meaning and form in a way that may sound simplistic but that I hope will prove nonetheless exact.

To say that poetry and theology are indistinguishable at a certain point in the poem is not to say that they should be indistinguishable in our analysis. As obvious as this remark sounds, there is still a great deal of critical confusion about the difference between what Dante believed and what we believe. Nowhere is this clearer than in discussions of Dante's allegory or "figural typology." Sometimes the word "allegory" is used to describe what *Dante* thought he was doing: writing a poem patterned on the Bible, for which a divine privilege was claimed in the Middle Ages. Because "allegory" is also a general literary term, however, others speak of it as though it were a formal characteristic of the poem, comparable to other examples of literary allegory. Erich Auerbach's otherwise masterly essay, "Figura," illustrates the confusion by first celebrating the mimetic power of Dante's representation, which is presumably a literary judgment, and then claiming to have found "the solid historical grounding" for this judgment in the theory of figural representation. It is as if the earlier critical perception required the medieval theory of *figura* in order to be validated or, conversely, as if the theological theory were somehow established by the power of Dante's poetry. The fact remains that any modern reader would accept Auer-

bach's literary judgment, but no modern reader could possibly accept the theory in which it is presumably grounded. This confusion, pervasive in Dante studies, can be resolved only by showing *how* a medieval conception of theological allegory can be reconciled to a formal pattern and so be made accessible to any reader, without theological presuppositions. In my effort to show how theological meaning and poetic form are, in at least one instance, inseparable, I shall also have something to say concerning the *form* of theological allegory.

To begin with an abstract form is to proceed in a manner that is the reverse of what one might expect of a cultural historian. The coherence of Dante's poem is often taken to be a reflection of the coherence of his faith, which we take as the primary cultural reality, but the formula might well be reversed, by suggesting that the apparent coherence of Dante's belief is at least in part a projection of the coherence of his poem. The reversal is not meant to be cynically de-constructive; there are good historical grounds for maintaining a certain reversibility of terms. In a culture which called its central principle "the Word," a certain homology between the order of things and the order of words is strongly implied. This is another way of stating what Kenneth Burke has referred to in another context as the "logological" principle. If theology is words about God, wherein linguistic analogies are used to describe a transcendent divinity, then "logology" is the reduction of theological principles back into the realm of words. What ensures the possibility of the reversal is the central tenet of Christianity, the doctrine of the Word, according to which language and reality are structured analogously. We need not privilege either pole: thematics (that is, theology) and poetics might conceivably be joined in such a way as to offend neither historical understanding nor contemporary skepticism, for in either case, we are discussing a coherence that is primarily linguistic. The traditional problem of poetry and belief would then be shifted onto a philosophical plane. Does the order of language reflect the order of reality or is "transcendent reality" simply a projection of language? What we had always taken to be a problem of Dante criticism turns out to be the central epistemological problem of all interpretation.

The formal aspect of the poem that I have chosen to discuss is Dante's rhyme scheme, *terza rima.* Its significance has rarely been questioned because it has seemed too obviously to represent the Trinity. While this may be true, it tells us very little. For one thing, virtually everything represents God in this poem; the abstraction is so remote as to be meaningless. For another, and perhaps more importantly, a verse scheme is necessarily temporal, or at least a spatial representation of time. It is not self-evident that a temporal scheme could serve to represent a timeless deity.

Dante derived his rhyme scheme especially for the ***Divine Comedy.*** It is very simply expressed: ABA, BCB, CDC, etc. Some critics believe it to have been adapted from previously existing verse forms, sirvente, sestina or sonnet, but most of their discussions are clearly attempts to deduce influence from metric analogies. In any case, the *terzina* is characterized by a basically triadic structure, like the sirvente, and by a forward *entrelacement,* like both the sirvente and the sestina. Unlike the sestina, however, the rules for closure are not inherent in the form: the *terzina* as a metric pattern could theoretically go on forever and must be arbitrarily ended.

It is this open-endedness that has moved some theorists to object that pure *terza rima* does not exist, since it would have to violate its own rules in order to begin or end. So it is with Dante's *terzina,* which has a dyadic beginning and end. In each canto, it begins and ends with what are sometimes called *rime rilevate*. The rhyme A in the scheme ABA, BCB, CDC . . . appears only twice, rather than three times, while at the end, the last rhyme, Z, also appears only twice: XYX, YZY, Z. A and Z (or Alpha and Omega, to hint at a more accurate theological analogy) are *rime rilevate,* arbitrary beginnings and endings for an otherwise autonomous and infinite forward movement, whose progress is also recapitulation. So *terza rima* may be characterized as a movement that begins and ends arbitrarily. This heterogeneity of the form would seem to be incompatible with the idea that it might represent the Trinity.

Not only was Dante's rhyme form unique, but his organization of tercets into *canti* was also a formal innovation, transforming the arbitrary element of versification into a higher formal exigency. Since his verses are hendecasyllables, each of his *terzine* consists of 33 syllables. So too, each of his *cantiche* consists of 33 *canti,* if we except the first canto as prologue to the rest. We have then a formal structure which suggests a certain homology between the versification and the formal divisions of the poem. The 33 syllables of a *terzina* are mirrored in the 33 *canti* of a *cantica* and the three *cantiche* thus represent a kind of cosmic tercet, an encyclopedic representation of the number three.

> **Not only was Dante's rhyme form unique, but his organization of tercets into *canti* was also a formal innovation, transforming the arbitrary element of versification into a higher formal exigency.**
>
> —*John Freccero*

We are familiar with this kind of numerology from Dante himself who, in the *Vita Nuova,* refers to the mystic power of the number three and its square, nine.

Here, however, I should like to stress not the static value of divisions by the number three, but rather the reconciliation of motion that *terza rima* implies: a forward motion, closed off with a recapitulation that gives to the motion its beginning and end. Any complete appearance of a rhyme, . . . BA BCB . . . , incorporates at the same time a recall to the past and a promise of the future that seem to meet in the *now* of the central rhyme.

The formal pattern of interlocking rhymes arbitrarily closed off in a way that is symmetrical with its beginning becomes more significant when we reflect for a moment on its thematic counterpart, the forward motion of the pilgrim toward a goal which is, at the same time, the narrative's logical point of departure. Readers have for centuries noted innumerable correspondences between the three *cantiche,* constituting retrospective recalls over the course of the poem, the most familiar of which, perhaps, is the recurrence of the word *stelle* at the end of each of them. So far as I know, however, Singleton's essay on the "Vistas in Retrospect" is the only full treatment of the subject at both the lexical and thematic levels. Singleton brilliantly illustrates the manner in which the theme proceeds by a gradual unfolding that is recaptured en route in a series of retrospectives that range from the minute (the retrospective gloss on the word *ruina,* for example) to the cosmic (as in the backward glance of the pilgrim from the Gemini in the starry heaven). The final recapitulation is at the same time the logical justification for the poem's beginning, the transformation of the pilgrim into the author, whose story we have just finished reading. When Singleton paradoxically suggests that the story must be read from the ending, as well as from the beginning, he confirms the analogy we have drawn between the movement of the verse and the movement of the theme.

Perhaps the most astonishing parallel between the theme and the formal pattern is established by the dramatic action of the poem, the pilgrim's path. The geometric representation of forward motion which is at the same time recapitulatory is the spiral. Whatever thematic importance we wish to attach to the spiral path in Dante's story (and I have said elswhere what I take that importance to be), it happens to be a geometric synthesis of the contradictory theses that are presented temporally by the verse pattern and thematically by the story line. From a purely geometric standpoint, the first two *cantiche* are replicas of each other, with the cavity of Hell inversely symmetrical with the Mount of Purgatory, while the representation of Paradise recapitulates both of those shapes with the celestial rose mirroring the Godhead and the surrounding angels "come clivo in acqua . . . si specchia" (**Par.** XXX.109-110). The geometric complexities of the spiral theme are spatial analogues of the temporal paradox of *terza rima,* forward motion which recapitulates the beginning in the end.

We have seen that both the verse pattern and the theme proceed by a forward motion which is at the same time recapitulatory. I should now like to suggest that this movement also can serve as the spatial representation of narrative logic, particularly autobiography. The paradoxical logic of all such narratives is that beginning and end must logically coincide, in order for the author and his *persona* to be the same. This exigency, analogous to what Kenneth Burke in another context refers to as "the Divine tautology," takes the form, "I am I, but I was not always so." The whole of temporal sequence in such a narrative, then, is generated by some form of negation introduced into the principle of identity and then refined away. Logically, autobiography is a sequential narrative that moves toward its own origin. If that statement seems paradoxical, it is no more so than the premise of all autobiography—that one can judge one's own life as though that life were concluded. The ending of such a story implies its beginning, for the *persona's* experience must be concluded before the author's voice (and hence the story) can come into existence. The paradox of continuity/discontinuity in the formal representation of *terza rima* is matched by the paradox of continuity/discontinuity involved in the logic of autobiographical narrative: I am I, but I was not always so.

Thus far, we have traced a pattern in three conceptual orders: the formal, the thematic, and the logical. *Terza rima,* Dante's theme, and the logic of autobiographical narrative all may be represented as forward motion that moves toward its own beginning, or as a form of advance and recovery, leading toward a final recapitulation. All that is required in order to move from the realm of poetics to the realm of theology in this context is to assert that the pattern we have been describing has a *necessary* rather than arbitrary justification. Thus far we have been dealing with a formal characteristic of the poem that is discernible to any reader; the theological leap requires only that we ascribe this pattern, not simply to the poem, but to metaphysical reality. Notice, however, that our description of the pattern in either case remains the same. Doubtless Dante believed that his verse pattern reflected some transcendent reality, while a contemporary skeptic might claim that the verse pattern is constitutive of that imagined reality. Since we are dealing with a linguistic coherence, however, we need not decide that issue.

Let us turn now to the "theologizing" of this formal pattern. I shall begin with the theological counterpart of the logical structure of autobiography, because it is so clear. The narrative structure we have been describing, like the verse pattern, privileges the *ending,* the moment of closure and makes it coincide with the beginning. This logical reversal is theologically the movement of *conversion,* of death and resurrection. The Christian theme of conversion satisfies the contrary exigencies of autobiography by introducing a radical discontinuity into the sequence of a life thanks to which one can tell one's life story as though it were true, definitive, and concluded. Death in life is closure in the story, but it is thanks to a spiritual resurrection that the story can be told. It was Augustine who set the pattern for this Christian thematization of narrative structure in his *Confessions,* although it might equally well be said that it was the Christian theme that gave rise to the narrative. The logic of definitive autobiography demands conversion, just as conversion, death, and resurrection imply the continuity/discontinuity of the autobiographic form. In this case, the formal pattern and the theology of conversion are identical.

The analogy between this Augustinian pattern and Dante's story is evident in the gap that separates pilgrim and poet. It is further reinforced by about twenty-three addresses to the reader, each of which suggests a progressive movement toward a goal that is the poem's beginning: the pilgrim's story leads to the establishment of the author's status as storyteller, so that the story of the **Divine Comedy** is in part the story of how the story came to be written. The addresses to the reader create a chronological illusion, leading us to understand the evolution of the pilgrim as preceding the telling of the story. In fact, however, the experience of the pilgrim and the telling of the story are one and the same: pilgrim and author are *dialectically* related by the action of the story, for the narrative voice is created by the action of the protagonist in the very act of interrupting it. It is only at the poem's ending that the retrospective illusion is completed, when pilgrim and poet become one. If we were to represent that dialectic in logical form, we would have to describe it as a movement forward in time that is simultaneously a recapitulation. That Dante thinks of this movement as a series of conversions can scarcely be doubted. The ending of the **Inferno** is marked by a literal conversion, a turning upside-down of the pilgrim and his guide, providing a continuity and discontinuity in spatial terms as well as in spiritual terms. The second part of the journey also ends in a *conversion,* with the theological motifs of sanctifying grace whose presence has been convincingly demonstrated by Singleton. Finally, in the transition between nature and supernature, the whole of the universe is turned to mirror the image of God surrounded by his angels.

The theology of conversion perfectly illustrates the tautological argument of autobiography: "I am I, but it was not always so." Here again, I must make reference to Singleton's work on the **Purgatorio,** where he explores the attempts in the Middle Ages to describe conversion, death, and resurrection, in Aristotelian terms, as a movement toward form. Logically, conversion implies a destruction of a previous form and the creation of a new form. Like the process of autobiography, conversion begins with *two* subjects: the sinner who *is* and the saint who *will be,* like the pilgrim who *is* and the author who will be. The evolution of the sinner is toward destruction, the evolution of the saint is toward regeneration. Logically, the movement is twofold, chronologically it is one, for the first step toward salvation is the first away from sin. Like the dialectics of the poem, wherein pilgrim and narrator are created at the same time, conversion is a *dialectic* of death and resurrection. We may observe in passing that this theological paradox is illustrated in the poem by the symmetry and asymmetry of Hell and Purgatory. The center of the universe is no space-occupying place in the coordinates of moral theology, but simply the logical zero-point of a moral dialectic that leads from mountain-top to mountain-top, from the Prologue scene to the ending of the **Purgatorio.** When the pilgrim says "Io non mori' e non rimasi vivo" (**Inf.** XXXIV.25), he indicates a purely logical point that marks the destruction of an anterior form and the beginning of the generation of a new form, sanctifying grace. From the standpoint of theology, the two processes take place together.

We have discussed the theology of autobiographic structure. It remains for us now to discuss the theology of the movement represented in the formal pattern of both the verse and the pilgrim's path. *Conversion* is the technical term used by theologians to describe the transformation of the Old Testament into the New. That transformation is precisely in the form we have been describing, forward motion toward recapitulation. This movement is the essence of the Christian theory of history referred to by the early Greek fathers of the Church as ἀνακεφαλαιώσις, or *recapitulation.* Irenaeus is the church father most often associated with the theory, which is defined by a modern theologian in words which might equally well describe *terza rima*:

> It means not just flowing backward to the beginning, but movement forward in time as the integration of the beginning in the end, and this is the significance of the movement forward itself, insofar as it is at once in time and above time.

The word itself, ἀνακεφαλαιώσις, comes from Ephesians 1:10, where Christ is described as "the fullness of time." We are told that the eternal plan of the Father was realized by the Son: "and this His good pleasure He purposed in Him, to be dispensed in the fullness of time: to *re-establish* [recapitulate] all things in Christ, both those in the heavens and those on earth." Thus, Christ *is* the recapitulation, the fulfillment of the promise and the return to the beginning, as is said in the Gospel of John: "In the beginning was the Word."

This theory of history is the foundation of Biblical Allegory, God's way of writing narrative, with things rather than signs. It is what Dante called the Allegory of Theologians. According to it, Christ, as the fullness of time, recapitulates all of the preceding history and gives to it its moment of closure. The New Testament must be understood as the fulfillment of the Old, which is to say, its ending. Thus history is the movement of time away from the Word and back to the Word, with all of the persons and events having their own autonomy, yet functioning prefiguratively as signs of their own truth: "di lor vero umbriferi prefazii" (**Par.** XXX.78). The moment of reversal was referred to as the *conversio* of the Old Testament into the New. Christian history or Biblical allegory (they are one and the same) move in the same way as *terza rima*.

Dante gives us only one clue as to the significance of his verse form. The forward movement of *terza rima* is interrupted in the **Paradiso,** where the name of Christ, *Cristo,* appears in rhyme only with itself. It must not be imagined that this is merely pietistic reticence—the name of God, the Holy Spirit and of Mary all appear in rhyme at some point or other in the text. Even if it were, however, we should have to ask why rhyme would be inappropriate for the name of Christ. The answer must be that rhyme *is* the movement of temporality and Christ transcends time. The *now* of the Christ event is underscored even in the tenses of verbs in the **Paradiso** with latinisms "ciò che . . . fatto avea prima, e poi era fatturo" (VI.82-83), said of the eagle, or again, Ripheus and Trajan, who lived in faith, "quel d'i passuri, e quel d'i passi piedi" (XX.105). The three-fold appearance of "Cristo" in the tercet points unmistakably to a recapitulation of past, present, and future in His transcendence. Finally, the name of Christ rhymes with itself twelve times in the **Paradiso,** as if to underscore the zodiacal all-inclusiveness of the fullness of time.

The appearance of the name of Christ three times in a tercet suggests a further elaboration of Biblical allegory which may be worth mentioning here. I have said that Old Testament time should be regarded as the unfolding of time toward its fullness, the New Testament, which is in a sense a recapitulation of all that went before. This structure is the basis of what is usually called figural typology or, to use the language of St. Paul, of the difference between the Letter and the Spirit. The Spirit is the end-term, the moment of closure, the New Testament that gives meaning to the Old. Yet this moment was transcendent—it is the New *and External* Testament, which means that it has three hypostases in time: past, present and future. From this consideration, born in the tradition, no doubt, when it became clear that the fullness of time was not in fact the end of the world, there arose a further elaboration of Christian allegory—the so-called four-fold theory, which should be understood as one plus three: the literal, fulfilled by the Christ-event in history (allegory in the past), the Christ-event in the individual soul (allegory in the present or tropological sense) and finally, the Second Coming (allegory in the future or anagogic sense). In the interstices between the first coming and the second, there is the founding of the Church and the work of the Redemption of individual souls, but history properly speaking is concluded with the first coming.

With reference to the time after the Crucifixion, the word *recapitulatio* has a history in the Latin West. As originally used in the Greek church, it suggested above all universal restoration, a theory that survives in Latin exegesis in the idea of Christ as the New Adam. In the West, with the Donatist Tychonius, it comes to have a more specialized meaning, as one of the seven rules for the interpretation of Scripture. A recapitulation is made when a Biblical writer speaks simultaneously of both the type and the anti-type, the promise and the fulfillment. It was in this form that the term was passed on to the Latin West, through the extensive paraphrase made of Tychonius' remarks by Augustine in the *De doctrina christiana*. Like the story of the **Divine Comedy,** Christian history is a forward motion toward an end-term which is the beginning: "In the beginning was the word . . . and the word was made flesh."

We have examined a formal pattern in Dante's work and have explored theological parallels, ancient and medieval thematizations of that pattern. I do not by any means wish to suggest that these theological motifs are "solid historical grounding" for Dante's poetics, as does Auerbach in his search for an historical valorization of his critical judgement. On the contrary, I should like to suggest quite the reverse: the theological principles that seem to underlie Dante's formal pattern are themselves in turn derived from literary principles. The Christian theory of recapitulation is derived from linguistic categories. If one wished to trace the origins of the use of the word ἀνακεφαλαιῶσις, it would surely be in the realm of rhetoric. Both the orator Lysias and Aristotle use the word to mean a verbal summary, or the summation of a statement: "rerum congregatio et repetitio," to use the definition of Quintilian. It would seem that the theory of history derives from the attempt to superimpose linguistic closure on the realm of temporality, transforming entropy, what Augustine would call fallen time, into formal discourse, the time redeemed. If it is possible to see in Dante's literary form a reflection of his theological beliefs, then it is equally possible to see in that theology the projection of literary forms.

Of all of the Fathers of the Church, Augustine, orator and Bishop, was most aware of the analogy between the realm of words and the Theology of the Word. His discussion of the rule of recapitulation in the *De doctrina christiana* moves from an understanding of the term as a literary device to its application to Biblical exegesis. There is no conflict in his mind between literary interpretation and salvation history; on the contrary, poetry was for him the emblem of intelligibility in the cosmos. Just as meter gave a pattern and a regularity to the otherwise open-ended flow of our words, so God's providential intent gave meaning to the flow of time. History itself might be said to be God's poem, saved from both the timeless eternity of the Platonists and the death of the fall by the Word, through whom the time was redeemed. In such a plan, human lives are the syllables, ordered to one another according to the meter of Providence, and death is no more than the syntactic silence necessary for meaning to emerge.

One passage from the *Confessions* might well serve as a recapitulation of all that I have said. It is so suggestive for understanding the homologies in Dante's poem that Dante might well have had it in mind. It occurs as an illustration of the nature of time:

> Suppose that I am going to recite a song (*canticum*) that I know. Before I begin, my faculty of expectation is engaged by the whole of it. But once I have begun, as much of the song as I have removed from the province of expectation and relegated to the past now engages my memory, and the scope of the action which I am performing is divided between the two faculties of memory and expectation, the one looking back to the part which I have already recited, the other looking forward to the part which I have still to recite. But my faculty of attention is present all the while, and through it passes what was the future in the process of becoming the past. As the process continues, the province of memory is extended in proportion as that of expectation is reduced, until the whole of my expectation is absorbed. This happens when I have finished my recitation and it has all passed into the province of memory.

This discussion of the nature of time conforms exactly to the movement of *terza rima.* If we think of the second of the triple rhyme as the *now* of recitation, it is equally divided between the memory of repetition and the anticipation of the third and last rhyme of the series. Augustine refers to the *canticum* as known by heart, which is another way of referring to its tautological character. The ending is the beginning, for recitation is the performance, or unfolding, of a text previously known in its entirety. As in the act of speech, we move from the intentionality of the speaker to the performance of the speech, syllable by syllable, until it is completely sounded in time. The silence that follows the speech exactly corresponds to the silence that preceded it. Time, in such a context, is impressed, like syntax, into the service of significance.

This, of course, is the central metaphor of Christian history. God's Word, pre-existing for all time, is recited by all of history until, in the fullness of time, it is made flesh. The human spirit, which repeats this action with its three faculties of memory, attention, and expectation (or, to use later Augustinian terminology, memory, intelligence, and will) reflects, in this respect, the Trinity of Father, Son, and Holy Spirit. It is in the *now* of the Word, the Logos, that the present moment becomes all-encompassing.

Augustine's passage on the nature of time goes on to express the series of homologies, of ever-increasing dimension, from the syllabic to the autobiographical to the eschatological:

> What is true of the whole song is also true of all its parts and of each syllable. It is true of any longer action in which I may be engaged and of which the recitation of the song may be only a small part. It is true of a man's whole life, of which all his actions are parts. It is true of the whole history of mankind, of which each man's life is a part.

Whether the grounding of Dante's poem is in the formal, syllabic structure of its cantos or in the *canticum* of the universe, its rhyme scheme remains the same. It begins and ends in duality, for there can be no memory in the first instant nor any further expectation at the last. Like the Hegelian dialectic, its modern analogue, *terza rima* represents a model for the synthesis of time and meaning into history.

Robert Pogue Harrison (essay date 1987)

SOURCE: "Comedy and Modernity: Dante's Hell," in *Modern Language Notes,* Vol. CII, No. 5, December, 1987, pp. 1043-58.

[*In his essay, Harrison demonstrates that Guido's monologue in* Inferno XXVII *expresses Dante's comic world-view, in which earthly life is viewed as Hell.*]

For years I have wondered what T. S. Eliot had in mind when he began "The Love Song of J. Alfred Prufrock" with two tercets from the speech of Guido da Montefeltro in *Inferno* XXVII. How much did he know, or how much did he intuit, about the unique status of that canto in the *Divine Comedy* and its appropriateness as a frame for the dramatic monologue? Even if the young poet actually intended his Prufrock poem to become the modernist manifesto that it now represents for us, did he know, and did he expect his reader to realize, that from the perspective of a rigorous theology of history, *Inferno* XXVII stands as Dante's broad critique of the modern era? Indeed, the only such critique in Dante's *Commedia*? The question asks about far more than mere authorial intent, but if we begin our inquiry with an affirmative answer—and that is only a beginning—then the least we can say is that the import of Eliot's epigraph has gone largely unexplored in the extensive scholarship that surrounds the poem:

> *"S'i' credesse che mia risposta fosse*
> *a persona che mai tornasse al mondo,*
> *questa fiamma staria sanza più scosse;*
>   *ma però che già mai di questo fondo*
> *non tornò vivo alcun, s'i' odo il vero,*
> *sanza tema d'infamia ti rispondo."*
>
> (ll. 61-66)

["If I thought my answer were to one who might return to the world, this flame would flicker no more; but since no one has ever returned alive from these depths, if what I hear is true, without fear of infamy I answer you."]

The epigraph, we are told, signals that Prufrock inhabits a private hell of sorts and that, as modern readers, we too inhabit his hell, his isolation from the world of the living, and that by hearing or overhearing the soliloquy we are complicitous with the voice that speaks in it. One must wonder, though, because even if its *raison d'etre* stops there, the epigraph accidentally evokes an extraordinary context for the poem's paradigmatic modernism, and literature is the one realm where accidentality invariably implies coincidentality, or where an intersection of texts means an algebra of

relations and ontodependencies that authorial intent rarely circumscribes.

In his *Glossary of Literary Terms,* M. H. Abrams states that modernist literature "subvert[s] . . . basic conventions . . . by breaking up the narrative continuity, departing from the standard ways of representing characters, and violating the traditional syntax and coherence of narrative language." In *Inferno* XXVII, the "modern" status of Guido da Montefeltro is portrayed precisely through his soliloquy's subversion of a "traditional syntax" in the sense described by Abrams, and not by accident; furthermore, Guido draws us into a psychic "stream of consciousness" that Dante apparently also took as the mark of a modern subject. While we have traditionally perceived the (superficial) ways Prufrock is linked by identity to Guido, we have yet to understand how and why Guido, in Dante's text, figures in every respect as a proto-Prufrock. In other words, if one had cause to wonder how much T. S. Eliot could have known or intuited about Dante's agenda in *Inferno* XXVII when he chose his epigraph from there, one may have even more reason to wonder how much Dante himself knew or intuited about the agenda that we call modernism when he gave voice to that contemporary of his.

The latter is the question that interests me here, for, posed in the right way, it asks about the very historicity of Dante's poem—both as an artifact reflecting its epoch as well as an ideological reflection on the nature of epochs. It is in the interdependence of these two dimensions that Dante's poem turns uncanny in the canto of Guido da Montefeltro. To be sure, the moment the poem ceases to be uncanny it ceases to be the poem Dante brought into being; it becomes something else—a "treasure" in our cultural patrimony, a heyday for philologists, a "divine" comedy, in any case a mummification. T. S. Eliot has said that Dante and Shakespeare share the modern world between them, but once again, while we have seen with easy retrospection what is modern "about" Dante, we have yet to uncover the implicit and proleptic vision of modernity—Prufrock's modernity—in Dante's own text. The prospect may strike us as absurd when we think of the epochal abyss separating Dante from the alienated world and consciousness of a Prufrock, and yet in *Inferno* XXVII we have a preview of a typically "modern" drama in its familiar versions. Here I will try to show that for Dante the drama, as it takes shape in Guido's monologue, is fundamentally "comic," in the broad historical sense conveyed by the title of his poem. Establishing the link between comedy and modernity will help disclose the peculiar hell of Dante's world view—not merely his *Inferno*—and its ominous extension into the modern era.

Dante meets the shade of Guido da Montefeltro in the eighth ring of the eighth circle of Hell. The sinners here are each enveloped in a flame—a "tongue" of fire through which he or she speaks and which probably symbolizes his or her abuse of the Pentecostal gift of truthful speech. Guido inhabits this moral zone along-side the epic hero Ulysses, with whom he is juxtaposed in such a way as to set up the terms for a historical, rhetorical, and moral comparison. The fact that Dante devoted an entire canto to both characters, whose sins are presumably identical, indicates the particular importance of the issues raised by this ambiguous area of hell. Dante's *Inferno* abounds with paired sinners (Paolo & Francesca, Farinata & Cavalcante, Ugolino & Ruggieri, et al.) but in no other case is a pair separated by a canto. The gap between one canto and another delineates an abyss, a historical crevice, that separates the modernity of Guido da Montefeltro from the antiquity of Ulysses, and our purpose is to chart its contours in order to discover yet another abyss that lies buried beneath it and separates the two cantos together from the critical project that engages us here. We begin with Ulysses' speech in *Inferno* XXVI. A preliminary remark, however, will be helpful. In the encounter with Ulysses it is Virgil who addresses the hero and bids him to speak; by contrast, the pilgrim will address his contemporary Guido in the next canto. Both sinners, upon request, embark upon monologues in which they recount the circumstances of their death. Ulysses' speech begins as follows:

> *"Quando*
> *mi diparti' da Circe, che sottrasse*
> *me più d'un anno là presso a Gaeta,*
> *prima che sà Enea la nomasse,*
> *né dolcezza di figlio, né la pieta*
> *del vecchio padre, né 'l debito amore*
> *lo qual dovea Penelopè far lieta,*
> *vincer potero dentro a me l'ardore*
> *ch'i' ebbi a divenir del mondo esperto*
> *e de li vizi umani e del valore;*
> *ma misi me per l'alto mare aperto*
> *sol con un legno e con quella compagna*
> *picciola da la qual non fui diserto.*
>
> (ll. 90-102)

["When I had departed from Circe, who held me more than a year near Gaeta, before Aeneas named it so, neither fondness for son, nor pity for my old father, nor the love I owed Penelope to make her happy, could conquer within me the burning urge I had to gain experience of the world, and of human vices and valor; but I set out upon the high sea with just one boat and those few companions by whom I had not been deserted."]

Ulysses and his men set sail westward and in their old age they reach the straits of Gibraltar, the edge of the known world where the "pillars of Hercules" signal to men to venture no further. With a rhetorical *tour de force* Ulysses persuades his men to continue the westward course into the unpeopled world:

> *"O frati," dissi, "che per cento miglia*
> *perigli sieta giunti a l'occidente,*
> *a questa tanto picciola vigilia*
> *d'i nostri sensi ch'è del rimanente*

> *non vogliate negar l'esperienza,*
> *di retro al sol, del mondo sanza gente*
> *Considerate la vostra semenza:*
> *fatti non foste a viver come bruti,*
> *ma per seguir virtute e canoscenza."*
>
> (ll. 112-120)

["O brothers," I said, "who have passed through a hundred thousand dangers to reach the West, do not deny to the short vigil that remains of our senses the experience of the unpeopled world behind the sun. Consider your natures: you were not made to live like brutes, but to follow virtue and knowledge."]

Enflamed by this "orazion picciola," the mariners set out on a southwest course into the southern hemisphere. After five months they approach a superhuman mountain (of Purgatory, we are to assume). "We rejoiced," says Ulysses to Virgil, "and our joy quickly turned to grief." A storm rises from the mountain and sinks the ship.

The Ulysses canto is one of the most glossed and over-glossed of Dante's *Commedia* and if I limit myself to certain essential remarks it is because I am interested primarily in its juxtaposition with the next canto. Ulysses' speech is in the high style, as befits a lofty epic subject matter. Its narrative contains a decisive beginning (the departure westward), a middle (the decision at Gibraltar to continue), and an end (the shipwreck). In orthodox Aristotelian fashion, a series of actions sustains the narrative coherence, actions that occur in purely external settings: Gaeta, the straits of Gibraltar, the open sea, the mountain and so forth. Ulysses neither interrupts the sequence of events nor troubles it with narrative qualifications in the first person; furthermore he displays, in his "orazion picciola," a mastery of the rules of classical rhetoric by artfully employing such conventions as the captatio benevolentiae, amplificatio, hyperbole, etc. In short, the formal resolution of the speech as a whole represents a rhetorical adequation to the moral magnitude of this epic hero.

This moral magnitude is embodied in Ulysses' courage to brave the unpeopled world in a spirit of self-reliance, undertaking a "mad flight" beyond all prescribed bounds. From one perspective the voyage appears as a quest for a utopia beyond the bounds of human temporality and its law of generation and decay. Neither pity for father (past), nor fondness for son (future), nor love for Penelope (present) could check the desire to follow the sun over the horizon—to transcend, in his old age, the linear finitude of human time and place himself on the sun's cyclical course of eternal rebirth. In this version of the hero's death—which Dante, it seems, invented—Ulysses shows none of his traditional nostalgia for the human community but only for the transcendent return, the diurnal *nostos,* of the rising sun.

From another perspective, Ulysses' desire for helioeternity appears as a nostalgia for the world outside of language, or better, *prior* to language. Just as he rejects the generational grammar of Ithaca, so too he prides himself on having been at Gaeta *before* Aeneas gave that place its name. Ulysses portrays himself as an ante- as well as anti-Aeneas, repudiating the "pieta del vecchio padre" that commits Aeneas to a destiny of filial obligation. Piety in this (Virgilian) sense means accepting the generational linearity that holds one in the finite span between father and son; it means, in short, upholding the sacred law of the *domus,* or household. It cannot hurt to recall, since Dante scholarship seems to have overlooked it here, that Aeneas' entire providential and divinely assisted journey has but one essential purpose: to transport the household gods of Troy to a new land (*Aeneid,* I, 100). What is crucial here is that the law of the household, of the Penates, would seem to hold sway over Aeneas' acts of name-giving. Compared to Ulysses' flight into the unnamed world, the successful voyage of Aeneas from Troy to Italy represents a topological domestication of the West through the act of naming wild and unpeopled places. Ulysses' desire for the world prior to its domestication in the name makes his reference to Gaeta ironic and even disdainful, for we know that Aeneas named that place after his own nursemaid—a figure of pure domesticity. The world of language and the language of the world become in this sense the piety of the domestic, a piety Ulysses rejects as he passes beyond the last sign into the nameless.

The tragic grandeur of Ulysses gives way in the next canto to the small contemporary stature of Guido da Montefeltro. Here too we will look first at the monologue's stylistic features and then at the moral portrait of the speaker. But first the context: Guido, an ex-Ghibelline general, has overheard the exchange with Ulysses and calls out to Virgil, asking him whether his native land of Romagna is still fraught with civil strife. Virgil bids Dante to answer this voice, which speaks his modern and provincial language. The pilgrim informs Guido of the ongoing conflicts between the petty lords of his region and then beseeches the flame to identify himself so that news of him may reach world of the living when Dante returns there. Guido hesitates. His monologue begins with a preamble in two tercets that became the epigraph of the Prufrock poem. Guido them proceeds to describe the circumstances of his life and death, telling how in his old age he repented for his sins and became a Franciscan friar, and how Pope Boniface VIII later came to him for advice to destroy the town of Penestrino, promising him absolution in advance for the sin such counsel would entail. Fear of Boniface leads Guido to provide the counsel, but absolution turns out to be a false promise, for upon his death the devil claims Guido's soul from St. Francis with an irrefutable logic about free will and repentence. Thus Guido finds himself in the eighth ring of *Malebolge,* enveloped in a flame. The following verses provide a sample of the speech that comes forth from the tip of that shivering tongue of fire:

> *"Io fui uom d'arme, poi fui cordigliero,*
> *credendomi, sì cinto, fare ammenda;*

> *e certo il creder mio venìa intero,*
> *se non fosse il gran prete, a cui mal prenda!,*
> *che mi rimise ne le prime colpe;*
> *e come e quare, voglio che m'intenda.*
> *Mentre ch'io forma fui d'ossa e di polpa*
> *che la madre mi diè, l'opere mie*
> *non furon leonine, ma di volpe.*
> *Li accorgimenti e le coperte vie*
> *io seppi tutte, e sì menai lor arte*
> *ch'al fine de la terra il suono uscìe.*
> *Quando mi vidi giunto in quella parte*
> *di mia etade ove ciascun dovrebbe*
> *calare le vele e raccoglier le sarte,*
> *ciò che pria mi piacea, allor m'increbbe,*
> *e pentuto e confesso mi rendei;*
> *ahi miser lasso! e giovato sarebbe."*

(ll. 67-84)

["I was a man of arms, then I was a friar, believing that so girt I would make amends; and surely my belief would have worked out had it not been for the great priest—may he be damned!—who drew me back into my former sins; and how and why I want you to hear. When I had the form of flesh and bones given me by my mother, my deeds were not lion-like but like the fox. The wiles and covert paths, I knew them all and so mastered their art that the rumors reached the ends of the earth. When I saw myself arrive at that age when each should drop the sails and gather in the shrouds, that which used to please me now grieved me, so contrite and confessant I gave myself up to God; O miserable me! and it would have availed."]

A stylistic comparison of the two soliloquies immediately reveals the historical as well as psychological chasm that divides the two speakers. We saw how Ulysses gave plasticity to his narrative through a series of logically ordered actions lodged in purely external settings. With Guido, on the other hand, we immediately move into a landscape of interiority, along the byways of a soul ridden with anxieties. The dramatic events are strictly psychological: conversion, repentence, *psychomachia,* regret, self-justification and so forth. No external setting organizes the soliloquy, only the drama of self-consciousness fraught with fears and misgivings. Unlike the Ulysses speech, we have in the monologue a central psychological "subject," where the narrative follows the same reflexive motion of the subjective self-consciousness that defines it. It begins with the event of conversion, retreats into a description of Guido's prior life as a man of arms, and then once again comes round to the conversion. The monologue is fraught with interruptions—*parenthetical clauses* ("and surely my belief would have worked out"; "O miserable me! and it would have availed"); with *invectives* ("were it not for the great priest—may he be damned!—") and with *hypothetical constructions* ("If I believed that my response were to one . . ."; "if what I hear is true . . ."). In short, it follows a "stream of consciousness" that continuously turns back upon itself in a series of self-reflexive qualifications and fragmentations that remind us of modernist techniques of mimetic disorganization. If modernist literature "breaks up the narrative continuity" and "violates the traditional syntax and coherence of narrative language" (Abrams), Guido's speech, placed conspicuously alongside Ulysses' classical performance, represents precisely such a subversion of standard literary conventions—a rhetorical *contaminatio,* to use a category Dante had in mind in this canto.

But these stylistic features are indissociably linked to a psychology that is no less "modern" in nature, especially if we are Hegelian enough to believe that consciousness becomes increasingly reflexive and interiorized through the succession of epochs. Ulysses clearly has no eye for the inward gaze that sees the self in its intangible interiority. It even seems out of place to speak of Ulysses in terms of "self," for the concept implies a self-conscious subject inherently split and objectified unto itself with the attendant alienations that go with this split to define the spirit of our modern era. Guido, on the other hand, reveals in his anxieties a consciousness that has turned in on itself in an almost exasperated reflexivity of conscience and guilt. In essence, Guido draws us into the same psychological horizon of subjectivity in which Prufrock sets out to make a visit. The "unhappy consciousness" belongs equally to both, and in both their soliloquies we are meant to follow the inner coils of a self at odds with itself.

Guido's modernity lies in this psychological selfhood. Before examining Dante's implicit conception of the relation of this selfhood and modernity, let us first take a closer look at the moral constitution of the interiority that envelops Guido in its shadows of anxiety. The key to it lies in Guido's capacity for bad faith. I use the term in a technical, Sartrean sense to mean the act of willful self-deception whereby the self freely persuades itself to believe what it knows is not true. *Mauvaise foi* in this sense allows the individual to conceal from himself the responsibility of his unconditional freedom, and is therefore linked ultimately to fear. Guido's case is typical. How could this "fox" and master of wiles allow himself to be deceived by a Pope who needs his superior counsel? It seems rather that Guido's fear of Boniface triggers the mechanism of self-deception whereby Guido falls for the very trick he recommends to his trickster, for in effect Guido prescribes to Boniface a strategy of which he himself is the master, and of which he will become the victim, namely a strategy of bad faith: "lunga promessa con l'attender corto / ti farà triunfar ne l'alto seggio" (ll. 110-1) ["A long promise and short keeping will make thee triumph in the high seat"]. But Guido provides this counsel on the basis of Boniface's own "long promise" to him—the long promise of everlasting life among the blessed through absolution. But again, it is not Boniface who can deceive Guido. This master of deceit can be deceived only by his own willful self-deception, motivated by fear.

Likewise Guido's repentance and conversion, his donning of the Franciscan robe, are motions undertaken in bad faith and fear—the fear of eternal damnation. "Io fui uom d'arme, poi fui cordigliero." The symmetry of the verse and the continuity between its two terms in the "poi," already belie Guido's conversion as a mere change of costume from the military uniform to the religious robe. The distinctive feature of authentic conversion—the case of Paul or Augustine—is the radical discontinuity between the pre-conversion and post-conversion self. But Guido *believed* that a gesture in bad faith could make amends, for he has a peculiar ability to make (himself) believe: "Io fui uom d'arme, poi fui cordigliero, / *credendomi,* sì cinto, fare amenda; / e certi il *creder* mio venia intero. . . ." The verb "credere" punctuates Guido's monologue with an ironic resonance and in each instance refers to what Guido believes without really believing. The most striking instance occurs in the preamble to his speech—T. S. Eliot's famous epigraph—where once again Guido persuades himself to believe a falsehood: "S'i' credesse che mia risposta fosse / a persona che mai tornasse al mondo. . . ." In order to allay his fear of infamy and his paranoia about preserving appearances, Guido here construes the pilgrim's transitivity as a deception. He is willing to believe what he has heard about hell ("s'i' odo il vero . . .") so as not to believe that his confession to this interlocutor entails a public disclosure of his private shame.

The devil who comes to claim Guido's soul at his death exposes these ruses with an irrefutable logic: "'ch'assolver non si può chi non si pente, / né pentere e volere insieme puossi / per la contradizion che nol consente'." ["'for he who has not repented cannot be absolved, nor can he repent and will together, since the law of contradiction does not allow it'."] One cannot repent and will simultaneously, for the freedom of the will lies in the will's responsibility for its own freedom. Bad faith wants to circumvent the logic of this freedom, and even in hell Guido continues to displace responsibility onto Pope Boniface, the "gran prete, a cui mal prenda!"

The freedom of the will lies in the will's responsibility for its own freedom. For Dante, this freedom is the incontrovertible facticity of Guido's "modernity" with regard to Ulysses. Broadly speaking, it consists in the personal option between salvation or damnation, an option closed off to Ulysses and his pre-Christian era. But we have seen that Ulysses is always ahead of himself and likes to reach places before others do. Not only does he arrive at Gaeta before Aeneas, but he also approaches at the mountain of Purgatory before the only other living person does, and that person is the pilgrim Dante. Thus Ulysses ventures into the horizon of personal salvation before its advent in time and shatters against this absolute limit of linear, historical temporality. In this respect his shipwreck appears as the very paradigm of tragedy, where the hero shatters against the inexorable dictates of fate and necessity. Ulysses' succinct utterance, "We rejoiced, and our joy quickly turned to grief," practically transliterates the classical definition of tragedy as a story that "begins in happiness and ends in sorrow." But while Ulysses can assume this tragic grandeur in *Inferno* XXVI because of his exclusion from personal salvation, Guido da Montefeltro finds himself included in the scheme of salvation history and for that reason excluded from the spirit of tragedy. Guido, in other words, figures on the Christian stage of "comedy" and its happy ending. To fully grasp this logic, which links the Christian era to comedy, we must take a step back into the medieval conceptions of tragedy and comedy that underlie Dante's thinking about historical epochs.

Theories of tragedy during the Middle Ages derived either directly or indirectly from the *Poetics* of Aristotle. We now know that this text was available either through the Latin translation of William or Moerbeke or through Herman the German's translation of Averroës' middle commentary on the *Poetics.* The latter in particular was an important source of diffusion for the concept of *hamartia* that lies at the center of all theories of the tragic even during the Middle Ages. While we tend to translate *hamartia* as "tragic flaw," it appears as the word for sin in the Greek Bible and is translated as *peccatum* in the Vulgate. Both Moerbeke and Herman translate the word as *peccatum,* and it is in this Judeo-Christian context of original sin and personal sin that Dante will ground his vision of the Christian era as the anti-tragic, or comic era. Let us briefly see what is at stake here.

In Averroës' middle commentary on the *Poetics,* tragedy is described as the representation of the fall of a *just* man at the hands of adverse fortune: "ex imitatione virtutum ad imitatione adversae fortunae, in quam probi lapsi sunt." Tragedy requires that a just man, a *probus,* be brought down by the adverse and indifferent forces of fate. The subjective innocence of the hero shattering against an inexorable objective order of fate dramatizes the universal *hamartia* of man, which we can now better define as human fallibility in the rigorous sense of impotence in the face of necessity. If we choose to translate *hamartia* as "guilt," and there are good reasons to do so, we must understand by guilt a universal condition of fallibility or fallenness that remains independent of subjective or personal responsibility. Seen in this way, the concept is not far removed from the category of original sin, at least insofar as this category was interpreted by Christian doctrine, which conceived it as an objective state of fallenness transmitted to all men and women independently of subjective responsibility. In theological terms, original sin is *natural* and not *personal.*

The purpose of Christ's advent in history was precisely to undo the tragic terms of *hamartia* and to liberate men from its inexorable destruction. The impotence of the personal will in the face of universal guilt comes to an end as Christ redeems man's nature of natural sin and transfers it to his or her person, which now retains a tendency toward sin but with the possibility of being saved through what the Church Fathers called the "superabundant merits" of Christ on the Cross. Guilt, in other words, is transferred from the objective order of fate to the subjective order of man's free will. Men

and women now have the choice of an eventual justification that depends on the individual's decision to expiate his sins through the salvific sacrifice of Christ. Thus if the formula for tragedy required the representation of the objective "guilt" of the "just man," Christianity prepares the way for comedy by allowing for a justification of the guilty man. Salvation becomes above all a personal affair, and the essence of Christian comedy becomes tied to the drama of individual free will. Thus St. Augustine can write: "That offence [original sin] was committed when all mankind existed in one man, and it brought universal ruin on mankind; and no one can be rescued from the toils of that offence, which was punished by God's justice, unless the sin is expiated *in each man singly* by the grace of God."

It is in terms of the single soul's progress from guilt to innocence, then, that we must understand the deeper meaning of Dante's title: *La Commedia.* Commenting on the meaning of comedy in his "Letter to Can Grande," Dante states: "a principio horribilis et foetida est, quia *Infernus,* in fine prospera, desiderabilis et grata, quia Paradisus." The poem is comic not simply because it begins with a representation of hell and ends with that of paradise, but because its "subject matter" deals with the personal subject in his or her paradoxical freedom to become an obedient *subiectum* of God's moral order, that is to say, to progress like a pilgrim from a state of guilt to one of grace: "Et si totius operis allegorice sumpti subiectum est homo prout merendo et demerendo per arbitrii libertatem est iustitiae premiandi et puniendi obnoxius. . . ." The subject of the allegory is the individual man who through the exercise of free will earns the reward or the punishment of divine justice. The subjective will, which in tragedy remains neutralized, has here become the central protagonist of a moral drama destined for comedy, condemned to comedy, insofar as the Incarnation has turned salvation or damnation into personal options. The essence of comedy for Dante is precisely this historical liberation of free will, and his *Commedia* figures as an extended allegory of that liberation.

> **It is in terms of the single soul's progress from guilt to innocence . . . that we must understand the deeper meaning of Dante's title *La Commedia.***
>
> **—*Robert Pogue Harrison***

In the broadest of terms, then, the "comic" horizon inhabited by Guido is that of subjective freedom with regard to divine justice. But let's pause a moment and reflect on the nature of this freedom. How much liberation from universal determination does it actually entail? The impossible paradox of Christianity is that, while it affirms the freedom of personal will, it fails to empower the will with freedom of self-determination. For in the Christian framework the will is free only to accept or reject God's law, but that law is as absolute and objective as the fateful forces that bring about the downfall of the tragic hero. Within the economy of Christian faith, the difference amounts to the certitude of salvation for the person who exercises his "free will" under a set of rigorous constraints and guidelines. Thus we have the beginning of an epoch of "tutelage," to use Kant's expression, in which virtue amounts to obedience and the personal will is denied even its tragic alternative. Indeed, Dante's *Inferno* (and also his *Paradiso*) is an imaginary testimony of the ultimate impotence of the will in the face of God's moral and comic order. More importantly, when subjective freedom turns into an autonomous self-legislation whereby the self presumes to ground itself solely on the basis of its own freedom, Dante, as the guardian of faith, will commit that sinner to the "blind prisonhouse" of his Inferno. The case of Guido. At bottom Dante rejects and even terrorizes human freedom. The degree to which he affirms the comic freedom of the soul to subject itself to God's justice is also the degree to which he condemns its perversion as a law unto itself. Such perversion is what is truly "modern" about Guido. As we shall see, Guido's true modernity consists in the paradoxical manner by which he freely exploits his subjective freedom and at the same time submits his conscience to the Christian superego that brings on anxieties about transgression.

(Historically, Christianity opened the way to modern secular freedom, but it could not properly survive its advent, precisely because it defines freedom in terms that ultimately neutralize freedom's resources, leaving itself vulnerable, in turn, to the reverse phenomenon, namely the neutralization of Christianity by secularization. If we believe theorists like Immanuel Kant (*What Is Enlightenment?*) or even Martin Heidegger, the history of the modern era has a single theme: man's attempts to ground himself in the law of his free subjectivity. The modern era, we are told, is founded upon a new concept of freedom: "To be free now means that, in place of the certitude of salvation, which was the standard for all truth, man posits the kind of certitude by virtue of which and in which he becomes certain of himself as the being that thus founds itself upon itself." The secularism that Heidegger describes here does not simply negate Christian law, however much it may repudiate the tutelage of that law, for it is precisely Christianity's invitation to a paradoxical personal freedom that liberates man from that same law. To quote from the Heidegger passage once more: "The history of [secular] modern mankind . . . was *mediately* prepared by Christian man. . . . The *saeculum,* the 'world' through which something is secularized in the celebrated 'secularization,' does not exist in itself or in such a way that it can be realized simply by stepping out of the Christian world." Christianity, in other words, prepares the way for the process of secularism that alienates modern men from Christianity.)

In Guido da Montefeltro we can discern the passage from so-called "Christian man," oriented toward the certitude of salvation, to the man of the modern era who "comes of age," to use Kant's expression, and strives for self-reliance. A careful look at Guido's psychology shows that his bad faith is actually underscored by a positive faith in his own resources—his circumspection, his efficacy, and his shrewd art of manipulation. In his distraught psychology, reflected by his interrupted and self-reflexive narrative that no longer takes its cues from objective norms of style, and in the exercise of his personal freedom in repeated gestures of bad faith, we witness a state of subjectivity that has already turned in on itself, enclosed itself within its interiority, and, from within that interiority, seeks control over its own transcendent destiny. For in the final analysis Guido *truly* believed that on the basis of his own resources he could negotiate the terms of his afterlife. His damnation after death revealed that, from the perspective of the Christian God, the faith he placed in himself was altogether misplaced.

But to negotiate the terms of one's destiny by relying solely upon one's own resources, was this not the project of Guido's counterpart Ulysses? And is Guido not dialectically juxtaposed to the grand figure of Ulysses with his self-doubts and insecure wavering between contradictory alternatives? How do we account for the interplay of differences and identities? In the following manner perhaps: in Guido we witness the Christian anxieties of a soul at the threshold of a new freedom, a historical era beyond the legislations of faith. It is impossible to determine where or when this era begins—with Renaissance humanism, with the Enlightenment, with positivism, with Nietzsche's dictum "God is dead," or with the advent of modern technology? The indetermination of this epochal event—the advent of modernity—finds its figure in the indeterminate psychic interiority of Guido da Montefeltro. Guido is the figure in whom the passage from piety to self-reliance reveals its manifold tensions in a soul that will never again recover the openness or externality of freedom, will never recover, that is, the open sea of Ulysses, precisely because the experience of Christianity determines its historicity. Is this what Dante meant to convey in these cantos? Who is to say? We have only the text, which sets up a deliberate contrast between the nautical imagery in Guido's speech with the "mad flight" of Ulysses across forbidden seas. In verses 79-81 Guido speaks of the appropriateness of pulling down the sails when one reaches old age; but we have seen that this anti-Ulyssean piety in the face of death was only apparent and not substantial. More importantly, for Guido the nautical imagery is precisely that—imagery—while Ulysses seeks the active externality of a nautical journey as such. It is in Guido's metamorphosis of Ulysses' nautical activism into a negative psychic image that a historical abyss between them opens up most forcefully. If Ulysses reaches places in their raw external givenness, before their domestication in the name, and if Aeneas subdues the wildness of the world with his pious, topological nomenclature, Guido exasperates the progress by seeking the space of psychic symbolization, where the transcendent externality of Ulysses' world moves inward, beyond the line of signifiers, and becomes imaginally dense. Ulysses' open sea has become Guido's stream of consciousness.

And yet Guido inhabits the same moral space as Ulysses in Dante's text. The paradox is that Guido's modernity consists in those aspects of his personage that differentiate him from Ulysses on the one hand, and identify him with Ulysses on the other. In the encounter with Ulysses Virgil warned Dante not to speak since the Greek hero might disdain his modern language; but when Guido calls out to Virgil in the next canto, he has overheard the exchange with Ulysses in his own provincial dialect: "O you to whom I address my voice and who were just now speaking Lombard, saying 'Now you may go, I urge you no more'. . . ." Guido in effect translates the high style and foreign speech of Ulysses into his own modern grammar, and in this translation a number of the historical distinctions that set him off from Ulysses are morally collapsed. An essentialism is at work here whereby the differentiations Dante articulates between the two characters are reduced to sameness from the perspective of He (or he) who damns them together.

The adjacency of the two sinners is crucial to the portrait of Dante's contemporary, for it would seem that Ulysses haunts the unconscious of Guido. The former looms as a powerful archetype of fascination that reveals the intimate secret of Guido's timid fantasies, namely, self-reliance with a good conscience. But Ulysses' daring and good faith in himself can represent only the great *myth* of a modern psychology such as Guido's, or even Prufrock's for that matter, for it would seem that the historical experience of Christianity has condemned modernity to bad faith irrevocably. In this respect T. S. Eliot's conversion in mid-life seems like an emblem of unresolved tensions at the heart of modernity, an emblem that adds to the tensions rather than pointing to their resolution. This much, in any case, is certain: the figure of Ulysses exerts a peculiar fascination not only on Guido da Montefeltro in *Inferno* XXVII but on the modernist writer as well. We need only think of Tennyson's canonical "Ulysses" poem, of James Joyce's modernist epic with the same title, and of Ezra Pound's *Cantos* patterned on the wandering hero's descent into the underworld to realize that Ulysses remains the privileged figure of modernist literature. This much is also certain: that Dante's critique of Guido's modernity in *Inferno* XXVII entails a critique of the fascination which Ulysses' humanism and self-reliance exert both on Guido and Dante's reader. Ulysses is meant to fascinate and to remain in hell. Such are the rules of this macabre comedy.

Patrick J. Gallacher (essay date 1989)

SOURCE: "The Conversion of Tragic Vision in Dante's *Comedy*," in *Romanic Review*, Vol. LXXX, No. 4, November, 1989, pp. 607-25.

[*The following essay elucidates the process of "demonic epiphany" in Dante's* Divine Comedy *whereby tragic heroes recognize their sin and suffer shame on the way to achieving greatness of soul.*]

An important feature of the recognition scene in tragedy is a moment of harrowing shame which Northrop Frye in his *Anatomy of Criticism* has called the demonic epiphany. When Oedipus and Othello fully recognize their tragic mistakes, the humiliation of exposure is perhaps the keenest aspect of their misery. Such moments are especially painful but also most illuminating both for the fictional characters and those who see the play or read the narrative; for this moment powerfully unifies the theme and action and offers a simultaneous perception of all the ideas and incidents. What Frye does not say, but what I think is true, is that this moment of greatest shame effects a passage to tragic vision and final eloquent self-acceptance, itself related to a certain kind of innocence. What we value in tragedy is the revealing tension between the hero's responsibility and those forces beyond his control. If the hero must bear all the responsibility, he becomes a moralistic cliché. If he is totally without responsibility, he is a victim, not a hero, like Willie Loman in *Death of a Salesman* or any of his numerous relations in naturalistic drama and fiction. Consequently, the recognition of a tragic hero is, simultaneously but in different respects, an acceptance and rejection of shame. The kind of innocence he achieves depends on the fact that, having acknowledged the precise degree of his own responsibility, he is caught up in a vision of what lay beyond his control—chance, the gods, or fate. In short, tragic shame, propelled by painful intellectual clarity, proceeds to a kind of innocence and, finally, to a greatness of soul, or magnanimity.

If such a structure is archetypal, always present in literature with appropriate variations, regardless of time and place, it should appear in some form in medieval literature. For some readers, an excellent medieval example of the tragic hero's transcendence of shame would be the conduct of Farinata degli Uberti in the *Inferno,* who rejects the shame of Hell itself. But what Frye calls the demonic epiphany in tragedy modulates into something different in the *Divine Comedy.* The literary structure itself, in a sense, undergoes a conversion.

The transcendence of shame and the assimilation of magnanimity that Dante, as a character, experiences takes place most explicitly in a conversion scene at the end of the *Purgatorio* and at certain moments in the *Paradiso.* Moreover, not only does Dante himself experience this transcendence of shame, but he witnesses significant instances of the same development in others. In regard, then, to both Dante and selected characters, I wish to trace in the poem a nuanced acceptance and rejection of shame as a process that varies and finally transforms the demonic epiphany into comic vision. I shall briefly summarize the medieval pattern of this process and trace its development in three sections: Cantos VIII, IX, and X, of the **Inferno**; Cantos XXX to XXXIII of the **Purgatorio**; and Cantos I, IX, and XVII of the **Paradiso**.

Question 144 of the Secunda Secundae of the *Summa Theologiae* of Aquinas contains the basic elements of a medieval recognition scene. First of all, the element of public witnessing which constitutes the demonic epiphany for Northrop Frye also defines shame for Aquinas. He observes that just as honor denotes witnessing or attestation to someone's excellence, so too reproach, the fear of which is shame, or *verecundia,* denotes witnessing to a person's defect. The more weighty a person's witnessing is considered to be, the more does he make another person ashamed. Insofar as shame is the result of a disgraceful act, it is not a virtue. Since, however, the fear of reproach can prevent disgraceful acts, shame is laudable, although a more perfect motive characterizes the person who acts out of love for the good.

The most important aspect of the discussion of shame in Aquinas, since he does not really consider shame a virtue, is what might be called the "refusal of shame" and concerns those situations in which a person is unjustly an object of public disapproval and suffers, so to speak, the externals of a demonic epiphany. The wise and virtuous man will despise the ignominy to which he is falsely subject, because he does not deserve it. This sense of violated worthiness and contempt for injustice is synonymous with disdain or indignation, terms in which the negative prefixes, together with the etymological root of "dignus," or "worthy," emphasize the repudiation of blame. Quoting Aristotle's *Ethics,* IV, iii, Aquinas observes that this disdain of unjust opprobrium is a characteristic of the magnanimous man. Aquinas applauds this magnanimous refusal of shame, which is closely related, I believe, to the tragic hero's realization that beyond his own fragility and fallibility lies the exoneration of a more encompassing truth. Quoting from *Acts,* V, 41, Aquinas says that the Apostles went from the presence of the council, rejoicing that they were accounted worthy to suffer reproach for the name of Jesus. In the medieval tradition, then, there is the possibility of exultation in an external context of shame, a magnanimity which disdains public opinion on the basis of a mysterious higher truth. Although the triumph of the tragic hero over shame, which he deserves, is obviously different from the analogous experience of the innocent, nevertheless the liberating effect of a greater vision is an important point of similarity.

Insofar as it is a virtue, shame is defined as a mean between shamelessness and excessive shame, or *inordinatus stupor.* The confusion of this latter experience corresponds archetypally, I believe, to that segment of the recognition scene where bewilderment overcomes the tragic hero and demands a search for a new pattern of explanation. In Dante, however, the bewilderment that seeks an explanation is itself transformed into a wonder or admiration directed towards the providen-

tial order of the universe itself. In the **Comedy,** Dante eventually goes through something like the deserved shame of the tragic hero and the bewilderment or *stupor* that demands a new pattern of explanation. Finally, through repentance and grace, he achieves the restored innocence of redemption. This, in turn, causes the magnanimity which triumphs over shame and issues in an eloquence that is first prayer and then, in an important sense, the **Comedy** itself. This process takes place by stages, by the challenges and reinforcements that result from the various encounters of the journey.

With Dante's response to the insolence of Filippo Argenti in Canto VIII of the **Inferno,** this process begins on an almost instinctual level. The latter's insolence is a reverse image of an audacity which will characterize the authentic transcendence of shame. Argenti's sudden appearance effectively prevents deliberation and his arrogant question to Dante—"Chi se' tu che vieni anzi ora?" ("Who are you that come before your time?" VIII:33), by assuming that Dante belongs in Hell, attempts a public witnessing to a defect, which is the essence of shame. Answering that if he comes, he does not remain, Dante asks for the identity of the questioner, who in his shame refuses this request: "Vedi che son un che piango" ("You see that I am one who weeps" VIII, 36). Dante's realization that he is addressing Filippo Argenti occurs simultaneously with an awareness of his own relative moral worth. In contrast to Argenti's foolish insolence, Dante's just indignation foreshadows the basic structure of the scenes that follow and is a first hint of that magnanimity that will eventually be his. Dante's disdain—applauded by Virgil's exclamation, "Alma sdegnosa, / benedetta colei che 'n te s'incinse!" ("Indignant soul, blessed is she who bore you," VIII:44-45)—arises from a just evaluation of his own moral worth as compared to that of Argenti and expresses his refusal of the public opprobrium implicit in the latter's insolence. The allusion to Christ and the Virgin in Virgil's statement, by providing a figural authority, makes Dante's indignation exemplarily Christian.

But as tragedy and Dante's **Comedy** teach us, moral worth is dauntingly relative; and because nature in relation to grace has a kind of ontological insufficiency, there is a symbolic justification of Virgil's shame in the next scene. The opprobrium of the demons before the gate of Dis witnesses to a defect in even the most perfect human nature. After first moderating their "gran disdegno" (VIII:88), they send him back to Dante with his "occhi a la terra e le ciglia . . . rase / d'ogne baldanza . . ." ("his eyes upon the ground and his brows . . . shorn of all boldness," VIII:118-19). In Canto IX, which continues this scene, the public humiliation of Virgil induces a state of confusion—akin to the *stupor* mentioned by Aquinas—and reduces his legendary eloquence to a bewildered stammering: "Pur a noi converrà vincer la punga," / cominciò el, "se non . . . Tal ne s'offerse" ("Yet we must win this fight," he began, "or else . . . such did she offer herself to us!" IX, 7-8). Benvenuto da Imola's commentary on this passage confirms the elements of shame and confusion that make up a demonic epiphany.

The encounter with the Furies and the threat of Medusa—who suggests an experience of *inverecundia,* the shamelessness of complete moral insensitivity—further witness to the limitations of Virgil. Such shamelessness is the emotional equivalent of the moral petrification and refusal of meaning that, according to John Freccero, is the essential significance of Medusa. At this point, some explanatory action representing a higher truth is needed to dissipate the confusion and advance the journey. Such an action is the arrival of the heavenly messenger who embodies the magnanimous disdain of grace towards the evil that can shame the best of nature's efforts.

Although the superior power he represents is rendered to hearing and sight by several memorable images—*"un fracasso d'un suon, pien di spavento"* ("a crash of fearful sound" IX:65); *"dinanzi polveroso va superbo"* ("haughtily drives onward in its cloud of dust" IX:71)—the most telling sign of magnanimity is the almost languid boredom of his manner:

> *Dal volto rimovea quall' aere grasso,*
> *menando la sinistra innanzi spesso;*
> *e sol di quell' angoscia parea lasso.*

> (He was clearing the gross air from before his face
>   often moving his left hand before him,
>   and only with that annoyance did he seem weary.)
>   (IX:82-84)

Dante's exclamation—"Ahi quanto me parea pien di disdegno!" ("Ah how full of disdain he seemed to me!" IX:88)—foreshadows an eventual and thorough assimilation of this contempt for evil. Since the angel's eloquent rebuke of the demonic insolence derives from his participation in divine magnanimity—"quella voglia / a cui non puote il fin mai esser mozzo" ("that Will / which can never be thwarted of its end," IX:94-95), it provides the pattern by which Dante's own progress in grace will exhibit an articulate disdain for evil. Since Virgil does not participate in the realm of grace, he cannot himself assimilate this distinctively Christian pattern of dispensing with shame, dramatically asserted by the angel and embodied by Cunizza and Folco in the *Paradiso,* and eventually by Dante himself.

The encounter with Farinata, with its interaction of shame and eloquence regarding the "art of returning," offers the clearest analogue in the *Inferno* of the tragic recognition scene. His magnanimity, when he rises up to look at Dante—"col petto e con la fronte/ com' avesse l'inferno a gran dispitto" (X:35-36) ("with chest and brow thrown back as if he had great scorn of Hell")—is so daunting, only the angel's eloquent disdain of evil in the previous canto puts the scene in proper perspective and accounts for Dante's splendidly modest reaction. We expect that Farinata's contempt for Dante's ancestors—"quasi sdegnoso" ("as if in dis-

dain," X:41); "ond' ei levò le ciglia un poco in suso" ("whereupon he raised his brows a little," X:45); and finally, "per due fiate li dispersi" ("twice over I scattered them," X:48)—will certainly reduce Dante to shame, confusion, and silence. His reply, however, is surprising in its self-possessed, concise understatement:

> *"'ei fur cacciati, ei tornar d'ogne parte"*
> *rispuos' io lui, "l'una e l'altra fiata;*
> *ma i vostri non appreser ben quell' arte."*

> ("If they were driven forth, they returned from
>   every quarter, both times," I answered him,
>   "but yours have not learned that art well.")
>   (X:49-51)

Not at all abashed by Farinata's rebuke, Dante counters by witnessing to the faint-heartedness of the degli Uberti. The ludicrous appearance and disappearance of Cavalcante reveals a shame that is static and inward-looking and that does not become transcendence of any kind. His behavior calls attention to the dignity of Farinata's acceptance both of Dante's rebuke and the shame of his family's behavior: "S'elli han quell' arte," disse, "male appressa, / ciò mi tormenta più che questo letto" ("And if," he said . . . , "they have ill learned that art, that fact torments me more than this bed" X:77-78).

Although we cannot speak of an innocence in Farinata like that achieved by the tragic hero, there is a lack of self-concern and an exultation in his disdain for Hell that is, in its context, admirable and that Dante approves. Not only does Farinata, in effect, accept shame for his posterity's failure to learn the art of returning, but the structure of the poem allows him to participate in a vision that goes far beyond his own immediate situation. Having a knowledge of the future, Farinata tenders an obscure prediction of Dante's exile from Florence, the fulfillment of which will teach him "quanto quell' arte pesa" ("how much that art weighs" X:81). Although the art in question is that of returning to Florence, in this poem about a journey that is primarily a moral return, such an art would imply the whole process of conversion that Dante must yet go through. For Dante, the art of returning entails not only the painful acceptance of shame demanded of the tragic hero, but also a return to the world of time and history. Farinata's statement, in which he accepts shame for the guilt of his family and predicts hardship for Dante, testifies to the tragic principles of personal responsibility and the forces beyond one's control; and the wary resolution of his own character is the *figura* of Dante's gradual conversion. This is not to exonerate Farinata: he is, after all, in Hell. His quite brief prophecy, however, embodies a variation of tragic vision. When Cacciaguida, in *Paradiso* XVII, clarifies this obscure prediction of Dante's exile in the context of providential order, he is completing a vision that Farinata participates in by having begun; and Dante can gain access to this order only by the designated art of returning. However, for Farinata, as for the typical tragic hero, the time for effective action is over. The comic modification of this structure, however, requires a return to the world of challenges and responsibilities from which the protagonist has withdrawn.

The acceptance and transcendence of shame within a recognition scene receive their most extensive expression in *Purgatorio* XXX to XXXIII. In this sequence, Dante displays at first a marked absence of magnanimity, in contrast to the scene in the *Inferno,* where the spirited exchange with Farinata reflects a natural sense of honor. Because the supernatural truths of Beatrice render him radically powerless, Dante must earn a new magnanimity, in accordance with the Christian virtue of humility and the explicit issue of grace. There is also a further point of contrast. As I have observed, the tragic hero realizes that in spite of his obvious guilt, he is also, in a sense, innocent. Dante, on the other hand, realizes that although he is emphatically less blameworthy than those in the dead world—so much so that Virgil has pronounced him crowned and mitred, secure to follow his own pleasure (XXVII: 139-42)—an encounter with shame on a level of deeper spiritual expectations lies ahead. The guilt of the tragic hero derives from the grave violation of some basic human imperative, like Othello's murder of his wife or Lear's abandonment of his daughter. Dante's guilt, on the other hand, is in the failure to achieve a providential destiny by his disregard of natural gifts, love, and grace, a motif that dominates his most poignant experience and transcendence of shame.

In the transition from shame to magnanimity, from the rejection to the affirmation of self, love plays a key role. In Canto XXX, it is the physical recollection of this love, sensed by an occult power, that Dante desires to communicate to Virgil, only to find him gone. This disappearance, in turn, emphasizes the fact that the recognition scene will engage a love that goes beyond the experience of reason, and hence, the structures of tragedy as well. As Charles Singleton says, the second of Dante's three conversions occurs in this sequence where Beatrice is especially associated with the supernatural love of charity. Furthermore, just as, according to Aquinas, the greater dignity of the person administering the rebuke increases the shame, so the love that Dante has for Beatrice brings to bear an additional power to humiliate. In fact, Beatrice's shaming rebuke of Dante resonates with the hierarchy of love associated with her literal and allegorical nature.

Dante's own personal demonic epiphany—his humiliation of exposure—begins with Beatrice's command that he look at her—"Guardaci ben!" (XXX, 73), an act that shame makes almost impossible. His acknowledgment of the order, within which her reprimands take place, will liberate him from shame and confusion, and endow him with a sense of magnanimity. By immediately questioning his worthiness to be in Eden, her ironic inquiry—"Come degnasti d'accedere al monte?" (XXX:74)—makes her a kind of gatekeeper and recalls the function of the demons before the city of Dis. The

next question—"non sapei tu che qui è l'uom felice?" ("Did you not know that here man is happy?" XXX:75)—by recalling the central motif of the Boethian *Consolation of Philosophy,* mocks Dante's willful refusal to pursue true happiness. As subsequent remarks indicate, Beatrice's ironic question designates as a gratuitous childish perversity Dante's failure to proceed from philosophical awakening to the wisdom of faith. When Dante grasps this, the humiliation of exposure intensifies: refusing the gaze of Beatrice, he cannot bear even to look at himself:

> *Li occhi mi cadder giù nel chiaro fonte;*
> *ma veggendomi in esso, i trassi a l'erba,*
> *tanta vergogna mi gravò la fronte.*

> (My eyes fell down to the clear fount,
> but, seeing myself in it, I drew them back to the grass,
> so great shame weighed on my brow . . .)
> (XXX, 76-78; my italics)

The pity of the angels, who take his side like the comic equivalent of a tragic chorus, calls attention to the confusion of shame: "Donna, perché sì lo stempre?" ("Lady, why do you so confound him?" XXX, 96). Her answer includes the epistemological fact that the angelic intelligence totally and immediately grasps its object, but the human mind, to achieve its goal, must experience confusion as part of a graduated process of discursive understanding. Moreover, the hierarchy of vision in the poem must be paralleled by the appropriate hierarchy of emotions through which shame, intensified here by love, becomes magnanimity. Dante's confusion here, like Virgil's before the gate of Dis, corresponds to Aquinas's *inordinatus stupor* and is essential to the recognition process. Beatrice emphasizes not only Dante's own responsibility and the advantages he had from nature, but also the more serious failure of refused graces, "che sì alti vapori hanno a lor piova, / che nostre viste là non van vicine" ("which have for their rain vapors so lofty that our sight goes not near thereto" XXX, 113-14). The imagery here of *vapori* and *viste* confirm, I believe, the direction of my argument. The vapors that cannot be seen point to the forces that lie beyond human control: the benevolence of grace, which is the correlative of fate in tragedy. The inability to see calls attention to the shame that keeps Dante from looking either at Beatrice or himself but also anticipates that greater vision that will come with repentance and increase with grace.

Having catalogued his falls from virtue, Beatrice asks Dante for acknowledgment at the beginning of Canto XXXI. The description of his inaudible reply—a simple yes—continues the theme of confusion by a double reference ("Era la mia virtù tanto *confusa*") ("my power was so *confounded*" XXXI, 7); "Confusione *e paura insieme miste,*" ("*confusion* and fear together mingled" XXXI, 13) and leads to further humiliation.

The contrast between young and mature birds (61-63), by calling attention to Dante's failure to learn from experience, further intensifies the motif of shame and the absence of magnanimity, for the contrast reveals Dante as morally childish. Dante's lack of anything like magnanimity at this stage is emphasized by the juvenile demeanor of his shame—"Quali fanciulli, *vergognando*, muti / con li occhi a terra stannosi" ("As children stand *ashamed* and dumb, with eyes on the ground" XXXI, 64-65; my italics).

The next stage in his experience of shame requires that he raise his head and "face" his accuser, an action that parallels his meeting with the traitor, Bocca, in the **Inferno.** Beatrice's mocking words force him to confront further the experience of looking and being looked at—"alza la barba / e prenderai più doglia riguardando" ("lift up your beard and you will receive more grief through seeing" XXXI: 69). The first terzina devoted to the beard imagery points to a vehement struggle with shame equal to that of any tragic hero:

> *Con men di resistenza si dibarba*
> *robusto cerro, o vero al nostral vento*
> *o vero a quel de la terra di Iarba,*
> *Ch'io non levai al suo comando il mento . . .*

> (With less resistance is the sturdy oak
> uprooted, whether by wind of ours,
> or by that which blows from Iarbas' land
> than at her command I raised my chin . . .)
>   (XXXI: 70-73; my italics)

The storm imagery, used to mark his avoidance of the full shame of being looked at, testifies to the emotional depths of the struggle. This uprooting of the oak as a "debearding" calls attention to the implied accusation of moral beardlessness: "e quando per la *barba* il viso chiese, / ben connobi il velen de l'argomento" ("and when by the *beard* she asked for my face, well I knew the venom of the argument" XXXI, 74-75; my italics). This powerful image recalls Dante's own furious attempt, in *Inferno,* XXXII, to extract a confession of identity from the treacherous Bocca, who, seized by the hair, still keeps his eyes down, as Dante is doing here:

> *Io avea già i capelli in mano avvolti,*
> *e tratti glien' avea più d'una ciocca,*
> *latrando lui con li occhi in giù raccolti . . .*

> ("I had already twisted his hair in my hand
> and had yanked out more than one tuft,
> he barking and with his eyes kept close down . . ."
>   (*Inf.* XXXII:103-105)

At first glance, what links the two scenes are anatomically similar images of shame—the lowered eyes and the forcible raising of the head by hair or beard. But this resemblance introduces a more pointed dialectic. The treacherous, imprisoned up to their necks in ice—"livide, insin là dove appar *vergogna*" ("livid up to where the hue of *shame* appears" l. 34; my italics)—anticipate the visual nature of Dante's own shame-filled reaction to Beatrice: "Perché cotanto in noi ti spec-

chi?" ("Why do you gaze so much on us?" XXXIII, 54). By promising to tell their story, Dante has regularly elicited a response from the damned; but when he offers fame here, Bocca, who embodies the most deadening shame in the poem, belligerently asserts his preference for anonymity, for the transcendence of shame requires an avowal of identity.

Dante's reply, when he learns that it is Bocca, has an indignation which characterizes his own rhetoric of blame throughout the **Comedy,** but which becomes fully explicit only after his own acceptance and transcendence of shame:

> *"Omai," diss' io, "non vo' che più favelle,*
> *Malvagio traditior; ch'a la tua onta*
> *io porterò di te vere novelle."*

> ("Now," said I, "I do not wish you to speak more,
> accursed traitor, for to your *shame*
> will I carry true news of you.")
>   (XXXII:109-11; my italics)

Returning to the **Purgatorio,** we observe that Dante, unlike Bocca, willingly raises his eyes, for the first time since Beatrice's rebuke began. Seeing Beatrice now, he realizes that his emotions have undergone a profound reversal for he now hates most what once he loved most. The final anguish of the scene comes to him through combined sight and judgment as, according to the measured process of the journey, he perceives that death and transfiguration (XXXI, 76-84) have made Beatrice only more beautiful. She now surpasses her former self more than when in life her beauty gave him "sommo piacer" (XXXI, 52), and her beauty, precisely because it incarnates the highest values of natural and supernatural, most reveals his unworthiness and represents the deepest cause of his shame. His grasp of these implications—"Tanta riconoscenza" (XXXI, 88) stuns him into unconsciousness. But the acknowledgement has begun the transformation of shame, for when he revives, he is being helped by Matelda to walk through and drink of the river, Lethe.

Although eliminating a memory of the fault might seem to eliminate the shame as well, Dante still retains some of its effects, as we shall see. He is led into the dance of the four fair ones—the cardinal virtues—who promise to bring him to the eyes of Beatrice. The pain of looking and being looked at, the demonic epiphany of tragedy, is transformed in this comic structure into a pleasure that will have its ultimate fulfillment in the Beatific Vision. Tragic vision, we might say, like the four pagan virtues, can bring us to the eyes of Beatrice; but only the theological virtues can provide the surpassing experience of supernatural understanding:

> *Merrenti a li occhi suoi; ma nel giocondo*
> *lume ch'è dentro aguzzeranno i tuoi*
> *le tre di là che miran più profondo.*

> (We will bring you to her eyes; but in the joyous
> light which is within them the three on

the other side, who look deeper, shall quicken yours.)
(XXXI: 109-111)

The love that was made painful by shame becomes at once a passionately amorous gaze and a spiritual vision of the Incarnation. Dante's transcendence of shame will go beyond that of Farinata, the tragic hero, to a strengthening and joyous contemplation which, in turn, makes possible a final return to action. After the Theological Virtues exhort him to a visual abandon which is the opposite of the self-enclosed and thwarted gaze of shame—"Fa che le viste non risparmi" ("See that you spare not your gaze" XXXI, 115)—Dante experiences the release from emotional inhibition that accompanies the transcendence of shame, looking fervently and unself-consciously into the eyes of his exalted beloved:

Mille disiri più che fiamma caldi
strinsermi li occhi a li occhi rilucenti . . .

(A thousand desires hotter than flame
held my eyes on the shining eyes . . .)
(XXXI: 118-19)

The thousand desires are not simply a conventional hyperbole: Beatrice represents here, according to Charles Singleton, happiness itself, which having been clearly seen, overcomes the dispersion of human appetite—the thousand desires—and focuses them into a unity. Just as the demonic epiphany proceeds to a tragic vision of reality, Dante's gaze into Beatrice's eyes—*"che pur sopra 'l grifone stavan saldi"* ("that remained ever fixed on the griffin" XXXI, 120)—meets the central mystery of the Christian comedy, the Incarnation. The object of tragic vision is the mystery of a universe in which the most gifted lose their moral integrity and succumb to a ruinous evil. The object of Dante's vision, the Incarnation, is the means by which history as tragedy takes a profoundly hopeful turn, the implications of which for his personal life and for the general human condition pervade the entire poem.

Although what Dante sees of the Griffon in the eyes of Beatrice is expressed in the most general terms—"or con altri, or con altri reggimenti" ("now with the one, now with the other bearing" XXXI, 123), this vision of the Incarnation has a significance that provides a further parallel with the vision of the tragic hero. The archetypal dilemma, once again, is that if the forces beyond man's control are excessive, he loses his identity and becomes a victim. If the entire burden of action is his own, the result is a Horatio Alger, moralistic tract. Just as great tragedy always steers between these two extremes, Dante's formulation of the analogous structure in the Christian economy is similarly balanced. In *Paradiso* VII, Beatrice states the providential alternatives occasioned by Adam's fall. God could simply pardon the offense of Adam and presumably do away with evil in history; or man could be left to cope with evil exclusively in terms of his own initiative (*Paradiso* VII, 91-93). The Incarnation as a solution to this problem preserves man's identity and dignity; and just as the sinister forces beyond his control are part of the tragic hero's vision, so in the recognition structure of the *Comedy*, there is a pervasive mystery of generous love:

che più largo fu Dio a dar sé stesso
per far l'uom sufficiente rilevarsi,
che s'elli avesse sol da sé dimesso . . .

(for God was more bounteous in giving Himself
to make man sufficient to uplift himself again,
than if He solely of Himself had remitted . . .)
(*Par.* VII, 115-17)

It is precisely the refusal of this magnanimous and challenging dispensation, of both autonomy and support, that Dante stands accused of in his encounter with Beatrice in the *Purgatorio.*

Having beheld the Griffon remain still in itself and in its image changing, he is ready for the next phase of his conversion. His witness of the allegorical dramatization of Church history, involving the transformation of the chariot, the harlot and the giant, and the eagle, reminds us of that return to the historical and the temporal that must follow Dante's transcendence of shame. In fact, when the pageant is finished and Beatrice invites Dante to draw near and speak with her, the focus is on such reinvolvement, which recalls Farinata's art of returning. Dante has not yet completely overcome his shame, and like Perceval, who does not ask the meaning of the Grail procession, he is immersed in an awed silence. Beatrice asks him why he does not inquire about the meaning of what he has seen (XXXII:23-24). Once more like Virgil before the gate of Dis and like himself before his confession in Canto XXXI, Dante speaks only with difficulty. He is like those whose reverence before their superiors is so entire *"che non traggon la voce viva ai denti"* "that they do not bring the voice whole to their lips [sic] (XXXIII:27)" In their previous verbal exchange, she was at pains to intensify his confusion. Now, in giving him his commission, his role in the active life to which he, unlike the tragic hero, must return, she explicitly urges him to substitute a resolute and decisive speech for the dreamy, unfocused discourse of his fear and shame:

Ed ella a me: "Da tema e da vergogna
voglio che tu omai ti disviluppe,
sì che non parli più com' om che sogna.

(And she to me, "From fear and from shame,
I wish that you henceforth divest yourself,
So that you may no more speak like one who is
dreaming.)
(XXXIII; 31-33; my italics)

This reinvolvement is substantially the *Comedy* itself.

To bring the motif of shame into a concluding focus, we must remember the double point of view in the *Comedy*: that of the Dante who has already taken the journey and is writing the poem; and that of the voyager, who knows only what has been shown to him at any given time. The commission that Beatrice gives Dante the pilgrim to speak out will be repeated by Cacciaguida and manifested most explicitly in the prayer of the poet with which the *Paradiso* begins. This prayer is perhaps the most resolute and powerful statement of Dante's intention in the *Comedy* and in itself embodies a memorable refusal of shame. However, to understand its power, we must look at, in addition to Cacciaguida's discourse, the speeches of Cunizza and Folco in *Paradiso* IX, who embody a victory over shame that, having inspired the pilgrim, can sustain the poet.

Cunizza and Folco speak with an easy sense of obstacles overcome, which contrasts with the prayer at the beginning of the *Paradiso* which evokes the irascible appetite's response to the difficult. Both appear in the sphere of Venus, the last one affected by the shadow of the earth (IX, 118-119). Cunizza, notorious for her amorous intrigues, has so overcome her shame that her exquisite disdain for earthly reputation startles the reader:

> *Cunizza fui chiamata, e qui refulgo*
> *perché mi vinse il lume d'esta stella . . .*

> (I was called Cunizza, and I am refulgent here
> because the light of this star overcame me.)
> (IX: 32-33)

By naming herself and laying stress on the place of her manifestation, the sphere of Venus, she specifies the failures of her temporal life. But even here, her choice of words asserts a triumph of *refulgo* over *mi vinse*. She is resplendent now in spite of her defeat, and joy has completely replaced shame:

> *ma lietamente a me medesma indulgo*
> *la cagion di mia sorte, e non mi noia;*
> *che parria forse forte al vostro vulgo.*

> (But I gladly pardon in myself the reason of my lot,
> and it does not grieve me—which might perhaps
> seem strange to your vulgar herd.)
> (IX:34-36)

The last line shows an appealing scorn for the superficiality and gossip of public disapproval. Moreover, displaying an autonomy that further underlines the transcendence of shame, she forgives herself. Further on in the same Canto, Folco, the next speaker, affirms the universal order of providential love which complements Cunizza's emphasis on the social world. His admission to fault goes beyond Cunizza's, when, placing himself in an historical company of illicitly ardent lovers, he almost boasts that none of them burned more than he. In both of these characters, there is a kind of innocent and winning shamelessness:

> *Non però qui si pente, ma si ride,*
> *non de la colpa, ch'a mente non torna,*
> *ma del valor ch'ordinò e provide.*

> (Yet here we repent not, but we smile,
> not for the fault, which returns not to mind,
> but for the Power that ordained and saw.)
> (IX:103-5)

Still focusing on a love that goes beyond the self in its narcissistic shame, he emphasizes the wonder created by the metamorphosis of shame's bewilderment:

> *Qui si remira ne l'arte ch'addorna*
> *cotanto affetto, e discernesi 'l bene*
> *per che 'l mondo di sù quel di giù torna.*

> (Here we contemplate the art which
> so much love adorns, and we discern the good
> by reason of which the world below again
> becomes the world above.)
> (IX:106-8)

No longer shamed or confused, they are nevertheless eternally astonished by the great love that adorns the craftsmanship of providence and by the mystery of the good which transforms the world below into the world above: the wonder of how the ontological good, present even in the sinner, is made pervasive and drawn to its archetypal cause. In these two characters, the demonic epiphany of tragedy is entirely transformed into its transcendently comic counterpart.

In contrast to such ease but, in a sense, informed and made intelligible by it, is Dante's prayer in *Paradiso* I. A final effect of the transformation of shame is present in the return from contemplation to action. This development comes as a response to Cacciaguida's prophecy of Dante's exile in *Paradiso* XVII, a prophecy that fulfills and validates the limited vision of Farinata. The concrete application of the transcendence of shame comes with Dante's statement about his own role in the shaming of the unjust. While Dante himself will be blameless in his exile (XVII, 52-54), its worse circumstance will be his new companions who will reject him, to their shame, not his—"ella, non tu, n'avrà rossa la tempia" ("their brows, not yours, shall redden for it" XVII, 66). Dante's response to his great-great-grandfather's prophecy is linked to his composition of the *Comedy.* In the fact of exile and in his subsequent experience, Dante will encounter an unjust public witnessing to a defect; but he will not only refuse this shame but will also assign it where it belongs. The desire for truth and fame come together in his speech here, as they do in the prayer at the beginning of the *Paradiso,* as he responds that only the truth of his songs can prevent the loss of Florence from causing further dispossession. If he tells what he has seen in his journey through Hell, Purgatory, and Paradise, it will be bitterly offensive to many. Once again we are struck by the transformation of the tragic hero's eloquence— a boldness asserted in a context of unjust opprobrium:

> *"e s'io al vero son timido amico,*
> *temo di perder viver tra coloro*
> *che questo tempo chiameranno antico."*

("and if I am a timid friend to the truth,
  I fear to lose life among those
  who shall call this time ancient.")
                                        (XVII, 118-20)

Refusing the unjust shame, he will in turn shame the unjust; and his public witnessing will extend to furthest posterity. Although Dante simply intends to tell the truth, Cacciaguida's voice predicts the shaming consequences of Dante's poetry:

*indi rispuose: "Coscienza fusca
  o de la propria o de l'altrui* vergogna
  pur sentirà la tua parola brusca.

(then it replied, "A conscience dark,
  either with its own or with another's *shame,*
  will indeed feel your speech to be harsh.")
                                        (124-26; my italics)

Public witnessing to a defect elicits a personal judgment: the innocent will ignore it, but the guilty must scratch where they itch.

The speaker of the prayer in *Paradiso* I, 19-30, has assimilated this experience with Cacciaguida. Dante the poet is, perhaps notoriously, free from false modesty, and although there are many passages that manifest this in the poem (e.g., himself among the three great poets of antiquity), this first Canto of the *Paradiso,* which has an emphasis of place, can provide a concluding statement about the final transcendence of shame and the return from contemplation to action. The passage is remarkable in its combination of deep spirituality, resolute humanism, and an unabashed self-assertion that is the opposite of shame. Significantly, in relation to the structure of both tragedy and comedy that we have been describing, the prayer contains a fully self-conscious sense of equilibrium between responsibility and the forces beyond one's control. Here it is a balance between what the Divine Apollo is being asked to do and what, on his part, the petitioner resolves:

*O divina virtù, se mi ti presti
  Tanto che l'ombra del beato regno
  segnata nel mio capo io manifesti,
  Vedra'mi al piè del tuo diletto legno
  venire, e coronarmi de le foglie
  che la materia e tu mi farai* degno.

(O divine power, if you do so lend yourself to me
  that I may show forth the image of the blessed realm
  which is imprinted in my mind,
you shall see me come to your beloved tree
  and crown me with those leaves
  of which the matter and you shall make me *worthy.*)
                                        (I, 22-27; my italics)

Bold confidence and a sense of need for divine grace are equally present here. The word *degno* both embodies the pilgrim's victory over shame and echoes the many examples of the poet's indignation in the poem. This confi-

dence has been anticipated by the commanding use of the reflexive verb—*coronarmi:* you will see me *crown myself,* an autonomy that recalls both Cunizza's self-forgiveness and the incarnational ability to raise oneself ("sufficiente rilevarsi," *Paradiso* VII, 116). Finally, the presence of this motif in the prayer is generalized in Dante's compelling affirmation of Christian humanism:

*Sì rade volte, padre, se ne coglie
  per triunfare o cesare o poeta,
  colpa e vergogna de l'umane voglie*

(So rarely, father, are they gathered,
  for triumph of caesar or of poet—
  fault and shame of human wills—)
                                        (I, 28-30)

The fact that great political and poetic success occurs so seldom is the shame of the human will. Such an assertion could not be in greater contrast to the final stage of tragedy. For all its humane magnificence, tragic vision remains practically ineffectual compared to Dante's invitation to historical engagement. And yet there is an important sense in which the two visions are complementary. The poignancy of Farinata's situation, from Dante's point of view, consists in the excellence not only of what he was but also of what he could have been. But the great Ghibelline's disregard for his own pain and his persistent concern for the magnanimity of his offspring point to what the human spirit is capable of, those political and cultural achievements to which Dante exhorts the reader.

The demonic epiphany, the shame which the tragic hero overcomes by acceptance and vision, is an element of literary structure, which, I hope to have shown, has an important manifestation and variation in the *Divine Comedy.* Public witnessing to a defect in these works causes a confusion which, if endured and examined, can lead to a greater understanding of both the human condition and the universe itself. The development of this motif in the *Divine Comedy* employs a worldview that is different from that of the tragic hero, but that shares a sense of both personal responsibility and mysterious forces beyond human control. Dante's encounters with Argenti, the Furies, the Angel, Farinata, Bocca, Beatrice, Cunizza, Folco, and Cacciaguida, represent a varied pattern of the acceptance and refusal of shame that becomes focused in his prayer for the accomplishment of his providential destiny. The rejection of self experienced in shame is transformed into magnanimous affirmation.

FURTHER READING

Bibliography

Freccero, John. "Selected Bibliography." In *Dante: A Collection of Critical Essays,* pp. 181-82. Englewood Cliffs: Prentice-Hall, Inc., 1965.
  Bibliography follows final chapter.

Criticism

Abrams, Richard. "Illicit Pleasures: Dante among the Sensualists (*Purgatorio* XXVI)." *Modern Language Notes* 100, No. 1 (January 1985): 1-41.

Argues that the method of the *Comedy* is a sort of dance of veils, seducing the reader to aspire to the beyond.

Ahern, John. "Dante's Slyness: The Unnamed Sin of the Eighth Bolgia." *Romanic Review* LXXIII, No. 3 (May 1982): 275-91.

Calls the sin of slyness *"astutia"* rather than "Fraudulent Counsel," as it has been translated, and explores the *Divine Comedy* in light of this new reading.

Baranski, Zygmunt G. "Re-viewing Dante." *Romance Philology* XLII, No. 1 (August 1988): 51-76.

Surveys a dozen books on Dante published outside North America from 1982-83.

Eliot, T. S. "Dante." In *Selected Essays,* pp. 199-229. Harcourt, Brace and Company, 1950.

Comments on the "polysemous" nature of Dante's poetry, which Eliot contends makes it readable as both allegory and story.

————. "Dante." In *The Sacred Wood,* pp. 159-71. Metheun and Co., Ltd., 1964.

Defends Dante's "philosophical" poetry and its treatment of emotions against the charge of French poet Paul Valery that poetry should stir an emotional "state."

Ferrante, Joan. *The Political Vision of the Divine Comedy.* Princeton: Princeton University Press, 1984, 392 pp.

Delineates Dante's views on the separation of church and state. Chapter topics include: Hell as the "Corrupt Society"; Purgatory as "Society in Transition"; and Paradise as the "Ideal Society."

Franke, William. "Dante's Address to the Reader and its Ontological Significance." *Modern Language Notes* CIX, No. 1 (January 1989): 117-27.

Investigates Erich Auerbach's premise that Dante's addresses to the reader invite a "new relationship" between the author and audience while creating an overarching structure in the poem.

Freccero, John, ed. *Dante: A Collection of Critical Essays.* Englewood Cliffs: Prentice-Hall, Inc., 1965, 182 p.

Collection of fourteen essays by noted Dantists examining the author's works from a variety of perspectives.

Freccero, John. "Infernal Irony: The Gates of Hell." *Modern Language Notes* IC, No. 4 (September 1984): 769-86.

Examines the mimetic "visions" of the *Comedy,* according to Pauline and Augustinian definitions.

Hollander, Robert. "Tragedy in Dante's *Comedy.*" *The Sewanee Review* XCI, No. 2 (Spring 1983): 240-60.

Explains Dante's use of both high and low aspects of poetry in the *Divine Comedy.*

Shapiro, Marianne. "On the Role of Rhetoric in the *Convivio.*" *Romance Philology* XL, No. 1 (August 1986): 38-64.

The first article to examine the *Convivio* without comparison to other works of Dante. Endeavors to reveal how Dante regarded rhetoric, as a science and heuristic for poetry.

Additional coverage of Dante's life and career is contained in the following sources published by Gale Research: *Classical and Medieval Literature Criticism,* **Vols. 3, 18;** *DISCovering Authors: British***;** *DISCovering Authors: Canadian***;** *DISCovering Authors: Most-studied Authors Module***;** *DISCovering Authors: Poets Module***; and** *World Literature Criticism Supplement.*

Odysseus Elytis
1911-1996

(Also transliterated as Elýtis; born Alepoudelis, also transliterated as Alepoudhélis) Greek poet, essayist, and critic.

INTRODUCTION

An internationally acclaimed poet considered among the foremost Greek literary figures of the twentieth century, Elytis celebrated the splendors of nature while affirming humanity's ability to embrace hope over despair. Combining his interest in surrealism with lyrical evocations of Greek landscape, history, and culture, Elytis created poems that exalt the virtues of sensuality, innocence, and imagination while striving to reconcile these attributes with life's tragic aspects. Through his rejection of rationalism, Elytis suggested that truth resides in mystery, and he endeavored to establish parallels between the physical and spiritual worlds by blending elements of mythology, pantheism, anthropomorphism, and Christianity. A recipient of the 1979 Nobel Prize in literature, Elytis was cited by the Swedish Academy for writing "poetry which, against the background of Greek tradition, depicts with sensuous strength and intellectual clearsightedness modern man's struggle for freedom and creativity."

Biographical Information

The youngest of six children, Elytis was born in Iráklion, Crete, to a wealthy industrialist and his wife. He attended primary and secondary schools in Athens before enrolling at the University of Athens School of Law. As a youth, Elytis spent his summer vacations on the Aegean Islands, absorbing the seaside atmosphere that deeply informs the imagery of his verse. Also essential to Elytis's poetic development was his attraction to surrealism, which he developed during the late 1920s through the works of French poet Paul Éluard. In 1935, after leaving law school, Elytis displayed several visual collages at the First International Surrealist Exhibition in Athens and began publishing poems in various Greek periodicals.

During the fascist invasion of Greece in 1940 and 1941, Elytis served on the Albanian front as a second lieutenant in Greece's First Army Corps. The heroism he witnessed amid the tragedy and suffering of combat is reflected in his long poem *Azma iroikó ke pénthimo yia ton haméno anthipologhaghó tis Alvanías* (*Heroic and Elegiac Song for the Lost Second Lieutenant of the Albanian Campaign*). Following the publication of *Heroic and Elegiac Song,* Elytis ceased producing poetry for more than a decade, immersing himself in civic and cultural affairs. From 1948 to 1953, during the civil strife in Greece, Elytis lived in Paris, where he studied at the Sorbonne and wrote

articles in French for *Verve* magazine. After returning to Greece, Elytis published *To áxion estí* (*The Axion Esti*), which received both the National Poetry Prize and the National Book Award in 1960. Elytis died following a heart attack on March 18, 1996, in Athens.

Major Works

Elytis's early poems are light and sensual. His first collection of verse, *Prosanatolizmi* (*Orientations*), which focuses on the beauty of the Aegean landscape, emphasizes the significance of erotic forces in the progression of natural and human events. These poems also display Elytis's affinity for such surrealistic devices as the portrayal of supernatural occurrences, exploration of the unconscious, and personification of abstract ideas and natural phenomena. His poems became more erotic with each collection. *Ilios protos* (*Sun the First Together with Variations on a Sunbeam*) was interpreted by Andonis Decavalles as a catalog of "the seven stages in a girl's erotic experience and growth." *Sun the First* also touches on suffering and the need to transcend it, a theme that frequently reappears in later works. The long poem *Heroic and Elegiac Song* centers on the death of a young Greek soldier whose transfiguration and resurrection serves as an affirmation of justice and liberty. The poem advances Elytis's concerns with the merging of physical and spiritual existence and pays tribute to those individuals who resist oppression and defend freedom.

Elytis's later poems, which are often elaborately structured, combine the idyllic innocence and beauty of his early works with the painfully achieved wisdom of *Heroic and Elegiac Song*. In these later poems, Elytis examines the triumph of hope over despair, the union of spirit and flesh, and the richness of Greek culture and tradition. *The Axion Esti,* which is perhaps Elytis's best known work, is an intricately structured cycle alternating prose and verse. Indebted for much of its tone, language, symbolism, and structure to the liturgy of the Greek Orthodox Church, *The Axion Esti* combines Christian elements and Grecian culture in an effort to reconcile life's dichotomies. *Maria Neféli (Maria Nephele)*, another significant work in Elytis's canon, consists of a series of antiphonal passages between a liberated woman, who functions as a symbol of the individual in contemporary society, and an intelligent and mature poetic persona. This work further illuminates Elytis's preoccupation with humanity's ability to attain harmony amid the chaos of the modern world.

Critical Reception

Criticism of Elytis's poetry, though sparse, has for the most part been laudatory. Much of it centers on analysis and interpretation, which has proved challenging since his poetry varies significantly from one collection to the next in terms of theme, language, structure, and style. Several critics have attempted to place Elytis within a more established poetic tradition, comparing his works to that of such poets as Walt Whitman, Dylan Thomas, and William Blake. As Decavalles noted "We cannot afford not to think of Blake, his innocence, his experience and his eventual marriage of heaven and hell. Elytis's progress has been identical, even to the point of his turning himself into the prophet of a new Paradise." Even so, Elytis is decidedly a Greek poet as Greece "for which he had always felt the most soul-stirring devotion, an almost sensual yearning for physical possession," according to Vincenzo Rotolo, is the most predominant feature of his poetry. It is the common thread that binds his early and more recent poetic works and distinguishes Elytis from other great poets.

PRINCIPAL WORKS

Poetry

Prosanatolizmi [*Orientations*] 1936
Ilios o protos, mazi me tis parallayies pano se mian ahtidha [*Sun the First Together with Variations on a Sunbeam*] 1943

Asma iroikó ke pénthimo yia ton haméno anthipologh-aghó tis Alvanías [*Heroic and Elegiac Song for the Lost Second Lieutenant of the Albanian Campaign*] 1945
I kalosíni stis likoporiés [*Kindness in the Wolfpasses*] 1946
To áxion estí [*The Axion Esti*] 1959
Éxi ke miá típsis yia ton ourano [*Six and One Regrets for the Sky*] 1960
To fotódhendro ke i dhekáti tetárti omorfiá [*The Light Tree and the Fourteenth Beauty*] 1971
O ílios o iliátores [*The Sovereign Sun: Selected Poems*] 1971
To Monograma [*The Monogram*] 1971
Thánatos ke anástasis tou Konstandínou Paleológhou [*Death and Resurrection of Constantine Paleologhos*] 1971
Ta ro tou erota [*The Ro of Eros*] 1972
O fillomandis [*The Leaf Diviner*] 1973
Ta eterothali [*The Stepchildren*] 1974
Maria Neféli: Skiniko piima [*Maria Nephele*] 1978
Tria piimata me simea evkerias [*Three Poems Under a Flag of Convenience*] 1982
Imeroloyio enos atheatou Apriliou [*Diary of an Invisible April*] 1984
O mikros naftilos [*The Little Mariner*] 1985
Krinagoras 1987
Ta elegía tis Oxópetras [*The Elegies of Jutting Rock*] 1991

Other Major Works

Ho Zographos Theophilos [*The Painter Theophilos*] (criticism) 1973
Anihta hartia [*The Open Book*] (essays) 1974
I mayia tou papadiamandhi [*The Magic of Papadiamantis*] (essays) 1978
Anafora ston Andrea Embiriko [*Report to Andreas Embirikos*] (prose) 1980
To Domatio me tis ikones [*The Room of Images*] (notebooks) 1986
Ta Dimosia ke ta idiotika [*Public and Private Matters*] (prose) 1990
I idiotiki odos [*Private Way*] (prose) 1990
En lefko [*In White*] (prose) 1992

CRITICISM

Hans Rudolph Hilty (essay date 1960)

SOURCE: "Odysseus Elytis: A Contemporary Greek Poet," in *Nette Zürcher Zeitung,* July 17, 1960, pp. 59-63.

[*In the excerpt below (an article especially liked by Elytis himself), Hilty explores Elytis's relationship to French surrealists and its impact on his use of traditional Greek themes and images in his poetry.*]

Elytis (born Odysseás Alepoudhélis) is descended from an old family native to Lesbos and was born in 1911 in Iráklion, Crete—where, by the way, Kazantzakis also first saw the light of day (1883). He grew up in Athens and began studying law in 1930, but soon felt himself drawn more to writing and to art. He was particularly captivated by the expressive world of the French surrealists. He translated Lautréamont, Éluard, Jouve and Lorca into modern Greek, wrote studies on modern art, traveled, then settled for a time in Paris in 1948; and without this expedition into the wide-open spaces, without the element of an open and expanding intellectual curiosity, his poetry would be inconceivable. His roots in the singular nature of his homeland remained strong, however, as was demonstrated during the war, when, following his return from the front, he became a poet of the Greek Resistance through his works *Heroic and Elegiac Song for the Lost Second Lieutenant of the Albanian Campaign* and the **"Albaniad,"** both of which could only be circulated by hand in manuscript form until the end of the Occupation. Those roots are no less evident in the general mood and tone of all his poems, which evoke the atmosphere of the Aegean landscape with passionate power. The broad perspective of an open mind and a vital, concrete bond with the archetypal gestures of life, magical surrealism and unbroken Hellenic substance merge in this poetry to form painfully illuminating images of Mediterranean existence.

Take, for example, the poem **"Body of Summer,"** which gave the German collection its title:

A long time has passed since the last rainfall was
  heard
Above the ants and the lizards
Now the sky burns endlessly
The fruit trees paint their mouths
The pores of the earth very slowly open
And beside the trickling and syllabic waters
A huge plant stares straight into the sun.

Who is this who sprawls on the far beaches
Stretched on his back, smoking the smokesilver
  olive leaves
Crickets warm themselves in his ears
Ants scurry to work on his chest
Lizards glide in the long grasses of his armpits
And through the seaweed of his feet a wave lightly
  passes
Sent by that small siren who sang:

"O naked body of summer, burnt
And eaten away by oil and salt
Body of rock and the heart's tremor
Great fluttering in the willow's hair
Breath of basil on the curly groin
Filled with starlets and pine needles
Profound body, vessel of day!"

The slow rains come, the pelting hail,
The shores pass by, flogged by the claws of the
  wintry wind

That with savage billows lowers in the sea-depths
The hills plunge into thick udders of clouds
But behind all this you smile unconcernedly
And find again your deathless hour
As once more you are found on the beaches by the
  sun
And amid your naked vigor by the sky.

The landscape is perceived by the poet as archaically harsh and glaring—considering Elytis's birthplace, one is tempted to say "Cretan"—and man does not appear here as lord of creation, as the measure of all things. Human "Morphé," human form is, to be sure, assumed by the forces of the landscape and of time: the summer, the earth, youth, memory. But man, for his part, is scarcely anything other than a lens, in which the burning force of the landscape and of time is refracted—a reflection, and perhaps a deceptive one. It becomes apparent that whenever Elytis introduces man into the landscape, he almost always resorts to questioning inversions:

What can you face and what can you wear
Dressed in the music of grass and how do you
  proceed
Amid the sage and the heather . . .
On your lips there is a taste of storm—But where
  have you wandered
All day long with the hard reverie of stone and
  sea . . .

The age of the sea within your eyes
And on your body the sun's vigor—what was I
  looking for
Deep within sea-caverns amid spacious dreams . . .

In the unquestionable process of landscape and time, man is a disruptive, painful question—there is the Act, in which man can participate directly in the unquestionableness of nature:

It was April, I remember, when I felt for the first
  time your human weight
Your human body of clay and corruption
As on our first day on earth
It was the festival of the amaryllis . . .

To be sure, Elytis never speaks of love in the present, but rather always in the form of memory. Memory, however, can incorporate not only things past but also things future; every utterance about paradise lost engenders the hope for a paradise to be regained. "Echo" is both a favorite word and a key word in Elytis's poems. Sky and sea, sea and land, landscape and man, man and woman, and also the ecstasies of time—past, present and future—stand opposite one another in an echo-relationship: the one the echo and reflection of the other. The oeuvre of this Greek poet is a canon of such echoes and reflections. Hence, the singularity of his images: they are never pale, always colorful, vivacious; but as soon as they begin to coalesce into something tangible, they flicker out again. It is in this flickering realm that Elytis finds his most beautiful poetic signatures: "earth of Boeotia brightened by the wind," "dressed in the music of grass," "dust of maiden dreams," "a clover of light on your breast."

In the poetry of Lorca, of Ungaretti, of Quasimodo and of Montale, and in recent Hebrew poetry from Israel, there can be found related poetic emanations of Mediterranean life. Precisely such a juxtaposition of thematically similar literary phenomena, however, serves to clarify and delineate the Greek's highly individual poetic profile: it is more expansive and inclusive, with longer lines and multi-layered images. A characteristic feature of the Greek language is that, even in the hands of modern Greek poets, it has preserved a secret affinity to the epic narrative; something of the flow of Homeric verse, something beyond any kind of classicism, is discernible in Cavafis and Elytis.

The most exact parallels to Elytis's poetic images are found, not in the work of other lyric poets, but rather in the essays of Albert Camus. In "Noces" ("Nuptials") there are sentences which sound like rational prose paraphrasings of verses by Elytis:

> Here, I leave order and moderation to others. The great free love of nature and the sea absorbs me completely. In this marriage of ruins and springtime, the ruins have become stones again, and losing the polish imposed on them by man, they have reverted to nature. To celebrate the return of her prodigal daughters Nature has laid out a profusion of flowers . . . How many hours have I spent crushing absinthe leaves, caressing ruins, trying to match my breathing with the world's tumultuous sighs! Deep among wild scents and concerts of somnolent insects, I open my eyes and heart to the unbearable grandeur of this heat-soaked sky. It is not easy to become what one is . . .

It would be idle to ask whether Elytis and Camus knew each other or not. What is involved here is by no means anything such as literary "inheritance" or "adaptation," but rather a correspondence between the world experience of two poets of identical age in the midst of the selfsame Mediterranean landscape. For Elytis, the concept "echo" is the key; Camus uses "marriage" in the same sense: "marriage of ruins and springtime," "marriage of light." And where Camus discerns beneath the unbearable vastness of the gleaming sky the summons "to become what one is," Elytis says the following, taken from his poem **"Laconic"**:

> Ardor for death so inflamed me that my radiance
>   returned to the sun,
> And it sends me back into the perfect syntax of
>   stone and air.
> Well then, he whom I sought *I am.*

Here some mention of myth must be made. Ancient Greek history is certainly present on occasion in Elytis's poetry. In the poem **"Shape of Boeotia"** he asks about the fate of Thebes:

> What has become of the orchestra of nude hands
>   below the palaces

> The mercy that rose like the smoke of holiness
> Where are the gates with archaic birds that sang
> And the clang of metal that daybroke the terror of
>   the people
> When the sun entered like a triumph
> When fate writhed on the lance of the heart
> And the civil strife of birdsong raged
> What has become of the immortal March libations
> Of Greek traceries on the watery grass

> Brows and elbows were wounded
> Time from too much sky rolled crimson
> Men advanced
> Laden with lament and dream.

But the poet avoids the names of the Greek myths, and he avoids above all throughout his oeuvre the names of Greek gods and heroes. It would therefore be an unjustified Hellenization if, for example, in the verses just cited, one were to replace "the sun" with "Helios." There is no mythology in Elytis's poetry, but this does not mean that for him there are no gods. Turning to Camus once again, we find on the page following the passage previously quoted, this commentary:

> Those who need myths are indeed poor. Here the gods serve as beds or resting places as the day races across the sky. I describe and say: "This is red, this blue, this green. This is the sea, the mountain, the flowers." Need I mention Dionysus to say that I love to crush mastic bulbs under my nose?

Only in one selection from the volume *Körper des Sommers,* namely, the poem **"The Sleep of the Valiant (Variation),"** are there classical Greek concepts which have remained untranslated: the three concepts "Hades," "kairos" and "arete." These have proven untranslatable, and it is precisely in this poem—which, like Elytis's magnificent Resistance poems, stems from the theme of Greece's struggle for freedom—that an allusion to the Greek national spirit seems justified. In the poem, arete takes on human form:

> One drop of clear water, hanging courageously over
>   the abyss, they named Arete, and gave her a
>   lean, boyish body.

> All day now young Arete descends and labors hard
>   in those places where the earth was rotting out
>   of ignorance, and where men inexplicably had
>   committed their dark iniquities.

This Arete is no classical goddess of valor in the heroic mold, but rather a little girl with a slender, boyish body who labors the whole day through at what has been neglected. Similarly, Jean Anouilh's Antigone in the play of the same name is no heroine of tragic grandeur, but instead a stubborn young girl, "the skinny little thing sitting back over there and saying nothing"; but she alone will defy Creon. The parallel is exact. Anouilh's Antigone is to Sophocles's heroine as Elytis's Arete is to the Arete or Virtus of classical antiquity.

The fact that this transformation has taken place in the work of a Greek poet, writing in Greek and on Greek soil, in precisely the same fashion as in the work of a French playwright is interesting enough. In regard to Elytis's entire accomplishment, the image of this "little Arete" attests anew to the fact that Hellenic substance lives on in modern Greek literature with a vitality which increases in direct proportion to the decisive subjugation of classicism. In the process of this transformation, the regenerative power of life becomes apparent in the transformation of language and in the transformation of human ideals—and in the capacity for creative communication. Understood in these terms, Odysseus Elytis can rightfully be considered the most representative poet of present-day Greece. And understood in these terms, the oft-repeated twaddle contrasting "tradition and modernity" collapses as soon as we come upon a genuine work of art.

Andonis Decavalles (essay date 1975)

SOURCE: "Eros: His Power, Forms and Transformations in the Poetry of Odysseus Elytis," in *Odysseus Elytis: Analogies of Light,* edited by Ivar Ivask, University of Oklahoma Press, 1975, pp. 45-58.

[*Below, Decavalles explores one of Elytis's principle themes, the "progressive story of Eros's nature . . . his external and internal discoveries in the process of building a world at once natural, human esthetic, earthly and universal, timely and timeless, finite and infinite, mortal yet immortal."*]

I have conceived my figure between a sea that comes to view right behind the whitewashed little wall of a chapel and a barefoot girl with the wind lifting her dress, a chance moment I struggle to capture, and I waylay it with Greek words.

If I spoke at the beginning about a girl and a chapel, at the risk of sounding less than serious, I had my reasons. I would have liked to draw that girl into the chapel and make her my own, not to scandalize anyone, but to confess that the eros is one, and also to make more dense the poem I wish to make out of the days of my life.

I would then see pomegranate branches sprouting from the iconostasis, and the wind singing at the little window together with the sea-wave, when the South Wind, blowing stronger, would help that wave jump over the stone parapet. Once, such a parapet touched my naked body, and I felt my innards purified, as if the lime, with its disinfectant qualities, had passed through all the folds of my heart. This is why I was never afraid of the wild look of the Saints, like anybody who ever reached the inapproachable: I knew that I was just enough to decode the Laws of my imaginary republic and to reveal that that was the seat of innocence. Do not take this as arrogance. I do not speak about myself. I speak for anyone who feels like myself but does not have enough naïveté to confess it.

If there is, I think, for each one of us a different, a personal Paradise, mine should irreparably be inhabited by trees of words that the wind dresses in silver, like poplars, by men who see the rights of which they have been deprived returning to them, and by birds that even in the midst of the truth of death insist on singing in Greek and on saying "eros, eros, eros!"

(*Open Book*)

To speak of Eros in Elytis's poetry, Eros in the fullness of his meaning, is tantamount to excluding very little. Elytis the poet has been above all Elytis the lover of the beauty in his "girls" and in nature, particularly that Aegean world of purity, serenity and love. He has been the lover of life and its poetry, of the tangibles and the intangibles, of earth and its ascent to the sky, and has ultimately been forced to become the passionate defender of them all. Eros has been the force that has driven both his life and pen, the earthly yet transcending power that has aspired to accomplishing the happy marriage of earth and heaven. We cannot afford not to think of Blake, his innocence, his experience and his eventual marriage of heaven and hell. Elytis's progress has been identical, even to the point of his turning himself into the prophet of a new Paradise. Their differences lie, of course, in their different times and worlds. In the place of Blake's northern New Jerusalem there is Elytis's sun-drenched Aegean, the day and its light, the summer and its noon and a youth that never ends. Much like Blake, Elytis shaped his own personal myth. Onto his pagan and Christian inheritances, the coexistent and inseparable products of the same racial genius, the same frame of mind, he put his own creative stamp. With the exception of the all-ruling sun, his divinities have stayed nameless in an animistic world. They are the natural and the inner forces that once gave birth to ancient myth.

The passage quoted above, a retrospective self-portrait, contains almost the entire essence of Elytis. Commenting and expanding on its parts, we could give a picture of the whole; for Elytis, like most significant poets and creators, has had one basic story to tell, the progressive story of Eros's nature, his longings, his advancement and conquests and his external and internal discoveries in the process of building a world at once natural, human, esthetic, earthly and universal, timely and timeless, finite and infinite, mortal yet immortal. The taking of that girl into that whitewashed chapel by the sea brings together the pagan and the Christian worlds in the purity of the erotic act, with Dionysian pomegranates of fertility and ecstasy sprouting from the iconostasis. It is this purity which counts, the sacredness of Eros, the transformation of what was wrongly deemed sin into virtue, Arete, and the concomitant raising of the earth to the heights of the sky or heaven (the Greek *ouranós* means both). In the process the poet-lover is not frightened by the wild-looking, ossified faces of the saints. Those faces, after all, have in them the familiarity of the barren and rocky Greek soil.

Our gothic century has not ingratiated us with beauty. Beauty has long been out of fashion and respect, much as has been goodness, the other half of that blessed ancient couple, *kalón* and *agathón.* We have long abided with the anguished Baudelairean version of beauty, and it is certainly a solace to witness in Elytis a rejuvenation of that old pair under the cascading light of a sovereign sun, to rediscover an Eros of beauty in both matter and spirit, in both body and soul. A declared Platonist, Elytis, in his own manner, has stood faithfully by Diotima's words, yet with a slight but significant difference. If, for the somewhat dualistic Diotima, the beauty of the body was there to lead the way to the beauty of the soul, the same is true for Elytis; but the body is not left behind. The two types of beauty exist as one.

Who have been the lovers in Elytis, his erotic males and females? The dominant lover has certainly been the poet himself, representing as well all the honest lovers of his kind, the human and the elemental. His universal alter ego has been the sun, a sun that stood active on both sides of Plato's divided line. And how else could it be in a world primarily visual, one of images, of parallels embracing in a constant fruitional and fructifying exchange? As for his beloved ones, we have mentioned the "girls"—for the most part anonymous, archetypal, occasionally called Myrto (for the myrtle and its sexual connotation in one of Archilochus's fragments), or Marina for her sea association, or Helen or Eva. Other lovers, alternating with the girls, are the sea, the mother earth, the boats, the pomegranate trees, the islands (Santorini above all), Greece, a "sunray" in "her" variations of colors, "drops of pure water" turning into maids (Arete is one of them), the Virgin Mary as Panayia or Evangelistra (Our Lady of the Annunciation) or the Unfading Rose, and incarnated abstractions such as Hope, Purity, Freedom and the Platonic Ideas.

No short survey could adequately cope with the immense variety of Eros's pervasive presence in Elytis's work. As we enter his world, Eros or "Erotas" greets us from the opening page, as the initial word in the very first of his "First Poems" in the collection *Orientations,* the poem entitled **"Of the Aegean."** Here Eros is framed by the standard elements of his setting:

> Love
> The archipelago
> And the prow of its foam
> And the seagull of its dream
>
>   . . . . .
>
> Love
> Its song
> And the horizons of its voyage
> And the echo of its nostalgia
>
>   . . . . .
>
> Love
> Its ship
> And the freedom from care of its etesian winds
> And the jib of its hope
>
>   . . . . .
>
>   (*The Sovereign Sun*)

The only sorrow that at times reaches this early, erotic world of Elytis, the only "cloud" of darkness upon it, is the absence of the beloved, as in the "Climate of Absence," with its "knot of sorrow" and the torment of memory. But even here "hope" is always present to disperse the sadness with happiness and fulfillment.

Widely known and very popular among Elytis's earliest poems has been the epigrammatic, Platonic quatrain in which the girl grows as an incarnation of Ideas: "Prior to my eyes you were the light / Prior to Eros you were Eros himself / And when the kiss took you / You became Woman." The same motif is repeated in the **"Windows to the Fifth Season,"** wherein the poet says of the girl, "How beautiful she is! She has taken on the form of that thought which feels her when she feels it devoted to her." As for the power of the erotic embrace: "Two arms are waiting. An entire earth supports itself on their elbows. An entire poetry on their expectation." And then, as if in sympathetic magic, nature is creatively affected by the girl's beauty: "In the touch of your palms the fruit will repose that hovers now without purpose. In the translucent abutment of your body's stature, trees will find the long-lived fulfillment of their whispered isolation. In your first freedom from care herbs will multiply like hopes. Your presence will cool the dew." As for Eros himself, the creator, he too has to be given form: "And when the sky runs under the bridges of our woven hands . . . we shall create the form of love lacking from these visions / It is then we shall / To the ritual of difficult dreams a sure restoration." In the later works *The Axion Esti* and the *Six and One Remorses for the Sky* the dreams will be restored to "take their revenge upon reality."

Eros aspires to rise, to ascend to sky/heaven—a transcendence which finds its earliest fullest, most traditional, most Platonic-Dantesque version in the early **"Orion,"** one of Elytis's very few night poems. Let us notice, by the way, that in contrast to most love poets Elytis is a daytime, noontime lover. In **"Orion"** the world comes to terms with bitterness as night falls and is liberated from noise and worry. "Our head is in the hands of God." A prayer transforms the heights, we become "the descendants of the perishable tears," we leave behind us our earthly skin, and "our foreheads neighbor the stars." A shower of light dresses every notion in the air, which brings our "hope" closer to serenity. Our souls advance to their meeting with heaven. The pure moment shines. Within us "silence is dissolved," and memory rolls into "an uninhabited chaos, when we granted ourselves to an unbelievable shore, a shore of light shades, once dreamed of through tears . . . We detached ourselves from our weight as we detached ourselves from sin." Our new dream "palpitates pure. An invisible hand pulls our own to where Calm becomes an innocent heaven where the soul masters itself unchangeable."

Furtively present in several of Elytis's early love poems is a sense of sin, sin which is to be purified. As if to cancel the quasi-metaphysical, traditionally spiritual ascent in **"Orion,"** the poet in his **"Anniversary"** poem posits an earthly, a marine paradise within human, earthly access "Where a man may go / Who is nothing else but a man."

The poet himself brought his life "To this spot that struggles / Always near the sea / Youth on rocks, breast / To breast against the wind" to grow there from childhood to manhood and to learn from the elements, where "A few years, a few waves" are a "Sensitive rowing / In the bays surrounding love." It should be noticed that here as well as in several other instances, youth and erotic growth, erotic adolescence and its earthly teleology involve a sea-journey, on which the poetlover, "a stone pledge to the watery element," sails "Further off than the islands / Lower than the waves," where "hope is resplendent with all its dolphins / The sun's gain in a human heart" and where the eyes can certainly uphold "infinity."

In its concern for the heights and depths in the erotic sea-journey of exploration and discovery, **"The Clepsydras of the Unknown"** prophesies a union of opposites, a constant, insistent Heraclitean/neo-Platonic expectation: "A day will come when the cork will imitate the anchor / and will steal the taste of the deep / A day will come when their double self will be united." In moments of quandary the poet painfully wonders what might be the key of that "other gate," the gate to that "other world." Is it Eros? Life is certainly measured with pulses, joy and "desperate gesticulations." Toil is needed. Youth passes, despair prevails, but there also comes the promise of sunrise to discard darkness. Merry lips kiss girls, a boat sets sail full of songs, and there are "marble mansions of naked women / Each one of them was once a drop of water / Each one now is light." Swarms of erotic visions follow: "Earth is simple and leading / Layers of kindness, one by one, like florins cut in the sun / in the lips, in the teeth, one by one, the sins / Of life are peeled into goods." Noon brings callings of purity; the poet is ready "to go out to the white gates of noon, to ring with voices the blue bells of resurrection / And all the cold islands will set their hair afire and promenade / With innocent flames and pebbles the erotic open seas." The day, then, whose "nocturnal past" is "purified" by the dawn, comes into its full glory. "Darkness owes me light," the poet exclaims, contemplating the "Blond day, reward of the sun and of eros." Twenty-one short subsequent pieces, under the title "Serenities," are "earthly fragments of happiness," poems of love, of admiration and praise of girls and nature in their mutual exchange and fruition that render Death "useless."

In contrast to the Apollonian clarity and equanimity of **"Anniversary"** and **"The Clepsydras,"** the orgiastic **"Dionysus"** brings a high sensualism, lust, inebriation and frenzy, and teems with monsters and wild beasts. This is one of Elytis's richest pieces, one of Asiatic splendor, with its "swift schooners of desire," with the expectations of "eternity' in sight, with women that "beautify clarity," with rainbows sailing through crystal skies and sending amber boats down to earth.

In the longish **"Concert of the Hyacinths"** we overhear the intimate whisperings, the complaints and admonitions, of a lover to his beloved. He is her initiator into the world of Eros and its mysteries. This and other early poems by Elytis bring to mind the "carpe diem" tradition, yet without the traditional simplicity that reached its highest sophistication in John Donne. The lover's complaint here concerns his beloved's dangerous playfulness, her high airs, her irresponsibility, her remoteness and her disregard of the value and depth of his feelings and of her own power. "You leave and disappear, conquering your presence, creating a divine solitude, a turbulent and incomprehensible happiness . . . I did nothing else but what I found and imitated in You!" He proclaims her "the only reality," but hastens to add, "When you leave those who are assimilated within nonexistence and offer yourself again as a mortal woman, I awaken in your transformation from the beginning . . . Do not play any longer. Cast the ace of fire. Break open the human geography."

Sun the First came out in 1943, during the time of the Nazi Occupation of Greece, when the war experience was already past. Might we assume that the poems in this book were conceived in an earlier day? Or were they a reaction to darkness with recollected light? War does not appear in them, nor does its ugly immediate aftermath; but there is, to some extent, a maturity born of the Greek war experience, an awareness of suffering in life and of the need to transcend that suffering. Eros in these poems widens his embrace beyond the Aegean innocence to reach a world less private. The cure for evil lies in the recollection of that bright Aegean sun. As if in retrospect, the poet says:

> I spoke of love, of the rose's health, the sunray
> That alone finds the heart straightway
> Of Greece that walks the sea with surety
> Of Greece that takes me on voyages always
> To naked snow-glorious mountains
>
> I give my hand to justice
> Translucent fountain, spring on the mountain
>   summit
> My sky is deep and unchanging
> Whatever I love is born unceasingly
> Whatever I love is always at its beginning.

> (*The Sovereign Sun*)

Wasn't Ezra Pound, too, to exclaim in Pisa, "What thou lovest well remains"? Justice and heroic Greece herself now enter the gallery of Elytis's loved ones. The closer familiarity with suffering and pain, even death, evokes a greater effort from Eros. "Pain rounds the good cape / No voice gets lost in the bays of the sky."

In an art that had achieved a better mastery of its means through compact simplicity and meaningful selectivity, the poems in *Sun the First* reproduce in a more sculpturesque manner the quintessence of the Aegean world found in *Orientations*. The love of a girl and of nature brings the poet to enter the surrounding procreative processes more deeply. He becomes another element, a driving force, to fructify and aid the world creatively, to help it achieve its physical and supernal function, its destination and rebirth. Negatives are turned into positives ("I know the night no longer that is a night only"), and inimical elements are now viewed as contributory to that creation in which Eros is the primum mobile. Yeats's "Adam's Curse" comes to mind as we read the concluding poem of this group: "With what stone, what blood, what iron / What fire we are made." We poets, says Elytis, may be called idealists, woolgatherers or visionaries when "our arms open under an all-white Idea" which we entreat but which "never descends." However, "the desire's vision wakes up in flesh one day / And where, before, a naked wilderness shone / A City is now laughing, as beautiful as you wanted it." This initial plea for the poet-creator was eventually to develop into a passionate self-defense in Elytis's later poetry.

Closer to his erotic theme and very ingeniously conceived is the seven-poem sequel to *Sun the First* entitled *Variations on a Sunbeam* The *Variations* are the colors of the spectrum, slightly shuffled in their order and increased in number from six to seven—Elytis's ever-present mystical number (there are seven heavens in Greek tradition)—to serve his symbolism. The colors of the sunray, we easily realize, are the seven stages of the day from dawn to evening; but they are also the seven stages in a girl's erotic experience and growth, from the birth of Eros in her virginal girlhood to his decline at the end of her youth. The "red" is for her lips: "Your mouth speaks with four hundred roses / Beats the trees, raptures all the earth / Pours into her body the first shuddering." The "green" represents physical greenness or immaturity, "the girl who has not yet entered eros fully / But keeps in her apron an acrid grove of fruit"; the lover tells her: "My girl / I have an untouched grass in my heart / A rain of newborn trefoil / And a cascade that has not yet pounced / It lies deeper, lower, it will pounce / Like a wild beast of day upon your April." The "yellow" is that of the day as it approaches fullness, of girls with uncovered breasts that "Go and blow gibbets of fire with trumpets in the threshing floors / Burn hay, melt gold coins . . ." We reach the climax when the girl, inebriated by the sun, consents to be called the "Orange Girl" and is surrounded by the "seven heavens glittering" and by crystals and swallows. Her inebriation seizes the vine, the heron and the whole world, all of them whispering her secret name further and further. She is now told that "No one knows you as the kiss does." Through the "light blue" color of her eyes the poet contemplates the sky, the stars and Hope, in an ascent to the heights; and the "deep blue," being the color of infinity, indicates the depths revealed. The wind acquires deep-blue lips, the girl's glance grows endless, the blue of the sea becomes a revealing light, and the poet sees "a deep-colored bird drunk with the riddle of her embrace." The cycle closes with a Baudelairean "violet," the mournful color of the evening and of death.

One would not expect the erotic element to have a major part in the *Heroic and Elegiac Song for the Lost Second Lieutenant of the Albanian Campaign* (1945). The theme here is the acquaintance with, the knowledge, conquest and transcendence of death. The brilliant Aegean is for the hero a world now lost but affectionately recollected, a solace in the midst of suffering. The hero was indeed a lover once: "Love was so huge within him," and "In the arms of bitter-orange girls at night / He would soil the large garments of the stars." Yet even the hero's ascent to heaven in part XII has an erotic touch in an idealistic, solemn sense. Eros again enhances the ascent: "With a morning stride on the growing grass / He ascends alone and blazing with light . . . / Flower tomboys wave to him secretly / And speak to him in high voices that turn to mist on the air / Even the trees bend toward him lovingly"; and the crystal bells tolling in part XIII "tell of him who burned in life / . . . / who was not given time to weep / For his deep longing for the Love of life." The last part, a Gloria, with a vision of Liberty shining in the firmament, transforms the erotic aspect: "Rainbow-beaten shores fall into the water / Ships with open sails voyage on the meadows / The most innocent girls / Run naked in men's eyes / . . . / He is continually ascending; / Around him those passions glow that once / Were lost in the solitude of sin." The Liberty that the hero's sacrifice accomplishes brings a purification of passions, along with a resurrection and a life reborn.

It took several years of silence, meditation and study for that rebirth to find its elements and form. A poetic "genesis" was needed, however, if that life was to rise from darkness into life again, a recollection, an introspection, a sense that the restoration of things lost would be worth our effort, our love and our praise, worth our life. This restoration required a deeper awareness of all that was involved. Eros, above all else, was again the Demiurge, and *The Axion Esti* (1959) is, in fact, an account of Eros's doings: his shaping the world anew; his battle with hatred, enmity, misunderstanding and their darkness; his victory, justification and praise. Like the biblical God, the poet-lover is the vocal shaper of the Aegean universe as a world without and a world within, physical and spiritual, a microcosm that is a macrocosm, "THIS WORLD / this small world the great!" Platonically, the poet is "still tied to heaven." He identifies himself as "the One I really was, the One of many centuries ago / the One still verdant in the midst of fire" (we get here a triple reference: to Plotinus, to the burning bush in which God appeared to Moses on Mt. Sinai, and of course to Greece's eternal youth despite her age), and he creates in obedience to the sun, whose axis is in him and whose voice, like Fate above the poet's crib, comes "like memory become the present," like Hesiod's and Plato's Mnemosyne. The world to be created is "written" in the poet's entrails and thus takes form as a self-projection. And since creation is a battle against chaos in which one is to use "his own weapons," the poet's weapons at the outset are "Pomegranates or Zephyrs or Kisses."

Light is already present when the earth is created, first as a female, as a woman's naked body shaped in an erotic embrace: "the curves gentle / one inside the other / *land masses that made me feel / the smell of earth like understanding.*" The constant exchange in later Elytis, the interfusion of the concrete with the abstract, of the esthetic with the ethical, of the physical with the mental, the deeper common identity of *kalón* and *agathón,* presents us with a moment of joyous exultation as the poet-creator shapes and populates the earth:

There, alone, he placed
> white marble fountains
> mills of wind
> tiny pink cupolas
> and tall perforated dovecotes

Virtue with its four right angles
And since he thought it beautiful for each to be in
another's arms
> the large watering troughs filled with love
> the cattle lowered their heads, gently, calves
> and cows
> as though the world held no temptations
> as though knives were yet unknown

Eros with its purity in an Eden.

The sea is created next and is likewise a female, the equivalent of purity, "innocent and tremulous like a vineyard / deep and unscarred like the sky's other face, / *A drop of soul amidst the clay.*" And in the midst of the sea he plants the islands, "little worlds in [his] image and likeness." The names of the plants and herbs he creates next are "*Secret syllables through which I strove to utter my identity.*" The sun tells him at this point: "Good, . . . you know how to read / and you'll come to learn a great deal / if you study the Insignificant in depth," echoing Blake's "To see a World in a Grain of Sand."

Next the girls are created, shaped in the image of "red jugs lined up on the quay / . . . / Maidens beautiful and naked and smooth like pebbles / with that touch of black in the delta of the thighs / . . . / some upright sounding the Conch / others spelling out in chalk / words strange and enigmatic: / ROES, ESA, ARIMNA / NUS, MIROLTAMITY, YELTIS," anagrams of Eros, Sea, Marina, Sun, Immortality and Elytis—in short, no less than the essentials of the poet's erotic-spiritual paradise.

Wilderness, too, will have to be encountered, conquered, made fertile and thereby transcended: "But first you will see the wilderness and give it your own meaning . . . / The wilderness will precede your heart / and then again the wilderness will follow it." In the process, positives need to be drawn out of negatives: "night after night / *I sought whiteness to the utmost intensity / of blackness, hope to the point of tears / joy to the outer limit of despair.*" Through this ascetic exercise purity is reached, purity that is "the same on the slopes as in your entrails"; and as the sun heats mint, lavender, verbena, his "light threads of silver / falling from the heights" become the "cool hair of a girl I saw and wanted / Tangible woman / 'Purity,' he said, 'is she' / and full of yearning I caressed the body / kisses teeth to teeth; then one inside the other." Eros with Purity, and in that embrace Good and Evil meet at a point reminiscent of Eliot's "still point of the turning world."

Finally, necessity, too, the "other element," the "monstrous Duty" with its "four voids," the concern for the other people, the experience with the "black men," the enemies, would have to be confronted, accepted, understood and transcended by the Sun of Justice that becomes human, becomes the poet himself. "Necessity" is that

which takes us into the second section of *The Axion Esti,* "The Passion"—the poet's and the world's war experience which turned the poet into a fighter and eventually a missionary of his world and message. In darkness and suffering, the soul, taken unawares, is temporarily disoriented, until it discovers the redeeming value of its experience. In his loneliness the poet sings of himself as a single swallow still unable to bring in the difficult spring. There is fighting on the mountains and fighting at sea, where, miraculously, however, "Small craft rounding the cape / suddenly turn over and vanish, / emerge again among the clouds / on the other side of the deep." In this small craft's re-emergence is symbolized the spirit of an entire people, the brave fighters conquering death with death, and of the poet's own spirit in a pattern of death and resurrection so prominent in Elytis. At the center of it all, the poet wonders where he can find his "soul, the four-leaf tear" and appeals to the "Intelligible sun of Justice" (recalling Plato's *Republic?*) not to forget his country.

Several parts of this section of *The Axion Esti* turn into a passionate self-defense by the poet against the charges of the "young Alexandrians":

> "Look," they said, "the naive tourist of the
> century—so insensitive:
> when the rest of us mourn, he rejoices

> · · · · ·

> A man with no friend
> or follower,
> who trusts his body only
> and looks for the great mystery inside the
> sun's thorny leaves, this is he,
> the outcast of the century's marketplaces!

> · · · · ·

> The antichrist and callous satanist of the
> century!"

Possessed of a world view diametrically opposed to the modern existential anguish, Elytis has been attacked by those who have failed to see the depth below his surface, to realize his tragic awareness and the world-redeeming qualities of his Eros and his Purity. As Plato himself believed, one does not cure evil with evil, nor sorrow with sorrow. The noblest remedy is Eros, Love. Recollecting his youth, the poet exclaims:

> Good for you, my first youth and untamed lip,
> You who taught the storm's pebble
> and in the midst of squalls talked back to the
> thunder

> · · · · ·

> I'm clean from end to end.
> and in the hands of Death a useless vessel,
> bad prey in the claws of the brutal.

He laments the loss of that youth, and his voice grows softer and nostalgic in what sounds like a love complaint to God, he tells Him how to His creation he brought "lasting Rose," that quintessence of virginal girlhood and femininity as well, which has always been more human, more intimate and accessible to the Greek Orthodox Christian than the awesome and remote Holy Trinity. Then, in what sounds like a love complaint to God, he tells Him how to His creation he brought his own, as a gift to a gift, but that God's creation, with the element of evil contained in it, destroyed the poet's creation, his pure world of dream.

> I ROUSED the sensual pleasures early,
>
> . . . . .
>
> I flung the darkness on the bed of love
>   with worldly things naked in my mind,
>
> . . . . .
>
> and once again gave birth to the visible.

God's response is a restoration: "You blew and my entrails yearned, / one by one the birds came back to me!" The recovery ushers in a new joy with which the earthliness of the Aegean world rises now to a quasi-metaphysical level, from mortality to deification, where the poet assumes an almost sacred mission to serve what is new, to worship the innocent, the naked, the virginal creatures. His chastity will have the "purity of the instinct" of reproduction, ready to pass the test of sin, which in turn will be purified. There the "eleventh Commandment" will emerge from his eyes: "Either this world or none other shall be."

The prose "Prophetic" that follows foretells of the time when "Many years after Sin—which they called Virtue in the churches and gave it their blessing—and after the storm—which will be given birth by the mind of man—will have swept relics of old stars and cobwebbed corners of the heavens, then Creation . . . shall shudder." Hades shall be shaken by the sun, a sign that "the time has come for dreams to take their revenge." This ascent, this glory, must first be preceded by a descent into the abyss of darkness. The "way up" will follow the "way down." First, "beauty will be surrendered to the flies of the Marketplace." The men of power will be dethroned, and against all will sail forth "the gunboats of Love." And in the superb and inspired conclusion, the poet foresees the coming of new creators to a new Eden.

> And then the last of men will say his first word: that the grass shall grow tall and that woman shall rise at his side like a sun's ray. And again he will worship the woman and lay her upon the grass, as was ordained. And dreams will take their revenge, and they will sow generations forever and ever.

The "Meadows of Bliss" will eventually appear, emerging from the breast of the poet himself, who will then advance into "a far and sinless country," accompanied by airy creatures with trees walking by his side, a world of transcendence where, like Christ returning to Jerusalem, he will be welcomed with "Hosanna to the coming one!" and proclaimed "holy, holy / He, the conqueror of Hades and the savior of Eros," for

> Now it is the hand of Death
>   that grants the gift of Life
> and sleep does not exist
>
> . . . . .
>
> Forever forever and now and now the birds sing
>   PRAISED BE the price paid.

The third and final section of *The Axion Esti* is its triumphant "Gloria," a hymn to all the elements that compose the new Paradise, the things worthy of praise, all set in a piece of exquisite beauty and harmony of imagery, music and symbolic devices. We would naturally again expect the position and role of Eros to be central in this creation of an ideal-yet-earthly world out of the insignificant yet beautiful things in nature and in man, this union of the physical with the spiritual, of the earthly with the universal. This hymn to an earthly heaven is interspersed with salutations to the Girl, the Female and femininity, echoing the Orthodox Church's "Salutations" to the Virgin in the Mass of "The Akathist Hymn": "Hail Girl Burning and hail Girl Verdant / Hail Girl Unrepenting, with the prow's sword / . . . / Hail O Wild One of the depth's paradise / Hail O Holy One of the islands' wilderness." particularly expressive is the passage delineating the archetypal variety of femininity:

> THE GIRLS, blue grass of utopia
> the girls, those Pleiades led astray
>   the girls, those Vessels of the Mysteries
> full to the brim yet bottomless
>
>   Astringent in the dark yet marvelous
> carved out in light yet all darkness
>   turning on themselves like a lighthouse
> the sun-devouring, the moon-walking

Light is praised, human creation, the power of the sun, the islands, the sea, the winds, the house on the shore, sun's inebriation, noon, sleep, love, the girls, marriage, family, the living and the dead—in short, all things of the "now," which are also the things "forever."

Contemporary with, and in a sense parenthetical to *The Axion Esti,* the *Six and One Remorses for the Sky* (1960) was to contrast the longer poem's declarative, solemn, triumphant, often lyrical voice with some few private meditations and whisperings, yet within the same climate. The poet's remorses are for a sky, the transcendent summit of his Eros, which had lost its earlier innocence through the poet's and the world's war and postwar experience. These poems are inner questionings and efforts to pass from a common and personal sense of guilt to a new and liberated awareness, to draw from experience a new knowledge and hope and so help a new sky—now more emphatically an inner one—attain a new purity on a higher and more conscious spiritual level.

In **"Beauty and the Illiterate"** the poet comes to learn of a feminine beauty of a different kind: the deeper beauty of the suffering soul, a beauty beyond matter, beyond even life itself, the beauty born out of love's tears. The **"Autopsy"** reveals in the poet's corpse elements and substances testifying to his erotic life and foretelling and promising the fertility of the land: "We shall have early fruit this year." Among the things springing from **"The Sleep of the Valiant,"** who sacrificed their lives to the noble cause of life, is "One drop of clear water, hanging courageously over the abyss, they named Arete, and gave her a lean, boyish body." **"The Other Noah"** is the poet himself considering what is to be saved in the Ark of his asceticism "for lust to begin its holy career." Among the things found and saved are *"bread, longing, love . . ."* As in *The Axion Esti,* an ascent is to follow a downfall, when "the holy day of sensual pleasure may emit its fragrance, / That the Lady, Bearer of Verdure, may ascend naked the stream of Time" accompanied by "The trills of Paradise." The **"Seven Days for Eternity"** are seven short lyrical pieces, considerably erotic and transfigurative, which serve as steps leading again toward a resurrection and paradisiacal blessedness.

Praise of his more recent *Monogram* (1971) pertains primarily to its accomplishment as an art form, the ingenuity of its prosody and its intricate "mathematical" structure. Its thematic content and imagery—where the lonely "I" of the lover addresses softly, affectionately, nostalgically, the ghostly "You" of a lost and recollected beloved now summoned back to enter a paradise to be born within—mark, to some extent, a return to the poet's earlier, idyllic world, enhanced by a craft that has perfectly mastered the simplicity of depth. In its twilight world, the word *agape* (not in the Western theological sense of the term) replaces the word *eros,* and the lover's speech has a hallucinatory quality in addressing a Beatrice-like figure raised to the realm of Ideas. Natural, earthly beauty is still present and is viewed now in the more ethereal light of the beyond.

The pieces in *The Light Tree and the Fourteenth Beauty* (1971) might be called fragments of the new paradise. They are generally lighter, less lonely and less nostalgic in mood than those in *The Monogram.* The sky of Palm Sunday brings a young girl who "paused without reason leaving her blouse unbuttoned." In **"The Girl the North Wind Brought"** the poet is seeking a little chapel as a respite from the wilderness, when the girl appears in a shower of signs and oracles, again Beatrice-like, a recollection "as beautiful as can be," an apparition longed for but elusive and soon to disappear. **"Three Times the Truth"** presents the poet's search for the "Something else [that] must be found," leading first to the discovery that inner man is "Nobody Nobody!" and soon devolving into a version of the Lord's Prayer:

Our Father who art in heaven I who have loved I who have kept my girl like a vow who could even catch the

sun by its wings like a butterfly *Our Father* I lived on nothing.

The poet then concludes by stressing again the simplicity of his Paradise: "Until at last I felt and let them call me crazy that out of nothing is born our Paradise."

In his *Open Book* (1974) speaking at length about the significance and value of dreams for poetry—a value that surrealism was to take ample advantage of—Elytis recounts some of his own revelatory dreams, and we suspect that some of the poems in *The Light Tree* are essentially dream-poems in nature. In **"On the Republic"** (another name for his Paradise), for example, the poet builds a Temple out of "four stones and a little sea-water" and sits there waiting. As noon approaches, much as in Mallarmé's "L'après-midi d'un faune," he falls asleep and is visited by a dream (a wet dream) that mixes the four horses of the Apocalypse with a bearded man approaching sexual intercourse with a woman. The dream transforms the world as the poet awakens. In another poem he beckons a thirteen-year-old **"Little Green Sea"** (the Ionian Sea of his childhood), wanting to sleep "secretly" with her and find in her embrace "Broken stones: the words of God / Broken stones: fragments from Herakleitos." As for **"The Light Tree"** poem, that tree (we suspect, a sunray), grown in his backyard, bursts suddenly into blossom through the moisture of his spit, bringing the answer of "truth" to all of his childhood questionings with regard to the meaning of the world and the end of happiness. Evil times have intervened, he finds his beloved island now deserted, and he wonders what has happened to that tree "Now when no one mourns the nightingales and all write poems."

In attempting to detect Eros's steps through a bird's-eye view in the expanse of Elytis's verse, we have certainly missed a great deal. We have seen numerous sights shining bright and different, yet springing from the same ground, illumined and nurtured by the same core of light. They are enlivened by a highly active Eros, who has stood at the heart of Elytis's verse from its very beginning. Other themes and forces have been related to that one theme and force, of which they become extensions in the widening of its meaning and creative functions. In terms of origins, Elytis's Eros was already present in the Hesiodic *Theogony* as "that fairest among the deathless gods, who unnerves the limbs and overcomes the mind and wise counsels of all gods and all men within them," but with one significant exception: rather than overcoming, this new Eros has continued composing and creating. Also, according to Sappho (to whom our poet owes much), Eros was the child of Uranus, the Sky; hence his constant longing to rise, with earth, to his father's realm. Elytis's Platonism further expanded the concept and functions of Eros. For Plato's Eros—a daimon rather than a god, by the way—the beauty of the body was to serve as tinder, as bait for the higher aspiration, the beauty of the soul. In Elytis, as we have already remarked, there is a longing for a comparable ascent, a transcendence of matter into spirituality; but for him the two worlds are far from being mutually exclusive. They are together and inseparate, the one an extension of the other and its spiritual completion.

In Plato, there stood behind Eros, leading the soul downward into the depths, the spirit of memory, Mnemosyne, the recollection of an ancient, prenatal happiness in the company of the gods, a eudaimonia we lost when we entered time. The pain of that loss was to spur us toward the recovery of that world of eternal purity. Elytis, too, is full of recollection of a perfect world, not prenatal but earthly, his Aegean, the loss of which causes him his utmost pain; and the effort of his verse is to recover this world imaginatively and to transcend it. Seen in this light, his poetry reflects three gradual stages, the first being that of an innocent, erotic youth in the arms of an Aegean blessedness. The next stage brings the loss of that world and its purity, the loss of youth, the ugly experience of war and the taste of death, where that early world is passionately recollected as a solace. The third stage draws from this experience the elements not only for the recovery of that lost world, but its spiritual justification and transcendence as well. The value of suffering is discovered, together with the heroic and the tragic elements in life. Not only the heavenly heights, but the depths, too, are reached, and all this for the building of a new paradise, as intuitive as the early one, yet also highly conscious. Opposites are reconciled and unified in the light of recollection of that splendid old summer, the realm of the Sun, of Beauty and of Eros, where now Purity and a sun-like Justice are triumphant. This is his paradise within.

Orientations and *Sun the First* expressed the first stage. Elytis may later have discredited that early poetry of his from an artistic viewpoint, but we beg to disagree with him to some extent. Some of his loveliest and most cherished poems are in those early collections. The solid foundations of his entire creation are already present. The *Heroic and Elegiac Song* brought in the second stage, that of loneliness, pain and estrangement, with its simultaneous effort to transcend that state through understanding and recollection. The years of silence that followed were also years of meditation and study, as well as years of worldly experience, during which Elytis's intuitive familiarity with his Greekness evolved into a deeper, more intellectual awareness of its ancient, Byzantine and modern tradition and wealth—elements now thoroughly assimilated by his lyrical genius and his prevalent view of life. Time and its tragicality entered his world, and with them came maturity. His symbols gained in breadth and scope. The product was *The Axion Esti,* the core of his work, which in its three parts encompasses all three stages: a "Genesis" to rebuild the universality of the Aegean world, "The Passion" to come to terms with time and experience and set the foundations for a resurrection, and the concluding "Gloria," singing the praise of the resulting new world of Purity and Love, which the *Six and One Remorses* then further refine. As for Elytis's more recent books, they have all centered more or less on his concern for the building of this new inner paradise. Eros had built that first world, in all its innocence, but then vanished for a time in the archetypal, heroic descent into darkness, the archetypal Nekyia. But he remained active even there—in the dark where gold shines, to borrow from Pound—regathering his cosmogonic resources for a new and more powerful rise, a rise full of wisdom.

Edmund Keeley (essay date 1975)

SOURCE: "The Voices of Elytis's *The Axion Esti,*" in *Odysseus Elytis: Analogies of Light,* edited by Ivar Ivask, University of Oklahoma Press, 1975, pp. 81-6.

[*Keeley argues that Elytis's* The Axion Esti *follows in the tradition of earlier twentieth-century Greek poets such as Angelos Sikelianos, and examines the various voices present in the poem.*]

The response of Greek readers to Odysseus Elytis's most ambitious poem, *The Axion Esti,* has been ambivalent during the fifteen years since it appeared in Athens in late 1959 to end more than a decade of silence by a poet then considered to be Greece's best hope among the "younger" generation of poets to follow George Seferis. Though the poem earned the First National Award for Poetry in 1960 and was widely read during the years that followed, the attitude of leading critics remained mixed. A similar ambivalence was also evident in the response of English-speaking readers to the two sections of the poem that appeared in this country and England during the 1960s. For those brought up on the post-Eliot/Pound mode—or on the Cavafis/Seferis mode—the poem was seen to be excessively rhetorical and subjective, at times too obviously programmatic in its formal and thematic projections, at other times too obscure.

Given a commitment to these anti-rhetorical modes, one could find ample ground for regarding the poem as overblown in many of its parts, perhaps even in its central intentions. But this is not the only commitment that governs modern poetry, certainly not so in the case of the modern Greek tradition. Those readers familiar with twentieth-century Greek poetry can discern a direct line from the rhetorical modes of Palamás and Sikelianós to those of *The Axion Esti,* modes that are as characteristic of Greek verse in this century as the more frugal, controlled expression of Cavafis and Seferis. There is now increasing evidence in the response of English-speaking readers, particularly the younger poets in this country, that the poem speaks with power to those who turn (or return) to the surrealist movement of the early twentieth century for their principal inspiration.

My argument here is that there is no single mode in the poem but several modes and a variety of voices—some more objective and dramatic than others, some more effective than others, but serving to shape an impressive poetic statement in their totality—and that even the most subjective and rhetorical of the poem's voices really should be judged within a relevant context: that phase of the modern Greek tradition which foreshadows Elytis's use of an enlarged first-person, his most controversial voice. For those English-speaking readers without access to the work of Palamás and Sikelianós, it may be helpful to approach the poem not with reference to the post-Eliot/Pound mode but with reference to those poets in our tradition who engaged in an enterprise parallel to Elytis's, specifically Walt Whitman and Dylan Thomas. Both these poets project a first-person voice that usually manages to transcend the

subjective and rhetorical trappings that come with it, sometimes in a manner that anticipates Elytis's first-person
speaker in portions of *The Axion Esti.* When Whitman
sings, in "Song of Myself, 16," that

> I am of old and young, of the foolish as much as
> the wise,
> Regardless of others, ever regardful of others,
> Maternal as well as paternal, a child as well as a
> man,
> Stuff'd with the stuff that is coarse and stuff'd
> with the stuff that is fine,
> One of the Nation of many nations, the smallest
> the same and the largest the same,
> A Southerner soon as a Northerner . . .

his large first-person voice is meant to rise above the
subjective syntax and to speak for the nation, for the
proposed national sensibility that the "I" is intended to
represent; and it is partly the rhetorical tone of the passage that forces the reader to accept this grand design.

Elytis attempts the same kind of representation through
his first-person speaker in several of the Psalms of part
two, "The Passion," for example in Psalm III:

> RICHES you've never given me,
> devastated as I've always been by the tribes of the
> Continents,
> also glorified by them always, arrogantly!

or in Psalm V:

> MY FOUNDATIONS on mountains,
> and the people carry the mountains on their
> shoulders
> and on these mountains memory burns
> like the unconsumed bush.

Here the first-person voice speaks for the nation more
than for the self: those riches never given, and the devastation by "tribes of the Continents," are attributes that
belong not so much to a personal as a national predicament; and "my foundations" become the country's foundations when the mountains that hold them are raised on
the shoulders of "the people." The rhythm, as in Whitman,
is that of a rhetorical progress from "I" as persona to "I"
as metaphor for a general sensibility.

In those instances when Elytis's first-person voice speaks
in a more overtly personal context, his mode appears closer to that of Dylan Thomas, whose work also reveals a
parallel handling of imagery. The opening lines of Thomas's "Fern Hill," for example, remind us of lines in part
one, "The Genesis":

> Now as I was young and easy under the apple
> boughs
> About the lilting house and happy as the grass was
> green,
> The night above the dingle starry,
> Time let me hail and climb

> Golden in the heydays of his eyes,
> And honored among wagons I was prince of the
> apple towns
> And once below time I lordly had the trees and
> leaves
> Trail with daisies and barley
> Down the rivers of the windfall light.

"The Genesis" opens as follows:

> IN THE BEGINNING the light And the first hour
> when lips still in clay
> try out the things of the world
> Green blood and bulbs golden in the earth
> And the sea, so exquisite in her sleep, spread
> unbleached gauze of sky
> under the carob trees and the great upright
> palms
> There alone I faced
> the world
> wailing loudly

Both poets offer a persona who speaks out of personal
past history, childhood in the case of Thomas and infancy
in the case of Elytis. But the objective of this personal
evocation is to provide a context for the creation of the
brave new world that each persona discovers during the
innocence of his early life. The focus is not on autobiographical detail but on those elements that make the world
surrounding the persona green and golden, before the
progress of time intrudes to bring a consciousness of the
fall from grace—the knowledge of death in Thomas and of
evil in Elytis—that changes early Eden into the harsher
world of later years. The subjective voice again serves a
broader, metaphoric vision; the rhetorical tone, even the
conceits ("prince of the apple towns," "unbleached gauze
of sky") again seem appropriate in elevating the ordinary
to the level of wonder, specifically, the wonder that comes
with "trying out the things of the world" in a state of
innocence.

These parallels illustrate two forms of the first-person
voice in *The Axion Esti,* forms that fall between what
Palamás called the personal and the temporal, or "lyricism
of the *I*" and "lyricism of the *we*." When Elytis allows the
personal, or the self, to dominate the more general group
consciousness, he is clearly less successful, as in Psalm
X of "The Passion," where the persona's defensiveness
under attack by "the young Alexandrians" seems to border on paranoia. And he is also less successful when his
persona takes on the role of prophet, turning from the recreated world before him to visionary abstractions (e.g., "I
see the coherence of secret meanings," or "Blessed, I say,
are the potent ones who decipher the Undefiled"), as in
passages of the Reading called "Prophetic" and in the late
Psalms. The first-person voice appears inevitably to speak
with the greatest conviction and force when it is discovering or celebrating or even challenging the symbols of
"this small world the great" that are rooted in the Greek
reality, whether of landscape, recent history or literary
tradition—all of which evoke a shared, group response
and therefore transcend the overly hermetic.

The same criterion applies to the first-person voice of the numerous intricate Odes of "The Passion," a voice that is in one sense the most subjective and rhetorical that we hear in *The Axion Esti* but that is at the same time the most formal, confined within the limits of a lyrical frame created by strict metrics and frequent refrains. It is a voice clearly meant to sing, and we permit it some of the license this intention presupposes. But again, to the extent that the rhetorical "I" of these Odes "takes the shape of my native country" (as the poet himself puts it in Ode j), it escapes an excess of self-consciousness and promotes some of the finest lyrics that Elytis has written. To the extent that it speaks privately or with a tone of self-righteousness ("Betrayed, I remained on the plain, alone, / Stormed, I was taken in the castle, alone, / The message I raised I endured alone!") or through slogans ("In the desolate and empty city / only the hand remains / To paint across the great walls / BREAD AND FREEDOM") or in "prophetic" abstractions ("But then, at the sixth hour of the erect lilies, / When my judgment will make a crack in Time, / The eleventh Commandment will emerge from my eyes: . . ."), it rings rather hollow, the product not so much of the poet's mature, liberated spirit as of his programmatic attempt to present grand themes.

A related esthetic can be brought to bear on the more objective voices that emerge in *The Axion Esti,* and they are several. One index of the sophistication of this poem, of the progress in method that occurred during the years of silence that preceded it, resides in the poet's "dramatic manner of expression" (to use the phrase Seferis offered in designating what he had learned first of all from reading Eliot's *The Waste Land*)—an expression that often finds embodiment in characters some distance from the poet himself and his persona. The first such character to appear is "the One I really was, the One of many centuries ago, / the One still verdant in the midst of fire, the One still tied to heaven" in "The Genesis," a kind of alter ego who acts as the creator of the infant poet's green world. This voice utters some of the best lines in the poem, lines that are effective exactly because they evoke a recognizable landscape, a poetic image of Greek reality, while at the same time dramatizing the infant poet's emerging sensibility:

> And ample the olive trees
> > to sift the light through their fingers
> > that it may spread gently over your sleep
> and ample the cicadas
> > which you will feel no more
> > than you feel the pulse inside your wrist
> but scarce the water
> > so that you hold it a God and understand the
> > > meaning of its voice
> and the tree alone
> > no flock beneath it
> > so that you take it for a friend
> > and know its precious name
> sparse the earth beneath your feet
> > so that you have no room to spread your roots
> > and keep reaching down in depth
> and broad the sky above
> > so that you read the infinite on your own

The experiment in dramatic expression extends, in "The Passion," to a series of prose poems called Readings, where the speaking voice is essentially that of a narrator, though the narrative focus shifts from the point of view of a participant in the action to that of a more distant observer and, finally, to that of the "poet-prophet" mentioned above. The voice is most alive in the early Readings, when Elytis succeeds in creating a tone that is organically related to his subject and to the image of experience he wishes to project, without the intrusion of explicitly subjective overtones. In the First and Second Readings, for example, the unidentified narrator, a soldier participating in the historical moments described (both during the Albanian campaign of 1940-41), speaks in a colloquial language that provides verisimilitude in that particular context and that also subtly echoes the colorful demotic of a great nineteenth-century narrator, General Makriyánnis, whose *Memoirs* described the Greek War of Independence and its aftermath. The relation of World War II to earlier Greek history in terms of an engaged perspective is thus established by narrative tone as much as by the kind of direct allusion—too direct for my taste—that invokes heroes out of the past to travel in the company of our contemporary soldiers. In the best of the Readings, tradition becomes an organic element of the language celebrating tradition.

The voice in the concluding section of the poem, "The Gloria," is perhaps the most consistently effective in *The Axion Esti.* Here the poet overtly assumes the stance of celebrant, but in general he allows the world he is celebrating to speak for itself. Except for the refrains "PRAISED BE" and "HAIL," he remains outside the context he projects, and the refrains simply establish a frame of intention, a celebrative tone, for his evocation of all that he finds in "this small world the great" which is most worthy of praise. The proof of worthiness is left to the images created, without any subjective pressure from poet or persona; the value of the world rendered depends on the degree to which we the readers find the various images of it convincing—and most of them prove to be so. This suggests a truly liberated strategy, one that serves to invoke the best of Elytis's early work but now reinforced by a mature command of plotting, of decorum and aptness in the progression from one image to the next, values sometimes slighted in the early Elytis. Perhaps more important, in some passages of this section, the poet succeeds—as his predecessor Seferis so often does—in conveying the mythological dimension that pervades the details of contemporary life in Greece without pressing the case through overt comment or allusion to literary sources. In the following passage, for example, gods and heroes from the Greek past are brought subtly into the contemporary landscape by way of a sudden metaphor linking a tree trunk with the goddess of fertility and vegetation who presumably animates it, by way of a compound epithet, and a name carrying echoes of Homer, and the intermingled whispering of deities and the natural element they inhabit, all made to seem casually at home in the island world that the poet is celebrating:

> The white and porous middle of day
> the down of sleep lightly ascending

the faded gold inside the arcades
and the red horse breaking free

Hera of the tree's ancient trunk
the vast laurel grove, the light-devouring
a house like an anchor down in the depths
and Kyra-Penelope twisting her spindle

The straits for birds from the opposite shore
a citron from which the sky spilled out
the blue hearing half under the sea
the long-shadowed whispering of nymphs and
maples

Throughout most of this final section of the poem, Elytis is observing first of all, observing and re-creating, selecting details that will move the reader to a recognition and letting any attendant thematic or ideological overtones come as they may. The picture is all, and when it is right, it can startle the reader with a new perspective on the hauntingly familiar:

PRAISED BE the wooden table
the blond wine with the sun's stain
the water doodling across the ceiling
The philodendron on duty in the corner . . .

PRAISED BE the heatwave hatching
the beautiful boulders under the bridge
the shit of children with its green flies
a sea boiling and no end to it . . .

THE ISLANDS with all their minium and
lampblack
the islands with the vertebra of some Zeus
the islands with their boat yards so deserted
the islands with their drinkable blue volcanoes

The only faltering in "The Gloria" is that which we have seen in other sections: a weakness for vague abstraction in those few moments when the poet attempts to rise above the world before him to the region of absolutes and general principles. In the closing lines of this section, he juxtaposes representations of the "Now" and the "Forever" in a sort of coda to the whole poem. Neither plane, as rendered here, moves the heart or even the mind to the kind of discovery effected by the specific images we have seen. And this rhetorical mode of evocation serves to diffuse and intellectualize what has so far been poetically concrete:

Now the hallucination and the mimicry of sleep
Forever forever the word and forever the astral Keel

Now the moving cloud of lepidoptera
Forever the circumgyrating light of mysteries

Now the crust of the Earth and the Dominion
Forever the food of the Soul and the quintessence . . .

Now the amalgam of peoples and the black Number
Forever the statue of Justice and the great Eye . . .

The poem ends: "and Forever this small world the Great!" Indeed. But as the best passages in the poem demonstrate, the eternal dimensions of this small world are most convincingly established when the greatness of it is celebrated with a lower case "g." This is the poet's strongest impulse in the poem, and it is what makes *The Axion Esti* both a major stage in the poet's development and a major contribution to the modern Greek tradition in poetry.

Vincenzo Rotolo (essay date 1975)

SOURCE: "The 'Heroic and Elegiac Song for the Lost Second Lieutenant of the Albanian Campaign': The Transition from the Early to the Later Elytis," in *Odysseus Elytis: Analogies of Light,* edited by Ivar Ivask, University of Oklahoma Press, 1975, pp. 75-9.

[*In the following excerpt, Rotolo argues that the* Heroic and Elegiac Song for the Lost Second Lieutenant of the Albanian Campaign *marks a transition in Elytis's poetry, the war between Italy and Greece heightening his love for his native land and forcing upon him a wider consciousness, at once more human and more political.*]

The poetry of Odysseus Elytis prior to the *Ázma iroikó ke pénthimo yia ton haméno anthipolohaghó tis Alvanías (Heroic and Elegiac Song for the Lost Second Lieutenant of the Albanian Campaign)* has long engaged the critics' attention. In addition to those who stubbornly rejected all innovation, even Marxist criticism, which in Greece more than anywhere was rooted in the then current concept of socialist realism, was unkindly disposed toward Elytis's first compositions. He was even stigmatized as a "Sunday" poet. Though the supporters of modern poetry had accepted the technical novelties of his language, they had stereotyped him as an aristocratic, solitary poet who could only sing lyrically of the beauty of nature and life. This conventional frame managed to stand even after *Ílios o prótos (Sun the First*; 1943), but with the *Heroic Song* (1945) it completely broke down. Those critics who had sustained him felt they had been betrayed (many years later they were to complain of a yet more clamorous "betrayal" in *The Axion Esti*), and they reproached him for deserting his world of blissful youth. But here a preliminary remark should be made.

Elytis's early poetical works, later collected in *Prosanatolizmí (Orientations*; 1939), have certain definite features that reappear in the already-mentioned *Sun the First.* As regards technique, the main innovation is in the use of language, which constitutes one of the most personal and most successful adaptations in European poetry of the dictates of "automatic writing," with linguistic and structural implications going far beyond a well-learned lesson. In Elytis, an extraordinary linguistic sensibility succeeds in reconciling the absolute freedom of lexical and semantic transcription of the world of the unconscious with the discipline of a man who shows meticulous care for the language he uses. As regards content, the most prominent feature is the vast range of sensations and notations with which the poet expresses his relationship with the outside world and with his own self. The contemplation of the natural beauty of Greece and of the Aegean in particular, a point on which critics have dwelled considerably, is indeed an expression of a state of ecstasy, of exultation with life; but it also conceals a heartfelt need to seek to commune with nature because of the impossibility of communicating with "the others." Man, in Elytis's poetry, is either absent or no more than an indistinct, shadowy figure. Even in his early phase, the poet knows full well the notes of gloom, the heavy presence of darkness, even though he strives to counter them with light, with the sun. Elytis's youthful attitude is therefore due to his own personal difficulty of finding human contacts rather than to any real desire to avoid them. (At most, one might speak of a certain political disengagement, then quite common, in a period when extremely few intellectuals denounced, for example, the dramatic situation of victims of political persecution struggling for better social justice.)

With the war between Italy and Greece, the poet comes to maturity. This war not only snatches him away from his solitary life, thrusting him into a wider human context; it also enables him to acquire a political conscience by showing him that the rights of the weak are being trampled underfoot by the strong and powerful. The *Heroic Song* is therefore not so much a turning point as a continuation of what the poet has already set out to do. There is also another much stronger thread connecting the early Elytis to the later poet—Greece. The Greece for which he had always felt the most soul-stirring devotion, an almost sensual yearning for physical possession, now in the dramatic expreience of war takes on an unwonted appearance, sorrowful and afflicted, yet at the same time proud.

The transition from the early to the later Elytis may be traced not only contextually in the *Heroic Song* but also in some parts of the poems of *I kalosíni stis likooporiés (Kindness in the Wolfpasses)* and *The Axion Esti.* The first of these two, though published in 1946, draws its genesis from the atmosphere of war, reproducing the conflict between opposing values where choice, though forced, is categorical and relatively easy. *Kindness* has to face the enemy with its own arms and give battle. And the poet has to accept the fact that he must bid farewell to the diversions and childish fancies that previously satisfied him. In the collision with reality, the dream-world in which his poetry had been submerged disintegrates into a nebula where fragments may still be seen of the old carefree simplicity, relived in the recalling of a legend. An analogous situation is to be found in *The Axion Esti.* Here, too, the innocents are trapped with no way of escape. There is no alternative but to fight, each with his own weapons. And in actual fact, when the Greeks have to face the brutal and absurd Fascist aggression, no man can any longer be tempted by idle recreation. Lethargy is jolted into action. Even the scenic background is abruptly transformed. Gone is the sea spray playing on shells and polished stones, gone is the splendor of light and color; now there are bloody battles on gloomy, snow-topped mountains. Elytis had already used these mountains in a poem in *Sun the First,* in which he identified Greece with her bare and gloriously snowy peaks. The scenery of the *Heroic Song* is full of mountains; even when they are not explicitly mentioned, their looming, solemn presence can be felt, protecting or threatening.

Man, in Elytis's poetry, is either absent or no more than an indistinct, shadowy figure.

—*Vincenzo Rotolo*

The *Heroic Song* is densely packed with emblematic values skillfully inserted into an organic, linear structure. The very title of the "song," with its two adjectives, encompasses the work's compound nature: something halfway between a threnody and a short epic poem. Of the threnody it has the lamentations, the pining regret, the exaltation of life passed by; it makes some use of formulae and modules taken from folk poetry, adapted to Elytis's own style and language. Of the epic poem it has the mythical fable-like quality, the wish to extract a cathartic teaching from the drama of the fallen soldier, the idealization of the protagonist. The lack of realistic tone in the poem is scarcely surprising, considering Elytis's esthetic conceptions. The situations are not wholly materialized; they are presented in brief glimpses, in impassioned suggestions evoked from the world of the unconscious.

The *Heroic Song* contains fourteen poetical compositions, each corresponding to a moment in the life—and death—of the extraordinary protagonist. These fourteen sections are not connected in time or place, but are interlinked through an inner affinity and through oneiric memory. The sections vary in both content and tone, leading to inevitable comparisons with a symphony. One might also be put in mind of the various scenes of a dream-vision reproduced in a series of apparently disconnected film frames skillfully stitched together by a montage expert.

At least four main sequences may be distinguished in the poem: 1) the antefact, including sections I-II, which present the Greek-Albanian landscape in an ever-stronger foreboding of death, and section III, in which the outbreak of war is recounted; 2) the death of the protagonist (section IV); 3) the consequences of his death, including the poet's shock at what has happened (V-VI), the mother's desperation as seen against the background of the death scene (VII), the diminution of the entire world through the Second Lieutenant's death (VIII-X) and the punishment of those guilty of his death (XI); and 4) the transfiguration and resurrection of the fallen Second Lieutenant (XII, XIV), with an interpolated lament for his unfinished life (XIII).

Let us examine those sections most deserving of note. The first line ("There where the sun first dwelt") of section I foretokens the drama in its re-evocation of the country scenery, which takes on a nostalgic connotation in the twofold reference to place and time, "there" and "first." The contrast with the present is strongly expressed in line

11, which begins with the adverb "now" (repeated in the next line), and initiates a series of somber, distressful images: the spreading shadow has now obscured the sun forever.

In section II the transformation is announced by the adverb "now," placed conspicuously as the first word of the first line: "Now in muddy waters an agitation arises." The waters are no longer still, as they were in line 14 of section I, and are no longer clear; *now* they are muddy because *now* there is agitation. The identity is, in fact, total: now = agitation. The trepidation for the morrow is well-tendered in the urgent series of impassioned metaphoric images. The shattered peace of the country-side is contrasted with the soldiers' unwavering purpose, which is expressed in their war-cry, "fire or the sword." The expression in lines 19-20, "Something evil / Shall flame up," returns in a slightly altered form in the penultimate line of section II, where it is no longer generic but is instead directed against a specific object, the aggressors.

The conflict becomes reality in section III, and man smiles in vain, indifferent to his destiny in the face of death, which approaches with the dull roar of the big guns and which leaves behind it destruction and smoke. All is plunged into darkness, despite the efforts of the sun to break through. The technical composition of this section differs from that of the others, which come in compact units of varying length (occasionally separated by single lines or couplets). Here there are six short three-line strophes, each containing a complete logical meaning or image. The last two strophes are exceptional in that they are linked, if only by the antithesis of day and night, the images which dominate the fifth and sixth strophes respectively.

The scene is dominated in section IV by the body of the fallen soldier, stretched out on "his scorched battle-coat." The sudden presentation of the dead protagonist is unusual and extremely effective. The first two strophes are rich in original metaphors and similes, whose purpose is to convey the real meaning of the lieutenant's death. But the most powerful strophe is the third, depicting as if in a hasty uncompleted sketch the lifeless figure, of which only a few clear details are presented: the empty helmet, the mud-soiled blood, the "half-finished" arm and especially the "small bitter well" boring into the forehead. The use of modular repetitions and refrains gives the final strophe the air of a funeral dirge.

In accordance with lamentation technique, the re-evocation in section VI opens on a mythical, legendary tone. Three long strophes develop the motif suggested by the first sentence of each. Structurally the sentences follow the same pattern of verb-adjective-noun, the verb and noun remaining unchanged and the adjective always different: "He was a handsome lad," "He was a sturdy lad," "He was a valiant lad." While in the first two strophes the re-evocation recalls a distant, almost timeless age, the last, developing the opening and closing line, refers to his wartime experiences until his death. A series of metaphors gives another glimpse of the body, which is the "silent

shipwreck of dawn"; the mouth is a "small songless bird," the hands "wide plains of desolation" (i.e., city squares). In section VII, two prosopopoeiae in the form of the female characters Suffering and Solitude (in the first and second strophes respectively) prepare the way for the highly emotive scene of the mother in mourning-weeds. Less convincing are the closing lines which overemphatically declare that it is the lot of mothers to weep and of men to fight, almost implying that courage may be an end in itself, in contrast with the ideal values personified in the protagonist.

The eleventh section is divided into three strophes (the first two containing eleven lines each, the third containing three) and is devoted to the enemies, "Those who committed evil." Each of the three strophes starts with this isolated hemistich. Tormented and appalled at their evil-doing, the enemies vanish in a dark cloud. The second strophe has been rightly said to re-echo klephtic poetry, though in a personal and of course modern way. It is true that some denunciations may seem too harsh, especially today, considering that they involve an entire country with no distinction between the political responsibilities of the leaders of the Fascist dictatorship and the Italian people, reluctantly forced into becoming aggressors toward a kindred people. However, this has little importance from the point of view of art. What is important is that these lines genuinely re-echo popular feeling prevalent in Greece at that tragic point in time, when the decision to defend to the death was taken not out of a sense of nationalistic hatred or antagonism but as an option for justice, liberty and democracy.

In the last three sections (XII-XIV) the hero ascends to heaven saluted by birds and men whom he recognizes as brothers in a cosmic embrace, while crystal bells herald the coming of Easter. The good and innocent hero, dead *ante diem,* has redeemed himself by his sacrifice. Not only do his person and his tragedy belong to a higher sphere, but his country, too, is finer than all others. His country is the land where once the sun dwelt and where one day it will return to shine. It is the land of justice, the land of beauty, the land of passion. Elytis thus consciously and organically develops his ethical conception of Greece and Grecism, even though it is tied to a particular case chosen as a symbol of an historic moment. Later, in *The Axion Esti,* Elytis's magnum opus, he provides a further and more explicit structure, both diachronic and synchronic, of the most significant events and moments of the Greek world.

As to the style and language of the **Heroic Song,** a few remarks may suffice. On the whole, if we compare the poem with Elytis's previous and subsequent work, we find confirmation of the boldness of certain stylistic techniques and of the creative richness of his language. Among the most frequent stylistic devices, the metaphor is particularly noteworthy. Bearing in mind that Elytis's choice of language is instinctively disposed toward figurative uses, thus creating innumerable metaphors, only the most notable will be pointed out. Classifying them according to the two elements being compared, these are: a) syntactically dependent metaphors (using the genitive in Greek) such as "famine of joy," "crumbs of heaven" and "branch of oblivion"; b) juxtaposed metaphors such as "hermit rocks," "gipsy anemones," "cloud months," "sickle moon" and "tomboy flowers"; c) appositional metaphors, including "garden, odeon of flowers" and "mouth, small bird"; and d) compound metaphors, such as *aloghovouno* (mountain/horse), *sinefolíkena* (clouds/she-wolf), *nerantzokóritsa* (girls/bitter oranges) and *horiatomouzmouliá* (medlartree/peasant). Lexically there are some interesting linguistic formations, such as the compounds *foradhopoúles* (young mares), *thampóhrisa* (of tarnished gold), *ghalazovoló* (to irradiate with blue) and *iridhohtipiménos* (struck by the iris). Syntactically we encounter again a curious peculiarity of Elytis's language, namely, that of using an intransitive verb with an object in the accusative (as, for example, "a flag *flapped* aloft *earth and water*," "black centuries about him *bay* with skeletons of dogs *the hideous silence*"). These violations of the normal rules produce bizarre and powerful effects, which in the final analysis sustain the poet's tendency toward figurative language, enhancing his linguistic genius and his creative fantasy with unexpected properties.

George Economou (review date 1981)

SOURCE: "The Two Voices of Odysseus Elytis," in *The Washington Post Book World,* September 6, 1981, pp. 8, 14.

[*In the following review, Economou explores the two narrative voices present in* Maria Nephele *and compares Elytis's Maria to Dante's Beatrice.*]

That The Nobel Prize for Literature creates a specialized, sometimes ephemeral, industry for translators and publishers is a fact of modern literary history. It is also true that a good deal of poetry of the 1979 recipient of the prize, the Greek poet Odysseus Elytis, while not popular in this country at that time, was fairly widely translated and available to those who make it their business to know the international literary scene. The publication of an English-language version of his **Maria Nephele,** therefore, can be as easily regarded as part of a continuity of interest as it can an inevitability in the wake of his award by the Swedish Academy.

Published in Athens in 1978 and started 18 years before, *Maria Nephele* represents an important advance in Elytis' development as a poet both in its form and its subject matter. The growth that results from the setting and meeting of new challenges has become as prominent a trait of the poet's career as some of the personae, landscapes and modes that typify the body of his work. Elaborately structured like his **The Axion Esti** (1959), which figured so importantly in the Nobel citation, **Maria Nephele** relies more on colloquial language and makes greater use of the urban situation than any previous Elytis work.

The poem is divided into three main parts, each comprised of seven pairs of poems in which the personae of Maria Nephele (Maria Cloud) and an Antiphonist (the poet) "say" and "respond" to each other's convictions on subjects ranging from philosophy, poetry and love to recent political events. Each of these 42 poems is concluded with an italicized epigrammatic statement which hangs from it like a distillated drop of insight. For example, at the end of a poem entitled **"The Waterdrop"** (a recurring motif in Elytis' work) comes the line, "*In the village of my language Grief is called the Radiant Lady.*" In addition, there are a prologue, two interludic songs, and an epilogue. The parts of this whole are closely, often serially, interrelated and unified through various thematic correspondences and are animated by a large number of literary and mythological references and allusions. All of this has been ably explicated and annotated by translator Athan Anagnostopoulos in the introduction and notes to his strictly literal version of the poem.

But the true dynamic of the poem lies neither in its structure nor in its allusiveness. It is, rather Elytis' ability to compact and unite the work's elements into a single, comprehensive myth that makes its experience significant. In an interview published in *Books Abroad* in 1975, Elytis explained his interest in finding the sources of his neo-Hellenic world by keeping "the mechanism of mythmaking" rather than the traditional mythical figures. This mechanism, mastered and exploited so effectively and lyrically in his previous work, in fact nourished **Maria Nephele** in a new way. Maria Nephele, the complex feminine mediator between the contemporary world and the poet, has her roots in Marina, the enigmatic girl of the Aegean with "the taste of tempest" on her lips in a poem Elytis published in 1939. As she says in the closing lines of her dialogue with the poet-Antiphonist in the prologue, which is titled **"The Presence."**

> And from the many tempests I returned
> among the people self-exiled!

So now she comes in the form of a young radical speaking for the world-view of a new, alienated generation to lead him into a new awareness out of which he forges a tribute to their mutual endurance. The mythic model that comes to mind is that of the epic journey to the other world, especially Dante's *Comedy,* when one considers Elytis' revelation that he met a young woman in real life that provided him with the basis for the mythical figure of the poem. A kind of Beatrice, she confronts and tests the poet's commitments and leads him through previously uncharted territory, forcing the poet to show the other side of himself. This territory, represented by the usually clashing world-visions of the two personae, also forces the reader to show other sides of himself through an ingenious strategy of poetic thinking: To read this antiphonal work is to become involved in the dialectic of the encounter, and the reader's interpretations must synthesize the oppositions of the two voices. . . .

Karl Malkoff (review date 1987)

SOURCE: "Poetry with an Accent," in *American Book Review,* Vol. 9, No. 1, January-February, 1987, pp. 22-3.

[*In the review below, Malkoff examines Olga Broumas's literal translations in the collection* What I Love: Selected Poems of Odysseus Elytis, *and concludes that the translations, though problematic and inconsistent at times, are still "interesting" and of some value.*]

New translations of poems (which, like most of those selected by Olga Broumas for **What I Love,** have been recently rendered into English by more than competent translators) promise something new. In this respect, Olga Broumas, for better and for worse, does not disappoint. She informs us at the outset that she intends to preserve the strangeness, the foreignness of Elýtis's texts. It ought to be, she asserts, "English with an accent."

This raises basic questions. In the very first poem, **"Sun the First,"** a critical sentence is translated: "I don't know anymore the night." Clearly, English with an accent. Broumas's line indeed follows the original word order. To the Greek reader, however, this order is natural and idiomatic, as other translators have more or less made clear (Edmund Keeley and Philip Sherrard: "I no longer know the night"; Kimon Friar: "I know the night no longer"). Sometimes the point of reproducing Elýtis's foreign accent seems to make sense. For example, another section of **"Sun the First"** begins, "Day shiny shell of the voice you made me by. . . ." The ambiguous positioning of "shiny" between "Day" and "shell" reflects the fact that in Greek adjectives may come before or after the nouns they modify. On the other hand, in poems like **"Helen,"** when we read, "With her existence alone / she annihilates off [sic] half the people," it is difficult to avoid at least considering the possibility that the choice of language is uninformed rather than intentional, possibly a confusion generated by the expression "finishes off." This is not the place to answer the question of what the translator's chief goal ought to be: the most literal possible (yet still idiomatic) reproduction of the text, the freer attempt to reproduce as nearly as possible the impact the work has made in the original, or a refusal to allow the translation to make what ought to seem strange familiar. But Olga Broumas's translations provocatively raise that question.

Somewhat more disturbing to the reader who, having been assured that "Line by line, the poems nearly match their original," is willing to give up the idiomatic are the liberties Broumas seems to take in the "literal" translation of certain words. The first of the prose poems—surely suitable material for the literalist—of **"The Hyacinth Symphony"** is a striking example of this. Here the night is "drawing her naked body" while in the original it "dreams" it (*onirevetai*); here the night has many "composers" while in the original it has many "compasses" (*piksides*); here an anchor "regales the depths" while in Greek it "leads" them (*ivemonevei*). It is *not* that such variance is never acceptable in translation (it may sometimes be preferable); it is simply that if Broumas claims to offer the literal, it is difficult to justify these departures.

Having gotten the worst of it off my chest, and without denying some lack of confidence in the text produced by the contradictions cited above, I nonetheless had a certain amount of pleasure reading this volume. First of all, whether one agrees with it entirely or not, Broumas has a point. Not only is Elýtis a speaker of Greek rather than English, he is also a surrealist, who sees the world in terms of its odd juxtapositions which the rational, conscious mind attempts to smooth out, to rationalize, just as, Broumas might say, the conventional translator is a rationalizer of the strangeness of other languages and the unique approaches to reality those other languages contain. On at least some occasions, she captures Elýtis's special music with accuracy and intensity (I am thinking of a poem like **"The Kite,"** from the **Maria Nefele** sequence: "In the bath next door the faucets open / face down on my pillow / I watched the immaculate white fountains splashing me; / how beautiful my god how beautiful / foot-trampled on the ground / to still hold in my eyes / such mourning for the distant past.")

Second, although Sam Hamill's "Afterword" seems at first glance an attempt to give the appearance of predetermined purpose to a relatively accidental selection of poems—the theme of love, cited in the title, is ubiquitous in Elýtis—the fact is that Hamill does point to a particular characteristic of Elýtis's work which is effectively highlighted by Broumas's translations. Hamill writes: "Like the presocratics Elýtis is far more interested in the origins and sources of mythology (in the *mechanism,* to use his own term), than in the figures themselves." All poets make myths, more or less, but this aspect of the poet's art is of special importance to Elýtis's poetic powers. From the body-island of **"Sun the First"** to the girl-cloud of **Maria Nefele,** Elýtis's ability to see the relationships between microcosm and macrocosm, between inner reality and outer, as literal rather than metaphorical bonds, is lucidly on display and is revealed as one of the essential components of man's myth-making capacities.

To answer the question implied at the very start of this review (why another translation of these poems?): Elýtis is a major poet, expressing with clarity and passion one of the sensibilities of modern Greece. He not only *deserves* a variety of perspectives on his work, he *needs* them, so that in turn its various dimensions can be emphasized for English-speaking readers; to get them all at once, that reader must learn Greek. Olga Broumas's translation is not without its flaws, but it is interesting work and unmistakably sheds light on the original poetry.

Andonis Decavalles (essay date 1988)

SOURCE: "Time versus Eternity: Odysseus Elytis in the 1980s," in *World Literature Today,* Vol. 62, No. 1, pp. 22-32.

[*In the excerpt below, Decavalles examines* Three Poems under a Flag of Convenience, *suggesting that the collection effectively captures Elytis's transcendental vision and the transformative powers of art.*]

When we turn to the **Three Poems under a Flag of Convenience** (1982), we may possibly understand the evoked *efkerías* (opportunity, convenience) as another chance, another try to admonish and so to break the isolation, the increased loneliness always extant in Elytis's admonitions. In their unity and sequence the three poems here, each divided into seven parts, bear the individual titles **"The Garden Sees," "The Almond of the World,"** and **"Ad Libitum."** The viewing garden is obviously the paradise-oriented angle of vision, detecting through sunny lucidity and projecting through instantaneous revelations life's real essence and truth. The "almond of the world" must be that real essence and truth itself, Elytis's equivalent of Plato's *to agathon,* yet bitter at times, as almonds are. As to the phrase "ad libitum," ironically enough, instead of pleasurable ease it expresses the strain in a losing battle of the poet's identity against the odds that time has brought.

No less the *vates* that he has always been, the poet has the garden's eye detect and reveal ingredients of his transcendental creed and its salvatory potential, as yet unfortunately ignored by those to be rescued.

> 1. Maybe
> > if we except Anchorites
> > I might be the last player
> > to exercise his rights
>
> > > presumption
>
> > > I don't understand
> > > what profit means
>
> a Panselinos who paints though God does not exist
> and proves exactly the opposite
>
> > > stream
>
> > what water
> > blue with sparks
>
> beyond the barrier of the Sirens' sound
> signals to me
>
> > > leaping
>
> > > come on
>
> somewhere
>
> > > Perfection lies completed
> > > and lets a rivulet roll up to here

Art makes real the unreal; it even creates God where He does not exist. Perfection is *there,* accomplished for those who care for it. There are always its "raging" messages, one after another, but "what to do / no one knows." As to the future:

> > So what will happen when
> sometime social struggles stop when inventions
> obsolete themselves when all demands are satisfied
>
> > > void

> inside which will fall those (serves them right)
> who turn the wheel for the sake of the Wheel
>
> > dazzle
>
> > we others
>
> shall commence to live initiates in the body's
> > Sanskrit
> essentially and metaphorically speaking

We are the microcosms of a macrocosm, a universe made of "antimatter," and there are "a million signs / omega zeta eta [i.e., *zoe* or 'life'] / and if these don't form a word for you / tomorrow / will be yesterday forever." If the words will raise life to its affirmation, then "at a second level wars will recur / without anyone's being killed / there are sufficient reserves of death," where war gains its Heraclitan meaning. The garden then "starts off the countdown / withering / acme / waking / a young woman's breast is already / an article of the future's Constitution."

It is in this spirit that the poem unfolds to its end with the belief that "the decay of time at last will turn against it." The urging comes with a reference to Oedipus's reaching his transcendence at Colonus.

> . . . advance
> > you encounter the famous grove of Colonus
> > you follow Oedipus
>
> > > coolness
> > > peace
> > > nightingales
> suddenly daybreak
> > the cock on the weathervanes
> > it's you in the church
> > the icon-screen superb with pomegranate trees
>
> Kore stepping on the waves
> a gentle westerly
> > > wafts
>
> > your hand copies
> > > the Inconceivable.

But this is not easy. As the second poem states:

> *the almond of the world*
> > is deeply hidden
> > > and still unbitten
> a myriad possibilities shudder
> around us which we idiots wouldn't
> > > even touch
>
> we never understood how pigeons think
> two hand-spans above our head
> > > what we have lost already is in play

No doubt, "*the almond of the world* / is bitter and there's no way / you can find it unless / you sleep half outside of sleep." That he himself has strived for.

at night
      when I speak as if to stir up constellations
in the upper embers for a moment the face
      is formed that God
      would give me if he knew
      how much the earth in truth cost me
in desperation
      in "it was destined" whispered variously at
        night
          in cypresses
          centuries old like poems
during the making of which I was disrealized.

Though his strife has caused him isolation and loneliness, and despite the dislike he may have encountered, he would not give up. He would continue his "course / against this society / against inhibiting idiocy." Poetry needs to produce a spark in its fruit, for "something surely / must surreptitiously have been subtracted / from the terraqueous globe / for it to pant so / to turn pale / and for mourning to spread itself." The sad truth is that "Even if you have it all / something's always lacking / it's enough the Integral not be accomplished / and Fortune feel fortunate."

Man's longing for perfection is always plagued by limited potential, as was earlier expressed in *The Light Tree.* "We always sought / precisely that which cannot be—one of heaven's sins which led to the *Six and One Remorses.* As you strive to cut "the almond of the world," you have your hand scorched and end up writing "some white / poems on the black page." Further on are implications of Plato's notion of our preexistence, forgotten upon birth, to be recollected and regained in a lifelong struggle: "man is as if coming from elsewhere / and so he sounds out of tune / with a memory all fragmented." Loneliness is the price, with only instantaneous gratifications.

all alone
      I am hanging
          since Heraclitus' time
like *the almond of the world*
      from a branch of the North Aegean
      an ancient fisherman with his trident
      who has known many gales until there:
      sometime the moment arrives

the waters around him become
          brilliant
          chilly
          rosy
      he squints his eyelids
          it's because the reflection
          all absolute beauty
shows with whom it briefly had with no intention
  on his part
          a confidential meeting.

An expectation of a kind of afterlife can be seen in the lines "axiomatically I am living beyond the point where I find myself / besides / continuing along my mother / you will meet me even after death." Such still-inherent hope for spiritual timelessness, for eternity, carries on in dialectical

fashion its desperate battle against increasing doubts and questionings as we reach the third poem, **"Ad Libitum,"** which represents a more pragmatic encounter with and consideration of temporal reality. Much as in *The Axion Esti,* the poet begins here by defining his personal yet ethnic and historical identity, but with a more painful awareness of the present and the future.

I am alpha years old and European to the middle
      of the Alps or Pyrenees
      I never never touched the snow

      there's not one who can represent me
      war and peace ate at me on both sides
      what remained endures still

          till when
          friends

      must we lift up the excommunicated past
      filled with kings and subjects

          myself
          I feel like a seduced cypress

to whom not even a tombstone remained
only empty plots rocks stone-enclosures
and the inconsolable northwind
beating yonder on the factories' high walls

      all of us enclosed there we work as
      elsewhere in History

          the

          Future

years say spilled crude oil
set ablaze

          help

      Rintrah roars and shakes
      his fires in the burdend air

my unfortunate allalone *one*

          what's to become of you
five or six zeroes on the side will eat you up

          and it is finished
there already now
      Authority dresses as Fate and whistles to
      you
          Ad libitum.

Never before has Elytis spoken in a language of such stark and hopeless pragmatism about time's advance and the accompanying physical, mental, and moral decline, where death is in view. Rilke had wished one's death to be individual, chosen, one's own, in agreement with the identity of his soul. Here instead we read:

fortunately the ambient wind has no memory
it persists in smelling of rose
and in punishing you
while you die wretchedly

ready in line behind the others
for passport control
with an airline bag on your shoulder

You resist such impersonal, mechanical, mass departure, where "you call to mind your limits / always in the dark / conducted by a ground-stewardess / completely uninterested in your personal luck." The air-flight scenery and much else was part of Maria Nefeli's world as well, but in that poem was eventually redeemed through the revelation of Maria's deeper purity and victimized innocence and through the poet's still-solid faithfulness, whereas here it remains unpurified and unredeemed. The "girl" in this poem seems to have lost her old, gratifying nature, remaining strange and indifferent as to the traveler's movement toward "the cryings of birds-of-prey / and the complete petrification / wherein you shall be enlisted / thee little one / how can you magnified by thought / defy natural phenomena."

The poet had been deemed a "phenomenon" by those who heard at night a pen scratching "like a cat on the closed / door of the Unknown" guarded by "infamous / personae turpi." The victims of our times, "amid revolutions and wars we all grew up / that's why on our foreheads / the mark of the bullet not shot / at all times continues to cause death." Confronting such despairing circumstances, the "final conclusion" asks:

what can one say

until we become men whom health does not bore
some Beauty will be traveling in space
camouflaged never struck by anyone

an idol that still

knows to preserve the olive-tree's aspect
among the Scythians
and that will be restored to us
like a lovely echo from the
Mediterranean
smelling still of a deepsea goat

one for the other Odysseus
upon a raft

centuries now

I cry out in Greek and no one answers me

it is that no one knows any more
what noon reflection means
how and whence leans omega to alpha
who finally disunites time

Ad libitum.

How much hope is there still left for time's transcendence? The highly unexpected and puzzling postscript reads: "P.S. But there is a different version: don't believe me / the more I age the less I understand / experience untaught me the world." Is this only an ironic joke, or a moment's mood, or a way to say that negation too has not been overlooked or omitted? Or does it express the poet's utter bitterness for the lack of response he feels he has received? Or does it say that even he himself has not been left untouched by doubt as to the validity, the truth, of his message? The fact remains that even if this postscript comes gently, sotto voce, as an epilogue, an afterthought, it is still the last word of the poem, its conclusion, with an emotional precedent in the **"Exit"** of *The Little Seafarer*.

Jeffrey Carson (review date 1992)

SOURCE: "Elegiac Elytis: 'Elegies of Jutting Rock'," in *World Literature Today*, Vol. 66, No. 3, Summer, 1992, pp. 445-46.

[*In the following review, Carson examines the influences on Elytis's elegies, focusing specifically on the "eternal values" of Elytis's verse: love, awe, and redemption.*]

Odysseus Elytis's eightieth birthday, on 2 November 1991 was widely celebrated in Greece. Literary journals undertook dedicatory issues, television and radio produced special programs, concerts were given. Elytis answered us with the best gift of all, a new volume of poems, *Ta eleyía tis Oxópetras* (*The Elegies of Jutting Rock*), his fourth since his Nobel Prize in 1979.

Jung suggests that the artist in old age must reverse the expansions of youth and focus on what is most meaningful and permanent. The aged Rembrandt's sitters radiate a dim halo of inner, unnatural light, and Titian's later backgrounds smolder with sanguine brushstrokes. The old Yeats climbs in his last works toward a joyful simplicity based on reality's archetypes, and the euphonious Stevens grows harsher in his imagination's recasting of memory and desire. Beethoven's mysterious late quartets plumb imagination and introspection as a deliverance from the tragedy of experience, and Bach wrote fugues in his last year that to this day no one is sure how to execute. With the concentration and ardent assurance of his recent period, Elytis joins this group.

In his collected prose Elytis, describing his paradise, invokes the *kore* poetry and "birds which even amid the truth of death insist on warbling in Greek and on saying 'eros,' 'eros,' 'eros.'" Elytis's first great poem, **"Anniversary"** (from his 1939 book *Prosanatolizmí* (*Orientations*) is a meditation on death.) Eros and thanatos continue to be his theme. The Elegies, however, are not "about" death; rather, Elytis peers through death to eternal values as he used (and continues) to peer through pelagic waters and crisp ethers. Thus the title is apt, since an elegy is a lyric whose formal lament meditates on the death of a person or the tragedy of existence and finds solace in the contemplation of eternal values. "Jutting Rock" translates the Greek *Oxópetra,* the name of a deserted rocky promontory on the island of Astypalaea; the poet has in mind the sound and image rather than the place.

Elytis is doing nothing else than trying more concretely than ever to get into words the ultimate diaphaneity he has always attested. The difficulties of the book are not in the writing but in the subject. That is why Elytis has developed, yet again, a new style, different from the many he has previously found useful.

For a model, Elytis took Hölderlin's elegies, which deal with the impossible ideal and golden youth. The look of Hölderlin's lines and techniques of construction deliberately recall Pindar, always one of Elytis's exemplars. (Like Elytis, Pindar thinks perceptually, not conceptually, and, with one exception, no two of his elaborate meters are identical.)

In the third Elegy, **"Cupid and Psyche,"** Elytis remembers how Hölderlin transformed his love for a real girl into poetry (called "Diotima"), and, like Hölderlin, he affirms that "within the Futile and the Nothing" exists "that unascertained something": this is the thesis of all fourteen of the Elegies. "Cupid" in Greek is *Eros*; *Psyche* is the word for "Soul." Their story was probably first told in Apuleius' Latin romance *The Golden Ass* (after 125 A.D.). After the girl Psyche lost her god-lover by looking at him, Venus set her many tasks, one of which was to bring back from Persephone a box containing Beauty; opening it, Psyche found nothing; Cupid eventually married her. In Plato's *Symposium* Socrates says that the priestess of Mantinea, Diotima, taught him his metaphysic of Eros. The disastrous end of Hölderlin's love affair with Susette Gontard (whom he called "Diotima") upset his fragile psyche; when he heard of her death in 1802, he went mad. Caught permanently in the "Harpy's claws" of madness, Hölderlin, who was Swabian, often signed his name "Scardanelli."

Elytis calls Dionysios Solomos "my master" and often invokes him in his poetry, always heroically. Solomos (1798-1857) is the founder of modern Greek poetry. Born on the Ionian island of Zakynthos, then part of Italy while most of Greece belonged to Turkey, he was educated in Italian, and so he did not know the purist Greek in which other writers waxed poetic. Though he never visited the Greek mainland, he proved that the spoken language was capable of great subtlety and exaltation in a poetry of national, ethical, and stylistic struggle. In his verse romantic emotion is controlled by exquisite diction, rigorous form, and undoubted sincerity. Because he was forging something new, he completed little, but every one of his fragments has seeded much Greek poetry. The short poem "Glory," for example, on the Ottoman slaughter of the populace of tiny Psara, showed how the demotic tongue could rival Simonides for grave brevity: "On the deepblack ridge of Psara / Glory walking in solitude / meditates on the bright young heroes / and on her hair she wears a wreath / woven of the scanty grasses / remaining on that desolate land."

Solomos's most famous longer poems are "The Hymn to Liberty" (whose first stanzas are the Greek national anthem), "On the Death of Lord Byron," and his masterpiece, the fragmentary work "The Free Besieged," in which the starving Greeks of Missolonghi heroically resist the Turks during the War of Independence. In his great 1985 sequence **The Little Seafarer** Elytis imagines the poet's spirit at Missolonghi, and in a set of epiphanies called "Snapshots" he recalls a visit to Solomos's house: "Late afternoon in Akrotiri, at the old house of Dionysios Solomos. In front of the large, round, stone table in the garden. Awe and silence. And also a muffled, strange consolation." These words are the starting point for **"Awe and Devastation of Solomos."**

What Yeats called Byzantium and Pound Ecbatana, Elytis calls **"Lost Commagene,"** which in daily life is unattainable. Commagene was a small Hellenistic kingdom founded in 162 B.C. in northern Syria, later annexed to Roman Syria by Vespasian. Eupalinus of Megara built the underground aqueduct on Samos—a remarkable engineering feat—during the reign of Polycrates (d. 522 B.C.). (Possibly the association was triggered by the founder of Commagene's capital [150 B.C.], King Samos.)

The concluding elegy, **"The Last of Saturdays,"** allows an ascension into the pellucid sea depths and sunlight of the other side. Socrates was warned by invisible powers to prepare for the ascension by writing poems. The line "the stone and the tomb and the soldier" refers to icons of the Resurrection. This is the Elegies' permanent principle of hope, tragically metaphorical. The last line is "Death the sun without sunsets." The last line, that is, of **The Elegies of Jutting Rock**; Elytis is still writing, and, as he has said, there is a different version waiting to be built on Homer's beaches.

FURTHER READING

Biography

Gregory, Dorothy M. T. "Odysseus Elytis." in *European Writers,* Vol 13, edited by George Stade, pp. 2955-988. New York: Scribner, 1983.
> Provides an overview of Elytis's background and influences; contains selected bibliography.

Criticism

Elytis, Odysseus. "Nobel Lecture, 8 December 1979." *Georgia Review* XLIX, No. 1 (Spring 1995): 99-104.
> Translation of Elytis's acceptance speech upon his receipt of the Nobel Prize in literature in 1979.

Friar, Kimon. "Introduction." In *The Sovereign Sun,* pp. 3-44. Philadelphia: Temple University Press, 1974.
> A detailed introduction to Elytis's poetry.

Green, Peter. "The Poets' Greece." *The New York Review of Books* XXVII, No. 11 (June 26, 1980): 40-44.

Discusses Elytis's poetry in the context of modern Greek literature.

Hamill, Sam. "A Paradise of One's Own: Odysseas Elytis." *Georgia Review* XLIX, No. 1 (Spring 1995): 105-10.
Examines the insights that shape Elytis's poetry.

Jouanny, Robert. "Aspects of Surrealism in the Works of Odysseus Elytis." *Books Abroad* 49, No. 4 (Autumn 1975): 685-89.
Discusses the influence of surrealism on modern Greek poetry.

Malkoff, Karl. "Eliot and Elytis: Poet of Time, Poet of Space." *Comparative Literature* 36, No. 3 (Summer 1984): 238-57.
Compares Elytis's *The Axion Esti* to T. S. Eliot's *Four Quartets,* and presents evidence of similarities in theme and in form.

Additional coverage of Elytis's life and career is contained in the following sources published by Gale Research: *Contemporary Authors,* Vols. 102, 151; *Contemporary Literary Criticism,* Vols. 15, 49, 100; *DISCovering Authors: Poets Module*; and *Major 20th-Century Writers.*

Anne Finch
1661-1720

(Full name: Anne Kingsmill Finch, Countess of Winchilsea)
English poet and playwright.

INTRODUCTION

A poet of the early eighteenth century, Anne Finch composed in a variety of contemporary forms, including the verse epistle, the Pindaric ode, the fable, and occasional poetry, exploring issues of authorship, love, friendship, and nature. Her nature poetry celebrates the beauty of the country, especially in contrast to the superficial frivolity of London society, while her love poetry praises married life rather than the attentions of a lover. Finch defended the appropriateness of women writing and often adapted the conventions of male Augustan writers to female experiences and themes. Though rarely adopting the satirical tone of Alexander Pope or Jonathan Swift, Finch was nonetheless encouraged in her craft by these literary figures.

Biographical Information

Born the youngest of three children to upper-class parents in Hampshire, Anne Kingsmill had lost her father, mother, and stepfather by the age of seven. While little is known about her childhood, it is believed that her upbringing was entrusted to her mother's brother. Well-educated and carefully nurtured to be suitably married, she was appointed a Maid of Honor in 1683 to Mary of Modena, Duchess of York and later queen consort of James II. At court she met an attendant to the Duke of York, Heneage Finch, whom she married in 1684. They evinced a contented mutual love uncharacteristic of their sophisticated age, and he became a source of inspiration and support for Finch's creative endeavors. Using the pen name "Ardelia," Finch wrote a number of love poems to her husband, whom she styled "Dafnis" in her poetry. In 1688, the Finches were forced to retire from public life after refusing to take the oath of allegiance to William III. For a time the Finches relied on the generosity of various members of their families until they made their permanent home at Eastwell in Kent, where Heneage Finch succeeded his nephew in title after the latter's death in 1712. At Eastwell, an estate removed from the activities of London, the couple devoted themselves to intellectual interests and enjoyed the pleasures of rural life, an unconventional attitude to hold during a time when life divorced from the bustle and excitement of court and town was considered "a living entombment." Eastwell's seclusion and idyllic surroundings afforded Finch intense delight and provided the inspiration for much of her nature poetry. Her early

poetry appeared anonymously in songbooks and miscellanies, or circulated in manuscript form among her friends and acquaintances. After the success of her poetic description of the effects of depression in "The Spleen" and with the continued encouragement by her husband, Finch anonymously published *Miscellany Poems on Several Occasions* in 1713. Though she never published another collection, she continued to write and share her manuscripts with her family and friends until her death in 1720.

Major Works

Finch's *Miscellany Poems on Several Occasions* and her unpublished manuscript poems record the insights of a creative aristocratic woman. The majority of her poems are characterized by such themes as gender and politics. Marginalized through politics and her desire to write, Finch recognized the difficulties of an eighteenth-century woman assuming the public voice of a poet, while insisting that intellectual pursuits were not the prerogative of men. She commemorated the beauty of nature in "Nocturnal

Reverie," "The Tree," "The Bird," and "Petition for an Absolute Retreat," the latter poem also suggesting her escape from political turmoil. In a similar vein, "Ardelia's Answer to Ephelia" lauds the value of rural retirement while criticizing the pretentiousness of London society and female vanity. In "The Introduction," "Circuit of Apollo," "Ardelia's Answer to Ephelia," and "To the Nightingale," she asserted the validity of women writing. In taking up the pen to write love poetry, she countered the tradition of arranged marriages and male infidelity by celebrating conjugal love in poems to her husband, though she criticized mercenary marriages in other poems. Her greatest eighteenth-century success, "The Spleen," examines both a generalized public understanding of the condition and treatment of melancholy and her private suffering.

Critical Reception

Although Finch's *Miscellany Poems on Several Occasions* was published anonymously, it was widely known as the work of the Countess of Winchilsea by those in literary circles. Pope, Swift, and Nicholas Rowe praised her poetry, though Pope also satirized her as one of the "female wits" of the age. Finch's popularity declined in the late eighteenth century until 1820 when William Wordsworth inserted seventeen of her poems in a private anthology that he had compiled, proposing Finch as one of the few poets since John Milton to incorporate fresh images of nature. Following Wordsworth's assessment, many critics of Finch tended to see her as a precursor to Romantic poets rather than as a participant in Augustan culture. With the discovery and publication of some of Finch's manuscript poems in the twentieth century, other critics have emphasized Finch's connection to the seventeenth century metaphysical poetry of John Donne. In addition, many critics have pointed out Finch's position among the circle of female authors including Katherine Philips and Aphra Behn. Most often, Finch is seen not as a minor Augustan poet overshadowed by Pope and John Dryden, but as a major voice in women's literature of the eighteenth-century.

PRINCIPAL WORKS

Poetry

Miscellany Poems on Several Occasions, Written by a Lady, 1713 1713
The Poems of Anne, Countess of Winchilsea 1903
Poems by Anne, Countess of Winchilsea 1928
Selected Poems of Anne Finch: Countess of Winchilsea 1979
Poems by Anne Finch 1980; published in journal *Women's Studies: An Interdisciplinary Journal*
Anne Finch, Countess of Winchilsea, Selected Poems 1987

CRITICISM

John Middleton Murry (essay date 1931)

SOURCE: "The Countess of Winchilsea," in *Countries of the Mind: Essays in Literary Criticism,* Oxford University Press, 1931, pp. 166-80.

[*In the following excerpt, Murry describes Finch as a poet of emotions rather than one of ideas, pointing specifically to her love of nature and of her husband.*]

In 1664, when Anne Finch was three, her mother died; and seven years later her stepfather, Sir Thomas Ogle, died also. No doubt she lived with some of her many connexions, who naturally brought her up to be married, and little besides. There is a perceptible tinge of resentment against such an education in her poetry; and seeing that her dreamland was one

> Where no dowry e'er was paid,
> Where no jointure e'er was made . . .

and that none of her childhood connexions, save one, have any place in her poetry, we may imagine that she was none too happy as a girl. There seem to have been no childish recollections on which she loved to dwell, although she was precisely the kind of woman who might have been expected to do so: and the very fervour of her devotion to Mary of Modena, to whom she became a Maid of Honour in 1683, suggests that the fatherless and motherless girl found in her royal mistress an object of which her affection had previously been starved. And this perhaps will explain the persistence with which her loyal lover, Colonel Heneage Finch, Captain of Halberdiers and Gentleman of the Bedchamber in the same Royal Household, had to woo her—in days when eligible suitors were not lightly put aside—before

> his constant passion found the art
> To win a stubborn and ungrateful heart.

I like to fancy—and fancy here may legitimately be indulged—that two at least of Mary of Modena's Maids of Honour, Anne Finch and that Mistress Anne Killigrew whom Dryden immortalized, formed with their royal mistress something of a feminine cabal. They were, I think, a little down on men, and perhaps the notorious liaison between the Duke of York and yet a third Maid of Honour, Catherine Sedley—what simple and lovely names!—made them adopt, as it were in defence of their mistress, a distinctly chilly attitude to wooers. Anyhow Anne Finch was no heiress; and we cannot suppose that she aimed higher than the son and uncle of an Earl. Besides which, it is clean contrary to what we know of her character to suppose that she put him off in hope of something better. And what we know of Colonel Heneage Finch makes it certain that she could not have hoped for a goodlier man or a more loving husband. The probabilities are that she was, though not quite 'stubborn and ungrateful', as she afterwards made out in the self-abasement of love, discouraging and superior towards his advances. Beautiful I am positive she was, but alas! a little of the blue-stocking and a little of the man-hater, and she did not believe in making herself too agreeable. However, the Colonel persisted, and she at last relented. The flag once lowered, came down with a run, for in the register of marriage dated May 14, 1684, in which the Colonel truthfully described himself as a 'bachelor aged about 27 years', Anne Kingsmill declared that she was a 'spinster aged about 18 years', which was five years too little. *Corruptio optimi pessima,* will say the feminists at this shocking defection: but I, like Richard Burton in like circumstances, declare roundly that I admire her for it. There should be no half-measures in love, and if Anne Kingsmill went to extremes at the moment she first indulged in feminine arts, it was due not to misplaced enthusiasm, but lack of practice.

There can have been, in the whole history of love, few happier marriages than this one, even though it was childless. Thirty-nine years later, when Anne Finch had been dead three years, the Earl of Winchilsea (as Colonel Finch unexpectedly became) wrote against the date of his marriage in a little private diary, meant for no eyes but his own and God's, 'Most blessed day'. There is no gainsaying such evidence, even by the professional cynic; but it really does no more than confirm the witness of the poems themselves. If it is not real happy married love that speaks in the most intimate of them then one man's ear for the voice of true emotion is hopelessly at fault. The situation was, of course, a little unusual for an aristocratic couple in those days; though probably the fashionable literature of the time leads us to think it rather more unusual than it actually was. Certainly, Ardelia (for that was her poetical name for herself, given with an obvious, and probably just, allusion to 'ardent') was whimsically aware of a certain abnormality about the whole proceeding—a husband who

> by tenderest proof discovers
> They err who say that husbands can't be lovers,

and a wife who positively shocks Parnassus by demanding inspiration for a love-poem to her legal lord and master. Indeed, it seems to be true that Colonel Finch found separation even harder to bear than she did. For when she was at Tunbridge Wells for the waters in the summer of 1685, in pursuit of assuagement for her melancholy or spleen, he felt so lonely that he urged her to return. It was she who had to be firm, as appears by the only decipherable stanza of her reply:

> Daphnis, your wish no more repeat
> For my return, nor mourn my stay,
> Lest my wise purpose you defeat,
> And urged by love I come away.
> My own desires I can resist,
> But blindly yield if you persist.

This was in 1685, the year after the marriage. Anne Finch had left the service of Mary of Modena; but the Colonel retained his posts in the Duke of York's Household. So they lived at Westminster, honourably situated, though not affluent, through the brief and troubled reign of their master. It was, we may guess, in Westminster, while James was still Duke of York, that she heard 'unpaid sailors, and hoarse pleaders brawl'. When James became King and in control of the Treasury, the sailors had no need to clamour for their pay. He was, she declares in her elegy on his death,

> Open to all; but when the seaman came,
> Known by his face and greeted by his name,
> Peculiar smiles and praises did impart,
> To all his prowess and desert:
> All had his willing hand, the seaman had his heart.
> He, born an Islander, by nature knew
> Her wooden walls her strength, her guard the naval
>   crew.

Yet another contrast she noted, as a member of a Royal Household well might do, between the reigns of the Merry Monarch and his more conscientious brother, and she gives us a glimpse of her own past anxieties, when she writes:

> Weep ye attendants who composed his train
> And no observance spent in vain
> Nor ever with uneasy fears
> Contracted needful debts and doubted your arrears.

But the halcyon days of paid sailors and paid salaries were soon over. Three brief years and all was lost. James and his queen went into exile, and the Finches, their faithful servants, into disgrace and poverty. They became 'gentlefolk in reduced circumstances'. In some verses commiserating with Colonel Finch upon his gout, Ardelia explains that he was

> Not rich enough to soothe the bad disease
> By large expenses to engage his stay,
> Nor yet so poor to fright the gout away.

For many years he refused to take the oath of allegiance to William of Orange, and thus debarred himself for his honour's sake from all places of profit and emolument under the Crown. Instead of a soldier he became perforce a student of warfare, and in **"The Invitation to Daphnis"** we are given a glimpse of him poring over the maps of Mons and Namur. Retirement was forced upon them, but they were fit for retirement. They were dependent upon the kindness of their family and friends; but their family and friends were kind. And though one may easily gather from Ardelia's poems that at first the position of poor relation was trying, one gathers with no less certainty that the young Earl of Winchilsea behaved towards them as a sympathetic kinsman should behave. At last the unexpected happened; the young Earl died leaving no direct heir, and Colonel Finch succeeded to the title. He put on flesh—the notebook records his being weighed at sixteen stone—became one of the studious antiquaries of the time, and in 1717 was elected President of their learned Society. Three years later, on August 5, 1720, the Countess of Winchilsea died. In her latter years she had published anonymously her **Miscellany Poems,** and consorted with the great wits of the age, Swift, Pope, Gay, and Arbuthnot. It was said that either Pope or Gay satirized her in *Three Hours after Marriage* as a blue-stocking with the itch for scribbling, and she was also said to have given offence to Gay in particular by saying that his *Trivia* showed that 'he was more proper to walk before a chair than to ride in one'. All this dubious gossip is uninteresting. What she was her poems sufficiently declare; and, if we set her poetical gift aside, we find in her and her husband a very perfect example of a type which, though it grows rarer, is assuredly not yet extinct in the English aristocracy: true ladies and true gentlemen who do not willingly provide paragraphs for the gossip-columns, nor take up postures innumerable in the illustrated weeklies: on their estates, in town, in the Royal Household itself, which they generally serve at some time in their lives, they live sequestered; secret charities, unpaid services, flow from them; and the love and honour of a countryside flows to them. Their felicity is enviable, but not envied, because they have deserved it: in word and deed, in courtesy and kindness, they remember that *noblesse oblige.*

Anne Finch was truly religious. She tasted early the mutability of human fortunes; and as Bossuet said of Queen Henrietta Maria, 'Elle-même a su profiter de ses malheurs et de ses disgrâces plus qu'elle n'avait fait de toute sa gloire'. The **"Fragment"** plainly records the process of her soul, and in many other of her poems are unmistakable traces of a genuine contemplative piety. The good Bishop Ken was her friend and spiritual guide. Thus, though in virtue of the nature-mysticism which utters itself in **"A Nocturnal Reverie"** she has intelligibly been called the precursor of the English Romantics, she is romantic with an essential difference. There is no trace of pantheism in her attitude. That had to wait for Rousseau before it declared itself. And that same **"Nocturnal Reverie"**, which by the depth and directness of its nature-emotion so clearly anticipates the Romantic revival, contains at the end a line which makes clear the distinction between the Countess of Winchilsea's creed and that of her more famous successors. In such a moment of rapture, she says, 'the free soul'

> Joys in the inferior world, and thinks it like her
>   own.

Doubtless, the Countess wrote the line to guard herself against being misunderstood by other people and by herself. We have only to compare the thought of the concluding lines of the **"Reverie"** with that of Wordsworth's "Tintern Abbey" to understand the distinction between orthodoxy (which we may, if we know what we are about, call classicism) and romanticism in the matter of nature-poetry. The world of nature, though she loved deeply, was still the inferior world for the Countess; the soul did not inhabit there. Only there were moments when it could delude itself into believing that it did. In her 'recovered moments' she remembered that she must wait 'till heaven be known in heaven'. The 'ineffable recess' was not approached even in the most ecstatic of her earthly thoughts.

But she was in no real danger of sacrificing this life to the next. She was acute in her own self-knowledge, and was quite able to distinguish a mood of depression from a spiritual discontent. Her curious Pindaric poem **"The Spleen"**, which is said to have been judged the best account of that elusive infirmity by eighteenth-century doctors, shows that she had discovered for herself or inherited the sane psychology of the orthodox tradition. If Cowper or Smart had had her religious wisdom they would have been spared much·suffering, and we might have gained much poetry. It is the spleen, she says, and not true religion which causes morbid religious fear.

> By thee Religion, all we know
>   That should enlighten here below,
>   Is veiled in darkness and perplexed,
> With anxious doubts and endless scruples vexed,
> And some restraint implied from each perverted text
> Is but thy niggard voice disgracing bounteous
>   heaven.

That is religious sanity, condemning Puritanism; and the Countess's religion was so sweet and wholesome that she could on occasion, as in the last lines of **"The Apology"**, be whimsical about it.

The genuine love of nature and the genuine Christian piety which controlled it both distinguished the Countess of Winchilsea from contemporary poets. Though it is not true that religion and the love of nature are necessarily allied (for religion can become predominantly intellectual), it probably is true that a genuine nature-emotion is in some sort religious: so that we may say that if the Countess of Winchilsea had not been pious she would have been a pantheist. It was a very good thing that she was not: for pantheism requires a stronger nature than hers to bear it out to the end. Orthodoxy remained her support, and nature her solace. Thereby she found much happiness, nor was she often tempted to overtax her poetic strength.

That was not great, but it was real. At her best she has an exquisite sense of nuance, and a simple felicity in expressing it. Such phrases as

> Silent as a midnight thought . . .

or

> Softer than love, softer than light
> When just escaping from the night . . .

linger like fragrance in the memory. They are a woman's phrases; and they have a peculiar perfection of femininity. For a slightly different and perhaps even more characteristic nuance, of beauty tinged with malice, we may admire the two astonishing lines from **"The Spleen"**:

> Nor will in fading silks compose
> Faintly the inimitable rose.

That is the *ne plus ultra* of feminine poetry; a perfect example of the Countess of Winchilsea's lovely gift, quintessentially hers because it is shot with her own contempt for

The dull manage of a servile house.

I may be wrong; but I am inclined to believe that those lovely lines had an interesting sequel. They are the jewel of **"The Spleen"**; but that poem contains another striking phrase:

Now the Jonquille o'ercomes the feeble brain;
We faint beneath the aromatic pain.

It has been already noticed, I think first by Sir Edmund Gosse, that Pope borrowed the phrase for his famous line:

Die of a rose in aromatic pain.

But what I suspect is that Pope's line came wholly from **"The Spleen"**; and that he, with his notable flair for the excellent, combined in his memory the two memorable phrases—

Faintly the inimitable rose . . .

and

Faint beneath the aromatic pain

to make his more spectacular, but less lovely, line.

Exquisite is the word for Ardelia at her best. She had a genius for the intangible. Surely nothing, in its kind, was ever better than **"A Sigh"**:

Gentlest air, thou breath of lovers,
  Vapour from a secret fire,
Which by thee itself discovers,
  Ere yet daring to aspire.

Softest note of whispered anguish,
  Harmony's refinedest part,
Striking, whilst thou seemst to languish,
  Full upon the hearer's heart.

Safest messenger of passion,
  Stealing through a crowd of spies,
Which constrain the outward fashion,
  Close the lips and guard the eyes.

Shapeless sigh! we ne'er can show thee,
  Formed but to assault the ear;
Yet, ere to their cost they know thee,
  Every nymph may read thee here.

It *is* a sigh, drawn out to a lovely, silvery music, lingering on the air, gay and tender, a song, if ever one were, for a lover to listen to his mistress singing in a shadowy candle-lighted room to the sound of a harpsichord. And the same strange, simple, and impalpable gift of identifying her music with her theme shines out unmistakably in her little poem to the nightingale. I do not think there can

be any doubt that she wrote it while actually listening to the nightingale's song, or that she was speaking the simple truth when she said:

This moment is thy time to sing,
This moment I attend to praise
And set my numbers to thy lays.
Free as thine shall be my song,
As thy music short or long.

Enchanting is the simplicity with which she captures the veritable voice, the authentic thrill.

She begins. Let all be still!
  Muse, thy promise now fulfil!
Sweet, oh sweet, still sweeter yet!
Can thy words such accents fit,
Canst thou syllables refine,
Melt a sense that shall retain
Still some spirit of the brain?
'T will not be! then change thy note;
  Let division shake thy throat . . .

There is nothing in it? I am not sure that there is not everything. I can but leave it to the delight of others whose ear for poetry is not wholly unattuned to mine. But that the Countess of Winchilsea had a subtle and instinctive understanding of some of the rarest effects of poetical 'music' seems to me indubitable: and for a sort of external corroboration of this opinion I would call in evidence the fact that for the 'musical' theme of her **"Nocturnal Reverie"** she went unerringly to the lovely antiphon of the final scene of *The Merchant of Venice*, 'On such a night . . .'

These are the pinnacles of the Countess of Winchilsea's poetic achievement. **"The Sigh"** and **"The Nightingale"** and **"A Nocturnal Reverie"** at least should be in every anthology. And, for yet another example of what I have called her sense of the nuance, and one that has the added interest of showing that her preoccupation with the elusive was conscious, there are the beautiful lines which Wordsworth admired and extracted from an unequal poem:

Deep lines of honour all can hit,
Or mark out a superior wit;
Consummate goodness all can show
And where such graces shine below:
But the more tender strokes to trace,
To express the promise of a face
When but the dawnings of a mind
We from an air unripened find,
Which, altering as new moments rise,
The pen or pencil's art defies;
When flesh and blood in youth appears
Polished like what our marble wears;
Fresh as that shade of opening green
Which first upon our groves is seen;
Enlivened by a harmless fire
And brightened by each gay desire;
These nicer touches would demand
A Cowley's or a Waller's hand . . .

But, beautiful as it is, it gives us a glimpse of the Countess of Winchilsea's weakness as a poet. She is inclined to be diffuse, to add touch after touch, forgetful of her main design. In this she reminds us of another exquisite minor poet, John Clare. That is only to say, what no one would have doubted, that the Countess of Winchilsea *is* a minor poet. But major poets are few, and minor poets of so delicate an individuality are not very numerous. We certainly cannot afford that a mind so gracious, and a talent so delightful, should any longer be a victim of the iniquity of oblivion.

The genuine love of nature and the genuine Christian piety which controlled it both distinguished the Countess of Winchilsea from contemporary poets.

—John Middleton Murry

The same self-knowledge that is apparent in the sanity of her religion is revealed also in her power of detachment from her own poetry. Sometimes, it is true, she carries self-depreciation too far, and she may be suspected rather of seeking to divert criticism than of speaking the truth from her heart when she declared of some estimable and forgotten contemporary authoress that she

> Of each sex the two best gifts employed
> The skill to write, the modesty to hide.

If anything is certain upon internal evidence it is that Ardelia did not believe that a woman ought to be ashamed of being a writer. Modesty was thrust upon her by a masculine convention. She accepted the convention, but she did not like it. And though she was glad of the fact that she had kept her poetry to herself and her intimates, she does not allow it to be thought that she was glad of the necessity.

'It is still a great satisfaction to me [she wrote in later years], that I was not so far abandoned by my prudence, as out of mistaken vanity, to let any attempts of mine in poetry show themselves while I lived in such a public place as the Court, where everyone would have made their remarks on a versifying Maid of Honour; and by far the greater number with prejudice if not contempt'.

Perhaps, if her verses had been more in accord with the fashion of the day, she would not have been so reticent. Although she was witty, and although she could be quite effectively satirical, she was not particularly interested in being either. The attitude must have made her quite formidable as a young lady in the society of her day. Wit in a woman could be accepted, and returned, if possible, in kind; but to know that a woman could be witty, and yet rather despised her wit, must have been alarming. It called for all Colonel Finch's good-humoured pertinacity to fight his way past the barrier which a kind heart and an original mind had set about themselves. And she for her part was quite acutely aware that her mode in poetry was not that of the moment. She imagines the fashionable critic objecting,

> Oh, stun me not with these insipid dreams,
> The eternal hush, the lullaby of streams;
> Which still (he cries) their even measures keep
> Till both the writers and the readers sleep . . .

'Insipid dreams' is, very precisely, what the wits of town would have called her best poetry. Its tenuous, intangible beauty would have escaped them. 'Insipid' probably would have been the name even for those lines which I prefer to Pope's 'improvement' of them. (It was the age of 'improvers'; and Ardelia occasionally made efforts to 'improve' herself.) 'Insipid', certainly, would have been the word for most of her loveliest lines: the pellucid couplet on first love—

> That oft I sighed, ere yet I knew the cause,
> And was a lover ere I dreamed I was . . .

or on a calm sea—

> For smooth it lay as if one single wave
> Made all the sea, nor winds that sea could heave.

'Insipid' above all the prayer, which she knew had been granted, of her **"Petition for an Absolute Retreat"**:

> Give me there (since Heaven has shown
> It was not good to be alone)
> A partner suited to my mind,
> Solitary, pleased, and kind;
> Who partially may something see
> Preferred to all the world in me.

But 'insipid' would have been their name for Wordsworth also, whose genius finally created the taste for the delicate emotional simplicity which he enjoyed in her work. This simplicity is the simplicity of distinctly felt emotion. The Countess of Winchilsea's contemporaries were less interested in distinct emotions than in distinct ideas. Neither alone is sufficient to make great poetry; but great poetry was not being written in the Countess of Winchilsea's day. Hers, at the best, was authentic poetry of distinct emotion; and that will keep it sweet for many years to come.

Reuben A. Brower (essay date 1945)

SOURCE: "Lady Winchilsea and the Poetic Tradition of the Seventeenth Century," in *Studies in Philology*, Vol. XLII, No. 1, January, 1945, pp. 61-80.

[*In the following excerpt, Brower situates Finch's poems within the metaphysical traditions of John Milton and John Donne.*]

There is little likelihood that present-day readers will regard Anne as a member of the Romantic family unhappily born before 1798. Nevertheless, it is unfortunate that the preface to the standard edition of the poems should so exaggerate Lady Anne's "romantic" qualities. Dr. Reynolds, like most writers on the pre-Romantics, is only too eager to find intimations of Wordsworth in the poetry of the eighteenth century. Yet she shows quite clearly in her preface that Lady Anne was no voice crying in the wilderness of Augustan England. On the contrary, it appears that Lady Winchilsea was acquainted with the leading writers of her day, with Prior, Swift, Pope, Gay, and Rowe. The affinities between much of her poetry and that of Prior and Gay is obvious; while the majority of her poems exhibit one or more typically Augustan qualities: the characteristic neatness and plainness of verse structure, the social and aristocratic tone, the religious solemnity and high morality, and the inevitable fondness for the satirical attitude.

If Lady Winchilsea is "prophetic," in poems such as **"Fanscombe Barn," "The Petition for an Absolute Retreat"** and **"A Nocturnal Reverie,"** she is prophetic of Thomson, Young, Gray, and Akenside, rather than of Wordsworth. Even so, "prophetic" is an awkward term; for blank-versifying, melancholy reflection, night meditations, and even accurate natural images can be found in various poems which were published in Anne's lifetime or very shortly after her death, from Cowley and Flatman to Philips, Pomfret, Parnell, and William Ramsay. Pope himself, as Dr. Leavis has pointed out [in *Revolution,* 1936] anticipates "the eighteenth-century meditative-melancholic." As Dr. Leavis has also reminded us, Pope has affinities with the Metaphysicals. But it is still convenient to call Pope an "Augustan," though in using the term we must remember that the poetry written between 1700 and 1730 is more varied in equality than is often assumed.

If we look at the work of a poet born twenty or thirty years before Pope, we shall see even more clearly the mélange of poetic strains. We shall see indeed how completely seventeenth- and eighteenth-century elements merge. It is for this reason that Lady Winchilsea is an interesting figure to a student of the English poetical tradition. Lady Winchilsea's status as an amateur and the ease with which she lent herself to diverse influences make her a nice case for studying a change in poetic taste. While she is a child of the Restoration (she was born in 1661), she also belongs to the world of the Great Compromise, the majority of her published poems being written during the reigns of James and of William and Mary. Her nearest contemporaries are Prior and Pomfret, a significant pair, if we consider the mixture in Lady Anne's work of the Restoration social manner and the love of an "absolute retreat." But though she frankly admired the great writers of the Restoration, she was a country lady before she was a lady-in-waiting; and her piety and love of simple things were hardly products of the Court of Charles II.

We should look for her social and literary forbears among aristocratic ladies such as the Countess of Pembroke and Elizabeth Cary, Viscountess Falkland, ladies who also cultivated piety and poetry and learning. Like earlier bluestockings, Lady Winchilsea writes mainly for aristocratic friends and relations and discreetly circulates her poems in manuscript form. Publication is an afterthought, coming only when a reputation has been established in polite circles. In her poetry as in her way of living, Anne looks both before and after. She pines for a sweet retreat, but also for the "sence and Nature . . . of Dryden, Etheridge, or Lee," and for the worldly glories of Restoration literature. It is a still more interesting fact that her poetry shows connections also with the then old-fashioned Metaphysicals. Before looking at the evidence for this connection, we should recall that though obsolescent, Metaphysical poetry still enjoyed some popularity during Lady Anne's childhood, and even in the eighties when she was writing her earlier poems. Inglorious minors such as Flatman and Ayres were very likely writing Metaphysical poetry in the 1670's and 1680's. Cleveland must have been much read, to judge by the republication of his poems in 1677, 1687, and 1699. Cowley was most certainly read and imitated. And it was in 1681 that the *Miscellaneous Poems* of Marvell were first published.

Without yielding to the pleasant temptation of making a "post-Metaphysical" out of a "pre-Romantic," we may point out certain Metaphysical elements in a fairly large number of Lady Winchilsea's poems. These elements deserve some scrutiny as showing both the continuity of poetic tradition in the seventeenth and eighteenth centuries and the change in sensibility which was gradually taking place. There are in Lady Anne's poetry traces of the conceit, of the combination of "levity and seriousness," and of the union of lyricism with the diction and movement of speech,—characteristics which are so well illustrated in Donne, Herbert, and Marvell. These familiar features of the Metaphysical style can be seen in **"An Invocation to Sleep."** The poem starts in a manner which has an Elizabethan-Petrarchan ancestry:

> How shall I wooe thee gentle rest,
> To a sad Mind, with cares oppress'd?

Quite like the sonneteers the poetess says she can offer Sleep her head, if not her "overburthen'd" Heart. But the sugared sweets of Elizabethan song have been adulterated by introducing the accents of speech. The flavor of the following lines is definitely seventeenth century; it is also definitely not Augustan (as the term is used of Pope):

> Nor do I think, that heretofore
> Our first great Father, gave thee more,
> When, on a flow'ry bank, he lay,
> And did thy strietest Laws obey:
> For, to compose his lovely Bride,
> He yielded not alone his side,
> But, if we judge by the event,
> Half of his heart too, with itt went,
> Which, waken'd drew him soon away
> To Eve's fair bosome, where itt lay,
> Pleas'd to admitt his rightfull claim
> And tending, still, tow'rds whence itt came.

These lines are less simply serious than is the introduction; they are touched with humour and wit. There is, for example, the half-serious "proof" of the similarity between her case and Adam's. And the fairly elaborate, if subdued, conceit (the divided heart) has a Metaphysical quality, as can be seen by comparison with Cleveland's lines "Upon an Hermaphrodite":

> Adam, till his rib was lost,
> Had both sexes thus engrossed.
> When Providence our Sire did cleave,
> And out of Adam carved Eve,
> Then did man 'bout wedlock treat,
> To make his body up complete.

Anne's fancy is certainly subdued when compared with the outrageous ambiguities and the flaunting irreverence of Cleveland's hard and clipped lines. Humour has softened the invention; and the politeness of "compose his lovely Bride," "yielded," "fair bosome," and "pleas'd" contrasts sharply with the indecent dispatch of "cleave" and "carved." The firm outlines of the seventeenth-century manner are slowly dissolving in gentility and tenderness. And yet a minor poetess can still avail herself of the seventeenth-century conventions. She can play with her sadness. Her mood still presents a refreshing contrast with the deadly solemnity of eighteenth-century nocturnal meditations.

There is only one complete poem by Lady Winchilsea which we might confidently include in a collection of Metaphysical verse, the lines **"On Affliction"**:

> Wellcome, what e're my tender flesh may say,
>   Welcome affliction, to my reason, still;
> Though hard, and ruged on that rock I lay
>   A sure foundation, which if rais'd with skill,
>   Shall compasse Babel's aim, and reach th'
>   Almighty's hill.
>
> Wellcome the rod, that does adoption shew,
>   The cup, whose wholsome dregs are giv'n me here;
> There is a day behind, if God be true,
>   When all these Clouds shall passe, & heav'n be
>   clear,
>   When those whom most they shade, shall shine
>   most glorious there.
>
> Affliction is the line, which every Saint
>   Is measur'd by, his stature taken right;
> So much itt shrinks, as they repine or faint,
>   But if their faith and Courage stand upright,
>   By that is made the Crown, and the full robe of
>   light.

It would be hard to deny that these lines are reminiscent of George Herbert, though there is no evidence, aside from the title, of any direct indebtedness. In particular, we miss the real, if mild conflict of Herbert's internal debates. What reminds us of Herbert is the architectural imagery and the personal allegory presented through Biblical allusions. By contrast we can see in the banality and warm sentiment of

"There is a day behind, if God be true," an anticipation of the hymn style of Cowper.

> Much of "The Spleen" like most of Anne's other consciously "serious" poetry does not anticipate the Romantics or recall the Metaphysicals; it is perfectly characteristic of the poetry of melancholy being written at the turn of the century.
>
> —*Reuben A. Brower*

It is the third stanza which shows that the poem belongs to the Metaphysical tradition. The Metaphysical features hardly call for demonstration: the geometrical flavor of the "line" figure, the seemingly paradoxical logic of the "shrinking measure," and the bold double shift of the "line" metaphor to that of "the Crown, and the full robe of light." In a commonsense reading of the lines, we might suppose that affliction increases when Christians "repine and faint," and decreases when they are courageous. But as in Donne, the paradoxical inversion is not a mere paradox, since it corresponds to the realities of faith and experience. And again, as in both Donne and Herbert, this suprising turn of thought is reserved for the conclusion of the poem. The objective, generalizing form of statement used in this stanza is also an inheritance from Metaphysical poetry, the shift from the second person to the third person indicating a change from a personal to a more detached view of the experience.

The same close union of wit and seriousness is hard to match elsewhere in Anne's poetry, though a fair number of Metaphysical conceits can be found. In the long Pindaric ode, **"Upon the Death of Sir William Twisden,"** we find a laborious Cowleyesque account of Parliamentary affairs (Sir William had lost his seat in Parliament to an inferior candidate):

> Well did we in our far applauded Kent . . .
> Make him our choice, the Whole to represent;
> The worthyest pattern of the publick Mind.
> Who, when alas! we more Fanatick grew,
> A heavyer Immage of our Country drew
> (Like to a fault, in every altered part)
> A rough ill wrought Dessign, a work of Flemish Art.

In **"To the Nightingale,"** there is a conceit which shows less superficial Metaphysical qualities: the subtle analysis of thought, the compression effected by unexpectedly combining the concrete with the abstract:

> Canst thou Syllables refine,
> Melt a Sense that shall retain
> Still some Spirit of the Brain,
> Till with Sounds like these it join.

The union in this poem of "rapture" and cool gaiety is also notable, a mixture of qualities which has been overlooked by rather too fervent admirers of the poem.

At the close of **"The Absolute Retreat,"** in lines of a superficially "Wordsworthian" cast, Lady Anne introduces a conceit of a common Metaphysical type:

> But as those, who Stars wou'd trace
> From a subterranean Place,
> Through some Engine lift their Eyes
> To the outward, glorious Skies;
> So th' immortal Spirit may,
> When descended to our Clay,
> From a rightly govern'd Frame
> View the Height, from whence she came;
> To her Paradise be caught,
> And things unutterable taught.

The telescope image is of a type which can be found repeatedly in religious poetry of the seventeenth century, being used by Milton, Marvell, Donne, and many other writers. There is also in these lines a faint imprint of the Metaphysical way of thinking in verse: note, for example, the neat ambiguity of "rightly govern'd Frame," and the Platonic character of the whole figure. The conventional seventeenth-century quality of the passage may be further brought out by comparison with some lines from another minor poet, Arthur Wilson:

> *Man is a thing of nought!* yet from above
> There beams upon his soul such rays of love,
> As may discover by *Faith's* optic, where
> The Burning Bush is, though not see HIM there,
> The meekest man on earth did only see
> His shadow shining there, it was not HE.
> And if that great soul, who with holy flame,
> And ravish'd spirit to the Third Heav'n came,
> Saw things unutterable, what can we
> Express of those things that we ne'er did see?

"*Faith's* optic" and the identical "things unutterable" of course do not indicate any direct connection between the two poems; such coincidences merely show that Lady Winchilsea at times writes in the idiom of the mid-seventeenth century. But her telescope figure, despite its derivation, presents a contrast with more purely Metaphysical conceits. It is relatively open, loose in texture, nearer to the illustrative similes of the neo-classical type. Wilson's "optic" figure has by comparison more of the enigmatic quality of Metaphysical poetry.

We can find a more interesting example of the Metaphysical style in a famous couplet from **"The Spleen"**:

> Now the *Jonquille* o'ercomes the feeble Brain;
> We faint beneath the Aromatick Pain.

A comparison of the second line with the well-known parallels in Dryden, Pope, and Shelley will clarify Anne's place in poetical tradition, showing in particular that she is nearer to Donne than to the Romantics. The pungency of "faint beneath the Aromatick Pain" can be felt only in context, since the line comes as a climax to a passage describing in Platonic terms the rebellion of the senses against the soul:

> Falsly, the Mortal Part we blame
> Of our deprest, and pond'rous Frame,
> Which, till the First degrading Sin
> Let Thee, its dull Attendant, in,
> Still with the Other did comply,
> Nor clogg'd the Active Soul, dispos'd to fly,
> And range the Mansions of it's native Sky.
> Nor, whilst in his own Heaven he dwelt,
> Whilst Man his Paradice possest,
> His fertile Garden in the fragrant East,
> And all united Odours smelt,
> No armed Sweets, until thy Reign,
> Cou'd shock the Sense, or in the Face
> A flusht, unhandsom Colour place.
> Now the *Jonquille* o'ercomes the feeble Brain;
> We faint beneath the Aromatick Pain,
> Till some offensive Scent thy Pow'rs appease,
> And Pleasure we resign for short, and nauseous
> Ease.

The flicker of wit in "Aromatick Pain" can now be sensed; in fact, the phrase is a good example of the *discordia concors* which Dr. Johnson considered characteristic of Metaphysical poetry. But the richness of the expression can only be appreciated if it is set beside the tame replica, "nauseous Ease." Here is the bare union of opposites, with little of the suggestiveness of the metaphor in "Aromatick." "Aromatick" does not stand merely as a negative to "Pain," but evokes also a positive sensuous quality, due to the connections with "Jonquille" and "faint." We might be tempted to say that the contrast between "Aromatick Pain" and "nauseous Ease" is the contrast between the wit of the seventeenth century and the wit of the eighteenth century. Certainly in "Aromatick Pain" we have a good example of Metaphysical writing, in the union through metaphor of paradox, sensuous suggestion, and seriousness of thought. This seriousness is the seriousness of a religious and philosophical idea which is experienced, not merely entertained. The paradox has its basis in Christian belief; and the sensuous value of the metaphor is an index of the individuality and sensitivity of the believer's experience.

We can see a good example of wit divorced from this thoughtfulness and vividness of sense impression, if we compare Lady Anne's lines with their probable original in Dryden's *Annus Mirabilis*:

> Amidst whole heaps of spices lights a ball,
> And now their odours arm'd against them fly:
> Some preciously by shatter'd porc'lain fall
> And some by aromatic splinters die.

The "shocking" quality of these lines is a thousand times more evident. Dryden, challenging the reader to play a game of making impossible combinations of words, mints a series of Clevelandisms. The contrasts which result are too various for the reader to absorb at one time: aromatic *vs.* splinters, odours *vs.* armed, odours *vs.* fly (i. e. shoot), preciously *vs.* fall, and so on. As we can see, Anne introduces some of the same contrasts (note "united Odours" and "armed Sweets"); but the effect of her lines is less impersonal and less obviously surprising. Dryden's crackling lines are a good exhibition of later seventeenth-century fancy, of fancy for fancy's sake. The oppositions are bold,—but we might say,—purely "verbal." The reader has to remind himself forcibly that "aromatic" refers to a kind of fragrance.

If we turn to the Pope couplet which is related to these two passages, we shall see some truth in Dr. Leavis's contention that Metaphysical wit was more congenial to Pope that to Dryden:

> Or quick effluvia darting thro' the brain,
> Die of a rose in aromatic pain.

In this couplet at least Pope achieves some closeness of connection between the surprising metaphor and the underlying philosophic idea. (The context in the *Essay on Man* should be recalled.) Though the *Essay on Man* is a classic collection of ideas which are entertained rather than experienced, in this particular passage Pope seems more fully engaged than usual by the thought he is versifying. Unlike the "bright sparkles" of Dryden's quatrain, Pope's metaphor is not easily separable from the "prose sense": Pope makes us feel through his metaphor what life would be like if we were so intensely sensitive. And though Pope's thought has for him little of the personal value which Lady Anne's beliefs have for her, his way of thinking in metaphor brings him with Lady Anne nearer to Donne than to Dryden. But if we now compare again the parallel passages from Pope, Dryden, and Lady Winchilsea, we shall see that Lady Winchilsea's lines have the fullest combination of Metaphysical qualities.

The "romantic" element in Lady Winchilsea's poetry— and in that of other early Augustans—may be gauged in part by contrasting her "Jonquille" lines with a passage from Shelley's *Epipsychidion*. The lines are particularly apt for our purpose because they are so purely Shelleyan:

> And from the moss violets and jonquils peep,
> And dart their arrowy odour through the brain,
> Till you might faint with that delicious pain.

The essential difference is between "faint with that *delicious* pain" and "faint beneath the *Aromatick* Pain." We have left, in Dryden's phrase, "the cool shades of wit" for a sensuous reverie "like echoes of an antenatal dream." Without denying that Shelley's lines may be admired, we must note the loss of a critical attitude which results from the change in the key adjectives. With "delicious," "faint" takes on a quality of sweet indulgence which was barely perceptible in Anne's use of the word. In place of a mere suggestion of faintness we are now offered a full romantic swoon. There is also a marked difference in Ardelia's and Shelley's attitude to "fainting," for Lady Anne is on the side of the angels; she is scornful of mortals who cannot stand up against the assaults of "armed sweets." Indulgence is for her a sin; for Shelley, an opportunity. The comparison does not show us that Lady Anne was an incipient Romantic, but that Shelley, like Wordsworth, read Anne "Romantically." A Shelleyesque reader might also find an exquisite sensuousness in the lines which Mr. Murry so much admires:

> Nor will in fading Silks compose
> Faintly th' inimitable *Rose* . . .

But these lines are less mono-chromatic than they appear out of context. Read in the original stanza, they are touched with a light tone of scorn for ladies who spend their time on embroidery and painting.

Much of **"The Spleen"** like most of Anne's other consciously "serious" poetry does not anticipate the Romantics or recall the Metaphysicals; it is perfectly characteristic of the poetry of melancholy being written at the turn of the century. *All is Vanity, Life's Progress,* and *Some Reflections* are thoughtful, not as Donne's *Third Satire* is "thoughtful," but in the sense in which the word is used of the moral and religious verse of Flatman, Prior and Young. But on occasion, as in the "jonquille" lines, Lady Winchilsea could be thoughtful without excluding wit and freshness of sense perception. She could also be thoughtful without being unctuous, as in **"Ardelia to Melancholy"** and **"On Myselfe,"** poems in which the accent of thoughtful speech marks the style as much closer to Donne and Ben Jonson than to Prior and Young:

> Good Heav'n, I thank thee, since it was design'd
> I shou'd be fram'd, but of the weaker kinde . . .
> > **"On Myselfe"**

> At last, my old inveterate foe,
> No opposition shalt thou know.
> > **"Ardelia to Melancholy"**

The lines **"On Affliction,"** already quoted, show the same union of thoughtfulness and conversational tone; and **"An Invocation to Sleep"** and **"The Losse"** have more than a trace of the same style. All these poems show that it was still possible at the close of the seventeenth century to write of self and the "greater facts" without assuming a tone of grandiloquence.

In the eighteenth century the poetry of religious meditation and moral reflection merged with the poetry of natural description in a composite type which is illustrated by countless poems from "The Seasons" to "The Task." To this poetic family belong Lady Winchilsea's two most famous pieces, **"The Petition for an Absolute Retreat"** and **"A Nocturnal Reverie."** Critics interested in the origins of the Romantic movement have usually chosen to isolate one common feature of all these eighteenth-century reflective poems, the fact that the high musings always have a natural setting. But we must observe that though "Nature" is always there, she plays a bewildering number of roles.

As I have already remarked, it is hardly necessary to prove at length that Lady Winchilsea's "Nature" and Wordsworth's represent quite different experiences. But it is worth nothing that in the attitudes toward physical nature and in the combination of natural description with contemplation Lady Anne's poetry has marked affinities with poetry of the seventeenth century. A clue to the literary genealogy of Lady Winchilsea's "nature poetry" is offered by a charming passage from **"The Absolute Retreat"**:

> All, but the *Forbidden Tree*,
> Wou'd be coveted by me;
> Grapes, with Juice so crouded up,
> As breaking thro' the native Cup;
> Figs (yet growing) eandy'd o'er,
> By the Sun's attracting Pow'r;
> Cherries, with the downy Peach,
> All within my easie Reach;
> Whilst creeping near the humble Ground,
> Shou'd the Strawberry be found
> Springing wheresoe'er I stray'd,
> Thro' those Windings and that Shade.

These lines show what Wordsworth meant by citing Anne as one of the few eighteenth-century poets who had an "eye steadily fixed upon the object." Impressions of natural things are presented with some sense of immediacy. But a reader familiar with Marvell's "Garden," will recognize that these lines are not entirely original:

> What wond'rous Life in this I lead!
> Ripe Apples drop about my head;
> The Luscious Clusters of the Vine
> Upon my Mouth do crush their Wine;
> The Nectaren, and curious Peach,
> Into my hands themselves do reach;
> Stumbling on Melons, as I pass,
> Insnar'd with Flow'rs, I fall on Grass.

The similarity of the grape images and the close parallel of the lines riming in *Reach . . . Peach* indicate quite certainly a recollection of Marvell's poem. These similarities are important not as proving the "source" of Lady Anne's lines, but as showing the orientation of much of Lady Winchilsea's "nature poetry." She retains in many passages attitudes which are distinctly those of the seventeeth century, as may be easily illustrated from Marvell and Milton.

John Buxton (essay date 1967)

SOURCE: "The Countess of Winchilsea," in *A Tradition of Poetry*, Macmillan, 1967, pp. 162-70.

[*In the following excerpt, Buxton discusses the importance of nature in Finch's poetry and sees her as a precursor to the Romantics.*]

[Finch] herself, with no masculine tradition of the active life to make discontent, with no household to manage, and no children to care for, might yet have found time hang heavy on her, had she not taken endless pleasure in the life of the countryside. Once, on a visit to Eastwell in July 1689, she took too long a walk in the park, drawn (she said) by 'romantic notions', and got a lift home again 'in a water-cart driven by one of the underkeepers in his green coat, with a hazelbough for a whip'. She turned the incident into a burlesque, merrily laughing at herself for so unromantic a homecoming. She loved the park, which she thought the finest in England, so much that she felt her gift of poetry unequal to the task of its description: if only it had been otherwise, she would surely have exalted its fame above Denham's *Cooper's Hill.* In any event, as she told Pope, she always found it difficult to praise well what she admired. But when in 1702 Lord Winchilsea (her nephew) undertook various improvements at Eastwell she celebrated the occasion in verse. Among these works was the conversion of a mount, that typically Elizabethan feature of a large garden, into a terrace:

> So lies this hill, hewn from its rugged height,
> Now levelled to a scene of smooth delight,
> Where on a terrace of its spoils we walk
> And of the task and the performer talk.

She preferred the distant, unimpeded view which the new terrace gave to surveying elaborately formal knots from the elevation of the mount, just as she preferred the enlarged windows which were inserted in the old house at the same time. In these things she shared the taste of the coming age rather than of that which had passed.

Fifty years before, Andrew Marvell had written his longest poem in compliment to Lord Fairfax, about the house and gardens and park at Nunappleton in Yorkshire. But he preferred the military precision of formal gardening and would not have liked the new landscaping which Lord Winchilsea was bringing to Eastwell; and he never gave any hint that he had looked beyond the confines of the park to 'beauteous fields and scattered woods', or to the remote moorlands in the distance. Yet it is Marvell's poetry that Lady Winchilsea's most often recalls, not because Marvell's tense power of phrase and precise brilliance of imagery lack virility—far from it—but because in an age of fanaticism Marvell remained a balanced and civilized being, one who appreciated the art of living so well that he could declare a cause 'too good to have been fought for'. His achievement was the greater partly because it was so much more difficult in the 1650s than in the 1700s, for a man than for a woman, to refuse to be diverted by the trivialities of political passion.

Marvell's *Garden,* or the park of Appleton House, where he found seclusion from the turmoils of the time, are not unlike the ideal world which Lady Winchilsea describes in her **"Petition for an Absolute Retreat"**. They wrote in similar situations; Marvell when he had joined Lord Fairfax in retirement after his refusal to lead Cromwell's armies against the Scots, Lady Winchilsea when she had accompanied her husband after his refusal to come to terms with 'the Glorious Revolution'. If Marvell had found himself where

Grapes with juice so crowded up
As breaking through the native cup,
Figs, yet growing, candied o'er
By the sun's attracting power,
Cherries, with the downy peach,
All within my easy reach,

he would not have thought himself a stranger, though he
and his hostess would not have agreed about the company they wished to keep. To Marvell

Two paradises 'twere in one
To live in paradise alone.

But Lady Winchilsea included in her **"Petition"** this:

Give me there (since heaven has shown
It was not good to be alone)
A partner suited to my mind,
Solitary, pleased, and kind;
Who, partially, may something see
Preferred to all the world in me.

Marvell, nostalgic for the primal innocence of Eden, must
dissent from the longings of Eve and her daughters.

"The Petition for an Absolute Retreat" is one of the
longest and most ambitious of Lady Winchilsea's poems;
it is also one of the best. Like many of her poems it is
addressed to a friend (here, to the Countess of Thanet,)
whose company she would welcome in her retreat from the
world of fashion. It was that world with its talk of business, and wars, its news and rumours, its exotic dishes
and extravagant dress, its attitudes and affections—in a
word, its vanity, that she rejected. Not there could she feel
at home, but on some quiet estate in the country. She was
thoroughly English in her tastes and preferred the peace
of the garden to the frivolity of London, preferred also (we
may be sure) country clothes to London finery, so that to
her smart acquaintance she was

so rustic in her clothes and mien,
'Tis with her ungenteel to be seen.

We might imagine her, in our own day, dressed in a tweed
suit, a Henry Heath hat and flat-heeled shoes, busy about
her herbaceous borders, a flower-basket on her arm and
secateurs in her hand, arranging the flowers in the house,
and managing her household with calm competence, yet
finding time to be well read and to enjoy the conversation
of her friends and guests.

She wrote **"The Petition"** at a time of distress when all
she wished was to creep away from the hostile world
which had caused this. Later, when she had recovered her
spirits, she could gaily deride that world with a sharpness
of perception which suggests Jane Austen. **"Ardelia's
Answer to Ephelia"**, who had invited her to come to her
in town, like **"The Petition"**, could only have been written
by a woman. She disclaims any bent for the satire and
detraction that were all the rage: she had not, she says
(and we may believe her), enough ill-nature joined to her

wit. She portrays Almeria as another Melantha, to whose
distaste, when they go on an expedition, she presently
stops the coach for, of all things, to go into a church. The
scene is drawn with delightful felicity. We are shown
Almeria fluttering at the windows of her coach in her
eagerness to attract attention. Thus

the gay thing, light as her feathered dress,
Flies round the coach, and does each cushion
press;
Through every glass her several graces shows,
This, does her face, and that, her shape expose
To envying beauties and admiring beauxs.
One stops and, as expected, all extols,
Clings to the door and on his elbow lolls,
Thrusts in his head, at once to view the fair
And keep his curls from discomposing air,
Then thus proceeds—
'My wonder it is grown
To find Almeria here, and here alone.
Where are the nymphs that round you used to
crowd.
Of your long courted approbation proud,
Learning from you, how to erect their hair,
And in perfection all their habit wear,
To place a patch in some peculiar way,
That may an unmarked smile to sight betray,
And the vast genius of the Sex display?'
'Pity me then (she cries) and learn the fate
That makes me porter to a temple gate.'

And Almeria gives her beau a portrait of the wretched
Ardelia: she is most tiresomely uninterested in Almeria's
efforts to make something of her; disdains her advice on
how to dress, or where to shop; fails to remark on the
excellence of the tea she is given to drink; refuses to
prefer the latest plays to those of dull old authors like
Dryden, Etherege, and Lee. Besides, Ardelia has such out
of date ideas on feminine beauty or masculine wit, is so
Puritanical, so boorish. This contrast of sense and sensibility has lost nothing of its freshness or point; and the
author of *Miscellany Poems on several occasions, written by a Lady, 1713,* deserves to be remembered with the
author of a novel 'by a Lady' which was published in
three volumes in 1811.

As with Jane Austen, Lady Winchilsea's comments on
vain women have a feminine sharpness of rebuke quite
unlike what we find in Congreve or Pope. She felt that
such as Almeria were a disgrace to her sex, and thought
it undignified that men should find them amusing. In a
poem which she wrote when on a visit to Tunbridge Wells
in 1706, where she discovered an affectation of surprise at
a young man being in love, she gave some advice to the
young ladies:

For every fop lay not the insnaring train,
Nor lose the worthy to allure the vain,
Keep at due distance all attempts of bliss,
Nor let too near a whisper seem a kiss.
Be not the constant partner of a swain,
Except his long address that favour gain;

Nor be transported when some trifle's view
Directs his giddy choice to fix on you.

The Ephelia who had invited Ardelia to visit London was probably a member of the Thynne family of Longleat, but if such invitations were unacceptable, invitations to their magnificent house in Wiltshire were welcome. In an epistle to Lady Worsley 'who had most obligingly desired my corresponding with her by letters', Ardelia briefly mentions the famous house

Which above metaphor its structure rears,

but chiefly commends the gardens with their fountains, terraces, and lawns, in order to compliment Lord and Lady Weymouth (the parents of the newly married Lady Worsley) on the taste they had there shown in laying out the gardens in the new Dutch style. Lady Winchilsea felt more at ease in commenting on the gardens, as she did even at Eastwell, than on the house and its contents, especially in view of the reputation as a connoisseur deservedly enjoyed by Viscount Weymouth's son Henry, the Theanor of Ardelia's poems. His excellent taste (she tells us)

Italy has wrought
In his refined and daily heightened thought,
Where poetry or painting find no place
Unless performed with a superior grace.

And perhaps she took the greater pleasure in strolling through the newly improved grounds with her host and hostess, when

Twas paradise in some expanded walk
To see her motions and attend his talk.

However, though she eschewed the harder labour of describing Longleat, she did attempt a description of one of the tapestries in the house in a poem addressed to Henry Thynne; and in another she rebuked the painter of an illdrawn picture of his wife. She knew the Henry Thynnes at Longleat, and she also visited them at their house at Leweston in Dorset from which she dated a letter in 1704 to Lady Worsley, enclosing a fragment of a Pindarick ode in which she compared Longleat to Armida's Castle. This was particularly apt, because it was almost certainly Henry Thynne who translated literally to her those passages from Tasso which she turned into verse.

Lady Winchilsea showed her poems to Henry Thynne for criticism, as she says in some lines addressed to his daughter (who married Lord Hertford in 1715) where she requests her to

look with favour on Ardelia's muse,
And what your father cherished, still excuse.
Whenever style or fancy in them shines,
Conclude his praise gave spirit to those lines.

Lady Hertford inherited her father's critical judgment, for in 1728 James Thomson dedicated to her his *Spring* which (he said) 'grew up under her encouragement'; and she also befriended Savage and Shenstone. But Lady Winchilsea in a poem addressed to her when she had engaged Eusden 'to write upon a wood, enjoining him to mention no tree but the aspen and no flower but the king-cup' light-heartedly asserted a romantic liberty for the poet against the patron,

For we're all wronged if Eusden is confined.

This poem well illustrates the incipient romanticism which Wordsworth so much valued in Lady Winchilsea's poetry. In it she mischievously invents the kind of poem which the poet laureate would have written but for Lady Hertford's prescribed limitations.

Had Eusden been at liberty to rove,
Wild and promiscuous he had formed your grove
Of all the sons of earth that ever grew,
From lightsome beech down to the sable yew,

and she goes on to name lime, hazel, sycamore, maple, cedar, pine, juniper, hawthorn, holly, oak, birch, and ash. She even pretends to despise Lady Hertford's chosen tree which

Is but the rattle to some peevish wind.

Her own love of trees is often apparent, and though Wordsworth could not have read this poem . . . one of his favourites was that entitled **"The Tree"**, in which she gives thanks for its shade and shelter, and prays that its end may come at last through the wind and not the axe. She had a particular reason, other than that of romantic sentiment, for disliking the felling of trees. Some years before she first came to Eastwell the then Earl of Winchilsea felled a grove of oaks, 'and gave the first blow with his own hands', John Aubrey records. 'Shortly after, the Countess died in her bed suddenly, and his eldest son, the Lord Maidstone, was killed at sea by a cannonbullet'. This was in the Battle of Sole-Bay on 28 May 1672. He was serving on board the *Royal Charles* and his son Charles was born four months later. The association of the felling of the oaks with the deaths of her husband's mother and brother must have been very well known to her, and she alludes to it in the poem which she wrote on the improvements made by the fourth Earl, that same Lord Maidstone's son, from which I have already quoted. This story too, though it is not very likely that Wordsworth knew it, would have pleased the romantic taste for the supernatural.

John F. Sena (essay date 1971)

SOURCE: "Melancholy in Anne Finch and Elizabeth Carter: the Ambivalence of an Idea," in *The Yearbook of English Studies,* Vol. I, 1971, pp. 108-19.

[*In the following excerpt, Sena compares Finch's description of melancholy in "The Spleen" with contemporary medical accounts.*]

The physical disability and psychological perturbations of melancholy were well known to one of the foremost women poets of the eighteenth century, Anne Finch, Countess of Winchilsea. As a victim of the malady, her description of its effects were first-hand and specific, with none of the generalities born of vague knowledge. In an early poem on the subject, **"Ardelia to Melancholy"**, Lady Winchilsea compares herself to a fortress and melancholy to an 'inveterate foe', a tyrant trying to scale her. She employs the 'useless arms' of diversion—music, mirth, friendship, and poetry—but her many 'troops of fancy' have failed her, yielding her 'Captive to her adversary'. She concludes despairingly: 'The Fort is thine, now ruin'd, all within, Whilst by decays without, thy Conquest too, is seen' (l. 41). In **"A Song on Griefe"**, she again uses martial imagery to describe her futile struggle against the debilitating effects of melancholy. Grief, like melancholy, is a military enemy who, with his 'close Allie', fear, leaves no 'state' untouched. She finally capitulates to the 'great Monark', who will establish his seat in her soul and write his title in her heart:

> To thee, great Monark, I submitt,
> Thy Sables, and thy Cypresse bring,
> I own thy Pow'r, I own thee King,
> Thy title, in my heart is writt,
> And 'till that breaks, I ne'er shall freedom gett.

Lady Winchilsea begins her best-known poem on the subject, **"The Spleen"** (1701), by describing the malady as '*Proteus* to abus'd Mankind' (l. 2). No one can find the cause of the affliction, she writes, nor can one 'fix thee to remain in one continued Shape' (l. 4). By speaking of melancholy in these terms, Lady Winchilsea is echoing the sentiments of contemporary physicians who frequently compared the disease to Proteus, the shape-changing god of the sea, because its manifestations were always changing, continuously shifting from one part of the body to another, while constantly mimicking other diseases. To Sydenham it was of 'protean form and chameleon-like' ["Epistolary Dissertation," *Works*, Vol. 2], while Robert James, compiler of one of the period's most popular medical dictionaries, referred to the spleen as a 'Proteus-like Disorder' ["Hypochondriacus Morbus," *A Medical Dictionary*, 1745]. Underlying its various forms, however, was the notion expounded by the Countess and contemporary physicians alike that melancholy was a mixed malady of body and mind, causing the sufferer physical pain and the psychological disorders of anxiety, grief, and fear without cause.

Although melancholic attacks could occur at any hour of the day, night-time was frequently associated with the malady's more gruesome and terrifying manifestations. The delusions, the frightful and hideous hallucinations, experienced by those in the throes of a nocturnal melancholic seizure were realistically and vividly set forth by Anne Finch in **"The Spleen"** (ll. 11 ff.):

> On Sleep intruding dost thy Shadows spread,
> Thy gloomy Terrours round the silent Bed,
> And croud with boading Dreams the Melancholy
>   Head;

> Or, when the Midnight Hour is told,
> And drooping Lids thou still dost waking hold,
> Thy fond Delusions cheat the Eyes,
> Before them antick Spectres dance,
> Unusual Fires their pointed Heads advance,
> And airy Phantoms rise.

Purcell attributed the terrifying and lugubrious dreams of melancholics to the theory that one usually dreams of what has made a deep impression on one's consciousness the day before; thus 'since those who are far gone in this Distemper, do generally think of what is Melancholy, Dreadful, and Perplexing; they are therefore molested with Terrible and frightful Dreams' [*A Treatise of Vapours*]. Nicholas Robinson, a Fellow of the Royal College of Physicians and author of the comprehensive *A New System of the Spleen, Vapours, and Hypochondriack Melancholy* (1728), concurred that melancholics were denied the comforts and benefits of restful sleep: 'In the Night Time they are affrighten'd with many absurd, fearful, and phantastick Visions, that crowd about their Eyes, and disturb their Slumbers. . . .' Dr John Armstrong, a physician more interested in poetry than medicine, in *The Art of Preserving Health* (1744), graphically described (ll. 93 ff.) a nocturnal melancholic vision in terms not unlike Lady Winchilsea's depiction of the horrors awaiting a splenetic at night:

> Sour melancholy, night and day provokes
> Her own eternal wound. The sun grows pale;
> A mournful visionary light o'erspreads
> The cheerful face of nature: earth becomes
> A dreary desert, and heaven frowns above.
> Then various shapes of curs'd illusion rise:
> Whate'er the wretched fears, creating fear
> Forms out of nothing: and with monsters teems
> Unknown in hell.

The delusions described by Lady Winchilsea and Armstrong, if exacerbated, according to William Battie, could result in insanity. In fact, Battie, perhaps the century's leading authority on mental disorders, included the terms 'spleen' and 'melancholy' among the names for madness. At the basis of his conception of madness was the notion of a 'deluded imagination'. A 'deluded imagination' would cause one to receive sensory impressions which bore little resemblance to the objects perceived, and this phenomenon frequently occurred during 'black November days' and 'easterly winds', conditions traditionally associated with melancholy in the eighteenth century [*Treatise on Madness*, 1757]. Thus in describing the 'antick Spectres', 'Unusual Fires', and 'airy Phantoms' encountered by a melancholic at night, Anne Finch was expressing a contemporary view which found little that was admirable or pleasurable in the spleen.

Lady Winchilsea is quick to assail the association between melancholy and genius, a theory which tended to make the spleen a fashionable, even a desirable, affliction. [Sir Richard] Blackmore, in 'An Essay Upon the Spleen', [in *Essays Upon Several Subjects*, Vol. 2, 1716-17] observed that:

It is for this Reason, that as some to procure Reputation, personate the Characters of good or bad Men, and are Hypocrites in Vertue or Vice, as the one or the other grows in Fashion; so many, to be thought Men of Parts and Ingenuity, lay claim, out of meer Ostentation, to the Power of the Spleen in their Complexion, to which they have no manner of Title; nor are there Instances wanting in the fair Sex, who pretend to this reputable Distemper of the Spirits, with the same Vanity that others affect the Beauty of an unsanguine and sickly Countenance.

Matthew Green, who versified medical concepts in *The Spleen* (1737), wrote that a primary cause of the spleen is mistaking the malady for wit:

> Or see some poet pensive sit,
> Fondly mistaking spleen for wit,
> Who, tho' short-winded, still will aim
> To sound the epic trump of fame.

Thus Lady Winchilsea observes that feigning melancholy affords the fool and dullard a means of claiming brilliance: 'The *Fool,* to imitate the Wits, / Complains of thy pretended Fits' (l. 64) and serves as a rationalization for the ill-tempered husband, the intemperate imbiber, and the playful coquette (ll. 90-111). She feels, however, that those who cultivate the malady for its association with intellectual acumen and its alleged ability to explain unconventional behaviour must be renounced, for they are contributing to its popularity and deference. They are turning a grave disease into a 'maladie imaginaire', a mere snobbish affectation. In actuality, she has found the spleen to be inimical to art: it has impaired her intellectual activity and stultified her imaginative and creative powers (ll. 74-89).

Rationalizing intellectual posing, intractability, intemperance, and foppery, however, are but the innocuous uses of the spleen: more direful are the results of melancholy on religion. Not only does it cause confusion and doubt in the devout, but it is the very source of religious inspiration for the Puritans:

> Whilst *Touch* not, *Taste* not, what is freely giv'n,
> Is but thy niggard Voice, disgracing bounteous
>   Heav'n.
> From Speech restrain'd, by thy Deceits abus'd,
> To Deserts banish'd, or in Cells reclus'd,
> Mistaken Vot'ries to the Pow'rs Divine,
> Whilst they a purer Sacrifice design,
> Do but the *Spleen* obey, and worship at thy
>   Shrine.
>
>   (l. 121)

In associating melancholy with dissenting circles, Lady Winchilsea is echoing a relationship common in the period. In *Spectator* (No. 494) Joseph Addison describes the reception of a student by a 'very famous Independent minister, who was head of a college in those times', Dr Thomas Goodwin, the man who attended Oliver Cromwell on his deathbed and later became President of Magdalen College. Puritans, Addison alleges, measure morality and

sanctity by 'a sorrowful countenance . . . eaten up with spleen and melancholy'; mirth and pleasantry are to them marks of a carnal disposition. A youth appearing before Dr Goodwin for an examination was received at the door by a dour servant who conducted him to a room darkened at noonday, with only a single candle burning. He was led from these melancholic surroundings to a second chamber 'hung with black, where he entertained himself for some time by the glimmering of a taper, until at length the head of the college came out to him, from an inner room, with half a dozen nightcaps upon his head, and religious horror in his countenance'. Instead of being asked to display his Latin and Greek, the youth was only asked if he were prepared for death. Addison concludes by asserting that the 'cheerfulness' and 'serenity' of religion should be stressed and the gravity and austerity of the Puritans eschewed.

Physicians also described the association between melancholy and Puritanism, as well as the baleful effects of the malady on religious in general. Sir Richard Blackmore asserted that when the spleen attacked a religious person it produced 'superstitious fears' and 'hypochondriacal Enthusiasm'. Like Addison, he felt that the 'amiable and delightful' side of religion should be stressed: 'And hence it comes to pass, that so many morose, rigid and melancholy Persons unhappily bring Dishonour on the Practice of Vertue, by tempting others to look upon Religion, which in itself is most amiable and delightful, as an unlovely and frightful Object' ["An Essay upon the Spleen"]. Nicholas Robinson concurred with this judgement, observing that when melancholy afflicted one of a religious cast, fear and presumption resulted, 'the latter most properly is call'd Enthusiasm . . .' [*A New System of the Spleen,* 1728]. This type of individual, according to Robinson, mistaking his whims and fantasies for supernatural inspiration, believes himself a divinely ordained saint, commissioned to reform the impious and unbelieving world. Enthusiasts 'are elevated to the highest Degree of Familiarity with their Maker: They are his Viceroys, chosen Saints and Servants, sent on especial Errands, to reclaim the unbelieving World'. Dr Cheyne added to the indictment of the Puritans by asserting that those who allow a melancholic disposition to create a 'Disgust or Disrelish of worldly Amusements and Creature-Comforts . . .' are frequently religious hypocrites, devoid of piety and devoutness [*An Essay of Health and Long Life,* 1724].

The Countess of Winchilsea suggests that a splenetic employ all the arts of contemporary medicine to overcome the affliction: liquor, music, and nostrums ('The Spleen', ll. 128-37). In prescribing these remedies she was restating poetically medical concepts that were permeating the Augustan air. Music was frequently considered to be an excellent antidote to melancholic passions. Robinson, in endorsing the therapeutic value of music, cites Plato's contention that music has as great an influence over the mind as air has over the body. As medicines purge the body of gross humours, Robinson adds, music purges the soul of gloomy thoughts. Matthew Green, who, although not a physician himself, assimilated medical doctrines in *The Spleen* (1737), also recommends music as a melancholic curative (l. 141). In addition to music, liquors and wine were popular remedies for melancholia. John Purcell, after extensively cataloguing curative medicines for the spleen, advises taking French wine during these remedies. Francis Fuller, a leading exponent of exercise in the treatment of melancholy, asserts [in *Medicina Gymnastica,* 1705] that a 'Cordial' is a more effective cure for the malady than the most sophisticated medicines, and cites the medical history of a servant who found alleviation from hysteric fits by taking wine as substantiation. Ephraim Chambers, author of a popular encyclopedia of the period, advises melancholics to imbibe 'old claret or Madeira, or water with a little brandy or rum . . .' ["Hypochondriac," *Cyclopedia*]. If good health could not be restored by music and liquors, a more artificial method, it was felt, must be employed. A wide range of purgatives, vomits, and drugs were thus recommended for the treatment of melancholy. Purcell frequently prescribed cardus water, powder of vipers, spirit of sal ammoniac, and chalybeat, but found that root of black hellebore was the most efficacious drug. To restore the tone and elasticity of body fibres, Dr Cheyne [in *The English Malady,* 1733] recommended bitters, aromatics, and chalybeats. John Wesley in *Primitive Physic* (1747), a homespun medical book which blends popular myths with advice gleaned from the writings of Dover, Mead, Cheyne, Sydenham, and Boerhaave, suggested tincture of valerian as an antidote for nervous disorders. Wesley recommended that the tincture be prepared by cutting six ounces of valerian root gathered in June, beating it in a mortar, mixing it with white wine, and allowing it to stand for three weeks. It should then be filtered through paper and 'Taken with as much as will lie on a shilling of the Powder of Misletoe, twice a day, when the stomach is most empty . . .'. Sir John Elliot, in his medical handbook listing the symptoms and cures of diseases arranged alphabetically, combines recommendations from Cheyne and Wesley in advising that castor, valerian, bitters, and chalybeats be administered for the spleen [*The Medical Pocket-Book,* 1784]. Thus the choice of drugs seemed to depend largely on the medical predilections of the physician; however, underlying the use of nostrums was the constant notion that drugs are a last resort in treating melancholy, a means used when all else has failed. By recommending music, liquor, and drugs as splenetic curatives, Lady Winchilsea is reflecting, not merely personal remedies, but the collective medical wisdom of her age.

Anne Finch's treatment of melancholy in **"Ardelia to Melancholy"**, **"A Song on Griefe"**, and particularly in **"The Spleen"**, thus exemplifies one contemporary attitude toward the malady. To those of her persuasion, melancholy was an affliction which destroyed one's physical health and mental tranquility, disrupted the rational process, stifled artistic creativity, stultified the imagination, and filled one's life with fear and sorrow. The disease was debilitating and enervating, rendering the sufferer sluggish and slow, dilatory and capricious, and subject to terrifying and absurd hallucinations. Ultimately, the affliction could terminate in insanity. Lady Winchilsea's conception of melancholy seems kin to Thomas Gray's 'black Melancholy', which excludes everything that is pleasurable in the present and removes all hope for happiness in the future.

Katharine Rogers (essay date 1979)

SOURCE: "Anne Finch, Countess of Winchilsea: An Augustan Woman Poet," in *Shakespeare's Sisters: Feminist Essays on Women Poets,* edited by Sandra M. Gilbert and Susan Gubar, Indiana University Press, 1979, pp. 32-46.

[*In the following excerpt, Rogers discusses Finch's depiction of women and her use of eighteenth-century poetic forms.*]

Anne Finch, Countess of Winchilsea (1661-1720), is important not only as a gifted poet but as a unique example—a poet who was both a woman and an Augustan. In many ways a typical Augustan, she wrote in all the traditional genres, from flippant songs to ponderous Pindaric odes. Yet because she was a woman, her poems are subtly different from those of her male contemporaries. She shows a distinctive sincerity in her love poetry, a distinctive standard in her satire, a distinctive simplicity in her response to nature, and a distinctive freedom from the Augustan writer's obligation to make public statements.

Generally speaking, this difference is not a matter of conscious outlook and aims. Winchilsea shared many characteristic Augustan attitudes, such as distrust for the mob and a sophisticated acceptance of human weaknesses coupled with suspicion of human grandiosity. She consistently upheld reason—not only her satire on irrational deviations, but her devotion to her husband is rational, as well as her religion and her appreciation of nature. There is a reasonable basis for all her feelings, and none are expressed with sentimentality or "enthusiasm." Her love poems are restrained and her nature poems precise. She wrote in the usual Augustan verse forms, particularly heroic couplets, although she was less prone to smartly decisive antithesis than John Dryden or Alexander Pope.

As an Augustan writer who was also a woman, Winchilsea faced peculiar problems. Of course women authors have always written in a masculine tradition, but the Augustan period was especially male-oriented. For one thing, the poet saw himself as a public figure—celebrating national events, reprehending the vices of society, relating personal experience to universal moral principles. And women were confined, by their opportunities and experience and what was assumed to be their capacity, to private social life and the domestic sphere: they were not, supposedly, qualified to pronounce on the Use of Riches or the Reign of Dullness. For another, the poet was following in the footsteps of the Roman poets, who wrote from a conspicuously male point of view.

This is particularly evident in the genre of the love lyric. For the Roman erotic poets, love for a woman was a superficial feeling based on desire. It could be intensely pleasurable, though surprisingly often it was painful—but in any case it was classed with such sensual pleasures as drinking. Often love and drinking are balanced against the higher pleasure of friendship, which is always assumed to exist between men. Women appeared in this poetry only as more or less unworthy love objects, existing for the amusement of men.

Love poets of the Restoration and early eighteenth century followed this convention unquestioningly. Almost without exception, the love poems of John Wilmot, Earl of Rochester, Sir Charles Sedley, William Wycherley, and Matthew Prior (an almost exact contemporary of Winchilsea) are addressed to mistresses, not wives, and mistresses who are usually transient and never taken seriously. By definition they are beautiful (otherwise no one could love them); the only possible variations are that they may or may not be "kind" (that is, willing to sleep with the poet without marriage), and they may or may not be constant (until he is ready to move on). The woman appears always as a generalized sex object, never individualized enough to be identifiable. Wycherley even argues that an ex-mistress has no right to reproach him for leaving her, for it is she who has changed, not he: he has remained "true to Love and Beauty" in leaving her for a younger woman.

Because the Restoration poets wrote in reaction against the fatuous idealization of much Renaissance love poetry, their erotic verse is frequently hostile, showing the lover vilifying his mistress or relieving his frustrations by raping her. The characteristic Restoration mood is total cynicism: honor and faithfulness are stupid, since women and men inevitably cheat each other. The fact that "The Imperfect Enjoyment" (resulting from impotence) was a favorite theme in this poetry shows both the total physicality of the love involved and its chronically unsatisfactory nature. The poet Rochester constantly associates love with negative feelings. Not pleasure, but pain is its sure proof—"Kind jealous doubts, tormenting fears, / And anxious cares" provide the only reliable evidence. Even his relatively positive poems on love reveal a negative undertone. The love lyrics he exchanged with his wife led to the conclusion that she had better treat him with scorn and coldness lest she lose his love.

Prior, writing some years later than the Restoration rakes, softened their attitude. But his affection for "Chloe," his long-term mistress, is superficial and patronizing. "On Beauty" would seem to flatter women by paying tribute to their power. However, this power is equated with beauty (as if that were a woman's only significance), and the triumph it produces is hardly complimentary: Chloe has shown her power by drawing him away from every important concern, from "Ambition, Business, Friendship, News, / My useful Books, and serious Muse." Her beauty has made him submit to sit with her and talk "Of Idle Tales, and foolish Riddles."

Now how could a woman function in such a tradition? For one thing, unless she was prepared to cast off her reputation publicly like Aphra Behn, she was shut out by its licentiousness. Obviously, she could not write to her lovers as the men could write to their mistresses. Nor could she treat love as a trivial amusement, since it was not a pastime for her but a central focus of her life. The only man a respectable woman could write to was her husband,

and in those days of mercenary arranged marriages she might well not find him a suitable inspiration. Winchilsea was fortunate in this respect—she and her husband loved each other deeply—so that she could write to him as passionately as the men did to their mistresses. More so, in fact, since the relationship she was celebrating was so much more significant.

In **"To Mr. F. Now Earl of W."** she cleverly makes use of the conventions to express her own deeper feelings. Her husband is away and has asked her to greet him on his return with a poem. In typical Augustan manner, she appeals to the Muses, who are ready to assist until they discover, to their amazement and shock, what she is asking them to do—to help her express love for her husband! No, they cannot lend their aid to such an outlandish enterprise. No beau in the coffee houses "That wore his Cloaths with common Sense" (notice how the sly equation of reason with dressing suggests the beau's superficiality) could excuse "mention of a *Spouse*."

The Muses all send excuses, but Urania, the muse of heavenly love, tells the poet in confidence that heartfelt love can be expressed without the Muses' inspiration. So Winchilsea relies on her own feelings, realizing that to express tenderness for one you truly love requires no aid of Muse or convention. However, considering how unfashionable such endearments are, she decides to reserve them until her husband comes home and she can confide them to him privately—when they too can enjoy "that Pleasure . . . Of stollen Secresy" which makes all the "fancy'd Happiness" of illicit lovers.

Winchilsea did express her love openly in another poem to her husband, in which she dispensed entirely with classical convention. She opens with passionate simplicity: "This to the Crown, and blessing of my life, / The much lov'd husband, of a happy wife." Notice, first of all, the mutuality of their feeling: she loves him, and he has made her happy. Their love is of paramount importance, and it gives, as love should, perfect happiness. She expresses her appreciation for his "constant passion," which conquered her initial resistance (perhaps she had resented the generally exploitative and superior attitude of contemporary men in love), and now flouts fashionable convention by combining the status of a husband with the attentive passion of a lover. For his sake she will even undertake "What I in women censure"—presumably, conforming to the accepted female role of frivolity and fashionable accomplishments. What emerges here is a real relationship, based on deep love, involving mutual concessions (his efforts to win her "stubborn, and ungratefull heart," her yielding to convention to please him), and irradiating both their lives equally.

Always preserving Augustan form and Augustan restraint in these poems to her husband, Winchilsea achieved an unusually personal, genuine tone simply by looking at their actual relationship directly. Her expression of uncomplicated wholehearted pleasure in the company of a loved spouse, free of pretentiousness in feeling or diction, is unique in her period. A good example is **"An Invitation to**

Dafnis," in which she urges him to leave his study and take a walk in the fields with her. Light Augustan wit precludes any air of sentimentality. Dafnis, immersed in military history, must not:

> . . . plead that you're immur'd, and cannot yield,
> That mighty Bastions keep you from the feild,
> Think not tho' lodg'd in Mons, or in Namur,
> You're from my dangerous attacks secure.

He must come with her into a natural field, where:

> The Cristall springs, shall murmure as we passe,
> But not like Courtiers, sinking to disgrace;
>
> . . . . .
>
> But all shall form a concert to delight,
> And all to peace, and all to love envite.

Even when Winchilsea was writing on more modish themes, she introduced a refreshing feminine point of view. Considering men's constant complaints that marriage is a ball and chain, oppressive to the natural freedom of the male, it is nice to see a woman making exactly the same claim in **"The Unequal Fetters."** Accepting for the moment the Restoration attitude toward love, Winchilsea shows how unfair it is to women. To love would be worth our while, she opens—if we could stop time and preserve youth. But since we women must lose the beauty which has won your hearts, and since we know you will then seek it in new faces, to love is but to ruin ourselves—not through seduction, but through empty marriages. She, for her part, will remain as free as Nature made her, will not allow herself to be caught in matrimony, a male invention that restricts women far more than men:

> Mariage does but slightly tye Men
>   Whil'st close Pris'ners we remain
> They the larger Slaves of Hymen
>   Still are begging Love again
> At the full length of all their chain.

Happily, Winchilsea herself had escaped this dilemma by a marriage which, founded on a deeper feeling, did not turn into a galling yoke; but here she looked at marriage in general as it prevailed in her time. She claimed natural freedom as opposed to artificial institution just as the men did, but, considering contemporary marriage law, with much better reason. Like the typical Restoration wit, she saw how hypocritical and restrictive the institution was; unlike him, she saw and protested against its particular unfairness to women.

In her **"Epilogue to the Tragedy of Jane Shore,"** Winchilsea was inspired by the whore's progress of Jane to contrast the lifetime courses of women and men. A beautiful young woman dwindles to fine and well-dressed, then to "well enough," and finally to merely good—which means she is no longer admired and has nothing to do but retire. A man, on the other hand, can pass from "pretty fellow" to witty freethinker to politician, and "Maintains some

figure, while he keeps his breath." While she makes no comment on this disproportion—it would be out of place in the flippancy of a neoclassical epilogue—the unfairness of valuing a woman in terms of her beauty alone is implicit. Both these feminist protests are playful, but significant in that their subjects would never have occurred to a male writer.

Like any Augustan poet, Winchilsea satirized deviations from reason. But her enforced detachment from the fashionable world—attributable mostly to her sex—sharpened her ability to see where accepted social norms diverged from reason.

—Katharine Rogers

As a woman, Winchilsea could not treat love and marriage as flippantly as did men for whom they were a minor part of life; respectively, pastime or dull obligation. Because it was impossible for a woman to be comfortable in the convention, she could not follow it without question as they did. This inability proved to be fortunate, in view of its limitation and superficiality: the men's poems might be highly accomplished, but were rarely more. Generally the men were less interested in the women they claimed to love than in the cleverness with which they expressed their feelings. Almost never dealing with permanent or profound relationships, they had often to resort to obscenity or empty paradox in an attempt to give their songs liveliness and individuality. Isolated from this convention by her sex, Winchilsea was in a manner forced to be original. She looked directly at her feelings and described them sincerely, and thereby produced poems which were not only distinctively natural but refreshingly free of the superficiality and cynicism which tainted most love poetry in her time.

"Ardelia's Answer to Ephelia" likewise shows Winchilsea's personal adaptation of a popular Restoration form, derived ultimately from Horace (Book I, Satire ix) and more recently from Boileau (Third Satire). The poet meets a fool who aims at being socially pleasing, who takes possession of him or her for a long tedious time. A contrast with Rochester's "Timon" will bring out the distinctive characteristics of Winchilsea's satire. Rochester's Timon, like Winchilsea's Ardelia, is taken in tow by a pretender to wit and fashion, who drags him home to dinner. First the forcible host reads poor Timon an insipid libel and insists Timon wrote it, in spite of his protest that he "never rhymed but for my pintle's [penis's] sake." The company at dinner consists of bullies who pretend to wit and, even worse, the host's wife, a faded beauty who retains nothing of youth but affectation and shows her stupidity by insisting on an idealistic view of romantic love. They praise a string of bad plays, commending them for the very qualities which any person of taste would recognize as faults. At length the discussion degenerates into a fight, and Timon escapes.

In contrast to Rochester's consistent detraction—there is nothing positive in his poem—Winchilsea judges the follies she satirizes against clear moral and rational ideals. She rejects the Town because she finds it uncongenial to friendship as well as to intellectual fulfillment. And she explicitly disavows detraction, the staple of Rochester's poem. She will not fit into fashionable society, she says, because she cannot supplement her wit with the ill nature necessary "To passe a gen'rall censure on mankind," to sneer at unsophisticated young people as foolish and at moral people as dull, to cheapen the genuine heroism of a soldier or the genuine inspiration of a poet. In contrast, most Restoration writers agreed with Rochester's assumption that wit has to be linked with cynicism, slashing universal criticism, and obscenity: whenever Rochester needed a simile, a phallic image leapt to his mind.

Almeria takes Ardelia in tow as Timon's host did him, but there is a significant difference between the two objects of satire. While both are fools, Timon's host is a fool because he aims at but cannot achieve true fashion; Almeria, on the other hand, is a fool because she conforms perfectly to the model of a sophisticated Restoration lady. Timon judges the fools as an insider, one who has mastered and consummately practices society's standards of wit and breeding. Ardelia prides herself on being an outsider from a society whose rules she considers immoral and irrational.

Almeria is an accomplished lady of fashion, much like a female Timon. She has the same talent for seeing faults: "she discerns all failings, but her own." Yet to one's face she is effusively complimentary: she embraces Ardelia, protests she has pined hourly for her company, and insists she come to dine, though in fact she considers her an old-fashioned prude. Almeria never stops slandering the absent, but when the subject is present, she maintains "'tis want of witt, to discommend." After dinner they ramble about in Almeria's coach to see the fashionable sights—or, actually, "any thing, that might the time bestow." Ardelia stops to enter a church, thus forcing Almeria to be, as she puts it, "Porter to a Temple gate." But Almeria does not waste her time: she "Flys round the Coach" in order to display herself to the best advantage to any passing beau.

Almeria lists Ardelia's many faults to one of these fops, and thereby exposes herself, since she represents contemporary fashion in contrast to Ardelia's Right Reason. Ardelia not only "Dispises Courtly Vice," but insists "That sence and Nature shou'd be found in Plays," and therefore prefers the earlier Restoration masters, Dryden, Etherege, and Wycherley, to contemporary sentimental drama. (Note that Winchilsea lists the good playwrights, while Rochester named only to pillory.) Moreover, Ardelia has no interest in Almeria's most absorbing concern— those trifles on which most women built their egos, as indeed convention encouraged them to. Almeria prides herself on judgment shown in such things as placing "a

patch, in some peculiar way, / That may an unmark'd smile, to sight betray, / And the vast genius of the Sex, display." She is mortified that Ardelia drank tea without a single "complement upon the cup," even though Almeria had braved a storm at sea in order to get her first choice of the china on an incoming ship. Instead of gratefully attending when Almeria advised her about clothing shops, Ardelia cut her off with "I deal with one that does all these provide, / Having of other cares, enough beside."

They rush from the church to Hyde Park, lest they should "loose e're night, an hour of finding fault." There Almeria points out an "awk'ard creature," but when Ardelia looks for some monster she sees a lovely though undeveloped girl. Almeria proceeds to sneer at the gifted translator Piso (Lord Roscommon)—how can anyone consider him a wit when he makes no artful compliments on a lady's dress or new coach, never cries down a play for the fun of it, and refuses to praise every novelty? Almeria then greets her "best of friends" in a voice that carries across the park; Ardelia agrees that this woman has a mind as beautiful as her person. But instead of being gratified, Almeria is clearly put out by this praise of her dear friend; and she immediately confides that the woman is disgracefully in love. Finally Almeria sees the most ridiculous creature of all—a poetess ("They say she writes, and 'tis a common jest"). Ardelia asks whether the poet is conceited or spiteful. Otherwise, what is wrong with a woman's writing? At length Ardelia manages to escape, to return to the country the next day.

Like any Augustan poet, Winchilsea satirized deviations from reason. But her enforced detachment from the fashionable world—attributable mostly to her sex—sharpened her ability to see where accepted social norms diverged from reason. As an outsider, she was better qualified to evaluate the ideals of the dominant group. Moreover, isolation from Restoration fashionable circles kept her free of the withering cynicism that made Rochester's satires (as well as his love poems) so negative. She had no patience with vice or folly, and she could appreciate the slashing satire of Wycherley (whom Almeria detested for his exposure of hypocritical women)—but she had clear standards of positive morality which included charity and kindness.

Winchilsea could satirize women very sharply, but her satire is always modified by the fact that it comes from a right-minded woman rather than a male censor of the sex. Thus, she avoided patronizing generalizations and expected women to meet a universal human standard rather than a specifically "feminine" one. She showed herself, as Ardelia in the **"Answer"** or the speaker in **"On Myselfe,"** as one with sufficient rational morality to despise the frivolity charged to women, to value what is truly important, and, if necessary, to live on her own resources. Moreover, she pointed out that society pressed women to be foolish: they are "Education's, more then Nature's fools" (**"The Introduction"**). Small-minded Almeria conforms to conventional standards; it is Ardelia who is the social misfit. Finally, Winchilsea saw follies primarily as a waste of women's time and resources, rather than as an annoyance to men. Ardelia scorns shopping not because it is expensive or takes her away from home and family, but because she is more interested in intellectual pursuits.

Winchilsea was keenly aware of the niggling details that clog women's lives—necessary details that are piled on them, and the expansion and overemphasis on these details made by those who wish to distract women from more significant occupation. Her **"Petition for an Absolute Retreat"** is, like Andrew Marvell's "The Garden" and John Pomfret's "The Choice," a celebration of rational, virtuous retirement in nature, a common Augustan theme. But while Pomfret wants company, Winchilsea would exclude idle visitors, probably because women were obligated to entertain whoever came, while men could generally escape constant attendance (as Pomfret implies he would). Male authors of the period constantly twitted women for idle visiting; it took a woman to point out that it was a tiresome burden imposed by society's views of ladylike behavior. For the same reason, Winchilsea specifies that her table will not only be simply provided (as is usual in these poems), but "spread without my Care." Unlike male authors, women had to supervise their own housekeeping.

Pomfret would include female company in his ideal retreat—sometimes a man needs to relax in the sweet softness of women's conversation—but only in an incidental way. He specifies that he will not have a wife, but an obliging female neighbor who can provide occasional companionship without scandal. Winchilsea would have congenial friends of both sexes, primarily of course her husband:

> Give me there (since Heaven has shown
> It was not Good to be alone)
> A *Partner* suited to my Mind,
> Solitary, pleas'd and kind;
> Who, partially, may something see
> Preferr'd to all the World in me.

She proceeds to draw a blissful picture of a world in which a man and wife are all in all to each other.

This looks like a direct refutation of a passage in Marvell's "The Garden," the prototype for both "retreat" poems. Describing his idyllically peaceful garden and comparing it to Eden, Marvell rudely charged that in the original Eden "man . . . walked without a mate," until God made the mistake of adding a female help, as if a helpmate could be needed in a perfect place. That Marvell could put this piece of extreme and irrelevant misogyny into a pleasing philosophical poem, and that it could be accepted without question by generations of readers, dramatically demonstrates the need for a female voice in poetry.

Winchilsea's explicit feminism appears usually in connection with the plight of the woman poet. (The attitudes of her contemporaries are exemplified on the one hand by *Three Hours After Marriage*, by Pope, John Gay, and John Arbuthnot, in which a woman is pilloried for being a writer; and on the other by Prior's epilogue to a play of female authorship, in which he declares that a woman's writing must be praised because she belongs to the beau-

tiful sex.) More than any other eighteenth-century writer, Winchilsea adverted to the difficulties of the female author, from the petty details that distracted her to the widespread assumption that it was presumptuous for a woman to write poetry. She was unusually outspoken in maintaining that a creative woman has a right to express herself because it is wrong to force anyone to bury a talent. Far from apologizing for taking time to fulfill herself by writing, she roundly declared that the approved feminine occupations were unworthy of an intelligent person. Her description of the foolish pseudo-arts to which women were expected to devote themselves is withering: to

> . . . in fading Silks compose
> Faintly, th'inimitable *Rose,*
> Fill up an ill-drawn *Bird,* or paint on Glass
> The *Sov'reign's* blurr'd and undistinguish'd Face,
> The threatening *Angel,* and the speaking *Ass.*
> ("The Spleen")

Her **"Introduction,"** written for a manuscript collection of her poems not published by her but wistfully left for publication, argues her right to be a poet. Starting with the common Augustan attack on various sorts of carping critics, she soon closes in on the charge all critics will find: her verses are "by a Woman writt." It is a general feeling that "a woman that attempts the pen" is "an intruder on the rights of men," that women should devote their minds to "Good breeding, fassion, dancing, dressing, play."

> To write, or read, or think, or to enquire
> Wou'd cloud our beauty, and exaust our time,
> And interrupt the Conquests of our prime;
> While the dull mannage, of a servile house
> Is held by some, our outmost art, and use.

In other words, men do not want women wasting their time and energy on anything that does not contribute to their usefulness to men, whether as sexual objects or household managers; nor do they want them to rise above trivia, lest they develop ideas of their own. She goes on to prove women's ability to write by some biblical examples, which may not appear very convincing today but seemed called for in an age when the Bible was constantly used to keep woman in her place. But Winchilsea's confidence falters when she considers the present state of women, and she comes to a depressing conclusion. Debarred from education, instead positively trained and expected to be dull, few women can rise above the mass. And if one is pressed by "warmer fancy, and ambition" to try, she cannot help wavering: "So strong, th'opposing faction still appears, / The hopes to thrive, can ne're outweigh the fears." She concludes that she had best keep her Muse's wing "contracted," keep her verses to herself and a few friends, not aspire to laurel groves but remain in her absolute retreat.

Such expressions of discouragement, and even more her occasional disparagement of her vocation as a feminine foible or disclaimers that her works would merit publication even if she were not a woman, show that Winchilsea was not completely at ease in her unconventional role. Consistently, however, she insisted not only that she was a serious poet, but that poetry was the most important thing in her life. In **"Ardelia to Melancholy,"** she lists the various remedies for depression that she has vainly tried: first, social mirth; second, friendship; last, writing poetry. When that failed, she knew further struggles were useless. She was chronically plagued by depression, to which her difficulties and ambivalence as a woman poet may have contributed. Certainly it affected her most painfully by undermining her confidence as a poet. When depressed, she feared that her poetry was degenerating, and even that those who decried her writing as "An useless Folly, or presumptuous Fault" might be right (**"The Spleen"**).

Defending a woman poet against the unthinking sneers of Almeria, who follows fashion by viewing a female poet as a ridiculous object, Winchilsea asks: "Why shou'd we from that pleasing art be ty'd, / Or like State Pris'ners, Pen and Ink deny'd?" Thus, she makes a bold equation between the legal restrictions on a prisoner (who is either guilty or imprisoned by what all would agree was a violation of traditional English liberty) and the customary restrictions on a woman, imposed simply because of her sex. Winchilsea was particularly concerned with liberty—not the public liberty so constantly cited in British literature, freedom from autocracy and oppressive laws; but rather the domestic liberty which was harder to establish, especially for a woman, freedom from the petty restrictions of convention and trivial obligations. Declining Ephelia's invitation to London, she suggests that the country be "Our place of meeting, love, and liberty." They cannot express their thoughts and affection amid the fashionable conventions operating in London. In the **"Absolute Retreat"** she petitions that "the World may ne'er invade . . . My unshaken Liberty." Liberty was not a feature of Marvell's or Pomfret's similar retreats.

Considering the importance of liberty to Winchilsea, one is tempted to read her tale **"The Bird and the Arras"** as an allegory. A bird is caught in a room and mistakes the pictured scene on a tapestry for a real one, but, trying to alight on a tree, only beats herself against the flat surface. She rises to the pictured sky, seeing the pictured birds apparently flying there and glorying in her ability to rise above them. But then she strikes the ceiling and plummets to the ground. She flutters around "in endlesse cercles of dismay" until a kind person directs her out the window "to ample space the only Heav'n of Birds." The bird imprisoned in a man-made room suggests a woman imprisoned in man-made conventions; the bird which makes doomed efforts to rise through the ceiling, the poet who "wou'd Soar above the rest" of her sex, only to be "dispis'd, aiming to be admir'd" (**"The Introduction"**).

Limitation seems to have had a special meaning for Winchilsea: it was not the Augustans' decorous acceptance of human limits, but the Romantics' painful awareness of the discrepancy between human beings' aspirations and achievement. Her poem **"The Nightingale"** anticipates Keats's "Ode" and Shelley's "To a Skylark" in its suggestion that the bird has a freedom and joy impossible to human self-consciousness. The poet aims to imitate the song of the nightingale, to compose a song as freely self-expressive as the bird's—for "Poets, wild as thee, were born, / Pleasing best when unconfin'd, / When to Please is least design'd." She aspires to unite the music of the bird with human awareness. But of course the attempt fails. The poem ends with a typical Augustan turn and moral, but the ideas of unfulfillable aims and of the loss when humans give up their natural freedom remain. It is the Romantic yearning to burst limits, perhaps occurring to Winchilsea because a woman was made particularly aware of the restrictions on human beings. An outsider by sex, as later pre-Romantics were outsiders by temperament, she anticipates the Romantic artist's yearning for something beyond the physical, social world in which she must live.

Winchilsea's **"Nocturnal Reverie"** has been seen as a pre-Romantic work ever since Wordsworth singled it out for praise. But actually the poem is Augustan in attitude and technique. It opens with the classical references that naturally sprang into educated eighteenth-century minds and proceeds to a series of beautifully exact bits of description characteristic of Augustan appreciation of nature. She describes the thin clouds that flit across the moon, the alteration in colors under moonlight—the foxglove is still recognizably red, though its hue is blanched—the greater clarity of odors and sounds at night, the swelling haystacks visible only as masses, the large approaching shape which frightens her until the sound of forage being chewed reassures her that it is only a horse. Winchilsea achieves her effects through precise detailing, not through suggestive appeals to passion or imagination; and her use of metaphor is subdued to the point that it is barely visible. Intense as her appreciation is, she perceives physical creatures as such, making no attempt to inflate them into some higher significance. The focus is consistently on her conscious reflecting mind—from her classical allusions in the first lines, through her moral observation on the glowworms ("trivial Beauties watch their Hour to shine"), to the direct description of her own mental state which ends the poem. She is stirred not to ecstasy, but to generalizing from her sensory impressions.

Description of the animals' activity at night leads her to delicate sympathy: "Their shortliv'd Jubilee the Creatures keep, / Which but endures, whilst Tyrant-*Man* do's sleep." She is not deprecating obvious cruelty (as Pope did in "Windsor Forest"), nor even any specific oppression, but just the restrictions imposed on domestic and wild animals by man's dominion. The poet, too, enjoys an unaccustomed liberty in this peaceful solitary scene. In the subdued moonlight, she feels free from the distractions of day and able to respond to the spiritual influences which speak to her true nature; her "free Soul" can feel at home even "in th'inferiour World." The soul's affinity and longing for Heaven is of course a traditional religious idea, but one thinks also of the imprisoned bird finally escaping into "ample space."

What is most distinctive in Winchilsea's poem is its personal quality. When the Augustans related physical nature to human concerns, they typically thought in terms of large moral or national issues. Pope's "Windsor Forest" includes some lovingly precise nature description, but uses it as a springboard to celebrate the destiny of Great Britain. He starts his poem not with personal response but with an invocation followed by descriptive details neatly organized to support a generalization—"order in variety we see"—and usually reinforced with a stock simile. He appreciates English oaks not because they are impressive in themselves but because they will be used to build the mighty British navy. His description of reflections in a river,

> The watery landskip of the pendant woods,
> And absent trees that tremble in the floods;
> In the clear azure gleam the flocks are seen,
> And floating forests paint the waves with green,

is beautiful in its way; but it does not equal Winchilsea's simple, honest attempt to convey what such reflections actually look like: "When in some River, overhung with Green, / The waving Moon and trembling Leaves are seen."

Pope as well as Winchilsea finds observation of nature conducive to religious thoughts, but he seems to be expressing the state of Man in general rather than that of a particular person. Happy the man who retires to these shades to study or practice benevolence, who

> Bids his free soul expatiate in the skies,
> Amid her kindred stars familiar roam,
> Survey the region, and confess her home!

The distinction is subtle, since of course Winchilsea assumed that her feelings were representative; but her closing lines are unmistakably more personal: they grow out of her own feelings as accumulated in the poem, and are free of pompous diction and grandiloquent generalization.

Ann Messenger   (essay date 1986)

SOURCE: "Selected Nightingales" in *His and Hers: Essays in Restoration and Eighteenth-Century Literature,* The University Press of Kentucky, 1986, pp. 71-83.

[*In the following excerpt, Messenger discusses the literary tradition of poet as nightingale and the dualisms— such as art and nature or humans and animals—that underscore Finch's "To the Nightingale."*]

"To the Nightingale" begins with a command to the bird to sing so that the poet can write the lyrics for its music. The poet makes some comparisons between the bird and poets in general. When the bird begins to sing, the poet or the Muse attempts twice to match it with words but fails in the attempt. With a quick sour-grapes reversal, the poet attacks the frivolity of the nightingale, who is neglecting the serious business of nest-building, and concludes with a rueful analysis of the motivation for that attack.

One can readily see how this would appeal to the Romantic Wordsworth or Coleridge: the admiration for the beauty of the bird's song; the humbling, even the humiliation, of the mere human being before the wondrous powers of nature; and, above all, what one could call the "expressive" theory of poetic creativity: "Cares do still their Thoughts molest, / And still th'unhappy Poet's Breast, / Like thine, when best he sings, is plac'd against a Thorn." (I will return to that rather curious masculine pronoun.) Alluding to the myth of Philomela, Lady Winchilsea claims a most un-Augustan source for inspiration: personal pain. Pope sometimes claimed that moral pain goaded him into writing satire, but that is not at all the same thing. This sounds more like Coleridge in "Dejection"—except that there he claims that pain kills his creativity—but he creates a poem about that very notion. Lady Winchilsea could be writing in a similarly autobiographical vein here: there were many circumstances in her life that caused her considerable pain. And yet this is of course a conventional reference to the classical myth of Philomela and to the equation of singer, either bird or person, with poet. It is not necessary to choose between convention and autobiography, to label this line Augustan or Romantic. It is both. . . .

Lady Winchilsea's poem has similarities to and differences from both [Richard] Crashaw's and [Ambrose] Philips's poems ["Musicks Duell" and "Fifth Pastoral," respectively]. In historical terms, it has both metaphysical and Augustan elements. Like all her predecessors, she pits human being against bird. But the terms of the contest differ: words are to be matched with music, not music with music. Each artist is to perform in her own natural and characteristic medium. The most radical difference is in the outcome— Lady Winchilsea's nightingale wins. It is the only one I have found in the nightingale contest poems of the period to do so. The possibility of a victorious bird is suggested in Sylvester's translation of DuBartas, the Fifth Day of the First Week, but the outcome of the contest is not described. Lady Winchilsea's victorious bird is, it seems, original. And, again as far as I have been able to discover, hers is the only nightingale contest poem written by a woman.

The poem begins with the poet's command to the bird to sing: "Exert thy Voice, sweet Harbinger of Spring!" The command suggests human superiority. Yet the poet is attuned to the bird: this is the appropriate time for the bird to sing and the poet is prepared not only to write the words but also to heap praise on the skillful singer. Their relationship does not begin as a contest. Instead, a partnership is suggested, words to be tailored to fit the music. After all, birds and poets have much in common: both are wild creatures; both sing best when they are suffering, when the breast is placed against a thorn.

At this point, Lady Winchilsea uses a masculine pronoun for "th'unhappy Poet," which raises a number of questions and possibilities. It is probably not a typographical error: the 1713 volume, which is well printed and lists only a few obvious errors as errata, prints "he." One cannot take it as the poet trying to disguise her sex, for the 1713 title page proclaims that the poems are by "a Lady." One could pass it off as a slip of some sort; most eighteenth-century poets were men, and "poet . . . he" would almost write itself. But Lady Winchilsea was more careful of detail than that.

The idea of speech as a uniquely human attribute and, indeed, the idea of the limitations of speech recur frequently in Lady Winchilsea's poems.

—Ann Messenger

The picture is further complicated by the facts of nightingale life. The male nightingale, who arrives in England in the spring, several days before the female, is responsible for the famous song, while only the female builds the nest. Whether Lady Winchilsea knew these facts is debatable. She lived in the country, in Kent, where nightingales nested regularly, and might have had accurate information about their habits. But the males and females look very much alike, and some naturalists at the time believed that the females sang. Besides, the story of Philomela and the whole tradition in poetry made the singing nightingale female. In Lady Winchilsea's poem, the bird is consistently "she" and is scolded for neglecting the nest-building, which is in fact the female's job.

If we had a male nightingale and a female poet in this poem, which would reverse the pronouns but fit the facts, we would see a male figure rejecting partnership in favor of a contest and defeating the female who offers words for his music. One could take the poem, then, as expressing Lady Winchilsea's sense of the woman poet's lot, her subordinate position, her inferior abilities due perhaps to her inadequate education. In other poems, such as **"The Spleen"** and **"The Appology,"** she speaks disparagingly of her poetic powers; in **"Mercury and the Elephant"** and **"The Introduction,"** among others, she shows, directly and indirectly, the scorn of men for female poets. The defeated female poet in **"To the Nightingale,"** in other words, is consistent with some of Lady Winchilsea's other images of women. This reading is strengthened by the fact that **"To the Nightingale"** actually shows only the Muse being defeated, not overtly the poet to whom the masculine pronoun is applied, for the Muse provides the words which the nightingale "outflies." And Muses are always female.

With the bird a female, however, and the poet a male, we have a different story. The bird is always "she" in the poem and in the tradition. The poet is "he," if we forget for the moment the matter of the female Muse who supplies the words but could be dismissed as a mere convention. This allocation of the sexes contradicts the natural facts but fits the pronouns—the facts of the poem—and it would not be the first time that Lady Winchilsea had adopted a male persona. This reading turns the tables on the whole nightingale tradition in which male poet defeats

female bird—here, female bird defeats male poet. It would be a sweet and subtle revenge.

Disregarding the question of sex, however, there remains the inescapable fact that the nightingale is a bird and the poet is a human being. That becomes the problem. After the initial and brief assumption of human superiority when the poet commands the bird to sing, the proposed partnership and the similarities of bird and poet suggest the unity of all creation that informs Crashaw's poem. Indeed, similarity had been the basis of the various relationships between human beings and nightingales even before Crashaw. Shakespeare, in Sonnet 102, compares himself to a nightingale and claims that he has equally good sense when he, like the bird, ceases to sing so as not to bore the listener. Spenser, for whom great poets *are* nightingales, laments harmoniously with the bird at midnight. Sidney too, in various Eclogues, asks Philomela to help him express his sorrow and comments on the similar reasons for silence in the nightingale and in man. And in his poem called simply "The Nightingale," Sidney and the bird share the sorrows of love, though his are worse, he claims, because he is deprived of his lady while she just had too much of her man; there is an element of rivalry here as the poet measures his male suffering against Philomela's womanlike complaints. But even when there was overt rivalry, as in Crashaw's poem, unity and similarity continued to inform the relationship.

But unity and similarity vanish in Lady Winchilsea's poem when the bird begins to sing and the partnership dissolves into a contest. Oneness is an illusion; difference, dualism, prevails. We have moved into Ambrose Philips's world of human separateness, but not into his world of the superiority of art to nature, for when Lady Winchilsea's poet calls on the Muse for help ("Muse, thy Promise now fulfill!"), the call is not answered. The bird "outflies" the Muse. Defeated by nature, the human poet then asserts the superiority not of art, as in Philips, but of human values, specifically the work ethic, over the simple beauty of the bird's song: "Trifler, wilt thou sing till *June?* / Till thy Bus'ness all lies waste, / And the Time of Building's past!" Here the question of the bird's and the poet's sex arises again. Although women in the eighteenth century did not build "nests," they were certainly supposed to look after the nests provided by their husbands. Even noble ladies were expected to direct the servants, to engage in "the dull mannage, of a servile house." Anything that distracted them from those duties came under heavy fire, especially when the distractions took such unfeminine forms as reading and writing. The *Spectator* papers, for example, though at times advocating the education of women, kept up a steady stream of disparagement of those women whose learning interfered with their housekeeping (for example, Numbers 242, 328, 606). When Lady Winchilsea's male poet, then, chides the nightingale for neglecting her nest and wasting her time with idle song, "he" voices a common sentiment, one from which she herself had suffered. "He" deserves to be defeated by the bird.

On another level, calling the bird a "trifler" is sour grapes, and Lady Winchilsea, with her human self-consciousness, knows it, as the last six lines indicate. Here she holds the human poet up to ridicule, mocking his claim to superiority over the bird. But the human poet is not therefore simply inferior to the bird. He, or she, is different. The poet has "Speech / Unlike what thy Forests teach," something that sets human beings apart from the rest of creation.

"To the Nightingale" is part of an ancient and ongoing tradition. Like all pastoral poems which celebrate nature, it is a work of high and conscious art. . . . Lady Winchilsea has refreshed the tradition by bending it to the expression of her own complex, coherent, and unique thought.

—Ann Messenger

By asserting that speech defines the human, Lady Winchilsea was taking sides in a complex debate. In her time as in ours, mankind was difficult to define. When some thinkers claimed that beasts had reason and a form of speech, possessed souls, and could even look forward to a life after death, perhaps on Mars, the traditional boundaries were clearly being threatened. Orthodox theologians rejected such ideas and clung to the immortal soul and its manifestations in reason and speech as the distinguishing characteristics, while the new scientists rejected the old ideas of analogies and resemblances between man and nature in favor of a neutral and objective approach. Lady Winchilsea, then, is both scientifically up to date (and not metaphysical or Romantic) in her sense of the separateness of humanity from the rest of the creation, and theologically conservative in her assignment of speech as the distinguishing characteristic of the human. And yet the conservative definition tends to imply the superiority of the human. John Ray, Ben Jonson, and Bishop Wilkins, for example, agreed that speech was peculiar to man and beyond the capacities of inferior beasts. Lady Winchilsea's poem is thus profoundly ironic when the artless music of the mere bird defeats the poet's highest and most human skill, the art of speech. She affirms differentness, but she leaves open the question of human superiority.

The idea of speech as a uniquely human attribute and, indeed, the idea of the limitations of speech recur frequently in Lady Winchilsea's poems. Most often she uses the word "syllables" to indicate human speech, implying, I think, that, though language may differentiate man from beast, it is not a simple gift of God but a human construct, capable of being analyzed into its component parts, and that, as a human construct, it has limited powers. In the nightingale poem, she asks if the Muse can "refine" her presumably rough-and-ready syllables to make them a suitable accompaniment for the bird's music. Elsewhere, in **"A Letter to the Same Person"** (her husband), she finds

herself unable to express the fullness of her love and concludes:

> But since the Thoughts of a Poetick Mind
> Will never be to Syllables confin'd;
> And whilst to fix what is conceiv'd, we try,
> The purer Parts evaporate and dye:
> You must perform what they want force to do,
> And think what your ARDELIA thinks of you.

Lady Winchilsea's most anthologized poem, **"A Nocturnal Reverie,"** contains another example. She describes the sights, sounds, and fragrances of the night in which the spirit feels "a sedate Content" (l. 39), when "silent Musings urge the Mind to seek / Something too high for Syllables to speak . . ." (ll. 41-42).

This example, and less indirect lines here and in other poems, indicate not only that speech differentiates human beings from the rest of the creation, but also that the possession of an immortal soul, which speech implies, is their highest glory. Indeed, many times Lady Winchilsea speaks of heaven as the true home of the human soul. The idea appears indirectly in **"A Nocturnal Reverie,"** when the soul grows quiet and "Joys in th'inferiour World, and thinks it like her Own." The emphasis is on "thinks"; the world of the soul is not the world of the nonhuman creation, though it is refreshing to pretend that it is, to rest temporarily from the burdens of humanness. The animals have no such burdens because they have no heavenly home, as Lady Winchilsea implies at the end of a short poem called **"The Bird and the Arras."** The bird in this poem has flown into a room in which an arras covers a wall; the arras depicts a grove of trees, and does it so well that the bird is deceived. She flies up into the tapestry trees and bumps her head on the ceiling, then tries again and dashes herself against a windowpane. Finally, someone opens the window and shoos the bird out: "some kind hand directs the certain way / Which through the casement an escape affords / And leads to ample space the only Heav'n of Birds." Birds belong to a lower order of creation, or at least a different order; they have no souls, no heaven beyond the sky. This essential difference underlies **"To the Nightingale"** as well and is part of the reason why the human poet, male or female, cannot participate in the music of the bird.

The poet scolds the bird for neglecting her nest, and the poem concludes with an analysis of the sour-grapes reaction to defeat:

> Thus we Poets that have Speech,
> Unlike what thy Forests teach,
> If a fluent Vein be shown,
> That's transcendent to our own,
> Criticize, reform, or preach,
> Or censure what we cannot reach.

The song of the bird *is* superior; the poet "cannot reach" it. Must one then close the open question and conclude that nature is superior to art and that humanity is shockingly inferior to the beasts? The dualism is there, as in

Philips's pastoral, and he, following the usual Augustan impulse to make judgments, judged that art and humanity are superior. The issue, as I have indicated, was complex, and the debate about it took various forms. But Lady Winchilsea's poem does not adopt the common form of a simple dichotomy between art and nature, nor does she make a simple choice between them. In another poem [**"An Invitation to Dafnis"**], she does make such a choice—but that choice is part of the wit of the invitation to her husband to leave his books and come for a walk in the fields with her. In **"To the Nightingale"** she makes no choice in the sense of a value judgment; instead, at the end of the poem, she emphasizes the separateness of the human world with its propensity to make moral judgments, to "Criticize, reform, or preach," which birds never do. And she criticizes biased, self-interested human judgments: "Or censure what we cannot reach." The poet implicates herself—or the "he" persona—in that criticism. She has been typically human in her attack on the bird. She, who had thought that the worlds of bird and poet, of animal and man, were alike, and had proposed a partnership, has been proved wrong, and proved human, by her defeat.

Other dualisms besides those of art and nature and man and beast underlie the argument of **"To the Nightingale,"** dualisms that are part of the philosophical assumptions and critical vocabulary of the period. Passion is set over against Reason, as the poet who writes from personal pain suddenly turns practical and scolds the nightingale for delaying its nest-building. Wit and judgment, as Locke defined them, shape the argument of the poem: wit, the faculty which consists in the assemblage of ideas, makes the poet see herself as akin to the bird, while judgment, which lies in separating carefully, shows her that she belongs to a different order of being. The dualisms and the progression from partnership to contest and defeat show that the poem comprehends two opposing sensibilities without reconciling their differences, without closing all the questions. Perhaps the tragedy is that the differences between all the twos cannot be reconciled, something that Lady Winchilsea knew but that Wordsworth had to find out.

"To the Nightingale" is part of an ancient and ongoing tradition. Like all pastoral poems which celebrate nature, it is a work of high and conscious art. Like all the nightingale contest poems, it has something to say about the relationship between the contestants. And, like all good poems, it is also original and new. Lady Winchilsea has refreshed the tradition by bending it to the expression of her own complex, coherent, and unique thought.

Marilyn L. Williamson (essay date 1990)

SOURCE: "Orinda and Her Daughters," in *Raising Their Voices: British Women Writers, 1650-1750,* Wayne State University Press, 1990, pp. 64-133.

[*In the following excerpt, Williamson surveys the role of the woman writer as presented in Finch's poetry.*]

[Finch] was resolutely ladylike and therefore a natural daughter of Orinda [Katherine Philips], and so she is consistently defensive about her writing. In **"Mercury and the Elephant,"** which began her *Miscellany Poems, on Several Occasions, Written by a Lady,* she uses a fable to represent the predicament of the woman writer. Just as the god Mercury cannot be bothered with the quarrels of an elephant and a wild boar, so men can hardly be troubled with what women write:

> What Men are not concern'd to know:
> For still untouch'd how we succeed,
> 'Tis for themselves, not us they *Read*;
> Whilst that proceeding to requite,
> We own (who in the Muse delight)
> 'Tis for our Selves, not them, we *Write.*

The tone is light and self-deprecating but also ironic about godlike males; the defense of writing for each other leaves women relatively invulnerable to male criticism, but also incapable of affecting the male audience.

More touching are two suppressed works: **"The Introduction"** and the preface to the manuscript folio. **"The Introduction"** describes women's past achievements. Presenting an amalgam of biblical incidents, it praises women who sang to celebrate the bringing of the Ark into Jerusalem, the women greeting the victorious David with songs, and, most of all, Deborah:

> A Woman here, leads fainting Isreal on,
> She fights, she wins, she tryumphs with a song,
> Devout, Majestick, for the subject fitt,
> And far above her arms, exalts her witt,
> Then, to the peacefull, shady Palm withdraws,
> And rules the rescu'd Nation, with her Laws.

Winchilsea saw her contemporaries as greatly diminished from that heroic tradition because, like Cavendish, she despaired at women's lack of education:

> How are we fal'n, fal'n by mistaken rules?
> And Education's more then Nature's fools,
> Debarr'd from all improve-ments of the mind,
> And to be dull, expected and dessigned;
> And if some one, wou'd Soar above the rest,
> With warmer fancy, and ambition press't,
> So strong, th'opposing faction still appears,
> The hopes to thrive, can ne're outweigh the fears.

Her resolve, therefore, was to keep her muse retired: during her lifetime she achieved her status as an heir to Orinda by keeping her most transgressive poetry for private circulation.

The preface to the folio shows how self-conscious Winchilsea was about Orinda's model, how she used many of the same psychological strategies, even in a manuscript volume, and therefore how deeply ingrained those habits of mind were. First, she explained that she did not expect her scattered efforts at poetry to be attended to, but that through circulation in manuscript, they had "grown by the partiality of some of my friends, to the formidable appearance of a Volume." She never expected, she said, to "reatch Orinda's prayse"; she never wrote any of her poems for publication; indeed, she had almost stopped writing when she and Finch moved to Eastwell, but his nephew, their host, and the beauty of the place inspired her muse: "But now, having pleaded an irresistable impulse, as my excuse for writing, which was the cheif design of this Preface, I must also expresse my hopes of excaping all suspition of vanity, or affectation of applause from itt." She was sensible to the laws of poetry defined by Aristotle, Horace, Rapin, Despreaux, Roscommon, Dryden, and how imperfect her poetry appeared in light of literary theory. Yet she hoped her poetic subjects were inoffensive. She wrote, she said, little of love, using Orinda as a model: "Tho' I must confesse, the great reservednesse of Mrs. Philips in this particular, and the prayses I have heard given her upon that account, together with my desire not to give scandal to the most severe, has often discourag'd me from making use of it." In writing plays too she followed Orinda: "and mine, tho' orginals, I hope are not lesse reserv'd." Finally, in a moving passage [quoted in Lawrence Lipking, "Aristotle's Sister," *Critical Inquiry,* Vol. 10, September 1983], she told how she used poetry as a stay against melancholy and isolation, "achieving, through sharing the emotions of loneliness and abandonment, a momentary sense of not being alone."

> And indeed, an absolute solitude (which often was my lott) under such dejection of mind, cou'd not have been supported, had I indulg'd myself (as was too natural to me) only in the contemplation of present and real afflictions, which I hope will plead my excuse, for turning them for releif, upon such as were immaginary, & relating to Persons no more in being. I had my end in the writing, and if they please not those who will take the pains to peruse them, itt will be a just accusation to my weaknesse, for letting them escape out of their concealment; but if attended with a better successe, the satisfaction any freind of mine, may take in them, will make me think my time past, not so unprofitably bestowed, as otherwise I might.

Although she frequently asserted poetry's private uses for her, Winchilsea was more ambitious (in the manuscript poems) for women poets and for herself than first appears. She modestly insisted upon the limitations of her own talent in **"The Appology,"** "Each Woman has her weakness; mine indeed / Is still to write tho' hopelesse to succeed," but in an early verse she saw the poetry of a friend as reviving the strain of Sappho and surpassing Orinda:

> Since our own Age is happily possesst
> Of such a genius, in a Female Breast,
> As gives us Faith for all those wonders told,
> Producing New, to justify the old.
> Then we'll no more submitt, but (in your name)
> To Poetry renew our Ancient Claime;
> Through itts retirement, we'll your worth persue,
> And lead itt into Public Rule and View.
>
> . . . . .
>
> And whilst Orinda's part you far transcend,
> I proudly bear that of her glorious Friend,

Who though not equaling her lofty Witt,
Th' occasion was, of what so well writt.

The friend, Mrs. Randolph, had represented Winchilsea bearing the mantle of Cowley. The compliments are exaggerations, but supportive nonetheless.

"The Circuit of Appollo" belongs to the genre of "sessions" of the poets and offers judgments about Winchilsea herself and several contemporaries. The poem is based on the terms of the Salic Law of Wit, which generally excludes women from writing, just as they are excluded from the French throne. Only Apollo may make exceptions to the law for truly extraordinary talent, and he usually makes one exception at a time. Here Apollo judges Aphra Behn for her morals, a general attitude toward the end of the century, and yet her art is praised:

> He [Apollo] lamented for Behn o're that place of
>   her birth,
> And said amongst Femens was not on earth
> Her superior in fancy, in language, or witt
> Yet own'd that a little too loosly she writt.

The other poets, Alinda, Laura, Valeria, and Winchilsea herself as Ardelia, are all judged as worth the bays. But Apollo, noting the outcome of the Judgment of Paris, decides to divide the laurels among all four. The poem is wittily cynical about Apollo's judgment and about women at the end, but it also refuses the dictate of the Salic Law of Wit that there could be only one approved woman poet at a time. The effect of the poem is a witty spoof of the entire idea of the Salic Law of Wit. Winchilsea's description of herself is characteristically self-effacing:

> Ardelia, came last as expecting least praise,
> Who writt for her pleasure and not for the bays,
> But yett, as occasion, or fancy should sway,
> Wou'd sometimes endeavour to passe a dull day,
> In composing a song, or a Scene of a Play
> Not seeking for Fame, which so little does last,
> That e're we can taste itt, the Pleasure is Past.
> But Appollo reply'd, tho' so careless she
>   seemd,
> Yett the Bays, if her share, wou'd be highly
>   esteem'd.

Apollo's attitude admits, on behalf of Winchilsea, that she truly enjoyed the recognition of her achievements, despite her lifelong concealment of her poetry. This exaggerated modesty seems to be a form of undoing because Winchilsea was very much aware, when she wrote about Pope, of how any poet seeks fame:

> For none have writ (whatever they pretend)
> Singly to raise a patron or a friend;
> But whatsoe'er the theme or object be,
> Some commendation to themselves foresee.

Occasionally Winchilsea's religious fervor made her ambitious. She did not publish her most devout religious poetry, probably because it would have seemed enthusiastic.

Here, in a poem from the Wellesley Manuscript, she would better Dryden because of divine inspiration:

> My temper frail and subject to dismay
> Be steadfast there spiritualiz'd and gay
> My low Poetick tendency be rais'd
> Till the bestower worthily is prais'd
> Till Dryden's numbers for Cecilia's feats
> Which sooth depress inflame and shake the breast
> Vary the passions with each varying line
> Allow'd below all others to outshine
> Shall yeild to those above shall yeild to mine
> In sound in sense in emphasis Divine.

Because she herself went to such lengths to tread a narrow line between asserting herself as a poet and being modest as a woman, Winchilsea blamed women poets for the social scorn they earned because they were too public, wrote spiteful verse, or otherwise made social spectacles of themselves. Here [in **"Ardelia's Answer to Ephelia"**], she depicts Ardelia's conversation with a fashionable lady:

> They say she writes, and 'tis a common jest.
> Then sure sh' has publickly the skill professt,
> I soon reply, and makes that gift her pride,
> And all the world, but scribblers, does deride;
> Setts out Lampoons, where only spite is seen,
> Not fill'd with female witt, but female spleen.
> Her florish'd name, does o're a song expose,
> Which through all ranks, down to the Carman, goes.
> Or poetry is on her Picture found,
> In which she sits, with pained lawrel crown'd.
> If no such flyes, no vanity defile,
> The Helyconian balm, the sacred oyl,
> Why shou'd we from that pleasing art be ty'd,
> Or like State Pris'ners, Pen and Ink deny'd?

There is possible irony in the mention of *spleen* because her poem by that name made Winchilsea famous as "the Author of **'The Spleen'**." Still, women who kept proper limits, as Winchilsea herself did, should not be criticized for writing. If the character Phoebe Clinket in *Three Hours After Marriage* is modeled on Winchilsea, that is a true irony of literary history, for one of Phoebe's main concerns is getting her work published. The character is probably a composite of many women writers, with a good deal of Cavendish in her, and the satiric concentration on ambition shows the accuracy of Winchilsea's judgment about her world.

Even if her modesty did keep her from publishing much of her verse that is most interesting today, some of Winchilsea's protests about fame seem psychological strategies. **"The Spleen"** had been published in 1701, and was a great success; and after that she could publish as its author. Although she may have vainly longed for Pope's praise of her *Miscellany* in 1713, she enjoyed the esteem of many important contemporaries. But, as Ann Messenger has said [in "Publishing without Perishing," *Restoration*, Vol. 5, Spring 1981], her defenses of the privilege of writing are complex and, I would add, quite like Orinda's. Winchilsea undoes her deviancy by acknowledging it and satirizes women's activities as Cavendish did in *Sociable Letters*:

> My Lines decry'd, and my Employment thought
> An useless Folly, or presumptuous Fault:
>   Whilst in the *Muses* Paths I stray
> Whilst in their Groves, and by their secret Springs
> My Hand delights to trace unusual Things,
> And deviates from the known, and common way;
>   Nor will in fading Silks compose
>   Faintly th'inimitable *Rose,*
> Fill up an ill-drawn *Bird,* or paint on Glass
> The *Sov'reign's* blurr'd and undistinguish'd Face,
> The threatening *Angel,* and the Speaking *Ass.*

We will return later to her satire on fashionable, contemporary women.

The very selection of poems to be published in *Miscellany* and those to be preserved in manuscript is a defense strategy in itself. For, if one studies, as Ann Messenger has, the kinds of poems Winchilsea published and those she suppressed, one sees that many of the poems that fit Lipking's definition of a female poetic remain in manuscript: virtually all the poems that are shaped to the self, are about her life, are about other women or being a woman, are suppressed. This is especially true for the Wellesley manuscript, which is full of personal occasional verse. Published are many fables, thirty-four of eighty-six poems in the volume. The fable, a popular genre of the period, afforded opportunities to translate or imitate famous male writers and was "an appropriately humble form for a women to use" [Ann Messenger, "Publishing Without Penshins"]. The fable also provided protection for the author: it has inherent distancing that allows its author a range of comments and tones. As Messenger suggests, an insight into how Winchilsea used fables lies in **"The Critick and the Writer of Fables."** The poet has tired of Pindarics and would use fables to teach and to delight: some will be translated, but the fables will be simple and pleasant. The critic dislikes fables, and so the poet offers epic verse, which the critic also scorns. The critic also rejects the pastoral, but endorses satires. The poet tries to get the critic to accept a pluralistic muse, but the critic is scornful of those diverted with ease. Just as scornful of the critic was Winchilsea.

Other genres represented in volume of 1713 are songs, biblical translations, pastorals, Pindarics, a parody of Milton, **"The Spleen"** (already published), and **"The Hurricane,"** based on a storm of November 1703. . . . There are also a very few love poems addressed to Winchilsea's husband. The generalization that applies to most of these poems is that they offend practically no reader within Winchilsea's society. Her political convictions, her deviant views about women, her many poems about personal relationships and about herself, even some of her poems of married love, all waited in manuscript three centuries for readers.

The themes that mark Winchilsea as a descendent of Orinda can be easily discerned in the published volume, however. Although she suppressed several more personal poems addressed to women friends, several were published in 1713. Winchilsea was especially fond of the theme of inexpressible love, which resolves her most familiar friend-ship poem ["**Friendship Between Ephelia and Ardelia**"]:

> *Eph.* This indeed, tho' carry'd high,
>   This, tho' more than e'er was done
>   Underneath the rolling Sun,
>   This has all been said before.
>   Can *Ardelia* say no more?
> *Ard.* Words indeed no more can shew:
>   *But 'tis to love, as I love you.*

"**To the Painter of an Ill-Drawn Picture of Cleone, the Honorable Mrs. Thynne**" is really a friendship poem in which Winchilsea criticizes the painting of Cleone in order to define an ideal of womanhood. The painter has made Cleone look too aggressive: the picture resembles a virago or an Amazon, who would never have captured Theanor's heart. The poem resolves as did the previous one to Ephelia: neither the painter nor the poet could capture "what Nature in Cleone's Face has writ."

In one of her better known and most interesting poems, "**The Petition for an Absolute Retreat**," Winchilsea blends the favorite themes of retreat from the world, friendship, married love, and politics. The poem is inscribed to "Catherine Countess of Thanet," who seems to have given the Finches refuge during the difficult period after the flight of James II in 1688. The poem fairly bursts with the emotions Winchilsea must have experienced in that moment, but its conventions also lie squarely in the retirement tradition. It begins with the desire for an absolute retreat in which the speaker's existence would be very like that of the Golden Age: all would be simple, old, and natural, expressing "unaffected Carelessness." As heaven has shown the way, the speaker asks for a partner who will also abandon wealth and pride. But these pleasures are those of youth. By means of the figure of an old oak, the poem modulates to the plight of the poet when blasted by a storm over "all the *British* State." In this peril Winchilsea had the comfort of Arminda, a wonderful friend:

> To Woman ne'er allow'd before,
> What Nature, or refining Art,
> All that Fortune cou'd impart,
> Heaven did to *Arminda* send;
> Then gave her for *Ardelia's* Friend:
> To her Cares to Cordial drop,
> Which else had overflow'd the Cup.

As friendship is the support of humankind, the speaker hopes for a friend in the retreat also. The poem shows that if Crassus and Sertorius had been content to remain in retreat, Crassus in his cave and Sertorius in the Fortunate Isles, both would have found peace and rest. It ends in a vision of the soul finding the joy of paradise. Winchilsea's retirement because of politics echoes that of Cavendish, and indeed they have other common qualities.

Winchilsea combined political and personal themes with her celebration of rural England and its aristocracy in a poem addressed to Arminda's daughter, "**A Poem for the Birth-day of the Right Hon**^BLE **the Lady Catherine Tuf-**

ton.**" Here Serena is celebrated, first for her family "In whom our Britain lets us see / What once they were, and still should be"; then for her personal attributes: honor, wit, goodness, and grace. The poem concludes with a vision of Serena as a bride, bestowed by Hothfield, the Thanet country house, and continuing the aristocracy of England:

> Of Fathers, the long-fram'd Design,
> To add such Splendour to their Line,
> Whilst all shall strive for such a Bride
> So Educated, and Ally'd.

. . . . .

Winchilsea's emphasis on education is probably unusual in this kind of poetry, but her second adjective about alliance is surely mainstream. Because of her conservatism and her attitudes as a woman, the social implication of her poetry is extremely complex, especially because she circulated her poems privately.

Part of her cluster of individual attitudes was Winchilsea's celebration of domestic happiness. She is more satiric than Cavendish, but like her in making her own marriage an ideal to which others should strive. Two poems in **Miscellany** idealize the relationship of married love. The first, "**To Mr. F. Now Earl of W.**," satirizes the contemporary world for denigrating married love. When Winchilsea appeals to the Muses for inspiration, they are dismayed to discover her subject:

> The hasty Summons was allow'd;
> And being well bred, they rose and bow'd,
>   And said, they'd poste away;
> That well they did *Ardelia* know,
> And that no Female's Voice below
>   They sooner wou'd obey.

Only Urania counsels the poet that she need but look in her heart and write. Winchilsea concludes that Flavis alone should hear her love, for if the world so despises married love, it should remain a mystery. The second poem, "**A Letter to the Same Person**," reverts to Winchilsea's favorite assertion of the inexpressibility of love; yet in passing it pays tribute to the importance of poetry in the life of love:

> Love without Poetry's refining Aid
> Is a dull Bargain, and but coarsely made;
> Nor e'er cou'd Poetry successful prove,
> Or touch the Soul, but when the Sense was Love.

Other and more moving tributes Winchilsea kept in manuscript.

If she conformed to many of the attitudes of the Orinda tradition and her society, Winchilsea was like all of Orinda's daughters in raising a highly distinctive voice. Her special subject was the spleen and the use of poetry to deal with it. "**The Spleen**" was much admired in its time, and has frequently been reprinted since then. The poem is a fascinating mixture of psychological and physical analysis, personal confession, and social satire. The poem is remarkable in taking the affliction seriously and renders its symptoms graphically, including the affected senses as the victim is made nauseous by certain odors. In addition, the work acknowledges the social dimension of disease, how it may spread by imitation. This kind of fashion can turn its trivial side to domestic quarrels or the fop, but it may be serious as religious despair. The two central sections are structured similarly in moving from domestic scenes to affectations and then to serious artistic and religious depression. These sections are flanked by an introduction that deals with symptoms and a conclusion that dismisses cures. It is an impressive performance, and the confession embedded at its center only establishes the speaker's authority.

Winchilsea did not publish another moving poem she wrote about the same affliction, probably because it was too personal: **"Ardelia to Melancholy."** The speaker calls melancholy her "old inverterate foe," and the poem is almost a personal continuation of the end of **"The Spleen"** because one remedy for melancholy after another is rejected as ineffective. The poet has tried music and distracting arts, only to experience more intense pain. (The Wellesley manuscript contains a fascinating account of what we would call the use of music therapy for depression.) Friendship is no remedy, either, and the breaking of friendship only causes greater pain:

> Freindship, I to my heart have laid,
> Freindship, th' applauded sov'rain aid,
> And though that charm so strong wou'd prove,
> As to compell thee, to remove;
> And to myself, I boasting said,
> Now I a conqu'rer sure shall be,
> The end of all my conflicts, see,
> And noble tryumph, wait on me;
> My dusky, sullen foe, will sure
> N'er this united charge endure.
> But leaning on this reed, ev'n whilst I spoke
> It pierc'd my hand, and into pieces broke.
> Still, some new object, or new int'rest came
> And loos'd the bonds, and quite disolv'd the
>   claim.

Even poetry, the last resort, is no equal to depression, "and heav'n, alone, can sett me free." It seems very likely that, with the extent of Winchilsea's conformity and conflicting need to use her talent, the anger that occasionally surfaced in her work and that Mary Chudleigh understood and analyzed, turned into Winchilsea's melancholy. If anger and depression are identified as significant women's problems today, we may see that in Chudleigh, Winchilsea, and others studied here, they have been women's problems for hundreds of years; and women have raised their voices about the predicaments that spawn the conditions for centuries without being heard, but they have raised their voices nonetheless.

Many of the other poems that Winchilsea left in manuscript are also those that are the personal expression of

her life. There are several love poems addressed to her husband, such as **"A Letter to Dafnis April: 2nd 1685."** In this poem she draws a magic circle in which he is her only audience: "You know who writes; and I who 'tis that reads." She was not, therefore, flaunting her inexpressible love for him publicly, as other women might. She could express at once her love and the boundary dividing the private and the public.

Although she was as critical of superficial women as was Cavendish, Winchilsea had a social approach to their predicament that Cavendish lacked.

—Marilyn L. Williamson

In addition to frank comments on the difficulties of being a woman writer that we have already seen, Winchilsea wrote many unpublished poems about women. There are sixteen poems in the Wellesley manuscript alone either addressed to women, or about them, or both. There are more poems of friendship, but there are also poems that are critical of female contemporaries. In **"On Myselfe"** Winchilsea contrasted herself with other women whose lives are consumed with trifles:

> Good Heav'n, I thank thee, since it was design'd
> I shou'd be fram'd, but of the weaker kinde,
> That yet, my Soul, is rescued from the Love
> Of all those trifles, which their Passions move.
> Pleasures, and Praise, and Plenty haue with me
> But their just value. If allow'd they be,
> Freely, and thankfully as much I tast,
> As will not reason, or Religion wast.
> If they're deny'd, I on my selfe can Live,
> And slight those aids, unequal chance does give.
> When in the Sun, my wings can be display'd,
> And in retirement, I can bless the shade.

The spirit is very much that of Orinda and the retirement discourse: a stoic determination to survive a possibly hostile world through a conscious self-sufficiency, a stubborn unwillingness to depend on what the world offers. Like Cavendish, Winchilsea held no brief for most women's lives, not did she believe that most of them had the slightest sympathy for her purposes. The set piece for these views is **"Ardelia's Answer to Ephelia,"** in which the speaker is a bookish, old-fashioned woman from the country and satirizes her friend Almeria. The latter is fashionable, full of affectations in dress and in taste of all kinds, including fancy china and tea. She envies other women's beauty and is insensitive to the virtues and accomplishments of Piso, "who from the Latin, Virgil frees." Almeria betrays the confidences of friends and makes fun of a woman poet. Ardelia cannot wait to bid her good-bye and head for the country:

We parted thus, the night in peace I spent,
And the next day, with haste and pleasure went
To the best seat of fam'd and fertile Kent.
Where lett me live from all detraction free
Till freind, and Foe, I treat with such dispite
May I no scorn, the worst of ills, excite.

It is difficult to escape the conclusion that even if their political fortunes had not forced them into the country, both Cavendish and Winchilsea were too strong-minded and independent to tolerate life in London.

Winchilsea was acutely attuned to the taste and attitudes of her age, and, despite her individual perspectives, tried to hew as carefully as possible to what she thought would be socially and artistically acceptable.

—Marilyn L. Williamson

Although she was as critical of superficial women as was Cavendish, Winchilsea had a social approach to their predicament that Cavendish lacked. For Winchilsea women were "Education's more then Nature's fools." Winchilsea had a social vocabulary in which to view women's problems that Cavendish never developed because of her allegience to Nature. So despite Winchilsea's own happy marriage, she understood that the institution was manmade as an unequal relationship:

Free as Nature's first intention
Was to make us, I'll be found
Nor by subtle Man's invention
Yeild to be in Fetters bound.
By one that walks a freer round.

Mariage does but slightly tye Men
Whil'st close Pris'ners we remain
They the larger Slaves of Hymen
Still are begging Love again
At the full length of all their chain.

Winchilsea frequently satirized both surly husbands and shrewish wives, as in **"Reformation"** or **"The Spleen,"** where she was quite evenhanded. An interesting example of her attitude toward marriage is **"A Tale"** from the Wellesley manuscript. There on a wager a man will give an apple to dominant wives and a horse to submissive ones. The bet is that he will return with four horses and no apples. He finds mostly shrews until he comes upon a woman who appears to be bullied by her mate. The gambler is about to award the horse when the wife begins to berate her husband about which horse to choose! They are promptly awarded an apple. At the end Winchilsea apologizes for the story, but counsels women to serve their desires by being loving to their mates. Then in closing she also sees clearly that some women may suffer without remedy in marriage:

But if we meet some manly brute
  Whose power is all his pride
Nor love nor tears nor mild dispute
  Can stem the boysterous tide.

Silently suffering to the Grave
  Must be our wretched fate
Eve when she made herself a slave
  Determin'd all our fate.

When her work is taken as a whole, Winchilsea fits consistently into the Orinda tradition and into Lipking's definition of a woman's poetic. How accurate his definition is may be shown by how many of the poems that were shaped by her life and self Winchilsea believed she could never publish. It is also clear why modern critics have found Winchilsea to be a typical Augustan, even if her nature poetry attracted Wordsworth. She was acutely attuned to the taste and attitudes of her age, and, despite her individual perspectives, tried to hew as carefully as possible to what she thought would be socially and artistically acceptable. That we are beginning to understand how far her vision exceeded the bounds she herself accepted is a tribute to the legacy she left unpublished and unacknowledged for hundreds of years.

Jean Mallinson (essay date 1990)

SOURCE: "Anne Finch: A Woman Poet and the Tradition," in *Gender at Work*, edited and introduced by Ann Messenger, Wayne State University Press, 1990, pp. 34-76.

[*In the following excerpt, Mallinson discusses how Finch's position on the margins of eighteenth-century society influenced her poetry.*]

The relation of literary theory to practice in the Restoration and early eighteenth century is problematical and variously interpreted. The fact that Anne Finch was a woman writer attempting to adapt her talents to a literary tradition from which women's voices were almost absent made her position as a writer in her time idiosyncratic. If Earl Miner is correct in seeing in the Restoration a shift from the private and coterie to the public mode, and if critics of the period are right in their consensus that satire sets the dominant tone in the literature of the time, then Anne Finch's work is marginal to the literature of her age. She was not a satirist; in a prose statement she dissociated herself from satire's underhandedness and lack of charity. There is a satirical edge to her fables, epistles, and occasional poems; her life in retirement from the *beau monde* provided a distance across which she could view it with an ironic eye. But the themes of power, pretentiousness, and corruption in the public spheres of politics, established institutions, and high society, which provide the substance of much neoclassical satire, were not her concerns. When she turns her pen to the fates of kingdoms and monarchs, she expresses her sense of these affairs in older modes like the extended emblem. Satire is an aggressive mode, out for the kill or at least the exposé, and Anne Finch's sense of irony, which often included herself, undercuts the fiction of authority which satire requires.

Thus temperament, and the voice which expresses temperament, influence a poet's choice of genre, which Frank Kermode [*The Genesis of Secrecy*, 1979] calls the first of the "constraints which shadow interpretation." And for a woman poet in the late seventeenth century there was a condition prior to the constraints of genre: the constraint of being a woman. The fact that Anne Finch turns repeatedly in poems to her concern with her vocation as a poet who is also a woman suggests that it constitutes an essential knot which she by turns entwines, embellishes, or attempts to untie. The combination woman/poet presents at various times a paradox, a mystery, a scandal, an oxymoron, and a triumph. This concern haunts her poetry, sometimes on the periphery, as a distraction or obstacle which must be dealt with before she can get to her theme, sometimes, as in **"The Appology,"** as her subject itself. In these ironic lines she disarms anxiously anticipated criticism by belittling her accomplishments as a poet and at the same time using received opinion about women—"Each Woman has her weakness"—to argue her case for her persistence in writing poetry:

> 'Tis true I write and tell me by what Rule
> I am alone forbid to play the fool
> To follow through the Groves a wand'ring Muse
> And fain'd Idea's for my pleasures chuse
> Why shou'd it in my Pen be held a fault
> Whilst Mira paints her face, to paint a thought
> Whilst Lamia to the manly Bumper flys
> And borrow'd Spiritts sparkle in her Eyes
> Why shou'd itt be in me a thing so vain
> To heat with Poetry my colder Brain. . . .

The paired comparisons which express her ironic deprecation of her choice of folly point to the higher value of her unfeminine predilections, but the use of rhetorical questions rather than assertions suggests that her weakness is not likely to be viewed with sympathy by those to whom the poem is addressed.

There is a telling passage about her poetic aspirations enclosed in the formal epistle, **"To the Honorable the Lady Worsley at Longleate,"** an extended compliment to a style of life and writing and a concentrated topographical poem in the vein of Marvell's "Upon Appleton House":

> Cou'd but the Witt that on her paper flows
> Affect my Verse and tune itt to her Prose
> Through every Line a kindly warmth inspire
> And raise my Art equal to my desire
> Then shou'd my Hand snatch from the Muses store
> Transporting Figures n'ere expos'd before
> Somthing to Please so moving and so new
> As not our Denham or our Cowley knew.

The "Cou'd but . . . Then" construction in this passage points to the tension in her poetry between ambition and accomplishment, but her longing to outdo the esteemed Denham and Cowley suggests the scope of her ambition.

"An Epistle From Ardelia to Mrs. Randolph in answer to her Poem upon Her Verses" gives Anne Finch the occasion to claim for her sex their ancient rights to poetry—not in her own name, for her defensive mask of modesty forbids her to do so, but in the name of a sister poet:

> Madam,
>   till pow'rfully convinc'd by you,
> I thought those Praises never were Their due,
> Which I had read, or heard bestow'd by Men
> On Women, that have ventur'd on the Pen.
> But now must yeild (pursuaded by your stile)
> That Lesbian Sapho's might all hearts beguile.
> The vanquish'd Pindar, now I must beleive
> Might from Corrina's Muse new Laws receive,
> Since our own Age is happily possest
> Of such a genius, in a Female Breast,
> As gives us Faith for all those wonders told,
> Producing New, to justify the old.
> Then we'll no more submitt, but (in your name)
> To Poetry renew our Ancient Claime;
> Through itts retirement, we'll your worth persue
> And lead itt into Public Rule and view. . . .

The formal complexity of these lines shows Anne Finch's mastery of the subtleties of neoclassical style. This brief poem is a compliment enclosed in an epistle which also encompasses a panegyric to friendship and—in the lines quoted—a manifesto of women's ancient rights to poetry.

The lovely, varied lyric, **"Melinda on an Insippid Beauty In imitation of a fragment of Sapho's,"** combines the old *memento mori* theme with the equally old conceit concerning the poet's fame after death to make a poem which is the boldest statement Anne Finch ever ventured about the worth of her poetic endeavors. It accords with what we know of her temperament that she could make such a strong assertion only through the persona of Sappho, acknowledged paradigm of women poets:

> You, when your body, life shall leave
> Must drop entire, into the grave;
> Unheeded, unregarded lye,
> And all of you together dye;
> Must hide that fleeting charm, that face in dust,
> Or to some painted cloath, the slighted Immage
>   trust,
> Whilst my fam'd works, shall throo' all times
>   surprise
> My polish'd thoughts, my bright Ideas rise,
> And to new men be known, still talking to their
>   eyes.

This brief poem has great formal beauty. It imitates in its changing line length the movement of its thought from the confinement of death to the freedom of living in spirit after death, through poetry. The poet, as she often does, balances the poem on a contrast between the conventional image of the feminine and her own sense of poetic vocation, but this lyric is free from defensiveness. It states with clear authority, without question, condition, or qualification, her expectation of poetic renown. It is characteristic of her ironic wit that she envisions her triumph, immortality through her poems, in terms of feminine conquest—"And to new men be known, still talking to their eyes."

Finch's misgivings about the worthwhileness of "scribbling" are common to all authors on occasion, but there is a shudder in the words "grotesque and trivial, shun'd by all," which can be linked to her apprehension, expressed in other poems, that her deviance in being a woman writer will cause her to be despised and condemned by the world.

—*Jean Mallinson*

In spite of such affirmations as the one expressed in this poem, it remains true that Anne Finch's poetic vocation marked her, in her time, as eccentric. . . . [Literature] was still considered the province of men, and women ventured into their territory with trepidation and at the risk of scorn. Anne Finch availed herself of various stratagems for surviving as an eccentric—a versifying lady. One device, as in the lyric just quoted, was to speak through the voice of a recognized and lauded paradigm like Sappho. Another was to make common cause with fellow eccentrics. This she does humorously in the **"The Circuit of Appollo,"** a whimsical description of a contest among women poets, probably modeled on Suckling's "A Session of the Poets," and seriously in such poems as the epistle to Mrs. Randolph discussed above and in her lines **"To a Fellow Scribbler,"** an intricate extended emblem. Written in a poetic convention which links its author with early seventeenth-century poets, it expresses forcefully Anne Finch's anxiety lest, after all, "we rhiming fools" may have spent life in "vain flourish":

Unless we solidly indite,
Some good infusing while we write,

. . . . .

We like that tree and hedge be found,
Grotesque and trivial, shun'd by all,
And soon forgotten when we fall.

Her misgivings about the worthwhileness of "scribbling" are common to all authors on occasion, but there is a shudder in the words "Grotesque and trivial, shun'd by all," which can be linked to her apprehension, expressed

in other poems, that her deviance in being a woman writer will cause her to be despised and condemned by the world.

Another tactic is to describe oneself as deviant in a way which allows such eccentricities as the writing of poetry. By presenting herself in a number of poems as melancholy, a prisoner of Spleen, Anne Finch provided an image of herself which gave a certain licence to her odd persistence in following her Muse. That she did indeed suffer from this malady is documented by Reynolds. In her poems, her fits of depression are linked in various ways to her writing of poetry. In **"Ardelia to Melancholy"** she invokes poetry as an attempted cure for the "dusky, sullen foe" which acts the Tyrant in her "darken'd breast." In **"The Spleen"** her malady is described as inimical to her poetic powers:

O'er me alas! thou dost too much prevail:
I feel thy Force, whilst I against thee rail;
I feel my Verse decay, and my crampt Numbers fail.
Thro' thy black Jaundice I all Objects see,
  As Dark, and Terrible as Thee,
My Lines decry'd, and my Employment thought
An useless Folly, or presumptuous Fault.

"The Spleen" is a Pindaric ode composed in neoclassical style, to which this set piece of confession is incidental. But these lines do suggest that her moods of melancholy undermine her confidence in her "Employment," her poetic vocation. The notions of "Folly" and "Fault" are elaborated in the justly famous passage in which she declares her choice of eccentricity and eloquently justifies it in comparison with the accomplishments which social conventions encourage in women:

Whilst in the *Muses* Paths I stray,
Whilst in their Groves, and by their secret Springs
My Hand delights to trace unusual Things,
And deviates from the known, and common way;
  Nor will in fading Silks compose
  Faintly th' inimitable *Rose,*
Fill up an ill-drawn *Bird,* or paint on Glass
The *Sov'reign's* blurr'd and undistinguish'd Face,
The threatning *Angel,* and the speaking *Ass.*

This lovely passage presents an image in miniature of Anne Finch's achievements as a poet. It expresses in fine epitome her own sense of her dubious rarity, her resolute refusal of conventional womanly accomplishments, the whole couched in a style which displays her mastery of the refinements of neo-classical poetic convention, especially in her choice of epithets and her striking nouns which capture both the image and the type.

The source of the strength which enabled her to make such a daring refusal was her clear sense of vocation. Underneath the apologies, justifications, brooding inquiries, and rueful jests lies her unquenchable delight in writing. She tried to give it up, but by her own account she found herself to be "like those imperfect penitents, who are ever relenting, and yett ever returning to the same offences . . . till at last (like them) wearied with uncertainty, and irresolution, I rather chuse to be harden'd in an errour, then to be still att the trouble of endeavering to over come itt: and now, neither deny myself the pleasure of writing, or any longer make a mistery to that of my friends and acquaintance, which does so little deserve itt." The personal narrative of conflict and self-doubt suggested by this passage can only be inferred from her words. What is clear is that some of her best poetry arises out of the very conflict between aspiration and denial, between poetic vocation and social convention, which is expressed with such restraint in this prose passage.

Carol Barash (essay date 1991)

SOURCE: "The Political Origins of Anne Finch's Poetry," in *Huntington Library Quarterly,* Vol. LIV, No. 4, Fall, 1991, pp. 327-51.

[*In the following excerpt, Barash discusses the relationship between gender and politics in Finch's poetry.*]

Like so many of the poems written to and about English monarchs between the public execution of Charles I in 1649 and the death of his granddaughter, Queen Anne, in 1714, Finch's **"Elegy on the Death of King James"** suggests the awkward relationship between the embattled monarch's material body and the authority of poetry which attempts to uphold the *idea* of monarchy even as it attacks one or more of the living claimants to the throne. By the late seventeenth century, and particularly in light of the inability of the last of the Protestant Stuarts—James II's daughters, Mary II and Anne—to produce living heirs, political writing emphasized questions of reproduction and the body, which overlapped with problems of gender and sexuality as well. Since praising James II after his death could easily be read as opposition to William III and therefore treasonable, elegies on James's death were often dedicated to his daughter Anne who was, after her cousin William, next in line for the crown.

Surprisingly there are no such gestures of self-protection in Finch's poem to James; nor did she, like so many women writers of the period (Whig and Tory alike) claim protection as a woman under the banner of Princess—soon to be Queen—Anne. Instead, the title-page appellation "By a Lady" seems in 1701 to have been a device used by Finch simultaneously to assert class privilege and to gain both sexual and political protection. As non-jurors, Finch and her husband were in a precarious political and economic situation from the time of their banishment from court in 1688 to his inheritance of the Winchilsea title and lands in 1712. Finch used the title "By a Lady" to imply that she was writing neither for profit nor for party, but from the vantage point of one outside political and economic contests.

The first two stanzas of the poem suggest the ways in which the speaker's fate as a poet is bound up with that of the late king:

If the Possession of Imperial Sway,
   Thou hadst by Death, unhappy Prince,
   resign'd,
   And to a Mournful Successor made way,
Whil'st all was Uncontested, all Combin'd:
How had the Streets? How had the Palace rung,
   In Praise of thy acknowledg'd Worth?
What had our Numerous Writers then brought
   forth?
    What Melancholly Dirges had they sung?
    What Weeping Elogies prepar'd

    . . . . .

   But Royal *James,* tho' none shall pay this
   Verse,
   Bred in a Land not Honour'd with thy Herse;

    . . . . .

    Yet shall a free disinterested Muse,
In chosen Lines, perform that Task,
Which does an abler Writer ask;
   But abler Writers will the Work refuse:
And where, Alas! 'twill but the Feather cost,
The Noblest Subjects for the Pen, are lost.

Finch here reveals the preoccupation of women writers of this period with the profit they can reasonably expect from their published works. Her speaker claims that she will receive no payment for her elegy because she lives in a country in which even the former king's body is not welcome: "Royal James . . . none shall pay this Verse / Bred in a land not honour'd with thy Herse." She must nevertheless praise the king because "abler Writers will the Work refuse." The elegy, metonymically, carries the king's body from birth, through his early military triumphs, to his defeat and death. The "Noblest Subjects" of the last line quoted above figure in the stories of both James himself and those among his political "subjects" with courage to praise him publicly after his death.

Finch uses James's death to situate herself, publicly, as author and political subject. For Katherine Philips, Margaret Cavendish, Aphra Behn, Anne Finch, and others, the community of heroic women included not merely noble women, but women who patterned their own lives on a model of female heroism and female political agency, and who therefore were forced to defend their embattled monarchs in print. By 1688 to inscribe oneself publicly as a woman writer was to inscribe oneself as a heroic woman as well. Grief in this context becomes a form of political action akin to fighting beside James:

  O you who in his frequent Dangers stood,
And Fought to Fence them at the Expense of
  Blood,
    Now let your Tears a heavier Tribute pay,
    Give the Becoming Sorrow Way:
    Nor bring bad Parallels upon the Times,
   By seeking, thro' mistaken Fears,
To Curb your Sighs, or to Conceal your Tears;

'Twas but in *Nero*'s Days, that Sighs and Tears
were Crimes.

After several awkward attempts to draw analogies between James's situation and the stories of excluded monarchs from Latin historians, Finch's elegy focuses on Mary of Modena's grief:

> But draw the Vail, nor seek to paint the Grief,
> Which knows no Bounds, nor Meditates relief;
> *Maria* weeps with unexhausted Tears;
> No Look that Beauteous Face, but sorrow, wears:
>   And in those Eyes, where Majesty was seen
>   To warn Admirers, and Declare the Queen,
> Now only reigns incurable Distress,
>   Which, Royal *James,* thy Faithful Consort
>   shows,
> Who, by her Different Grief, does too Confess,
>   That now, Alas! she the Distinction knows
> 'Twixt Weeping for thy Loss, or with thee for thy
>   Woes.

>   . . . . .

> A Grave is all, she with her *James* can share,
> And were it not for what he left, her Care,
> How soon would she descend, and be his Consort,
>   there.

As in Behn's and Barker's poems about Mary of Modena, Mary's haunting eyes announce that she is queen. Just as the attraction between the female speaker and Mary of Modena is described in bodily terms, James's political opposition is represented as a sexual threat. Finch's poem imagines Mary wishing to die, that she might live "Securely by [James's] unmolested side." In death James's body is no longer threatened with violation or rape; his corpse rests "unmolested."

The last stanza of Finch's elegy shifts perspectives again, turning away from Mary of Modena and her dead husband to address an allegorical female "Britain":

> Oh *Britain!* take this Wish before we cease:
> May Happier Kings procure thee Lasting Peace;
>   And having Rul'd the[e] to thy own Desire,
>   On thy Maternal Bosom late expire,

>   . . . . .

> Oh *Britain!* may thy Days to come be Fair,

>   . . . . .

> May no Intestine Broils thy Intrails tear.

The manuscript version of the second line reads "Rightful" rather than "Happier" kings. In 1701 the phrase "Rightful Kings" would likely have been read as an attack not only on William III—who was in the eyes of James's supporters the *unrightful* king—but also on Anne, who was beginning to use maternal symbolism to justify her potential rule.

Finch displaces the symbolically feminine from Anne to an allegorical figure for the English people, whose political "desire" is for "lasting Peace." We are left at the end of this passage with the vivid and bodily contrast between Britain's peaceful "Maternal Bosom" and the political conflicts which threaten to "tear" her "Intrails." The poet herself is linked to this maternal figure for England in "[bringing] forth" the poetry others shun (line 7). The poem's stated ambitions change once more in the final lines, which express the speaker's wish for a simple and virtuous existence, parallel to Mary of Modena's but devoted to "the Pen" rather than to God:

> Whilst for my self, like Solitary Men,
>   Devoted only to the Pen
>   I but a Safe Retreat amidst thee crave
> Below the Ambitious World, and just above my
>   Grave.

The poem ends with her asking for a "Safe Retreat," a place where she and her writings will be protected from political turmoil, where she will have the same access to poetic language as politically oppositional male poets. The "retreat" of Finch's famous **"Petition for an Absolute Retreat"** is thus from the first a political retreat, a rhetorical stance from which she can continue to praise the Stuarts in their absence.

The manuscript version, **"Upon the Death of King James the Second,"** extends the overlap of political and religious identifications embodied for Finch in the last of the Stuart monarchs. The elegy to James is the last poem in the Finch manuscript now owned by the Folger Library; the elegy completes a section of poems titled "Aditional Poems cheifly upon Subjects Devine and Moral" [*sic*], which includes several poems addressed to members of the royal family. Manuscript changes in at least two places suggest Finch's shifting sense of herself as a political writer. At line 66, the manuscript has been changed from "whilst Your Reccords" to "whilst our Reccords shall have place." Whereas the earlier version stresses James as the subject of political history, the change to the first-person plural suggests Finch's identification with those who use panegyric poetry as a form of political rhetoric.

The manuscript also includes seventeen lines, not included in the published version, which considerably heighten the political pitch of the poem. Lines 102-5, with their echo of Milton's *Lycidas,* are crossed out, as are twelve lines following line 115 and two lines following line 142. The most substantial change, that of the twelve canceled lines, can be partially reconstructed:

> And if one had reveal'd his Private Life
> How had it been of all our Pens the Strife
> [line illegible]
> Of vanquishing [half line illegible]
> Had thus the Conqueror (tho with Teares Bewayl'd
> That words were wanting e're his Ardour fail'd)
> But inward rais'd his too [word illegible] Thought
> Age and [word missing] Ambition 'twoud have
>   Wrought

In his own Breast a Rebel Work'd to Find
Where such embattl'd troops of Vices grew
[So?] the Subduer did at Length subdue
Who forward bent his Course, but left that war
    behind.

The passage seems to suggest that James's private life
would have reinforced his heroic public deeds, and that
poets would have strived to imitate him. A battle is displaced from poets to the "Conqueror['s] . . . own Breast,"
where "Rebel . . . troops" struggle to "subdue" him.

A page was torn out of the manuscript at this point, and
the pages subsequently renumbered, suggesting that the
poem might once have continued further in this vein.
These lines may have been canceled because they en-
act—both within James's heart and between poets—the
public contest between James II and his nephew and
son-in-law William III. Beginning by recounting the intemperance of Elizabeth's troops who, according to Finch's
note in the published editions, brought "the Custom of
Excessive Drinking . . . out of Holland," the canceled lines
edge dangerously close to comparing the excesses of
English soldiers in Holland to those characteristic of another Dutch "conqueror," William III, seeming to pose
William's intemperance against the heroic ideal embodied
in James II.

The pair of canceled lines describing Mary of Modena's
eyes are also concerned with the Stuarts as ideal monarchs. They elaborate a picture of the queen as perfectly,
almost fiercely, heroic:

(Lest Ruin'd by their complicated Charms
Mankind had laid on Fate their unprevented Harms)

The idea that the heroic woman can wound her enemies
with her perfect self-control—particularly with her ideally
beautiful eyes—is a common topos in women's political
writing of the late seventeenth century, a tradition which
Finch recalls but then rejects in the more volatile political
climate of 1701.

That Mary of Modena remained an ideal for Finch is clear
from the elegy she wrote after Mary's death in 1718.
Similar in structure to Killigrew's "The Discontent," Finch's
"On the Death of the Queen" is a pastoral dialogue between two nymphs—Lamira, and Finch's persona, Ardelia.
Ardelia likens the dead queen to Urania, goddess of justice from the Golden Age of Ovid's *Metamorphoses,* and
a type of ideal woman:

URANIA she to all prefer'd . . .
As if all vertues of the polish't mind
All excellencies of the female kind
All win[n]ing graces in Urania join'd
As if perfection but in her was seen
And Her least dignity was England's Queen.

She compares Urania to other heroic women, portraying
her as the ideal *femme forte* able, like Portia, to "[inflict]
wounds which did her firmness prove." By wounding

herself Portia proved herself worthy of sharing the secret
of the plot on Julius Caesar's life. Finch seems similarly to
maim herself in order to be a political poet worthy of the
respect of her male peers.

**The publishing of *Miscellany Poems* in
1713 marks the single most important
moment in Finch's construction of herself
as a poet of emotional rather than political
and religious extremity.**

—*Carol Barash*

Ardelia so profoundly identifies with Mary that her grieving body imitates the queen's: "sad ARDELIA mourn'd
URANIA'S Death / In sighs which seem'd her own expir-
ing breath." She imagines herself finally as if she were the
queen's widow:

this sad divorce
From her to whom my self I had resign'd
The Sovereign Mistress of my vanquish't mind
Who now survive but to attend her hearse
With dutious tribute of recording verse.

This passage presents the same configuration of monarch,
poet, and political poetry as that found in Finch's elegy
to James II: poetry becomes a "hearse," the vehicle which
brings the body of the exiled queen back to England.
Although Finch seems to have wanted to suppress her
early pastoral poems about life as an attendant at Mary's
court—one of them is completely scratched out in a manuscript of poems from that period—near the end of her own
life she looked back on that time as paradise, Mary's
unblemished beauty and devotion like "Eve e'er innocence she lost" (Wellesley manuscript).

During the reign of Queen Anne, from 1702 to 1714, wom-
en responded to the construction of Anne as "guiding
mother" of England and the Anglican Church in at least
three ways. By inscribing themselves as Anne's dutiful
daughters, writers such as Mary Astell, Mary Chudleigh,
and Sarah Fyge Egerton attached their own poetic ambitions to Anne's political and military triumphs. In contrast,
Delarivier Manley used scandalous narratives to assert
the political authority of the female monarch, but at the
same time suggested the dangers for women writers of
basing the queen's authority on tropes of her innocence
and passivity.

Finch, finally, used her training in the English and classical traditions to bury her sympathy to the Stuarts in myths
of a private female self. Finch splits her identification as
a woman writer from her political identification, projecting
her political alienation on to haunting myths of a female
voice cut off from history and from others, fused with the

landscape, and at the same time alone in both body and mind. In Finch's numerous poems about birds, she depicts her female speaker as both empowered and entrapped by her chosen solitude. **"The Bird and the Arras,"** for instance, finds her attempting to fly out of a castle in which she is confined, and finally bloodying herself against a clear but nevertheless closed window.

The political upheaval which is recast as gender warfare in Finch's best-known poem, **"The Spleen,"** returns in the context of women's friendship in **"The Petition for an Absolute Retreat."** **"The Petition"** begs for a place free from the cumbersome rituals of entertaining in favor of a place in which nature abundantly provides.

> Grapes, with Juice so crouded up,
> As breaking thro' the native Cup;
> Figs (yet growing) candy'd o'er,
> By the Sun's attracting Pow'r;
> Cherries, with the downy Peach,
> All within my easie Reach.

Just as the two nymphs together mourn for Mary of Modena in **"On the Death of the Queen,"** the power of female friendship imaginatively rescues Ardelia from storms of political upheaval in **"The Petition"**:

> Back reflecting let me say,
> So the sad *Ardelia* lay;
> Blasted by a Storm of Fate,
> Felt, thro' all the *British* State;
>
> . . . . .
>
> Faded till *Arminda's* Love,
> (Guided by the Pow'rs above)
>
> . . . . .
>
> With Wit, from an unmeasured Store,
> To Woman ne'er allow'd before.

At the end of the poem, Finch's speaker soars to a vantage point above earth and heaven, a position from which the political and religious controversies of her own time are rendered irrelevant.

In the context of Finch's *Miscellany Poems* of 1713—a volume which she and her husband helped to see into print—**"The Petition for an Absolute Retreat"** seems far less political, far more tame than it becomes in relation to Finch's use of similar tropes in elegies to James II and Mary of Modena. Throughout *Miscellany Poems* we find Finch remaking her earlier political tropes as emotional ones.

"A Fragment," a small poem near the back of *Miscellany Poems,* provides a clue to the process of Finch's political self-censorship. The poem titled **"A Fragment"** is not actually a fragment. The title refers to what the poem's protagonist, Ardelia, has become since the banishment of James and Mary in 1688:

> So here confin'd, and but to female Clay,
> *ARDELIA'S* Soul mistook the rightful Way:
> Whilst the soft Breeze of Pleasure's tempting Air
> Made her believe, Felicity was there;
> And basking in the warmth of early Time,
> To vain Amusements dedicate her Prime.
> Ambition next allur'd her tow'ring Eye;
> For Paradice she heard was plac'd on high,
> Then thought, the Court with all its glorious Show
> Was sure above the rest, and Paradice below.

The speaker replaces her earlier belief in the court as an earthly paradise with a contemplation of God in heaven:

> Retirement, which the World *Moroseness* calls,
> Abandon'd Pleasures in Monastick Walls:
> These, but at distance, towards that purpose tend,
> The lowly Means to an exalted End;
>
> . . . . .
>
> Pity her restless Cares, and weary Strife,
> And point some Issue to escaping Life;
> Which so dismiss'd, no Pen or Human Speech
> Th'ineffable Recess can ever teach:
> Th'Expanse, the Light, the Harmony, the Throng,
> The Bride's Attendance, and the Bridal Song,
> The numerous Mansions, and th'immortal Tree,
> No Eye, unpurg'd by Death, must ever see,
>
> . . . . .
>
> Observe but here the easie Precepts given,
> Then wait with chearful hope, till Heaven be
>   known in Heaven.

In Finch's early poems, Ardelia is imaginatively fused with her queen and mistress Mary of Modena. In a similar manner, the private retreat which Finch creates for Ardelia in *Miscellany Poems* allows her protagonist to pursue God as both palpable and ideal. Ardelia's "absolute retreat" is similarly an idealized place from which Finch can mock the customs of the world around her and plead the special case of the individual believer.

The publishing of *Miscellany Poems* in 1713 marks the single most important moment in Finch's construction of herself as a poet of emotional rather than political and religious extremity; here the ideal of the heroic woman is translated into patterns of negativity which link Finch's work to later women writers such as Emily Dickinson, Christina Rossetti, and indeed Virginia Woolf herself. It is no coincidence that Finch attempted this translation when she did. In 1713 Queen Anne was quite ill, and many believed her death imminent. The Treaty of Utrecht ending the War of the Spanish Succession gave England control of the transatlantic slave trade; many in England believed the treaty's other concessions too great a price to pay for peace. Supporters of the Old Pretender believed this was their moment to return the exiled Stuarts to England, and Finch's family were among those preparing to assist James Francis Edward Stuart reclaim what they considered his birthright.

Miscellany Poems, of course, mentions none of this, but subtly and repeatedly reworks a myth of female community initiated by Katherine Philips—and most vigorously and materially enacted by Finch and other women at court with Mary of Modena—into a politically oppositional community of pro-Stuart women. The title page of *Miscellany Poems,* with its ornamental device of two female nymphs crowning one another with palm and laurel wreaths, emphasizes women's community as a source of female poetic authority. The nymphs look rather like Amazons, their breasts hidden in shadow if not cut off. In contrast, in the device drawn for an earlier Finch manuscript, the female poet is depicted alone, surrounded by arms which have no hands. Although she is exiled, she looks directly out at the reader—she is a fearless heroic woman, not a nymph.

The warrior woman is similarly translated into the woman poet in Finch's pseudonym Ardelia, a name which comes from Philips's poems about the Society of Friendship between Orinda and Lucasia. In Finch's early manuscripts she calls herself "Areta," suggesting a conflation of Ares, Roman god of war, and Arethusa, a nymph in the train of the chaste Diana, to whom Mary of Modena was often compared. Ardelia, in contrast, is the female form of "ardelio," Latin for a meddler or busybody. If Finch's speaker burns ardently with transgressive political desires, those desires are on the verge of being ironized as the individual woman's private emotional concerns.

Finch was not, finally, the deist Wordsworth wanted her to be. The Wellesley manuscript of Finch's later poetry, as well as Finch correspondence in the Bodleian Library, shows Finch struggling with the boundaries between Anglican and Anglo-Catholic understandings of religious ritual for the rest of her life and her late poems are quite explicit in approaching heaven as the bride of Christ. Indeed, the religious verse found in Finch's last manuscript is, in terms of sexual and religious politics, far more important and far more apiece with her earlier works than has been previously noted. While the relationship between women's political voice and the body of monarchy is displaced on to a variety of private emotional landscapes in Finch's poetry, we can nevertheless see residual tensions, gestures of self-division and self-censorship, as well as the political stakes in her movement toward the hauntingly individual lyric voice for which Wordsworth valued her.

Barbara McGovern (essay date 1992)

SOURCE: "'Nature Unconcern'd': Nature Poems and Humanistic Sensibilities," in *Anne Finch and Her Poetry: A Critical Biography,* The University of Georgia Press, 1992, pp. 78-88.

[*In the following excerpt, McGovern argues that Finch's nature poetry emphasizes the role of human agents in nature.*]

Of the more than 230 poems [Anne Finch] wrote . . . only about half a dozen are devoted primarily to descriptions of external nature, and these, with the exception of the two just named, are not among her better poems. Yet invariably these have been the poems included in standard anthologies. A few recent anthologies of women's literature have offered a more representative selection of her work, as have the small collections of her poetry that Denys Thompson and Katharine Rogers have edited. The popular image of Finch that still exists today, however, is that of a nature poet.

> **Wordsworth's praise . . . resurrected Finch's name from the obscurity that befell any pre-nineteenth-century English woman writer. But for nearly two hundred years it has distorted the general perception of her as a poet and thwarted recognition of the depth, the quality, and the diversity of her work.**
>
> **—*Barbara McGovern***

The reason for this continued misrepresentation of her work is that until recently her reputation has rested almost entirely upon Wordsworth's celebrated remark in his 1815 supplementary essay to the preface of the *Lyrical Ballads* that

> excepting the **'Nocturnal Reverie'** of Lady Winchilsea, and a passage or two in the 'Windsor Forest' of Pope, the poetry intervening between the publication of the 'Paradise Lost' and 'The Seasons' does not contain a single new image of external nature, and scarcely presents a familiar one from which it can be inferred that the eye of the Poet had been steadily fixed upon his object, much less that his feelings had urged him to work upon it in the spirit of genuine imagination.
>
> (*Prose*)

Wordsworth's praise has been a mixed blessing. It resurrected Finch's name from the obscurity that befell any pre-nineteenth-century English woman writer. But for nearly two hundred years it has distorted the general perception of her as a poet and thwarted recognition of the depth, the quality, and the diversity of her work. It is therefore essential that her few nature poems be placed within a proper literary context.

Wordsworth's remark has set the tone for critics, anthologists, and literary historians throughout the nineteenth and much of the twentieth century. It has caused Finch to be analyzed, anthologized, and categorized almost exclusively as a nature poet and precursor of Wordsworthian Romanticism. Edmund Gosse, for example, who discovered the folio manuscript of her poems in 1884, heralds her as a misplaced poet whose "temper was . . . foreign to the taste of her own age and who was possibly "the first of the new romantic school" (*History*). Reynolds declares in

The Learned Lady in England, 1650-1760, that Finch "delicately foreshadowed tastes that ruled in the romanticism of a century later," and in the lengthy introduction to the still-standard edition of her poems, Reynolds makes repeated comparisons between Finch and Wordsworth, declaring some of her verses to be "exactly Wordsworthian in substance and mood" and maintaining that "Wordsworth's strong interest in Lady Winchilsea is justified by the law of affinities."

Finch frequently expresses the belief that redemptive value lies not with nature but with the artistic creations of men and women.

—Barbara McGovern

The misjudgment in representing such a richly diverse poet as a nature poet and Romantic precursor is doubly ironic, for under close examination even those few poems that deal with external nature are less Romantic and far more a product of her age than Wordsworth's comments might lead one to suppose. **"A Nocturnal Reverie,"** her most widely anthologized poem since the eighteenth century, is a case in point.

There is much in **"A Nocturnal Reverie"** to recommend it as Romantic. The setting is rustic, dark, and secluded, and when the persona begins to speak of her serenity in the midst of nature, one senses all the proper movements for some Wordsworthian recollected tranquility. The poem recalls the opening scene in act V of Shakespeare's *Merchant of Venice,* in which Lorenzo and Jessica exchange a series of imaginative musings on the beauty of nature, each beginning with the phrase "In such a night." Finch's poem, however, is something of a tour de force, its entire fifty lines a single sentence constructed around clauses that begin, "In such a night . . . when. . . ." The descriptions are specific and contain numerous visual, auditory, and olfactory images of nature. Moreover, the scene is a nocturnal one, with night transforming the appearance of everything, so that the imagination of the reader is fully engaged. All is thinly veiled, clouded, and hidden in shadows, suggesting an air of Gothic mystery that would appeal to the Romantic sensibility:

> In such a *Night,* when passing Clouds give place,
> Or thinly vail the Heav'ns mysterious Face;
> When in some River, overhung with Green,
> The waving Moon and trembling Leaves are seen;
>
> . . . . .
>
> When darken'd Groves their softest Shadows wear,
> And falling Waters we distinctly hear;
> When thro' the Gloom more venerable shows

> Some ancient Fabrick, awful in Repose. . . .

There are other suggestions of Wordsworthian Romanticism in the poem as well. The mood is reflective. Nature, the poet tells us, can renew the weary spirit, can calm the confusion and rage that torment the human soul. Furthermore, the dichotomy between the social world and the natural world is emphasized. Nature's serenity is marred by man: the kine are able to feed contentedly only because they are temporarily "unmolested," and all of nature's creatures enjoy their "shortliv'd Jubilee" only "whilst Tyrant-*Man* do's sleep" (line 38). Lastly, there is even the suggestion that nature possesses transcendental attributes:

> But silent Musings urge the Mind to seek
> Something, too high for Syllables to speak.

But these very lines, when taken in the context of what follows them, demonstrate the essential difference between Finch and Wordsworth:

> Till the free Soul to a compos'dness charm'd,
> Finding the Elements of Rage disarm'd,
> O'er all below a solemn Quiet grown,
> Joys in th' inferiour World, and thinks it like her
>   Own. . . .

A comparison of these lines with the conclusion of Wordsworth's "Ode: Intimations of Immortality from Recollections of Early Childhood" is revealing. While the "meanest flower that blows" may cause Wordsworth to have "Thoughts that do often lie too deep for tears," Finch's response to nature is quite different. Wordsworth is inspired to "thoughts" that turn inward and seeks meaning within himself, whereas Finch, as a devout Anglican, is inspired to seek beyond herself, to look to heaven for meaning. Moreover, she is dealing not with nature in a generalized sense but with nature at a specific time and place. It is not *any* grove, any meanest flower, that can bring relief from life's pressures and a chance to refresh oneself: it is this particular time and place—a night such as this in this very setting. And the poet is well aware that such retreats from life's cares are temporary at best ("Till Morning breaks, and All's confus'd again" [line 48]). In such moments of respite, the poet tells us, she seeks to speak "Syllables" that will articulate her sense of a divinity beyond herself, but such musings cannot be expressed. Here is a thoroughly orthodox and rational approach. One may be seduced into a false illusion that man and nature are one; one even, "in such a Night," occasionally "Joys in th' inferiour World, and thinks it like her Own." But the soul's source is elsewhere, and Finch knows ultimately that the world of nature is but an "inferiour" world.

It is notable that in his supplement to the preface, what Wordsworth specifically notes in his praise of Finch is, in addition to her fresh images of external nature, her "feelings" and "genuine imagination," though of course the concept of these terms, as Wordsworth understood them, would have been foreign to her. Wordsworth, like Finch, is concerned with the process of perceiving nature, as well as the ability of nature to infuse one with a transcendent spirit. For him it is not simply that nature is invested with value. In Finch's poetry there are moral implications to nature as well, as can be seen in some of her pastoral poems, such as **"The Change."** The difference is that for her there is an irreconcilable dualism that exists between man and nature, so that nature and the human soul remain two separate realities. The dualism that Ann Messenger finds inherent in the argument of **"To the Nightingale"** ["Selected Nightingales," *His and Hers*, 1986] is present in all of Finch's nature poems, including **"A Nocturnal Reverie."**

There are other characteristics of **"A Nocturnal Reverie"** that mark it as decidedly not Romantic in a Wordsworthian or Shaftesburian sense. As with all Finch's nature and pastoral verse, it is men and women, not nature in the abstract, who are the focus of the scene. At the center of the poem is a lovely, brief tribute to her friend Lady Salisbury, whose beauty and virtue withstand "the Test of every Light" (line 20). Moreover, the careful control and sense of containment that the heroic couplets supply are another reminder that here are rational, moralistic reflections, not the ecstatic soarings of a free Romantic spirit. There is also humor in the poem, and even social satire. The glowworms are likened to "trivial Beauties" who similarly wait for twilight to appear, realizing that it is their most favorable hour to shine. Even the quasi-Gothic description quoted above is immediately undercut by a touch of whimsy and mild self-irony. An unidentified figure, "Whose stealing Pace, and lengthen'd Shade we fear," appears upon the darkened pasture, but reality checks the rampant and foolish imagination of the frightened sojourners, for they recognize that the threatening intruder is but a harmless grazing horse, noisily chewing forage.

All nature can do, Finch believes, is provide a temporary retreat from the world so that the spirit can renew itself. Moreover, the poem's conclusion is a reminder that daylight brings a return to everyday activities and a renewed pursuit of those often illusive but nevertheless attainable joys of life:

> Our Cares, our Toils, our Clamours are renew'd,
> Or Pleasures seldom reach'd, again pursu'd.

Wordsworth, incidentally, deleted four lines from the poem when he prepared for Lady Mary Lowther in 1818 a manuscript of works by women poets, including sixteen Finch poems. Two of the lines are the only mildly satirical ones in the entire poem:

> When scatter'd Glow-worms, but in Twilight fine,
> Shew trivial Beauties watch their Hour to shine.

The other two lines Wordsworth deleted are the tribute to Lady Salisbury. Neither satire nor poetic compliments to female friends appear to have pleased him.

The ideal retreat is the subject of another of Finch's well-known nature poems, **"The Petition for an Absolute Retreat."** It contains many instances of what Wordsworth referred to as the poet's eye being "steadily fixed upon his object." In its celebration of simplicity and naturalness, as

well as in its style, it bears similarities to Robert Herrick's verse. . . . Finch's debt to Herrick is especially evident in the following passage:

> Cloath me, Fate, tho' not so Gay;
> Cloath me light, and fresh as *May*:
> In the Fountains let me view
> All my Habit cheap and new;
> Such as, when sweet *Zephyrs* fly,
> With their Motions may comply;
> Gently waving, to express
> Unaffected Carelessness:
> No Perfumes have there a Part,
> Borrow'd from the *Chymists* Art. . . .

When placed alongside the final lines of Herrick's "Delight in Disorder," the resemblance is striking:

> A winning wave, deserving note,
> In the tempestuous petticoat;
> A careless shoestring, in whose tie
> I see a wild civility;
> Do more bewitch me than when art
> Is too precise in every part.

Both poems convey a similar idea: Finch would have her garments yield to the breezes in much the way that Herrick would have his lady's clothing yield to the movement of her body, and both poets scorn the cosmetic arts in preference for naturalness. Both poems also contain a tone that is distinctively light and charming and that reflects simplicity in style. The meter and rhyme of the last four lines in the Finch passage recall the closing lines of "Delight in Disorder," with four words in those lines echoing key words in the Herrick passage: "waving," "carelessness," "part," and "art."

"The Petition for an Absolute Retreat" also bears some similarity to Andrew Marvell's "Garden," as Reuben Brower has already noted. But while both poems are reflective, Finch's, unlike Marvell's, describes a real retreat that is truly a part of the natural world, rather than an abstract meditative state. For her, moreover, nature provides an object lesson, an understanding of reality that Marvell's poem lacks. Thus a withered oak becomes for her a *memento mori*, and the temporary retreat, as in **"A Nocturnal Reverie,"** provides the means for renewing her spiritual self and for viewing both "the Height, from whence she came," and the paradise that awaits her (line 277). But the principal way in which her poem differs from Marvell's is in her sense of society. Finch's poem is thoroughly peopled. In lines 8-21, for instance, she describes what she is retreating from and what sort of people she wants to join her, and lines 164-201 contain a lengthy passage in praise of friendship and a tribute to her friend Arminda, whom she would have join her. Furthermore, in lines 104-05 Finch appears to be directly answering Marvell, who, in the eighth stanza of "Garden," rounds off his description of paradise with this startling assertion:

> But 'twas beyond a mortal's share
> To wander solitary there:

Two paradises 'twere in one
To live in paradise alone.

In her description of her retreat, Finch also evokes the Garden of Eden, but her paradise is incomplete without a mate:

Give me there (since Heaven has shown
It was not Good to be alone)
A *Partner* suited to my Mind,
Solitary, pleas'd and kind;
Who, partially, may something see
Preferr'd to all the World in me;
Slighting, by my humble Side,
Fame and Splendor, Wealth and Pride.

Finally, she devotes the conclusion of this section to praise of human love as the gift heaven has given to bring people closer to God.

For Finch, then, it is human beings that provide the spiritual continuity and depth to life, even in a rustic retreat. For this reason, the men and women in her poems seem always to be set against a temporary background of nature, rather than within it.

A similar focus upon people is evident in her poems on nature as it is manifested in the English garden. Much has been written about the early eighteenth-century movement in gardening. Relevant here is Maynard Mack's reminder that what the eighteenth century meant by "natural," which implied "not oppressively trammeled or corseted by man, yet always conspicuously responding . . . to human pleasure and human need," was different from the later Romantic sense of the word (*Garden*).

Finch frequently expresses the belief that redemptive value lies not with nature but with the artistic creations of men and women. Those poems of hers that deal with gardening ultimately praise not so much the gardens as the gardeners. In **"Upon My Lord Winchilsea's Converting the Mount in His Garden to a Terras,"** for example, Finch honors her husband's nephew, whose new landscaping of Eastwell both refined nature and corrected the aesthetic errors of his ancestors. In his wisdom, the young Charles "Removes a Mountain, to remove a fault," a mountain that long had stood "concealing all the beautys of the Plaine" (34, lines 8, 10). Lord Winchilsea's innovations are bold, and as Finch describes them, they reveal the sense of vast design that was to become the hallmark of such renowned eighteenth-century landscape artists as Capability Brown:

So lies this Hill, hew'n from itts rugged height,
Now levell'd to a Scene of smooth delight,
Where on a Terras of itts spoyles we walk,
And of the Task, and the performer talk;
From whose unwearied Genius Men expect
All that can farther Pollish or Protect;
To see a sheltring grove the Prospect bound,
Just rising from the same proliffick ground,
Where late itt stood. . . .

In designing the gardens and remodeling the house, Charles has employed Augustan principles of design, so that "gracefull simetry, without is seen, / And Use, with Beauty are improv'd within" (lines 53-54). Yet throughout the poem, and again in its conclusion, the poet stresses that her intent is primarily to honor the lord of this estate. It is he, after all, whose art has controlled nature and brought it into harmony with Augustan aesthetic principles, using form and reason to impose order upon his world.

In their sense of rustic retirement as displacement, in their concern with shade and darkness, and in their recurrent images of circuitous wandering and straying in lonely haunts, Finch's nature poems display traits that several feminist critics have identified as characteristic of a feminine poetics.

—Barbara McGovern

"To the Honorable the Lady Worsley at Longleat" is another honorific poem whose praise of an estate's gardens similarly becomes a tribute to the gardener who designed them. And here, again, it is not the mansion that is singled out for description but the grounds of the estate, for it is they that most fully reflect the lord of this estate as an artist/creator. The poem is addressed to Lady Worsley, Finch's friend and the niece of her husband, and it contains much hyperbolic praise of her. But the laudatory verses to her father, the Viscount Weymouth, are the true nexus of the poem. Weymouth has laid out the gardens in Dutch fashion, and the descriptive passages of the flowered labyrinths, terraced landscapes, and Italian-style fountains and cascades are a tribute to his genius. He has "th' original improv'd," and by doing so, has made of this lovely setting a Garden of Eden (54, line 72). But, the poet writes, paradise did not get its name from the beauty and fruitfulness of external nature, but from Adam and Eve, "th' accomplish'd Pair / That gave the Title and that made itt fair" (lines 107-08). Thus, what makes a garden a paradise, what gives meaning to nature, is not the physical beauty or lushness of the place but the moral and spiritual attributes of the men and women who inhabit it. And that is why, whether in the gardens of Longleat or the gardens of Eden,

'Twas Paradice in some expanded Walk
To see Her motions, and attend his Talk.

But if human beings remain at the heart of Finch's poetry, one must yet be careful to avoid too loosely applying such terms as "Augustan" to her, as if there were a single, monolithic world view or eighteenth-century humanistic tradition. Finch is a woman, and while the intent of this chapter has been to differentiate her nature poems from a

Romantic framework and to define specific ways in which her conceptualization of nature differs from Wordsworth's, something must be added. For once such distinctions have been made, one is still left with an impression that there is a feminine quality about her descriptions of nature that makes them, if not compatible with a Romantic sensibility, at least inconsistent with the values of order, cohesiveness, systematic structure, and light that are traditionally associated with the Enlightenment.

In their sense of rustic retirement as displacement, in their concern with shade and darkness, and in their recurrent images of circuitous wandering and straying in lonely haunts, Finch's nature poems display traits that several feminist critics have identified as characteristic of a feminine poetics.

Charles H. Hinnant (essay date 1994)

SOURCE: "'My Old Inveterate Foe': Poems of Melancholy and Grief," in *The Poetry of Anne Finch: An Essay in Interpretation,* University of Delaware Press, 1994, pp. 197-226.

[*In the following excerpt, Hinnant describes how melancholy is associated with patriarchal power structures in Finch's poems.*]

One of the striking features of the poems that Finch devoted to melancholy is their absorption in suffering—as if depression itself was being embraced as a substitute for a lost existence. While it is true that she does not refer explicitly to political issues in these poems, it is difficult not to link her obsessive preoccupation with melancholy, loss, mourning, care, and the spleen with the abdication of James II and the subsequent arrest of her husband. Indeed, court politics and political disappointment provide a source for the insights and imagery of these poems. Moreover, in the "Preface" that she originally intended to publish before her miscellany volume, Finch writes of the "melancholy thoughts which possess me, not only for my own, but much more for the misfortunes of those to whom I owe all imaginable duty and gratitude"; and she goes on to confess that "an absolute solitude (which was often my lott) under such dejection of mind, cou'd not have been supported, had I indulg'd myself (as was natural to me) only in the contemplation of present and real afflictions." Such a dejection may only become supportable when political trauma is absorbed into the subject's private mythology of suffering.

Finch's dejection in **"Ardelia to Melancholy"**—the one poem explicitly devoted to the subject—is reflected in her concern, not with the causes of melancholy, but with the sense of paralysis it produces. The poem consists of an enumeration of the remedies that the speaker has undertaken to alleviate this malady:

> At last, my old inveterate foe,
> No opposition shalt thou know.

> Since I by struggling, can obtain
> Nothing, but encrease of pain,
> I will att last, no more do soe,
> Tho' I confesse, I have apply'd
> Sweet mirth, and musick, and have try'd
> A thousand other arts beside,
> To drive thee from my darken'd breast,
> Thou, who hast banish'd all my rest.
> But, though, sometimes, a short reprieve they gave,
> Unable they, and far too weak, to save;
> All arts to quell, did but augment thy force,
> As rivers check'd, break with a wilder course.

> Freindship, I to my heart have laid,
> Freindship, th' applauded sov'rain aid,
> And thought that charm so strong wou'd prove,
> As to compell thee, to remove;
> And to myself, I boasting said,
> Now I a conqu'rer sure shall be,
> The end of all my conflicts, see,
> And noble tryumph, wait on me;
> My dusky, sullen foe, will sure
> N'er this united charge endure.
> But leaning on this reed, ev'n whilst I spoke
> If pierc'd my hand, and into peices broke.
> Still, some new object, or new int'rest came
> And loos'd the bonds, and quite dissolv'd the claim.

> These failing, I invok'd a Muse,
> And Poetry wou'd often use,
> To guard me from thy Tyrant pow'r;
> And to oppose thee ev'ry hour
> New troops of fancy's, did I chuse.
> Alas! in vain, for all agree
> To yeild me Captive up to thee,
> And heav'n, alone, can sett me free.
> Thou, through my life, wilt with me goe,
> And make ye passage, sad, and slow.
> All, that cou'd ere thy ill gott rule, invade,
> Their uselesse arms, before thy feet have laid;
> The Fort is thine, now ruin'd, all within,
> Whilst by decays without, thy Conquest too, is
>   seen.

What is most striking about these remedies—"Sweet mirth and musick," "Friendship," and "Poetry"—is that they are among those that are most prominently emphasized in treatises like Robert Burton's *Anatomy of Melancholy.* The failure of these remedies is linked to the speaker's sense of the hopelessness of her condition. There is nothing pleasurable in her experience of melancholy—nor does she seek to explain it in terms of any discernible cause. To the readiest clichés of both the fashionable votary and the empiric, she replies, "Heav'n alone, can sett me free."

Melancholy is thus envisaged as a power that is beyond rational comprehension and control. It can hardly be a coincidence that Finch's representation of this power as a cruel tyrant reproduces melancholy outside—rather than inside—the mind. As a major figure in Finch's mythology of pain and suffering, the tyrant provides her with a figural means of imagining in palpable yet general terms the source of her sorrow and grief. To identify her melancholy with this saturnine conqueror is not to contemplate it with detachment but, instead, to confront the awareness that one may be a prey to delusion yet utterly powerless to drive it from one's mind. With Finch, melancholy takes on a material form, because it is expressed through an imagery of conquest and domination—and because domination is an easily representable state, with natural ties to politics and patriarchy. In giving embodiment to this state, Finch resorts to the figure of address—the trope through which a poet or orator invests an absent, deceased, or voiceless entity with the animate faculty of hearing. What the figure of address conjures up here is a sinister vision uneasily hypostatized by being summoned up from the depths of the speaker's memory. It does not speak, and yet its silence—by being ascribed to the speaker's past history—is given an authority that is more terrifying than if it had actually replied to her. To address this silent and "sullen foe" is to assume the virtual disappearance of a receptive audience—and thus to be radically different from the kind of speaker who composes a letter to a sympathetic auditor in a world of friendly voices. Melancholy's silence takes the reader out of that world of friendly voices and thrusts him or her into a specular reflexiveness that makes a toy of human thought. Indeed, the speaker's long-deferred decision to break her own silence is seen as the direct outcome of her reluctant decision to renounce worldly pleasures and aspirations—all of which are portrayed as having been rendered inutile by her "old inveterate foe." Ardelia, having discovered that "by struggling," she "can obtain / Nothing but encrease of pain," has decided to make a total submission to this mysterious and sinister figure.

The address to melancholy, concentrated in the opening lines, not only sets the scene but controls the meaning throughout. The dramatic appeal of the poem's action comes from the contrast between the hope initially raised by the remedies that Ardelia has adopted on the one hand, and the quiet dignity with which she admits their inefficacy on the other. Ardelia, resigned to her plight, seems to recognize the essential impoverishment of her world. It is perhaps for this reason that both the animation of melancholy and the highly patterned action conform to Colerige's description of "allegory" as "a translation of abstract notions into a picture language, which is itself nothing but an abstraction from objects of the senses" [*Lay Sermons*]. In fact, one is given, in this two-fold process of abstraction, a precise account of the movement by which melancholy seems to empty the world of meaning and value. In this sense, the allegory of **"Ardelia to Melancholy"** is related to what Paul de Man [in *Blindness and Insight,* 1983] has called a "renunciation of nostalgia and the desire to coincide" and "the unveiling of an authentically temporal destiny." Allegory offers a linguistic and structural correlative to the speaker's anguished decision to renounce all worldly ties; and this renunciation, in turn, produces a sense of time that is the reverse of what desire engenders. In striking contrast to the perception of fleeting time evoked in the love song **"Quickly Delia,"** the speaker in **"Ardelia to Melancholy"** tells her dusky con-

queror, "Thou, through my life, wilt with me goe, / And make yᵉ passage, sad, and slow." The poem's prosody participates in the same depressive logic: its tempo, unlike the heightened rhythms of the Restoration amatory lyric, is stately, funereal and deliberately retarded.

To experience time as a retarded and funereal movement is synonymous with being imprisoned within it—a perspective that informs the image of the "Fort" that is "ruin'd" in the closing lines of the poem. The link between time and space is suggested by the image of a soul enclosed within the confines of a spatial enclosure while its body "decays without." The image situates the speaking voice of the poem, since that voice is produced—at least as far as the reader is concerned—by the sounds that the reader may imagine escaping from the fort. In this particular construction of the lyrical voice as subject, the speaker establishes herself as an autonomous and stable entity only by a kind of submission to her conqueror—a submission that protects her against the nightmarish possibility of an even worse kind of suffering, namely, the greater pain involved in prolonging the futile struggle against melancholy. It is precisely this kind of immolation, suffering and masochistic self-abasement to which women have sometimes been regarded as being especially susceptible. Ardelia's renunciation is portrayed as a yielding to a forgiving yet punishing paternal figure, who must be both sought and placated. Yet it could be argued that immolation is not really what the poem is dramatizing: what this commonplace observation may overlook is the satisfaction implicit in the act of renunciation itself. The speaker's aim may be self-defense, not surrender—that is, a way of protecting herself against melancholy by declaring her submission to its power. A strategy that depends upon the denial of remedies may be viewed as the surest means of recovering what such a strategy denies. Indeed, the irony of a subject who seeks to escape melancholy by giving in to it is inscribed in the fictive situation of the poem. For this kind of submission enables the speaker to establish herself in a centered world of focus and purpose, in which the syntax of her address to melancholy has acquired the armature of logic and lucid rationality.

Yet, it would be utterly perverse to overlook the implications of the imagery of self-abasement in **"Ardelia to Melancholy."** The dual and contradictory consciousness of self that is projected in the poem can be linked to Hegel's "unhappy consciousness" and, behind it, to a religious meditation on alienation. The references to "heav'n" and to the soul as a fort in submission to a cruel tyrant are traditionally tied to a belief in a "first breach with Heav'n" (**"The Appology,"** l. 17) which engendered the loss of an initial state of happiness. It goes without saying that this typology is not made explicit in the poem: the speaker is in bondage to melancholy not Satan. Yet her bondage appears to be irremediable and without limits: it is the substitution of an emptiness for plenitude—a tragic manner of being incapable of resisting evil, except by submitting to it with dignity.

There is, furthermore, another dimension of the poem that supports a theological interpretation. This dimension can be found in the contrast—deemed essential to the speaker's argument—between the unity of purpose implied in the phrase "my old inveterate foe" and the multiplicity inherent in the remedies to which the speaker resorts. Instead of opposing one unity with another, the speaker opposes a unity with a fractured multiplicity that never moves beyond the confines of a set of particulars. Melancholy is an unchanging entity; but "a thousand other arts" (l. 6), "a new object, or new int'rest" (l. 27), and "new troops of fancy's" (l. 33) are divided and dispersed. The enumeration of ever new objects or new interests is an enumeration that can be continued indefinitely, without ceasing to be a repetition rather than a rebirth. Indeed, one might wonder if the value implied in the adjective "new" is not in fact intended to convey a familiarity or satiety that leads to its own downfall. For what could be more corrupt for a remedy aspiring to a rejuvenation than turning to a repetition that leads to no permanent transformation? If a unity can only be conquered by another unity, then there is no conquest possible—since the declared purpose of the remedies is to overwhelm the one in order to escape the tyranny of melancholy by dint of an infinite multiplication of novelties and pleasures. Enumerative repetition is what disrupts the strategy at the crucial moment when the speaker hopes, by means of friendship, to achieve a decisive victory over melancholy:

> But leaning on this reed, ev'n whilst I spoke
> It pierc'd my hand, and into pieces broke.
> Still, some new object, or new int'rest came
> And loos'd the bonds, and quite disolv'd the claim.

Instead of suggesting the sense of an opposition between a dominant and totalizing power and its opponent, this passage suggests a hidden link—a perverse connection—between the infinite repetition of novelties and the melancholy that they ostensibly contest. The "unhappy consciousness" in Hegel's succinct account of this process, [in *Phenomenology of Spirit*] "takes itself to be merely the Changeable," while "the Unchangeable is, for it, an alien Being."

"Ardelia to Melancholy" thus suggests a more complex and hidden relationship between the speaker and her plight than the one it ostensibly projects. The cruel tyrant is an ambivalent figure of patriarchal power—the bestower of both suffering and despair; but he is accompanied in the poem by an equally threatening and insidious power—the speaker's own imagination. What Finch as a poet wants to explore is what links these two figures—how they are bound together—and what is the twisted and perverse complicity between them.

Another group of poems—"An Invocation to Sleep," "To Death," "The Losse," and "A Song on Greife"—are not addressed to melancholy directly, yet are closely related to "Ardelia to Melancholy" in their preoccupation with mourning, loss, care, and suffering. "An Invocation to Sleep," for example, belongs to the popular category of poems devoted to sleep but also resembles "Ardelia to Melancholy" in its implicit recognition of the failure of the speaker's efforts to find a respite from her woes;

> How shall I wooe thee gentle rest,
> To a sad Mind, with cares opress'd?
> By what soft means, shall I invite
> Thy Pow'rs into my Soul to night?
> Yett, Gentle sleep, if thou wilt come,
> Such darknesse shall prepare the Room,
> As thy own Pallace ouerspreads,
> (Thy Pallace, stor'd with peaceful Beds)
> And Silence too, shall on thee waite
> Deep, as in the Turkish State;
> Whilst, still as Death, I will be found,
> My arms, by one another bound;
> And my dull lidds, so clos'd shall be
> As if allready seal'd by thee.
> Thus, I'll dispose the outward part,
> Wou'd I cou'd quiet too my Heart.
> But in its overburthen'd stead
> Behold I offer thee, my head;
> My head, I better can command,
> And that, I bow beneath thy hand.

The effectiveness of the poem lies in the fact that this premonition of failure is accompanied by a refusal to lament. The combination of a sense of defeat and an equally rigorous sense of dignity suggests that Finch recognized what Emily Dickinson conveyed in affirming that "Safe Despair it is that raves / Agony is frugal" [*Final Harvest,* 1961].

Like the address to melancholy, the invocation to sleep presupposes, in theory at least, a turning away from the world and its cares and distractions in order to address a voiceless entity. Yet no real personification occurs in the poem; far from inviting visualization—let alone sensory perception—sleep differs from melancholy in being featureless as well as voiceless. This is undoubtedly a major element in the strategy of the poem, since the invocation—a calling forth rather than a simple address—leaves the reader uncertain whether the animation that the invocation presupposes is fictive or mimetic and whether sleep can be summoned forth or comes only when ignored. This uncertainty is central to the understanding of sleep embodied in the poem. Although the speaker appears to seek in "gentle rest" the kind of renewal that will liberate her from the "cares" of a flawed world, it seems clear that sleep is never the phenomenon that it seems. Sleep is at once an experience that gives new life, for example, the birth of Eve (l. 25), and an experience that is akin to death, for example, in sleep's two-fold attributes of impending arrival and indefinite deferral.

Between the two extremes of life and death, sleep appears as a third way—one that incorporates elements of both. The speaker begins by describing the elaborate ritual she undertakes in order to prepare for the arrival of sleep. The ritual is futile, yet the image of a recumbent woman preparing for sleep by enfolding her arms in a dark and silent room conveys a sense of torpor that is clearly different from full consciousness. The progress of the speaker is a movement from daylight awareness to a "Turkish State" that is clearly meant to be understood as a kind of spiritual death. Yet because this spiritual death fails to bring an end to the "cares" that prevent her from achieving sleep, such a state proves to be as self-defeating as Ardelia's quest for novelty. There comes a point at which she is no longer satisfied with the indeterminancies of a state of limbo and yearns to possess the "kinder Death" that will supply its "place" (l. 38).

Of particular difficulty in **"An Invocation to Sleep"** is the bold, yet puzzling, comparison of the speaker to "our first great Father" (l. 22), who obeyed sleep's "strictest laws" (l. 24) in lending not only "his side" (l. 26) but "Half of his Heart" (l. 28) to "compose his lovely Bride" (l. 25). Intended to demonstrate what Adam "gave" (l. 22) to sleep in order to participate in the creation of Eve, the poem suggests that sleep is associated in some way with an exchange in which self-sacrifice achieves its own reward. Yet the contrast between the deep sleep of the primordial patriarch and the "cares" that beset the female subject of the poem probably betrays—although in a far more concealed fashion—the poem's debt to the same religious discourse that informs **"Ardelia to Melancholy."** Indeed, one might argue that the dejection at the heart of the speaker's quest for sleep is not directed at a specific object at all but at an archaic and lost domain—the secret and unattainable horizon of all her aspirations and desires.

Nevertheless, the speaker persists in seeing sleep as a respite from her cares—and is thus perhaps best described as blind, because her effort to woo sleep is at once intensely appealing and delusive. The juxtaposition of head and heart is self-defeating, and the poem reveals the absurdity of the project in its literalization of the metaphor of "head":

> Wou'd I cou'd quiet too my Heart.
> But, in its overburthen'd stead
> Behold I offer thee, my head;
> My head, I better can comand,
> And that, I bow beneath thy hand.

Her failure is made even more apparent in her appeal to the "surer Friend, tho' with harsher face" (l. 38); for death, envisaged in this way as an anticipated horizon, is never really a terminus ad quem but only the displaced name of a temporal predicament: death functions in the poem, not as a privileged moment at the end of a lifetime of cares— the point of arrival at a state of tranquility—but at what is endlessly deferred, namely, the recognition of a failed project that has itself become the source of its own woes.

"To Death" was described by Myra Reynolds as belonging to Finch's "religious" poems, but it seems more appropriate to link it to **"Ardelia to Melancholy"** and **"An Invocation to Sleep."** What distinguishes **"To Death"** from poems that are explicitly devotional in their orientation is not its secular outlook but the absence in the poem of any suggestion that Finch envisages death as a means of access to heaven. It is also true that in **"To Death"** there are no explicit references to the poet's dejection or cares. Yet the poem resembles **"Ardelia to Melancholy"** and **"An Invocation to Sleep"** in the attitude that the speaker adopts toward the subject of her address:

> O King of Terrors, whose unbounded Sway
> All that have Life, must certainly Obey;
> The King, the Priest, the Prophet, all are Thine,
> Nor wou'd ev'n *God* (in Flesh) thy Stroke decline.
> My Name is on thy Roll, and sure I must
> Encrease thy gloomy Kingdom in the Dust.
> My soul at this no Apprehension feels,
> But trembles at thy Swords, thy Racks, thy
>   Wheels;
> Thy scorching Fevers, which distract the Sense,
> And snatch us raving, unprepar'd from hence;
> At thy contagious Darts, that wound the Heads
> Of weeping Friends, who wait at dying Beds.
> Spare these, and let thy Time be when it will;
> My Bus'ness is to Dye, and Thine to Kill.
> Gently thy fatal Sceptre on me lay,
> And take to thy cold Arms, insensibly, thy Prey.

In **"Ardelia to Melancholy," "An Invocation to Sleep,"** and **"To Death,"** the speaker seeks to acknowledge her subjection to the object of her address—to embrace it— to absorb it, as it were, into her very being. Like melancholy, moreover, death is envisaged as a patriarchal signifier—a cruel tyrant who demands total submission; but since death's realm is seen as unlimited—extending even to *"God* (in Flesh)"—there is no suggestion that the speaker might ever have expected to avoid death. Her petition to this "King of Terrors" is rather to be exempted from his "Swords," his "Racks," and his "Wheels"; and this petition is what provides a clue to the affinity of this poem on death with Finch's other poems on melancholy. For a person trapped in depression, death can come to seem like an escape from anguish, including the anguish generated by the prospect of dissolution itself. But what may produce this respite is not the prospect of future glory or of redemption from a sinful nature but rather of a new dignity within this existence. Because the speaker seeks to look death in the face and tries to confront her mental anguish honestly, she hopes to achieve a new state of mind—not necessarily one of religious transcendence, but definitely one that is disillusioned, serene, and even businesslike in its attitude toward its destiny. . . .

The poem that first established Finch's reputation—**"The Spleen, A Pindarick Poem"**—has apparently undergone an irreversible decline in critical esteem. Widely admired throughout the eighteenth century, it was devalued in favor of her more spontaneous nature poems in the nineteenth century and has continued to be ignored in the twentieth. There are a number of reasons for this critical disregard. An appreciation of the lyric qualities of the irregular Pindaric ode has never been the strong suit of twentieth-century formalist criticism. Nor has criticism that has been preoccupied with themes of interest to women found much comfort in the apparent orientation of the poem—its evocation of what was still regarded at the beginning of the eighteenth century as 'a female malady.' The tendency of this criticism has been to overlook texts that appear to embody patriarchalist distortions of reality and to concentrate instead upon what are held to be representations of authentic female experience. This, in turn, suggests that the most important source of the poem's neglect lies in Finch's own ambiguous attitude toward the medical materials that she develops in the poem. While few readers have any difficulty appreciating **"The Unequal Fetters"** or **"The Introduction"** because of their assertions of a specifically female difference, **"The Spleen"** poses greater interpretive challenges because Finch is simultaneously writing within and subverting a late seventeenth-century tradition of medical discourse.

The reader who chooses to look beyond the poem's neglect and consider its possible convergence with feminist concerns has a warrant for doing so in Finch's own words. Far from accepting the notion that women were especially susceptible to hysteria or melancholy, Finch ridicules the readiness of contemporary medical practitioners to take advantage of this belief. In her fable **"For the Better,"** imitated from Roger L'Estrange, a quack tells a male patient, "Your Voice, your Pulse, your Face, / Good Signs afford and what you seem to feel / Proceeds from Vapours, which we'll help with Steel" (ll. 15-17). "No more of Vapours, your belov'd Disease," the patient answers without hesitation, "Your Ignorance's Skreen, your *What-you-please,* / With which you cheat poor Females of their Lives, / Whilst Men dispute not, so it rid their Wives" (ll. 20-23). In the ironic scepticism of these lines, Finch clearly differs from the perspective that prevails, for example, in Pope's "gloomy Cave of *Spleen.*" In fact, she suggests that the intervention or the so-called expert—and his supposed knowledge of the female psyche—has everything to do with the constitution of power, both within the family and within society. Rather than being affirmed as a natural and inherently debilitating female malady, "the vapours" are treated as a social construct, a category produced for the specific purpose of individual aggrandizement and social domination. Finch develops the same kind of revisionary reinterpretation of the female malady in **"The Spleen,"** only this time the vocabulary itself is travestied:

> In the Imperious *Wife* thou Vapours art,
> Which from o'erheated Passions rise
> In Clouds to the attractive Brain,
> Until descending thence again,
> Thro' the o'er-cast, and show'ring Eyes,
> Upon her Husband's soften'd Heart.

For centuries, medicine had explained the disease in precisely these terms—as the hungry up-and-down wanderings of the uterus or as the poisonous and corrupt "Vapours" rising from a diseased womb. Finch parodies this highly metaphoric discourse of female physiology, but now it is the "Imperious *Wife*" rather than the quack or devious husband who employs it as an instrument of domination and discipline. Power comes from below, yet the consequence seems equally destructive and pernicious:

> He the disputed Point must yield,
> Something resign of the contested Field;
> Till Lordly *Man,* born to Imperial Sway,
> Compounds for Peace, to make that Right away,
> And *Woman,* arm'd with *Spleen,* do's servilely Obey.

If **"The Spleen"** is an ironic poem like **"For the Better,"** its irony is directed, not at the abuses of medical discourse, but rather at the power addressed by that discourse. This power is not so much natural or cultural as ambiguous: it manifests itself in a wider range of natural symptoms than melancholy or grief, but it is no less resistant to rational explanation. As a poet, Finch was free of the obligation to theorize—and therefore free of the obligation to conform to "the collective medical wisdom of her age." **"For the Better"** and **"The Spleen"** are distinguished from medical opinion in Finch's time by the manner in which they interpret such phenomena—namely, as a discourse to be questioned and possibly understood rather than as a pathology to be corrected. **"The Spleen"** goes beyond **"For the Better"**: the former includes—through its distinction between "the dull Pretence" and the reality—the latter's critique of the "Vapours" as a cultural construction. But **"The Spleen"** goes beyond this critique by basing its ironies on an imagery that puts the very distinction between affectation and reality in doubt. As Finch envisages the spleen, it is neither a natural category nor a cultural fiction but a power that precedes and thus internalizes both.

FURTHER READING

Biography

McGovern, Barbara. *Anne Finch and Her Poetry: A Critical Biography.* Athens, Georgia: The University of Georgia Press, 1992, 278 p.

> A detailed study of Finch's life and literary career with close readings of her major groups of poems.

Criticism

Hinnant, Charles H. *The Poetry of Anne Finch: An Essay in Interpretation.* Newark: University of Delaware Press, 1994, 289 p.

> Identifies the major genres of Finch's poetry and analyzes representative pieces.

Mermin, Dorothy. "Women Becoming Poets: Katherine Philips, Aphra Behn, Anne Finch." *ELH, A Journal of English Literary History* LVII, No. 2 (Summer 1990): 335-55.

> Describes the conditions under which these eighteenth-century women developed subjects for poetry and achieved literary success.

Messenger, Ann. "Publishing Without Perishing: Lady Winchilsea's *Miscellany Poems* of 1713," *Restoration: Studies in English Literary Culture* V, No. 1 (Spring 1981): 27-37.

> Traces Finch's literary life from her earliest poems to her decision to become a "she-author" and publish *Miscellany Poems.*

Rogers, Katharine M. "Finch's 'Candid Account' vs. Eighteenth-Century Theories of the Spleen," *Mosaic* XXII, No. 1 (Winter 1989): 17-27.

Argues that Finch's account of depression in "The Spleen" unites her own emotional experience with empirical observations.

Additional coverage of Finch's life and career is contained in the following source published by Gale Research: *Literature Criticism from 1400 to 1800,* Vol. 3.

Frances Ellen Watkins Harper
1825-1911

(Born Frances Ellen Watkins; also wrote as Effie Afton)
American poet, novelist, essayist, and short story writer.

INTRODUCTION

Harper, a celebrated orator and social activist, was one
of the most popular black poets of the nineteenth century. Her works are considered transitional. While she
wrote against slavery, she also broke away from the
purely propagandistic mode of the anti-slavery poet,
becoming one of the first African American writers to
focus on national and universal issues. Today, in the
canon of American literature, she is considered an
important abolitionist poet whose works possess greater
historic than artistic significance.

Biographical Information

Born of a free mother in the slave state of Maryland,
Harper was raised by an aunt and uncle after her mother's early death and educated at her uncle's school for
free blacks. Her first job at age thirteen was caring for
the children of a bookseller; there she began composing
poems and reading the popular literature of the period.
Intent on living in a free state, Harper moved to Ohio
where she worked as a sewing teacher. A subsequent
move to Little York, Pennsylvania to teach elementary
school acquainted her with the Underground Railroad—
a loosely organized network of abolitionists who helped
fugitive slaves to escape north—and she quickly aligned
herself with the anti-slavery movement. Her first abolitionist speech was a marked success. Preaching social
and political reform and moral betterment, Harper spent
the next several years lecturing against slavery and offering readings from her *Poems on Miscellaneous Subjects* (1854). She supported the rebellion of John Brown
and, as he awaited execution, Harper lived with his wife
to lend moral support. Married to a farmer when she was
thirty-five, Harper retired from public life and bore a
child. Her husband died four years later, and she returned to lecturing. With the conclusion of the Civil War
and the enforcement of the Emancipation Proclamation,
her speeches shifted to Reconstruction themes stressing
the divisive effects of racism as well as the need for
temperance, domestic morality, and education for black
Americans. Ignoring the advice of friends, and despite
failing health and dwindling financial resources, Harper
continued to speak before black and racially mixed audiences, often without a fee, throughout the still dangerous
South. Until the end of her career she remained active
in such religious and social organizations as the Wom-

en's Christian Temperance Union and the American
Woman Suffrage Association. She died at age eighty-
five in Philadelphia.

Major Works

Harper's first publication, *Forest Leaves* (c. 1845), a collection of poetry and prose, has not been preserved. Her
next book of poetry, *Poems on Miscellaneous Subjects*
was her most popular book, selling several thousand copies in at least twenty editions. Containing her most-
acclaimed abolitionist poem, "Bury Me in a Free Land,"
it firmly established Harper's literary reputation. Imitative of the works of Henry Wadsworth Longfellow and
John Greenleaf Whittier, the poems in the volume are
primarily anti-slavery narratives. *Moses: A Story of the
Nile* (1869) and *Sketches of Southern Life* (1872) are
considered Harper's best works, though they were not as
well known as *Poems on Miscellaneous Subjects*. Published almost fifteen years after her first collection, *Moses*
chronicles the Hebrew patriarch's life, stressing the personal sacrifices he made in order to free the Israelites.

Most critics consider this a non-racial work, but the poem's emphasis on leadership and self-sacrifice is consistent with Harper's often-stated hopes for black leadership and unity. *Sketches of Southern Life,* a collection of poems, is narrated by ex-slaves Aunt Chloe and Uncle Jacob. With wit and charm they provide a commentary on the concerns of Southern blacks: family, education, religion, slavery, and Reconstruction. These narratives are written in African-American vernacular speech.

Critical Reception

During her career, Harper was extremely popular with both black and white audiences. Most critics believe that her popularity as an orator was largely responsible for the favorable reception of her poetry. As for her aesthetic abilities, the vernacular speech of the narrators in *Sketches of Southern Life* has been praised by some critics who recognize it as a forerunner of the dialect verse used by James Edwin Campbell, Daniel Webster Davis, and Paul Laurence Dunbar. Others, including Jean Wagner, argue that Harper's "language and humor are far from being authentically of the people." Though critics do not agree on Harper's artistic importance, twentieth-century literary scholars generally recognize her importance as an historic figure in African-American poetry. She has been described variously as an early feminist, one of the first African-American protest poets, and, in the words of Patricia Liggins Hill, "a major healer and race-builder of nineteenth-century America."

PRINCIPAL WORKS

Poetry

*†*Forest Leaves* (poetry and prose) c. 1845
**Eventide* [under pseudonym Effie Afton] (poetry and prose) 1854
**Poems on Miscellaneous Subjects* (poetry and essays) 1854
Moses: A Story of the Nile 1869
Poems 1871
Sketches of Southern Life 1872
‡*Atlanta Offering: Poems* 1895
Idylls of the Bible 1901
The Poems of Frances E. W. Harper 1970
Complete Poems 1988

Other Major Works

*"The Two Offers" (short story) 1859
"The Colored Woman of America" (essay) 1878
Iola Leroy; or Shadows Uplifted (novel) 1892

Minnie's Sacrifice; Sowing and Reaping; Trial and Triumph: Three Rediscovered Novels by Frances E. W. Harper (novels) 1994

*Works before 1860 were published under Harper's maiden name, Frances Ellen Watkins.

†There are no extant copies of Harper's first collection *Forest Leaves,* also referred to as *Autumn Leaves.*

‡Contains *The Sparrow's Fall and Other Poems* and *The Martyr of Alabama and Other Poems.*

CRITICISM

William Lloyd Garrison (essay date 1854)

SOURCE: Preface to *Poems on Miscellaneous Subjects,* by Frances Ellen Watkins, Merrihew & Thompson, 1857, pp. 3-4.

[*Garrison, an American abolitionist and civil libertarian, founded the antislavery journal* Liberator *and was co-founder of the American Anti-Slavery Society. In the following excerpt from his preface to the first edition of Harper's* Poems on Miscellaneous Subjects, *originally published in 1854, he implies that Harper's verse should not be judged by overly strict standards but rather as the work of a deserving apprentice poet. While Garrison believes that Harper demonstrates talent, he also suggests that she needs encouragement and cultivation.*]

There are half a million free colored persons in our country. These are not admitted to equal rights and privileges with the whites. As a body, their means of education are extremely limited; they are oppressed on every hand; they are confined to the performance of the most menial acts; consequently, it is not surprising that their intellectual, moral and social advancement is not more rapid. Nay, it is surprising, in view of the injustice meted out to them, that they have done so well. Many bright examples of intelligence, talent, genius and piety might be cited among their ranks, and these are constantly multiplying.

Every indication of ability, on the part of any of their number, is deserving of special encouragement. Whatever is attempted in poetry or prose, in art or science, in professional or mechanical life, should be viewed with a friendly eye, and criticised in a lenient spirit. To measure them by the same standard as we measure the productions of the favored white inhabitants of the land would be manifestly unjust. The varying circumstances and conditions of life are to be taken strictly into account.

Hence, in reviewing the following [*Poems on Miscellaneous Subjects*], the critic will remember that they are written by one young in years, and identified in complexion and destiny with a depressed and outcast race, and who has had to contend with a thousand disadvantages from earliest life. They certainly are very creditable to her, both in a literary and moral point of view, and indicate the possession of a talent which, if carefully cultivated and properly encouraged, cannot fail to secure for herself a poetic reputation, and to deepen the interest already so extensively felt in the liberation and enfranchisement of the entire colored race.

Benjamin Brawley (essay date 1937)

SOURCE: "Literature, 1895-1890," in *The Negro Genius: A New Appraisal of the Achievement of the American Negro in Literature and the Fine Arts,* Dodd, Mead & Company, 1937, pp. 100-23.

[*Brawley is considered one of the most influential critics of Harlem Renaissance literature. An educator, historian, and clergyman, Brawley's literary contributions are largely concerned with black writers and artists, and with black history. In the following excerpt, Brawley briefly describes and compliments Harper's books of poetry.*]

Frances E. W. Harper (1825-1911) was distinctly a minor poet, though sometimes her feeling flashed out in felicitous lines. To account for her reputation one must recall that she was more than a writer. For six years before the Civil War she was an anti-slavery agent in the East, and for more than three decades thereafter a lecturer in the South on temperance and home-building. Her prime concern was with moral and social reform.

Frances Ellen Watkins was born of free parents in Baltimore. When she was three years old her mother died, and at thirteen she had to earn her own living. When grown to womanhood she served for three years as a teacher in Ohio, but an incident of the year 1853 led her to devote herself to effort for freedom. Maryland passed an act forbidding free Negroes from the North to come to the state on penalty of being imprisoned and sold into slavery. A man who unwittingly violated this statute was sold into Georgia. Endeavoring to escape, he hid himself behind the wheel house of a boat bound for the North, but was discovered and remanded to slavery. He then died of exposure and hardship. "Upon that grave," said Miss Watkins, "I pledged myself to the anti-slavery cause." She became interested in the work of the "underground railroad" and in 1854 was engaged as a lecturer by the Anti-Slavery Society of Maine. In 1860, in Cincinnati, she married Fenton Harper, who died just four years later. After the war she worked under the auspices of the Woman's Christian Temperance Union. Her manner in her speeches was dignified; she made few gestures and was never theatrical.

Mrs. Harper's poems were the ornaments of her public addresses. Because she most frequently printed them in paper-back booklets that sold for a quarter or even less, it is now difficult to find copies of her work, while the rearrangements and the different editions offer the bibliographer a genuine problem. William Still, who wrote the

Introduction to the novel, *Iola Leroy,* published in 1892, enumerated five previous publications—*Forest Leaves, Miscellaneous Poems, Moses: A Story of the Nile, Poems,* and *Sketches of Southern Life.* Of the first of these no copy is known to exist. *Poems on Miscellaneous Subjects* appeared in 1854 and by 1871 was in the twentieth edition. *Moses* was in the second edition in 1869, appeared in enlarged form in 1889, and was the chief piece in a collection entitled *Idylls of the Bible* (1901), though it must be said that this hardly lives up to its name. *Poems,* first appearing as a new collection in 1871, was enlarged more than once and by 1895 made a beautiful booklet of ninety pages, more firmly bound than usual. *Sketches of Southern Life,* first issued in twenty-four small pages in 1872, was enlarged in 1896.

With the exception of *Moses* and some shorter pieces on biblical subjects, Mrs. Harper's poems were mainly a reflection of the life of the Negro. In her loose, flowing meters she showed the influence of Longfellow and Felicia Dorothea Hemans. The secret of her popularity is to be seen in such lines as the following from **"Bury Me in a Free Land"**:

> Make me a grave where'er you will,
> In a lowly plain or a lofty hill;
> Make it among earth's humblest graves,
> But not in a land where men are slaves.

Of the Emancipation Proclamation she wrote:

> It shall flash through coming ages,
>   It shall light the distant years;
> And eyes now dim with sorrow
>   Shall be brighter through their tears.

Of little children she said:

> I almost think the angels
>   Who tend life's garden fair,
> Drop down the sweet white blossoms
>   That bloom around us here.

In *Sketches of Southern Life* the speaker is Aunt Chloe, who recalls various experiences, among them the selling of her two boys away from their parents and the later happy reunion of the family. *Moses,* intended as a religious epic, records different incidents in the life of the lawgiver in what was an attempt at blank verse. Of the shorter pieces on biblical subjects **"Vashti"** stands out with something of distinction.

> She leaned her head upon her hand
>   And heard the King's decree—
> "My lords are feasting in my halls;
>   Bid Vashti come to me.
>
> "I've shown the treasures of my house,
>   My costly jewels rare,
> But with the glory of her eyes
>   No rubies can compare.

"Adorn'd and crown'd I'd have her come,
   With all her queenly grace,
And mid my lords and mighty men
   Unveil her lovely face.

"Each gem that sparkles in my crown,
   Or glitters on my throne,
Grows poor and pale when she appears,
   My beautiful, my own!"

. . . . .

She heard again the King's command,
   And left her high estate;
Strong in her earnest womanhood,
   She calmly met her fate,

And left the palace of the King,
   Proud of her spotless name—
A woman who could bend to grief
   But would not bow to shame.

J. Saunders Redding (essay date 1939)

SOURCE: "Let Freedom Ring," in *To Make a Poet Black,*
McGrath Publishing Company, 1968, pp. 19-48.

[*In* To Make a Poet Black *Redding provides a scholarly
appraisal of black poetry, including a historical overview as well as biographical information about individual
poets. In the following excerpt from that book, originally
published in 1939, Redding discusses Harper's attempts
to broaden the scope of African-American verse in her*
Poems on Miscellaneous Subjects *and other collections.*]

In 1854, while Douglass was climbing in importance as
the spokesman and ideal of the Negro race, there appeared
in Philadelphia a thin volume called *Poems on Miscellaneous Subjects,* by Frances Ellen Watkins. The title is
significant, for it indicates a different trend in the creative
urge of the Negro. Except for Jupiter Hammon and Phillis
Wheatley, Negro writers up to this time were interested
mainly in the one theme of slavery and in the one purpose
of bringing about freedom. The treatment of their material
was doctrinal, definitely conditioned to the ends of propaganda. A willful (and perhaps necessary) monopticism had
blinded them to other treatment and to the possibilities in
other subjects. It remained for Miss Watkins, with the
implications in the title of her volume, to attempt a redi-
rection.

The writers did not immediately follow the lead. William
Wells Brown, for an instance, only partly rejected doctrinal
treatment in his later work. It was not until the late sixties,
following the war, that Douglass's speeches rang changes
on his material. Novels, short stories, and essays, though
milder than the dozens of slave biographies, autobiographies, and "accounts" published earlier, were still infected
by the deadly virus when Charles Chesnutt began his

literary career at the turn of the century. But attempts had
been made to bring about a truer artistic outlook.

> **In one sense [Harper] was a trail blazer,
> hacking, however ineffectually, at the
> dense forest of propaganda and striving
> to "write less of issues that were
> particular and more of feelings
> that were general."**
>
> **—*J. Saunders Redding***

In 1861 Mrs. Harper (Frances Ellen Watkins) wrote to
Thomas Hamilton, the editor of the *Anglo-African,* a
monthly journal that had been established the year before: "If our talents are to be recognized we must write
less of issues that are particular and more of feelings that
are general. We are blessed with hearts and brains that
compass more than ourselves in our present plight. . . .
We must look to the future which, God willing, will be
better than the present or the past, and delve into the
heart of the world."

It seems that Hamilton was influenced by this admonition. He did his best to make his magazine a broad cultural organ for black American expression, a Negro-
manned duplicate of the *North American Review* or the
Atlantic Monthly. In the very nature of things at that
time he could not succeed, but one meets in the pages of
the *Anglo-African* articles and essays on the theater, on
agronomy, on literature, and on the colonization movement, sermons on many subjects, and a few stories without the predominant bias. Now and then the work of this
kind hit the farthest extreme, as in most of the work of
Phillis Wheatley.

To what degree Frances Ellen Watkins followed her own
advice can be judged from her writings. In one sense she
was a trail blazer, hacking, however ineffectually, at the
dense forest of propaganda and striving to "write less of
issues that were particular and more of feelings that were
general." But she was seriously limited by the nature and
method of her appeal. Immensely popular as a reader ("el-
ocutionist"), the demands of her audience for the sentimental treatment of the old subjects sometimes overwhelmed her. On the occasions when she was free "to
delve into the heart of the world" she was apt to gush with
pathetic sentimentality over such subjects as wronged
innocece, the evils of strong drink, and the blessed state
of childhood.

Poems on Miscellaneous Subjects was published when
Miss Watkins was twenty-nine years old. It is evident from
the poems in this volume that she had not thought out the
artistic creed later indited to Thomas Hamilton. Her topics are slavery and religion, and these first poems mark
her as a full-fledged member of the propagandist group.

The volume sold ten thousand copies within five years and was reprinted three times before her next work, *Moses, A Story of the Nile,* appeared in 1869. *Sketches of Southern Life* came in 1873 and her fourth volume, published without date, was called *The Sparrows Fall and Other Poems.*

At first she was sometimes tense and stormy, as in **"Bury Me In a Free Land"**:

> I ask no monument, proud and high,
> To arrest the gaze of the passer-by;
> All that my yearning spirit craves
> Is bury me not in a land of slaves.

After *Moses* Miss Watkins tended more frequently to the maudlin. Her later volumes show her of larger compass but of less strength than does the first. Though she held conventional views on most of the social evils of the day, at her best she attacked them in a straightforward manner. A few lines from **"The Double Standard"** show her method:

> Crime has no sex and yet today
>   I wear the brand of shame;
> Whilst he amid the gay and proud
>   Still bears an honest name.
>
>   . . . . .
>
> Yes blame me for my downward course,
>   But Oh! remember well,
> Within your homes you press the hand
>   That led me down to hell.
>
>   . . . . .
>
> No golden weights can turn the scale
>   Of justice in His sight;
> And what is wrong in woman's life
>   In man's cannot be right.

Miss Watkins wrote a great many sentimental ballads in obvious imitation of the ballads which appeared with monotonous regularity in *Godey's Lady's Book* and other popular monthlies. The ballad form was well suited to some of her material and was an excellent elocutionary pattern. Even now the recitation of the piece **"The Dying Bondman"** has not lost its effectiveness.

> By his bedside stood the master
> Gazing on the dying one,
> Knowing by the dull gray shadows
> That life's sands were almost run.
>
> "Master," said the dying bondman,
> "Home and friends I soon shall see;
> But before I reach my country,
> Master write that I am free;
>
> Give to me the precious token,
> That my kindred dead may see—

> Master! write it, write it quickly!
> Master write that I am free!"
>
>   . . . . .
>
> Eagerly he grasped the writing;
> "I am free!" at last he said.
> Backward fell upon the pillow.
> He was free among the dead.

Practically all the social evils from the double standard of sex morality to corruption in politics were lashed with the scourge of her resentment. Her treatment of these topics never varied: she traced the effects of the evil upon some innocent—a young and dying girl, as in **"A Little Child Shall Lead Them,"** or a virtuous woman, as in **"The Double Standard,"** or a sainted mother, as in **"Nothing and Something."** But her treating these evils at all entitles her to respect and gratitude as one who created other aims and provided new channels for the creative energies of Negro writers.

In some of Miss Watkins's verse one thing more is to be noted especially. In the volume called *Sketches of Southern Life* the language she puts in the mouths of Negro characters has a fine racy, colloquial tang. In these poems she managed to hurdle a barrier by which Dunbar was later to feel himself tripped. The language is not dialect. She retained the speech patterns of Negro dialect, thereby giving herself greater emotional scope (had she wished or had the power to use it) than the humorous and the pathetic to which it is generally acknowledged dialect limits one. In all of her verse Miss Watkins attempted to suit her language to her theme. In *Moses* she gives her language a certain solemnity and elevation of tone. In her pieces on slavery she employs short, teethy, angry monosyllables. Her use of dialectal patterns was no accident. She anticipated James Weldon Johnson. . . .

In general Miss Watkins was less confined than any of her contemporaries. Her poetry can be grouped under four heads—religious poems, traditional lyrics of love and death, antislavery poems, and poems of social reform, of which the antislavery group is not the largest. Her poetry was not unduly warped by hatred. Like Horton, whom she probably knew in his later years, she gave to some of her pieces a lightness of touch that was sadly lacking in most of the heavy-footed writing of her race. A great deal of her poetry was written to be recited, and this led her into errors of metrical construction which, missed when the poems are spoken, show up painfully on the printed page. In all but her long, religious narrative, *Moses,* simplicity of thought and expression is the keynote.

She was the first Negro woman poet to stand boldly forth and glory in her pride of race, but she was not too vindicative. Her ambition to be the pivot upon which Negro writers were to turn to other aims, to compass more than themselves in their racial plight, was not accomplished. But before her death in 1911, the movement of which she had been the first champion had a brief and brilliant revival.

Joan R. Sherman (essay date 1974)

SOURCE: "Frances Ellen Watkins Harper, 1824-1911" in *Invisible Poets: Afro-Americans of the Nineteenth Century,* University of Illinois Press, 1974, pp. 62-74.

[*In the following essay, Sherman explains that while the poems in Harper's early collections may seem maudlin to modern readers, Harper should nonetheless be remembered as a black poet who broke away from purely racial protest themes to treat other national issues of significance.*]

In an 1859 essay, "Our Greatest Want," Miss Watkins declared that neither gold, intelligence, nor talent were the most pressing needs of her people; rather, "We want more soul, a higher cultivation of all spiritual faculties. We need more unselfishness, earnestness and integrity. . . . We need men and women whose hearts are the homes of a high and lofty enthusiasm, and a noble devotion to the cause of emancipation, who are ready and willing to lay time, talent and money on the altar of universal freedom." No sounder description of the virtues Miss Watkins herself possessed was ever written, although journalists from Maine to Alabama, fellow abolitionists, and contemporary historians acclaimed her unsparing dedication to humanity and honored her as the equal of Bishop Daniel Payne and Frederick Douglass in her contributions to race advancement.

Frances Ellen Watkins was born in Baltimore in 1824, the only child of free parents. When her mother died in 1828 she went to live with her aunt and soon became a student in the academy of her uncle, William J. Watkins. Here daily Bible readings, composition practice, and Watkins's zealous abolitionist teachings shaped her young mind. At the age of fourteen Miss Watkins left school to work as housekeeper and seamstress in the home of a Baltimore bookstore proprietor. She continued her education in his library and wrote poems and articles that were published in local newspapers during the 1840's. Miss Watkins left Baltimore in 1850 for Union Seminary, a vocational school near Columbus, Ohio, founded by the African Methodist Episcopal Church and later absorbed into Wilberforce University. Here she instructed classes in embroidery and plain sewing until 1852, when for a year she taught fifty-three "unruly children" in Little York, Pennsylvania.

In Little York Miss Watkins was deeply moved by "the poor, half-starved, flying fugitive[s]" traveling the Underground Railroad and by the story of a free Maryland black man who was kidnapped and sold into slavery in Georgia. She now pledged herself to the antislavery cause, "to use time, talent, and energy in the cause of freedom." In 1854 Miss Watkins lived at the Underground Railroad Station in Philadelphia. That summer she visited the antislavery office in Boston and there published her first volume of poems, *Poems on Miscellaneous Subjects* (with a preface by William Lloyd Garrison). In August at a public meeting in New Bedford, Miss Watkins delivered her first lecture, "The Elevation and Education of Our People," and in September, 1854, the Maine Anti-Slavery Society hired her to lecture throughout New England for the next eighteen months. After a visit to the fugitives in Canada in September, 1856, Miss Watkins added Ohio and New York to her lecture circuit and was soon engaged by the Pennsylvania Anti-Slavery Society as lecturer and agent for eastern Pennsylvania and New Jersey from October, 1857, to May, 1858. From 1854 until 1860 Miss Watkins took to the podium in more than eight states, usually daily but often two or three times a day, in the cause of emancipation. She attracted large, enthusiastic audiences, for her fragile, dainty figure and dignified manner belied her power to kindle abolitionist fervor in the hearts of both races. Piercing black eyes dominated her dark African features, and her handsome face radiated the vitality and resolute passion of a charismatic orator. She recited her poetry, demanded liberty for the slave and righteousness from the nation with graceful gestures and in a strong, clear, musical voice. Her wit, reason, sincerity, and eloquence impressed every auditor. In short, she was "a magnificent type of woman, physically and mentally."

Miss Watkins's sympathetic identification with the bondsmen and her tragic sense of the impending crisis grew steadily. She wrote to William Still, "I have lived in the midst of oppression and wrong, and I am saddened by every captured fugitive in the North; a blow has been struck at my freedom, in every hunted and down-trodden slave in the South; North and South have both been guilty; and they that sin must suffer." In letters to Still, with whom she corresponded from 1854, Miss Watkins sent money for the fugitives and pleaded for more work of any kind that she might do for their welfare. She lived in Still's Philadelphia home with Mrs. John Brown for the two weeks preceding Brown's execution in 1859, and afterward she wrote letters and sent packages to the martyrs still in prison.

Miss Watkins retired from public life for a few years when she married Fenton Harper, a widower, in Cincinnati on November 22, 1860, and bought a small farm near Columbus for their home. They had a daughter, Mary, who became a Sunday School teacher and volunteer social worker. Mary never married, but lived with Mrs. Harper and died about two years before her. Fenton Harper died on May 23, 1864, and in October Mrs. Harper returned to the lecture circuit with a speech on "The Mission of the War." Until 1865 she lectured in New England; then, except for a few months in Philadelphia (fall, 1867), she traveled until 1871 at her own expense through thirteen Southern states. In the South Mrs. Harper lived with the freedmen in "the old cabins of slavery" and spoke at Sunday schools, day schools, churches, town meetings, in homes and village squares, on the same daily and two-a-day schedule as before the War. Her only income was from sparse collections taken at meetings and from sales of new poetry, *Moses, A Story of the Nile* (1869) and *Poems* (1871), and reprints of *Poems on Miscellaneous Subjects,* which reached a twentieth edition in 1871. Speaking in an Alabama brush arbor or before the legislature of South Carolina, Mrs. Harper exhorted the freedmen to be independent, responsible citizens, to gain education and land, to build strong families and homes based on mutual respect and Christian morality. Her lectures were broad in scope: "National Salvation," "Enlightened Motherhood," "The Colored Man as a Social and Political Force," "Racial Literature," "The Mission of the War and the Demands of the Colored Race in the Work of Reconstruction." Although in poor health and often depressed by the ignorance and indifference of the freedmen, Mrs. Harper labored for six years with a crusader's zeal, with infinite compassion and faith to bring about the elevation of the race. "After all," she wrote in 1870, "whether they encourage or discourage me, I belong to this race, and when it is down I belong to a down race; when it is up, I belong to a risen race."

After 1871 Mrs. Harper also wrote and lectured in support of many nationwide social and moral reform movements, for it was a "privilege," she said, to be "sister to the human race." For forty years after making Philadelphia her permanent home in February, 1871, she worked with a dozen organizations on behalf of education, women's and children's rights, and temperance. In 1872 she organized and was assistant superintendent of a YMCA Sabbath school in Philadelphia. She served as lecturer and officer in the National Association of Colored Women, the National Council of Women of the United States, the American Association of Educators of Colored Youth and Author's Association. From about 1875 to 1882 Mrs. Harper was superintendent of the Philadelphia and Pennsylvania chapters of the National Women's Christian Temperance Union, Colored Branch. Without remuneration she headed the Northern United States WCTU activities from 1883 to 1890 and continued as an organizer, field worker, and lecturer for them until 1896. For this service her name was placed on the Red Letter Calendar of the World WCTU in 1922. In addition, Mrs. Harper wrote and worked for the African Methodist Episcopal Church, which "adopted" her—she was a Unitarian—and frequently paid homage to her selfless labors.

During these busy years, Mrs. Harper published new poetry in *Sketches of Southern Life* (1872) and in three verse pamphlets, *Light Beyond the Darkness, The Sparrow's Fall and Other Poems,* and *The Martyr of Alabama,* all of which were later included in *Atlanta Offering* (1895). Mrs. Harper was the first woman of her race to publish a short story, "The Two Offers" (1859), and a novel, *Iola Leroy* (1892). Her celebrity as an author, lecturer, and reformer was virtually unsurpassed in her day; however, like other black poets and most race leaders, soon after her death her volumes of poetry were out of print and her deeds all but forgotten. She died of heart disease at the age of 87 on February 20, 1911, and, after a funeral service at the First Unitarian Church, she was buried in Eden Cemetery, Philadelphia, on February 24. For her contributions to literature and human welfare Mrs. Harper deserves to be honored anew among the healers and builders of nineteenth-century America.

Mrs. Harper's Poetry

As the most popular black poet before Dunbar, Mrs. Harper earned enough from sales of twenty-five-cent pamphlets and slim volumes of verse to support herself and to buy the three-story house at 1006 Bainbridge Street, Philadelphia, from which her later works were published. Although most of her poetry, and the best of it, was written by 1872, new titles and reprints continued to appear at least until 1901. She shifted the thematic emphasis of her poetry from volume to volume; nevertheless, from 1854 through 1901 her subjects remain religion, race, and social reform. Mrs. Harper's verse is frankly propagandist, a metrical extension of her life dedicated to the welfare of others. She believed in art for humanity's sake:

> Let me make the songs for the people,
>   Songs for the old and young;
> Songs to stir like a battle-cry
>   Wherever they are sung.

Her poems were "songs to thrill the hearts of men / With more abundant life," "anthems of love and duty" for children, and songs of "bright and restful mansions" for the "poor and aged" (**"Songs for the People,"** 1894). Except for *Moses* (1869) and *Sketches of Southern Life* (1872), which will be considered later, Mrs. Harper's lyric and narrative poetry varies little in form, language, or poetic technique.

Her numerous religious poems embrace both New and Old Testament ideologies and imagery, honoring their respective God heroes, a gentle Redeemer and a fiery Jehovah. The former brings "comfort, peace and rest," "changes hearts of stone/ To tenderness and love" through grace, and offers a "crown of life" hereafter to all who trust in him. This God of light and mercy appears in several early poems like **"That Blessed Hope"** and **"Saved by Faith"** (1854), in poems of the middle years when, following the loss of her husband in 1864, Mrs. Harper seems preoccupied with death (twelve of the twenty-six selections in *Poems* [1871] concern dying or life after death), and in the 1890's the same God of love dominates some two dozen poems such as **"The Refiner's Gold," "The Sparrow's Fall," "The Resurrection of Jesus,"** and **"Renewal of Strength."** Mrs. Harper's fervid commitment to Christian virtues and her faith in a "gloryland" are moving, but poetically more interesting is her allegiance to a dynamic warrior God who "hath bathed his sword in judgement," who thunders in "whirlwinds of wrath" or swoops with a "bath of blood and fire" to redress injustice in *this* world. It is the God of the Israelites who will free her people, as in **"Ethiopia"** (1854):

> The tyrant's yoke from off her neck,
>   His fetters from her soul,
> The mighty hand of God shall break,
>   And spurn the base control.

>   . . . . .

> Secure by night, and blest by day,
>   Shall pass her happy hours;
> Nor human tigers hunt for prey
>   Within her peaceful bowers.

Then, Ethiopia, stretch, O stretch
  Thy bleeding hands abroad!
Thy cry of agony shall reach
  And find redress from God.

In poems like **"Lines"** (1857), **"Retribution"** (1871), and **"The Martyr of Alabama"** (1894), Mrs. Harper invokes the God of Moses not only as a militant redeemer, but also as the scourge of men and nations who "trample on His children." She wrote to John Brown in prison in 1859: "God writes national judgements on national sins." Thus when men of Cleveland returned a young fugitive girl to slavery to "preserve the union," Mrs. Harper prophesied the coming chaos in one of her best poems, **"To the Union Savers of Cleveland"** (1860). These are the last five of eleven stanzas:

    There is blood upon your city,
      Dark and dismal is the stain;
    And your hands would fail to cleanse it,
      Though Lake Erie ye should drain.

    There's a curse upon your Union,
      Fearful sounds are in the air;
    As if thunderbolts were framing
      Answers to the bondsmen's prayer.

    Ye may offer human victims,
      Like the heathen priests of old;
    And may barter manly honor
      For the Union and for gold.

    But ye can not stay the whirlwind,
      When the storm begins to break;
    And your God doth rise in judgment,
      For the poor and needy's sake.

    And, your sin-cursed, guilty Union
      Shall be shaken to its base,
    Till ye learn that simple justice
      Is the right of every race.

Mrs. Harper seldom shows such righteous indignation as gives power to this poem, and even less often is she bitter or cynical. However, these emotions do invigorate such poems as **"The Bible Defense of Slavery"** (1854), **"The Dismissal of Tyng"** (1857), and **"A Fairer Hope, A Brighter Morn"** (LBD) in which the poet denounces white "prophets of evil" who weave phantom fears of miscegenation out of their own guilt in order to oppress the race they formerly enslaved.

In many other poems on racial themes, such as **"Eliza Harris"** (1853) and **"The Slave Auction"** (1854), Mrs. Harper describes the anguish of slave mothers, the heroism of black men, and the suffering of fugitives and captives. As in most abolitionist verse, emotions of fear, pain, and pity are generic, like the situations, detached from both poet and poetry. Without Mrs. Harper's dramatic recitations they remain superficial, sentimental period pieces. On the other hand, when the poet speaks in her own

voice, as in **"Bury Me in a Free Land"** (1858), true passion is felt, and the poem succeeds:

    Make me a grave where'er you will,
    In a lowly plain, or a lofty hill;
    Make it among earth's humblest graves,
    But not in a land where men are slaves.

      . . . . .

    I'd shudder and start if I heard the bay
    Of bloodhounds seizing their human prey,
    And I heard the captive plead in vain
    As they bound afresh his galling chain.

      . . . . .

    I ask no monument, proud and high,
    To arrest the gaze of the passers-by;
    All that my yearning spirit craves,
    Is bury me not in a land of slaves.

More objective and intellectual than the abolitionist verses are Mrs. Harper's postwar appeals for freedmen's rights. Although often militantly urgent in tone, they express conciliatory sentiments. **"Words for the Hour"** (1871) is addressed to **"Men of the North"**:

    'Tis yours to banish from the land
      Oppression's iron rule;
    And o'er the ruin'd auction-block
      Erect the common school.

    To wipe from labor's branded brow
      The curse that shamed the land;
    And teach the Freedmen how to wield
      The ballot in his hand.

"An Appeal to the American People" (1871) reminds white Americans of the black soldiers' heroism, chides them for ignoring these "offerings of our blood," and appeals to their manhood, Christian principles, and honor to see justice done in the nation. There are no suggestions of black separatism in these poems; rather, the poet optimistically envisions racial brotherhood and national progress, as in **"The Present Age"** (SF):

    Blame not the age, nor think it full
    Of evil and unrest;
    But say of every other age,
    "This one shall be the best."

    The age to brighten every path
    By sin and sorrow trod;
    For loving hearts to usher in
    The commonwealth of God.

As black and white work together for mutual betterment, their souls must be pure and their hearts consecrated to Christian morality and social welfare. In some three dozen "reform" ballads Mrs. Harper weeps for families ruined by King Alcohol, and she gushes over innocent children and helpless women threatened or ruined by a sinful world. Her lecture audiences were captivated by these catalogues of human frailty which now seem maudlin. Nevertheless, such ballads on issues of national concern represent a unique and significant movement by a black poet, a breaking away from exclusively racial protest themes to write "more of feelings that are general . . . and delve into the heart of the world." The "slavery of intemperance," Mrs. Harper wrote, "is a curse in the home, a menace to the Church, a blight to the State, a fretting leprosy in the national house," against which we must "consecrate, educate, agitate, and legislate." In **"The Drunkard's Child"** (1854) a boy dies of neglect in his besotted father's arms. A ruined bride, mother, and child regain happiness through "the gospel and the pledge" in **"Signing the Pledge"** (1888); a dozen unsuspecting people are destroyed by drink in the melodramatic **"Nothing and Something"** (1888); and a typical alcoholic father repents at the sight of his child's empty Christmas stocking in **"The Ragged Stocking"** (1889):

Stony drink is a raging demon,
  In his hands are shame and woe,
He mocketh the strength of the mighty
  And bringeth the strong man low.

. . . . .

Then I knelt by this little stocking
  And sobbed out an earnest prayer,
And rose with strength to wrestle
  And break from the tempter's snare.

Mrs. Harper was also an outspoken champion of women's rights. In **"A Double Standard"** (SF) a deceived young girl speaks:

Crime has no sex and yet today
  I wear the brand of shame;
Whilst he amid the gay and proud
  Still bears an honored name.

. . . . .

No golden weights can turn the scale
  Of Justice in His sight;
And what is wrong in woman's life
  In man's cannot be right.

Other oppressed women are victims of economic injustice, as in **"Died of Starvation"** (1854), or martyrs to man's pride like Vashti, Queen of Persia. Occasionally Mrs. Harper projects her own moral and spiritual strength into biblical heroines, creating appealing individuals, warm, courageous, loving women who transcend the cause they espouse. In poems like **"Rizpah, the Daughter of Ai"** (1857), **"Ruth and Naomi"** (1857), **"Mary at the Feet of Christ"** (1871), and **"Vashti"** (1870), emotions tied to specific crises arc conveyed in simple, direct language, giving the poems a vibrant immediacy as well as lasting human validity.

Most of Mrs. Harper's religious, racial, and reform verse resembles the typical nineteenth-century work in Rufus W. Griswold's *Female Poets of America* (1848, 1873), possessing by today's standards more cultural and historical than aesthetic value. Generally her diction and rhymes are pedestrian; the meters are mechanical and frequently dependent on oral delivery for regularity, and the sentiments, however genuine, lack concreteness and control. However, Mrs. Harper attains notable artistic success with *Moses: A Story of the Nile* (1869) and the Aunt Chloe poems in *Sketches of Southern Life* (1872). *Moses,* a forty-page narrative in blank verse recounting the career of Israel's leader, was no doubt inspired by the Emancipation and Lincoln's death. Through a dramatic dialogue of Moses and Charmian, the poet describes Moses' departure from the Pharaoh's court. Then her narrative moves briskly through the Old Testament story to Moses' death. Mrs. Harper handles the blank verse skillfully, bringing the biblical events to life with vivid imagery:

Then Moses threw his rod upon the floor,
And it trembled with a sign of life;
The dark wood glowed, then changed into a thing
Of glistening scales and golden rings, and green,
And brown and purple stripes; a hissing, hateful
Thing, that glared its fiery eye, and darting forth
From Moses' side, lay coiled and panting
At the monarch's feet.

In grisly detail, the ten plagues descend on Egypt: "every fountain, well and pool / Was red with blood, and lips, all parched with thirst, / Shrank back in horror from the crimson draughts / "; frogs "crowded into Pharaoh's bed, and hopped / Into his trays of bread, and slumbered in his / Ovens and his pans." The horrors continue, until

    for three long days, nor saffron
Tint, nor crimson flush, nor soft and silvery light
Divided day from morn, nor told the passage
Of the hours; men rose not from their seats, but sat
In silent awe. That lengthened night lay like a
  burden
On the air,—a darkness one might almost gather
In his hand, it was so gross and thick.

The poet conveys Moses' complex emotions and strong personality through his actions. In the final chapter she admirably evokes the mingled sense of pride and sorrow felt by the Israelites, "reaching out unconscious hands" to keep him. She portrays the solitude of Moses and his mixed feelings of regret and joy as "He stood upon the highest peak of Nebo, / And saw the Jordan chafing through its gorges . . . the ancient rocks / That dripped with honey . . . the vines opprest / With purple riches, the fig trees fruitcrowned / Green and golden"—a scene of peace and beauty which prepares Moses' "ransomed soul" for the even fairer land of "crystal fountains" to which "a troupe of fair young angels" soon conveys him. The poem's elevated diction, concrete imagery, and formal meter harmoniously blend to magnify the noble adventure of Moses' life and the mysterious grandeur of his death. Mrs. Harper maintains the pace of her long narrative and its tone of reverent admiration with scarcely a pause for moralizing. *Moses* is Mrs. Harper's most original poem and one of considerable power.

She shows a similar talent for matching technique and subject in the charming series of poems which make up most of *Sketches of Southern Life* (1872). Aunt Chloe, the narrator, is a wise, practical ex-slave who discusses the war and Reconstruction with earthy good humor, as Uncle Jacob, a saintly optimist, counsels prayer, "faith and courage." These poems are unique in Mrs. Harper's canon for their wit and irony; the colloquial expressions of Aunt Chloe's discourse form a new idiom in black poetry which ripens into the dialect verse of Campbell, Davis, and Dunbar in the last decades of the century. **"The Deliverance"** in sixty stanzas describes antebellum plantation life and the departure of young master for war:

> And I said to Uncle Jacob
>   'Now old Mistus feels the sting.
> For this parting with your children
>   Is a mighty dreadful thing.'
>
> Mistus prayed up in the parlor
>   That the Secesh all might win;
> We were praying in the cabins,
>   Wanting freedom to begin.

Among the slaves, great rejoicing and praise of Lincoln greet the Yankee victory,

> But when old Mistus heard it,
>   She groaned and hardly spoke;
> When she had to lose her servants,
>   Her heart was almost broke.

Aunt Chloe chides the freedmen for selling their votes for three sticks of candy and gloats over the man who "sold out for flour and sugar; / The sugar was mixed with sand." But she is at last an optimist, admitting that most of the freedmen know "freedom cost too much" to be given away for profit or pleasure. In shorter sketches like **"Learning to Read,"** antagonism of the "Rebs" to the freedmen's progress is quietly but firmly overcome by trickery or hard work. The Aunt Chloe series is successful because a consistent, personalized language and references to everyday objects give authenticity to the subjects while directly communicating the freedmen's varying attitudes of self-mockery, growing self-respect, and optimism without sentimentality. Serious issues sketched with a light touch are rare in Mrs. Harper's work, and it is unfortunate that Aunt Chloe's fresh and lively observations were not enlarged.

Mrs. Harper wrote a great quantity of poetry during half a century, all of it in moments snatched from her public life as lecturer and reformer. Possibly *Moses* and *Sketches* were composed during her brief marriage, only four years out of eighty-seven that might be called leisure time. Her race protest and reform verse, combined with her lectures, were effective propaganda; she takes honors as well for the originality and harmony of poetic form and language in *Moses* and the innovative monologues of Aunt

Chloe. In short, Mrs. Harper's total output is the most valuable single poetic record we have of the mind and heart of the race whose fortunes shaped the tumultuous years of her career, 1850-1900.

Frances Smith Foster (essay date 1993)

SOURCE: "Doers of the Word, The Reconstruction Poetry of Frances Ellen Watkins Harper," in *Written By Herself: Literary Production by African American Women, 1746-1892*, Indiana University Press, 1993, pp. 131-53.

[*Foster is a noted literary historian in the area of African-American literature. She is the author of* Witnessing Slavery: The Development of the Antebellum Slave Narrative; *the editor of* A Brighter Coming Day: A Frances Ellen Watkins Reader *and* Minnie's Sacrifice; Sowing and Reaping; Trial and Triumph: Three Rediscovered Novels *by Frances E. W. Harper; and the coeditor of* The Oxford Companion to African-American Literature. *In the following excerpt, Foster describes the themes and poetic techniques that Harper used in the poetry she wrote during the Reconstruction Era. Foster points out the degree to which Harper makes statements applicable to contemporaneous issues of race and sex, incorporates her own experiences into her poetry, and adheres to the literary aesthetics of her contemporaries.*]

For African American writers the "quest for a usable past" had a special urgency. They knew that by confronting that past and its literary stereotypes, they could affect their present condition and help shape the American future. African American writers took it as their social responsibility as well as their literary right to revise history, report the present, and envision a future in which their people and their people's contributions and potentials would be fully appreciated. In terms of literary techniques, for example, this meant expanding their subjects, creating new characters, and experimenting with genre and style. Some chose to concentrate upon nonfiction and journalism. Others contributed to the American literary transformation by writing fiction and poetry that conveyed the attitudes and experiences of their people in ways more true to the ways in which those attitudes and experiences were expressed among themselves. Frances Ellen Watkins Harper chose to do both.

Harper was not a new literary voice. During the antebellum era, writing as Frances Ellen Watkins, she had produced numerous letters, essays, and poems as well as what is generally considered the first published short story by an African American. Harper's literary reputation had been greatly influenced by the popularity of particular poems such as **"The Slave Mother," "Eliza Harris,"** and **"Bury Me in a Free Land"**; by her own indefatigable efforts as an abolitionist; and by the general tendency to associate blacks and their literature with slavery. Her poems, though never exclusively devoted to topics of race or slavery, had been recognized as providing, along with the spirituals and the slave narratives, the most authentic rendition of the slave's point of view available to nineteenth-century readers.

Like Whittier, Stowe, Douglass, and many others of her time, Frances Harper based most of her writings upon incidents and themes which her readers could acknowledge as "real." She wrote of heroic historical figures, of pressing contemporary issues, and of timeless moral and philosophical ideals. For Harper, literature was one of the many tools necessary to create a better world. As an antislavery lecturer and a member of the Underground Railroad, she had covered thousands of miles carrying her messages of abolition, Free Produce, women's rights, and other reform issues to audiences throughout the free states. During her travels, Harper strategized with local and national leaders, interviewed fugitive and ex-slaves, and witnessed the conditions under which free women and men lived. With the money that her books and appearances generated, she further supported the causes to which she devoted her voice and pen. It was entirely in keeping with Harper's activist poetics that immediately after the War between the States had ended, she went to the South to determine what could be done to aid the freedpeople and to bind the nation's wounds.

From 1864 to 1871 Frances Harper crossed and recrossed the South, visiting every state but Arkansas and Texas, teaching and lecturing to Southern audiences and recording her impressions for Northern readers. The time that she spent in the deep South was a period of physical danger, intellectual challenge, and intense self-discovery. The poverty was beyond any she had previously experienced, but the hospitality, optimism, and hard work of most blacks and many whites surpassed her expectations. There Harper found "ignorance to be instructed; a race who needs to be helped up to higher planes of thought and action; and whether we are hindered or helped, we should try to be true to the commission God has written upon our souls." There Harper rededicated herself to her literature and her causes. On February 20, 1871, Harper wrote, "I am standing with my race on the threshold of a new era, and though some be far past me in the learning of the schools, yet today, with my limited and fragmentary knowledge, I may help the race forward a little."

The texts of most of Frances Harper's Reconstruction lectures are not available. Apparently she was too busy traveling and speaking to write them out. Some of her words were recorded by news reporters and a few lectures such as "The Colored Woman of America" were reprinted almost verbatim in periodicals. Other lecture titles, such as "The Mission of War," "The Work before Us," and "The Colored Man as Social and Political Force," suggest that her general themes were the same as those in her letters to William Still. It is these letters—some of which were published in Northern papers and others which Still included in his book, *The Underground Rail Road* (1871)— that most directly inform us of Harper's Reconstruction concerns.

Frances Harper generally developed two themes in her Reconstruction lectures. One was that the future of the nation depended upon the ability of its citizens to unite behind a common goal. She argued, "Between the white people and the colored there is a community of interests, and the sooner they find it out, the better it will be for both parties"; yet, Harper continued, "that community of interests does not consist in increasing the privileges of one class and curtailing the rights of the other, but in getting every citizen interested in the welfare, progress and durability of the state." Her other theme, and the one that increasingly dominated her published writings, was that the Emancipation had opened a new era—a time for blacks, particularly black women, to "lift up their heads and plant the roots of progress under the hearthstone."

The poems and letters that appeared in the press and the fact that the earliest existing text of *Moses: A Story of the Nile,* published in 1869, is marked as the second edition suggest that the indefatigable Mrs. Harper did continue to write during her Southern tour. However, we have no new collection of poems until fifteen years after *Poems on Miscellaneous Subjects* first appeared. Then in rapid succession, Frances Harper published three collections: *Moses: A Story of the Nile* (1869), *Poems* (1871), and *Sketches of Southern Life* (1872).

Frances Harper's activities and interests are more important to the subject of her Reconstruction poetry than simple biographical context alone. To Harper, literature was not separate from life. Her writing was but one of the ways in which she sought to live her convictions and to work for the betterment of the world within which she lived and the people with whom she identified. In her earliest extant prose piece, "Christianity" (ca. 1853), she enunciated her aesthetic convictions by saying that literature is an "elegance" achieved by toil of pen and labor of pencil. Its purpose is "to cultivate the intellect, enlighten the understanding, give scope to the imagination, and refine the sensibilities." But, she also admonished, it is important only to the extent that it inspires individuals to high and noble deeds. Over the years she reaffirmed this idea in several texts. For example, Jenny, Harper's fictive self in her **"Fancy Etchings"** series (1873), tells her Aunt Jane:

> Aunty I want to be a poet, to earn and take my place among the poets of the nineteenth century; but with all the glowing enthusiasms that light up my life I cannot help thinking, that more valuable than the soarings of genius are the tender nestlings of love. Genius may charm the intellect, but love will refresh the spirit.

Wanting to "earn and take [her] place among the poets of the nineteenth century" indicates a recognition of a tradition to be entered, a standard to be surpassed, a "genius" to be expressed. But personal satisfaction and public acclaim are secondary objectives. Jenny continues, "It is just because our lives are apt to be so hard and dry, that I would scatter the flowers of poetry around our paths; . . . I would teach men and women to love noble deeds by setting them to the music, of fitly spoken words."

Frances Harper's commitment to a pragmatic poetics did not exclude concern with literary techniques or experimentation with genre and style. It was during her travels throughout the war-torn South and as a part of her Reconstruction efforts that she created one of her most experimental texts. *Moses: A Story of the Nile* is transitional between the structure that Harper had used in poems such as **"Ruth and Naomi"** (1856) and **"The Two Offers"** (1859), and that she would use again in the novel *Iola Leroy* (1892). Each of these works begins, as does *Moses,* with a dialogue between two major characters that is interrupted by an omniscient narrator who describes or interprets for the reader. The first eight stanzas of *Moses* alternate between the words of Moses and his adopted mother, Charman. But here she prefaces these first stanzas with the name of the speaker and thereby frames the dialogue as dramatic scenes. She restages the life and times of the Jewish leader who led his people from slavery in seven hundred lines of blank verse. Her characters and the scenes she creates reenact the Bible story in ways that are obviously useful for the religious inspiration and instruction of women and children and, as such, entirely in keeping with notions of "women's literature" and "women's concerns." At the same time, in *Moses,* as in many other biblically and classically inspired poems by African American women, the central participants are women and the themes are applicable to the contemporary issues of race and sex.

Frances Harper revises the Old Testament story to make manifest its relevance in two major ways. First, she subordinates the unique circumstances of Moses's life and focuses instead upon the decision that he makes to sacrifice his immediate pleasures and privileges in order to help his race. Second, she gives the women larger, more active parts in the liberation story. The Old Testament mentions the women only in terms of their roles in preserving the infant's life and summarizes Moses' childhood by noting that "the child grew," was taken "unto the Pharoah's daughter, and he became her son" (Exod. 2:10). Frances Harper invents a childhood characterized by deep love and devotion between Moses and his two mothers. She presents these women as strong, intelligent, and morally courageous and suggests that Moses' heroism was nurtured by their examples.

The first part of *Moses* echoes Harper's earlier depictions of idealized motherhood and the grief of separation in poems such as **"Eliza Harris"** and **"A Mother's Heroism,"** **"The Slave Mother"** and **"The Slave Auction."** She emphasizes the separation theme by entitling the first section **"The Parting."** Her opening scene depicts the conversation between adoptive mother and son. Moses's salutation emphasizes Charmian's high rank, goodness, and generosity as well as his personal esteem for her:

> Kind and gracious princess, more than friend,
> I've come to thank thee for thy goodness,
> And to breathe into thy generous ears
> My last and sad farewell. . . .

Despite his personal attachment to her, he can no longer live "in pleasure" in her household while his people "faint in pain." Charmian, on the other hand, calls him "my son"

and tries to dissuade him from a decision that she believes will make his life less comfortable and his future less secure. Charmian, as we learn from her argument, is a noble and loving woman who defied the law and braved her father's wrath to save the infant Moses' life. She succeeded because of her steadfast determination to protect with her own the life of that child. As her narrative indicates, Charmian has inherited this strength and courage from her own mother and it is this resemblance to his beloved wife that vanquishes her father's anger and resolve. The Pharoah's words are quoted by Charmian to Moses:

> Charmian, arise,
> Thy prayer is granted; just then thy dead mother
> Came to thine eyes, and the light of Asenath
> Broke over thy face. Asenath was the light
> Of my home; the star that faded out too
> Suddenly from my dwelling, and left my life
> To darkness, grief and pain, and for her sake,
> Not thine, I'll spare the child.

Harper shows that although Charmian is not Moses' biological mother and is, in fact, of another "race," she sincerely and unequivocally loves Moses as her son. She has rescued him from drowning in the Nile and from the death decree of her father, the Pharoah, and this, she declares, makes him

> Doubly mine; as such I claimed thee then, as such
> I claim thee now. I've nursed no other child
> Upon my knee, and pressed upon no other
> Lips the sweetest kisses of my love. . . .

Moses is fond of Charmian, but he would not forswear his race in order to live with her. During their conversation, Charmian recognizes in Moses a nobility, courage, and self-sacrifice that surpasses her own, and before "the grandeur of the young man's choice, / . . . she bowed / Her queenly head and let him pass." In Frances Harper's version of the Old Testament story, Charmian, the foster mother of Moses, claims as much, if not more, of the reader's sympathies as does her son, the ostensible protagonist. Charmian's was a claim and a devotion that Moses recognized and to which he responded. However, Moses could not accept an individual freedom while others of his race were excluded from similar experiences. He chose the greater needs of his race over the smaller pleasures of his personal affinities. This dilemma is one that Harper pursues from a slightly different perspective later in her novel, *Iola Leroy.* Then Iola, Henry, and Dr. Latimer all repeat, in almost the same words, Moses' decision to reject the offers of "adoption" into the dominant society and to "share the futures of my race."

Harper again enhances the role of women and, in this instance, privileges women's writing with the insertion of a poem she calls **"Miriam's Song."** In the Old Testament after the crossing of the Red Sea, "Moses and the children of Israel" sang a song of victory and thanksgiving that detailed the destruction of the enemy and celebrated a God who evoked "fear and dread." Moses' song gets nineteen verses, then in one quick mention, we learn that Miriam, "the prophetess, the sister of Aaron" led the women in dancing and singing Moses' song (Exod. 15:1-21). Miriam was sister to both Aaron and Moses, and Harper chooses to identify her not with Aaron but with Moses, the heroic leader. Harper increases the halo effect created by Miriam's close kinship with the heroic leader by describing Miriam's great joy and having Miriam "live the past again" as she reviews her role in protecting and nurturing Moses. As in the biblical version, Miriam leads the women in music, dance, and songs of celebration, but in Harper's account, **"Miriam's Song"** is not the repetition of a refrain from Moses' song. It is "another song of triumph" that is heard to rise over the first song and to change both the tune and the tenor of the occasion. Instead of celebrating the details of destruction, **"Miriam's Song"** contrasts the past with the present and emphasizes the Passover when "Egypt wakes up with a shriek and a sob / To mourn for her first-born and dead." In *Moses: A Story of the Nile,* women have been crucial actors in bringing this moment to pass and a woman now becomes its poet and historian. Harper emphasizes Miriam's perspective by setting the song apart from the rest of the text and presenting it as a separate poem with its own distinctive rhythm and rhyme patterns. **"Miriam's Song"** interrupts the narrative, it identifies individual ambition and pride as increasing the suffering of an entire nation, and it illustrates two of Harper's themes, the pain and grief of divided families and the opportunity for each individual to assist in the eventual triumph of good over evil. In focusing upon Miriam and her song, Harper implicitly makes a case for women's active participation in politics and she gives a biblical precedent for women as poets and social analysts.

In her characterization of Moses' mother, Frances Harper merges feminist and racial themes. It was the mother's ancestral stories that gave Moses his strong identification with his race. In vivid imagery Harper depicts the scene of the young children, gathered, fascinated and inspired, around the woman as she related what Moses calls "the grand traditions of our race that float, / With all their weird and solemn beauty, around / Our wrecked and blighted fortunes." It was his mother, Moses asserts, who instilled in her children their hope of freedom and their understanding of the necessity of their faith and obedience to God's will as conditions of that moment when ". . . the God our fathers loved and worshiped, / Would break our chains, and bring to us a great / Deliverance."

In *Moses: A Story of the Nile* Frances Harper creates an allegorical piece from Judeo-Christian mythology that reinterprets the roles of women and women's stories but does so in a distinctively African American manner. The subtitle, **"A Story of the Nile,"** suggests, for example, the whole of Africa and not simply the small area indicated by "Egypt." It also shifts the focus from the hero to the situation, thus implying that the story is larger than that of one individual, one family, or even one nation. Just as Phillis Wheatley did with "Goliath of Gath" nearly a hundred years earlier, with *Moses* Frances Harper chose a subject and emphasized details that invite comparisons with the conditions of African American people. Were there more texts by African American women writers available, I might be able to chronicle a continuous progression from Wheatley to Harper. As it stands, I can assert that the literary model did exist and that in *Moses,* as with her other biblically and classically inspired poems, Frances Harper claimed her legacy by asserting the contemporaneousness of history and its applicability to issues of race and sex.

The roots of *Moses* grew not only from the African American women's literary tradition, but also from the more general folk culture. As Kenny Williams points out [in *They Also Spoke: An Essay on Negro Literature in America,* 1970], Harper's *Moses* is her "most ambitious and her most symbolic work. . . . it never mentions the Negro's position in America nor the problems which immediately occurred as a result of the Emancipation Proclamation; yet it is quite obvious that the poem is an attempt to use the story of Moses very much as the poets of the spirituals had done in order to emphasize the need for a racial leader." Williams's suggestion that *Moses* is a symbolic work in the tradition of "the poets of the spirituals" is insightful and is easily corroborated by many elements of Harper's poetry. Perhaps the most obvious is the Moses motif, itself, a staple in African American cultural, as it was in Harper's personal mythology. Spirituals such as "Go Down, Moses," "On the Rock Where Moses Stood," "Deep River," and "Steal Away" emphasize the liberation, escape, and vindication themes that her own *Moses* echoes. And Harper's emphasis upon the attitudes and roles of women find precursors in such ancestral songs as "Mary, Don't You Weep" as it conflates the Old and New Testament mythologies and invites the woman to take courage from her knowledge of similar moments in history.

However, we find other possible sources for themes and images in Harper's poem in the African American secular folk tradition. For example, Harper's characterization of Moses' mother as not only the culture bearer but also the nurturer of resistance resembles similar imagery in songs such as "De Ole Nigger Driver." In this piece, the narrator recalls his mother's teachings about the oppression of his people and the sources of that oppression when he says,

> Fust ting my mammy tell me,
>   O, gwine away!
> Tell me 'bout de nigger driver,
>   O, gwine away!
> Nigger driver second devil,
>   O, gwine away!

And, as Moses did with the Egyptian overseer, the narrator decides

> Best ting for do he driver,
>   O, gwine away!
> Snock he down and spoil he labor,
>   O, gwine away!

In African American folklore, the Moses figure was well established as a literal and symbolic device. Harper's

Moses is the liberator of both the Old Testament and of the spirituals. Moreover, Moses in African American folk culture is androgynous. Moses is also Harriet Tubman, the African American woman of the antebellum Underground Railroad. Tubman, like Moses, had escaped the fate of her enslaved people. And, like Moses, Tubman refused to bask in the luxury of her individual freedom while her people remained enslaved. Moses symbolized the sacrificing of personal gain, the risking of personal safety for the good of one's people. In a speech at the Eleventh Woman's Rights Convention on May 10, 1866, Harper explicitly identified Harriet Tubman with the Old Testament Moses when she said: "We have a woman in our country who has received the name of 'Moses,' . . . —a woman who has gone down into the Egypt of slavery and brought out hundreds of our people into liberty."

In referring the overwhelmingly white Protestant delegates to the Eleventh Woman's Rights Convention to the Jewish Moses and the black Harriet Tubman, Frances Harper was mediating between cultures. She was reminding them that the Old Testament stories directly condemned racial oppression and she was requiring them to absorb African American symbology into their frames of reference. Harper's poem, then, resonates with multiple allusions and would have sparked interest and identification with a variety of readers ranging from the newly literate to the more experienced and well educated. Several news accounts indicate that Harper recited *Moses: A Story of the Nile* to "large and delighted" audiences. While these reporters do not indicate their personal awareness that the poem had any particular relevance to current issues, on at least one occasion Frances Harper explicitly identified its contemporary application. During the Woman's Rights Convention, after identifying Harriet Tubman as a Moses, Harper expanded the definition of those needing to be saved to include not just black slaves but also white women of leisure. Harper said:

> While there exists this brutal element in society which tramples upon the feeble and treads down the weak, I tell you that if there is any class of people who need to be lifted out of their airy nothings and selfishness, it is the white women of America.

Her words echo those that Harriet Jacobs used as an epigraph to *Incidents in the Life of a Slave Girl* when she quoted Isaiah's warning to the "careless daughters."

Moses: A Story of the Nile is a Reconstruction poem in other ways. To the antebellum symbolism of a black Moses, Harriet Tubman, Frances Harper added a second, modern day Moses. Harper, like many other nineteenth-century blacks, called Abraham Lincoln "Moses." In a letter to William Still dated April 19, 1869, Harper writes:

> Moses, the meekest man on earth, led the children of Israel over the Red Sea, but was not permitted to see them settled in Canaan. Mr. Lincoln had led up through another Red Sea to the table land of a triumphant victory, and God has seen fit to summon for a new era

another man. It is ours then to bow to the Chastener and let our honored and loved Chieftain go [quoted in *The Underground Railroad*].

Postbellum readers would recognize **Moses: A Story of the Nile** as a call to all citizens of the United States to choose the larger social good over their own personal gain. The African American oral tradition had long since established Egyptian bondage as a metaphor for American slavery and the abolitionist movement had taught many whites to recognize this. Therefore, **Moses** as a symbolic retelling of African American history would be clear to many. At the same time, this poem would not unduly disturb those readers who wished to concentrate upon the building of a united nation and ignore its past mistakes. Moral decisions that faced the reunited states also included the proper relationship between individual aspirations and community responsibilities. If the term, "the Gilded Age," had not yet been applied, the manifestations of such an era were fast becoming evident. As the story of an individual who renounced material success, identified with the downtrodden, and accepted the tasks assigned him by his God, Moses could also serve as a model for American society at large.

As a writer who saw her art as means of educating and uplifting, Harper was careful to choose figures who were familiar to and instructive for the greatest number of readers. As a teacher, she recognized the inclusiveness of the Moses symbol that made it effective as a text in day and Sabbath schools. In focusing her first major postbellum work upon a figure as well established in African American folk culture as Moses, Frances Harper increased the significance of her poem for African American readers. However, her message was one of renewal and rededication for all people of good will. It made it easier to see, for example, the work of the Freedmen's Bureau and the American Missionary Society as enacting contemporary versions of the biblical story. The teachers, nurses, and social workers who left their homes and loved ones to join the survivors in the devastated South could identify with Moses, as individuals who answered God's call to prepare a way out of the wilderness into the Promised Land.

In 1871, Frances Harper published **Poems,** her second Reconstruction volume. It does not obviously continue the Reconstruction themes and the bold experimentation with form of **Moses: A Story of the Nile,** but presents a number of poems that in style, theme, and subject echo those of her antebellum best-seller, **Poems on Miscellaneous Subjects.** Since many of the selections in **Poems** had been published separately before and during the war, it might seem more fitting to consider this work as a miscellaneous collection rather than a sustained new work. However, in his essay "The South in African American Literature: 1877-1915," Dickson D. Bruce, Jr., makes a point worth heeding here. Bruce notes that post-Reconstruction black poets organized their books with "easily recognizable structural principles" designed to appeal to a diverse readership [*CLA Journal,* Vol. 31, 1987]. To understand the poet's intention, one must consider the effect of the entire volume, the order of its poems and its dominant tone, as well as the themes and subjects of individual poems. While Bruce's concern is with a slightly later group of writers, his idea holds true for Harper as well. In fact, since Harper was a precursor to and model for those writers and since she exercised great authority over the composition of her books, indeed published and distributed most of them herself, it is altogether reasonable to suggest that Harper's *Poems* may have set the pattern that Bruce finds common during the period of his study.

The individual works in *Poems* generally focus on three subjects: motherhood, death, and public celebration. Though these are not new subjects for Harper, her Reconstruction social and artistic ideals inspired modifications and additions, especially in tone and theme. For example, in *Poems* she writes about infants and children not as objects of pathos but as sources of love and faith. As in her earlier volumes, Harper still idealizes motherhood, but to the fugitive mother running with infant in arms and to the sorrowful slave mother being auctioned away from her child she adds a new figure, a mother who says, "Hope and joy, peace and blessing, / Met me in my firstborn child."

Many of the death poems in this volume also focus upon divided families, especially those created by dying mothers or children. Again, however, Harper modifies her antebellum images. Rather than the kinds of poems that appeared in her antebellum collection, **"The Slave Mother"** grieving over her imminent parting with her child or even the central figure in **"The Slave Mother, a Tale of Ohio"** choosing to kill her infant rather than see it return to slavery, this volume offers other, less tragic separations. **"The Dying Mother"** with her last words blesses her children, comforted by the knowledge that her husband and family remain together, that God will watch over them, and that they will be united in "the brighter world above." From the horrific and unnatural experiences that slavery created, Harper's poems now turn to the redemptive suffering of divinely ordained separations.

The new poems about children, the death poems, and the celebratory poems of public experiences such as **"The Fifteenth Amendment," "Lines to Miles O'Reilly,"** and **"President Lincoln's Proclamation of Freedom"** establish a Reconstructive ideal, that of heroic effort, sacrifice, and courage rewarded or continued through new life.

Poems has about twice as many death poems as did Harper's earlier collection. In her introduction to *The Complete Poems of Frances Ellen Watkins Harper,* Maryemma Graham suggests that this may be a response to Frances Harper's own fragile health and to her husband's death in 1864, less than a decade before. It is quite likely that personal grief was a factor. Furthermore, such an autobiographical perspective also suggests reasons for the unusually high number of pieces that celebrate infants and children. When *Poems on Miscellaneous Subjects* appeared in 1854, its author was a single woman. During her brief marriage to Fenton Harper, Frances Harper had become mother to Mary and stepmother to her widowed spouse's three children. This could account for works such as **"To a Babe Smiling in Her Sleep," "The Mother's Bless-**

ing," and **"Thank God for Little Children."** Reading the poems from an autobiographical perspective enhances their meaning in the context of the total volume.

In general, *Poems* strikes a more mature, contemplative, but hopeful tone than the earlier collection. This shift undoubtedly reflects Harper's personal experiences, but it also mirrors the Reconstructive social spirit with which Harper aligned herself. And this perspective, I believe, is more in keeping with the relationship Harper maintains between her life and her art. Since the early days when she dedicated her life to public service, Frances Harper did not usually allow her private life to diverge from her public stance. Her literature is remarkably formal in that it does not divulge her own feelings or allude to her own life except, as in the example of her being ousted from the Philadelphia streetcars or in her letters from the South to abolitonist friends and the reading public, when her experiences illustrated larger social themes. From this perspective, the more general sorrow over the deaths of countless soldiers and of Abraham Lincoln which Harper shared with her readers was as important as Harper's own motherhood and widowhood in shaping the new emphases upon life and death in this volume.

Poems concludes with **"Light in Darkness,"** a work that can be read as representative of the collection and of the hopeful period within which it was published. In the heavily iambic rhythm and ABCB-rhymed stanzas that typify other poems in this collection, the narrator of "Light in Darkness" declares that even though "We've" lost much due to mistakes and bad choices, and we have been punished for our sins, there is, nonetheless, "room to build holy altars / Where our crumbling idols lay." The poem suggests that the loss of material goods and the assault upon their spirits are actually gifts for which "the chastening angel" might be thanked because from the "shadows" of their suffering they could more clearly see "the light and beautiful visions." The poem becomes a metaphor for the experiences of the Civil War period. In the concluding stanza, the narrator credits poetry for making survival easier and foreshadows the words of Jenny in **"Fancy Etchings"** some five years later:

> Our first view of the Holy City
>   Came through our darken'd years,
> The songs that lightened our sorrows,
>   We heard 'mid our night of tears.

Frances Harper's third Reconstruction volume, *Sketches of Southern Life,* was published in 1872. It is a small volume of poetry—only nine poems—but its small size belies its great significance. *Sketches* summarizes Frances Harper's earlier themes and anticipates her later writings. It is a true benchmark in her own poetic career and a touchstone for African American literature. *Sketches* combines the themes of *Moses* and of *Poems* while returning to the stylistic experimentation of the earlier work. *Sketches* continues Harper's earlier emphasis on female characters and their perspectives, explores further possibilities concerning civil rights, social responsibilities, and spiritual progress, and it initiates a bold new direction in African

American poetics. As Maryemma Graham concludes, *"Sketches of Southern Life,* . . . shows a mature poet at her best. It is both a culmination of the formal structure Harper had used in her earliest poetry and an incorporation of a vernacular mode."

Sketches echoes the dramatic narrative technique with which Harper was experimenting in *Moses* and earlier works. In fact, as Graham indicates, *Moses* and *Sketches* "may be seen as complementary texts. For Harper, they represent an intellectual exploration into the meaning and nature of freedom. Taken together they form an important link in the evolution of the quest or journey motif in African American autobiographical, poetic and fictional discourse." While the biblical sources, the theme, the characterizations, and even the structure of *Moses* bear some resemblance to earlier writing, equally important are the ways in which that text reflects Harper's Reconstruction ideas and anticipates *Sketches of Southern Life,* a work that consciously and clearly incorporates elements of African American folk culture and was intended to contribute to the Reconstruction of American literature.

Sketches of Southern Life articulates Frances Harper's basic Reconstruction theme that the future of the nation depended upon the ability of its citizens to unite behind a common goal. Poems such as **"Learning to Read"** and **"Church Building"** promote community effort in establishing the institutions whereby individuals may reach their highest development. Finally, *Sketches* anticipates Harper's later work. Many of its ideas, situations, characters, and techniques reappear and are reworked in later poems such as **"Dialogue on Women's Rights"** and in her novel, *Iola Leroy.*

The remainder of my discussion of the Reconstruction poetry of Frances E. W. Harper will center on *Sketches* as I seek to demonstrate three ideas which basically apply to all three books: (1) Frances Harper wrote as a popular poet with a clear sense of the aesthetics and concerns of popular literature. (2) She did not limit herself to simply imitating the popular poetry of the day but instead experimented with form, character, and language. (3) *Sketches,* like Harper's other collections, not only shares characteristics with nineteenth-century American popular literature in general, but represents the literature of other African American women writers of that era.

Sketches of Southern Life begins with a poem of appreciation to **"Our English Friends"** for their support of the American anti-slavery struggle. It includes several poems told by one persona, Aunt Chloe, and it concludes with two poems titled respectively, **"I Thirst"** and **"The Dying Queen."**

The first poem, dedicated to **"Our English Friends,"** acknowledges the international readership that Harper anticipated for this volume. From the earliest extant published book by an African in the American colonies through the slave narratives, the earliest novels by African Americans, and up to Harper's own time, England had provided an enthusiastic reception for African American literature.

Moreover, during the antebellum period, British abolitionists had worked to block an effort to enlist England in support of the Confederacy and Harper, of course, was well aware of this. There was an important difference, however, between this poem and antebellum works, such as William and Ellen Craft's narrative, that heralded the British as the antithesis of Americans, as those who proclaimed a monarchy but offered freedom while those who spoke of democracy deliberately maintained slavery. **"Our English Friends"** does not play up the irony of an Old World monarchy that nurtured democratic movements more fervently than the New World republic which had declared its independence in pursuit of equal rights for all. The slave era is portrayed, instead, as a time of mortal affliction, when "Slavery full of wrath and strife, / Was clutching at the Nation's life." The brave Britons had reached out to this nation in its "hour of need," and the poet, on behalf of the country itself, thanks them for their nobility and courage, for putting their love of freedom ahead of "paltry gain," for encouraging and supporting the winning cause. In speaking not as a member of a freed race but as a citizen of a revived country, the narrator aligns herself and the freedpeople with the best elements of United States society, those individuals who had recognized the peril and righteously fought to overcome it.

The title of the penultimate poem, **"'I Thirst,'"** evokes the Crucifixion as related in John 19:28-30 when Jesus said "I thirst," drank the vinegar, and died. In this way, biblical scholars tell us, Jesus fulfilled the final prophecy and his mission was completed. He was allowed to die. As she had done in *Moses,* Harper writes this as a drama which she embellishes with the details that suit her immediate goals. **"'I Thirst'"** is a dialogue between two voices, one longs for death to end earthly suffering and the second rebukes that longing. The second voice reminds the first that death is God's decision as to when human work has ended and that until God had determined that they had fulfilled their obligations, each individual must rely upon the "living fount" within for renewal of strength and restoration of faith.

The final poem, **"The Dying Queen"** recounts the last moments of a woman who chooses to die as she had lived, with her eyes wide open. The epigraph of this poem is "I would meet death awake." Although the resolution is different, the words echo those of Cleopatra, the African Queen, who also had "met the battle's shock, / And born the cares of state." Both Harper's and Shakespeare's dying queens reject the death scene urged upon them by friends and dictate their own terms upon which they would meet death.

"Our English Friends," "'I Thirst,'" and **"The Dying Queen"** frame the series of poems that obviously inspired the volume's title. This structure, which defines the context within which the Aunt Chloe narratives will be read, anticipates similar strategies by writers such as Joel Chandler Harris, Charles Chesnutt, Thomas Nelson Page, and Octavia Albert. The first and the last two poems in the volume not only separate the "Aunt Chloe" section but their tone and narrative personae establish a relational distance wherein the writer and the personae in the framing poems stand closer to the reader as they all become the audience for the world being depicted in the middle section. Such a relationship allows greater freedom in the Aunt Chloe series to sketch with all its peculiarities and without omitting the abuse and pain of her slave experiences, a history that is both individual and social but a history not intended to implicate all readers. The framing poems "balance" the volume and mediate between the Aunt Chloe voice and that of the book as a whole. At the same time that it balances, the volume also privileges Aunt Chloe's voice. Since two-thirds of the poems and the title itself relate to Aunt Chloe and her friends, the variety within the remaining three poems emphasizes the priority of that single subject.

The "Aunt Chloe" poems form at once an autobiography of an ex-slave woman and a history of slavery and Reconstruction as narrated by that woman. Whereas Harper's antebellum poetry often told stories about slaves, in these poems a slave speaks for herself. Aunt Chloe is the voice of the slave mother, heretofore only seen from a distance, now being heard and understood from her own perspective.

The opening poem, which serves as the exposition to the overall saga, is a revised slave narrative. The Civil War and the constitutional amendments that followed it had made the proclamation of humanity less an issue than the quality of character that these new citizens possessed. Thus Harper's narrator did not need to begin with "I was born" and other attestations of being. Like Elizabeth Keckley, Harper assumed the task of demonstrating the potential of newly freed slaves to become responsible and contributing citizens. Chloe, like Elizabeth, concentrates on the incidents that molded her character. Chloe begins with her separation from her children. As in many slave narratives, their sale was not a deliberately punitive action in response to any inadequacy or guilt of the enslaved, but the result of the insolvency that the master's death exposed.

As Keckley had implied in her work, white women were also victimized by slave economics. When Aunt Chloe heard that her children had been sold, her first impulse was to ask her mistress to intercede. She undoubtedly knew that the widowed woman had no legal power, but she quickly learned that the news of her insolvency had reduced her mistress to tears and that she was emotionally incapable of helping Chloe with her crisis. Here, Harper reverses the situation in much abolitionist literature. Instead of an Angelina Grimke or a Lydia Maria Child or any other white woman describing the sufferings of black women, the ex-slave woman is the one who reports the sufferings of white females in the antebellum South.

The poem is not about the plight of women, however. It is about a particular group of women, American slave women as represented by Aunt Chloe. Chloe is a part of a community. Her fellow slaves warn her of the impending sale, they sympathize with her in her grief, and they rejoice with her in their freedom. Their stories are used to supplement Chloe's personal experiences and to provide a context within which the protagonist can be better understood.

Aunt Chloe identifies her feelings when her children were sold away, suggests that the slaves had a mutual support system, and describes the development of the faith that allowed her to survive that separation. When her fellow slaves whispered to her that her children had been sold, Chloe says:

> It seemed as if a bullet
> > Had shot me through and through,
> And I felt as if my heart-strings
> > Was breaking right in two.

The importance of the slave community to Chloe's survival stands in stark contrast to accounts in the slave narratives by men, whose protagonists were usually alienated from mothers, friends, or support systems; they were, in Phillis Klotman's words, "running men." However, Frances Harper's depiction is quite in keeping with the accounts by slave women discussed earlier. As was the case with Harriet Jacobs, the women sympathized with and supported one another; and as with Jacobs, the protagonist prefers to remain within the community. She leaves only to insure the safety and survival of herself and her family.

The second poem, **"Deliverance,"** is a sixty-stanza history of Chloe's life from the sale of her children until the present telling. Chloe's frequent use of the first-person plural encourages the reader to see her experiences as representative of those of other slaves as well. The poem's three subplots exemplify the themes of retribution, release, and responsibility. Retribution, or the "justice in the kingdom," ultimately comes after liberation, but it is also manifested in the reversals that the slaves witness during slavery. For example, Aunt Chloe, whose sons have been sold from her, sees her mistress lose her son to war. In a scene ironically reminiscent of the parting between Moses and Charmian, Mister Tom chose his higher calling (i.e., joining the Confederate forces) over the tearful entreaties of his loving mother who would keep him safe at home. Chloe's acknowledgment of the woman's suffering may well have been the attitude of Moses' mother toward Charmian's grief. Chloe says, "'Now, old Mistus feels the sting, / For this parting with your children / Is a mighty dreadful thing.'" But as certainly as Moses' mother was not overly troubled by the Egyptian princess's loss, Chloe recognizes her mistress's suffering without misunderstanding the differences in their circumstances. Though the grief of separation is a "mighty dreadful thing," the "now" and the "old" that describe "Mistus" suggest the satisfaction of retribution realized.

In telling the story of the slaves' release from bondage, Harper focuses on the liberator more than on any active participation of the liberated. Like the children of Israel during the plagues and the Passover, the slaves "were praying in the cabins, wanting freedom to begin" while a noble and courageous individual carried out the liberation. In **"Deliverance,"** not only does Harper identify

Abraham Lincoln as the Moses figure but she implies that he is a second Christ. When the news comes that the South has been defeated, the former slaves "just poured our prayers and blessings / Upon his [Lincoln's] precious head." Their jubilation brings to mind the scene in *Moses* after the Red Sea has destroyed the pursuing army. Like the Israelites, the slaves just "laughed, and danced, and shouted, / And prayed, and sang, and cried." Lincoln's assassination was "one awful sorrow," one that aroused an immediate desire for someone else to "be the Moses of all the colored race." However, the emancipated people must learn that with freedom comes great responsibilities, and the subsequent poems demonstrate that the freed slaves, like the children of Israel, could not rely upon Moses to bring them to the promised land.

This third theme, responsibility, supplements the acclamation of a divinely inspired liberator with attention to the subsequently important roles of the liberated. Leaders can open the way, but the journey is ultimately made by the followers. The poem rejects the subordination of one to the other and suggests that those who follow might at some point need to lead. It does assert the necessity of each doing what one can. The final section of **"Deliverance"** concentrates upon the importance of intelligent suffrage and the roles that women can play to insure clean politics even when disenfranchised. By listing several cases wherein men misused their votes and by contrasting their stupidity with the strong and corrective actions of their wives, Harper demonstrates that lack of political rights is not necessarily lack of power and that enfranchisement based solely upon gender is incorrect and dangerous to the country's reconstruction.

The final stanza makes the lesson of **"Deliverance"** clear. Though there are still too many who don't know the facts and obligations of their liberation and though liberation, especially that of women, has not been complete, it is vital to "rally round the cause"—for each individual must recognize that

> . . . their freedom cost too much
> Of blood and pain and treasure,
> For them to fool away their votes
> For profit or for pleasure.

"Aunt Chloe's Politics," "Learning to Read," and **"Church Building"** are shorter poems that elaborate on the three issues that Harper believed would make a reconstructed nation strong: equal rights, education, and spirituality. The final poem of the sequence, **"The Reunion,"** serves as the narrative denouement. It completes the circle by moving from Chloe's communal experiences back to her more personal story. The social achievements of learning to read, participating in community development, and acquiring her own property are most satisfying when shared with loved ones. The promise of reunification contained in the first poem fulfilled, this postbellum slave narrative closes with the vision of a unified family in a home "that will hold us all." Reunited with her children and now a proud grandmother, the slave, Aunt Chloe, has become "Mrs. Chloe Fleet," woman and citizen.

To Frances Harper, as to many nineteenth-century writers, "songs for the people" should be "sweet anthems of love and duty," and her desire was to inspire that "deeper sense of justice and humanity" in as many people as she could. Like nineteenth-century women, particularly, Frances Harper resisted the trend toward secular materialism and wrote with a firm grounding in militant Christianity. Such literary goals were shared by nineteenth-century American readers. They expected their literature to record, argue, or exhort, to point out the lessons in their everyday experiences, to be a weapon with which to defend good, to expose hypocrisy, and to abolish evil. However, readers in the mid-nineteenth century were by and large, as Roy Harvey Pearce states [in *The Continuity of American Poetry,* 1971], "literate but not literary, thinking but not thoughtful, caught up in the exhilarating busyness of day-to-day life." Therefore, as Pearce concludes, "the rule was this: that the poet who would reach the great audience had, willy-nilly, to cut himself down to its size. Such a cutting down . . . implies also the production of an art in some respects different in kind from high art, and to be judged and valued accordingly." The privileging of utility over pleasure and of inclusiveness over exclusivity not only required a particular kind of writing but it encouraged the merging of oral and written forms.

One way in which Harper achieved this—incorporating folk symbology into her writing—has already been discussed. Another method is that described by Pearce. Harper adapted her writing to the "great audience" and created popular art. Not only did she intend her work to be printed, but like Dickens, Twain, and others, Frances Harper gave public readings that were exceptionally well received. It could be said of her poetry as Theodore Parker said of Emerson's works, that they were "published before they were printed; delivered by word of mouth to various audiences." From her presentations, if from nothing else, Frances Harper knew that nineteenth-century readers preferred poems with rhythms and rhymes that were easy to memorize and to recite. Other requirements for popular poetry included familiar verse forms such as the sonnet and the ballad, simple and didactic metaphors, and readily comprehensible and prosaic word order. When one recognizes this, then the fact that Harper's poetry often sounds better in recitation than it scans may be attributed to factors other than what later critics decided were errors in her construction of meter.

Frances Harper was also adhering to aesthetics of postbellum popular literature in writing literature that was designed to appeal to a broad spectrum of American society. Frances Harper was herself a radical civil rights activist, who had a clear-eyed and realistic perspective of difficulties: particularly of the poverty, the abuse, and the devastation that permeated the postbellum South. However, Harper chose to mitigate with humor the misery of slavery and the atrocities of Reconstruction and to emphasize themes of progress, unity, and determination. For example, in **"Deliverance,"** the key poem of *Sketches.* Harper devotes four stanzas to the disappointment of the Johnson era, but she treats it ultimately as merely an aggravating interruption of the nation's progress:

> But everything will pass away—
>   He went like time and tide—
> And when the next election came
>   They let poor Andy slide
>
> But now we have a President,
>   And if I was a man
> I'd vote for him for breaking up
>   The wicked Ku-Klux Klan.

The rhythm is lively and light, but within these lines, Harper acknowledges the unwillingness of Andrew Johnson to support Reconstruction efforts, the failure of the country to allow women to vote, and the existence of the Ku Klux Klan. Her audience may well have noticed her gentle derision in referring to the former president as "poor Andy," especially when contrasted to her consistent references to Abraham Lincoln as "Mister Lincoln" and to the next line which says "But now we have a President." In other writings of the same period Harper does not treat the vicious Ku Klux Klan so gently, but in this poem her use of the term "wicked" deflects the controversy that more forceful adjectives would have engendered.

Certainly her colleagues in the suffrage movement would appreciate the irony of Aunt Chloe, the narrator who is competent to recite history but not to vote; the contrast in **"Deliverance"** between the men who sold their votes for three sticks of candy or for white sand topped with sugar and their wives who brought them back in line; and the declaration that despite their inability to vote, "we women radicals" had nonetheless defeated Curnel Johnson's election efforts. These are all obviously critical statements. Yet they are made with wit and humor and with the clear implication that things are getting better, thereby encouraging the assent of less radical but politically important readers.

As she did in **Moses,** Harper chooses characters that a wide and diverse group would recognize but with which the freed slaves would be particularly familiar. For example, there is a biblical precursor to Aunt Chloe that strengthens the poem's applicability to the Reconstruction era. In the New Testament, Paul's first letter to the Church at Corinth came during a time when various groups were trying to establish their own places within the emerging Christian society. The Corinthian congregation included a woman named Chloe. Paul's letter came in response to information from Chloe's people about certain factions; he was writing to revive their unity and to assure that each individual was accorded proper respect. Readers who associated the New Testament Chloe with Harper's would recognize similarities in the current American situation and that of Corinth. They would remember that Paul began his letter by asserting Christian equality. The Corinthians were "called to take their place among all the saints everywhere who pray to our Lord Jesus Christ; for he is their Lord no less than ours" (1 Cor. 1:2). Readers could even have compared Paul's literary aesthetic and Harp-

er's, for Paul, too, wrote "not with any show of oratory or philosophy, but simply to tell you what God has guaranteed" (1 Cor. 2:1).

A second connection that would have been made by nineteenth-century readers is that between Frances Harper's Aunt Chloe and Harriet Beecher Stowe's. Both Harper and Stowe based their characters on cultural types. In the *Key to Uncle Tom's Cabin,* Stowe argued that she drew upon personal accounts and contemporary literature for her people and incidents. But while the mammy figure may have been a part of contemporary literature or even of African American culture, Stowe's Aunt Chloe was a caricature. As Trudier Harris explains in *Mammies and Militants,* the Southern mammy figure had begun as a complex literary rendition of a type, but quickly began to degenerate. Harris says:

> Mammy's self-respect was lost in groveling before and fawning upon her mistress, master, and young white charges. Her loyalty became self-effacement and her affection anticipated the exaggeration of the minstrel tradition. Her piety and patience worked more often than not in favor of the whites, and her tyranny was most ruthless when it was exercised over other Blacks.

Harriet Beecher Stowe's *Uncle Tom's Cabin* was one of the early examples of this, and Frances Harper's Aunt Chloe was an early African American response. Harper's own familiarity with Harriet Stowe's work is well established. In the 1850s, she had written a poem **"To Mrs. Harriet Beecher Stowe"** that praised Stowe's abolitionist efforts, and she had based at least two earlier poems, **"Eliza Harris"** and **"Eva's Farewell,"** upon characters from *Uncle Tom's Cabin.* Perhaps Harper did not take on Stowe's depiction of the mammy earlier because she did not wish to lessen the abolitionist value of the novel, or perhaps at that time Frances Harper herself, a freeborn, middle-class black woman, was not sufficiently knowledgeable about slave women of the rural South. But as her letters document, Harper's postwar experiences in the South gave her a new appreciation of and respect for these women. And her postbellum resolve, which was shared by most African Americans, to become even more aggressive in articulating African American realities from the perspective of African Americans gave a new urgency and new direction to her feminist concerns. Thus, it is not entirely coincidental that the experiences and attitudes of Harper's Aunt Chloe revise several of those of Stowe's character.

Several critics have recognized Harper's experimentation with language in **Sketches.** J. Saunders Redding, for example, notes that "In all her verse [Harper] attempted to suit her language to her theme. In **Moses** she gives her language a certain solemnity and elevation of tone. In her pieces on slavery she employs short, teethy, angry monosyllables. Her use of dialectal patterns [in **Sketches**] was no accident." While a few critics have misjudged Harper's language as "dialect," it is more appropriately recognized, as Redding notes, as "dialectal patterns." Harper's folk characters speak with "a fine racy, colloquial tang." Eschewing misspellings and linguistic signals that befuddle the reader and constrain the speaker within preconstruct-ed dialectical boundaries of pathos and humor, Frances Harper avoided the problems that ensnared Paul Laurence Dunbar and worried James Weldon Johnson.

Paul Lauter [in his article, "Is Frances Ellen Watkins Harper Good Enough to Teach," *Legacy*, Vol. 5, 1988] has pointed out that Harper's language was "clearly a conscious and . . . political choice." Lauter describes Harper's technique and distinguishes it from that of Harriet Stowe in the following analysis of **"Aunt Chloe's Politics"**:

> Here, however, [Harper] wishes to draw a shrewd and upright woman of the people who is not, like Stowe's Aunt Chloe, distanced from her audience, white or middle-class black, by the "color," so to speak, of her language. Like most Americans, this Aunt Chloe uses some slang—like "honey-fugle round," to cajole or wheedle, and "a heap"—some non-standard grammar—"have took it"—and the mock ignorance of the savvy: "I don't know very much About these politics." Harper carefully establishes in the third line—"Though I think that some who run 'em"—Aunt Chloe's control of standard, informal English before, in the next to last line—"Though I thinks a heap of voting"—she presents her using a specifically Southern black locution. Aunt Chloe's language is, I believe, designed to legitimate her keen political commentary.

Frances Watkins Harper was an innovator among African American writers. According to Joan Sherman in *Invisible Poets: African Americans of the Nineteenth Century*:

> in every decade since 1850, Harper's work remains the prototype of black poetry. As early as 1871 she forgave the oppressor and combined her appeals for civil rights with a confident vision of racial brotherhood. During the last two decades of the century she leads the poets in uplifting verse, directed not only at raising black moral, educational, and economic status, but also at reforming the national evil of alcoholism and the double standard of sex.

Frances Harper was an innovator among American writers generally. At least a dozen years before Walt Whitman's essay "The Poetry of the Future," Frances Harper was writing along the lines that Whitman visualized. In his 1881 manifesto, Whitman called for a poetry that would "arouse and initiate more than to define or finish." He called for epic poetry about the "real history of the United States," works that would sum up "the tremendous moral and military perturbations of 1861-5, and their results." According to Whitman, the new poetry would recognize that "the real, though latent and silent bulk of America, city or country, presents a magnificent mass of material, never before equalled on earth," and that "Poetry of the Future" would unite "closer and closer not only the American States, but all nations, and all humanity." Exhorted Whitman, "That, O poets! is not that a theme worth chanting, striving for? . . . Perhaps the most illustrious culmination of the modern may thus prove to be a signal growth of joyous, more exalted bards of adhesiveness, identically

one in soul, but contributed by every nation, each after its distinctive kind."

Frances Harper anticipated Whitman in her use of the Civil War and its aftermath as her subject. Her choice of black American farmers was more radical than Whitman probably intended but it did give voice and visibility to a "real, though latent and silent bulk of America." As she sang songs of her "distinctive kind" she also emphasized the unification of the peoples of the United States.

Melba Joyce Boyd (essay date 1994)

SOURCE: "'Neath Sheltering Vines and Stately Palms: The Radical Vision of Frances Ellen Watkins Harper" and "The Dialectics of Dialect Poetry: Frances Harper's *Sketches of Southern Life*," in *Discarded Legacy: Politics and Poetics in the Life of Frances E. W. Harper, 1825-1911*, Wayne State University Press, 1994, pp. 56-78, 147-166.

[*Boyd is a poet, a professor, and a scholar of African-American studies. Her book,* Discarded Legacy, *is a historical study of Harper's life and works. In the following excerpt from this work, Boyd offers a thematic and stylistic survey of Harper's verse in* Poems on Miscellaneous Subjects *and* Sketches of Southern Life.]

"Ethiopia"

> "Let bronze be brought to Egypt, let Ethiopia
> hasten to stretch out her hands to God."
> Psalm 68:31

Yes! Ethiopia yet shall stretch
  Her bleeding hands abroad;
Her cry of agony shall reach
  The burning throne of God.

The tyrant's yoke from off her neck,
  His fetters from her soul,
The mighty hand of God shall break,
  And spurn the base control.

Redeemed from dust and freed from chains
  Her sons shall lift their eyes;
From cloud-capt hills and verdant plains
  Shall shouts of triumph rise.

Upon her dark, despairing brow,
  Shall play a smile of peace;
For God shall bend unto her wo,
  And bid her sorrows cease.

'Neath sheltering vines and stately palms
  Shall laughing children play,
And aged sires with joyous psalms
  Shall gladden every day.

Secure by night, and blest by day,
    Shall pass her happy hours;
Nor human tigers hunt for prey
    Within her peaceful bowers.

Then Ethiopia! stretch, oh! stretch
    Thy bleeding hands abroad;
Thy cry of agony shall reach
    And find redress from God

Frances E.W. Harper, 1854
Poems on Miscellaneous Subjects

One month after Frances Harper delivered her first lecture on behalf of the antislavery cause, her second book of poetry and essays, *Poems and Miscellaneous Subjects,* was published by J. B. Yerrinton & Son in Boston. In 1857, the second edition was published by Merrihew & Thompson in Philadelphia with an introduction by William Lloyd Garrison. Many of these poems appeared in her first book, *Forest Leaves,* as well as in abolitionist periodicals. She had already acquired some literary notice, but this second book dramatically expanded her reputation. She emerged as the bronze muse of the abolitionist movement.

While confirming her talent and her artistic future, William Lloyd Garrison's introduction insinuates limitations in Harper's poetry. In a patronizing tone, he qualifies her poetry by asking the audience to consider her circumstances.

> Hence, in reviewing the following *Poems,* the critic will remember that they are written by one young in years, and identified in complexion and destiny with a depressed and outcast race, and who has had to contend with a thousand disadvantages from earliest life. They certainly are very credible to her, both in literary and moral point of view, and indicate the possession of a talent which, if carefully cultivated and properly encouraged, cannot fail to secure for herself a poetic reputation, and to deepen the interest always so extensively felt in the liberation and enfranchisement of the entire colored race.

On September 2, 1854, a similar review of Harper's work by William Still of Philadelphia appeared in the Canadian "colored" newspaper, *The Provincial Freeman.* But Still's statements are more enthusiastic than Garrison's. Still's article contains the emerging Afroamerican cultural perspective. His critique considers Harper's poetry an achievement for a literary tradition outside of the leisure class:

> It may not be amiss to state here, that Miss Watkins has been constantly engaged as school teacher and seamstress during the time of writing this book, and consequently has only had the privilege for study of such leisure hours as fall the lot of those in her calling. But according to the judgment of several able critics who have examined the manuscript, I think I may take the liberty to predict that it may rank as high, if not higher, than any production of the kind ever published in this country by a colored person.

[Sept. 2, 1854]

Though Garrison and Still respectfully promote Harper's work, the implications of this book are more profound than either of them realized. The thematic range of *Poems on Miscellaneous Subjects* challenges repressive cultural and political practices by attacking racist and sexist beliefs. Harper confronts American social, political, and cultural systems of repression. The "miscellaneous" format of the book centers around human suffering; and when the holistic context of that format is considered, one can more appropriately perceive and appreciate the poet's complexity. *Poems on Miscellaneous Subjects* refracts Harper's radical vision, and these themes determine her political and literary direction.

Poems on Miscellaneous Subjects is a "colored" prism. Through graphic portrayals, Harper conveys the traumatic feelings of the enslaved. Her imagery focuses on the experience rather than the issue of slavery. This shift in poetic perspective is extremely important because it engages slavery as a concrete reality rather than as an intellectual abstraction. At the same time, Harper's abolitionist poetry reveals how racism and sexism interact. Focusing on the perspective of the slave woman exposes the oppressive nature of the white patriarchal slave society. Many of these abolitionist poems emanate from the destruction of the family, whereby the slave mother is physically and emotionally abused, and her children are destined for debased servitude.

Poetry about poverty in Charles Dickens's England and about alcoholism throughout American society extend beyond the boundaries of social segregation and provide contexts for shared human experiences. Poems about male/female relationships and gender attitudes extend common, tragic themes that affect most western women. These social themes consider realities that cross racial and class lines. Still's decision to showcase Harper's **"Died of Starvation"** as part of his review of *Poems on Miscellaneous Subjects* demonstrates Harper's literary influences and her influence on the reading interests of the abolitionist audience. The epigraph reads, "See this case, as touchingly related in *Oliver Twist* by Dickens."

Sadly crouching by the embers,
    Her famished children lay;
And she longed to gaze upon them,
    As her spirit passed away.

But the embers were too feeble,
    She could not see each face,
So she clasped her arms around them—
    'Twas their mother's last embrace.

This parallels the desolate experience found in another poem in *Poems on Miscellaneous Subjects,* **"The Slave Mother"**:

They tear him from her circling arms,
    Her vast and fond embrace:
Oh! never more may her sad eyes
    Gaze on his mournful face.

No marvel, then, these bitter shrieks
　Disturb the listening air:
She is the mother, and her heart
　Is breaking in despair.

The reading of a book of poetry, like the reading of a poem, is not a linear experience. The collective consciousness of the book renders relationships capable of transforming past perceptions of reality by revealing patterns and parallels that are imperceptible to most people because of social and cultural conditioning. These two poems associate women in the lower class of Victorian England with women in the slave class in nineteenth-century America. Conversely, this parallel demonstrates Harper's continental consciousness. America's social investment in economic disparity is directly related to its postcolonial inheritance of British class values. Both portrayals of the disenfranchised are qualitatively and definitively class-associated experiences from the perspective of lower-class women.

Derived from the oral folk tradition, the ballad was the poetic form Frances Harper preferred for most of her abolitionist poems. They are folk poems, poetic slave narratives adapted from Underground Railroad stories about runaways, from reports she heard from escaped slaves, or from scenes she witnessed with her own eyes. The narrative voice of the black slave woman characterizes the poems **"The Slave Mother," "Eliza Harris,"** and **"The Slave Mother: A Tale of Ohio."** Dialogue personalizes and provides an opportunity for the slave to testify.

"Eliza Harris," a poetic abstraction of Harriet Beecher Stowe's novel *Uncle Tom's Cabin,* was first published in William Lloyd Garrison's *Liberator* (1853). It reappeared in *Frederick Douglass' Paper* on December 23 of the same year.

Like a fawn from the arrow, startled and wild,
A woman swept by us, bearing a child;
In her eye was the night of a settled despair,
And her brow was o'ershaded with anguish and
　care.

She was nearing the river—in reaching the brink,
She heeded no danger, she paused not to think;
For she is a mother—her child is a slave—
And she'll give him his freedom, or find him a
　grave!

The publication of this poem in both papers aggravated an already existing antagonism between the two abolitionist camps. A stern letter from the Garrisonians to the *Frederick Douglass' Paper* charged the poem **"Eliza Harris"** had been presented in *Frederick Douglass' Paper* as if the poem had been especially written for the publication. The letter argued that the poem had originally appeared in the *Liberator*. The *Frederick Douglass' Paper* responded by admitting to a technical error. The response also includes an apology to Harper and an appeal that she continue to submit literature to their publication.

Despite this debate and the differences between Douglass and Garrison, Harper remained unaffected by their disputes and was able to work politically with them both. Undoubtedly, her prominence as a political figure prevented any unreasonable appeal from either of them. Most certainly, their reserve and respect for Harper's uncle, William Watkins, protected the poet from an exclusive alignment with either editor.

Significant changes occurred in **"Eliza Harris"** from the time it was first published in the 1853 antislavery publications. In the first version the rhyme and rhythm are not thematically coordinated or tightly metered. Additionally, the point of view shifts, which conflicts with the narrative and disrupts the visual development of the imagery. The graphic depiction of plot in the second version is more succinctly synchronized with the rhythm and rhyming techniques, producing a smoother and more subtle interplay of poetic devices. The political statement is entwined to heighten dramatic tension and to underscore social horror. The critical difference between the two versions lies in the endings. The second version is extended with an additional stanza that cyclically completes and unifies the poem by focusing on the mother and the child in both the first and last stanzas.

But she's free!—yes free from the land where the
　slaves
From the hand of oppression must rest in the grave.
Where bondage and blood, where scourges and
　chains,
Have placed on our banner indelible stains.

Did a fever ever burning through bosom and brain,
Send a love-like flood through every vein,
Till it suddenly encoded 'neath a healing spell,
And you know, oh! the joy, you know you were
　well.

The revised version reads:

But she's free!—yes, free from the land where the
　slave
From the hand of oppression must rest in the grave;
Where bondage and torture, where scourges and
　chains
Have plac'd on our banner indelible stains.

The bloodhounds have miss'd the scent of her way;
The hunter is rifled and foil'd of his prey;
Fierce jargon and cursing, with clanking chains,
Make sounds of strange discord on Liberty's plains.

With rapture of love and fullness of bliss,
She plac'd on his brow a mother's fond kiss:—
Oh! poverty, danger and death she can brave,
For the child of her love is no longer a slave!

This poem underwent another structural transition when it was anthologized in 1981 in *Black Sister* under the title, **"She's Free."** The poem was transformed into a sonnet by deleting some lines and rearranging others. Hence, the narrative was edited into an alien form, creating a visual disruption in the imagery and an aural disorientation in the sound. There is no historical indication that the poet made these alterations because the poem was not published or collected in this form during the poet's lifetime.

Admiration for Stowe's political contribution to abolitionism is enshrined in a poem entitled, **"To Mrs. Harriet Beecher Stowe."** It applauds the power of the novel that is credited for raising the consciousness of thousands of Americans. The ending lines are indicative of a prevailing radical Christian reception of Stowe's novel:

> The halo that surrounds thy name
>   Hath reached from shore to shore
> But thy best and brightest fame
>   Is the blessing of the poor.

This poem appeared in *Frederick Douglass' Paper* (February 3, 1854), but was not later collected. In the same issue, a review of Dickens's "Christmas Number of Household Words" appeared. The reviewer notes: "Some we have read; but all we mean to read, for we always expect great things of Mr. Dickens, and are rarely disappointed." The presence of Harper, Stowe, and Dickens on the same page exemplifies the cross-cultural influences on and of abolitionist literature. Reportedly, Dickens praised Stowe's *Uncle Tom's Cabin* and was very critical of American slavery.

"The Slave Mother: A Tale of Ohio" is based on a real slave narrative, a famous case which brought attention to the severity of slavery and to what ends a mother would go to save her children from that fate. But unlike **"Eliza Harris,"** a fictional character who escapes, the unnamed slave mother of Ohio is captured after she kills one of her children. The poem begins with the mother's voice, but an omniscient narrator weaves the persona's thoughts with foreboding anticipation of bounty hunters tracking her trail. Resigned to her inevitable capture, as foreshadowed by warnings and flashing visions, the slave mother is persuaded by her desperation to deliver her children from slavery through death.

> I will save my precious children
>   From their darkly threatened doom,
> I will hew their path to freedom
>   Through the portals of the tomb.

But the poet does not trust the audience's logic and does not simply conclude with the tale's deadly ending. The last lines define the mother's action as a *"deed of fearful daring,"* and then raises the rhetorical question, and through call and response challenges the audience to join the fight against the true cause of the crime:

> Do the icy hands of slavery
>   Every pure emotion chill?

Toni Morrison's novel, *Beloved,* invokes the ghost of this child, who returns, not to haunt the community, but to obtain understanding for the meaning of her death. Frances

Harper's poem blames the inhumanity of slavery for the death and supplies this alternative perspective for compassionate understanding.

> They snatched away the fatal knife,
>   Her boys shrieked wild with dread;
> The baby girl was pale and cold,
>   They raised it up, the child was dead.
>
> Sends this deed of fearful daring
>   Through my country's heart no thrill,
> Do the icy hands of slavery
>   Every pure emotion chill?
>
> Oh! if there is any honor,
>   Truth or justice in the land,
> Will ye not, us men and Christians,
>   On the side of freedom stand?

"The Slave Auction," one of Harper's most famous poems, begins with stanzas that present slavery as an extension of an inhumane economic system. The moral disgrace of dealing human life directs attention to the emotional humiliation and devastation of those being bartered. This imagery conveys the harshness and inhumanity of slave dealers. In direct and chilling language the poem describes and accuses:

> The sale began—young girls were there,
>   Defenseless in their wretchedness,
> Those stifled sobs of deep despair
>   Revealed their anguish and distress.
>
> And mothers stood with streaming eyes,
>   And saw their dearest daughters sold;
> Unheeded rose their bitter cries,
>   While tyrants bartered them for gold.
>
> And woman, with her love and truth—
>   For those in sable forms may dwell—
> Gaz'd on the husband of her youth,
>   With anguish none may paint of tell.
>
> And men, whose sole crime was their hue,
>   The impress of the Maker's hand,
> And frail sad shrinking children, too,
>   Were gathered in that mournful band.

"The Slave Auction" evokes an emotional response via graphic description and elicits the trauma of being sold at a slave auction. The interplay between low pitch and elongated syllables creates a slow rhythm which produces a haunting echo. The poem revolves around the image of the "sable" woman as the first stanza opens with African women internalizing the sexist dehumanization of their nakedness in the human marketplace. The second stanza expands the image with anguished children being abducted from their screaming mothers. This terrorizing destruction of the family is further dramatized as the husbands of these women are divorced from them by a bill of sale. The fourth stanza, the climax, shifts the perspective of the poem to the *"shrinking children"* who foreshadow the future. This image foregrounds the end of the poem, which is a direct appeal to the audience. She attempts to engage their empathy by connecting a death in the family to their emotional response to **"The Slave Auction."** Through such comparison, the poem establishes a parallel between the two situations and depicts slavery as an agonizing existence, grimmer than grief and crueler than death.

> Ye who have laid your love to rest,
>   And wept above the lifeless clay,
> Know not the anguish of that breast,
>   Whose lov'd are rudely torn away.
>
> Ye may not know how desolate
>   Are bosoms rudely forced to part,
> And how dull and heavy weight
>   Will press the life-drops from the heart.

This poem appeared simultaneously in *Frederick Douglass' Paper* (September 22, 1854) and in **Poems on Miscellaneous Subjects.** It is one of the most often referenced abolitionist poems, and the one from this collection that has been repeatedly anthologized. It is considered a classic and has managed to maintain a position for the poet in Afroamerican poetry.

Poems that focus on enslaved men praise heroic acts of resistance, rebellion, and escape, thereby contradicting prevailing propaganda about the "contented slave" and preordained stereotypes of the "docile" negro. These poems advocate the defiance of black men and the innate spirit of freedom. In concurrence with egalitarian feminist views, Harper advocated strong convictions about male character. While she confronted woman's sexual oppression and maternal agony during slavery, she praised bondmen defying punishment and death in order to maintain their integrity or to acquire freedom.

"The Tennessee Hero," based on *"an actual incident in 1856,"* evokes the voice of a dead slave, an unheralded hero. The poem's epigraph reads: *"He had heard his comrades plotting to obtain their liberty, and rather than betray them he received 750 lashes and died."* **"The Tennessee Hero"** champions one man's resistance against sanctioned tyranny, and at the same time it counters the racist perception that black men do not inherently possess ethical principles.

It is an inspirational poem written to remember and herald such character. An imagined dialogue between the slave and his assailants creates drama and tension in the poem. The hero's defiance defines resistance to tyranny as natural, necessary, and spiritual:

> "I know the men who would be free;
>   They are the heroes of your land,
> But death and torture I defy,
>   Ere I betray that band.
>
> And what! oh, what is life to one,
>   Beneath your base control?

> Nay! do your worst. Ye have no chains
>   To bind my free-born soul."
>
> They brought the hateful lash and scourge,
>   With murder in each eye.
> But a solemn vow was on his lips—
>   He had resolved to die.
>
> Yes, rather than betray his trust,
>   He'd meet a death of pain;
> T'was sweeter far to meet it thus
>   Than wear a treason stain!
>
> Like storms of wrath, of hate and pain,
>   The blows rained thick and fast;
> But the monarch soul kept true
>   Till the gates of life were past.
>
> And the martyr spirit fled
>   To the throne of God on high,
> And showed his gaping wounds
>   Before unslumbering eye.

Likewise, **"A Mother's Heroism"** exalts political activism as commensurate with individual integrity. This poems salutes the white abolitionist Elijah P. Lovejoy, editor and publisher of an antislavery newspaper, as a martyr. Killed in 1837 by a proslavery mob in Alton, Illinois, his mother is quoted in the epigraph: "When the mother of Lovejoy heard of her son's death, she said, 'It is well! I had rather he should die so than desert his principles.'"

> From lip and brow the color fled—
>   But light flashed to her eye:
> "'Tis well! 'tis well!" the mother said,
>   "That thus my child should die."
>
> "'Tis well that, to his latest breath,
>   He pleaded for liberty;
> Truth nerved him for the hour of death,
>   And taught him how to die."
>
> "It taught him how to cast aside
>   Earth's honors and renown;
> To trample on her fame and pride,
>   And win a martyr's crown."

The paradoxical **"The Fugitive's Wife,"** considers the conflicting response to a freedom tale. A slave woman simultaneously mourns and rejoices her husband's escape from slavery. Like an early blues poem, a countertheme of bitter abandonment undercuts this ballad of celebration. A heavy, forlorn rhythm that rises and then falls on a down beat at the end of each stanza develops this contrast. The woman bemoans the loss of her husband, whose *"manly pride"* was too frail to sustain the *"grief and pain"* of enslavement. But the ambivalent slave woman consoles her heartbreak with compassion for his motivations, and confirms his right to take flight:

> He strained me to his heaving heart—
>   My own beat wild with fear;

I knew not, but I sadly felt
  There must be evil near.

He vainly strove to cast aside
  The tears that fell like rain:—
Too frail, indeed, is manly pride,
  To strive with grief and pain.

Again he clasped me to his breast,
  And said that we must part:
I tried to speak—but, oh! it seemed
  An arrow reached my heart.

"Bear not," I cried, "unto your grave,
  The yoke you've borne from birth;
No longer live a helpless slave,
  The meanest thing on earth!"

Harper's preference for the ballad form had direct bearing on the practicality of her art. She was not a poet removed from her work as political activist, but rather, her poetry was inclusive of her activism, an integral part of her lectures and writing. The overriding purpose of her poetry was to challenge the power of evil and greed.

The ballad form embraces the natural lyrical patterns of nineteenth-century mass culture, and with its flexible meter, it coincides well with the elocutionary format. Weaving her poems into the context of her lectures, she adhered to the elocutionary style of William Watkins, whose beliefs and praxis she emulated and improvised. The abolitionist platform amplified her stature as a nationally recognized intellectual and poet. Moreover, her activism intensified her poetic themes. **"The Dying Bondman"** demonstrates this development in her poetic craft. The subtle ambience is achieved through a more complex rhythm and a more subtle manipulation of diction, while the dramatic tension transcends simplistic romanticism by juxtaposing irony and pathos.

By his bedside stood the master
Gazing on the dying one,
Knowing by the dull grey shadows
That life's sands were almost run.

"Master," said the dying bondman,
"Home and friends I soon shall see;
But before I reach my country,
Master write that I am free;

Give to me the precious token,
That my kindred dead may see—
Master! Write it, write it quickly!
Master write that I am free!"

Eagerly he grasped the writing;
"I am free!" at least he said.
Backward fell upon the pillow
He was free among the dead.

Such imagery intends to disturb audiences by supplanting benign abstract perceptions of slavery with horrifying concrete experiences. By focusing on personal experiences of slaves, Harper's poetry humanizes the appeal for justice. The physical and cultural distance that contributed to northern indifference to southern slavery was bridged by such storytelling. Harper ingrains memory with this imagery, and reinforces these images with subliminal sound devices and the power of rhyme.

FEMINIST POETRY

The abolitionist movement gave impetus to the feminist movement, and as an abolitionist-feminist, Harper's poetry bonds the two movements through the compounded oppression of black women in slavery. But sexist repression is pervasive, and Harper's feminist poems addressed to the "free public" extend and educate the black and white communities. The poem, **"Report,"** advises young men, *wed not for beauty*" for it will *"fade in your eyes."* But rather, select a woman with *"actions discreet, manners refined,"* and who is *"free from deceit."* In the poem **"Advice to the Girls,"** Harper cautions,

Wed not a man whose merit lies
  In things of outward show,

but one who is *"free from all pretense"* and *"at least has common sense."*

This "light verse" is tuned by precise, taut phrasing which complements the fundamental common sense and tried truths conveyed in the lines. The regularity and simplicity of rhythm and the even, *a b a b* terminal rhyme scheme encase these poetic thoughts for easy memorization, recall, and reflection. But **"The Contrast"** offers a more serious lesson.

This poem criticizes the hypocrisy of sexism. It tells the story of a woman disgraced for her involvement in a love affair, while the man, a person of position and wealth, is assured impunity and marries another in a proper ceremony.

None scorned him for his sinning,
  Few saw it through his gold;
His crimes were only foibles,
  And these were gently told.

The poem provides a typical Victorian twist to this all-too-common scenario. In the second part of the poem, marked by a distinct break, the man stands undaunted at the altar, when a vision of "the other woman's" funeral flashes in his mind and shocks his consciousness. The scorned woman is dead. The superimposition of the funeral over the wedding provides contrasting imagery to emphasize the tragedy resulting from an endorsed double standard society.

Harper revises this theme and plot in a later poem, **"A Double Standard,"** which replaces tragic resignation with a transcendent, feminist consciousness. Instead of committing suicide, the shunned woman testifies against the privileged position of the man, repudiates social condemnation, and chooses life renewed through spiritual redemption. Like Eve, she was tempted by the *"adder's hiss."* Like the Samaritan woman, condemned for her alleged infidelity, her lips were pressed to stone. Harper engages the image of Jesus Christ, who defended the Samaritan woman, as the persona's feminist advocate. The poem promotes forgiveness and transcendence as a mechanism to reverse Victorian, patriarchal, and religious persecution. Additionally, the call-and-response pattern in the repetition and the refrain of questions encourages the audience to affirm the poem's position against injustice and to speak out against hypocrisy.

> Would you blame him, when you drew from me
>   Your dainty robes aside,
> If he with gilded baits should claim
>   Your fairest as his bride?
>
> Would you blame the world if it should press
>   On him a civic crown;
> And see me struggling in the depth,
>   Then harshly press me down?
>
> Crime has no sex and yet today
>   I wear the brand of shame;
> Whilst he amid the gay and proud
>   Still bears an honored name.
>
> Can you blame me if I've learned to think
>   Your hate of vice a sham,
> When you so coldly crushed me down,
>   And then excused the man?

RELIGIOUS POETRY

To man, guilty, fallen and degraded man, she shows a fountain drawn from Redeemer's veins; there she bids him wash and be clean. She points to Mount Zion, the city of the living God, to an innumerable company of angels, to the spirits of just men made perfect and to Jesus, the mediator of the new Covenant, and urges him to rise from the denigration of sin, renew his nature, and join with them.

Harper's essay, "Christianity," ridicules the material and intellectual arrogance of man's civilized history and denotes the frivolity of illusion and the pitfalls of power while emphasizing the living presence and vision of God. Harper's spiritual beliefs underlined her feminist and abolitionist convictions. Radical Christianity constituted a spiritual system and defined a cosmic order that facilitated her political principles. Since the spirituality of orthodox Christianity had more often than not been corrupted by the economic and social designs of the white patriarchal culture, the poet used her writing to reveal the philosophical contradictions in theological dogma and its impact on everyday experience.

Published in *Poems on Miscellaneous Subjects,* "Christianity" articulates a theoretical Christian premise similarly espoused by the African Methodist Episcopal church. It does not represent the doctrine of this church, but it does articulate Harper's early religious views and a belief similar to that of most radical abolitionists. She envisions Christianity as the only infallible system for spiritual survival in man's contrived and debased society.

Likewise, the poem, **"Bible Defense of Slavery,"** evidences the difference between *"Mount Zion, the city of the living God"* and the New Egypt, in the United States. The poem attacks a book of the same title that distorts biblical text in order to support the institution of slavery. Published in 1851, the book employs pseudoscientific logic to prove Caucasian supremacy. It conversely promotes "a plan of national colonization to the entire removal of the free blacks." Like William Watkins, Harper strongly opposed the colonizationists and advocated civil rights for people of color in the United States.

The poem aptly indicts the book's racist, religious appeal by identifying the contradictions and explaining that such thoughts and proposals endanger the moral and social integrity of the country. Through comparison, Harper references Sodom and Gomorrah (Genesis 13:10) whose wicked citizens were destroyed by God, concluding that denigration will be answered on Judgment Day (Matthew 10:15). The poem forewarns of the treachery of church and state:

> A "reverend" man, whose light should be
>   The guide of age and youth,
> Brings to the shrine of Slavery
>   The sacrifice of truth!
>
> For the direst wrong by men imposed,
>   Since Sodom's fearful cry,
> The word of life has been unclosed,
>   To give your God the lie.
>
> Oh! when ye pray for heathen lands,
>   And plead for their dark shores,
> Remember Slavery's cruel hands
>   Make heathens at your doors!

"Ethiopia" is drawn from Psalms 68:31, "Let bronze be brought to Egypt; let Ethiopia hasten to stretch out her hands to God." This biblical epigraph, the theological foundation of the African Methodist Episcopal church, becomes the symbolic connection between American abolitionism with black Christianity. An inspirational poem, it is a finely woven ballad infused with Eden-like imagery and envisioned deliverance in the promised land.

Other religious poems, like **"Saved by Faith," "The Dying Christian," "The Syrophenician Woman"** (based on Mark 7:24-30), **"That Blessed Hope," "Eva's Farewell,"** and **"The Prodigal's Return"** (Luke 15:11-32) are based on or related to biblical text and render a more modern interpretation of these stories. Harper's poetry emphasizes the spirit of Jesus as a soothing source of peace and transcendence as a favored theme in her religious poetry; but again, the feminist dimension expands the presentation of biblical text in order to recenter gender in religious belief and practice.

Of her religious poems in *Poems on Miscellaneous Subjects,* **"Ruth and Naomi"** and **"Rizpah, The Daughter of Ai"** contain the most impressive adaptations of biblical texts. Based on Ruth, one of two books in the Bible by and about women, **"Ruth and Naomi"** flows with a delicate lyricism characterized by subtle, oblique rhyme affecting the soft end rhymes. In this poem, Harper demonstrates her adeptness with rhythm and internal structural devices. Almost all of the vowel sounds in the following stanzas are short and light, except during the lowering of mood with words like "fell," "pale," and "farewell."

> Like rain upon a blighted tree,
>   The tears of Orpah fell,
> Kissing the pale and quivering lip,
>   She breathed her sad farewell.
>
> But Ruth stood up, on her brow
>   There lay a heavenly calm;
> And from her lips came, soft and low,
>   Words like a holy charm.
>
> I will not leave thee, on thy brow
>   Are lines of sorrow, age and care;
> Thy form is bent, thy step is slow,
>   Thy bosom stricken, lone and scar.

"Rizpah, The Daughter of Ai" (2 Samuel 3:7) demonstrates similar grace and lilt:

> She sprang from her sad and lowly seat,
> For a moment her heart forgot to beat,
> And the blood rushed up to her marble cheek
> And a flash to her eye so sad and meek.
>
> The vulture paused in his downward flight,
> As she raised her form to its queenly height,
> The hyena's eye had a horrid glare
> As he turned to his desert lair.
>
> The jackal slunk back with a quickened tread,
> From his cowardly search of Rizpah's dead;
> Unsated he turned from the noble prey,
> Subdued by a glance of the daughter of Ai.
>
> Oh grief! that a mother's heart should know,
> Such a weary weight of consuming wo,
> For seldom if ever earth has known
> Such love as the daughter of Ai has known.

"Vashti" from *Poems,* 1871, one of Harper's later and most exemplary religious poems, deserves attention. Characteristic of her feminist revisions of biblical interpretations and her views on intemperance, the poem focuses on the banishment of a queen of Persia because she refuses to be disgraced by her king's demand that she unveil before a drunken crowd of men. The king wishes to display her beauty as his prize possession. Defending her self-respect, she exclaims:

> "I'll take the crown from off my head
>   And tread it 'neath my feet
> Before their rude and careless gaze
>   My shrinking eyes shall meet.
>
> "A queen unveil'd before the crowd!—
>   Upon each lip my name!—
> Why, Persia's women all would blush
>   And weep for Vashti's shame!"

This act of resistance is met with patriarchal protest by the king's counselors:

> "The women, restive 'neath our rule,
>   Would learn to scorn our name,
> And from her deed to us would come
>   Reproach and burning shame."

The king is encouraged to dethrone and banish the queen *"From distant Jud to Ethiop,"* the massive expanse of this ancient kingdom. In addition to Harper's portrayal of this repressive patriarchal act fueled by drunkenness, the inclusion of geographical detail illuminates black African historical presence, a critical contrast against the conscious exclusion of Africa from orthodox religious teachings and from some versions of the Bible.

"Vashti" further extends the poet's feminist Christian vision, as **"Ruth and Naomi"** and **"Rizpah, The Daughter of Ai"** reflect in her earlier work. Structurally and thematically, **"Vashti"** expresses the poet's best forum, as her visionary depth expands and enhances her skill. Her religious poetic productions consistently reflect the poet's most impressive work.

On a more philosophical level, this poem attempts a simplification of abstract religious concepts through poetic expression. In particular, **"Youth in Heaven"** (from *Poems*) translates the metaphysics of Emanuel Swedenborg (1688-1722), a Swedish physicist turned spiritualist, who speculated on the spatial and temporal dimensions of heaven. He defined the universe as an organic hierarchy that could be mathematically measured (or approximated) as the finite and the infinite. The all-encompassing God, according to Swedenborg, is composed of "three degrees of being," that is, love, wisdom, and creative energy. This poem also relates to Harper's conversion to Unitarianism, as the Swedenborgians held ideological beliefs similar to those of the Unitarian church. In the United States the Unitarians were staunch supporters of the Underground Railroad and the abolitionist movement. Harper's involvement with Unitarianism developed through her political affiliations.

In **"Youth in Heaven,"** Harper explains very plainly, that life is a procession, whereby death is the passage or entry into eternal life. The poem suggests a reversal of the aging process as the planet evolves in darkness toward death; the motion of the heavens reverses that rotation, moving towards light. Hence, in heaven,

the eldest of the angels
    Seems the youngest brother there.

Likewise, Harper images Goethe's death around a similar theme that dominated his work. In her poem, **"Let the Light Enter! The dying words of Goethe"** (*Poems*), Goethe identifies *"light"* as the energy by which life enters into heaven:

Gracious Savior when our day dreams
    Melt and vanish from the sight,
May our dim and longing vision
    Then be blessed with light, more light.

Light energizes the motion of death that moves the spirit through the dark, finite, four-dimensional sphere into the infinite, ethereal realm. The spiritual world interfaces the physical, mortal planet, whereby death provides a transition into the afterlife.

These poems were useful to Harper as a Sunday school teacher because they demystify the concept of eternal life. Harper's aesthetic strategy is the application of poetics to inspire faith, and to access the obscure and abstract. Unlike most nineteenth-century black poets who inundated their poetry with Greek references for a select audience, Harper used simple language and lucid imagery to explain and to clarify.

TEMPERANCE POETRY

If mind is more than matter, if the destiny of the human soul reaches out into the eternities, and as we sow so must we reap, then bad as was American slavery the slavery of intemperance is worse. Slavery was the enemy of one section, the oppressor of one race, but intemperance is the curse of every land and the deadly foe of every kindred, tribe and race which falls beneath its influence.

Frances Harper wrote essays and lectures against alcoholism, which she considered another form of slavery and a serious social issue that affected all classes. Temperance was a key issue of Christian abolitionists and radical feminists, and it found favor with Harper's poetry. Like her Dickensian poem concerning class repression in England, her dedication to the temperance movement relates to her broader social vision. Before the end of the nineteenth century, alcoholism had become one of the most destructive forces in oppressed communities of color in the United States, preying on their desperate conditions.

"The Drunkard's Child" dramatizes a pathetic scene in order to accentuate the devastating impact of alcoholism on the family:

He stood beside his dying child,
    With dim and bloodshot eye;
They'd won him from the haunts of vice
    To see his first born die.

He came with a slow and staggering tread,
    A vague, unmeaning stare,
And, reeling, clasped the clammy hand,
    So deathly pale and fair.

Like **"Died of Starvation"** and **"The Slave Mother: A Tale of Ohio,"** **"The Drunkard's Child"** ends with death. The dramatic pursuit of the poem is to capture audience imagination, to engage its empathy, and to enlist its moral outrage. Aesthetic dismissal of a poem often uses resistance to sentimentality as a common excuse. It is a response to tragedy, which is more characteristic of women's writing. Apparently this affronts aesthetic distance or male "objectivity." But as evidenced in Stowe's *Uncle Tom's Cabin* and many other nineteenth-century women's writing, the purpose of the literature is to instigate a compassionate response in thought and action. Harper conveyed this romanticism from the lectern to sway the subjective receptivity of the audience. Death offers deliverance until an indifferent society changes.

He clasped him to his throbbing heart,
    "I will! I will!" he said;
His pleading ceased—the father held
    His first born and his dead.

. . . . .

DIALECT POETRY

Harper's adaptation of natural speech patterns does not rely on the excessive use of apostrophies to convey sound differences. The thrust of the rhythm provides an authentic musical quality inherent in the syntax. The poetic line is used as a gauge of rhythmic variations, expanding or contracting the meter in order to facilitate the natural inclination of the expression. The line responds to the sound rather than to a rigid metrical formula. Expressions like, *"honey-fugle round"* and *"like an egg is full of meat,"* determine a rhythm that is more reflexive relative to the syntax of the dialect than it is to the poetic line. The rhythm of the oral speech pattern takes precedence, resonating in an improvisational response to the ballad structure that contains the overall thrust of the poem's aural impact. Hence, when Harper uses conventional spellings, the words do not resound as standard voice pronunciations.

Particular syntactical features germane to black dialect, even today, like subject-verb agreement, colloquial expressions, and biblically coded symbolism, contribute to structural and thematic cohesion. The impetus of the energy is affected through the thematic frame of imagery, and its rhythmic resonance is amplified by an authentic voice. Harper's poem transcends the technical technique of nineteenth-century literature by activating a synergistic plane of aural intersection. This intersection is dependent on the convergence of sound patterns that interact beyond any single word or syllable; hence, Harper's critical departure from conventional dialect.

Harper's personae speak fluidly and critically about enslavement, the Civil War, literacy, religion, and electoral politics. *Sketches of Southern Life* speaks to the people in their memory and about their especial American identity. For these and other reasons, Aunt Chloe of *Sketches* constitutes an indelible character. She speaks a fusion of the standard and the dialect. Her literacy has modified her dialect, but since her purpose was to learn to read the Bible and not to master the King's English, her narrative represents a natural adjustment. Her diction is less affected, and her syntax to an even lesser extent. Unlike the slave narratives that were tightly edited for the benefit of white readers, Harper's *Sketches of Southern Life* is a fresh and marvelous expression that stands independently without the intimidation of cultural imperialist considerations.

THE POEM

Sketches of Southern Life is the slave narrative of Aunt Chloe, an elderly ex-slave woman who explains her trials during bondage, exclaims the joys of deliverance, and reveals the political conflicts that arise during Reconstruction. She relays her determination to learn to read, and the community's efforts to build a church. The poem ends cyclically and appropriately with the first reunion of Chloe's family since her sons were sold away from her during slavery.

The long poem begins with the tension of tragedy and the promise of peace. The experience expressed by Aunt Chloe's language and point of view determines the tone and setting. While the ballad provides a flexible framework wherein variations in Chloe's speech pattern are modulated by the drama in the imagery and the *a b c b* rhyme pattern, the consistency of the subject-verb conjugation combined with the vernacular dialect assure a folk pronunciation. The first section of the poem is subtitled, "Aunt Chloe," and it begins with reflections of her most traumatic slave experience and a typical Harper theme, the selling of her children away from the plantation. The first-person pronoun and the capitalization of all the letters in "REMEMBER" emphasize the influence of oral history.

> I REMEMBER, well remember,
>   That dark and dreadful day,
> When they whispered to me, "Chloe,
>   Your children's sold away!"

The dialogue between Aunt Chloe and her cousin Milly explains the nature and cause of this disaster, as the master of the plantation has died and left his wife in debt. Milly empathizes with Chloe, explaining how her son Saul was likewise sold away by the old master. Pinioned by depression, Chloe "*waste*[s]" into a "*shadow,*" and turns "*to skin and bone,*" until Uncle Jacob advises her to take her troubles to the Lord, who lightens her load and redeems her soul:

> "You'll get justice in the kingdom,
>   If you do not get it here."

The reiteration of the image of the heart appears in the second stanza,

> And I felt as if my heart-strings
>   Was breaking right in two.

Likewise the Mistus is crying in the big house "*like her heart would break,*" and Uncle Jacob warns Chloe "*your poor heart is in the fire.*" In folk culture there is an integral connection between the heart and the spirit. The "old folks" believe the spirit lives in the heart. Hence, Chloe's sorrow had emaciated her body and her soul, until she was lingering on the edge of death.

When Uncle Jacob speaks, the imagery of the poem becomes Christlike:

> And he told me of the Savior,
>   And the fountain in His side.

It should also be noted that "master" when used to reference the slaveholder, is not capitalized, unlike when referencing Jesus, "*the blessed Master's feet.*" After Chloe prays, the biblical reference to the stone being rolled from Jesus' tomb is used to symbolize the uplifting of her spirit and the salvation of her soul:

> And I felt my heavy burden
>   Rolling like a stone away.

Resurrected, her new consciousness elevates her to a higher cosmic plane, one of spiritual enlightenment.

Chloe's rebirth demonstrates how spirituality contributed to the survival of the slave. Religion was a source of replenishment, relieving the agony of suffering through transcendence, but not through resignation to maltreatment. Chloe is sustained by the God of justice during her plight, but her understanding of that does not preclude justice on earth. The biblical and folk references reflected in names and in the dialogue are culturally characteristic and enhance the folk diction.

"The Deliverance," the second part of *Sketches,* carries Chloe's narrative through the Civil War, the abolition of slavery, the death of Lincoln, the retrenchment of Reconstruction, and the enactment of the Fifteenth Amendment. It is the longest section in the poem. Chloe discusses several historical events interwined with personal experiences and political convictions. But Chloe's portrayal of plantation life is not particularly gruesome. In fact, the new master, Mister Thomas, is described as "*kind at heart,*" with a judicious disposition. The contrast between the cruel master and the benevolent slaveholder suggests that the "kind" master profited because his slaves were more cooperative.

> He kept right on that very way
>   Till he got big and tall,
> And ole Mistus used to chide him,
>   And say he'd spile us all.
>
> But somehow the farm did prosper
>   When he took things in hand;
> And though all the servants liked him,
>   *He made them understand.*

The ambiguity of the slave/master relationship, as Harper portrays it here, avoids a simplistic, didactic reduction of "white" as completely bad and "black" as completely helpless. With regards to the consistency of diction, words like "*spile*" and "*mistus*" as opposed to "spoil" and "mistress" contribute to the presence of dialect and to the subtle underplay of oblique rhyme, as in the case of "*chide*" and "*spile*." Likewise, the dynamic imagery inherent in the dialect contributes to the imaginative expressions.

The war intervenes and Mister Thomas, no matter how kind at heart, is still a Confederate advocate. He explains to his mother, who

> looked on Mister Thomas
> With a face as pale as death,

that he wished he had been at the battle at Fort Sumter. Now, the "*mistus*" must contend with the same pain imposed on the slave mother.

> "I was thinking, dearest Thomas,
>   'Twould break my very heart
> If a fierce and dreadful battle
>   Should tear our lives apart."

Aunt Chloe expresses sympathy for old Mistus as she relays Mister Thomas's departure, but the encroaching agony of this mother and son, is intuitively scrutinized:

> But somehow I couldn't help thinking
>   His fighting must be wrong.

and that,

> For I felt somehow or other
>   We was mixed up in that fight.

Chloe recognizes the pendulum of reciprocity:

> How old Mistres feels the sting,
> For this parting with your children
>   Is a mighty dreadful thing.

Uncle Jacob tells Chloe that slavery is doomed, and that the war will be the slave's retribution. Like his biblical antecedent, Jacob symbolizes persistence and endurance. While Mistress "*prayed up in the parlor*," the slaves

> were praying in the cabins,
>   Wanting freedom to begin,

and when the Yankee troops arrived,

> the word ran through the village
>   The colored folks are free—
> In the kitchens and the cabins
>   We held a jubilee.

The dramatic tension of these stanzas is constructed by a progressive upbeat that moves toward the climax of the last lines, and the last word, "*jubilee.*"

> And he often used to tell us,
>   "Children, don't forget to pray;
> For the darkest time of morning
>   Is just 'fore the break of day."

> Well, one morning bright and early
>   We heard the fife and drum,
> And the booming of the cannon—
>   The Yankee troops had come.

> When the word ran through the village,
>   The colored folks are free—
> In the kitchens and the cabins
>   We held a jubilee.

The high spirit of the jubilee sequence is eclipsed by the death of President Lincoln, and the dismal failure of his successor, Andrew Johnson, who they hoped would be "*the Moses / Of all the colored race.*" Again the Mosaic motif surfaces in Harper's script. But Johnson fails to acquiesce to the biblical allusion while the Rebels resist black, postwar independence.

The elliptical curve of Afroamerican language is characteristic of Chloe's narrative. She rarely speaks directly to describe or to delineate the literal, but rather she alludes to effects and ramifications. Concerning Johnson's alleged attempt to address Rebel tyranny, Chloe says:

> Cause I heard 'em talking ''bout a circle
>   That he was swinging round.

But subsequently, Johnson loses the election, and Chloe elicits a common Afroamerican expression (that is still vividly active in contemporary speech) to reference Johnson's electoral defeat: "*They let poor Andy slide.*")

Chloe praises President Grant

> for breaking up
> The wicked Ku-Klux Klan.

and the narrative proceeds with a series of critical observations about suffrage and the black vote. She explains that selling one's vote is a treacherous act, and relates three examples of men selling out. She also includes the political attitudes and actions of the women, responding to such selfish irresponsibility. Notwithstanding, Harper's position on the Fifteenth Amendment renders some disappointment with the irresponsible voting practices of some black men.

When John Thomas Reeder sold his vote to buy some flour and meat, his wife, Aunt Kitty, threw them away and scolded him for being so cheap, and likewise "*voting for the wrong side.*" David Rand's treachery was highlighted by his stupidity, when he sold his vote for sugar that turned out to be sand. The superficial level of white sugar is associated with Rands' shallow intelligence. In both instances, the vote is considered priceless by the wives; both of these images reemerge in *Iola Leroy*.

Lucinda Grange harassed her husband, Joe, when she discovered he had sold his vote, and told him to either take the "*rations*" back or if he voted wrong, "*To take his rags and go.*" Such volatile reactions on the part of the women are intensified in the ensuing stanza, whereby the election is crucial to the defeat of the rebel candidate and the possibilities for the radical party. The inclusion of the pronoun "we" is collective and inclusive as the political perspective of the poet and the community.

> I think that Curnel Johnson said
>   His side had won the day,
> Had not we women radicals
>   Just got right in the way.

In contrast to the travesties of Reeder, Rand, and Grange, John Slade is exemplified as a man of integrity,

> And we've got lots of other men
>   Who rally round the cause.

Chloe concludes the section of the story on an encouraging note for the transcendent black man:

> And yet I would not have you think
>   That all our men are shabby;
> But 'tis said in every flock of sheep
>   There will be one that's scabby.

> I've heard, before election came
>   They tried to buy John Slade;
> But he gave them all to understand
>   That he wasn't in that trade.

> And we've got lots of other men
>   Who rally round the cause,
> And go for holding up the hands
>   That gave us equal laws.

> Who know their freedom cost too much
>   Of blood and pain and treasure,
> For them to fool away their votes
>   For profit or for pleasure.

"Aunt Chloe's Politics" is the third part of the poem and is the shortest—only five stanzas. Speaking metaphorically, Chloe's expressions sustain the aural consistency of the poem. She cuts critically into the diabolical motives of politicians with sardonic similes, the latter of which can be found in Shakespeare:

> I've seen 'em honey-fugle round,
>   And talk so awful sweet,
> That you'd think them full of kindness,
>   As an egg is full of meat

Her political concern is for the future, in particular, "*we want to school our children.*" This active concern and sacrifice on the part of the freedwomen was observed and reported by Harper in her letters and essays. Likewise, Chloe's politics do not accept or exempt responsibility according to color. She states matter-of-factly that:

> When we want to school our children
>   If money isn't there,
> Whether black or white have took it,
>   The loss we all must share.

> And this buying up each other
>   Is something worse than mean,
> Though I thinks a heap of voting,
>   I go for voting clean.

The pragmatic vision of Aunt Chloe, like many freedwomen, coincides with Harper's black feminist perspective. These women do not have the vote but many realize that the value of electoral politics is the power and protection it could give. This sequence of *Sketches* does not include the historical action, but rather intersects thematically with the progressive thrust of Chloe's story.

The sequence, **"Church Building"** exemplifies the apex of spiritual confirmation and engages the social, political, and religious convergence of Christianity for the Afroamerican community. Uncle Jacob, the religious leader of the community, advises them to build "*a meeting place.*" This opening stanza indicates the historical experience of the church during slavery, a place where the slaves met under the auspices of spiritual and political communion.

The poor but conscientious community manages to salvage savings from their wages until the church becomes a reality. Uncle Jacob's death is forecasted with greying anticipation, "*But his voice rang like a trumpet,*" the sound of Gabriel calling him home to heaven. The rolling of the *o*'s inside the internal and terminal rhyme pattern reinforces the musical simile, while the dialect modulates the rhythm. Uncle Jacob's passing into "*the promised land,*" has a deliberate ring. After the deliverance from slavery the people never crossed the River Jordan, as they were beset by the tyranny of the Ku Klux Klan and unkept promises from the federal government. Uncle Jacob tells them to keep the faith,

> "Children you meet me
> Right in the promised land,

which unfortunately still resides only in heaven.

> "For when I'm done a moiling
>   And toiling here below,
> Through the gate into the city
>   Straightway I hope to go."

"Learning to Read" addresses the quest for literacy during and after slavery. Slave illiteracy was often enforced through legislation, and for the most part, nineteenth-century Americans as a whole were illiterate. Harper's advocacy of Afroamerican education was an extension of her own specialized preparation by her abolitionist uncle for survival in a hostile society. Harper's strenuous academic training was regarded as a political weapon against the confabulations of the American power brokers advocating racist/sexist legislation, cultivating cultural chauvinism, distorting biblical text, and thereby undermining the possibilities of a participatory democracy.

Chloe conveys the historical connection between slave society and Confederate resistance to Freedman schools even after slavery:

> Our masters always tried to hide
>   Book learning from our eyes.

The popular belief of the slave holding class was that an educated slave was a discontented slave, which was not an especially astute observation since literate slaves were not dependent on plantation propaganda for insight or information. In fact, the impact of David Walker's *Appeal* on Nat Turner encouraged the enactment of antiliteracy legislation. But intellectual isolation did not necessarily obstruct visionary possibilities for escape through the labyrinth of lies that strengthened the mental chains of slavery, as well as the vicissitudes of national politics that veiled the self-determination of the newly freed during Reconstruction.

Aunt Chloe relays the tales of Uncle Caldwell and Ben Turner who pursued reading during slavery despite the threat of punishment. Caldwell

> took pot liquor fat
>   And greased the pages of his book
> And hid it in his hat.

This maneuver deluded his overseers who would not suspect that these *"greasy papers"* were part of a library.

Turner, like Tom in *Iola Leroy,* who one also associates with Nat Turner, had *"heard the children spell,"* memorized their words, and learned to read through aural association. A point to observe here is how the oral orientation of the culture can become a pedagogical technique for literacy. Sound identification internalized before visual recognition of written transcription, to some extent disrupts dialect interference because tonal distinctions are differentiated before the visual symbol is cognitively processed. *Sketches* is a text that benefits this learning strategy, with the infusion of dialect interrelating with a predominance of standard spelling in folk rhythms.

Chloe also says, *"I longed to read my Bible,"* but because she is *"rising sixty,"* most folks say it is too late. But Chloe considers her age as an incentive and does not stop studying until she can read the *"hymns and Testament."* After she learns to read, she acquires her own place, thereby connecting literacy to self-sufficiency, as well as to spiritual independence. The feminist attitude about education, work, and autonomy is conveyed in the following image:

> Then I got a little cabin
>   A place to call my own—
> And I felt as independent
>   As a queen upon her throne.

The last section of *Sketches* is **"The Reunion."** The ending cyclically rounds the long poem into its resolution with the reunion of Chloe and her son Jake. The reunion fulfills Uncle Jacob's prophecy and demonstrates Harper's belief in the cosmic justice. The thematic thrust of the ending invigorates vision, sustained by faith, focused on family. Chloe's son returns asking for *"Missis Chloe Fleet."* She recognizes his voice and turns to embrace Jake. Her metaphor for joy is derived from the Twenty-third Psalm, as she exclaims:

> What gladness filled my cup!
> And I laughed, and just rolled over.

Jake explains how he, like so many other freed slaves, was determined to find his family. Likewise, he reports the circumstances of his brother Ben, Chloe's second son:

> "Why, mammy, I've been on your hunt
>   Since ever I've been free,
> And I have heard from brother Ben,—
>   He's down in Tennessee.
>
> "He wrote me that he had a wife,"
>   "And children?" "Yes, he's three."
> "You married, too?" "Oh no, indeed,
>   I thought I'd first get free."

The intense dialogue between mother and son in the preceding stanzas contains tight, lyrical control through brevity, drama, and dense imagery. In only two stanzas we come to understand how, where, and why Chloe's family is alive and prospering. The following lines contrast her good fortune with the demise of the *"Mistus"* and the death of *"Mister Thomas."*

> I'm richer now then Mistus
>   Because I have got my son;
> And Mister Thomas he is dead,
>   And she's got nary one.

Chloe culminates the denouement with a suggestion to *"write to brother Benny"* and to tell him *"he must come this fall."* She declares they will make her cabin big enough to *"hold us all."* The poem ends with a final request to collect her entire family before she dies, thus the encircling of the children, a necessary ritual before the passage through death into heaven. Chloe compares her spirit to Simeon, who helped Jesus bear the burden of the cross on the road to Mount Calvary. But she must reunite with her offspring before she can pass into peace.

> Tell him I want to see 'em all
>   Before my life do cease.
> And then, like good old Simeon,
>   I hope to die in peace.

CONCLUSION

Sketches of Southern Life is one of the first works of American literature that appreciates the dynamics of Afroamerican folk language and culture. More than any other Harper poem, *Sketches* embodies the source and force of slave resistance. Harper's class sensitivity, which was an outgrowth of her own experiences with economic uncertainty and social strife, and her expansive perspective, which was the consequence of her ongoing interactions with grass roots activists and radical political activity, developed the creative insight necessary to write a poem reflective of the strength and beauty of the people she served and the complexity and dynamics of the history they prevailed.

Carla L. Peterson (essay date 1995)

SOURCE: "'Whatever Concerns Them, as a Race, Concerns Me': The Oratorical Careers of Frances Ellen Watkins Harper and Sarah Parker Remond," in *"Doers of the Word": African-American Women Speakers and Writers in the North (1830-1880),* Oxford University Press, 1995, pp. 119-45.

[*In the following excerpt, Peterson analyzes the cultural contexts surrounding Harper's poetry, seeing her writing as an "experimental activity" that appropriated the nineteenth-century discourse of sentimentality and broke down social distinctions between public and private spheres.*]

Poetry—in both its recited and printed forms—was . . . an experimental activity for Watkins Harper, serving as a structural frame through which she could fashion herself in the public role of poet-preacher in order to articulate her vision of nineteenth-century America. In accordance with Unitarian literary theory, in which the British novelist Maria Edgeworth and poet Felicia Hemans were put forth as models of good taste, Watkins Harper conceived of poetry as moral and didactic preaching in which originality was less important than the ability to create character in the reader. In particular, sentimentality became a mode whose purpose was not to unleash an excess of emotion in the reader but rather to channel feelings toward benevolent and moral ends, develop Christian character, and forge social bonds that would commit the individual reader to work for the betterment of society. Thus, Watkins Harper's poetry was designed to rationalize the emotions in order to encourage her audience's social activism.

In appropriating sentimentality to fashion her poetic discourse, Watkins Harper was of course working with a mode that had come to dominate antebellum literary discourse. Relying on contemporary modernist norms, early twentieth-century critics have tended to devalue her work because of this very sentimentalism and didacticism. In *To Make a Poet Black,* for example, Saunders Redding condemns Watkins Harper both for being "a full-fledged member of the propagandist group," indulging in "particular" rather than "general" feelings, and for allowing herself to be "overwhelmed" by "the demands of her audience for the sentimental treatment of the old subjects" and thus "gush with pathetic sentimentality." His comments further suggest that Watkins Harper's popularity—her

acquiescence to the taste of her nineteenth-century public—was a sign of artistic weakness which "led her into errors of metrical construction." Such evaluations dehistoricize Watkins Harper's poetry, ignoring the cultural work it performed. It is only recently that revisionist scholarship on sentimental culture has been able to place Watkins Harper's poetry in its proper cultural context that would help us understand her enormous popularity in the nineteenth century. . . .

[It] may be noted here that sentimentality in America was an outgrowth of the ideology of separate spheres that sought to establish a strict dichotomy between the public male sphere and the domestic female one. Written largely by and for women, sentimentality took as its main subject such domestic themes as the family, the home, motherhood, and childhood. More specifically, according to Philip Fisher [in *Hard Facts: Setting and Form in the American Novel,* 1985], sentimentality occupied itself with the socially weak and helpless whose plight was most often inscribed upon the body, rendering it a highly bodied form. Such a pitiable portrayal of the weak was designed to evoke feelings of pathos in the reader, to create, in Fisher's words, "an inward and empathetic emotional bond." Yet, if sentimentality initially seemed to locate itself within the private worlds of domesticity and feeling, in the hands of many writers—both white and black—it quickly extended itself to more public and political themes. Much sentimental literature, in fact, illustrates the extent to which the public comes to infiltrate and inhabit the domestic, thereby politicizing it, and conversely the degree to which metaphors of domesticity are appropriated to express the political, thereby domesticating it. Ultimately, sentimentality's demand that its readers respond with compassion and sympathy to the plight of the oppressed dictated, as Fisher has noted, a "public" extension of the reader's private self out toward the other. It is important to note, however, that in the case of many black writers, Watkins Harper included, their reading public was conceptualized not merely as female but also as male; and at all times their goal remained the public one of stirring moral conscience in order to effect social change.

An analysis of one of Watkins Harper's earliest poems, **"The Syrophenician Woman,"** may serve to illustrate some of the ways in which sentimental discourse is deployed in her poetry. The poem inaugurates her earliest volume of poetry available to us, *Poems on Miscellaneous Subjects,* first published by a Boston house, J. B. Yerrinton and Sons, in 1854 and then in a slightly enlarged edition by a Philadelphia printer, Merrihew and Thompson, in 1857 (there are no extant copies of *Forest Leaves* [1845], which Still has named as Watkins Harper's first published collection). The selection of **"The Syrophenician Woman"** as a first poem is revealing, since several other poems in the collection (**"Eliza Harris," "The Dying Christian,"** and **"Ethiopia"**) appear to have been written earlier. But **"The Syrophenician Woman"** is a highly appropriate inaugural choice as it encapsulates themes and techniques that recur throughout Watkins Harper's poetry and illustrates her early awareness of poetry as experimental activity.

Cast as a narrative, Watkins Harper's poem focuses on the Syrophenician woman as the weak and oppressed subject whose plight is designed to evoke the reader's compassion. It is a revision of the New Testament story told in Mark 7 of the mother who begs Jesus to cast out unclean spirits from her daughter. The theme of the fallen woman is common in Watkins Harper's poetry, yet it is present here only indirectly—as the biblical source of poetic inspiration. Although the biblical verses might well resonate in the reader's ear, Watkins Harper's poem actually depicts the mother's attempt to save her (ungendered) child from death by hunger. The poem universalizes the themes of hunger and poverty, but it also allows those readers who so choose to apply these circumstances to the specific historical experience of African Americans; and it remains possible that such experiences were evocative of Watkins Harper's own childhood as well. As in Mark's account, Watkins Harper's woman remonstrates with the Lord who at first fears "wast[ing] the children's bread" but then acknowledges her moral superiority. She thus takes on a preacherly function, becoming the voice of moral conscience itself. Finally, the poem also illustrates the basic thrust of Watkins Harper's narrational strategies. For if the poet initially positions the Syrophenician woman as a first-person narrator, in the third stanza she becomes a character in a third-person narrative, distanced from the reader and mediated by the interposition of an authoritative narrator who, in telling her story, seeks to stir the moral conscience of her readers just as the woman had Jesus': "With a purpose nought could move, / And the zeal of woman's love, / Down she knelt in anguish wild—."

Like **"The Syrophenician Woman,"** many of Watkins Harper's other antebellum poems also insist on a reconfiguration of the categories of public and private. Her poetry functions, then, on one level as "public" poetry that narrates multiple social histories through the characterization of representative types: slavery in **"The Slave Mother"** and **"The Slave Auction,"** temperance in **"The Drunkard's Child,"** poverty in **"Died of Starvation,"** appropriate marriage choices in **"Report"** and **"Advice to the Girls,"** female sexuality and the double standard in **"The Contrast,"** and finally, Reconstruction racial uplift work in her poems of the 1870s. On occasion it may also represent, very indirectly, the "private" history of Watkins Harper's own life in which feelings stemming from the autobiographical facts of orphanhood or death find covert emotional expression as, for example, in **"The Dying Christian"**: "She faded from our vision, / Like a thing of love and light; / But we feel she lives for ever, / A spirit pure and bright."

Yet in Watkins Harper's poems the public-private dichotomy finds itself repeatedly deconstructed. Thus, if the public history of African Americans is seen most often to unfold within the "private" familial sphere, the poems' depiction of the slave mother's or the fugitive's wife's fate, for example, historicizes African-American family life and demonstrates the degree to which it is never "private." These characters are representative because history has inscribed itself on their bodies; yet Watkins Harper's

narrational strategy is one that, unlike the sentimental discourse of the dominant cultural, seeks carefully to deemphasize the African-American body and focus instead on emotional response. In addition, as the poems' narrating persona, Watkins Harper empowered herself to comment upon their events, thus giving public voice to her own private opinions. And, in availing herself of contemporary public poetic conventions to portray her own private emotions, concerning orphanhood and death, for example, she was able to make public her deepest feelings while simultanenously veiling them behind the anonymity of conventional poetic discourse. Finally, just as other African-American writers sold their slave narratives or spiritual autobiographies after delivering antislavery speeches or sermons, so Watkins Harper sold her books of poems to the audiences that had come to hear her lecture. In this sense her poetry can be interpreted as autobiography, as an indirect account of an individual life.

If such poetry relied on sentimental discourse in order to call attention to the plight of the weak and the oppressed while refusing to scrutinize their bodily form, it was also designed in public performance to rationalize the speaker's body. To achieve these goals, Watkins Harper made use of an "aesthetics of restraint" whose chief "coping strategies," in Buell's words, were "narrative and meter"; in this aesthetics, emotion is contained "within formal limits conceded themselves to be limited" [Introduction to *Selected Poems of Henry Wadsworth Longfellow*]. Indeed, as critics like Frances Smith Foster, Maryemma Graham, and Patricia Liggins Hill have noted, Watkins Harper most often chose the narrative mode over the lyric, implicitly suggesting her desire to avoid the lyric, traditionally associated with the spontaneous expression of emotion. In Watkins Harper's poetry, passion is subdued and rationalized by means of narrativization. In order to narrate different nineteenth-century "public" and "private" histories, Watkins Harper relied on highly conventional poetic forms just as she utilized highly traditional rhetorical modes in her public speaking; it was perhaps the very traditionalism of her verse that made publication with a mainstream press possible and ensured her popularity throughout the nineteenth century. Specifically, the poetic forms she appropriated were the ballad and the hymn, and in the Reconstruction period, the epic as well, all three of which are ancient poetic modes grounded in incontrovertible forms of narrative authority and designed to bring together in community the disparate elements of the audience.

In appropriating the ballad form, Watkins Harper turned to the work of such contemporary poets as Longfellow who had adapted the European ballad to American subjects. In its origins the ballad grew out of oral folk culture as the product of an anonymous author who voices the concerns of the community; in addition, in the British tradition the broadside ballad came into being as a vehicle for political expression. As she made use of the ballad form, Watkins Harper invoked its oral, communal, and political functions in order to recount diverse social histories embedded in nineteenth-century American culture at large. In these ballads, plots unfold around social themes as characters interact with one another, often by means of dialogue, while Watkins Harper as narrator intervenes on occasion to provide authorial judgments and reinforce the moral point of the poem, as, for example, in **"The Slave Auction"**: "Ye who have laid your love to rest, / And wept above their lifeless clay, / Know not the anguish of that breast, / Whose lov'd are rudely torn away." Rather than view such authorial commentary as a sign of excessive sermonizing and didacticism, we should recognize its important function as a vehicle that enabled Watkins Harper to authorize, and make public, her own personal opinions on social issues. It also encouraged her in other poems to become the poetic protagonist and speak out directly in her own voice as, for example, in **"Free Labor"**: "I wear an easy garment, / O'er it no toiling slave / Wept tears of hopeless anguish, / In his passage to the grave."

Watkins Harper's awareness of the need to temper personal political passion through narrative control is articulated in her poem **"A Mother's Heroism,"** which depicts Elijah Lovejoy's mother's reaction to the news of her son's death: "It seemed as if a fearful storm / Swept wildly round her soul; / A moment, and her fragile form / Bent 'neath its fierce control." Watkins Harper's personal convictions about mob violence are here projected onto the poetic protagonist. But speech enables Lovejoy's mother to regain control of her emotions and consequently to articulate a narrative of liberty: "' 'Tis well! 'tis well!' the mother said, / 'That thus my child should die. / 'Tis well that, to his latest breath, / He plead for liberty; / Truth nerved him for the hour of death, / And taught him how to die.'" If narrative here is a means of emotional and physical containment, allowing Lovejoy's mother's "fragile form" ultimately to resist the "fearful storm's" "fierce control" in order to impose its own control, so is Watkins Harper's conventional use of the ballad's formal elements—the four-line stanza composed of alternating iambic tetrameter and trimeter lines, whose brevity makes metrical substitutions difficult, and an ABAB (or ABCB) rhyme scheme that need not be technically perfect. In its origin, the simplicity and regularity of this stanzaic form served the purposes of memorability and popular appeal in oral folk culture. In Watkins Harper's poems the conventionality and formal limitations of the ballad stanza further served the poet's imperative of emotional restraint.

Familiarity with the ballad enabled Watkins Harper to experiment with another verse form not usually encompassed under the rubric of poetry—the hymn, whose stanzaic form is identical to that of the ballad. For, like other contemporary Unitarians and abolitionists such as Lowell, Longfellow, and Whittier, Watkins Harper wrote poems that are hymnal in nature and intent. As public poetry designed for oral performance and to move the entire congregation, the hymn is grounded in a literary philosophy of simplicity and clarity. As Isaac Watts, the great English hymn writer, whose compositions were freely adapted by American Unitarians, admitted: "In many of these composures, I have just permitted my verse to rise above a flat and indolent style . . . because I would neither indulge any bold metaphors, nor admit of

hard words, nor tempt the ignorant worshipper to sing without his understanding" [Quoted in Donald Davie, *English Hymnology in the Eighteenth Century,* 1980].

It was Watkins Harper's genius to take the hymn form beyond religious exaltation to social appeal and, in the Reconstruction period, to political argument. Thus, **"That Blessed Hope"** speaks in traditional language of the poet's desire to join Christ in Heaven: "Help me, amidst this world of strife, / To long for Christ to reign, / That when He brings the crown of life, / I may that crown obtain!" But other poems directly address current social and political conditions in a discourse that, unlike that of the ballad, does not center on representative types but rather is given to reflective commentary that will stir the readers' moral conscience and commit them to social action. **"Ethiopia,"** for example, predicts God's deliverance of this nation's sons from slavery—"Redeemed from dust and freed from chains, / Her sons shall lift their eyes"—while **"Bible Defence of Slavery"** specifically attacks the American churches' support of slavery and the hypocrisy of their missionary efforts abroad: "Oh! when ye pray for heathen lands, / And plead for their dark shores, / Remember Slavery's cruel hands / Make heathens at your doors!" If the hymn verse in its simplicity and regularity was designed, like the ballad, to appeal to popular understanding, it also enabled Watkins Harper once again to contain her own political passion within formal limits and thereby legitimate the radicalness of her political stance.

Watkins Harper's poems also appeared, of course, in printed form, thus allowing her to abstract herself from the public's gaze and invert that strategy of looking away adopted by Greenfield's audience in order to appreciate her music as "sounds right sweet." Published singly in newspapers, the poems were also brought together in book form, making it possible to read the poetic volume as a continuous narrative and seek out links between the poems. Although we have no way of knowing to what extent Watkins Harper was able to control her own publication process, we may nonetheless speculate as to how the sequence of poems in each volume might add to our understanding of both her social ideology and her methods of appealing to contemporary audiences. Like the collected volumes of Lydia Sigourney and other contemporary white women poets, none of Watkins Harper's volumes may be said to form a progressive linear narrative; instead, they appear to resist strict organization. But the poems within each volume, as well as from volume to volume, are unified by a common ethos—evangelical Unitarianism—and by the recurrent emergence of related themes; moreover, the positioning of the first and last poems of each volume as well as the additions made from edition to edition function as a kind of cultural statement.

If there is a particular structural principle operative in Watkins Harper's two surviving antebellum collections of poems, I suggest that it is a framing device in which the first and last sets of poems tend to constellate around a particular topic, or in which the last poems function as a kind of counterweight to the first. Thus, the initial and final poems of the 1854 *Poems on Miscellaneous Sub-*

jects focus for the most part on the topic of slavery, while those of the central section are concerned with multiple themes—death, temperance, marriage, female sexuality, and so forth. Such a framing device tends to foreground the material of the frame itself rather than that which is placed inside it. In this instance it embeds within the frame some of Watkins Harper's most personal concerns—death, orphanhood, the social construction of women's sexual and marital roles—allowing these to recede somewhat from the reader's line of vision. But it also points to the presence of a common thread that unites all these social issues—the perversion of power relations between strong and weak, whether between master and slave, man and woman, or rich and poor—of which slavery remained for Watkins Harper the most egregious. The dominance of slavery in Watkins Harper's thinking is further reinforced by the addition of a new group of poems at the end of her 1857 edition of *Poems on Miscellaneous Subjects,* almost all of which focus on this one topic—**"The Tennessee Hero," "Free Labor," "Lines," "The Dismissal of Tyng,"** and **"The Slave Mother (A Tale of the Ohio)."**

The very last poems of both the 1854 and 1857 editions of *Poems on Miscellaneous Subjects,* however, explicitly seek to link the social oppression of women within the "private" sphere to larger political issues. They portray women whose lives are constrained, even destroyed, by male political action, be it American slavery or other forms of bondage. Thus, **"Eva's Farewell,"** a retelling of the death of Stowe's Eva, who refuses to live any longer within the context of Southern slavery, concludes the 1854 edition, while **"The Slave Mother (A Tale of the Ohio),"** a poetic account of Margaret Garner's murder of her child in Ohio in 1856, is appended to the 1857 edition. Finally, two biblical poems, **"Rizpah, the Daughter of Ai"** and **"Ruth and Naomi,"** complete the 1857 volume. If **"Ruth and Naomi"** recounts the well-known story of female friendship in which the widowed Naomi exiles herself from the land of Moab and returns to Bethlehem accompanied by her faithful daughter-in-law Ruth, **"Rizpah, the Daughter of Ai"** narrates a much less familiar story. Turning to the biblical account of Joshua's conquest of Canaan, it retells from the woman's point of view Rizpah's sorrow over David's sacrifice of her sons to the Gibeonites as a penance for Saul's betrayal. All four poems thus illustrate how from biblical times to the present women within the supposedly protected domestic sphere have been made to suffer as a consequence of male political actions.

Watkins Harper's poems, as we have noted, occasionally served as accompaniments to her speeches. Indeed, in Watkins Harper's canon verse and lectures cannot be considered isolated aesthetic objects that exist separately from one another but must be viewed as coextensive not only with each other but with her essays and fiction as well. Poems and prose interact continuously as social concerns find their way equally, and often in exact detail, into both forms. As Frances Foster has shown, for example [in *A Brighter Coming Day: A Francis Ellen Watkins Harper Reader,* 1990], Watkins Harper's description of

"the stain of blood and tears upon the warp and woof" of cloth made by slave labor is woven into both her poem **"Free Labor"** and her 1855 "Free Labor Movement" speech; and her antebellum praise of Moses in the essay "Our Greatest Want"—"I like the character of Moses"— is later developed in her postbellum epic. Aunt Chloe's Reconstruction political efforts in *Sketches of Southern Life* are echoed by the fictional character of Aunt Linda in *Iola Leroy* (1892), just as the poetic hero's martyrdom in "A Story of the Rebellion" is embodied in the slave Tom in the same novel. Watkins Harper's appeal to the "women of America" to demand justice for the Negro in her 1892 speech "Woman's Political Future" is reiterated in the 1895 poem "An Appeal to My Countrywomen," and the 1895 poem "Only a Word" is actually embedded in a later essay, "True and False Politeness" (1898). Throughout the volumes, poems on slavery and temperance make concrete the abstract propositions set forth in the speeches and essays. And finally, Watkins Harper's belief in the redemptive power of Jesus Christ reverberates as a constant theme in all her writings, poetry and prose.

FURTHER READING

Bibliography

Miller, Ruth, and Peter J. Katopes. "Modern Beginnings." In *Black American Writers: Bibliographic Essays I: The Beginnings Through the Harlem Renaissance and Langston Hughes,* pp. 133-60. New York: Saint Martin's Press, 1978.

Descriptive bibliography of Harper's works and relevant secondary sources.

Whiteman, Maxwell. Introduction to *Poems on Miscellaneous Subjects,* by Frances Ellen Watkins. 1857. Reprint. Philadelphia: Historic Publications, 1969, 48 p.

Bibliography of works and principal sources of biographical and bibliographic information.

Yellin, Jean Fagan, and Cynthia D. Bond. "Frances Ellen Watkins Harper." In *The Pen Is Ours: A Listing of Writings by and about African-American Women before 1910 with Secondary Bibliography to the Present,* pp. 80-101. New York: Oxford University Press, 1991.

Lists all of Harper's works including magazine and anthology listings for publication of individual poems and letters. Also includes over one hundred entries of writings about her.

Biography

Bacon, Margaret Hope. "'One Great Bundle of Humanity': Frances Ellen Watkins Harper (1825-1911)." *The Pennsylvania Magazine of History & Biography* CXIII, No. 1 (1989): 21-43.

Historical biography praising Harper for her abolitionist and humanitarian activities.

Brawley, Benjamin. "Three Negro Poets: Horton, Mrs. Harper, and Whitman." *The Journal of Negro History* II, No. 4 (October 1917): 384-92.

  Briefly mentions Harper as a popular poet in the mid-nineteenth century, whose writing "was best when most simple."

Brown, Hallie Q. "Frances Ellen Watkins Harper." In *Homespun Heroines and Other Women of Distinction,* pp. 97-103. 1926. Reprint. Freeport, N. Y.: Books for Libraries Press, 1971.

  Biographical sketch focusing on Harper's career as an orator and her work with the Underground Railroad.

Dannett, Sylvia G. L. "Freedom Lectures." In *Profiles of Negro Womanhood: Volume I, 1619-1900,* pp. 94-109. New York: M. W. Lads, 1964.

  Biography and critical commentary. Dannett's praise for Harper's poetry and the novel *Iola Leroy* are secondary concerns in the essay.

Majors, M. A. "Frances E. W. Harper." In *Noted Negro Women: Their Triumphs and Activities,* pp. 23-7. Chicago: Donohue & Henneberry, 1893.

  Contains laudatory remarks about Harper's character and career. Majors cites supporting information from book entries and journal reviews on the oratorical and literary career of Harper and on her qualities of high morality and civic consciousness.

Robinson, William H., Jr. "Frances E. W. Harper." In *Early Black American Poets: Selections with Biographical and Critical Introductions,* pp. 26-38. Dubuque, Iowa: Wm. C. Brown, 1969.

  Selection of Harper's poetry, with a short biographical introduction to her life and works.

Sherman, Joan R. "Frances Ellen Watkins Harper." In *African-American Poetry of the Nineteenth Century: An Anthology,* pp. 112-45. Urbana: University of Illinois Press, 1992.

  Selection of eleven of Harper's poems, with notes and a short biographical introduction.

Still, William. "Frances Ellen Watkins Harper." In *The Underground Railroad,* pp. 755-80. 1871. Reprint. New York: Arno Press and The New York Times, 1968.

  Biographical essay. Still, a contemporary and personal friend of Harper, includes excerpts of letters written to him by Harper and newspaper reviews of her lectures.

Criticism

Barksdale, Richard, and Keneth Kinnamon. "The Struggle Against Slavery and Racism, 1800-1860: Frances Watkins Harper." In *Black Writers of America: A Comprehensive Anthology,* pp. 224-25. New York: Macmillan, 1972.

  Declares Harper a mediocre poet and inferior prose writer whose exposure as a lecturer led to her success as a writer.

Boyd, Melba Joyce. "Discarded Legacy: The Critical Mistreatment of the Literature by Frances E. W. Harper." *Drumvoices Revue* 3, Nos. 1 & 2 (1993-94): 129-38.

  Disagrees with earlier critics of Harper, such as Benjamin Brawley and Vernon Loggins, citing the need for recognition of Harper's aesthetic contributions.

Hill, Patricia Liggins. "'Let Me Make Songs for the People': A Study of Frances Watkins Harper's Poetry." *Black American Literature Forum* 15, No. 2 (Summer 1981): 60-5.

  A chronological, thematic discussion of Harper's poetry.

Riggins, Linda N. "The Works of Frances E. W. Harper." *Black World* 22, No. 2 (December 1972): 30-6.

  Briefly analyzes selected poems in light of their social contributions.

Additional coverage of Harper's life and career is contained in the following sources published by Gale Research: *Black Literature Criticism*; *DISCovering Authors: Multicultural Authors Module*; *DISCovering Authors: Poets Module*; **and** *Twentieth-Century Literary Criticism,* **Vol. 14.**

Philip (Arthur) Larkin
1922-1985

English poet, novelist, essayist, and critic

INTRODUCTION

A major poet of the post-World War II period, Larkin attempted to capture ordinary experience in realistic and rational terms. Larkin's poetry both avoids romanticizing experience and moves away from the abstract, experimental language of Eliot and the modernists. Although Larkin's poetry follows the cadences of everyday "plain speech," it is composed in strict meters and forms. It is executed in the poet's own voice, which can be self-deprecatingly humorous or cynical, thoughtful or softly humorous. To some critics, his poetry, reflective of the life of a near-recluse, seems too grim, "bleak, if not black," but to Clive James, "It made misery beautiful. . . . the voice was unmistakable."

Biographical Information

The son of Eva Day and Sydney Larkin, a city treasurer, Larkin was born in Coventry, England. While he claimed that his childhood was happy, he was extraordinarily shy, due in part to his stammering and near-sightedness, which went unnoticed for a long time. In 1940 he began undergraduate studies at St. John's College at Oxford, where he formed close friendships with Kingsley Amis and John Wain, and wrote and published poems in student literary magazines. It was at Oxford that he finally felt that he was among peers, that he could excel, and he did. After completing his degree in English with high honors, Larkin took a post as librarian in Shropshire, and the two years that followed were so productive for Larkin that he composed his first two volumes of verse and his two novels. In 1955 Larkin moved to Hull to become university librarian at the Brynmor Jones Library. There he established the solitary, private lifestyle for which he became well-known, avoiding participation in literary circles and refusing public appearances. With the publication of *The Less Deceived,* his critical reputation took seed, and he was honored with many awards in his lifetime. Larkin remained at Hull for thirty years, writing poetry and criticism in the evenings, and travelling little, until he died in 1985 at 63 after surgery for throat cancer. His *Collected Poems* continue to be a bestseller in Britain; and his popularity, especially since his death, has brought him acclaim as England's "unofficial poet-laureate" and the "poet laureate of the common man."

Major Works

Before Larkin moved to Hull, he wrote and published *The North Ship* (1946) and a pamphlet, *XX Poems* (1951), which

he published himself. The former book is widely considered to reflect the poet's early influences, W. H. Auden and W. B. Yeats; the latter, his emergent mature voice. "I felt for the first time," he said, "that I was speaking for myself." In his next work, *The Less Deceived* (1955), the poet expressed his lifelong need to expose false ideals and illusions. *The Whitsun Weddings* (1964) has been said to express the prosperity of Britain's post-war mass culture and is colored by a wide range of tones. In *High Windows* (1974), the poet, ever cynical and introspective, had now entered middle-age and was poised to look at death, or, as he wrote in the final lines of "High Windows," eternity. After *High Windows* Larkin wrote no new poetry except for the famous "Aubade." *Required Writing* (1983) is a compilation of prose written between 1955 and 1982. One who could not "live a day without jazz," Larkin contributed music reviews to the *Daily Telegraph,* which were collected in *All What Jazz* (1970). His two novels, *Jill* (1946) and *A Girl in Winter* (1947), featuring naive, female protagonists, were for Larkin "oversized poems." *Collected Poems* (1988) appeared posthumously, edited by fellow "Movement" poet Anthony Thwaite, who decided to include some of Larkin's unpublished verse to demonstrate his editorial ability, his development as an artist, and problems he solved over days, months, or even a decade, in various verses.

Critical Reception

Larkin has been viewed largely as a gloomy poet, misanthropic, and pessimistic about human endeavors. Although the author of only four volumes of verse, these, along with his two novels, continue to be reprinted, and Larkin finds British rivals only in Ted Hughes and Dylan Thomas. His accessible style, which often uses concrete images to move to symbolic celebration and expression of freedom, as well as the first-person speaker of many of his poems, have won him his following over the years. He is the "urban modern man, the insular Englishman," as Seamus Heaney remarked in *Critical Inquiry,* whose "tones are mannerly but not exquisite, well-bred but not mealy-mouthed. If his England and his English are not as deep as Hughes's or as solemn as Hill's, they are nevertheless dearly beloved."

PRINCIPAL WORKS

Poetry

The North Ship 1946; revised edition, 1966
XX Poems 1951
The Fantasy Poets No. 21: Philip Larkin 1954
The Less Deceived 1955; revised edition, 1958
The Whitsun Weddings 1964
High Windows 1974
Collected Poems 1988; revised edition, 1989

Other Major Works

Jill (novel) 1946
Girl in Winter (novel) 1947
All What Jazz: A Record Diary 1961-71 (essays) 1970; revised edition, 1985
Required Writing: Miscellaneous Pieces 1955-1982 (essays) 1983; revised edition, 1984
Selected Letters: 1940-1985 1993

CRITICISM

Ian Hamilton (interview date 1964)

SOURCE: "Four Conversations," in *The London Magazine,* Vol. IV, No. 6, November, 1964, pp. 71-77.

[In the following interview, Larkin discusses his attitudes towards modernist poetry, as exemplified in a number of his own poems.]

[HAMILTON]: *I would like to ask you about your attitude to the so-called 'modernist revolution' in English poetry; how important has it been to you as a poet?*

[LARKIN]: Well, granted that one doesn't spend any time at all thinking about oneself in these terms, I would say that I have been most influenced by the poetry that I've enjoyed—and this poetry has not been Eliot or Pound or anybody who is normally regarded as 'modern'—which is a sort of technique word, isn't it? The poetry I've enjoyed has been the kind of poetry you'd associate with me, Hardy pre-eminently, Wilfred Owen, Auden, Christina Rossetti, Williams Barnes; on the whole, people to whom technique seems to matter less than content, people who accept the forms they have inherited but use them to express their own content.

You don't feel in any way guilty about this, I imagine; would you see yourself as rebelliously anti-modern—you have talked about the 'myth-kitty' and so on . . .

What I do feel a bit rebellious about is that poetry seems to have got into the hands of a critical industry which is concerned with culture in the abstract, and this I do rather lay at the door of Eliot and Pound. I think that Eliot and Pound have something in common with the kind of Americans you used to get around 1910. You know, when Americans began visiting Europe towards the end of the last century, what they used to say about them was that they were keen on culture, *laughably* keen—you got jokes like 'Elmer, is this Paris or Rome?' 'What day is it?' 'Thursday.' 'Then it's Rome.'—you know the kind of thing. This was linked with the belief that you can order culture whole, that it is a separate item on the menu—this was very typically American, and German too, I suppose, and seems to me to have led to a view of poetry which is almost mechanistic, that every poem must include all previous poems, in the same way that a Ford Zephyr has somewhere in it a Ford T Model—which means that to be any good you've got to have read all previous poems. I can't take this evolutionary view of poetry. One never thinks about other poems except to make sure that one isn't doing something that has been done before—writing a verse play about a young man whose father has died and whose mother has married his uncle, for instance. I think a lot of this 'myth-kitty' business has grown out of that, because first of all you have to be terribly educated, you have to have read everything to know these things, and secondly you've got somehow to work them in to show that you are working them in. But to me the whole of the ancient world, the whole of classical and biblical mythology means very little, and I think that using them today not only fills poems full of dead spots but dodges the writer's duty to be original.

You are generally written up as one of the fathers of this so-called Movement; did you have any sense at the time of belonging to a group with any very definite aims?

No sense at all, really. The only other writer I felt I had much in common with was Kingsley Amis, who wasn't really at that time known as a writer—*Lucky Jim* was published in 1954—but of course we'd been exchanging letters and showing each other work for a long time, and I think we laughed at the same things and agreed largely about what you could and couldn't write about, and so on. But the Movement, if you want to call it that, really began when John Wain succeeded John Lehmann on that B.B.C. programme; John planned six programmes called *First Readings* including a varied set of contributors—they weren't all Movementeers by any means. It got attacked in a very convenient way, and consequently we became lumped together. Then there was an article in *The Spectator* actually using the term 'Movement' and Bob Conquest's *New Lines* in 1956 put us all between the same covers. But it certainly never occurred to me that I had anything in common with Thom Gunn, or Donald Davie, for instance, or they with each other and in fact I wasn't mentioned at the beginning. The poets of the group were Wain, Gunn, Davie and, funnily enough, Alvarez.

To what extent, though, did you feel consciously in reaction against Thomas, the Apocalypse, and so on?

Well, one had to live through the forties at one's most impressionable time and indeed I could show you, but won't, a lot of poems I wrote that you wouldn't—well, that were very much of the age. I wrote a great many sedulous and worthless Yeats-y poems, and later on far inferior Dylan Thomas poems—I think Dylan Thomas is much more difficult to imitate than Yeats—and this went on for years and years. It wasn't until about 1948 or 9 that I began writing differently, but it wasn't as any conscious reaction. It's just that when you start writing your own stuff other people's manners won't really do for it.

I would like to ask you about reviews of your work; do they bore you, do you find any of them helpful? In general, how do you react to what is said about you?

Well, one can't be other than grateful for the kind things that are said. They make you wish you wrote better. Otherwise one tries to ignore it—critics can hinder but they can't help. One thing I do feel a slight restiveness about is being typed as someone who has carved out for himself a uniquely dreary life, growing older, having to work, and not getting things he wants and so on—is this so different from everyone else? I'd like to know how all these romantic reviewers spend their time—do they kill a lot of dragons, for instance? If other people do have wonderful lives, then I'm glad for them, but I can't help feeling that my miseries are over-done a bit by the critics. They may retort that they are over-done by me, of course.

You usually write in metre, but now and then you have rather freer poems. I wonder if you have any feeling of technical unrest, of being constricted by traditional forms. Do things like syllabics, projective verse, for instance, have any interest for you?

I haven't anything very original to say about metre. I've never tried syllabics; I'm not sure I fully understand them. I think one would have to be very sure of onself to dispense with the help that metre and rhyme give and I doubt really if I could operate without them. I have occasionally, some of my favourite poems have not rhymed or had any metre, but it's rarely been premeditated.

I'd like to ask you about the poem "Church Going," which has been taken fairly generally as a kind of 'representative attitude poem, standing for a whole disheartened, debunking state of mind in post-war England. How do you feel about that poem, do you think that the things that have been said about it are true? How do you feel about its enormous popularity?

In a way I feel what Hardy is supposed to have said about *Tess*; if I'd known it was going to be so popular I'd have tried to make it better. I think its popularity is somewhat due to extraneous factors—anything about religion tends to go down well; I don't know whether it expresses what people feel. It is of course an entirely secular poem. I was a bit irritated by an American who insisted to me it was a religious poem. It isn't religious at all. Religion surely means that the affairs of this world are under divine superveillance, and so on, and I go to some pains to point out that I don't bother about that kind of thing, that I'm deliberately ignorant of it—'Up at the holy end', for instance. Ah no, it's a great religious poem; he knows better than me—trust the tale and not the teller, and all that stuff.

Of course the poem is about going to church, not religion—I tried to suggest this by the title—and the union of the important stages of human life—birth, marriage and death—that going to church represents; and my own feeling that when they are dispersed into the registry office and the crematorium chapel life will become thinner in consequence. I certainly haven't revolted against the poem. It hasn't become a kind of *Innisfree,* or anything like that.

I have the feeling about it—this has been said often enough, I suppose—that it drops into two parts. The stanza beginning 'A serious house on serious earth it is' seems significantly different in tone and movement to the rest of the poem and it is almost as if it sets up a rejoinder to the attitudes that are embodied in the first part. And that the first part is not just about religious belief or disbelief, it's about the whole situation of being a poet, a man of sensibility, a man of learning even, in an age like ours—that it is all this exclusiveness that is being scoffed at in the first half—it is seriousness in general. Somehow the final stanzas tighten up and are almost ceremonial in their reply to the debunkery; they seem to affirm all that has been scoffed at, and are deliberately more poetic and dignified in doing so. In this sense it seems a debate between poet and persona. *I'd like to know if you planned the poem as a debate.*

Well, in a way. The poem starts by saying, you don't really know about all this, you don't believe in it, you don't know what a rood-loft is—Why do you come here, why do you bother to stop and look round? The poem is seeking an answer. I suppose that's the antithesis you mean. I think one has to dramatize onself a little. I don't arse about in churches when I'm alone. Not much, anyway. I still don't know what rood-lofts are.

A number of poems in **The Less Deceived** *seem to me to carry a final kick in the head for the attitudes they have* *seemed to be taking up. In a poem like "Reasons for Attendance," say, where you have that final 'Or lied'; somehow the whole poem doubles back on itself. What I want to know is how conscious you are of your poems plotting a kind of elaborate self-imprisonment. Do you feel, for instance, that you will ever write a more abandoned, naïve, kind of poetry where you won't, as it were, block all the loopholes in this way? I think this is why I prefer* The Whitsun Weddings *book, because it doesn't do this anything like as confidently.*

Well, I speak to you as someone who hasn't written a poem for eighteen months. The whole business seems terribly remote and I have to remember what it was like. I do think that poems are artificial in the sense that a play is artificial. There are strong second act curtains in poems as well as in plays, you know. I don't really know what a 'spontaneous' poem would be like, certainly not by me. On the other hand, here again I must protest slightly. I always think that the poems I write are very much more naïve—very much more emotional—almost embarrassingly so—than a lot of other people's. When I was tagged as unemotional, it used to mystify me; I used to find it quite shaming to read some of the things I'd written.

I didn't mean that there is not strong personal feeling in your poems, or that they don't have a strong confessional element. But what I do rather feel is that many of them carry this kind of built-in or tagged-on comment on themselves, and I wonder if you feel able to dispense with this. I can see how this might mean being less alert, in a way, less adult and discriminating even. It's probably a stupid question.

It's a very interesting question and I hadn't realised I did that sort of thing. I suppose I always try to write the truth and I wouldn't want to write a poem which suggested that I was different from what I am. In a sense that means you have to build in quite a lot of things to correct any impression of over-optimism or over-commitment. For instance, take love poems. I should feel it false to write a poem going overboard about someone if you weren't at the same time marrying them and setting up house with them, and I should feel bound to add what you call a tag to make it clear I wasn't, if I wasn't. Do you see what I mean? I think that one of the great criticisms of poets of the past is that they said one thing and did another, a false relation between art and life. I always try to avoid this.

I would like to ask you about your novels, and why you haven't written any more.

Well, because I can't. As I may have said somewhere else, I wanted to be a novelist. I wrote one, and then I wrote another, and I thought, This is wonderful, another five years of this and I'll be in the clear. Unfortunately, that was where it stopped. I've never felt as interested in poetry as I used to feel in novels—they were more theatrical, if you know what I mean, you could do the strong second-act curtain even better. Looking back on them, I think they were over-sized poems. They were certainly

written with intense care for detail. If one word was used on page 15 I didn't re-use it on page 115. But they're not very good novels. A very crude difference between novels and poetry is that novels are about other people and poetry is about yourself. I suppose I must have lost interest in other people, or perhaps I was only pretending to be interested in them.

There was a review recently in the Times Literary Supplement *which gave this portrait of you as being some kind of semi-recluse, almost, deliberately withdrawing from the literary life, not giving readings, talks, and so on. I wonder to what extent this withdrawal from literary society is necessary to you as a writer; given that it is true, that is.*

I can't recall exactly what the *TLS* said, but as regards readings, I suppose I'm rather shy. I began life as a bad stammerer, as a matter of fact. Up to the age of 21 I was still asking for railway tickets by pushing written notes across the counter. This has conditioned me against reading in public—the dread that speech failure might come back again. But also, I'm lazy and very busy and it wouldn't give me much in the way of kicks. I think if there is any truth in this rumour or legend, it's because I do find literary parties or meetings, or anything that considers literature, in public, in the abstract rather than concretely, in private, not exactly boring—it is boring, of course—but unhelpful and even inimical. I go away feeling crushed and thinking that everyone is much cleverer than I am and writing much more, and so on. I think it's important not to feel crushed.

Following on, really, from the last question, I was going to ask you about that poem, "Naturally the Foundation Will Bear your Expenses . . ."

Well, that was rather a curious poem. It came from having been to London and having heard that A had gone to India and that B had just come back from India; then when I got back home, happening unexpectedly across the memorial service at the Cenotaph on the wireless, on what used to be called Armistice Day, and the two things seemed to get mixed up together. Almost immediately afterwards *Twentieth Century* wrote saying that they were having a Humour number and would I send them something funny, so I sent that. Actually, it's as serious as anything I have written and I was glad to see that John Wain has picked this up, quite without any prompting from me, in an article in *The Critical Quarterly.* Certainly it was a dig at the middleman who gives a lot of talks to America and then brushes them up and does them on the Third and then brushes them up again and puts them out as a book with Chatto. Why he should be blamed for not sympathising with the crowds on Armistice Day, I don't quite know. The awful thing is that the other day I had a letter from somebody called Lal in Calcutta, enclosing two poetry books of his own and mentioning this poem. He was very nice about it, but I shall have to apologise. I've never written a poem that has been less understood; one editor refused it on the grounds, and I quote, that it was 'rather hard on the Queen'; several people have asked what it was like in

Bombay! There is nothing like writing poems for realizing how low the level of critical understanding is; maybe the average reader can understand what I say, but the above-average often can't.

I wonder if you read much foreign poetry?

Foreign *poetry?* No!

Of contemporary English poets, then, whom do you admire?

It's awfully difficult to talk about contemporaries, because quite honestly I never read them. I really don't. And my likes are really very predictable. You know I admire Betjeman. I suppose I would say that he was my favourite living poet. Kingsley Amis I admire very much as a poet as well as a novelist; I think he's utterly original and can hit off a kind of satiric poem that no-one else can (this is when he is being himself, not when he's Robert Graves). Stevie Smith I'm very fond of in a puzzled way. I think she's terribly good but I should never want to imitate her. Anthony Thwaite's last book seemed very sensitive and efficient to me. I think one has to be both sensitive and efficient. That's about as far as I can go. I don't mean I dislike everyone else, it's just that I don't know very much about them.

What about Americans?

I find myself no more appreciative of Americans. I quite liked Lowell's *Life Studies* but his last book was all about foreign poets—well, I think that is the end; versions of other people's poems are poor substitutes for your own. Occasionally one finds a poem by Donald Justice or Anthony Hecht, but I don't know enough about them to comment. Actually, I like the Beat poets, but again I don't know much about them. That's because I'm fond of Whitman; they seem to me debased Whitman, but debased Whitman is better than debased Ezra Pound.

Do you have many poems you haven't collected? Are you more prolific than you seem to be?

I'm afraid not. There was a whole period between *The North Ship* and *The Less Deceived* which produced a book with the portentous title of *In the Grip of Light,* which went round the publishers in the middle and late forties, but thank God nobody accepted it. Otherwise I hardly ever finish a poem that I don't publish.

*One final, rather broad question. How would you characterize your development as a poet from **The North Ship** to **The Whitsun Weddings**?*

I suppose I'm less likely to write a really bad poem now, but possibly equally less likely to write a really good one. If you can call that development, then I've developed. Kipling said somewhere that when you can do one thing really well, then do something else. Oscar Wilde said that only mediocrities develop. I just don't know. I don't think I want to change; just to become better at what I am.

Anthony Thwaite (essay date 1970)

SOURCE: "The Poetry of Philip Larkin," in *The Survival of Poetry: A Contemporary Survey,* Faber and Faber, 1970, pp. 37-55.

[*In the following essay, Thwaite weaves Larkin's own commentary on his work into a chronological overview of his corpus.*]

There is a certain irony about sitting down to write a critical paper on the poetry of Philip Larkin, when one remembers some remarks of Larkin's about 'poetry as syllabus' and 'the dutiful mob that signs on every September.' Larkin needs no prolegomena, no exegesis: there is no necessary bibliography, no suggested reading, except the poems themselves. In a straightforward Wordsworthian sense, he is a man speaking to men (though his detractors might put it that he is too often simply a chap chatting to chaps). Although few of the poems need any background knowledge beyond that which any reader of English may be supposed to command, when such knowledge is necessary Larkin himself has generally provided it, in his rare but always relevant and commonsensical statements about his work. Beyond that, I can only stand witness to my conviction that he is our finest living poet— and not in any *'Victor Hugo, hélas'* sense—and go on to draw out and underline what seem to me to be his themes, his special voice and his peculiar excellences.

Although Larkin made little impact as a poet until the publication of *The Less Deceived* in 1955, when he was 33, he had started to write and to publish much earlier. In a fugitive essay in the Coventry arts magazine, *Umbrella* (Vol. I, No. 3, Summer 1959), he spoke of writing ceaselessly in his schooldays: 'now verse, which I sewed up into little books, now prose, a thousand words a night after homework.' His first publication, apart from the school magazine of King Henry VIII School in Coventry, was a poem in *The Listener* of November 28th 1940, when he was 18. This (titled **'Ultimatum'**) was one of four poems he had sent in the summer of 1940:

'I was astonished when someone signing himself J.R.A. wrote back saying that he would like to take one (it was the one I had put in to make the others seem better, but never mind).'

Here, as so often, the late J. R. Ackerley showed himself to be a perceptive judge; during his quarter of a century as literary editor of *The Listener,* that periodical probably published more good poetry than any other in England. As it has never been reprinted, it is worth noting this consummately Audenesque piece:

> But we must build our walls, for what we are
> Necessitates it, and we must construct
> The ship to navigate behind them, there.
> Hopeless to ignore, helpless instruct
> For any term of time beyond the years
> That warn us of the need for emigration:
> Exploded the ancient saying: Life is yours.

For on our island is no railway station,
There are no tickets for the Vale of Peace,
No docks where trading ships and seagulls pass.
Remember stories you read when a boy
—The shipwrecked sailor gaining safety by
His knife, tree trunk, and lianas—for now
You must escape, or perish saying no.

Later appearances were in the Fortune Press's anthology, *Poetry From Oxford in Wartime,* edited by William Bell in 1944, and in his own first volume of poetry, **The North Ship,** published by the Fortune Press in July 1945. In the republished version of **The North Ship,** Larkin wrote a characteristically wry and humorous account of the book's original struggle for birth, assisted by that same L. S. Caton (the owner of the Fortune Press) who makes fleeting and protean appearances in several of Kingsley Amis's novels, for Amis's own first book of poems, *Bright November,* was published by the same press and no doubt with some of the same attendant difficulties. Later, in 1946, the Fortune Press published Larkin's first novel, *Jill,* a book which had a minor underground reputation at Oxford when I was an undergraduate in the early and mid-1950s: it was difficult to get copies at that time (though I think it has never actually been out of print), and those few there were were passed round and read with great respect and interest, not chiefly for the authentic-feeling atmosphere of 1940 Oxford but for the extraordinary way in which Larkin manages to present the central character's growing and gradually enveloping fantasy about 'Jill' with a clear narrative and realistic dialogue. This is not the place to deal properly with *Jill,* or with its more professional successor, *A Girl in Winter,* published by Faber in 1947; but they mark the brief flowering of Larkin the novelist, and both of them are so memorable that one can imagine him having staked out, if he had continued, an area and a reputation comparable with, say, Forster's up to *Howards End.*

The North Ship is now gently and self-deprecatingly dismissed by Larkin. Indeed, I want to make no great claims for it. It is interesting in the way that any considerable poet's juvenilia are interesting, with a phrase here, a line there, suggesting or prefiguring what was to come. Larkin has written:

Looking back, I find in the poems not one abandoned self but several—the ex-schoolboy, for whom Auden was the only alternative to "old-fashioned" poetry; the undergraduate, whose work a friend affably characterized as "Dylan Thomas, but you've a sentimentality that's all your own"; and the immediately post-Oxford self, isolated in Shropshire with a complete Yeats stolen from the local girls' school.

I find few traces of Auden; certainly nothing as Audenesque as **'Ultimatum,'** though **'Conscript'** has something of 'In Time of War' about it, particularly the first two stanzas:

The ego's county he inherited
From those who tended it like farmers; had

All knowledge that the study merited,
The requisite contempt of good and bad;

But one Spring day his land was violated;
A bunch of horsemen curtly asked his name,
Their leader in a different dialect stated
A war was on for which he was to blame . . .

I can find nothing at all of Dylan Thomas; perhaps the friend whom Larkin quotes was commenting on poems which did not in fact get selected for **The North Ship.** It is true that a good deal of *Poetry Quarterly* and *Poetry London* in that 1943-53 decade was taken up with Dylanism, and it might be thought surprising that Larkin escaped it; but as he has said:

'Wedding-Wind' is the only completely happy poem of Larkin's, the only one in which there is a total acceptance of joy.

—Anthony Thwaite

'The principal poets of the day—Eliot, Auden, Dylan Thomas, Betjeman—were all speaking out loud and clear, and there was no reason to become entangled in the undergrowth . . . except by a failure of judgement.'

Admiration for Dylan Thomas didn't then, and doesn't now, necessarily carry in its wake base imitation.

But of Yeats there is a predominance in **The North Ship**:

'Not because I liked his personality or understood his ideas but out of infatuation with his music . . . In fairness to myself it must be admitted that it is a particularly potent music, pervasive as garlic, and has ruined many a better talent.'

Larkin has said that the edition of Yeats's collected poems he had at the time was the 1933 one, so that he 'never absorbed the harsher last poems.' This might be guessed from such lines as these:

Let the wheel spin out,
Till all created things
With shout and answering shout
Cast off rememberings;
Let it all come about
Till centuries of springs
And all their buried men
Stand on the earth again.
　　A drum taps: a wintry drum.

For the first time I'm content to see
What poor mortar and bricks
I have to build with, knowing that I can

Never in seventy years be more a man
Than now—a sack of meal upon two sticks.

The beauty dries my throat.
Now they express
All that's content to wear a worn-out coat,
All actions done in patient hopelessness,
All that ignores the silences of death,
Thinking no further than the hand can hold,
All that grows old,
Yet works on uselessly with shortened breath.

Yet though these poems are derivative, their technique is generally quietly assured; their infatuation is self-aware enough to stop short of mere pastiche. And here and there another voice comes through:

This is your last, meticulous hour,
Cut, gummed; pastime of a provincial winter.

Only a name
That chimes occasionally, as a belief
Long since embedded in the static past.

To show you pausing at a picture's edge
To puzzle out the name, or with a hand
Resting a second on a random page.

The cadences are mellifluous, but not in a middle-Yeatsian way; and the sense of time, its preciousness and its passing, is there. Four lines from **'Songs: 65° N.'** directly point forward to **'Next, Please'** in *The Less Deceived,* where they are put more sharply in focus:

I am awakened each dawn
Increasingly to fear
Sail-stiffening air,
The birdless sea.

(*The North Ship*)

Only one ship is seeking us, a black-
Sailed unfamiliar, towing at her back
A huge and birdless silence. In her wake
No waters breed or break.

(*The Less Deceived*)

In the 1966 re-publication of *The North Ship,* Larkin included an additional poem 'as a coda.' Rather, it is a prelude. In his preface to the Faber edition, he tells how in early 1946 he began to read Hardy's poems, having known him before only as a novelist: 'as regards his verse,' Larkin says:

I shared Lytton Strachey's verdict that "the gloom is not even relieved by a little elegance of diction." This opinion did not last long; if I were asked to date its disappearance, I should guess it was the morning I first read "Thoughts of Phena At News of Her Death."

Larkin's added poem (**"XXXII"** in the re-published *The North Ship*) first appeared in the little pamphlet, *XX Poems,* which Larkin brought out at his own expense in 1951.

(There were 100 copies of this pamphlet, most of them—as ruefully described by Larkin—sent to well-known literary persons, the majority of whom failed even to acknowledge it, presumably because he had under-stamped the envelopes at a time when the postal charges had just been increased. It was still possible to order it in early 1954, as I did through Blackwells in Oxford, and to pay 4/6d for it. Its present dealers' value has been quoted at £20.) The first stanza of the new poem immediately establishes not just the new presence of Hardy (it is in fact much less like Hardy than the Yeatsian pieces are like Yeats) but a new way in Larkin of finding and using material. The observation is exact, the framing of mood and incident within description makes a perfect fit:

Waiting for breakfast, while she brushed her hair,
I looked down at the empty hotel yard
Once meant for coaches. Cobblestones were wet,
But sent no light back to the loaded sky,
Sunk as it was with mist down to the roofs.
Drainpipes and fire-escape climbed up
Past rooms still burning their electric light:
I thought: Featureless morning, featureless night.

What Hardy taught Larkin was that a man's own life, its suddenly surfacing perceptions, its 'moments of vision,' its most seemingly casual epiphanies (in the Joycean sense), could fit whole and without compromise into poems. There did not need to be any large-scale system of belief, any such circumambient framework as Yeats constructed within which to fashion his work: Larkin has dismissed all that as the 'myth-kitty.' Like Parolles in *All's Well,* he seems to say: 'Simply the thing I am shall make me live.' As Larkin himself put it in a radio programme on Hardy:

When I came to Hardy it was with the sense of relief that I didn't have to try and jack myself up to a concept of poetry that lay outside my own life . . . One could simply relapse back into one's own life and write from it.

Looking again at **'Waiting for breakfast,'** one sees that what it turns into is an address to the Muse, though in no sense that that habitual Muse-invoker, Robert Graves, would accept. The 'I' of the poem has spent the night with a girl, and his mood is one of almost surprised disbelief that he is so happy:

Turning, I kissed her,
Easily for sheer joy tipping the balance to love.

Yet whatever sparks the poet into writing poems doesn't seem to start from such a mood. 'Perfection of the life, or of the work': one is pushed back to Yeats again, to the sort of conundrum he poses there. Will absorption in the girl and in the happiness she seems to bring stifle his poems?

Are you jealous of her?
Will you refuse to come till I have sent
Her terribly away, importantly live
Part invalid, part baby, and part saint?

This is the first poem of Larkin's maturity, and it links interestingly with the earliest poem in *The Less Deceived*: 'Wedding-Wind,' which also dates from 1946. But there is one large difference. The voice of the poem here is in no useful sense that of the poet: a woman on the morning after her wedding night is wonderingly turning over the fact of her happiness, with the force of the high wind 'bodying-forth' not only the irrelevance of such violent elements to the new delight she has found, but also the way in which the whole of creation seems somehow to be in union with her state:

> Can it be borne, this bodying-forth by wind
> Of joy my actions turn on, like a thread
> Carrying beads? Shall I be let to sleep
> Now this perpetual morning shares my bed?
> Can even death dry up
> These new delighted lakes, conclude
> Our kneeling as cattle by all-generous waters?

'Wedding-Wind' is the only completely happy poem of Larkin's, the only one in which there is a total acceptance of joy. Perhaps that is why it is liked by some people who otherwise find him too bleak a poet for their taste. Yet it is happy, joyous, without being serene: it implies, in its three closing questions, the impermanence of the very happiness it celebrates, the possibility of its being blown and scattered, made restless as the horses have been and

> All's ravelled under the sun by the wind's blowing.

The poem's three questions remind one of the three questions at the end of 'Waiting for breakfast,' suggesting that the balance of 'sheer joy' can as easily be tipped in the other direction.

This emotional wariness, which can too easily—and inaccurately—be labelled as pessimism, is at the roots of Larkin's sensibility. Its fine-drawn expression can be found in most of the poems in *The Less Deceived* and *The Whitsun Weddings*. And it is at this point, when Larkin in 1946 wrote 'Waiting for breakfast' and 'Wedding-Wind,' that it seems unprofitable to go on examining his poems in a supposed chronological order of composition; for from now on the personality is an achieved and consistent one, each poem re-stating or adding another facet to what has gone before. Critics who tried to sniff out 'development' when *The Whitsun Weddings* followed nine years after *The Less Deceived,* or who showed disappointment when they found none, were wasting their time or were demonstrating that Larkin was at no time their man. The sixty-one poems in these two books, and the handful that have appeared in periodicals since, make a total unified impact. There have been rich years and lean years (Larkin's remark that he writes about four poems a year shouldn't be taken too literally in any statistical sense), but only quantitatively.

Yet though there has been no radical development in Larkin's poetry during these years, the number of tones and voices he has used has been a great deal more varied than some critics have given him credit for. The 'emotional

wariness' can in some of the poems be better defined as an agnostic stoicism, close to the mood (though not to the origin of that mood) of Arnold's 'Dover Beach.' And what he is both agnostic and stoical about is time, the passing of time, and 'the only end of age': death. Indeed, if it had not been used perfectly properly for another literary achievement (and in any case Larkin might reject it as being too presumptuously resonant), 'The Music of Time' could serve as a title for all Larkin's post-1946 poetry.

> **I sometimes think that the most successful poems are those in which subjects appear to float free from the preoccupations that chose them, and to exist in their own right, reassembled—one hopes—in the eternity of imagination.**
>
> —*Philip Larkin*

There are poems in which time, and death as the yardstick of time, are seen in an abstract or generalized context: 'Ignorance,' 'Triple Time,' 'Next, Please,' 'Nothing to be Said,' 'Going,' 'Wants,' 'Age.' They are abstract or generalized in that they don't start from some posited situation, though their language and imagery are concrete enough: the street, sky and landscape of 'Triple Time,' the 'armada of promises' of 'Next, Please,' the quickly shuffled references ('Small-statured cross-faced tribes / And cobble-close families/In mill-towns on dark mornings') of 'Nothing to be Said.' All our hours, however we spend them,

> advance
> On death equally slowly.
> And saying so to some
> Means nothing; others it leaves
> Nothing to be said.

This great blankness at the heart of things has to be endured—that is what I meant by stoicism. We bolster up our ignorance, and make ourselves able to bear our long diminution and decay, by being busy with the present and—when we are young—dreaming about the future:

> An air lambent with adult enterprise.

So, too, we look at the past, and cling to and preserve those bits of it that belong to us, which we call our memories. It is no accident that of the jazz which Larkin regards with such enthusiasm, it is the blues that he writes about with most feeling (in his prose pieces, that is; for example, in his record reviews in the *Daily Telegraph.* Only one poem, 'For Sidney Bechet,' celebrates this 'natural noise of good'). For the blues are thick with the searchings and regrets of memory.

In an often-quoted statement made in 1955, Larkin said:

'I write poems to preserve things I have seen/thought/felt (if I may so indicate a composite and complex experience) both for myself and for others, though I feel that my prime responsibility is to the experience itself, which I am trying to keep from oblivion for its own sake. Why I should do this I have no idea, but I think the impulse to preserve lies at the bottom of all art.'

More recently, commenting on *The Whitsun Weddings* in the Poetry Book Society Bulletin, he wrote:

'Some years ago I came to the conclusion that to write a poem was to construct a verbal device that would preserve an experience indefinitely by reproducing it in whoever read the poem.'

Though he went on to qualify this, the 'verbal pickling' (as he put it) is seen to be the process at work in many of his best and best-known poems: in his two most sustained efforts, **'Church Going'** and **'The Whitsun Weddings,'** and also in **'Mr Bleaney,' 'Reference Back,' 'I Remember, I Remember,' 'Dockery and Son,'** and elsewhere. All of these start from some quite specifically recalled incident which becomes, through the course of the poem, 'an experience' in the sense intended by Larkin in that prose note. A casual dropping-in to a deserted church; a long train-journey on Whit Saturday; the taking of new lodgings; a visit home to one's widowed mother; another train-journey, which takes one through one's long-abandoned birthplace; a visit in middle age to one's old college at Oxford—these 'human shows' inhabit an area Hardy would have recognized, and each both preserves the experience and allows it to move out into other areas not predicted by the casually 'placing' opening lines. Indeed, in several of them the placing, the observation, is steadily sustained for a great part of the poem, as if the 'impulse to preserve' were determined to fix and set the moment with every aspect carefully delineated, every shade faithfully recorded. I remember Larkin writing to tell me, when I was about to produce the first broadcast reading (in fact the first public appearance) of **'The Whitsun Weddings,'** that what I should aim to get from the actor was a level, even a plodding, descriptive note, until the mysterious last lines, when the poem should suddenly 'lift off the ground':

> there swelled
> A sense of falling, like an arrow-shower
> Sent out of sight, somewhere becoming rain.

'Impossible, I know,' he said comfortingly; though I think that first reader (Gary Watson) made a very fair approximation to it.

If **'The Whitsun Weddings'** is a poem of one carefully held note until the very end, **'Church Going'** is more shifting in its stance and tone. Both poems are written in long, carefully-patterned rhyming stanzas (Larkin once said to me that he would like to write a poem with such elaborate stanzas that one could wander round in them as in the aisles and side-chapels of some great cathedral), but whereas each ten-line stanza of **'The Whitsun Weddings'** seems caught on the pivot of the short four-syllable second line, pushing it forward on to the next smooth run, the nine-line stanza of **'Church Going'** is steady throughout, the iambic pentameter having to hold together—as it successfully does—the three unequal sections: the first two stanzas, easy, colloquial, mockingly casual; then the four stanzas of reflection and half-serious questioning, becoming weightier and slower as they move towards the rhetorical solidity of the final stanza's first line:

> A serious house on serious earth it is. . . .

'Church Going' has become one of the type-poems of the century, at the very least 'the showpiece of the "New Movement",' as G. S. Fraser put it; much discussed in every sixth-form English class and literary extension-course, anthologized and duplicated, so that I sometimes feel it has become too thoroughly institutionalized and placed. Larkin has quoted Hardy's supposed remarks (on *Tess*) on the subject: 'If I'd known it was going to be so popular, I'd have tried to make it better,' and one senses a wry surprise in that, as one does in his comment that after it was initially published in the *Spectator* (after first being lost, and then held in proof, for about a year), he 'had a letter from one of the paper's subscribers enclosing a copy of the Gospel of St John':

> In fact it has always been well liked. I think this is because it is about religion, and has a serious air that conceals the fact that its tone and argument are entirely secular.

Here Larkin is perfectly properly fending off the common misconception that it is a 'religious' poem. It is not so, in any dogmatic or sectarian sense. It dips not even the most gingerly of toes into metaphysics, makes not even the most tentative gestures towards 'belief' ('But superstition, like belief, must die'). What it does do is to acknowledge the human hunger for order and ritual (such as go with 'marriage, and birth, / And death, and thoughts of these'), and to recognize the power of the past, of inherited tradition, made emblematic in this abandoned piece of ground,

> Which, he once heard, was proper to grow wise in,
> If only that so many dead lie round.

But **'Church Going'** is not a perfect poem, though a fine one, and it is not Larkin's best. Donald Hall has maintained that it would be a better one if it were cut by a third, and without accepting that kind of drastic surgery (American editors have a reputation for being the 'heaviest' in the world, leaning on their authors in a way that has more to do with power than with support) it is fair to say that it has some amusing but distracting divagations—particularly in the middle section—of a sort which one doesn't find in the equally circumstantial but more unified **'Whitsun Weddings.'** That Irish sixpence, for example—many readers don't know whether they are supposed to laugh here or not (many do in any case); but if the ruined church which started the poem off was in Ireland, as Larkin in a broadcast said it was, wouldn't it make a difference? Does he mean to demonstrate the sort of unthinking piety that agnostics hold to out of habit, or is he chalking up another mild self-revelatory bit of schoolboyish japing, as in the mouthing of 'Here endeth' from the lectern? (What Larkin intends of *that* performance comes out very clearly in his Marvell Press recording.) One doesn't know; and in a poem so specific this is a flaw.

To go on about the Irish sixpence at such length may well seem absurdly trivial, but the uncertainty it suggests is not unique in the poem. One has the feeling that Larkin knows more than he chooses to admit, with the pyx brought in so effortlessly and the rood-lofts sniggeringly made much of: naming them implies knowledge of what they are, and one doesn't need to be a 'ruin-bibber, randy for antique' to recognize such things. They are part of one's general store of unsorted knowledge, like knowing who A. W. Carr or Jimmy Yancey (or, indeed, Sidney Bechet) were. Here, without much relish, I am drawn into mildly deploring what might be called the Yah-Boo side of Larkin's work—a side not often apparent, which he shares sporadically with his admired (and admiring) fellow-undergraduate and old friend from St John's, Kingsley Amis. (Incidentally, *XX Poems* was dedicated to Amis, and Amis dedicated *Lucky Jim* to Larkin.) The 'filthy Mozart' type of jeer is never given the extended outing with Larkin that it is with Amis, and one has to be aware of personae and so forth, but the edgy and gratuitous coarseness of 'Get stewed. Books are a load of crap' and 'What does it mean? Sod all' have always made me wince a bit. This might show a feeble prudishness in me, but rather I feel that Larkin's poems can get by without such manly nudging.

It could be argued that these things are part of Larkin's apt contemporary tone; certainly he has such a tone, more usefully heard in **'Mr Bleaney,' 'Toads,' 'Toads Revisited,' 'Reasons for Attendance,' 'Poetry of Departures,'** and most startlingly in **'Sunny Prestatyn.'** In this last poem the calculated violence seems exactly and inevitably matched with the brutalizing of the language: those lunging monosyllables are dead right—and 'dead' is right too. 'A hunk of coast' is drawn into the stabbing words that follow—'slapped up,' 'snaggle-toothed and boss-eyed,' 'Huge tits and a fissured crotch,' 'scrawls,' 'tuberous cock and balls,' 'a knife / Or something to stab right through.' Like the faded photographs that must lie behind **'MCMXIV,'** like the medieval figures in **'An Arundel Tomb'** that 'Time has, transfigured into . . . untruth,' the blandishments of the girl on the poster have (with the help of human agency) been reduced to the wrecks of time. As in the lines of the body, in **'Skin,'** she is the end-product

> Of the continuous coarse
> Sand-laden wind, time.

'Sunny Prestatyn' is the most extreme of Larkin's poems about diminution, decay, death. Elsewhere, he more often brings to them what—in a review of Betjeman's poems—he has called 'an almost moral tactfulness.' **'Faith Healing,' 'Ambulances,' 'Love Songs in Age,' 'At Grass,' 'An Arundel Tomb,'** the more recent and uncollected **'Sad**

Steps'—all, with perhaps the exception of the last, stand at a reserved but certainly not unfeeling distance from their ostensible subjects. In the broadcast I have already quoted from, Larkin said:

'I sometimes think that the most successful poems are those in which subjects appear to float free from the preoccupations that chose them, and to exist in their own right, reassembled—one hopes—in the eternity of imagination.' And he went on to say, introducing **'Love Songs in Age'**:

'I can't for the life of me think why I should have wanted to write about Victorian drawing-room ballads: probably I must have heard one on the wireless, and thought how terrible it must be for an old lady to hear one of these songs she had learnt as a girl and reflect how different life had turned out to be.' 'How different life had turned out to be'—here time is shown as the gradual destroyer of illusions. Like the advertisement hoardings in **'Essential Beauty,'** showing us serenely and purely 'how life should be,' the old sheet music summons up and sets blankly before us two things: that lambent air which the future promised, and that present which has hardened 'into all we've got / And how we got it.' (**'Dockery and Son.'**) Christopher Ricks (who has written particularly well on Larkin) has pointed out how in **'Love Songs in Age'** the three sentences of the poem gradually narrow down, from the expansive openness of the first, with its careful proliferation of detail and its almost mimetic lyricism ('Word after sprawling hyphenated word'), through the briefer concentration on 'that much-mentioned brilliance, love,' to the blank acknowledgement that love has indeed not solved or satisfied or 'set unchangeably in order':

> So
> To pile them back, to cry,
> Was hard, without lamely admitting how
> It had not done so then, and could not now.

That last sentence, so much less serpentine than the others, seems the last brief twist of the knife.

Ricks has also pointed out one of the hallmarks of Larkin's style: those negatives which define the limits and shades of the world, and which coldly confront our flimsy illusions. *Un, in, im, dis*—with such small modifiers Larkin determines the edges of things, which blur into

> the solving emptiness
> That lies just under all we do.

So we find *unfakable, unspoilt, undiminished, unmolesting, unfingermarked, unhindered, unchangeably,* set against *unsatisfactory, unlucky, unworkable, unswept, uninformed, unanswerable, unrecommended, untruthful* and *untruth. Imprecisions, imperfect, incomplete* and *inexplicable* jostle with *disbelief, disproved, disused* and *dismantled.* They seem to share something—in their modifying, their determination to record an exact shade of response rather than a wilder approximation—with another hallmark: those compounds which one begins to find as early as the poems in *The North Ship. Laurel-surrounded, fresh-peeled, branch-arrested, Sunday-full, organ-frowned-on, harsh-named, differently-dressed, luminously-peopled, solemn-sinister*—there are over fifty others in *The Less Deceived* and *The Whitsun Weddings* alone.

Compound-formations bring Hopkins to mind, though his are of course a good deal more strenuous and draw more attention to themselves than Larkin's. Yet Hopkins is, perhaps curiously, a poet Larkin much admires. Indeed, though he has been at some pains to admit how narrow his tastes in poetry are, Larkin's acknowledged enthusiasms show a wider range of appreciation than he seems to give himself credit for. Without at all being a regular pundit in the literary papers, he has written with warmth and depth about not only Hardy but also William Barnes, Christina Rossetti, Wilfred Owen, and among living poets, Auden (pre-1940), Betjeman and Stevie Smith. Not much of a common denominator there, and of them all it is only Hardy who seems to have left any trace on Larkin's own work, and that in no important verbal way. In fact Larkin is very much his own poet. His impressment into the Movement, in such anthologies as Enright's *Poets of the 1950s* and Conquest's *New Lines,* did no harm and may have done some good, in that it drew attention to his work in the way that any seemingly concerted action (cf. The Group) makes a bigger initial impact than a lone voice. But really he shares little with the 'neutral tone' of what have been called the Faceless Fifties: anonymity and impersonality are not at all characteristics of his work, and the voice that comes across is far more individual than those of such properly celebrated poets as Muir, Graves and R. S. Thomas, to pick three who have never (so far as I know) been accused of hunting with any pack or borrowing anyone's colouring.

The case against Larkin, as I have heard it, seems to boil down to 'provincialism' (Charles Tomlinson), 'genteel bellyaching' (Christopher Logue), and a less truculent but rather exasperated demur that any poet so negative can be so good (A. Alvarez). Well, he is provincial in the sense that he doesn't subscribe to the current cant that English poets can profitably learn direct lessons from what poetry is going on in Germany or France or Hungary or up the Black Mountain: poetry is, thank heaven, a long way from falling into an 'international style,' such as one finds in painting, sculpture, architecture and music, and such validly 'international' pieces as I *have* seen (e.g. in concrete poetry) are at best peripherally elegant and at worst boring and pointless. 'Genteel bellyaching' and 'negative' are really making the same objection, the first more memorably and amusingly than the second. There is a sense in which Larkin does define by negatives; I have made the point already. He is wary in front of experience, as who should not be: one doesn't put in the same set of scales Auschwitz and the realization that one is getting older, or the thermo-nuclear bomb and the sense that most love is illusory. Yet the fact that Larkin hasn't, in his poems, confronted head-on the death camps or the Bomb (or Vietnam, or Che Guevara) doesn't make him, by definition, minor. His themes—love, change, disenchantment, the mystery and inexplicableness of the past's survival and

death's finality—are unshakably major. So too, I think, are the assurance of his cadences and the inevitable rightness of his language at their best. From what even Larkin acknowledges as the almost Symbolist rhetoric of

> Such attics cleared of me! Such absences!

to the simple but remorseless

> They show us what we have as it once was,
> Blindingly undiminished, just as though
> By acting differently we could have kept it so

is a broad span for any poet to command. And those haunting closing lines to many poems (**'Church Going,' 'The Whitsun Weddings,' 'No Road,' 'Next, Please,' 'Faith Healing,' 'Ambulances,' 'Dockery and Son,' 'An Arundel Tomb,' 'Sad Steps'**—the list becomes long, but not absurdly so): they have an authentic gravity, a memorable persistence. I think that Larkin's work will survive; and what may survive is his preservation of 'the true voice of feeling' of a man who was representative of the mid-20th century hardly at all, except in negatives—which is, when you come to think about it, one way in which to survive the mid-20th century.

Calvin Bedient (essay date 1974)

SOURCE: "Philip Larkin," in *Eight Contemporary Poets,* Oxford University Press, 1974, pp. 69-94.

[*In the essay below, Bedient praises Larkin's poetic voice, claiming "[h]is achievement has been the creation of imaginative bareness, a penetrating confession of poverty."*]

English poetry has never been so persistently out in the cold as it is with Philip Larkin—a poet who (contrary to Wordsworth's view of the calling) rejoices not more but less than other men in the spirit of life that is in him. Frost is a perennial boy, Hardy a fighter, by comparison. The load of snow, soiled and old, stays on the roof in poem after poem and, rubbing a clear space at the window, Larkin is there to mourn once again a world without generative fire. Well, it is just as he knew it would be, though now and then something surprising—a sheen of sunlight, some flutter of life—almost makes him wish for a moment that he could frolic out of doors.

Not that Larkin has wholly a mind of winter. A neighbourly snowman, he sometimes wears his hat tipped jauntily, and smiles and makes you laugh. Notice the drooping carrot nose in the mockingly titled **'Wild Oats'**:

> About twenty years ago
> Two girls came in where I worked—
> A bosomy English rose
> And her friend in specs I could talk to.
> Faces in those days sparked
> The whole shooting-match off, and I doubt

If ever one had like hers:
But it was the friend I took out,

And in seven years after that
Wrote over four hundred letters,
Gave a ten-guinea ring
I got back in the end, and met
At numerous cathedral cities
Unknown to the clergy. I believe
I met beautiful twice. She was trying
Both times (so I thought) not to laugh . . .

In fact this is more lively than (say) the typical poem in *The Oxford Book of English Verse.* A witty and amiable snowman, then, with a clown's rueful sense of himself, and a clown's way of asking a genial tolerance for, indeed an easy complicity in, his ancient familiarity with defeat.

Yet where the clown, however little and stepped on, is indefatigably hopeful, Larkin is unillusioned, with a meta-physical zero in his bones. Larger than his world, outside it, he bears it before him, in chagrin, like a block of ice. While the clown is merely done to, Larkin in a sense does in the world, denying it every virtue in advance. Behind the paint a countenance of stone . . . .

This dismissal of the world, at the same time as it ensures his nullity, is a proud, self-affirming act. Yet at times his complaint against life is precisely that it has never attempted to lure him. Its very indifference, its failure to have any use for him, makes him want to reject it. 'Life is first boredom', he writes in **'Dockery and Son'**, speaking of his own life but (so overwhelming is the tedium) generalizing, too. And in **'I Remember, I Remember'**, he elaborates devastatingly:

By now I've got the whole place clearly charted.
Our garden, first: where I did not invent
Blinding theologies of flowers and fruits,
And wasn't spoken to by an old hat.
And here we have that splendid family

I never ran to when I got depressed,
The boys all biceps and the girls all chest,
Their comic Ford, their farm where I could be
'Really myself'. I'll show you, come to that,
The bracken where I never trembling sat,

Determined to go through with it; where she
Lay back, and 'all became a burning mist'.
And, in those offices, my doggerel
Was not set up in blunt ten-point, nor read
By a distinguished cousin of the mayor,

Who didn't call and tell my father *There
Before us, had we the gift to see ahead* . . .

Yet it is just this accident of temperament that brings Larkin into line with contemporary history—not with its actual resilience and stubborn energy but with its conta-gious fears: his very cells seeming formed to index the withering of the ideal, of romance, of possibility, that characterizes post-war thought. If Larkin is not merely admired but loved, it is partly because, finding poetry and humour even in sterility, he makes it bearable: he shows that it can be borne with grace and gentleness. He arrived at the right time to blend in with the disenfranchised youth of the Second World War ('At an age when self-importance would have been normal', he writes in the Preface to his novel *Jill,* 'events cut us ruthlessly down to size'). And although his depression, like Hardy's, is as if from before the ages, he has continued to seem the poet mid-century England required, his dogged parochialism reflecting the shrunken will of the nation, his bare details the democratic texture of the times.

Larkin's distinction from other nihilists lies in his domestication of the void: he has simply taken nullity for granted, found it as banal as the worn places in linoleum.

—Calvin Bedient

Larkin's distinction from other nihilists lies in his domes-tication of the void: he has simply taken nullity for grant-ed, found it as banal as the worn places in linoleum. Other nihilists, by comparison, are full of emotional and techni-cal protest. With frighteningly poised hysteria, a Donald Barthelme dips his readers into a whirlpool of received pretensions that have just been dissolved by parody; a Robert Lowell is tragically grand, a Samuel Beckett sav-agely sardonic, a Harold Pinter sinister as a toyed-with knife . . . Larkin is plain and passive. Yet these qualities, far from letting him down, prove almost as striking as brilliant inventiveness—striking for their very simplicity. Characteristically Larkin presents not a 'world elsewhere' but life 'just here', denuded of libido, sentiment, obvious imaginative transvaluation. Like Hardy and Frost he uses imagination precisely in order to show what life is like when imagination is taken out of it.

'This was Mr Bleaney's room. He stayed
The whole time he was at the Bodies, till
They moved him'. Flowered curtains, thin and
    frayed,
Fall to within five inches of the sill,

Whose window shows a strip of building land,
Tussocky, littered. 'Mr Bleaney took
My bit of garden properly in hand'.
Bed, upright chair, sixty-watt bulb, no hook

Behind the door, no room for books or bags—
'I'll take it' . . .

In everything except effect, Larkin is thus the weakling of the current group of nihilists, or the pacifist, the one who never stands up to the niggling heart of existence, throwing down even the stones of fantasy, technical dazzle, fierce jokes—the devices of an adventurous imagination—as being in any case useless against the Goliath of the void. His achievement has been the creation of imaginative bareness, a penetrating confession of poverty.

This achievement came only with difficulty, Larkin respecting bareness so much and misapprehending the function of imagination so greatly that at first he tried to keep the two apart, like honour from shame. Imagination? The dubious water spilling over the dam the world erects in front of the ego. From the beginning Larkin was the sort of young man, old before his time, whose stern wish is to put aside childish things. 'Very little that catches the imagination', he says in *The London Magazine* of February 1962, 'can get its clearance from either the intelligence or the moral sense'. 'There is not much pleasure', he adds, 'to be got from the truth about things as anyone sees it. . . . What one does enjoy writing—what the imagination is only too ready to help with—-is, in some form or other, compensation, assertion of oneself in an indifferent or hostile environment, demonstration . . . that one is in command of a situation, and so on'. The imagination, moreover, is a fetishist, 'being classic and austere, or loading every rift with ore . . . with no responsible basis or rational encouragement'.

Larkin's problem, then, has been to write in the grim countenance of these views, with their pride in naked endurance, their fierce modesty—his limited output no doubt confessing to the difficulty. And if at first he took up fiction as well as poetry, it was because of its traditional alliance with 'the truth about things'. His fiction became the exercise ground of his lucidity. Both *Jill* (1946) and *A Girl in Winter* (1947) creep coldly to their conclusions. Though necessarily works of imagination—works *conceived*—their conceptions are unexcited, even numb. Imagination, they imply, is nugatory, a nail scratching a dream on ice. And so they labour against themselves. Virtually nothing happens to their youthful protagonists; crocuses doomed to fill with snow, they have only to sense futility to give way to it. The pale Oxford undergraduate in the first learns from a visit to his home town, recently bombed, 'how little anything matters', 'how appallingly little life is'. Then a dream tells him that, 'whether fulfilled or unfulfilled', love dies. This is enough to destroy his desire for the innocent Jill. He decides to die, as it were, before his death, so as to die as little as possible. In *A Girl in Winter,* too, wartime lends plausibility to a disillusionment that in fact seems pursued. And again the most ordinary relationships fail, as if there were something radically wrong with the human heart. The heroine, Katherine, finally repudiates 'the interplay of herself and other people'. With resolution, not in self-pity, beyond calling back, even gratefully, she steps out into a lucid solitude. At the close she envisions the 'orderly slow procession', as of an 'ice floe', of her permanently frozen desires: 'Yet their passage was not saddening. Unsatisfied dreams rose and fell about them, crying out against their implacability, but in the end glad that such order, such destiny, existed. Against this knowledge the heart, the will, and all that made for protest, could at last sleep'. And so she

chooses to abstain from life, convinced that the fruit is anyway infested.

Given not only these passive protagonists but a starved-sparrow manner and a merely *determined* disenchantment, totally lacking in the passion either of truth or regret, the novels could not help seeming too long, indeed superfluous after the drain pipes, the snow. Larkin had yet to see that his thorough disbelief in adventure—even a Beckett shows a taste for mock adventure—necessitated the briefest of literary forms, and that the surest way to make the humanly sterile emotionally forceful is to place it in the midst of a poem, where, dwarfed by the glorious remembrances of the medium, it can have a shivering significance.

Meanwhile his poetry was the lyrical run-off of his lucidity. The poems in **The North Ship** (1946) treat the same themes as the novels—a world eaten through at the root by time, the wisdom of taking 'the grave's part', the failure of love—with all the runaway outcry that the novels stiffly restrained. Seeking at once the altitudes of the great lyrists of his youth, Yeats and Dylan Thomas, Larkin rises too high for his leaden themes:

> I was sleeping, and you woke me
> To walk on the chilled shore
> Of a night with no memory,
> Till your voice forsook my ear
> Till your two hands withdrew
> And I was empty of tears,
> On the edge of a bricked and streeted sea
> And a cold hill of stars.

And again:

> And in their blazing solitude
> The stars sang in their sockets through the night:
> 'Blow bright, blow bright
> The coal of this unquickened world'.

So Larkin sings as the blade comes down, is ardent about the ice in the fire of youth. Fulsomely embracing poetry as a legitimized form of 'compensation', he wrote as if it were unnecessary to be sensible in it, permissible to speak of 'bricked and streeted' seas or of stars that, while blazing, begged to be ignited. A remarkable discrepancy: the novels prematurely grizzled, the poems puerile.

Larkin had yet to reconcile the supposed unpleasure of truth with the pleasure of imagination. This he was now to do abruptly, being one of those poets who undergo an almost magical transformation between their first and second volume. It was Hardy who showed him that imagination could treat 'properly truthful' themes truthfully yet with acute delicacy, deliberate power. Never mind that Hardy's poems are greyly literal: they get into you like a rainy day. 'When I came to Hardy', Larkin says, 'it was with the sense of relief that I didn't have to try and jack myself up to a concept of poetry that lay outside my own life—this is perhaps what I felt Yeats was trying to make me do. One could simply relapse back into one's own life and write from it'. Again: 'Hardy taught one to feel . . . and he taught one as well to have confidence in what one felt'.

In truth, Larkin's themes belong to that great negative order of ideas that has always proved the most potent in art. We cannot help ourselves: we home to tragedy— optimism in art commonly leaving us feeling deprived of some deeper truth. Nothing is of more initial advantage to a poet than a horizon of clouds. For pathos makes us irresistibly present to ourselves, silhouettes us against a backdrop of fate, renders us final for the imagination. And to achieve it Larkin, as he now saw, had only to 'feel'— feel simply, without exaggeration. This itself meant that he had to measure ordinary life, life as he knew it, with the rigour of regret. In his novels he had passed beyond protest into a limbo of resignation. In *The North Ship,* on the other hand, he had exhibited a preposterous surprise and anguish—as if sterility were not, after all, the scene on which his blind rose every morning. Now he needed to find a manner at once warm and cold, steeped in futility but not extinguished by it. He had to open bare cupboards that would speak of all that might have been in them.

And so he does in his second volume, *The Less Deceived* (1955), and again in his third and most recent, *The Whitsun Weddings* (1964). Here is **'As Bad as a Mile'**:

> Watching the shied core
> Striking the basket, skidding across the floor,
> Shows less and less of luck, and more and more
>
> Of failure spreading back up the arm
> Earlier and earlier, the unraised hand calm,
> The apple unbitten in the palm.

What redoubtable depths of acceptance in the calm of that unraised hand. Even so, the close-up of the unbitten apple proves affecting: if the poem is stoic about the end, it is without prejudice to the pleasure preceding it; it is stoic with regret. What is more, here Larkin brings the lofty literary sorrow of *The North Ship* down from 'black flowers', 'birds crazed with flight', and wintry drums, to the level of the everyday, where, no longer diffuse, it can be felt like pain in a vital organ. And, neither egoistic nor fetishistic, imagination has now become only a way the truth has of entering us all at once, swiftly and completely, in a context of value. Far from being an evasion of the truth, it is a hammer for the nail, the poignancy secreted in the prosaic.

Larkin's poems now take on the brute force of circumstantial evidence. Like sour smoke, the odour of actual days hangs about them. They have an unusual authenticity; they form a reliving. Even when the naming is general, it can have bite:

> Home is so sad. It stays as it was left,
> Shaped to the comfort of the last to go
> As if to win them back. Instead, bereft
> Of anyone to please, it withers so,
> Having no heart to put aside the theft

> And turn again to what it started as,
> A joyous shot at how things ought to be,
> Long fallen wide. You can see how it was:
> Look at the pictures and the cutlery.
> The music in the piano stool. That vase.

The final articles are as blunt as pointing fingers and, with the adjective *that,* the series ends in a conclusive jab. It amounts to instant trial and conviction. The vase stands exposed, empty as the atmosphere around it, coldly reduced to its potential function—a failure, a thing without love.

Many of Larkin's poems, however, have the specific density of descriptive detail—often autobiographical. Consider the first portion of **'Dockery and Son'**:

> 'Dockery was junior to you,
> Wasn't he?' said the Dean. 'His son's here now'.
> Death-suited, visitant, I nod. 'And do
> You keep in touch with—' Or remember how
> Black-gowned, unbreakfasted, and still half-tight
> We used to stand before that desk, to give
> 'Our version' of 'these incidents last night'?
> I try the door of where I used to live:
>
> Locked. The lawn spreads dazzlingly wide.
> A known bell chimes. I catch my train, ignored.
> Canal and clouds and colleges subside
> Slowly from view. But Dockery, good Lord,
> Anyone up today must have been born
> In '43, when I was twenty-one.
> If he was younger, did he get this son
> At nineteen, twenty? Was he that withdrawn
>
> High-collared public-schoolboy, sharing rooms
> With Cartwright who was killed? Well, it just shows
> How much . . . How little . . . Yawning, I suppose
> I fell asleep, waking at the fumes
> And furnace-glares of Sheffield, where I changed,
> And ate an awful pie, and walked along
> The platform to its end to see the ranged
> Joining and parting lines reflect a strong
>
> Unhindered moon . . .

Here again pleasure and truth meet effortlessly. How casually the lawn and then the moon, both unhindered in beauty, set off hindered humanity. The detail is at once natural (though 'Death-suited' forces perception) and resonant. The poem has the simple fascination of an honestly reported life—even suggesting the moment to moment flow of consciousness. It possesses also a humble appeal of personality, a tone as unpressingly intimate as the touch of a hand on one's arm.

So it was that Larkin took the path of Edward Thomas, of Frost, of Hardy, and became a poet who looks at ordinary life through empty, silent air. His poems now sprang like snow-drops directly from the cruel cast of things, yet in themselves attaining beauty. And just as they now found their pathos in everyday things, so the void now spoke, in part, where day by day Larkin heard it, in the trite though sometimes pert and piquant language of the streets. Here was a language as sceptical as it was hardy, soiled with disappointment. Of a certain billboard beauty, 'Kneeling up on the sand / In tautened white satin', Larkin writes:

> She was slapped up one day in March.
> A couple of weeks, and her face
> Was snaggle-toothed and boss-eyed;
> Huge tits and a fissured crotch
> Were scored well in, and the space
> Between her legs held scrawls
> That set her fairly astride
> A tuberous cock and balls
>
> Autographed *Titch Thomas,* while
> Someone had used a knife
> Or something to stab right through
> The moustached lips of her smile.
> She was too good for this life . . .

By contrast, Larkin's words will not be too good for this life. They make room not only for the colloquial 'Or something' but—sympathetically—for words betraying the fascinated disgust of adolescent sexual emotion. Still, Larkin's regret that anything *should* be too good for this life shines through his contempt for the meretricious poster. He makes the common words sorrier than they know.

Larkin thus renews poetry from underneath, enlivening it with 'kiddies', 'stewed', 'just my lark', 'nippers', 'lob-lolly men', 'pisses', 'bash', 'dude', and more of the same. And yet his manner rises easily from the slangy to the dignified; its step is light, its range wide. Here it is as vernacular caricature, amused at itself:

> When getting my nose in a book
> Cured most things short of school,
> It was worth ruining my eyes
> To know I could still keep cool,
> And deal out the old right hook
> To dirty dogs twice my size . . .

A degree up from this we find the almost aggressive slang of the poem on the billboard girl. Then comes the perky, street-flavoured simplicity of **'Toads'**, **'Wild Oats'**, **'Send No Money'**, or **'Self's the Man'**:

> Oh, no one can deny
> That Arnold is less selfish than I.
> He's married a woman to stop her getting away
> Now she's there all day . . .

A step higher and the style rises from self-consciousness and begins to leave the street:

> Talking in bed ought to be easiest,
> Lying together there goes back so far,
> An emblem of two people being honest . . .

This is the plain style of most of Larkin's poems. And this plainness is sometimes heightened by rhythmical sculpturing, syntactical drama, or repetition, as in **'MCMXIV'**:

> Never such innocence,
> Never before or since,
> As changed itself to past
> Without a word—the men
> Leaving the gardens tidy,
> The thousands of marriages
> Lasting a little while longer:
> Never such innocence again . . .

Whatever its degree of formality, the peculiarity of Larkin's style is an eloquent taciturnity: it betrays a reluctance to use words at all. If, as **'Ambulances'** says, a 'solving emptiness . . . lies just under all we do', then Larkin's words, as if preparing to be swallowed up, will make themselves as lean as they can—nothingness, they assert, will not fatten on them. Indeed, they seem to have soaked a long age in a vinegar that dissolves illusions. Such is the impression they make in **'As Bad as a Mile'**, and here again in **'Toads Revisited'**:

> Walking around in the park
> Should feel better than work:
> The lake, the sunshine,
> The grass to lie on,
>
> Blurred playground noises
> Beyond black-stockinged nurses—
> Not a bad place to be.
> Yet it doesn't suit me . . .

The short lines and clipped syntax suggest an almost painful expenditure of language. A head with a wagging tongue, they say, is time's fool. Larkin, of course, also writes in somewhat freer rhythms, as at the end of **'An Arundel Tomb'**. But he always counts before he pays, and his more expansive effects bank on their moving contrast with his usual, slightly tough laconicism.

Larkin's laconicism also conveys the poverty of the sayable. That 'Life is slow dying', it implies, 'leaves / Nothing'—or almost nothing—'to be said'. He says little because he sees too much. Like Ted Hughes, he feels pressed back into himself by a vision of an unjustified and unjustifiable reality, but where this has finally provoked Hughes into desperate garrulity, it has all but frozen Larkin's mouth—two slender volumes since 1946; two interruptions of silence.

If Larkin relies on traditional form, it is partly out of the agreement of numbness and caution that we find in his style. Why seek new forms, he seems to ask, when there is nothing new under the sun? In any case, 'Content alone interests me', he says. 'Content is everything'. Like a man freezing to death in a snowstorm, refusing to be distracted by the beauty of the flakes, he resolves to be lucid to the last, his mind on the truth alone. And, paradoxically precisely this is why he writes in form. For, by virtue of its familiarity, traditional form, skilfully used, is all but transparent. (Only experiments, antiformalists, and writers of verse make an *issue* of form.) At its finest, prosody is anyway meltingly one with the content; and Larkin is frequently a fine craftsman. So nothingness stares out of

Larkin's poems undistracted, with a native starkness. Even the bodily warmth conveyed by rhythm is often restrained by nicely calculated metrical irregularity.

The impression of falseness is sometimes just as strong when Larkin sets his imaginative paints aside and attempts serious thought. Indeed, without much exaggeration it might be said that he is only poised and intelligent with particulars—abstractions tend to spill out of his hands.

—*Calvin Bedient*

Yet form has also for Larkin its traditional function: not modest after all, it is an attempt at the memorable. If he writes, the reason is to silence death, if only with the fewest possible words. In a statement contributed to D. J. Enright's anthology, *Poets of the 1950's,* Larkin says: 'I wrote poems to preserve things I have seen / thought / felt (if I may so indicate a composite and complex experience) both for myself and for others, though I feel that my prime responsibility is to the experience itself, which I am trying to keep from oblivion for its own sake. Why I should do this I have no idea, but I think the impulse to preserve lies at the bottom of all art'. Nihilist though he is, he thus raises against nothingness—like every other literary nihilist, if more moderately—the combined plea and protest of his constructions, with their exemplary inner necessity, their perfection.

In sum, his forms are at the same time sorry to be there and insistently there. In his use of words and form alike, Larkin both defies and skulks before his nihilistic 'content', like an animal that, while shrinking back, offers to fight.

So it was that, without betraying his scruples, Larkin became a poignant and cohesive poet, his means the functional intelligence of his ends. More sophisticated writers have chided him for his poetic provinciality, but he is right, I think, to be as simple as he is. His poetry seems not only the necessary expression of his temperament but the very voice of his view of things, the pure expression of his aim—his purpose being not to make sterility whirl but precisely to make it stand still, freed from confusion, from the human fevers that oppose it. Far from adhering piously to English poetic tradition, he uses it for his own ends. The result, in any case, is a poetry of mixed formality and informality, mixed severity and charm, mixed humour and pathos, that carries a unique personal impress—a poetry that, for all its conservatism, is unconsciously, inimitably new.

Even *The Less Deceived* and *The Whitsun Weddings,* however, are somewhat subject to the 'poetic' toning up of *The North Ship,* and poems corrupted by self-pity appear side by side with the mature poems just described. A void with an ashen pallor—how resist rouging it, giving it dramatic visibility? Regret, in any case, touches us so nearly that it slips at the slightest urge into self-commiseration. At his weakest Larkin exploits this readiness for sorrow-suckling, for the histrionic; he tries for pathetic *effects.*

Of course, when a poem is so delightful as **'Days'**, criticism hesitates:

> What are days for?
> Days are where we live.
> They come, they wake us
> Time and time over.
> They are to be happy in:
> Where can we live but days?
>
> Ah, solving that question
> Brings the priest and the doctor
> In their long coats
> Running over the fields.

But those men in their long coats are too easy to summon over the fields: they border on the animated cartoon. Throwing us on the wretchedness of being passive before them, in need of them, they are more melodramatic than the truth. For all that its subject is 'days', the poem places itself so far from the quotidian that it can say, can picture anything without fearing contradiction from itself. The often admired **'Next, Please'** also steps off from life into self-pity. The poem figures expectancy as a 'Sparkling armada of promises' that leaves us 'holding wretched stalks / Of disappointment'. But whatever were we waving at those ships? In the intoxication of its chagrin, the piece neglects propriety and probability. Even the final stanza, though grand, begets uneasiness:

> Only one ship is seeking us, a black-
> Sailed unfamiliar, towing at her back
> A huge and birdless silence. In her wake
> No waters breed or break.

This is a trifle too awesome, Death in makeup. Another admired poem, **'No Road'**, begins:

> Since we agreed to let the road between us
> Fall to disuse,
> And bricked our gates up, planted trees to screen us,
> And turned all time's eroding agents loose,
> Silence, and space, and strangers—our neglect
> Has not had much effect.
>
> Leaves drift unswept, perhaps; grass creeps
>   unmown;
> No other change . . .

What is really 'unmown' is the conceit—its leaves, grass, bricks, and trees lacking specific reference as metaphors. As in **'Next, Please'**, the vehicle is too much an end in itself. All three poems are rhetorical, written in emotional generality. Like still other pieces, including **'Whatever**

Happened?', 'Age', 'Triple Time', 'Latest Face', 'If, My Darling', and 'Arrivals, Departures', they stand at a remove from the literal, on a swaying rope bridge of tropes, dramatic but ill-supported.

Yet virtual fact is liable to the cosmetic impulse, too, as witness so ostensibly autobiographical a poem as **'Church Going'**. The first two stanzas, it is true, are everything these other poems are not:

> Once I am sure there's nothing going on
> I step inside, letting the door thud shut.
> Another church: matting, seats, and stone,
> And little books; sprawlings of flowers, cut
> For Sunday, brownish now; some brass and stuff
> Up at the holy end; the small neat organ;
> And a tense, musty, unignorable silence,
> Brewed God knows how long. Hatless, I take off
> My cycle-clips in awkward reverence,
>
> Move forward, run my hand around the font.
> From where I stand, the roof looks almost new—
> Cleaned, or restored? Someone would know: I don't.
> Mounting the lectern, I peruse a few
> Hectoring large-scale verses, and pronounce
> 'Here endeth' much more loudly than I'd meant.
> The echoes snigger briefly. Back at the door
> I sign the book, donate an Irish sixpence,
> Reflect the place was not worth stopping for.

Pungently detailed, this has a wonderful air of verisimilitude and candour. Except for 'Someone would know: I don't', the lines are free of padding, and the symbolism, as in the brownish flowers and 'Here endeth', is like an afterthought to the forcefully literal. Compare the middle of the poem, with its speculation about the time when churches will be out of use:

> Shall we avoid them as unlucky places?
>
> Or, after dark, will dubious women come
> To make their children touch a particular stone;
> Pick simples for a cancer; or on some
> Advised night see walking a dead one?
> Power of some sort or other will go on
> In games, in riddles, seemingly at random;
> But superstition, like belief, must die,
> And what remains when disbelief has gone?
> Grass, weedy pavement, brambles, buttress, sky,
>
> A shape less recognizable each week,
> A purpose more obscure. I wonder who
> Will be the last, the very last, to seek
> This place for what it was; one of the crew
> That tap and jot and know what rood-lofts were?
> Some ruin-bibber, randy for antique,
> Or Christmas-addict, counting on a whiff
> Of gowns-and-bands and organ-pipes and myrrh? . . .

It is hard to say what is more forced here—the questions, or the assertions that 'power of some sort or other will go on' and that the church will be 'less recognizable each week', or the effort to imagine 'the very last' to seek its purpose. Like the consciously colourful detail at the close, all this is essentially idle, a fabrication. The poem picks up again as Larkin confronts the church in discovery and wonder:

> A serious house on serious earth it is,
> In whose blent air all our compulsions meet,
> Are recognized, and robed as destinies . . .

But the effect is partly to make us regret all the more the triviality of the middle stanzas.

The impression of falseness is sometimes just as strong when Larkin sets his imaginative paints aside and attempts serious thought. Indeed, without much exaggeration it might be said that he is only poised and intelligent with particulars—abstractions tend to spill out of his hands. When he thinks, he often seems to be frowningly struggling to create a philosophical intricacy and importance. Here he is in **'Lines on a Young Lady's Photograph Album'**:

>   . . . Those flowers, that gate,
> These misty parks and motors, lacerate
> Simply by being over; you
> Contract my heart by looking out of date.
>
> Yes, true; but in the end, surely, we cry
> Not only at exclusion, but because
> It leaves us free to cry. We know *what was*
> Won't call on us to justify
> Our grief, however, hard we yowl across
>
> The gap from eye to page . . .

With 'Yes, true', you can virtually hear his voice leaving its natural home in particulars, growing thin and subject to confusion. As if driven to manufacture complexities, the lines suddenly snarl up what had been plain from the descriptive life of the poem. To say that the past leaves us 'free to cry' is to make a false conundrum of what has already been said simply: that it excludes us. The truly subtle idea in the passage—namely, that the past is forlorn because *excluded from us*—is obscured by the fussy thought. And meanwhile grace and measure are abandoned—'yowl' being especially awkward, an attempt to bring the blanched thought back into poetic animation.

'Dockery and Son' similarly gravels in 'philosophy'. Why, asks the speaker, did Dockery

>   . . . think adding meant increase?
> To me it was dilution. Where do these
> Innate assumptions come from? Not from what
> We think truest, or most want to do:
> Those warp tight-shut, like doors. They're more a
>   style
> Our lives bring with them: habit for a while,
> Suddenly they harden into all we've got
>
> And how we got it; looked back on, they rear
> Like sand-clouds, thick and close, embodying

For Dockery a son, for me nothing,
Nothing with all a son's harsh patronage . . .

Reasoning this through is at first like trying to put on a shirt with sewn sleeves—and finally we can only *grant* that such assumptions are 'innate' or distant from what we 'think truest'. (Innate assumptions are usually not all we have but what we wish we had: eternal life, supreme importance, a guiltless being. . . .) The simile of the sand-clouds is slipshod also. Until the last line, we are far from the brilliant beginning.

In the final stanza of **'Deceptions'**, the self-pity that permits such laxity lies still more forward, spoiling an even more exquisite poem. At the same time, it compares weakly with the epigraph from Mayhew's *London Labour and the London Poor,* a statement of bald power almost beyond art itself: 'Of course I was drugged, and so heavily I did not regain my consciousness till the next morning. I was horrified to discover that I had been ruined, and for some days I was inconsolable, and cried, like a child to be killed or sent back to my aunt'. The stanza comments:

> Slums, years, have buried you. I would not dare
> Console you if I could. What can be said,
> Except that suffering is exact, but where
> Desire takes charge, readings will grow erratic?
> For you would hardly care
> That you were less deceived, out on that bed,
> Than he was, stumbling up the breathless stair
> To burst into fulfilment's desolate attic.

The final phrase, 'fulfilment's desolate attic', bears a Johnsonian indictment, irrevocably disabused, of the delusions of desire. But even granting the romantic assumption that the seducer made too much of his desire, what is its brief match flame compared to the conflagration of the girl's young life? We can hardly care either that the girl was the less deceived. The poem treats the misreading of desire as a tragedy. But nothing it says or implies supports so extravagant and self-condoling a view.

Yet, serious as they are, Larkin's defects are easily outbalanced by his virtues. Thus, though he may abandon an imaginary scene for questionable thought, he is also likely to have put us into that scene with as piercing a dramatic immediacy as any poet now writing. We have witnessed this in **'Church Going'** and **'Dockery and Son'**; and here is the first stanza of **'Deceptions'**:

> Even so distant, I can taste the grief,
> Bitter and sharp with stalks, he made you gulp.
> The sun's occasional print, the brisk brief
> Worry of wheels along the street outside
> Where bridal London bows the other way,
> And light, unanswerable and tall and wide,
> Forbids the scar to heal, and drives
> Shame out of hiding. All the unhurried day
> Your mind lay open like a drawer of knives.

Imagination, said Emerson, is a sort of seeing that comes by 'the intellect being where and what it sees', and this happy definition highlights what is remarkable in the stanza. For the lines virtually *are* the original moment, as well as a beauty beyond it and compassion for it. 'Print', it is true, is lost in ambiguity (footprint? a picture-shape on the wall?) and indefinite in relation to the light described later; and 'scar' rather rushes a fresh wound. But almost everything else tells keenly—'The brisk brief / Worry of wheels' poignantly commenting on the girl's inconsolateness, 'bridal London' on her social ruin; 'Light, unanswerable and tall and wide' being unimprovable; and the simile of the drawer of knives, though risking melodrama, properly savage.

We touch here on gifts more specialized than the dramatic imagination, gifts for epithet and metaphor. Of course, in their own way, these too are dramatic, restoring a primal power to the language. We are all bees trapped behind the spotted glass of usage till the poet releases us to the air. And so Larkin releases us in these lines of **'Coming'**:

> On longer evenings,
> Light, chill and yellow,
> Bathes the serene
> Foreheads of houses.
> A thrush sings,
> Laurel-surrounded
> In the deep bare garden,
> Its fresh-peeled voice
> Astonishing the brickwork . . .

'Chill and yellow' and 'fresh-peeled' are especially happy inventions. So again at the beginning of a recent poem, **'Dublinesque'**: 'Down stucco side-streets, / Where light is pewter. . . .' In another recent poem, **'The Cardplayers'**, the trees are—magnificently—'century-wide'. Spring, in the poem of that title, is 'race of water, / Is earth's most multiple, excited daughter'. Delightful in **'Broadcast'** is the 'coughing from / Vast Sunday-full and organ-frowned-on spaces'. And what could be at once more homely and endearing than the 'loaf-haired secretary' of **'Toads Revisited'**?

Larkin's imagination has also, of course, a turn for wit. At times he instinctively inhibits the sobbing in his strings by playing staccato. Consider the lover in **'Lines on a Young Lady's Photograph Album'**:

> From every side you strike at my control,
> Not least through these disquieting chaps who loll
> At ease about your earlier days:
> Not quite your class, I'd say, dear, on the whole . . .

Or take the comic candour of **'Annus Mirabilis'**:

> Sexual intercourse began
> In nineteen sixty-three
> (Which was rather late for me)—
> Between the end of the *Chatterley* ban
> And the Beatles' first LP . . .

Next time around the parenthesis reads, 'Though just too late for me', which gives the playfulness a fine grimace.

These poems have the good grace of self-irony, a civilized lightness. Better still is the comedy—vigorous with universal truth—in **'Toads'** and **'Toads Revisited'**. With rising bravura the first begins:

> Why should I let the toad *work*
>   Squat on my life?
> Can't I use my wit as a pitchfork
>   And drive the brute off?
>
> Six days of the week it soils
>   With its sickening poison—
> Just for paying a few bills!
>   That's out of proportion . . .

The second, with toad-eating helplessness, concludes:

> No, give me my in-tray,
> My loaf-haired secretary,
> My shall-I-keep-the-call-in-Sir:
> What else can I answer,
> When the lights come on at four
> At the end of another year?
> Give me your arm, old toad;
> Help me down Cemetery Road.

Entertaining though they are, these are works of the full imagination, more quickened than compromised by caricature. They are true and touching as well as spirited. One would be tempted to call the poisoning toad and the pitchfork the best comic conceit in modern poetry were not that of the old toad on Cemetery Road consummate to the point of tears. We are not far here from the world of fairy tales and have only to hear of Cemetery Road to fancy that, like the way through the woods to Grandmother's house, it has existed in the imagination for ever.

An unusual poet, reminding us on the one hand of the grand classical tradition and on the other of Beatrix Potter and Dorothy Parker, and all the while sounding like no one so much as himself! And Larkin has still other virtues. To begin with, there is, as we have seen, the instinctive adjustment of his means to his end, so that, for instance, he is one of the most pellucid of poets because nothing to him is more self-evident than nothingness. Then the unconscious rightness of his forms, **'Toads'** being, for example, appropriately restless in alternating uneven trimeters and dimeters, **'Toads Revisited'** properly more settled in its trimeters; **'Toads'**, again, troubled with alternating off-rhyme and **'Toads Revisited'** calmer in off-rhymed couplets, full rhyme kept in reserve for the *entente cordiale* of 'toad' and 'Road'. There is the frequent perfection of his metrical spacing; the easy way his words fall together; the tang and unsurpassed contemporaneity of his diction and imagery; the fluent evolution of his poems. There is also his beautifully mild temper and his tenderness for those pushed 'To the side of their own lives'. Nor finally should we fail to add his facility at opening that scepticism about life which everyone closets in his bones.

Still, only at his best does Larkin make us grateful for what a human being can do with words. It is above all in **'Coming'**, **'Toads'**, **'Toads Revisited'**, **'At Grass'**, **'Here'**, **'The Whitsun Weddings'**, and **'An Arundel Tomb'** (with two fairly recent poems, **'High Windows'** and **'To the Sea'**, pressing near) that he puts experience under an aspect of beauty, gracing and deepening it with the illusion of necessary form and producing the privileged sensation—perhaps illusory, perhaps not—of piercing through to a truth. It is in these poems, too, that, at once detached and concerned, he most frees us from self-pity without destroying feeling.

With the exception of **'Here'** and **'Toads'**, these pieces display an exquisite stoic compassion for the littleness, the fragility, indeed the unlikelihood, of happiness. Even in **'Here'**, however, tenderness is implicit in the perception, the diction, the syntax. For instance, in 'Isolate villages, where removed lives / Loneliness clarifies', the lives are considerably enfolded by the clause at the same time that the line break removes and isolates them. But such tenderness is like water under ice. Where life is as raw, insufficient, and essentially lonely as it is in **'Here'**, better (so the poem implies) keep yourself inwardly remote, like the 'bluish neutral distance' of the sea. Though **'Here'** is all one travelling sentence till it brakes in short clauses at the end, 'Swerving east, from rich industrial shadows' out finally to the 'unfenced existence' of the sea, emotionally it is one continuous 'freeze', since each successive 'here' is as barren, as without self-justification, as the rest. **'Here'** leads us as far from ourselves, as far into objective reality, as we can go—to the sea that has nothing for us, 'Facing the sun, untalkative, out of reach'—then leaves us there, all but freed from desire and too well schooled by the accumulated evidence, too guarded, to be appalled. The poem is a masterpiece of stoicism.

The equally fine **'Coming'** is as remarkable for its original conception as for the felicity (already sampled) of its similes. Indeed, the two prove inseparable in the second half of the poem:

> It will be spring soon,
> It will be spring soon—
> And I, whose childhood
> Is a forgotten boredom,
> Feel like a child
> Who comes on a scene
> Of adult reconciling,
> And can understand nothing
> But the unusual laughter,
> And starts to be happy.

Throwing us back into the vulnerable heart of childhood, into an ignorance not ignorant enough, the simile redeems an inevitably romantic subject by abrading it, complicating it with domestic truth. Nor could any comparison be at once so unexpected and convincing, giving exactly, as it does, the situation of being drawn into an emotion neither understood nor trusted yet beyond one's power to refuse, since the moment it comes it reveals itself as all, nearly all, of what was needed. The poem, if complete in itself, is also an expressive elaboration of its most poignant word, 'starts'. Too doubting and perplexed for rhyme or a long line, as slender as the inchoate joy it evokes, it is like the 'chill and yellow' light described at the outset, lyrically lovely yet inhibited—its recurring two beats like a heart quickened but still at the tentative start, the mere threshold, of happiness.

There is nothing tentative about **'At Grass'**, which celebrates the profound peace, the cold joy, in the relinquishment of labour and identity. The retired racehorses in the poem have stolen death from itself:

> The eye can hardly pick them out
> From the cold shade they shelter in,
> Till wind distresses tail and mane;
> Then one crops grass, and moves about
> —The other seeming to look on—
> And stands anonymous again . . .

The early, strenuous days of the horses, full of 'Silks at the start' and 'Numbers and parasols', are later evoked with the same classical directness as this shaded scene, which has a clarity that leaves nothing between us and the subject. Like the horses the poem exists quietly, is envyingly 'at ease' in a pace slowed often enough by stressed monosyllables to seem tranced beyond all care. The rhyme, too, is spaced out placidly, making the stanzas like the 'unmolesting meadows'. (It does, however, cause an awkward syntactic inversion at the close: 'Only the groom, and the groom's boy, / With bridles in the evening come.') Because of its distanced subject and because the horses have both lived out and outlived their swiftness, the poem takes the sickness out of the desire for oblivion, offering in place of weariness a paradise of shade.

An even more exquisite poem is **'An Arundel Tomb'**, which begins:

> Side by side, their faces blurred,
> The earl and countess lie in stone,
> Their proper habits vaguely shown
> As jointed armour, stiffened pleat,
> And that faint hint of the absurd—
> The little dogs under their feet.

The lines rise to the ceremony of their occasion. So 'Side by side', each syllable royally weighted, is balanced by the four syllables of 'their faces blurred', the two phrases equal and graceful in their partnership but immobile as the effigies they describe. Through rhyme, the third line offers its arm to the second as they move in iambic procession. Then the time-softened long *i* stiffens into the short one, and the little dogs break into the sentence like an afterthought (which in fact they may originally have been). Modelled and exact in its rhythms, lovely, fresh, and affecting in its detail, tender in its deeply deliberated tone, holding the slow centuries in its hands, the poem is indeed very lovely, very moving. Unfortunately, it has need to be in order to humble its one defect: its manipulation of the subject for the sake of pathos. Nothing 'with a sharp tender shock' that the earl and countess are holding hands, the poet says:

> They would not think to lie so long.
> Such faithfulness in effigy
> Was just a detail friends would see:
> A sculptor's sweet commissioned grace
> Thrown off in helping to prolong
> The Latin names around the base . . .

But why would they not think to lie so long? If Larkin denies them intention, it is evidently to press his own, which is to view faithful love through the ironic and brittle glass of accident. One balks at this, censures it, and at the same time acknowledges, 'This is Larkin's most beautiful poem'.

Less exquisite but more substantial than **'An Arundel Tomb'**, **'The Whitsun Weddings'** is distinguished for ease, poise, balance, and inclusiveness.

It has even more of England in it than **'Here'**, similarly taking us by train through the country and making its breadth and variety, its unfolding being, our own. The very movement is that of a leisurely if inexorable journey, the lines frequently pausing as if at so many stations, yet curving on in repeated *enjambements* past scenes swiftly but timelessly evoked, as though the stanzas themselves were the wide windows of a moving train:

> All afternoon, through the tall heat that slept
>   For miles inland,
> A slow and stopping curve southwards we kept.
> Wide farms went by, short-shadowed cattle, and
> Canals with floatings of industrial froth;
> A hothouse flashed uniquely: hedges dipped
> And rose: and now and then a smell of grass
> Displaced the reek of buttoned carriage-cloth
> Until the next town, new and nondescript,
> Approached with acres of dismantled cars . . .

This is deft, light in depiction but strongly evocative. And the English themselves are as vividly present as their towns and countryside, indeed man himself is here in his several ages: the children in the platform wedding parties frowning as 'at something dull', the young men 'grinning and pomaded', the brides' friends staring after the departing trains as 'at a religious wounding', the married couples themselves boarding the carriages in distraction, the uncles shouting smut, the fathers looking as if they had 'never known / Success so huge and wholly farcical', and the mothers' faces sharing the bridal secret 'like a happy funeral'.

And the poet? By chance, he himself is there on the train that Whitsun as the eternal witness of the contemplative artist, inward with what he sees yet outside it precisely to the extent that he sees it. Single amid the married couples in the carriage, he is yet caught up by them, caught up *with* them ('We hurried towards London'), quickened into a sense of physical existence in time. On the other hand, with his indisplaceable knowledge of failure, absence, endings, he is the loneliness of contemplation lucid before the happy blindness of the body and its emotions. He knows he might well envy this happiness and yet he dwarfs it:

> Now fields were building-plots, and poplars cast
> Long shadows over major roads, and for
> Some fifty minutes, that in time would seem
> Just long enough to settle hats and say
>   *I nearly died.*
> A dozen marriages got under way.
> They watched the landscape, sitting side by side
> —An Odeon went past, a cooling tower,
> And someone running up to bowl—and none
> Thought of the others they would never meet
> Or how their lives would all contain this hour.
> I thought of London spread out in the sun,
> Its postal districts packed like squares of wheat:
>
> There we were aimed. And as we raced across
>   Bright knots of rail
> Past standing Pullmans, walls of blackened moss
> Came close, and it was nearly done, this frail
> Travelling coincidence; and what it held
> Stood ready to be loosed with all the power
> That being changed can give. We slowed again,
> And as the tightened brakes took hold, there
>   swelled
> A sense of falling, like an arrow-shower
> Sent out of sight, somewhere becoming rain.

The poem throughout links beginnings to ends, ends to beginnings—as in its wedding parties 'out on the end of an event / Waving goodbye', its mingling of generations, and the stops and starts of the journey itself. And here at the close, at the same time that it gives the energy of life and the fruition of time their due, even as arrows speed and rain promises germination, it also makes us aware of inevitable dissolution, as arrows fall and rain means mould, dampness, the cold, the elemental. Like certain romantic poems—'The Echoing Green', 'Kubla Kahn', 'Intimations of Immortality', 'Among School Children'—the poem thus brings together, irreducibly, life in its newness and power and life in its decline and end. Nowhere else in his work (though **'To the Sea'** marks a near exception) is Larkin so irresistibly drawn out to observe with an emotion close to happiness the great arena of life in its diversity and energy, undeluded though he is, doomed though he feels the energy to be.

'Poetry', St.-John Perse remarks, 'never wishes to be absence, nor refusal'; and certainly in ***The Whitsun Weddings*** Larkin grants it the presence of the world, as he grants the world its presence. Yet even apart from ***The Whitsun Weddings*** we would be without Larkin's poems the poorer by that much presence and that much love. Poet though he is of the essential absence of life from itself, he yet makes himself present as regret that it must be so; and for all his defeatism it is easy to find him a sympathetic figure as he stands at the window, trying not to cloud it with his breath, mourning the winter casualties, concerned to be there even though convinced beyond all argument that, like everything else, his concern is gratuitous.

Lolette Kuby (essay date 1974)

SOURCE: "Style and Language," in *An Uncommon Poet for the Common Man: A Study of Philip Larkin's Poetry,* 1974, pp. 19-42.

[*Below, Kuby examines Larkin's place among British poets, specifically his relationship to the modernist school.*]

Facets of Larkin's style point to several progenitors. In many ways his differences from the modern tradition resemble Ben Jonson's differences from his own contemporaries. Both tend to avoid extended metaphor, strings of similes, and other rhetorical elaborations which in Jonson's time were called 'conceits', or 'bravery' of language. The poems of both have prose sense and a ready surface intelligibility due, in part, in both cases, to the fact that the poems are organized by rational rather than by emotional or imagistic sequences. Both express themselves succinctly, attempting, as Jonson put it, "what man can say / In a little", the poetic impulse being toward reduction and condensation rather than expansion and extension ["Epitaph on Elizabeth, L.H."]. Neither depends on single, striking lines and memorable phrases to carry the meaning. Jonson's couplets, even the final couplets of epigrams, do not explain the poem. And of Larkin, G. S. Fraser says [in *Vision and Rhetoric,* 1959]: "[the] poem moves us as a complex whole. . . . There is nothing, or almost nothing, that we 'apprehend' in the poem before we have 'comprehended' it. There are no single lines and images that flash out at us." Moreover, he is a moralist like Jonson who

> makes of his theater a kind of complicated moral machine for projecting human behavior onto a screen so constituted as to reveal the true nature of that behavior, a nature always kept hidden by the distorted perspectives of mundane interests and commitments.
>
> [John Hollander, *Ben Jonson,* 1961]

From Jonson one traces many of Larkin's general qualities through Dryden and Pope, the Augustans, down through the early nineteenth century poet, Praed, whom Larkin admires and whose best poems are "vers de société" written in the Augustan vein and character sketches reminiscent of the *Spectator Papers*:

> Some public principles he had
> But was no flatterer, no fretter
> He rapped his box when things were bad,
> And said "I cannot make them better!"
>
> [Praed, "Quince"]

What accounts perhaps more for Larkin's admiration of Praed are a number of poems in the form of gossipy verse letters, a species of less profound dramatic monologue which satirize the prejudices or mannerisms of the fictional writer. In "The Talented Man", for example, a young woman claims to be enchanted with a "clever, new, poet" whose talent, she avers, compensates for his physical unattractiveness: "He's lame,—but Lord Byron was lame, love, / And dumpy,—but so is Tom Moore." Yet, she concludes, he has a defect for which talent cannot compensate:

P.S.—I have found, on reflection,
One fault in my friend,—*entre nous*
Without it, he'd just be perfection;—
Poor fellow, he has not a *sou:*

Larkin, too, writes a type of dramatic monologue, though less obviously sarcastic, far more complex than Praed's, and directed to the middle class as opposed to the leisured, fashionable, late Augustan sophisticates and their provincial imitators whom Praed addressed.

Praed's poetry, according to Kenneth Allott [in *Selected Poems of Winthrop Mackworth Praed,* 1953], contains exactly that world which Wordsworth says he ignores:

The things which I have taken, whether from within or without, what have they to do with routs, dinners, morning calls, hurry from door to door, from street to street, on foot or in carriage; with Mr. Pitt or Mr. Fox, Mr. Paul or Sir Francis Burdett, the Westminster election or the borough of Honiton? . . . What have they to do . . . with a life without love?

It may come as a surprise then, one of those unsettling critical contradictions, to find Larkin's name linked also with Wordsworth's. There is, however, some resemblance to both poets. Robert Spector and Christopher Ricks say correctly that "Larkin is committed to portraying life in the language of people, presenting the ordinary in an unusual way" [Spector, "A Way to Say What a Man Can See," *Saturday Review,* Vol. XLVIII, Feb. 13, 1965]. "They have a Wordsworthian subject, the ordinary sorrow of man's life" [Ricks, "A True Poet," *N.Y. Review of Books,* Vol. III, Jan. 14, 1965]. Certainly Larkin, like Words-worth, presents the ordinary sorrows of ordinary life, and his tone (perhaps better defined as undertone) is like Wordsworth's, tender and serious. With some exceptions, it is without Praed's briskness and assertiveness, soft while Praed's is loud. And his vocabulary, like Wordsworth's, is highly suggestive, whereas Praed's is highly denotative. On the other hand, Larkin's wry humor and self-mockery, utterly absent in Wordsworth, are found in Praed:

Our love was like most other loves;—
A little glow, a little shiver,
A rose-bud, and a pair of gloves,
Some hopes of dying broken-hearted;
A miniature, a lock of hair,
The usual vows, and then we parted.
["The Belle of the Ballroom"]

Most unlike Wordsworth, however, is Larkin's treatment of the ordinary. No matter how average Wordsworth's characters are, or how simple their pursuits, they come "trailing clouds of glory". That combination of the ordinary and the glorious is what makes Wordsworth Wordsworth. He invests triviality with a luminescence derived from a spiritual universe. Larkin's universe is bleak if not black. His vision is more like Frost's than Wordsworth's, and uncannily like Hardy's.

Among the Victorians, there is a resemblance of Larkin to Browning, though, indeed, disregarding the Aesthetes, there is a resemblance to the moral seriousness which distinguishes Victorian novels and poetry alike. "Seriousness", [A. O. J.] Cockshut says of George Eliot, was one of her "key words, and is, in general, a word indicating a thread of continuity between eightteenth century piety . . . firmly based on a religious faith . . . and the unreligious morality of George Eliot" [*The Unbelievers,* 1966]. As much could be said of Larkin. In fact he says it himself at the end of **"Church Going"**:

A serious house on serious earth it is,
In whose blent air all our compulsions meet,
Are recognised, and robed as destinies.
And that much never can be obsolete,
Since someone will forever be surprising
A hunger in himself to be more serious.

With Browning Larkin shares not only moral seriousness but the method of revealing it through dramatic monologue. The speakers in **"Mr Bleaney"**, **"Self's the Man"**, **"Dockery and Son"**, to mention a few, expose their limitations, their self-centeredness, the flaws in their morality or vision in much the same way Browning's "Bishop" or "duke" or "Fra Lippo Lippi" do by dramatizing their personalities in response to a situation, idea, or event.

But it is Hardy that occupies a special place among Larkin's literary forebears. Lumping Larkin together with the 'Poets of the Fifties' again, [D. J.] Enright says they "represent a revival of a tradition associated with Hardy and kept alive only through the vigour and persistence of poets like Robert Graves" [*Conspirators and Poets,* 1966]. Similarities of other poets of the Fifties to Hardy is debatable, but Larkin admits his strong influence. After **The North Ship,** he says, "I looked to Hardy rather than Yeats as my ideal, and eventually a more rational approach, less hysterical and emphatic, asserted itself". Though there remains some 'Yeatsian music' in Larkin's poetry, it occurs as climax or emphasis in contrast to preceding more halting conversational rhythms. A comparison of several lines of Larkin's **"Mr Bleaney"** with several lines from "Sailing to Byzantium" reveals that the music in both depends, to a great extent, on the frequent repetition of identical vowel sounds (in Larkin's case, nine high front vowels, (i), in a total of forty syllables; and in Yeats' case, six mid back vowels, (o), in the same number of syllables), and on the close correlation between poetic meter (varied iambic) and prose meter (closely approximating varied iambic). In the following scansion, primary prose stresses are below the line, and those indicating the patterned meter above:

But if he stood and watched the frigid wind
Tousling the clouds, lay on the fusty bed
Telling himself that this was home, and grinned,
And shivered, without shaking off the dread . . .

O sages standing in God's holy fire
As in the gold mosaic of a wall,
Come from the holy fire, perne in a gyre,
And be the singing-masters of my soul.

This passage, however, is not typical of Larkin's later style which is less regular metrically and less repetitive of sound:

Fall to within five inches of the sill,

Whose window shows a strip of building land,
Tussocky, littered. "Mr Bleaney took
My bit of garden properly in hand".
Bed, upright chair, sixty-watt bulb, no hook

Behind the door, no room for books or bags—
"I'll take it". So it happens that I lie . . .

From Hardy, Larkin may have learned colloquialness, restraint of lyricism, and the inclusion within the poem of its motivating setting or situation (although many of Larkin's later poems, **"Next, Please"**, **"Going"**, **"Wants"**, are thoughts with no situational specifics, and some that precede Hardy's influence, **"XXXII"**, **"XX"**, present, as Hardy's often do, stage settings for the poetic action). Also, occasionally, direct echoes of Hardy's language or imagery can be traced. For example, the dialogue in Hardy's "Two Houses":

"—Will the day come",
Said the new one, awstruck, faint,
"When I shall lodge shades dim and dumb—"

"—That will it, boy;
Such shades will people thee . . ."

sounds like the dialogue in Larkin's **"Send No Money"**:

Tell me the truth, I said,
Teach me the way things go.

So he patted my head, booming *Boy*
There's no green in your eye.

In the same poem Hardy uses a house to represent a human being upon whom others "print . . . their presences". Larkin uses the same image in **"Home is So Sad"** in which a house, like a person, is "Shaped to the comfort of the last to go / As if to win them back". Again, echoing Hardy's "The Minute Before Meeting":

And knowing that what is now about to be
Will all *have been* in O, so short a space!
I read beyond it my despondency.

Larkin says in **"Triple Time"**:

This is the future furthest childhood saw
And on another day will be the past,
A valley cropped by fat neglected chances.

And again, Larkin's

Life is first boredom, then fear.
Whether or not we use it, it goes,
And leaves what something hidden from us chose,
And age, and then the only end of age.

is reminiscent of Hardy's "He Abjures Love":

—I speak as one who plumbs
Life's dim profound,
One who at length can sound
Clear views and certain.
But—after love what comes?
A few saw vacant hours,
And then, the Curtain.

What the above quotations make clear, beyond similarities of style, mood, diction, is that either Hardy had a profound influence on Larkin's view of life, or that Larkin found mirrored in Hardy a startling coincidence to his own view. For Larkin, as for Hardy, it is a view of the "tragic groundwork of existence".

Although the poems of both appeared when their respective era's doubts and anxieties were widely, if not universally, felt, their negativism (Hardy's expression of the 'breakdown of Victorianism', and Larkin's of the emptiness of the mechanical age, which is, in fact, a continuation and intensification of the same breakdown) is singled out for critical reproach. Hardy became extremely sensitive to what he felt was both misreading and adverse moral judgment, and in *Winter Words* (1928) devoted a section of his preface to denying the allegation that he was an unrelieved pessimist whose "anecdotes and episodes . . . reveal a perverse preoccupation with 'life's little ironies' and a prepossession with gloom". Larkin's critics sound a variation on the same theme: "typical of a younger group of self-snubbers and self-loathers. . . . It is another turn on that *petty* bitterness about life" [M. L. Rosenthal, The Modern Poets, 1960]; "determinedly and successfully glum" [Enright]. Interestingly, the terms of critical approbation applied to one, can, with little alteration, apply to the other:

Life's meaningless and man's ignorance are in some obscurely moving way *celebrated* by being recorded.
["Undeceived Poet," *London Times Literary Supplement*, Vol. LXIII, March 12, 1964]

Its chief characteristic is a 'satisfying flatness'. It is 'satisfying' because it presents the interesting spectacle of a mind continually probing and exploring; while its 'flatness' is produced by the persistent pressure of the Spirit of Negation.
[A. C. Ward, *Twentieth-Century English Literature 1901-1960,* 1964]

Larkin would not quarrel with Hardy that "the road to a true philosophy of life seems to be in humbly recording diverse readings of its phenomena as they are forced on us by chance or change" [Harold Child, *Thomas Hardy,* 1916]. Their poems do not present, perhaps do not derive from, a unified philosophy. But both have a habitual way of looking at things which certainly amounts to a philosophy. They share an anguished view of an unspiritual universe in which the terms 'good' and 'evil' have no applicability outside of the small cage of man's cranium, and in only one small portion of even that. Nature, history, society, the other portion of man himself move in accordance with an inexorable and unconscious law whose goal, it seems, is nothing less absurd than movement itself. Hardy's idea of a "Vast Imbecility", a "neutral Spinner of Years", a "sightless Mother", occurs in Larkin too. But whereas Hardy conceived of nature as blind Will seeking only its own perpetuation, Larkin sees it as blind cycles, caring not for its own preservation but moving through endless revolutions of generation and extinction that "shift to giant ribbing, sift away". To Larkin, it is not so much in conflict with man's reason as with man's ability to conceive the impossible—his idealism. In contrast with Hardy, it is the idealizing capacity of man's mind not his reason that makes him a "freak of nature".

Larkin's negativism is, if anything, more pervasive than Hardy's, but then the times in which he lives are more negative. Certain strengths of Hardy's world which occur in his poetry and novels, in Larkin's world no longer exist. The ruins of an old Roman Theater and an old Roman road, traces of the Napoleonic Wars, folk customs and superstitions, the permanence of natural objects, ponds, rocks, trees, were to Hardy poignant reminders of the individual's oblivion in time and of the absence of moral progress in nature; but they were also evidence of continuity and of man's identification with his past. Larkin too sees nature as non-evolving, but sees the environment as having changed for the worse. The very landscape of the twentieth century bespeaks an insuturable cut from the past: "I leant far out, and squinnied for a sign / That this was still the town that had been 'mine' / So long." Event is not anchored in place as it so forcefully is in Hardy's poems; memory loses its referent in the external world, while the quick and easy transportability of things and the extreme mobility of people further intensifies the sense of disconnection: "Hurrying to catch my comet", "traffic all night north", we "met at numerous Cathedral cities". Not living in a fully mechanized, technological society, Hardy, in his world, was surrounded by artifacts that retained the values of durability and association with human personality, though even at that time Rilke (whose life span corresponds to the later fifty years of Hardy's) could say [in a letter to von Hulewicz, quoted in Stephen Spender, *The Struggle of the Modern*, 1963]:

> For our grandfathers, a house, a fountain, a familiar tower, their very clothes, their coat, was infinitely more, infinitely more intimate. . . . The lived and living things, the things that share our thoughts, these are on the decline and can no more be replaced.

In Larkin's world, Rilke's prediction has come completely true. The 'decay of values' applies not only to moral and religious values but to the universal cheapening and vulgarization of those material things that are prized or desired. The sleazy quality of objects built not to last; the "comic Ford", "Cheap suits, red kitchen-ware, sharp shoes", the saucer-souvenir" are the artifacts which surround Larkin.

Hardy sets his characters down in geological time, time measured by the formation of the moors and hills, Stonehenge, the Bible. Larkin's characters measure time by a photograph album, a train ride, an old phonograph record. The quality of eternal permanence about the places and things in Hardy's world has given way to a madly accelerated tempo in which present things, experiences, places, ideas 'turn to past'. Larkin's world partakes actively of oblivion, emphasizes death.

In a sense, the negativism of Larkin's view is greater because his characters do not willingly succumb. Often Hardy's poems sink under the pressure of a pre-vision, the dark shape of the universe which exists in Hardy's mind and of which the poems are small exterior models. He boxes his personae into contrived situations which seem superimposed upon reality and not ordinarily experienced in the terms in which he presents them by the average life. And he freezes them in Laocoön-like anguish which offers no possibility of escape from their author's labels, "Time's Laughingstocks" and "bond-servants of chance". Larkin, by recreating the building processes rather than the accomplished model of a dark universe, presents to the realist no easy exit. Whatever cynicism and despair is expressed grows out of situations so mundane and universal; misinterpreted laughter, a room that signifies penury, routine domesticity, an invitation to a houseparty, that no one fails to recognize them. Within these situations the embattled minds of his personae grapple with questions of free will and fate, neither one of which is accepted as the final answer. No sooner is one emotion or idea proposed as the truth, then it grimaces at the speaker with the leer of a lie. No sooner is another discarded as a lie then it buds into a small truth. Both in their mental vacillations and in the audacious humor with which they often confront despair, Larkin's characters resist the idea of their own victimization which Hardy's characters too often appear to welcome. What keeps Larkin's poems afloat is that continuous, convoluted movement of minds which press through self-deception, rationalization, recrimination, and defense, exposing the partiality of every 'position', toward what the poems discover as the fundamental ambiguity—man's fate and his will.

Perhaps the broadest definition of the Movement, one that would include Larkin, is to call it exactly what Dylan Thomas is not (in fact Thomas is a frequent favorite target of theirs). Larkin's poetry is not visionary, vatic, subjective, emotional, or wordy. It continues that strain of British poetry that emphasizes thoughtfulness, plain language, moral consciousness, and reason. It is skeptical rather than optimistic: it sees the universe as physical process rather than as sacred harmony; and it sees humanity as small, unheroic, selfish, anxious, pathetic, and conflicted. Its plainness of language and reasonableness of style reflect skepticism in a way that lyricism and poetic diction cannot. Larkin regards his own worst fault as "lack of resonance". To the extent that resonance in poetry implies lyricism, one can see that Larkin's 'lack' is an inescapable part of his unillusioned view; for irrespective of the meaning of the words involved, the *sound* of resonance, its musical and rhythmic force, is the nonsemantic sound of faith, optimism, harmony.

The reason behind Larkin's plain style, what may be called its "raison d'éthique", is implicit in his poems and is based upon the condition of the world as he sees it. Orwell made a statement of that condition in the mid 1940's:

> Since about 1930 the world has given no reason for optimism whatever. Nothing is in sight except a welter of lies, hatred, cruelty and ignorance, and beyond our present troubles loom vaster ones which are only now entering the European consciousness. It is quite possible that man's major problems will never be solved.

> [Kenneth Allsop, *The Angry Decade,* 1958]

Rejection of a style that employs eloquence, exhalted emotionalism, baroque diction, is less a rejection of these rhetorical items *per se* than it is a recognition that they imply optimism and hope. They ring false to contemporary poetic sensibility. They seem an attempt to will into existence, or to shout into existence through sheer power of voice, universal harmony that does not exist. In Larkin's poems there is little of the type of resonance heard in Thomas's "Heads of the characters hammer through daisies; / Break in the sun till the sun breaks down" to cover the roar of what is to Larkin cosmic emptiness: "Oh attics cleared of me. Oh absences!"

That is not to say that there is no lyricism in Larkin's poems, but his persistent refusal to allow the individual voice to be swallowed by eternal harmonies is reflected in their dialogical mode as well as in their imagery. Moustached women, puking boys, cart-ruts in mud-lanes resist transformation into something wonderful and strange. And the perplexed, argumentative, searching talk of the poems: "It may be that through habit these do best", "The difficult part of love is being selfish enough", "Too subtle that, too decent too. Oh hell", unlike the voice of celebration or reverie is a sour, off-key note in the close harmony of the spheres. Yet when Larkin's voices move from the idiosyncracies of speech with maximal voice print into the lyrical endings of *The Whitsun Weddings,* **"Dublinesque"**, or **"At Grass"**, the movement is felt by contrast to be of great weight and significance, inherently both a loss and a gain which the paradoxical life-death imagery of the closing of the poems reinforces.

Perhaps both Hardy's influence and the unavoidable truth of Orwell's statement are accountable for the fact that Larkin has skipped over or rejected the more startling innovations in English literature as practiced by Pound, Eliot, Sitwell, Joyce—the leaders of the Poetic Revolution. Although he is associated with a group of poets called the 'New Formalists' or 'New Traditionalists', Larkin's brand of modernism seems less a throw-back to earlier principles, as the term 'neo' would imply, than new growth on an old traditional tree, with differences resulting naturally in its adaptation to new forces in the environment. The more radical departures of the Poetic Revolution—the disappearance of a clear element of rational meaning; cryptic, esoteric, and erudite allusions; disconnected collage of images; eccentric vocabulary—are not characteristics of Larkin's poetry. 'Modern' elements that do appear—irregular meter, diminished melodiousness, irony, puns, and idiomatic language—while promoted by Pound, Eliot, *et al.,* certainly are not innovations.

Structurally, Larkin's poems combine the traditional and the modern. He occasionally writes in a manner that resembles free verse, but the form is never entirely freed. For example, **"Water"**, which is metrically and syllabically free, retains strict stanza divisions that conform to thought moving logically:

> If I were called in
> To construct a religion
> I should make use of water.
>
> Going to church
> Would entail a fording
> To dry, different clothes.

"Coming", which is as close as Larkin gets to free verse, employs a basic five syllable line and three rhymed pairs, two of them widely separated, in a poem of nineteen lines: "reconciling / nothing", "evenings / sings", "serene / scene".

For the most part, however, his poems are basically iambic, basically rhymed, and basically stanzaic; and his most telling formal characteristic is to free the poems from these bases. Formal tension exists not only between prose and poetic meter, but between symmetry and asymmetry throughout the poem. For example, freed rhythm might return to the iambus as a touchstone:

> Well, useful to get that learnt.
> In my wallet are still two snaps
> Of bosomy rose with fur gloves on.
> Unlucky charms, perhaps.
>
>   (**"Wild Oats"**)

Or stanza divisions will be strictly even but conclude in a run-on line so that the stanza's conventional function of thought or image shift is combined with non-stanzaic continuity:

> . . . Surely, to think the lion's share
> Of happiness is found by couples—sheer
>
> Inaccuracy, as far as I'm concerned.
>   (**"Reasons for Attendance"**)

Or slant rhyme or the repetition of final consonants only will settle into hard rhyme:

> The lake, the sunshine,
> The grass to lie on, . . .
>
> Blurred playground noises
> Beyond black-stockinged nurses—
> Not a bad place to be.
> Yet it doesn't suit me.
>
>   (**"Toads Revisited"**)

But it is Larkin's language rather than his forms that breaks most sharply with the modernisms practiced not only by the leaders of the Poetic Revolution but by their successors, Empson, Auden, Thomas, who are alike, as different from each other they are in other respects, in employing a language composed of extraordinary phrases, uncommon words, and confounding combinations of ordinary words. Although Larkin states that The Movement, "if it had any real core at all, was essentially a reversion to the virtues of the thirties", and that his own poetic education was "in the Auden tradition—objective, outward-looking, political, materialist, unpretentious", his language is of the variety "kept alive by Graves" [Judith Anne Johnson, unpubl. thesis]. And it is [Robert] Graves, after all, who most vocally attacks modernist language as "cloacinal ranting, snook-cocking, pseudo-professional jargon" and "incrustations of nonsense . . . double talk" ["These be your Gods"]. Whether or not The Movement was a reversion to "something of the style of Empson" [Johnson thesis] as Larkin says, in view of certain other of his statements it seems he would have to agree with [Charles] Tomlinson that Empson's "development has consisted largely of a retreat into style. . . . The object of the poems tends to disappear, as in the early Letter II and the later Bacchus with its crossword puzzle approach and its six pages of notes, and we are left with a handful of conceits" ["Poetry Today," *The Modern Age,* 1961]. Tomlinson's objection to Empson's style may be more specifically directed against Empson's choice and combination of words:

Roll not the abdominal wall; the walls of Troy
Lead, since a plumb-line ordered, could destroy.
Roll rather, where no mole dare sap, the lawn,
And ne'er his tumuli shall tomb your brawn.

Larkin's own disenchantment with Auden is largely an exasperation with linguistic conundrums. Auden changed, Larkin says [in "What's Become of Wystan," *The Spectator,* Vol. CCV, July 15, 1960],

from a social poet full of energetic, unliterary knockabout and unique lucidity of phrase [to one who is] too verbose to be memorable.

For some time he has insisted that poetry is a game, with the elements of a crossword puzzle; it is 'luck of verbal playing'. One need not be a romantic to suspect that this attitude will produce poetry exactly answering to that description.

It is unfortunate that Robert Conquest dragged out the banner, "the language of men", to wave over the poets in *New Lines.* It was already soiled when Wordsworth used it, and is by now so tattered and splattered as to make the poets who march under it indistinguishable. The language of men is, after all, all language, and if Conquest meant by that phrase the words and rhythms of average conversation then he means a language that has been attributed to Pope, Browning, Frost, Wordsworth, Whitman, and many others. The phrase unquestionably applies to Larkin but it does little to indicate his uniqueness or the nature of his linguistic break with modernism. Larkin writes poetry which communicates primarily to the mind, not to the intellectual mind, but to the understanding, the mind that apprehends idea in experience. To do so requires a language that derives from thought rather than from dream or from the Freudian or Jungian unconscious. It cannot be a language which by its very nature resists being understood. It is exactly that language which defenders of modernism object to. In an oblique negative reference to The Movement, Spender says:

Poetry itself is invaded by the prose idea, the reaction against what is dismissed as a period of 'experiment'. The reaction is called 'consolidation' or the revival of 'traditionalism', or 'correctness' or 'clarity'. But of course behind these labels is the assumption that it is possible to be clear in a period of confusion, that it is possible to be traditional when the line of tradition has been fragmented, that it is possible to consolidate the 'experiments' of Joyce.

A similar explanation is offered by G. S. Fraser for Surrealistic poetry such as the following by J. F. Hendry:

Cast in a dice of bones I see the geese of Europe
Gabble in skeleton jigsaw, and their battered anger
Scream a shark-teeth frost through splintering earth
     and lips.

"The obscurity of our poetry", Fraser says, "its air of something desperately snatched from dream or woven round a chime of words, are the results of disintegration, not in ourselves but in society" [Quoted by Tomlinson].

The point of Larkin's "traditionalism", "correctness", "clarity", to use Spender's words, is not that these are formalist "causes célébres" but that they are the means of writing communicative poetry. The point of Joyce's (novels), Pound's, Eliot's, often Thomas's and Yeats's, the post Symbolists' and Surrealists' poetry is that in their search for the prophetic, or mystical, or subconscious-tapping word, the word which in some way was to harmonize or reintegrate cultural disintegration, they tended to compound that disintegration. Not only were their results often not understandable with reference to experience but their efforts led to highly subjective poems which were finally understood only by the writer. On this score, Larkin comments [in *All What Jazz,* 1970]:

Modernism, whether perpetrated by Parker, Pound or Picasso . . . helps us neither to enjoy nor endure. It will divert us as long as we are prepared to be mystified or outraged, but maintains its hold only by being more mystifying and more outrageous.

One trend of Modernism, typified by Joyce and Thomas (following Hopkins), has been the baroque piling up of words with the aim of arriving at the 'whatness', or 'essence', or 'inscape' of whatever is perceived or felt:

After the funeral, mule praises, brays,
Windshake of sailshaped ears, muffle-toed tap
Tap happily of one peg in the thick
Grave's foot.
     [Dylan Thomas, "In Memory of Ann Jones"]

With futurist onehorse balletbattle pictures

Ben Dollard's voice barreltone . . . Croak of
vast manless moonless womoonless marsh.
(Lines from *Finnegan's Wake* and *Ulysses*)

The search for the right word, the perfect word, is, in these examples, part of the piece itself, a component of the finished product. Larkin's traditionalism, or what may be called 'classicism' in this respect, is that the search for the word goes on outside the poem. The process of groping, paring away, discarding, comparing remains in the author's mind. What appears in the poem is the final word, convincing because it is decisive:

Then begins
A snivel on the violins: . . .

or

On me your voice falls as they say love should,
Like an enormous yes.

or

Beneath it all, desire of oblivion runs:
Despite the artful tensions of the calendar.

Even these fragments expose by comparison with the quotations from Thomas and Joyce a quality of frenzied search for the always elusive word. In contrast, Larkin's language demonstrates the usability of usual words. The ease and simplicity of his language implies faith in the communicability of words existing in the common idiom which, in spite of the poems' expressions of despair, resignation, or absurdity, serves as a reintegration of values.

Larkin also diverges from the effect on its language of the Poetic Revolution's loudly proclaimed reaction against Victorian 'narcissism', and 'romantic egotism'. Again the reaction tended to become an exaggeration and extension of the fault elaborately hidden behind a surface of new techniques. No Victorian carried narcissism or subjectivity so far as Joyce, Pound, or Yeats in their inventions of language so private and symbolic images so personal as to be indecipherable even to a highly educated audience. The outer limits of egotism are reached in *Finnegan's Wake* which insists that all men learn one man's language; in Pound's *Cantos* in which the images insist, "it is so because I say it is so, no referential proof necessary"; and in those of Yeats's poems which refer to privately invented mythology.

Larkin's language avoids just such subjectivity. His most personal poems are universalized by speaking in the vernacular. He obviously eschews sentimentality and the other 'excesses' that fill the Victorian *Golden Treasury,* but he does not make the modern error of confusing sentimentality with subjectivity. Though sentimentality seems egotistically to assume that the writer's own emotions will be shared by all, its success with the public proves that it is quite right in that assumption. In one sense sentimentality

is the farthest extreme from subjectivity since what it taps into is the norm of a universal or cultural pat response with none of the complications of individual responses. Stock response is evoked by the use of the most commonplace language and the most commonplace images possible. In **"I Remember, I Remember"**, as elsewhere, Larkin counters sentimentality on its own grounds. In contrast with Modernists who escape sentimentality by using private languages and esoteric imagery, he shows stock response to be false by presenting an alternative viewpoint in common language. In doing so he revalidates the effectiveness of the language men speak:

Our garden first: where I did *not* invent
Blinding theologies of flowers and fruits,
And *wasn't* spoken to by an old hat.
And here we have that splendid family

I never ran to when I got depressed,
The boys all biceps and the girls all chest.

One of the possible pitfalls of language as simple as Larkin's is pointed out by [David] Daiches [in *The Present Age in British Literature,* 1965]:

A superficial clarity may be the result of depending too heavily on shop-worn words and idioms which *appear* to have a poetic meaning but which in fact on repeated and careful reading can be seen to lack all precision, and individuality.

Larkin often uses "shop-worn words" as the above quotation and the one following indicate:

No, I have never found
The place where I could say
This is my proper ground,
Here I shall stay;
Nor met that special one
Who has an instant claim
On everything I own
Down to my name.

(**"Places, Loved Ones"**)

But the meanings of the poems do not ride on individual words. Phrasing, the unique turn of thought, dialectic between thoughts, and fluctuations in tone of voice renew shop-worn words. At any rate the pitfall of clarity is less dangerous, and certainly less an affront to the reader, than the pit that is emptied of meaning once the riddle of diction is removed.

Larkin also departs from modernist practices that attend closely to Pound's warning, "go in fear of an abstraction". **"Days"**, **"Ignorance"**, **"Places, Loved Ones"**, **"Next, Please"**, among many others, are full of abstract language:

Always too eager for the future, we
Pick up bad habits of expectancy.
Something is always approaching: every day
Till then we say.

(**"Next, Please"**)

Strange to know nothing, never to be sure
Of what is true or right or real,
But forced to qualify *or so I feel,*
Or, *Well, it does seem so:*
Someone must know.

                                        (**"Ignorance"**)

Such abstract language is appropriate to the subject which
is the Never Happened, the Always Wished For, the tragic
discrepancy between the ideal and the real.

Larkin's reversion to pre-modernist use of language allows him to achieve, in addition to objectivity and commu-
nicativeness, tonal range. Using as his base a median,
conversational English, he can ascend and descend without climbing too high or dropping too low. Slight modulations suffice to create dramatic shifts in mood and tone.
In **"Wedding Wind"**, for example, rising emotion is suggested without exaggeration by the lines: "Shall I be let to
sleep / Now this perpetual morning shares my bed?" because they have been preceded by the easy prosiness
of "a stable door was banging, again and again / . . .
and I / Carry a chipped pail to the chicken-run". In **"Church
Going"**, for another example, a tone of flippancy, "some
brass and stuff / Up at the holy end", is altered to one of
gravity, "A serious house on serious earth it is", without
departing radically from the linguistic norm of the poem:
"Wondering what to look for; wondering, too, / When churches fall completely out of use / What we shall turn them
into".

Larkin's language may be called both democratic and moral.
It is democratized by its intelligibility to the general reading public, and moral in not "blarneying its way'. It is not
the language of the intellectual elite, nor that of the confidence man. It is morality that 'squats' in the language of
the poems which, as Larkin puts it in another context in
"Toads", "will never allow me to blarney / My way to
getting / The fame and the girl and the money / All at one
sitting", and which, in an important way, separates it from
the language of the Poetic Revolution.

The second most important aspect of Larkin's 'traditionalism' is his shifting away from another Modernist dogma—the absolute importance placed on concreteness,
'thinginess', or *Dinglichkeit*. Pound decreed that the
vehicle of poetry was to be things: objects, whether taken
from dream, fancy, or reality, were to stand in for states
of mind or emotion. Pound's contemporary English Symbolists, the Imagists, the later Surrealists, and virtually all
poetry since then, as the following recent examples show,
have served that principle with unquestioning allegiance.
Presentation of idea without its embodiment in the 'objective correlative' of a Thing practically vanished from
poetry:

The month of the drowned dog. After long rain the
        land
Was sodden as the bed of an ancient lake,
Treed with iron and birdless. In the sunk lane
The ditch—a seep silent all summer—
                        [Ted Hughes, "November"]

White, these villages. White
their churches without altars. The first snow
falls through a grey-white sky
and birch-twig whiteness turns
whiter against the grey. White
the row of pillars.
                [Charles Tomlinson, "In Connecticut"]

The disappearance of the speech of thought, as such, and
its replacement by what in a broad sense must be called
'description' contributes, along with experiments in language, to the obfuscation of meaning in modern poetry. Except in the greatest of *Dinglichkeit* poetry such as
"Prufrock", the importance of tone of voice in the dramatization of human personality has been usurped by
things. In Larkin's poems, tone of voice, above all, is
important. He verifies human personality by liberating
speech from things. He can write lines in which not a
'thing' appears:

Therefore I stay outside
Believing this; and they maul to and fro,
Believing that; and both are satisfied,
If no one has misjudged himself. Or lied.
                        (**"Reasons for Attendance"**)

Parting, after about five
Rehearsals, was an agreement
That I was too selfish, withdrawn,
And easily bored to love.

                                        (**"Wild Oats"**)

Not that Larkin avoids imagistic writing, but he brings it
into conjunction with that straight speech of thought-
without-pictures which is all but absent in modern tradition but which is part and parcel of the tradition before
1914. Larkin's descriptions are vivid and accurate:

Flowered curtains, thin and frayed,
Fall to within five inches of the sill,
Whose window shows a strip of building land,
Tussocky, littered.

                                        (**"Mr Bleaney"**)

But description is there for the purpose of grounding
a state of mind in reality. The poem goes on to what
is humanly important, a question, an answer, a speculation:

Telling himself that this was home, and grinned,
And shivered, without shaking off the dread
That how we live measures our own nature.

The great emphasis on things in modern poetry seems
to spring from the same source as the fear of the failure
of language. In a world of dissolving values, things—
the sensible properties of sheer materiality—become
the bases of psychic security. Yet, paradoxically, things
are emptied of psychic value. Fear seems evident in
such statements as the following [by William Dickey,
"Poetic Language," *Hudson Review*, Vol. XVII, 1964-
65]:

This ability to see is neither easy nor usual, and it represents one of the most important ways in which the floating world of poetic language can be given a persistent human relevance, a persistent reference back to the solidities of existence.

That statement refers to Ciardi's lines in "Person to Person":

> Morning glories, pale as a mist drying
> fade from the heat of the day, but already
> hunchback bees in pirate pants and with peg-leg
> hooks have found and are boarding them.

Similarly, [Anne] Stevenson praises Elizabeth Bishop's "pre-occupation with the surfaces of things", and with "what can be suggested by a selection and presentation of surface" [*Elizabeth Bishop,* 1966]. Typical of the resulting poetry are these lines from "Fish":

> his brown skin hung in strips
> like ancient wallpaper,
> and its pattern of darker brown
> was like wallpaper:
> shapes like full-blown roses
> stained and lost through age.

And Rosenthal says of Tomlinson [in *The New Poets,* 1967], comparing him with Larkin to the latter's disadvantage:

> The mood, the readiness for perception, requires a certain restraint of personality . . . so that the eye . . . may be as responsive as possible. . . . Tomlinson holds the advantage of making his poem a discovery of concrete phenomenon.

Rosenthal's example of Tomlinson's "eye" is:

> A house, the wall-stones, brown,
>   The doubtful light, more of a mist than light
> Floating at hedge-height through the sodden fields
>   Had yielded, or a final glare
> Burst there, rather, to concentrate
>   Sharp saffron, as the ebbing year—.

Larkin himself comes in for both praise or censure depending upon how closely he conforms to the contemporary critical bias in favor of 'things'. Rosemary Dean praises the authenticity of "bleached / Established names on sunblinds" [Commonweal, Vol. LXXXI, Dec. 25, 1964]. And Enright applauds the concreteness of "the reek of buttoned carriage seats". Starting with a similar premise, Rosenthal censures "Here" because, he says:

> It is as though Larkin had suddenly remembered his gloomy tenets and snapped himself out of delighted absorption in reality . . . in the excitement of sense-awareness as Williams might have done.

In its fear of the absence of shared values or of universally similar states of mind, modern poetry's attempts to find a common objective ground in the things of the external world has tended to become more subjective on less common

ground. Ciardi's striving for concreteness in the image of bees quoted above, for example, results in the subjectivity he probably was trying to avoid. To some eyes, bees may look hunchbacked, and in the "impossible endlessness of observation" the balloon-shaped protrusions of fuzz on their legs may be seen as resembling pirate pants [A. Alvarez, *The Shaping Spirit,* 1958]. But they may also be seen as resembling harem pants, or Dutchboy pants, or what have you. The critical question must be: what has made Ciardi see them as pirate pants and not as something else which fancy can equally justify? How does the meaning of the poem—if it has a meaning beyond fanciful, imagistic simile—justify that particular fancy? How is significance built out of the image he has chosen? Another question must be: beyond the rather far-fetched visual resemblance, what is there about the nature of bees and the act in which they are engaged which is like the act of pirates? Though they 'board' their object and carry off something from it, it is difficult to think of a life activity that cannot be seen in the same way. And unlike pirates, they neither ravage nor destroy. The nautical word "board" is used in an effort to validate the metaphor by extending it, but it remains, along with the peculiar vision of "Morning glories" as ships, arbitrary and subjective.

The resemblance between these fragments by Hughes, Tomlinson, Bishop, and Ciardi to the touchstone of imagist poetry, the complete fragment, Pound's "Station of the Metro": "The apparition of these faces in the crowd; / Petals on a wet, black bough", is that they are provocative sensory stimuli which evoke in the reader an emotion or idea that may or may not be the one the author buried in the image. Larkin's reintroduction of thought into the surface of the poem produces a symbiotic relationship between idea and image which recreates connectedness between the internal and external world, not only of the speaker, but of the reader. The lines from **"Mr Bleaney"**, quoted above, show how Larkin picks out of the event or environment those details which contribute to an experience that involves not only seeing, but cognition. With few exceptions (**"Age"**, **"If, My Darling"**), Larkin's imagery is not psyche symbolizing itself, projecting from itself a subjective psychological landscape, but verifiable reality to which mind and mood react. The terms of the poetic image testify to a certain state of mind; but approached through the additional avenues of tone of voice and articulated thought, the state of mind verifies the image, disallowing idiosyncratic sight.

One other by-product of the modern slogan "no ideas but in things" which Larkin avoids is the tendency for emphasis on concreteness to deteriorate into emphasis on sight at the expense of the other senses. The modern poet keeps his eyes open. He is visually aware of his environment. When Donald Hill praises Richard Wilbur's "close disinterested observation", he means his visual perceptiveness—his ability to describe that which is seen. When Rosenthal finds that Larkin's **"Send No Money"** suffers from "the obvious fact that its mood is anchored in no justifying referent . . . a voice without a body; there is no dive into the specifics of observation", he is saying that the poet has not embodied his mood in the visual properties of a concrete object. When Stevenson approves Elizabeth Bishop for the "accuracy of her perceptions", she means the accuracy of her eyes.

"Dinglichkeit" in Larkin's poems is not confined to the visual properties of things. There is not only a mind that thinks about what the eyes see, but also olfactory, auditory, and kinesthetic senses. Concreteness includes smell:

> A smell of grass
> Displaced the reek of buttoned carriage cloth.

> Within the terminate and fishy-smelling
> Pastoral of ships

taste:

> I changed, / And ate an awful pie

> The boy puking his heart out in the Gents

sound:

> An uncle shouting smut

> That note you hold, narrowing and rising

touch:

> Their heads clasped abruptly

> sensing the smoke and sweat,
> The wonderful feel of girls

and motion:

> Palsied old step-takers,
> Hare-eyed clerks with the jitters

> . . . as the tightened brakes took hold, there swelled
> A sense of falling.

Larkin is more accurately described as a non-conformist to modernism than as a traditionalist. His poems sound modern: they capture contemporary sensibility and deal with contemporary problems. In his non-conformism, he avoids esoteric language of all kinds—that which is privately invented, and that which is taken from less known classics, mythology, religion. He also avoids over-burdening his poems with 'things' at the expense of thought and tone of voice. At bottom his non-conformism is a return to communicative poetry: there is someone talking and the assumption of someone listening and understanding. It implies faith both that there *is* an audience and that the audience shares a common tongue viable enough to communicate the full range of experience.

Merle Brown (essay date 1977)

SOURCE: "Larkin and His Audience," in *The Iowa Review,* Vol. VIII, No. 4, Fall, 1977: 117-33.

[*Here, Brown focuses on Larkin's "absences," not solely as symbols from nature, but as referents for his audience.*]

Readers of Philip Larkin's poetry keep writing about it, even though they recognize how simple and clear it is, because they also sense that its most distinctive aspect is indefinable, not just in criticism of the poetry but in the poetry itself. Because this aspect of Larkin's poetry seems by its very nature to be inexpressible, it needs speaking of in as many ways as possible, if the very sense of it is not to lapse. It seems that only the obvious can be said of Larkin, and that everyone who has written on him has said it again and again, in one way or another, since it is as simple and clear as a glass of water. Yet, because it cannot be defined, doubts remain as to whether either his most sympathetic critics, like John Wain, David Timms, and Alan Brownjohn, or his more severe, like Colin Falck, Donald Davie, and Calvin Bedient are responding to what makes Larkin's poetry of distinctive value.

Of Larkin himself, however, there can be no doubt. His choice of **"Absences"** as his own favorite poem for the anthology, *Poet's Choice,* as early as 1962, indicates that even then he had a sure sense of the indefinable aspect of his poetry that gives it its value. For **"Absences"** comes closer than any other of Larkin's poems to being explicit about what is inexplicable.

> Rain patters on a sea that tilts and sighs.
> Fast-running floors, collapsing into hollows,
> Tower suddenly, spray-haired. Contrariwise,
> A wave drops like a wall: another follows,
> Wilting and serambling, tirelessly at play
> Where there are no ships and no shallows.

> Above the sea, the yet more shoreless day,
> Riddled by wind, trails lit-up galleries:
> They shift to giant ribbing, sift away.

> Such attics cleared of me! Such absences!

John Press uses **"Absences,"** in a recent article, as an instance of those of Larkin's poems which "evoke a world transcending the contingencies and imperfection of daily existence," a world "whose nature can be hinted at by the medium of images drawn from the inexhaustible realm of nature—sun, moon, water, sky, clouds, distance" ["The Poetry of Philip Larkin," *The Southern Review,* Vol. XIII, Jan. 1977]. Donald Davie's unarguable claim that Larkin buys "sympathy with the human, at the price of alienation from the nonhuman" should insure that Press is not misheard as saying that **"Absences"** is a nature poem, a poem sympathetic with the nonhuman [*Thomas Hardy and British Poetry,* 1973]. For Press says only that Larkin *uses* images from nature, and it is clear that the phrase, "the inexhaustible realm," is the critic's, not the poet's. Press is, however, wrong to attribute a transcending world to the poet. Larkin himself is more precise. He says of the poem [in *Poet's Choice*]:

> I fancy it sounds like a different, better poet than myself. The last line, for instance, sounds like a slightly unconvincing translation from a French symbolist.

If **"Absences"** does evoke a transcendent world, it is only in the shape of an unconvincing translation. That is what

Larkin likes about the poem. What remains, in the place of that disbelieved, denied world, is the indefinable aspect of his poetry to which I have been pointing. The poem is "cleared of me," the biographically identifiable ego is absent from it. Yet it is no world, natural or supernatural. It is a very human attending and exclaiming; it is nothing, that unobjectifiable, un-delimitable act of observing, thinking, and speaking. The act itself cannot be seen or heard; in truth, it cannot even be thought, because to think it is to objectify it, to treat it as a mental object or fact, whereas its essential nature, as an act that arches over and assimilates both self and world, is to be irreducible to that which is other than itself, to the posited, to the factual. There is, however, nothing superhuman, Teutonic, or metaphysical about it, even though it is no part of the world as it is thought about in the *Tractatus*. By alliterating "absences" with "attics," Larkin calls attention to its humanness, even its commonness. It is awesome only in the sense that it is invulnerable, but it is available to any and all who will simply pull back from the existent world and live the invisible, inaudible, inarticulate attending aspect of their humanity along with whatever else they may have to do and suffer in the real, existent human and nonhuman world. Larkin is very careful to help his audience hear the last line in just this, the proper way. The conspicuous alliteration in the last line of the first stanza insures that, as the absence of all human beings is being affirmed, their presence as the indefinable act of viewing the sea as free of all human beings is gently suggested. The sea is made to remind one of a funhouse, with its collapsing floors, its tiltings and drops, its playfulness. The indefinable aspect of the poem, the saving, indefinable aspect of humanity, to which even the vast images of the sea and the sky are inadequate, is safe and homey. It has nothing to do with the fearfulness of nihilism or existentialistic absurdity. It is that absolute security into which the poem leads one to retreat from the meaninglessness of existence, of everything objective, whether ideal or real.

It is not otherworldly, only nonworldly. The "yet more shoreless day" does, of course, have its shores, as does everything in the objective world, whatever its expanse. Even the final exclamation, "Such absences!", is pressed into a delimited shape by the verbal imagining of the undelimitable nothing who does not give himself up even to the poem as object, offering it as a self-consuming artifact, to be broken down along with all selves as entities, and assimilated into the perfect freedom of being invisibly pleased. In such freedom, there is no respect for persons, there is no hierarchic stratification, one and all are anonymous. The most authentic statement Larkin has made outside his poetry is: "I think it's important not to feel crushed" [*The London Magazine,* Vol. IV, No. 6, Nov. 1964]. That is the essence of the inexplicable freedom that gives his poems their distinctive value. However silly Larkin is willing to make himself seem within his poems, he is never crushed, because he has his true life in that undelimitable, uncrushable act of attending, of imagining, of speaking. His poems make an appeal, it is true, as though Larkin were an entertainer, who would as a result be subject to anxieties concerning the ups and downs of audience response. If the appeal fails, however, the loss is the read-

er's, not Larkin's, for he is never fully engaged in any objective situation or encounter, whereby he might be hurt or crushed. The same sort of aloofness indeed is what he offers to all, not as a way of life, but as an aspect of whatever way of life one may be connected with. It is easy of access, and priceless because invulnerable.

"Solar," a poem in Larkin's most recent volume, **High Windows,** is enough like **"Absences"** to indicate how steady his fidelity has been. It is quite clearly "a slightly unconvincing translation from a French symbolist."

> Suspended lion face
> Spilling at the centre
> Of an unfurnished sky
> How still you stand,
> And how unaided
> Single, stalkless flower
> You pour unrecompensed.
>
> The eye sees you
> Simplified by distance
> Into an origin:
> Your petalled head of flames
> Continuously exploding.
> Heat is the echo of your
> Gold.
>
> Coined there among
> Lonely horizontals
> You exist openly.
> Our needs hourly
> Climb and return like angels.
> Unclosing like a hand,
> You give for ever.

Actually, this poem is an unconvincing translation not of a French symbolist, but of the final poem in Thom Gunn's *Moly,* "Sunlight." Gunn works to be precise about the sun in its nonhuman remoteness and otherness, and yet he also strives to be precise about the exact nature of the sun as an image of our desires. The poem ends in a highly individual address to the sun taken doubly, as it is and as it "outlasts us at the heart."

> Great seedbed, yellow centre of the flower,
> Flower on its own, without a root or stem,
> Giving all colour and all shape their power,
> Still recreating in defining them,
>
> Enable us, altering like you, to enter
> Your passionless love, impartial but intense,
> And kindle in acceptance round your centre,
> Petals of light lost in your innocence.

Although Gunn seems to be in accord with Alvarez's claim that "since Freud the late Romantic dichotomy between emotion and intelligence has become totally meaningless," he is emphasizing the stress between what one knows and what one desires ["The New Poetry, or Beyond the Gentility Principle," *The New Poetry,* 1962]. It is the pain of holding the known and the desired up against each other that gives "Sunlight" its power. That power, moreover, is enhanced by the way Gunn's sunlight refracts light coming to him from "Burnt Norton IV" ("After the kingfisher's wing / Has answered light to light, and is silent, the light is still / At the still point of the turning world") as well as from the last canto of the *Paradiso*. Gunn's "Sunlight" disproves Donald Davie's claim that, along with its violation of the non-human, mass industrialization and suburbanization has so damaged the traditional language of celebration that images like water and wheat have lost their poetic potency.

For Larkin, on the contrary, no object, not even the sun, deserves such adoration. He accepts the debasement of all objects and images and uses even the supreme object, the sun, in such a way as to reduce it to mere words in the service of his special kind of human freedom. That freedom entails a recognition that one cannot rely on anything outside himself as an origin, as a source of value, and that, if one separates himself off from his needs and from those aspects of himself which are visible, which "exist openly," he himself can be that which no object, real or ideal, can be, inviolably self-originative. To accomplish this, one must split himself as intelligence off from his needs and emotions. Larkin is willing to do it in order to be uncrushable. When he snaps out "Sod all" or "Books are a load of crap," when he reduces "essential beauty" to a picture slapped up on a billboard, he is not just being mean and nasty, but is insisting that all objects are ultimately unconvincing.

In **"Solar,"** instead of a beholding of the sun with adoration, Larkin offers the hilarious shenanigans of a verbal artist whipping the silly sun about with metaphorical abandon, shaking it like a baby toy. The word "Solar" itself makes the sun small, shrunken by commerce and science. It is just something hung up there, suspended in a room with no furniture, a naked bulb, but magical, without wires. It may be a "lion face," but it is a comic one, spilling like a sack of wheat, pouring like a salt shaker. "Continuously exploding" set against "petalled head of flames" is all show, fireworks. The sun's gold is coined, it is just legal tender, solar coinage. The sun, at bottom, is like a picture on a billboard, an illuminated hand unclosing over and over, to which we send our needs and receive them back, unchanged. In its dismissiveness, its mildly sad contempt, the poem is jovial. There is hidden laughter at the loss of one more source of security, for there is such security in one's own self-source. Larkin feels that modernist jazz must be all wrong, because it comes across so clearly as not "the music of happy men" [*All What Jazz*]. If Larkin's poetry is at times tedious and irritating, it is not because of its chronic sadness, but because of what lies behind it, making it a sham sadness, that is, its gaiety, its jollity, won without effort and held to so jauntily.

In the introduction to the 1966 reprint of his pre-poetic volume of verse, *The North Ship,* Larkin says he woke up poetically when he realized that Hardy's "Thoughts of Phena At News of Her Death" was not a gloomy poem. He also admits that, because the volume of Yeats which so influenced *The North Ship* stopped at "Words for Music

Perhaps," he "never absorbed the harsher last poems." If Larkin did, in his maturity, overcome Yeats's influence and write under Hardy's, just as important is the fact that the gaiety which charges Larkin, as it nowhere charges Hardy, resembles that of late harsh poems of Yeats like "Lapis Lazuli," which ends:

> There, on the mountain and the sky,
> On all the tragic scene they stare.
> One asks for mournful melodies;
> Accomplished fingers begin to play.
> Their eyes mid many wrinkles, their eyes,
> Their ancient, glittering eyes, are gay.

Yeats says it and aspires to it; Larkin does it. There is nothing heroic in Larkin, because it requires no effort. The heroic aspect of "Lapus Lazuli" comes from Yeats's feeling that that gaiety is out of his reach, that he is still tied to the natural, dying animal.

It bears repeating, I think, to say that Larkin does not write symbolic poems, only unconvincing translations of them. There are no objective correlatives in his poetry. The sun of **"Solar"** is shown up as deserving dismissal, as incapable of bodying forth indefinable value. Just so, the sea and "shoreless day" of **"Absences,"** instead of symbolizing mental spaciousness, are made to seem amusingly confined and inadequate, in comparison to the illimitable act of seeing them so. Many of Larkin's poems elude the crushing condescension of unsatisfied critics by crushingly dismissing each and every symbol as inadequate. Alvarez, who quite regularly has the courage to appear in vulnerable ways, called the last poem of *The Less Deceived,* **"At Grass,"** (which Larkin considers his first good poem), "a nostalgic re-creation of the Platonic (or *New Yorker*) idea of the English scene, part pastoral, part sporting. His horses are *social* creatures of fashionable race meetings and high style." Alvarez's dismissive tone echoes crudely the delicately dismissive tone of Larkin himself, in the very poem Alvarez is dismissing, **"At Grass."** It is true that the two horses of the poem are better off at grass than when winning races. At grass they have a freedom not unlike that which is the joy of Larkin's poetry. They stand anonymous, they

> Have slipped their names, and stand at ease,
> Or gallop for what must be joy,
> And not a fieldglass sees them home,
> Or curious stop-watch prophesies:
> Only the groom, and the groom's boy
> With bridles in the evening come.

Alvarez moves away from the poem uncomprehendingly as a result of placing it next to Hughes's "A Dream of Horses." If it is placed next to "A Blessing" by James Wright, the exquisite edge of **"At Grass"** will become available, if still invisible. Wright and a friend enter a field where two Indian ponies "come gladly out of the willows" to welcome them. There is a genuine encounter, where the nonhuman and the human momentarily fuse in a joy so delicate that it cannot quite bear the triumph of the poem's ending:

Suddenly I realize
That if I stepped out of my body I would break
Into blossom.

In **"At Grass,"** Larkin does not approach the horses, but keeps his distance, the eye just barely picking "them out / From the cold shade they shelter in." If the horses were being offered as representative of a perfect human joy, if a fusion of the human and nonhuman did occur, then the edge of that moment would turn ironically against the poet, who as author of this poem is not slipping his name but making it, winning the poetry race in England. Larkin, however, is aware that by putting these horses into his poem, he is halting their escape into perfect invisibility and anonymity, their "going down the long slide / To happiness, endlessly." He is holding them up, a catch, still alive, but corralled within the fence of the poem. Their joy, their freedom, is entirely dependent on the groom and the groom's boy, who "With bridles in the evening come." Even if the reader is merely puzzled by the last two lines, that will be enough to pull him away from the horses, and the poem itself, as objectified, into that condition of aloneness which is identical with oblivion, an identification almost made explicit in the curious little poem, **"Wants,"** also printed in *The Less Deceived*. What often seem like endings that qualify the rest of the poem, the poet turning on himself and getting the whole truth out so that the poem is perfect, are really working in the opposite way, like trick endings which will insure that the reader not take the poem, or the existence within "the garden" of the poem, too seriously. Imagine a dismissive wave of the hand fading out of sight, and you can sense a generosity in Larkin not matched by Marvell, even if their wit is comparable. Larkin wants to be sure that no reader takes his images too seriously. Highly-wrought language, a dazzle which might draw a reader swooning and yet alert into the imaginative experience of a poem, as a refuge where he could live happily apart from the pressures of the daily grind, Larkin will never imperil a reader with such a gawdy trap. What Larkin would share with his reader, ultimately, is the act of dismissing all images, all symbols, all realizations, all artifacts, the world itself, as inadequate, as inferior to the freedom of looking, imagining, thinking dismissively.

What makes not just Larkin's poems, but also his ataraxic stance, his sustained act of looking, imagining and thinking dismissively, so unstable is that there is only one form of response appropriate to them. Larkin has said that, of "the two tensions from which art springs . . . the tension between the artist and his material, and between the artist and his audience . . . the second of these has slackened or even perished," during the past seventy-five years or so, in the works of those artists and poets known as modernists. Although some poets do unquestionably write poems with no sense of how they will be heard, I should have thought that this was characteristic, not of modernist poets, but of romantic or neo-romantic poets. Modernist poets, in contrast, are, if anything, excessively concerned with their audience. They sense an extreme diversification of the ways in which poetry and art are being responded to, not just hostile ways along with sympathetic ones, but,

even more challenging, ways which come out of radically different life conceptions. In both *The Wasteland* and *Mercian Hymns,* the difficulty of the poetry results from its being responsive to conflicting modes of reading, to what, in the visual-auditory experience of poetry, is like a multiple perspectivism in the visual arts. Much of the genius of Eliot and Hill goes into their shaping the poetry so precisely that the unique way in which each hears his words is realized in sharp and often opposing relation to alternate ways in which those words can be heard. As a result, much of the delight of modernist poetry comes from hearing it in several ways at once, in the poet's own unique way, in the ways from which he has differentiated his own, and in one's own way. The poetry is made to allow for, even to encourage and thrive on, multiple modes of hearing and responding. Such charged vitality—in contrast to the relaxed vitality Larkin admires—is not quite the same as Empsonian ambiguity, Wheelwright's polysignificance, or even Umberto Eco's notion of the open work, for it emphasizes the poet's own unique mode of listening as the creative edge of the poem that evokes and keeps alive all the alternate and opposed ways of listening. In modernist poetry the reader feels responsible for listening as the poet listens, but this requires that he also listen in ways the poet sets himself against, and, ultimately, also in his own way.

The strain of creating such polyphonic poetry must lead even the strongest of modernist poets to the verge of disintegration and breakdown. For weaker aspirants it has no doubt led to what Larkin erroneously describes as typically modernist products, "poems resembling the kind of pictures typists make with their machines during the coffee break, or a novel in gibberish, or a play in which the characters sit in dustbins." Collapsing great modernist works, as Larkin does here, with weak evasions from the strain of the modernist predicament into a single junkheap seems, however, to be itself a perilously evasive move. It is, however, consistent with the poetry Larkin writes, a poetry for a single audience, which listens in a single way determined by Larkin as his way. Claiming falsely that all modernist poetry is like so much, say, of Robert Creeley's, not heard at all, Larkin feels even righteous about writing a poetry which is preeminently hearable, in a single, soporific way, indifferent to all other ways, especially thoughtful, reflective, critical ways. The aim is pleasure in the form of ease and comfort. One is invited to set aside his larger, human self in its relations with others and with the complexities of his actual situation and to assume the dream-identity of a single, secure audience, a fictitious cloud of unknowing that takes on real existence only as that into which actual readers and listeners escape. Collingwood was warning forty years ago that entertainment could become so important a part of a person's day that he would cease to live at all except in a make-believe way.

There is, in sum, a weakness in the generosity with which Larkin offers poems that will not disturb his readers. The unstableness of his achievement, moreover, stems from its dependence on his readers' being generous in the same way. The poem **"Wants"** suggests that Larkin is aware of the instability of the conditions of his poetry:

Beyond all this, the wish to be alone:
However the sky grows dark with invitation-cards
However we follow the printed directions of sex
However the family is photographed under the
    flagstaff—
Beyond all this, the wish to be alone.

Beneath it all, desire of oblivion runs:
Despite the artful tensions of the calendar,
The life insurance, the tabled fertility rites,
The costly aversion of the eyes from death—
Beneath it all, desire of oblivion runs.

The latent appeal of the poem is that one accept the not quite stated identification of being alone and being in oblivion without reflecting on it or criticizing it. The condition of oblivious aloneness is, to be sure, a delicate one, is, indeed, an aspect of that aloof, dismissive attentiveness which is the inner value of all Larkin's poetry. To be alone but aware of being alone is the painful state of loneliness. In truth, one is not really alone, since he has doubled up into an inner society of being alone and being aware of it. The real aloneness which one desires is an oblivious aloneness, a condition in which others are unaware of one and one is himself unaware of himself as well as of others. The self, moreover, of which one would be unaware is not just the self as one entity among many in the objective world, but also that unidentifiable, unobjectifiable, larger self which is the sustained act of looking at everything dismissively. In the condition of oblivious aloneness, that is, one is dismissive even of one's quintessential dismissiveness.

One is not, of course, to think about this condition, only to experience it, and Larkin, writing from within this condition as from an impregnable fortress, lures the reader who wants what he has with a strikingly subtle technique. At bottom, the technique is the casual lightness of the assertorial tone of the middle three lines of both stanzas. The alternatives to oblivious aloneness are presented not as irritants that make one want to escape into that state and not as attractions in spite of which one wants to make that escape, but as items waved aside and dismissed as negligible. As a result, unless one has read against the grain of the poem, by its end one is himself in the state of oblivious aloneness, unable to remember exactly what it is that he is now beneath and beyond. Properly read, therefore, six of the ten lines of the poem are so forgettable as to be forgotten by the end of the poem: friends, love, family, living with care in time and in thoughtful relation to one's mortality, all such matters are as nothing compared to the comfort of ataraxic aloofness. To think of them would, in fact, destroy the poetic experience, a crucial part of which is the condition of obliviousness.

If a reader begins to fuss, recognizing that there is no hint in the poem that the nature of any of these aspects of living as a human being in the world has been experienced or even thought about by the large, untouchable, uncrushable self dismissing them, so that the dismissal is totally uncompelling and unconvincing, then one will be breaking the implicit contract of the poem, the assumption that the reader shares the poet's wants and will raise no questions if the poem fulfills them. Larkin's own response to such a reader of bad faith is implicit in the following comment which he made in his interview with Ian Hamilton:

> There is nothing like writing poems for realizing how low the level of critical understanding is; maybe the average reader can understand what I say, but the above-average often can't.

His "average reader" is, in my terms, one who keeps the faith, holding to the contract, submissively. His "above-average" reader is one who raises questions. In Larkin's terms, to raise questions is to read without understanding, to lack the generosity necessary for the reading of his poetry. He remains invulnerable, no matter what the carping of the critic. Yet that critic raises questions because he has read the poems not only with sympathetic understanding, but also with a reflective, critical understanding of their limitations. His discomfort with the poems, his not understanding them Larkin's way, coincides with his understanding them truthfully.

Even though all Larkin's poems share the instability of being dependent on his actual readers' willingness to occupy unquestioningly the passive position he has reserved for them, it is possible to distinguish the more successful from the less. The more successful will be those poems in which the devices used to bring the reader up to the ataraxia of the poet are inconspicuous. For if the reader notices the devices, as devices, he will become more rather than less alert, a ruinous turn for such poetry. Also, those poems will weather best in which Larkin has most effectively hidden the troublesome moral implications inherent in the dismissive attentiveness into which he would lure his audience, for his sort of euphoria cannot tolerate anything worrisome.

On the grounds, then, of the effective concealment of tricks in the means and of moral disturbances in the end, it should be evident that **"Here,"** the opening poem of ***The Whitsun Weddings,*** will prove more durable than the title poem of that volume. Both poems depend on strategies and a moral flaw which must go unnoticed, if the reader is to enjoy the oblivious aloneness of the poems fully. Above all, readers must be kept from puzzling about the nature of the act of observing which is the basis of both poems. That critics of **"Here"** have already come close to such puzzling without actually lighting on it is a sign that it has the better chance of surviving undamaged.

The very obviousness of the main device of **"Here"** has perhaps kept it unnoticed. Grammatically, the first nine lines are a compound dangling modifier. The grammatical "error" goes unnoticed, however, because what dangles grammatically does in truth modify an unspecified, unspecifiable act of aloof attentiveness into which the reader obliviously escapes. Once there, once at one with that anonymous act, he will almost certainly ride out the poem in comfort. Although no critic has to my knowledge noted this quirk in grammar in relation to the invisible act of unreflective awareness, only one, Calvin Bedient, has betrayed a failure to experience it by improperly specifying it as taking place on a train [*Eight Contemporary Poets,* 1974]. A casual reading should bring out the inappropriateness of such placement.

"Here"

    Swerving east, from rich industrial shadows
    And traffic all night north; swerving through fields
    Too thin and thistled to be called meadows,
    And now and then a harsh-named halt, that shields
    Workmen at dawn; swerving to solitude
    Of skies and scarecrows, haystacks, hares and
      pheasants,
    And the widening river's slow presence,
    The piled gold clouds, the shining gull-marked mud,

    Gathers to the surprise of a large town:
    Here domes and statues, spires and cranes cluster
    Beside grain-scattered streets, barge-crowded water,
    And residents from raw estates, brought down
    The dead straight miles by stealing flat-faced
      trolleys,
    Push through plate-glass swing doors to their
      desires—
    Cheap suits, red kitchen-ware, sharp shoes, iced
      lollies,
    Electric mixers, toasters, washers, driers—

    A cut-price crowd, urban yet simple, dwelling
    Where only salesmen and relations come
    Within a terminate and fishy-smelling
    Pastoral of ships up streets, the slave museum,
    Tattoo-shops, consulates, grim head-scarfed wives;
    And out beyond its mortgaged half-built edges
    Fast-shadowed wheat-fields, running high as hedges,
    Isolate villages, where removed lives

    Loneliness clarifies. Here silence stands
    Like heat. Here leaves unnoticed thicken,
    Hidden weeds flower, neglected waters quicken,
    Luminously-peopled air ascends;
    And past the poppies bluish neutral distance
    Ends the land suddenly beyond a beach
    Of shapes and shingle. Here is unfenced existence:
    Facing the sun, untalkative, out of reach.

Though Larkin does ride a train in other poems, in this one, his swerving from "traffic all night north" suggests that his vehicle is a bus, turning off the M-1 in the direction of Hull. The "harsh-named halt" would not be a railway station, but a sheltered bus stop. The vehicle needn't have halted at the halt, however, so it could as well be a car. What is important, however, is the lack of specification, a lack intended to help one feel unseen as he views the scene.

A more sensitive error is John Wain's saying that Larkin's life is one of those "removed lives // Loneliness clarifies," for it nudges one in the right direction, even though it does not bring him to oblivious aloneness, which is altogether superior to anything involving loneliness ["Engagement or Withdrawal? Some Notes on the Work of Philip Larkin," *Critical Quarterly,* Vol. VI, 1964]. Loneliness is a social condition, for the lonely are set apart from the "cut-price crowd"; whereas, as oblivious and alone, Larkin or you or me, any and all aloof, anonymous observers, are secure and at home, though radically alienated, wherever they may be, in the city or in an isolate village. The lonely, it is true, are closer to the alone than the crowd is; that is why they come after the crowd in the movement of the poem, which is meant to lead the reader in a gentle swerve to that condition in the objective world which most nearly resembles the condition of the unobjectifiable act of observing which accompanies invisibly the lines of the poem from beginning to end.

Donald Davie commits an even more sensitive error in suggesting that Larkin has been imprecise in the lines "Here leaves unnoticed thicken, / Hidden weeds flower, neglected waters quicken." Larkin, he claims, does clearly notice the leaves, and so forth, so how can he call them unnoticed? Perhaps, Davie speculates, he meant to say that they go unnoticed by that "cut-price crowd." But Larkin is not so sloppy as that. What does not get mentioned throughout the poem, the unmentionable anonymous act of noticing, that is the only noticing the leaves get. Larkin himself does not notice them, for he has slipped his name by the time he is at one with that act of noticing. These lines, moreover, are part of Larkin's subtly non-symbolic technique of luring his reader unreflectively into a oneness with that hidden act of negligent noticing. In the last stanza he is simply setting down what is seen, just as he did in the other three stanzas, and what he sees does not in fact seem as interesting, at least in its details, as what has already been observed. But the tone rises, as though something important is happening. Larkin effects the rise in tone mainly by beginning the three sentences of the stanza (the other sentence of the poem covers the other three stanzas) with the title word "Here." "Here" by the end of the poem is "bluish neutral distance," is "unfenced existence: / Facing the sun, untalkative, out of reach." The proper response to that is a brief, bemused "Hm, so what?" after which one goes about his business, without further thought. This casual, dismissive attitude is what is truly unfenced, even if "bluish neutral distance" comes closer to such freedom than anything else in the objective world does.

Davie, however, almost blows the poem apart with his last comment on it:

> In Larkin's poem one detects a perverse determination that the ultimate ("terminate") pastoral shall be among the cut-price stores, and nowhere else. And the pity felt for the denizens of that pastoral, the "residents from raw estates," is more than a little contemptuous.

From the start of the poem, Larkin's aim has been to ease his reader into the condition of that true "Here" which is nowhere, that hovering, unspecifiable attending with which the reader is to identify himself unawares. From such an unlocatable locus, the attitude taken toward every object, toward everything objectifiable, not just toward that "cut-price crowd," will be a mixture of pity and contempt. Except that, in principle, every member of that crowd might himself be truly at one with the uncrushable act of observing dismissively, so that, as part of that act, one may be enjoying a false sense of superiority by looking down, as he does, upon the crowd. Even so, it is Larkin who has lured him into that falseness, by contrasting the movement of the observing as a "swerving" to the straight line of the "traffic all night north," and then emphasizing the straightness of the crowd by having it "brought down / The dead straight miles by stealing flat-faced trolleys." He is the one who has made one feel different from and superior to the crowd. He might well weasel, if confronted with this, saying that he did not really mean the contrast, that it was only a manner of speaking. Even admitting the truth of that, one may wonder if it is necessary to the sense of the value of unfenced attending that it be kept in constant contrast to the fenced quality of everything seen, imagined, or thought. One might even wonder whether it isn't a moral uneasiness which makes Larkin come out of the sure comfort of his aloof attentiveness to write poems. Perhaps he writes them so that he can feel superior to them. Or perhaps his comfort is unstable enough to need the reassurance of the belief that others are also of his way of thinking. Perhaps, however, **"Here"** would not have given rise to any questions at all, if Davie had not come at it with the idea that Larkin values the human scene more than the nonhuman scene. The truth, rather, is that Larkin values the human seeing as equally superior to the human and the nonhuman scenes. His weakness is that, because of the oblivious nature of that seeing, he must keep his preference itself hidden, so that it is imperative that his critics keep making mistakes.

Although **"The Whitsun Weddings"** was intended by Larkin as the centerpiece of *The Whitsun Weddings,* it is vulnerable as **"Here"** is not, and, for that matter, as its own counterparts in *The Less Deceived* and *High Windows,* **"Church Going"** and **"The Building"** are not. Because of his deep revulsion for the objective, existent world, Larkin cannot put himself as an identifiable human being into a poem except as an object of revulsion or at least as the butt of his anonymous mockery. In contrast to what he does in those other poems, in **"The Whitsun Weddings,"** Larkin puts himself into the poem as an individual, observable entity, but without the slightest hint of mockery or revulsion. Even worse, toward the end of the poem, because attention is called to the breadth of the "I"'s awareness, in contrast to the self-absorption of those just married, and because of the ostentatious metaphorical flourish with which the poem ends, this "I," who as an entity existent within the objective world of the poem must have limits like its every other entity, is presented as possessing, as a poet, the value which only the illimitable, anonymous act of attending dismissively can have. As a result, the poem is tainted by smugness.

Instead of remaining safely hidden as in **"Here,"** in **"The Whitsun Weddings"** Larkin recklessly seats himself in a train heading south for London. In his characteristic way of noticing things, he first flattens nature with nature violated by industry, ("Wide farms" and "short-shadowed cattle" with "canals with floatings of industrial froth" and "acres of dismantled cars,") and then proceeds to view the wedding participants in the same way he has viewed nonhuman nature and its man-caused violations. The participants are all presented as types ("The fathers with broad belts under their suits / And seamy foreheads; mothers loud and fat," and so forth) just as animals are noticed according to species and cars lumped together as dismantled. The first direct reference to the brides and bridegrooms, "Fresh couples climbed aboard," might rather be a reference to cattle, and "A dozen marriages got under way" is a manner of speaking more fit for fruit than individual human beings. In themselves, such references scarcely warrant remark, since they are typical of Larkin's attitude toward every object and entity in the existent world.

In this poem, however, they do deserve remark, because of the presence alongside them of the poet himself as just one more such entity who inexplicably and undeservedly escapes any and all dismissive glances and remarks. The reader cannot but observe Larkin looking and looking without ever being looked upon in return. Out the window, as the train leaves another station, he sees girls

> In parodies of fashions, heels and veils,
> All posed irresolutely, watching us go,
>
> As if out on the end of an event
>   Waving goodbye
> To something that survived it.

The "as if" is just a hint that perhaps nothing of a wedding does survive the event. The hint is corroborated two stanzas later; with all the couples aboard, the weddings have turned into "a dozen marriages." The real moral problem, however, does not lie in Larkin's cynicism, but in his observing without being observed. The "us," of course, of "watching us go" is impersonal, referring to the whole train; if those on the platform focus at all, it will be on the married couple they have just seen off. Larkin is in a situation like that of Dante, in the thirteenth canto of the *Purgatorio,* where he and Vergil come upon those doing penance for their envy. They are seated in a row with their backs against the mountainside, the eyelids of each sewn together, so that they cannot see others, about whom they would then say belittling, cynical things, out of envy. Dante turns away from the view, because to him it seems a moral outrage to be looking at others without being looked back upon in turn. Though he may be proud, there is no streak of envy in Dante. In contrast, Larkin keeps staring at people who are unaware he is looking at them and who do not, as a result, gaze back at him. The anonymous, illimitable act by which the "cut-price crowd" of **"Here"** is dismissively attended to is, in essence, invisible and unobservable. In **"The Whitsun Weddings,"** however, Larkin takes on the sovereign privileges of such invisible, unnameable observing even though he also presents himself as a visible, existent, individual entity. He should have recognized that such a hybrid is inadmissible in poetry the likes of his. By bringing the act of attending into the scene, he has unknowingly committed an obscenity, in the sense that he has brought on stage what by its nature must occur offstage.

The vice is compounded by the self-congratulatory professionalism of the end of the poem.

A dozen marriages got under way.
They watched the landscape, sitting side by side
—An Odeon went past, a cooling tower,
And someone running up to bowl—and none
Thought of the others they would never meet
Or how their lives would all contain this hour.
I thought of London spread out in the sun,
Its postal districts packed like squares of wheat:

There we were aimed. And as we raced across
  Bright knots of rail
Past standing Pullmans, walls of blackened moss
Came close, and it was nearly done, this frail
Travelling coincidence; and what it held
Stood ready to be loosed with all the power
That being changed can give. We slowed again,
And as the tightened brakes took hold, there
  swelled
A sense of falling, like an arrow-shower
Sent out of sight, somewhere becoming rain.

It is stated as a fact that not one of the dozen couples gave a moment's thought to any of the others. After the statement, however, its unsettling grounds are provided, inadvertently: "I thought of London spread out in the sun, / Its postal districts packed like squares of wheat." The thoughtlessness of the twelve couples is not, then, a fact, but rather the claim of this thoughtful "I", who is calling attention to his own attentiveness by way of contrast with all those others, who are much like cattle, self-absorbed, looking without seeing. The unsettling aspect of this contrast can be sensed even in John Wain's praise of it:

> The human actors in this scene, who will set up homes and mate and keep the human spectacle going, are unreflective: their world is the concrete and the immediate; if we are to have any such things as 'art'— whether poetry or any of the other arts—their actions need to be completed and interpreted by a brooding imaginative vision playing over them from a point of detachment. In a sense the poet's involvement is greater than theirs. . . .

The trouble in the passage lies in the turn from art, poetry, a brooding imaginative vision, to "the poet's involvement," at which point one realizes that Wain is speaking in praise of his friend at the expense of all those others. If Larkin, as I believe, is making for himself, within the poem, the very same claim which Wain makes for him, then the last six lines of the poem should be read as follows. Sad it may be, but no significant change has occurred to the married couples. The specialness, the joy, the sacredness of the weddings does not survive the event. The show, the fireworks, the "arrow-shower," turns to rain. It fructifies, there are droppings of human babes, the populace grows and grows, naturally and thoughtlessly, like wheat. The couples copulate, reproduce, and in time will be fathers and mothers on station platforms, waving goodbye to their just married off-spring. But the rain which the arrow-shower becomes is also the tears of us superior people, who observe "the association of man and woman / In daunsinge, signifying matrimonie— / A dignified and

commodious sacrament" and think of the unchanging cycle: "Feet rising and falling. / Eating and drinking. Dung and death" [T. S. Eliot, "East Coker I"]. The change that truly gives power is not that of marriage, but that of poetry. Consider, as the example of the poem, the change from the weary worker whose "three-quarters-empty train" pulled out "about / One-twenty on the sunlit Saturday" to the "I" of this ending, loosing from his magnificently broad vision this grand metaphorical display. From just a weary one he has huffed and puffed till he is so big as to include all of England from Hull to London, all of London, and indeed a vision of all of life too. It is a very fine thing to be a poet.

Larkin, it is true, wrote the poem for the comfort of his audience, unreflective viewers rather than unreflective actors and carping critics. In the long run, however, even his own audience will prefer his unpretentious poems, those in which Larkin does not make the mistake of trying to define what is indefinable, of exhibiting what cannot be put on exhibit, that impersonal, invisible, never even quite audible act of observing dismissively.

Richard Brookhiser (review date 1989)

SOURCE: A review of *Collected Poems,* in *The American Spectator,* Vol. XXII, No. 10, October, 1989, pp. 46-8.

[*In the following review of* Collected Poems, *Brookhiser examines the language and content of Larkin's poems, concluding that "his world looks severly limited."*]

The **Collected Poems** of Philip Larkin, editor, jazz critic, and librarian at the University of Hull, have appeared four years after his death in a volume edited by Anthony Thwaite. The first thing that strikes the reader is the photograph of Larkin on the jacket, which is notable for its aggressive ugliness. *Aggressive* implies will, and I use the word advisedly. We are not responsible for our baldness or our wrinkles, which God gives us, but we can choose our glass frames. Larkin's—black, square, heavy— look like a prop from a Monty Python sketch on chartered accountancy, or a spare pair of General Jaruzelski's. He wanted, in other words, to look this way. It suggests the attitude he brought to his art, his career, his life—I'm the way I am, and if you don't like it, who asked you?—the attitude responsible for shaping the slim output preserved in this book.

The chief benefit of Mr. Thwaite's selection is that it will put Larkin in the bookstores. I live in Manhattan, supposedly the publishing and bookselling capital of the country. But I remember the time I had, a few years back, trying to get all of Larkin's individual volumes together. It took months, and I never did find a copy of **The Less Deceived.** Now we can lay hands on him.

Apart from this, the volume is a curious enterprise. "Many poems," the flap copy boasts, "are collected here for the first time." But with a poet as severe and self-censoring as Larkin that is not necessarily a good thing. In an introduction to a reissue of **The North Ship,** his first volume, Larkin recalled a "hint" one of his literary mentors had given him years earlier: "Yesterday I destroyed about two thousand poems that mean nothing to me now." Larkin obviously didn't destroy the poems that are here exhumed, but that doesn't mean they are any good. If anything, Larkin should have destroyed a number of the poems he did publish.

One use for the clunkers is a game of Spot the Influence. Here is Auden pottiness, there is a whiff of Yeats.

> What lover worries much
> That a ghost bids them touch?
> *A drum taps: a wintry drum*

For technicians, they provide a study of development. It's good to see the young man who is satisfied with

> But we are pledged to work alone,
> To serve, bow, nor ask if or why

becoming the older man capable of

> Why should I let the toad *work*
> Squat on my life?

The poems are arranged in chronological order, with an appendix of early poems at the end. Pieces that have been previously published are identified by volume initials. The best thing a curious nonspecialist can do is begin with **"At Grass,"** the twenty-first poem in the book and the first good one, then read on, ignoring all poems labeled TNS (for **The North Ship**) and skipping the appendix entirely.

Larkin began writing as the last bright, clear-aired peak of English poetry, the high modernism of Eliot, Yeats, and Pound started to recede to landmark distance. His problem was what to do next. It's been everyone's problem for fifty years.

One course he might have taken, which is an option open to all poets at all times, would have been to write "poetically"—to model his work on the rhythm and the ring of some great predecessor. This method is probably responsible for more bad poetry than any other. Sometimes, the style of genius is simply unique: Yeats's music, of all the high moderns, was most elusive—so much so that not even he always got it right. Even if a style is classical and replicable, what the imitator gains over his model in skill he is sure to lose in freshness, unless he brings some transforming element of his own to the task.

Another possibility, one which many of the great revivers of the language have thought themselves to be exploring, is plain speaking. If trying to write like a poet leads you astray, then write like a man. Eliot spoke of purifying the "dialect of the tribe"; John Dryden shucked off Baroque magnificence and encrustation. But the most dogged apostles of plain speaking who also happened to be Titans were probably William Wordsworth in England and Walt Whitman here. Don't make faces at me, they say, I'm only telling you how the leech gatherers/roughs talk.

Of course, no one actually talked like Wordsworth or Whitman. What they were really doing, when they were writing at their best, was partaking of that experience which every great poet shares, and around which critics write and write without ever quite explaining it, when the passion for truth lifts a man up to beauty. You know it when you see it done. If you don't, the future will; it's all the future will have to see, because everything else will have fallen by the wayside.

But plain speaking is not only a means of self-hypnosis for geniuses, it is a good way of getting honest, modest work done, and this, after a few youthful fumbles, is the path Larkin chose to pursue. That doesn't mean his best poems aren't crafted. A little looking uncovers elaborate skeins of rhymes or half-rhymes, sometimes running through quite long stanzas. But Larkin is almost never interested in drawing attention to his labor. Conversational rhythms and enjambments smudge the outlines. When he does give us something unmistakably structured, it's usually in the jog trot of hymns and jingles: forms for which familiarity has bred indifference. These little packages he fills with his bitterest sentiments, so as to profit by the contrast.

> They fuck you up, your mum and dad.
>   They may not mean to, but they do.
> They fill you with the faults they had
>   And add some extra, just for you.

Metrically, it could be Hallmark, but don't look for it on Mother's Day.

And what, with his consonances and his glasses, did Larkin write about? The answer is surprising, but unavoidable. Larkin was a love poet.

The love comes in two kinds. There is a vein of affection for things and creatures that, perhaps because they can't be held responsible for failing to return it, never flags. **"At Grass"** is a description of old racehorses.

> Do memories plague their ears like flies?
> They shake their heads. . . .
> Almanacked, their names live they
> Have slipped their names, and stand at ease,
> Or gallop for what must be joy.

Larkin may turn these feelings to furniture, to old clothes, to a dead hedgehog. So Robert Herrick wrote about his lares and penates.

Big-L love means love of other people, and this is trickier. In fact, it is impossible. We have already seen what a mess parents make of it. Larkin's men and women don't do any better.

> Parting, after about five
> Rehearsals, was an agreement

That I was too selfish, withdrawn,
And easily bored to love.
Well, useful to get that learnt.

The closest a couple in Larkin's poems come to love is not a real couple at all, but a pair of centuries-old stone effigies.

> Such plainness of the pre-baroque
> Hardly involves the eye, until
> It meets his left-hand gauntlet, still
> Clasped empty in the other; and
> One sees, with a sharp tender shock,
> His hand withdrawn, holding her hand.

The poem **"An Arundel Tomb"** ends with the line, "What will survive of us is love." But, in offering the thought, Larkin first tells us that it is only "almost true"; that is, false. The gesture we set so much store by was only an artistic detail:

> A sculptor's sweet commissioned grace
> Thrown off in helping to prolong
> The Latin names around the base.

Loveless lives can make us as depressed as a bachelor considering a rented room.

> . . . how we live measures our nature,
> And at his age having no more to show
> Than one hired box should make him
>   pretty sure
> He warranted no better.

Sometimes, as in **"Love Songs in Age"** or **"Faith-Healing,"** the contemplation of lovelessness breaks out in real rage. But there is nothing to be done about it.

> Life is first boredom, then fear.
> Whether or not we use it, it goes
> And leaves what something hidden from
>   us chose.

If you don't like it, who asked you?

Here and there, rarely, we get a glimpse of a third mood, a rapture higher than affection and, unlike love, fulfilled. Where jazz was concerned, Larkin was what is called a moldy fig: a fan of jazz before be-bop got to it, and he writes in one poem of Sidney Bechet that "On me your voice falls . . . / Like an enormous yes" (you won't find a better phrase-long definition). Or nature, in its impersonal totality, gives a similar lift: ". . . that high-builded cloud / Moving at summer's pace." But summer ends, or the record does, and we're back in the hired box: forerunner of the box we never vacate.

It is only fair to a poet who moves us to consider him on his own terms. But it's only fair to us to consider him on ours as well. Get a few steps back from Larkin's seductive plain speaking, and his world looks severely limited: whether by the fate of his character, as he would say, or by choice, as of glass frames, as I would, doesn't matter. He does us the favor, however, of not trying to be us. He lived in a kind of perpetual four o'clock in the morning, and that's what he presents. When we hit that hour, as we regularly do, he is there, to show us around.

J. D. McClatchy (review date 1989)

SOURCE: "Songs of a Curmudgeon," in *The New York Times Book Review,* May 21, 1989, pp. 24-5.

[*The following review commends poet Anthony Thwaite for including much of Larkin's unpublished work in* Collected Poems, *thereby revealing the careful editing and revising Larkin performed, and the deliberation with which he practiced his craft.*]

Once, some years ago, when he was asked what he thought about the prospect of becoming Britain's poet laureate, Philip Larkin replied, "I dream about that sometimes—and wake up screaming. With any luck they'll pass me over." They didn't. The story goes that in 1984, by which time he had long been the most admitted poet of his generation in England, Larkin was offered the laureate's post—and refused it. Perhaps by then he knew his health was precarious. (He died of throat cancer on Dec. 2, 1985, at the age of 63.) But the refusal was also characteristic.

Larkin seemed to have led a life of refusals. He was an unmarried university librarian in a provincial town who described himself as looking "like a balding salmon," and who was used to renting rooms at the top of a house. He shied from publicity, rarely consented to interviews or readings, cultivated his image as right-wing curmudgeon and grew depressed at his fame. His art, too, refused both the glamorous technical innovations and myth-mongering of Modernism as well as the will to transcendence that empowered many of his peers. He preferred to write, in clipped, lucid stanzas, about the failures and remorse of age, about stunted lives and spoiled desires. "Desolation," he once remarked, "is for me what daffodils were for Wordsworth." But from such refusals he fashioned a rich body of work likely to stand as the most enduring of mid-century British poetry.

The publication of his *Collected Poems,* then, is an auspicious event, but one accompanied by some controversy. Larkin left ambivalent instructions about his unpublished work. One clause in his will asks that it be destroyed; another clause gives his executors some discretion in the matter. To the consternation of purists, one of those executors, the poet Anthony Thwaite, has fortunately decided to ignore Larkin's doubts. Of the book's 242 poems, 83 appear in print here for the first time. This swells the small output considerably, and may alter an opinion of Larkin—who published just four volumes of verse, one per decade—as a skimpy miniaturist.

Mr. Thwaite has made other decisions that will annoy other purists. The book is arranged chronologically but the early writing, from before 1946, is placed last, to one side of the poet's mature poems. And Mr. Thwaite has made only a "substantial selection" from Larkin's prodigious early work. With the later work, though the original order of each book's contents is listed in an appendix, we lose in this volume the canny force of Larkin's own arrangements, the juxtaposition of tones and themes. But to compensate, because of this edition's precise dating, we can now watch Larkin work out a problem over several adjacent poems, written within months of one another. In any case, whatever reservations some readers may have, Mr. Thwaite has done his task with an exemplary fastidiousness, and he has given us a fascinating and indispensable text.

I turned first to the "new" poems. They range from apprentice exercises of the late 1930's to occasional squibs from Larkin's last years. The general impression one takes away from reading them in bulk is an increased respect for Larkin's editorial judgment. None of these suppressed poems will detract from his reputation, but little here will add to it. There are, though, a few surprises—among them several marvelous poems, most of them late (the already famous **"Aubade"** and the haunting **"Love Again"** are two of them). And some unfinished poems from his notebooks, including **"The Dance"** from 1963-64, a sweet-and-sour narrative in a dozen 11-line stanzas which, if completed, would have stood with the poet's best.

The earliest poems—"pseudo-Keats babble," Larkin once called them—date from his schooldays, and their pastiche soon gives way to more serious imitations, demonstrating how thoroughly he absorbed the strongest initial influences on his imagination, Auden and Yeats. The menaced tone and vivid rhythms of Auden pulse in lines from a 1941 poem, **"Observation"**:

> Only in books the flat and final happens,
> Only in dreams we meet and interlock,
> The hand impervious to nervous shock,
> The future proofed against our vain suspense. . . .
>
> Range-finding laughter, and ambush of tears,
> Machine-gun practice on the heart's desires
> Speak of a government of medalled fears.

This was soon after replaced by the austere plangencies of Yeats; warnings yielded to yearnings, and it is Yeats's voice that dominates Larkin's first collection, *The North Ship* (1945). But one is also struck now by tentative, muffled versions of what we have come to recognize as Larkin's own distinctive voice. Even with its affected teenage weariness, his apprentice sonnet **"Nothing Significant Was Really Said"** sounds a note we will hear clearly throughout his career. "What was the rock my gliding childhood struck, / And what bright unreal path has led me here?"

Even more curious is to discover startling anticipations. A poem from 1943, **"A Stone Church Damaged by a Bomb,"** seems now like a practice effort for the more famous **"Church Going"** of 1954. In **"Spring Warning,"** written in 1940 and published in Larkin's school magazine, the troubling onset of spring is greeted by some who, mutter-

ing they are neither simple nor great enough to *feel,* "refuse the sun that flashes from their high / Attic windows." The phrase, of course, anticipates the great poem Larkin wrote a quarter-century later, **"High Windows,"** the title poem of his final collection. It is both ironic and rueful about the brave new world of easy sex the young seem joylessly to enjoy, and the poet wonders about the happiness his elders once thought he'd laid claim to just by being young. But, in the eerie last stanza, his speculation drifts into a memory, an image that accuses what it laments:

> Rather than words comes the thought of high windows:
> The sun-comprehending glass,
> And beyond it, the deep blue air, that shows
> Nothing, and is nowhere, and is endless.

The stark revelation of this endless nothing that overlooks and underlies experience is strangely offset by the nearly religious hush of the rhetoric. It is not the opposition between categories of knowledge—a relentless self-scrutiny on the one hand, and the perspectives of memory and desire on the other—that animate Larkin's best poems, but the tension between them.

The small book that first brought Larkin to prominence as a poet, and established his particular reputation, was *The Less Deceived* (1955). He chose that title, he once explained in a letter, for its "sad-eyed realism." The deception he conjured in order to cast it out was largely a self-deception: that romantic love or good intentions can save us from "singleness." What art exalts as "the individual," Larkin reminds us, is only isolation. The best poems in his two major collections, *The Whitsun Weddings* (1964) and *High Windows* (1974), return to this work of disenchantment. The tone of later poems is darker, often more embittered, but throughout both books he casts a cold eye on love that always promises to solve and satisfy:

> Truly, though our element is time,
> We are not suited to the long perspectives
> Open at each instant of our lives.
> They link us to our losses: worse,
> They show us what we have as it once was,
> Blindingly undiminished, just as though
> By acting differently we could have kept it so.

The pathos of Larkin's work lies in that link with his losses, in his sense of having been obscurely betrayed. "Elsewhere underwrites my existence," he writes. The lost paradise of innocence obsesses him and his poems. Only because of the forlorn; noisy, mean clutter of our lives does this innocence seem a "solving emptiness" for which we hunger and are sickened by.

"Larkin's poetry is a bit too easily resigned to grimness don't you think?" Elizabeth Bishop once wrote to Robert Lowell. It is true that his range is rather narrow, but within its confines is a beguiling variety of tones and forms. He never repeats himself to make the same point, and his poems are more readily memorized than those of almost any other postwar poet. His wit can be at once mordantly satirical and unnervingly sadhearted:

> Sexual intercourse began
> In nineteen sixty-three
> (Which was rather late for me)—
> Between the end of the Chatterley ban
> And the Beatles' first LP.

Larkin first wanted to be a novelist, and early on wrote two novels that still give wry pleasure. His poems, too, are built from finely observed details and portraits of the England of council flats and tea towels.

Thomas Hardy, the poet from whom Larkin learned the most, said it was his melancholy satisfaction to have died before he was out of the flesh, to have taken the ghost's view of things. "To think of life as passing away is a sadness; to think of it as past is at least tolerable." Perhaps Larkin viewed this world so astutely because he wrote as if from the other side. And when most of the flashier, more blustery contemporary literature has passed away, his poetry—ghostly, heartbreaking, exhilarating—will continue to haunt.

FURTHER READING

Bibliography

Kuby, Lolette. "Bibliography." In *An Uncommon Poet for the Common Man: A Study of Philip Larkin's Poetry,* pp. 181-90. Paris: Mouton, 1974.
    A detailed bibliography citing some of Larkin's lesser-known works.

Biography

Jacobson, Dan. "Profile 3: Philip Larkin." *The New Review* I, No. 3 (June 1974): 25-9.
    A profile based on biographical questions, with some literary commentary.

Motion, Andrew. *Philip Larkin: A Writer's Life.* New York: Farrar, Straus Giroux, 1993, 570 p.
    A teacher at Hull, literary executor to Larkin, and friend, the author states that the poet lived simply, "in the strictest sense, a writer's life," so that he could concentrate on his craft.

Criticism

Heaney, Seamus. "Now and in England." *Critical Inquiry* III, No. 3 (Spring 1977): 483-88.
    Considers Larkin's language as "rational music," "rational light," comparing it to that of many of his English forebears.

Kissick, Gary. "They Turn on Larkin." *The Antioch Review* LII, No. 1 (Winter 1994): 64-70.
    Explores "Larkin-bashing" in the wake of the publication of his letters and Andrew Motion's biography. Kissick cites Larkin's racism, misogyny, and "confused and morose" attitudes toward sex.

Kuby, Lolette. *An Uncommon Poet for the Common Man: A Study of Philip Larkin's Poetry.* Paris: Mouton, 1974, 190 p.
    Comprehensive overview placing Larkin among his contemporaries.

Martin, Bruce. *Philip Larkin.* Boston: Twayne Publishers, 1978, 166 p.
    Approaches Larkin from two perspectives: American New Criticism and the British "men of letters."

Osterwalder, Hans. *British Poetry between the Movement and Modernism: Anthony Thwaite and Philip Larkin.* Heidelberg: Carl Winter, 1991, 299p.
    Re-evaluates Larkin's work vis-a-vis his own anti-modernist stance and the French symbolists.

Perloff, Marjorie. "What to Make of a Diminished Thing." *Parnassus: Poetry in Review* XIX, No. 2 (1994): 9-30.
    Reviews *Selected Letters of Philip Larkin* and *Philip Larkin, A Writer's Life,* providing a less harsh appraisal of Larkin's right-wing tendencies than Kissick's article.

Phillips, Robert. "The Art of Poetry XXX." *The Paris Review* XXIV, No. 84 (Summer 1982): 45-72.
    Interview in which Larkin speaks of his personal life and development as a writer.

Whalen, Terry. "Philip Larkin's Imagist Bias: His Poetry of Observation." *Critical Quarterly* XXIII, No. 2 (Summer 1981): 29-46.
    Aligns Larkin with the Imagists as "a poet of sensation and impression."

Additional coverage of Larkin's life and career is contained in the following sources published by Gale Research: *Concise Dictionary of British Literary Biography, 1960 to Present; Contemporary Authors,* Vols. 5-8R, 117; *Contemporary Authors New Revision Series,* Vol. 24; *Contemporary Literary Criticism,* Vols. 3, 5, 8, 9, 13, 18, 33, 39, 64; *Dictionary of Literary Biography,* Vol. 27; *DISCovering Authors: British; DISCovering Authors: Most-Studied Authors Module; DISCovering Authors: Poets Module;* and *Major Twentieth-Century Writers.*

Ogden Nash
1902-1971

(Full name Frediric Ogden Nash) American poet and playwright.

INTRODUCTION

Nash enjoyed one of the largest audiences of this century, attracting readers from all walks of life with his insightful, satirical view of human nature and human foibles. His biting wit was tempered by humor and sensitivity, enabling him to tread lightly over touchy subjects, including the behavior of other people's children, social affectations, and illness. Nash's unique style is characterized by his willful disregard for grammatical and spelling rules, and his deliberate mis-spelling of words to force a rhyme, such as spelling diapers "diopes" to rhyme with "calliopes." Many of Nash's poems have been so widely quoted, they have reached near-proverbial status. "Candy / Is dandy, / But liquor / Is quicker," and "If called by a panther, / Don't anther" are two Nash poems that are so familiar to the public that they are often attributed to "Anonymous." While the unconventional nature of his verse has denied him the status of a "serious" poet, Nash remains one of the most read and quoted poets of this century.

Biographical Information

Born in Rye, New York, to a family of old Southern stock, Nash was raised along the Eastern Coast as his father's import-export business frequently moved the family from state to state. This nomadic childhood resulted in Nash's unique accent, which was part Southern drawl, and part New Englander. Nash attended St. George's School in Newport, Rhode Island, and Harvard University for one year, 1920-1921. Forced to drop out to earn his living, Nash tried his hand at several professions, including teaching at his alma mater, St. George's, and a brief, unsuccessful stint as a bond salesman. By 1925 Nash had settled into a career in advertising with the publishing house Doubleday, Page, later to become Doubleday, Doran. During this time, Nash attempted to write serious poetry, "sonnets about beauty and truth" in the tradition of Byron, Keats, and Shelley. It was while writing advertising copy at Doubleday, Doran, Nash found his poetic voice. His poem "Spring Comes To Murray Hill" was jotted down in a fit of procrastination and later sent to the *New Yorker* magazine, which published it in 1930. The poem exhibited all the traits that were to become Nash's characteristics: the whimsical tone, the outrageous mis-spellings and mis-pronunciations. Also present was Nash's characteristic theme—the trivial, often-overlooked details of life in the city, viewed through a cynical, almost curmudgeonly perspective.

Nash married Frances Leonard in 1931. His new roles of husband and father influenced his poetry as his initial crustiness softened into musings over his two small daughters, beginning with *Happy Days*. In 1936, Nash moved with his family to Hollywood where he wrote screenplays for MGM. During that time he produced *The Shining Hair* with Jane Murfin, *The Feminine Touch* with George Oppenheimer and Edmund L. Hartman, as well as *The Firefly*. None of these met with much success, and a somewhat discouraged Nash returned to the East Coast in 1942. One good thing came out of his time in Hollywood, however, and that was his friendship with S. J. Perelman, with whom he collaborated on the book and lyrics for *One Touch of Venus,* a smash hit during Broadway's 1943 season. In the 1950s and 1960s, Nash began writing children's poetry in addition to his whimsical verses for adults. *Parents Keep Out: Elderly Poems for Youngerly Readers, The Christmas That Almost Wasn't,* and *Custard the Dragon* are a few of his works addressed to children, partly influenced by his grandchildren, even as grandfatherly ruminations entered his verses for adults. Another topic that occurred with increasing frequency in Nash's later years was mild complaints about sickness and aging, always with a comic bent. Indicative of his position in American poetry, Nash was a member of both the American Academy of Arts and Sciences and the National Institute of Arts and Letters. Nash died in 1971 in Baltimore, Maryland.

Major Works

Nash published his first poem, "Spring Comes to Murray Hill," in the *New Yorker* magazine in 1930. His first collections of poems, *Hard Lines* (1931) and *Free Wheeling* (1931), established Nash's reputation as an original, witty, and whimsical creator of humorous verse with wonderful insight into human nature. In 1933 Nash wrote *Happy Days,* which introduced new themes of matrimony, household crises, and fatherhood. Throughout the 1930s and 1940s, Nash continued to produce collections in the same characteristic style that distinguished his verse, including *The Primrose Path* (1935), *The Bad Parents' Garden of Verse* (1936), *I'm a Stranger Here Myself* (1938), *Good Intentions* (1942), and *Many Long Years Ago* (1945). Nash collaborated on the smash Broadway musical *One Touch of Venus* in 1944, co-authoring the book and lyrics with S. J. Perelman. During the remainder of his career, Nash continued to write whimsical verse for adults, and began to write children's poetry as well, such as *The Christmas That Almost Wasn't* (1957), *Custard the Dragon* (1959), *The Adventures of Isabel* (1963), and *The Mysterious Ouphe* (1965).

Critical Reception

Although Nash was largely ignored by most critics in his lifetime, he was well liked by the public. Nash's ability to delight his readers through comical and entertaining verses often obscured the technical virtuosity required to produce them. Nash admitted to having "intentionally mal-treated and man-handled every known rule of grammar, prosody, and spelling"; after Nash's death, a *New York Times* obituary by Albin Krebs suggested that, despite this disregard for convention, Nash's verse reveals "a carefully thought-out metrical scheme and a kind of relent-less logic." Critics in more recent years have begun to re-evaluate Nash's reputation, noting that, throughout his career, Nash demonstrated great flexibility and versatility of the English language in volume after volume. Moreover, his social and political satirical skills have earned him comparisons to the great eighteenth-century satirists Al-exander Pope and Jonathan Swift.

PRINCIPAL WORKS

Poetry

Hard Lines 1931
Free Wheeling 1931
Happy Days 1933
The Primrose Path 1935
The Bad Parents' Garden of Verse 1936

I'm a Stranger Here Myself 1938
The Face is Familiar: The Selected Verse of Ogden Nash 1940; revised edition, 1954
Good Intentions 1942; revised edition, 1956
The Ogden Nash Pocket Book 1944
Many Long Years Ago 1945
The Selected Verses of Ogden Nash 1946
Versus 1949
Family Reunion 1950
The Private Dining Room, and Other New Verses 1953
The Pocket Book of Ogden Nash 1954
You Can't Get There From Here 1957
Verses From 1929 On 1959
Everyone but Thee and Me 1962
Marriage Lines: Notes of a Student Husband 1964
An Ogden Nash Bonanza. 5 Vols. 1964
The Animal Garden 1965
Funniest Verses of Ogden Nash: Light Lyrics by One of America's Favorite Humorists 1968
The Scroobious Pip [with Edward Lear] 1968
There's Always Another Windmill 1968
New Comic Limericks: Laughable Poems [with others] 1969
Bed Riddance: A Posy for the Indisposed 1970
The Old Dog Barks Backwards 1972
I Wouldn't Have Missed It: Selected Poems of Ogden Nash 1972
Custard and Company 1980
A Penny Saved Is Impossible 1981
Ogden Nash's Zoo 1986

Other Major Works

Cricket of Carador [with Joseph Alger] (juvenilia) 1925
Born In a Beer Garden; or, She Troupes to Conquer [with Christopher Morley, Cleon Throckmorton, and others] (satire) 1930
Nothing but Wodehouse [editor] (short stories) 1932
Four Prominent So and So's [music by Robert Armbruster] (libretto) 1934
The Firefly (screenplay) 1937
The Shining Hair [with Jane Murfin] (screenplay) 1938
The Feminine Touch [with George Oppenheimer and Edmund L. Hartman] (screenplay) 1941
One Touch of Venus [with S. J. Perelman] (libretto) 1943
Ogden Nash's Musical Zoo [music by Vernon Duke] (libretto) 1947
Parents Keep Out: Elderly Poems for Youngerly Readers (juvenilia) 1951; enlarged edition, 1962
The Moon Is Shining Bright as Say: An Anthology of Good-Humored Verse [editor] (poetry) 1953
The Boy Who Laughed at Santa Claus (juvenilia) 1957
The Christmas That Almost Wasn't (juvenilia) 1957
I Couldn't Help Laughing: Stories Selected and Introduced by Ogden Nash [editor] (short stories) 1957
Custard the Dragon (juvenilia) 1959
Beastly Poetry (juvenilia) 1960
A Boy Is a Boy; The Fun of Being a Boy (juvenilia) 1960
Scrooge Rides Again (juvenilia) 1960
Custard the Dragon and the Wicked Knight (juvenilia) 1961
Everybody Ought to Know: Verses Selected and Intro-

duced by Ogden Nash [editor] (poetry) 1961
Girls Are Silly (juvenilia) 1962
The New Nutcracker Suite and Other Innocent Verses (juvenilia) 1962
The Adventures of Isabel (juvenilia) 1963
A Boy and His Room (juvenilia) 1963
The Untold Adventures of Santa Claus (juvenilia) 1964
The Mysterious Ouphe (juvenilia) 1965
The Cruise of the Aardvark (juvenilia) 1967
Santa Go Home: A Case History for Parents (juvenilia) 1967

CRITICISM

Lisle Bell (review date 1931)

SOURCE: "Verses That Click," in *New York Herald Tribune Books,* Vol. 7, No. 19, January 18, 1931, p. 5.

[*In the following review of* Hard Lines, *Bell comments on Nash's creative vocabulary and structure in his poetry, as well as his position in relation to "traditional" poets.*]

When a new poet comes along, the least a reviewer can do is to find method in his madness—and write a paragraph on the technique of it. This—now that our chortles of enjoyment have partially subsided—we shall undertake.

Briefly and specifically, what Ogden Nash does is to take words apart to see what makes them tick, and put them together so that they click. And not necessarily in the condition in which he found them. Any one who is under the impression that the English language is not sufficiently flexible should study **Hard Lines.** It demonstrates that our mother tongue can be made to behave in a manner hardly becoming a mother, but irreproachably amusing. Here the English language is not only flexible; it is double-jointed, ambidextrous, telescopic, kaleidoscopic, and slightly demented. If this isn't flexibility, then a coil spring made out of piano wire is a ramrod.

Mr. Nash proves the poetic possibilities of words which have been lying around untouched since the days of Chaucer and Spenser. Also the poetic possibilities of words which are so young that they are still wearing—as he spells it—"diopes." (Pronounced to rhyme with "calliopes.")

In his more casual moods, Mr. Nash is a philosophic first cousin of Sam Hoffenstein, but deeper down we find more than a trace of Walt Whitman. If you don't believe it, read the poem entitled **"I Want New York."** A very definite attitude toward life underlies the most skittish of the verses; they have a flavor apart from their pattern and from their infectious novelty. One begins to suspect that there is a vein of thoughtfulness behind the verbal pastiche, and one's suspicions are verified on the last page—a poem entitled **"Old Men":** . . .

People expect old men to die,
They do not really mourn old men.
Old men are different. People look
At them with eyes that wonder when.
People watch with unshocked eyes . . .
But the old men know when an old
    man dies.

Lisle Bell (review date 1935)

SOURCE: "Goofy Gallopings in Verse," in *The New York Herald Tribune Books,* Vol. 11, No. 24, February 17, 1935, p. 2.

[*In the following review of* The Primrose Path, *Bell praises Nash's trailblazing verse and examines several themes present in the collection.*]

Opposite the title page of **The Primrose Path** there is a list of "other books by Ogden Nash" and one of them, we observe with mild surprise, is **The Primrose Path.** If there were some other author we'd call this a discrepancy, but with Mr. Nash one can't be certain. Quite possibly he devotes all his spare time to primrose pathfinding, and for the sake of a little privacy he may have a hidden primrose path from which the public is excluded—though that would be a crime.

A Daniel Boone on the fantastic frontiers of rhyme, Mr. Nash nonchalantly blazes trails of prosody which are rapidly hacked into highways by his imitators. But he has a goofy gallop in verse which leaves the copyists far behind. We'd rather watch Nash on his piebald Pegasus than Lady Godiva on a white horse. His performance is like that of the fellow who leaped into the saddle and dashed off in all directions. He goes neatly over social hedges and takes political ditches in his stride, and so—mind if we borrow your pencil, mister?—here's a straight tip: Put two berries and a half on Nash to win. It's in the book!

The Primrose Path is wider, longer and roomier than the previous Nash models. It has everything except a center of gravity—poems of appreciation, of indignation, of the animal kingdom and of the fireside. There are also "poems to be pinned to the calendar," from which category we quote a seasonal excerpt. It appears in Mr. Nash's **"Song for the Saddest Ides."**

Citizen? Resident? Married? Single?
Living together, or don't you mingle?
Blessed events? If so, please state
Change of status, its nature and date.
Royalties? Rents? Commissions? Fees?
If none, explain their absence, please.
And let there be no legal flaw
In Deductions Authorized by Law.

Salaries? Wages? Sale of Property?
Here comes the Notary, hippety-hop-
    pety!

Raise your hand and take your oath
To tell the truth or bust. Or both.

Phyllis McGinley (review date 1936)

SOURCE: "Evolution of a Benedick," in *Saturday Review,*
October 10, 1936, p. 15.

[*Below, McGinley reviews* The Bad Parent's Garden of
Verse *in verse, imitating Nash's style.*]

In those unthinkable days of yore
When Ogden Nash was a bachelor,
He wrote no rhymes and he found no reason
To hymn the results of the mating season.
In cynical stanzas he used to scoff Spring
  And slander scions and sneer at offspring,
  Boast how a crib won only dismay from
   him,
  And plead with the stork to keep away
   from him.
  Yes, wry were the themes that he used to
   rhyme on
  For Mister Schuster and Mister Simon.

But look what happens to attitudes lyrical!
Then came the deluge, then the miracle.
Before you could say, "I bet you daren't,"
Ogden Nash had become a parent.
Indeed, undaunted by teething trouble,
He went and became a parent, double.

How the bells rang out with joy and
 elation,
How word went flashing across the nation,
How news spread foreign and news spread
 local!
For any parent is pretty vocal,
But where is the man wouldn't crow aloud,
With daughters and copy at once endowed?

So now he sings more gay than he uster
 For Mr. Simon and Mr. Schuster,
And strings his harp as a father should
To praise the pleasures of parenthood.

Hurrah, Mr. Nash, for your writings laughable!
We liked you surly, we love you affable,
And think your poems designed for the nursery
Almost the best in your bulging versery.
(There's one, especially, you might brag on,
Concerning Belinda who owned a dragon;
We also discovered ourselves in stitches
Over the lady who ate up witches.)

And, fine, Mr. Nash! you're not so silly as
Many another Pater Familias,
For you see flaws as well as perfection
In little gazelles of your own selection.
And we like your remarks on tending and feeding

them;
And, thank God, most the poems in this book
 scan, and aren't
  made up of the kind of lines that used to be
  funny but now
  we get eyestrain from reading them.
And since that's a thing that we're filled with
 delight about,
We're glad that you had some daughters to write
 about.

Louis Untermeyer (review date 1938)

SOURCE: "Inventory of Nash: 1938," in *Saturday Review,*
June 4, 1938, pp. 6-7.

[*In the following review, Untermeyer offers criticism of
Nash's technique, contending that the rhyme scheme and
long, asymmetrical lines obscure serious themes in his
poetry.*]

Ogden Nash has been both over-praised and underrated;
his stock has gone up and down and up again; his highs
are often confused with his lows. Nevertheless, in a rapidly changing world and a nervously fluctuating market,
he has always had more orders than he could fill. Although highly salable, his work is interesting to brows of
all altitudes; it is intelligent and always unpredictable.
Nash is, therefore, something of a phenomenon as poet
and producer, and he merits a more detailed stock-taking
than he has received.

There are, first of all, Nash's two most obvious characteristics. Both of them are curiosities in technique: the long,
asymmetrical lines, and the elaborately inexact rhymes.
One or two fanatical source-hunters have found the
origin of Nash's lengthy eccentricities in Gilbert's "Lost
Mr. Blake." But an unprejudiced comparison will show
that the two styles have nothing in common. Apart from
the almost opposite idioms, Gilbert's lines are consistently
long and fairly regular, while Nash's line-lengths vary
from two to sixty-two syllables; Nash's unmatched and
unscannable lines are his own, a distinct technical departure. Nevertheless, I do not think they are particularly
effective. Their charm is the frail charm of the unexpected;
with each repetition the surprise is a little less surprising—so much so that when Nash, after hundreds of pur-
posefully shapeless verses, printed a few poems in traditional meters, his readers were really surprised. In [*I'm a
Stranger Here Myself*] as in the preceding *The Bad Parents' Garden of Verse,* the keenest as well as the most
comical verses are those in which the rhythm is regular
and the lines quite orthodox in shape. I would be disposed
to put the "invention" of the irregular line on the debit
side.

The rhymes are another matter. Here the reader is constantly and incredibly assaulted by a shock which is partly esthetic and partly galvanic. A rhyming word is usually
a preparation for another rhyming word; Nash delights the

reader with the pleasure of inexactitude, with words that rhyme reluctantly, with words that nearly-but-do-not-quite rhyme, with words which never before had any relation with each other and which never again will be on rhyming terms. These distortions are at their best when they are their worst. What reader can fail to be startled when confronted with a poem which begins:

> Oh, sometimes I sit around and think, what would you do if you were up a dark alley and there was Caesar Borgia,
>
> And he was coming torgia,
> And brandished a poisoned poniard,
> And looked at you like an angry fox looking at the plumpest rooster in a boniard?

Such rhymes are as delightful as they are astonishing; they are like apparently improvised speeches in which the errors are more lively—and more likable—than the prepared accuracies. I should say that Nash's calculated recklessness in rhyme belongs definitely on the credit side.

Nash has been applauded for his industry and his verbal ingenuities. Both are virtues, but they become vices with Nash. For one thing, he writes too much. At first his work seems amazing; then it becomes amusing; after too many repetitions of the same effects, it descends to the mechanical. The present volume contains almost three hundred pages; were it half as long it would be twice as good. Productiveness not only compels Nash to pad but to pretend. He has to pretend to be funnier than he really is, or to be funny when he wants to be serious, or to give a "snap" to a title which might better have been casual or non-committal. I feel he is working too hard when he forces himself to such titles as **"To Bargain, Toboggan, To-Woo!" "Boop-Boop-Adieup, Little Group!" "Man Bites Dog-Days," "Where There's a Will, There's Velleity," "Little Miss Muffet Sat on a Prophet," "Barmaids Are Diviner than Mermaids."** Working overtime and straining too often put much of Nash's output on the debit side.

But the rest of Nash belongs on the sunny side of the ledger. His verse always makes good reading; often it is the best light verse written in America today. The territory might be extended to include England, for, with the possible exception of A. P. Herbert, there is no one here or abroad who can surpass the straight-faced absurdity of **"Adventures of Isabel,"** the sensible nonsense of **"Curl Up and Diet,"** the clipped but devastating disposals of **"Fellow Creatures."** Nash's *The Bad Parents' Garden of Verse,* and in particular **"The Tale of Custard the Dragon,"** proved he could be as nimble and original as A. A. Milne; page after page in the present volume proves he can take the leap from childlike fancy to social satire in one effortless stride. It is hard for me to understand why no musician, manager, or theatrical producer has made Nash supply book and lyrics for a series of native comic operas, especially since there seems to be an almost hopeless search for librettists with imagination.

It is in this realm, the realm of incalculable imagination, that Nash is happiest and at his highest. Time and again he begins inconsequentially, with a wisp of an idea, or with no thought at all. Once upon a time, he mumbles to himself, there was a man named Mr. Strawbridge. Strawbridge rhymes with drawbridge and so the poem not only is about Mr. Strawbridge who wanted a drawbridge, but about what kind of a drawbridge would please him best. He wanted it because he wanted to interfere with traffic; on his house he had a veranda built (rhyming with Vanderbilt) so that he could look at the Atlantic Ocean,

> But he said sometimes on Sundays and holidays he couldn't see the Atlantic for the motorists,
> And he said he'd rather see the former than the latter even though they were handsome and respectable Kiwanians and Lions and Rotarists,

And so the poem goes wildly on from one mad fantasy to another—and all because the name of Strawbridge popped into Nash's oddly proportioned mind.

Nonsense and criticism elbow each other in Nash; he is a crazy story-teller one moment, a satirist the next, a wit who takes to clowning to correct pretense and expose hypocrisy. Playfully but incisively he makes his summaries with the deceptive calm of the following "tribute":

> How courteous is the Japanese;
> He always says, "Excuse it, please."
> He climbs into his neighbor's garden,
> And smiles, and says, "I beg your pardon";
> He bows and grins a friendly grin,
> And calls his hungry family in;
> He grins, and bows a friendly bow:
> "So sorry, this my garden now."

Such moments occur frequently enough to lift Nash above his own pleasant insanities; they are funny, but they are wryly, seriously humorous. Some day the committee which gratifyingly awarded a Pulitzer Prize to Morrie Ryskind, George S. Kaufman, and the Gershwins for "Of Thee I Sing" will give Nash that honor for adding a new approach, a new style, and a new meaning to American social verse. This will be as much a surprise to the committee as it will be to Mr. Nash.

Edward Larocque Tinker (review date 1942)

SOURCE: "Lines By Ogden Nash," in *New York Times Book Review,* November 29, 1942, p. 16.

[*In the following review of* Good Intentions, *Tinker comments upon Nash's insight into human nature and his ability to succinctly, accurately, and wittily incorporate those observations into his poems.*]

To present an adequate picture of the blithe, careless quality of Ogden Nash's rib-tickling poems one would have to be another Ogden Nash—and he is *sui generis.* He takes his fellow man, and woman, apart in his new collection of vivacious verse [*Good Intentions*]—the first in four years—with engaging cheerfulness and an insight into their foibles that is almost uncanny. This deep and mellow understanding of human nature pervades his work and gives substance to what otherwise might be only frothy, funny verse.

Few of the perennial bores have escaped his stabbing pen, and his portrait of the "man who when he bares his breast to life it comes back to him all covered with welts, because everything that happens to him is much worse than the same thing happening to any one else . . . Other people with indigestion just have indigestion, but his indigestion ranks somewhere between appendicitis and cholera" is life-like.

His particular enmity is reserved for the horny-handed enthusiast who always encores the most boring numbers. His head should be amputated and brought to him on a silver platter, and it might be well, he adds, to cut it off twice.

His wit is a perennial spring, but he is a poet by *force majeure,* for he has mangled, masticated and maltreated every known rule of grammer, prosody and spelling. When a word proves recalcitrant he attacks it brutally, applies an anesthesia, performs an appendectomy or lops off a limb, and the result is such Nashian rhymes as snuffle and uffle (awful), Autumn and tautumn (taught 'em), and "parsley is gharaley."

Mr. Nash is encyclopedic in his interests, for he has collected his reactions to such diversified topics as skinks, skunks, ganders, termites and octopi; osteopaths, editors, doctors and big executives; serenades, allergies and assorted chocolates.

His genius for arresting the attention by a single line— "Sally Rand needs an extra hand," for instance—is as infallible as that of the FBI in arresting criminals. No one could refrain from reading a poem which began "Roses are things which Christmas is not a bed of"; your curiosity would certainly be aroused by a lady whose "one eye looks like Goya and the other paranoia"; and you would be forced to agree with an author who confesses "I prefer charity to hospitality, because charity begins at home but hospitality ends there." His definition of September as the month that "makes you glad to get back where you were glad to get away from" has the accuracy and succinctness of a Webster grown whimsical in his cups.

Good Intentions has one serious poem to serve as a foil for the others—**"Heil, Heilige Nacht!"**—an ironic and deeply felt indictment of war at Christmas time. It sounds like a funeral-bell tolling in the midst of a jazz number, but its sincerity and restrained bitterness give it real emotional power.

But as the book, with this exception, is the gayest and most amusing of the season, this appreciation should end on a lighter note, and there is none better than Mr. Nash's sidelight on the city in which we live:

> *Here men walk alone*
> *For most of their lives,*
> *What with hydrants for dogs*
> *And windows for wives.*

Russell Maloney (review date 1945)

SOURCE: "Ogden Nash Nosegay," in *The New York Times Book Review,* October 14, 1945, p. 4.

[*In the following review of* Many Long Years Ago, *Maloney describes Nash as a poet of the cynical generation produced by the Depression, who possesses the ability to make readers laugh at the foibles and inconveniences of modern life.*]

Many long years ago it was, indeed—fifteen, I believe—that Ogden Nash's first published writing appeared in The *New Yorker.* It was the immortal lyric entitled **"Spring Comes to Murray Hill,"** which contained the couplet:

> *The Pilgrims settled Massachusetts in 1620 when they landed on a stone hummock.*
> *Maybe if they were here now they would settle my stomach.*

The depression had produced a poet. Since then Ogden Nash has been, at one time or another, a magazine editor, Hollywood writer and musical-show librettist, but students yet unborn will find him listed in their History of English Literature as a poet.

Nash is the laureate of a generation which had to develop its own wry, none-too-joyful humor as the alternative to simply lying down on the floor and screaming. His ragged verse is remarkably like Ring Lardner's unpruned prose in effect—a catalogue of the annoying trifles that constitute our contemporary civilization, set down with a friendly leer. Lardner wrote about prohibition, golf, the stock market, Americans traveling abroad, million-dollar prizefights and similar nostalgic nuisances; Nash runs the gamut from the depression to Hitler, touching upon such disparate subjects as detective stories, crooners, the theatre-ticket shortage, Father's Day, knitting, colds, fruit salad, bankers, the circus, rain, strong drink, marriage and children's parties.

Many Long Years Ago is a sort of retrospective volume, representing Nash's published work to date. Any but the most well-read and retentive-minded Nash fan would find it difficult to separate the early verse from the recent. Both rejoice the innocent reader's heart with their leisurely tempo and indifference to formal scansion and their miraculous quasi-rhymes. Further, Nash is one of the rare people who can make a pun and make you like it. He can write sentimental rhymes about his children and make you like those, too. In short, he can do almost anything in the poet line, and he has been doing it for fifteen years.

A hair-spring sense of outrage is Nash's most valuable bit of professional equipment. He can be as angry at marshmallow or whipped cream on a salad as at an absconding banker, and as mad at the absconding banker as at Hitler. He is an urbane and articulate Donald Duck, an Alexander Pope with a hangover, a Rabelais whom you could introduce to your sister.

Times Literary Supplement (review date 1949)

SOURCE: "Nash as Only Nash Can," in *Times Literary Supplement*, December 9, 1949, p. 811.

[*In this review, the critic lauds Nash's abilities as an ironist and philosopher, in addition to his talent as a humorist.*]

Although it is impossible to appreciate all the subtleties and refinements of Mr. Ogden Nash's humour without some knowledge of the domestic habits of the Americans, or at least of the *New Yorker*'s attitude to them, the welcome given on this side of the Atlantic to his two previous collections of nonsense rhymes and cautionary tales in verse would certainly seem to justify a separate English edition of his latest one [*Versus*]. Mr. Nash's English readers will be delighted by it, for once again he proves himself to be a most ingenious and amusing critic of human frailty and absurdity. It would be a mistake, however, to think of him merely as a funny man; like Mr. Thurber, he has a Democritean streak which entitles him to the respect due to a philosopher, albeit a laughing one. His philosophy is that of the ironist rather than that of the satirist. "Well," he says,

> I have learned that life is something about which you
>   can't conclude anything except that it is full of
>   vicissitudes,
> And where you expect logic you only come across
>   eccentricitudes.

The vicissitudes and eccentricitudes of domestic life, as they affect a gentle, somewhat bewildered man of forty-five, are responsible for the vicissitudes and eccentricitudes of the form as well as the substance of his verses. Like a clown, he is most endearing when he is most deeply involved in them, for, as he remarks:

> Humour depends on the point of view,
> It's a question of what is happening to who.

And to illustrate this profound truth he reminds us that

> If the puppy is ill on your new tuxedo,
> Why, naturally, you don't laugh, but he do.

We may indeed laugh at him as the victim of circumstance—of the people upstairs

> Who when their orgy at last abates
> Go to the bathroom on roller-skates,

of the awful Miss Hopper, the "Polterguest," of uninflammable petrol-lighters, of child-pianists, of "bobby-soxers," of relatives' prescriptions, of the rainy house-party and "the girl who does Ruth Draper"; but we also laugh with him because, by describing these personal experiences with detachment, he gives them universal validity. Even when he invites us to join him as a spectator of other people's behaviour—the grown-up man trying to outwit a duck, the diners-out who "cry 'Garçon' after the school of Stratford-atte-Bowe or New Rochelle," the golfer or the commuter—his irony is always gentle: at the most it may tickle, but it is incapable of lacerating the heart.

At times even this teasing instrument is laid aside; in such cautionary tales as **"The Outcome of Mr. Buck's Superstition"** and **"The Confessions of Count Mowgli de Sade"** Mr. Nash is content merely to describe a situation and leave it to the judgment of his readers' sense of the ludicrous. His drollery is so immediately affecting that it is easy to underestimate and even to overlook what it owes to technical virtuosity. Humpty Dumpty would certainly have approved of Mr. Nash's command of language: but the liberties he takes with words and syntax and rhyme—liberties which only a highly literate clown would dare to take—may conceal from a casual reader the remarkable range and skill of his metric. It is not too much to say that there are very few poets who could not learn something from a study of his verse, especially his modulations of rhythm and his half-rhymes; and, in doing so, add profit to their pleasure.

Lloyd Frankenberg (review date 1950)

SOURCE: "In Nick-of-Time Rhyme," in *The New York Times Book Review*, November 19, 1950, p. 4.

[*Below, Frankenberg analyzes Nash's theme of family as addressed in* Family Reunion, *and comments upon his irregular use of meter.*]

At first glance there is no resemblance between *Family Reunion,* Ogden Nash's latest collection of verses, and T. S. Eliot's play of some years back, *The Family Reunion.* With second sight, however, and something of a shiver, I have apprehended the striking of at least one identical theme: "I regret that before people can be reformed they have to be sinners."

The theme is struck, yes; so hard it never shows its head again. For Nash's development of this theme is another story; a plangent tangent: "And that before you have pianists in the family you have to have beginners."

Nash's development is always another story. It may be the story of the little boy who didn't believe in Santa Claus, and how the reindeer got even with him. It may be a gripping adventure, like eating outdoors in the dark:

> *If your half-broiled chicken leaps about,*
> *That's half the excitement of eating out;*

If you dust it with sugar instead of salt,
It's everyone's fun and nobody's fault;
And if anything flies in your mouth, perchance,
Why, that is mystery, that's romance!

This particular story (**"Out Is Out"**) winds up at the cleaner's. Nash's sense of direction is unerring, if unnerving. "Two roads diverged in a yellow wood," Robert Frost once said, "And sorry I could not travel both. . . ." But Nash does travel both. He sets forth blithely, putting his worst foot forward, no excess baggage on his mind or at his back, and fetches up in the opposite direction. **"The Trouble With Women Is Men,"** he concludes.

As to which is his worst foot, they're hard to choose between. I can barely distinguish one from another: unshod iambic, stumbling trochee, on-the-loose anapaestic, or stopped-dead-in-its-tracks spondee. Often, like centipedes, they all turn up in the same line, which lends variety and the challenge: "You scan it." Is Nash plodding the long hard road back from free verse? Yet only a serious student of prosody, one surmises, could fall so flat so frequently, on his own dead pan. And he always has a nick-of-time rhyme:

I will pen me my memoirs.
Ah, youth, youth! What euphorian days them was!
I wasn't much of a hand for the boudoirs,
I was generally to be found where the food was.

Then, just to show us he can do it with both ears shut, he will come up with a metre that is as smooth as it is idiotic:

Oh, a home as mute as a bell that's clapperless
Is forlorn as an Indian in Indianapolis.

It was a good idea to bring together in one volume Nash's verses, many old and some new, on the subjects of children:

Hail, third-born infant of my friend,
Thou rosy extra dividend!
What mirth enlivens thy vicinity,
Thou handsome example of masculinity!
Thou rugged atom, thou hairless he-man,
Potential President or G-man!

their pets:

Tell me, O Octopus, I begs.
Is those things, or is they legs!
I marvel at thee, Octopus;
If I were thou, I'd call me Us.

and their parents:

There was an old miser named Clarence,
Who simonized both of his parents.
"The initial expense,"
He remarked, "is immense,
But I'll save it on wearance and tearance."

For anyone benighted enough not to possess a copy of Nash, this is a good one to begin the study of a poet whose themes, as I have suggested earlier, sometimes clash with Eliot's. Those who have one, or two, even three (I've lost count) of his previous books, will find here, among old favorites, many that will become their new.

David McCord (review date 1951)

SOURCE: "Nashsense Under One Roof," in *The Saturday Review*, February 10, 1951, p. 18.

[*In the excerpt below, McCord praises* Family Reunion *as a collection that appeals to all ages, and feels that it is representative of the body of Nash's work.*]

It may be assumed that Ogden Nash is America's No. 1 family man. The title of **Family Reunion** therefore suggests a selection of the master's work as closely knit as the poet's knitting allows, with the notion in mind that any member of any family can read it with comfort and delight. The present selection which Mr. Nash has made fully lives up to this happy expectation. There are verses here for father, for mother, and verses about children and about various animals domestic, feral, and in between. I should not say that the verses about children are also *for* children, though I am not really sure that the whole book is not addressed to children as much as to beleaguered parents. I for one have never been quite satisfied with any previous selection of Mr. Nash's verse as representing the total area of his paper work. Somehow the present volume, assembled as it were under one leaky roof, is the volume for which one reader at least has been waiting. Some day the critics will either divide Mr. Nash's output into the bachelor and parent categories or else discover that by some osmotic process they are all for one and one for all. Just now it is too early to say.

In one sense **Family Reunion** is a series of selections. I had forgotten, if I ever knew, that Nash had written more than one verse about dogs, but he has. People who think that he is all froth and frivolity might do well to consider **"For a Good Dog."** It is a best of breed; so poignantly felt that the reader may find it difficult to turn again to lighter things. Or take the really beautiful **"Tin Wedding Whistle."** For honest sentiment controlled (as so many moderns fear it and cannot control it) give me the humorist with his guard for the moment down.

The animal and nature verses, apart from the three or four dog poems, are a little book in themselves. I hope some day that Mr. Nash's publisher will find his collective self in the mood to put all these and more together under one cover, with plenty of appropriate illustrations. No one save Belloc on a much smaller scale has ever approached them. No, not even the early A. P. Herbert, whose influence like that of Belloc is here mildly traceable in scattered pages.

But for all this trace—or any other, like that of Hoffenstein—any rereading of Nash (and this book is mostly rereading) but increases one's astonishment at the genuine originality of his voice and method. In the small world of light verse, as I have been at some pains to study it, he and he almost alone constantly seems to be saying things that have never been said before. Such as:

> In far Tibet
> There live a lama,
> He got no poppa,
> Got no momma,
>
> He got no wife,
> He got no chillun,
> Got no use
> For penicillun,
>
> He got no soap,
> He got no opera,
> He don't know Irium
> From copra . . .
>
> He got no teeth,
> He got no gums,
> Don't eat no Spam,
> Don't need no Tums . . .
>
> Indeed, the
> Ignorant Have-Not
> Don't even know
> What he don't got. . . .

If anyone has ever written anything like that before my name is Edward Lear. And curiously enough in all such marvelous writing there is for me the distant and gentle undertone of sadness, from which true nonsense is perhaps never entirely separated. But when Mr. Nash consciously tries his hand at nonsense where many of the words are freshminted nonsense, too, he comes a cropper. "Jabberwocky" succeeds where Nash's **"Geddondillo"** does not. I see nothing funny in

> Appetency lights the corb of the
>   guzzard now,
> The ancient beveldric it otley
>   lost . . .

This is not even as successful as the T. S. Eliot imitations of Lear. Thackeray could do it and one or two others. *Finem respice.*

The main thing is that we have Ogden Nash, nearly always his own unstudied self. In this evil world and at this evil hour, his voice is something beyond price.

> A husband at a lecture
> Twitches his architecture.

Nash defies a lecture or a book review or quibbling or even the will not to read him. You are simply a part of this family reunion. We all are.

Lewis Nichols (review date 1953)

SOURCE: "In Nashion Fashion," in *The New York Times Book Review,* April 12, 1953, p. 10.

[*Here, Nichols contends that in* The Private Dining Room *Nash's style and subject matter matures, and, in an interview with the poet, discusses the factors that influenced his development.*]

Mr. Nash notes the symptoms of middle age: he defends trains, he welcomes the arrival in the house of a son-in-law "to chew the fat with." Salad dressing comes under his eye—he likes it simple—and parents and children, and there is a summation of all the clichés about dogs and their owners which should end that subject forever. Obviously the only kind of poetry that counts, and at its best.

Poetry?

"What I do is pick up poetry and bash its brains against the sidewalk," said Mr. Nash the other day.

At 50, a date he acquired simultaneously with a grandchild, he now describes himself as a "middle-aged writer of light verse." There is, perhaps, a little less hair on the top of him and the beginnings of a little more front to the body of him, but there is no lament about the old days. Mr. Nash ages properly—viz. the beginning of bashed poetry entitled **"Peekaboo, I Almost See You"**:

> *Middle-aged life is merry, and I love to lead it,*
> *But there comes a day when your eyes are all right but*
> *   your arm isn't long enough to hold the telephone*
> *   book where you can read it,*
> *And your friends get jocular, so you go to the oculist,*
> *And of all your friends he is the joculist.*
> *So over his facetiousness let us skim,*
> *Only noting that he has been waiting for you ever since*
> *   you said good evening to his grandfather clock*
> *   under the impression that it was him.*

"About five years ago I decided I was getting along," he said. "The umpires at ball games began to look like good guys. I grew conscious of the passing of time. But I'm not alone in this. There are a good many of us."

As to the origins of Ogden Nash, middle-aged writer of light verse: he is not what he planned to be, away back in the mists of antiquity.

"I used to write serious poetry," he said. "The poems were pretty bad—more bathos than pathos. I just learned to add more bathos still."

The hiatus between *Versus* and *Dining* has been due to what clearly constitute major vices—lecturing and lyric writing for the theatre. He began the latter when the late Kurt Weill dropped him a note asking would he be interested in doing the lyrics for "One Touch of Venus." That was a hit and fine, but Mr. Nash caught himself the virus and apparently can't shake it, even though more recent efforts have not been hits and fine.

"I say now I won't have anything more to do with the theatre, but I don't know what I'd say if anyone asked me. I like doing lyrics. They're like verse, yet not like it. When they come off you get a wonderful feeling."

In *The Private Dining Room* are sundry by-products of lecture tours, including a note that trains always get where they're going along about daybreak. "That almost killed me till I learned the lecturer's trick of being able to take a nap anywhere, any time. Nap, bath and nip are the salvation of the lecturer."

From the vantage point of a middle-elder statesman, Mr. Nash finds the present and immediate future state of American humor writing not in the best of condition.

"There are many more prohibitions than there used to be, taboos, things you can't say. Also, all the bright kids get gobbled up by advertising or TV, so the magazines don't get the stuff they did. The kids themselves are unsettled. The old way was to laugh off unsettlement. Now all the brilliance seems to go into despair."

Craftsman at work: As he wanders about the country Mr. Nash jots down ideas on the covers of those paper-bound detective stories he deems good enough to take home. Later, at leisure, he works them out. **"Peekaboo"** took an hour and a half, others in the present volume took months.

Included in the volume there also is a sport, a white elephant, a proof that even middle age is not free of literary ups and downs. It is a verse called **"Next!"** About fossils, it has a tag line—"It's kind of fun to be extinct"—which Mr. Nash admires. He sent it to every editor he had ever known, and they all sent it back immediately. It here gains publication.

"I said the hell with them," Mr. Nash remarked. "I still like it."

David McCord (review date 1957)

SOURCE: "A Cache of Ogden Nash," in *The New York Times Book Review*, June 9, 1957, p. 7.

[*Below, American poet David McCord evaluates Nash's highly original voice and inventive genius, and compares Nash to other established American poets such as Robert Frost, E. B. White, e. e. cummings, and W. H. Auden.*]

Perhaps you can't get there from here, but in Ogden Nash's company you will reach any number of pleasant destinations. You will also reach an inevitable conclusion, if you have not come to it years and lines ago: Nash is a genuine original voice, and such voices in any literature are rare. Consider the living American writers who combine in high degree wit with poetry or poetry with wit.

Who are those with established reputations? Robert Frost, E. B. White, Ogden Nash, Thornton Wilder, James Thurber, E. E. Cummings, W. H. Auden, Morris Bishop. A very small company, and under these limitations not easily expanded. A few lines, fewer sentences, sometimes but a few words chosen blindfold from the mature work of any of these men are sufficient to establish the authorship. However much a poet or prose writer may perfect and enhance his skill, he will never achieve a truly original voice. He must be born with it.

Now one of the blessings of original voice, particularly in the poet, is that the assembled work in convenient book lengths reveals the total writer—that is the whole is greater than the sum of the parts. If Nash reads well in the magazines, he reads even better in his books as Frost does, as Auden does. The quality or density (of the poet) may vary, but not the voice, not the man. You are in his total company; an individual is talking. And if you happen to like him, you have companionship all the way. Ogden Nash is the most cheerful of all companions, and even when he falters now and then, or overreaches, one does not mind.

The latest Nash, of more than 100 pieces, is one of his best. Liking his quatrains, one reader regrets that this volume contains so few. Take **"Birthday on the Beach"**:

> *At another year*
> *I would not boggle*
> *Except that when I jog*
> *I joggle.*

It is true that a few of the scalpel studies of the Miss Rapunzel Fitts or Porteous Burnham sort appear controlled from the beginning by the concluding pun or dénouement. Keats wrote of "stretched meter"; Miss Rapunzel suffers from "tetched" meter. Yet in verse after verse Mr. Nash is still tilting with habits, quirks, crazes, obsessions, foibles and the like, at the grass roots of our society. He is still miraculously funny about things that drive us nuts.

He is human: *"How did I get so old so quick?"* Regretful: *"The Audubon that I audubin."* Wishful: *"And the best part of any guest / Is the last part out the door."* Serious: *"This great country, which wants all its children to go to college but is distrustful of its adults with college degrees."*

Certainly his inventive genius for the unpackaged rhyme was never better. Why, then, does he several times drop to the level of the little masters of the imprecise précis with football-footfall, hickory-history, manhood-canned goods amid a true-rhyme setting? But what of it, when there is plenty of privacy-Godivacy, definite-chef-in-it surprise!

> *And you shall be as precious, love,*
> *As a mermaidsk from Murmansk,*
>
> *And I will tend the customers, love,*
> *In a suit with two prupantsk.*

There is one pr. revelations in this book. The more important of them is **"A Tale of the Thirteenth Floor,"** a grim and marvelous ballad beyond Kipling, Service, Marquis—even beyond Nash. May the Gunga Din boys from here to Ultima Thule demagnetize their tape and take this on!

> So I'll stash one cache of Ogden Nash
> Under my dead-spring bed.
> Where the sea lies calm round date and palm
> I shall drift with his verse I've read,
> To the Musial chime of the squeeze-play rhyme,
> For the Island of Done and Said.

Ben Ray Redman (review date 1957)

SOURCE: "An Antidote to Miltown," *Saturday Review,* June 29, 1957, p. 24.

[*In the following review of* You Can't Get There From Here, *Redman reiterates critics' inability to analyze or categorize Nash's verse, while emphasizing his skill in the traditional verse forms that are often overshadowed by his renowned unconventional style.*]

Nash the Man and Nash the Poet are well on their way to becoming Nash the Institution. A generation of readers has grown up that would find it hard to imagine a world without Nash, a world without his jagged lines, his inversions (no less famous than many religious conversions), his wry rhymes, and his polymorphic prosody. This being so, it is high time that his work was made the subject of Definitive Criticism. But criticism of what kind, what school? Ah, there's the rub!

The historical-comparative school might give him a working over as a jovial Juvenal. The psychoanalytic school could have a Roman holiday with his confessed likes and dislikes, his fears, joys, and obsessions, all of which, of course, may be traced to traumatic experiences that he tripped over before the age of three, or earlier. One Nash on the couch might well prove worth a gross of ordinary recumbent poets. The technical-metrical school could drive itself quite mad by trying to define his poetic devices, and distempers. And the New Critics, now not so new? How I should like to see what they would do to and with him, if he were turned over to them bound but not gagged! I can imagine some of the erudite, recondite, hermetic, crabbed, jargonized products of their "close readings." How useful it would be to have profound studies of Nash's poetic strategy, his texture, his ambiguities and ambivalences, his dichotomies! And if the New Critics were a bit rough with him, who could blame them? Has not he himself, in this new book, hit them where it hurts most—in the vocabulary?

> Some words, like ugly courtiers,
> Should lag behind the portieres.
> Here's two such hippotomi:
> Ambivalence, dichotomy.
> I deprecate their prevalence,
> Dichotomy, ambivalence.

> Why do the learned quarterlies
> Such couthless cant immortalize?

Were there but space enough and time, I might attempt criticism along one of the lines I have suggested. But I must content myself with being curt and reportorial. The essential fact is that there is as much first-rate Nash, and as little second-rate Nash, in this book as in any of his earlier volumes. Nothing is stale, nothing is withered; the laurels are still in the woods, flourishing and uncut. The old master shows no signs of weariness. His pitching arm is as strong as ever, his control as sure. But he has—yes, he has—mellowed. He hates less, likes more, and has extended his area of tolerance. He, who never suffered fools otherwise than madly, is now as often as not willing to let them go their ways with only a gentle chiding. He is practising coexistence with folly, foible, and fad, on a scale that he would have found impossible when he was merely a bachelor, and later only a husband and a father. But now he is a grandfather. *Non sum qualis eram. . . .*

In a way it is a pity that this tolerance should invade his spirit at this particular moment in American history. When I reviewed his preceding book, *The Private Dining Room,* I spoke of him as a seeing-eye dog in the country of the blind. How well he served for years in that capacity! And now what an opportunity is offered him in a tranquilized America! He could, if he would, remain our one wholly anxious citizen; he could serve us as the antidote to Miltown and its similars. He could open eyes, glazed by happy pills, to the realities of our existence. And, indeed, it must be said, in all fairness, that during the rest of the time his verse does not suffer. A dozen poems prove that he is still a keen disliker; his dealings with Miss Nancy Mitford show that he can slit a silly neck as prettily as ever. The gift of eloquent brevity is still his.

This book demonstrates again what fit readers have long known: there is much more to Nash than the famous Nash tricks and trademarked practices. He is as skilful in regular verse forms as in his own, God-forbid-that-it-be-imitated, style. Read **"Don't Be Cross Amanda," "Exit, Pursued by a Bear," "The Buses Headed for Scranton,"** and **"A Tale of the Thirteenth Floor,"** if you would test his range.

Happy baby-sitting, Grandpa!

Louis Hasley (essay date 1971)

SOURCE: "The Golden Trashery of Ogden Nashery," in *The Arizona Quarterly,* Vol. 27, 1971, pp. 241-50.

[*In the following excerpt, Hasley examines the literary merits of Nash's poetry, evaluating themes, seriousness of subject matter, consistency in composition and editing, and Nash's elaborately artificial voice of naïveté.*]

A well of poor English undefiled. A fountain of fizz, fun, and frolic. A Christmas tree under a colored light wheel.

Plus gentle admonitions about the *p*'s and *q*'s of this world. . . .

In undertaking to write about the poems of Ogden Nash, I think one may be excused, if not exonerated, for thus trying to seize in metaphor some breath of the poet's spirit. For in the world of humorous literature he is *sui generis,* almost without lineage; certainly we have little critical tradition to account for how he came to be. That is, if you take the world of literature to exclude the writers of bad verse, including "the sweet singer of Michigan," Julia Moore, whose verses inspired his artfully distorted syntax, gnarled rhythms, and mangled rhymes. Not since Lewis Carroll, I suppose, has any versifier gathered such a universal readership among both ordinary and discriminating readers. And probably no poet has had so many imitators.

I have been able to locate only a few of the poems of Julia Moore, but from them I can readily see that her flights were homely sentimental effusions notable for irregularities of rhythm, cliché expressions, awkward inversions, and inept rhymes. While Nash has sidestepped the homespun and the sentimental, he uses the same devices as Julia Moore, the good-humorous effect resulting principally from exaggeration. In his work, the irregularities are wild, the clichés are altered, the inversions are extreme; and the rhymes, elaborately contrived, often become outrageous word distortions. Bonus additions are redundancy and vernacular grammar. All these devices characteristically appear under a carefully assumed naïveté of expression and even manage at times to have an integral appropriateness.

> O Duty,
> Why hast thou not the visage of a sweetie or a cutie?
> Why displayest thou the countenance of the kind of
>   conscientious organizing spinster
> That the minute you see her you are aginster?
> Why glitter thy spectacles so ominously?
> Why art thou clad so abominously?
> Why art thou so different from Venus
> And why do thou and I have so few interests mutually
>   in common between us? . . .

("Kind of an Ode to Duty")

Merely to mention, however, the characteristic Nash techniques as outlined above is narrowly misleading; for he shows impressive resourcefulnes in avoiding stereotype. On some occasions he writes in conventional modes, which means dropping the playful and the lightly satirical to write the pure lyric or to add a didactic note to the prevailing humorous tenor of his verse.

Ogden Nash is thoroughly imbued with American life, liberty, and the pursuit of happiness. His verse tells us that he has an unflagging love of the American way of comfortable living. He sees from a reasonably high and cushy middle-class perch. We are not fooled when we observe in his poems a criticism of the people who enjoy a high standard of living. The genial cynicism is such that it shows both a self-awareness and an engagingly candid self-indulgence. He is an amiable bystander who would be unhappy if the passing parade yielded no foibles for him to toy with. Of course no reader is asking that he don sackcloth and ashes, and he is not about to do so . . .

Nash at his best is good indeed. He has adroitly blended the rhythms of prose and the varying line lengths of free verse with end-rhyming that is customarily alien to free verse. . . . The often grotesque rhymes, the prose rhythms, and the widely varying line lengths blend to form a caricature of conventional versification.

—Louis Hasley

The late Thomas Sugrue called Nash "the little man's laureate," not in the sense of championing underdog causes, but as dealing with universal themes at an easily accessible level. Anyone who has been in love, or yearned to be; who has lived with parents, or spouse, or children; who has had some smattering of parties, dinners, or almost any kind of social life; or who has been fascinated by language will catch the bright gleam of his own thoughts and experiences in Nash's verse.

What may at first seem a serious limitation in range is the absence of some aspects of American life. Aside from a few dozen short, conventional, humorous poems, describing such members of the animal kingdom as pig, rabbit, oyster, phoenix, grass-hopper, and smelt, there is little reflection of Nature—no rural life, no landscape, no world of mountains, rivers, forests. Nash stays near the drugstore, the theater, and the night club; that is, his world is that of the representative humorist in this mid-half of the twentieth century. That world is the life of the city, of structured society, ritual entertainment, and organized leisure. So that in terms of contemporary American life, which is predominantly urban, the exclusions seem now of little moment, except for the grimmer aspects represented by war, industrialism, and social injustice, subjects which are left to the Black Humorists for whatever drops of humor can be wrung out of the dark cloth of our time.

> The country was made first,
> Yes, but people lived in it and rehearsed,
> And when they finally got civilization down,
> Why, they moved to town.

("The City")

Food, taxis, cocktails, language, love, the common cold, the theater, travel, conscience, money, birthdays, card games, weather, football, matrimony—these topics and others, take his exuberant fancy. But the exuberance is seldom bubbly. More characteristically it is introspective, taking the form of a psychological process which is based on close observation of some subject that is commonly considered unimportant. Though it is marked by surface nonsense, it may be interpenetrated by a satiric common sense. Yet there is a range from poems expressing a serious, if covert, theme, to other poems that are arbitrarily, coyly playful—mere play—poems that make no attempt to reflect life or its texture, but accomplish only a momentary, sensuous tickle or tease, as in the expert limerick **"Requiem"** (don't ask why the title):

> There was a young belle of old Natchez
> Whose garments were always in patchez.
> When comment arose
> On the state of her clothes,
> She drawled, When Ah itchez, Ah scratchez!

In a serious assessment of a poet with an overgenerous spirit of fun, the question of how much the content weighs in judging quality must be faced. No precise rule can be laid down; only a rough guide that goes something like this: the lighter the content, the greater the burden carried by the form. Language being an intellectual vehicle of meaning, we readily conclude that the poem must have *some* content, cannot be mere gibberish. It may, however, briefly forego discursive content if it can supply a psychological reflection of mood, which is itself a kind of content, even if it is expressed surrealistically. Moreover, a subject matter is not in itself necessarily heavy or light. Nuclear physics can be treated lightly, humorously; humor can be treated heavily, philosophically. What matters in determining lightness or heaviness is the poet's attitude and the details in which his attitude is embodied.

The practice of literary criticism yields supporting evidence for the relative importance of content. The "heavier" critics rarely undertake to deal with light verse poets. They may even demand a view of reality unmarked by humor. One remembers Matthew Arnold's refusal to give the highest rank to that great poet-humorist, Chaucer, because of a lack of "high seriousness." Of course, other critics do not give the same overwhelming importance to content; different schools of criticism place different values on the proper proportions of substance and form. But *no* literary critic will denominate as literature **"The Ballad of Beautiful Words,"** a mere series of discrete words without predication and arranged in rhymed stanzas. For years this affront to literature was proudly printed periodically in a large metropolitan newspaper. As a "poem," it possessed only form in the shape of technique, or device, and was entirely without substance.

Of course there are no scales on which to weigh content. How account for—*can* we account for—the rather high place in literature of Lewis Carroll's *Alice in Wonderland*? Right off, assuming its highly skillful form, it won't do to maintain that it is the political and social allegory of Victorian England that satisfies the requirement of content; for such allegory has become a labored irrelevancy and is largely inaccessible to today's reader. What then? Not realism, for the story is a dream. But precisely so. Dreams are a part of life, a significant part whether or not we can determine accurately their meanings. The haunting lunacy of Alice's dream is disquietingly and amusedly seen as reflective of our own psychological processes, a lunacy and inconsecutiveness by no means confined to dreams.

The relevance of this reasoning to the poems of Ogden Nash should be clear. Its application is not always complimentary; certainly it is not always derogatory.

First of all, he is a very prolific poet. He has kept the presses warm with volume after volume. Every so often he publishes a selected volume which omits many previously published poems. Despite the selectivity, he could well afford to be much more selective. Many of the poems, even of those that survive the winnowing, evidence hasty composition and lax standards. One can only conclude that Nash sometimes scamps the arduous polishing needed to create a fully satisfying poetic experience. Not infrequently the reader perceives, not that the basic technique should have been different, but that Nash has not used well his own technique. The confident reader (brash, if you prefer) may feel that he knows how Nash should have said it to achieve a surer result.

This is particularly true of occasional rhymes which, instead of being expertly awkward, are awkwardly awkward. There exists a strong imperative for exact rhymes in light verse, and the lighter the verse the stronger the imperative. Not that Nash's rhymes must be conventionally exact. They should be *un*conventionally exact; and he should not allow the Eastern provincialism of pronouncing *Canada* to rhyme with *janitor,* a kind of offense of which he is guilty more than a few times. Where his poems betray such weaknesses of form, the literary needle registering the charge scarcely quivers.

If it were always so, this essay would not have been written. For Nash at his best is good indeed. He has adroitly blended the rhythms of prose and the varying line lengths of free verse with end-rhyming that is customarily alien to free verse. When not metrical, each couplet, often each line, moves like a prose sentence to a strong pause or full stop at the end. The often grotesque rhymes, the prose rhythms, and the widely varying line lengths blend to form a caricature of conventional versification.

Some indefatigable counter has declared that the number of syllables per line in Nash varies from two to sixty-two. The vast majority of his rhymes occur in couplets. Of course many poems follow regular metrics and regular stanza forms in almost every variety, more than a few of them parodying the tone and cadence of established works of literature. Something of this is suggested through titles, such as **"Tarkington, Thou Should'st Be Living in This Hour,"** **"Correction:** *Eve* **Delved and** *Adam* **Span,"** and **"All, All Are Gone, the Old Familiar Quotations,"** as well as in clichés, whether oral or written, as in **"A Dog's Best Friend Is His Illiteracy"** and **"You Bet Travel Is Broadening."**

Amidst the elaborately artificial naïveté so much employed by Nash, his use of clichés cannot escape attention. Probably no other writer of literary stature has employed so many. If the unsophisticated reader is uneasy about this because he has been taught to avoid clichés, let him become enlightened as to their use in humor. They have been tellingly used by James Thurber, Robert Benchley, and probably every modern humorist you can name, including Frank Sullivan, whose fictional character, Doctor Arbuthnot, is a cliché expert, a collector of clichés. Nash himself (in a letter to me dated September 25, 1958) has put his finger precisely on the explanation for the effective use of clichés. "The trick is," he wrote, "that it must be somebody else's cliché and not the author's own." What that means is that the author keeps the cliché he uses from being considered naturally his own by a satirical, sophisticated context, or by an artful alteration in its phrasing. In one delightful poem of twenty-four lines, **"The Visit,"** he manages seventeen clichés, a few of which are found in these lines:

> She welcomes him with pretty impatience
> And a cry of Greetings and salutations! . . .
> Snug as a bug, the cup he waits
> That cheers but not inebriates. . . .
> And now he whispers, a bit pajamaly,
> That he's fed to the teeth with his whole fam damily,
> Perhaps she'll forgive an old man's crotchet
> And visit Bermuda on his yachat.

There is a considerable amount of mild didacticism in Nash's verse. Some part of it rises to the level of social criticism. A gift for epigrammatic summation is suggested by these lines:

> It is easier for one parent to support seven children
> than for seven children to support one parent.

> Women would rather be right than reasonable.

> Never befriend the oppressed unless you are prepared
> to take on the oppressor.

> Frankness consists in having your back bitten right to
> your face.

In such poems as reveal an unfaltering finesse there is usually a sufficient insight into individual thought or behavior patterns, or into social mores, to satisfy the reader who asks for a worthy, memorable, and enduring experience. The fact that Nash is one of the most quotable of poets supports the judgment that he is frequently master of harmoniously effective combinations of language and meaning.

Not surprisingly, the meaning is often only adequate and the pleasure lies in the language. Tortured rhymes of great ingenuity abound (Buddha, shouldha; *savoir-faire*, back of a chair; house the pup in, to dress up in; waiter, potater). So, too, examples of tortured grammar and word order (let one suffice): "The driest point in America is not Death Valley, but a man with lots of important work on his desk's throat." Puns are scarce, but other forms of wordplay are frequent if not constant. ("Today I am a swashbuckler, would anybody like to buckle any swashes?" "Ye clergymen, draw near and clerge. . . ." "Who wants my jellyfish / I'm not sellyfish!") Because his own practice has the special purpose of humor, it is not inconsistent of

him to satirize the popular substitution of *like* for *as*: "Like the hart panteth for the water brooks, I pant for the revival of Shakespeare's *Like You Like It*." Nonsense neologisms are found in **"Your Lead, Partner, I Hope We've Read the Same Book,"** in which he tells of inventing Amaturo, a card game:

> The deck has seven morkels
> Of eleven guzzards each,
> The game runs counterclockwise,
> With an extra kleg for dreech,
> And if you're caught with a gruice,
> The score reverts to deuce.

Nonsense coinages nevertheless are rare in Nash. So, too, is fantasy:

> And as for being lazy, I know one robin that held
>   down two jobs at once just so his younger brother
>   (their parents had passed away uninsured) could
>   get to be a transport pilot,
> But if you mentioned it he was modest as a buttercup
>   or a vilot. . . .

Almost all of Nash's devices reveal some form of deliberate naïveté and therefore the reader appeal is, at least in good part, a flattering feeling of superiority. Such a device is circularity.

> My attention has recently focussed
> Upon the seventeen-year locust.
> This is the year
> When the seventeen-year locusts are here,
> Which is the chief reason my attention has been
>   focussed
> Upon the seventeen-year locust.

How much of "the real Ogden Nash" is revealed in his poems? In the use of point of view, he tends to identify with the "I" or the poet speaking in the poem. He is capable, however, of writing on both sides of a quarrel in different poems, as in those dealing with the battle of the sexes. For example, contrary to custom, he takes the point of view of the woman in **"The Trouble with Women Is Men."** And in **"If Fun Is Fun, Isn't That Enough?"** he argues that no humorist is totally trustworthy.

> They'll sell their birthright every time
> To make a point or turn a rhyme.

> This motto, child, is my bequest:
> There's many a false word spoken in jest.

One feels sure, however, that when Nash is not writing as a humorist, he is writing out of honest attitudes and convictions. The occasional "straight" poem from his pen can be an unadulterated joy. **"Listen"** (beginning "There is a knocking in the skull") is a metaphysical poem worthy of Emily Dickinson. **"A Lady Thinks She Is Thirty"** is a pure lyric holding strains of seventeenth-century love poetry. The tightly held compassion in the six-line **"Old Men"** bursts forth in the closing couplet:

People watch with unshocked eyes;
But the old men know when an old man dies.

In **"A Carol for Children"** we catch a glimpse of an underlying religious reverence. It is a rare and sober note in Nash that reveals a sense of nostalgia for a time when faith was strong:

Two ultimate laws alone we know,
The ledger and the sword—
So far away, so long ago,
We lost the infant Lord.

From even a mere dozen of Nash's poems chosen at random, a reader could hardly fail to observe that, while Nash sees and enjoys the misfortunes, the ineptitudes, and the chicanery of men, he is not greatly exercised by the debit side of existence. In short, he is an optimist. Not a cheap one, but a cheerful one. While he is no professional celebrant of our country right or wrong, the detached and optimistic observer shows clear in the following lines from **"Look What You Did, Christopher!"**:

The American people,
With grins jocose,
Always survive the fatal dose.
And though our systems are slightly wobbly,
We'll fool the doctor this time, probly.

Reviewing Nash's first volume of verse in the *Saturday Review of Literature* in 1931, William Rose Benét declared that it was "about as good a picture of his life and times as others have spent volumes on." Now, umpteen volumes later, the picture has taken on additional richness and detail and continues to delight as well as to provide some confections for reflection. The well-read will be rewarded by many allusions to song and character and story worked deftly into the fabric of the poetic experience. Varying elements of didacticism, never heavy, often merely playful, tease the ruminative mind. In his meanings, he seldom has depth, though there is more than the casual reader might think—more than a little of it social criticism. In his form and technique he has made a contribution to humorous literature—not momentous, perhaps, only ineradicable. Too much of him read at a sitting can indeed cloy. But read a little at a time, he provides unique and continuing delectation.

Grace. Gaiety. Charm. The artfully, quaintly naïve. Bounce. The puckish. The fantastic. The frivolous. These furnish some of the pleasures we get from what one of his inspired book blurbs called "The Golden Trashery of Ogden Nashery."

Reed Whittemore (essay date 1972)

SOURCE: "End of the Old Vaudeville," in *The New Republic*, Vol. 167, No. 15, October 21, 1972, p. 33.

[*In the following excerpt, Whittemore singles out Nash for his distinct verse and voice, the qualities by which Whit-* temore measures 20th-century poets, and describes Nash's legacy to the genre of American light verse.]

If we are to measure poets by their distinctiveness—and for better or worse the achieving of distinctiveness is the *raison d'être* for most 20th-century American poetry—it simply won't do to think of Ogden Nash as a minor figure. He is as distinctive as Cummings, and will perhaps be around as long as Cummings. He was slightly younger but not much, and his death in 1971 left us with acres of Ogden Nashery as well as with a clear—maybe too clear—vision of how the art of light verse should be perpetrated. He created a body of work that went triumphantly against the prevailing esthetic of poetry as a lofty, Sextus-Propertius affair, and he stuck with his creation for nearly forever, thereby becoming the chief poetic practitioner of the grand mundane in our country's most successful literary magazine, *The New Yorker*. *The New Yorker* has published good and important works by most of America's most highly thought-of sobersides, but it would nonetheless have been a nothing venture without its comedians. Nash was, forever, its chief verse comedian. Nash was the one who kept reminding *New Yorker* readers—who might otherwise have been scared away by the flavor of compressed elegance characteristic of the "serious" poetry its editors favored—that verse could be relaxed and topical. In other words Nash was the one who practically singlehandedly kept the verse department of the magazine in the business that the rest of the magazine was in, of commenting with intelligence, wit and asperity upon the contemporary American scene—its fads and fashions, its promotional and rhetorical excesses, its varied social and cultural crises. His contributions were too often on the cute side, and one could argue that a greater satirical severity toward America's multitudinous morasses—in a magazine that has always had after all the most serious of literary and critical aspirations—would have been in order; but Nash could hardly have been expected to carry the whole burden here. What he did he did well, and in so doing he not only kept American verse more open and various in its aims and interests than it otherwise would have been, but also kept *The New Yorker* on a track from which its artier verse contributors constantly wished to remove it.

Nash's new volume is work from the last three or four years of his life. Some of it is not particularly good Nash; all of it wears thin, as does Cummings' work, if read in big hunks; but it is all sufficiently sharp and sufficiently attuned to contemporary occasions to suggest that Nash's feel for the here and now did not diminish in old age. Nor did his wit. There are even some surprising brief pieces in which he abandons his lifelong pose of Look-I-Can-Write-Worse-Verse-Than-You-Can, and easily qualifies as a *good* comic poet!

Archibald MacLeish (essay date 1972)

SOURCE: Introduction to *I Wouldn't Have Missed It: Selected Poems of Ogden Nash*, Little, Brown, and Company, 1972, pp. vii-ix.

[*In the excerpt below, MacLeish argues that Nash did not write "light verse," but rather invented a unique, inimitable form that represented his times.*]

Ogden Nash's admirable obituary in the *New York Times* appeared under the heading "Master of Light Verse Dies." There are three things wrong with those five words. Nash's most important and most characteristic work is not in "verse." It is not "light." And his mastery, which was real enough, had nothing to do with a combination of the two. It consisted in the invention of a form, uniquely his own, which defied all the categories and, far more than that, altered the sensibility of his time: a form like the magic shoes in a Celtic tale which enable the wearer to enter an untraveled world—the untraveled world, in Nash's case, of the infinite banalities of the contemporary city.

Eliot had discovered that world with the aid of the ironic meters he borrowed so brilliantly from Laforgue, but only the sophisticated knew of his famous journey. Nash settled there and then went back to fetch his readers. His colloquial couplets in rhymed prose with their honest grins and innocent disguises gave him entrance everywhere. And once his foot was in the door his readers had no choice but listen. He was a humorist, wasn't he?—the author of delightful little jingles like "Candy / Is dandy / But liquor / Is quicker"? What risk was there in letting *him* in? *He*'d never tell you things you didn't want to know— show you your time as a Waste Land where Long Island used to be.

But of course he would and did, and to call the consequences "light verse" is hardly fair to anyone. For one thing the term is inaccurate. "Verse" is one of the vaguest words in the language except when it is used to make a distinction between verse and prose. When that happens it becomes a term of art, precise as are all such instruments. Verse as distinguished from prose is a form of composition founded on the *line*. Even what used to be called "free" verse—particularly what used to be called "free" verse—is composed of lines. In prose the basic element of structure is the sentence; in verse the sentence makes its peace with the line or the whole thing collapses. In prose the hearing ear pays no attention to the line's end at the margin of the page; in verse it is the line's end the ear is waiting for.

Apply all this to Nash's characteristic form. It has no *lines* in the verse sense; the line's end is a typographical accident with Nash and it is the sentence—the infinitely extensible sentence—which bears the burden. The hearing ear pays no more attention to the line's end in the print of his pieces than it would in a newspaper column. Nothing in the whole device suggests the structure of verse but the rhymes, and the rhymes are not used as verse would use them. They are not used, that is to say, to establish an enlarging counterpoint to the rhythm of the lines. They are used, instead, to force the sentences into couplets, or other combinations, which are often as funny as the assonances are outrageous. It is not the sound they play on but the sense. Or unsense. They are instruments of meaning. Often of zany meaning. But often, too,

of new and impossible associations which can blow the mind.

Ogden Nash, though not a satirist in the Swiftian sense, had a satirist's concern for the humanity of human creatures.

—Archibald MacLeish

That is one objection to the term: it is inaccurate. The other is the implication. "Light verse" carries a demeaning connotation. It implies that the art of poetry has its Macy's basement where a kind of secondrate excellence is the criterion. And this, of course, is an affront to poetry. There is only one kind of poetry: poetry. The art has no departments. It does not help that newspaper reference to "light verse" to explain that what is meant by "light verse" is verse with a sense of humor—as though poetry, which knows everything about mankind, knew nothing about human laughter. Who laughed at life the longest? Was it Shakespeare himself? Or Chaucer? Or Catullus? Or Li Po? Nash knew all this as well as anyone. And I suspect, although I do not know, that it had a good deal to do with his invention of a form which was *not* "light verse": a form which would enable him to examine the inanities of his time in a colloquial language most men understood because, like Molière's astonished character, they spoke it themselves.

In any case, and whatever the rationalization, Nash's first *New Yorker* publication shows how the form began. It was a piece written in 1930, when Mr. Herbert Hoover's Plateau of Permanent Prosperity had collapsed into the Great Depression carrying a generation with it—most painfully, a generation of the young. Nash was twenty-eight, a failed prep school teacher, a failed bond salesman, and a failed sonneteer, supporting himself, if that is the term, by composing advertising copy for a New York publisher. He was approaching the age at which a young man's commitment to art can no longer survive on hope. After thirty, failure begins to taste of finality and it becomes harder and harder to try again. But as one approaches thirty things have a way of happening. And they did for Ogden Nash in his grubby office on that 1930 afternoon. He found himself—or, if not precisely himself, then a form of language he could speak. It fell into half a dozen more or less rhymed couplets, which he might well have called (but didn't) "Portrait of the Artist as a Young Man," and it changed his life. It ended the failure, began a considerable literary success and, more astonishing than either, altered—or began to alter—the relation of his contemporaries to the time in which they lived:

I sit in an office at 244 Madison Avenue
And say to myself You have a responsible job,
  havenue?
Why then do you fritter away your time on this
  doggerel?

*If you have a sore throat you can cure it by using
a good goggeral. . .*

A portrait certainly, but a portrait in the Cinquecento manner with a glimpse of the city in the background. Or, if not a glimpse, then a whiff. If one doesn't see Murray Hill beyond the copywriter's head as he leans from his window the way one sees the Duomo beyond the Saint, one can at least smell it: that penetrating pharmaceutical scent of face powder and sex which pervades the metropolises of our cosmetic civilization. The gargle taints the afternoon and it is that breath of antiseptic which puts the figure in the foreground at the center of its time. Even the young man's hope is somehow sterile—even the defeated artist's pain. The drugstore on the corner can take care of everything and that longing for the long-unwritten poem is no worse—or better—than a brief sore throat.

Mean it? With those hilarious rhymes? Of course he didn't mean it. He was laughing—had to be. Anyway Mr. Ross of the *New Yorker* published it, and the *New Yorker,* in its early years, was a humorous magazine. Also Ogden Nash soon joined the staff of the *New Yorker.* But still the question hung there. Did he? Didn't he? In any case he continued to work the same vein with the same sharp tool and the tool grew more and more effective as he went along until now, with the whole range of his work before us, we begin to see. Americans of the last quarter of the century—particularly young Americans—know better than their predecessors what was happening in those fusty years. They know what Nixon thought the country was, and what he tried to do to it—almost did. They understand what their fathers and their elder brothers didn't understand: that the rot of the Seventies came *out* of the society, not *down* on it from a crew of subversives at the top. And understanding that, they can see what a man who probed the intimacies of such a time with outrageous rhymes and comical couplets might have been up to. They may even conclude that Ogden Nash, though not a satirist in the Swiftian sense, had a satirist's concern for the humanity of human creatures. And they may come to read [*I Wouldn't Have Missed It*] not for the laughs but for the tears—and for the love.

George W. Crandell (essay date 1989)

SOURCE: "Moral Incongruity and Humor: The 'Good Bad' Poetry of Ogden Nash," in *Studies In American Humor,* Vol. 7, 1989, pp. 94-103.

[*In the excerpt below, Crandell examines the relationship between humor and art in Nash's poetry.*]

For some readers, the term "humorous poetry" is an oxymoron. "Poetry" denotes something serious, while "humorous," by definition, means just the opposite. Equating "serious" with "good" and "humorous" with "bad," the same individuals use "humorous" in a pejorative sense to distinguish writing that has some of the formal characteristics of poetry, rhyme and meter for example, but which

lacks the seriousness of lyric, narrative or dramatic verse. Likewise, the terms *vers de société* and "light verse" have sometimes been used synonymously with "humorous poetry" to denote a type of writing lacking both seriousness and significant aesthetic value.

This line of argument has even been carried to the point of dissociating humor and art. Immanuel Kant, for example, commenting on the "humorous manner," perceives a qualitative difference between humor and art such that the creative act of humor "belongs rather to pleasant than to beautiful art, because the object of the latter must always show proper worth in itself, and hence requires a certain seriousness in the presentation, as taste does in the act of judging" [*Critique of Judgment,* translated by J. H. Bernard, 1892]. Similarly, Christopher Wilson argues that "art and humour have comparable form but differ in the significance of their raw materials," art, unlike humor, being "constructed from serious stuff" [*Jokes: Form, Content, Use, and Function,* 1979].

Even among writers of "light verse" the serious/humorous characterization is a important one, significant enough, in fact, that American humorist and poet Ogden Nash made the distinction between serious and humorous poetry the basis of his art. Nash confesses that he gave up hope of becoming a "serious" poet after the fashion of Browning, Swinburne or Tennyson, and so "began to poke a little bit of fun at [himself], . . . accentuating the ludicrous side of [what], at first had been attempts at serious poetry" [*Ogden Nash,* in an interview in *Conversations,* edited by Roy Newquist, 1967]. Early in his career, Nash decided "that it would be better to be 'a good bad poet than a bad good poet.'"

Nash's self-depreciating remarks may be seen as a defensive strategy similar to that employed by professional comedians studied by Seymour and Rhonda Fisher: "The comic defends himself against the accusation of badness by systematically proving that what is good and bad exists only in the eye of the beholder" [*Pretend the World Is Funny and Forever: A Psychological Analysis of Comedians, Clowns, and Actors,* 1981]. The comic asserts his own goodness by convincing "people that good and bad, like all classificatory schemes, are relative and that they may, in fact, blend meaninglessly to each other."

Although Nash uses the term "good-bad poet" jokingly and disparagingly, it characterizes two distinctive features of his work. The "good-bad" distinction serves equally well to describe 1) Nash's divided persona, the poet-fool, who, as we shall see, may be "good" or "bad" depending upon the perspective from which he is viewed, and 2) Nash's concern with problems of morality. An examination of these two characteristic features of Nash's work ultimately reveals that, in Nash's view, moral and aesthetic categories alike are relative. . . .

In the guise of the poet-fool, Nash, following the pattern of historical and literary antecedents, is both truth-teller and buffoon. As soothsayer, Nash imparts a kind of folk wisdom, or "horse-sense" to use Walter Blair's term [*Native American Humor,* 1937], as when Nash's speaker reminds parents, "Many an infant that screams like a calliope / Could be soothed with a little attention to its diope." In a society in which royal courts have given way to democratic institutions, the poet-fool in Nash's twentieth-century, American society is an ordinary figure, but one with a special talent for expressing proverbial wisdom. The basis for the truth told by Nash's poet-fool is Nash's observation of people, his habit of "noting human traits and characteristics you might see in an elevator, at the dinner table, at a party or a bridge game" [Nash, in *Conversations*]. Like the professional comedian, Nash is someone who "prowls around looking for new patterns and new insights about how people behave" [*Pretend the World Is Funny and Forever*]. Many of Nash's poems begin with an observation, for example: "The camel has a single hump; / The dromedary two." From that starting point, Nash proceeds in a manner that again mirrors the method of some professional comedians who then "come up with a twist that highlights the relativity or absurdity of that perspective," as in **"The Camel"**:

> The camel has a single hump,
> The dromedary two,
> Or else the other way around,
> I'm never sure are you.

Many of Nash's poems about animals follow the same pattern; the poet-fool presents us with one perspective of the animal and then comments upon that view. One example, **"The Turtle,"** serves not only to show this pattern, but also to illustrate Nash's economical expression, and his dexterous manipulation of sound to compliment the sense of the poem:

> The turtle lives twixt plated decks
> Which practically conceal its sex;
> I think it clever of the turtle
> In such as fix to be so fertile.

Notice how slowly, like a turtle, the reader voices the first line, slowed by the series of nine phonological stops (/t/, twice each in "turtle" and "twixt"; /p/, /t/, and /d/, all in "plated"; and /d/ and /k/ in "decks"). The difficulty the reader experiences is perhaps not unlike that of the turtle trying to be fertile.

In making observations about animals, Nash's poet-fool often reveals a truth about himself, usually a foible or moral weakness characteristic of human nature in general. The spectator watching the camel reveals his ignorance. The observer of the turtle, we may speculate, imagines copulating turtles, while the person who defines the cow displays a delightful naivete: "The cow is of the bovine ilk; / One end is moo, the other, milk."

As Nash himself confesses and as these poems illustrate, Nash is primarily concerned with "human nature, particularly the relationships between men and women, the relationships of humans to the world in which they live and their attempts to cope with it." In defining **"The Perfect Husband,"** for example, Nash observes: "He tells you when you've got on too much lipstick, / And helps you with your girdle when your hips stick." Similarly, the poet-fool offers advice to parents about how to care for **"The Baby"**: "A bit of talcum / Is always walcum."

At the same time that Nash's poet-fool expresses sage advice, the ludicrous form of his maxims belittles and ridicules the speaker. In particular, the phonological incongruity of rhymes such as "calliope/diope" and "talcum/walcum" give the impression of an undereducated buffoon. Pretentiousness, suggested for example by the classification "bovine ilk" in **"The Cow,"** is comically deflated by the speaker's innocent definition that follows it. The expression of wisdom, the incongruous sound effects, the comic deflation, all serve to endear the poet-fool to his audience.

In the endearing figure of the poet-fool, Nash found the mask from behind which he could express himself. In an interview with Roy Newquist [in *Conversations,* 1967], Nash comments on the persona he discovered: "In the verse I have a sort of disguise I can assume so that I'm not so vulnerable. . . . . Therefore I was able to hide behind this mask, keeping people from knowing whether I'm ignorant or just fooling around." Having discovered this mask ("mask" comes from the Arabic *maskhara,* meaning clown, or buffoonery), Nash proceeded to speak. The voice that emerges from behind the mask is that of an ironic moralist, exposing the absurdity of moral distinctions, and blurring the supposedly clear lines demarcating good and evil. . .

The poet-fool occupies an "objective" position, detached "from any moral conflict," and thus is able to comment, truthfully and objectively, on the relativity of "good" and "bad." From this standpoint, the poet-fool typically exposes the relativity of moral values by holding up two incongruous images representing the extremes on a moral continuum and viewing them, as it were, from its objective "point of indifference," or *punctum indifferens.* In **"It Must Be the Milk,"** for example, Nash observes "how much infants resemble people who have had too much to drink" by comparing the way that infants and intoxicated people walk:

> Yet when you see your little dumpling set sail across
>   the nursery floor,
> Can you conscientiously deny the resemblance to
>   somebody who is leaving a tavern after having
>   tried to leave it a dozen times and each time
>   turned back for just one more?
> Each step achieved
> Is simply too good to be believed;
> Foot somehow manages to stay put;
> Arms wildly semaphore,
> Wild eyes seem to ask, Whatever did we get in such
>   a dilemma for?

The similarity of toddlers and inebriates might be dismissed as coincidental if the speaker did not expose to view other likenesses which also serve to erode the distinction between pure and impure:

Another kinship with topers is also by infants exhibited,
Which is that they are completely uninhibited,
And they can't talk straight.
Any more than they can walk straight;

In these images, the incongruous and humorous pairing of "tots and sots" serves to blur the moral distinction between innocence and sullied experience. By suggesting a likeness between the infant and the drunk, Nash means to point out that good and evil are relative terms that depending on one's moral perspective can be applied to the same behavior, just as uncoordinated walking may be perceived as reprehensible and adorable: "in inebriates it's called staggerin' but in infants it's called toddling." Likewise, talking characterized by "awful" pronunciation and "flawful" grammar may be perceived from morally opposite perspectives: "in adults, it's drunken and maudlin and deplorable, / But in infants it's tunnin' and adorable."

Nash's pattern of observation exhibited here is similar to the creative act that Arthur Koestler terms "bisociation," that is, "the perceiving of a situation or idea . . . in two self-consistent but habitually incompatible frames of reference" [*The Act of Creation,* 1964]. Here the idea, walking, is "bisociated" with the two frames of reference—the child and the drunk. As Koestler also remarks, "It is the clash of the two mutually incompatible codes, or associative contexts, which explodes the tension," and so results in a comic effect.

As we have seen in **"It Must Be the Milk,"** Nash typically pairs two incongruous elements to blur the distinction between opposites, especially objects representing moral extremes. In a similar fashion, Nash pairs candy and liquor, in **"Reflection on Ice-Breaking,"** to comment on the relative appropriateness of types of courtship behavior:

Candy
Is dandy
But liquor
Is quicker.

Incongruous as candy and liquor may be, Nash nevertheless compels us to see both objects as means to an end. Ice-breaking is Nash's euphemism for seduction, and liquor is the more efficient of the two means to that end. In pairing candy and liquor, Nash contrasts a deliberate, manipulative and speedy means of coercion with a romantic, socially acceptable method of wooing. But by reminding his audience that both liquor and candy ultimately have the same end, and by suggesting that love can be bought, with either a drink or a box of candy, Nash calls conventional notions of acceptability into question.

The pattern of pairing incongruous ideas in **"It Must Be the Milk,"** and **"Reflection on Ice-Breaking"** is duplicated in **"Portrait of the Artist as a Prematurely Old Man."** In this poem, Nash demonstrates how action and inaction are relative terms with respect to sinful behavior. In another variation on the theme of moral relativity, Nash points out the absurdity of distinctions between activity and passivity when both have sinful consequences. Nash begins by identifying two kinds of sin:

One kind of sin is called a sin of commission, and that is very important,
And it is what you are doing when you are doing something you ortant,
And the other kind of sin is just the opposite and is called a sin of omission and is equally bad in the eyes of all right-thinking people, from Billy Sunday to Buddha,
And it consists of not having done something you shuddha.

In this example, the idea of sin is perceived in incompatible frames of reference, "doing something you ortant," and its opposite, "not having done something you shuddha," or more simply: doing and not doing. The incongruous pairing of action and inaction has the intended effect of showing the absurdity of human behavior and its consequences. Ironically, intentional sinful actions are fun, hence "good" from the speaker's perspective, while unintentional sinful actions are not fun, hence "bad.": "Sins of commission . . . must at least be fun or else you wouldn't be committing them," but

"You didn't get a wicked forbidden thrill
Every time you let a policy lapse or forgot to pay a bill;
You didn't slap the lads in the tavern on the back and loudly cry Whee,
Let's all fail to write just one more letter before we go home, and this round of unwritten letters is on me.
No, you never get any fun
Out of the things you haven't done."

In exposing the absurdity of a world in which sinners who commit sins are rewarded by having fun, Nash's persona may be said to satisfy, vicariously, the audience's desire to voice or act out anarchistic impulses, as when Nash's speaker advises that sins of commission are preferable to sins of omission: "If some kind of sin you must be pursuing, / Well, remember to do it by doing rather than by not doing." Similarly in **"Reflection on Ice-Breaking,"** Nash's poet-fool speaks for lovers whose principal motivation is the immediate gratification of physical desire. In another poem, **"Epistle to the Olympians,"** Nash writes from the perspective of a child-adult to give voice to the child's objections to the seemingly arbitrary rules of conduct that govern the behavior of adults in disciplining children. In a pattern familiar to the reader, Nash pairs incongruous ideas, showing how, from the moral perspective of parents, "big" and "little" are relative terms.

When one mood you are in,
My bigness is a sin:
"Oh what a thing to do
For a great big girl like you!"
But then another time
Smallness is my crime;
"Stop doing whatever you're at;
You're far too little for that!"

In the vicarious, anarchistic role of wish-fulfiller, the poet-fool paradoxically serves as a stabilizing force in an otherwise unstable world. By defining the boundaries of what is proper, "Oh what a thing to do / For a great big girl like you!" and "Stop doing whatever you're at; / You're far too little for that!" the poet fool thus has "the effect of encouraging the stability of a system by preventing it from consistently going too far in any one extreme direction" [*Pretend the World Is Funny and Forever*]. Nash's **"Epistle to the Olympians,"** even illustrates how the poet may call for a modification to the seemingly arbitrary moral code (defined by the extremes of bigness and smallness) that governs proper behavior:

> Kind parents, be so kind
> As to kindly make up your mind
> And whisper in accents mild
> The proper size for a child.

In the school of American letters, Ogden Nash is the class-clown. As the eccentric who dares to say what his "classmates" are afraid, unwilling or incapable of saying, he is an object of admiration and a source of delight. But as the deviant one who defies authority and mocks convention, he is the "bad boy" and an object of ridicule.

In assessing Nash's place in literature, we could note how closely his work matches a standard definition of humor such as C. Hugh Holman's [in *A Handbook to Literature*, 4th edition, 1980]: "Humor implies a sympathetic recognition of human values and deals with the foibles and incongruities of human nature, good-naturedly exhibited," or we could observe the degree to which his work confirms the work of scholars in the social sciences studying humor. The first approach fails to take into account almost thirty years of research into the nature of humor and laughter. Among social scientists and increasingly among literary critics, the move is "away from universal theories based on a single and too-simple definition of what all humor is, toward well-focused questions about aspects of humor" [Paul Lewis, *Comic Effects: Interdisciplinary Approaches to Humor in Literature*, 1989]. The latter approach, it seems, offers greater potential for understanding the complexity and multifarious nature of humor, including humorous poetry.

In the present examination, we have seen how Nash's humorous work is characterized by concerns with "good" and "bad." The persona through which Nash speaks is a divided figure who like historical and literary poet-fools combines "good" (expressing folk wisdom) and "bad" (subverting the regular rules of rhyme and meter) in a single figure, the poet-fool. Likewise, Nash's typical method of presentation often focuses on problems of "good" and "bad." From a point of indifference, poised objectively between "good" and "bad," the poet-fool then pairs incongruous objects for the purpose of exposing the relativity of moral distinctions. In these two characteristic aspects of Nash's humor, we can observe other parallels to points established by recent humor research and summarized by Paul Lewis.

Lewis points out, first of all, that "humorous experiences originate in the perception of an incongruity: a pairing of ideas, images or events that are not ordinarily joined and do not seem to make sense together." The starting point for many of Nash's humorous poems, as we have seen, is an incongruous pairing of objects or ideas: infant/drunk, candy/liquor, activity/inactivity, bigness/smallness.

Secondly, Lewis points out that "in most cases humor appreciation is based on a two-stage process of first perceiving an incongruity and then resolving it." In the poetry of Ogden Nash, resolution is achieved by means of the single concept through which each incongruous element is perceived. While readers may at first be perplexed by the incongruity of a drunk and an infant, the confusion is resolved by noting how much alike they are when they walk.

Third, "humor is a playful, not a serious, response to the incongruous." The incongruities that Nash points out to us are neither frightening, nor so complex that we are unable to solve the riddle of the poem. The poet-fool's playful antics, the deliberate mocking of poetry's rules of meter and rhyme, for example, remind the reader that the commonsensical wisdom of the speaker is offered in fun.

Fourth, Lewis remarks that "the perception of an incongruity is subjective, relying as it does on the state of the perceiver's knowledge, expectations, values and norms." As Lewis' comments suggest, the appreciation of Nash's humor depends upon a set of shared values between speaker and audience. Nash's great popularity for nearly four decades from the early 1930s to the early 1970s suggests that large audiences identified with the values expressed by Nash's persona. The explanation may be that the value shared, that which allows the audience to perceive the incongruity as humorous, is often the fact of being human. Nash's **"The Hippopotamus"** illustrates how the perception of incongruity may be subjective depending upon one's perspective:

> Behold the hippopotamus!
> We laugh at how he looks to us,
> And yet in moments dank and grim
> I wonder how we look to him.
> Peace, peace, thou hippopotamus!
> We really look all right to us,
> As you no doubt delight the eye
> Of other hippopotami.

Finally, Lewis writes that "because the presentation of a particular image or idea as a fitting subject for humor is based on value judgments, the creation and use of humor is an exercise of power: a force in controlling our responses to unexpected and dangerous happenings, a way of shaping the responses and attitudes of others." As we have already seen, Nash repeatedly exposes the relativity of values by blurring the supposedly clear lines demarcating good and bad, an action that has consequences both morally and aesthetically. By defining the limits of acceptable behavior, the poet-fool exerts a powerful influence in defining both a standard of morality and a criterion of art.

FURTHER READING

Bibliography

Crandell, George W.   *Ogden Nash: A Descriptive Bibliography.* Metuchen, N. J.: The Scarecrow Press, Inc., 1990, 466 p.

 Complete bibliography of Nash's publications, excluding reprintings in periodicals and anthologies.

Criticism

Bacon, Leonard. "A Self-Appointed Love-Child." *Saturday Review* X, No. 14 (October 21, 1933): 197, 202.

 A verse review of *Happy Days.*

"Come Mr. N., Are You Men or Are You Milne?" *The New York Times Book Review* (October 4, 1936): 4.

 Finds fault with Nash's long poems.

"Criminal Hyminal." *The North American Review* II, No. 1 (Spring 1965): 58.

 This review praises Nash in verse imitative of his style.

Disch, Tom. "With the Best of Intentions." *Times Literary Supplement* (February 3, 1984): 118.

 Presents an overview of Nash's career and poetic hallmarks.

Frankenberg, Lloyd. "Father Nash's Mother Goose." *The New York Times Book Review* (November 10, 1957): 39.

 Review of Nash's Christmas poem *The Christmas That Almost Wasn't.*

Kermode, Frank. "Maturing Late or Simply Rotted Early?" *The Spectator* (September 24, 1994): 36-37.

 Review of selected poems, which examines Nash's relevancy today.

Merriam, Eve. "Children's Book World." *Book World* (December 24, 1967): 10.

 Expresses disappointment with Nash's children's verse, calling it tired and condescending.

Nordell, Rod. "Ogden Nash's Latest." *The Christian Science Monitor* 49, No. 162 (June 6, 1957): 11.

 Reviews *You Can't Get There From Here* and explores the wide range of subject matter that fills Nash's poetry.

"Roaring 50s." *Time* LXI, No. 16 (April 13, 1953): 112, 114.

 Argues that Nash's themes mature in *The Private Dining Room.*

"White-Collar Laureate." *Time* LVII, No. 1 (January 1, 1951): 62.

 Comments on Nash's themes of domestic confusion and parenting, describing him as the voice of the average American.

Additional coverage of Nash's life and career is contained in the following sources published by Gale Research: *Contemporary Authors,* **Vols. 13-14, 29-32R;** *Contemporary Authors New Revision Series,* **Vol. 34;** *Contemporary Authors Permanent Series,* **Vol. 1;** *Contemporary Literary Criticism,* **Vol. 23;** *Dictionary of Literary Biography,* **Vol. 11;** *DISCovering Authors: Poets Module; Major Authors and Illustrators for Children and Young Adults; Major Twentieth-Century Writers;* **and** *Something About the Author,* **Vols. 2, 46.**

Gary Snyder
1930-

(Full name Gary Sherman Snyder) American poet, essayist, translator.

INTRODUCTION

Snyder is a Pulitzer Prize–winning poet whose work, strongly influenced by Buddhism, deals with the natural world and ecological concerns. Snyder made his poetic debut at the Six Gallery in San Francisco in 1955, at what has come to be known as the "coming out party" for the Beat Generation poets. Although he lived in Japan, studying Zen Buddhism, during much of the Beat period, he has been linked personally and professionally with Beat writers such as Allen Ginsberg and Jack Kerouac. While much of the Beat writing is characterized by a rejection of literary tradition, Snyder's work embodies the influence of literary giants such as T. S. Eliot, Walt Whitman, and Ezra Pound. In addition to winning the Pulitzer Prize for his 1974 poetry collection, *Turtle Island,* he has also been honored with the Bollingen Prize for Poetry and the John Hay Award for Nature Writing.

Biographical Information

Snyder was raised on small farms, first in Washington and later in Oregon, and held jobs as a logger, seaman, and fire-lookout. His interest in American Indian culture led him to acquire degrees in literature and anthropology at Reed College. He began graduate studies in linguistics at Indiana University, and then transferred to University of California at Berkeley, where he studied Oriental languages. During the early 1950s, Snyder became involved with the Beat community. Just as the Beat poets were gaining national attention, Snyder moved to Japan, where he became actively involved in Zen Buddhism. He subsequently returned to California, where he lived and worked in rural areas. Since 1985, he has been a professor of creative writing at the University of California at Davis.

Major Works

Snyder's writing is strongly influenced by his understanding of Native American culture, Asian culture (primarily Japan and China) and the environment. His early writing—such as his first book, *Riprap*—reflects an appreciation for the hard work of rural life and the bond it produces with nature. *Myths & Texts,* his next collection, is a long, highly allusive lyrical poem divided into three sections: "Logging," "Hunting," and "Burning." *The Back Country* (1967), divided into five sections—"The Far West," "The Far East," "Kali," "Back," and translations of work by the Japanese poet Miyazawa Kenji—reveals the influence of

East and West on both the style and content of Snyder's poetry. His subsequent major collections—*Regarding Wave* (1969), *Turtle Island* (1974) and *Axe Handles* (1983)—continue to develop the themes and concerns introduced in his early collections. His *Mountains and Rivers Without End* (1996) is an ongoing lyrical series, begun in the 1950s. In addition to his poetry, Snyder has published a number of nonfiction works, most notably *Earth House Hold* (1969), *The Old Ways* (1979), and *The Real Work* (1980), collections of essays that relate to his poetry thematically.

Critical Reception

Snyder has been regarded by some critics and other poets as an heir of the Emersonian tradition because of his concern both for the natural and the spiritual worlds. Critical response to Snyder's works has been mixed. Upon publication of *Riprap,* some reviewers perceived Snyder as simplistic and overrated. Yet others commented favorably on the clarity and exactness of *Riprap's* spare poems. *Myths & Texts* has been regarded as superior to *Riprap* in literary merit: it is more tightly constructed, unified, and expansive. While Snyder shows more certainty and control in *Turtle Island,* it has also been criticized for being polemical.

PRINCIPAL WORKS

Poetry

Riprap 1959
Myths & Texts 1960
The Firing 1964
Hop, Skip, and Jump 1964
Nanoa Knows 1964
Riprap and Cold Mountain Poems 1965
Six Selections From Mountains and Rivers Without End
  1965
A Range of Poems 1966
Three Worlds 1968
The Blue Sky 1969
Regarding Wave 1970
Manzanita 1971
Plute Creek 1972
*The Fudo Trilogy: Spel against Demons, Smokey the Bear
  Sutra, The California Water Plan* 1973
Turtle Island 1974
All in the Family 1975
Smokey the Bear Sutra 1976
Songs for Gaia 1979
Axe Handles 1983
Left Out in the Rain 1986
Mountains and Rivers Without End 1990
No Nature 1992

Other Major Works

Earth House Hold: Technical Notes and Queries to Fellow Dharma Revolutionaries (prose) 1969
The Old Ways: Six Essays (prose) 1977
He Who Hunted Birds in His Father's Village: The Dimensions of a Haida Myth (prose) 1984
Passage Through India (autobiography) 1983
The Practice of the Wild (prose) 1996

CRITICISM

Thomas J. Lyon   (essay date 1970)

SOURCE: "The Ecological Vision of Gary Snyder," in *Kansas Quarterly,* Vol. 2, No. 2, Spring, 1970, pp. 117-24.

[*In the following excerpt, Lyon considers Snyder's poetry strongly rooted in the ecology of the American West.*]

The limitations of White/Western thought have also been limned, for serious Western writers, by the presence of the Indian, who lasted long enough in the West to be the model of primitive ecology and religious responsibility to earth. But the critique has not been simple-minded. Frank Waters, to name perhaps the deepest student of the Indian among writers, has long been recommending a supra-rational, supra-emotional synthesis between cultures, making finally an ecologically responsible civilization and psychically whole persons; the Western writer's ability to take the Indian seriously has resulted in real trailbreaking.

> **In common with most of the poetic generation that has rebelled against the formulaic Eliot rhetoric and intellectual abstraction, Snyder writes a solid line, but the special quality in his diction, the personal voice, lies in his knowledgeable selection of objects. They are things he has worked with and felt the grain of.**
>
> —*Thomas J. Lyon*

It may be—I almost believe it—that the West's great contribution to American culture will be in codifying and directing the natural drive toward ecological thought: a flowering of regional literature into literally world-wide attention and relevance. Now, after all this prologue, I come to my subject, the poet Gary Snyder, for as Snyder begins to emerge as an important force in the ideas and art of America, he shows signs of embodying the Western ecological vision in a culturally viable form. His writing is popular, certainly, and as I hope to show, it is valid in deeper, permanent ways.

The first thing that strikes one about Snyder's poetry is the terse, phrase-light and article-light diction, the sense of direct *thing*-ness. In common with most of the poetic generation that has rebelled against the formulaic Eliot rhetoric and intellectual abstraction, Snyder writes a solid line, but the special quality in his diction, the personal voice, lies in his knowledgeable selection of objects. They are things he has worked with and felt the grain of, and thus known better than good-sounding "poet's" catalogs:

> Rucksack braced on a board,
>   lashed tight on back.
> sleeping bags, map case, tied on the
>   gas tank
> sunglasses, tennis-shoes, your long tan
>   in shorts
> north on the west side of Lake Biwa
> Fukui highway still being built,
>   crankcase bangd on rocks—
>   pusht to the very edge by a
>   blinded truck
>   I saw the sea below beside my knee:
> you hung on and never knew how close.

Experience is not elaborately prepared for, in the Snyder poetics, just handed over: "Woke once in the night, pissed,

/ checkt the coming winter's stars / built up the fire" opens a poem and puts the reader in the mountains without any pastoral-tradition framing. This is the "near view" of the Sierra that John Muir wanted so much and knew that conventional art didn't give. Snyder's open directness moves toward solving one of Muir's and other transcendentalists' great dilemmas: how to talk about things, especially wild ones, without harming their integrity by language; how to preserve and communicate suchness without falling into an arch aesthetic distance between subject and object, a romantic decoration that destroys the very wholeness, which is wildness, one loved and wanted to convey somehow. The thin line of poetic truth between overstatement and private code requires first of all respect for things, letting them stand free instead of being marshaled into line for a mental performance. Snyder apparently recognizes the lover's paradox in writing ("each man kills the thing he loves"), and turns back on his own mind with good humor:

> foxtail pine with a
> clipped curve-back cluster of tight
>   five-needle bunches
>   the rough red bark scale
> and jigsaw pieces sloughed off
>   scattered on the ground.
> —what am I doing saying "foxtail pine"?

The comment might be on alliteration and rolling rhythm, as well as on the general deceit of naming: the poem moves beyond nature love to a focus on relation, among Snyder and his poem and the tree, and the ironic mode of the final question enters dimensions of richness quite beyond simple appreciation, if such a thing is simple. The openness of Snyder's seemingly casual presentation of objects, then, should not be mistaken for naïvete. The freshness of youth in his perceptions seems to be the result of having passed through a midstage of poeticizing and returned to the primal, simultaneous brotherhood-inseparateness of all objects. This is the wild world which Thoreau intuitively saw great poetry aiming at. Leaving it in integrity requires only pointing, and here Snyder's long Zen training provides the exact discipline needed. But the poet can also bring himself in and show the paradoxical nature of knowledge (and the poignant human consciousness of separateness) by levels of irony. So we have Snyder writing,

> When
> Snow melts back
>   from the trees
> Bare branches   knobbed pine twigs
>   hot sun on wet flowers
> Green shoots of huckleberry
> Breaking through the snow.

on the one hand, and

> A clear, attentive mind
> Has no meaning but that
> Which sees is truly seen.
> No one loves rock, yet we are here.

on the other. The inclusiveness resulting is literally "part" and "parcel" of the ecological vision. Tingeing the Zen core with irony, though it is far from his only technique, is one of Snyder's singular contributions to modern poetry, a byproduct of the connection he has knitted in his life between East and West. In a sense, Snyder is moving westward in the way that Whitman meant for us to do, the total effect of his final synthesis being, to use one of his essay titles, a "Passage to More than India."

Snyder shows his naturalness and American-West roots most obviously in his colloquial, object-laden language, but another and perhaps more important consonance with the wilderness world can be felt in his verse rhythms. "I've just recently come to realize that the rhythms of my poems follow the rhythm of the physical work I'm doing and the life I'm leading at any given time," he wrote in 1959, and many of his poems are tuned so closely to muscular and breath paces that they seem quite as spontaneous as his analysis implies. A bit of **"Riprap,"** which grew out of building trails on slick granite in the Sierra will illustrate this:

> Lay down these words
> Before your mind like rocks,
>   placed solid, by hands
> In choice of place, set
> Before the body of the mind
>   in space and time:
> Solidity of bark, leaf, or wall
>   riprap of things:
> Cobble of milky way,
>   straying planets,
> These poems, people,
>   lost ponies with
> Dragging saddles—
>   and rocky sure-foot trails.

There are some fine rhythms starting from non-human wilderness, too, where the birds and other animals seem almost to have written the poem by themselves.

> Birds in a whirl, drift to the rooftops
> Kite dip, swing to the seabank fogroll
>
>   . . . . .
>
> The whole sky whips in the wind
> Vaux Swifts
> Flying before the storm
> Arcing close hear sharp wing-whistle
> Sickle-bird

Snyder flirts with meter and with internal rhyme and alliteration, clearly, but the forming principle is not external. He once described formal poetry as "the game of inventing an abstract structure and then finding things in experience which can be forced into it," identifying this kind of writing with the rationalistic philosophy-culture of the West—of civilization—and then stated his preference for wilderness: "the swallow's dip and swoop, 'without east or west.'" The basic direction of his prosody is that of his image-selection: to go beyond the midstage to the consciously primitive, where there is no "east or west." Since we are both an unconscious, animal process and a conscious intellect, Snyder's poetics can be seen as an attempt at continuous self-transcendence, a leading through ego-borders into the wild. Self, ego, is at work in nature-love, as it is more obviously in nature-hate, as it is also in cultural typologies and forms for poetry. The ultimate meanings in Snyder's poetry, deeply revolutionary meanings in the sense of consciousness-changers, putting man in a different place from where he thought he was all these years, can be sensed very clearly in his formal poetics alone. His work is therefore organic rather than contrived, and although this can be said of many contemporary poets and indeed marks the fundamental direction of modern American poetry, the special virtue in Snyder's work is that he has created or allowed to develop a form that grows so rightly out of *wild* things, and which leads the reader uncannily ahead to a wild point of view. This is the technique of the ecological sense which goes past both the primitive and primitiv*ism,* into something else, in certain poems the ecstatic ecology of wholeness. Then to keep the sense of mind—"all the junk that goes with being human," as Snyder wrote once—alive along with the transparent eyeball, is art. Snyder's best poems, in my opinion, are the ones that move through these levels of apprehension, keeping the whole thing alive and total, finally conveying the great molecular interrelatedness, yet not as a static "thing," not even as a "poem," sweated out, but with the rhythmic feel of the unworded wild truth.

Sherman Paul (essay date 1970)

SOURCE: "From Lookout to Ashram: The Way of Gary Snyder," in *Critical Essays on Gary Snyder,* G. K. Hall & Co., 1991, pp. 58-80.

[*In the following excerpt, Paul reveals correlations between personal events in Snyder's life and his development as both a poet and an environmentalist.*]

I know of no one since Thoreau who has so thoroughly espoused the wild as Gary Snyder—and no one who is so much its poet. His root metaphor, the "back country," covers all that Thoreau, explicitly or implicitly, meant by the "wild." "Poetry and the Primitive," one of the recent essays collected in *Earth House Hold* (1969), is his most important statement and the resolution of much of his work, an essay comparable in import, though not in distinction of style, to Thoreau's "Walking." Thoreau's essay, originally a lecture called "The Wild," is testamentary, and so is Snyder's, though his is not terminal. It does not conclude a life but draws a phase of life to conclusion and, in this way and by the affirmation of writing, announces a new departure at a deeper depth of realization. The two essays that follow it, "Dharma Queries" and "Suwa-no-se Island and the Banyan Ashram," record his vows and practice, and the latter begins his life anew with his marriage to Masa Uehara, whom he celebrates in *Regarding Wave* (1969), his latest book of poems.

Earth House Hold, spanning the years 1952 to 1967, provides an excellent introduction to a poet whose poetry, because of its autobiographical nature and allusions to Oriental and American Indian lore, is not always readily available. Its title feelingly translates "ecology," a science that Paul Shepard and Daniel McKinley consider subversive—subversive, and urgent, in respect to the attitudes and ends of overly technological civilization. Its subtitle, "Technical Notes & Queries to Fellow Dharma Revolutionaries," suggests this revolutionary character, and as a manual for revolution, it offers a way (of thought and action) and indicates the studies and disciplines that, in the author's experience, lead us back to the back country where we may enjoy "Housekeeping on Earth." As "Dharma" implies, this revolution turns on truth; it is what Emerson called a silent revolution of thought, and the thought, much of it, is Oriental, the "primal thought" spoken of in Whitman's "Passage to India." The revolutionaries are spiritual seekers whom Snyder, not without humor, now addresses as guerrillas. He once called them "Dharma-hobos" (in 1956) and Jack Kerouac, in the title of a novel relating his meeting and experience with Snyder, called them "Dharma-bums" (in 1958). Kerouac even prophesied a "rucksack revolution" and in his novel Japhy Ryder (Gary Snyder) says: "Think what a great world revolution will take place when East meets West finally, and it'll be guys like us that start the thing. Think of millions of guys all over the world with rucksacks on their backs tramping around the back country and hitchhiking and bringing the word down to everybody." The revolutionary here—in the 1950's—is one who withdraws from society; he "signs off," as Thoreau would say, and becomes a saunterer, a holy-lander. Bum, for Kerouac, translates *bhikkhu,* monk; hopping freights and hitch-hiking are in keeping with a free life of voluntary poverty. Or, in the phrase Snyder uses to characterize his friend Nanao Sakaki—a phrase that also characterizes him and reminds one of Bash—the revolutionary may be a "wanderer and poet," whose only moral imperative "in this yuga," as Snyder declares for himself in the first journal, is to communicate. Now, at the end of the 1960's, as the subtitle indicates, this social passivity, so much in the grain of Eastern thought, is disclaimed; "revolutionary" has the meaning of the 1960's and the goal of revolution is represented for Snyder in the I. W. W., slogan, "Forming a new society within the shell of the old." Snyder's book begins where Kerouac's *The Dharma Bums,* a book about individual salvation, ends. It reflects the changing lifestyle, the increasing activism and communitarianism, of the past decade, and its quiet confidence and sense of vast tributary support (mostly out of the past—Snyder dates some essays and poems from the time of the earliest cave paintings) are noteworthy. It may be described briefly as a development from lookout to ashram.

Earth House Hold begins in the back country which was also Snyder's boyhood world. Though he was born in San Francisco (in 1930), his formative years were spent in the Pacific Northwest. During the depression, his family tried dairy-farming in Washington, and, after 1942, lived in Portland, Oregon, where he attended Reed College. The

Northwest is his personal geography: the low country of "Nooksack Valley," where, sitting in "a berry-pickers cabin / At the edge of a wide muddy field / Stretching to the woods and cloudy mountains," the smell of cedar reminds him of "our farm-house, half built in '35"; and the high country of the mountain wilderness of the North Cascades which he first entered in his youth. This landscape, especially the mountain wilderness, is aboriginal, like the "Fur Countries" that had early rejoiced Thoreau and the "*great west* and *northwest* stretching on infinitely far and grand and wild" that he later said qualified all of his thoughts—"That is the only America I know . . . That is the road to new life and freedom . . . That great northwest where several of our shrubs, fruitless here, retain and mature their fruits properly." Wilderness of this kind, Snyder reminds us, as much from personal experience as from historical report, is what Americans confronted on the frontier. Here was "a vast wild ecology" that was "mind-shaking." For Americans, nature, he says, meant wilderness, an "untamed realm of total freedom—not brutish and nasty, but beautiful and terrible." And it meant the Indian, whose ways Snyder, like Thoreau, seriously studied (his bachelor's thesis, "The Dimensions of a Myth," treats the Haida) and whose ghost, he says in the portentous manner of Lawrence, "will claim the next generation as its own."

Snyder possessed this primitive landscape in many ways, among them by learning woodcraft as a boy, mountain climbing as a youth, and working in the forest as a trail-maker, logger, and lookout in his early manhood. And while he was possessing it, he was, as a student of folklore, mythology, religion, and Oriental languages, extending and deepening its meanings, transforming the back country into a spiritual domain. By the time he goes to Crater Mountain Lookout in 1952, the back country has become the "Buddha land," a place of spiritual enlightenment to which one ascends by means of the disciplines he practices there. Crater Mountain becomes "Crater Shan," another Cold Mountain, whose namesake Han-shan wrote the "Cold Mountain" poems that Snyder later translated, poems defining the back country as a condition of being: "Freely drifting, I prowl the woods and streams / And linger watching things themselves. / Men don't get this far into the mountains." All high places become one and have this significance, as later, when climbing in the Glacier Peak Wilderness Area, Snyder recalls Cold Mountain and imagines himself a Tibetan mountaineer, a Japanese woodcutter, and an exiled Chinese traveler. The nature he enters is universal, like that Thoreau said he entered on his daily walk: "I walk out into a nature such as the old prophets and poets, Menu, Moses, Homer, Chaucer, walked in. You may name it America, but it is not America . . . There is a truer account of it in mythology than in any history of America. . . ."

For the back country is *back*. It is reached by going back to what Peter Levi, in a recent review of Snyder's poetry, called the "sources" ("Snyder's work is a restoration of the sources, a defence of the springs," awakening in us a sense of a "lost dimension of life"). And back is *down*, a descent, as William Carlos Williams spoke of it, to the fertile chaos, the very "mother stuff" of our being, to the unconscious from which, Snyder believes, we can reconstruct, by means of meditation, whatever aspects of previous cultures we desire. Like the primitive wilderness—the "naked" world where both Thoreau and Snyder believe we are most alive—the sources are still there, a deeper down where love is rooted and creative forces play, the *nature* that is always woman ("no human man can belong to mountains except as they are nature, and nature is woman"). Here the mind is untamed and the "seeds of instinct," to use Thoreau's phrase, are nurtured (for a true culture, Thoreau remarked, does not "tame tigers"). It is a darkness, too, perhaps like the "back" where Coyote lives ("His house was back in the back of the hills") or the "Deep North" of Bash's last journey, the "other shore," or the world after death, the back country of Snyder's "Journeys" that one enters only by dying. Finally, as wilderness and unconscious, outer and inner equivalents, the back country is *beyond*—beyond society, civilization and its discontents ("I did not mean to come this far," Snyder writes in "Twelve Hours out of New York,"—"baseball games on the radio / commercials that turn your hair—"). It is the "old, dirty countries," the backward countries he has wandered in, places where the old traditions are still living, and places like Suwa-no-se Island where the primitive communal life he now advocates can be lived.

Earth House Hold—the very title declares it—records this deepening awareness of the significance of the back country. In it, one follows the random course of (a) life, sees it nurturing a poet, focusing and concentrating itself. The concluding essays, the most recent, comprise a platform or program, and are ardently didactic. But the early journals are exercises in recording one's life, part of a discipline of being. In this, they remind one of the journals of Emerson and Thoreau. The young man to whom they introduce us—they give us our first and earliest glimpse of Snyder—is already pursuing the way and is wholly intent on overseeing and shaping his perceptions; this, perhaps, accounts for the impersonal quality of the personal in Snyder's work and distinguishes him from the other autobiographical (confessional) poets of his generation. The journals are the work of a Zennist and a poet, a poet who has learned much about form from Pound but more, I think, from Chinese and Japanese poetry.

The first part of "Lookout's Journal," that covering the summer of 1952 on Crater Mountain, is the best of all the journals in *Earth House Hold*. In none of the others is the experiment in form and the experience so fully realized. It is, I think, a more daring work than any of the early poems collected in *Riprap* (1959)—larger, more open, able to contain, substantively and formally, more experience. The trajectory of experience it presents passes through *the* experience which, unrecorded, is of the kind given in the carefully wrought Poundian-cadenced poem of purification, clarity, and serenity commemorating the following summer's lookout, **"Mid-August at Sourdough Mountain Lookout,"** the initial poem of *Riprap*:

> Down valley a smoke haze
> Three days heat, after five days rain
> Pitch glows on the fir-cones

Across rocks and meadows
Swarms of new flies.
I cannot remember things I once read
A few friends, but they are in cities
Drinking cold snow-water from a tin cup
Looking down for miles
Through high still air.

This might be called a satori poem. It fulfills the need recorded in the first journal: "to look within and adjust the mechanism of perception." And it reminds one of Thoreau's realization at Walden ("Both place and time were changed, and I dwelt nearer to those parts of the universe and to those eras in history which had most attracted me") and of Emerson's reliance on the power of prospects.

The journal gives the essential particulars of experience that contributed to such attainment. It begins in late June, at the Ranger Station, with the following brief entry:

Hitchhiked here, long valley of the Skagit. Old cars parked in weeds, little houses in fields of braken. A few cows, in stumpland.

Ate at the "parkway cafe" real lemon in the pie
   "—why don't you get a jukebox in here"
   "—the man said we weren't important enough"

One probably notices first the abbreviated syntax—an expression of economy, one that tells us that the traditional syntax isn't essential enough and telegraphs a quick grasp of things, like sumi painting. We are given objective fragments, but even in this simplest entry they are arranged and placed on the empty space of the page. Like a haiku poem, they work by means of the art of omission, by what they suggest. They tell of arrival but indicate the journey (compare this entry with Kerouac's account in *The Dharma Bums*) and give the sense of increasing sparseness and emptiness. We are in the back country now, old cars in the weeds, little houses, a few cows in the stumpland, a place not important enough—frequented and commercial enough—for a jukebox but still backward enough, in its values, as Hemingway would have noted, to serve unadulterated lemon pie. As Snyder pointed out in reviewing a book of prose translations of Chinese poems, "any irregular line arrangement creates a manner of reading and a rhythm, which is poetical." So here. The entry is a poem. The balanced cadence of "Old cars parked in weeds, little houses in fields of braken" is artful.

Each entry is a formal design, a field of experience, in which the poet intends the fragments (thoughts, perceptions, notations of objects) to relate, become whole. The unity of the entry is often the unspoken ground to which all refer, as in the following:

Granite creek Guard station 9 July
   the boulder in the creek never moves
      the water is always falling
         together!
A ramshackle little cabin built by Frank Beebe the
   miner.

Two days walk to here from roadhead.
   arts of the Japanese: moon-watching
                        insect-hearing

Reading the sutra of Hui Neng.

   one does not need universities and libraries
   one need be alive to what is about

saying "I don't care"

The ground, here, is the resolve to pursue the way; the entry is really very intense and builds to the attitude of not caring about the "world" below. The poet is still struggling with—perhaps rehearsing—the "complete and total choice" he made about this time to relinquish a "professional scholar's career in anthropology" and set himself loose "to sink or swim as a poet." The entry begins with the poet's play (the rhythmic capitalization of the location) and with a haiku poem appropriate to resolute thought, and it moves associatively from the isolated little cabin of a miner to the meditative arts practiced in seclusion by the Japanese, to his own discipline (reading the sutra) and thoughts (the recognition of a Zen truth about learning), and determined statement of choice. . . .

The unity of *Riprap* is essentially one of stillness, and that of *Myths & Texts* is thematic. The unity of *The Back Country* depends upon the notion of travel and the metaphoric force of the title, but neither secures it so much as the presence of memory which now begins to fill some of the poems. This is a third volume of poems, and so its ground is familiar to poet and reader and, in a sense, recovered. Now experience is compounded by remembering and deepening of life. Though the book, especially the opening section, "Far West," contains poems that might have been included in *Riprap,* its dominant tone is of another kind. There is agitation in *Riprap,* but it is resolved by a course of action, the journey to Japan. Now, much that the poet has carried with him on his travels is admitted, as in **"Looking at Pictures to be Put Away"**:

Who was this girl
In her white night gown
Clutching a pair of jeans

On a foggy redwood deck.
She looks up at me tender,
Calm, surprised,

What will we remember
Bodies thick with food and lovers
After twenty years.

And as he continues to travel, still by working aboard ship, he begins to ponder in **"7.IV.64,"** and not with the levity the poem intends, his place in life:

all my friends have children
& I'm getting old. at least enough to be
a First Mate or an Engineer.
now I know I'll never be a Ph.D.

What is now admitted in the poems, and we realize was hitherto almost wholly excluded, is the poet's experience of love. The more he travels the more he is possessed by thoughts of love and friendship, and by a sense of loss, by the memory of innocent desire with which he first knew them. Back, mirror-imaged, may be a reflection of this.

Friendship is a minor strain, best represented in **"August on Sourdough, A Visit from Dick Brewer"** and **"Rolling in at Twilight."** The gesture of the poem itself, which names the friend and fixes forever an exemplary act, testifies to Snyder's feelings for the deep and open relationship of youth. In the first poem Dick Brewer "hitched a thousand miles" to see the poet, who, in turn, loaned him his poncho; in the second, Phil Whalen has laid in some groceries against the poet's probable arrival.

Love is the major strain and is first presented here in **"After Work"**:

> The shack and a few trees
> float in the blowing fog
>
> I pull out your blouse,
> warm my cold hands
>   on your breasts.
> you laugh and shudder
> peeling garlic by the
>   hot iron stove.
> bring in the axe, the rake,
> the wood
>
> we'll lean on the wall
> against each other
> stew simmering on the fire
> as it grows dark
>   drinking wine.

Love here is a prized part of a steady continuum of living whose sensations the poet fully savors and deeply appreciates. It is depicted as a homecoming. And it is as simple and directly physical and without haste as the poem, for the poet who transfers the rhythm of his experience to the poem knows the values of relation and contrast, the care of the husbandman, and is as confident of the pleasures of love as of other goods of life, the food to come, the wine, the enveloping warmth and darkness.

This poem is among the new poems in the latest edition of *The Back Country*. Along with the concluding poem of section one, **"For the Boy Who Was Dodger Point Lookout Fifteen Years Ago,"** it introduces the theme of loss and longing that before was not broached until the poems for Robin in section two. This concluding poem is explicitly retrospective. A head note tells us that the poet, now hiking alone in the Olympic mountains, remembers a trip in the same area many years before with his first wife (an experience treated in another poem, **"Alysoun,"** which begins section three). The poem is for the boy-lookout and for the boy the poet had been. It describes the mountain meadows and from the vantage of the lookout, to which the poet has climbed to talk with the lonely boy, the

tableau of Alison (Robin) bathing naked in a pond. From this distance she is "Swan Maiden," merely a lovely icon as well as significant mythmotif. For what is important is the meeting of poet and lookout "in our / world of snow and flowers"—the representation of friendship as perhaps higher and purer than love. . . .

Like Lawrence and Williams before him, to cite only two of the pioneer modern writers with whom he stands, Snyder would redress our culture by restoring the vital and the feminine, by voyaging historically and psychically to Pagany, and by charting for us new contours of feeling.

—*Sherman Paul*

In section two, "Four Poems for Robin" carry this theme. They tell of the lonely poet who remembers in his body ("I remember your cool body / Naked under a summer cotton dress") and now knows that in the "pointless wars of the heart" he lost the "grave, awed intensity" of young love: ". . . what the others All crave and seek for; We left it behind at nineteen." . . .

With section three, "Kali," the theme of love becomes more prominent. As a way of designating his travels, "Kali" stands for India; the section includes the poems on India that are counterparts of "A Journey to Rishikesh & Hardwar" in *Earth House Hold*. But Kali is the Mother Goddess, and many poems, variously, praise her. The opening poem to Alison acknowledges her as the first of many Kalis in the poet's experience. There are poems of the whorehouse and of erotic adventure and of marital celebration (Snyder married Joanne Kyger in 1960). But all—and this is invariably true of Snyder's treatment of love—are tender and reverential. Love for him, as other poems here on darkness and drunkenness suggest, is a dark ecstatic mystery. . . .

And as the other love poems of the last section show he has learned much on the way. **"Across Lamarck Col"** not only confesses his fault ("your black block mine") but the fact that all subsequent love affairs assert his loss, his fidelity to original feeling. And another fine poem, as good in its complexity as **"August Was Foggy"** is in its simplicity, realizes the equation of mountain = nature = woman. **"Beneath My Hand and Eye the Distant Hills, Your Body"** is a geography, geology, aesthetics, and metaphysics of love in which abstractions are used to deny themselves and yield the solvent feeling of experience. In this poem, Snyder shows as well as anywhere what it is that he has gone in search of and brought back from the East.

His most recent work, ***Regarding Wave,*** celebrates the world-as-woman and love as its ever-generative force, the spirit that moves him to poetry and now to marriage and fatherhood. The title and essential ideas of the book are glossed in **"The Voice as a Girl,"** a part of the essay, "Poetry and the Primitive." He explains here what he tries to convey in the poems: that, for him, the universe is alive and enters his body as breath, thereby enabling him to sing out "the inner song of the self"; that poetry is such inspired speaking, a response of the self that is deeper than ego to the touch of the world. The attitude he wishes to present is not that of the Western tradition of the Muse and Romantic Love, though its notion of "woman as nature the field for experiencing the universe as sacramental" is all of the primitive tradition that is left to us. Not woman as nature but nature as woman is what he sings—not a particular woman divinized, as in the cult of Romantic Love, but the Goddess herself. The Goddess Vak. "Poetry is voice, and according to Indian tradition, voice, vak (vox)—is a Goddess. Vak is also called Sarasvati, she is the lover of Brahma and his actual creative energy. . . ." Sarasvati means "the flowing one"; and "as Vak is wife to Brahma ('wife' means 'wave' means 'vibrator' in Indo-European etymology) so the voice, in everyone, is a mirror of his own deepest self." Such is the meaning of *Regarding Wave,* the poet's reverential praise of the continual creation in which he humbly and gratefully participates.

It is always difficult to write a poetry of praise. None of the poems in this book is especially epiphanic. Snyder's achievement is not in single poems but in the sustained feeling and quality of the book as a whole. The book is well unified by a three-part structure that may be considered wave-like, by a wave-like line and stanza, by the breath-phrasing of the line, not unusual with Snyder, but emphasized here, and by its singleness of theme. The wave is to Snyder's apprehension of nature what the leaf is to Goethe's—it is the ur-phenomenon. He celebrates it variously: in ocean, river, sands, pebbles, clouds; in flow and process and growth; in ecology and food chains. And against this celebration of organic creation, he sets a counter-theme of spoliation and violation of the female. The book begins with an invocation to the wave.

> Ah, trembling spreading radiating wyf
>   racing zebra
> catch me and fling me wide
> To the dancing grain of things of my mind!

and ends with the prayerful awareness of the still flowing wave in all things:

> The Voice
> is a wife
>   to
>
> him still.

And the book is especially well unified by its occasion, the fullness of the new life, a primitive, "archaic" life, he has found with Masa Uehara at the ashram on Suwa-no-se Island, their marriage there (with which account the superb last essay of *Earth House Hold* ends), and the birth of their child out of the sea of the womb. In **"It was When,"** a catalog (or Whitmanian litany) of sexual consummations, he tells how "we caught"—and

> Waves
>   and the
>   prevalent easterly
>   breeze
>   whispering into you
>   through us,
>   the grace.

In **"The Bed in the Sky,"** he turns from the cold outdoors, where he feels he ought to stay to watch the moon, to the indoor warmth of bed and wife and the stirring child in her belly. **"Kai, Today"** announces the sea-birth of his son, and **"Not Leaving the House,"** tells of the change this advent has brought: "From dawn til late at night / making a new world of ourselves / around this life."

This is not a book of travel nor of place, though the third section is largely devoted to the "burning island." Place is important but finally indifferent. What matters in this account of working in the elements of sea and land, of planting seeds and caring for new life, is that the current of the universal being has flowed through him and he has become, more selflessly, a servant of life. And something hitherto unattained has at last been attained: the wish of the lookout who long ago noted in his first journal, "Or having a wife and child, living close to the ocean, with skills for gathering food." This book commemorates the taking up housekeeping on earth.

From lookout to ashram. From Walden, we might say, to Fruitlands. The imperative throughout is Thoreau's: "Every man is tasked to make his life, even in its details, worthy of the contemplation of his most elevated and critical hour." But the direction is Alcott's: from solitude to society, from the individual to the family. Meditation is a seeing into the self that entails its acting out, and this action, Snyder says, in "Buddhism and the Coming Revolution," is "ultimately toward the true community (sangha) of 'all beings.'" The revolution—or transformation—he calls for is to be made in family life, for its agency is love and "love begins with the family and its network of erotic and responsible relationships." To change the form of family life is to alter society radically, at its root. And Snyder's Edenic vision of "ecological balance, classless society, social and economic freedom" is as radical for our society as the matrilineal communal family that he believes enables it—the "family as part of the divine ecology."

The feelings to which this familial-social vision answers are neither unfamiliar nor radical. Literature, and the literature of youth, has always reported them. Snyder, whose writing tells nothing of his past family life, tells in "Passage to More Than India" of his own discovery, at 18, in a community house, of "harmony and community with fellow beings." This too, much later, is what he found ideally at the Banyan Ashram on Suwa-no-se Island. Such feelings, like so much that is considered radical, are conservative—conserving essential and full humanity—and Snyder is right to connect them with occult traditions and a persistent Great Subculture. What is radical now is not merely the repudiation of present social forms ("the modern family is the smallest and most barren that has ever existed"; "the traditional cultures are in any case doomed") but the search for social solutions in the past, the distance back being, perhaps, the measure of this. Snyder is radical because he holds, as he says, "the most archaic values on earth" and because he tries to advance them by realizing them anew in his life and his work. Yet there is nothing archaic in his appropriation of them: they are his (and ours) by right of modern psychology and anthropology as well as meditation. No more than Thoreau, can he be put down as a primitive: "I try to hold both history and wilderness in my mind," he says, "that my poems may approach the true measure of things and stand against the unbalance and ignorance of our times."

This declaration addresses our fearful centralizing technology and the sovereignty of the present that speeds it on; and it is noteworthy because it announces again, for still another generation, the great theme and major work of our time, the restoration of culture in its true measure. Like Lawrence and Williams before him, to cite only two of the pioneer modern writers with whom he stands, Snyder would redress our culture by restoring the vital and the feminine, by voyaging historically and psychically to Pagany, and by charting for us new contours of feeling.

We should not expect him by himself to work this great change. This is the mistake of those who confuse poetry with politics, critics like Peter Levi, who says that we need Snyder's poetry but adds that "his medicine is not going to cure anything. . . ." His work is political because it bears witness; on this account one respects the ways it combines autobiography and utopia. We should accept his optimism—can an ecological conscience be created in time to save a devastated universe?—as a condition of the work, as an act of faith founded on profound basic trust. It is not the register of social naivete. The distance from lookout to ashram is long and difficult; it is not easy for us to enter the back country nor find the archaic springs. We cannot expect literature to cure us, only to hearten us by showing us new and true possibilities and how much may be achieved in life and art by conscious endeavor. Snyder's work, already a substantial achievement, does this. And it may be especially heartening to us because in it an American poet has finally turned to the Orient and shown how much of America might yet be discovered in a passage to India.

Bert Almon (essay date 1977)

SOURCE: "Buddhism and Energy in the Recent Poetry of Gary Snyder," in *Mosaic: A Journal for the Comparative Study of Literature and Ideas,* Vol. XI, No. 1, Fall, 1977, pp. 117-25.

[*In the following essay, Almon explores the influence of Buddhist metaphysics on Snyder's work.*]

For all its attention to the physical world, the poetry of Gary Snyder has always had a metaphysical dimension. He once called poetry "a riprap (cobbled trail) over the slick rock of metaphysics," but metaphysics can also provide a trail over the slick rock of the poetry, providing a path where we might see only a difficult physical terrain. I will put aside the important matter of the influence of American Indian spirituality on Snyder's work and investigate the Buddhist context. Snyder's interest in Zen Buddhism is well-known: he is the poet who spent years in Japan studying it. While much of the material in recent works, such as *Regarding Wave* (1970) and *Turtle Island* (1974), may certainly be clear without a knowledge of Buddhism, some is not, and Snyder's fundamental opposition to industrial civilization can be clarified by understanding the Buddhist influence.

Zen is one of the schools of the Mahayana branch of Buddhism prevalent in Buddhist countries outside of Southeast Asia. It is a very special school, one minimizing philosophy and emphasizing direct experience. Western readers familiar only with the Zen tradition—the Zen master stories, the *koan* exercises—may not be aware of certain basic Mahayana concepts. The Mahayana schools have an ideal of active compassion that extends to all living beings: even the grass should be led to enlightenment by the Bodhisattva, the "enlightenment being" who vows to deliver the whole universe. The Bodhisattva practices *upaya,* "skillful means," stratagems and teachings fitted to the various beings he wishes to deliver. For the enlightened mind, the world is a state of being beyond all conflicts and oppositions. As Snyder puts it in "Four Changes," an important essay in *Turtle Island*: ". . . at the heart of things is some kind of serene and ecstatic process which is beyond qualities and beyond birth-and-death." This state of nirvana is not accessible to most of us, and we experience *samsara,* the world of birth-and-death. On this relative level of being, the universe is conceived of as a dynamic realm of interdependent and transient phenomena. Living beings are temporary groupings of elements of this flux, a conception that Snyder translates into the terms of Western physics: ". . . we are interdependent energy-fields of great potential wisdom and compassion . . ." he says in "Four Changes." He puts it this way in the "Introductory Note" of the same collection: "The poems speak of place, and the energy-pathways that sustain life. Each living being is a swirl in the flow, a formal turbulence, a 'song.'" In Snyder's work, the concept of interdependence is translated into ecological terms, and the conception of the world as flux is rendered in terms of physics: the world is a dynamic field of energy. Modern physics shows no interest in the potential wisdom and compassion of energy fields certainly. Science is an instrument of understanding and altering the world. Archimedes is with us yet, even if he may soon have no world to move. Ecology, on the other hand, is one science that does concern itself with wisdom. The ecologist knows how serious the consequences of acting without foresight and compassion can be. Ecological compassion is not a matter of sentimental humanitarianism, just as Snyder's notion of compassion does not rule out taking life, to sustain life.

But the poems in *Riprap,* and many in *Myths & Texts,* do not convey a world of flux. The poems are often contemplative: meditations set in stable landscapes, even if the poet laments transience and notes the passage of birds. Sherman Paul has said that "The unity of *Riprap* is essentially one of stillness. . . ." and I must agree with that insight ["From Lookout to Ashram," Part 2, *Iowa Review*, Vol. I, Fall 1970]. Zen awareness and Zen detachment permeate the early poems. Often they evoke quiet landscapes and sweeps of geological time. The scenes are *composed*, and composed very skillfully. The art of *sumi* painting comes to mind: vistas of clouds and mountains, a human figure or two almost lost in the mist, birds flying off into limitless space, all done in a few strokes. Not the intricate hum of transient elements in the void. And even the poems in *Myths & Texts*, though they describe logging and hunting, more often deal with contemplation than action.

There are transitional poems in *The Back Country*, but the striking change comes with *Regarding Wave*. Instead of a panoramic view of mountains or valleys, the poems frequently offer a world placed under the microscope. And rather than contemplation, the attitude is involvement. The proper analogy with painting would be the *tanka* art of Tibet, which arouses and transforms psychological energies through a blaze of color: processes instead of scenes. Consider the opening of the first poem ("Wave") in the book:

> Grooving clam shell,
>   streakt through marble,
> sweeping down ponderosa pine bark-scale
>   rip-cut tree grain
>   sand-dunes, lava flow

The dynamism of wave-forms is traced even in static objects. Physics and Mahayana Buddhism would agree that there are no stable objects, merely the illusion of stability. One of the objects of Buddhist meditation is to achieve awareness of impermanence in all aspects of reality, external and internal. The poetry of *Regarding Wave* often deals with what "Wave" calls ". . . the dancing grain of things / of my mind!" The "dancing grain" is a fine metaphor, and the activity of dancing is one of Snyder's favored means of conveying a dynamic world. Running water is another recurrent image used in the book. And the poet adopts the standard meditation strategy of imagining the physical world permeated with the sounds of the *Dharma* (Buddhist teachings) in several poems. In **"Regarding Wave,"** the *Dharma* is "A shimmering bell / though all," and the slopes of the hills are said to flow. **"All the Spirit Powers Went to Their Dancing Place"** turns the very landscape into sound: "Hills rising and falling as music, long plains and deserts as slow quiet chanting."

The style of *Regarding Wave* tends toward the break-up of straight-forward description and narration. The lines frequently take the form of image clusters: phrases and single words replacing the extended utterance as the unit of expression. (I say "extended utterance" because Snyder's terseness sometimes led him to avoid the complete sentence in the early poems.) The images themselves often evoke minute particulars, such as seeds, sand grain, thorns, or bark-scales. The world is examined with a close-up lens. Not that the images are always visual. Tactile, auditory, gustatory, olfactory and kinesthetic impressions are prominent and heighten the impression of involvement.

I will return to the matter of involvement in a moment, but I should mention that *Turtle Island* reverses these stylistic trends. We still come upon lines like "Snow-trickle, feldspar, dirt." But the poet is more concerned with narrative, even exposition, and the style is therefore more conventional, less concerned with rendering the flow of process. Social criticism and the desire to come to terms with Western America take precedence over the dancing grain of things. There are poems like **"On San Gabriel Ridges"** which would easily fit into *Regarding Wave,* but in the later volume Snyder is engrossed with the anecdotal and didactic, and the writing reflects those intentions. The sweep of evolution (300,000,000 years go by in one poem) and the workings of the American political system get more attention than the intricate dynamics of sand grains.

Snyder's Buddhist training has been in the Zen school, but his philosophical position is now influenced by the Vajrayana sect, whose outlook he discusses in *Earth House Hold*. Vajrayana (literally, "The Diamond Vehicle") is a Tantric school, predominant in Tibet before the Chinese invasion of 1959, and still widely practiced in the Himalayan region. Tantra is an approach found in Hinduism as well as Buddhism. The Tantric method is to involve the practitioner with the very reality that most Hindu and Buddhist sects seek detachment from: the world of birth-and-death, the realm of the passions. The key is to transform this reality rather than to escape from it. The attitude toward the emotions in Vajrayana Buddhism is particularly important: passions are aroused and transmuted, not repressed. Anger and desire, for example, can be made instruments of enlightenment. They are changed from poisons into wisdom. Readers who assume that Buddhism is a religion of passivity and kindness may be puzzled by Snyder's ferocity in some of the *Turtle Island* poems. Anger can be a teaching method (consider the Zen master and his stick), and it can also be transmuted into compassion. Better, it is one of the possible forms of compassion, as in the polemics of the ecology movement.

Snyder's **"Spel Against Demons"** is a good example of the role of wrath in his poetry. The poem originally appeared with **"Smokey the Bear Sutra"** and **"The California Water Plan"** in a limited edition entitled *The Fudo Trilogy*. It alone was reprinted in *Turtle Island*. "Fudo" is the Japanese name for a Mahayana deity called "Achala" or "Acala" in Sanskrit. His iconography and the *sadhana* (ritual of worship, visualization and invocation) devoted to him are described in **"The California Water Plan."** The deity represents the struggle against evil and is sometimes called the Lord of Heat. His imagery is summed up in Alice Getty's *The Gods of Northern Buddhism*: "His appearance is fierce and angry. The sword in his right hand is to smite the guilty and the lasso in his left to catch and bind the wicked." He is associated with fire: "Behind him is a glory of flames, symbolizing the destruction of Evil. . . ." Snyder's Smokey the Bear is fancifully presented as a form of Achala, or Fudo, and the **"Smokey the Bear Sutra"** is a droll parody of Buddhist scriptures. **"Spel Against De-**

mons" is also modeled on a Buddhist literary form, the *dharani.*

A *dharani* is a charm or spell, usually invoking a Buddha or Bodhisattva. Although D. T. Suzuki gives examples of the form in his well-known *Manual of Zen Buddhism,* the *dharani* represents a magical dimension of Buddhism which has received little attention in the West. **"Spel Against Demons"** attacks "The release of Demonic Energies in the name of / the People" and "The stifling self-indulgence in anger in the name of / Freedom." Mindless terrorism is denounced as ". . . death to clarify / death to compassion." The poem represents anger without rancor: "The poem calls upon Achala to bind "demonic killers" with his diamond noose and describes this deity ". . . who turns Wrath to Purified Accomplishment." The poem ends with a Sanskrit *mantra,* a power-formula—the "spel" of Achala.

It is not, then, contradictory for Snyder to include poems of anger and denunciation (**"The Call of the Wild," "Steak," "Control Burn"**) in the same section of *Turtle Island* that contains the warm family scenes of **"The Bath"** and the compassionate descriptions of **"The Dead by the Side of the Road."** The Vajrayana tradition embraces a life-giving exploitation of anger: some of the meditation masters of the Vajarayana were willing to use wrath and even force as teaching tools. The sensuous delight in the flesh that Snyder conveys in **"The Bath"** is equally respectable. The body is not the "running sore" for Vajrayana that it is for the Southern branch of Buddhism, the Theravada. Mindless craving is condemned, but the power of the senses is power that the spiritual life can harness.

The anger usually has a compassionate thrust. And the outrage Snyder feels often grows out of the abuse of living creatures that many religions ignore: animals and trees. The theoretical scope of Buddhist compassion is unlimited. The object of compassion is any living being, not just human beings. The Buddhist, like the North American Indian, gives a kind of equality to ". . . the other people—what the Sioux Indians called the creeping people, and the standing people, and the swimming people . . ." (*Turtle Island,* "The Wilderness"). Many of Snyder's "people" are birds, coyotes, whales, insects or even plants. It is easy to dismiss this sympathy as sentimental pantheism but Snyder knows that the ecological crisis grows out of such attitudes. His problem as a poet of the whole range of living beings is to create poems in which animals and plants appear as autonomous presences, not as mere symbols for human feelings or concepts. Naturally, the terms used are anthropomorphic, but anthropomorphism is a problem only for a world view that assumes an absolute gulf between man and other beings. Buddhism provides what Robinson Jeffers would call a transhuman perspective. The aim is not to raise the supposedly lower orders to a human level, but to see all beings as co-citizens in a community of life. Snyder assumes that the artist can imaginatively enter into the lives of other organisms and speak for them. In "The Wilderness," he says: "I wish to be a spokesman for a realm that is not usually represented in intellectual chambers or in the chambers of government." According to Snyder, the

way to be such a spokesman is to create paintings, dances or songs to express an interpretation of other beings.

Snyder is perhaps most skilled at interpreting birds: *Myths & Texts* contains some fine descriptions of them, and poems such as **"The Wide Mouth"** in *Regarding Wave* (depicting a sparrow) and **"The Hudsonian Curlew"** in *Turtle Island* are high points in the books. Deer, bears and coyotes get attention also. Plants present the biggest challenge: they are the basis of any ecological system, the "proletariat" on which other living beings feed, directly or indirectly, but they are very static characters, clearly. Snyder managed action in his early poems on plant life by describing forest fires and logging, and in *Regarding Wave* he deals with the dissemination of seeds by wind and water and on the fur of mammals. The distribution of seeds reminds us that plants have an active role in the shifting pattern of life.

Plants from the base of what in "Four Changes" Snyder calls ". . . a vast and delicate pyramid of energy-transformations. "Those transformations usually take the form of eating and being eaten. Food is one of Snyder's favorite themes. Many of the poems in his books deal with eating, and sometimes on an Odyssean scale. For example, *The Back Country* ends, not with the mythical splendors of **"Through the Smoke Hole,"** but with **"Oysters,"** a poem about hunting and eating the shellfish. The implied theme of the poem is the abundance of nature. Poems like **"Shark Meat"** in *Regarding Wave* create an awareness of the interdependence of all phenomena. The shark traveled far to become part of a feast on Suwa-no-se Island.

> Miles of water, Black current,
> Thousands of days
>   re-crossing his own paths
>   to tangle our net
>   to be part of
>   this loom.

And **"The Hudsonian Curlew"** in *Turtle Island* evokes the complexity of the physical world in which such birds live, then goes on to present the eating of them as an incorporation of their being into the eater: "dense firm flesh, / dark and rich, / gathered news of skies and seas." Eating becomes a reverential act, rather than a brutal necessity. Snyder is probably more indebted to North American Indian attitudes toward hunting and eating in this poems than he is to the Buddhist tradition. Buddhism teaches gratitude toward food—acknowledgement that it represents a loss of life—and that attitude is common among the American Indians, but Buddhism also encourages vegetarianism in order to minimize suffering. It is mindfulness of the interconnections involved in eating which Snyder draws from Buddhism. On the question of vegetarianism he takes the side of the primitive hunter who believes that humility, gratitude and acts of propitiation expiate the blame for eating meat or taking furs. Snyder does see Buddhism and American Indian attitudes as compatible, and both are influences in the poems. In **"One Should Not Talk to a Skilled Hunter about What is Forbidden by the Buddha"'** (which invokes a Zen master's

authority in the title), Snyder describes a Buddhist ceremonial in honor of a gray fox which is to be skinned:
chanting the *Shingyo,* or *Heart Sutra,* a text often recited
to the dying and at funerals. Another poem in *Turtle
Island,* **"The Dead by the Side of the Road,"** presents the
use of animals killed by accident. The ceremony described,
offering corn meal by the dead body, is North American
Indian. The Buddhist tradition that meat not killed by or
specifically for one can be eaten without blame, and the
conclusion of the poem is an act of mindfulness in the
Buddhist sense: it emphasizes that some blame does attach to human beings for building highways across animal
trails. The Buddhist and North American Indian elements
in Snyder's poems are more likely to reinforce than contradict each other.

Both traditions condemn thoughtless murder of any creature. The poems in *Turtle Island* reject such killing.
"Steak" condemns those who eat grain-fattened beef
without realizing the cost to the land or acknowledging
the suffering of the animals. The poem concludes with an
image of the live cattle which are being fattened-up:

> Steaming, stamping,
> long-lashed, slowly thinking
> with the rhythm of their
> breathing,
> frosty—breezy—
> early morning prairie sky.

The key word is "thinking." We prefer not to realize that
cattle are sentient beings, capable of suffering.

The greatest anger in *Turtle Island* is reserved for wanton
killing for mere gain or comfort, a different matter from
eating to sustain life. **"The Call of the Wild"** is particularly effective, with its acid portrait of the man who has
coyotes trapped because they make noise, and its terse,
disgusted chronicle of the city hippies who move to the
country but sell their cedars because someone tells them
that "Trees are full of bugs." The anger is tempered with
awareness and compassion that reduce the potential for a
self-righteous tone. In **"I Went into the Maverick Bar"**
the speaker disguises himself as a middle American ("My
long hair was tucked up under a cap / I'd left the earring
in the car.") and observes the mores of his countrymen
with some sympathy. I am reminded of the Bodhisattva
named Vimalakirti, who was famed for going into brothels
and taverns in order to practice compassion. He always
appeared to be one of the revelers, but only as a form of
upaya, skillful means. One of the most interesting poems
in *Turtle Island* is **"Dusty Braces,"** in which the poet
acknowledges the influence of his wandering, land-
destroying ancestors and gives them "nine bows," a traditional form of homage in Buddhism. But acknowledging
his *karma*—the formative influences on him—doesn't mean
that he accepts the destructive ways of those ancestors.

The indignation recorded in *Turtle Island* reaches a climax
in **"Mother Earth: Her Whales,"** a denunciation of the
"robots" who ". . . argue how to parcel out our Mother
Earth / To last a little longer." This poem, like "Toward

Climax" later in the book, strikes me as a good prose essay
mysteriously incarnated as a bad poem. **"Mother Earth:
Her Whales"** has too many discordant elements: a manifesto calling for an uprising of "otters, wolves and elk,"
lyrical passages describing the lives of the whales themselves, rhetorical denunciations of the "robots" at the
Stockholm Conference on the Environment, fragments of
ballads, and historical sketches. A reader can share the
disgust and yet feel that the poem is not successful. Prose
might have been a better vehicle for conveying the sense
of outrage.

This particular poem does make it clear that the poet
wants to take on all exploitative civilizations:

> how can the head-heavy power-hungry politic
>   scientist
> Government   two world   Capitalist-Imperialist
> Third World   Communist   paper-shuffling male
>   non-farmer   jet-set   bureaucrats
> Speak for the green of the leaf? Speak for the soil?

The technological abuses of Western civilization are envied by the non-Western nations: the instrumental approach—pragmatism and exploitation—is shared by many
developing as well as developed nations. The energy crisis has shown that this approach is ultimately self-defeating. It breaks down those "energy-pathways" that sustain
life. And energy in the narrow sense, mere fuel, can be
exhausted.

Technically-advanced societies, and those aspiring to such
status, regard energy as a means of controlling, altering
and exploiting the natural world. The environment is a
mass of raw material to be exploited. For Mahayana Buddhism, the world is a dynamic process to be interpreted
through contemplation, or even transmuted (as in Vajrayana)—not cut-down, burned-out, torn-up or strip-mined.
In Zen monasteries the ideal is to waste nothing, not even
a drop of water. The Buddhist approach is one of gratitude
for what one receives, while the industrial approach is to
devise ways of getting more. One of Snyder's themes in
Turtle Island is exploitation and wanton destruction. Much
of the wrath can be accounted for by the shameless way
in which governments that very slowly awoke to public
pressure for environmental protection measures have moved
quickly to give up those measures whenever they interfere
with the need for energy. A shortage of energy in the
limited sense—fuel—justifies further damage to the ". . .
vast and delicate pyramid of energy-formations" which
makes life possible. The real sources of energy are the sun
and the mental energy within the mind. Opposed to these
sources is the **"Liquid Metal Fast Breeder Reactor,"** which
Snyder sees as "Death himself," a source of contamination
likely to heighten the environmental damage already done
by conventional approaches to creating industrial energy.
The poet insists that "We would live on this Earth /
without clothes or tools!" But this is not possible without
vast transformations in our way of life, of course, and the
prose essays in *Turtle Island* are meant to encourage
such changes. His commentary on "As for Poets" declares
that ". . . there is another kind of energy, in every living

being, close to the sun-source, but in a different way. The power within. Whence? 'Delight.' The delight of being alive while knowing of impermanence and death, acceptance and mastery of this." Such power, he says, ". . . will still be our source when coal and oil are long gone, and atoms are left to spin in peace." He defines "Delight" in terms of Mahayana metaphysics, though he draws the term from William Blake, who said that "Energy is Eternal Delight." It is interesting to note that Herbert V. Guenther, seeking a term for the *Karmamudra* experience of sexual ecstasy in Tantric Buddhism, hit upon Blake's "Eternal Delight" also [*The Life and Teaching of Naropa,* 1963]. For Snyder, Delight grows out of a perception of the world as a luminous, interdependent reality, which can be perceived as serene and joyful when observed without dualistic thinking:

> Delight is the innocent joy arising
> with the perception and realization of
> the wonderful, empty, intricate,
> inter-penetrating,
> mutually-embracing, shining
> single world beyond all discrimination
> or opposites.

In **"Charms"** *(Turtle Island),* Snyder follows the Tantric tradition in suggesting that "The beauty of naked or half-naked women" evokes this perception of ". . . the Delight / at the heart of creation." There are other ways of evoking Delight, and the celebration of animals, plants and birds is one means of summoning up a joy in the energy of things. The flux of physical reality need not be perceived as a conflict if there is no desire to conquer or exploit it. And even the passion of anger can be plowed back into "Fearlessness, humor, detachment," genuine forms of power.

Charles Molesworth (essay date 1983)

SOURCE: "The Political and Poetic Vision of *Turtle Island*" in *Gary Snyder's Vision,* University of Missouri Press, 1983, pp. 144-56.

[*In the following essay, Molesworth discusses the political and poetic viewpoints of Snyder's Pulitizer-prize-winning work,* Turtle Island.]

We can take Snyder's *Turtle Island* as the most complete expression of his political and poetic vision, not only because it is his most recent finished volume, but also because it contains the fullest mediations of the themes and concerns of all his work. I propose to look at the book as incorporating three mediations. First, *Turtle Island* serves Snyder with a chief metaphor for a physical environment and a utopian vision. As he puts it in the "Introductory Note," Turtle Island is the "old / new name for the continent, based on many creation myths of the people who have been living here for millennia." The metaphor of the continent floating on the back of a giant turtle serves as a cosmogonic emblem of archaic knowledge and future hopes: "Hark again to those roots, to see our ancient solidarity, and then to the work of being together on

Turtle Island." This work, another version of the real work, extends beyond North America to "the earth, or cosmos even," because Turtle Island is another version of the "idea found world-wide" of a "serpent-of-eternity," the *uroboros* familiar to all students of world mythology. Turtle Island thus combines the immanent awareness of a space occupied for thousands of years with the historically transcendent space of the planet reimagined as the seat of the species.

Snyder is less concerned with interior states than with environmental harmony.

—Charles Molesworth

Secondly, Snyder uses Turtle Island as a way of mediating between an ethics of responsibility and an ethics of ultimate ends. I take these terms from Max Weber's well-known essay "Politics as a Vocation" (1918) [reprinted in *From Marx to Weber: Essays in Sociology,* 1946]. Weber distinguishes between these two "fundamentally differing and irreconcilably opposed" senses of value, since those who formulate or pursue ultimate ends are unlikely to take pragmatic consequences into consideration. But Weber is quick to add that the ethics of ultimate ends need not produce actions that deny or evade all consequences, and likewise the ethics of responsibility should not be equated with "unprincipled opportunism." Snyder includes in *Turtle Island* a section, called "Plain Talk," of prose essays, the most extended of which is "Four Changes." This essay contains "practical and visionary suggestions" and is the fullest statement in expository prose of Snyder's aims and beliefs. Here he advances several radical ideas: the world's population should be cut in half, alternative family structures should be explored, the world should be divided into "natural and cultural boundaries rather than arbitrary boundaries" (thereby eliminating nation-states and most existing political structures), we should seek a reliance on unobtrusive technologies and energy sources, and so forth. The arguments for each proposal mix appeals to scientific and technological fact and research with attacks on the ideology of consumption and private property. All of the proposals, however, are for a new ethics, and this new ethics stands in relation to our current ethical standards and behavior in a way that is based on both immediate responsibilities and ultimate ends.

The third major mediation in *Turtle Island* presents a sense of the lyric poem that has dominated literature for the last century and a half, together with a future model of the lyric poem as more committed to enhancing an awareness of cosmic scale and cosmic forces and the need of the community to heighten and preserve such awareness: "The common work of the tribe." The dominant current model of the lyric poem originated with the postromantic sense of the isolated artist and the autotelic theories of aesthetic experience. This model was made more or less canonic by such anthologies as F. T. Palgrave's *Golden Treasury* (1861) and by such critical studies, some generations later, as I. A. Richard's *Principles of Literary Criticism* (1925). Snyder is indebted to this model, as is virtually every postromantic poet, and his riprap poetics can be seen in part as an extreme development of one aspect of the art-lyric, the dictum against ornate or merely decorative imagery. But Snyder's more recent work is set against several other dicta of the art-lyric, chiefly the strict avoidance of intellectual content and didactic intentions. Snyder attempts to celebrate the common work of the tribe, and so his poetry has a didactic role, as well as a concern for group consciousness and social value (although more often of a desired rather than an actual sort) that mitigates against the art-lyric's concentration of the single, exacerbated sensibility. In a poem like **"Anasazi,"** which opens *Turtle Island,* there is little or no trace of an observing subject or a lyrical ego; everything is subordinated to an almost phenomenological rendition of the Anasazi's tribal existence. More like an ethnographic field report than an art-lyric, this poem relies on an understood valuation that praises any social grouping that relates harmoniously to its physical environment. The ending of the poem blocks out in stark imagery the tribe's conditions of existence, and the ambiguity of reference equates the landscape with the tribe itself:

> trickling streams in hidden canyons
> under the cold rolling desert
>
> corn-basket   wide eyed
>   red baby
>   rock lip home,
>
> Anasazi

The "streams" can be the water that nourishes the Indians' crops or metaphorically the Indians themselves; the corn-basket can contain either the cereal that is the staple of their diet or their infants; their homes are made in and of the rock lip, the "clefts in the cliffs." The poem does not directly address any inner state or dramatize any emotional tension; it records and names rather than enacts or addresses its subject matter. It applies to us only insofar as we can see ourselves as products of, and preservers of, a physical environment.

Each of these three mediations helps to center Snyder's poetry and to support the other two; the mediation of poetic ends is, however, perhaps the most important. Snyder has talked about shamanistic songs and about the use of poetry and art that extends back to the Pleistocene era. Though the anthropological evidence is slim in these matters, there is a social use for poetry that extends beyond that of the art-lyric and the privatized reader. Some of this use function was once partly fulfilled by epic poetry, and today some have suggested it is fulfilled by advertising copywriters, who are the most successful, or at least widespread, mediators of our common dreams and our social reality. But Snyder returns to some of the functions of epic poetry while preempting the role of advertising. Here, from *The Old Ways,* is a description, written in

1975, of the new model of poetry Snyder envisions:

> We're just starting, in the last ten years here, to begin to make songs that will speak for plants, mountains, animals and children. When you see your first deer of the day you sing your salute to the deer, or your first red-wing blackbird—I saw one this morning! Such poetries will be created by us as we reinhabit this land with people who know they belong to it; for whom "primitive" is not a word that means past, but *primary,* and *future.* They will be created as we learn to see, region by region, how we live specifically (plant life!) in each place. The poems will leap out past the automobiles and TV sets of today into the vastness of the Milky Way (visible only when the electricity is turned down), to richen and humanize the scientific cosmologies. These poesies to come will help us learn to be people of knowledge in this universe in community with the other people—nonhuman included—brothers and sisters.

For me the key term here is "salute," for that is the mode of address in the Anasazi poem quoted above. Salutation involves recognition but also a well-wishing, a call to and for the forces of health and safety. Salutation, of course, also has a social dimension, and it communizes both its speaker and the person addressed. By this complex act of naming, well-wishing, and social placement, Snyder is less concerned with interior states than with environmental harmony. Learning to live "specifically . . . in each place" means knowing the plant life, knowing how the immediate physical environment makes available and uses its weather, soil, and other conditions to produce food, and this knowledge is necessary for the community to sustain its biological life as well as its cultural identity. Such localism and regionalism are not grounded in xenophobia or philistinism; rather they draw on and lead to a scientific understanding of the importance of place. Thus, Snyder's new poetry is as likely to include facts as it is to draw on so-called primitive or archaic knowledge and culture.

The second section of *Turtle Island* begins with a poem called **"Facts,"** and in its ten numbered prose sentences it moves as far from the model of the art-lyric as would seem possible. Here are some samples:

1. 92% of Japan's three million ton import of soybeans comes from the U.S.

2. The U.S. has 6% of the world's population; consumes 1/3 the energy annually consumed in the world.

    . . . . .

6. General Motors is bigger than Holland.

7. Nuclear energy is mainly subsidized with fossil fuels and barely yields net energy.

These formulations can be further understood, beyond their self-explanatory factuality, in the larger contexts of Snyder's recurrent concerns. But such an integration into a larger vision does not make **"Facts"** a good poem. Certainly no argument will convince a reader who expects or desires an art-lyric to like **"Facts."** Thomas Parkinson [in "The Theory and Practice of Gary Snyder," *Journal of Modern Literature,* Vol. 2, No. 3, Winter 1971] has identified two modes in Snyder, one that is "measured, dramatic, definite . . . in design, formal, and contemplative," and another that is "fluent, wise, witty, mediative and hortatory." For Parkinson the first mode is clearly the best, while the second produces work that is "prepoetic." *Prepoetic,* of course, would also describe most oral poetry, primitive chants, mantras, and other forms that, from the perspective of the art-lyric, lack the dramatic and contemplative features we associate with postromantic poetry. **"Facts"** can be seen as prepoetic not only because it lacks a dramatic or formal structure but because it clearly reads as prose and uses the language of mundane reality in nonstylized ways. But Snyder bids us to recall all the specificity of our world of prose; not every song can be a salutation, yet each poem can address a fact that informs the community about an essential aspect of its identity. By including the prepoetic (or the unpoetic, though this word has been largely outlawed since W. C. Williams objected to Wallace Stevens's use of it in describing Williams's poetry), Snyder at the very least implicitly acknowledges that a chant or song will not of itself alter social reality.

Another way to see **"Facts"** is to recognize that Snyder's ethics of responsibility does not get obscured by an ethics of ultimate ends, that the pressures and constraints of a very real social structure create an inescapable obligation to keep a vision alive with actual consequences. Another poem, from the first section of *Turtle Island,* is closer to the art-lyric tradition, and its dramatic, anecdotal structure might be seen by a programmatic avant-gardist as old-fashioned. This is **"I Went into the Maverick Bar,"** which vividly captures the despairing lack of social possibility that is a minor but important theme counterpointing Snyder's utopian vision.

> I went into the Maverick Bar
> In Farmington, New Mexico,
> And drank double shots of bourbon
> 　　　　backed with beer.
> My long hair was tucked up under a cap
>
> I'd left the earring in the car.
> Two cowboys did horseplay
> 　by the pool tables,
> A waitress asked us
> 　where are you from?
> a country-and-western band began to play
> "We don't smoke Marijuana in Muskokie"
> And with the next song,
> 　a couple began to dance.
>
> They held each other like in High School dances
> 　in the fifties;
> I recalled when I worked in the woods
> 　and the bars of Madras, Oregon.
> That short-haired joy and roughness—
> 　America—your stupidity.

> I could almost love you again.
> We left—onto the freeway shoulders—
> 　under the tough old stars—
> In the shadow of bluffs
> 　I came back to myself,
> To the real work, to
> "What is to be done."

The allusion to Lenin's revolutionary tract in the last line of the poem, along with the use of what is one of Snyder's key phrases, "the real work," poses this anecdote on an edge of ambiguity that in many ways resembles that prized in the art-lyric. Yet the ambiguity here—the unspecified commitment, the feelings of rejection and fear mingled with nostalgia and fondness—actually dissolves with the phrase "I came back to myself." Here Snyder realizes how far his values are from those of many of his ordinary fellow citizens, but he also realizes he must and will maintain those values. Unlike the art-lyric, which traditionally strives for an image of closure that focuses and yet heightens ambiguity, this poem closes with an opening vista of resolution to pursue an ethically formed, intellectually shaped goal.

The most important supposition of the art-lyric, namely that momentary emotion, heedless of larger consequences, has a self-justifying truth grounded in its very intensity, is here embodied in the flow of the verse. The dancing couple breaks in on the song celebrating repression, and this triggers the memories of work and class-affiliation, which are then shattered by an image impacted with contradictory emotional values ("short-haired joy and roughness"); this causes the speaker's consciousness to crest with a large abstract image, followed by the unconcealment of his emotional conflict. As a phrase, "I could almost love you again" refuses to indulge its lyric impulses, and instead the poem turns away from the immediately present community to a larger, less present, but more "real" commitment. So the verse, with its dashes and line breaks, not only enacts the process of discovery but also registers the speaker's self-denial and self-correction. The poem is about promise-within-failure, and it must take its recognition of the "common work of the tribe" away from the immediate source of its song.

Much of the tension present in **"I Went into the Maverick Bar"** pervades the whole of *Turtle Island.* The book is divided into four sections, three of poetry and one of prose. The sections of poetry—"Manzanita," "Magpie's Song," and "For the Children"—could respectively be considered a poetry of prayer and ritual, a poetry of instruction, and a poetry of hope. But this sort of classification will not hold firmly, and it is better to see each section as containing some poems from each of the three modes, though dominated by a specific set of concerns. Perhaps we can best see this organization, loose as it is, by looking closely at the shape and subjects of one section, nothing some exceptions, and then glancing at the other two sections. In the section called "Manzanita," for example, the first two poems, **"Anasazi"** and **"The Way West, Underground,"** are clearly salutations, the second being a poem about bears that recalls the Coyote poem that opened *The Back Country.* Then there is a poem that reads very like a doxology from a religious ritual: **"Without,"** which argues that singing is "the proof of the power within." This poem announces one of the volume's chief themes, that all energy must be internally graceful in order to be truly powerful. Harmony relies on the path having "no / end in itself" but rather recircling in both inner and outer realms. The poem is written in simple language, virtually without imagery, and draws on the philosophical bent we saw in *Regarding Wave* (for which it could serve as a fitting epigraph). Other poems in this section, namely **"The Great Mother," "No Matter, Never Mind,"** and **"Prayer for the Great Family,"** resemble **"Without,"** and together they can be read as Snyder's creation hymn and doxology. As a group they strongly influence the feeling of this section as one preoccupied with prayer and ritual. There is even an exorcism poem, **"Spel against Demons,"** which contributes to this feeling. In turn this feeling pervades a poem like **"The Bath,"** with its refrain of *"This is our body"* and its description of an ideal erotic and familial union among Snyder, his wife, and his sons, Kai and Gen. The exceptions to this dominant mood are poems such as **"I Went into the Maverick Bar," "Front Lines,"** and **"The Call of the Wild."** With a little ingenuity we could see these three poems as broken rituals, places where the "common work of the tribe" breaks down into alienation and mistrust. **"Front Lines"** recalls the poems in the "Logging" section of *Myths & Texts,* and here we see a

> bulldozer grinding and slobbering
> Sideslipping and belching on top of
> The skinned-up bodies of still-live bushes
> In the pay of a man
> From town.

Since Snyder has written this poem before, and generally better, the best reading of its inclusion here would argue that the problem of alienated labor has not gone away, and recognition of the problem is demanded even in a group of primarily celebratory poems.

The last two poems in the section contribute to the salutational atmosphere. The poem that lends the section its title, **"Manzanita"** is clearly a song of plant life that mediates between Coyote as a mythical figure and the plant itself, with its transformative power and its connections to the net of what Snyder calls "ethnobotany," the use of vegetative life in human culture. "The longer you look / The bigger they seem," says the last stanza of the poem, describing the manzanita bushes. This poem then concludes by citing the etymology of the plant's name, "little apples." The final poem, **"Charms,"** looks back to the mode of **"The Song of the Taste"** in *Regarding Wave,* but its subject is the "dreamlike perfection / of name-and-form" incorporated in female beauty. Snyder says that such beauty evokes "the Delight / at the heart of creation" and even avers that he could be "devastated and athirst with longing / for a lovely mare or lioness, or lady mouse." To the vegetable kingdom of **"Manzanita"** this poem exuberantly adds the animal kingdom, and where **"Manzanita"** is local and specific, **"Charms"** is universal; where the one celebrates the immediate physical environment,

the other makes a hymn to a utopian sense of "another world," the Deva Realm as Snyder calls it. Read together the two lyrics not only help to complete our sense of Snyder's new poetry but they also show how the reinhabitation of the land will be aided by songs of knowledge and community. In a sense both of these poems are postpolitical, since they speak to a consciousness built of a total harmonization of man with nature and man with man.

What separates Snyder from many traditional poets is his refusal to appropriate the nonhuman (or natural) realm as no more than a dramatic or illustrative backdrop to the "tension of human events." This is what gives Snyder a legitimate claim to be operating as much outside or beyond the contexts of traditional literary values as any other contemporary poet.

—Charles Molesworth

As a section, then, "Manzanita" is heavily weighted with poems that salute principles of harmony and growth, though there are also poems, such as **"Front Lines,"** that try to face up to the "Rot at the heart / In the sick fat veins of Amerika." The book's next section, "Magpie's Song," has several longer poems that seem concerned with conveying information, somewhat in the manner of Thoreau's natural historian who is content to let a fact flower into a truth. **"Mother Earth: Her Whales," "Straight-Creek—Great Burn,"** and **"The Hudsonian Curlew"** take delight in descriptions of natural processes and rhythms and seek little metaphoric resonance beyond the awareness of immanent order and shapeliness. Again, this feeling is determined in part by the section's opening poem, **"Facts,"** but it is also counterpointed by an ethical longing or predilection that arises in some of the shorter poems. I am thinking here of the conclusions to poems like **"Ethnobotany"** ("Taste all, and hand the knowledge down") and **"Up Branches of Duck River"** ("hold it close / give it all away"). These ethical principles are, as I have suggested, sometimes versions of a Buddhist-like wisdom and sometimes a practical field-knowledge. This particular mediation, between ultimate ends and local responses, has been a goal of Snyder's poetry all along, of course, though it seems to be more self-conscious and more aesthetically successful in *Turtle Island* than in, say, *Riprap.* In this section's closing poem, **"Magpie's Song,"** Snyder begins with a specific place and time and then alludes glancingly to the tutelary or totemic figure of Coyote, but here the creature is seen naturalistically. One might expect the following figure of the magpie to also operate in a naturalistic manner, but instead the poem ends with a message of hope and the poet's integration of and with natural forces and his own disciplined mind.

Six A.M.
Sat down on excavation gravel
by juniper and desert S.P. tracks
interstate 80 not far off
    between trucks
Coyotes—maybe three
    howling and yapping from a rise.

Magpie on a bough,
Tipped his head and said,

   "Here in the mind, brother
Turquoise blue.
I wouldn't fool you.
Smell the breeze
It came through all the trees
No need to fear

What's ahead
Snow up on the hills west
Will be there every year
be at rest.
A feather on the ground—
The wind sound—

Here in the Mind, Brother,
Turquoise Blue"

The magpie's instruction recalls the Rinzai sense of the mantras that are to be found in the patterns that result from natural forces: the blowing snow, the sounding wind. The poet has been fraternalized by this initiation or instruction scene, and the jeweled mind corresponds once more with the jeweled net of interconnected systems. The Amerindian West and the Buddhist East are brought together as the local and the cosmic open to one another.

The third and final section of poetry in **Turtle Island** is called "For the Children" and obviously deals with that new sense of the primitive that Snyder strives to establish, the primitive as both "primary" and "future." But the section also contains one of Snyder's boldest historical poems, **"What Happened Here Before,"** which moves, in a little over three pages, from 300 million years ago to the present. The *here* refers to the area around Snyder's homestead in the Sierra Nevadas, and the poem ends with the challenge: "WE SHALL SEE / WHO KNOWS / HOW TO BE." This challenge refers to the ethos of Snyder and the reinhabitants of Turtle Island, with their specific knowledge of county tax rates and local history as well as of their cosmic and prehistoric vistas, as opposed to the people who pilot the "military jets [that] head northwest, roaring, every dawn." Preceding this poem in the section is **"Tomorrow's Song,"** which begins with the radical notion that because America "never gave the mountains and rivers, / trees and animals, / a vote," it has "slowly lost its mandate." This is Snyder's most challenging, most "untraditional" notion, that animals and trees should be represented by government and accorded rights. Part of his hope for the preservation of the wilderness and natural resources, this notion may also be seen as Snyder's final mediation between his reverence for nature and his social-

ist-humanist political vision. Snyder says that "We look to the future with pleasure" since we can "get power within / grow strong on less," and in this new political-natural order he imagines a people living on Turtle Island who will be "gentle and innocent as wolves / as tricky as a prince." By inverting the Hobbesian sense of man as predatory and by playfully invoking Machiavelli's *The Prince*, Snyder redraws two of the Western political tradition's main metaphors and uses them to redefine what he means by being "At work and in our place." The real work is knowing what is to be done, but knowing also the ground—in all the senses of the word—on which it can be done. **"Tomorrow's Song"** is Snyder's salute to the future and contains one of his fullest descriptions of the ethos of Turtle Island.

The poem that lends its title to this last section of poetry, **"For the Children,"** concludes with a simple testament of faith, a gesture that catches up elements of salutation and instruction to form a final set of ethical principles.

In the next century
or the one beyond that
they say,
are valleys, pastures,
We can meet there in peace
if we make it.

To climb these coming crests
one word to you, to
you and your children:
Stay together
learn the flowers
go light

Political community, reverence for nature, and an ascetic gracefulness—all of Snyder's values are reflected in these three injunctions. The simplicity of the diction and the images recalls Blake, and the whole tradition of the literary ballad, in which a sophisticated poet adopts a simple framework to say something that is at once primitive and essential. Snyder's "one word" is the equivalent of what Kerouac called the "final lesson," and in each case the sublime is domesticated, brought home by bodily knowledge and mental harmony.

Taken together, and with the remarkable prose essays as well, the three sections of poetry in **Turtle Island** form a whole that advances Snyder's work well beyond the objectivist poetics of the early books and the political suppositions of *Earth House Hold*. Supplemented with the essays of *The Old Ways*, some of which are contemporary with **Turtle Island,** Snyder's vision is as full and distinctive as that of any of his contemporaries, including the slightly earlier generation of Lowell, Berryman, and Jarrell. Only Olson, I believe, compares with him in terms of a mythic imagination, and only Levertov has as broad and deep a political consciousness. But can Snyder claim for his art (or can his readers claim on his behalf) any authority other than that of the aesthetic realm? Take his notion that trees and animals should be represented in Congress. While this neatly ties together his ecological awareness and his political concerns, can the average reader see it as anything but an amusing conceit? Perhaps we can glimpse through this "literary" notion, this play with metaphors and contexts, a twitting of the serious tradition of representative democracy. Or can we better see it as a serious critique of representational government if we realize that banks and corporations command a share of representative power in our legislatures, and they are no more capable of speaking for themselves, without human mediation, than are trees and animals? If humans can find a way to define the rights of a corporation, why can they not do the same for the forest?

As for **Turtle Island** as a literary work, its language goes against the grain of several canonic tenets of modernism, and it flies in the face of once fashionable styles such as confessionalism. Like much genuinely innovative work, Snyder's poetry resorts to some quite ancient strategies and rhetorical gestures. Without the resplendent imagery of neo-surrealism, or the tight dramatic irony of academic poetry, or the display of an exacerbated sensibility, Snyder has reduced and yet enlarged the range of the lyric poem. But only a reader with at least a political awareness, if not a like-minded political will, can extensively respond to that range. Snyder has not solved the problem (how could he?) that animated so much of the theory of the autotelic art-lyric in the first place, namely, should not the extra-literary considerations of political or ethical belief be separated from the judgment of a poem on purely literary grounds? Snyder's work implicitly rejects the autotelic, formalist solution which said that only strictly structural and technical criteria should determine the worth of a poem, "as poem." This rejection is etched in the apparent lack of formal expertise in much of his poetry (though in fact his prosody can be quite sophisticated if judged from a nontraditional vantage point). Whether his language use can bring about a broad revival of, or even limited respect for, such forms as a poetry of salutation or instruction is an intriguing possibility. As early as the 1952 "Lookout's Journal" in *Earth House Hold,* Snyder asked:

> —If one wished to write poetry of nature, where an
> audience?
> Must come from the very conflict of an attempt to
> articulate
> the vision poetry and nature in our time.
> (reject the human; but the tension of
> human events, brutal and tragic, against
> a non-human background? like Jeffers?)

It is to the credit of **Turtle Island,** and the whole of Snyder's work, that he has not rejected the human, and indeed has avoided Jeffer's solution by refusing to subordinate the human to the nonhuman. On the other hand, what separates Snyder from many traditional poets is his refusal to appropriate the nonhuman (or natural) realm as no more than a dramatic or illustrative backdrop to the "tension of human events." This is what gives Snyder a legitimate claim to be operating as much outside or beyond the contexts of traditional literary values as any other contemporary poet. What **Turtle Island** finally mediates is the tension in mythical speculation that sees the world as supported and yet free-floating. Literature in such a mediation can try to be both self-grounded and ethically normative. But no modern poet would ever think such a dual burden could be easily lightened. Snyder says in the closing poem of **Turtle Island** that

> A Mind Poet
> Stays in the house.
> The house is empty
> And it has no walls.
> The poem
> Is seen from all sides,
> Everywhere,
> At once.

We have to realize the "house" is both the cosmos and the imagination, and that a poem whose perspective is panoptic and omnipresent can be understood both as an art-lyric poised on the vanishing point of self-reflective irony and as a cosmic hymn of all-embracing belief. Here Snyder's vision, or at least his desire for a healing vision, is as full as possible.

Robert Schultz and David Wyatt (essay date 1986)

SOURCE: "Gary Synder and The Curve of Return," in *The Virginia Quarterly Review,* Vol. 62, No. 4, Autumn, 1986, pp. 681-94.

[*In the following excerpt, Schultz and Wyatt, summarize Snyder's early work and provide in-depth coverage of* Axe Handles.]

Published when he was 29, Snyder's first book [**Axe Handles**] empties the mind of the "damned memories" that clog it in an ascesis that marks the beginning of his quest. In **Riprap** (1959) he turns from America toward the East and begins the motion out and away that will preoccupy him for 15 years. **Myths & Texts** (1960) promotes Snyder's emerging vision of process in a dialectical structure which resolves that all form is a momentary stay, "stresses that come into being each instant." In a world where "It's all falling or burning" the experience of place is only a fiction, and there can be therefore nothing to return to. **Mountains and Rivers Without End** (1965-) will contain 25 sections and is as yet unfinished. This may prove the major work of Snyder's career, though, as in Pound's *Cantos,* the poet can seem more committed to the theory than the poetry of this poem. The theory holds, in Snyder's words, that "every poem in **Mountains and Rivers** takes a different form and has a different strategy." A poem built upon the impulse of turning away from its own realized structures, **Mountains and Rivers** would seem a work about journeys, about "Passing / through." Its fascination however with what Snyder has called the "focal image" and with a realm above the Blue Sky also reaches toward permanence. These growing tensions as well as the poem's quality as a running rumination on all that Snyder holds dear place it at this point beyond any developmental model of Snyder's career.

The Back Country (1968) is in this argument the pivotal book, the one most openly engaged with Snyder's own history of turning. What begins as a reprise of *Riprap*—in **"Far West"** Snyder amasses his reasons for moving and forgetting—proceeds by discovering an opposing impulse to return and remember. A poem like **"Dodger Point Lookout"** bears comparison to "Tintern Abbey" in its acceptance of meaning as a function of elapsed time. The return of the poet to a beloved spot five years later "brings it all back," and he admits that the conserving power of memory is what keeps him "sane."

Regarding Wave (1970) shores up the position gained in *The Back Country* by valorizing a new and conserving pattern—the wave—capable of storing and releasing the energy which Snyder had earlier discovered in the stream. A book about **"What's Meant by Here,"** *Turtle Island* (1974) registers Snyder's emerging commitment to a structure that stays in place. Homesteading replaces hitchhiking as the privileged human activity as Snyder's act of settlement in California expands into a sense of stewardship over the entire planet.

This rapid summary brings us back to *Axe Handles,* Snyder's first book of poems in nearly a decade and one in which he celebrates the whim and wisdom of middle age. In *Axe Handles* Snyder begins with work around the house and ends with journeys. Travel is now seen as the venturing out from a hearth, and thus the controlling metaphors ("Loops" and "Nets") are of structures that return or contain.

Axe Handles is divided into three parts, "Loops," "Little Songs for Gaia," and finally "Nets," which itself contains four sections. At first glance, the book may seem too intricate or arbitrary in its structure, but with further reading sections and subsections reveal important groupings of Snyder's current concerns. The book follows the poet's movement of mind as he attempts to discover a coherence among commitments that are personal, familial, and cultural in scope.

"True Night," the book's central poem and the concluding poem of the first section, most succinctly dramatizes the choice Snyder has made in favor of returning and settling. But the poems which surround it show the full content of the poet's choice. *Axe Handles* is a declaration of affiliations to an ideal of "home," an ideal that has grown in Snyder's imagination to include the full range of a life's attachments, from the most personal and local to the most public and distant. At the personal level, Snyder takes firm possession of his own biography, noting memories which reveal patterns of self-definition (**"Look Back," "Soy Sauce," "Delicate Criss-crossing Beetle Trails Left in the Sand"**). He writes of family and community with ideals of mutual support and teaching (**"Changing Diapers," "Painting the North San Juan School"**). He writes about the possibilities and limitations of government (**"Talking Late with the Governor about the Budget"**). He returns again and again to the mooring certainties of hard physical labor (**"Working on the '58 Willys Pickup," "Getting in the Wood"**). And, as ever, he writes with great

attention to a natural order seen through the particularities of his home region (the book is dedicated "To San Juan Ridge").

Memory, family, community, teaching, government, and natural process: the subjects of *Axe Handles* necessarily involve Snyder in time and recurrence. The poet who began by relishing the obliterating sense of timelessness as he peered down alone through miles of air from Sourdough Lookout now gives special emphasis to the loops of cultural transmission, and *Axe Handles* begins with a coincidence which dramatizes for Snyder the "craft of culture." His son has asked for a hatchet handle, and while carving it with an axe Snyder remembers with a shock of recognition the Chinese phrase, "When making an axe handle the pattern is not far off." The lesson, first read in Ezra Pound and then studied again under Snyder's Japanese teacher, Chen, is now lived by the poet, and he writes:

> . . . I see: Pound was an axe,
> Chen was an axe, I am an axe
> And my son a handle, soon
> To be shaping again, model
> And tool, craft of culture,
> How we go on.

The book's second poem reinforces the theme, as the spirit of Lew Welch returns from the dead to tell Snyder: ". . . teach the children about the cycles. / The life cycles. All the other cycles. / That's what it's all about, and it's all forgot." And indeed, subsequent poems deal with integrities created by recurrence: the water cycle; the life cycle of a Douglas fir; loops of personal memory that illuminate present moments; and a pilgrimage of return to Japan to renew ties with Masa's family and, incidentally, to crisscross the path of Snyder's own earlier travels. . . .

Imbued with a sense of nature's rigor, Snyder has chosen to live apart from what he takes to be the extravagance of his contemporaries. He frets comically about the $3.50 worth of kerosene required to soak his fence posts and wonders at the amount of fuel burned in displays of power by air defense jets. His alarm at our civilization's utter dependence upon a diminishing oil supply, in fact, arises in no fewer than five poems, making it one of the book's most insistent concerns. In **"Alaska"** he describes a trip to the oil pipeline, where he read the question, "Where will it all end?" spray-painted on the elevated tube. Later, dozing with his colleagues in a small plane, he suddenly noticed out the window "the mountains / Soaring higher yet, and quite awake."

The eerie presence of those mountains, immense and watchful, looms for Snyder as a premonition of inevitable retribution. According to the poet's sense of natural law, unnatural acts call forward inevitable consequences, and in several poems Snyder sounds a note of judgment. In **"Money Goes Upstream,"** he is in a lecture hall, daydreaming about greed and corruption. Money, he thinks, is "an odd force . . . in the world / *Not* a power / That seeks to own the source." It behaves unnaturally—"It dazzles and it slips us by. / It swims upstream." Therefore, those who place it too near the center of their lives become unmoored, possessed. Against this insidious influence Snyder poses his own ability to summon the corrective presence of nature:

> I can smell the grass, feel the stones with bare feet
>   though I sit here shod and clothed
>   with all the people. That's my power.

This power is two-fold: Snyder's firsthand knowledge of nature and its sufficiencies inoculates him from avarice, and his ability to summon what is not present keeps him ever close to the natural law from which he borrows his authority.

Snyder could hardly have traveled farther from his early absorption with moments of pure vision or sensation to the instinct for teaching—and judgment—so apparent in *Axe Handles.* The former experience is solitary and held out of time by its novelty and intensity, while "passing on" is communal and temporal. yet the poet still holds that our most fundamental knowledge is discovered in moments of experience which stand out of time. And, as if to reaffirm this fact, Snyder includes at the center of *Axe Handles* a sequence of lyrics which presents a gallery of such moments.

"Little Songs for Gaia," issued in an earlier version as a Copper Canyon Press chapbook (1979), is addressed to the earth goddess of Greek mythology. In it Snyder descends from the more general point of view which allows him to be discursive elsewhere in the book to write here with an unmixed particularity. The ecological point of view expressed in *Axe Handles* has grown out of a thousand individual experiences, and here Snyder reestablishes contact, zooming down to the thing, itself:

> Red soil—blue sky—white cloud—grainy granite,
>   and
> Twenty thousand mountain miles of manzanita.
>   Some beautiful tiny manzanita
>   I saw a single, perfect, lovely,
>   manzanita
>   Ha.

Snyder, like Antaeus, renews his strength by touching ground, and that is what he does in this middle section, absorbed in description of his home region and his daily domestic life.

Elsewhere in the book readers may sometimes balk at Snyder's prose-like rhythms, which often conform only to the poet's clipped, trochaic manner of speech. But "Little Songs for Gaia" features some of the most accomplished lyric writing of Snyder's career whether he is presenting a dream of corn goddesses or a deer hit by a car:

> Dead doe lying in the rain
>
>   on the shoulder
>   in the gravel

> I see your stiff leg
>
>   in the headlights
>   by the roadside
>
> Dead doe lying in the rain

The circularity of this brief lyric fixes our attention, beginning and end, on the unfortunate deer, with the assonance of the spondee, "Dead doe," hammering home the image. In between, the four prepositional phrases are exactly parallel in rhythm, relentlessly locating the dead animal. And in between them, the kernel sentence, "I see your stiff leg," particularizes the doe efficiently and with poignance.

Elsewhere, Snyder even uses end rhyme to good effect:

> Log trucks go by at four in the morning
>   as we roll in our sleeping bags
>   dreaming of health.
> The log trucks remind us,
>   as we think, dream and play
>
> Of the world that is carried away.

The surprise of the closural rhyme, which suddenly links the family's dreams and play with eventual loss, is largely responsible for the power of this brief lyric. Contributing to the effect, three consecutive anapests speed the final line, creating a sense of the poet's world quickly slipping away.

"Little Songs for Gaia" is made of glimpses—heightened moments of perception or feeling communicating an intimacy of contact with things which spices and sustains the life of the poet. Everywhere in this section Snyder is intent upon the particular and absorbed in the moment, attending to everything as to the flickers' call: "THIS! / THIS! / THIS! / in the cool pine breeze."

Snyder moves back from knowing to doing in the book's final section, "Nets," in which each of the four clusters of poems forms a rather loosely organized Poundian "ideogram." Taken together, these four clusters portray the "nets" of contemplation and activity in which Snyder is currently enmeshed.

The first, a bridge from the Gaia sequence, presents Snyder active and reverent in a natural world that flashes glimpses of deity. Walking a Yellowstone meadow, for instance, he observes its graceful creatures and ambiguously records the perception of a goddess-like presence:

> And I saw: the turn of the head, the glance of the
>   eye, each gesture, each lift and stamp
>
> Of your high-arched feet.

Part II of "Nets" probes the possibilities and shortcomings of government. Snyder is skeptical (he seems to long for a more expansive governmental perspective when he notes that "The great pines on the Capitol grounds [in Sacramento] / Are less than a century old"), but he is willing to participate, and former California governor Jerry Brown, who appointed Snyder to the state Arts Council, is a sympathetic character in the book. Adding another piece of the cultural puzzle, part III juxtaposes "civilization" with more primitive ways of life, marking chiefly their differing relationships to the ecosystems which support them. . . .

The allegiances pledged in **Axe Handles** are many—to family, community, culture, and planet. And to make such pledges Snyder has turned considerably from his earlier conception of the world as "all change, in thoughts, / As well as things" (**"Riprap"**). Within this earlier view, the poet's only recourse was to attempt to fix in words moments plucked out of the careering flux.

In *Axe Handles* there are many heightened moments seized out of time by language, but these are now seen to take their place within a broader continuity. Snyder still prizes moments when the self loses itself entirely in sensation, and a poem like **"Getting in the Wood"** shows how that early experience of transcendence survives into its new context. This passage in mid-poem contains no subject because the self is utterly absorbed in its work:

> The lean and heave on the peavey
> that breaks free the last of a bucked
>   three-foot round,
>   it lies flat on smashed oaklings—

Departing from the usual subject-predicate structure, Snyder's noun phrase presents only the effort itself and the object worked upon, with internal rhyme and skillfully managed rhythms communicating the strain of the job. The poet is happily lost in what he elsewhere calls the "relentless clarity at the heart of work," an experience which is for Snyder virtually a kind of meditation. At peace in his work, his attention is enthralled by "Wedge and sledge, peavey and maul, / little axe, canteen, piggy-back can / of saw-mix gas and oil for the chain, / knapsack of files and goggles and rags."

Snyder could be writing about his early logging days in a poem like this, which captures in words the grit and strain of sensation. But the distance he has traveled since those early days is revealed in the final stanza, in which the task at hand is shown to be a collective one, and in which Snyder emphasizes the continuities of family and community which the work helps to develop:

> the young men throw splits on the piles
> bodies hardening, learning the pace
> and the smell of tools from this delve
> in the winter
> death-topple of elderly oak.

This is a community task, with the young men learning and hardening to the jobs they will inherit when their elders pass, like the toppled oak. Here is the sense of continuity and cultural transmission which Snyder has acquired as a husband, father, and homesteader, a sense

which has changed him over the course of his career from *dharma* hitchhiker to domestic visionary.

Jody Norton (essay date 1987)

SOURCE: "The Importance of Nothing: Absence and its Origins in the Poetry of Gary Synder," in *Contemporary Literature,* Vol. XXVIII, No. 1, Spring, 1987, pp. 41-66.

[*In the excerpt below, Norton discusses Snyder's use of imagery.*]

In his early wilderness poetry, Gary Snyder builds absences into the structure, imagery, and syntax of his texts in order to inscribe the essential Zen Buddhist perception of the identity of *sunyata* (Emptiness) and *tathata* (suchness, objective reality) in the form itself of each poem.

In the West, we are accustomed to conceiving the world dualistically. We define both material objects and ideas in terms of binary oppositions (rough/smooth, good/evil). We oppose the real to the ideal, valorizing one at the expense of the other or, with Plato, redefining the one *as* the other. Buddhism subverts such definitional projects by questioning the capacity of abstract thought to comprehend or articulate reality in any except misleading ways. Mind (Oneness), being inseparable from itself, cannot be understood in dualistic terms (Absolute/conditional, for example).

Gary Snyder's poems sheer away from abstractions, delineating the material world boldly in series of concrete images. Matter-of-fact as they appear, however, Snyder's lyrics depend as much on what they omit as on what they include. Honeycombing his poems with syntactical and structural ellipses, and refusing to fully determine his imagery, Snyder seeks to disrupt our complacent relation to our own experience by short-circuiting our customary ways of dividing and conquering that experience, the chief of which is language.

Grammars, books on usage, manuals of style, and the like seek to make language systematic and reasonable. When conventionally required elements are omitted from linguistic structures, be these structures lines, sentences, or poetic forms, they become unreasonable, and their meanings are consequently problematized. But Snyder's procedures are aimed at more than merely confounding the understanding. His purpose is to use the grammatical, syntactical, and semantic spaces that permeate even language, the model for all structuralist enterprises, to make possible a kind of immediate knowing that language is not theoretically designed to produce.

Because language must make provisional use of names, Zen Buddhist teachings refer to an ultimate reality, by one word or another, in attempting to help the student of Zen to his own direct spiritual experience. But such words do not mean, in the ordinary sense, because the "meaning" they intend escapes enclosure within any particular term. To speak of the One as though it were an entity among other entities is precisely (and wrongly) to *constitute* it as such an entity. Snyder thus avoids any explicit reference to an Absolute.

> **Never fully present, Snyder's poems enable, rather than provide, an indefinite number of actualizations—actualizations that the reader can produce only by refusing to be merely the receiver of the text.**
>
> —*Jody Norton*

By eliding the solitary speaker as well as the One in many of his poems, Snyder follows Buddhism in tacitly asserting the illusory nature of the self. Elision of the subject is often accompanied by a replacement of verbs with verbals. Use of these two forms of ellipsis enables the poet to present activity not in terms of an "I" who takes action but simply as action that is taking place.

Wishing, however, to avoid simply substituting an inverted hierarchy for the one he seeks to put in question (nothingness for objective reality, let us say, or Absence for Presence), Snyder fills his poems with palpable natural imagery—earth, plants, animals—which is strongly sensuous but at the same time generic in its conception. This generalization of imagery accomplishes two ends: it denies the reality of individuation (the proper) without refusing particularity (the common), and it implies that the embodied experience of the poem is neither personally nor historically unique.

Never fully present, Snyder's poems enable, rather than provide, an indefinite number of actualizations—actualizations that the reader can produce only by refusing to be merely the receiver of the text. The poems demand that their reader exceed rational and discursive approaches and engage his imagination, and ultimately his intuition, actively in the completion of the poetic experience.

Snyder's poetry incorporates, in addition to the Buddhist (non)conception of the Void, which constitutes its unstated ontological ground, numerous elements of the poetics and stylistic procedures of the shih poetry of T'ang Dynasty China and the Japanese haiku. Snyder combines these assumptions and practices with his own experience, imagination, and voice to compose a characteristic elliptical mode, whose aim is to make form not an extension, but an expression, of content.

Julie Martin (essay date 1987)

SOURCE: "The Pattern Which Connects: Metaphor in Gary Snyder's Later Poetry," in *Western American Literature:*

Quarterly Journal of the Western Literature Association, Vol. XXII, No. 2, Summer, 1987, pp. 99-123.

[*In the following excerpt, Martin uses feminist theory to analyze Snyder's complex metaphors.*]

With one or two exceptions, critical readings of Gary Snyder's poetry have argued that he makes little use of metaphor. On this point critics have taken their lead from Thomas Parkinson, whose comments in 1968 seem to have set the trend for many later readers ["The Poetry of Gary Snyder," *Southern Review,* Vol. 4]. Following Parkinson's emphasis there have been several very useful commentaries which I do not wish to question here. The problem with this kind of analysis is, however, that it tends to overlook the appearance in the poetry of structures which I can only term metaphoric. This is particularly clear in the later poetry, which has so far received rather scant critical attention.

Robert Kern has shown how Snyder's use of syntax and open forms is intrinsic to the "ecological consciousness" which the poetry proposes. My reading suggests that the use of metaphoric structures is as important in this respect. The view which Snyder once rather whimsically called the "Avatamsaka ("Power Wreath") jewelled-net-interpenetration-ecological-systems-emptiness-conciousness", (*The Old Ways*), is surely his most significant contribution to the reconciliation of personal, political and religious models. And in the later poetry this view of things is often most clearly expressed by means of metaphoric structures.

The Avatamsaka model has been discussed at some length—what has been variously called Snyder's "ecological consciousness," or his idea of "interbirth," "True Communionism," and so on. But it is still useful to identify its main features. In a paper given at the Ethnopoetics conference in 1975, Snyder made what I consider to be his most intriguing comment on the subject:

> From the standpoint of the 70's and 80's it serves us well to consider how we relate to those objects we take to be outside ourselves—non-human, non-intelligent, or whatever.

The phrase "objects we take to be outside ourselves" refers here to everything which, in an epistemology of oppositional relations, is habitually defined as "other." From the position of phallocentric culture then, this has meant: nature, women, "other" races, animals, the body, the "primitive," etc. The corollary of this sort of division is an idea of the individual (person, species, community, etc.) as being a self-contained unit, existing in opposition to other such entities.

Working as I do in apartheid South Africa, one is confronted every day with some of the political implications of this sort of binarism. In Snyder's work this aspect is an important one, but his analysis does not originate in a study of ideology. His critique of oppositional epistemology derives largely from his studies in ecology, systems biology and Buddhism. These disciplines also propose an alternative view which informs the poetry. Recent work in ecology and biology has shown that the relation of an individual organism to its environment is that of one open system to another, and that to conceptualize these systems as being "closed," in competition, or in opposition to each other, is to falsify the necessary exchange between them. Buddhism similarly stresses the deficiency of a dualist model in which the skin-bound observer is separated from a world to which s/he stands in opposition. . . .

One of Snyder's earliest metaphors for this pattern of interdependence is the "vast 'jewelled net'" in which all are "interborn," an image from the Avatamasaka sutra of Hua-Yen Buddhism. His later work proposes further metaphors (the Great Family, the goddesses Vak and Gaia, etc.) but the same emphasis remains.

[Charles] Altieri has called the concept of interbirth or Communionism Snyder's fundamental religious insight [*Enlarging the Temple,* 1979]. [Charles] Molesworth goes a step further when he examines it as an innovative political term [in *Gary Snyder's Vision,* 1983]. This seems more accurate, since for Snyder the religious, political and personal are not meaningfully separable domains: each informs the other. In *Earth House Hold* he criticized the "ultimately uncompassionate and destructive" tendency of institutional Buddhism to "ignore the inequalities and tyrannies of whatever political system it found itself under." In rejecting an epistemology of binary oppositions, the poetry and prose question both some of the fundamental assumptions of Western metaphysics and their ideological manifestations. Snyder recognizes in the epistemological error which opposes "self" and "other" an implicit hierarchy with "us" at the top. This allows for the systematic exploitation of "other" for whatever gains, and has (in religious terms) frequently led to the denigration of physical, material, worldly things, in favor of what is "otherworldly." Like several other writers, Snyder considers this error to be at the root of the present ecological crisis. Consequently his work seeks to articulate a metaperspective on dualistic oppositions: what might be called a systems view.

In this essay I will also call it a *metaphoric view* of things. However, in order to do so I must define some terminology. "Metaphor" as it is ordinarily understood denotes a transfer of meaning from one semantic domain to another. This is the first sense in which I will use the term. As several critics have pointed out, this transfer indicates a relation of, say, "tenor" and "vehicle" that seems inappropriate to the state of undifferentiated or ecological consciousness that many of Snyder's poems seek to evoke. . . .

Other critics have made similar comments about Snyder's "distrust" of metaphor (for example Altieri and [Dan] McLeod). It should be clear that he has good reason to be wary of the kind of metaphoric transfer that appears in the writings of many Western mystics, and of the metaphors and symbols characteristic of so much Romantic and Modern poetry. . . .

Regarding Wave is probably Snyder's most successful articulation of the theme of interdependence. As the syntactically ambiguous title suggests, the collection is directly concerned with the potentially revolutionary significance of experiencing oneself as a participant in a dynamic universe. Both structurally and thematically the book reflects Snyder's preoccupation with the goddess Vak who becomes the focusing metaphor.

In *The Old Ways* Snyder alludes to the tradition of Sanscrit poetics, according to which poetry originates in the sound of running water and the wind in the trees. According to this idea, human language (and particularly the poet's use of voice) derives from "the sense of the universe as fundamentally sound and song," that is, from an experience of Voice. This Voice is the goddess Vak (or Sarasvati, "the flowing one"). She is associated with rhythmic pattern, and is described as "the universe itself as energy, the energy of which all sub-energies are born." As the flyleaf of *Regarding Wave* suggests, the linking of energy, sound and the feminine which Vak represents is precisely what Snyder is aiming for in the collection. The poetry is presented as the vehicle of a vision of the community or interdependence of all phenomena. According to this all things are perceived in terms of their participation in Vak—that is, in energy (what I call here "waveness") and sound ("voice"). This view is articulated most clearly in the poems **"Wave"** and **"Regarding Wave"** which frame the seminal first three sections of the book, Regarding Wave I, II and III.

Snyder's first discussion of Vak appears in the essay "Poetry and the Primitive" in *Earth House Hold,* where "Voice" is presented as one of the Buddhist Three Mysteries. The section "The Voice as a Girl" emphasizes the significance of the goddess Vak with respect to the notion of "woman as nature the field for experiencing the universe as sacramental." In *Regarding Wave* the correspondence of "woman" and "nature"—Vak and the pattern of interpenetrating energies—is made repeatedly.

This emphasis centers on the correspondence of "wave . . . wife" in the opening poem, **"Wave,"** which presents the mind's apprehension of pattern or "waveness." The poem is, in [Roman] Jakobson's terms, a strikingly metaphoric piece. Appropriately, the structure serves to convey the quality of this pattern and the interrelatedness of phenomena which it implies, as well as the orientation of the perceiver that this order of experience requires. Like many of the others in *Regarding Wave* this poem is a celebration, in this case a celebration of the mind's interaction with the patterned texture of the world—"those objects we take to be outside ourselves." Playing with the phonetic expectations set up by the core word ("wave"), the poem proposes the correspondences that may be perceived to exist, at many levels, between apparently separate natural phenomena. The final climactic invocation calls for the speaker to be caught and thrown out of the narrow selfhood, his imaginary autonomy, into the "dancing grain" of the world, the pattern of the "wave." Significantly, the pattern dances, not only in "things" out there, but in the mind of the poet as well. In this way, the last two lines make explicit the relative status of mind and objects that the poem proposes. The corollary of perceiving the waveness of all phenomena is both a recognition of their interrelatedness, and a sense that the human "I" is also a participant in this environment.

***Regarding Wave* is probably Snyder's most successful articulation of the theme of interdependence. As the syntactically ambiguous title suggests, the collection is directly concerned with the potentially revolutionary significance of experiencing oneself as a participant in a dynamic universe.**

—*Julie Martin*

The significance of these aspects of the poem becomes clear when it is read in the context of the rest of the collection. For the poems that follow, **"Wave"** functions as the primary source of imagery and subject matter, the association of the feminine with water, the sea and rhythmic process being made repeatedly. The purpose of this is, on the one hand, to confirm the connection of "wife," the maternal sea, with energy and voice, and consequently with fertility and creation. At the same time, the possibility of sexual union with the feminine "other" reveals, metaphorically, the possible interpenetration of mind and Mind, the voice of the poet and the Voice of the Goddess which the concluding lines of **"Wave"** suggest. It is therefore appropriate that the central experiences in *Regarding Wave* should be those of love-making, marriage, conception and birth, and that these should take place in a non-hierarchic island community.

The thematic cohesion of the collection makes for a structure that is not accounted for by what is usually written about Snyder's work, although some of his own statements are very explicit. In *The Real World* he compares the structure of his poetry with that of the raga and tala in Indian music:

> These give me a model, analogous in some senses to my own work, of a longer range sense of structuring with improvisatory possibilities taking place on a foundation of a certain steadiness that runs through it. So one poem has of itself the periodicity of a line, one structuring, and a number of poems to get a scene together will form a construct that is like one whole melodic thing. The model that underlies that also is the sense of the melodic phrase as dominating the poetic structure.

Regarding Wave is the clearest example of this sort of construct, and appropriately so, given its major concerns. The structure remarkably resembles that of a piece of music composed of repetitions around a single note or theme. This prevalence of parallels, contrasts and repetitions (phonetic, syntactic, lexical) makes it in Jakobson's terms a highly metaphoric document: the elements are usually combined by virtue of their similarity.

I describe the collection as a single document deliberately. While several poems (such as **"Wave," "Seed Pods,"** etc.) are certainly metaphoric in this way, patterning of this kind is more marked across the collection as a whole. This means that a single poem simply cannot function fully as a separable, discrete item, since the "longer range sense of structuring" demands that it be read in relation to the others to which it is connected. Each poem (like a living organism) is necessarily an "open system." Particularly with respect to the use of metaphor, the single poem is not the main focus, as this comment from Snyder asserts [in a letter dated August 20, 1984]:

> As for metaphor, the definition (and use) of metaphor can be vastly shrunk or expanded. Almost all the poems in *Regarding Wave* respond to a subtle underlying thematic metaphor. The same for all my other books. Metaphor is not trotted out as a short term device section by section in poems but amounts to subtle controlling imagery that binds whole cycles of poems together.

After **"Wave,"** the most obvious poem for discussion is **"Regarding Wave."** Snyder's frequent claim that a text should be a "scoring" for an oral performance is particularly applicable to a poem such as this, being as it is an account of "Voice." A text that is metaphorically cohesive as this one (or **"Wave"**) is, functions very much like a piece of music in which themes are repeated and varied. However it is only when the two poems are considered together (the second informed equally by the connections that have been established in the intervening poems) that their full sense begins to appear. . . .

In the earlier poem Snyder examined the texture of natural objects and the sense of correspondence this evokes. The focus is close, the attention to the "dancing grain" suggesting the flow of matter at a molecular level. This is reversed in **"Regarding Wave."** The field of vision has widened. The "flow" is now perceived on an extended scale, recalling the earlier poetry and its similarity to Chinese landscape painting. Nevertheless the concerns of the two poems, the acts of mind they represent, are very similar. The later poem serves to establish that the relations in **"Wave"** remain: after the climactic central events (the birth of Kai and the new life this brings) "The Voice / is a wife / to // him still." In order to be understood this sentence draws on the correspondences between "wave" and "wife" that the first poem establishes and subsequent poems reinforce. This information serves to clarify the reference to "wave" in the title of a poem ostensibly concerned with "Voice."

The appended parallel reading of the two poems reveals their structural, phonetic, lexical, thematic correspondences at a glance. It should be clear that the coherence of each depends on its relation to the other. In framing the "Regarding Wave" sections of the book, these poems inform the others, defining the patterns according to which they are to be read. The effect of this metaphoric patterning is a linguistic mimesis of a metaphoric view of things—that is, mimesis of the omnipresent patterned grain—with which the poems are concerned. Similarly, the interdependence which attention to grain and wave reveals is reflected in the open system which the poems together comprise. However, instead of being in any sense distinct from, or in opposition to, nature (which mimesis would usually imply), the mind which makes these linguistic patterns, and the voice which sings the songs, are seen as participants in a Voice and a Pattern that includes this mind, these poems, and yet goes beyond them.

So far I have used terms such as "framing," "open system" and "cohesion" without comment. Both poems exhibit a highly cohesive verbal structure, which nevertheless resists closure. By the most inconclusive of conclusions Snyder seeks in each case to extend the experience of reading the poem into a deeper interaction with "those things we take to be outside ourselves," and therefore with Self, Vak, Mind. The speaker's invocation at the end of **"Wave"** is extended in **"Regarding Wave"** in the linguistically more dramatic transition from English to mantra. . . .

It should be sufficient here to note that mantra is often described as the closest human articulation of mystic sound—Snyder's "shimmering bell / through all." In concluding a poem (and a cycle of poems) in this way, Snyder is doing something rather unusual, which is at the same time very appropriate. Since the function of a mantra is precisely the dissolution of dualistic oppositions, the use of mantra in the poem invites the reader to participate, not in ideas *about* Vak, the interdependence of "self" and "universe," but rather in direct experience of these.

If the encounter with wilderness in Snyder's earlier poems signified on the intrapsychic level meeting with unconscious areas of the self, then making love with the feminine represents another aspect of the same process:

> As Vak is wife to Brahma . . . so the voice, in everyone, is the mirror of his deepest self.

In **Regarding Wave,** however, because the voice-wave-wife is experienced as permeating all phenomena, the epiphany is not only an intrapsychic event. It involves rather "becoming one" with whatever is considered to be *outside* the self: a participatory universe. In Buddhist terms, the integration of self implies reintegration into Self, interpenetration with that "other" from which one is never really separable.

The highly orchestrated first three sections of the collection are followed by poems that are very different in structure, although they are also concerned with patterns of metaphoric correspondence. The poems in "Long Hair" involve a movement outwards from the climactic personal intensity of those in "Regarding Wave." The first, **"Revolution in the Revolution in the Revolution"** proposes an essential connection between interbirth and revolutionary consciousness, at the center of which are the mantric

"seed syllables" of the previous poem. By connecting the relations that have already been established between Vak (waveness, energy, power) and the rather different expectations one is likely to have about the power of revolutionary liberation, the concluding lines suggest that their origin is, in an important sense, the same:

> & POWER
> comes out of the seed-syllables of mantras

Given its position in the sequence of the collection, the transvaluation of both religious and political terminology that the poem explores is significant. The linguistic fusion in "True Communionism" provides an important context for the earlier descriptions of "personal" epiphany.

In the poems that follow, grain and wave are recalled, their repetition remaining the basis of the metaphoric structure. But since the "Regarding Wave" poems explicitly celebrated a sense of the personal correspondence with these, such correspondences are now implicit. It seems to be enough to describe the **"Running Water Music"** itself:

> Clear running stream
>   clear running stream
>
> Your water is light
>   to my mouth.
> And a light to my dry body
>
>   your flowing
> Music,
>   in my ears. free,
>
> Flowing free!
> With you
>   in me.

The poems in "Target Practice," the final section of *Regarding Wave,* are not haiku, but they do show the apparently effortless condensation that is characteristic of the form, and for the same reasons. . . .

Like much of Snyder's early poetry and its Oriental models, these poems depict a reunion with "those things we take to be outside ourselves." As in other Zen poems, this is done by pointing without explanation at the material thing itself and so reducing the opposition of subject-object. In this collection, however, the reading of these brief metonymic pieces is informed by the more extended descriptions of intensely perceived correspondences in the poems that have preceded them. Given the sense of interdependence of things which the other poems in the collection suggest—with metaphoric patternings, repetitions, parallels—it is now enough to return with delight to any apparently insignificant fragment. . . .

Following *Regarding Wave, Turtle Island* makes explicit the political implications of the idea of sacramental interdependence, or the interpenetration of the self, or individual organism, and the community of objects ostensibly external to it. In contrast with the recurrent correspondence of wave-wife, the central image here is of the Earth as Mother, and the enormity of her destruction by patriarchal-technological culture. The concerns are, nevertheless, a continuation of the earlier ones. The present ecological crisis is shown to be a direct consequence of "otherworldly" (and often patriarchal) metaphysics, and the Cartesian oppositions with which these are linked. Assuming that religious or mystical positions may not be ideologically neutral, Snyder examines the political meaning of religious doctrines, in particular those which promote potentially exploitative attitudes towards whatever is conceived as "other."

With respect to form, *Turtle Island* is obviously very different from the metaphorically patterned *Regarding Wave.* It also differs from Snyder's early poetry, with its tendency to avoid metaphor and symbol. Here the political, spiritual, personal concerns of the poetry are informed by several important metaphors, what Altieri would probably call "myths." These include "Amerika," "Turtle Island" and "the Great Family," and involve repeated references to a symbolic feminine. As the Introductory Note indicates, the book's title works as a focusing metaphor. In identifying the turtle with the serpent-of-eternity, Snyder establishes from the beginning its identity with primal creative energy that precedes differentiation: the ouroboros biting its tail.

> The poems speak of place, and the energy-pathways that sustain life. Each living being is a swirl in the flow, a formal turbulence, a "song." The land, the planet itself, is also a living being—at another pace.

The relation established here between the turtle, "place" and "energy-pathways" is significant. Whereas in *Regarding Wave* the energy of Vak is omnipresent, vibrating in "every hill," "every leaf," *Turtle Island* suggests that this resource is largely hidden, the energy buried within the land, beneath the recent accretions of civilized culture. In proposing ways of access to this buried power, the poems attempt to regain those aspects of experience that Western culture has tended to deny. In this context, "a sense of place" means being "grounded" to the maternal Earth, and perception of the complex interdependencies of things involves a sense of oneself as being part of her family. . . .

In the nine years between the publication of *Turtle Island* and that of *Axe Handles,* Snyder seems to have evolved a style that is not as vulnerable to the kinds of critical objection which the earlier collection raised. Like *Regarding Wave,* then, this collection is more obviously homogeneous than *Turtle Island.* However, in contrast with the high degree of metaphoric patterning that was evident in the former, many of the poems in *Axe Handles* recall Snyder's earliest poetry, through the use of metonymy. They are to this extent, like those that Kern discussed, "focused metonymically on things contiguous in the world, and not on language in the poem" ["Recipes, Catalogues, Open Form Poetics," *Contemporary Literature,* Vol. 18, No. 2, 1977]. Clear examples of this are poems such as **"Fence Posts," "So Old"** and **"Removing the Plate of the Pump on the Hydraulic System of the Backhoe."**

However, this tendency is not uniform, and the informing structure of the book as a whole is metaphoric. The title, cover picture ("The Snow Goddess") and the suggestive naming of the book's three sections ("Loops," "Gaia," "Nets") make this clear. These function as the controlling metaphors which define the context in which the "metonymic" poems are to be read. More importantly, these are very explicit metaphors for a perception of the world and of history which is itself (in Jakobson's terms) metaphoric. Each of the key metaphors refers to patterns of correspondence and interrelatedness—the sort of "mythic" thinking that Levi-Strauss identified with the metaphoric pole of discourse. The effect of this is similar to that in the later sections of *Regarding Wave.* In each case the metaphoric structure of the collection as a whole conditions the way in which individual, metonymic poems are to be read. In so doing, these metaphors develop on those in *Turtle Island,* in a more explicit attempt to "go beyond" dualistic thinking. In what follows I will discuss each of the three central metaphors which structure the collection and within which the poems in *Axe Handles* take shape.

The first section of the book is called "Loops." If the poems in *Turtle Island* communicated a "sense of place," of the buried energies within the land itself, then *Axe Handles* proposes a particular sense of *time* or *timing* and of tradition. This is contrasted with the pace and "ungroundedness" of contemporary American civilization. The alternative modes are conveyed either syntactically, phonetically, or by means of the arrangement or "scoring" of the words on the page.

Snyder has frequently used the idea of "looping back" to indicate a recursive sense of history and tradition. The metaphor implies at many levels a reconnection with origins, "the old ways," and a recognition of continuity with ancient tradition. This sense of being a participant in and bearer of culture or tradition is one consequence of the recognition that the individual is necessarily a participant in a collective system. The view is intrinsic to Snyder's sense of role as a poet, as the title poem and this collection, more than his previous work, acknowledge. From one point of view this orientation involves the attempt to use poetry as a vehicle to "get back to the Pleistocene," as a connecting "loop" to the roots of poetry in song and ritual observance. From another point of view, Snyder frequently writes that ecological sanity, and therefore political sense, require reassessment of our cultural roots, and attempting to relearn some of the "Old Ways" by which people lived for thousands of years before the comparatively recent accretion of high technology culture.

Many of the poems (and not only in the "Loops" section) are concerned in different ways with "looping back": a return to Japan, to Piute mountain where he worked twenty-five years before, the looping back of plant and animal life to their origins. The loops to Snyder's own past recall a time of relative solitude, in contrast with the family and other concerns in which he is now involved: "Today at Slide Peak in the Sawtooths / I look back at that mountain / twenty-five years. Those days / When I lived and thought all alone."

The title poem, **"Axe Handles,"** is a record of a significant epiphany arising from a response to manual work on one fairly ordinary occasion. Its placing is important in several ways. As in *Turtle Island* and *Regarding Wave,* the first poem in the collection informs the reading of the others. In this case, the epiphany arises in the recognition that the axe is at once a real tool, and a powerful metaphor by which the interdependence of old and new may be perceived.

> And I see:
> Pound was an axe,
> Chen was an axe, I am an axe
> And my son a handle, soon
> To be shaping again, model
> And tool, craft of culture,
> How we go on.

In the course of the poem the axe becomes metaphoric. A semantic transfer of some kind is certainly taking place, but this is not quite the kind that one usually expects. The process whereby a new handle is shaped from an existing one, works here as a metaphoric vehicle which is used to clarify something about the transmission of culture (here the tenor). In this poem, however, the metaphor is one where the vehicle is not separable from the tenor. This is because the shaping of the axe handle (and the father's communication of this to the son) is itself an example of the sort of process for which it is a metaphor: in this sense both "model and tool." This is rather similar to what happens in a number of the poems (compare, for example, **"Wave"** in *Regarding Wave*). The device seems to be a meaningful feature of the poetry, representing an attempt to avoid the dualistic split that other sorts of metaphor may imply, where the tenor and vehicle are clearly separable domains.

As the title of the collection indicates, the metaphor suggests a way of reading the poems that follow—as "axe handles." As such they are artifacts that may work as tools in their own right, as well as models for what is to follow. This is because they themselves have been "shaped" from and are connected to numerous precedents.

Clearly then, "Loops" represents the possibility of a cyclic sense of time which belongs to the metaphoric or mythic way of thinking. . . .

The final section of *Axe Handles* is called "Nets." Even more so than "Loops," the metaphor "Nets" is a multivalent word for Snyder, and for the subculture by whom his work has been received. It appears in his work as early as *Earth House Hold,* where the "jewelled net" of INDRA is used as a metaphor for the mythic or metaphoric notion of "interbirth" or "Communionism." *Axe Handles* resumes the explicit attention to this perception of things that *Regarding Wave* initiated. "Nets" as it is used in *Axe Handles* recalls the central metaphor in **"Shark Meat,"** where the shark that had fouled the fishermen's nets is eaten by the islanders. In this context, given the appropriate rituals—enough time, attention, reverence—activities like hunting, fishing and eating other animals are not problematic. If "the real work is eating each other," then the meaning of "net" as that by which animals are trapped is clearly significant. The relation it implies between man and animal is shown to be one instance of the phenomenon of interdependence, the web of reciprocity. Elsewhere Snyder calls it "the shimmering foodchain."

This attitude towards "those things we take to be outside ourselves" is illustrated in the poem **"Geese Gone Beyond."** As in *Turtle Island,* hunting as it is described here is accompanied by ritual behavior, recalling ancient practice: "I kneel in the bow. . . ." This prepares the reader for the shooting itself, in which there is no sense of violation, or personal animosity—"A touch across, / the trigger. . . .". The function of these lines is to diminish the sense of *personal* responsibility: the syntax works to give the action a very different status from what it would have had in, say, "I pull the trigger." It seems, too, as though the first bird is in some sense a conscious participant. The bird flies up, as though acknowledging what is to happen: "The one who is the first to feel to go." This interpretation is reinforced by the poem's title, **"Geese Gone Beyond"** which alludes to an idea of "Gone Beyond Wisdom" introduced on the flyleaf of *Regarding Wave.* Its use here suggests that in shooting the geese the narrator is acting as a vehicle for *their* transcendence, and thereby (to the extent that he has "become one" with them) for his own as well. As in **"Shark Meat"** and **"The Hudsonian Curlew,"** the human is understood to be a necessary agent in the animals' cycle of birth and death: killing in this way for food is an acknowledgement of our interdependence, human and non-human, in the living web.

As early as his B.A. thesis in 1951, with its fascination with the Muse and the Mother Goddess, Snyder gives emphasis to a theme which has been continuous in his work. This theme is the mythic significance of Woman as *"the totality of what can be known"* [my emphasis]. As Snyder indicated in a letter, the goddess as metaphor represents more for him than the reverse image of a patriarchal deity. It is rather a crucial metaperspective on oppositional or dualistic epistemology:

> We only divide the world up into two sets—such as essential and karmic, or noumenal and phenomenal, or wisdom and compassion, temporarily for arriving at certain kinds of clarity. But in the uncompromisingly non-dualistic Buddhist view which is an experiential view, not merely abstract and philosophical, these divisions are really just means and the world is one. Or as Yamada Roshi says, "not even one." There are such terms in esoteric Buddhism as the garbha (womb) realm and the vajra (thunderbolt) realm. But all of these are studied to the point of dissolving the dualism, even while maintaining a healthy understanding of the multiplicities by which things function. Prajna paramita is the "perfection" of a kind of wisdom that goes beyond such distinctions as being/nonbeing yin/yang essential/phenomenal or even wise/ignorant, or even enlightened/unenlightened. The wisdom that has done this is the wisdom that has "gone beyond". . . . But to make the circle interesting, the esoteric Buddhist tradition represents the wisdom that goes beyond all

dualisms as . . . a goddess. I find this charming. For "wisdom that has gone beyond," "illusion and wisdom both have been left behind."

This sense of "woman" or the goddess as symbolic of totality needs to be spelled out in this way because it is confusing for obvious reasons. A similar difficulty arises with Snyder's use of "nature" to signify, not an alternative to "culture," but the whole biosphere, the whole earth. In the later work, the culminating expression of this theme is the goddess Gaia—a metaphor for the attempt to go beyond dualistic oppositions, and for a metaphoric view of the world. In Gaia, "the great biosphere being," both "woman" and "nature" as *totality* are simultaneously evoked.

The metaperspective this represents is wholly fitting to the character of this ancient divinity. In Greek mythology, Gaia is the primal Earth Goddess, the Great Mother, and in terms of the idea of "looping back," she is clearly appropriate in Snyder's symbolic system. As the oldest Greek deity, both in mythic and probably in historical terms, she stands firstly for the earth and for values contrary to those associated with patriarchal religion and culture. Secondly, however, as mother of Uranus, existing before the discrimination into sexes, she is, symbolically, the mother out of whom these contrary values are born.

In addition, the name of Gaia has come to be associated with the concept of the "network" in recent years. Two environmental scientists, James Lovelock and Sydney Epton, have in the last ten years evolved a fairly influential model which they call The Gaia Hypothesis [Lovelock, *Gaia: A New Look at Life on Earth,* 1979]. In this model (from which Snyder borrowed the name) "Gaia" is the name for:

> a complex entity involving the earth's biosphere, atmosphere, oceans and soil; the totality constituting a feedback or cybernetic system which seeks an optimal physical and chemical environment for life on this planet.

It follows that in whatever sense she is understood, Gaia represents both "the whole network," and the originating source of its life. Consequently the energy she embodies is both primarily undifferentiated and an image of the transcendence of oppositional relations.

In *Axe Handles,* "Little Songs for Gaia" is centered between "Loops" and "Nets," serving to emphasize the role of Gaia as the one who binds these elements together: a net is made of loops, while it is mythically the work of the goddess to weave the disparate threads of the net or web together. The songs in this central section, rather like those in "Target Practice," evoke the simplicity of a state of consciousness "beyond transcendence." The following poem is a good illustration of the sense of correspondence this characteristically involves for Snyder.

> 24.IV.40075, 3.30 PM,
>   n. of Coaldale, Nevada,
> A Glimpse through a Break
> in the Storm of the Summit
>   of the White Mountains

>   O Mother Gaia
> sky cloud gate milk snow
>   wind-void-word
>   I bow in roadside gravel

The moment of its occurrence carefully documented, the epiphany which this poem records is an intense recognition that "at one level there are no hierarchies of qualities in life." For this reason the monosyllabic elements in the second line are equally weighted—evenly paced with equal spaces between. This is followed by a characteristic hyphenating of words, conveying a paradoxical interrelation of "wind," "void," and "word." Contrary to what might have been expected, neither the first line (invocation) nor the last (ritualized response) are separated from the rest: weaver of the net of correspondences, "Mother Gaia" is wholly immanent in the world of interpenetrating phenomena—they are in fact one and the same. At the same time she represents that which transcends and is beyond the particular scene. Similarly, the human perceiver's awed response is to a world in which he is participant as well as observer: the ritual bow "in roadside gravel" is an indication at once of a delighted recognition of the goddess "out there," and at the same time of his own part in the magic system. In *The Old Ways* Snyder alludes to this order of experience, with regard to its scarcity in contemporary "civilization":

> Not that special, intriguing knowledges are the real point: it's the sense of the magic system; the capacity to hear the song of Gaia at *that* spot, that's lost.

The body of Snyder's work suggests that momentary epiphanies of the kind the poem (and others in *Axe Handles*) presents are valuable. But this value depends on the extent that they are seen to be surrounded not, as in Eliot or Stevens, by "waste sad time" or its equivalent. The context is rather an everyday one, in which the Goddess, and the sacramental metaperspective she represents, continue to be accessible in the rhythm of the most everyday activities. . . .

Snyder's project is a similar one. His response to the problem of "other" is Buddhist and ecological. As other critics have noted, his work proposes a mode of perception that transcends or "goes beyond" dualism. For this reason the earlier poetry notably avoided metaphor and symbol. Surprisingly, however, metaphor and structures of metaphoric pattern and correspondence are used in the later work for precisely the same purpose: to suggest a necessary inter-dependence between the individual and "those things we consider to be outside ourselves." In the collections I have discussed, metaphor works to reveal Snyder's sense of the pattern which connects, producing a context of complex correspondences in which the individual, often metonymic, poems are to be read.

This makes for poetry that contradicts some of the critical observations that have been made about it. Altieri, for example, sees some of the poems in *Regarding Wave* as an extension of Williams' objectivism ["Process as Plenitude"]. Elsewhere he discusses the main features of this orientation. Using Jakobson's model of metaphor and metonymy, he argues that two main traditions in modern poetry derive from different strategies for approaching the metonymic image and transcending its limits. The first, essentially symbolist, tradition ("mythmakers" like Yeats, Eliot, Stevens) assumes that the mind requires informing universals if it is to be satisfied in experience, and so it funds in metonymy a cause for despair. For the second tradition (Williams, for example) metonymy is a step in the right direction because "the source of despair is not metonymy itself but the dream that consciousness can find unifying structures" [Altieri, "Objective Image and Act of Mind in Modern Poetry, *PMLA,* Vol. 91, 1977].

There is, however, a crucial difference between Snyder's use of metaphor and metonymy and either of the trends which Altieri describes. In his case, the context in which a wheelbarrow (or anything else) is perceived is a universe of necessary correspondences, mutual interpenetration, in which all things are wave-patterned, an expression of the Goddess: all things, even the inanimate, have Buddha-nature. Given this, it is irrelevant for the human perceiver to construct "unifying structures." As Molesworth's comment about metaphor suggested, the poet's work is rather to recognize and make explicit a metaphoric connection which *already exists* between the various elements. Instead of being a "mythmaker," s/he is a "myth handler-healer," restoring the connections that have been disrupted by divisive mental habit.

The social and political implications of recognizing the pattern which connects are extensive, as writers in other fields have shown. Snyder's work draws attention to the ideological consequences of our habitual binary thinking, and the poetry returns again and again to examples of this in Western technological culture. This political incentive is certainly a crucial aspect of his spiritual, ecological, personal perspective. But problems do seem to arise from putting the poetry to work for political ends. I would agree with other commentators that this is most evident in *Turtle Island,* although my sense of the problem is slightly different. I also think that the problems are not confined to *Turtle Island.*

In rejecting a dualistic model, Snyder's project is to write poetry that proposes an alternative to binary thinking. And yet, to the extent that it involves placing the self in opposition to an exploitative, oppressive ideology, the "alternative" view is in danger of becoming its mirror-image. This becomes particularly clear in the choice of metaphors. So for example the angry depiction of "Amerika" in *Turtle Island* is a rather two-dimensional oversimplification, and some of the "natural" metaphors verge on sentimentality, as Kern and Altieri have shown. [Anthony] Wilden states the problem in general terms [in *System and Structure,* 1972] as follows:

> We canot destroy the master simply by taking his place; we have to make him irrelevant—and that means to reduce his mastery by transcending the oppositional relationship in which we find ourselves in a negative identification with him. To destroy exploitative mastery

we must do more than become the negative complement of the master, his mirror-image. . . .

The most significant area in this respect for Snyder is the metaphoric complex he calls "the Goddess"—which includes Vak, "Mother Earth" and Gaia. Snyder's Goddess connects nature, woman, and all the other unfortunates that appear on the wrong side of the divide in a binary epistemology. The intention in this focus is clearly very different from that which has motivated the simultaneous exploitation of women, nature, other races, animals, etc. It is, quite explicitly, an attempt to heal the damage caused by these attitudes and to propose the mythic feminine as an image of totality. This image of the feminine achieves its clearest expression in *Axe Handles,* with its celebration of Gaia and of the world in which she is perceived. As metaphor, Gaia represents a perspective that is clearly of a higher logical type than those which either welcome or bemoan an identification of the "feminine" with "nature," and represent the goddess as the reverse image of the "masculine," "patriarchal" god. As such, the metaphor is a powerful image of totality. Even so, the post-feminist reader is likely to ask whether it is possible to associate woman and nature metaphorically without calling up the patriarchal-technological viewpoint which made this connection an exploitative one. Although I do find Gaia an effective metaphor, I think that the poetry shows very little self criticism on this subject, and little sense of the problems inherent in making such connections.

I have argued that in the later work the use of metaphor, and specifically metaphors associated with the Goddess, is an important way of pointing to the jewelled network of connecting pattern. And yet the poems themselves insist on their provisional nature: even at its best, poetry remains a kind of pointer, since the Way to the Pattern must finally be one that has no map. Snyder's version of the Buddhist idea of the Pathless Path, the Gateless Gate appears in *Regarding Wave* in the poem **"The Way is Not a Way."** In this context, hitting the target or finding the pattern must involve, paradoxically, **"Looking for Nothing"**—as the first poem in "Target Practice" indicates. Significantly, this point of view reveals the Goddess after all:

> Look in the eye of a hawk
> The inmost ring of a log
>
> The edge of the sheath and the
> Sheath—where it leads—
>
> River sands.
> Tara "Joy of
> Starlight"
>   thousand—
>   eyed.

Julie Martin (interview date 1990)

SOURCE: "Coyote-Mind: An Interview with Gary Snyder," in *TriQuarterly,* Vol. 79, Fall, 1990, pp. 148-72.

[*In the following interview, Snyder discusses the influence of his past on his work and the evolution of his ideas on nature and Buddhism.*]

[Martin]: *I'd like to start by talking about origins and influences. You've spoken about your childhood before, but what I'm interested in is your experience of growing up in a politically conscious environment: your family was involved in IWW politics. Can you say something about that?*

[Snyder]: Well it was a Washington State thirties Depression household, as many households were, in the rural territory just north of Seattle, predominantly settled by Scandinavians with a few Japanese-American households doing truck farming. Our family tradition was radical politics on both sides, particularly on my father's side because my grandfather was an active IWW and socialist speaker and thinker. Then my father was active during the thirties with the League of Unemployed Voters and other left-wing, labor-oriented groups of the time. My mother was sympathetic with those ideas, had essentially the same politics and was for her time very much of a feminist.

The effect of that was for there to be a certain kind of political conversation around the house, certain opinions about the Depression and the economy which I grew up with, a high degree of critical attitude towards some of the more unthinking aspects of the society, and a very critical attitude towards Christianity and the Church. My mother is a militant atheist, my father was a nonmilitant atheist. That combined with the fact of our poverty and the fact that we worked very hard to keep things going, gave me what you might call a kind of working-class, left-wing outlook, from an early age. It involved a certain literary outlook too, because my mother was a student in writing at the University of Washington, and when she was younger she read quite a bit. She wasn't reading during the Depression—I don't think we had any books. So we started going to the public libraries.

Does that background have a significant influence on the way you've constructed your life here at Kitkitdizze [California] which seems to be a political choice of a kind?

In some sense it certainly feeds into it. Growing up in a rural situation where we kept chickens and cows, cut a little firewood, had an outhouse, makes this kind of life very comfortable for me. That is to say I had many of the skills and attitudes already. I don't think this is an exceptional life, in other words. This is just another way that people live. I like living in the city, and I like living this way too. I don't do it for ideological reasons, or because I think the world is going to come to an end, or civilization is going to collapse and we ought to be self-sufficient.

So you do it because . . . ?

I do it because I like to live this way! I'd live this way even if civilization were going to last [*laughs*]. But there is a little difference in attitude which I and my present neighbors bring to it from my father's generation, I think. This generation of back-to-the-land people is very clear on wanting to establish a long-range relationship to a place, and not take it as such an easy thing to move on to another place: to slow down that traditional white-American mobility, which is also rural mobility in many cases, and take the idea of commitment to a place more seriously. So there's a difference in attitude there. That could be said to be somewhat political.

In what respects is this way of living affected by the wider context of capitalist America that you're situated in?

It's affected in absolutely every detail, like everything else is. We live in the same economy, we use the same monetary system, we have to make our living however we can. Being a rural person in America—or anywhere else in the developed world—is in no way to be out of the economy. It's true that there's a small amount of income that comes through what you might call subsistence, through foraging, through gathering, that is nontaxable [*laughs*], which is not counted as income. All of a hunter-gatherer's income is nontaxable, so to speak. So we are to a tiny extent growers and foragers. We could be much more than we are, but it's economically not feasible. There's a higher degree of efficiency to be part of the economy than to opt out of it. In other words, growing food costs you more than buying food at the market.

It's a peculiar feature of a more complex economy that there are economic strategies by which you can live in a rural situation without being engaged in rural production. You just happen to do your work in a rural location, rather than an urban location. But there's very little difference from doing your work in a suburb of New York. It's just a matter of where you choose to live.

You are talking about a First World economy, though. Many of the "alternative life-styles" that are possible here in the United States simply aren't an option where I come from [Capetown, South Africa].

I'm sure they are possible where you come from. I'm sure somebody who was skilled in writing and computer programming could live just as well away from town as in town, because of the decentralization of the information economy.

But that presupposes a high degree of skill and privilege . . .

I'm sure there are writers in South Africa who don't live right in the middle of downtown, who live out in the country. It requires a little more ingenuity sometimes, but people all over the developed world are doing it—in Scandinavia, England, Wales, Scotland and many other places. You have to spend more time thinking about tools and maintenance, but it's never accurate to say "You can do this but other people can't." I run into that periodically. That is actually not a sensible way of putting it. The fact is, you can if you want to. Anyone can live like this if they're willing to put out the time and energy. But it's also a matter of what the nature of your work is. There are a lot of people who opt for a lower income to be able to live here. They could make better money if they lived in the city.

Would you say that the way you teach is affected by your attitudes towards authoritarian structures?

I don't think it is. I just teach in as directly communicative a way I can. I also expect a lot from students. As a teacher I'm authoritarian . . . you have to be.

That's what a "teacher" is?

Sure. It's a great work—make people get the idea that there are higher standards than what they've been accustomed to, and that improves their sense of what can be done. I think of that as being part of the older cultural milieu, the milieu of student and teacher.

Which models do you have in mind? Where do they come from?

From Buddhist teaching, kiva instruction, from apprenticeship rituals, from my own appreciation of that approach in teachers, and from my understanding of learning—how people learn.

The sort of literature teaching you're doing now must be very different from your own literary training in the fifties, which would have meant New Criticism.

Everything has gone through a lot of changes since then. That was one side of my literary training. The other side was anthropological, where I was exposed to other literary traditions, and to the sense of nonelite cultural features, understanding that all cultures have literature, and that it is not at all necessarily dominated by an elite class: folklore, mythology, folk-song.

That position obviously informs your discussion of the Haida myth, "He Who Hunted Birds in His Father's Village," in your B.A. thesis. Several critics have seen the thesis as a sort of storehouse of ideas and images that have been basic to your later writing. Do you see it like that?

Yes. What I brought together in the thesis were a lot of interests that I'd been exploring. It was a way of trying to synthesize a lot of diverse interests, some of which I'm still exploring. There are other things that are not particularly part of me these days. Obviously it gave me a good push.

So what stays with you now? Which things are you still exploring?

Well, I'm still interested in the question of the role of myth and nonmyth, the play between direct understanding and perception as against point of view shaped by cultural structures, direct experience as against hearsay, direct experience and any kind of experience mediated by opinion or ideology of preconditions. Unmediated experience—

it's an interesting thing. That's what Zen is pointing to: unmediated experience.

So your Zen practice and your interest in anthropology are going in the same direction. On the subject of myth and nonmyth, you wrote at that time that "The function mythology serves in primitive culture is desperately needed in contemporary society." That was the early fifties. Would you still put it like that?

You see you have to say two things at once. This is the interesting part. We have to say that we need myth. And then you also have to say that you need to get to the end of myth. Myth can be understood as a kind of *provisional* ordering of the situation to get the territory at least clear enough so you can begin to work on it. In a so-called primitive culture, myth works to give a shape and a wholeness to a wide range of behaviors and institutions. Sometimes it's extraordinarily shapely and very well constructed in some way: one symbol informs another symbol, and such a society has tremendous strength. However, the way mythologies work is by no means always benign. And so we have another way of speaking about myth, which is to speak of it as superstition, prejudice, preconceptions, blinders on the eyes, blinders on the mind, views and opinions which trap people. So mythology, images, can be used in more ways than one. We need to be able to discriminate between visions that liberate and visions that enslave, myths that liberate and myths that do not.

In your thesis you emphasized the mytheme of the supernatural wife, and stressed the idea of "Woman" as mythic image of "the totality which can be known." Can you comment on what this view of a mythic Woman has involved in your work?

Yes, there are a number of feminine images that overlap in there. The phenomenal world as female, as illusion, is one.

Maya.

Yes. The phenomenal world as the totality of that which may be known, as a *magna mater,* or the goddess of nature, is another. The two are one and the same, though. The phenomenal world is either illusion or it's not illusion, depending on how you look at it. Either way, it is given in some traditions a feminine imagery.

Those are images, I'm quite sure, that are projected by men. The phenomenal world, as both what can be known and what cannot be known, can be seen in a *nongendered* way as the Tao. In Vajrayana and Hindu symbolic metaphysics they actually switch the genders back and forth, and in Hinduism the masculine is seen as the quiescent and the feminine as the active. In some schools of Buddhism, the universe as illusion is seen as the feminine and the universe as insight or wisdom is seen as the masculine, and sometimes that's switched. The more you get into it, the less important the gender imagery becomes. In Zen, the terminology is "host and guest"—it doesn't matter which gender you're talking about. You're talking about the interplay of the apparently dichotomous nature of the universe, and the fact that it's actually not dichotomous. It's one. And yet it plays back and forth between emptiness and phenomena, in time and out of time, the karmic fabric and the essential position, without time.

So I'm not as much interested in the *genderization* of those things. But I see the *use* of gender imagery in India in its poetic mythology and Tibet in its poetic mythology as charming—and sometimes useful. You might say that in a bhakti tradition, a devotional tradition, they tend to concretize their imagery into gender and have goddesses and gods. And in a gnostic tradition, a jnana tradition, a wisdom tradition, they would prefer not to see it as gender-tied imagery.

In terms of your own work, would you see yourself as making use of both traditions, bhakti and jnana? There's a lot of goddess mythology in your poems.

Certainly.

I'm thinking particularly of the goddess Gaia. When you write about Gaia it seems to indicate some sort of identification with those eco-feminists and deep ecologists who have been using the term in the last decade or so.

I took Gaia from the beginning as a very useful, charming way of giving a word to the biosphere. Gaia is not all of the phenomenal universe, nor does it refer to an illusory realm. It refers to something very limited and very specific: the biosphere on Planet Earth. So it's not talking about "matter" or "nature," but about one particular organism and its history.

Is the use of a goddess as image for the biosphere a strategic choice, a counter to patriarchal mythologies?

It's historic. Because the "ge" is what we have for "geology." I wouldn't support it for *too* long, because you get into trouble as soon as you ask "Now what's the opposite of Gaia?" or "What's the male of Gaia?"

And then?

Solar energy? O.K. . . . now solar energy is coming in and doing all this stuff with chemicals and making life. That's O.K., but you don't want to pursue those images very long. It gets too literal. So I take it as a nonliteral image, and I wrote a few poems called "Songs for Gaia," more interested in developing the scale of the image than anything literal. You know, "How large an image of life can you think of? How large an organism can you imagine? But I get really bored with all these New Age types that go around holding Gaia conferences all the time now, as though they were talking about something real [*laughs*].

You would see the term as a provisional myth, in other words.

Yes. And also it's an interesting scientific fact, or possibly scientific fact.

That's Lovelock's Gaia Hypothesis.

Yes. Better that people should not get too carried away with talking about archetypes and stuff when they're talking about Gaia, and should stay with the interesting question of "How large an organism is life?" and "How does an organism of that scale work if it works? What is the chemistry of it?" That's much more interesting. Too many of these people want to jump over the details of biology right back into mythology before they've got themselves grounded in it. So I backed off from the use of the term *Gaia,* except as an interesting metaphor. I presume the hypothesis to have some use as a hypothesis. But talking about the planet as Gaia per se will not do the planet a lot of good though [*laughs*]. You still have to find a course of action, a program. Do something active: "Where do we go from here?"

What about the more general connection of "woman" and "nature"?

That's a good question. Carolyn Merchant (who wrote *The Death of Nature*) and I were talking about that. There are definitely two schools of feminist thought about it. Ynestra King, for example, wants to eliminate all gendered references to nature. She says that doesn't help women. It just makes them look fecund and Great Mothery, and it keeps them in the kitchen. Then there's another imagery which is certainly very deeply established in thought and lore: metaphors drawn from some obvious observations of seeds being planted and sprouting, birth processes in nature, which suggest an analogy with women's bodies and their roles in culture. I don't know if hunter-gathering people ever got so deeply fertility- and goddess-oriented as did agrarian people. In agriculture there is the very clear metaphor of scratching the ground, poking a hole, and then dropping a seed in it, covering it up and watching it sprout. It becomes very easy to see the sun and the sky as some kind of fertilizing force, and the earth as a womb which holds the seed and then brings it out. Hunter-gathering people do not genderize nature in the way that early agrarian cultures do.

How useful can that sort of early agrarian metaphor be for late twentieth-century people?

Well, you can take "woman" to mean "generative force," assigning more of the reproductive role to the female than to the male, which is the way that some people might see it. (There is some biological truth in this. In some animals the female has a more nurturing capacity than the male.) And *then* you can continue the image and say "our mother Earth," and say "We shouldn't destroy our mother Earth." So it becomes ecological language. To be more precise, "We shouldn't destroy our mother Earth and our father—whatever the father is." If there are forces at work, and there are two of them, we need both of them [*laughs*]. So . . . I'm just playing with these things still myself. We should respect the wholeness of the enterprise, the familiarity, the complementarity of the whole organic process.

You referred to two trends in feminist thought about the metaphoric association of "woman" and "nature." Would you agree that it is precisely that association that has legitimized the oppression of women?

Clearly, in some cases.

You also spoke of a "male projection."

For some of it . . .

I'm interested in the differences between the way, say, radical feminists might write about "woman and nature," and their responses to the use of similar terminology by male writers. Adrienne Rich, for example, has been very critical of the celebration by male writers of what they would call "the feminine." Any comments? To what extent is your use of such terminology conditioned by your gender?

Well, I'm sure it is. I think it's tedious to get too involved in trying to figure out those arguments. I mean everyone has an agenda.

As well as a gender . . . Would you call yourself a feminist?

I don't think it would be appropriate for a man to call himself a feminist. There are many women who wouldn't call themselves feminists. So it's a role that's appropriate for women, and I support feminists, although I don't support all feminists. I don't support feminists who are just out there to buy into the capitalist system and become managers. That seems like a very revisionary form of feminism. I don't necessarily support a feminism of women's uniqueness, either. I *do* feel that the force of feminism in, for example, Japanese culture is very important, is in some ways truly revolutionary, and is more unsettling to the culture than industrialization and modernization have been.

What about the questions feminism raises for Zen Buddhism, which has traditionally been very much a male line?

Zen teaching seems to be able to incorporate women easily, as in a lot of places in the States. What's interesting to hear is what Zen women who practice Buddhism have to say, their views towards Buddhist practice and towards feminism. There are some women who will say (having come from a feminist background), that they came to Buddhism because they needed a study of who they really were, without preconceptions, without a feminist or an antifeminist agenda. To ask yourself "What is my nature really like?" without the presumption that it's going to be particularly female or male: to go beyond the gender side of the question and just look at what *is*, to observe what your mind and psyche does. So they found Buddhism very refreshing in its freedom from preconceptions about the way the mind is. Buddhism teaches that the mind is the mind, and that the difference between a woman's mind and a man's mind at deeper levels is absolutely zero. So when Buddhism is doing what it should be doing, it helps us all equally, before race or gender, in establishing an insight into our own nature.

And it may be that that insight includes some understanding of this part of me, this component which you might call feminine. That calls for some acknowledgment, and I need not be afraid of it or ashamed of it. And the same for men too—there has to be a place where they can acknowledge what part of their makeup is generated by their gender.

By their socialization into that gender?

Prior to socialization. Well, socialization into the gender, but also, you know, there are forces at work that are prior to socialization. You see it in the difference between different girls and different boys. Some girls will be frilly and feminine from the very beginning. Some won't. And I see it around here, we all see it: we've seen mothers who are handling chain saws and driving trucks, whose daughters won't touch them. They simply won't do that. There is a character that you're born with, and there are tendencies that are prior to what your parents have socialized you into. There are definitely tendencies amongst girls to do certain things in certain ways, and there are tendencies in boys to do certain things, *prior* to socialization. *Then* socialization can enforce certain things or play down certain things. But you're not dealing with a totally blank slate.

With regard to gender, Buddhism would seem then to reject the idea that differences such as "male" and "female" indicate fixed essences, fixed givens.

Buddhism would say that the male/female differences are real enough, but on a fairly illusory level, and that our essential nature is free of that. After all, our essential nature is the nature of rocks and trees, and there are no men and women there [*laughs*]. So gender has very little do with the essential insights, and in *koan* study, and the primary awakening called *satori,* and the subsequent insights that people have. The way women grasp *koans* and the way men grasp *koans* is absolutely the same—there's no difference at all. There's no gender difference.

There are some sides of Buddhist mythology that do put women down, it's true. And in some traditions those lines may be quoted from time to time, and in other traditions they won't. Zen has *always* held that there's no difference between men and women with respect to practice.

But historically that's not how monasteries have been run.

No, because the *society* has not supported that. The Buddhists say women and men are equal in their capacity for achieving enlightenment. But the society is not sending them equal numbers of men and women, for other reasons, for reasons that are already established in the society at large.

As I understand it, the version of Buddhist practice that you're developing at the Ring of Bone Zendo emphasizes this place, this experience. You don't want it to be an Asian import.

Yes, North American. The other thing we're trying to do is to keep ourselves, so to speak, local. In that sense we're more orthodox, more Asian than many of the Zen centers that have been established, in the usual modern mode of establishing a center which caters to rootless and alienated people that come and go, and bring their problems, who are sampling the smorgasbord of therapies and possibilities for themselves in modern urban life. Most Zen centers draw on the alienated, educated members of the upper middle class. They also tend to carry on traditional Japanese Buddhist forms without any critical thought. That is the way that new cults worked in Rome.

In Rome?

That's the way that new religions functioned in Rome in the second and third century A.D., as symptomatic of the breakdown of the fabric of society: contending alien cults in a collapsing society. That's not a very interesting place to be [*laughs*]. What's more interesting to me is something which is quite a bit deeper. First of all, what happens when you begin to have something a little more like a real community, and you can look at the possibilities of a sort of "post-revolutionary socialism," or what Paul Goodman calls "a natural society"?

What does that mean in particular? Can you give some examples?

It means a society in which people live in one place for a good number of years; it means that they know each other personally on a first-name basis; it means that they know a *considerable* amount of the personal history of the individuals concerned; it means that they know their own family history, and that they keep in touch with their parents; it means that they are engaged in their community in one or another ways by serving on committees, formal and informal committees; it means that they do not expect everybody to do what they do—a community in its own nature cannot be homogeneous.

As would be the case in an intentional community.

We're talking about a *natural* community.

And you'd see an intentional community as being artificial.

An intentional community can enforce a point of view. A natural community is a *culture.* Consequently, points of view are formed almost subliminally, over the long run, by the totality of the experiences that people go through, and by the songs and the stories that they tell each other. So on many levels such a place is, so to speak, selfmotivating. So that's a natural community, a symptom of a natural society.

I don't think that Buddhism can function in a way that's truly beautiful, truly interesting, until it has a natural society as its ground. *Then* the truly existential problems become the problems you're dealing with. You get the politics out of the way by having a sane society. *Then*

you can begin to work on the really *refined* study of the mind. This is what I've understood from working in Asia, that *that* is what Buddhism was doing at its best. We are in an era of tremendous social and political breakdown. Buddhism is not the cure for that, although it may be of help. But it can only be *one* of the kinds of measures.

So that's why I divide my time between what you may call culture-building, community-building and Buddhist teaching. It would be really easy to live in the city and teach at a Zen center and do nothing but Buddhist teaching. I wouldn't want to do it that way. I'd rather go out and start working in the neighborhoods as much as I could, because I think you have to work the ground for a Buddhist society first. You can't just leave your society the way it is and say "We offer this as one of the teachings." You've got to help the society get its feet on the ground before those teachings can begin to flourish.

You've talked about "getting the politics out of the way," and yet that seems to be premised on an idea of radical social transformation, at the local level at least. You also used the term "post-revolutionary." Would you call yourself a revolutionary?

I'd call myself a post-revolutionary! [*Laughs.*] I guess I'd call myself a revolutionary in the sense that I can clearly envision situations, actually practical social structures, that are well beyond and *after* the kinds of conditions that people are living under now. And I can recognize that those possibilities are real, not impractical, not utopian. But it will take some drastic changes before we can get there. I'm *not* sure that deliberately applied drastic changes will necessarily get you where you want to go. So I'm a little bit cautious about proposing programs. There are a few things I do propose.

Such as?

Don't move. That's very revolutionary. That's why it catches people by surprise. They can't figure out why it's revolutionary for a long time [*laughs*]. It takes a while to start seeing that it is.

I suppose my questions make it clear that I see your work as often being explicitly ideological, political. Would you agree with this reading?

I imagine that my work is political in the sense of its engagement in issues of import regarding the manner of the directions of our societies, and issues of import in the manner of fundamental ethical attitudes. *That's* where it is political, like Blake was political. And I don't expect some of the things that I propose poetically, so to speak, to make sense, maybe, for decades. So that's poetic politics, where what you launch are challenges and suggestions that don't make sense, or don't begin to add up for a long, long time.

Politics is also just drama. I know people who do politics as their art form, who are actually very clear about that:

"I could write poetry, I could be a painter. I like to do street theater, I like to do politics as theater. This is my theater." There are a lot of people who do that. So it's not interesting, really, to separate art and politics: politics *is* a kind of theater in which the stage is your own society, as you go back and forth on it. So ecological politics is mountains-and-fields theater. It's a large-scale theater of the surface of the planet. Gaia is a theatrical device. The mother goddess is another mask of theater.

To be used for as long as it serves its purpose?

Yes, as long as it plays. And how it plays, and what happens when it plays, is fun to watch. And the stakes are real. The stakes *are* real. The stakes have to do with a kind of sustained viability in its diversity, without utopian or perfectionistic expectations. It would just be nice if we could keep going [*laughs*].

You made a comment in **Turtle Island** *that has stuck with me as a puzzle: "Knowing that nothing need be done, is where we begin to move from." What did you mean, exactly?*

Yes, that's a Buddhist point. Lots of people have asked me about that. In the larger scale, things *will* take care of themselves. It's obviously human hubris to think that we can destroy the planet, can destroy life. It's just another exaggeration of ourselves. Actually we can't. We're far too small.

Really?

The time scale is far too large, and the resistance of cellular life is far too great. Lovelock is very interesting on this, on the extraordinary resilience of cells. But that's no excuse. That would be no excuse for doing things poorly. A kind of bottom line is that all human activity is as trivial as anything else. We can humbly acknowledge that and excuse ourselves from exaggerating our importance, even as a threat, and also recognize the scale and the beauty of things. And *then* go to work.

Don't imagine that we're doing ecological politics to save the world. We're doing ecological politics to save ourselves, to save our souls. It's a *personal* exercise in character and in manners. It's a matter of etiquette. It's a matter of living right. It's not that the planet requires us to be good to it. It's that we must do it because it's an esthetic and ethical choice.

Would you say, then, that there's a lot of hysterical scare about? What about the ozone hole?

Those issues are all real. Those issues are all real, but they're not total. And the power of the universe far surpasses any damage we can do it.

One response to the ecological crisis that you have been associated with is the deep ecology movement, or what you have referred to as "depth ecology." Can you say something about this?

"Deep ecology" is not my term, it's Arne Naess's term. It just means, to my notion, people who are serious about ecology, and aware of the larger-scale importance of the whole array of creatures and processes in the biosphere, and don't rate human beings as being necessarily the most interesting or the most important part of that. So that's where they are: non-anthropocentric, and they call it biological egalitarianism. I don't think that there's any shame in being a human being, and being pro-human. I think we should take that as being part of the turf. We're not *forced* to practice human guilt, feel guilty about being a human being, any more than you need to have any other guilt about who you are [*laughs*]. But still they have a lot of good points to make: that rough distinction of resource-management ecology as shallow ecology and long-term, life-respecting strategies for the benefit of all, as deep ecology, is important. So that's deep ecology.

"Depth ecology" is a term that I'm working with now. I developed it when I started trying to do an ecological and etymological myth analysis of the widely distributed sub-Arctic study of the girl who married a bear. My method of analysis of that story came out of what I would call depth ecology, which is going to be in my book. The term would refer to a territory where myth or folklore or shamanic constructions have to do with the way you treat creatures, whether or not you kill them or don't kill them. How do you kill a bear? What do you do with a bear when you've killed it? Who eats it, who doesn't eat it? What part of the bear do women and children eat, what part do old men eat? That's . . . depth ecology [*laughs*].

So your understanding of ecological work is something very different from environmentalism.

One would do environmentalist work in the sense of dealing with little issues as they came up—we all do that— whereas the ecological view is a larger-scale view, one that is more biological. You can be an environmentalist without knowing anything about biology, just as you can be a politician without any knowledge of anthropology [*laughs*].

I'm thinking particularly of Murray Bookchin's critique of what he calls "mere environmentalism."

Yes, I know pretty much what Murray would say. Part of it is just exercises in terminologies. I don't put people down for working on issues, especially if they win something. Whether or not they understand the larger picture, we have to be grateful for people who get out there and save a marsh. The same would be true of any political affairs. So what's the use of putting them down? They're working within their abilities . . . and that's wonderful.

You mentioned earlier that your upbringing led you to be critical towards Christianity, and you've often written about the connection you see between Western metaphysics and the current ecological crisis. Can you see any ways that the work you're involved in, in Buddhism particularly, might benefit from Christian or Occidental religious traditions?

That's an interesting question. Of course Western Buddhists, coming out of Western culture and being probably from Christian or Jewish backgrounds, are already bringing those things into Buddhism, by virtue of their personalities and their background. So there's already some kind of exchange there, I'm sure.

My own view is that Buddhists can profit from, but wouldn't necessarily want to emulate, an understanding of the Christian concern for history, and the historical fact of the Christian concern for personality, as a kind of leavening factor in the evolution of Buddhist thought. I think that the Buddhists also have to admire the commitment of certain Christian sects, such as the Quakers, to *peace,* and the Christian idea of witness and bearing witness as a matter of conscience. It has its pitfalls from a Buddhist standpoint, pitfalls of over ego-stimulation. But that side of Christian engagement is admirable. It certainly can be learned from. Buddhists can learn from, or at least take note of, the section of the Church that is doing liberation theology. Buddhism has been quiescent, socially, for much of its history, and what and how it becomes more active in the social sphere is going to be very interesting. I'm sure it will, because in the West everybody gets more social. And also the power makes a difference: political action, political involvement, makes a difference in a pluralistic democracy, whereas in a traditional Asian culture there's very little direct political action possible.

Would you see your work as a counter to that traditional quiescence?

Yes, well what I see is . . . an interesting vision proposed by Mahayana Buddhism that hasn't been acted out much, hasn't been actualized much. I think that it may be the destiny for Western Buddhists to try to make the effort of *actualizing* what Buddhists say they can do in terms of actual life in society.

Can you be more specific?

Part of the actualization of Buddhist ethics is, in a sense, to be a deep ecologist. The actualization of Buddhist insights gives us a Buddhist economics, an economics not based on greed but on need, an ethic of adequacy but simplicity, a valuation of personal insight and personal experience over possessions. What I like most about Buddhism really is its fearlessness. So much of what warps people is fear of death and fear of impermanence. So much of what we do is simply strategies to try and hold back death, trying to buy time with material things. So at its best Buddhism provides people with a way of seeing their own frailty: you need less in the way of material objects and fortresses around yourself.

I'd like to talk about what you meant in **Turtle Island** *by the phrase "bringing a voice from the Wilderness, my constituency." What does this say about your role as Buddhist, ecologist, poet? You've written elsewhere about correspondences between "wilderness" and "the unconscious."*

I think I'd just like to leave that because as an image it generates enough as it is. It's something that is quite adequate, once suggested.

It finds its own way? O.K. Perhaps we can just talk about "voice." In **Regarding Wave** *the central metaphors, as I see it, derive from images associated with the goddess Vak, or Voice. Is the concept of Vak, or "the voice of the Dharma," still useful to you now?*

Vak is just another way for referring to speech. I haven't done anything further with Sanskrit language theory or mantra theory. In Buddhism, though, they say the sense of hearing, the vehicle of sound, is the clearest and easiest and most appropriate vehicle for enlightenment. We proceed to learn from the sense of sound better than from any other sense, in the very specific terms of Zen enlightenment. So that's why *Kuan Yin's* name means "observe the sounds." That's very clearly stated in Vajrayana mythology. It also says that the present *kalpa* is presided over by *Amitabha,* whose color is red and who resides in the West. *Amitabha's* active compassion emanation in the material universe is *Avalokiteshvara,* "observe the sound, learn by hearing" [*laughs*]. And that's exactly what happens: sound is essentially your path in.

It's a different point, although it's related, that literature and poetry are fundamentally oral, because language is oral, and writing is secondary. I understand that some of the French intelligentsia don't believe that, but they really have it backwards. In fact one of Derrida's biggest weaknesses is his insistence on theorizing from written texts. A whole lot of what he's trying to say falls apart if you go back to orality. There's a Jesuit teacher who's written on this . . .

Walter Ong, Orality and Literacy? *He does mention Deconstruction near the end.*

Yes, that's it.

If, as Taoism at least proposes, "The Way which can be spoken is not the Way," how (or why) write poems (or even sing them)? Can you say something about what seems to be the paradox of composing a Zen poem: how to give expression to an experience which is pre-symbolic, pre-verbal?

What you quoted was the first line of the first chapter of the *Tao te Ching,* which is often translated as "The Way which can be spoken of is not the true Way." That may not be the only translation. The translation I prefer treats the second "Tao" as a verb, and would translate as "The Way which can be *followed* is not the true or correct Way," which puts a different twist on it. Anyway, I don't think it's correct that "that which can be said" is automatically not true. To the contrary, in Zen we find that that which *cannot* be said is not complete. If you have an understanding and cannot express it, then your understanding is not yet complete. The act of expressing clarifies your understanding of it. However, the nature of that expression may not be clear and transparent to everybody, which is why Zen literature is not easy to follow. But that's what it is. So the person who has a Zen eye can understand it.

> I feel that the primary mode of existence of poetry is in speech and performance, and that writing is its secondary mode of existence. . . . By thinking that way and by practicing that way I do make a connection in my own poetics with a very broad tradition of poems, the pre-literate and oral traditions.
>
> —*Gary Snyder*

I think in general it's dangerous to propose . . . there's been a lot of mischief that has proceeded from the idea that the truth cannot be said. It gets people off the hook too easily.

Inscrutable silences?

Exactly. A Zen teacher won't accept that, absolutely won't accept it. You go before a Zen teacher and he says "Well what is *mu*? What is the non-dual essence of the mind?" And you just sit there and smile beatifically. He'll say, "Come on, get off it." [*Laughs.*]

How does this idea of "the Way which can be followed" relate to what you said earlier about teachers, the value of an authoritarian teaching tradition?

Well, you have to learn how to go on a way before you quit following it.

Charles Olson wrote in the sixties about the need for poetry to get rid of "the lyrical interference of the ego, of the subject and his soul." Would this describe what you're attempting to do?

Yes, I'm not interested in being a consistent poet speaking voice, speaking for my own sentiments and sensibilities.

Because?

Because it's not interesting, it's like talking about yourself.

And what is interesting?

Talking about your non-self! [*Laughs.*] When a bird flies across from one tree to another tree, you can be the bird flying across from one tree to another tree. You don't have to *think* about the bird, how you feel about the bird. No difference between self and universe. So just shortcut that illusion.

But "self" informs the way you read the bird.

But you don't have to encourage it. Which isn't to say that sometimes poems aren't written in the first person. The point is not to let yourself be the main character of what you're thinking. If the sense of self is too narrowly located, then people sound like they're talking about themselves all the time.

Do you evolve conscious strategies other than your formal Zen practice for developing this sort of attitude?

Zen practice is not limited to sitting on a cushion in a zendo. That becomes a habit of life, that's true.

The poem "What Have I Learned" describes a lifetime's knowledge of how to use certain "tools." It's clear that the term means many things in this context: "What have I learned / but the proper use for several tools . . . ." Can you say more about this?

I was thinking of such tools as language, the library . . .

Your word processor?

No, more general: the whole fact of the stored body of information which is accessible to us at any time—you go up to the library—which means all of the referencing and information research skills.

The poem refers to "passing it on." Is that what you see yourself passing on?

Not quite exactly. What one hopes to pass along is the living experience of being in each moment.

You've spoken about the oral roots of literature, and Vak as speech. How important is oral performance for your poetry?

I enjoy reading my own and others' poems aloud. If somebody other than myself did it that would be O.K. I feel that the primary mode of existence of poetry is in speech and performance, and that writing is its secondary mode of existence. That's where it's been put *down*, where it's been kept. Just like a play: you know when you read a play that its full mode of existence would be in performance. Still, you know that you can get something out of it by reading the script. So a poem is a kind of script—at least it can sometimes be that way; I think of a poem in that way. By thinking that way and by practicing that way I do make a connection in my own poetics with a very broad tradition of poems, the pre-literate and oral traditions.

To what extent does the sort of poetics you have in mind imply a rejection of the dominant Western literary tradition?

It doesn't reject the *poems*. There's some excellent poetry there. It rejects the limitations that it has imposed on us: the elitist limitations, transforming itself into an academic discipline, where its works are kept in libraries.

Do you have any suggestions for people who are working in a primarily literate culture and want access to oral tradition so as to incorporate some of its features in their own poetry?

That is something that we've been just making up as we went along, and there's been a lot of exchange back and forth between people in drama, storytellers, and some traditional native people, and the artists who've been doing it. It's very lively now. Performance poetry is being done all the time in New York, Los Angeles and San Francisco. You go to a lot of theater and performance and get a sense of what's happening, of what can be done. You try things out. Try things out in your living room.

More specifically, do you have any advice for writers who are experimenting with forms that don't reproduce the old relation between reader and writer?

We did an event at Green Gulch Farm, a branch of San Francisco Zen Center, a year ago last April, where we had a poetry creation right in the zendo, with a great deal of randomness and unpredictability, à la John Cage. It's fun, but it's not memorable. The writer-reader is the singer-hearer relationship. Traditionally you break down the line between the singer and the hearers with responses or choruses where people join in the chorus, sing together. There's a play that goes back and forth between the singer and the hearers, with the singer or singers who occupy the central territory invading the territory of the audience, including the audience in their territory and then backing out again. I have no problem with that. I have no problem with the singer-hearer, reader-writer relationship. It's a voluntary association. Nobody is forced to be a reader or a hearer and so I would not call it a model of oppression. You can walk out if you want to. In fact it has a good free-market analogy. It's the market: pay and enjoy, or don't buy. You go down the alleys and lanes of a fair, and you go in to find which jugglers you want to see. The writer or the artist has no complaint. People either come to hear her wares or they don't.

With the free-market analogy in mind, how would you respond to the criticism that your work tends to be too esoteric, too dependent on allusions that most readers will not get?

Some does, some doesn't. Some of my writing is more esoteric, some is less. I try to put in something for everybody.

And who is your audience?

The primary audience is people born since 1925, living in California, Oregon, Washington, British Columbia and Alaska.

That's pretty regional.

That's primary. That's where the people live who can get a sense of what the inside levels are. People can read it in other places, but they'll miss some.

Why that date?

Because that's when the zeitgeist becomes . . . the zeitgeist of this particular zeit [*laughs*] . . . that's *this* zeit, this time frame.

*I was recently reading the poem **"Front Lines"** with some of my students in South Africa, most of whom were born in the sixties. I told them I was going to be seeing you, and asked if I should pass on any questions. [Snyder laughs loudly.] After a highly charged account of ecosocial exploitation, the poem ends with the words "And here we must draw / our line." The students' response was "That's fine. But if we accept your critique, what do we do?"*

Well the bio-regional program is very good. That is the one that says "First, don't move, and second, find out what that teaches you." It means you have to learn local history, local economics: not just in the abstract, but as it affects you locally. You're asking "How are we related to the economy exactly, detail by detail?" I know exactly how much gravel is worth. I know how the price of timber has fluctuated over the last fifteen years. There are a lot of instructive things you learn about how you're related to the economy. I can't know what South African students are faced with, but if they feel they have a right to be where they are at all, then they should be there and they should take it on as a serious obligation. They should think up where they want to raise their children, and then they should provide a place for their children. That doesn't necessarily mean in the country. A few things then: one is place, one is your mind. That means meditation in one form or another, as a nonstressful, nonhysterical lifetime process, just a habit of life. A third thing is to have a craft, have a skill, have *one thing* that you can do. If it's something you can do with your hands, all the better. Have a *real* skill, for the sake of yourself, and for the sake of others. Those are very fundamental. I would say that political sanity and engagement can in part come out of a curriculum like that. Not one hundred percent. If a person as a matter of career has chosen the life of a political warrior, then that involves some other kinds of action.

We were speaking this morning before the interview about pressure on writers to conform to ideological positions that are considered to be "politically correct." Would you mind repeating some of what you said?

It seems to me, by my (by no means thoroughly researched) historical information, that putting a high degree of importance on the fine points of doctrine, and on the idea of the correct line, the correct doctrine, comes into Occidental culture in a big way with the Catholic Church and its various councils in which it declared certain positions heretical or false. The importance that they placed on that, and the inability to accept these poetically different versions, or different aspects of the same truth, and the continual seeking-out, arguing-out of doctrinal points has dominated much of Christian thought. This means that the possession of, or the adherence to, a correct line, now seems to take precedence over action or meditation or prayer, in a big way. I see it continuing right into the old

Communist Party's paranoid obsession with the correct line, and you know radical movements today for which there can be no diversity regarding the line. It's what is going on right now with the feminists and deep ecologists and Murray Bookchin, all arguing about what's the vanguard and what's the right line. Murray Bookchin's main complaint is that he's not the vanguard. He wants to be the vanguard and he's mad because Earth First! is the vanguard, and so he has to criticize Earth First! all the time [laughs]. That is elevating the theory over the practice, and it need not be done that way. There are other ways to accomplish clarification of doctrine without being so intellectual or abstract about it. The whole thing is an Occidental neurosis.

At the same time there is surely a place for vigilance. Having grown up in South Africa, I'm aware of the possibilities for unwittingly internalizing the dominant ideology, while attempting to articulate something that is an alternative to it, which is outside it. Are you conscious of that in your work? Do you deliberately work against it?

Yes, I certainly try to watch out for it. It's a danger on the Buddhist level-I mean, that really is on the level of understanding what it is that's affecting you, understanding how you are shaped, understanding what the deeper levels of your opinions and thoughts and feelings are. Those things are so unconscious. You also have to find out what the dominant ideology is, and how it changes. That's tricky. It isn't just that you set yourself against it, because if you set yourself too totally against it, you can't talk to it. If you don't understand how indoctrinated you are, then there's no communication possible. That takes a certain coyote-mind.

Trickster?

Yes, coyote-mind can understand both sides of a question anytime. *Really* understand them [laughs].

Is that a way of approaching Zen's non-dualism?

Yes.

How would these questions relate to the problems of a program focused on celebrating "woman as nature"?

O.K., let's see how a program celebrating woman as nature is unwittingly buying into the dominant ideology. For one thing it might involve organizing a group of people to be an audience to celebrate something that is given an authority above them. Structurally it's no different from celebrating the flag. So instead of looking to content you look at form, and the form is the form of masses elevating authority. That's acting within the dominant ideology.

And yet you've written poems that could be described as celebrating woman as nature?

Oh I might have done that once or twice [laughs], as an exercise, and as I felt like it. But I can also look back and say "Well, maybe I was just reproducing . . . the Fourth of July or something," reproducing a *form* which is more insidious than one might have thought. Those are interesting questions.

Patrick D. Murphy (essay date 1992)

SOURCE: "Of Wildness and Wilderness in Plain Language: The Practice of the Wild," in *Understanding Gary Snyder,* University of South Carolina Press, 1992, pp. 154-66.

[*In the following excerpt, Murphy discusses the ecological impact of Snyder's writing.*]

Since the publication of **Axe Handles** Snyder has continued to address the central problem of civilization but in a more diversified way. He has written poetry, given poetry readings, written prose, and begun teaching as a permanent member of a university faculty. His latest published volume is a work qualitatively superior and more significant than any other prose volume he has published. *The Practice of the Wild* is a sophisticated yet clear, complex yet uncomplicated, unified book about *knowing how to be* in this world. In one of the early reviews of this book, Ray Olson claims that Snyder's essays "constitute the finest wisdom (and also ecological) literature of our time" [*Booklist,* September 15, 1990].

Earth House Hold has been his only prose volume treated critically in its own right and remains the prose most often quoted, with perhaps the exception of the essay "Four Changes" at the end of **Turtle Island.** Yet *Earth House Hold* is not a unified work but a selection of discrete pieces that work together because of the life and mind behind them; a full appreciation of this collection is to some extent dependent on the reader's knowledge of Snyder's poetry. *The Practice of the Wild* functions on a different level of organization, being thematically unified by a discussion of the interrelationships of the meanings of freedom and responsibility, wilderness and wildness, humanity and nature, mind and body, conscious and unconscious, and knowledge and action.

It has been inaccurately defined as "nature writing," compared time and again with Thoreau's *Walden,* and discussed in terms of primitivism and nostalgia. But the Anglo-American tradition of nature writing has tended to be based on a sense of the author's alienation and distance from the natural world and a male desire to be reunited with something felt to be missing or lost. Thoreau had to leave Concord and go to the woods to try his two-year experiment of simple living by Walden Pond and in so doing embodied the romantic notions of human alienation from nature and nostalgic yearning to return to some Edenic ideal.

Snyder is concerned instead with people conducting practice in place. As he remarked in an interview with David Robertson conducted while Snyder was completing *The Practice of the Wild,* "I hope that the book I am now writing will be stimulating to a broad range of people and provide them with historical, ecological, and personal visions all at the same time. I would like to see the book be political in the sense of helping people shape the way they want to live and act in the world" ["Practicing the Wild," *Critical Essays on Gary Snyder,* 1990].

The Practice of the Wild leaps beyond the traditional limitations of the genre of nature writing. This is ecological writing in its fullest sense and treats in detail ideas that Snyder could only present in outline in his poems. And while the volume is optimistic, it is not idealistic in the sense of being utopian or naive. Robertson's comment to Snyder is pertinent here: "One of the things I like so much about your prose writing is your ability to lay out a vision of life as it ought to be, at the same time recognizing very hardheadedly that actual life is rooted in ambiguity and frustration over uncompleted goals." Robertson may in part be responding to Snyder's recognition reiterated since the early 1970s, first to Ekbert Faas and then to numerous other interviewers including Robertson, that "we are entering into a really critical age. Things are bad and they are going to get worse." But, as Snyder maintains throughout *The Practice of the Wild,* he also knows that they can get better.

The first section of *The Practice of the Wild,* "The Etiquette of Freedom," begins with the notion of a "compact" as one of the forms of proper relationships among all entities who inhabit this earth. Snyder realistically recognizes that these arrangements include predatory as well as symbiotic, mutually beneficial ones. In what humans consider the wild reaches of the world, nonhuman creatures work out their lives in relationships that are conditioned first and foremost by the various food chains of their bioregions. To date, as Snyder points out, contemporary humans are the worst example of creatures disrupting their own and other creatures' food chains. To counter this process Snyder emphasizes the need to educate people so that they will work to cease "causing unnecessary harm" to other beings as well as to themselves.

From the notion of "compact," Snyder moves to an investigation of the popular American dream of "wild and free" and describes that dream in terms of a freedom that is achieved only when people recognize the real conditions of existence in which they participate. A crucial component of those conditions is "impermanence," which Americans in particular seem to fear, given their attitudes toward aging and dying. To realize freedom, Snyder argues, people are going to have to begin to build a civilization that can come to terms with and sustain "wildness." Suspecting that his readers do not have a very good sense of such terms as "Nature, Wild, *and* Wilderness," Snyder elaborates the derivations and definitional developments of these three words.

What people have for centuries termed the "wild" is that which has an ecosystem sufficiently flexible that humans who have not previously participated in it may enter it and survive. In contrast, contemporary cities are so inflexible and closed that wild vegetation and animals haven't a chance and generally rarely venture in. It is important to remember, however, that human beings at various histor-

ical moments developed within and as functioning parts of wild ecosystems.

Snyder then relates language to body, swerving around the popular Western tendency to separate mind and body or to perceive them as in contradiction with one another. He points out that "language is a mind-body system that coevolved with our needs and nerves," i.e., it is psychic *and* physical, since the psyche is part of the body. And poetry enters the picture as one of the ways in which language can serve the re-education of human beings to their own wild origins.

Having developed the idea of wild ecosystems and the wildness that must be reasserted along with recovering wilderness, Snyder turns his attention to conceptions of place. He emphasizes here the ways in which peoples relate to the land by means of an understanding of locale, region, and community. He begins with a position shared by Wendell Berry and numerous Native Americans: non-Native Americans are a set of rootless, un-placed and displaced peoples, and this condition is fundamentally unhealthy; it produces dis-ease. Snyder starts with a concept of home as hearth and moves to an understanding of region based on local specifics and on one's apprehension of that region as a living, interactive place, not a national or governmental abstraction composed of dotted lines on a distorted map.

The "commons" is a European practice of setting aside land for communal activities, and Snyder applies this idea to the sharing of "natural areas." Various forms of commons can be found around the world, including in Japanese farming villages. In the United States, commons were a rare feature of the East but did turn up in the West, due to climate and topography, and have been developed perhaps most fully in relationship to equitable access to water. Snyder believes that it is absolutely necessary to return to a system of commons and that this system needs to be used worldwide and should be extended to include such aspects of the biosphere as the air and the oceans. On the land, Snyder thinks that the greatest hope for recovering the commons lies in instituting localized bioregional governments and community practices. Fundamentally, "bioregionalism is the entry of place into the dialectic of history. Also we might say that there are 'classes' which have so far been overlooked—the animals, rivers, rocks, and grasses—now entering history." Snyder renders these claims concrete by relating the way he and others who inhabit San Juan Ridge are learning their place and their role in that place.

In this section of *The Practice of the Wild* Snyder turns his attention to manifestations of bioregional practice in terms of the cultural specifics of peoples and what the healthier cultures have in common. He draws on his experiences in Asia as well as North America to develop his points. In Alaska, Snyder finds significant parallels between the means by which the Inupiaq are attempting to raise their children and the practices of the San Juan Ridge school back home. One of the issues that Snyder discusses here is the relationship between oral transmissions and written transmissions of cultures. In a literate society, he notes, "books are our grandparents," because in oral cultures it is the elders who transmit the cultural lore and values by means of stories.

Such considerations lead Snyder into meditations on nature writing, nature as a book, and an ecology of language. Snyder claims that grammars, like metaphors, are ways of interpreting reality, and that "tawny grammars" come from nature itself in its myriad manifestations. Snyder's point is not so much to argue for the organic and evolutionary character of language as to deflate the homocentric egotism of those who like to imagine "language as a uniquely human gift."

Tom Clark, writing about *The Practice of the Wild* as a whole, claims that "the essays are deployed poetically, less like steps in an argument than as spokes radiating around a single, urgent, central theme: the need for re-establishing those traditional practices of wilderness that once linked humanity in a single, harmonic chord with the animals, plants, lands and water" ["Essays that Echo Thoreau," *San Francisco Chronicle,* September 16, 1990]. "Good, Wild, Sacred" can be seen as being structured in the same way. Snyder begins with this triad of key concepts, centered on "wild," and works through a series of reflections on historical and present-day experience. He speaks of the contradiction within an "agrarian theology" that holds that humans render themselves more holy by "weeding out" the wild from their own nature, at the same time that their having done the same to cattle and pigs has altered those animals from "intelligent and alert in the wild into sluggish meat-making machines." In the process of attempting to elevate themselves, humans have degraded nature and reduced natural intelligence. Snyder necessarily rejects any theology based on a separation of the physical and the spiritual and speaks approvingly here of Native American beliefs that connect land and spirit.

From the spiritual practices of North America's inhabitory peoples, Snyder then turns to what he has learned about spirit and place from the aboriginal people of Australia. In particular, he focuses on the ways in which their stories about themselves as people are intimately tied to the land in which they live. In that land exist certain sacred places, some of which he was privileged to visit. He was told that some of those places were defined as "teaching spots" and some as "dreaming spots." This experience prompts him to mediate on "dreamtime," which he believes "is the mode of the eternal moment of creating, of being, as contrasted with the mode of cause and effect in time." Differentiating between the linear time frame that dominates Western thought and the dream time of aboriginal peoples leads Snyder to think of Buddhism, particularly the Avatamsaka Sutra, and the practices of Japan's aboriginal people, the Ainu. Snyder reflects sadly on the fact that in present-day Japan so little of the Ainu and Shinto practices in relation to the sacredness of land remain.

Toward the end of the essay, Snyder circles back to the North American present and eventually to the land in which he lives, where the essay started. He makes an extremely important point that runs counter to much of European and American thinking that has been current for centuries: "It is not nature-as-chaos which threatens us, but the State's presumption that *it* has created order"; and, further, "Nature is orderly. That which appears to be chaotic in nature is only a more complex kind of order."

The essay "Blue Mountains Constantly Walking" is heavily dependent for its meaning on Snyder's deep and abiding philosophical, spiritual, and aesthetic debts to Japan and Buddhism. Snyder begins the essay by talking about Dogen, the thirteenth-century Buddhist monk, and his "Mountains and Waters Sutra," delivered in 1240. He then links Dogen's attention to mountains to the practices of Buddhist pilgrimages and attitudes about sacred mountains, such as Mt. Hiei.

Snyder not only provides historical information about such pilgrimages but also includes personal experience. It is useful to remember that while Snyder was in Japan he took vows with the Yamabushi monks, as he describes some of that initiation here. The Yamabushi are a sect of mountain ascetic monks, and Snyder reminds his reader that "in East Asia 'mountains' are often synonymous with wilderness," particularly since they are the terrain impervious to wilderness-destroying agriculture. But mountains cannot be understood properly in a vacuum, since they enter into relationship with the rest of nature. Dogen's sutra is, after all, about "mountains *and* waters," because, as Snyder observes: "mountains and rivers indeed form each other: waters are precipitated by heights, carve or deposit landforms in their flowing descent, and weight the offshore continental shelves with sediment to ultimately tilt more uplifts." Poems in *Regarding Wave* are informed by this attitude as can be noted when Snyder remarks here that a mountain range is sometimes referred to "as a network of veins on the back of a hand," an image which also appears in *Regarding Wave.* What is most important, however, is not the ability to make associations among the different aspects of nature—mountains like veins, bodies like streams; it is being able to realize that there is no *nature* as an entity but only *naturing,* a process of interaction and mutual transformation. Solidity consists of energy transformations in an apparent, but only apparent, period of stasis.

According to Clark, "Ancient Forests of the Far West" comprises "the crowning component of this stirring, thoughtful field report on the tenuous state of the wild in our time." Interestingly enough, Snyder uses as epigraph for this essay the same lines from Exodus that he quotes in **"Logging 2"** of *Myths & Texts.* Thus he explicitly loops back to poetry written nearly forty years earlier. In the opening section of the essay he loops back even farther to youthful experiences growing up and working in those Far West forests. This essay provides one of the clearest pictures Snyder has presented of the events behind the poetry of the "Logging" section of *Myths & Texts* as well as early poems, such as **"The Late Snow & Lumber Strike of the Summer of Fifty-four"** in *Riprap.*

Snyder uses these personal memories as a way of detailing an appropriate type of logging, selective and sensitive to the bioregion and to the individual trees that are dying. From this lesson of the right way to do things, Snyder switches to the history of U.S. forest management, as well as to an analysis of the ecological specifics of the ancient western forests. Snyder notes that "the forests of the maritime Pacific Northwest are the last remaining forests of any size left in the temperate zone" worldwide. And he details the history of the loss of corresponding forests in the Mediterranean and East Asia before returning to the threats that the surviving forests face from the U.S. government and its various agencies. Snyder speaks lovingly and respectfully of the forests of his own region and the need and ways to protect them. This essay ends with a determined anger in which the tasks of Snyder and reader alike are delineated: "We must make the hard-boiled point that the world's trees are virtually worth more standing than they would be as lumber, because of such diverse results of deforestation as life-destroying flooding in Bangladesh and Thailand, the extinction of millions of species of animals and plants, and global warming. . . . We are all endangered yokels."

Paths and trails have served writers as metaphors for an entire series of human activities, both spiritual and physical, for centuries. In this essay Snyder participates in this tradition by developing his own literal and metaphoric senses of these terms. He also introduces the concept of "networks" to distinguish between two aspects of an individual's life. As Snyder sees it, community is grounded in place, while work is often grounded in associations that take one beyond place into a network of people engaged in the same or related tasks. As a result "networks cut across communities with their own kind of territoriality." The problem for Snyder is that in the present day people often relate only to their network and fail to establish themselves in their community as well.

Snyder turns to Asia to develop a notion related to path and trail—that of "way," which includes the idea of path but extends it to an entire perception of being, to the realms of philosophies, religions, and ideologies. One of the ways that people travel is that of art, which Snyder discusses in terms of the relationship between tradition and creativity. This in turn brings him back to a relationship addressed at the beginning of *The Practice of the Wild*, which is that of freedom and responsibility. Manifestations of this relationship can be thought of in terms of discipline and spontaneity, as well as models and innovation. Snyder here resorts again to Buddhism and the various means by which its masters have tried to teach the relationship of the tradition, discipline, and path of Buddhist practice and individual experience—the last marked by the distinction between prescribed forms of meditation and the individual experiencing of enlightenment. Snyder concludes that "there are paths that can be followed, and there is a path that cannot—it is not a path, it is the wilderness. There is a 'going' but no goer, no destination, only the whole field." And, then, he immediately departs the realm of metaphor to talk about his own experience, which led him to study Zen in Japan, as well as to return to the United States as the place to practice what he had learned. Snyder ends with a warning about the relation-

ships of freedom and responsibility, discipline and spontaneity, tradition and innovation: "But we need paths and trails and will always be maintaining them. You must first be on the path, before you can turn and walk into the wild."

In "The Woman Who Married a Bear" Snyder brings together tradition and innovation, myth and experience, with a popular Native American tale of intersexuality between humans and other animals. He begins with the mythical story. Then, rather than explaining the tale, he begins to relate the history of bears in North America. This too becomes a story as Snyder retells with more realistic details rather than mythic ones the bear-human marriage myth. Like any good myth, Snyder's story educates readers about the world, specifically about the lives of bears and their relationship to their environment. Then, with his version of the story ended, Snyder relates the source of the tale and a little information about the Native American woman who told it, followed by a suggestion of the ubiquity of bear-human stories through references to Greek mythology.

The reader may keep waiting for Snyder to analyze the story, but he never does. Instead, he ends with another story, about a Native American bear dance he witnessed in 1977. What is revealed here, rather than claimed or explained, is the power that myth can carry in the present day and the ways by which it can help bridge the gap between animal and human that, as the story of the woman who married a bear suggests, once did not exist.

"Survival and Sacrament" serves as Snyder's conclusion to *The Practice of the Wild*. It begins on an ominous note by warning of the terrifying difference between death and the "end to birth," that is, between an individual's death and the end of the coming into being of an entire species. Since their arrival in North America white human beings have been not only witnesses but also the cause of the "end to birth" of countless species at an ever-increasing rate with no conception of the suffering involved or the long range effects on the ecosystems of this continent and the entire planetary biosphere. Snyder points out that excessive human reproduction, particularly in the past three hundred years, is a crucial dimension of this problem.

Snyder opens his conclusion with a warning, but he ends it with a promise of covenant. That promise begins with the argument that a true human quest "requires embracing the other as oneself" and that a movement in the world is growing that recognizes just such a necessity. This necessity does not take the form of developing a more advanced civilization, as one might expect, but of developing a wilder culture, a "culture of the wilderness." This phrase encapsulates a dual recognition. One, nature is always a social construct in terms of the limits of human understanding and interaction with the rest of the world; two, society is always a natural construct arising in relation to and on the basis of natural conditions of existence. Snyder closes his book with a discussion of "Grace," both as prayer and behavior, as a socially constructed natural act which recognizes that "eating is a sacrament." To approach eating with respect is to recognize human integration with the rest of the world in which people live and die, and in which people cause other beings to live and die as well, either necessarily or capriciously. By this emphasis on grace Snyder has returned to the beginning of *The Practice of the Wild,* teaching his readers about a particular form of the "etiquette of freedom," one which recognizes and gratefully affirms human responsibility.

Helen Vendler (essay date 1995)

SOURCE: "American Zen: Gary Snyder's *No Nature,*" in *Soul Says: On Recent Poetry,* The Belknap Press of Harvard University Press, 1995, pp. 117-29.

[*In the following excerpt, Vendler discusses the concept of self in Snyder's poetry.*]

Gary Snyder is more widely known as an ecological activist than as a poet, and indeed the jacket copy on his *No Nature: New and Selected Poems* makes a heavy-handed pitch to the ecologically minded sector of his audience: "We are a people, as this century ends, desperate to recapture the feeling of being at home in the world. *No Nature* offers us guidance along this path. Snyder's poems invite us to observe nature carefully, and to see ecology, bioregionalism, and sustainable culture as intrinsically bound to our own human fate." This offers us Snyder as guru, and it is a role he has not avoided. "My political position," he has written, "is to be a spokesman for wild nature. . . . And for the people who live in dependence on that." Gurus may live by their messages alone, but poets do not. And though Snyder has earned the seriousness of his views, which he presents not only in political debates over the fate of the California landscape, for instance, but also in the example of his own frugal way of living, his moral seriousness by itself would not earn him the title of poet. But he has also changed what we consider the lyric self to be.

Modern dismantlers of the notion of selfhood have pointed out that each of us is less a "unified self" than a site traversed by the discourses to which we have been exposed. The amalgam of multiple discourses in you "is" you; consciousness is coextensive with the languages in which it is conceived. The free-will or constructivist version of this idea gives you some agency in picking and choosing your discourses, whereas the determinist version finds you helplessly passive in your absorption of the discourses of your cultural and environmental moment.

There is an element of plain common sense in all this; of course one's selfhood is bounded by the available discourses of conceptualization during one's existence—a fact that ought to prevent the sort of anachronistic blame that accuses the Bible of "sexism" or Shakespeare of "racism." But a more acute question follows: what would a self that really believed itself to be just a site of crisscrossing transient discourses (and no more than that) sound like

when it opened its mouth? It would have to sound both more provisional and more self-effacing than the encapsulated "I" that has represented, successively, the Christian soul, the rationalist self, and the Freudian ego. It would know that it once did not exist, and would soon not exist again; it would be less anxious about the lifelong continuity of selfhood than was, say, Wordsworth. It would have to be self-conscious about the discourse realm in which it was moving at any given moment, and of its exits and entrances as it moved from one realm to another.

Such a self would not regard itself as distinct from other matter in the universe. It would be part of nature, but not in the pantheistic way that projected a soul into nature. Instead, the self would be situated in an unremarkable continuity with other inorganic and organic clusters of natural forms. It would not occupy a position superior to other beings but would see itself in a horizontal landscape, touching other beings left and right. It would know that it constitutes its world by means of its own limited perceptual apparatus, but it would also acknowledge that the world seems to us a solid given thing, and that it impresses itself upon us in realist guise.

What would this sort of selfhood look like in lyric? It would look like Gary Snyder. And how did a poet born in 1930, the contemporary of the confessional poets (Plath, Sexton) and the prophetic poets (Ginsberg, Rich), think up this selfless self and its distinctive style of writing? The complete answer will not appear until we know more of Snyder's life (there is as yet no biography), but the central experience from which his adult poetry derives seems to be his study of Zen Buddhism, both as a young man and then during the twelve years (1956-1968) when he lived mostly in Japan, studying with Zen masters. . . .

A committee of which I was a member awarded the 1975 Pulitzer Prize to Snyder's *Turtle Island,* and I recall wondering at the time who the person was who sang these impersonal songs. Here, for example, is the now famous poem **"The Real Work"** (about rowing with friends by Alcatraz, as the epigraph tells us):

> sea-lions and birds,
> sun through fog
> flaps up and lolling,
> looks you dead in the eye.
> sun haze;
> a long tanker riding light and high.
> sharp wave choppy line—
> interface tide-flows—
> seagulls sit on the meeting
> eating;
> we slide by white-stained cliffs.
>
> the real work.
> washing and sighing,
> sliding by.

There's an impersonal "you" here and an amorphous "we," but no "I." Instead, the reader meets a montage of noun phrases, and along with them come verbals in *-ing*: the sun lolling, the tanker riding, the tideflows meeting, the seagulls eating, the "real work" of the sea washing and sighing, the "real work" of the observers sliding by. A hidden hand has taken a good deal of trouble to arrange these and other visual and aural effects, bringing about what the poet Alan Williamson has called "little defiant rescues of pure momentariness from the grid of generalized time that is built into grammar itself." But the cinematographer of this scene prefers to obscure himself, letting us follow his "camera eye" alone, just as the moralist of this poem, defining what "the real work" is, prefers to couch it in metaphorical rather than conceptual terms.

This method of composition was named metaphorically by Snyder himself in his first volume as "riprap"—the stone cobble laid on a mountain trail to prevent erosion: "Lay down these words / Before your mind like rocks." It is painstaking and heavy work. The poetics of riprap owes something to Pound's notion of the poem as sculpture, and to Pound's phrasal organization, but Snyder, more than Pound, is attached to syntactic effects as well as phrasal ones. In **"The Real Work"** there are real sentences: the sun looks you in the eye, the seagulls sit, and the rowers slide by cliffs. That is, there is statement and closure as well as timeless phrasal presentation of visual effects. The morality of the end echoes Keats's "moving waters at their priestlike task / Of pure ablution round earth's human shores," but Keats would not have written in terms of the easygoing "sliding by."

Back in 1975, I preferred the elegantly arranged cinematographic poems in ***Turtle Island*** to the heavy-handed protest poems, and I still do. Here is an example of the latter:

> How can the head-heavy power-hungry politic
>   scientist
> Government   two-world Capitalist-Imperialist
> Third-world Communist paper-shuffling male
>   non-farmer   jet-set bureaucrats
> Speak for the green of the leaf? Speak for the soil?
> (Ah Margaret Mead . . . do you sometimes dream
>   of Samoa?)

There was more of this sort of political-tract boilerplate in the eight volumes from which ***No Nature*** has been selected. And there were failed attempts to speak with a tribal voice, as in **"Praise for Sick Women,"** a poem not collected here that was printed in the influential 1960 Donald Allen anthology *The New American Poetry*. **"Praise for Sick Women"** begins with an unfortunate reminiscence of Pound ("The female is fertile, and discipline / (contra naturam) only / confuses her") it continues with an attempt to represent early tribal views which considered menstruation unclean:

> Where's hell then?
> In the moon.
> In the change of the moon:
> In a bark shack
> Crouched from sun, five days,
> Blood dripping through crusted thighs.

Inept though this is, it is suggestive of the sort of experiment Snyder wanted to make.

Snyder's Buddhism has always existed in sharp and productive tension with his inherited socialist utopianism and its negative consequence, bitter political protest.

—Helen Vendler

A list of poetic imperatives in the mature Snyder would go something like this: to reenter the archaic, but not in such a way as to sound foolish; to utter protests, but not in such a way as to become solely a propagandist; to efface "personality" in favor of a mostly perceptual being-in-the-world; to arrange words like cobble ("granite; ingrained / with torment of fire and weight"; to use restraint in tone and form alike. Snyder does wonderful things with and within these imperatives. He often registers the passage of time with an impersonality full of wonder: the vividly appreciative evolutionary poem **"What Happened Here Before"** traces the geological and ecological changes in the California landscape from three hundred million years ago till 1825, retelling each epoch, sometimes in the present tense, sometimes in the past. Three hundred million years ago: "soft sands, muds, and marls." Eighty million years ago: "warm quiet centuries of rains . . . / volcanic ash . . . piles up the gold and gravel." Three million years ago: "ground squirrel, fox, blacktail hare, ringtail, bobcat, bear, / all came to live here." Forty thousand years ago: "And human people came with basket hats and nets." This part of the poem closes with the nineteenth-century gold rush:

> Then came the white man: tossed up trees and
>   boulders with big hoses,
>   going after that old gravel and the gold.
> horses, apple-orchards, card-games,
>   pistol-shooting, churches, county jail.

For the duration of such a poem, we are given, on loan, a time-sense that we ourselves may live in rarely, but that Snyder lives in always—the opulent time-sense of a luxuriously unfolding evolutionary dynamic in which we are very late comers. When reproached for the "impracticality" of his ideas on how to live, Snyder is fond of pointing out that he is in synchrony with the large evolutionary picture, whereas his critics live too narrowly in the present: "It's only a temporary turbulence I'm setting myself against. I'm in line with the big flow . . . 'Right now' is an illusion too." In poems like **"What Happened Here Before,"** Snyder takes on the archaic tribal role of storyteller, but instead of telling cosmological tribal myths of sky gods and earth women, he relates our commonly accepted narrative of geological and evolutionary change in successive phases ("I was there to see it") of exquisitely chosen detail, musically modulated into what are, it is not too much to say, lovable stanzas.

The later Snyder can allow himself a relaxed political diction, as in a poem dedicated to Jerry Brown, **"Talking Late with the Governor about the Budget,"** where, "tired of the effort / Of thinking about 'the People,'" he leaves the building and sees overhead the moon, a planet, and a star, "And east, over the Sierra, / Far flashes of lightning— / Is it raining tonight at home?" The glimpses of personal feeling here—of weary Arts Council efforts in unpromising directions, and of momentary homesickness—are nevertheless chastened by the presence of the regal and imperturbable processes of the cosmos. Politics cannot be everything to Snyder. His Buddhism has always existed in sharp and productive tension with his inherited socialist utopianism and its negative consequence, bitter political protest. Insofar as Buddhism proclaims such engagement a form of illusion, Snyder knows that he should not let it disturb his inner quiet: "To take the struggle on without the least hope of doing any good." Asked whether poetry makes anything happen, Snyder once replied, "Well in that sense poetry does no more than woodchopping, or automobile repair, or anything else does because they're all equally real." And so he drives himself resolutely back from protest to his poetic function: to be a link in the transmission of what there is to be seen and known in the world. (He remarks, suggestively, in one interview, "My father . . . was a smart man, a very handy man, but he only knew about fifteen different trees and after that he was lost. I wanted more precision; I wanted to look deeper into the underbrush.") He wants to be a channel for what he calls, in the early poem of that name, **"High Quality Information."** It is the earnest and eager poem of a young man, and in it Snyder makes clear that much must be repressed in order for the new imperatives to arise:

> A life spent seeking it
> Like a worm in the earth,
> Like a hawk. Catching threads
> Sketching bones
> Assessing where the road goes.
> Lao-tzu says
> To forget what you knew is best.
> That's what I want;
> To get these sights down,
> Clear, right to the place
> Where they face
> Back into the mind of my times.
> The same old circuitry
> But some paths color-coded
> *Empty*
> And we're free to go.

To forget what you knew; to color-code some of your mental paths "Empty" and never go down them again: this resolve accounts for some of what is missing in Snyder's work.

Snyder is not unaware of the dangers in taking too remote and geological a view of human affairs. He voices that danger in the poem **"Word Basket Woman,"** commenting on the American poet nearest him in ecological vision, Robinson Jeffers:

> Robinson Jeffers, his tall cold view
> quite true in a way, but why did he say it
> as though he alone
> stood above our delusions, he also
> feared death, insignificance,
> and was not quite up to the inhuman beauty
> of parsnips or diapers, the deathless
> nobility at the core of all ordinary things.

Because Snyder fears the tonal extremes of prophetic denunciation and an indifferent Olympianism, because he wants to include parsnips and diapers, the tonal range he allows himself in his best poetry is rather narrow: it runs from curious observation to cheerful enjoyment to genial hospitality. Because he is so steady in his self-control, the more denunciatory and chaotic moments in the poetry strike the reader as off key. Yet one suspects that chaos may be more "natural" to Snyder than order, the mid-range tonality more "controlled" than spontaneous. This control can be seen in the tightness of his poetic structures.

There is an obsessive concern with arrangement in Snyder's best work—a concern one wants to call "Japanese"—as all the cobbles in the riprap begin to take on mutual relations like those between the famous stones in the Ryoan-ji garden. The stones that we repair to, in a visual zigzag, as we traverse **"Surrounded by Wild Turkeys,"** a beautiful late meditation on parental and filial generations, are the words "call," "pass," "through," and "like":

> Little calls as they pass
> through dry forbs and grasses
> Under blue oak and gray digger pine
> In the warm afternoon of the forest-fire haze;
>
> Twenty or more, long-legged birds all alike.
>
> So are we, in our soft calling,
>
> passing on through.
>
> Our young, which trail after,
>
> Look just like us.

The other "stones" successively placed in the poem are its gentle adjectives: "little," "blue," "gray," "warm," "long-legged," "soft." They make up the tonal climate. In many poems, Snyder represents himself and his family as leading what one must call a mammalian life, really not much different in its needs and instincts from the herd life of bears or sheep; but here he extends the comparison even to birds. Of course, even Snyder's organic sympathies have limits; he is not likely to compare himself and his family to a hive of termites. But a poem like **"Surrounded by Wild Turkeys"** (in which the baby turkeys "trailing" after their parents confer their verb on Snyder's mental image of his own children) suggests a way of being in the world—unassuming, honest, untranscendent, selfdeprecating, tender, and open to delight—which is quietly exemplary, without aggressively urging itself on others.

Formally, Snyder has stuck pretty conclusively to his main tools—noun phrases, present participles, an emphasis on the visual, and a care for musical phrasing. Every so often, he'll do something deliberately striking, as in a Zen poem of earthly revelation. This poem bears an enormous title, and is dated from an origin over forty thousand years ago, when human life first appeared on earth:

> 24:IV:40075, 3:30 PM,
> N. OF COALDALE, NEVADA, A GLIMPSE THROUGH A
>   BREAK IN THE STORM OF THE SUMMIT
>   OF THE WHITE MOUNTAINS
>
> O Mother Gaia
>
> sky cloud gate milk snow
>
> wind-void-word
>
> I bow in roadside gravel

This is a densely constructed poem of both vertical and horizontal orientation. Mother Gaia, the earth, is found on the highest hierarchic level; sky, snow, and summit on the next level down; wind and discourse below that, while the humble disciple on the humble pebbles defines the lowest level. So much for the "vertical plot." The "horizontal plot" of landscape does not, and cannot, exist at the highest level, that of conceptuality: there, Mother Gaia lives alone. Below her, we see the broad horizontal revelation described in the title: a gate opens in the milky clouded sky, and one glimpses a snowy summit. (Naturally, the gate opens in the middle of the scene, framed by cloud-milk in the proximate position, by sky and snow in the remote position.) The horizontal plot at the next level, expressed in words linked by hyphens, tells us that the natural "word" of the universe (the wind) and the real word of human discourse, cannot be separated from the Buddhist void, the gap in meaning, occupying the same place in the "discursive plot" on this level as the glimpsed gate in the "higher" visual plot preceding it. Finally, the last horizontal plot presents the human figure "I" on the left, balanced by the humbling gravel on the right. This is a poem that takes up the challenge of the pagan and Christian shaped lyric and renews the form, while renewing as well the classical apostrophe to the genius loci in the theophany, or manifestation of the god or goddess.

Snyder is one of the many modernist poets to have brought English lyric into conjunction with Chinese and Japanese poetry. The long history of Western fascination with "the Chinese written character as a medium for poetry" (Pound

out of Fenollosa) has reached its apogee with Snyder, if only because Snyder (unlike Amy Lowell, Pound, Stevens, Williams, Rexroth, and others) really knows Japanese and Chinese. His economy and fastidiousness in poetry would please, I should think, not only the ghosts of American Imagism and Objectivism but also those Zen masters with whom he studied; they would recognize the metaphorical weight borne by his apparently artless visual lists, and the historical passion distilled into the words retelling his evolutionary chronicles.

Snyder is one of the many modernist poets to have brought English lyric into conjunction with Chinese and Japanese poetry.

—Helen Vendler

In this way, Snyder offers a worthy counter-possibility to the American passion for explanatory confession. His poems convey remarkably little about his own views of his psyche. Perhaps he doesn't believe he has one—or, at least, one available to reliable inspection. He compels his reader into a rather shocking redefinition of what makes an interesting poem—a definition that goes not only against the confessional norm prevalent in Western lyric since the *Vita Nuova,* and the witty metaphysical poetry that has been the chief lyric rival to the confessional strain, but also against the third major stream of lyric, the "nature poetry" where one might think to locate him. What would the providential Emerson of "The Rhodora," the yearning Frost of "Birches," or the stern Jeffers of Big Sur make of the unembarrassed opening of Snyder's **"Right in the Trail,"** a humorous but admiring poem about bear droppings:

> Here it is, near the house,
> A big pile, fat scats,
> Studded with those deep red
> Smooth-skinned manzanita berries,
> Such a pile! Such droppings,
> Awesome.

Snyder's attempt to see as a Native American might, his de-Christianized gaze, his Buddhist reverence for all life, are the efforts authenticating the stanzas of his nature poems, good and bad alike, and make for his indubitable originality. Especially in the nature poems, we see the suppression of a confessional and introspective self, and the adoption of a self that is perceptually alive, one which allows the discourses appropriate to successive phenomena to appear through him, as through a medium, on the page.

The losses in adopting such an attitude, with its allied formal techniques, are real. The volatility, anguish, and self-questioning of the passionate self, together with certain of its appropriate vocabularies and tropes, vanish. The stories of Snyder's four marriages (and the three divorces) go untold, as does his loss, by divorce, of his father (the cause, perhaps, of his attachment first to Rexroth and next to a succession of Zen masters). The quite fantastic confection that is Snyder's life (measured against the American male norm) makes him a genuine American eccentric, living naked with his naked family (as a visitor reports in the Sierra Club book), and building not only a house but also a Zen meditation hall for himself and his neighbors. His life may be his greatest work of art. Its raggednesses (such as every life must possess) have been pruned and espaliered; the beautiful and chastely decorated Japanese-style timber house, the fine plain utensils, the orderly division of the days and months into travel time and work time, the neatness of all his visual arrangements—these are the outward signs of an inner discipline that may work to hold some disorder at bay. One must respect Snyder for keeping the constraint equal to the disorder. His discretion about personal suffering suggests that the chaos and violence he attacks in the industrial world outside his careful precincts of pastoral retirement may be in part a projection from within, causing that occasional disequilibrium in tone that mars some of his poems.

Snyder remarked in an interview that he could sing approximately two hundred folk songs by heart. The simplicity of oral poetry is what he aims to preserve in his far more tersely organized written poetry. "The poem or the song," he says revealingly, "manifests itself as a special concentration of the capacities of the language and rises up into its own shape." Such a poem rebukes, by its authenticity, poems of no compactness, of no individual shape: "There is an intuitive aesthetic judgment that you can make that in part spots phoniness, spots excess, spots the overblown, or the undersaid, the unripe, or the overripe." Snyder usually walks the tightrope between these extremes with a clearly judged balance; the true poem, he has said, walks "that edge between what can be said and that which cannot be said." It is just that fine edge that is missing in his prose: "If we are lucky we may eventually arrive at a totally integrated world culture with matrilineal descent, free-form marriage, naturalcredit communist economy, less industry, far less population and lots more national parks." Yes, no doubt, but who will remember this paragraph in fifty years? It is a good thing we have poetry to protect us from expository prose at its most *bien pensant*. And although *No Nature* is annoyingly arranged (with some early poems stuck in the latter part, interrupting what is otherwise a chronological order) it is good to have most of Gary Snyder's poems available in one volume. He has been claimed by virtuous ecology, but let us claim him for virtuous poetry, too; by getting rid of "too much ego interference, too much abstract intellect, too much striving for effect," he has constructed in verse a remarkable self resolutely different from the perennial lyric "I," a self in which archaic and modern discourses alike can meet. Of course, it then takes Snyder's genius to make riprap of them, until they make a trail for us into his myths and texts.

FURTHER READING

Biography

Steuding Bob. *Gary Snyder*. Boston: G. K. Hall & Co., 1976, 175 p.

Reflects on Snyder as a poet and provides an in-depth view of his major writing.

Criticism

Altieri, Charles. "Gary Synder's *Turtle Island*: The Problem of Reconciling the Roles of Seer and Prophet." *Boundary 2* IV, No. 3 (Spring 1976): 761-77.

Discusses the relationship between seer and prophet, and their relevance to this piece of work.

Bartlett, Lee. "Gary Snyder's *Myths & Texts* and the Monomyth." *Western American Literature: Quarterly Journal of the Western Literature Association* XVII, No. 2 (Summer 1982): 137-48.

Reveals how *Myths & Texts* mirrors the basic structure of the classic model of the monomyth: separation, initiation, and return.

Carpenter, David A. "Gary Snyder's Inhumanism, from *Riprap* to *Axehandles*." *South Dakota Review* XXVI, No. 1 (Spring 1988): 110-38.

Claims Snyder follows Robinson Jeffers in a tradition that does not see humanity as central to existence.

Holaday, Woon-Ping Chin. "Formlessness and Form in Gary Snyder's *Mountains and Rivers Without End*." *Sagetrieb: A Journal Devoted to Poets* 5, No. 1 (Spring 1986): 41-51.

Examines this particular piece of work from the vantage point of an environmentalist and reaches a conclusion far different from most critical opinions of this work.

Lavazzi, Tom. "Pattern of Flux: Sex, Buddhism, and Ecology in Gary Snyder's Poetry." *Sagetrieb: A Journal Devoted to Poets* 8, Nos. 1 and 2, (Spring and Fall 1989): 41-68.

Purports that Snyder's desire in all of his poetry is to institute change of mind and worldview, not to overthrow social-political institutions.

Murphy, Patrick D. *Critical Essays on Gary Snyder*. Boston: G. K. Hall & Co., 1990, 262 p.

Offers an in-depth view of the many aspects of Snyder's work from a variety of noted Snyder scholars.

———. *Understanding Gary Snyder*. University of South Carolina Press, 1992, 186 p.

Provides an intensive view of all of Snyder's work from his first pieces to his most recent publications.

Whalen-Bridge, John. "Spirit of Place and Wild Politics in Two Recent Snyder Poems." *Northwest Review* 29, No. 3 (1991): 123-31.

Considers Snyder's embrace of urban environments
in "Walking the New York Bedrock" and "Buildings."

Additional information on Snyder's life and career can be found in the following sources published by Gale Research: *Contemporary Authors,* **Vols. 17-20R;** *Contemporary Authors New Revision Series,* **Vol. 30;** *Contemporary Literary Criticism,* **Vols. 1, 2, 5, 9, 32;** *Dictionary of Literary Biography,* **Vols. 5, 16, 165; and** *DISCovering Authors: Poets Module.*

Cathy Song
1955-

American poet.

INTRODUCTION

Song is an award-winning poet whose work draws on not only her rich Korean and Chinese ancestry but her experiences as a woman in America. Song herself has maintained that the world she creates in her poetry transcends her ethnic and regional background and resists classification as "Asian American" or "Hawaiian" writing. Her verses, which have appeared in numerous magazines and anthologies, are collected in the three volumes, *Picture Bride; Frameless Windows, Squares of Light*; and *School Figures.*

Biographical Information

Song was born August 20, 1955, in Honolulu, Hawaii. Her father, Andrew, was a second-generation Korean American; her mother, Ella, came to Hawaii from China as a "picture bride," her marriage to Song's father having been arranged through an exchange of photographs. During high school and college, Song became interested in writing, and during this time she was encouraged in her efforts by the noted poet and biographer John Unterecker. Song graduated from Wellesley College with a degree in English literature in 1977. She went on to earn a master's degree in creative writing from Boston University in 1981. Her first volume of poetry, *Picture Bride,* published in 1983, draws heavily on her family's experiences and earned Song the prestigious Yale Series of Younger Poets Award as well as a nomination for the National Book Critics Circle Award. While living in Boston, Song married Douglas McHarg Davenport, a medical student. As he was completing his residency in Denver, Song completed her second book of poetry, *Frameless Windows, Squares of Light,* which was published in 1988. In 1993 Song won the Hawaii Award for Literature and the Shelley Memorial Award from the Poetry Society of America. The following year she published her third collection of poetry, *School Figures.* Song now lives and teaches in Honolulu.

Major Works

Uniting Song's body of work is her abiding focus on family. The moral ties that bind women to children and parents, to their community, to tradition, and to the land are continuously interwoven throughout her poems. In the ti-

tle poem of *Picture Bride,* for example, Song recalls the story of her grandmother, who at age twenty-three had come from Korea to the United States in order to marry a many who knew her only from a photograph. *Frameless Windows, Squares of Light* continues the theme of family history and relationships. "The Tower of Pisa" concerns the poet's father, an airline pilot whose life she describes as "one of continual repair." "Humble Jar" is written in praise of her mother, a seamstress. Song again treats the theme of womanhood in "A Mehinaku Girl in Seclusion," in which a girl, her coming of age signaled by her first menstruation, is removed from her tribe for three years and "married to the earth." In *School Figures* Song again casts the stories of her family in verse. Both "A Conservative View" and "Journey" explore the challenges faced by her parents, while "Sunworshippers" recalls her mother's advice against self-gratification. The thoughts, feelings, and impressions couched in each of Song's poems—whether quietly coming to terms with the death of a father or sitting amid the clatter of dishes and the chatter of family members during dinner—are transformed into the poet into universal images, transcending labels of race, gender, or culture.

Critical Reception

Song's focus on familial images, evoking both the particular and the universal, has received much attention from critics. Gayle K. Fujita-Sato has argued that *Picture Bride* "describes both a personal history and a paradigm for analysing multicultural writing. In its portrayal of specific places and histories that is at the same time a portrayal of cultural synthesis and pluralism, *Picture Bride* defines a kind of 'third-world' writing." Richard Hugo has emphasized Song's quiet restraint, observing: "Song's poems are flowers—colorful, sensual and quiet—offered almost shyly as bouquets to those moments in life that seemed minor but in retrostpect count the most." Similarly, the reviewer for the *Washington Post Book World* stated that there is "a good deal of quiet music in [Song's] portraits of individuals who endure unlived lives." The restraint of many of Song's poems has led to some negative appraisals. Robert B. Shaw has detected a "meandering repetitiousness" in some of her works, and Jessica Greenbaum, writing of the poems in *Frameless Windows, Squares of Light*, charged that some pieces "lack the freshness of articulation we expect from good poetry." Other critics, including Fujita-Sato and Patricia Wallace, have explored the connections between Song's poetry and her Asian American heritage. The image of Song's grandmother looms large in these studies, for, as Lee Kyhan has stressed, Song "readily recognizes in the story of her grandmother a fortitude and a strength of character that she somehow hopes to make relevant to her own predicament as a modern Asian-American woman."

PRINCIPAL WORKS

Poetry

Picture Bride 1983
Frameless Windows, Squares of Light 1988
School Figures 1994

Other Major Works

"Beginnings (For Bok Pil)" (short story) 1976; published in the journal *Hawaii Review*
Sister Stew [editor; with Juliet Kono] (poetry and prose) 1991

CRITICISM

Richard Hugo (essay date 1983)

SOURCE: "Foreword," in *Picture Bride*, Yale University Press, 1983, pp. ix-xiv.

[*In 1982, acclaimed American poet Richard Hugo selected Song as the recipient of the prestigious Yale Series of Younger Poets Award, presented each year to an American poet under the age of 40 who has not previously published a collection. Below, Hugo praises Song's quiet strength, her sensuous language, and her efforts to incorporate and understand her heritage through her poetry.*]

The final line of Cathy Song's book, **Picture Bride,** reads "Someone very quiet once lived here." This poem, **"The Seamstress,"** is about someone Song knows, or has fictionalized (and knows), and now speaks for. Parts of the poem, including the final line, might be said to apply to Song herself, the poet who "lived here." In Cathy Song's quietude lies her strength. In her receptivity, passive as it seems, lies passion, a passion that is expressed in deceptive quiet and an even tone. She receives experiences vividly and without preset attitude. Her senses are lucky to have remained childlike and reception appears to be a complete act. It would not be complete, however, without the poems.

Each section of the book is named for a flower, and Song's poems are flowers—colorful, sensual and quiet—offered almost shyly as bouquets to those moments in life that seemed minor but in retrospect count the most.

Song finds artistic kinship with two visual artists: the modern American painter, Georgia O'Keeffe, and the nineteenth-century Japanese printmaker, Kitagawa Utamaro. In one poem she pays homage to Utamaro's work; in another she concentrates on a single print, the details of which she has absorbed with such affection that finally she does more than describe. She presents as decades ago Ezra Pound wisely advised poets to do.

While Song admires Utamaro and finds the women in his prints creatures that she can recreate, she identifies with O'Keeffe's work. **"From the White Place"** is dedicated to her, and a sequence of five poems, **"Blue and White Lines after O'Keeffe,"** is based on five of her floral paintings. Song's personal relationship with O'Keeffe's work is as deep as her admiration of Utamaro's work.

Through empathy Song speaks for other women in some poems (**"The Youngest Daughter," "Lost Sister," "The Seamstress"**). She recreates these women just as she recreated the woman in Utamaro's print. On the other hand, Song's relation to O'Keeffe's paintings is allied to those poems in which Song speaks for and creates herself (**"Waialua," "Blue Lantern," "For My Brother," "The White Porch"**).

Taste and touch are strong elements in the poems, although it is our sight that is most often engaged. And at times the sensuous and the sensual are inseparable.

> But there is this slow arousal.
> The small buttons
> of my cotton blouse
> are pulling away from my body.
> I feel the strain of threads,
> the swollen magnolias

heavy as a flock of birds
in the tree. Already,
the orange sponge cake
is rising in the oven.
I know you'll say it makes
your mouth dry
and I'll watch you
drench your slice of it
in canned peaches
and lick the plate clean.

"The White Porch"

With her quiet tone Song engages a wide variety of experiences from the ecstatic to the distasteful. She accommodates experiential extremes with a sensibility strengthened by patience that is centuries old, ancestral, tribal, a gift passed down.

In the poem **"Stray Animals,"** a young couple tries to "trick nature" as the poem puts it. They make love, but want no children. However, nature "slipped in"

like the small animal
who began appearing then;
we attracted her with the heat
of our blue fire.

Since they are poor and have "nothing to spare," the couple refuses "the stray cat" admittance. They keep the cat out as they tried to keep the child out of their lives. The cat is like the developing child:

. . . I imagined the slight pressure
of her body, persistent as guilt,
on the other side of the door.
At night, we tried to muffle
her human noises with thick cushions
but the sound, cradled
in the iced trees, moaned through.

The cat is killed by a "blind vehicle," and later they see "someone stoop to wrap / the stunned pieces in an old sheet." The unwanted child grows now in the mother, and the mother has faith that, though she and her husband tried to trick nature once, nature will not try to trick them in return. Her husband's "large, untrained hands"

. . . will come to trust
themselves enough to guide
our frightened child through water,
out from the darkness of a dream.

Nature, as always, remains huge and neutral. And all experience becomes natural: some stray animals rejected so others can survive, stray animals killed because vehicles are blind, things done by us for each other (someone even tends to the remains of the cat), and children brought home safely even though they were once unwanted. We are all stray animals. This poem, perhaps more than any other in this collection, demonstrates a deep conviction held by Song: what you receive belongs to you and becomes what you are.

Song does not shrink from the hard realities of the societal and familial traps set for women. In **"Lost Sister,"** she pays tribute to one who rebelled against China's systematic repression of women by immigrating. Perhaps Song pays special tribute to her lost sister because the psychic price of her rebellion was great and the rebellion failed. The rebel finds herself in the new land,

But in another wilderness,
the possibilities,
the loneliness,
can strangulate like jungle vines.

Being a stranger in a new culture can lead to the most outrageous fear of things unknown: "A giant snake rattles above, / spewing black clouds into your kitchen." And the demands of change are too much.

You find you need China:
your one fragile identification,
a jade link
handcuffed to your wrist.

The would-be rebel loses all chance for individual identity. Like her mother in China, she has "left no footprints." Sad as that failure seems, in her effort to rebel she still put an ocean between herself and that past and at least created an "unremitting space" others can cross or fill.

The familial trap is also harshly realized. In **"The Youngest Daughter,"** for some time a woman has been caring for her sick mother. The woman sometimes suffers migraines and the mother in turn cares for her. The situation is cheerless.

The sky has been dark
for many years.

. . . . .

It seems it has always
been like this: the two of us
in this sunless room,
the splashing of the bathwater.

The daughter must bathe the mother. Though things seem better than usual on this day, once we see through her eyes we find the situation hardly wholesome.

She was in a good humor,
making jokes about her great breasts,
floating in the milky water
like two walruses,
flaccid and whiskered around the nipples.
I scrubbed them with a sour taste
in my mouth, thinking:
six children and an old man
have sucked from these brown nipples.

A recurring theme in *Picture Bride* is a sometimes hidden but relentless desire for escape. **"The Youngest Daughter"** shows that freedom is momentarily known in the sudden dramatics available to the visual imagination.

She knows I am not to be trusted,
even now planning my escape.
As I toast to her health
with the tea she has poured,
a thousand cranes curtain the window,
fly up in a sudden breeze.

This desire to escape takes a delightfully fanciful turn in the poem **"Primary Colors"** when babies escape their parents, "sailing by in their runaway carriages, / having yanked the wind / out from under their mothers."

Song has learned the strength of quiet resolve. As a poet she has discovered how hard work and the long act of writing and rewriting pay off if one remains passionately committed.

—*Richard Hugo*

If we accept Cathy Song's background as it comes through the poem **"Leaving"** and through bits and pieces of other poems, we may sense the origin of, and even the necessity for, her passive/receptive sensibility. She need not rave or struggle. She has learned the strength of quiet resolve. As a poet she has discovered how hard work and the long act of writing and rewriting pay off if one remains passionately committed.

Cathy Song's poems do more than simply return to us a world vividly received. The world is *her* world and she alone has the artistic license to illuminate it. Some of her poems show a psychic and social range that, if much wider, would require a larger form than modern poetry with its inherited limitations can provide. Possibly a large work of fiction will be hers to write in the years ahead. For now, she offers her luminous world with candor and generosity.

Washington Post Book World **(review date 1983)**

SOURCE: A review of *Picture Bride,* in *Washington Post Book World,* August 7, 1983, pp. 4-5.

[*In the following, the critic offers a favorable review of Song's first collection,* Picture Bride, *praising the "quiet music" and "scrupulous craftsmanship" evident in her poems.*]

Picture Bride is . . . a first book, not surprising given that Cathy Song is only 27; the work won the 1982 Yale Series of Younger Poets competition, open to any American under 40 who has not previously published a volume of poetry. The judge for this contest was the late Richard Hugo, a man whose own work is robust and earthy. It is clear that

he was responsive to language different from his own, since the words that most readily come to mind in describing Song's work are delicacy, sensitivity, restraint, elegance, control.

I am reminded as I read these touching poems of two quite disparate writers, Maxine Hong Kingston and Robert Lowell. Kingston, in *China Men,* provides loving portraits of her forebears who settled in the New World from China, and Cathy Song, for her part, gives novelistic descriptions of the migration of her grandparents from Korea to Hawaii, and of their life in that unfamiliar setting. And Robert Lowell? *Picture Bride* is a kind of gentle *Life Studies,* a series of sketches of family members as seen through the observant eyes of a child. Unlike Lowell, however, Song is almost wholly without irony:

By evening, it was raining hard.
Grandfather and I skipped supper.
Instead, we sat on the porch
and I ate what he peeled
and cleaned for me.
The scattering of the delicate
marine-colored shells across his lap
was something like what the ocean gives
the beach after a rain.

This is not poetry of ideas but of gestures and voices. We are given some memorable portraits, especially of women. There is, for example, the bride of the title poem, arriving in Hawaii from Korea to meet a stranger, 13 years older than she, who is her husband. There is a lonely woman, suffering from migraine, who is trapped in a life of caring for her old mother:

It seems it has always
been like this: the two of us
in this sunless room,
the splashing of the bathwater.

We meet the poet's taut father, "the burning cigarette / dangling from his mouth / is the fuse to the dynamite," and her young mother, who seems nervous except when cooking.

Her hands would assume a certain confidence
then, as she rubbed and patted butter
all over a turkey as though
she were soaping and scrubbing up a baby.

There is a good deal of quiet music in these portraits of individuals who endure unlived lives and of the more fortunate who find outlets for their passion and art. Song, herself obviously devoted to the most scrupulous craftsmanship (there are no excesses in these poems, no unpolished corners), is especially acute in describing various modes of expression, whether growing orchids, preparing vegetables, or, in a stunning poem called **"The Seamstress,"** sewing perfect seams:

It seems I have always lived
in this irregular room, rarely needing

to see beyond the straight seams that fit neatly,
the snaps that fasten securely in my mind.
The world for me is the piece of cloth
I have at the moment beneath my hands.

From the cloth in her own confident hands, Cathy Song
has fashioned something wondrous and fine.

Perhaps the best measure of how successful this recognition, this painting, has been, is the way a consciousness of past, of art, of character and of flowers, nature, come so easily together here. And the way, in the last poem, **"The Seamstress,"** present and past are brought together in her art: "The world for me is a piece of cloth / I have at the moment beneath my hands. / I am not surprised / by how little the world changes."

Richard Jackson   (review date 1986)

SOURCE: "The Geography of Time," in *American Book Review,* Vol. 8, No. 2, January-February, 1986, pp. 19-20.

[*The following review of* Picture Bride *focuses on Song's metaphor of flowers as it is used to produce "a poetry of description and recognition."*]

Cathy Song's *Picture Bride* contains a poetry of adjectives: the frames of the past and present are delicately described, the major metaphor being flowers, in an attempt not to escape but to be reframed, or, in terms of the book's predominant metaphor, rerooted, repotted. Thus, a poem about her mother, **"A Pale Arrangement of Hands"** (note the flower reference), is spoken from the perspective, late in the book, of a girl whose vision, through a series of conflicts and allegiances, has come to include that of the mother in a sort of Stevensian double vision. Curiously enough, another set of images, this one associated with seas and oceans, tends to underscore just such a set of connections among the characters and times of this geography, all the while suggesting a limitless expanse, the kind one finds *within* the flowers of Georgia O'Keeffe, one of Song's influences. And for Song . . . escapes . . . do not motivate the book because they have already been made—her grandmother's from Korea to a man who waited "turning her photograph" for someone to fill it (**"Picture Bride"**), her own self admitting a lover to her room on the sly (**"The White Porch"**), even the babies and flowers that seem to be "hiding somewhere / threatening to break loose" (**"Primary Colors"**). Hers, then, is a poetry of description and recognition. The whole book, divided into five parts named for flowers, suggests a progression of moods (Black Iris, Sunflower, Orchids, Red Poppy, White Trumpet Flower), slowly, from a somewhat dark, impoverished past towards the bright, triumphant present to which it is connected. **"Blue and White Lines After O'Keeffe,"** a poem that duplicates the book's structure, ends with these lines spoken by Song and the painter:

> It has taken me all these years
> to realize that this is what I must do
> to recognize my life.
> When I stretch a canvas
> to paint the clouds,
> it is your spine that declares itself:
> aching,
> your arms stemming out like tender shoots
> to hang sheets in the sky.

Gayle K. Fujita-Sato   (essay date 1988)

SOURCE: "'Third World' as Place and Paradigm in Cathy Song's *Picture Bride*," in *MELUS,* Vol. 15, No. 1, Spring, 1988, pp. 49-72.

[*In the excerpt below, Fujita-Sato explores how* Picture Bride *"descibes both a personal history and a paradigm for analysing multicultural writing" through poems that draw on the cultural traditions of Song's ancestors as well as her own contemporary American upbringing to produce a unique blend representative of her heritage.*]

Cathy Song's *Picture Bride* won the Yale Series of Younger Poets award in 1982. Her second book, *Frameless Windows, Squares of Light,* appeared in 1988. Song is Korean and Chinese-American. Born in Honolulu in 1955, she attended the University of Hawaii and Wellesley College, where she received a B.A. in 1977. In 1981, she received an M.A. in creative writing from Boston University. In the summer of 1987, she returned to live in Hawaii with her husband, son, and daughter. *Picture Bride* furnishes a rich text for the study of relationships among ethnicity, culture, and writing. Through an analysis of the book's organization and image patterns, followed by close readings of several key poems, I attempt to show how *Picture Bride* describes both a personal history and a paradigm for analysing multicultural writing. In its portrayal of specific places and histories that is at the same time a portrayal of cultural synthesis and pluralism, *Picture Bride* defines a kind of "third world" writing.

Through the title poem **"Picture Bride,"** Song begins her book with an attempt to learn more about her paternal Korean grandmother. Of the scant information she already has—her grandmother's age when she left Korea for Hawaii, the port she sailed from, the name of the sugar plantation where her husband worked, and his age—only the first item is presented as fact in the poem's single declarative sentence. The remaining lines being questions, the poem is thus mostly speculation. Yet the process of searching is inevitably a process of constructing, for even the few details Song uses to pose questions create complex impressions of her grandmother's new surroundings and of the woman herself:

> And when
> she arrived to look
> into the face of the stranger
> who was her husband,
> thirteen years older than she,

did she politely untie
the silk bow of her jacket,
her tent-shaped dress
filling with the dry wind
that blew from the surrounding fields
where the men were burning the cane?

Such a question, reminiscent of [Maxine Hong] Kingston's method in the first chapter of *The Woman Warrior,* is already an answer even as it is being posed. Song, too, wants "ancestral help," to have a grandmother's life "branching into" hers (Kingston). Every image, whether speculation or fact, becomes part of an evolving picture. The writer who seeks ancestral help wills and writes that help into being.

Not only this strategy of construction through inquiry but the subject itself of picture brides is common in Asian-American literature that concerns the recovery of familial and communal histories. Picture brides was a method of arranging marriages used by Japanese and Korean immigrants before the war. Usually a man would ask his parents or relatives to find a prospective bride, and the couple then exchanged photographs of themselves. When marriage was agreed upon, an official ceremony was held in the home country before the woman departed to join her husband. In many cases the picture bride's arrival was the couple's first face-to-face meeting.

The title poem, **"Picture Bride,"** thus clearly invites interpretation of the book as Asian-American literature. Although only this first of thirty-one poems is about literal picture brides, the majority concern marriage, motherhood, traditional women's roles in both Asian and American society, images of women in the art of Georgia O'Keeffe and Kitagawa Utamaro (eighteenth-century Japanese *ukiyo-e* artist), and the nature of artistic creation. The book's title thus includes as subjects the ancestors and descendents of literal picture brides, their culture, and their role in producing that culture. This is an extension of what "picture bride" designates, a kind of enlargement and reshaping of a phenomenon, and it suggests another meaning of the title as referring to a creative process in general. "Picture bride" in this second, expanded sense refers to the process of interpreting and representing phenomena, as when, for example, Song pictures women's various activities—applying lipstick, putting paint to canvas, buttering a turkey—as different kinds of artistry. Song's distinction between completed pictures and the process of picturing can be described as a difference between "third world" as place and "third world" as paradigm. Operating in both kinds of "third worlds," *Picture Bride* depicts Asian-American culture as well as the process of synthesis that creates culture.

"Third world" in the socio-economic sense refers to a body of social institutions, patterns of group behavior, religious and secular rituals, ideologies, and so forth, created when two or more cultures intersect. The usefulness of such a term rather than "ethnic community" is the implied emphasis on newness and intercultural relations. "Third" refers not to rank or priority, but to a process of combining one thing and another to get a third. "Third world" in the paradigmatic sense designates the "place" where the forms and expressions of culture originate. It is the inner space of imagination and modes of thinking where the process of synthesis that creates ethnic cultures occurs. Since this process is continuous, the paradigmatic sense of "third world" also destabilizes our socioeconomic sense of "third world." The term thus designates a particularly constituted place but also the fact that it is continually evolving.

Picture Bride illustrates both kinds of "third worlds." There are numerous pictures of particular people and places: portraits of artists (Song, O'Keeffe, Utamaro, sculptors, musicians, dancers, seamstresses) and family members, in settings that include pineapple fields and backyard porches in Hawaii, flower shops in Mexico City and tailor shops in Pusan, New England snow and New Mexico desert, a contemporary American Chinatown and the pleasure quarters of Edo. In one poem, Song recalls her father's subscription to *National Geographic* and how as a child she "feasted / on those pictures of the world" (**"Leaving"**). It was not much different when she began to write: "everything was edible" (**"Hotel Genève"**). *Picture Bride* recreates that plenitude for the reader's consumption; it is a feast of pictures colored by the particularities of Song's experience.

In the second part of this paper I will examine the interconnectedness of both senses of "third world" through close readings of several poems. At this point, however, I would like to focus on the paradigmatic sense. An overview of what and how Song synthesizes is provided by the picture motif, embroidered through scattered images such as the reference to *National Geographic,* but expressed directly and compactly through the title poem and section titles. The title poem which refers to an Asian-American socio-economic phenomenon, and the section titles which refer to flower paintings by O'Keeffe, form two structural frames that emphasize, relative to each other, a distinction between Asia and America and between the socio-economic and the artistic. But the contents of the poems thus framed also break down these frames.

For instance, **"Picture Bride"** is less about an arranged marriage per se than a meditation on how to acquire knowledge of the past. Likewise, a section title like "Black Iris" suggests the theme of origins shared by all the poems included under it. In her autobiographical book, *Georgia O'Keeffe* (more will be said later regarding its influence on Song), the painter describes her repeated though unsuccessful attempt to paint the black iris as it was just beginning to bloom. In Song's book, the "Black Iris" section comes first, and it contains besides the title poem which seeks knowledge of an ancestor's arrival in Hawaii, poems that trace an event or idea back to a point of origin, such as **"Easter: Wahiawa, 1959"** which revisits a scene from early childhood through the perspective of an adult. Song's "Black Iris" poems, like O'Keeffe's "Black Iris" painting, are about beginnings.

What results, then, from the interlocked frameworks provided by the book's title and section titles, is a structure embodying synthesis. **"Picture Bride"** refers explicitly to a socio-historical phenomenon but says more about interpretation and imagination of events. The section titles, borrowed from paintings, suggest an emphasis on creation and expressive forms, but in some sections the poems grouped under these titles emphasize socio-historical concretes. The organization of the book thus presents a structure of crossing categories, or a structure of pluralism and synthesis.

As a point of entry into this structure and its more detailed elaboration in various poems, we can return to the image concluding **"Picture Bride"**:

> . . . [D]id she politely untie
> the silk bow of her jacket,
> her tent-shaped dress
> filling with the dry wind
> that blew from the surrounding fields
> where the men were burning the cane?

A billowing dress, animated by winds from new surroundings, representing change and newness, initiates the book's pervasive imagery of potential and fulfillment. A partial list includes: blank journals, canvases stretched for painting, ovens, bathtubs, baskets, bowls, bracelets, wedding bands, pockets bulging with marbles, papaya "boats" packed with "tiny black seeds / that resembled caviar" (**"Tribe"**), lapfuls of beans and eggshells, pillows, moons, sea shells, seeds, eggs, the bellies of clouds and planes and pregnant women, canned sardines "lined like slender bullets" (**"Blue and White Lines After O'Keeffe"**), sheets "stacked like envelopes or tortillas" (**"Hotel Genève"**), termites who "gorge their amber bodies on the brocaded silk" (**"The Seamstress"**), and spaces framed by telescopes, camera lenses, mirrors, fences, porches, windows, and hands. In these diverse shapes of filling and fulfillment, the process of creation is rendered imagistically. In addition, the images indicate that Song's language and subjects are filtered through ethnicity and culture, as in the image cluster silk/termites/papaya which signifies "Asian American home in Hawaii."

But these image patterns also raise questions about the nature of ethnicity in Song's writing. If her language and subjects arise from an Asian-American context, why are the five sections of *Picture Bride* named after paintings of flowers by O'Keeffe—"Black Iris," "Sunflowers," "Orchids," "Red Poppy," "The White Trumpet Flower"—which also title the sections of the centrally positioned poem, **"Blue and White Lines After O'Keeffe"**? As Stephen Sumida has pointed out regarding this poem,

> [i]t may seem odd that what is thus the central monologue of the book is not spoken by one of Song's grandmothers, mother, aunts, others of her community, or by herself, but by an artist [O'Keeffe] who is a sojourner or merely a visitor to most of those places named in the monologue, even though that visitor may be one gifted with a talent and genius for seeing. Without addressing this question, but judging by Song's poetic imagery and allusions, Richard Hugo stresses that Song is highly sensitive to the visual

and to the visual arts, an intimacy with O'Keeffe in this regard being vital to Song's imagination and sensibility.

Sumida observes that, as a dramatic monologue, **"Blue and White Lines"** is about the limits defining a speaker. Regarding the poem's third section in particular which is situated in Hawaii, he finds it "a perceptive, sensitive, and serious rendition of the visitor's point of view," something which "has scarcely any precedents in Hawaii's literature." He also suggests that the poem's five settings "map the artist's [O'Keeffe's] career." These issues—the role of visual arts in Song's poetry, Song's depiction of Hawaii, and her development as an artist—are clarified when *Picture Bride* is examined in detail against the painter's autobiographical book *Georgia O'Keeffe*.

O'Keeffe's flower paintings suggest the kind of synthesis underlying Song's response to the painter's work as a whole and operating in her poetry as a whole. O'Keeffe's oversize, large canvas flowers contradict ideas of delicacy, tenderness, modesty, shyness, and so forth associated with flowers when they are symbols of traditional femininity. At the same time, however, their brilliant tints and finely nuanced, often soft or velvety textures and colors are also consistent with the "woman as flower" image. O'Keeffe's flowers are thus equally radical and conservative, a balance interpreted by Song as fundamental to the painter's creativity and personal vision. In the final section of **"Blue and White Lines After O'Keeffe,"** which refers to details from the painter's earliest recollections of home, Song invents a dialogue between the painter and her mother that reconciles traditional and non-traditional ideas of women, and that recognizes the interdependence of departing and returning, invention and conservation:

> Dear Mother,
> you would not like it out here;
> in Abiquiu there are no flowers,
> not your kind of weather.
> I have lived without mirrors and without men
> for a long time now—
> but I can feel my own skin,
> how it is parched and crinkled like a lizard's.
>
> . . . . .
>
> Yet, I am here, Mother.
> I have come to rest at your feet,
> to be near the familiar scent of talc,
> the ticking of the china clock,
> another heartbeat.
> It has taken me all these years
> to realize that this is what I must do
> to recognize my life.
>
> When I stretch a canvas
> to paint the clouds,
> it is your spine that declares itself:
> arching,
> your arms stemming out like tender shoots
> to hang sheets in the sky.

O'Keeffe herself does not speak of reconciling with her mother's "kind of weather." Song's invention is thus quite revealing. Her assertion that O'Keeffe needed a combination of desert and parlor is indicative of her own creative processes, in particular her synthesis of disparate traditions. Song's many poems on marriage, maternity, and motherhood indicate that she did not, like O'Keeffe, desire a world "without mirrors and without men." On the other hand she found such a world capable of nurturing personal independence and artistic dedication, but perhaps this fact was not perceived until Song was able to inhabit radically different worlds, and then, like her imagined O'Keeffe, acknowledge the process whereby a daughter's paint canvas had its earlier form in mother's laundry.

In a personal interview, Song recalled that the book *Georgia O'Keeffe* appeared soon after her transfer to Wellesley, and she spoke of the impact the book had on her. All the O'Keeffe poems in **Picture Bride** sprang from this encounter. They were all written before she left Wellesley. In the interview Song also recalled that the original **Picture Bride** manuscript had no divisions. It was re-ordered and sectioned off with the advice of Kathleen Spivack when being prepared for submission. Song says it was probably Spivack who suggested the O'Keeffe paintings as section titles. On the one hand, this history of the book's organization might imply the O'Keeffe framework is superficial. On the other hand, the fact that Song did not originally propose the section titles does not in itself invalidate a comparison of the poet and the painter. For in fact, Song's various poems on O'Keeffe testify to the painter's significant presence in her writing.

O'Keeffe viewed *Blue Lines* as the painting which marked the start of her personal vision and style. With the work of several months assembled in one room, and recognizing in each one the influence of different teachers, she realized: "I have things in my head that are not like what anyone has taught me—shapes and ideas so near to me—so natural to my way of being and thinking that it hasn't occurred to me to put them down." Deciding to "start anew—to strip away what [she] had been taught," she worked only with charcoal and paper until black and white no longer sufficed and she found that she "needed blue." Blue was thus the first item in O'Keeffe's color vocabulary, and it is especially prominent in her many paintings of desert sky, several of which furnish the occasion for more explicit commentary on the meaning of the color blue:

> . . . [S]o when I started painting the pelvis bones I was most interested in the holes in the bones—what I saw through them—particularly the blue from holding them up in the sun against the sky as one is apt to do when one seems to have more sky than earth in one's world . . . They were most wonderful against the Blue—that Blue that will always be there as it is now after all man's destruction is finished.

Although O'Keeffe does not comment as explicitly about white, its prominent juxtaposition with blue in the paintings referred to, and her choice of subjects and titles such

as *From the White Place, The White Barn, White Patio with Red Door, I, The White Trumpet Flower, White Calico Flower,* and *White Camellia,* among others, indicate its parallel significance in her color vocabulary. The paintings which appear in *Georgia O'Keeffe* display a liberal use of white highlights—pinpoints of light, thin lines accentuating edges and contours, smudges of softer light, portions of canvas left unpainted between colored shapes. Her description of one of these white images implies that white, like blue, signifies the origins of creative expression:

> I was on a stretcher in a large room, two nurses hovering over me, a very large bright skylight above me . . . The skylight began to whirl and slowly become smaller and smaller in a black space. I lifted my right arm overhead and dropped it. As the skylight became a small white dot in a black room, I lifted my left arm over my head. As it started to drop and the white dot became very small, I was gone. A few weeks later all this became the *Black Abstraction.*

Considering the amount of blue and white in O'Keeffe's paintings and the significance she attaches to these colors, Song's phrase "blue and white lines after O'Keeffe" can serve as a shorthand reference to the totality of O'Keeffe's work. That it can also serve the same purpose for Song's poems seems warranted by the color vocabulary of **Picture Bride,** beginning with the book's blue cover and continuing to the image of "wedding dresses each white, dusty summer" concluding the final poem. There are blue bruises, Easter eggs, whiskers, towels, rooms, and porcelain plates, "blue lantern light." "blue fire," "blue flowered flannel," "the blue of the Pacific," "[t]he same blue tint / of the hydrangea in glass," and "walls of ice, blue and iridescent." White skin of varying textures and shades is evoked through images such as "rice paper" and "milky water," "dumpling cheeks and tofu skin," "bruised white / like the skin of lilies," "sliced shavings / of a pickled turnip," and "snow / in a country / of huge white solemn birds." Like O'Keeffe, Song also applies white to intensify and define, as in this rendition of a photograph of her father holding her newborn older sister—"the hot white light of Coral Gables / momentarily blinding the two of you / in a halo of light. The white / edges of your cotton undershirt / hazy as if on fire" (**"Father and Daughter."**)

Quite literally, Song's poems are composed of "blue and white lines." But as the foregoing list of images indicates, Song's blues and whites tend to be smaller, concrete objects rather than landscape, background, or outline as in O'Keeffe's paintings. Actually, the significant resemblance lies below the surface color. It is a matter of form and transformation, of what O'Keeffe called "singing shapes."

This term appears in O'Keeffe's description of how two objects, a barn shingle and a clam shell, inspired a series of paintings. Attracted to the "white shape of the shell and the gray shape of the weathered shingle," O'Keeffe says she first did "realistic paintings," then more abstract renditions involving just portions of both objects. When she returned to representing the whole shingle and shell, they emerged as condensed forms: "the shingle just a dark space that floated off the top of the painting, the shell just a single white shape under it." The objects had lost their identities as shingle and shell. O'Keeffe "forgot what they were except that they were shapes together—singing shapes."

"Singing shapes" is remarkably applicable to Song's word pictures in three ways. First, as the many examples already listed or quoted indicate, her imagery emphasizes volume—pockets, pillows, bathtubs, baskets. Second, it often connects two objects with dissimilar textures yet possessing some resemblance that makes the resulting image pair seem "natural"—papaya and boat, salmon and sandstone, sheets and tortillas. Song's responsiveness to volume and texture, and her preference for discrete objects (even an unbounded surface like "sandstone" becomes considerably shaped by its association with "salmon"), make "singing shapes" an appropriate name for her imagery.

The third sense in which the term is applicable, however, is the most significant one where creative synthesis and cultural pluralism are concerned. "Singing" as applied to O'Keeffe's barn shingle and clam shell refers to an inner core of existence that appears when objects are put in relation, or when they become "shapes together." "Singing," however, also implies more than shape. It implies that the inner core of existence is energy, revealed through form and inhabiting many forms. The same energy contained in the forms of shingle and clam is what allows them to vibrate or "sing" together. But it is O'Keeffe who sets these objects to singing because she can perceive objects as relationships of energy. In the same way, but through words rather than paint, Song synthesizes two previously unrelated objects and illuminates through this new product the nature of creativity as a fluid shaping and re-shaping of energy.

I have chosen four poems, together with references to three others, to illustrate how Song recasts her existence into "singing shapes" and how this synthetic process constitutes and constructs two kinds of "third worlds." In **"Blue Lantern"** and **"Easter: Wahiawa 1959,"** which recollect events from Song's childhood in Hawaii, the emphasis is on "third world" as place. The other selections, **"Hotel Genève"** which describes the acquisition of poetic language, and **"The White Porch"** which renders a domestic scene as a field of energy, emphasize "third world" as paradigm. I will begin with a discussion of **"Blue Lantern,"** move to **"Hotel Genève"** and **"The White Porch,"** and conclude with **"Easter, Wahiawa: 1959"** in order to show how the two meanings of "third world" are always interlocked in Song's poetry.

In **"Blue Lantern,"** the speaker addresses a man who was once her neighbor as she recollects an event they shared. As a young child she had listened each night to this neighbor's grandfather "mourning his dead wife," "her absence, / the shape of his grief / funnelled through the bamboo flute." His nightly ritual became her bedtime story. Because she had yet to experience such loss, his music of

grief was her comfort and pleasure. She "dreamed the music / came in squares, / like birthday chocolate, / through the window / on a blue plate." She listened as though "under water / in the blueness of [her] room," feeling "buoyant and protected." The grandfather's sorrow is also an expression of conjugal love, which the speaker likewise understands only obliquely and incompletely as she pictures her friend in his own bed, his "head making a slight / dent in the pillow." All that the music contains as an adult expression is first received from a child's perspective and later re-heard in its fullness through an adult's and poet's perspectives. Imagistically speaking, the music is transformed twice. First the "shape of grief" takes the shapes of chocolate, pretty plates, and familiar bedroom walls. But later, in retrospect, these shapes are replaced by another:

> It was as though the weight
> of his grief washed over
> the two of us each night like a tide,
> leaving our bodies beached
> but unbruised, white and firm like shells.

The speaker now consciously contains the music, or knowledge of grief, imparted by the grandfather. This inner transformation is rendered imagistically through a re-shaping of her body. Now hollowed and weathered like a shell, she has the same capacity for knowledge and expression as the bamboo flute. The association with literal music makes the image of white shells the quintessential "singing shape" in *Picture Bride.*

Yet the poem's emphasis is not on a general process but certain forces that shaped the speaker's body in a specified way. The poem's first image is the "blue lantern light" that hung "like a full moon" over the hedge separating the houses. Blue lamplight merges with blue walls and blue music that are both linked to blue ocean—the room is "buoyant," the music is a "tide." The production of a white shell occurs in this blue medium. The white shell we might interpret as knowledge of loss and survival, endurance and essence. The blue medium that teaches this knowledge is a particular arrangement of home, neighbors, and physical landscape. What is learned is related to how the various human and natural resources of this environment interact. For instance, there is a sense of extended family and communal teaching in the fact that the old man "played unknowingly / to the child next door." He plays for himself, but his personal "ritual of remembrance" becomes a community resource, adding to the speaker's wisdom. The speaker's art benefits, too, for the flutist was also a transformer of shapes, giving "shape" to grief by "funnelling" his wife's "absence" through the flute. The future poet absorbs both form and substance from her neighbor's daily ritual.

The poem further suggests that the social structure of extended family may be a key factor in developing a capacity for synthesis. There are numerous mergings between family and non-relatives (the old man is called "the grandfather"), between indoors and outdoors (bedroom resembles ocean), between self and others (the speaker is "stricken" by the music), between human and natural (lantern light is like moonlight), and of course between one concrete object and another. All of these mergings constitute the dynamic of "singing shapes." The last of these shapes is the white shell, but the first one, blue lantern, gives the poem its title. The blue lantern is precisely located above the hedge between the speaker's house and her neighbor's, and its light bathes the whole scene. If shells represent the products or shapes produced here, it is the lantern which represents the environment's shaping forces. The poem **"Blue Lantern"** situates the production of "singing shapes" in a specific place. The transformation of bodies into flutes and shells pays tribute to an episode from the past.

In "Hotel Genève" Song's recognition of resemblances between the objects sorrounding her then and now, such as between the tint of Mexican skirts "with fluted edges, / violet on challis" and "[t]he same blue tint / of the hydrangea in glass" before her on the kitchen table, signifies that she has developed a poet's language of correspondences.

—Gayle Fujita-Sato

"Hotel Genève" also narrates the meaning of an event from the past through the language of "singing shapes," but the emphasis here is on the acquisition of such language. In this recollection of Song's trip to Mexico City at age fourteen, the imagery of heat and moisture conjoin to portray the conversion of life into words.

The recollection is framed in the present tense of the poet writing at her kitchen table. It has just rained, bringing to mind how "[i]t was always raining / in Mexico City." Thus begins a series of connections the poet will retrace, as announced in her opening sentence: "There are these quiet resemblances." But these connections can be named only because the poet has acquired language, something she lacked in Mexico City:

> I kept a pristine journal then
> when anything white pleased me.
> I would fold secrets into each page
> as though I were wrapping
> jade fish into origami.
>
> But there were things
> I had no words for:
> the matrons in the morning
> who brought clean starched sheets
> stacked like envelopes or tortillas.
> I made no distinctions:
> for me, everything was edible.

In **"Hotel Genève,"** a mature poet unwraps these phenomena into words. Her recognition of resemblances between the objects surrounding her then and now, such as between the tint of Mexican skirts "with fluted edges, / violet on challis" and "[t]he same blue tint / of the hydrangea in glass" before her on the kitchen table, signifies that she has developed a poet's language of correspondences. In Mexico City, while her parents went walking and shopping, she "stayed behind, / trying to find the words to describe / the phenomena of the world / opening up before [her] / like an anemone." Now, the playful mirroring of "(ph)e-n-o-m-e-n-a" and "a-n-e-m-o-n-e" declares a poet's confidence in her art of linguistic correspondences.

A single sentence bridging the last two stanzas enacts the conversion of Mexico City's rain and sensory experience into the steam, or creative heat, now contained within the poet:

> Those afternoons alone,
> the light shuddered
> translucent upon my skin
> as I eased into the bath.
> The vapor condensed onto the mirror
> like the humid windows
> of the flower shops we had passed,
>
> like the kitchen window, now
> blurred with rain.
> Water everywhere
> this end of summer.
> I breathe in its smell,
> of things green and ferny.
> Tonight,
> I am filled with the steam
> my warm body gathered,
> wrapping the petals of itself
> in a white towel.

As an image of retention, this steam-filled body recalls the shell image from **"Blue Lantern."** But whereas the shells were discrete white shapes against a blue space, a relation emphasizing context, in **"Hotel Genève"** the poet's body *is* the larger context. Wrapped in a white towel, which absorbs moisture and heat or in other words "gathers steam," the body that emerged from the baths and rain of Mexico City is itself a new kind of wrapper or "clean" sheet. The poet is no longer pristine in the sense of lacking words, but she is so in the sense of possessing a new, articulate self, a new potential. The conversion of experience into words is symbolized by the softening and reshaping of "jade fish" into "things green and ferny." In the former kind of absorption, where "everything was edible" and "no distinctions" could be made, phenomena could only be contained intact, like jade fish wrapped in paper. The aspiring writer's journal was therefore pristine, because without absorption it could not really contain anything. A poet's kind of absorption, however, which can distinguish energy from form and see resemblances in different forms, can therefore dis-assemble, transform, and construct phenomena. The world can be "breathed in" and truly absorbed. The world is soft and malleable, not jade-like but "green and ferny."

"Hotel Genève" presents striking transformations of imagery and even includes a quite literal "singing shape"—

> [t]he women were beautiful
> and music floated out into the streets,
> leaving on the hems of their skirts:
> a flounce of fluted edges,
> violet on challis

—which resembles the description in "Blue Lantern" of shakuhachi music as "shavings of notes" that "floated" into the night. But "singing shapes" in "Hotel Genève" celebrate the acquisition of poetic language and vision, whereas in "Blue Lantern" they pay tribute to the place where this acquisition was nurtured.

The last two poems to be discussed, "The White Porch" and "Easter, Wahiawa: 1959," also highlight the difference between "third world" as paradigm and as place. The first poem is almost Edenic in its portrayal of tremendous latent energy and fertility. The second poem is also almost Edenic in its portrayal of the unqualified love and security the poet remembers from her earliest home. Together the poems remind us that a place in *Picture Bride* always describes a potential—the creative space inhabited by Song as ethnic writer.

Before turning to "The White Porch," it is useful to take a look at "From the White Place," which is dedicated to O'Keeffe. Set in New Mexico's desert, it presents O'Keeffe as an embodiment of sexual independence and creative power. The imagery is of exposure—to a relentless aridity the painter feels like "an arthritic who cannot sleep, / tormented by bones and joints," and to Stieglitz' camera, before which "she endured the inspections / of her bones and wrists." Song pictures O'Keeffe developing into an artist through this exposure. The first section of the poem, titled "Blue Bones: Ghost Ranch," presents the "lunar" and "pelvic" mountains which symbolize the source of O'Keeffe's creative energy. The second section, titled "Memories, Gallery 291," portrays O'Keeffe separating Stieglitz' photographs of her from her own sense of self. The brief third and final section, titled the same as the poem, distills the desert's shades and textures into the shape of O'Keeffe's new artistic voice. Song thus presents a condensed image of the "white place," a place where artistic vision begins, through O'Keeffe's and her own aesthetic of "singing shapes":

> *Out on the pink mesa,*
> *the soft sandstone glowed*
> *like the belly of a salmon.*
> *I began breathing for the first time today,*
> *knowing the first breath would hurt.*

Song's interpretation of O'Keeffe's physical independence, artistic integrity, and communion with primal energies are summarized here through imagery of aridity and spaciousness. Only the spaciousness is present in "The White Porch," but this is consistent with the fact that it is about Song's, not O'Keeffe's "white place." As discussed earlier, Song's invention in "Blue and White Lines" of a synthesis of desert and parlor as the necessary condition for O'Keeffe's creativity is more descriptive of herself than the painter, especially judging by the number of poems in *Picture Bride* concerned with parlors, marriage, and motherhood. The narrator of "The White Porch" is a pregnant wife. She is absorbed in laundry and meals, but she has the same responsiveness to her physical surroundings as the poet in "Hotel Genève." The creative heat within this pregnant woman, and her awareness of it, are no less intense than a poet's. If "Hotel Genève" demonstrates the acquisition of poetic language through the construction of stunning singing shapes, "The White Porch" focuses on the energy animating those shapes.

The poem contains two time frames, the present in which the speaker is waiting for her husband to come home for dinner, and the past in which the speaker waited for her lover's secret visits at night. Whereas those waits were marked by distraction and impatience, the woman is now serenely submerged in the slow passage of time:

> I wrap the blue towel
> after washing,
> around the damp
> weight of hair, bulky
> as a sleeping cat,
> and sit out on the porch.
> Still dripping water,
> it'll be dry by supper,
> by the time the dust
> settles off your shoes,
> though it's only five
> past noon. Think
> of the luxury: how to use
> the afternoon like the stretch
> of lawn spread before me.
> There's the laundry,
> sun-warm clothes at twilight,
> and the mountain of beans
> in my lap. Each one,
> I'll break and snap
> thoughtfully in half.
>
> But there is this slow arousal.
> The small buttons
> of my cotton blouse
> are pulling away from my body.
> I feel the strain of threads,
> the swollen magnolias
> heavy as a flock of birds
> in the tree. Already,
> the orange sponge cake
> is rising in the oven.

The main activity of the white porch is waiting, which becomes a metaphor for a point of view that sees the world as Edenic. Waiting for hair and laundry to dry, for cake to rise, for husband to arrive, is all a sensual pleasure. The longer wait for the baby's arrival is measured and savored by such afternoons. What could in another situation prove stifling—a domestic round of washing hair, hanging laundry, preparing dinner, having babies—is presented here as a context of powerful productivity and creativity. Pregnancy becomes a means of acquiring a larger sense of the world as potential. A lapful can be a mountain of beans. As a place characterized by radical enlargement, a place of fruition, heat, blossoming, spaciousness, and plenty, the white porch, so ordinary at first glance, is nothing less than Song's version of O'Keeffe's "white place," the reservoir of creative energy.

The white porch also designates a place of creativity. In the second meaning of O'Keeffe's "white place," this is where the artist's individual voice and viewpoint are shaped or exercised. As a symbol of home, family, and traditional women's roles, Song's white porch "contains" the entire range of subjects and themes in *Picture Bride*. All poems in the section containing **"The White Porch"** (section two) as well as four poems from sections one, four, and five (**"For My Brother," "Birthmarks," "A Dream of Small Children," "January"**) are about pregnancy and newborn children. The remainder of the poems from section one and a couple more from section five (**"A Pale Arrangement of Hands," "The Seamstress"**) deal with relationships among family members or lovers and emphasize the physical settings of households. The poems in section four, which generally concern aspects of Chinatowns and Chinese-American traditions, include the other poems' concerns with marriage and family. Of the poems not accounted for, there remain only the three on Utamaro, placed with **"Blue and White Lines"** in the book's third section. Since these poems refer to the world of Edo's "[t]eahouse waitresses, actresses, / geishas, courtesans and maids" (**"Beauty and Sadness"**), and their rituals of baths and dressing, they, too, are concerned with traditional women's roles and domestic settings. Thus, it can be said that in terms of subject matter, all the poems are contained in **"The White Porch."**

This domestic world contrasts with the desert world of O'Keeffe's "white place," but it also furnishes a medium for the development of artists. **"Pale Arrangement of Hands,"** for instance, is a daughter's portrait of her mother which implies not only that the daughter's poetry is rooted in her mother's skills (the poem opens with the association of daughter's and mother's hands), but that the mother's inner life cannot be fully articulated by the daughter's words, that a significant part of her expression exists in the untranslated medium of housework and child care. Being a mother, in other words, means having an expressive capacity different in certain respects from a poet's. It is the poem which is, in fact, a "pale" arrangement.

The poem opens with the same setting that represented creativity in **"Hotel Genève."** The speaker sits at the kitchen table listening to the rain and looking at her hands, "[t]heir knuckles, yellow white / like the tendons of a drumstick, / the skin pulled taut to make a fist." She remembers her mother's hands, how nervous they seemed when idle, how confident when they "rubbed and patted butter / all over a turkey as though / she were soaping and scrubbing up a baby." The image of linked hands asserts a connection between mother and daughter, but the emphasis is on the older woman's skill. Her hands are active; the speaker's hands resemble the efficiently managed turkey. The speaker in this idle moment is filled with her mother's activity. Wondering "what she would prescribe / in weather like this," the speaker recollects a typical rainy day and her mother's tactics (such as making carnations out of discarded tissue papers) for coping with "three mild lunatics / she found herself with . . . / in a chicken-coop house." The poet speaks with affectionate admiration of her mother's inventiveness and stamina. The final image in the poem adds a sense of awe and mystery as the speaker recognizes what "power" children wield when, refusing to nap or even pretending to nap, they deny their mothers peace and privacy:

> Lying still
> but alert, I listened from the next room
> as my mother slipped out of her damp dress.
> The cloth crumpling onto the bathroom floor
> made a light, sad sound.

This final image is richly suggestive yet reticent. The dress slipping to the floor articulates in a medium other than poetry. The daughter as poet catches her mother's expression while at the same time recognizing the limits of her ability to translate that "light, sad sound." The speaker thus both succeeds and fails to comprehend her mother, yet this doubleness attests to their equal relationship as artists.

The Wahiawa household pictured in **"A Pale Arrangement of Hands"** is one manifestation of the paradigm furnished by **"The White Porch."** The "chicken-coop house" where rain "fell like a fence" furnished not only a "comfortable geography" of tuna casseroles and television, but a creative space where the poet who later writes of "cloth crumpling" began her training as one of the "mild lunatics." She was the child "singing to herself, / a crinoline worn on her head like a shroud." The adult's recollection of rainy days in Wahiawa is a recognition of plenitude within confinement, the same dichotomy characterizing an ordinary porch rendered as the source of creative energy.

The fullest elaboration of the "white porch" paradigm is **"Easter: Wahiawa, 1959,"** the final poem to be discussed. Whereas in **"Pale Arrangement"** the theme of plenitude in confinement is central but understated, the poem functioning more directly as a portrait of the mother, in **"Easter"** this theme is explicitly developed as a personal and cultural legacy. Since **"Easter"** includes the socio-historical framework of Song's grandparents' immigration in addition to the aesthetic of "singing shapes," it offers a compact picture of "third world" as place and paradigm.

The poem is about a backyard Easter egg hunt almost cancelled by stormy weather.

> The rain stopped for one afternoon.
> Father brought out
> his movie camera and for a few hours
> we were all together
> under a thin film
> that separated the rain showers
> from that part of the earth
> like a hammock
> held loosely by clothespins.
>
> Grandmother took the opportunity
> to hang the laundry
> and Mother and my aunts
> filed out of the house
> in pedal pushers and poodle cuts,
> carrying the blue washed eggs.
> Grandfather kept the children
> penned in on the porch,
> clucking at us in his broken English
> whenever we tried to peek
> around him. There were bread crumbs
> stuck to his blue gray whiskers.

After these opening stanzas, the poem proceeds to a description of the egg hunt and then to a relation of Grandfather's history from an impoverished childhood in Korea through his years as plantation laborer in Hawaii and finally to his presiding over eager grandchildren at a family holiday. As the story proceeds, the primary symbol of "blue washed eggs" is continuously transformed. They first reappear subtly in grandfather's "blue gray whiskers" and his "clucking," then in "the sky, / a membrane of egg whites / straining under the weight" of an impending storm. They revert to their earlier stage of "simmering / in vinegar and blue color all morning," retreat further to become quail eggs "like gigantic pearls" which Grandfather hunted as a boy in Korea, re-emerge in the present as "basketfuls of sky blue eggs" which he can now afford to lavish on grandchildren, and finally come to rest in three eggs he peels for one granddaughter, the poet:

> I found three that afternoon.
> By evening, it was raining hard.

> Grandfather and I skipped supper.
> Instead, we sat on the porch
> and I ate what he peeled
> and cleaned for me.
> The scattering of the delicate
> marine-colored shells across his lap
> was something like what the ocean gives
> the beach after a rain.

As this final scene indicates, Easter in Wahiawa, 1959 yielded two treasures, one for the child and one for the adult reviewing the event years later. The yielding of treasures is represented in the imagery of breaking open. First eggshells scatter as storm clouds burst, completing the action hinted at earlier in grandfather's broken English and breadcrumbed whiskers and bringing the day's excitement to an end. This sequence is then suspended until it reaches its final completion when the poet "fully receives" the symbolic import of that shower of rain and eggshells, when she interprets the Easter eggs as a gift of love given freely to a child, a gift entailing no obligation or requiring any knowledge of the labor expended to bring that egg hunt into being. After learning as an adult of Grandfather's history, the poet can now perceive a fuller meaning of Easter 1959, when a secularized but nonetheless profoundly life-giving ritual was celebrated: Lovely blue eggs were "hidden" expressly for the child to find, an experience that, when perceived as such, provides an undiminished source of love, as demonstrated by the poet's receiving still more as she re-experiences the event many years later. That the adult earns or becomes worthy of this gift by becoming a conscious receiver is beautifully understated in the poem's conclusion. Like Easter eggshells, what scatters on the beach is understood as bounty not in a material sense but as a symbol of unrequested giving and unearned receiving.

The process of becoming a conscious receiver, such that the meaning of an Easter egg hunt is enlarged, is further illuminated when **"Easter"** is paired with another poem picturing the same household, plantation setting, and weather as entrapment. **"Leaving,"** as the title indicates, counterpoints Song's account of her return to a past event.

> Wahiawa is still
> a red dirt town
> where the sticky smell
> of pineapples
> being lopped off
> in the low-lying fields
> rises to mix
> with the minty leaves
> of eucalyptus
> in the bordering gulch.
>
> . . . . .
>
> We grew there
> in the steady rain
> that fell like a gray curtain
> through which my mother peered:
> patches of depression.

She kept the children under cover.
We built houses within houses,
stripping our parents' bed
of pillows and sheets,
erecting walls out of
The National Geographic
which my father had subscribed to
for years. We feasted
on those pictures of the world,
while the mud oozed
past the windows
knocking over the drab green leaves
of palm fronds
as we ate our spinach.

Song eventually leaves this confinement, where energies with no outlet create ingrown, sunless "houses within houses." Having left, however, she can return and displace *National Geographic* with her own experience-based pictures of the world, including' new constructions of the place she left. **"Easter,"** in fact, shows the extent to which confinement can be re-viewed positively. Grandfather keeps the children "penned in on the porch"; later he himself is "enclosed / by his grandchildren, / scrambling around him." This porch scene echoes the fencing of human activities by nature, the way rain literally frames the egg hunt. The narration as well as the narrative is also a matter of frames, since the poet's knowledge of her grandfather's life is enclosed in her reminiscing while at the same time providing the larger context enabling her to interpret or re-read the reminiscence. All of these figurative and literal enclosures are not felt as restrictions. The same constraining circumstances that lead inward to form "houses within houses" in one situation can, from another perspective, dissolve outward to the freedom of shoreline. Together, **"Leaving"** and **"Easter"** describe the poet's capacity for reconciling oppositions, for making one thing yield something else.

This capacity is therefore creative through transformation. It is the capacity of "singing shapes" as a point of view as well as a formal poetic technique. What on the level of imagery is transformation of one shape into another, is on the level of ideas a capacity for multiple perspectives. Ultimately, the same energy underlies both the imagery and the ideas, the technique and the vision. The eternal fund of creative energy represented by a "white place" is also the bountifulness of pregnancy or parental love and, more generally, the bountifulness of a generosity towards people and nature. And it is this sensibility of generosity that gives rise to the specific patterns of "singing shapes" that appear not only within individual poems, but throughout *Picture Bride* as a whole. For instance, the same transformation of eggs in "Easter" occurs across several poems: "egg- and bean-shaped contours" of clay pots (**"Waialua"**), "bodies . . . white and firm like shells" (**"Blue Lantern"**), "[b]asketfuls of plastic eggs / nestled in cellophane grass" (**"Primary Colors"**), "tiny black seeds / that resembled caviar" and "eggshells Father hollowed for whistles" (**"Tribe"**), "farmyard hens" (**"Lost Sister"**), a jade bracelet "cracked into thousand-year-old eggshells" (**"Spaces We Leave Empty"**), the "ripe ovaries" of whales

(**"A Dream of Small Children"**). These strands of seed, womb, and egg imagery are part of the book's pervasive imagery of potential and fulfillment initiated by the picture bride's "tent-shaped dress" in the first poem. Thus we come full circle with the picture bride motif, which summarizes the double nature of Song's "third world" poetry. The tent-shaped dress is an ethnically specific image of larger image patterns that include other ethnicities, cultures, geographies, and historical periods. The literal picture bride experience is part of Song's legacy, but in addition to being written about, it has become a model of poetic form and perspective.

> **Whether writing of her grandmother or Georgia O'Keeffe, Song has necessarily interpreted and re-invented them both. The physical, biological relation of one woman is not less or more important than the presence of the other as an artistic influence.**
>
> —*Gayle Fujita-Sato*

Before publication, the manuscript was titled "From the White Place" instead of "Picture Bride." But Song's original preference for a title emphasizing O'Keeffe's importance, and the publisher's choice emphasizing ethnicity (Song, telephone interview), are clearly not at odds. Whether writing of her grandmother or O'Keeffe, Song has necessarily interpreted and re-invented them both. The physical, biological relation of one woman is not less or more important than the presence of the other as an artistic influence. Neither the title poem nor the flower paintings that title the book's sections suffice in themselves as frameworks for what the poems contain. The aesthetic of "singing shapes" can be traced directly to O'Keeffe, but as it operates in *Picture Bride,* it is Song's aesthetic, reshaped to articulate her sensibility and represent her experience. A poem like **"Easter, Wahiawa: 1959"** demonstrates how Song's "picture bride" legacy emerges from, but also furnishes, a "white place."

The Wahiawa porch and the white porch are the same place viewed differently: "third world" as place and "third world" as paradigm. Together these two kinds of porches suggest a framework for reading ethnic writing. In such a framework, ethnicity can be understood as both a stable set of social institutions and ideologies and the "place" where these stabilities are perceived and articulated. A "third world" location is a point as well as a point of viewing characterized by synthesis. Such a place values pluralistic imagination and nurtures continual uncovering of the pluralistic underpinnings of societies shaped by different cultures and ethnicities. *Picture Bride* conjoins disparate traditions and celebrates those creations. It defines and invites a kind of "third world" living.

Jessica Greenbaum (review date 1988)

SOURCE: "Family Albums," in *The Women's Review of Books,* Vol. VI, No. 1, October, 1988, p. 19.

[*In this review of* Frameless Windows, Squares of Light, *Greenbaum criticizes Song's excessive use of metaphors and biographical information.*]

Cathy Song is a first-generation Asian-American whose heritage is Korean; she has lived all of her 33 years in Hawaii. Her first book, *Picture Bride,* won the 1982 Yale Younger Poets Prize. Rooted in Korean culture, much of *Picture Bride* was about the author's family history and relationships, delivering even-tempered poems whose power came partly from the way their strong images floated up from dreamy narratives. That voice is evident in *Frameless Windows,* although her successes here are fewer.

Often speaking in the second person, Song projects her sensibility onto her family members' history and tries to weave a lyric from the two. The book's first poem, **"The Day You Were Born"** (apparently about the speaker's father), opens

> There was an emptiness
>   Waiting for you. The night
>   your mother knew you existed,
>   she felt a flicker of sadness
>   for the life, no bigger than her
>   thumbnail . . .

The poem begins gracefully and engagingly enough, but quickly buckles under the weight of too many metaphors and unwieldy biographical information. The subject of the poem is described all in one breath as "her last child, the last flowering / before the pod, like a crippled hand / withered shut." Is the uterus a pod or a crippled hand? It can't be visualized as both at once—where was Song's editor? The poem bogs down further with the sticky description, "you who would be / his third son, his fifth child." When we arrive at the poem's concluding stanza, the drama is undermined by its clichés:

> Your father would die uneventfully
>   but your mother, perched on the
>   porch
>   with a piece of sewing on her lap,
>   would be there waiting
>   for a boy to walk home
>   in the late afternoon light,
>   dragging his leather satchel. . . .

Biography is reduced in this way to clichéd vignettes. **"Magic Island"** has the same problem: "Under each tree, / a study in small pleasures: / a boy, / half in sunlight, / naps with his dog; / a woman, / marking a page with a leaf, / squints up / to bite into an apple."

Telling other people's stories in their voices often results in a stiff, unlived-in feel that stymies this otherwise lithe poet.

> There was always something that needed fixing,
> a car on the blink,
> a jinxed washing machine,
> a high-strung garbage disposer.
> His life was one of continual repair.

In this, from **"The Tower of Pisa,"** a poem about Song's father, an airline pilot whose job stifles his real talents, the fifth line is more an emphatic prose statement than poetry. Later in the same poem she writes, "A boy who wanted nothing else / but to fly those gorgeous machines. / It was maddening, the inactivity . . ." Which is far from the freshness of articulation we expect from good poetry.

Song is at her best when she wrenches free of her responsibilities to family history. **"A Mehinaku Girl in Seclusion"** describes the three-year isolation of a tribal adolescent after her first menstruation. Delicately told in the subject's voice, it casts its own subtle spell:

> When the pequi fruit blossomed,
> I went into seclusion.
> A red flower
> dropped out of my body
> and stained the red dirt of the earth
> one color. With one color
> I became married to the earth.
> I went to live by myself
> in the hut at the end of the village.

There is far greater intimacy here than there is in Song's second-person descriptions of other subjects. And while Song is generous with all her subjects, we care more about the Mehinaku woman and her plight is more immediate for us.

> When the rain comes I slip out
> and circle the dirt plaza.
> I pause as if to drink at each door.
> At each door,
> the sound of the sleeping.
> I return before the first
> hint of light,
> return to hear
> the click of my spinning.

Song also writes well about her own specific memories. In **"Humble Jar,"** for instance, she describes her mother's sewing kit and button jar, at one point remembering "the ditto marker (a tiny replica of a pizza cutter)." Because we simultaneously picture this sewing tool and register the wit of its metaphor, it's a satisfying description. One wishes Song would keep her vision this acute. Instead the poem moves to watery lines like "She'd bring these out as if by magic." The poem takes a nice turn in the end but our attention and respect have been too far diluted.

By contrast, **"A Small Light"** sustains its power. A dreamy poem, it describes a treehouse from the perspective of each member of the family:

> When the man comes home he takes off his hat
> and looks up at the leaves of the tree.

The light anoints each leaf as it sinks into the sea.
The tree shimmers like a thousand mirrors,
the suddenness of birds in flight.
A child is sleeping in the house.
The house rises and falls with each breath
as if the house were made of cloth.
Tacked to the walls is the sound of the clock
which keeps the house from floating away.

But finally . . . [Song's new book] suffers from lack of intensity. . . . [It] lapses into circumscribed thought that eclipses the possible largesse of poetry.

Robert B. Shaw (review date 1989)

SOURCE: A review of *Frameless Windows, Squares of Light,* in *Poetry,* Vol. CLIV, No. 5, August, 1989, pp. 289-90.

[*In the review below, Shaw praises Song's treatment of family life, but echoes other critics in the opinion that Song's talent would better served by tighter composition and editing, curbing her tendency to "meander."*]

Family history has been a fertile source for poetry in America in recent years. It may be that in a society as heterogeneous as ours it is the only sort of history which seems real in a personal sense: in a melting pot there is no common national past, only many gradually blending stories. Cathy Song shows herself a resourceful historian of her family in [*Frameless Windows, Squares of Light*], her second book; she also shows herself aware of the tenuousness of what she is about. Can we, at this late date, compel our dead grandparents or our own infant selves to sit still to be photographed?

The poet's background has made her conscious of cultural diversity. She was born in Honolulu; her grandparents were immigrants from China. She takes note of the special features of this heritage dispassionately, imagining her grandfather meeting the boat that had brought his mail-order bride to him:

. . . his young man's eyes had scanned
the cargo of brides
who bowed before the grim life held out to them;
sucking in their breath
at the vision of their own faces
caught like orange blossoms
in the sad hands of laborers.
 . . . my grandmother stepping forward
to acknowledge her own face
was the last to give herself away.

Song's memories are shaped by the gravity and patience of an observant child, as when she recalls visiting this grandfather the day before he died:

The radio was on,
the dial set fuzzily between two channels.

He had been listening to the static
as though he were waiting to decipher
a message he would know
at the moment of his hearing it.
                                        "Living Near the Water"

One values her sensitivity and precision, whether she is remembering childhood play with her brother amid the hanging laundry:

invisible to the world in our tent,
our tepee, our magnificent hut:
the house of permanent press,
its cool damp walls of sheets and shirts
billowing around us
                                        "Tribal Scenes"

or, as in another poem, conducting an inventory of her mother's button collection:

She prized the leather ones,
braided and varnished
like the miniature strudels
my dolls secretly enjoyed with tea.
Her indestructible car coat
was on the third generation of these.
                                        "Humble Jar"

While Song renders details with great clarity, she is apt to leave somewhat in shadow larger patterns of relationship and of the sequence of events. Some of this blurring is intentional: in **"Tribal Scenes"** her memories of her and her brother's childhood are merged with views of her own two children playing, and a perception of continuities linking generations emerges. She sees the present moment as potential memory, the latest addition to the palimpsest that is the past. At moments her attempts to evoke this plasticity of time can disorient the reader. It should be said, too, that Song is not always as disciplined as one could wish in determining the length of her pieces. Her preference is for relaxed, conversational rhythms, and she tends to avoid striking effects of climax; the result is that we notice a meandering repetitiousness in a number of poems which circle round a single point rather than pursuing a linear path of argument. This can be true of poems containing fine passages—in fact, it is true of some of those I have quoted. I find myself hoping that the future will add to this poet's evident gifts a greater talent for compression.

Marilyn Kallet (review date 1990)

SOURCE: "Illuminating Kinship," in *Belles Lettres,* Vol. 6, No. 1, Fall, 1990, p. 31.

[*Below, Kallet reviews* Frameless Windows, Squares of Light *in a mixed light, describing some poems as expansive and lyrical, and others as rambling and flat. Kallet also notes how this volume complements* Picture Bride *and, taken together, the two works narrate the writer's life and family history.*]

Cathy Song's first book of poems, *Picture Bride,* was a family history and a lyrical, pared-down story of a woman writer's life. In it, Hawaiian-born Song creates a hospitable place in language where Korean, Chinese, Japanese, Hawaiian, and Asian-American cultures meet. The writing is spare, like the brushstrokes of a Japanese painting, and musical, like the melancholy notes of the *shakuhachi,* the Japanese flute that Song's grandfather played.

Song's latest book, *Frameless Windows, Squares of Light,* continues the work of "claiming" family for her album of poetry. Poems in the new volume are on the average longer than those in her previous collection, *Picture Bride*: at times they ramble, or the language goes flat. Of a beloved family dog, Song writes:

> He seemed content to wait
> at your side, forever
> if you had wished,
> for the soggy tennis ball
> to be thrown one last time
> across the yard.

Here language is untextured, not "worked."

Other poems are more detailed and lyrical. The world becomes musical, as in this poem about observing a snowfall:

> The woman who watched it, interpreted it.
> She likened it to something symphonic,
> the musical texture of the snow—
> a flurry of feathers in the downward descent, the
> unexpected updraft, fluty, almost fragrant,
> and then the insertion of the glacial pause,
> the oboe's lugubrious chill.

Water and wind weave a continuum, uniting generations. **"Living Near Water"** is a moving poem about the death of Song's grandfather, "the warm wind had passed through him; / flowing out through each of us, / the smell of the sea." Quiet intimacy is the hallmark of Song's poetry. She addresses many of her poems to "you," to family members, and implicitly to her readers. "You" and "he" refer variously to brother, to the young poet-narrator, to Song's father. (Unfortunately, having to decode the many pronouns sometimes proves burdensome.)

In their intimacy and quiet discursiveness, these poems cross boundaries between poetry and letters; poetry and journal-writing. At their weakest, they are private family letters; at their strongest, they are expansive, inclusive. There is a willingness to reveal more of the "shadow" side of family life than in *Picture Bride,* where Song depicted herself as a "little Buddha," calm, quiescent. *Frameless Windows* shows us the sadness permeating Song's childhood. Her parents "settle into sleep, / into unhappiness." Their quiet daughter all but disappears:

> Unnoticed, you sailed into the trees
> where the pull of the wind
> could release your name like a kite:
> calling yourself home,
> flinging the broken sound of it
> into the leaves.

"This is your name, / and a river runs through it." The power of naming brings Song's life back into focus.

Silence in a woman's life is charged, bearing what her culture expects of her, and what she claims for herself. The recent book reveals more about the complexities of silence and self-image for Song. In her honesty, Song unburdens herself of the expectation that any woman in this culture, especially a minority woman, is free of anger.

Picture Bride pays tribute to family and to art, to Georgia O'Keeffe's bright blossoms. *Frameless Windows, Squares of Light* suggests photographs, memories captured in stills; mystical pages that "float upward in the dark like luminous kites / waiting for the words to come in." Song's books complement each other: They are one life-story unfolding.

Patricia Wallace (essay date 1993)

SOURCE: "Divided Loyalties: Literal and Literary in the Poetry of Lorna Dee Cervantes, Cathy Song, and Rita Dove," in *MELUS,* Vol. 18, No. 3, Fall, 1993, pp. 3-19.

[*In the following excerpt, Wallace explores the balance between art and history in Song's poetry, recognizing the influence of the poet's multicultural background on her poetry.*]

The poems of the Hawaiian-born Cathy Song transform what seems simple or ordinary—including words themselves—by lifting things out of their ordinary settings. A Song poem then moves between the beautiful strangeness such transformations reveal and a sharp sense of dailiness and practical necessity which resists that power. I think of **"Humble Jar,"** from Song's second collection, *Frameless Windows, Squares of Light* (1988), as a kind of emblem for Song's poetic practices. The title derives from a mayonnaise jar in which an Asian American mother keeps a variety of buttons "for every emergency." Like [Lorna Dee] Cervantes's Virginia [in her poem "For Virginia Chavez"] or the women in "Cannery Town in August," the mother of Song's poem is someone whose life is not identifiable with "literature." She exists in the poem as a presence distinct from the poet, as someone whose life is evoked by and yet resists the poet's designs. The mother's life is as "oddly private" as the buttons she hides away in the jar: "She could easily have led / the double life of a spy." The poet uses her imaginative power to reveal what is hidden in the mother's life (hidden from American culture at large and from the poet in particular) and so to bring poetry and the mother's life closer together. Song wants to transform the "undervalued" life of the mother, to uncover its hidden beauty and power, and to open possibility. But this effort is countered by a knowledge, felt in the rhythms of the poem, of how much the mother has had to put aside.

Buttons are the poem's central image, and as Song uses it that image is wonderfully figurative and stubbornly literal; it unsettles any stable distinction between those categories. Words, like buttons, can be "useful yet undervalued"; they are a form of "common currency," like the commonplace white buttons the mother keeps in the jar, "unremarkable but reliable, / rescuing a garment at a moment's notice." Words can also be like the "less practical" buttons in the jar, distinguished from the ordinary. Separated from their "original setting (a cashmere coat, / a bottle-green evening gown)," these are endowed by their freedom from context with beauty and possibility:

> What remained was no longer a button
> but a relic—
> a coat of arms,
> a silver dollar—
> something you couldn't spend.

A poet like Song uses familiar words so that they are no longer strictly defined by previous use, so that they become more than counters, become "something you couldn't spend." Yet the poet's words are also bound up in common usage, where, like the mother's buttons, they repair or mend, or retrieve "a moment / out of a cluttered life."

So the poet-daughter and the mother of this poem mix the plain and the decorative together in their jar and poems. It's amusing to think of **"Humble Jar"** as Song's humble version of poetry's Grecian urn, as her way of insisting on the connections between art and daily life. To imagine a button jar (and a mayonnaise jar at that) as an icon for poetry bridges the apparent gap between domestic activities and the making of poems, and suggests that each is a form of creative shaping. This means the making of poetry is not innately superior to other activities, a conviction that also underlies a number of Cervantes's poems (for example, "Beneath the Shadow of the Freeway"), and many of Rita Dove's poems as well (especially "Dusting"). And we may think of [Ralph Waldo] Emerson, who suggested in "Self Reliance" that there can be "prayer in all action." Such equations are part of an implicit argument for the continuity between the poet's life and work and that of other men and women, for the continuity between literary and literal.

But such an argument is not untroubled in Song's poems, any more than it is in Cervantes's. The poet's identity as poet also sets her apart; she is empowered by words in a way the Asian American mother (or Virginia Chavez or the women at the California cannery) is not. Her imaginative transformations have a freedom from some of the unyielding conditions that accompany most people's work. The poet-speaker of **"Humble Jar,"** for example, transforms herself through button-art. She holds "flat disks of gold" to her ears "as if they were the earrings" her mother never wore, "offering them to a younger self, / a child's soft face in the mirror, / gazing back, almost beautiful." In this moment Song conflates her poet-self and her mother, unites them in the image of the face in the mirror, that "younger self" who is, ambiguously, mother and daughter at the same time. But this poetic unity isn't really stable. It leaves out too much that separates these two lives: the passage of time, the claims others (including the poet) have made on the mother's life, the things that have been put aside and cannot be retrieved. The conclusion of the poem briefly recaptures—for the instant of a camera click—a moment of the mother's youth, light with possibility ("The summer she wore that scalloped dress"), only to lose it in the final, heavily stressed repetitions, with their weight of *what is*:

> The summer she wore that scalloped dress,
> she turned and smiled for the camera,
> my father, for life that was certain to be glorious.
> Beginners, both of them, the blind leading the
> blind.

In both her books Cathy Song is occupied with the shifting relations (divided *and* intertwined) between a transient reality and the designs of language and art. Her first book, *Picture Bride* (1983), explores exactly these relations in two poems dedicated to the Japanese printmaker, Kitagawa Utamaro [**"Beauty and Sadness"** and **"Girl Powdering Her Neck"**]. Even more pertinent is the title poem of *Picture Bride,* where Song struggles with the limits of her own imaginative power and her own uses of language to render another person's life. **"Picture Bride"** begins with the gap between an image—explicitly, a photographic image—and the life that image claims to represent. The poem imagines a grandmother who, Song suggests, was chosen as a bride from such an image and summoned from Korea to Hawaii, where "a man waited, / turning her photograph / to the light when the lanterns / in the camp outside / Waialua Sugar Mill were lit." The poet tries to recover a fuller sense of the grandmother's life, to see beyond the boundaries of the photograph. But the making of images is also the poet's work, and the grandmother's life remains in crucial ways beyond the reach of the poem's images, unassimilable as a literary creation.

In both *Picture Bride* and *Frameless Windows, Squares of Light* Cathy Song is occupied with the shifting relations (divided *and* intertwined) between a transient reality and the designs of language and art.

—*Patricia Wallace*

Although **"Picture Bride"** begins with an assertion of likeness, part of an effort to bridge the distance between the poet's life and that of the grandmother ("She was a year younger / than I, / twenty-three when she left Korea"), everything that follows takes the shape of an unanswered question. This method of imaginative speculation that seeks to reconstruct an ancestral image is, Gayle K. Fujita-Sato points out, reminiscent of Maxine Hong Kingston's strategy in the opening chapter of *The Woman Warrior*. In each case a young Asian American woman tries to imagine the life of a female ancestor whose history has been erased or repressed. Kingston's chapter is titled "No Name Woman" and Song's grandmother is never identified by name, only by the anonymous category of "picture bride." But in Song's poem the emphasis falls on the way each effort to "fill in" the picture of the grandmother runs up against her unavailability to the poet's imaginative designs. The solidity of each detail dissolves into questions until, in the conclusion, the grandmother seems simply to disappear from the poem itself:

> And when
> she arrived to look
> into the face of the stranger
> who was her husband,
> thirteen years older than she,
> did she politely untie
> the silk bow of her jacket,
> her tent-shaped dress
> filling with the dry wind
> that blew from the surrounding fields
> where the men were burning the cane?

The gesture of untying the "silk bow" of the "jacket" promises a revelation of what has been hidden—a fully embodied figure of the grandmother. But no sooner is the image made than it is unmade. As the dress fills with "dry wind" the grandmother evaporates. In the place we look for her we find only the wind and sugar cane fields; she disappears into a Hawaiian landscape (Waialua Sugar Mill fields) where powerful corporations often erased the presence of Asian American laborers, and from an American history which excludes mention of her and Asian American women like her. Like Cervantes in the conclusion to "Cannery Town in August," Song doesn't claim poetry has the power to overcome this erasure, any more than **"Humble Jar"** claims to restore the mother's youthful possibility. In an important way, **"Picture Bride,"** like other of Song's poems, refuses to separate the problems of language from the problems of culture. Yet the very uncertainty of Song's poetic structures honors the degree to which the grandmother's life is not a purely literary figuration.

Lee Kyhan (essay date 1994)

SOURCE: "Korean-American Literature: The Next Generation," in *Korea Journal*, Vol. 34, No. 1, Spring, 1994, pp. 20-35.

[*In the following excerpt, Kyhan explores the evolution of Korean-American literature in the twentieth century, focusing on the impact of gender and family traditions on Song's poetry. Kyhan positions Song within the scheme of this literature, and discusses her unique characteristics.*]

Quite a few second and third generation writers adamantly reject the hybrid or marginal implications of their identity, claiming allegiance to the American identity that they were born into, yet this too may likely be a defense mechanism against the tensions of identity crisis that are too painful to deal with in the open. Cathy Song is an interesting case in point. Song contends that she is merely "a poet who happens to be Asian-American" and coaches her readers to "look beyond the external characteristics of her life . . . to see the poet who molds images and meaning through words" [Debbie Murakami Nomaguchi, "Cathy Song: I'm a Poet who Happens to be Asian-American," *International Examiner*, 1984]. Again in an interview given in the *Honolulu Star-Bulletin* in 1983 shortly after the publication of *Picture Bride*, Song expressed her concern about the ethnocentric slant with which her readers and reviewers alike persistently interpret her poems. Yet, as evident in the predominantly 'oriental' flavor of her works, Song is in many respects typical of most next generation writers who have not been able to completely divorce themselves from their ethnic identity. . . .

Despite many similarities they share with other second generation and third generation immigrant writers, the next generation Korean-American writers express concerns that are particular to the Korean-American experience. First, one readily recognizes that the next generation writers exhibit an obsessive interest in and fascination with the story of their parents and grandparents, the first pioneer immigrants. Although the notion of "roots" is an important leitmotif prevalent throughout the next generation Korean-American literature, their preoccupation with the life of their immigrant forefathers is much more than a simple "root seeking" venture. Nor are they willingly embracing the cultural heritage of their immigrant forefathers as their own. As in Kim Ronyoung's *Clay Walls,* Peter Hyun's *Man Sei! The Making of a Korean Yankee,* Cathy Song's **Picture Bride,** Mary Paik Lee's *Quiet Odyssey,* Margaret Pai's *The Story of Two Yi-min,* Kumi Kilburn's "No Dogs and Chinese Allowed" to name a few, the next generation writers share a common project to somehow weave together the various life stories of their elders in a biographical novel, in the hopes that the experiences of first generation immigrants could somehow help them to better deal with their agonizing ambivalence towards their own hybrid identity. . . .

Cathy Song, the celebrated third generation poet, began her apprenticeship by writing short stories in her spare time but quickly moved away from that genre when she felt that they were "pure fantasy" and "merely a way of articulating dream wishes" (Nomaguchi). In her search for a purer medium of self-expression, Song discovered in writing poetry "an immediacy and intensity . . . which is lost in extended piece of writing like short stories or novels." Even in her later prose ventures like "Beginnings (for Bok Pil)," Song creates a distinctively poetic atmosphere, achieved in part by the deliberate abstinence from superfluous rhetoric and dialogue. She places much more emphasis on often banal yet memorable images that stimulate the reader's imagination. Exemplified in the poem below, Cathy Song, unlike her predecessors who are overtly conscientious of their Anglo-American readership, is also characteristic of the next generation writers in her unabashed and unapologetic use of colloquialism and Asian-centered images indigenous to her culture, which is evident in poems like **"Chinatown"**:

> *The children are the dumplings*
> *set afloat*
>
>   . . . . .
>
> *Wrap the children*
> *in wanton skins,*
> *bright quilted bundles*
> *sewn warm with five spices*
>
> *Jade, ginger root,*
> *sesame seed, mother-of-pearl*
> *& ivory. . . .*

For many who began writing when the feminist movement had come of age, literature afforded the medium through which one's identity, not only as an ethnic minority but also as a woman, could be reexamined and redefined. The task is understandably a formidable one. As Blicksilver points out, an ethnic woman writer will invariably confront alienation from the majority culture by virtue of her ethnic background, as was true of the first generation male writers, but she must also contend with alienation from her own ethnic group by virtue of her artistic sensibilities as a feminist writer. It is perhaps appropriate to note that few next generation writers claim to have written from a feminist platform. In their treatment of the life stories of their matriarchal forebears, the early picture brides, next generation women writers rarely betray bitterness or scorn towards what is unequivocally an example of the inequality of women inherent in the traditional Korean culture. Preoccupation of socio-cultural criticism is more evident in such Asian-American works as Maxine Hong Kingston's *The Woman Warrior.* On the contrary, through understanding and sympathy they hope to draw strength and wisdom from the remarkable life stories of their picture bride mothers and grandmothers. As Richard Hugo remarks of Cathy Song's poetry [in his introduction to **Picture Bride**], "in quietude lies her strength. In her receptivity, passive as it seems, lies passion, a passion that is expressed in deceptive quiet and an even tone." And it is perhaps in this fortitude through unobtrusive quietness that the contributions of their inherent Koreanness is most evident. . . .

> **Despite the pungent Korean and Korean-American aroma that permeates her work, Song remains an enigma of sort for Korean-American scholars because of her ardent resistance to any ethnic identification. Song, like many writers of her generation, may have become too "Americanized" to qualify as a Korean-American writer.**
>
> **—Lee Kyhan**

Cathy Song, perhaps the most well-known of the next generation Korean-American writers, was born in Hawaii in 1955. The first recognition of her literary talent came in 1982, when she won the Yale series of Younger Poets Competition among 625 entries, joining the ranks of previous Yale Younger Poets winners such as Adrienne Rich, W. S. Merwin, John Ashbery, and Muriel Rukeyser. Despite the pungent Korean and Korean-American aroma that permeates her works, Song remains an enigma of sort for Korean-American scholars because of her ardent resistance to any ethnic identification. Ch'oe Yon-hong feels that Cathy Song, like many writers of her generation, may have become too "Americanized" to qualify as a Korean-American writer. According to Shirley Lim [in a review of **Picture Bride,** in *MELUS* 15, No. 3, Fall 1983], Song had originally submitted her poems to Yale under the title "From the White Place," after a title of a poem in the collection dedicated to Georgia O'Keeffe, her aesthetic influence, but the title was later changed to **Picture Bride** reflecting a reordering of thematic emphasis possibly on the advice of her editors who were eager to capitalize on her ethnic background. In the *Picture Bride* Cathy Song takes us on a spiritual pilgrimage back to the time of her grandparents, the first Korean immigrants who had toiled on the sugar cane plantations of Hawaii at the turn of the century. The focus of course is on their suffering and sorrow, but what is absent in the poems are sentiments of pity or bitterness, usually evident in ethnic literature of this kind. Rather the reader encounters a sense of coziness and warmth of a child retelling the many stories of her family's past that she has been brought up on, like the situation portrayed in **"Easter: Wahiawa 1959"** in which retrospection is evoked by familiar faces brought together "under a thin film" of her father's movie camera.

As Richard Hugo points out, the ideas of "leaving" and "escaping" are dominant leitmotifs throughout Song's poems. In **"Primary Colors,"** the yearning to escape from the constraints imposed by parents is treated as a universal rebellion contemplated by all youth alike:

> Then the babies stormed the streets,
> sailing by in their runaway carriages,
> having yanked the wind
> out from under their mothers.

Perhaps for the offsprings of early laborer immigrants, this "universal rebellion" took on more meaning as they strived to escape the menial life of the first generation Korean-Americans and aspired for greater and better things in life. Song's rebellion is also directed against the image of woman of her grandmother's generation, hardened by demeaning labor and the subjugated roles imposed by traditional values:

> It seems I have always lived
> in this irregular room, rarely needing
> to see beyond the straight seams that fit neatly,
> the snaps that fasten securely in my mind.
> The world for me is a piece of cloth.
> I have at the moment beneath my hands.
>   **("Seamstress")**

In **"The Youngest Daughter,"** the restrictions of the older generations are mind-forged manacles of filial obligations dictated by the Confucian tradition. The young daughter is physically and emotionally drained by the never ending chores involved in nursing her ailing mother. She dreams of running away, despite the fact that she suspects that her mother "knows I am not to be trusted / even now planning my escape." In stoic dejection, she merely goes through the motions of her filial duties that have degenerated into meaningless rituals like a "toast to her health." Similarly, in **"The White Porch,"** the daughter finds her only moments of solace at night while her mother "slept in tight blankets," when she, like a heroine of fairly tales, lets her hair down to "smuggle" her imaginary lover into her room.

The theme of "leaving" is only the first stage of a larger theme that forms a cyclical pattern of *departure, reconciliation,* and the eventual *return.* Elaine Kim sees the central theme of Song's poems, which she calls a "consummately Korean-American theme," as being one of "exploring the relationship between the persona and her family, from whom she ventures forth and with whom she is eventually reconciled" ["Asian American Writers: A Bibliographical Review," *American Studies International,* 1989]. In so far as the reconciliation extends to her acceptance of her ethnic background, it can also be interpreted as a coming to terms with one's own ethnic identity as off-springs of those who came to this country as "strangers from a different shore."

The theme of "reconciliation with one's past" becomes prominent in poems like **"Lost Sisters."** The young Chinese picture bride flees from her life in China where "to move freely was a luxury / stolen from them from birth." She is intoxicated by her romantic vision of a new life in America where "there are many roads / and women can stride along with men." However, once in the States, she encounters still "another wilderness" in which "the possibilities, / the loneliness, / can strangulate like jungle vines." In her dejection and heightening sense of nostalgia, the young Chinese bride at once achieves a mysterious reunion with the very entity from which she has travelled across the ocean to escape:

> You find you need China:
> Your one fragile identification,
> a jade link
> handcuffed to your wrist.

Characteristic of Korean-American women writers of her generation, Cathy Song is fascinated with the story of her grandmother (to whom the title poem is dedicated), who, as one of the first picture brides, had travelled across the ocean for someone "whose name she had / only recently learned." Like Maxine Hong Kingston, who in *The Woman Warrior,* rummages through the discolored photographs of her mother to somehow draw courage and inspiration from the life story of her own mother, Cathy Song, too, readily recognizes in the story of her grandmother a fortitude and a strength of character that she somehow hopes to make relevant to her own predicament as a modern Asian-American woman:

> And when
> she arrived to look
> into the face of the stranger
> who was her husband,
> thirteen years older than she,
> did she politely untie
> the silk bow of her jacket
> her tent-shaped dress
> filled with the dry wind
> that blew from the surrounding fields
> where the men were burning the cane?
>   **("Picture Bride")**

And it is this inexplicable union with her immigrant forbearers that Cathy Song later termed "the intricacies of generations" and "the legacy of cycles."

FURTHER READING

Nomaguchi, Debbie Murakami. "Cathy Song: I'm a Poet Who Happens to be Asian American." *International Examiner* (May 2, 1984): 9.

    Much discussed interview with Song in which she de-emphasizes the effect her ethinicity has on her poetry.

Additional coverage of Song's life and career is contained in the following sources published by Gale Research: *American Women Writers,* **Vol. 5 supplement;** *Notable Asian Americans*; **and** *EXPLORING Poetry.*

Poetry Criticism
INDEXES

*Literary Criticism Series
Cumulative Author Index*

Cumulative Nationality Index

Cumulative Title Index

How to Use This Index

The main references

┌─────────────────────────────────────┐
│ **Calvino, Italo**   │
│   1923–1985 .... **CLC 5, 8, 11, 22, 33, 39,** │
│   **73; SSC 3** │
└─────────────────────────────────────┘

list all author entries in the following Gale Literary Criticism series:

BLC = *Black Literature Criticism*
CLC = *Contemporary Literary Criticism*
CLR = *Children's Literature Review*
CMLC = *Classical and Medieval Literature Criticism*
DA = *DISCovering Authors*
DAB = *DISCovering Authors: British*
DAC = *DISCovering Authors: Canadian*
DAM = *DISCovering Authors: Modules*
   DRAM: *Dramatists Module;* *MST*: *Most-Studied Authors Module;*
   MULT: *Multicultural Authors Module;* *NOV*: *Novelists Module;*
   POET: *Poets Module;* *POP*: *Popular Fiction and Genre Authors Module*
DC = *Drama Criticism*
HLC = *Hispanic Literature Criticism*
LC = *Literature Criticism from 1400 to 1800*
NCLC = *Nineteenth-Century Literature Criticism*
PC = *Poetry Criticism*
SSC = *Short Story Criticism*
TCLC = *Twentieth-Century Literary Criticism*
WLC = *World Literature Criticism, 1500 to the Present*

The cross-references

┌─────────────────────────────────────┐
│   See also CANR 23; CA 85-88;   │
│   obituary CA116   │
└─────────────────────────────────────┘

list all author entries in the following Gale biographical and literary sources:

AAYA = *Authors & Artists for Young Adults*
AITN = *Authors in the News*
BEST = *Bestsellers*
BW = *Black Writers*
CA = *Contemporary Authors*
CAAS = *Contemporary Authors Autobiography Series*
CABS = *Contemporary Authors Bibliographical Series*
CANR = *Contemporary Authors New Revision Series*
CAP = *Contemporary Authors Permanent Series*
CDALB = *Concise Dictionary of American Literary Biography*
CDBLB = *Concise Dictionary of British Literary Biography*
DLB = *Dictionary of Literary Biography*
DLBD = *Dictionary of Literary Biography Documentary Series*
DLBY = *Dictionary of Literary Biography Yearbook*
HW = *Hispanic Writers*
JRDA = *Junior DISCovering Authors*
MAICYA = *Major Authors and Illustrators for Children and Young Adults*
MTCW = *Major 20th-Century Writers*
NNAL = *Native North American Literature*
SAAS = *Something about the Author Autobiography Series*
SATA = *Something about the Author*
YABC = *Yesterday's Authors of Books for Children*

Literary Criticism Series
Cumulative Author Index

DA; DAB; DAC; DAM MST, MULT, POET, POP; WLCS
See also AAYA 7, 20; BW 2; CA 65-68; CANR 19, 42; DLB 38; MTCW; SATA 49

Anna Comnena 1083-1153 .... **CMLC 25**

Annensky, Innokenty (Fyodorovich) 1856-1909 **TCLC 14**
See also CA 110; 155

Annunzio, Gabriele d'
See D'Annunzio, Gabriele

Anodos
See Coleridge, Mary E(lizabeth)

Anon, Charles Robert
See Pessoa, Fernando (Antonio Nogueira)

Anouilh, Jean (Marie Lucien Pierre) 1910-1987 **CLC 1, 3, 8, 13, 40, 50; DAM DRAM; DC 8**
See also CA 17-20R; 123; CANR 32; MTCW

Anthony, Florence
See Ai

Anthony, John
See Ciardi, John (Anthony)

Anthony, Peter
See Shaffer, Anthony (Joshua); Shaffer, Peter (Levin)

Anthony, Piers 1934- .... **CLC 35; DAM POP**
See also AAYA 11; CA 21-24R; CANR 28, 56; DLB 8; MTCW; SAAS 22; SATA 84

Antoine, Marc
See Proust, (Valentin-Louis-George-Eugene-) Marcel

Antoninus, Brother
See Everson, William (Oliver)

Antonioni, Michelangelo 1912- .... **CLC 20**
See also CA 73-76; CANR 45

Antschel, Paul 1920-1970
See Celan, Paul
See also CA 85-88; CANR 33, 61; MTCW

Anwar, Chairil 1922-1949 .... **TCLC 22**
See also CA 121

Apollinaire, Guillaume 1880-1918**TCLC 3, 8, 51; DAM POET; PC 7**
See also Kostrowitzki, Wilhelm Apollinaris de
See also CA 152

Appelfeld, Aharon 1932- .... **CLC 23, 47**
See also CA 112; 133

Apple, Max (Isaac) 1941- .... **CLC 9, 33**
See also CA 81-84; CANR 19, 54; DLB 130

Appleman, Philip (Dean) 1926- .... **CLC 51**
See also CA 13-16R; CAAS 18; CANR 6, 29, 56

Appleton, Lawrence
See Lovecraft, H(oward) P(hillips)

Apteryx
See Eliot, T(homas) S(tearns)

Apuleius, (Lucius Madaurensis) 125(?)-175(?) **CMLC 1**

Aquin, Hubert 1929-1977 .... **CLC 15**
See also CA 105; DLB 53

Aragon, Louis 1897-1982 .. **CLC 3, 22; DAM NOV, POET**
See also CA 69-72; 108; CANR 28; DLB 72; MTCW

Arany, Janos 1817-1882 .... **NCLC 34**

Arbuthnot, John 1667-1735 .... **LC 1**
See also DLB 101

Archer, Herbert Winslow
See Mencken, H(enry) L(ouis)

Archer, Jeffrey (Howard) 1940- ..... **CLC 28; DAM POP**
See also AAYA 16; BEST 89:3; CA 77-80; CANR 22, 52; INT CANR-22

Archer, Jules 1915- .... **CLC 12**

See also CA 9-12R; CANR 6; SAAS 5; SATA 4, 85

Archer, Lee
See Ellison, Harlan (Jay)

Arden, John 1930-**CLC 6, 13, 15; DAM DRAM**
See also CA 13-16R; CAAS 4; CANR 31; DLB 13; MTCW

Arenas, Reinaldo 1943-1990 . **CLC 41; DAM MULT; HLC**
See also CA 124; 128; 133; DLB 145; HW

Arendt, Hannah 1906-1975 .... **CLC 66, 98**
See also CA 17-20R; 61-64; CANR 26, 60; MTCW

Aretino, Pietro 1492-1556 .... **LC 12**

Arghezi, Tudor .... **CLC 80**
See also Theodorescu, Ion N.

Arguedas, Jose Maria 1911-1969**CLC 10, 18**
See also CA 89-92; DLB 113; HW

Argueta, Manlio 1936- .... **CLC 31**
See also CA 131; DLB 145; HW

Ariosto, Ludovico 1474-1533 .... **LC 6**

Aristides
See Epstein, Joseph

Aristophanes 450B.C.-385B.C.**CMLC 4; DA; DAB; DAC; DAM DRAM, MST; DC 2; WLCS**
See also DLB 176

Arlt, Roberto (Godofredo Christophersen) 1900-1942**TCLC 29; DAM MULT; HLC**
See also CA 123; 131; HW

Armah, Ayi Kwei 1939-**CLC 5, 33; BLC; DAM MULT, POET**
See also BW 1; CA 61-64; CANR 21; DLB 117; MTCW

Armatrading, Joan 1950- .... **CLC 17**
See also CA 114

Arnette, Robert
See Silverberg, Robert

Arnim, Achim von (Ludwig Joachim von Arnim) 1781-1831 ...... **NCLC 5; SSC 29**
See also DLB 90

Arnim, Bettina von 1785-1859 .... **NCLC 38**
See also DLB 90

Arnold, Matthew 1822-1888**NCLC 6, 29; DA; DAB; DAC; DAM MST, POET; PC 5; WLC**
See also CDBLB 1832-1890; DLB 32, 57

Arnold, Thomas 1795-1842 .... **NCLC 18**
See also DLB 55

Arnow, Harriette (Louisa) Simpson 1908-1986 **CLC 2, 7, 18**
See also CA 9-12R; 118; CANR 14; DLB 6; MTCW; SATA 42; SATA-Obit 47

Arp, Hans
See Arp, Jean

Arp, Jean 1887-1966 .... **CLC 5**
See also CA 81-84; 25-28R; CANR 42

Arrabal
See Arrabal, Fernando

Arrabal, Fernando 1932- .... **CLC 2, 9, 18, 58**
See also CA 9-12R; CANR 15

Arrick, Fran .... **CLC 30**
See also Gaberman, Judie Angell

Artaud, Antonin (Marie Joseph) 1896-1948 **TCLC 3, 36; DAM DRAM**
See also CA 104; 149

Arthur, Ruth M(abel) 1905-1979 ...... **CLC 12**
See also CA 9-12R; 85-88; CANR 4; SATA 7, 26

Artsybashev, Mikhail (Petrovich) 1878-1927 **TCLC 31**

Arundel, Honor (Morfydd) 1919-1973**CLC 17**
See also CA 21-22; 41-44R; CAP 2; CLR 35;

SATA 4; SATA-Obit 24

Arzner, Dorothy 1897-1979 .... **CLC 98**

Asch, Sholem 1880-1957 .... **TCLC 3**
See also CA 105

Ash, Shalom
See Asch, Sholem

Ashbery, John (Lawrence) 1927-**CLC 2, 3, 4, 6, 9, 13, 15, 25, 41, 77; DAM POET**
See also CA 5-8R; CANR 9, 37; DLB 5, 165; DLBY 81; INT CANR-9; MTCW

Ashdown, Clifford
See Freeman, R(ichard) Austin

Ashe, Gordon
See Creasey, John

Ashton-Warner, Sylvia (Constance) 1908-1984 **CLC 19**
See also CA 69-72; 112; CANR 29; MTCW

Asimov, Isaac 1920-1992 **CLC 1, 3, 9, 19, 26, 76, 92; DAM POP**
See also AAYA 13; BEST 90:2; CA 1-4R; 137; CANR 2, 19, 36, 60; CLR 12; DLB 8; DLBY 92; INT CANR-19; JRDA; MAICYA; MTCW; SATA 1, 26, 74

Assis, Joaquim Maria Machado de
See Machado de Assis, Joaquim Maria

Astley, Thea (Beatrice May) 1925- ... **CLC 41**
See also CA 65-68; CANR 11, 43

Aston, James
See White, T(erence) H(anbury)

Asturias, Miguel Angel 1899-1974 **CLC 3, 8, 13; DAM MULT, NOV; HLC**
See also CA 25-28; 49-52; CANR 32; CAP 2; DLB 113; HW; MTCW

Atares, Carlos Saura
See Saura (Atares), Carlos

Atheling, William
See Pound, Ezra (Weston Loomis)

Atheling, William, Jr.
See Blish, James (Benjamin)

Atherton, Gertrude (Franklin Horn) 1857-1948 **TCLC 2**
See also CA 104; 155; DLB 9, 78, 186

Atherton, Lucius
See Masters, Edgar Lee

Atkins, Jack
See Harris, Mark

Atkinson, Kate .... **CLC 99**

Attaway, William (Alexander) 1911-1986 **CLC 92; BLC; DAM MULT**
See also BW 2; CA 143; DLB 76

Atticus
See Fleming, Ian (Lancaster)

Atwood, Margaret (Eleanor) 1939-**CLC 2, 3, 4, 8, 13, 15, 25, 44, 84; DA; DAB; DAC; DAM MST, NOV, POET; PC 8; SSC 2; WLC**
See also AAYA 12; BEST 89:2; CA 49-52; CANR 3, 24, 33, 59; DLB 53; INT CANR-24; MTCW; SATA 50

Aubigny, Pierre d'
See Mencken, H(enry) L(ouis)

Aubin, Penelope 1685-1731(?) .... **LC 9**
See also DLB 39

Auchincloss, Louis (Stanton) 1917-**CLC 4, 6, 9, 18, 45; DAM NOV; SSC 22**
See also CA 1-4R; CANR 6, 29, 55; DLB 2; DLBY 80; INT CANR-29; MTCW

Auden, W(ystan) H(ugh) 1907-1973**CLC 1, 2, 3, 4, 6, 9, 11, 14, 43; DA; DAB; DAC; DAM DRAM, MST, POET; PC 1; WLC**
See also AAYA 18; CA 9-12R; 45-48; CANR 5, 61; CDBLB 1914-1945; DLB 10, 20; MTCW

See also CA 73-76; DLB 75

Bierce, Ambrose (Gwinett) 1842-1914(?)
TCLC 1, 7, 44; DA; DAC; DAM MST; SSC 9; WLC
See also CA 104; 139; CDALB 1865-1917;
DLB 11, 12, 23, 71, 74, 186

Biggers, Earl Derr 1884-1933 .... **TCLC 65**
See also CA 108; 153

Billings, Josh
See Shaw, Henry Wheeler

Billington, (Lady) Rachel (Mary) 1942- **C L C 43**
See also AITN 2; CA 33-36R; CANR 44

Binyon, T(imothy) J(ohn) 1936- .... **CLC 34**
See also CA 111; CANR 28

Bioy Casares, Adolfo 1914-**CLC 4, 8, 13, 88; DAM MULT; HLC; SSC 17**
See also CA 29-32R; CANR 19, 43; DLB 113;
HW; MTCW

Bird, Cordwainer
See Ellison, Harlan (Jay)

Bird, Robert Montgomery 1806-1854**NCLC 1**

Birney, (Alfred) Earle 1904- **CLC 1, 4, 6, 11; DAC; DAM MST, POET**
See also CA 1-4R; CANR 5, 20; DLB 88;
MTCW

Bishop, Elizabeth 1911-1979 **CLC 1, 4, 9, 13, 15, 32; DA; DAC; DAM MST, POET; PC 3**
See also CA 5-8R; 89-92; CABS 2; CANR 26,
61; CDALB 1968-1988; DLB 5, 169;
MTCW; SATA-Obit 24

Bishop, John 1935- .... **CLC 10**
See also CA 105

Bissett, Bill 1939- .... **CLC 18; PC 14**
See also CA 69-72; CAAS 19; CANR 15; DLB
53; MTCW

Bitov, Andrei (Georgievich) 1937- ... **CLC 57**
See also CA 142

Biyidi, Alexandre 1932-
See Beti, Mongo
See also BW 1; CA 114; 124; MTCW

Bjarme, Brynjolf
See Ibsen, Henrik (Johan)

Bjornson, Bjornstjerne (Martinius) 1832-1910
TCLC 7, 37
See also CA 104

Black, Robert
See Holdstock, Robert P.

Blackburn, Paul 1926-1971 .... **CLC 9, 43**
See also CA 81-84; 33-36R; CANR 34; DLB
16; DLBY 81

Black Elk 1863-1950**TCLC 33; DAM MULT**
See also CA 144; NNAL

Black Hobart
See Sanders, (James) Ed(ward)

Blacklin, Malcolm
See Chambers, Aidan

Blackmore, R(ichard) D(oddridge) 1825-1900
TCLC 27
See also CA 120; DLB 18

Blackmur, R(ichard) P(almer) 1904-1965
CLC 2, 24
See also CA 11-12; 25-28R; CAP 1; DLB 63

Black Tarantula
See Acker, Kathy

Blackwood, Algernon (Henry) 1869-1951
TCLC 5
See also CA 105; 150; DLB 153, 156, 178

Blackwood, Caroline 1931-1996**CLC 6, 9, 100**
See also CA 85-88; 151; CANR 32, 61; DLB
14; MTCW

Blade, Alexander

See Hamilton, Edmond; Silverberg, Robert

Blaga, Lucian 1895-1961 .... **CLC 75**

Blair, Eric (Arthur) 1903-1950
See Orwell, George
See also CA 104; 132; DA; DAB; DAC; DAM
MST, NOV; MTCW; SATA 29

Blais, Marie-Claire 1939-**CLC 2, 4, 6, 13, 22; DAC; DAM MST**
See also CA 21-24R; CAAS 4; CANR 38; DLB
53; MTCW

Blaise, Clark 1940- .... **CLC 29**
See also AITN 2; CA 53-56; CAAS 3; CANR
5; DLB 53

Blake, Fairley
See De Voto, Bernard (Augustine)

Blake, Nicholas
See Day Lewis, C(ecil)
See also DLB 77

Blake, William 1757-1827 . **NCLC 13, 37, 57; DA; DAB; DAC; DAM MST, POET; PC 12; WLC**
See also CDBLB 1789-1832; DLB 93, 163;
MAICYA; SATA 30

Blasco Ibanez, Vicente 1867-1928 **TCLC 12; DAM NOV**
See also CA 110; 131; HW; MTCW

Blatty, William Peter 1928-**CLC 2; DAM POP**
See also CA 5-8R; CANR 9

Bleeck, Oliver
See Thomas, Ross (Elmore)

Blessing, Lee 1949- .... **CLC 54**

Blish, James (Benjamin) 1921-1975 . **CLC 14**
See also CA 1-4R; 57-60; CANR 3; DLB 8;
MTCW; SATA 66

Bliss, Reginald
See Wells, H(erbert) G(eorge)

Blixen, Karen (Christentze Dinesen) 1885-1962
See Dinesen, Isak
See also CA 25-28; CANR 22, 50; CAP 2;
MTCW; SATA 44

Bloch, Robert (Albert) 1917-1994 .... **CLC 33**
See also CA 5-8R; 146; CAAS 20; CANR 5;
DLB 44; INT CANR-5; SATA 12; SATA-Obit
82

Blok, Alexander (Alexandrovich) 1880-1921
TCLC 5; PC 21
See also CA 104

Blom, Jan
See Breytenbach, Breyten

Bloom, Harold 1930- .... **CLC 24, 103**
See also CA 13-16R; CANR 39; DLB 67

Bloomfield, Aurelius
See Bourne, Randolph S(illiman)

Blount, Roy (Alton), Jr. 1941- .... **CLC 38**
See also CA 53-56; CANR 10, 28, 61; INT
CANR-28; MTCW

Bloy, Leon 1846-1917 .... **TCLC 22**
See also CA 121; DLB 123

Blume, Judy (Sussman) 1938- ... **CLC 12, 30; DAM NOV, POP**
See also AAYA 3; CA 29-32R; CANR 13, 37;
CLR 2, 15; DLB 52; JRDA; MAICYA;
MTCW; SATA 2, 31, 79

Blunden, Edmund (Charles) 1896-1974 **C L C 2, 56**
See also CA 17-18; 45-48; CANR 54; CAP 2;
DLB 20, 100, 155; MTCW

Bly, Robert (Elwood) 1926-**CLC 1, 2, 5, 10, 15, 38; DAM POET**
See also CA 5-8R; CANR 41; DLB 5; MTCW

Boas, Franz 1858-1942 .... **TCLC 56**
See also CA 115

Bobette

See Simenon, Georges (Jacques Christian)

Boccaccio, Giovanni 1313-1375 ...**CMLC 13; SSC 10**

Bochco, Steven 1943- .... **CLC 35**
See also AAYA 11; CA 124; 138

Bodenheim, Maxwell 1892-1954 .... **TCLC 44**
See also CA 110; DLB 9, 45

Bodker, Cecil 1927- .... **CLC 21**
See also CA 73-76; CANR 13, 44; CLR 23;
MAICYA; SATA 14

Boell, Heinrich (Theodor) 1917-1985 **CLC 2, 3, 6, 9, 11, 15, 27, 32, 72; DA; DAB; DAC; DAM MST, NOV; SSC 23; WLC**
See also CA 21-24R; 116; CANR 24; DLB 69;
DLBY 85; MTCW

Boerne, Alfred
See Doeblin, Alfred

Boethius 480(?)-524(?) .... **CMLC 15**
See also DLB 115

Bogan, Louise 1897-1970 . **CLC 4, 39, 46, 93; DAM POET; PC 12**
See also CA 73-76; 25-28R; CANR 33; DLB
45, 169; MTCW

Bogarde, Dirk .... **CLC 19**
See also Van Den Bogarde, Derek Jules Gaspard
Ulric Niven
See also DLB 14

Bogosian, Eric 1953- .... **CLC 45**
See also CA 138

Bograd, Larry 1953- .... **CLC 35**
See also CA 93-96; CANR 57; SAAS 21; SATA
33, 89

Boiardo, Matteo Maria 1441-1494 .... **LC 6**

Boileau-Despreaux, Nicolas 1636-1711 . **LC 3**

Bojer, Johan 1872-1959 .... **TCLC 64**

Boland, Eavan (Aisling) 1944- .. **CLC 40, 67; DAM POET**
See also CA 143; CANR 61; DLB 40

Bolt, Lee
See Faust, Frederick (Schiller)

Bolt, Robert (Oxton) 1924-1995 ..... **CLC 14; DAM DRAM**
See also CA 17-20R; 147; CANR 35; DLB 13;
MTCW

Bombet, Louis-Alexandre-Cesar
See Stendhal

Bomkauf
See Kaufman, Bob (Garnell)

Bonaventura .... **NCLC 35**
See also DLB 90

Bond, Edward 1934- **CLC 4, 6, 13, 23; DAM DRAM**
See also CA 25-28R; CANR 38; DLB 13;
MTCW

Bonham, Frank 1914-1989 .... **CLC 12**
See also AAYA 1; CA 9-12R; CANR 4, 36;
JRDA; MAICYA; SAAS 3; SATA 1, 49;
SATA-Obit 62

Bonnefoy, Yves 1923-... **CLC 9, 15, 58; DAM MST, POET**
See also CA 85-88; CANR 33; MTCW

Bontemps, Arna(ud Wendell) 1902-1973**C L C 1, 18; BLC; DAM MULT, NOV, POET**
See also BW 1; CA 1-4R; 41-44R; CANR 4,
35; CLR 6; DLB 48, 51; JRDA; MAICYA;
MTCW; SATA 2, 44; SATA-Obit 24

Booth, Martin 1944- .... **CLC 13**
See also CA 93-96; CAAS 2

Booth, Philip 1925- .... **CLC 23**
See also CA 5-8R; CANR 5; DLBY 82

Booth, Wayne C(layson) 1921- .... **CLC 24**
See also CA 1-4R; CAAS 5; CANR 3, 43; DLB
67

Borchert, Wolfgang 1921-1947 .... **TCLC 5**
See also CA 104; DLB 69, 124

Borel, Petrus 1809-1859 .... **NCLC 41**

Borges, Jorge Luis 1899-1986**CLC 1, 2, 3, 4, 6,
8, 9, 10, 13, 19, 44, 48, 83; DA; DAB; DAC;
DAM MST, MULT; HLC; SSC 4; WLC**
See also AAYA 19; CA 21-24R; CANR 19, 33;
DLB 113; DLBY 86; HW; MTCW

Borowski, Tadeusz 1922-1951 .... **TCLC 9**
See also CA 106; 154

Borrow, George (Henry) 1803-1881 **NCLC 9**
See also DLB 21, 55, 166

Bosman, Herman Charles 1905-1951 **T C L C
49**
See also Malan, Herman
See also CA 160

Bosschere, Jean de 1878(?)-1953 ... **TCLC 19**
See also CA 115

Boswell, James 1740-1795 . **LC 4; DA; DAB;
DAC; DAM MST; WLC**
See also CDBLB 1660-1789; DLB 104, 142

Bottoms, David 1949- .... **CLC 53**
See also CA 105; CANR 22; DLB 120; DLBY
83

Boucicault, Dion 1820-1890 .... **NCLC 41**

Boucolon, Maryse 1937(?)-
See Conde, Maryse
See also CA 110; CANR 30, 53

Bourget, Paul (Charles Joseph) 1852-1935
TCLC 12
See also CA 107; DLB 123

Bourjaily, Vance (Nye) 1922- ....**CLC 8, 62**
See also CA 1-4R; CAAS 1; CANR 2; DLB 2,
143

Bourne, Randolph S(illiman) 1886-1918
TCLC 16
See also CA 117; 155; DLB 63

Bova, Ben(jamin William) 1932- ...... **CLC 45**
See also AAYA 16; CA 5-8R; CAAS 18; CANR
11, 56; CLR 3; DLBY 81; INT CANR-11;
MAICYA; MTCW; SATA 6, 68

Bowen, Elizabeth (Dorothea Cole) 1899-1973
**CLC 1, 3, 6, 11, 15, 22; DAM NOV; SSC 3,
28**
See also CA 17-18; 41-44R; CANR 35; CAP 2;
CDBLB 1945-1960; DLB 15, 162; MTCW

Bowering, George 1935- .... **CLC 15, 47**
See also CA 21-24R; CAAS 16; CANR 10; DLB
53

Bowering, Marilyn R(uthe) 1949- .... **CLC 32**
See also CA 101; CANR 49

Bowers, Edgar 1924- .... **CLC 9**
See also CA 5-8R; CANR 24; DLB 5

Bowie, David .... **CLC 17**
See also Jones, David Robert

Bowles, Jane (Sydney) 1917-1973 **CLC 3, 68**
See also CA 19-20; 41-44R; CAP 2

Bowles, Paul (Frederick) 1910- **CLC 1, 2, 19,
53; SSC 3**
See also CA 1-4R; CAAS 1; CANR 1, 19, 50;
DLB 5, 6; MTCW

Box, Edgar
See Vidal, Gore

Boyd, Nancy
See Millay, Edna St. Vincent

Boyd, William 1952- .... **CLC 28, 53, 70**
See also CA 114; 120; CANR 51

Boyle, Kay 1902-1992**CLC 1, 5, 19, 58; SSC 5**
See also CA 13-16R; 140; CAAS 1; CANR 29,
61; DLB 4, 9, 48, 86; DLBY 93; MTCW

Boyle, Mark
See Kienzle, William X(avier)

Boyle, Patrick 1905-1982 .... **CLC 19**

See also CA 127

Boyle, T. C. 1948-
See Boyle, T(homas) Coraghessan

Boyle, T(homas) Coraghessan 1948-**CLC 36,
55, 90; DAM POP; SSC 16**
See also BEST 90:4; CA 120; CANR 44; DLBY
86

Boz
See Dickens, Charles (John Huffam)

Brackenridge, Hugh Henry 1748-1816**N C L C
7**
See also DLB 11, 37

Bradbury, Edward P.
See Moorcock, Michael (John)

Bradbury, Malcolm (Stanley) 1932- **CLC 32,
61; DAM NOV**
See also CA 1-4R; CANR 1, 33; DLB 14;
MTCW

Bradbury, Ray (Douglas) 1920-**CLC 1, 3, 10,
15, 42, 98; DA; DAB; DAC; DAM MST,
NOV, POP; SSC 29; WLC**
See also AAYA 15; AITN 1, 2; CA 1-4R; CANR
2, 30; CDALB 1968-1988; DLB 2, 8;
MTCW; SATA 11, 64

Bradford, Gamaliel 1863-1932 ...... **TCLC 36**
See also CA 160; DLB 17

Bradley, David (Henry, Jr.) 1950- .. **CLC 23;
BLC; DAM MULT**
See also BW 1; CA 104; CANR 26; DLB 33

Bradley, John Ed(mund, Jr.) 1958- .. **CLC 55**
See also CA 139

Bradley, Marion Zimmer 1930-**CLC 30; DAM
POP**
See also AAYA 9; CA 57-60; CAAS 10; CANR
7, 31, 51; DLB 8; MTCW; SATA 90

Bradstreet, Anne 1612(?)-1672**LC 4, 30; DA;
DAC; DAM MST, POET; PC 10**
See also CDALB 1640-1865; DLB 24

Brady, Joan 1939- .... **CLC 86**
See also CA 141

Bragg, Melvyn 1939- .... **CLC 10**
See also BEST 89:3; CA 57-60; CANR 10, 48;
DLB 14

Braine, John (Gerard) 1922-1986**CLC 1, 3, 41**
See also CA 1-4R; 120; CANR 1, 33; CDBLB
1945-1960; DLB 15; DLBY 86; MTCW

Bramah, Ernest 1868-1942 .... **TCLC 72**
See also CA 156; DLB 70

Brammer, William 1930(?)-1978 .... **CLC 31**
See also CA 77-80

Brancati, Vitaliano 1907-1954 .... **TCLC 12**
See also CA 109

Brancato, Robin F(idler) 1936- .... **CLC 35**
See also AAYA 9; CA 69-72; CANR 11, 45;
CLR 32; JRDA; SAAS 9; SATA 23

Brand, Max
See Faust, Frederick (Schiller)

Brand, Millen 1906-1980 .... **CLC 7**
See also CA 21-24R; 97-100

Branden, Barbara .... **CLC 44**
See also CA 148

Brandes, Georg (Morris Cohen) 1842-1927
TCLC 10
See also CA 105

Brandys, Kazimierz 1916- .... **CLC 62**

Branley, Franklyn M(ansfield) 1915-**CLC 21**
See also CA 33-36R; CANR 14, 39; CLR 13;
MAICYA; SAAS 16; SATA 4, 68

Brathwaite, Edward Kamau 1930- .**CLC 11;
DAM POET**
See also BW 2; CA 25-28R; CANR 11, 26, 47;
DLB 125

Brautigan, Richard (Gary) 1935-1984**CLC 1,**

3, 5, 9, 12, 34, 42; DAM NOV
See also CA 53-56; 113; CANR 34; DLB 2, 5;
DLBY 80, 84; MTCW; SATA 56

Brave Bird, Mary 1953-
See Crow Dog, Mary (Ellen)
See also NNAL

Braverman, Kate 1950- .... **CLC 67**
See also CA 89-92

Brecht, (Eugen) Bertolt (Friedrich) 1898-1956
**TCLC 1, 6, 13, 35; DA; DAB; DAC; DAM
DRAM, MST; DC 3; WLC**
See also CA 104; 133; CANR 62; DLB 56, 124;
MTCW

Brecht, Eugen Berthold Friedrich
See Brecht, (Eugen) Bertolt (Friedrich)

Bremer, Fredrika 1801-1865 .... **NCLC 11**

Brennan, Christopher John 1870-1932**T C L C
17**
See also CA 117

Brennan, Maeve 1917- .... **CLC 5**
See also CA 81-84

Brentano, Clemens (Maria) 1778-1842**N C L C
1**
See also DLB 90

Brent of Bin Bin
See Franklin, (Stella Maraia Sarah) Miles

Brenton, Howard 1942- .... **CLC 31**
See also CA 69-72; CANR 33; DLB 13; MTCW

Breslin, James 1930-
See Breslin, Jimmy
See also CA 73-76; CANR 31; DAM NOV;
MTCW

Breslin, Jimmy .... **CLC 4, 43**
See also Breslin, James
See also AITN 1

Bresson, Robert 1901- .... **CLC 16**
See also CA 110; CANR 49

Breton, Andre 1896-1966**CLC 2, 9, 15, 54; PC
15**
See also CA 19-20; 25-28R; CANR 40, 60; CAP
2; DLB 65; MTCW

Breytenbach, Breyten 1939(?)- . **CLC 23, 37;
DAM POET**
See also CA 113; 129; CANR 61

Bridgers, Sue Ellen 1942- .... **CLC 26**
See also AAYA 8; CA 65-68; CANR 11, 36;
CLR 18; DLB 52; JRDA; MAICYA; SAAS
1; SATA 22, 90

Bridges, Robert (Seymour) 1844-1930**T C L C
1; DAM POET**
See also CA 104; 152; CDBLB 1890-1914;
DLB 19, 98

Bridie, James .... **TCLC 3**
See also Mavor, Osborne Henry
See also DLB 10

Brin, David 1950- .... **CLC 34**
See also AAYA 21; CA 102; CANR 24; INT
CANR-24; SATA 65

Brink, Andre (Philippus) 1935- **CLC 18, 36,
106**
See also CA 104; CANR 39, 62; INT 103;
MTCW

Brinsmead, H(esba) F(ay) 1922- .... **CLC 21**
See also CA 21-24R; CANR 10; CLR 47;
MAICYA; SAAS 5; SATA 18, 78

Brittain, Vera (Mary) 1893(?)-1970 . **CLC 23**
See also CA 13-16; 25-28R; CANR 58; CAP 1;
MTCW

Broch, Hermann 1886-1951 .... **TCLC 20**
See also CA 117; DLB 85, 124

Brock, Rose
See Hansen, Joseph

Brodkey, Harold (Roy) 1930-1996 .... **CLC 56**

See also CA 111; 151; DLB 130
Brodsky, Iosif Alexandrovich 1940-1996
See Brodsky, Joseph
See also AITN 1; CA 41-44R; 151; CANR 37;
DAM POET; MTCW
Brodsky, Joseph 1940-1996 **CLC 4, 6, 13, 36,
100; PC 9**
See also Brodsky, Iosif Alexandrovich
Brodsky, Michael (Mark) 1948- .... **CLC 19**
See also CA 102; CANR 18, 41, 58
Bromell, Henry 1947- .... **CLC 5**
See also CA 53-56; CANR 9
Bromfield, Louis (Brucker) 1896-1956**T C L C
11**
See also CA 107; 155; DLB 4, 9, 86
Broner, E(sther) M(asserman) 1930- **CLC 19**
See also CA 17-20R; CANR 8, 25; DLB 28
Bronk, William 1918- .... **CLC 10**
See also CA 89-92; CANR 23; DLB 165
Bronstein, Lev Davidovich
See Trotsky, Leon
Bronte, Anne 1820-1849 .... **NCLC 4**
See also DLB 21
Bronte, Charlotte 1816-1855 **NCLC 3, 8, 33,
58; DA; DAB; DAC; DAM MST, NOV;
WLC**
See also AAYA 17; CDBLB 1832-1890; DLB
21, 159
Bronte, Emily (Jane) 1818-1848**NCLC 16, 35;
DA; DAB; DAC; DAM MST, NOV, POET;
PC 8; WLC**
See also AAYA 17; CDBLB 1832-1890; DLB
21, 32
Brooke, Frances 1724-1789 .... **LC 6**
See also DLB 39, 99
Brooke, Henry 1703(?)-1783 .... **LC 1**
See also DLB 39
Brooke, Rupert (Chawner) 1887-1915 **T C L C
2, 7; DA; DAB; DAC; DAM MST, POET;
WLC**
See also CA 104; 132; CANR 61; CDBLB
1914-1945; DLB 19; MTCW
Brooke-Haven, P.
See Wodehouse, P(elham) G(renville)
Brooke-Rose, Christine 1926(?)- .... **CLC 40**
See also CA 13-16R; CANR 58; DLB 14
Brookner, Anita 1928- **CLC 32, 34, 51; DAB;
DAM POP**
See also CA 114; 120; CANR 37, 56; DLBY
87; MTCW
Brooks, Cleanth 1906-1994 .... **CLC 24, 86**
See also CA 17-20R; 145; CANR 33, 35; DLB
63; DLBY 94; INT CANR-35; MTCW
Brooks, George
See Baum, L(yman) Frank
Brooks, Gwendolyn 1917- **CLC 1, 2, 4, 5, 15,
49; BLC; DA; DAC; DAM MST, MULT,
POET; PC 7; WLC**
See also AAYA 20; AITN 1; BW 2; CA 1-4R;
CANR 1, 27, 52; CDALB 1941-1968; CLR
27; DLB 5, 76, 165; MTCW; SATA 6
Brooks, Mel .... **CLC 12**
See also Kaminsky, Melvin
See also AAYA 13; DLB 26
Brooks, Peter 1938- .... **CLC 34**
See also CA 45-48; CANR 1
Brooks, Van Wyck 1886-1963 .... **CLC 29**
See also CA 1-4R; CANR 6; DLB 45, 63, 103
Brophy, Brigid (Antonia) 1929-1995 **CLC 6,
11, 29, 105**
See also CA 5-8R; 149; CAAS 4; CANR 25,
53; DLB 14; MTCW
Brosman, Catharine Savage 1934- ..... **CLC 9**

See also CA 61-64; CANR 21, 46
Brother Antoninus
See Everson, William (Oliver)
Broughton, T(homas) Alan 1936- ..... **CLC 19**
See also CA 45-48; CANR 2, 23, 48
Broumas, Olga 1949- .... **CLC 10, 73**
See also CA 85-88; CANR 20
Brown, Alan 1951- .... **CLC 99**
Brown, Charles Brockden 1771-1810 **N C L C
22**
See also CDALB 1640-1865; DLB 37, 59, 73
Brown, Christy 1932-1981 .... **CLC 63**
See also CA 105; 104; DLB 14
Brown, Claude 1937- ... **CLC 30; BLC; DAM
MULT**
See also AAYA 7; BW 1; CA 73-76
Brown, Dee (Alexander) 1908- .. **CLC 18, 47;
DAM POP**
See also CA 13-16R; CAAS 6; CANR 11, 45,
60; DLBY 80; MTCW; SATA 5
Brown, George
See Wertmueller, Lina
Brown, George Douglas 1869-1902 **TCLC 28**
Brown, George Mackay 1921-1996**CLC 5, 48,
100**
See also CA 21-24R; 151; CAAS 6; CANR 12,
37, 62; DLB 14, 27, 139; MTCW; SATA 35
Brown, (William) Larry 1951- .... **CLC 73**
See also CA 130; 134; INT 133
Brown, Moses
See Barrett, William (Christopher)
Brown, Rita Mae 1944-**CLC 18, 43, 79; DAM
NOV, POP**
See also CA 45-48; CANR 2, 11, 35, 62; INT
CANR-11; MTCW
Brown, Roderick (Langmere) Haig-
See Haig-Brown, Roderick (Langmere)
Brown, Rosellen 1939- .... **CLC 32**
See also CA 77-80; CAAS 10; CANR 14, 44
Brown, Sterling Allen 1901-1989 **CLC 1, 23,
59; BLC; DAM MULT, POET**
See also BW 1; CA 85-88; 127; CANR 26; DLB
48, 51, 63; MTCW
Brown, Will
See Ainsworth, William Harrison
Brown, William Wells 1813-1884 ... **NCLC 2;
BLC; DAM MULT; DC 1**
See also DLB 3, 50
Browne, (Clyde) Jackson 1948(?)- .... **CLC 21**
See also CA 120
Browning, Elizabeth Barrett 1806-1861
**NCLC 1, 16, 61, 66; DA; DAB; DAC; DAM
MST, POET; PC 6; WLC**
See also CDBLB 1832-1890; DLB 32
Browning, Robert 1812-1889 **NCLC 19; DA;
DAB; DAC; DAM MST, POET; PC 2;
WLCS**
See also CDBLB 1832-1890; DLB 32, 163;
YABC 1
Browning, Tod 1882-1962 .... **CLC 16**
See also CA 141; 117
Brownson, Orestes (Augustus) 1803-1876
NCLC 50
Bruccoli, Matthew J(oseph) 1931- ... **CLC 34**
See also CA 9-12R; CANR 7; DLB 103
Bruce, Lenny .... **CLC 21**
See also Schneider, Leonard Alfred
Bruin, John
See Brutus, Dennis
Brulard, Henri
See Stendhal
Brulls, Christian
See Simenon, Georges (Jacques Christian)

Brunner, John (Kilian Houston) 1934-1995
CLC 8, 10; DAM POP
See also CA 1-4R; 149; CAAS 8; CANR 2, 37;
MTCW
Bruno, Giordano 1548-1600 .... **LC 27**
Brutus, Dennis 1924- ... **CLC 43; BLC; DAM
MULT, POET**
See also BW 2; CA 49-52; CAAS 14; CANR 2,
27, 42; DLB 117
Bryan, C(ourtlandt) D(ixon) B(arnes) 1936-
CLC 29
See also CA 73-76; CANR 13; INT CANR-13
Bryan, Michael
See Moore, Brian
Bryant, William Cullen 1794-1878 . **NCLC 6,
46; DA; DAB; DAC; DAM MST, POET;
PC 20**
See also CDALB 1640-1865; DLB 3, 43, 59
Bryusov, Valery Yakovlevich 1873-1924
TCLC 10
See also CA 107; 155
Buchan, John 1875-1940 ..... **TCLC 41; DAB;
DAM POP**
See also CA 108; 145; DLB 34, 70, 156; YABC
2
Buchanan, George 1506-1582 .... **LC 4**
Buchheim, Lothar-Guenther 1918- .... **CLC 6**
See also CA 85-88
Buchner, (Karl) Georg 1813-1837 . **NCLC 26**
Buchwald, Art(hur) 1925- .... **CLC 33**
See also AITN 1; CA 5-8R; CANR 21; MTCW;
SATA 10
Buck, Pearl S(ydenstricker) 1892-1973**CLC 7,
11, 18; DA; DAB; DAC; DAM MST, NOV**
See also AITN 1; CA 1-4R; 41-44R; CANR 1,
34; DLB 9, 102; MTCW; SATA 1, 25
Buckler, Ernest 1908-1984 .... **CLC 13; DAC;
DAM MST**
See also CA 11-12; 114; CAP 1; DLB 68; SATA
47
Buckley, Vincent (Thomas) 1925-1988**CLC 57**
See also CA 101
Buckley, William F(rank), Jr. 1925-**CLC 7, 18,
37; DAM POP**
See also AITN 1; CA 1-4R; CANR 1, 24, 53;
DLB 137; DLBY 80; INT CANR-24; MTCW
Buechner, (Carl) Frederick 1926-**CLC 2, 4, 6,
9; DAM NOV**
See also CA 13-16R; CANR 11, 39; DLBY 80;
INT CANR-11; MTCW
Buell, John (Edward) 1927- .... **CLC 10**
See also CA 1-4R; DLB 53
Buero Vallejo, Antonio 1916- ..... **CLC 15, 46**
See also CA 106; CANR 24, 49; HW; MTCW
Bufalino, Gesualdo 1920(?)- .... **CLC 74**
Bugayev, Boris Nikolayevich 1880-1934
See Bely, Andrey
See also CA 104
Bukowski, Charles 1920-1994**CLC 2, 5, 9, 41,
82; DAM NOV, POET; PC 18**
See also CA 17-20R; 144; CANR 40, 62; DLB
5, 130, 169; MTCW
Bulgakov, Mikhail (Afanas'evich) 1891-1940
TCLC 2, 16; DAM DRAM, NOV; SSC 18
See also CA 105; 152
Bulgya, Alexander Alexandrovich 1901-1956
TCLC 53
See also Fadeyev, Alexander
See also CA 117
Bullins, Ed 1935- ... **CLC 1, 5, 7; BLC; DAM
DRAM, MULT; DC 6**
See also BW 2; CA 49-52; CAAS 16; CANR
24, 46; DLB 7, 38; MTCW

See Simenon, Georges (Jacques Christian)
Desai, Anita 1937-**CLC 19, 37, 97; DAB; DAM NOV**
  See also CA 81-84; CANR 33, 53; MTCW; SATA 63
de Saint-Luc, Jean
  See Glassco, John
de Saint Roman, Arnaud
  See Aragon, Louis
Descartes, Rene 1596-1650 .... **LC 20, 35**
De Sica, Vittorio 1901(?)-1974 .... **CLC 20**
  See also CA 117
Desnos, Robert 1900-1945 .... **TCLC 22**
  See also CA 121; 151
Destouches, Louis-Ferdinand 1894-1961**C L C 9, 15**
  See also Celine, Louis-Ferdinand
  See also CA 85-88; CANR 28; MTCW
de Tolignac, Gaston
  See Griffith, D(avid Lewelyn) W(ark)
Deutsch, Babette 1895-1982 .... **CLC 18**
  See also CA 1-4R; 108; CANR 4; DLB 45; SATA 1; SATA-Obit 33
Devenant, William 1606-1649 .... **LC 13**
Devkota, Laxmiprasad 1909-1959 . **TCLC 23**
  See also CA 123
De Voto, Bernard (Augustine) 1897-1955 **TCLC 29**
  See also CA 113; 160; DLB 9
De Vries, Peter 1910-1993 **CLC 1, 2, 3, 7, 10, 28, 46; DAM NOV**
  See also CA 17-20R; 142; CANR 41; DLB 6; DLBY 82; MTCW
Dexter, John
  See Bradley, Marion Zimmer
Dexter, Martin
  See Faust, Frederick (Schiller)
Dexter, Pete 1943- ... **CLC 34, 55; DAM POP**
  See also BEST 89:2; CA 127; 131; INT 131; MTCW
Diamano, Silmang
  See Senghor, Leopold Sedar
Diamond, Neil 1941- .... **CLC 30**
  See also CA 108
Diaz del Castillo, Bernal 1496-1584 .... **LC 31**
di Bassetto, Corno
  See Shaw, George Bernard
Dick, Philip K(indred) 1928-1982**CLC 10, 30, 72; DAM NOV, POP**
  See also CA 49-52; 106; CANR 2, 16; DLB 8; MTCW
Dickens, Charles (John Huffam) 1812-1870 **NCLC 3, 8, 18, 26, 37, 50; DA; DAB; DAC; DAM MST, NOV; SSC 17; WLC**
  See also CDBLB 1832-1890; DLB 21, 55, 70, 159, 166; JRDA; MAICYA; SATA 15
Dickey, James (Lafayette) 1923-1997 **CLC 1, 2, 4, 7, 10, 15, 47; DAM NOV, POET, POP**
  See also AITN 1, 2; CA 9-12R; 156; CABS 2; CANR 10, 48, 61; CDALB 1968-1988; DLB 5; DLBD 7; DLBY 82, 93, 96; INT CANR-10; MTCW
Dickey, William 1928-1994 .... **CLC 3, 28**
  See also CA 9-12R; 145; CANR 24; DLB 5
Dickinson, Charles 1951- .... **CLC 49**
  See also CA 128
Dickinson, Emily (Elizabeth) 1830-1886 **NCLC 21; DA; DAB; DAC; DAM MST, POET; PC 1; WLC**
  See also AAYA 22; CDALB 1865-1917; DLB 1; SATA 29
Dickinson, Peter (Malcolm) 1927-**CLC 12, 35**
  See also AAYA 9; CA 41-44R; CANR 31, 58;

CLR 29; DLB 87, 161; JRDA; MAICYA; SATA 5, 62, 95
Dickson, Carr
  See Carr, John Dickson
Dickson, Carter
  See Carr, John Dickson
Diderot, Denis 1713-1784 .... **LC 26**
Didion, Joan 1934-**CLC 1, 3, 8, 14, 32; DAM NOV**
  See also AITN 1; CA 5-8R; CANR 14, 52; CDALB 1968-1988; DLB 2, 173; DLBY 81, 86; MTCW
Dietrich, Robert
  See Hunt, E(verette) Howard, (Jr.)
Dillard, Annie 1945- **CLC 9, 60; DAM NOV**
  See also AAYA 6; CA 49-52; CANR 3, 43, 62; DLBY 80; MTCW; SATA 10
Dillard, R(ichard) H(enry) W(ilde) 1937- **CLC 5**
  See also CA 21-24R; CAAS 7; CANR 10; DLB 5
Dillon, Eilis 1920-1994 .... **CLC 17**
  See also CA 9-12R; 147; CAAS 3; CANR 4, 38; CLR 26; MAICYA; SATA 2, 74; SATA-Obit 83
Dimont, Penelope
  See Mortimer, Penelope (Ruth)
Dinesen, Isak .... **CLC 10, 29, 95; SSC 7**
  See also Blixen, Karen (Christentze Dinesen)
Ding Ling .... **CLC 68**
  See also Chiang Pin-chin
Disch, Thomas M(ichael) 1940- ....**CLC 7, 36**
  See also AAYA 17; CA 21-24R; CAAS 4; CANR 17, 36, 54; CLR 18; DLB 8; MAICYA; MTCW; SAAS 15; SATA 92
Disch, Tom
  See Disch, Thomas M(ichael)
d'Isly, Georges
  See Simenon, Georges (Jacques Christian)
Disraeli, Benjamin 1804-1881 .... **NCLC 2, 39**
  See also DLB 21, 55
Ditcum, Steve
  See Crumb, R(obert)
Dixon, Paige
  See Corcoran, Barbara
Dixon, Stephen 1936- .... **CLC 52; SSC 16**
  See also CA 89-92; CANR 17, 40, 54; DLB 130
Doak, Annie
  See Dillard, Annie
Dobell, Sydney Thompson 1824-1874 **N C L C 43**
  See also DLB 32
Doblin, Alfred .... **TCLC 13**
  See also Doeblin, Alfred
Dobrolyubov, Nikolai Alexandrovich 1836-1861 **NCLC 5**
Dobyns, Stephen 1941- .... **CLC 37**
  See also CA 45-48; CANR 2, 18
Doctorow, E(dgar) L(aurence) 1931- **CLC 6, 11, 15, 18, 37, 44, 65; DAM NOV, POP**
  See also AAYA 22; AITN 2; BEST 89:3; CA 45-48; CANR 2, 33, 51; CDALB 1968-1988; DLB 2, 28, 173; DLBY 80; MTCW
Dodgson, Charles Lutwidge 1832-1898
  See Carroll, Lewis
  See also CLR 2; DA; DAB; DAC; DAM MST, NOV, POET; MAICYA; YABC 2
Dodson, Owen (Vincent) 1914-1983 **CLC 79; BLC; DAM MULT**
  See also BW 1; CA 65-68; 110; CANR 24; DLB 76
Doeblin, Alfred 1878-1957 .... **TCLC 13**
  See also Doblin, Alfred

See also CA 110; 141; DLB 66
Doerr, Harriet 1910- .... **CLC 34**
  See also CA 117; 122; CANR 47; INT 122
Domecq, H(onorio) Bustos
  See Bioy Casares, Adolfo; Borges, Jorge Luis
Domini, Rey
  See Lorde, Audre (Geraldine)
Dominique
  See Proust, (Valentin-Louis-George-Eugene-) Marcel
Don, A
  See Stephen, Leslie
Donaldson, Stephen R. 1947- **CLC 46; DAM POP**
  See also CA 89-92; CANR 13, 55; INT CANR-13
Donleavy, J(ames) P(atrick) 1926-**CLC 1, 4, 6, 10, 45**
  See also AITN 2; CA 9-12R; CANR 24, 49, 62; DLB 6, 173; INT CANR-24; MTCW
Donne, John 1572-1631**LC 10, 24; DA; DAB; DAC; DAM MST, POET; PC 1**
  See also CDBLB Before 1660; DLB 121, 151
Donnell, David 1939(?)- .... **CLC 34**
Donoghue, P. S.
  See Hunt, E(verette) Howard, (Jr.)
Donoso (Yanez), Jose 1924-1996**CLC 4, 8, 11, 32, 99; DAM MULT; HLC**
  See also CA 81-84; 155; CANR 32; DLB 113; HW; MTCW
Donovan, John 1928-1992 .... **CLC 35**
  See also AAYA 20; CA 97-100; 137; CLR 3; MAICYA; SATA 72; SATA-Brief 29
Don Roberto
  See Cunninghame Graham, R(obert) B(ontine)
Doolittle, Hilda 1886-1961**CLC 3, 8, 14, 31, 34, 73; DA; DAC; DAM MST, POET; PC 5; WLC**
  See also H. D.
  See also CA 97-100; CANR 35; DLB 4, 45; MTCW
Dorfman, Ariel 1942- ...... **CLC 48, 77; DAM MULT; HLC**
  See also CA 124; 130; HW; INT 130
Dorn, Edward (Merton) 1929- ... **CLC 10, 18**
  See also CA 93-96; CANR 42; DLB 5; INT 93-96
Dorsan, Luc
  See Simenon, Georges (Jacques Christian)
Dorsange, Jean
  See Simenon, Georges (Jacques Christian)
Dos Passos, John (Roderigo) 1896-1970 **C L C 1, 4, 8, 11, 15, 25, 34, 82; DA; DAB; DAC; DAM MST, NOV; WLC**
  See also CA 1-4R; 29-32R; CANR 3; CDALB 1929-1941; DLB 4, 9; DLBD 1, 15; DLBY 96; MTCW
Dossage, Jean
  See Simenon, Georges (Jacques Christian)
Dostoevsky, Fedor Mikhailovich 1821-1881 **NCLC 2, 7, 21, 33, 43; DA; DAB; DAC; DAM MST, NOV; SSC 2; WLC**
Doughty, Charles M(ontagu) 1843-1926 **TCLC 27**
  See also CA 115; DLB 19, 57, 174
Douglas, Ellen .... **CLC 73**
  See also Haxton, Josephine Ayres; Williamson, Ellen Douglas
Douglas, Gavin 1475(?)-1522 .... **LC 20**
Douglas, Keith (Castellain) 1920-1944**T C L C 40**
  See also CA 160; DLB 27
Douglas, Leonard

See Bradbury, Ray (Douglas)

Douglas, Michael
See Crichton, (John) Michael

Douglas, Norman 1868-1952 .... **TCLC 68**

Douglass, Frederick 1817(?)-1895 **NCLC 7, 55; BLC; DA; DAC; DAM MST, MULT; WLC**
See also CDALB 1640-1865; DLB 1, 43, 50, 79; SATA 29

Dourado, (Waldomiro Freitas) Autran 1926- **CLC 23, 60**
See also CA 25-28R; CANR 34

Dourado, Waldomiro Autran
See Dourado, (Waldomiro Freitas) Autran

Dove, Rita (Frances) 1952- **CLC 50, 81; DAM MULT, POET; PC 6**
See also BW 2; CA 109; CAAS 19; CANR 27, 42; DLB 120

Dowell, Coleman 1925-1985 .... **CLC 60**
See also CA 25-28R; 117; CANR 10; DLB 130

Dowson, Ernest (Christopher) 1867-1900 **TCLC 4**
See also CA 105; 150; DLB 19, 135

Doyle, A. Conan
See Doyle, Arthur Conan

Doyle, Arthur Conan 1859-1930 **TCLC 7; DA; DAB; DAC; DAM MST, NOV; SSC 12; WLC**
See also AAYA 14; CA 104; 122; CDBLB 1890-1914; DLB 18, 70, 156, 178; MTCW; SATA 24

Doyle, Conan
See Doyle, Arthur Conan

Doyle, John
See Graves, Robert (von Ranke)

Doyle, Roddy 1958(?)- .... **CLC 81**
See also AAYA 14; CA 143

Doyle, Sir A. Conan
See Doyle, Arthur Conan

Doyle, Sir Arthur Conan
See Doyle, Arthur Conan

Dr. A
See Asimov, Isaac; Silverstein, Alvin

Drabble, Margaret 1939- **CLC 2, 3, 5, 8, 10, 22, 53; DAB; DAC; DAM MST, NOV, POP**
See also CA 13-16R; CANR 18, 35; CDBLB 1960 to Present; DLB 14, 155; MTCW; SATA 48

Drapier, M. B.
See Swift, Jonathan

Drayham, James
See Mencken, H(enry) L(ouis)

Drayton, Michael 1563-1631 .... **LC 8**

Dreadstone, Carl
See Campbell, (John) Ramsey

Dreiser, Theodore (Herman Albert) 1871-1945 **TCLC 10, 18, 35; DA; DAC; DAM MST, NOV; WLC**
See also CA 106; 132; CDALB 1865-1917; DLB 9, 12, 102, 137; DLBD 1; MTCW

Drexler, Rosalyn 1926- .... **CLC 2, 6**
See also CA 81-84

Dreyer, Carl Theodor 1889-1968 ...... **CLC 16**
See also CA 116

Drieu la Rochelle, Pierre(-Eugene) 1893-1945 **TCLC 21**
See also CA 117; DLB 72

Drinkwater, John 1882-1937 .... **TCLC 57**
See also CA 109; 149; DLB 10, 19, 149

Drop Shot
See Cable, George Washington

Droste-Hulshoff, Annette Freiin von 1797-1848 **NCLC 3**
See also DLB 133

Drummond, Walter
See Silverberg, Robert

Drummond, William Henry 1854-1907 **TCLC 25**
See also CA 160; DLB 92

Drummond de Andrade, Carlos 1902-1987 **CLC 18**
See also Andrade, Carlos Drummond de
See also CA 132; 123

Drury, Allen (Stuart) 1918- .... **CLC 37**
See also CA 57-60; CANR 18, 52; INT CANR-18

Dryden, John 1631-1700 **LC 3, 21; DA; DAB; DAC; DAM DRAM, MST, POET; DC 3; WLC**
See also CDBLB 1660-1789; DLB 80, 101, 131

Duberman, Martin 1930- .... **CLC 8**
See also CA 1-4R; CANR 2

Dubie, Norman (Evans) 1945- .... **CLC 36**
See also CA 69-72; CANR 12; DLB 120

Du Bois, W(illiam) E(dward) B(urghardt) 1868-1963 **CLC 1, 2, 13, 64, 96; BLC; DA; DAC; DAM MST, MULT, NOV; WLC**
See also BW 1; CA 85-88; CANR 34; CDALB 1865-1917; DLB 47, 50, 91; MTCW; SATA 42

Dubus, Andre 1936- **CLC 13, 36, 97; SSC 15**
See also CA 21-24R; CANR 17; DLB 130; INT CANR-17

Duca Minimo
See D'Annunzio, Gabriele

Ducharme, Rejean 1941- .... **CLC 74**
See also DLB 60

Duclos, Charles Pinot 1704-1772 .... **LC 1**

Dudek, Louis 1918- .... **CLC 11, 19**
See also CA 45-48; CAAS 14; CANR 1; DLB 88

Duerrenmatt, Friedrich 1921-1990 **CLC 1, 4, 8, 11, 15, 43, 102; DAM DRAM**
See also CA 17-20R; CANR 33; DLB 69, 124; MTCW

Duffy, Bruce (?)- .... **CLC 50**

Duffy, Maureen 1933- .... **CLC 37**
See also CA 25-28R; CANR 33; DLB 14; MTCW

Dugan, Alan 1923- .... **CLC 2, 6**
See also CA 81-84; DLB 5

du Gard, Roger Martin
See Martin du Gard, Roger

Duhamel, Georges 1884-1966 .... **CLC 8**
See also CA 81-84; 25-28R; CANR 35; DLB 65; MTCW

Dujardin, Edouard (Emile Louis) 1861-1949 **TCLC 13**
See also CA 109; DLB 123

Dulles, John Foster 1888-1959 .... **TCLC 72**
See also CA 115; 149

Dumas, Alexandre (Davy de la Pailleterie) 1802-1870 .. **NCLC 11; DA; DAB; DAC; DAM MST, NOV; WLC**
See also DLB 119; SATA 18

Dumas, Alexandre 1824-1895 **NCLC 9; DC 1**
See also AAYA 22

Dumas, Claudine
See Malzberg, Barry N(athaniel)

Dumas, Henry L. 1934-1968 .... **CLC 6, 62**
See also BW 1; CA 85-88; DLB 41

du Maurier, Daphne 1907-1989 **CLC 6, 11, 59; DAB; DAC; DAM MST, POP; SSC 18**
See also CA 5-8R; 128; CANR 6, 55; MTCW; SATA 27; SATA-Obit 60

Dunbar, Paul Laurence 1872-1906 . **TCLC 2, 12; BLC; DA; DAC; DAM MST, MULT, POET; PC 5; SSC 8; WLC**
See also BW 1; CA 104; 124; CDALB 1865-1917; DLB 50, 54, 78; SATA 34

Dunbar, William 1460(?)-1530(?) .... **LC 20**
See also DLB 132, 146

Duncan, Dora Angela
See Duncan, Isadora

Duncan, Isadora 1877(?)-1927 .... **TCLC 68**
See also CA 118; 149

Duncan, Lois 1934- .... **CLC 26**
See also AAYA 4; CA 1-4R; CANR 2, 23, 36; CLR 29; JRDA; MAICYA; SAAS 2; SATA 1, 36, 75

Duncan, Robert (Edward) 1919-1988 **CLC 1, 2, 4, 7, 15, 41, 55; DAM POET; PC 2**
See also CA 9-12R; 124; CANR 28, 62; DLB 5, 16; MTCW

Duncan, Sara Jeannette 1861-1922 **TCLC 60**
See also CA 157; DLB 92

Dunlap, William 1766-1839 .... **NCLC 2**
See also DLB 30, 37, 59

Dunn, Douglas (Eaglesham) 1942- **CLC 6, 40**
See also CA 45-48; CANR 2, 33; DLB 40; MTCW

Dunn, Katherine (Karen) 1945- .... **CLC 71**
See also CA 33-36R

Dunn, Stephen 1939- .... **CLC 36**
See also CA 33-36R; CANR 12, 48, 53; DLB 105

Dunne, Finley Peter 1867-1936 ...... **TCLC 28**
See also CA 108; DLB 11, 23

Dunne, John Gregory 1932- .... **CLC 28**
See also CA 25-28R; CANR 14, 50; DLBY 80

Dunsany, Edward John Moreton Drax Plunkett 1878-1957
See Dunsany, Lord
See also CA 104; 148; DLB 10

Dunsany, Lord .... **TCLC 2, 59**
See also Dunsany, Edward John Moreton Drax Plunkett
See also DLB 77, 153, 156

du Perry, Jean
See Simenon, Georges (Jacques Christian)

Durang, Christopher (Ferdinand) 1949- **CLC 27, 38**
See also CA 105; CANR 50

Duras, Marguerite 1914-1996 **CLC 3, 6, 11, 20, 34, 40, 68, 100**
See also CA 25-28R; 151; CANR 50; DLB 83; MTCW

Durban, (Rosa) Pam 1947- .... **CLC 39**
See also CA 123

Durcan, Paul 1944- **CLC 43, 70; DAM POET**
See also CA 134

Durkheim, Emile 1858-1917 .... **TCLC 55**

Durrell, Lawrence (George) 1912-1990 **CLC 1, 4, 6, 8, 13, 27, 41; DAM NOV**
See also CA 9-12R; 132; CANR 40; CDBLB 1945-1960; DLB 15, 27; DLBY 90; MTCW

Durrenmatt, Friedrich
See Duerrenmatt, Friedrich

Dutt, Toru 1856-1877 .... **NCLC 29**

Dwight, Timothy 1752-1817 .... **NCLC 13**
See also DLB 37

Dworkin, Andrea 1946- .... **CLC 43**
See also CA 77-80; CAAS 21; CANR 16, 39; INT CANR-16; MTCW

Dwyer, Deanna
See Koontz, Dean R(ay)

Dwyer, K. R.
See Koontz, Dean R(ay)

Dye, Richard
See De Voto, Bernard (Augustine)

See also CA 33-36R; CANR 28; DLB 2, 28; DLBY 80
Fawkes, Guy
See Benchley, Robert (Charles)
Fearing, Kenneth (Flexner) 1902-1961 . **C L C 51**
See also CA 93-96; CANR 59; DLB 9
Fecamps, Elise
See Creasey, John
Federman, Raymond 1928- .... **CLC 6, 47**
See also CA 17-20R; CAAS 8; CANR 10, 43; DLBY 80
Federspiel, J(uerg) F. 1931- .... **CLC 42**
See also CA 146
Feiffer, Jules (Ralph) 1929- ..... **CLC 2, 8, 64; DAM DRAM**
See also AAYA 3; CA 17-20R; CANR 30, 59; DLB 7, 44; INT CANR-30; MTCW; SATA 8, 61
Feige, Hermann Albert Otto Maximilian
See Traven, B.
Feinberg, David B. 1956-1994 .... **CLC 59**
See also CA 135; 147
Feinstein, Elaine 1930- .... **CLC 36**
See also CA 69-72; CAAS 1; CANR 31; DLB 14, 40; MTCW
Feldman, Irving (Mordecai) 1928- ..... **CLC 7**
See also CA 1-4R; CANR 1; DLB 169
Felix-Tchicaya, Gerald
See Tchicaya, Gerald Felix
Fellini, Federico 1920-1993 .... **CLC 16, 85**
See also CA 65-68; 143; CANR 33
Felsen, Henry Gregor 1916- .... **CLC 17**
See also CA 1-4R; CANR 1; SAAS 2; SATA 1
Fenton, James Martin 1949- .... **CLC 32**
See also CA 102; DLB 40
Ferber, Edna 1887-1968 .... **CLC 18, 93**
See also AITN 1; CA 5-8R; 25-28R; DLB 9, 28, 86; MTCW; SATA 7
Ferguson, Helen
See Kavan, Anna
Ferguson, Samuel 1810-1886 .... **NCLC 33**
See also DLB 32
Fergusson, Robert 1750-1774 .... **LC 29**
See also DLB 109
Ferling, Lawrence
See Ferlinghetti, Lawrence (Monsanto)
Ferlinghetti, Lawrence (Monsanto) 1919(?)-
CLC 2, 6, 10, 27; DAM POET; PC 1
See also CA 5-8R; CANR 3, 41; CDALB 1941-1968; DLB 5, 16; MTCW
Fernandez, Vicente Garcia Huidobro
See Huidobro Fernandez, Vicente Garcia
Ferrer, Gabriel (Francisco Victor) Miro
See Miro (Ferrer), Gabriel (Francisco Victor)
Ferrier, Susan (Edmonstone) 1782-1854 **NCLC 8**
See also DLB 116
Ferrigno, Robert 1948(?)- .... **CLC 65**
See also CA 140
Ferron, Jacques 1921-1985 ....**CLC 94; DAC**
See also CA 117; 129; DLB 60
Feuchtwanger, Lion 1884-1958 .... **TCLC 3**
See also CA 104; DLB 66
Feuillet, Octave 1821-1890 .... **NCLC 45**
Feydeau, Georges (Leon Jules Marie) 1862-1921 .... **TCLC 22; DAM DRAM**
See also CA 113; 152
Fichte, Johann Gottlieb 1762-1814 **NCLC 62**
See also DLB 90
Ficino, Marsilio 1433-1499 .... **LC 12**
Fiedeler, Hans
See Doeblin, Alfred

Fiedler, Leslie A(aron) 1917- . **CLC 4, 13, 24**
See also CA 9-12R; CANR 7; DLB 28, 67; MTCW
Field, Andrew 1938- .... **CLC 44**
See also CA 97-100; CANR 25
Field, Eugene 1850-1895 .... **NCLC 3**
See also DLB 23, 42, 140; DLBD 13; MAICYA; SATA 16
Field, Gans T.
See Wellman, Manly Wade
Field, Michael .... **TCLC 43**
Field, Peter
See Hobson, Laura Z(ametkin)
Fielding, Henry 1707-1754 **LC 1; DA; DAB; DAC; DAM DRAM, MST, NOV; WLC**
See also CDBLB 1660-1789; DLB 39, 84, 101
Fielding, Sarah 1710-1768 .... **LC 1**
See also DLB 39
Fierstein, Harvey (Forbes) 1954- ... **CLC 33; DAM DRAM, POP**
See also CA 123; 129
Figes, Eva 1932- .... **CLC 31**
See also CA 53-56; CANR 4, 44; DLB 14
Finch, Anne 1661-1720 .... **PC 21**
See also DLB 95
Finch, Robert (Duer Claydon) 1900- **CLC 18**
See also CA 57-60; CANR 9, 24, 49; DLB 88
Findley, Timothy 1930- . **CLC 27, 102; DAC; DAM MST**
See also CA 25-28R; CANR 12, 42; DLB 53
Fink, William
See Mencken, H(enry) L(ouis)
Firbank, Louis 1942-
See Reed, Lou
See also CA 117
Firbank, (Arthur Annesley) Ronald 1886-1926 **TCLC 1**
See also CA 104; DLB 36
Fisher, M(ary) F(rances) K(ennedy) 1908-1992 **CLC 76, 87**
See also CA 77-80; 138; CANR 44
Fisher, Roy 1930- .... **CLC 25**
See also CA 81-84; CAAS 10; CANR 16; DLB 40
Fisher, Rudolph 1897-1934 . **TCLC 11; BLC; DAM MULT; SSC 25**
See also BW 1; CA 107; 124; DLB 51, 102
Fisher, Vardis (Alvero) 1895-1968 ...... **CLC 7**
See also CA 5-8R; 25-28R; DLB 9
Fiske, Tarleton
See Bloch, Robert (Albert)
Fitch, Clarke
See Sinclair, Upton (Beall)
Fitch, John IV
See Cormier, Robert (Edmund)
Fitzgerald, Captain Hugh
See Baum, L(yman) Frank
FitzGerald, Edward 1809-1883 .... **NCLC 9**
See also DLB 32
Fitzgerald, F(rancis) Scott (Key) 1896-1940
TCLC 1, 6, 14, 28, 55; DA; DAB; DAC; DAM MST, NOV; SSC 6; WLC
See also AITN 1; CA 110; 123; CDALB 1917-1929; DLB 4, 9, 86; DLBD 1, 15, 16; DLBY 81, 96; MTCW
Fitzgerald, Penelope 1916- ... **CLC 19, 51, 61**
See also CA 85-88; CAAS 10; CANR 56; DLB 14
Fitzgerald, Robert (Stuart) 1910-1985 **CLC 39**
See also CA 1-4R; 114; CANR 1; DLBY 80
FitzGerald, Robert D(avid) 1902-1987 **CLC 19**
See also CA 17-20R
Fitzgerald, Zelda (Sayre) 1900-1948 **TCLC 52**

See also CA 117; 126; DLBY 84
Flanagan, Thomas (James Bonner) 1923- **CLC 25, 52**
See also CA 108; CANR 55; DLBY 80; INT 108; MTCW
Flaubert, Gustave 1821-1880 **NCLC 2, 10, 19, 62, 66; DA; DAB; DAC; DAM MST, NOV; SSC 11; WLC**
See also DLB 119
Flecker, Herman Elroy
See Flecker, (Herman) James Elroy
Flecker, (Herman) James Elroy 1884-1915 **TCLC 43**
See also CA 109; 150; DLB 10, 19
Fleming, Ian (Lancaster) 1908-1964 . **CLC 3, 30; DAM POP**
See also CA 5-8R; CANR 59; CDBLB 1945-1960; DLB 87; MTCW; SATA 9
Fleming, Thomas (James) 1927- .... **CLC 37**
See also CA 5-8R; CANR 10; INT CANR-10; SATA 8
Fletcher, John 1579-1625 .... **LC 33; DC 6**
See also CDBLB Before 1660; DLB 58
Fletcher, John Gould 1886-1950 .... **TCLC 35**
See also CA 107; DLB 4, 45
Fleur, Paul
See Pohl, Frederik
Flooglebuckle, Al
See Spiegelman, Art
Flying Officer X
See Bates, H(erbert) E(rnest)
Fo, Dario 1926- .... **CLC 32; DAM DRAM**
See also CA 116; 128; MTCW
Fogarty, Jonathan Titulescu Esq.
See Farrell, James T(homas)
Folke, Will
See Bloch, Robert (Albert)
Follett, Ken(neth Martin) 1949- ..... **CLC 18; DAM NOV, POP**
See also AAYA 6; BEST 89:4; CA 81-84; CANR 13, 33, 54; DLB 87; DLBY 81; INT CANR-33; MTCW
Fontane, Theodor 1819-1898 .... **NCLC 26**
See also DLB 129
Foote, Horton 1916- **CLC 51, 91; DAM DRAM**
See also CA 73-76; CANR 34, 51; DLB 26; INT CANR-34
Foote, Shelby 1916- **CLC 75; DAM NOV, POP**
See also CA 5-8R; CANR 3, 45; DLB 2, 17
Forbes, Esther 1891-1967 .... **CLC 12**
See also AAYA 17; CA 13-14; 25-28R; CAP 1; CLR 27; DLB 22; JRDA; MAICYA; SATA 2
Forche, Carolyn (Louise) 1950- **CLC 25, 83, 86; DAM POET; PC 10**
See also CA 109; 117; CANR 50; DLB 5; INT 117
Ford, Elbur
See Hibbert, Eleanor Alice Burford
Ford, Ford Madox 1873-1939 **TCLC 1, 15, 39, 57; DAM NOV**
See also CA 104; 132; CDBLB 1914-1945; DLB 162; MTCW
Ford, Henry 1863-1947 .... **TCLC 73**
See also CA 115; 148
Ford, John 1586-(?) .... **DC 8**
See also CDBLB Before 1660; DAM DRAM; DLB 58
Ford, John 1895-1973 .... **CLC 16**
See also CA 45-48
Ford, Richard .... **CLC 99**
Ford, Richard 1944- .... **CLC 46**
See also CA 69-72; CANR 11, 47
Ford, Webster

TCLC 72
See also HW
Goodman, Paul 1911-1972 ...... **CLC 1, 2, 4, 7**
See also CA 19-20; 37-40R; CANR 34; CAP 2;
DLB 130; MTCW
Gordimer, Nadine 1923-**CLC 3, 5, 7, 10, 18, 33,
51, 70; DA; DAB; DAC; DAM MST, NOV;
SSC 17; WLCS**
See also CA 5-8R; CANR 3, 28, 56; INT CANR-
28; MTCW
Gordon, Adam Lindsay 1833-1870 **NCLC 21**
Gordon, Caroline 1895-1981**CLC 6, 13, 29, 83;
SSC 15**
See also CA 11-12; 103; CANR 36; CAP 1;
DLB 4, 9, 102; DLBY 81; MTCW
Gordon, Charles William 1860-1937
See Connor, Ralph
See also CA 109
Gordon, Mary (Catherine) 1949-**CLC 13, 22**
See also CA 102; CANR 44; DLB 6; DLBY
81; INT 102; MTCW
Gordon, N. J.
See Bosman, Herman Charles
Gordon, Sol 1923- .... **CLC 26**
See also CA 53-56; CANR 4; SATA 11
Gordone, Charles 1925-1995**CLC 1, 4; DAM
DRAM; DC 8**
See also BW 1; CA 93-96; 150; CANR 55; DLB
7; INT 93-96; MTCW
Gore, Catherine 1800-1861 .... **NCLC 65**
See also DLB 116
Gorenko, Anna Andreevna
See Akhmatova, Anna
Gorky, Maxim 1868-1936**TCLC 8; DAB; SSC
28; WLC**
See also Peshkov, Alexei Maximovich
Goryan, Sirak
See Saroyan, William
Gosse, Edmund (William) 1849-1928**TCLC 28**
See also CA 117; DLB 57, 144, 184
Gotlieb, Phyllis Fay (Bloom) 1926- .. **CLC 18**
See also CA 13-16R; CANR 7; DLB 88
Gottesman, S. D.
See Kornbluth, C(yril) M.; Pohl, Frederik
Gottfried von Strassburg fl. c. 1210- **C M L C
10**
See also DLB 138
Gould, Lois ....**CLC 4, 10**
See also CA 77-80; CANR 29; MTCW
Gourmont, Remy (-Marie-Charles) de 1858-
1915 .... **TCLC 17**
See also CA 109; 150
Govier, Katherine 1948- .... **CLC 51**
See also CA 101; CANR 18, 40
Goyen, (Charles) William 1915-1983**CLC 5, 8,
14, 40**
See also AITN 2; CA 5-8R; 110; CANR 6; DLB
2; DLBY 83; INT CANR-6
Goytisolo, Juan 1931- . **CLC 5, 10, 23; DAM
MULT; HLC**
See also CA 85-88; CANR 32, 61; HW; MTCW
Gozzano, Guido 1883-1916 .... **PC 10**
See also CA 154; DLB 114
Gozzi, (Conte) Carlo 1720-1806 .... **NCLC 23**
Grabbe, Christian Dietrich 1801-1836**N C L C
2**
See also DLB 133
Grace, Patricia 1937- .... **CLC 56**
Gracian y Morales, Baltasar 1601-1658**LC 15**
Gracq, Julien .... **CLC 11, 48**
See also Poirier, Louis
See also DLB 83
Grade, Chaim 1910-1982 .... **CLC 10**

See also CA 93-96; 107
Graduate of Oxford, A
See Ruskin, John
Grafton, Garth
See Duncan, Sara Jeannette
Graham, John
See Phillips, David Graham
Graham, Jorie 1951- .... **CLC 48**
See also CA 111; DLB 120
Graham, R(obert) B(ontine) Cunninghame
See Cunninghame Graham, R(obert) B(ontine)
See also DLB 98, 135, 174
Graham, Robert
See Haldeman, Joe (William)
Graham, Tom
See Lewis, (Harry) Sinclair
Graham, W(illiam) S(ydney) 1918-1986**C L C
29**
See also CA 73-76; 118; DLB 20
Graham, Winston (Mawdsley) 1910- **CLC 23**
See also CA 49-52; CANR 2, 22, 45; DLB 77
Grahame, Kenneth 1859-1932**TCLC 64; DAB**
See also CA 108; 136; CLR 5; DLB 34, 141,
178; MAICYA; YABC 1
Grant, Skeeter
See Spiegelman, Art
Granville-Barker, Harley 1877-1946**TCLC 2;
DAM DRAM**
See also Barker, Harley Granville
See also CA 104
Grass, Guenter (Wilhelm) 1927-**CLC 1, 2, 4, 6,
11, 15, 22, 32, 49, 88; DA; DAB; DAC;
DAM MST, NOV; WLC**
See also CA 13-16R; CANR 20; DLB 75, 124;
MTCW
Gratton, Thomas
See Hulme, T(homas) E(rnest)
Grau, Shirley Ann 1929-.. **CLC 4, 9; SSC 15**
See also CA 89-92; CANR 22; DLB 2; INT
CANR-22; MTCW
Gravel, Fern
See Hall, James Norman
Graver, Elizabeth 1964- .... **CLC 70**
See also CA 135
Graves, Richard Perceval 1945- .... **CLC 44**
See also CA 65-68; CANR 9, 26, 51
Graves, Robert (von Ranke) 1895-1985 **C L C
1, 2, 6, 11, 39, 44, 45; DAB; DAC; DAM
MST, POET; PC 6**
See also CA 5-8R; 117; CANR 5, 36; CDBLB
1914-1945; DLB 20, 100; DLBY 85;
MTCW; SATA 45
Graves, Valerie
See Bradley, Marion Zimmer
Gray, Alasdair (James) 1934- .... **CLC 41**
See also CA 126; CANR 47; INT 126; MTCW
Gray, Amlin 1946- .... **CLC 29**
See also CA 138
Gray, Francine du Plessix 1930- ..... **CLC 22;
DAM NOV**
See also BEST 90:3; CA 61-64; CAAS 2;
CANR 11, 33; INT CANR-11; MTCW
Gray, John (Henry) 1866-1934 ...... **TCLC 19**
See also CA 119
Gray, Simon (James Holliday) 1936- **CLC 9,
14, 36**
See also AITN 1; CA 21-24R; CAAS 3; CANR
32; DLB 13; MTCW
Gray, Spalding 1941-**CLC 49; DAM POP; DC
7**
See also CA 128
Gray, Thomas 1716-1771**LC 4, 40; DA; DAB;
DAC; DAM MST; PC 2; WLC**

See also CDBLB 1660-1789; DLB 109
Grayson, David
See Baker, Ray Stannard
Grayson, Richard (A.) 1951- .... **CLC 38**
See also CA 85-88; CANR 14, 31, 57
Greeley, Andrew M(oran) 1928- ..... **CLC 28;
DAM POP**
See also CA 5-8R; CAAS 7; CANR 7, 43;
MTCW
Green, Anna Katharine 1846-1935 **TCLC 63**
See also CA 112; 159
Green, Brian
See Card, Orson Scott
Green, Hannah
See Greenberg, Joanne (Goldenberg)
Green, Hannah 1927(?)-1996 .... **CLC 3**
See also CA 73-76; CANR 59
Green, Henry 1905-1973 .... **CLC 2, 13, 97**
See also Yorke, Henry Vincent
See also DLB 15
Green, Julian (Hartridge) 1900-
See Green, Julien
See also CA 21-24R; CANR 33; DLB 4, 72;
MTCW
Green, Julien .... **CLC 3, 11, 77**
See also Green, Julian (Hartridge)
Green, Paul (Eliot) 1894-1981**CLC 25; DAM
DRAM**
See also AITN 1; CA 5-8R; 103; CANR 3; DLB
7, 9; DLBY 81
Greenberg, Ivan 1908-1973
See Rahv, Philip
See also CA 85-88
Greenberg, Joanne (Goldenberg) 1932- **C L C
7, 30**
See also AAYA 12; CA 5-8R; CANR 14, 32;
SATA 25
Greenberg, Richard 1959(?)- .... **CLC 57**
See also CA 138
Greene, Bette 1934- .... **CLC 30**
See also AAYA 7; CA 53-56; CANR 4; CLR 2;
JRDA; MAICYA; SAAS 16; SATA 8
Greene, Gael .... **CLC 8**
See also CA 13-16R; CANR 10
Greene, Graham (Henry) 1904-1991**CLC 1, 3,
6, 9, 14, 18, 27, 37, 70, 72; DA; DAB; DAC;
DAM MST, NOV; SSC 29; WLC**
See also AITN 2; CA 13-16R; 133; CANR 35,
61; CDBLB 1945-1960; DLB 13, 15, 77,
100, 162; DLBY 91; MTCW; SATA 20
Greene, Robert 1558-1592 .... **LC 41**
Greer, Richard
See Silverberg, Robert
Gregor, Arthur 1923- .... **CLC 9**
See also CA 25-28R; CAAS 10; CANR 11;
SATA 36
Gregor, Lee
See Pohl, Frederik
Gregory, Isabella Augusta (Persse) 1852-1932
TCLC 1
See also CA 104; DLB 10
Gregory, J. Dennis
See Williams, John A(lfred)
Grendon, Stephen
See Derleth, August (William)
Grenville, Kate 1950- .... **CLC 61**
See also CA 118; CANR 53
Grenville, Pelham
See Wodehouse, P(elham) G(renville)
Greve, Felix Paul (Berthold Friedrich) 1879-
1948
See Grove, Frederick Philip
See also CA 104; 141; DAC; DAM MST

Grey, Zane 1872-1939 .. **TCLC 6; DAM POP**
See also CA 104; 132; DLB 9; MTCW
Grieg, (Johan) Nordahl (Brun) 1902-1943
TCLC 10
See also CA 107
Grieve, C(hristopher) M(urray) 1892-1978
CLC 11, 19; DAM POET
See also MacDiarmid, Hugh; Pteleon
See also CA 5-8R; 85-88; CANR 33; MTCW
Griffin, Gerald 1803-1840 .... **NCLC 7**
See also DLB 159
Griffin, John Howard 1920-1980 ..... **CLC 68**
See also AITN 1; CA 1-4R; 101; CANR 2
Griffin, Peter 1942- .... **CLC 39**
See also CA 136
Griffith, D(avid Lewelyn) W(ark) 1875(?)-1948
TCLC 68
See also CA 119; 150
Griffith, Lawrence
See Griffith, D(avid Lewelyn) W(ark)
Griffiths, Trevor 1935- .... **CLC 13, 52**
See also CA 97-100; CANR 45; DLB 13
Griggs, Sutton Elbert 1872-1930(?)**TCLC 77**
See also CA 123; DLB 50
Grigson, Geoffrey (Edward Harvey) 1905-1985
CLC 7, 39
See also CA 25-28R; 118; CANR 20, 33; DLB
27; MTCW
Grillparzer, Franz 1791-1872 .... **NCLC 1**
See also DLB 133
Grimble, Reverend Charles James
See Eliot, T(homas) S(tearns)
Grimke, Charlotte L(ottie) Forten 1837(?)-1914
See Forten, Charlotte L.
See also BW 1; CA 117; 124; DAM MULT,
POET
Grimm, Jacob Ludwig Karl 1785-1863**NCLC 3**
See also DLB 90; MAICYA; SATA 22
Grimm, Wilhelm Karl 1786-1859 .... **NCLC 3**
See also DLB 90; MAICYA; SATA 22
Grimmelshausen, Johann Jakob Christoffel von
1621-1676 .... **LC 6**
See also DLB 168
Grindel, Eugene 1895-1952
See Eluard, Paul
See also CA 104
Grisham, John 1955- .... **CLC 84; DAM POP**
See also AAYA 14; CA 138; CANR 47
Grossman, David 1954- .... **CLC 67**
See also CA 138
Grossman, Vasily (Semenovich) 1905-1964
CLC 41
See also CA 124; 130; MTCW
Grove, Frederick Philip .... **TCLC 4**
See also Greve, Felix Paul (Berthold Friedrich)
See also DLB 92
Grubb
See Crumb, R(obert)
Grumbach, Doris (Isaac) 1918-**CLC 13, 22, 64**
See also CA 5-8R; CAAS 2; CANR 9, 42; INT
CANR-9
Grundtvig, Nicolai Frederik Severin 1783-1872
NCLC 1
Grunge
See Crumb, R(obert)
Grunwald, Lisa 1959- .... **CLC 44**
See also CA 120
Guare, John 1938- . **CLC 8, 14, 29, 67; DAM
DRAM**
See also CA 73-76; CANR 21; DLB 7; MTCW
Gudjonsson, Halldor Kiljan 1902-
See Laxness, Halldor

See also CA 103
Guenter, Erich
See Eich, Guenter
Guest, Barbara 1920- .... **CLC 34**
See also CA 25-28R; CANR 11, 44; DLB 5
Guest, Judith (Ann) 1936- **CLC 8, 30; DAM
NOV, POP**
See also AAYA 7; CA 77-80; CANR 15; INT
CANR-15; MTCW
Guevara, Che .... **CLC 87; HLC**
See also Guevara (Serna), Ernesto
Guevara (Serna), Ernesto 1928-1967
See Guevara, Che
See also CA 127; 111; CANR 56; DAM MULT;
HW
Guild, Nicholas M. 1944- .... **CLC 33**
See also CA 93-96
Guillemin, Jacques
See Sartre, Jean-Paul
Guillen, Jorge 1893-1984 .... **CLC 11; DAM
MULT, POET**
See also CA 89-92; 112; DLB 108; HW
Guillen, Nicolas (Cristobal) 1902-1989 **C L C
48, 79; BLC; DAM MST, MULT, POET;
HLC**
See also BW 2; CA 116; 125; 129; HW
Guillevic, (Eugene) 1907- .... **CLC 33**
See also CA 93-96
Guillois
See Desnos, Robert
Guillois, Valentin
See Desnos, Robert
Guiney, Louise Imogen 1861-1920 **TCLC 41**
See also CA 160; DLB 54
Guiraldes, Ricardo (Guillermo) 1886-1927
TCLC 39
See also CA 131; HW; MTCW
Gumilev, Nikolai Stephanovich 1886-1921
TCLC 60
Gunesekera, Romesh 1954- .... **CLC 91**
See also CA 159
Gunn, Bill .... **CLC 5**
See also Gunn, William Harrison
See also DLB 38
Gunn, Thom(son William) 1929-**CLC 3, 6, 18,
32, 81; DAM POET**
See also CA 17-20R; CANR 9, 33; CDBLB
1960 to Present; DLB 27; INT CANR-33;
MTCW
Gunn, William Harrison 1934(?)-1989
See Gunn, Bill
See also AITN 1; BW 1; CA 13-16R; 128;
CANR 12, 25
Gunnars, Kristjana 1948- .... **CLC 69**
See also CA 113; DLB 60
Gurdjieff, G(eorgei) I(vanovich) 1877(?)-1949
TCLC 71
See also CA 157
Gurganus, Allan 1947- . **CLC 70; DAM POP**
See also BEST 90:1; CA 135
Gurney, A(lbert) R(amsdell), Jr. 1930- . **C L C
32, 50, 54; DAM DRAM**
See also CA 77-80; CANR 32
Gurney, Ivor (Bertie) 1890-1937 ... **TCLC 33**
Gurney, Peter
See Gurney, A(lbert) R(amsdell), Jr.
Guro, Elena 1877-1913 .... **TCLC 56**
Gustafson, James M(oody) 1925- ... **CLC 100**
See also CA 25-28R; CANR 37
Gustafson, Ralph (Barker) 1909- ..... **CLC 36**
See also CA 21-24R; CANR 8, 45; DLB 88
Gut, Gom
See Simenon, Georges (Jacques Christian)

Guterson, David 1956- .... **CLC 91**
See also CA 132
Guthrie, A(lfred) B(ertram), Jr. 1901-1991
CLC 23
See also CA 57-60; 134; CANR 24; DLB 6;
SATA 62; SATA-Obit 67
Guthrie, Isobel
See Grieve, C(hristopher) M(urray)
Guthrie, Woodrow Wilson 1912-1967
See Guthrie, Woody
See also CA 113; 93-96
Guthrie, Woody .... **CLC 35**
See also Guthrie, Woodrow Wilson
Guy, Rosa (Cuthbert) 1928- .... **CLC 26**
See also AAYA 4; BW 2; CA 17-20R; CANR
14, 34; CLR 13; DLB 33; JRDA; MAICYA;
SATA 14, 62
Gwendolyn
See Bennett, (Enoch) Arnold
H. D. .... **CLC 3, 8, 14, 31, 34, 73; PC 5**
See also Doolittle, Hilda
H. de V.
See Buchan, John
Haavikko, Paavo Juhani 1931- .. **CLC 18, 34**
See also CA 106
Habbema, Koos
See Heijermans, Herman
Habermas, Juergen 1929- .... **CLC 104**
See also CA 109
Habermas, Jurgen
See Habermas, Juergen
Hacker, Marilyn 1942- **CLC 5, 9, 23, 72, 91;
DAM POET**
See also CA 77-80; DLB 120
Haggard, H(enry) Rider 1856-1925**TCLC 11**
See also CA 108; 148; DLB 70, 156, 174, 178;
SATA 16
Hagiosy, L.
See Larbaud, Valery (Nicolas)
Hagiwara Sakutaro 1886-1942**TCLC 60; PC
18**
Haig, Fenil
See Ford, Ford Madox
Haig-Brown, Roderick (Langmere) 1908-1976
CLC 21
See also CA 5-8R; 69-72; CANR 4, 38; CLR
31; DLB 88; MAICYA; SATA 12
Hailey, Arthur 1920-**CLC 5; DAM NOV, POP**
See also AITN 2; BEST 90:3; CA 1-4R; CANR
2, 36; DLB 88; DLBY 82; MTCW
Hailey, Elizabeth Forsythe 1938- ..... **CLC 40**
See also CA 93-96; CAAS 1; CANR 15, 48;
INT CANR-15
Haines, John (Meade) 1924- .... **CLC 58**
See also CA 17-20R; CANR 13, 34; DLB 5
Hakluyt, Richard 1552-1616 .... **LC 31**
Haldeman, Joe (William) 1943- .... **CLC 61**
See also CA 53-56; CAAS 25; CANR 6; DLB
8; INT CANR-6
Haley, Alex(ander Murray Palmer) 1921-1992
**CLC 8, 12, 76; BLC; DA; DAB; DAC;
DAM MST, MULT, POP**
See also BW 2; CA 77-80; 136; CANR 61; DLB
38; MTCW
Haliburton, Thomas Chandler 1796-1865
NCLC 15
See also DLB 11, 99
Hall, Donald (Andrew, Jr.) 1928- **CLC 1, 13,
37, 59; DAM POET**
See also CA 5-8R; CAAS 7; CANR 2, 44; DLB
5; SATA 23
Hall, Frederic Sauser
See Sauser-Hall, Frederic

17, 25, 69; DA; DAB; DAC; DAM MST, NOV; SSC 9; WLC
See also CA 17-18; CAP 2; DLB 66; MTCW; SATA 50

Hewes, Cady
See De Voto, Bernard (Augustine)

Heyen, William 1940- .... **CLC 13, 18**
See also CA 33-36R; CAAS 9; DLB 5

Heyerdahl, Thor 1914- .... **CLC 26**
See also CA 5-8R; CANR 5, 22; MTCW; SATA 2, 52

Heym, Georg (Theodor Franz Arthur) 1887-1912 .... **TCLC 9**
See also CA 106

Heym, Stefan 1913- .... **CLC 41**
See also CA 9-12R; CANR 4; DLB 69

Heyse, Paul (Johann Ludwig von) 1830-1914 **TCLC 8**
See also CA 104; DLB 129

Heyward, (Edwin) DuBose 1885-1940 **T C L C 59**
See also CA 108; 157; DLB 7, 9, 45; SATA 21

Hibbert, Eleanor Alice Burford 1906-1993 **CLC 7; DAM POP**
See also BEST 90:4; CA 17-20R; 140; CANR 9, 28, 59; SATA 2; SATA-Obit 74

Higgins, George V(incent) 1939-**CLC 4, 7, 10, 18**
See also CA 77-80; CAAS 5; CANR 17, 51; DLB 2; DLBY 81; INT CANR-17; MTCW

Higginson, Thomas Wentworth 1823-1911 **TCLC 36**
See also DLB 1, 64

Highet, Helen
See MacInnes, Helen (Clark)

Highsmith, (Mary) Patricia 1921-1995**CLC 2, 4, 14, 42, 102; DAM NOV, POP**
See also CA 1-4R; 147; CANR 1, 20, 48, 62; MTCW

Highwater, Jamake (Mamake) 1942(?)- **C L C 12**
See also AAYA 7; CA 65-68; CAAS 7; CANR 10, 34; CLR 17; DLB 52; DLBY 85; JRDA; MAICYA; SATA 32, 69; SATA-Brief 30

Highway, Tomson 1951-**CLC 92; DAC; DAM MULT**
See also CA 151; NNAL

Higuchi, Ichiyo 1872-1896 .... **NCLC 49**

Hijuelos, Oscar 1951- **CLC 65; DAM MULT, POP; HLC**
See also BEST 90:1; CA 123; CANR 50; DLB 145; HW

Hikmet, Nazim 1902(?)-1963 .... **CLC 40**
See also CA 141; 93-96

Hildegard von Bingen 1098-1179 . **CMLC 20**
See also DLB 148

Hildesheimer, Wolfgang 1916-1991 .. **CLC 49**
See also CA 101; 135; DLB 69, 124

Hill, Geoffrey (William) 1932- **CLC 5, 8, 18, 45; DAM POET**
See also CA 81-84; CANR 21; CDBLB 1960 to Present; DLB 40; MTCW

Hill, George Roy 1921- .... **CLC 26**
See also CA 110; 122

Hill, John
See Koontz, Dean R(ay)

Hill, Susan (Elizabeth) 1942- . **CLC 4; DAB; DAM MST, NOV**
See also CA 33-36R; CANR 29; DLB 14, 139; MTCW

Hillerman, Tony 1925- . **CLC 62; DAM POP**
See also AAYA 6; BEST 89:1; CA 29-32R; CANR 21, 42; SATA 6

Hillesum, Etty 1914-1943 .... **TCLC 49**
See also CA 137

Hilliard, Noel (Harvey) 1929- .... **CLC 15**
See also CA 9-12R; CANR 7

Hillis, Rick 1956- .... **CLC 66**
See also CA 134

Hilton, James 1900-1954 .... **TCLC 21**
See also CA 108; DLB 34, 77; SATA 34

Himes, Chester (Bomar) 1909-1984**CLC 2, 4, 7, 18, 58; BLC; DAM MULT**
See also BW 2; CA 25-28R; 114; CANR 22; DLB 2, 76, 143; MTCW

Hinde, Thomas .... **CLC 6, 11**
See also Chitty, Thomas Willes

Hindin, Nathan
See Bloch, Robert (Albert)

Hine, (William) Daryl 1936- .... **CLC 15**
See also CA 1-4R; CAAS 15; CANR 1, 20; DLB 60

Hinkson, Katharine Tynan
See Tynan, Katharine

Hinton, S(usan) E(loise) 1950- **CLC 30; DA; DAB; DAC; DAM MST, NOV**
See also AAYA 2; CA 81-84; CANR 32, 62; CLR 3, 23; JRDA; MAICYA; MTCW; SATA 19, 58

Hippius, Zinaida .... **TCLC 9**
See also Gippius, Zinaida (Nikolayevna)

Hiraoka, Kimitake 1925-1970
See Mishima, Yukio
See also CA 97-100; 29-32R; DAM DRAM; MTCW

Hirsch, E(ric) D(onald), Jr. 1928- .... **CLC 79**
See also CA 25-28R; CANR 27, 51; DLB 67; INT CANR-27; MTCW

Hirsch, Edward 1950- .... **CLC 31, 50**
See also CA 104; CANR 20, 42; DLB 120

Hitchcock, Alfred (Joseph) 1899-1980**CLC 16**
See also AAYA 22; CA 159; 97-100; SATA 27; SATA-Obit 24

Hitler, Adolf 1889-1945 .... **TCLC 53**
See also CA 117; 147

Hoagland, Edward 1932- .... **CLC 28**
See also CA 1-4R; CANR 2, 31, 57; DLB 6; SATA 51

Hoban, Russell (Conwell) 1925- . **CLC 7, 25; DAM NOV**
See also CA 5-8R; CANR 23, 37; CLR 3; DLB 52; MAICYA; MTCW; SATA 1, 40, 78

Hobbes, Thomas 1588-1679 .... **LC 36**
See also DLB 151

Hobbs, Perry
See Blackmur, R(ichard) P(almer)

Hobson, Laura Z(ametkin) 1900-1986**CLC 7, 25**
See also CA 17-20R; 118; CANR 55; DLB 28; SATA 52

Hochhuth, Rolf 1931- .. **CLC 4, 11, 18; DAM DRAM**
See also CA 5-8R; CANR 33; DLB 124; MTCW

Hochman, Sandra 1936- .... **CLC 3, 8**
See also CA 5-8R; DLB 5

Hochwaelder, Fritz 1911-1986**CLC 36; DAM DRAM**
See also CA 29-32R; 120; CANR 42; MTCW

Hochwalder, Fritz
See Hochwaelder, Fritz

Hocking, Mary (Eunice) 1921- .... **CLC 13**
See also CA 101; CANR 18, 40

Hodgins, Jack 1938- .... **CLC 23**
See also CA 93-96; DLB 60

Hodgson, William Hope 1877(?)-1918 **T C L C 13**

See also CA 111; DLB 70, 153, 156, 178

Hoeg, Peter 1957- .... **CLC 95**
See also CA 151

Hoffman, Alice 1952- ... **CLC 51; DAM NOV**
See also CA 77-80; CANR 34; MTCW

Hoffman, Daniel (Gerard) 1923-**CLC 6, 13, 23**
See also CA 1-4R; CANR 4; DLB 5

Hoffman, Stanley 1944- .... **CLC 5**
See also CA 77-80

Hoffman, William M(oses) 1939-...... **CLC 40**
See also CA 57-60; CANR 11

Hoffmann, E(rnst) T(heodor) A(madeus) 1776-1822 .... **NCLC 2; SSC 13**
See also DLB 90; SATA 27

Hofmann, Gert 1931- .... **CLC 54**
See also CA 128

Hofmannsthal, Hugo von 1874-1929**TCLC 11; DAM DRAM; DC 4**
See also CA 106; 153; DLB 81, 118

Hogan, Linda 1947- ... **CLC 73; DAM MULT**
See also CA 120; CANR 45; DLB 175; NNAL

Hogarth, Charles
See Creasey, John

Hogarth, Emmett
See Polonsky, Abraham (Lincoln)

Hogg, James 1770-1835 .... **NCLC 4**
See also DLB 93, 116, 159

Holbach, Paul Henri Thiry Baron 1723-1789 **LC 14**

Holberg, Ludvig 1684-1754 .... **LC 6**

Holden, Ursula 1921- .... **CLC 18**
See also CA 101; CAAS 8; CANR 22

Holderlin, (Johann Christian) Friedrich 1770-1843 .... **NCLC 16; PC 4**

Holdstock, Robert
See Holdstock, Robert P.

Holdstock, Robert P. 1948- .... **CLC 39**
See also CA 131

Holland, Isabelle 1920- .... **CLC 21**
See also AAYA 11; CA 21-24R; CANR 10, 25, 47; JRDA; MAICYA; SATA 8, 70

Holland, Marcus
See Caldwell, (Janet Miriam) Taylor (Holland)

Hollander, John 1929- .... **CLC 2, 5, 8, 14**
See also CA 1-4R; CANR 1, 52; DLB 5; SATA 13

Hollander, Paul
See Silverberg, Robert

Holleran, Andrew 1943(?)- .... **CLC 38**
See also CA 144

Hollinghurst, Alan 1954- .... **CLC 55, 91**
See also CA 114

Hollis, Jim
See Summers, Hollis (Spurgeon, Jr.)

Holly, Buddy 1936-1959 .... **TCLC 65**

Holmes, Gordon
See Shiel, M(atthew) P(hipps)

Holmes, John
See Souster, (Holmes) Raymond

Holmes, John Clellon 1926-1988 ...... **CLC 56**
See also CA 9-12R; 125; CANR 4; DLB 16

Holmes, Oliver Wendell, Jr. 1841-1935**T C L C 77**
See also CA 114

Holmes, Oliver Wendell 1809-1894**NCLC 14**
See also CDALB 1640-1865; DLB 1; SATA 34

Holmes, Raymond
See Souster, (Holmes) Raymond

Holt, Victoria
See Hibbert, Eleanor Alice Burford

Holub, Miroslav 1923- .... **CLC 4**
See also CA 21-24R; CANR 10

Homer c. 8th cent. B.C.- ... **CMLC 1, 16; DA;**

Janowitz, Tama 1957- .. **CLC 43; DAM POP**
See also CA 106; CANR 52
Japrisot, Sebastien 1931- .... **CLC 90**
Jarrell, Randall 1914-1965**CLC 1, 2, 6, 9, 13, 49; DAM POET**
See also CA 5-8R; 25-28R; CABS 2; CANR 6, 34; CDALB 1941-1968; CLR 6; DLB 48, 52; MAICYA; MTCW; SATA 7
Jarry, Alfred 1873-1907 .. **TCLC 2, 14; DAM DRAM; SSC 20**
See also CA 104; 153
Jarvis, E. K.
See Bloch, Robert (Albert); Ellison, Harlan (Jay); Silverberg, Robert
Jeake, Samuel, Jr.
See Aiken, Conrad (Potter)
Jean Paul 1763-1825 .... **NCLC 7**
Jefferies, (John) Richard 1848-1887**NCLC 47**
See also DLB 98, 141; SATA 16
Jeffers, (John) Robinson 1887-1962**CLC 2, 3, 11, 15, 54; DA; DAC; DAM MST, POET; PC 17; WLC**
See also CA 85-88; CANR 35; CDALB 1917-1929; DLB 45; MTCW
Jefferson, Janet
See Mencken, H(enry) L(ouis)
Jefferson, Thomas 1743-1826 .... **NCLC 11**
See also CDALB 1640-1865; DLB 31
Jeffrey, Francis 1773-1850 .... **NCLC 33**
See also DLB 107
Jelakowitch, Ivan
See Heijermans, Herman
Jellicoe, (Patricia) Ann 1927- .... **CLC 27**
See also CA 85-88; DLB 13
Jen, Gish .... **CLC 70**
See also Jen, Lillian
Jen, Lillian 1956(?)-
See Jen, Gish
See also CA 135
Jenkins, (John) Robin 1912- .... **CLC 52**
See also CA 1-4R; CANR 1; DLB 14
Jennings, Elizabeth (Joan) 1926- .**CLC 5, 14**
See also CA 61-64; CAAS 5; CANR 8, 39; DLB 27; MTCW; SATA 66
Jennings, Waylon 1937- .... **CLC 21**
Jensen, Johannes V. 1873-1950 ...... **TCLC 41**
Jensen, Laura (Linnea) 1948- .... **CLC 37**
See also CA 103
Jerome, Jerome K(lapka) 1859-1927**TCLC 23**
See also CA 119; DLB 10, 34, 135
Jerrold, Douglas William 1803-1857**NCLC 2**
See also DLB 158, 159
Jewett, (Theodora) Sarah Orne 1849-1909
TCLC 1, 22; SSC 6
See also CA 108; 127; DLB 12, 74; SATA 15
Jewsbury, Geraldine (Endsor) 1812-1880
NCLC 22
See also DLB 21
Jhabvala, Ruth Prawer 1927-**CLC 4, 8, 29, 94; DAB; DAM NOV**
See also CA 1-4R; CANR 2, 29, 51; DLB 139; INT CANR-29; MTCW
Jibran, Kahlil
See Gibran, Kahlil
Jibran, Khalil
See Gibran, Kahlil
Jiles, Paulette 1943- .... **CLC 13, 58**
See also CA 101
Jimenez (Mantecon), Juan Ramon 1881-1958
TCLC 4; DAM MULT, POET; HLC; PC 7
See also CA 104; 131; DLB 134; HW; MTCW
Jimenez, Ramon

See Jimenez (Mantecon), Juan Ramon
Jimenez Mantecon, Juan
See Jimenez (Mantecon), Juan Ramon
Joel, Billy .... **CLC 26**
See also Joel, William Martin
Joel, William Martin 1949-
See Joel, Billy
See also CA 108
John of the Cross, St. 1542-1591 .... **LC 18**
Johnson, B(ryan) S(tanley William) 1933-1973
CLC 6, 9
See also CA 9-12R; 53-56; CANR 9; DLB 14, 40
Johnson, Benj. F. of Boo
See Riley, James Whitcomb
Johnson, Benjamin F. of Boo
See Riley, James Whitcomb
Johnson, Charles (Richard) 1948-**CLC 7, 51, 65; BLC; DAM MULT**
See also BW 2; CA 116; CAAS 18; CANR 42; DLB 33
Johnson, Denis 1949- .... **CLC 52**
See also CA 117; 121; DLB 120
Johnson, Diane 1934- .... **CLC 5, 13, 48**
See also CA 41-44R; CANR 17, 40, 62; DLBY 80; INT CANR-17; MTCW
Johnson, Eyvind (Olof Verner) 1900-1976
CLC 14
See also CA 73-76; 69-72; CANR 34
Johnson, J. R.
See James, C(yril) L(ionel) R(obert)
Johnson, James Weldon 1871-1938 **TCLC 3, 19; BLC; DAM MULT, POET**
See also BW 1; CA 104; 125; CDALB 1917-1929; CLR 32; DLB 51; MTCW; SATA 31
Johnson, Joyce 1935- .... **CLC 58**
See also CA 125; 129
Johnson, Lionel (Pigot) 1867-1902 **TCLC 19**
See also CA 117; DLB 19
Johnson, Mel
See Malzberg, Barry N(athaniel)
Johnson, Pamela Hansford 1912-1981**CLC 1, 7, 27**
See also CA 1-4R; 104; CANR 2, 28; DLB 15; MTCW
Johnson, Robert 1911(?)-1938 .... **TCLC 69**
Johnson, Samuel 1709-1784**LC 15; DA; DAB; DAC; DAM MST; WLC**
See also CDBLB 1660-1789; DLB 39, 95, 104, 142
Johnson, Uwe 1934-1984 .. **CLC 5, 10, 15, 40**
See also CA 1-4R; 112; CANR 1, 39; DLB 75; MTCW
Johnston, George (Benson) 1913- ..... **CLC 51**
See also CA 1-4R; CANR 5, 20; DLB 88
Johnston, Jennifer 1930- .... **CLC 7**
See also CA 85-88; DLB 14
Jolley, (Monica) Elizabeth 1923-**CLC 46; SSC 19**
See also CA 127; CAAS 13; CANR 59
Jones, Arthur Llewellyn 1863-1947
See Machen, Arthur
See also CA 104
Jones, D(ouglas) G(ordon) 1929- ...... **CLC 10**
See also CA 29-32R; CANR 13; DLB 53
Jones, David (Michael) 1895-1974**CLC 2, 4, 7, 13, 42**
See also CA 9-12R; 53-56; CANR 28; CDBLB 1945-1960; DLB 20, 100; MTCW
Jones, David Robert 1947-
See Bowie, David
See also CA 103
Jones, Diana Wynne 1934- .... **CLC 26**

See also AAYA 12; CA 49-52; CANR 4, 26, 56; CLR 23; DLB 161; JRDA; MAICYA; SAAS 7; SATA 9, 70
Jones, Edward P. 1950- .... **CLC 76**
See also BW 2; CA 142
Jones, Gayl 1949- .... **CLC 6, 9; BLC; DAM MULT**
See also BW 2; CA 77-80; CANR 27; DLB 33; MTCW
Jones, James 1921-1977 ...... **CLC 1, 3, 10, 39**
See also AITN 1, 2; CA 1-4R; 69-72; CANR 6; DLB 2, 143; MTCW
Jones, John J.
See Lovecraft, H(oward) P(hillips)
Jones, LeRoi .... **CLC 1, 2, 3, 5, 10, 14**
See also Baraka, Amiri
Jones, Louis B. .... **CLC 65**
See also CA 141
Jones, Madison (Percy, Jr.) 1925- .... **CLC 4**
See also CA 13-16R; CAAS 11; CANR 7, 54; DLB 152
Jones, Mervyn 1922- .... **CLC 10, 52**
See also CA 45-48; CAAS 5; CANR 1; MTCW
Jones, Mick 1956(?)- .... **CLC 30**
Jones, Nettie (Pearl) 1941- .... **CLC 34**
See also BW 2; CA 137; CAAS 20
Jones, Preston 1936-1979 .... **CLC 10**
See also CA 73-76; 89-92; DLB 7
Jones, Robert F(rancis) 1934- .... **CLC 7**
See also CA 49-52; CANR 2, 61
Jones, Rod 1953- .... **CLC 50**
See also CA 128
Jones, Terence Graham Parry 1942- **CLC 21**
See also Jones, Terry; Monty Python
See also CA 112; 116; CANR 35; INT 116
Jones, Terry
See Jones, Terence Graham Parry
See also SATA 67; SATA-Brief 51
Jones, Thom 1945(?)- .... **CLC 81**
See also CA 157
Jong, Erica 1942- . **CLC 4, 6, 8, 18, 83; DAM NOV, POP**
See also AITN 1; BEST 90:2; CA 73-76; CANR 26, 52; DLB 2, 5, 28, 152; INT CANR-26; MTCW
Jonson, Ben(jamin) 1572(?)-1637 .. **LC 6, 33; DA; DAB; DAC; DAM DRAM, MST, POET; DC 4; PC 17; WLC**
See also CDBLB Before 1660; DLB 62, 121
Jordan, June 1936- ...... **CLC 5, 11, 23; DAM MULT, POET**
See also AAYA 2; BW 2; CA 33-36R; CANR 25; CLR 10; DLB 38; MAICYA; MTCW; SATA 4
Jordan, Pat(rick M.) 1941- .... **CLC 37**
See also CA 33-36R
Jorgensen, Ivar
See Ellison, Harlan (Jay)
Jorgenson, Ivar
See Silverberg, Robert
Josephus, Flavius c. 37-100 .... **CMLC 13**
Josipovici, Gabriel 1940- .... **CLC 6, 43**
See also CA 37-40R; CAAS 8; CANR 47; DLB 14
Joubert, Joseph 1754-1824 .... **NCLC 9**
Jouve, Pierre Jean 1887-1976 .... **CLC 47**
See also CA 65-68
Joyce, James (Augustine Aloysius) 1882-1941
TCLC 3, 8, 16, 35, 52; DA; DAB; DAC; DAM MST, NOV, POET; SSC 26; WLC
See also CA 104; 126; CDBLB 1914-1945; DLB 10, 19, 36, 162; MTCW
Jozsef, Attila 1905-1937 .... **TCLC 22**

See also CA 116

Juana Ines de la Cruz 1651(?)-1695 ...... **LC 5**

Judd, Cyril
　See Kornbluth, C(yril) M.; Pohl, Frederik

Julian of Norwich 1342(?)-1416(?) .... **LC 6**
　See also DLB 146

Juniper, Alex
　See Hospital, Janette Turner

Junius
　See Luxemburg, Rosa

Just, Ward (Swift) 1935- .... **CLC 4, 27**
　See also CA 25-28R; CANR 32; INT CANR-
　32

Justice, Donald (Rodney) 1925- .. **CLC 6, 19,**
　102; DAM POET
　See also CA 5-8R; CANR 26, 54; DLBY 83;
　INT CANR-26

Juvenal c. 55-c. 127 .... **CMLC 8**

Juvenis
　See Bourne, Randolph S(illiman)

Kacew, Romain 1914-1980
　See Gary, Romain
　See also CA 108; 102

Kadare, Ismail 1936- .... **CLC 52**
　See also CA 161

Kadohata, Cynthia .... **CLC 59**
　See also CA 140

Kafka, Franz 1883-1924**TCLC 2, 6, 13, 29, 47,**
　53; DA; DAB; DAC; DAM MST, NOV;
　SSC 29; WLC
　See also CA 105; 126; DLB 81; MTCW

Kahanovitsch, Pinkhes
　See Der Nister

Kahn, Roger 1927- .... **CLC 30**
　See also CA 25-28R; CANR 44; DLB 171;
　SATA 37

Kain, Saul
　See Sassoon, Siegfried (Lorraine)

Kaiser, Georg 1878-1945 .... **TCLC 9**
　See also CA 106; DLB 124

Kaletski, Alexander 1946- .... **CLC 39**
　See also CA 118; 143

Kalidasa fl. c. 400- .... **CMLC 9**

Kallman, Chester (Simon) 1921-1975 **CLC 2**
　See also CA 45-48; 53-56; CANR 3

Kaminsky, Melvin 1926-
　See Brooks, Mel
　See also CA 65-68; CANR 16

Kaminsky, Stuart M(elvin) 1934- ..... **CLC 59**
　See also CA 73-76; CANR 29, 53

Kane, Francis
　See Robbins, Harold

Kane, Paul
　See Simon, Paul (Frederick)

Kane, Wilson
　See Bloch, Robert (Albert)

Kanin, Garson 1912- .... **CLC 22**
　See also AITN 1; CA 5-8R; CANR 7; DLB 7

Kaniuk, Yoram 1930- .... **CLC 19**
　See also CA 134

Kant, Immanuel 1724-1804 .... **NCLC 27**
　See also DLB 94

Kantor, MacKinlay 1904-1977 .... **CLC 7**
　See also CA 61-64; 73-76; CANR 60; DLB 9,
　102

Kaplan, David Michael 1946- .... **CLC 50**

Kaplan, James 1951- .... **CLC 59**
　See also CA 135

Karageorge, Michael
　See Anderson, Poul (William)

Karamzin, Nikolai Mikhailovich 1766-1826
　NCLC 3
　See also DLB 150

Karapanou, Margarita 1946- .... **CLC 13**
　See also CA 101

Karinthy, Frigyes 1887-1938 .... **TCLC 47**

Karl, Frederick R(obert) 1927- .... **CLC 34**
　See also CA 5-8R; CANR 3, 44

Kastel, Warren
　See Silverberg, Robert

Kataev, Evgeny Petrovich 1903-1942
　See Petrov, Evgeny
　See also CA 120

Kataphusin
　See Ruskin, John

Katz, Steve 1935- .... **CLC 47**
　See also CA 25-28R; CAAS 14; CANR 12;
　DLBY 83

Kauffman, Janet 1945- .... **CLC 42**
　See also CA 117; CANR 43; DLBY 86

Kaufman, Bob (Garnell) 1925-1986 . **CLC 49**
　See also BW 1; CA 41-44R; 118; CANR 22;
　DLB 16, 41

Kaufman, George S. 1889-1961**CLC 38; DAM**
　DRAM
　See also CA 108; 93-96; DLB 7; INT 108

Kaufman, Sue .... **CLC 3, 8**
　See also Barondess, Sue K(aufman)

Kavafis, Konstantinos Petrou 1863-1933
　See Cavafy, C(onstantine) P(eter)
　See also CA 104

Kavan, Anna 1901-1968 .... **CLC 5, 13, 82**
　See also CA 5-8R; CANR 6, 57; MTCW

Kavanagh, Dan
　See Barnes, Julian (Patrick)

Kavanagh, Patrick (Joseph) 1904-1967 C L C
　22
　See also CA 123; 25-28R; DLB 15, 20; MTCW

Kawabata, Yasunari 1899-1972 **CLC 2, 5, 9,**
　18; DAM MULT; SSC 17
　See also CA 93-96; 33-36R; DLB 180

Kaye, M(ary) M(argaret) 1909- .... **CLC 28**
　See also CA 89-92; CANR 24, 60; MTCW;
　SATA 62

Kaye, Mollie
　See Kaye, M(ary) M(argaret)

Kaye-Smith, Sheila 1887-1956 .... **TCLC 20**
　See also CA 118; DLB 36

Kaymor, Patrice Maguilene
　See Senghor, Leopold Sedar

Kazan, Elia 1909- .... **CLC 6, 16, 63**
　See also CA 21-24R; CANR 32

Kazantzakis, Nikos 1883(?)-1957 **TCLC 2, 5,**
　33
　See also CA 105; 132; MTCW

Kazin, Alfred 1915- .... **CLC 34, 38**
　See also CA 1-4R; CAAS 7; CANR 1, 45; DLB
　67

Keane, Mary Nesta (Skrine) 1904-1996
　See Keane, Molly
　See also CA 108; 114; 151

Keane, Molly .... **CLC 31**
　See also Keane, Mary Nesta (Skrine)
　See also INT 114

Keates, Jonathan 19(?)- .... **CLC 34**

Keaton, Buster 1895-1966 .... **CLC 20**

Keats, John 1795-1821 . **NCLC 8; DA; DAB;**
　DAC; DAM MST, POET; PC 1; WLC
　See also CDBLB 1789-1832; DLB 96, 110

Keene, Donald 1922- .... **CLC 34**
　See also CA 1-4R; CANR 5

Keillor, Garrison .... **CLC 40**
　See also Keillor, Gary (Edward)
　See also AAYA 2; BEST 89:3; DLBY 87; SATA
　58

Keillor, Gary (Edward) 1942-
　See Keillor, Garrison
　See also CA 111; 117; CANR 36, 59; DAM
　POP; MTCW

Keith, Michael
　See Hubbard, L(afayette) Ron(ald)

Keller, Gottfried 1819-1890**NCLC 2; SSC 26**
　See also DLB 129

Kellerman, Jonathan 1949- ... **CLC 44; DAM**
　POP
　See also BEST 90:1; CA 106; CANR 29, 51;
　INT CANR-29

Kelley, William Melvin 1937- .... **CLC 22**
　See also BW 1; CA 77-80; CANR 27; DLB 33

Kellogg, Marjorie 1922- .... **CLC 2**
　See also CA 81-84

Kellow, Kathleen
　See Hibbert, Eleanor Alice Burford

Kelly, M(ilton) T(erry) 1947- .... **CLC 55**
　See also CA 97-100; CAAS 22; CANR 19, 43

Kelman, James 1946- .... **CLC 58, 86**
　See also CA 148

Kemal, Yashar 1923- .... **CLC 14, 29**
　See also CA 89-92; CANR 44

Kemble, Fanny 1809-1893 .... **NCLC 18**
　See also DLB 32

Kemelman, Harry 1908-1996 .... **CLC 2**
　See also AITN 1; CA 9-12R; 155; CANR 6;
　 DLB 28

Kempe, Margery 1373(?)-1440(?) .... **LC 6**
　See also DLB 146

Kempis, Thomas a 1380-1471 .... **LC 11**

Kendall, Henry 1839-1882 .... **NCLC 12**

Keneally, Thomas (Michael) 1935- **CLC 5, 8,**
　10, 14, 19, 27, 43; DAM NOV
　See also CA 85-88; CANR 10, 50; MTCW

Kennedy, Adrienne (Lita) 1931- ..... **CLC 66;**
　BLC; DAM MULT; DC 5
　See also BW 2; CA 103; CAAS 20; CABS 3;
　CANR 26, 53; DLB 38

Kennedy, John Pendleton 1795-1870**NCLC 2**
　See also DLB 3

Kennedy, Joseph Charles 1929-
　See Kennedy, X. J.
　See also CA 1-4R; CANR 4, 30, 40; SATA 14,
　86

Kennedy, William 1928- ..**CLC 6, 28, 34, 53;**
　DAM NOV
　See also AAYA 1; CA 85-88; CANR 14, 31;
　DLB 143; DLBY 85; INT CANR-31;
　MTCW; SATA 57

Kennedy, X. J. ....**CLC 8, 42**
　See also Kennedy, Joseph Charles
　See also CAAS 9; CLR 27; DLB 5; SAAS 22

Kenny, Maurice (Francis) 1929- ..... **CLC 87;**
　DAM MULT
　See also CA 144; CAAS 22; DLB 175; NNAL

Kent, Kelvin
　See Kuttner, Henry

Kenton, Maxwell
　See Southern, Terry

Kenyon, Robert O.
　See Kuttner, Henry

Kerouac, Jack .... **CLC 1, 2, 3, 5, 14, 29, 61**
　See also Kerouac, Jean-Louis Lebris de
　See also CDALB 1941-1968; DLB 2, 16; DLBD
　3; DLBY 95

Kerouac, Jean-Louis Lebris de 1922-1969
　See Kerouac, Jack
　See also AITN 1; CA 5-8R; 25-28R; CANR 26,
　54; DA; DAB; DAC; DAM MST, NOV,
　POET, POP; MTCW; WLC

Kerr, Jean 1923- .... **CLC 22**
　See also CA 5-8R; CANR 7; INT CANR-7

See also CA 85-88

Konwicki, Tadeusz 1926- .... **CLC 8, 28, 54**
See also CA 101; CAAS 9; CANR 39, 59;
MTCW

Koontz, Dean R(ay) 1945- ..... **CLC 78; DAM NOV, POP**
See also AAYA 9; BEST 89:3, 90:2; CA 108;
CANR 19, 36, 52; MTCW; SATA 92

Kopit, Arthur (Lee) 1937-**CLC 1, 18, 33; DAM DRAM**
See also AITN 1; CA 81-84; CABS 3; DLB 7;
MTCW

Kops, Bernard 1926- .... **CLC 4**
See also CA 5-8R; DLB 13

Kornbluth, C(yril) M. 1923-1958 .... **TCLC 8**
See also CA 105; 160; DLB 8

Korolenko, V. G.
See Korolenko, Vladimir Galaktionovich

Korolenko, Vladimir
See Korolenko, Vladimir Galaktionovich

Korolenko, Vladimir G.
See Korolenko, Vladimir Galaktionovich

Korolenko, Vladimir Galaktionovich 1853-1921 .... **TCLC 22**
See also CA 121

Korzybski, Alfred (Habdank Skarbek) 1879-1950 .... **TCLC 61**
See also CA 123; 160

Kosinski, Jerzy (Nikodem) 1933-1991**CLC 1, 2, 3, 6, 10, 15, 53, 70; DAM NOV**
See also CA 17-20R; 134; CANR 9, 46; DLB
2; DLBY 82; MTCW

Kostelanetz, Richard (Cory) 1940- .. **CLC 28**
See also CA 13-16R; CAAS 8; CANR 38

Kostrowitzki, Wilhelm Apollinaris de 1880-1918
See Apollinaire, Guillaume
See also CA 104

Kotlowitz, Robert 1924- .... **CLC 4**
See also CA 33-36R; CANR 36

Kotzebue, August (Friedrich Ferdinand) von 1761-1819 .... **NCLC 25**
See also DLB 94

Kotzwinkle, William 1938- ..... **CLC 5, 14, 35**
See also CA 45-48; CANR 3, 44; CLR 6; DLB
173; MAICYA; SATA 24, 70

Kowna, Stancy
See Szymborska, Wislawa

Kozol, Jonathan 1936- .... **CLC 17**
See also CA 61-64; CANR 16, 45

Kozoll, Michael 1940(?)- .... **CLC 35**

Kramer, Kathryn 19(?)- .... **CLC 34**

Kramer, Larry 1935-**CLC 42; DAM POP; DC 8**
See also CA 124; 126; CANR 60

Krasicki, Ignacy 1735-1801 .... **NCLC 8**

Krasinski, Zygmunt 1812-1859 .... **NCLC 4**

Kraus, Karl 1874-1936 .... **TCLC 5**
See also CA 104; DLB 118

Kreve (Mickevicius), Vincas 1882-1954**TCLC 27**

Kristeva, Julia 1941- .... **CLC 77**
See also CA 154

Kristofferson, Kris 1936- .... **CLC 26**
See also CA 104

Krizanc, John 1956- .... **CLC 57**

Krleza, Miroslav 1893-1981 .... **CLC 8**
See also CA 97-100; 105; CANR 50; DLB 147

Kroetsch, Robert 1927-**CLC 5, 23, 57; DAC; DAM POET**
See also CA 17-20R; CANR 8, 38; DLB 53;
MTCW

Kroetz, Franz

See Kroetz, Franz Xaver

Kroetz, Franz Xaver 1946- .... **CLC 41**
See also CA 130

Kroker, Arthur (W.) 1945- .... **CLC 77**
See also CA 161

Kropotkin, Peter (Aleksieevich) 1842-1921
TCLC 36
See also CA 119

Krotkov, Yuri 1917- .... **CLC 19**
See also CA 102

Krumb
See Crumb, R(obert)

Krumgold, Joseph (Quincy) 1908-1980 **C L C 12**
See also CA 9-12R; 101; CANR 7; MAICYA;
SATA 1, 48; SATA-Obit 23

Krumwitz
See Crumb, R(obert)

Krutch, Joseph Wood 1893-1970 ...... **CLC 24**
See also CA 1-4R; 25-28R; CANR 4; DLB 63

Krutzch, Gus
See Eliot, T(homas) S(tearns)

Krylov, Ivan Andreevich 1768(?)-1844**N C L C 1**
See also DLB 150

Kubin, Alfred (Leopold Isidor) 1877-1959
TCLC 23
See also CA 112; 149; DLB 81

Kubrick, Stanley 1928- .... **CLC 16**
See also CA 81-84; CANR 33; DLB 26

Kumin, Maxine (Winokur) 1925- **CLC 5, 13, 28; DAM POET; PC 15**
See also AITN 2; CA 1-4R; CAAS 8; CANR 1,
21; DLB 5; MTCW; SATA 12

Kundera, Milan 1929- . **CLC 4, 9, 19, 32, 68; DAM NOV; SSC 24**
See also AAYA 2; CA 85-88; CANR 19, 52;
MTCW

Kunene, Mazisi (Raymond) 1930- .... **CLC 85**
See also BW 1; CA 125; DLB 117

Kunitz, Stanley (Jasspon) 1905-**CLC 6, 11, 14; PC 19**
See also CA 41-44R; CANR 26, 57; DLB 48;
INT CANR-26; MTCW

Kunze, Reiner 1933- .... **CLC 10**
See also CA 93-96; DLB 75

Kuprin, Aleksandr Ivanovich 1870-1938
TCLC 5
See also CA 104

Kureishi, Hanif 1954(?)- .... **CLC 64**
See also CA 139

Kurosawa, Akira 1910-**CLC 16; DAM MULT**
See also AAYA 11; CA 101; CANR 46

Kushner, Tony 1957(?)-**CLC 81; DAM DRAM**
See also CA 144

Kuttner, Henry 1915-1958 .... **TCLC 10**
See also Vance, Jack
See also CA 107; 157; DLB 8

Kuzma, Greg 1944-............................... **CLC 7**
See also CA 33-36R

Kuzmin, Mikhail 1872(?)-1936 ...... **TCLC 40**

Kyd, Thomas 1558-1594**LC 22; DAM DRAM; DC 3**
See also DLB 62

Kyprianos, Iossif
See Samarakis, Antonis

La Bruyere, Jean de 1645-1696 .... **LC 17**

Lacan, Jacques (Marie Emile) 1901-1981
CLC 75
See also CA 121; 104

Laclos, Pierre Ambroise Francois Choderlos de 1741-1803 .... **NCLC 4**

La Colere, Francois

See Aragon, Louis

Lacolere, Francois
See Aragon, Louis

La Deshabilleuse
See Simenon, Georges (Jacques Christian)

Lady Gregory
See Gregory, Isabella Augusta (Persse)

Lady of Quality, A
See Bagnold, Enid

La Fayette, Marie (Madelaine Pioche de la Vergne Comtes 1634-1693 .... **LC 2**

Lafayette, Rene
See Hubbard, L(afayette) Ron(ald)

Laforgue, Jules 1860-1887**NCLC 5, 53; PC 14; SSC 20**

Lagerkvist, Paer (Fabian) 1891-1974 **CLC 7, 10, 13, 54; DAM DRAM, NOV**
See also Lagerkvist, Par
See also CA 85-88; 49-52; MTCW

Lagerkvist, Par .... **SSC 12**
See also Lagerkvist, Paer (Fabian)

Lagerloef, Selma (Ottiliana Lovisa) 1858-1940
TCLC 4, 36
See also Lagerlof, Selma (Ottiliana Lovisa)
See also CA 108; SATA 15

Lagerlof, Selma (Ottiliana Lovisa)
See Lagerloef, Selma (Ottiliana Lovisa)
See also CLR 7; SATA 15

La Guma, (Justin) Alex(ander) 1925-1985
CLC 19; DAM NOV
See also BW 1; CA 49-52; 118; CANR 25; DLB
117; MTCW

Laidlaw, A. K.
See Grieve, C(hristopher) M(urray)

Lainez, Manuel Mujica
See Mujica Lainez, Manuel
See also HW

Laing, R(onald) D(avid) 1927-1989 .. **CLC 95**
See also CA 107; 129; CANR 34; MTCW

Lamartine, Alphonse (Marie Louis Prat) de 1790-1869**NCLC 11; DAM POET; PC 16**

Lamb, Charles 1775-1834 ..... **NCLC 10; DA; DAB; DAC; DAM MST; WLC**
See also CDBLB 1789-1832; DLB 93, 107, 163;
SATA 17

Lamb, Lady Caroline 1785-1828 ... **NCLC 38**
See also DLB 116

Lamming, George (William) 1927- **CLC 2, 4, 66; BLC; DAM MULT**
See also BW 2; CA 85-88; CANR 26; DLB 125;
MTCW

L'Amour, Louis (Dearborn) 1908-1988 **C L C 25, 55; DAM NOV, POP**
See also AAYA 16; AITN 2; BEST 89:2; CA 1-
4R; 125; CANR 3, 25, 40; DLBY 80; MTCW

Lampedusa, Giuseppe (Tomasi) di 1896-1957
TCLC 13
See also Tomasi di Lampedusa, Giuseppe
See also DLB 177

Lampman, Archibald 1861-1899 ... **NCLC 25**
See also DLB 92

Lancaster, Bruce 1896-1963 .... **CLC 36**
See also CA 9-10; CAP 1; SATA 9

Lanchester, John .... **CLC 99**

Landau, Mark Alexandrovich
See Aldanov, Mark (Alexandrovich)

Landau-Aldanov, Mark Alexandrovich
See Aldanov, Mark (Alexandrovich)

Landis, Jerry
See Simon, Paul (Frederick)

Landis, John 1950- .... **CLC 26**
See also CA 112; 122

Landolfi, Tommaso 1908-1979 .... **CLC 11, 49**

See White, Patrick (Victor Martindale)

Martin du Gard, Roger 1881-1958 **TCLC 24**
See also CA 118; DLB 65

Martineau, Harriet 1802-1876 .... **NCLC 26**
See also DLB 21, 55, 159, 163, 166; YABC 2

Martines, Julia
See O'Faolain, Julia

Martinez, Enrique Gonzalez
See Gonzalez Martinez, Enrique

Martinez, Jacinto Benavente y
See Benavente (y Martinez), Jacinto

Martinez Ruiz, Jose 1873-1967
See Azorin; Ruiz, Jose Martinez
See also CA 93-96; HW

Martinez Sierra, Gregorio 1881-1947**TCLC 6**
See also CA 115

Martinez Sierra, Maria (de la O'LeJarraga)
1874-1974 .... **TCLC 6**
See also CA 115

Martinsen, Martin
See Follett, Ken(neth Martin)

Martinson, Harry (Edmund) 1904-1978**C L C 14**
See also CA 77-80; CANR 34

Marut, Ret
See Traven, B.

Marut, Robert
See Traven, B.

Marvell, Andrew 1621-1678**LC 4; DA; DAB; DAC; DAM MST, POET; PC 10; WLC**
See also CDBLB 1660-1789; DLB 131

Marx, Karl (Heinrich) 1818-1883 . **NCLC 17**
See also DLB 129

Masaoka Shiki .... **TCLC 18**
See also Masaoka Tsunenori

Masaoka Tsunenori 1867-1902
See Masaoka Shiki
See also CA 117

Masefield, John (Edward) 1878-1967**CLC 11, 47; DAM POET**
See also CA 19-20; 25-28R; CANR 33; CAP 2; CDBLB 1890-1914; DLB 10, 19, 153, 160; MTCW; SATA 19

Maso, Carole 19(?)- .... **CLC 44**

Mason, Bobbie Ann 1940-**CLC 28, 43, 82; SSC 4**
See also AAYA 5; CA 53-56; CANR 11, 31, 58; DLB 173; DLBY 87; INT CANR-31; MTCW

Mason, Ernst
See Pohl, Frederik

Mason, Lee W.
See Malzberg, Barry N(athaniel)

Mason, Nick 1945- .... **CLC 35**

Mason, Tally
See Derleth, August (William)

Mass, William
See Gibson, William

Masters, Edgar Lee 1868-1950 **TCLC 2, 25; DA; DAC; DAM MST, POET; PC 1; WLCS**
See also CA 104; 133; CDALB 1865-1917; DLB 54; MTCW

Masters, Hilary 1928- .... **CLC 48**
See also CA 25-28R; CANR 13, 47

Mastrosimone, William 19(?)- .... **CLC 36**

Mathe, Albert
See Camus, Albert

Mather, Cotton 1663-1728 .... **LC 38**
See also CDALB 1640-1865; DLB 24, 30, 140

Mather, Increase 1639-1723 .... **LC 38**
See also DLB 24

Matheson, Richard Burton 1926- ..... **CLC 37**

See also CA 97-100; DLB 8, 44; INT 97-100

Mathews, Harry 1930- .... **CLC 6, 52**
See also CA 21-24R; CAAS 6; CANR 18, 40

Mathews, John Joseph 1894-1979 .. **CLC 84; DAM MULT**
See also CA 19-20; 142; CANR 45; CAP 2; DLB 175; NNAL

Mathias, Roland (Glyn) 1915- .... **CLC 45**
See also CA 97-100; CANR 19, 41; DLB 27

Matsuo Basho 1644-1694 .... **PC 3**
See also DAM POET

Mattheson, Rodney
See Creasey, John

Matthews, Greg 1949- .... **CLC 45**
See also CA 135

Matthews, William 1942- .... **CLC 40**
See also CA 29-32R; CAAS 18; CANR 12, 57; DLB 5

Matthias, John (Edward) 1941- .... **CLC 9**
See also CA 33-36R; CANR 56

Matthiessen, Peter 1927-**CLC 5, 7, 11, 32, 64; DAM NOV**
See also AAYA 6; BEST 90:4; CA 9-12R; CANR 21, 50; DLB 6, 173; MTCW; SATA 27

Maturin, Charles Robert 1780(?)-1824**NCLC 6**
See also DLB 178

Matute (Ausejo), Ana Maria 1925- .. **CLC 11**
See also CA 89-92; MTCW

Maugham, W. S.
See Maugham, W(illiam) Somerset

Maugham, W(illiam) Somerset 1874-1965
CLC 1, 11, 15, 67, 93; DA; DAB; DAC; DAM DRAM, MST, NOV; SSC 8; WLC
See also CA 5-8R; 25-28R; CANR 40; CDBLB 1914-1945; DLB 10, 36, 77, 100, 162; MTCW; SATA 54

Maugham, William Somerset
See Maugham, W(illiam) Somerset

Maupassant, (Henri Rene Albert) Guy de 1850-1893**NCLC 1, 42; DA; DAB; DAC; DAM MST; SSC 1; WLC**
See also DLB 123

Maupin, Armistead 1944-**CLC 95; DAM POP**
See also CA 125; 130; CANR 58; INT 130

Maurhut, Richard
See Traven, B.

Mauriac, Claude 1914-1996 .... **CLC 9**
See also CA 89-92; 152; DLB 83

Mauriac, Francois (Charles) 1885-1970 **C L C 4, 9, 56; SSC 24**
See also CA 25-28; CAP 2; DLB 65; MTCW

Mavor, Osborne Henry 1888-1951
See Bridie, James
See also CA 104

Maxwell, William (Keepers, Jr.) 1908-**CLC 19**
See also CA 93-96; CANR 54; DLBY 80; INT 93-96

May, Elaine 1932- .... **CLC 16**
See also CA 124; 142; DLB 44

Mayakovski, Vladimir (Vladimirovich) 1893-1930 .... **TCLC 4, 18**
See also CA 104; 158

Mayhew, Henry 1812-1887 .... **NCLC 31**
See also DLB 18, 55

Mayle, Peter 1939(?)- .... **CLC 89**
See also CA 139

Maynard, Joyce 1953- .... **CLC 23**
See also CA 111; 129

Mayne, William (James Carter) 1928-**CLC 12**
See also AAYA 20; CA 9-12R; CANR 37; CLR 25; JRDA; MAICYA; SAAS 11; SATA 6, 68

Mayo, Jim
See L'Amour, Louis (Dearborn)

Maysles, Albert 1926- .... **CLC 16**
See also CA 29-32R

Maysles, David 1932- .... **CLC 16**

Mazer, Norma Fox 1931- .... **CLC 26**
See also AAYA 5; CA 69-72; CANR 12, 32; CLR 23; JRDA; MAICYA; SAAS 1; SATA 24, 67

Mazzini, Guiseppe 1805-1872 .... **NCLC 34**

McAuley, James Phillip 1917-1976 .. **CLC 45**
See also CA 97-100

McBain, Ed
See Hunter, Evan

McBrien, William Augustine 1930- .. **CLC 44**
See also CA 107

McCaffrey, Anne (Inez) 1926-**CLC 17; DAM NOV, POP**
See also AAYA 6; AITN 2; BEST 89:2; CA 25-28R; CANR 15, 35, 55; DLB 8; JRDA; MAICYA; MTCW; SAAS 11; SATA 8, 70

McCall, Nathan 1955(?)- .... **CLC 86**
See also CA 146

McCann, Arthur
See Campbell, John W(ood, Jr.)

McCann, Edson
See Pohl, Frederik

McCarthy, Charles, Jr. 1933-
See McCarthy, Cormac
See also CANR 42; DAM POP

McCarthy, Cormac 1933- **CLC 4, 57, 59, 101**
See also McCarthy, Charles, Jr.
See also DLB 6, 143

McCarthy, Mary (Therese) 1912-1989**CLC 1, 3, 5, 14, 24, 39, 59; SSC 24**
See also CA 5-8R; 129; CANR 16, 50; DLB 2; DLBY 81; INT CANR-16; MTCW

McCartney, (James) Paul 1942- **CLC 12, 35**
See also CA 146

McCauley, Stephen (D.) 1955- .... **CLC 50**
See also CA 141

McClure, Michael (Thomas) 1932-**CLC 6, 10**
See also CA 21-24R; CANR 17, 46; DLB 16

McCorkle, Jill (Collins) 1958- .... **CLC 51**
See also CA 121; DLBY 87

McCourt, James 1941- .... **CLC 5**
See also CA 57-60

McCoy, Horace (Stanley) 1897-1955**TCLC 28**
See also CA 108; 155; DLB 9

McCrae, John 1872-1918 .... **TCLC 12**
See also CA 109; DLB 92

McCreigh, James
See Pohl, Frederik

McCullers, (Lula) Carson (Smith) 1917-1967
CLC 1, 4, 10, 12, 48, 100; DA; DAB; DAC; DAM MST, NOV; SSC 9, 24; WLC
See also AAYA 21; CA 5-8R; 25-28R; CABS 1, 3; CANR 18; CDALB 1941-1968; DLB 2, 7, 173; MTCW; SATA 27

McCulloch, John Tyler
See Burroughs, Edgar Rice

McCullough, Colleen 1938(?)-**CLC 27; DAM NOV, POP**
See also CA 81-84; CANR 17, 46; MTCW

McDermott, Alice 1953- .... **CLC 90**
See also CA 109; CANR 40

McElroy, Joseph 1930- .... **CLC 5, 47**
See also CA 17-20R

McEwan, Ian (Russell) 1948- .... **CLC 13, 66; DAM NOV**
See also BEST 90:4; CA 61-64; CANR 14, 41; DLB 14; MTCW

McFadden, David 1940- .... **CLC 48**

See also CA 104; DLB 60; INT 104

McFarland, Dennis 1950- .... **CLC 65**

McGahern, John 1934- **CLC 5, 9, 48; SSC 17**
See also CA 17-20R; CANR 29; DLB 14;
MTCW

McGinley, Patrick (Anthony) 1937- . **CLC 41**
See also CA 120; 127; CANR 56; INT 127

McGinley, Phyllis 1905-1978 .... **CLC 14**
See also CA 9-12R; 77-80; CANR 19; DLB 11,
48; SATA 2, 44; SATA-Obit 24

McGinniss, Joe 1942- .... **CLC 32**
See also AITN 2; BEST 89:2; CA 25-28R;
CANR 26; INT CANR-26

McGivern, Maureen Daly
See Daly, Maureen

McGrath, Patrick 1950- .... **CLC 55**
See also CA 136

McGrath, Thomas (Matthew) 1916-1990**CLC
28, 59; DAM POET**
See also CA 9-12R; 132; CANR 6, 33; MTCW;
SATA 41; SATA-Obit 66

McGuane, Thomas (Francis III) 1939-**CLC 3,
7, 18, 45**
See also AITN 2; CA 49-52; CANR 5, 24, 49;
DLB 2; DLBY 80; INT CANR-24; MTCW

McGuckian, Medbh 1950- ..... **CLC 48; DAM
POET**
See also CA 143; DLB 40

McHale, Tom 1942(?)-1982 .... **CLC 3, 5**
See also AITN 1; CA 77-80; 106

McIlvanney, William 1936- .... **CLC 42**
See also CA 25-28R; CANR 61; DLB 14

McIlwraith, Maureen Mollie Hunter
See Hunter, Mollie
See also SATA 2

McInerney, Jay 1955- ... **CLC 34; DAM POP**
See also AAYA 18; CA 116; 123; CANR 45;
INT 123

McIntyre, Vonda N(eel) 1948- .... **CLC 18**
See also CA 81-84; CANR 17, 34; MTCW

McKay, Claude... **TCLC 7, 41; BLC; DAB; PC 2**
See also McKay, Festus Claudius
See also DLB 4, 45, 51, 117

McKay, Festus Claudius 1889-1948
See McKay, Claude
See also BW 1; CA 104; 124; DA; DAC; DAM
MST, MULT, NOV, POET; MTCW; WLC

McKuen, Rod 1933- .... **CLC 1, 3**
See also AITN 1; CA 41-44R; CANR 40

McLoughlin, R. B.
See Mencken, H(enry) L(ouis)

McLuhan, (Herbert) Marshall 1911-1980
CLC 37, 83
See also CA 9-12R; 102; CANR 12, 34, 61;
DLB 88; INT CANR-12; MTCW

McMillan, Terry (L.) 1951-**CLC 50, 61; DAM
MULT, NOV, POP**
See also AAYA 21; BW 2; CA 140; CANR 60

McMurtry, Larry (Jeff) 1936-**CLC 2, 3, 7, 11,
27, 44; DAM NOV, POP**
See also AAYA 15; AITN 2; BEST 89:2; CA 5-
8R; CANR 19, 43; CDALB 1968-1988; DLB
2, 143; DLBY 80, 87; MTCW

McNally, T. M. 1961- .... **CLC 82**

McNally, Terrence 1939- .... **CLC 4, 7, 41, 91;
DAM DRAM**
See also CA 45-48; CANR 2, 56; DLB 7

McNamer, Deirdre 1950- .... **CLC 70**

McNeile, Herman Cyril 1888-1937
See Sapper
See also DLB 77

McNickle, (William) D'Arcy 1904-1977 **C L C
89; DAM MULT**

See also CA 9-12R; 85-88; CANR 5, 45; DLB
175; NNAL; SATA-Obit 22

McPhee, John (Angus) 1931- .... **CLC 36**
See also BEST 90:1; CA 65-68; CANR 20, 46;
MTCW

McPherson, James Alan 1943-... **CLC 19, 77**
See also BW 1; CA 25-28R; CAAS 17; CANR
24; DLB 38; MTCW

McPherson, William (Alexander) 1933- **C L C
34**
See also CA 69-72; CANR 28; INT CANR-28

Mead, Margaret 1901-1978 .... **CLC 37**
See also AITN 1; CA 1-4R; 81-84; CANR 4;
MTCW; SATA-Obit 20

Meaker, Marijane (Agnes) 1927-
See Kerr, M. E.
See also CA 107; CANR 37; INT 107; JRDA;
MAICYA; MTCW; SATA 20, 61

Medoff, Mark (Howard) 1940- ... **CLC 6, 23;
DAM DRAM**
See also AITN 1; CA 53-56; CANR 5; DLB 7;
INT CANR-5

Medvedev, P. N.
See Bakhtin, Mikhail Mikhailovich

Meged, Aharon
See Megged, Aharon

Meged, Aron
See Megged, Aharon

Megged, Aharon 1920- .... **CLC 9**
See also CA 49-52; CAAS 13; CANR 1

Mehta, Ved (Parkash) 1934- .... **CLC 37**
See also CA 1-4R; CANR 2, 23; MTCW

Melanter
See Blackmore, R(ichard) D(oddridge)

Melikow, Loris
See Hofmannsthal, Hugo von

Melmoth, Sebastian
See Wilde, Oscar (Fingal O'Flahertie Wills)

Meltzer, Milton 1915- .... **CLC 26**
See also AAYA 8; CA 13-16R; CANR 38; CLR
13; DLB 61; JRDA; MAICYA; SAAS 1;
SATA 1, 50, 80

Melville, Herman 1819-1891**NCLC 3, 12, 29,
45, 49; DA; DAB; DAC; DAM MST, NOV;
SSC 1, 17; WLC**
See also CDALB 1640-1865; DLB 3, 74; SATA
59

Menander c. 342B.C.-c. 292B.C. ..... **CMLC 9;
DAM DRAM; DC 3**
See also DLB 176

Mencken, H(enry) L(ouis) 1880-1956 **T C L C
13**
See also CA 105; 125; CDALB 1917-1929;
DLB 11, 29, 63, 137; MTCW

Mendelsohn, Jane 1965(?)- .... **CLC 99**
See also CA 154

Mercer, David 1928-1980**CLC 5; DAM DRAM**
See also CA 9-12R; 102; CANR 23; DLB 13;
MTCW

Merchant, Paul
See Ellison, Harlan (Jay)

Meredith, George 1828-1909 . **TCLC 17, 43;
DAM POET**
See also CA 117; 153; CDBLB 1832-1890;
DLB 18, 35, 57, 159

Meredith, William (Morris) 1919-**CLC 4, 13,
22, 55; DAM POET**
See also CA 9-12R; CAAS 14; CANR 6, 40;
DLB 5

Merezhkovsky, Dmitry Sergeyevich 1865-1941
TCLC 29

Merimee, Prosper 1803-1870**NCLC 6, 65; SSC
7**

See also DLB 119

Merkin, Daphne 1954- .... **CLC 44**
See also CA 123

Merlin, Arthur
See Blish, James (Benjamin)

Merrill, James (Ingram) 1926-1995**CLC 2, 3,
6, 8, 13, 18, 34, 91; DAM POET**
See also CA 13-16R; 147; CANR 10, 49; DLB
5, 165; DLBY 85; INT CANR-10; MTCW

Merriman, Alex
See Silverberg, Robert

Merritt, E. B.
See Waddington, Miriam

Merton, Thomas 1915-1968**CLC 1, 3, 11, 34,
83; PC 10**
See also CA 5-8R; 25-28R; CANR 22, 53; DLB
48; DLBY 81; MTCW

Merwin, W(illiam) S(tanley) 1927- **CLC 1, 2,
3, 5, 8, 13, 18, 45, 88; DAM POET**
See also CA 13-16R; CANR 15, 51; DLB 5,
169; INT CANR-15; MTCW

Metcalf, John 1938- .... **CLC 37**
See also CA 113; DLB 60

Metcalf, Suzanne
See Baum, L(yman) Frank

Mew, Charlotte (Mary) 1870-1928 .. **TCLC 8**
See also CA 105; DLB 19, 135

Mewshaw, Michael 1943- .... **CLC 9**
See also CA 53-56; CANR 7, 47; DLBY 80

Meyer, June
See Jordan, June

Meyer, Lynn
See Slavitt, David R(ytman)

Meyer-Meyrink, Gustav 1868-1932
See Meyrink, Gustav
See also CA 117

Meyers, Jeffrey 1939-........................**CLC 39**
See also CA 73-76; CANR 54; DLB 111

Meynell, Alice (Christina Gertrude Thompson)
1847-1922 .... **TCLC 6**
See also CA 104; DLB 19, 98

Meyrink, Gustav .... **TCLC 21**
See also Meyer-Meyrink, Gustav
See also DLB 81

Michaels, Leonard 1933- **CLC 6, 25; SSC 16**
See also CA 61-64; CANR 21, 62; DLB 130;
MTCW

Michaux, Henri 1899-1984 .... **CLC 8, 19**
See also CA 85-88; 114

Micheaux, Oscar 1884-1951 .... **TCLC 76**
See also DLB 50

Michelangelo 1475-1564 .... **LC 12**

Michelet, Jules 1798-1874 .... **NCLC 31**

Michener, James A(lbert) 1907(?)-1997 **C L C
1, 5, 11, 29, 60; DAM NOV, POP**
See also AITN 1; BEST 90:1; CA 5-8R; 161;
CANR 21, 45; DLB 6; MTCW

Mickiewicz, Adam 1798-1855 .... **NCLC 3**

Middleton, Christopher 1926- .... **CLC 13**
See also CA 13-16R; CANR 29, 54; DLB 40

Middleton, Richard (Barham) 1882-1911
TCLC 56
See also DLB 156

Middleton, Stanley 1919- .... **CLC 7, 38**
See also CA 25-28R; CAAS 23; CANR 21, 46;
DLB 14

Middleton, Thomas 1580-1627 **LC 33; DAM
DRAM, MST; DC 5**
See also DLB 58

Migueis, Jose Rodrigues 1901- .... **CLC 10**

Mikszath, Kalman 1847-1910 .... **TCLC 31**

Miles, Jack .... **CLC 100**

Miles, Josephine (Louise) 1911-1985**CLC 1, 2,**

14, 34, 39; DAM POET
See also CA 1-4R; 116; CANR 2, 55; DLB 48

Militant
See Sandburg, Carl (August)

Mill, John Stuart 1806-1873 .... **NCLC 11, 58**
See also CDBLB 1832-1890; DLB 55

Millar, Kenneth 1915-1983 .... **CLC 14; DAM POP**
See also Macdonald, Ross
See also CA 9-12R; 110; CANR 16; DLB 2; DLBD 6; DLBY 83; MTCW

Millay, E. Vincent
See Millay, Edna St. Vincent

Millay, Edna St. Vincent 1892-1950 **TCLC 4, 49; DA; DAB; DAC; DAM MST, POET; PC 6; WLCS**
See also CA 104; 130; CDALB 1917-1929; DLB 45; MTCW

Miller, Arthur 1915- **CLC 1, 2, 6, 10, 15, 26, 47, 78; DA; DAB; DAC; DAM DRAM, MST; DC 1; WLC**
See also AAYA 15; AITN 1; CA 1-4R; CABS 3; CANR 2, 30, 54; CDALB 1941-1968; DLB 7; MTCW

Miller, Henry (Valentine) 1891-1980 **CLC 1, 2, 4, 9, 14, 43, 84; DA; DAB; DAC; DAM MST, NOV; WLC**
See also CA 9-12R; 97-100; CANR 33; CDALB 1929-1941; DLB 4, 9; DLBY 80; MTCW

Miller, Jason 1939(?)- .... **CLC 2**
See also AITN 1; CA 73-76; DLB 7

Miller, Sue 1943- .... **CLC 44; DAM POP**
See also BEST 90:3; CA 139; CANR 59; DLB 143

Miller, Walter M(ichael, Jr.) 1923- **CLC 4, 30**
See also CA 85-88; DLB 8

Millett, Kate 1934- .... **CLC 67**
See also AITN 1; CA 73-76; CANR 32, 53; MTCW

Millhauser, Steven 1943- .... **CLC 21, 54**
See also CA 110; 111; DLB 2; INT 111

Millin, Sarah Gertrude 1889-1968 ... **CLC 49**
See also CA 102; 93-96

Milne, A(lan) A(lexander) 1882-1956 **TCLC 6; DAB; DAC; DAM MST**
See also CA 104; 133; CLR 1, 26; DLB 10, 77, 100, 160; MAICYA; MTCW; YABC 1

Milner, Ron(ald) 1938- **CLC 56; BLC; DAM MULT**
See also AITN 1; BW 1; CA 73-76; CANR 24; DLB 38; MTCW

Milnes, Richard Monckton 1809-1885 **NCLC 61**
See also DLB 32, 184

Milosz, Czeslaw 1911- **CLC 5, 11, 22, 31, 56, 82; DAM MST, POET; PC 8; WLCS**
See also CA 81-84; CANR 23, 51; MTCW

Milton, John 1608-1674 ..... **LC 9; DA; DAB; DAC; DAM MST, POET; PC 19; WLC**
See also CDBLB 1660-1789; DLB 131, 151

Min, Anchee 1957- .... **CLC 86**
See also CA 146

Minehaha, Cornelius
See Wedekind, (Benjamin) Frank(lin)

Miner, Valerie 1947- .... **CLC 40**
See also CA 97-100; CANR 59

Minimo, Duca
See D'Annunzio, Gabriele

Minot, Susan 1956- .... **CLC 44**
See also CA 134

Minus, Ed 1938- .... **CLC 39**

Miranda, Javier
See Bioy Casares, Adolfo

Mirbeau, Octave 1848-1917 .... **TCLC 55**
See also DLB 123

Miro (Ferrer), Gabriel (Francisco Victor) 1879-1930 .... **TCLC 5**
See also CA 104

Mishima, Yukio 1925-1970 **CLC 2, 4, 6, 9, 27; DC 1; SSC 4**
See Hiraoka, Kimitake
See also DLB 182

Mistral, Frederic 1830-1914 .... **TCLC 51**
See also CA 122

Mistral, Gabriela .... **TCLC 2; HLC**
See also Godoy Alcayaga, Lucila

Mistry, Rohinton 1952- .... **CLC 71; DAC**
See also CA 141

Mitchell, Clyde
See Ellison, Harlan (Jay); Silverberg, Robert

Mitchell, James Leslie 1901-1935
See Gibbon, Lewis Grassic
See also CA 104; DLB 15

Mitchell, Joni 1943- .... **CLC 12**
See also CA 112

Mitchell, Joseph (Quincy) 1908-1996 **CLC 98**
See also CA 77-80; 152; DLBY 96

Mitchell, Margaret (Munnerlyn) 1900-1949 **TCLC 11; DAM NOV, POP**
See also CA 109; 125; CANR 55; DLB 9; MTCW

Mitchell, Peggy
See Mitchell, Margaret (Munnerlyn)

Mitchell, S(ilas) Weir 1829-1914 ... **TCLC 36**

Mitchell, W(illiam) O(rmond) 1914- **CLC 25; DAC; DAM MST**
See also CA 77-80; CANR 15, 43; DLB 88

Mitford, Mary Russell 1787-1855 ... **NCLC 4**
See also DLB 110, 116

Mitford, Nancy 1904-1973 .... **CLC 44**
See also CA 9-12R

Miyamoto, Yuriko 1899-1951 .... **TCLC 37**
See also DLB 180

Miyazawa Kenji 1896-1933 .... **TCLC 76**
See also CA 157

Mizoguchi, Kenji 1898-1956 .... **TCLC 72**

Mo, Timothy (Peter) 1950(?)- .... **CLC 46**
See also CA 117; MTCW

Modarressi, Taghi (M.) 1931- .... **CLC 44**
See also CA 121; 134; INT 134

Modiano, Patrick (Jean) 1945- .... **CLC 18**
See also CA 85-88; CANR 17, 40; DLB 83

Moerck, Paal
See Roelvaag, O(le) E(dvart)

Mofolo, Thomas (Mokopu) 1875(?)-1948 **TCLC 22; BLC; DAM MULT**
See also CA 121; 153

Mohr, Nicholasa 1935- **CLC 12; DAM MULT; HLC**
See also AAYA 8; CA 49-52; CANR 1, 32; CLR 22; DLB 145; HW; JRDA; SAAS 8; SATA 8

Mojtabai, A(nn) G(race) 1938- **CLC 5, 9, 15, 29**
See also CA 85-88

Moliere 1622-1673 . **LC 28; DA; DAB; DAC; DAM DRAM, MST; WLC**

Molin, Charles
See Mayne, William (James Carter)

Molnar, Ferenc 1878-1952 .. **TCLC 20; DAM DRAM**
See also CA 109; 153

Momaday, N(avarre) Scott 1934- **CLC 2, 19, 85, 95; DA; DAB; DAC; DAM MST, MULT, NOV, POP; WLCS**
See also AAYA 11; CA 25-28R; CANR 14, 34; DLB 143, 175; INT CANR-14; MTCW;

NNAL; SATA 48; SATA-Brief 30

Monette, Paul 1945-1995 .... **CLC 82**
See also CA 139; 147

Monroe, Harriet 1860-1936 .... **TCLC 12**
See also CA 109; DLB 54, 91

Monroe, Lyle
See Heinlein, Robert A(nson)

Montagu, Elizabeth 1917- .... **NCLC 7**
See also CA 9-12R

Montagu, Mary (Pierrepont) Wortley 1689-1762 .... **LC 9; PC 16**
See also DLB 95, 101

Montagu, W. H.
See Coleridge, Samuel Taylor

Montague, John (Patrick) 1929- **CLC 13, 46**
See also CA 9-12R; CANR 9; DLB 40; MTCW

Montaigne, Michel (Eyquem) de 1533-1592 **LC 8; DA; DAB; DAC; DAM MST; WLC**

Montale, Eugenio 1896-1981 **CLC 7, 9, 18; PC 13**
See also CA 17-20R; 104; CANR 30; DLB 114; MTCW

Montesquieu, Charles-Louis de Secondat 1689-1755 .... **LC 7**

Montgomery, (Robert) Bruce 1921-1978
See Crispin, Edmund
See also CA 104

Montgomery, L(ucy) M(aud) 1874-1942 **TCLC 51; DAC; DAM MST**
See also AAYA 12; CA 108; 137; CLR 8; DLB 92; DLBD 14; JRDA; MAICYA; YABC 1

Montgomery, Marion H., Jr. 1925- .... **CLC 7**
See also AITN 1; CA 1-4R; CANR 3, 48; DLB 6

Montgomery, Max
See Davenport, Guy (Mattison, Jr.)

Montherlant, Henry (Milon) de 1896-1972 **CLC 8, 19; DAM DRAM**
See also CA 85-88; 37-40R; DLB 72; MTCW

Monty Python
See Chapman, Graham; Cleese, John (Marwood); Gilliam, Terry (Vance); Idle, Eric; Jones, Terence Graham Parry; Palin, Michael (Edward)
See also AAYA 7

Moodie, Susanna (Strickland) 1803-1885 **NCLC 14**
See also DLB 99

Mooney, Edward 1951-
See Mooney, Ted
See also CA 130

Mooney, Ted .... **CLC 25**
See also Mooney, Edward

Moorcock, Michael (John) 1939- **CLC 5, 27, 58**
See also CA 45-48; CAAS 5; CANR 2, 17, 38; DLB 14; MTCW; SATA 93

Moore, Brian 1921- **CLC 1, 3, 5, 7, 8, 19, 32, 90; DAB; DAC; DAM MST**
See also CA 1-4R; CANR 1, 25, 42; MTCW

Moore, Edward
See Muir, Edwin

Moore, George Augustus 1852-1933 **TCLC 7; SSC 19**
See also CA 104; DLB 10, 18, 57, 135

Moore, Lorrie .... **CLC 39, 45, 68**
See also Moore, Marie Lorena

Moore, Marianne (Craig) 1887-1972 **CLC 1, 2, 4, 8, 10, 13, 19, 47; DA; DAB; DAC; DAM MST, POET; PC 4; WLCS**
See also CA 1-4R; 33-36R; CANR 3, 61; CDALB 1929-1941; DLB 45; DLBD 7; MTCW; SATA 20

Moore, Marie Lorena 1957-

See Erdrich, Louise
Northrup, B. A.
　　See Hubbard, L(afayette) Ron(ald)
North Staffs
　　See Hulme, T(homas) E(rnest)
Norton, Alice Mary
　　See Norton, Andre
　　See also MAICYA; SATA 1, 43
Norton, Andre 1912- .... **CLC 12**
　　See also Norton, Alice Mary
　　See also AAYA 14; CA 1-4R; CANR 2, 31; DLB
　　8, 52; JRDA; MTCW; SATA 91
Norton, Caroline 1808-1877 .... **NCLC 47**
　　See also DLB 21, 159
Norway, Nevil Shute 1899-1960
　　See Shute, Nevil
　　See also CA 102; 93-96
Norwid, Cyprian Kamil 1821-1883 **NCLC 17**
Nosille, Nabrah
　　See Ellison, Harlan (Jay)
Nossack, Hans Erich 1901-1978 .... **CLC 6**
　　See also CA 93-96; 85-88; DLB 69
Nostradamus 1503-1566 .... **LC 27**
Nosu, Chuji
　　See Ozu, Yasujiro
Notenburg, Eleanora (Genrikhovna) von
　　See Guro, Elena
Nova, Craig 1945- .... **CLC 7, 31**
　　See also CA 45-48; CANR 2, 53
Novak, Joseph
　　See Kosinski, Jerzy (Nikodem)
Novalis 1772-1801 .... **NCLC 13**
　　See also DLB 90
Novis, Emile
　　See Weil, Simone (Adolphine)
Nowlan, Alden (Albert) 1933-1983 **CLC 15;**
　　DAC; DAM MST
　　See also CA 9-12R; CANR 5; DLB 53
Noyes, Alfred 1880-1958 .... **TCLC 7**
　　See also CA 104; DLB 20
Nunn, Kem .... **CLC 34**
　　See also CA 159
Nye, Robert 1939- .. **CLC 13, 42; DAM NOV**
　　See also CA 33-36R; CANR 29; DLB 14;
　　MTCW; SATA 6
Nyro, Laura 1947- .... **CLC 17**
Oates, Joyce Carol 1938- **CLC 1, 2, 3, 6, 9, 11,**
　　15, 19, 33, 52; DA; DAB; DAC; DAM MST,
　　NOV, POP; SSC 6; WLC
　　See also AAYA 15; AITN 1; BEST 89:2; CA 5-
　　8R; CANR 25, 45; CDALB 1968-1988; DLB
　　2, 5, 130; DLBY 81; INT CANR-25; MTCW
O'Brien, Darcy 1939- .... **CLC 11**
　　See also CA 21-24R; CANR 8, 59
O'Brien, E. G.
　　See Clarke, Arthur C(harles)
O'Brien, Edna 1936- **CLC 3, 5, 8, 13, 36, 65;**
　　DAM NOV; SSC 10
　　See also CA 1-4R; CANR 6, 41; CDBLB 1960
　　to Present; DLB 14; MTCW
O'Brien, Fitz-James 1828-1862 ..... **NCLC 21**
　　See also DLB 74
O'Brien, Flann .... **CLC 1, 4, 5, 7, 10, 47**
　　See also O Nuallain, Brian
O'Brien, Richard 1942- .... **CLC 17**
　　See also CA 124
O'Brien, (William) Tim(othy) 1946- . **CLC 7,**
　　19, 40, 103; DAM POP
　　See also AAYA 16; CA 85-88; CANR 40, 58;
　　DLB 152; DLBD 9; DLBY 80
Obstfelder, Sigbjoern 1866-1900 ... **TCLC 23**
　　See also CA 123
O'Casey, Sean 1880-1964 **CLC 1, 5, 9, 11, 15,**

88; DAB; DAC; DAM DRAM, MST;
WLCS
　　See also CA 89-92; CANR 62; CDBLB 1914-
　　1945; DLB 10; MTCW
O'Cathasaigh, Sean
　　See O'Casey, Sean
Ochs, Phil 1940-1976 .... **CLC 17**
　　See also CA 65-68
O'Connor, Edwin (Greene) 1918-1968 **CLC 14**
　　See also CA 93-96; 25-28R
O'Connor, (Mary) Flannery 1925-1964 **C L C**
　　1, 2, 3, 6, 10, 13, 15, 21, 66, 104; DA; DAB;
　　DAC; DAM MST, NOV; SSC 1, 23; WLC
　　See also AAYA 7; CA 1-4R; CANR 3, 41;
　　CDALB 1941-1968; DLB 2, 152; DLBD 12;
　　DLBY 80; MTCW
O'Connor, Frank .... **CLC 23; SSC 5**
　　See also O'Donovan, Michael John
　　See also DLB 162
O'Dell, Scott 1898-1989 .... **CLC 30**
　　See also AAYA 3; CA 61-64; 129; CANR 12,
　　30; CLR 1, 16; DLB 52; JRDA; MAICYA;
　　SATA 12, 60
Odets, Clifford 1906-1963 **CLC 2, 28, 98; DAM**
　　DRAM; DC 6
　　See also CA 85-88; CANR 62; DLB 7, 26;
　　MTCW
O'Doherty, Brian 1934- .... **CLC 76**
　　See also CA 105
O'Donnell, K. M.
　　See Malzberg, Barry N(athaniel)
O'Donnell, Lawrence
　　See Kuttner, Henry
O'Donovan, Michael John 1903-1966 **CLC 14**
　　See also O'Connor, Frank
　　See also CA 93-96
Oe, Kenzaburo 1935- **CLC 10, 36, 86; DAM**
　　NOV; SSC 20
　　See also CA 97-100; CANR 36, 50; DLB 182;
　　DLBY 94; MTCW
O'Faolain, Julia 1932- .... **CLC 6, 19, 47**
　　See also CA 81-84; CAAS 2; CANR 12, 61;
　　DLB 14; MTCW
O'Faolain, Sean 1900-1991 **CLC 1, 7, 14, 32,**
　　70; SSC 13
　　See also CA 61-64; 134; CANR 12; DLB 15,
　　162; MTCW
O'Flaherty, Liam 1896-1984 **CLC 5, 34; SSC 6**
　　See also CA 101; 113; CANR 35; DLB 36, 162;
　　DLBY 84; MTCW
Ogilvy, Gavin
　　See Barrie, J(ames) M(atthew)
O'Grady, Standish (James) 1846-1928 **T C L C**
　　5
　　See also CA 104; 157
O'Grady, Timothy 1951- .... **CLC 59**
　　See also CA 138
O'Hara, Frank 1926-1966 . **CLC 2, 5, 13, 78;**
　　DAM POET
　　See also CA 9-12R; 25-28R; CANR 33; DLB
　　5, 16; MTCW
O'Hara, John (Henry) 1905-1970 **CLC 1, 2, 3,**
　　6, 11, 42; DAM NOV; SSC 15
　　See also CA 5-8R; 25-28R; CANR 31, 60;
　　CDALB 1929-1941; DLB 9, 86; DLBD 2;
　　MTCW
O Hehir, Diana 1922- .... **CLC 41**
　　See also CA 93-96
Okigbo, Christopher (Ifenayichukwu) 1932-
　　1967 .... **CLC 25, 84; BLC; DAM MULT,**
　　POET; PC 7
　　See also BW 1; CA 77-80; DLB 125; MTCW
Okri, Ben 1959- .... **CLC 87**

See also BW 2; CA 130; 138; DLB 157; INT
138
Olds, Sharon 1942- .... **CLC 32, 39, 85; DAM**
　　POET
　　See also CA 101; CANR 18, 41; DLB 120
Oldstyle, Jonathan
　　See Irving, Washington
Olesha, Yuri (Karlovich) 1899-1960 .. **CLC 8**
　　See also CA 85-88
Oliphant, Laurence 1829(?)-1888 .. **NCLC 47**
　　See also DLB 18, 166
Oliphant, Margaret (Oliphant Wilson) 1828-
　　1897 .... **NCLC 11, 61; SSC 25**
　　See also DLB 18, 159
Oliver, Mary 1935- .... **CLC 19, 34, 98**
　　See also CA 21-24R; CANR 9, 43; DLB 5
Olivier, Laurence (Kerr) 1907-1989 . **CLC 20**
　　See also CA 111; 150; 129
Olsen, Tillie 1913- **CLC 4, 13; DA; DAB; DAC;**
　　DAM MST; SSC 11
　　See also CA 1-4R; CANR 1, 43; DLB 28; DLBY
　　80; MTCW
Olson, Charles (John) 1910-1970 **CLC 1, 2, 5,**
　　6, 9, 11, 29; DAM POET; PC 19
　　See also CA 13-16; 25-28R; CABS 2; CANR
　　35, 61; CAP 1; DLB 5, 16; MTCW
Olson, Toby 1937- .... **CLC 28**
　　See also CA 65-68; CANR 9, 31
Olyesha, Yuri
　　See Olesha, Yuri (Karlovich)
Ondaatje, (Philip) Michael 1943- **CLC 14, 29,**
　　51, 76; DAB; DAC; DAM MST
　　See also CA 77-80; CANR 42; DLB 60
Oneal, Elizabeth 1934-
　　See Oneal, Zibby
　　See also CA 106; CANR 28; MAICYA; SATA
　　30, 82
Oneal, Zibby .... **CLC 30**
　　See also Oneal, Elizabeth
　　See also AAYA 5; CLR 13; JRDA
O'Neill, Eugene (Gladstone) 1888-1953 **TCLC**
　　1, 6, 27, 49; DA; DAB; DAC; DAM DRAM,
　　MST; WLC
　　See also AITN 1; CA 110; 132; CDALB 1929-
　　1941; DLB 7; MTCW
Onetti, Juan Carlos 1909-1994 ... **CLC 7, 10,**
　　DAM MULT, NOV; SSC 23
　　See also CA 85-88; 145; CANR 32; DLB 113;
　　HW; MTCW
O Nuallain, Brian 1911-1966
　　See O'Brien, Flann
　　See also CA 21-22; 25-28R; CAP 2
Opie, Amelia 1769-1853 .... **NCLC 65**
　　See also DLB 116, 159
Oppen, George 1908-1984 ...... **CLC 7, 13, 34**
　　See also CA 13-16R; 113; CANR 8; DLB 5,
　　165
Oppenheim, E(dward) Phillips 1866-1946
　　TCLC 45
　　See also CA 111; DLB 70
Origen c. 185-c. 254 .... **CMLC 19**
Orlovitz, Gil 1918-1973 .... **CLC 22**
　　See also CA 77-80; 45-48; DLB 2, 5
Orris
　　See Ingelow, Jean
Ortega y Gasset, Jose 1883-1955 .... **TCLC 9;**
　　DAM MULT; HLC
　　See also CA 106; 130; HW; MTCW
Ortese, Anna Maria 1914- .... **CLC 89**
　　See also DLB 177
Ortiz, Simon J(oseph) 1941- .. **CLC 45; DAM**
　　MULT, POET; PC 17
　　See also CA 134; DLB 120, 175; NNAL

Orton, Joe .... **CLC 4, 13, 43; DC 3**
    See also Orton, John Kingsley
    See also CDBLB 1960 to Present; DLB 13
Orton, John Kingsley 1933-1967
    See Orton, Joe
    See also CA 85-88; CANR 35; DAM DRAM;
        MTCW
Orwell, George . **TCLC 2, 6, 15, 31, 51; DAB;
    WLC**
    See also Blair, Eric (Arthur)
    See also CDBLB 1945-1960; DLB 15, 98
Osborne, David
    See Silverberg, Robert
Osborne, George
    See Silverberg, Robert
Osborne, John (James) 1929-1994 **CLC 1, 2, 5,
    11, 45; DA; DAB; DAC; DAM DRAM,
    MST; WLC**
    See also CA 13-16R; 147; CANR 21, 56;
        CDBLB 1945-1960; DLB 13; MTCW
Osborne, Lawrence 1958- .... **CLC 50**
Oshima, Nagisa 1932- .... **CLC 20**
    See also CA 116; 121
Oskison, John Milton 1874-1947 .. **TCLC 35;
    DAM MULT**
    See also CA 144; DLB 175; NNAL
Ossoli, Sarah Margaret (Fuller marchesa d')
        1810-1850
    See Fuller, Margaret
    See also SATA 25
Ostrovsky, Alexander 1823-1886 **NCLC 30, 57**
Otero, Blas de 1916-1979 .... **CLC 11**
    See also CA 89-92; DLB 134
Otto, Whitney 1955- .... **CLC 70**
    See also CA 140
Ouida .... **TCLC 43**
    See also De La Ramee, (Marie) Louise
    See also DLB 18, 156
Ousmane, Sembene 1923- .... **CLC 66; BLC**
    See also BW 1; CA 117; 125; MTCW
Ovid 43B.C.-18(?) **CMLC 7; DAM POET; PC
    2**
Owen, Hugh
    See Faust, Frederick (Schiller)
Owen, Wilfred (Edward Salter) 1893-1918
    **TCLC 5, 27; DA; DAB; DAC; DAM MST,
    POET; PC 19; WLC**
    See also CA 104; 141; CDBLB 1914-1945;
        DLB 20
Owens, Rochelle 1936- .... **CLC 8**
    See also CA 17-20R; CAAS 2; CANR 39
Oz, Amos 1939- **CLC 5, 8, 11, 27, 33, 54; DAM
    NOV**
    See also CA 53-56; CANR 27, 47; MTCW
Ozick, Cynthia 1928- **CLC 3, 7, 28, 62; DAM
    NOV, POP; SSC 15**
    See also BEST 90:1; CA 17-20R; CANR 23,
        58; DLB 28, 152; DLBY 82; INT CANR-
        23; MTCW
Ozu, Yasujiro 1903-1963 .... **CLC 16**
    See also CA 112
Pacheco, C.
    See Pessoa, Fernando (Antonio Nogueira)
Pa Chin .... **CLC 18**
    See also Li Fei-kan
Pack, Robert 1929- .... **CLC 13**
    See also CA 1-4R; CANR 3, 44; DLB 5
Padgett, Lewis
    See Kuttner, Henry
Padilla (Lorenzo), Heberto 1932- ..... **CLC 38**
    See also AITN 1; CA 123; 131; HW
Page, Jimmy 1944- .... **CLC 12**
Page, Louise 1955- .... **CLC 40**

See also CA 140
Page, P(atricia) K(athleen) 1916- **CLC 7, 18;
    DAC; DAM MST; PC 12**
    See also CA 53-56; CANR 4, 22; DLB 68;
        MTCW
Page, Thomas Nelson 1853-1922 .... **SSC 23**
    See also CA 118; DLB 12, 78; DLBD 13
Pagels, Elaine Hiesey 1943- .... **CLC 104**
    See also CA 45-48; CANR 2, 24, 51
Paget, Violet 1856-1935
    See Lee, Vernon
    See also CA 104
Paget-Lowe, Henry
    See Lovecraft, H(oward) P(hillips)
Paglia, Camille (Anna) 1947- .... **CLC 68**
    See also CA 140
Paige, Richard
    See Koontz, Dean R(ay)
Paine, Thomas 1737-1809 .... **NCLC 62**
    See also CDALB 1640-1865; DLB 31, 43, 73,
        158
Pakenham, Antonia
    See Fraser, (Lady) Antonia (Pakenham)
Palamas, Kostes 1859-1943 .... **TCLC 5**
    See also CA 105
Palazzeschi, Aldo 1885-1974 .... **CLC 11**
    See also CA 89-92; 53-56; DLB 114
Paley, Grace 1922- **CLC 4, 6, 37; DAM POP;
    SSC 8**
    See also CA 25-28R; CANR 13, 46; DLB 28;
        INT CANR-13; MTCW
Palin, Michael (Edward) 1943- .... **CLC 21**
    See also Monty Python
    See also CA 107; CANR 35; SATA 67
Palliser, Charles 1947- .... **CLC 65**
    See also CA 136
Palma, Ricardo 1833-1919 .... **TCLC 29**
Pancake, Breece Dexter 1952-1979
    See Pancake, Breece D'J
    See also CA 123; 109
Pancake, Breece D'J .... **CLC 29**
    See also Pancake, Breece Dexter
    See also DLB 130
Panko, Rudy
    See Gogol, Nikolai (Vasilyevich)
Papadiamantis, Alexandros 1851-1911 **T C L C
    29**
Papadiamantopoulos, Johannes 1856-1910
    See Moreas, Jean
    See also CA 117
Papini, Giovanni 1881-1956 .... **TCLC 22**
    See also CA 121
Paracelsus 1493-1541 .... **LC 14**
    See also DLB 179
Parasol, Peter
    See Stevens, Wallace
Pareto, Vilfredo 1848-1923 .... **TCLC 69**
Parfenie, Maria
    See Codrescu, Andrei
Parini, Jay (Lee) 1948- .... **CLC 54**
    See also CA 97-100; CAAS 16; CANR 32
Park, Jordan
    See Kornbluth, C(yril) M.; Pohl, Frederik
Park, Robert E(zra) 1864-1944 ...... **TCLC 73**
    See also CA 122
Parker, Bert
    See Ellison, Harlan (Jay)
Parker, Dorothy (Rothschild) 1893-1967 **C L C
    15, 68; DAM POET; SSC 2**
    See also CA 19-20; 25-28R; CAP 2; DLB 11,
        45, 86; MTCW
Parker, Robert B(rown) 1932- **CLC 27; DAM
    NOV, POP**

See also BEST 89:4; CA 49-52; CANR 1, 26,
    52; INT CANR-26; MTCW
Parkin, Frank 1940- .... **CLC 43**
    See also CA 147
Parkman, Francis, Jr. 1823-1893 .. **NCLC 12**
    See also DLB 1, 30
Parks, Gordon (Alexander Buchanan) 1912-
    CLC 1, 16; BLC; DAM MULT
    See also AITN 2; BW 2; CA 41-44R; CANR
        26; DLB 33; SATA 8
Parmenides c. 515B.C.-c. 450B.C. **CMLC 22**
    See also DLB 176
Parnell, Thomas 1679-1718 .... **LC 3**
    See also DLB 94
Parra, Nicanor 1914- ...... **CLC 2, 102; DAM
    MULT; HLC**
    See also CA 85-88; CANR 32; HW; MTCW
Parrish, Mary Frances
    See Fisher, M(ary) F(rances) K(ennedy)
Parson
    See Coleridge, Samuel Taylor
Parson Lot
    See Kingsley, Charles
Partridge, Anthony
    See Oppenheim, E(dward) Phillips
Pascal, Blaise 1623-1662 .... **LC 35**
Pascoli, Giovanni 1855-1912 .... **TCLC 45**
Pasolini, Pier Paolo 1922-1975 . **CLC 20, 37,
    106; PC 17**
    See also CA 93-96; 61-64; DLB 128, 177;
        MTCW
Pasquini
    See Silone, Ignazio
Pastan, Linda (Olenik) 1932- **CLC 27; DAM
    POET**
    See also CA 61-64; CANR 18, 40, 61; DLB 5
Pasternak, Boris (Leonidovich) 1890-1960
    **CLC 7, 10, 18, 63; DA; DAB; DAC; DAM
    MST, NOV, POET; PC 6; WLC**
    See also CA 127; 116; MTCW
Patchen, Kenneth 1911-1972 ... **CLC 1, 2, 18;
    DAM POET**
    See also CA 1-4R; 33-36R; CANR 3, 35; DLB
        16, 48; MTCW
Pater, Walter (Horatio) 1839-1894 .. **NCLC 7**
    See also CDBLB 1832-1890; DLB 57, 156
Paterson, A(ndrew) B(arton) 1864-1941
    TCLC 32
    See also CA 155
Paterson, Katherine (Womeldorf) 1932- **C L C
    12, 30**
    See also AAYA 1; CA 21-24R; CANR 28, 59;
        CLR 7; DLB 52; JRDA; MAICYA; MTCW;
        SATA 13, 53, 92
Patmore, Coventry Kersey Dighton 1823-1896
    NCLC 9
    See also DLB 35, 98
Paton, Alan (Stewart) 1903-1988 **CLC 4, 10,
    25, 55, 106; DA; DAB; DAC; DAM MST,
    NOV; WLC**
    See also CA 13-16; 125; CANR 22; CAP 1;
        MTCW; SATA 11; SATA-Obit 56
Paton Walsh, Gillian 1937-
    See Walsh, Jill Paton
    See also CANR 38; JRDA; MAICYA; SAAS 3;
        SATA 4, 72
Paulding, James Kirke 1778-1860 ... **NCLC 2**
    See also DLB 3, 59, 74
Paulin, Thomas Neilson 1949-
    See Paulin, Tom
    See also CA 123; 128
Paulin, Tom .... **CLC 37**
    See also Paulin, Thomas Neilson

See also DLB 40
Paustovsky, Konstantin (Georgievich) 1892-
1968 .... **CLC 40**
See also CA 93-96; 25-28R
Pavese, Cesare 1908-1950 ... **TCLC 3; PC 13;
SSC 19**
See also CA 104; DLB 128, 177
Pavic, Milorad 1929- .... **CLC 60**
See also CA 136; DLB 181
Payne, Alan
See Jakes, John (William)
Paz, Gil
See Lugones, Leopoldo
Paz, Octavio 1914-**CLC 3, 4, 6, 10, 19, 51, 65;
DA; DAB; DAC; DAM MST, MULT,
POET; HLC; PC 1; WLC**
See also CA 73-76; CANR 32; DLBY 90; HW;
MTCW
p'Bitek, Okot 1931-1982**CLC 96; BLC; DAM
MULT**
See also BW 2; CA 124; 107; DLB 125; MTCW
Peacock, Molly 1947- .... **CLC 60**
See also CA 103; CAAS 21; CANR 52; DLB
120
Peacock, Thomas Love 1785-1866. **NCLC 22**
See also DLB 96, 116
Peake, Mervyn 1911-1968 .... **CLC 7, 54**
See also CA 5-8R; 25-28R; CANR 3; DLB 15,
160; MTCW; SATA 23
Pearce, Philippa .... **CLC 21**
See also Christie, (Ann) Philippa
See also CLR 9; DLB 161; MAICYA; SATA 1,
67
Pearl, Eric
See Elman, Richard
Pearson, T(homas) R(eid) 1956- .... **CLC 39**
See also CA 120; 130; INT 130
Peck, Dale 1967- .... **CLC 81**
See also CA 146
Peck, John 1941- .... **CLC 3**
See also CA 49-52; CANR 3
Peck, Richard (Wayne) 1934- .... **CLC 21**
See also AAYA 1; CA 85-88; CANR 19, 38;
CLR 15; INT CANR-19; JRDA; MAICYA;
SAAS 2; SATA 18, 55
Peck, Robert Newton 1928- ..... **CLC 17; DA;
DAC; DAM MST**
See also AAYA 3; CA 81-84; CANR 31; CLR
45; JRDA; MAICYA; SAAS 1; SATA 21, 62
Peckinpah, (David) Sam(uel) 1925-1984**C L C
20**
See also CA 109; 114
Pedersen, Knut 1859-1952
See Hamsun, Knut
See also CA 104; 119; MTCW
Peeslake, Gaffer
See Durrell, Lawrence (George)
Peguy, Charles Pierre 1873-1914 .. **TCLC 10**
See also CA 107
Pena, Ramon del Valle y
See Valle-Inclan, Ramon (Maria) del
Pendennis, Arthur Esquir
See Thackeray, William Makepeace
Penn, William 1644-1718 .... **LC 25**
See also DLB 24
PEPECE
See Prado (Calvo), Pedro
Pepys, Samuel 1633-1703 **LC 11; DA; DAB;
DAC; DAM MST; WLC**
See also CDBLB 1660-1789; DLB 101
Percy, Walker 1916-1990**CLC 2, 3, 6, 8, 14, 18,
47, 65; DAM NOV, POP**
See also CA 1-4R; 131; CANR 1, 23; DLB 2;

DLBY 80, 90; MTCW
Perec, Georges 1936-1982 .... **CLC 56**
See also CA 141; DLB 83
Pereda (y Sanchez de Porrua), Jose Maria de
1833-1906 .... **TCLC 16**
See also CA 117
Pereda y Porrua, Jose Maria de
See Pereda (y Sanchez de Porrua), Jose Maria
de
Peregoy, George Weems
See Mencken, H(enry) L(ouis)
Perelman, S(idney) J(oseph) 1904-1979 **C L C
3, 5, 9, 15, 23, 44, 49; DAM DRAM**
See also AITN 1, 2; CA 73-76; 89-92; CANR
18; DLB 11, 44; MTCW
Peret, Benjamin 1899-1959 .... **TCLC 20**
See also CA 117
Peretz, Isaac Loeb 1851(?)-1915 ... **TCLC 16;
SSC 26**
See also CA 109
Peretz, Yitzkhok Leibush
See Peretz, Isaac Loeb
Perez Galdos, Benito 1843-1920 .... **TCLC 27**
See also CA 125; 153; HW
Perrault, Charles 1628-1703 .... **LC 2**
See also MAICYA; SATA 25
Perry, Brighton
See Sherwood, Robert E(mmet)
Perse, St.-John .... **CLC 4, 11, 46**
See also Leger, (Marie-Rene Auguste) Alexis
Saint-Leger
Perutz, Leo 1882-1957 .... **TCLC 60**
See also DLB 81
Peseenz, Tulio F.
See Lopez y Fuentes, Gregorio
Pesetsky, Bette 1932- .... **CLC 28**
See also CA 133; DLB 130
Peshkov, Alexei Maximovich 1868-1936
See Gorky, Maxim
See also CA 105; 141; DA; DAC; DAM DRAM,
MST, NOV
Pessoa, Fernando (Antonio Nogueira) 1888-
1935 .... **TCLC 27; HLC; PC 20**
See also CA 125
Peterkin, Julia Mood 1880-1961 .... **CLC 31**
See also CA 102; DLB 9
Peters, Joan K(aren) 1945- .... **CLC 39**
See also CA 158
Peters, Robert L(ouis) 1924- .... **CLC 7**
See also CA 13-16R; CAAS 8; DLB 105
Petofi, Sandor 1823-1849 .... **NCLC 21**
Petrakis, Harry Mark 1923- .... **CLC 3**
See also CA 9-12R; CANR 4, 30
Petrarch 1304-1374 **CMLC 20; DAM POET;
PC 8**
Petrov, Evgeny .... **TCLC 21**
See also Kataev, Evgeny Petrovich
Petry, Ann (Lane) 1908-1997 ... **CLC 1, 7, 18**
See also BW 1; CA 5-8R; 157; CAAS 6; CANR
4, 46; CLR 12; DLB 76; JRDA; MAICYA;
MTCW; SATA 5; SATA-Obit 94
Petursson, Halligrimur 1614-1674 .... **LC 8**
Phaedrus 18(?)B.C.-55(?) .... **CMLC 25**
Philips, Katherine 1632-1664 .... **LC 30**
See also DLB 131
Philipson, Morris H. 1926- .... **CLC 53**
See also CA 1-4R; CANR 4
Phillips, Caryl 1958- .. **CLC 96; DAM MULT**
See also BW 2; CA 141; DLB 157
Phillips, David Graham 1867-1911 **TCLC 44**
See also CA 108; DLB 9, 12
Phillips, Jack
See Sandburg, Carl (August)

Phillips, Jayne Anne 1952-**CLC 15, 33; SSC 16**
See also CA 101; CANR 24, 50; DLBY 80; INT
CANR-24; MTCW
Phillips, Richard
See Dick, Philip K(indred)
Phillips, Robert (Schaeffer) 1938- .... **CLC 28**
See also CA 17-20R; CAAS 13; CANR 8; DLB
105
Phillips, Ward
See Lovecraft, H(oward) P(hillips)
Piccolo, Lucio 1901-1969 .... **CLC 13**
See also CA 97-100; DLB 114
Pickthall, Marjorie L(owry) C(hristie) 1883-
1922 .... **TCLC 21**
See also CA 107; DLB 92
Pico della Mirandola, Giovanni 1463-1494**LC
15**
Piercy, Marge 1936- **CLC 3, 6, 14, 18, 27, 62**
See also CA 21-24R; CAAS 1; CANR 13, 43;
DLB 120; MTCW
Piers, Robert
See Anthony, Piers
Pieyre de Mandiargues, Andre 1909-1991
See Mandiargues, Andre Pieyre de
See also CA 103; 136; CANR 22
Pilnyak, Boris .... **TCLC 23**
See also Vogau, Boris Andreyevich
Pincherle, Alberto 1907-1990 ... **CLC 11, 18;
DAM NOV**
See also Moravia, Alberto
See also CA 25-28R; 132; CANR 33; MTCW
Pinckney, Darryl 1953- .... **CLC 76**
See also BW 2; CA 143
Pindar 518B.C.-446B.C. ..... **CMLC 12; PC 19**
See also DLB 176
Pineda, Cecile 1942- .... **CLC 39**
See also CA 118
Pinero, Arthur Wing 1855-1934 ... **TCLC 32;
DAM DRAM**
See also CA 110; 153; DLB 10
Pinero, Miguel (Antonio Gomez) 1946-1988
CLC 4, 55
See also CA 61-64; 125; CANR 29; HW
Pinget, Robert 1919-1997 .... **CLC 7, 13, 37**
See also CA 85-88; 160; DLB 83
Pink Floyd
See Barrett, (Roger) Syd; Gilmour, David; Ma-
son, Nick; Waters, Roger; Wright, Rick
Pinkney, Edward 1802-1828 .... **NCLC 31**
Pinkwater, Daniel Manus 1941- .... **CLC 35**
See also Pinkwater, Manus
See also AAYA 1; CA 29-32R; CANR 12, 38;
CLR 4; JRDA; MAICYA; SAAS 3; SATA 46,
76
Pinkwater, Manus
See Pinkwater, Daniel Manus
See also SATA 8
Pinsky, Robert 1940-**CLC 9, 19, 38, 94; DAM
POET**
See also CA 29-32R; CAAS 4; CANR 58;
DLBY 82
Pinta, Harold
See Pinter, Harold
Pinter, Harold 1930-**CLC 1, 3, 6, 9, 11, 15, 27,
58, 73; DA; DAB; DAC; DAM DRAM,
MST; WLC**
See also CA 5-8R; CANR 33; CDBLB 1960 to
Present; DLB 13; MTCW
Piozzi, Hester Lynch (Thrale) 1741-1821
NCLC 57
See also DLB 104, 142
Pirandello, Luigi 1867-1936**TCLC 4, 29; DA;
DAB; DAC; DAM DRAM, MST; DC 5;**

SSC 22; WLC
See also CA 104; 153

Pirsig, Robert M(aynard) 1928-CLC **4, 6, 73;**
   DAM POP
   See also CA 53-56; CANR 42; MTCW; SATA
   39

Pisarev, Dmitry Ivanovich 1840-1868 N C L C
   25

Pix, Mary (Griffith) 1666-1709 .... **LC 8**
   See also DLB 80

Pixerecourt, Guilbert de 1773-1844NCLC **39**

Plaatje, Sol(omon) T(shekisho) 1876-1932
   TCLC 73
   See also BW 2; CA 141

Plaidy, Jean
   See Hibbert, Eleanor Alice Burford

Planche, James Robinson 1796-1880NCLC **42**

Plant, Robert 1948- .... **CLC 12**

Plante, David (Robert) 1940- CLC **7, 23, 38;**
   DAM NOV
   See also CA 37-40R; CANR 12, 36, 58; DLBY
   83; INT CANR-12; MTCW

Plath, Sylvia 1932-1963 CLC **1, 2, 3, 5, 9, 11,**
   14, 17, 50, 51, 62; DA; DAB; DAC; DAM
   MST, POET; PC 1; WLC
   See also AAYA 13; CA 19-20; CANR 34; CAP
   2; CDALB 1941-1968; DLB 5, 6, 152;
   MTCW; SATA 96

Plato 428(?)B.C.-348(?)B.C. ... **CMLC 8; DA;**
   DAB; DAC; DAM MST; WLCS
   See also DLB 176

Platonov, Andrei .... **TCLC 14**
   See also Klimentov, Andrei Platonovich

Platt, Kin 1911- .... **CLC 26**
   See also AAYA 11; CA 17-20R; CANR 11;
   JRDA; SAAS 17; SATA 21, 86

Plautus c. 251B.C.-184B.C. .... **DC 6**

Plick et Plock
   See Simenon, Georges (Jacques Christian)

Plimpton, George (Ames) 1927- .... **CLC 36**
   See also AITN 1; CA 21-24R; CANR 32;
   MTCW; SATA 10

Pliny the Elder c. 23-79 .... **CMLC 23**

Plomer, William Charles Franklin 1903-1973
   CLC 4, 8
   See also CA 21-22; CANR 34; CAP 2; DLB
   20, 162; MTCW; SATA 24

Plowman, Piers
   See Kavanagh, Patrick (Joseph)

Plum, J.
   See Wodehouse, P(elham) G(renville)

Plumly, Stanley (Ross) 1939- .... **CLC 33**
   See also CA 108; 110; DLB 5; INT 110

Plumpe, Friedrich Wilhelm 1888-1931T C L C
   53
   See also CA 112

Po Chu-i 772-846 .... **CMLC 24**

Poe, Edgar Allan 1809-1849NCLC **1, 16, 55;**
   DA; DAB; DAC; DAM MST, POET; PC
   1; SSC 1, 22; WLC
   See also AAYA 14; CDALB 1640-1865; DLB
   3, 59, 73, 74; SATA 23

Poet of Titchfield Street, The
   See Pound, Ezra (Weston Loomis)

Pohl, Frederik 1919- .... **CLC 18; SSC 25**
   See also CA 61-64; CAAS 1; CANR 11, 37;
   DLB 8; INT CANR-11; MTCW; SATA 24

Poirier, Louis 1910-
   See Gracq, Julien
   See also CA 122; 126

Poitier, Sidney 1927- .... **CLC 26**
   See also BW 1; CA 117

Polanski, Roman 1933- .... **CLC 16**

See also CA 77-80

Poliakoff, Stephen 1952- .... **CLC 38**
   See also CA 106; DLB 13

Police, The
   See Copeland, Stewart (Armstrong); Summers,
   Andrew James; Sumner, Gordon Matthew

Polidori, John William 1795-1821 . NCLC **51**
   See also DLB 116

Pollitt, Katha 1949- .... **CLC 28**
   See also CA 120; 122; MTCW

Pollock, (Mary) Sharon 1936-CLC **50; DAC;**
   DAM DRAM, MST
   See also CA 141; DLB 60

Polo, Marco 1254-1324 .... **CMLC 15**

Polonsky, Abraham (Lincoln) 1910- CLC **92**
   See also CA 104; DLB 26; INT 104

Polybius c. 200B.C.-c. 118B.C. ...... **CMLC 17**
   See also DLB 176

Pomerance, Bernard 1940-.... **CLC 13; DAM**
   DRAM
   See also CA 101; CANR 49

Ponge, Francis (Jean Gaston Alfred) 1899-1988
   CLC 6, 18; DAM POET
   See also CA 85-88; 126; CANR 40

Pontoppidan, Henrik 1857-1943 .... **TCLC 29**

Poole, Josephine .... **CLC 17**
   See also Helyar, Jane Penelope Josephine
   See also SAAS 2; SATA 5

Popa, Vasko 1922-1991 .... **CLC 19**
   See also CA 112; 148; DLB 181

Pope, Alexander 1688-1744 LC **3; DA; DAB;**
   DAC; DAM MST, POET; WLC
   See also CDBLB 1660-1789; DLB 95, 101

Porter, Connie (Rose) 1959(?)- .... **CLC 70**
   See also BW 2; CA 142; SATA 81

Porter, Gene(va Grace) Stratton 1863(?)-1924
   TCLC 21
   See also CA 112

Porter, Katherine Anne 1890-1980CLC **1, 3, 7,**
   10, 13, 15, 27, 101; DA; DAB; DAC; DAM
   MST, NOV; SSC 4
   See also AITN 2; CA 1-4R; 101; CANR 1; DLB
   4, 9, 102; DLBD 12; DLBY 80; MTCW;
   SATA 39; SATA-Obit 23

Porter, Peter (Neville Frederick) 1929-CLC **5,**
   13, 33
   See also CA 85-88; DLB 40

Porter, William Sydney 1862-1910
   See Henry, O.
   See also CA 104; 131; CDALB 1865-1917; DA;
   DAB; DAC; DAM MST; DLB 12, 78, 79;
   MTCW; YABC 2

Portillo (y Pacheco), Jose Lopez
   See Lopez Portillo (y Pacheco), Jose

Post, Melville Davisson 1869-1930 **TCLC 39**
   See also CA 110

Potok, Chaim 1929- . CLC **2, 7, 14, 26; DAM**
   NOV
   See also AAYA 15; AITN 1, 2; CA 17-20R;
   CANR 19, 35; DLB 28, 152; INT CANR-
   19; MTCW; SATA 33

Potter, (Helen) Beatrix 1866-1943
   See Webb, (Martha) Beatrice (Potter)
   See also MAICYA

Potter, Dennis (Christopher George) 1935-1994
   CLC 58, 86
   See also CA 107; 145; CANR 33, 61; MTCW

Pound, Ezra (Weston Loomis) 1885-1972CLC
   1, 2, 3, 4, 5, 7, 10, 13, 18, 34, 48, 50; DA;
   DAB; DAC; DAM MST, POET; PC 4;
   WLC
   See also CA 5-8R; 37-40R; CANR 40; CDALB
   1917-1929; DLB 4, 45, 63; DLBD 15;

MTCW

Povod, Reinaldo 1959-1994 .... **CLC 44**
   See also CA 136; 146

Powell, Adam Clayton, Jr. 1908-1972CLC **89;**
   BLC; DAM MULT
   See also BW 1; CA 102; 33-36R

Powell, Anthony (Dymoke) 1905-CLC **1, 3, 7,**
   9, 10, 31
   See also CA 1-4R; CANR 1, 32, 62; CDBLB
   1945-1960; DLB 15; MTCW

Powell, Dawn 1897-1965 .... **CLC 66**
   See also CA 5-8R

Powell, Padgett 1952- .... **CLC 34**
   See also CA 126

Power, Susan 1961- .... **CLC 91**

Powers, J(ames) F(arl) 1917-CLC **1, 4, 8, 57;**
   SSC 4
   See also CA 1-4R; CANR 2, 61; DLB 130;
   MTCW

Powers, John J(ames) 1945-
   See Powers, John R.
   See also CA 69-72

Powers, John R. .... **CLC 66**
   See also Powers, John J(ames)

Powers, Richard (S.) 1957- .... **CLC 93**
   See also CA 148

Pownall, David 1938- .... **CLC 10**
   See also CA 89-92; CAAS 18; CANR 49; DLB
   14

Powys, John Cowper 1872-1963CLC **7, 9, 15,**
   46
   See also CA 85-88; DLB 15; MTCW

Powys, T(heodore) F(rancis) 1875-1953
   TCLC 9
   See also CA 106; DLB 36, 162

Prado (Calvo), Pedro 1886-1952 ... **TCLC 75**
   See also CA 131; HW

Prager, Emily 1952- .... **CLC 56**

Pratt, E(dwin) J(ohn) 1883(?)-1964 **CLC 19;**
   DAC; DAM POET
   See also CA 141; 93-96; DLB 92

Premchand .... **TCLC 21**
   See also Srivastava, Dhanpat Rai

Preussler, Otfried 1923- .... **CLC 17**
   See also CA 77-80; SATA 24

Prevert, Jacques (Henri Marie) 1900-1977
   CLC 15
   See also CA 77-80; 69-72; CANR 29, 61;
   MTCW; SATA-Obit 30

Prevost, Abbe (Antoine Francois) 1697-1763
   LC 1

Price, (Edward) Reynolds 1933-CLC **3, 6, 13,**
   43, 50, 63; DAM NOV; SSC 22
   See also CA 1-4R; CANR 1, 37, 57; DLB 2;
   INT CANR-37

Price, Richard 1949- .... **CLC 6, 12**
   See also CA 49-52; CANR 3; DLBY 81

Prichard, Katharine Susannah 1883-1969
   CLC 46
   See also CA 11-12; CANR 33; CAP 1; MTCW;
   SATA 66

Priestley, J(ohn) B(oynton) 1894-1984CLC **2,**
   5, 9, 34; DAM DRAM, NOV
   See also CA 9-12R; 113; CANR 33; CDBLB
   1914-1945; DLB 10, 34, 77, 100, 139; DLBY
   84; MTCW

Prince 1958(?)- .... **CLC 35**

Prince, F(rank) T(empleton) 1912- .. **CLC 22**
   See also CA 101; CANR 43; DLB 20

Prince Kropotkin
   See Kropotkin, Peter (Aleksieevich)

Prior, Matthew 1664-1721 .... **LC 4**
   See also DLB 95

Ritsos, Giannes
See Ritsos, Yannis
Ritsos, Yannis 1909-1990 .... **CLC 6, 13, 31**
See also CA 77-80; 133; CANR 39, 61; MTCW
Ritter, Erika 1948(?)- .... **CLC 52**
Rivera, Jose Eustasio 1889-1928 ... **TCLC 35**
See also HW
Rivers, Conrad Kent 1933-1968 .... **CLC 1**
See also BW 1; CA 85-88; DLB 41
Rivers, Elfrida
See Bradley, Marion Zimmer
Riverside, John
See Heinlein, Robert A(nson)
Rizal, Jose 1861-1896 .... **NCLC 27**
Roa Bastos, Augusto (Antonio) 1917-**CLC 45;**
DAM MULT; HLC
See also CA 131; DLB 113; HW
Robbe-Grillet, Alain 1922- **CLC 1, 2, 4, 6, 8,**
10, 14, 43
See also CA 9-12R; CANR 33; DLB 83; MTCW
Robbins, Harold 1916- ... **CLC 5; DAM NOV**
See also CA 73-76; CANR 26, 54; MTCW
Robbins, Thomas Eugene 1936-
See Robbins, Tom
See also CA 81-84; CANR 29, 59; DAM NOV,
POP; MTCW
Robbins, Tom .... **CLC 9, 32, 64**
See also Robbins, Thomas Eugene
See also BEST 90:3; DLBY 80
Robbins, Trina 1938- .... **CLC 21**
See also CA 128
Roberts, Charles G(eorge) D(ouglas) 1860-1943
TCLC 8
See also CA 105; CLR 33; DLB 92; SATA 88;
SATA-Brief 29
Roberts, Elizabeth Madox 1886-1941 **T C L C**
68
See also CA 111; DLB 9, 54, 102; SATA 33;
SATA-Brief 27
Roberts, Kate 1891-1985 .... **CLC 15**
See also CA 107; 116
Roberts, Keith (John Kingston) 1935-**CLC 14**
See also CA 25-28R; CANR 46
Roberts, Kenneth (Lewis) 1885-1957**TCLC 23**
See also CA 109; DLB 9
Roberts, Michele (B.) 1949- .... **CLC 48**
See also CA 115; CANR 58
Robertson, Ellis
See Ellison, Harlan (Jay); Silverberg, Robert
Robertson, Thomas William 1829-1871**NCLC**
35; DAM DRAM
Robeson, Kenneth
See Dent, Lester
Robinson, Edwin Arlington 1869-1935**T C L C**
5; DA; DAC; DAM MST, POET; PC 1
See also CA 104; 133; CDALB 1865-1917;
DLB 54; MTCW
Robinson, Henry Crabb 1775-1867**NCLC 15**
See also DLB 107
Robinson, Jill 1936- .... **CLC 10**
See also CA 102; INT 102
Robinson, Kim Stanley 1952- .... **CLC 34**
See also CA 126
Robinson, Lloyd
See Silverberg, Robert
Robinson, Marilynne 1944- .... **CLC 25**
See also CA 116
Robinson, Smokey .... **CLC 21**
See also Robinson, William, Jr.
Robinson, William, Jr. 1940-
See Robinson, Smokey
See also CA 116
Robison, Mary 1949- .... **CLC 42, 98**

See also CA 113; 116; DLB 130; INT 116
Rod, Edouard 1857-1910 .... **TCLC 52**
Roddenberry, Eugene Wesley 1921-1991
See Roddenberry, Gene
See also CA 110; 135; CANR 37; SATA 45;
SATA-Obit 69
Roddenberry, Gene .... **CLC 17**
See also Roddenberry, Eugene Wesley
See also AAYA 5; SATA-Obit 69
Rodgers, Mary 1931- .... **CLC 12**
See also CA 49-52; CANR 8, 55; CLR 20; INT
CANR-8; JRDA; MAICYA; SATA 8
Rodgers, W(illiam) R(obert) 1909-1969**CLC 7**
See also CA 85-88; DLB 20
Rodman, Eric
See Silverberg, Robert
Rodman, Howard 1920(?)-1985 .... **CLC 65**
See also CA 118
Rodman, Maia
See Wojciechowska, Maia (Teresa)
Rodriguez, Claudio 1934- .... **CLC 10**
See also DLB 134
Roelvaag, O(le) E(dvart) 1876-1931**TCLC 17**
See also CA 117; DLB 9
Roethke, Theodore (Huebner) 1908-1963**CLC**
1, 3, 8, 11, 19, 46, 101; DAM POET; PC 15
See also CA 81-84; CABS 2; CDALB 1941-
1968; DLB 5; MTCW
Rogers, Thomas Hunton 1927- .... **CLC 57**
See also CA 89-92; INT 89-92
Rogers, Will(iam Penn Adair) 1879-1935
TCLC 8, 71; DAM MULT
See also CA 105; 144; DLB 11; NNAL
Rogin, Gilbert 1929- .... **CLC 18**
See also CA 65-68; CANR 15
Rohan, Koda .... **TCLC 22**
See also Koda Shigeyuki
Rohlfs, Anna Katharine Green
See Green, Anna Katharine
Rohmer, Eric .... **CLC 16**
See also Scherer, Jean-Marie Maurice
Rohmer, Sax .... **TCLC 28**
See also Ward, Arthur Henry Sarsfield
See also DLB 70
Roiphe, Anne (Richardson) 1935- .. **CLC 3, 9**
See also CA 89-92; CANR 45; DLBY 80; INT
89-92
Rojas, Fernando de 1465-1541 .... **LC 23**
Rolfe, Frederick (William Serafino Austin
Lewis Mary) 1860-1913 .... **TCLC 12**
See also CA 107; DLB 34, 156
Rolland, Romain 1866-1944 .... **TCLC 23**
See also CA 118; DLB 65
Rolle, Richard c. 1300-c. 1349 ...... **CMLC 21**
See also DLB 146
Rolvaag, O(le) E(dvart)
See Roelvaag, O(le) E(dvart)
Romain Arnaud, Saint
See Aragon, Louis
Romains, Jules 1885-1972 .... **CLC 7**
See also CA 85-88; CANR 34; DLB 65; MTCW
Romero, Jose Ruben 1890-1952 .... **TCLC 14**
See also CA 114; 131; HW
Ronsard, Pierre de 1524-1585 ... **LC 6; PC 11**
Rooke, Leon 1934- .. **CLC 25, 34; DAM POP**
See also CA 25-28R; CANR 23, 53
Roosevelt, Theodore 1858-1919 ..... **TCLC 69**
See also CA 115; DLB 47
Roper, William 1498-1578 .... **LC 10**
Roquelaure, A. N.
See Rice, Anne
Rosa, Joao Guimaraes 1908-1967 .... **CLC 23**
See also CA 89-92; DLB 113

Rose, Wendy 1948-**CLC 85; DAM MULT; PC**
13
See also CA 53-56; CANR 5, 51; DLB 175;
NNAL; SATA 12
Rosen, R. D.
See Rosen, Richard (Dean)
Rosen, Richard (Dean) 1949- .... **CLC 39**
See also CA 77-80; CANR 62; INT CANR-30
Rosenberg, Isaac 1890-1918 .... **TCLC 12**
See also CA 107; DLB 20
Rosenblatt, Joe .... **CLC 15**
See also Rosenblatt, Joseph
Rosenblatt, Joseph 1933-
See Rosenblatt, Joe
See also CA 89-92; INT 89-92
Rosenfeld, Samuel 1896-1963
See Tzara, Tristan
See also CA 89-92
Rosenstock, Sami
See Tzara, Tristan
Rosenstock, Samuel
See Tzara, Tristan
Rosenthal, M(acha) L(ouis) 1917-1996. **C L C**
28
See also CA 1-4R; 152; CAAS 6; CANR 4, 51;
DLB 5; SATA 59
Ross, Barnaby
See Dannay, Frederic
Ross, Bernard L.
See Follett, Ken(neth Martin)
Ross, J. H.
See Lawrence, T(homas) E(dward)
Ross, Martin
See Martin, Violet Florence
See also DLB 135
Ross, (James) Sinclair 1908- **CLC 13; DAC;**
DAM MST; SSC 24
See also CA 73-76; DLB 88
Rossetti, Christina (Georgina) 1830-1894
NCLC 2, 50, 66; DA; DAB; DAC; DAM
MST, POET; PC 7; WLC
See also DLB 35, 163; MAICYA; SATA 20
Rossetti, Dante Gabriel 1828-1882 . **NCLC 4;**
DA; DAB; DAC; DAM MST, POET; WLC
See also CDBLB 1832-1890; DLB 35
Rossner, Judith (Perelman) 1935-**CLC 6, 9, 29**
See also AITN 2; BEST 90:3; CA 17-20R;
CANR 18, 51; DLB 6; INT CANR-18;
MTCW
Rostand, Edmond (Eugene Alexis) 1868-1918
TCLC 6, 37; DA; DAB; DAC; DAM
DRAM, MST
See also CA 104; 126; MTCW
Roth, Henry 1906-1995 ..... **CLC 2, 6, 11, 104**
See also CA 11-12; 149; CANR 38; CAP 1;
DLB 28; MTCW
Roth, Philip (Milton) 1933-**CLC 1, 2, 3, 4, 6, 9,**
15, 22, 31, 47, 66, 86; DA; DAB; DAC;
DAM MST, NOV, POP; SSC 26; WLC
See also BEST 90:3; CA 1-4R; CANR 1, 22,
36, 55; CDALB 1968-1988; DLB 2, 28, 173;
DLBY 82; MTCW
Rothenberg, Jerome 1931- .... **CLC 6, 57**
See also CA 45-48; CANR 1; DLB 5
Roumain, Jacques (Jean Baptiste) 1907-1944
TCLC 19; BLC; DAM MULT
See also BW 1; CA 117; 125
Rourke, Constance (Mayfield) 1885-1941
TCLC 12
See also CA 107; YABC 1
Rousseau, Jean-Baptiste 1671-1741 ...... **LC 9**
Rousseau, Jean-Jacques 1712-1778**LC 14, 36;**
DA; DAB; DAC; DAM MST; WLC

See also AAYA 22; CDBLB 1789-1832; DLB 93, 107, 116, 144, 159; YABC 2

Scribe, (Augustin) Eugene 1791-1861 **N C L C 16; DAM DRAM; DC 5**

Scrum, R.
See Crumb, R(obert)

Scudery, Madeleine de 1607-1701 .... **LC 2**

Scum
See Crumb, R(obert)

Scumbag, Little Bobby
See Crumb, R(obert)

Seabrook, John
See Hubbard, L(afayette) Ron(ald)

Sealy, I. Allan 1951- .... **CLC 55**

Search, Alexander
See Pessoa, Fernando (Antonio Nogueira)

Sebastian, Lee
See Silverberg, Robert

Sebastian Owl
See Thompson, Hunter S(tockton)

Sebestyen, Ouida 1924- .... **CLC 30**
See also AAYA 8; CA 107; CANR 40; CLR 17; JRDA; MAICYA; SAAS 10; SATA 39

Secundus, H. Scriblerus
See Fielding, Henry

Sedges, John
See Buck, Pearl S(ydenstricker)

Sedgwick, Catharine Maria 1789-1867**N C L C 19**
See also DLB 1, 74

Seelye, John 1931- .... **CLC 7**

Seferiades, Giorgos Stylianou 1900-1971
See Seferis, George
See also CA 5-8R; 33-36R; CANR 5, 36; MTCW

Seferis, George .... **CLC 5, 11**
See also Seferiades, Giorgos Stylianou

Segal, Erich (Wolf) 1937- . **CLC 3, 10; DAM POP**
See also BEST 89:1; CA 25-28R; CANR 20, 36; DLBY 86; INT CANR-20; MTCW

Seger, Bob 1945- .... **CLC 35**

Seghers, Anna .... **CLC 7**
See also Radvanyi, Netty
See also DLB 69

Seidel, Frederick (Lewis) 1936- .... **CLC 18**
See also CA 13-16R; CANR 8; DLBY 84

Seifert, Jaroslav 1901-1986 .. **CLC 34, 44, 93**
See also CA 127; MTCW

Sei Shonagon c. 966-1017(?) .... **CMLC 6**

Selby, Hubert, Jr. 1928-**CLC 1, 2, 4, 8; SSC 20**
See also CA 13-16R; CANR 33; DLB 2

Selzer, Richard 1928- .... **CLC 74**
See also CA 65-68; CANR 14

Sembene, Ousmane
See Ousmane, Sembene

Senancour, Etienne Pivert de 1770-1846 **NCLC 16**
See also DLB 119

Sender, Ramon (Jose) 1902-1982**CLC 8; DAM MULT; HLC**
See also CA 5-8R; 105; CANR 8; HW; MTCW

Seneca, Lucius Annaeus 4B.C.-65 . **CMLC 6; DAM DRAM; DC 5**

Senghor, Leopold Sedar 1906-**CLC 54; BLC; DAM MULT, POET**
See also BW 2; CA 116; 125; CANR 47; MTCW

Serling, (Edward) Rod(man) 1924-1975**C L C 30**
See also AAYA 14; AITN 1; CA 65-68; 57-60; DLB 26

Serna, Ramon Gomez de la
See Gomez de la Serna, Ramon

Serpieres
See Guillevic, (Eugene)

Service, Robert
See Service, Robert W(illiam)
See also DAB; DLB 92

Service, Robert W(illiam) 1874(?)-1958**TCLC 15; DA; DAC; DAM MST, POET; WLC**
See also Service, Robert
See also CA 115; 140; SATA 20

Seth, Vikram 1952-**CLC 43, 90; DAM MULT**
See also CA 121; 127; CANR 50; DLB 120; INT 127

Seton, Cynthia Propper 1926-1982 .. **CLC 27**
See also CA 5-8R; 108; CANR 7

Seton, Ernest (Evan) Thompson 1860-1946 **TCLC 31**
See also CA 109; DLB 92; DLBD 13; JRDA; SATA 18

Seton-Thompson, Ernest
See Seton, Ernest (Evan) Thompson

Settle, Mary Lee 1918- .... **CLC 19, 61**
See also CA 89-92; CAAS 1; CANR 44; DLB 6; INT 89-92

Seuphor, Michel
See Arp, Jean

Sevigne, Marie (de Rabutin-Chantal) Marquise de 1626-1696 .... **LC 11**

Sewall, Samuel 1652-1730 .... **LC 38**
See also DLB 24

Sexton, Anne (Harvey) 1928-1974**CLC 2, 4, 6, 8, 10, 15, 53; DA; DAB; DAC; DAM MST, POET; PC 2; WLC**
See also CA 1-4R; 53-56; CABS 2; CANR 3, 36; CDALB 1941-1968; DLB 5, 169; MTCW; SATA 10

Shaara, Michael (Joseph, Jr.) 1929-1988**C L C 15; DAM POP**
See also AITN 1; CA 102; 125; CANR 52; DLBY 83

Shackleton, C. C.
See Aldiss, Brian W(ilson)

Shacochis, Bob .... **CLC 39**
See also Shacochis, Robert G.

Shacochis, Robert G. 1951-
See Shacochis, Bob
See also CA 119; 124; INT 124

Shaffer, Anthony (Joshua) 1926- .... **CLC 19; DAM DRAM**
See also CA 110; 116; DLB 13

Shaffer, Peter (Levin) 1926-**CLC 5, 14, 18, 37, 60; DAB; DAM DRAM, MST; DC 7**
See also CA 25-28R; CANR 25, 47; CDBLB 1960 to Present; DLB 13; MTCW

Shakey, Bernard
See Young, Neil

Shalamov, Varlam (Tikhonovich) 1907(?)-1982 **CLC 18**
See also CA 129; 105

Shamlu, Ahmad 1925- .... **CLC 10**

Shammas, Anton 1951- .... **CLC 55**

Shange, Ntozake 1948-**CLC 8, 25, 38, 74; BLC; DAM DRAM, MULT; DC 3**
See also AAYA 9; BW 2; CA 85-88; CABS 3; CANR 27, 48; DLB 38; MTCW

Shanley, John Patrick 1950- .... **CLC 75**
See also CA 128; 133

Shapcott, Thomas W(illiam) 1935-... **CLC 38**
See also CA 69-72; CANR 49

Shapiro, Jane .... **CLC 76**

Shapiro, Karl (Jay) 1913-... **CLC 4, 8, 15, 53**
See also CA 1-4R; CAAS 6; CANR 1, 36; DLB 48; MTCW

Sharp, William 1855-1905 .... **TCLC 39**

See also CA 160; DLB 156

Sharpe, Thomas Ridley 1928-
See Sharpe, Tom
See also CA 114; 122; INT 122

Sharpe, Tom .... **CLC 36**
See also Sharpe, Thomas Ridley
See also DLB 14

Shaw, Bernard .... **TCLC 45**
See also Shaw, George Bernard
See also BW 1

Shaw, G. Bernard
See Shaw, George Bernard

Shaw, George Bernard 1856-1950**TCLC 3, 9, 21; DA; DAB; DAC; DAM DRAM, MST; WLC**
See also Shaw, Bernard
See also CA 104; 128; CDBLB 1914-1945; DLB 10, 57; MTCW

Shaw, Henry Wheeler 1818-1885 .. **NCLC 15**
See also DLB 11

Shaw, Irwin 1913-1984 **CLC 7, 23, 34; DAM DRAM, POP**
See also AITN 1; CA 13-16R; 112; CANR 21; CDALB 1941-1968; DLB 6, 102; DLBY 84; MTCW

Shaw, Robert 1927-1978 .... **CLC 5**
See also AITN 1; CA 1-4R; 81-84; CANR 4; DLB 13, 14

Shaw, T. E.
See Lawrence, T(homas) E(dward)

Shawn, Wallace 1943- .... **CLC 41**
See also CA 112

Shea, Lisa 1953- .... **CLC 86**
See also CA 147

Sheed, Wilfrid (John Joseph) 1930-**CLC 2, 4, 10, 53**
See also CA 65-68; CANR 30; DLB 6; MTCW

Sheldon, Alice Hastings Bradley 1915(?)-1987
See Tiptree, James, Jr.
See also CA 108; 122; CANR 34; INT 108; MTCW

Sheldon, John
See Bloch, Robert (Albert)

Shelley, Mary Wollstonecraft (Godwin) 1797-1851**NCLC 14, 59; DA; DAB; DAC; DAM MST, NOV; WLC**
See also AAYA 20; CDBLB 1789-1832; DLB 110, 116, 159, 178; SATA 29

Shelley, Percy Bysshe 1792-1822 . **NCLC 18; DA; DAB; DAC; DAM MST, POET; PC 14; WLC**
See also CDBLB 1789-1832; DLB 96, 110, 158

Shepard, Jim 1956- .... **CLC 36**
See also CA 137; CANR 59; SATA 90

Shepard, Lucius 1947- .... **CLC 34**
See also CA 128; 141

Shepard, Sam 1943-**CLC 4, 6, 17, 34, 41, 44; DAM DRAM; DC 5**
See also AAYA 1; CA 69-72; CABS 3; CANR 22; DLB 7; MTCW

Shepherd, Michael
See Ludlum, Robert

Sherburne, Zoa (Morin) 1912-.......... **CLC 30**
See also AAYA 13; CA 1-4R; CANR 3, 37; MAICYA; SAAS 18; SATA 3

Sheridan, Frances 1724-1766 .... **LC 7**
See also DLB 39, 84

Sheridan, Richard Brinsley 1751-1816**N C L C 5; DA; DAB; DAC; DAM DRAM, MST; DC 1; WLC**
See also CDBLB 1660-1789; DLB 89

Sherman, Jonathan Marc .... **CLC 55**

Sherman, Martin 1941(?)- .... **CLC 19**

See also CA 116; 123

Sherwin, Judith Johnson 1936- .... **CLC 7, 15**
See also CA 25-28R; CANR 34

Sherwood, Frances 1940- .... **CLC 81**
See also CA 146

Sherwood, Robert E(mmet) 1896-1955T C L C
3; DAM DRAM
See also CA 104; 153; DLB 7, 26

Shestov, Lev 1866-1938 .... **TCLC 56**

Shevchenko, Taras 1814-1861 .... **NCLC 54**

Shiel, M(atthew) P(hipps) 1865-1947TCLC 8
See also Holmes, Gordon
See also CA 106; 160; DLB 153

Shields, Carol 1935- .... **CLC 91; DAC**
See also CA 81-84; CANR 51

Shields, David 1956- .... **CLC 97**
See also CA 124; CANR 48

Shiga, Naoya 1883-1971 ...... **CLC 33; SSC 23**
See also CA 101; 33-36R; DLB 180

Shilts, Randy 1951-1994 .... **CLC 85**
See also AAYA 19; CA 115; 127; 144; CANR
45; INT 127

Shimazaki, Haruki 1872-1943
See Shimazaki Toson
See also CA 105; 134

Shimazaki Toson 1872-1943 .... **TCLC 5**
See also Shimazaki, Haruki
See also DLB 180

Sholokhov, Mikhail (Aleksandrovich) 1905-
1984 .... **CLC 7, 15**
See also CA 101; 112; MTCW; SATA-Obit 36

Shone, Patric
See Hanley, James

Shreve, Susan Richards 1939- .... **CLC 23**
See also CA 49-52; CAAS 5; CANR 5, 38;
MAICYA; SATA 46, 95; SATA-Brief 41

Shue, Larry 1946-1985CLC 52; DAM DRAM
See also CA 145; 117

Shu-Jen, Chou 1881-1936
See Lu Hsun
See also CA 104

Shulman, Alix Kates 1932- .... **CLC 2, 10**
See also CA 29-32R; CANR 43; SATA 7

Shuster, Joe 1914- .... **CLC 21**

Shute, Nevil .... **CLC 30**
See also Norway, Nevil Shute

Shuttle, Penelope (Diane) 1947- .... **CLC 7**
See also CA 93-96; CANR 39; DLB 14, 40

Sidney, Mary 1561-1621 .... **LC 19, 39**

Sidney, Sir Philip 1554-1586 **LC 19, 39; DA;**
DAB; DAC; DAM MST, POET
See also CDBLB Before 1660; DLB 167

Siegel, Jerome 1914-1996 .... **CLC 21**
See also CA 116; 151

Siegel, Jerry
See Siegel, Jerome

Sienkiewicz, Henryk (Adam Alexander Pius)
1846-1916 .... **TCLC 3**
See also CA 104; 134

Sierra, Gregorio Martinez
See Martinez Sierra, Gregorio

Sierra, Maria (de la O'LeJarraga) Martinez
See Martinez Sierra, Maria (de la O'LeJarraga)

Sigal, Clancy 1926- .... **CLC 7**
See also CA 1-4R

Sigourney, Lydia Howard (Huntley) 1791-1865
NCLC 21
See also DLB 1, 42, 73

Siguenza y Gongora, Carlos de 1645-1700L C
8

Sigurjonsson, Johann 1880-1919 ... **TCLC 27**

Sikelianos, Angelos 1884-1951 .... **TCLC 39**

Silkin, Jon 1930- .... **CLC 2, 6, 43**

See also CA 5-8R; CAAS 5; DLB 27

Silko, Leslie (Marmon) 1948-CLC 23, 74; DA;
DAC; DAM MST, MULT, POP; WLCS
See also AAYA 14; CA 115; 122; CANR 45;
DLB 143, 175; NNAL

Sillanpaa, Frans Eemil 1888-1964 ... **CLC 19**
See also CA 129; 93-96; MTCW

Sillitoe, Alan 1928- ... **CLC 1, 3, 6, 10, 19, 57**
See also AITN 1; CA 9-12R; CAAS 2; CANR
8, 26, 55; CDBLB 1960 to Present; DLB 14,
139; MTCW; SATA 61

Silone, Ignazio 1900-1978 .... **CLC 4**
See also CA 25-28; 81-84; CANR 34; CAP 2;
MTCW

Silver, Joan Micklin 1935- .... **CLC 20**
See also CA 114; 121; INT 121

Silver, Nicholas
See Faust, Frederick (Schiller)

Silverberg, Robert 1935- CLC 7; DAM POP
See also CA 1-4R; CAAS 3; CANR 1, 20, 36;
DLB 8; INT CANR-20; MAICYA; MTCW;
SATA 13, 91

Silverstein, Alvin 1933- .... **CLC 17**
See also CA 49-52; CANR 2; CLR 25; JRDA;
MAICYA; SATA 8, 69

Silverstein, Virginia B(arbara Opshelor) 1937-
CLC 17
See also CA 49-52; CANR 2; CLR 25; JRDA;
MAICYA; SATA 8, 69

Sim, Georges
See Simenon, Georges (Jacques Christian)

Simak, Clifford D(onald) 1904-1988CLC 1, 55
See also CA 1-4R; 125; CANR 1, 35; DLB 8;
MTCW; SATA-Obit 56

Simenon, Georges (Jacques Christian) 1903-
1989 .. **CLC 1, 2, 3, 8, 18, 47; DAM POP**
See also CA 85-88; 129; CANR 35; DLB 72;
DLBY 89; MTCW

Simic, Charles 1938-.... **CLC 6, 9, 22, 49, 68;**
DAM POET
See also CA 29-32R; CAAS 4; CANR 12, 33,
52, 61; DLB 105

Simmel, Georg 1858-1918 .... **TCLC 64**
See also CA 157

Simmons, Charles (Paul) 1924-......... **CLC 57**
See also CA 89-92; INT 89-92

Simmons, Dan 1948- ..... **CLC 44; DAM POP**
See also AAYA 16; CA 138; CANR 53

Simmons, James (Stewart Alexander) 1933-
CLC 43
See also CA 105; CAAS 21; DLB 40

Simms, William Gilmore 1806-1870 NCLC 3
See also DLB 3, 30, 59, 73

Simon, Carly 1945- .... **CLC 26**
See also CA 105

Simon, Claude 1913- CLC 4, 9, 15, 39; DAM
NOV
See also CA 89-92; CANR 33; DLB 83; MTCW

Simon, (Marvin) Neil 1927-CLC 6, 11, 31, 39,
70; DAM DRAM
See also AITN 1; CA 21-24R; CANR 26, 54;
DLB 7; MTCW

Simon, Paul (Frederick) 1941(?)- ..... **CLC 17**
See also CA 116; 153

Simonon, Paul 1956(?)- .... **CLC 30**

Simpson, Harriette
See Arnow, Harriette (Louisa) Simpson

Simpson, Louis (Aston Marantz) 1923-CLC 4,
7, 9, 32; DAM POET
See also CA 1-4R; CAAS 4; CANR 1, 61; DLB
5; MTCW

Simpson, Mona (Elizabeth) 1957- .... **CLC 44**
See also CA 122; 135

Simpson, N(orman) F(rederick) 1919-**CLC 29**
See also CA 13-16R; DLB 13

Sinclair, Andrew (Annandale) 1935-. **CLC 2,**
14
See also CA 9-12R; CAAS 5; CANR 14, 38;
DLB 14; MTCW

Sinclair, Emil
See Hesse, Hermann

Sinclair, Iain 1943- .... **CLC 76**
See also CA 132

Sinclair, Iain MacGregor
See Sinclair, Iain

Sinclair, Irene
See Griffith, D(avid Lewelyn) W(ark)

Sinclair, Mary Amelia St. Clair 1865(?)-1946
See Sinclair, May
See also CA 104

Sinclair, May .... **TCLC 3, 11**
See also Sinclair, Mary Amelia St. Clair
See also DLB 36, 135

Sinclair, Roy
See Griffith, D(avid Lewelyn) W(ark)

Sinclair, Upton (Beall) 1878-1968 CLC 1, 11,
15, 63; DA; DAB; DAC; DAM MST, NOV;
WLC
See also CA 5-8R; 25-28R; CANR 7; CDALB
1929-1941; DLB 9; INT CANR-7; MTCW;
SATA 9

Singer, Isaac
See Singer, Isaac Bashevis

Singer, Isaac Bashevis 1904-1991CLC 1, 3, 6,
9, 11, 15, 23, 38, 69; DA; DAB; DAC; DAM
MST, NOV; SSC 3; WLC
See also AITN 1, 2; CA 1-4R; 134; CANR 1,
39; CDALB 1941-1968; CLR 1; DLB 6, 28,
52; DLBY 91; JRDA; MAICYA; MTCW;
SATA 3, 27; SATA-Obit 68

Singer, Israel Joshua 1893-1944 .... **TCLC 33**

Singh, Khushwant 1915- .... **CLC 11**
See also CA 9-12R; CAAS 9; CANR 6

Singleton, Ann
See Benedict, Ruth (Fulton)

Sinjohn, John
See Galsworthy, John

Sinyavsky, Andrei (Donatevich) 1925-1997
CLC 8
See also CA 85-88; 159

Sirin, V.
See Nabokov, Vladimir (Vladimirovich)

Sissman, L(ouis) E(dward) 1928-1976CLC 9,
18
See also CA 21-24R; 65-68; CANR 13; DLB 5

Sisson, C(harles) H(ubert) 1914- .... **CLC 8**
See also CA 1-4R; CAAS 3; CANR 3, 48; DLB
27

Sitwell, Dame Edith 1887-1964CLC 2, 9, 67;
DAM POET; PC 3
See also CA 9-12R; CANR 35; CDBLB 1945-
1960; DLB 20; MTCW

Siwaarmill, H. P.
See Sharp, William

Sjoewall, Maj 1935-............................. **CLC 7**
See also CA 65-68

Sjowall, Maj
See Sjoewall, Maj

Skelton, Robin 1925-1997 .... **CLC 13**
See also AITN 2; CA 5-8R; 160; CAAS 5;
CANR 28; DLB 27, 53

Skolimowski, Jerzy 1938- .... **CLC 20**
See also CA 128

Skram, Amalie (Bertha) 1847-1905TCLC 25

Skvorecky, Josef (Vaclav) 1924- CLC 15, 39,
69; DAC; DAM NOV

See also CA 61-64; CAAS 1; CANR 10, 34; MTCW

Slade, Bernard .... **CLC 11, 46**
See also Newbound, Bernard Slade
See also CAAS 9; DLB 53

Slaughter, Carolyn 1946- .... **CLC 56**
See also CA 85-88

Slaughter, Frank G(ill) 1908- .... **CLC 29**
See also AITN 2; CA 5-8R; CANR 5; INT CANR-5

Slavitt, David R(ytman) 1935- ...... **CLC 5, 14**
See also CA 21-24R; CAAS 3; CANR 41; DLB 5, 6

Slesinger, Tess 1905-1945 .... **TCLC 10**
See also CA 107; DLB 102

Slessor, Kenneth 1901-1971 .... **CLC 14**
See also CA 102; 89-92

Slowacki, Juliusz 1809-1849 .... **NCLC 15**

Smart, Christopher 1722-1771 .. **LC 3; DAM POET; PC 13**
See also DLB 109

Smart, Elizabeth 1913-1986 .... **CLC 54**
See also CA 81-84; 118; DLB 88

Smiley, Jane (Graves) 1949-**CLC 53, 76; DAM POP**
See also CA 104; CANR 30, 50; INT CANR-30

Smith, A(rthur) J(ames) M(arshall) 1902-1980 **CLC 15; DAC**
See also CA 1-4R; 102; CANR 4; DLB 88

Smith, Adam 1723-1790 .... **LC 36**
See also DLB 104

Smith, Alexander 1829-1867 .... **NCLC 59**
See also DLB 32, 55

Smith, Anna Deavere 1950- .... **CLC 86**
See also CA 133

Smith, Betty (Wehner) 1896-1972 .... **CLC 19**
See also CA 5-8R; 33-36R; DLBY 82; SATA 6

Smith, Charlotte (Turner) 1749-1806 **N C L C 23**
See also DLB 39, 109

Smith, Clark Ashton 1893-1961 .... **CLC 43**
See also CA 143

Smith, Dave .... **CLC 22, 42**
See also Smith, David (Jeddie)
See also CAAS 7; DLB 5

Smith, David (Jeddie) 1942-
See Smith, Dave
See also CA 49-52; CANR 1, 59; DAM POET

Smith, Florence Margaret 1902-1971
See Smith, Stevie
See also CA 17-18; 29-32R; CANR 35; CAP 2; DAM POET; MTCW

Smith, Iain Crichton 1928- .... **CLC 64**
See also CA 21-24R; DLB 40, 139

Smith, John 1580(?)-1631 .... **LC 9**

Smith, Johnston
See Crane, Stephen (Townley)

Smith, Joseph, Jr. 1805-1844 .... **NCLC 53**

Smith, Lee 1944- .... **CLC 25, 73**
See also CA 114; 119; CANR 46; DLB 143; DLBY 83; INT 119

Smith, Martin
See Smith, Martin Cruz

Smith, Martin Cruz 1942- ..... **CLC 25; DAM MULT, POP**
See also BEST 89:4; CA 85-88; CANR 6, 23, 43; INT CANR-23; NNAL

Smith, Mary-Ann Tirone 1944- .... **CLC 39**
See also CA 118; 136

Smith, Patti 1946- .... **CLC 12**
See also CA 93-96

Smith, Pauline (Urmson) 1882-1959**TCLC 25**

Smith, Rosamond
See Oates, Joyce Carol

Smith, Sheila Kaye
See Kaye-Smith, Sheila

Smith, Stevie .... **CLC 3, 8, 25, 44; PC 12**
See also Smith, Florence Margaret
See also DLB 20

Smith, Wilbur (Addison) 1933- .... **CLC 33**
See also CA 13-16R; CANR 7, 46; MTCW

Smith, William Jay 1918- .... **CLC 6**
See also CA 5-8R; CANR 44; DLB 5; MAICYA; SAAS 22; SATA 2, 68

Smith, Woodrow Wilson
See Kuttner, Henry

Smolenskin, Peretz 1842-1885 .... **NCLC 30**

Smollett, Tobias (George) 1721-1771 .... **LC 2**
See also CDBLB 1660-1789; DLB 39, 104

Snodgrass, W(illiam) D(e Witt) 1926-**CLC 2, 6, 10, 18, 68; DAM POET**
See also CA 1-4R; CANR 6, 36; DLB 5; MTCW

Snow, C(harles) P(ercy) 1905-1980**CLC 1, 4, 6, 9, 13, 19; DAM NOV**
See also CA 5-8R; 101; CANR 28; CDBLB 1945-1960; DLB 15, 77; MTCW

Snow, Frances Compton
See Adams, Henry (Brooks)

Snyder, Gary (Sherman) 1930-**CLC 1, 2, 5, 9, 32; DAM POET; PC 21**
See also CA 17-20R; CANR 30, 60; DLB 5, 16, 165

Snyder, Zilpha Keatley 1927- .... **CLC 17**
See also AAYA 15; CA 9-12R; CANR 38; CLR 31; JRDA; MAICYA; SAAS 2; SATA 1, 28, 75

Soares, Bernardo
See Pessoa, Fernando (Antonio Nogueira)

Sobh, A.
See Shamlu, Ahmad

Sobol, Joshua .... **CLC 60**

Soderberg, Hjalmar 1869-1941 ..... **TCLC 39**

Sodergran, Edith (Irene)
See Soedergran, Edith (Irene)

Soedergran, Edith (Irene) 1892-1923 **T C L C 31**

Softly, Edgar
See Lovecraft, H(oward) P(hillips)

Softly, Edward
See Lovecraft, H(oward) P(hillips)

Sokolov, Raymond 1941- .... **CLC 7**
See also CA 85-88

Solo, Jay
See Ellison, Harlan (Jay)

Sologub, Fyodor .... **TCLC 9**
See also Teternikov, Fyodor Kuzmich

Solomons, Ikey Esquir
See Thackeray, William Makepeace

Solomos, Dionysios 1798-1857 .... **NCLC 15**

Solwoska, Mara
See French, Marilyn

Solzhenitsyn, Aleksandr I(sayevich) 1918-**CLC 1, 2, 4, 7, 9, 10, 18, 26, 34, 78; DA; DAB; DAC; DAM MST, NOV; WLC**
See also AITN 1; CA 69-72; CANR 40; MTCW

Somers, Jane
See Lessing, Doris (May)

Somerville, Edith 1858-1949 .... **TCLC 51**
See also DLB 135

Somerville & Ross
See Martin, Violet Florence; Somerville, Edith

Sommer, Scott 1951- .... **CLC 25**
See also CA 106

Sondheim, Stephen (Joshua) 1930- . **CLC 30, 39; DAM DRAM**

See also AAYA 11; CA 103; CANR 47

Song, Cathy 1955- .... **PC 21**
See also DLB 169

Sontag, Susan 1933-**CLC 1, 2, 10, 13, 31, 105; DAM POP**
See also CA 17-20R; CANR 25, 51; DLB 2, 67; MTCW

Sophocles 496(?)B.C.-406(?)B.C. ... **CMLC 2; DA; DAB; DAC; DAM DRAM, MST; DC 1; WLCS**
See also DLB 176

Sordello 1189-1269 .... **CMLC 15**

Sorel, Julia
See Drexler, Rosalyn

Sorrentino, Gilbert 1929-**CLC 3, 7, 14, 22, 40**
See also CA 77-80; CANR 14, 33; DLB 5, 173; DLBY 80; INT CANR-14

Soto, Gary 1952- **CLC 32, 80; DAM MULT; HLC**
See also AAYA 10; CA 119; 125; CANR 50; CLR 38; DLB 82; HW; INT 125; JRDA; SATA 80

Soupault, Philippe 1897-1990 .... **CLC 68**
See also CA 116; 147; 131

Souster, (Holmes) Raymond 1921-**CLC 5, 14; DAC; DAM POET**
See also CA 13-16R; CAAS 14; CANR 13, 29, 53; DLB 88; SATA 63

Southern, Terry 1924(?)-1995 .... **CLC 7**
See also CA 1-4R; 150; CANR 1, 55; DLB 2

Southey, Robert 1774-1843 .... **NCLC 8**
See also DLB 93, 107, 142; SATA 54

Southworth, Emma Dorothy Eliza Nevitte 1819-1899 .... **NCLC 26**

Souza, Ernest
See Scott, Evelyn

Soyinka, Wole 1934-**CLC 3, 5, 14, 36, 44; BLC; DA; DAB; DAC; DAM DRAM, MST, MULT; DC 2; WLC**
See also BW 2; CA 13-16R; CANR 27, 39; DLB 125; MTCW

Spackman, W(illiam) M(ode) 1905-1990**C L C 46**
See also CA 81-84; 132

Spacks, Barry (Bernard) 1931- .... **CLC 14**
See also CA 154; CANR 33; DLB 105

Spanidou, Irini 1946- .... **CLC 44**

Spark, Muriel (Sarah) 1918-**CLC 2, 3, 5, 8, 13, 18, 40, 94; DAB; DAC; DAM MST, NOV; SSC 10**
See also CA 5-8R; CANR 12, 36; CDBLB 1945-1960; DLB 15, 139; INT CANR-12; MTCW

Spaulding, Douglas
See Bradbury, Ray (Douglas)

Spaulding, Leonard
See Bradbury, Ray (Douglas)

Spence, J. A. D.
See Eliot, T(homas) S(tearns)

Spencer, Elizabeth 1921- .... **CLC 22**
See also CA 13-16R; CANR 32; DLB 6; MTCW; SATA 14

Spencer, Leonard G.
See Silverberg, Robert

Spencer, Scott 1945- .... **CLC 30**
See also CA 113; CANR 51; DLBY 86

Spender, Stephen (Harold) 1909-1995**CLC 1, 2, 5, 10, 41, 91; DAM POET**
See also CA 9-12R; 149; CANR 31, 54; CDBLB 1945-1960; DLB 20; MTCW

Spengler, Oswald (Arnold Gottfried) 1880-1936 **TCLC 25**
See also CA 118

Spenser, Edmund 1552(?)-1599**LC 5, 39; DA;**

See also AAYA 15; CA 110; CANR 55

Stone, Robert (Anthony) 1937-**CLC 5, 23, 42**
See also CA 85-88; CANR 23; DLB 152; INT CANR-23; MTCW

Stone, Zachary
See Follett, Ken(neth Martin)

Stoppard, Tom 1937-**CLC 1, 3, 4, 5, 8, 15, 29, 34, 63, 91; DA; DAB; DAC; DAM DRAM, MST; DC 6; WLC**
See also CA 81-84; CANR 39; CDBLB 1960 to Present; DLB 13; DLBY 85; MTCW

Storey, David (Malcolm) 1933-**CLC 2, 4, 5, 8; DAM DRAM**
See also CA 81-84; CANR 36; DLB 13, 14; MTCW

Storm, Hyemeyohsts 1935- ...... **CLC 3; DAM MULT**
See also CA 81-84; CANR 45; NNAL

Storm, (Hans) Theodor (Woldsen) 1817-1888 **NCLC 1; SSC 27**

Storni, Alfonsina 1892-1938 . **TCLC 5; DAM MULT; HLC**
See also CA 104; 131; HW

Stoughton, William 1631-1701 .... **LC 38**
See also DLB 24

Stout, Rex (Todhunter) 1886-1975 ..... **CLC 3**
See also AITN 2; CA 61-64

Stow, (Julian) Randolph 1935- .. **CLC 23, 48**
See also CA 13-16R; CANR 33; MTCW

Stowe, Harriet (Elizabeth) Beecher 1811-1896 **NCLC 3, 50; DA; DAB; DAC; DAM MST, NOV; WLC**
See also CDALB 1865-1917; DLB 1, 12, 42, 74; JRDA; MAICYA; YABC 1

Strachey, (Giles) Lytton 1880-1932 **TCLC 12**
See also CA 110; DLB 149; DLBD 10

Strand, Mark 1934- **CLC 6, 18, 41, 71; DAM POET**
See also CA 21-24R; CANR 40; DLB 5; SATA 41

Straub, Peter (Francis) 1943- **CLC 28; DAM POP**
See also BEST 89:1; CA 85-88; CANR 28; DLBY 84; MTCW

Strauss, Botho 1944- .... **CLC 22**
See also CA 157; DLB 124

Streatfeild, (Mary) Noel 1895(?)-1986**CLC 21**
See also CA 81-84; 120; CANR 31; CLR 17; DLB 160; MAICYA; SATA 20; SATA-Obit 48

Stribling, T(homas) S(igismund) 1881-1965 **CLC 23**
See also CA 107; DLB 9

Strindberg, (Johan) August 1849-1912**TCLC 1, 8, 21, 47; DA; DAB; DAC; DAM DRAM, MST; WLC**
See also CA 104; 135

Stringer, Arthur 1874-1950 .... **TCLC 37**
See also CA 161; DLB 92

Stringer, David
See Roberts, Keith (John Kingston)

Stroheim, Erich von 1885-1957 ..... **TCLC 71**

Strugatskii, Arkadii (Natanovich) 1925-1991 **CLC 27**
See also CA 106; 135

Strugatskii, Boris (Natanovich) 1933-**CLC 27**
See also CA 106

Strummer, Joe 1953(?)- .... **CLC 30**

Stuart, Don A.
See Campbell, John W(ood, Jr.)

Stuart, Ian
See MacLean, Alistair (Stuart)

Stuart, Jesse (Hilton) 1906-1984**CLC 1, 8, 11, 14, 34**
See also CA 5-8R; 112; CANR 31; DLB 9, 48, 102; DLBY 84; SATA 2; SATA-Obit 36

Sturgeon, Theodore (Hamilton) 1918-1985 **CLC 22, 39**
See also Queen, Ellery
See also CA 81-84; 116; CANR 32; DLB 8; DLBY 85; MTCW

Sturges, Preston 1898-1959 .... **TCLC 48**
See also CA 114; 149; DLB 26

Styron, William 1925-**CLC 1, 3, 5, 11, 15, 60; DAM NOV, POP; SSC 25**
See also BEST 90:4; CA 5-8R; CANR 6, 33; CDALB 1968-1988; DLB 2, 143; DLBY 80; INT CANR-6; MTCW

Suarez Lynch, B.
See Bioy Casares, Adolfo; Borges, Jorge Luis

Su Chien 1884-1918
See Su Man-shu
See also CA 123

Suckow, Ruth 1892-1960 .... **SSC 18**
See also CA 113; DLB 9, 102

Sudermann, Hermann 1857-1928 .. **TCLC 15**
See also CA 107; DLB 118

Sue, Eugene 1804-1857 .... **NCLC 1**
See also DLB 119

Sueskind, Patrick 1949- .... **CLC 44**
See also Suskind, Patrick

Sukenick, Ronald 1932- .... **CLC 3, 4, 6, 48**
See also CA 25-28R; CAAS 8; CANR 32; DLB 173; DLBY 81

Suknaski, Andrew 1942- .... **CLC 19**
See also CA 101; DLB 53

Sullivan, Vernon
See Vian, Boris

Sully Prudhomme 1839-1907 .... **TCLC 31**

Su Man-shu .... **TCLC 24**
See also Su Chien

Summerforest, Ivy B.
See Kirkup, James

Summers, Andrew James 1942- .... **CLC 26**

Summers, Andy
See Summers, Andrew James

Summers, Hollis (Spurgeon, Jr.) 1916-**CLC 10**
See also CA 5-8R; CANR 3; DLB 6

Summers, (Alphonsus Joseph-Mary Augustus) Montague 1880-1948 .... **TCLC 16**
See also CA 118

Sumner, Gordon Matthew 1951- ...... **CLC 26**

Surtees, Robert Smith 1803-1864 .. **NCLC 14**
See also DLB 21

Susann, Jacqueline 1921-1974 .... **CLC 3**
See also AITN 1; CA 65-68; 53-56; MTCW

Su Shih 1036-1101 .... **CMLC 15**

Suskind, Patrick
See Sueskind, Patrick
See also CA 145

Sutcliff, Rosemary 1920-1992**CLC 26; DAB; DAC; DAM MST, POP**
See also AAYA 10; CA 5-8R; 139; CANR 37; CLR 1, 37; JRDA; MAICYA; SATA 6, 44, 78; SATA-Obit 73

Sutro, Alfred 1863-1933 .... **TCLC 6**
See also CA 105; DLB 10

Sutton, Henry
See Slavitt, David R(ytman)

Svevo, Italo 1861-1928 . **TCLC 2, 35; SSC 25**
See also Schmitz, Aron Hector

Swados, Elizabeth (A.) 1951- .... **CLC 12**
See also CA 97-100; CANR 49; INT 97-100

Swados, Harvey 1920-1972 .... **CLC 5**
See also CA 5-8R; 37-40R; CANR 6; DLB 2

Swan, Gladys 1934- .... **CLC 69**

See also CA 101; CANR 17, 39

Swarthout, Glendon (Fred) 1918-1992**CLC 35**
See also CA 1-4R; 139; CANR 1, 47; SATA 26

Sweet, Sarah C.
See Jewett, (Theodora) Sarah Orne

Swenson, May 1919-1989**CLC 4, 14, 61, 106; DA; DAB; DAC; DAM MST, POET; PC 14**
See also CA 5-8R; 130; CANR 36, 61; DLB 5; MTCW; SATA 15

Swift, Augustus
See Lovecraft, H(oward) P(hillips)

Swift, Graham (Colin) 1949- ...... **CLC 41, 88**
See also CA 117; 122; CANR 46

Swift, Jonathan 1667-1745 **LC 1; DA; DAB; DAC; DAM MST, NOV, POET; PC 9; WLC**
See also CDBLB 1660-1789; DLB 39, 95, 101; SATA 19

Swinburne, Algernon Charles 1837-1909 **TCLC 8, 36; DA; DAB; DAC; DAM MST, POET; WLC**
See also CA 105; 140; CDBLB 1832-1890; DLB 35, 57

Swinfen, Ann .... **CLC 34**

Swinnerton, Frank Arthur 1884-1982**CLC 31**
See also CA 108; DLB 34

Swithen, John
See King, Stephen (Edwin)

Sylvia
See Ashton-Warner, Sylvia (Constance)

Symmes, Robert Edward
See Duncan, Robert (Edward)

Symonds, John Addington 1840-1893 **NCLC 34**
See also DLB 57, 144

Symons, Arthur 1865-1945 .... **TCLC 11**
See also CA 107; DLB 19, 57, 149

Symons, Julian (Gustave) 1912-1994 **CLC 2, 14, 32**
See also CA 49-52; 147; CAAS 3; CANR 3, 33, 59; DLB 87, 155; DLBY 92; MTCW

Synge, (Edmund) J(ohn) M(illington) 1871-1909 ... **TCLC 6, 37; DAM DRAM; DC 2**
See also CA 104; 141; CDBLB 1890-1914; DLB 10, 19

Syruc, J.
See Milosz, Czeslaw

Szirtes, George 1948- .... **CLC 46**
See also CA 109; CANR 27, 61

Szymborska, Wislawa 1923-.............. **CLC 99**
See also CA 154; DLBY 96

T. O., Nik
See Annensky, Innokenty (Fyodorovich)

Tabori, George 1914- .... **CLC 19**
See also CA 49-52; CANR 4

Tagore, Rabindranath 1861-1941**TCLC 3, 53; DAM DRAM, POET; PC 8**
See also CA 104; 120; MTCW

Taine, Hippolyte Adolphe 1828-1893 . **NCLC 15**

Talese, Gay 1932-............................... **CLC 37**
See also AITN 1; CA 1-4R; CANR 9, 58; INT CANR-9; MTCW

Tallent, Elizabeth (Ann) 1954- .... **CLC 45**
See also CA 117; DLB 130

Tally, Ted 1952- .... **CLC 42**
See also CA 120; 124; INT 124

Tamayo y Baus, Manuel 1829-1898 **NCLC 1**

Tammsaare, A(nton) H(ansen) 1878-1940 **TCLC 27**

Tam'si, Tchicaya U
See Tchicaya, Gerald Felix

46
See also DLB 90
Tiger, Derry
See Ellison, Harlan (Jay)
Tilghman, Christopher 1948(?)- .... **CLC 65**
See also CA 159
Tillinghast, Richard (Williford) 1940-**CLC 29**
See also CA 29-32R; CAAS 23; CANR 26, 51
Timrod, Henry 1828-1867 .... **NCLC 25**
See also DLB 3
Tindall, Gillian 1938- .... **CLC 7**
See also CA 21-24R; CANR 11
Tiptree, James, Jr. .... **CLC 48, 50**
See also Sheldon, Alice Hastings Bradley
See also DLB 8
Titmarsh, Michael Angelo
See Thackeray, William Makepeace
Tocqueville, Alexis (Charles Henri Maurice Clerel Comte) 1805-1859 ...**NCLC 7, 63**
Tolkien, J(ohn) R(onald) R(euel) 1892-1973
  CLC 1, 2, 3, 8, 12, 38; DA; DAB; DAC; DAM MST, NOV, POP; WLC
  See also AAYA 10; AITN 1; CA 17-18; 45-48; CANR 36; CAP 2; CDBLB 1914-1945; DLB 15, 160; JRDA; MAICYA; MTCW; SATA 2, 32; SATA-Obit 24
Toller, Ernst 1893-1939 .... **TCLC 10**
See also CA 107; DLB 124
Tolson, M. B.
See Tolson, Melvin B(eaunorus)
Tolson, Melvin B(eaunorus) 1898(?)-1966
  CLC 36, 105; BLC; DAM MULT, POET
  See also BW 1; CA 124; 89-92; DLB 48, 76
Tolstoi, Aleksei Nikolaevich
See Tolstoy, Alexey Nikolaevich
Tolstoy, Alexey Nikolaevich 1882-1945**TCLC 18**
See also CA 107; 158
Tolstoy, Count Leo
See Tolstoy, Leo (Nikolaevich)
Tolstoy, Leo (Nikolaevich) 1828-1910**TCLC 4, 11, 17, 28, 44; DA; DAB; DAC; DAM MST, NOV; SSC 9; WLC**
  See also CA 104; 123; SATA 26
Tomasi di Lampedusa, Giuseppe 1896-1957
See Lampedusa, Giuseppe (Tomasi) di
See also CA 111
Tomlin, Lily .... **CLC 17**
See also Tomlin, Mary Jean
Tomlin, Mary Jean 1939(?)-
See Tomlin, Lily
See also CA 117
Tomlinson, (Alfred) Charles 1927-**CLC 2, 4, 6, 13, 45; DAM POET; PC 17**
See also CA 5-8R; CANR 33; DLB 40
Tomlinson, H(enry) M(ajor) 1873-1958**TCLC 71**
See also CA 118; 161; DLB 36, 100
Tonson, Jacob
See Bennett, (Enoch) Arnold
Toole, John Kennedy 1937-1969 **CLC 19, 64**
See also CA 104; DLBY 81
Toomer, Jean 1894-1967 ....**CLC 1, 4, 13, 22; BLC; DAM MULT; PC 7; SSC 1; WLCS**
See also BW 1; CA 85-88; CDALB 1917-1929; DLB 45, 51; MTCW
Torley, Luke
See Blish, James (Benjamin)
Tornimparte, Alessandra
See Ginzburg, Natalia
Torre, Raoul della
See Mencken, H(enry) L(ouis)
Torrey, E(dwin) Fuller 1937- .... **CLC 34**

See also CA 119
Torsvan, Ben Traven
See Traven, B.
Torsvan, Benno Traven
See Traven, B.
Torsvan, Berick Traven
See Traven, B.
Torsvan, Berwick Traven
See Traven, B.
Torsvan, Bruno Traven
See Traven, B.
Torsvan, Traven
See Traven, B.
Tournier, Michel (Edouard) 1924-**CLC 6, 23, 36, 95**
See also CA 49-52; CANR 3, 36; DLB 83; MTCW; SATA 23
Tournimparte, Alessandra
See Ginzburg, Natalia
Towers, Ivar
See Kornbluth, C(yril) M.
Towne, Robert (Burton) 1936(?)- ..... **CLC 87**
See also CA 108; DLB 44
Townsend, Sue 1946- ....**CLC 61; DAB; DAC**
See also CA 119; 127; INT 127; MTCW; SATA 55, 93; SATA-Brief 48
Townshend, Peter (Dennis Blandford) 1945-
  CLC 17, 42
See also CA 107
Tozzi, Federigo 1883-1920 .... **TCLC 31**
See also CA 160
Traill, Catharine Parr 1802-1899 ..**NCLC 31**
See also DLB 99
Trakl, Georg 1887-1914 .... **TCLC 5; PC 20**
See also CA 104
Transtroemer, Tomas (Goesta) 1931-**CLC 52, 65; DAM POET**
See also CA 117; 129; CAAS 17
Transtromer, Tomas Gosta
See Transtroemer, Tomas (Goesta)
Traven, B. (?)-1969 .... **CLC 8, 11**
See also CA 19-20; 25-28R; CAP 2; DLB 9, 56; MTCW
Treitel, Jonathan 1959- .... **CLC 70**
Tremain, Rose 1943- .... **CLC 42**
See also CA 97-100; CANR 44; DLB 14
Tremblay, Michel 1942- **CLC 29, 102; DAC; DAM MST**
See also CA 116; 128; DLB 60; MTCW
Trevanian .... **CLC 29**
See also Whitaker, Rod(ney)
Trevor, Glen
See Hilton, James
Trevor, William 1928- . **CLC 7, 9, 14, 25, 71; SSC 21**
See also Cox, William Trevor
See also DLB 14, 139
Trifonov, Yuri (Valentinovich) 1925-1981
  CLC 45
See also CA 126; 103; MTCW
Trilling, Lionel 1905-1975 ...... **CLC 9, 11, 24**
See also CA 9-12R; 61-64; CANR 10; DLB 28, 63; INT CANR-10; MTCW
Trimball, W. H.
See Mencken, H(enry) L(ouis)
Tristan
See Gomez de la Serna, Ramon
Tristram
See Housman, A(lfred) E(dward)
Trogdon, William (Lewis) 1939-
See Heat-Moon, William Least
See also CA 115; 119; CANR 47; INT 119
Trollope, Anthony 1815-1882**NCLC 6, 33; DA;**

DAB; DAC; DAM MST, NOV; SSC 28; WLC
See also CDBLB 1832-1890; DLB 21, 57, 159; SATA 22
Trollope, Frances 1779-1863 .... **NCLC 30**
See also DLB 21, 166
Trotsky, Leon 1879-1940 .... **TCLC 22**
See also CA 118
Trotter (Cockburn), Catharine 1679-1749**LC 8**
See also DLB 84
Trout, Kilgore
See Farmer, Philip Jose
Trow, George W. S. 1943- .... **CLC 52**
See also CA 126
Troyat, Henri 1911- .... **CLC 23**
See also CA 45-48; CANR 2, 33; MTCW
Trudeau, G(arretson) B(eekman) 1948-
See Trudeau, Garry B.
See also CA 81-84; CANR 31; SATA 35
Trudeau, Garry B. .... **CLC 12**
See also Trudeau, G(arretson) B(eekman)
See also AAYA 10; AITN 2
Truffaut, Francois 1932-1984 .. **CLC 20, 101**
See also CA 81-84; 113; CANR 34
Trumbo, Dalton 1905-1976 .... **CLC 19**
See also CA 21-24R; 69-72; CANR 10; DLB 26
Trumbull, John 1750-1831 .... **NCLC 30**
See also DLB 31
Trundlett, Helen B.
See Eliot, T(homas) S(tearns)
Tryon, Thomas 1926-1991 . **CLC 3, 11; DAM POP**
See also AITN 1; CA 29-32R; 135; CANR 32; MTCW
Tryon, Tom
See Tryon, Thomas
Ts'ao Hsueh-ch'in 1715(?)-1763 .... **LC 1**
Tsushima, Shuji 1909-1948
See Dazai, Osamu
See also CA 107
Tsvetaeva (Efron), Marina (Ivanovna) 1892-1941 .... **TCLC 7, 35; PC 14**
See also CA 104; 128; MTCW
Tuck, Lily 1938- .... **CLC 70**
See also CA 139
Tu Fu 712-770 .... **PC 9**
See also DAM MULT
Tunis, John R(oberts) 1889-1975 ...... **CLC 12**
See also CA 61-64; CANR 62; DLB 22, 171; JRDA; MAICYA; SATA 37; SATA-Brief 30
Tuohy, Frank .... **CLC 37**
See also Tuohy, John Francis
See also DLB 14, 139
Tuohy, John Francis 1925-
See Tuohy, Frank
See also CA 5-8R; CANR 3, 47
Turco, Lewis (Putnam) 1934- ...... **CLC 11, 63**
See also CA 13-16R; CAAS 22; CANR 24, 51; DLBY 84
Turgenev, Ivan 1818-1883 .... **NCLC 21; DA; DAB; DAC; DAM MST, NOV; DC 7; SSC 7; WLC**
Turgot, Anne-Robert-Jacques 1727-1781 **LC 26**
Turner, Frederick 1943- .... **CLC 48**
See also CA 73-76; CAAS 10; CANR 12, 30, 56; DLB 40
Tutu, Desmond M(pilo) 1931-**CLC 80; BLC; DAM MULT**
See also BW 1; CA 125
Tutuola, Amos 1920-1997**CLC 5, 14, 29; BLC;**

Vicar, Henry
See Felsen, Henry Gregor

Vicker, Angus
See Felsen, Henry Gregor

Vidal, Gore 1925-CLC 2, 4, 6, 8, 10, 22, 33, 72; **DAM NOV, POP**
See also AITN 1; BEST 90:2; CA 5-8R; CANR 13, 45; DLB 6, 152; INT CANR-13; MTCW

Viereck, Peter (Robert Edwin) 1916- . CLC 4
See also CA 1-4R; CANR 1, 47; DLB 5

Vigny, Alfred (Victor) de 1797-1863NCLC 7; **DAM POET**
See also DLB 119

Vilakazi, Benedict Wallet 1906-1947TCLC 37

Villiers de l'Isle Adam, Jean Marie Mathias Philippe Auguste Comte 1838-1889 **NCLC 3; SSC 14**
See also DLB 123

Villon, Francois 1431-1463(?) .... **PC 13**

Vinci, Leonardo da 1452-1519 ....**LC 12**

Vine, Barbara .... **CLC 50**
See also Rendell, Ruth (Barbara)
See also BEST 90:4

Vinge, Joan D(ennison) 1948-CLC 30; SSC 24
See also CA 93-96; SATA 36

Violis, G.
See Simenon, Georges (Jacques Christian)

Visconti, Luchino 1906-1976 .... **CLC 16**
See also CA 81-84; 65-68; CANR 39

Vittorini, Elio 1908-1966 .... **CLC 6, 9, 14**
See also CA 133; 25-28R

Vizenor, Gerald Robert 1934-CLC 103; DAM MULT
See also CA 13-16R; CAAS 22; CANR 5, 21, 44; DLB 175; NNAL

Vizinczey, Stephen 1933- .... **CLC 40**
See also CA 128; INT 128

Vliet, R(ussell) G(ordon) 1929-1984 **CLC 22**
See also CA 37-40R; 112; CANR 18

Vogau, Boris Andreyevich 1894-1937(?)
See Pilnyak, Boris
See also CA 123

Vogel, Paula A(nne) 1951- .... **CLC 76**
See also CA 108

Voight, Ellen Bryant 1943- .... **CLC 54**
See also CA 69-72; CANR 11, 29, 55; DLB 120

Voigt, Cynthia 1942- .... **CLC 30**
See also AAYA 3; CA 106; CANR 18, 37, 40; CLR 13,48; INT CANR-18; JRDA; MAICYA; SATA 48, 79; SATA-Brief 33

Voinovich, Vladimir (Nikolaevich) 1932-CLC 10, 49
See also CA 81-84; CAAS 12; CANR 33; MTCW

Vollmann, William T. 1959-... CLC 89; DAM NOV, POP
See also CA 134

Voloshinov, V. N.
See Bakhtin, Mikhail Mikhailovich

Voltaire 1694-1778. LC 14; DA; DAB; DAC; DAM DRAM, MST; SSC 12; WLC

von Daeniken, Erich 1935- .... **CLC 30**
See also AITN 1; CA 37-40R; CANR 17, 44

von Daniken, Erich
See von Daeniken, Erich

von Heidenstam, (Carl Gustaf) Verner
See Heidenstam, (Carl Gustaf) Verner von

von Heyse, Paul (Johann Ludwig)
See Heyse, Paul (Johann Ludwig von)

von Hofmannsthal, Hugo
See Hofmannsthal, Hugo von

von Horvath, Odon
See Horvath, Oedoen von

von Horvath, Oedoen
See Horvath, Oedoen von

von Liliencron, (Friedrich Adolf Axel) Detlev
See Liliencron, (Friedrich Adolf Axel) Detlev von

Vonnegut, Kurt, Jr. 1922-CLC 1, 2, 3, 4, 5, 8, 12, 22, 40, 60; DA; DAB; DAC; DAM MST, NOV, POP; SSC 8; WLC
See also AAYA 6; AITN 1; BEST 90:4; CA 1-4R; CANR 1, 25, 49; CDALB 1968-1988; DLB 2, 8, 152; DLBD 3; DLBY 80; MTCW

Von Rachen, Kurt
See Hubbard, L(afayette) Ron(ald)

von Rezzori (d'Arezzo), Gregor
See Rezzori (d'Arezzo), Gregor von

von Sternberg, Josef
See Sternberg, Josef von

Vorster, Gordon 1924- .... **CLC 34**
See also CA 133

Vosce, Trudie
See Ozick, Cynthia

Voznesensky, Andrei (Andreievich) 1933- CLC 1, 15, 57; DAM POET
See also CA 89-92; CANR 37; MTCW

Waddington, Miriam 1917- .... **CLC 28**
See also CA 21-24R; CANR 12, 30; DLB 68

Wagman, Fredrica 1937- .... **CLC 7**
See also CA 97-100; INT 97-100

Wagner, Linda W.
See Wagner-Martin, Linda (C.)

Wagner, Linda Welshimer
See Wagner-Martin, Linda (C.)

Wagner, Richard 1813-1883 .... **NCLC 9**
See also DLB 129

Wagner-Martin, Linda (C.) 1936- .... **CLC 50**
See also CA 159

Wagoner, David (Russell) 1926- CLC 3, 5, 15
See also CA 1-4R; CAAS 3; CANR 2; DLB 5; SATA 14

Wah, Fred(erick James) 1939- .... **CLC 44**
See also CA 107; 141; DLB 60

Wahloo, Per 1926-1975 .... **CLC 7**
See also CA 61-64

Wahloo, Peter
See Wahloo, Per

Wain, John (Barrington) 1925-1994 . CLC 2, 11, 15, 46
See also CA 5-8R; 145; CAAS 4; CANR 23, 54; CDBLB 1960 to Present; DLB 15, 27, 139, 155; MTCW

Wajda, Andrzej 1926- .... **CLC 16**
See also CA 102

Wakefield, Dan 1932- .... **CLC 7**
See also CA 21-24R; CAAS 7

Wakoski, Diane 1937- CLC 2, 4, 7, 9, 11, 40; DAM POET; PC 15
See also CA 13-16R; CAAS 1; CANR 9, 60; DLB 5; INT CANR-9

Wakoski-Sherbell, Diane
See Wakoski, Diane

Walcott, Derek (Alton) 1930-CLC 2, 4, 9, 14, 25, 42, 67, 76; BLC; DAB; DAC; DAM MST, MULT, POET; DC 7
See also BW 2; CA 89-92; CANR 26, 47; DLB 117; DLBY 81; MTCW

Waldman, Anne 1945- .... **CLC 7**
See also CA 37-40R; CAAS 17; CANR 34; DLB 16

Waldo, E. Hunter
See Sturgeon, Theodore (Hamilton)

Waldo, Edward Hamilton
See Sturgeon, Theodore (Hamilton)

Walker, Alice (Malsenior) 1944- CLC 5, 6, 9, 19, 27, 46, 58, 103; BLC; DA; DAB; DAC; DAM MST, MULT, NOV, POET, POP; SSC 5; WLCS
See also AAYA 3; BEST 89:4; BW 2; CA 37-40R; CANR 9, 27, 49; CDALB 1968-1988; DLB 6, 33, 143; INT CANR-27; MTCW; SATA 31

Walker, David Harry 1911-1992 .... **CLC 14**
See also CA 1-4R; 137; CANR 1; SATA 8; SATA-Obit 71

Walker, Edward Joseph 1934-
See Walker, Ted
See also CA 21-24R; CANR 12, 28, 53

Walker, George F. 1947- . CLC 44, 61; DAB; DAC; DAM MST
See also CA 103; CANR 21, 43, 59; DLB 60

Walker, Joseph A. 1935- .... CLC 19; DAM DRAM, MST
See also BW 1; CA 89-92; CANR 26; DLB 38

Walker, Margaret (Abigail) 1915- CLC 1, 6; BLC; DAM MULT; PC 20
See also BW 2; CA 73-76; CANR 26, 54; DLB 76, 152; MTCW

Walker, Ted .... **CLC 13**
See also Walker, Edward Joseph
See also DLB 40

Wallace, David Foster 1962- .... **CLC 50**
See also CA 132; CANR 59

Wallace, Dexter
See Masters, Edgar Lee

Wallace, (Richard Horatio) Edgar 1875-1932 **TCLC 57**
See also CA 115; DLB 70

Wallace, Irving 1916-1990 CLC 7, 13; DAM NOV, POP
See also AITN 1; CA 1-4R; 132; CAAS 1; CANR 1, 27; INT CANR-27; MTCW

Wallant, Edward Lewis 1926-1962CLC 5, 10
See also CA 1-4R; CANR 22; DLB 2, 28, 143; MTCW

Walley, Byron
See Card, Orson Scott

Walpole, Horace 1717-1797 .... **LC 2**
See also DLB 39, 104

Walpole, Hugh (Seymour) 1884-1941TCLC 5
See also CA 104; DLB 34

Walser, Martin 1927- .... **CLC 27**
See also CA 57-60; CANR 8, 46; DLB 75, 124

Walser, Robert 1878-1956 **TCLC 18; SSC 20**
See also CA 118; DLB 66

Walsh, Jill Paton .... **CLC 35**
See also Paton Walsh, Gillian
See also AAYA 11; CLR 2; DLB 161; SAAS 3

Walter, Villiam Christian
See Andersen, Hans Christian

Wambaugh, Joseph (Aloysius, Jr.) 1937-CLC 3, 18; DAM NOV, POP
See also AITN 1; BEST 89:3; CA 33-36R; CANR 42; DLB 6; DLBY 83; MTCW

Wang Wei 699(?)-761(?) .... **PC 18**

Ward, Arthur Henry Sarsfield 1883-1959
See Rohmer, Sax
See also CA 108

Ward, Douglas Turner 1930- .... **CLC 19**
See also BW 1; CA 81-84; CANR 27; DLB 7, 38

Ward, Mary Augusta
See Ward, Mrs. Humphry

Ward, Mrs. Humphry 1851-1920 .. **TCLC 55**
See also DLB 18

Ward, Peter
See Faust, Frederick (Schiller)

Warhol, Andy 1928(?)-1987 .... **CLC 20**

DLBY 83; MTCW

Westall, Robert (Atkinson) 1929-1993 **CLC 17**
See also AAYA 12; CA 69-72; 141; CANR 18; CLR 13; JRDA; MAICYA; SAAS 2; SATA 23, 69; SATA-Obit 75

Westlake, Donald E(dwin) 1933- **CLC 7, 33; DAM POP**
See also CA 17-20R; CAAS 13; CANR 16, 44; INT CANR-16

Westmacott, Mary
See Christie, Agatha (Mary Clarissa)

Weston, Allen
See Norton, Andre

Wetcheek, J. L.
See Feuchtwanger, Lion

Wetering, Janwillem van de
See van de Wetering, Janwillem

Wetherell, Elizabeth
See Warner, Susan (Bogert)

Whale, James 1889-1957 .... **TCLC 63**

Whalen, Philip 1923- .... **CLC 6, 29**
See also CA 9-12R; CANR 5, 39; DLB 16

Wharton, Edith (Newbold Jones) 1862-1937 **TCLC 3, 9, 27, 53; DA; DAB; DAC; DAM MST, NOV; SSC 6; WLC**
See also CA 104; 132; CDALB 1865-1917; DLB 4, 9, 12, 78; DLBD 13; MTCW

Wharton, James
See Mencken, H(enry) L(ouis)

Wharton, William (a pseudonym) CLC 18, 37
See also CA 93-96; DLBY 80; INT 93-96

Wheatley (Peters), Phillis 1754(?)-1784 **LC 3; BLC; DA; DAC; DAM MST, MULT, POET; PC 3; WLC**
See also CDALB 1640-1865; DLB 31, 50

Wheelock, John Hall 1886-1978 .... **CLC 14**
See also CA 13-16R; 77-80; CANR 14; DLB 45

White, E(lwyn) B(rooks) 1899-1985 **CLC 10, 34, 39; DAM POP**
See also AITN 2; CA 13-16R; 116; CANR 16, 37; CLR 1, 21; DLB 11, 22; MAICYA; MTCW; SATA 2, 29; SATA-Obit 44

White, Edmund (Valentine III) 1940- **CLC 27; DAM POP**
See also AAYA 7; CA 45-48; CANR 3, 19, 36, 62; MTCW

White, Patrick (Victor Martindale) 1912-1990 **CLC 3, 4, 5, 7, 9, 18, 65, 69**
See also CA 81-84; 132; CANR 43; MTCW

White, Phyllis Dorothy James 1920-
See James, P. D.
See also CA 21-24R; CANR 17, 43; DAM POP; MTCW

White, T(erence) H(anbury) 1906-1964 **C L C 30**
See also AAYA 22; CA 73-76; CANR 37; DLB 160; JRDA; MAICYA; SATA 12

White, Terence de Vere 1912-1994 ... **CLC 49**
See also CA 49-52; 145; CANR 3

White, Walter F(rancis) 1893-1955 **TCLC 15**
See also White, Walter
See also BW 1; CA 115; 124; DLB 51

White, William Hale 1831-1913
See Rutherford, Mark
See also CA 121

Whitehead, E(dward) A(nthony) 1933- **CLC 5**
See also CA 65-68; CANR 58

Whitemore, Hugh (John) 1936- .... **CLC 37**
See also CA 132; INT 132

Whitman, Sarah Helen (Power) 1803-1878 **NCLC 19**
See also DLB 1

Whitman, Walt(er) 1819-1892 . **NCLC 4, 31; DA; DAB; DAC; DAM MST, POET; PC 3; WLC**
See also CDALB 1640-1865; DLB 3, 64; SATA 20

Whitney, Phyllis A(yame) 1903- ..... **CLC 42; DAM POP**
See also AITN 2; BEST 90:3; CA 1-4R; CANR 3, 25, 38, 60; JRDA; MAICYA; SATA 1, 30

Whittemore, (Edward) Reed (Jr.) 1919- **CLC 4**
See also CA 9-12R; CAAS 8; CANR 4; DLB 5

Whittier, John Greenleaf 1807-1892 **NCLC 8, 59**
See also DLB 1

Whittlebot, Hernia
See Coward, Noel (Peirce)

Wicker, Thomas Grey 1926-
See Wicker, Tom
See also CA 65-68; CANR 21, 46

Wicker, Tom .... **CLC 7**
See also Wicker, Thomas Grey

Wideman, John Edgar 1941- **CLC 5, 34, 36, 67; BLC; DAM MULT**
See also BW 2; CA 85-88; CANR 14, 42; DLB 33, 143

Wiebe, Rudy (Henry) 1934- .. **CLC 6, 11, 14; DAC; DAM MST**
See also CA 37-40R; CANR 42; DLB 60

Wieland, Christoph Martin 1733-1813 **NCLC 17**
See also DLB 97

Wiene, Robert 1881-1938 .... **TCLC 56**

Wieners, John 1934- .... **CLC 7**
See also CA 13-16R; DLB 16

Wiesel, Elie(zer) 1928- **CLC 3, 5, 11, 37; DA; DAB; DAC; DAM MST, NOV; WLCS 2**
See also AAYA 7; AITN 1; CA 5-8R; CAAS 4; CANR 8, 40; DLB 83; DLBY 87; INT CANR-8; MTCW; SATA 56

Wiggins, Marianne 1947- .... **CLC 57**
See also BEST 89:3; CA 130; CANR 60

Wight, James Alfred 1916-
See Herriot, James
See also CA 77-80; SATA 55; SATA-Brief 44

Wilbur, Richard (Purdy) 1921- **CLC 3, 6, 9, 14, 53; DA; DAB; DAC; DAM MST, POET**
See also CA 1-4R; CABS 2; CANR 2, 29; DLB 5, 169; INT CANR-29; MTCW; SATA 9

Wild, Peter 1940- .... **CLC 14**
See also CA 37-40R; DLB 5

Wilde, Oscar (Fingal O'Flahertie Wills) 1854(?)-1900 **TCLC 1, 8, 23, 41; DA; DAB; DAC; DAM DRAM, MST, NOV; SSC 11; WLC**
See also CA 104; 119; CDBLB 1890-1914; DLB 10, 19, 34, 57, 141, 156; SATA 24

Wilder, Billy .... **CLC 20**
See also Wilder, Samuel
See also DLB 26

Wilder, Samuel 1906-
See Wilder, Billy
See also CA 89-92

Wilder, Thornton (Niven) 1897-1975 **CLC 1, 5, 6, 10, 15, 35, 82; DA; DAB; DAC; DAM DRAM, MST, NOV; DC 1; WLC**
See also AITN 2; CA 13-16R; 61-64; CANR 40; DLB 4, 7, 9; MTCW

Wilding, Michael 1942- .... **CLC 73**
See also CA 104; CANR 24, 49

Wiley, Richard 1944- .... **CLC 44**
See also CA 121; 129

Wilhelm, Kate .... **CLC 7**
See also Wilhelm, Katie Gertrude

See also AAYA 20; CAAS 5; DLB 8; INT CANR-17

Wilhelm, Katie Gertrude 1928-
See Wilhelm, Kate
See also CA 37-40R; CANR 17, 36, 60; MTCW

Wilkins, Mary
See Freeman, Mary Eleanor Wilkins

Willard, Nancy 1936- .... **CLC 7, 37**
See also CA 89-92; CANR 10, 39; CLR 5; DLB 5, 52; MAICYA; MTCW; SATA 37, 71; SATA-Brief 30

Williams, C(harles) K(enneth) 1936- **CLC 33, 56; DAM POET**
See also CA 37-40R; CAAS 26; CANR 57; DLB 5

Williams, Charles
See Collier, James L(incoln)

Williams, Charles (Walter Stansby) 1886-1945 **TCLC 1, 11**
See also CA 104; DLB 100, 153

Williams, (George) Emlyn 1905-1987 **CLC 15; DAM DRAM**
See also CA 104; 123; CANR 36; DLB 10, 77; MTCW

Williams, Hugo 1942- .... **CLC 42**
See also CA 17-20R; CANR 45; DLB 40

Williams, J. Walker
See Wodehouse, P(elham) G(renville)

Williams, John A(lfred) 1925- ..... **CLC 5, 13; BLC; DAM MULT**
See also BW 2; CA 53-56; CAAS 3; CANR 6, 26, 51; DLB 2, 33; INT CANR-6

Williams, Jonathan (Chamberlain) 1929- **CLC 13**
See also CA 9-12R; CAAS 12; CANR 8; DLB 5

Williams, Joy 1944- .... **CLC 31**
See also CA 41-44R; CANR 22, 48

Williams, Norman 1952- .... **CLC 39**
See also CA 118

Williams, Sherley Anne 1944- **CLC 89; BLC; DAM MULT, POET**
See also BW 2; CA 73-76; CANR 25; DLB 41; INT CANR-25; SATA 78

Williams, Shirley
See Williams, Sherley Anne

Williams, Tennessee 1911-1983 **CLC 1, 2, 5, 7, 8, 11, 15, 19, 30, 39, 45, 71; DA; DAB; DAC; DAM DRAM, MST; DC 4; WLC**
See also AITN 1, 2; CA 5-8R; 108; CABS 3; CANR 31; CDALB 1941-1968; DLB 7; DLBD 4; DLBY 83; MTCW

Williams, Thomas (Alonzo) 1926-1990 **CLC 14**
See also CA 1-4R; 132; CANR 2

Williams, William C.
See Williams, William Carlos

Williams, William Carlos 1883-1963 **CLC 1, 2, 5, 9, 13, 22, 42, 67; DA; DAB; DAC; DAM MST, POET; PC 7**
See also CA 89-92; CANR 34; CDALB 1917-1929; DLB 4, 16, 54, 86; MTCW

Williamson, David (Keith) 1942- ...... **CLC 56**
See also CA 103; CANR 41

Williamson, Ellen Douglas 1905-1984
See Douglas, Ellen
See also CA 17-20R; 114; CANR 39

Williamson, Jack .... **CLC 29**
See also Williamson, John Stewart
See also CAAS 8; DLB 8

Williamson, John Stewart 1908-
See Williamson, Jack
See also CA 17-20R; CANR 23

Willie, Frederick

See Lovecraft, H(oward) P(hillips)
Willingham, Calder (Baynard, Jr.) 1922-1995
CLC 5, 51
See also CA 5-8R; 147; CANR 3; DLB 2, 44;
MTCW
Willis, Charles
See Clarke, Arthur C(harles)
Willy
See Colette, (Sidonie-Gabrielle)
Willy, Colette
See Colette, (Sidonie-Gabrielle)
Wilson, A(ndrew) N(orman) 1950- ... **CLC 33**
See also CA 112; 122; DLB 14, 155
Wilson, Angus (Frank Johnstone) 1913-1991
CLC 2, 3, 5, 25, 34; SSC 21
See also CA 5-8R; 134; CANR 21; DLB 15,
139, 155; MTCW
Wilson, August 1945- **CLC 39, 50, 63; BLC;**
DA; DAB; DAC; DAM DRAM, MST,
MULT; DC 2; WLCS
See also AAYA 16; BW 2; CA 115; 122; CANR
42, 54; MTCW
Wilson, Brian 1942- .... **CLC 12**
Wilson, Colin 1931- .... **CLC 3, 14**
See also CA 1-4R; CAAS 5; CANR 1, 22, 33;
DLB 14; MTCW
Wilson, Dirk
See Pohl, Frederik
Wilson, Edmund 1895-1972 **CLC 1, 2, 3, 8, 24**
See also CA 1-4R; 37-40R; CANR 1, 46; DLB
63; MTCW
Wilson, Ethel Davis (Bryant) 1888(?)-1980
CLC 13; DAC; DAM POET
See also CA 102; DLB 68; MTCW
Wilson, John 1785-1854 .... **NCLC 5**
Wilson, John (Anthony) Burgess 1917-1993
See Burgess, Anthony
See also CA 1-4R; 143; CANR 2, 46; DAC;
DAM NOV; MTCW
Wilson, Lanford 1937- **CLC 7, 14, 36; DAM**
DRAM
See also CA 17-20R; CABS 3; CANR 45; DLB
7
Wilson, Robert M. 1944- .... **CLC 7, 9**
See also CA 49-52; CANR 2, 41; MTCW
Wilson, Robert McLiam 1964- .... **CLC 59**
See also CA 132
Wilson, Sloan 1920- .... **CLC 32**
See also CA 1-4R; CANR 1, 44
Wilson, Snoo 1948- .... **CLC 33**
See also CA 69-72
Wilson, William S(mith) 1932- .... **CLC 49**
See also CA 81-84
Wilson, Woodrow 1856-1924 .... **TCLC 73**
See also DLB 47
Winchilsea, Anne (Kingsmill) Finch Counte
1661-1720 .... **LC 3**
Windham, Basil
See Wodehouse, P(elham) G(renville)
Wingrove, David (John) 1954- .... **CLC 68**
See also CA 133
Wintergreen, Jane
See Duncan, Sara Jeannette
Winters, Janet Lewis .... **CLC 41**
See also Lewis, Janet
See also DLBY 87
Winters, (Arthur) Yvor 1900-1968 **CLC 4, 8,**
32
See also CA 11-12; 25-28R; CAP 1; DLB 48;
MTCW
Winterson, Jeanette 1959- **CLC 64; DAM POP**
See also CA 136; CANR 58
Winthrop, John 1588-1649 .... **LC 31**

See also DLB 24, 30
Wiseman, Frederick 1930- .... **CLC 20**
See also CA 159
Wister, Owen 1860-1938 .... **TCLC 21**
See also CA 108; DLB 9, 78; SATA 62
Witkacy
See Witkiewicz, Stanislaw Ignacy
Witkiewicz, Stanislaw Ignacy 1885-1939
TCLC 8
See also CA 105
Wittgenstein, Ludwig (Josef Johann) 1889-1951
TCLC 59
See also CA 113
Wittig, Monique 1935(?)- .... **CLC 22**
See also CA 116; 135; DLB 83
Wittlin, Jozef 1896-1976 .... **CLC 25**
See also CA 49-52; 65-68; CANR 3
Wodehouse, P(elham) G(renville) 1881-1975
CLC 1, 2, 5, 10, 22; DAB; DAC; DAM
NOV; SSC 2
See also AITN 2; CA 45-48; 57-60; CANR 3,
33; CDBLB 1914-1945; DLB 34, 162;
MTCW; SATA 22
Woiwode, L.
See Woiwode, Larry (Alfred)
Woiwode, Larry (Alfred) 1941- .... **CLC 6, 10**
See also CA 73-76; CANR 16; DLB 6; INT
CANR-16
Wojciechowska, Maia (Teresa) 1927- **CLC 26**
See also AAYA 8; CA 9-12R; CANR 4, 41; CLR
1; JRDA; MAICYA; SAAS 1; SATA 1, 28,
83
Wolf, Christa 1929- .... **CLC 14, 29, 58**
See also CA 85-88; CANR 45; DLB 75; MTCW
Wolfe, Gene (Rodman) 1931- **CLC 25; DAM**
POP
See also CA 57-60; CAAS 9; CANR 6, 32, 60;
DLB 8
Wolfe, George C. 1954- .... **CLC 49**
See also CA 149
Wolfe, Thomas (Clayton) 1900-1938 **TCLC 4,**
13, 29, 61; DA; DAB; DAC; DAM MST,
NOV; WLC
See also CA 104; 132; CDALB 1929-1941;
DLB 9, 102; DLBD 2, 16; DLBY 85; MTCW
Wolfe, Thomas Kennerly, Jr. 1931-
See Wolfe, Tom
See also CA 13-16R; CANR 9, 33; DAM POP;
INT CANR-9; MTCW
Wolfe, Tom .... **CLC 1, 2, 9, 15, 35, 51**
See also Wolfe, Thomas Kennerly, Jr.
See also AAYA 8; AITN 2; BEST 89:1; DLB
152
Wolff, Geoffrey (Ansell) 1937- .... **CLC 41**
See also CA 29-32R; CANR 29, 43
Wolff, Sonia
See Levitin, Sonia (Wolff)
Wolff, Tobias (Jonathan Ansell) 1945- . **C L C**
39, 64
See also AAYA 16; BEST 90:2; CA 114; 117;
CAAS 22; CANR 54; DLB 130; INT 117
Wolfram von Eschenbach c. 1170-c. 1220
CMLC 5
See also DLB 138
Wolitzer, Hilma 1930- .... **CLC 17**
See also CA 65-68; CANR 18, 40; INT CANR-
18; SATA 31
Wollstonecraft, Mary 1759-1797 .... **LC 5**
See also CDBLB 1789-1832; DLB 39, 104, 158
Wonder, Stevie .... **CLC 12**
See also Morris, Steveland Judkins
Wong, Jade Snow 1922- .... **CLC 17**
See also CA 109

Woodberry, George Edward 1855-1930
TCLC 73
See also DLB 71, 103
Woodcott, Keith
See Brunner, John (Kilian Houston)
Woodruff, Robert W.
See Mencken, H(enry) L(ouis)
Woolf, (Adeline) Virginia 1882-1941 **TCLC 1,**
5, 20, 43, 56; DA; DAB; DAC; DAM MST,
NOV; SSC 7; WLC
See also CA 104; 130; CDBLB 1914-1945;
DLB 36, 100, 162; DLBD 10; MTCW
Woollcott, Alexander (Humphreys) 1887-1943
TCLC 5
See also CA 105; 161; DLB 29
Woolrich, Cornell 1903-1968 .... **CLC 77**
See also Hopley-Woolrich, Cornell George
Wordsworth, Dorothy 1771-1855 .. **NCLC 25**
See also DLB 107
Wordsworth, William 1770-1850 .. **NCLC 12,**
38; DA; DAB; DAC; DAM MST, POET;
PC 4; WLC
See also CDBLB 1789-1832; DLB 93, 107
Wouk, Herman 1915- **CLC 1, 9, 38; DAM NOV,**
POP
See also CA 5-8R; CANR 6, 33; DLBY 82; INT
CANR-6; MTCW
Wright, Charles (Penzel, Jr.) 1935- **CLC 6, 13,**
28
See also CA 29-32R; CAAS 7; CANR 23, 36,
62; DLB 165; DLBY 82; MTCW
Wright, Charles Stevenson 1932- ... **CLC 49;**
BLC 3; DAM MULT, POET
See also BW 1; CA 9-12R; CANR 26; DLB 33
Wright, Jack R.
See Harris, Mark
Wright, James (Arlington) 1927-1980 **CLC 3,**
5, 10, 28; DAM POET
See also AITN 2; CA 49-52; 97-100; CANR 4,
34; DLB 5, 169; MTCW
Wright, Judith (Arandell) 1915- **CLC 11, 53;**
PC 14
See also CA 13-16R; CANR 31; MTCW; SATA
14
Wright, L(aurali) R. 1939- .... **CLC 44**
See also CA 138
Wright, Richard (Nathaniel) 1908-1960 **C L C**
1, 3, 4, 9, 14, 21, 48, 74; BLC; DA; DAB;
DAC; DAM MST, MULT, NOV; SSC 2;
WLC
See also AAYA 5; BW 1; CA 108; CDALB
1929-1941; DLB 76, 102; DLBD 2; MTCW
Wright, Richard B(ruce) 1937- .... **CLC 6**
See also CA 85-88; DLB 53
Wright, Rick 1945- .... **CLC 35**
Wright, Rowland
See Wells, Carolyn
Wright, Stephen Caldwell 1946- .... **CLC 33**
See also BW 2
Wright, Willard Huntington 1888-1939
See Van Dine, S. S.
See also CA 115; DLBD 16
Wright, William 1930- .... **CLC 44**
See also CA 53-56; CANR 7, 23
Wroth, LadyMary 1587-1653(?) .... **LC 30**
See also DLB 121
Wu Ch'eng-en 1500(?)-1582(?) .... **LC 7**
Wu Ching-tzu 1701-1754 .... **LC 2**
Wurlitzer, Rudolph 1938(?)- .... **CLC 2, 4, 15**
See also CA 85-88; DLB 173
Wycherley, William 1641-1715 **LC 8, 21; DAM**
DRAM
See also CDBLB 1660-1789; DLB 80

Wylie, Elinor (Morton Hoyt) 1885-1928
　　TCLC 8
　　See also CA 105; DLB 9, 45
Wylie, Philip (Gordon) 1902-1971 ... **CLC 43**
　　See also CA 21-22; 33-36R; CAP 2; DLB 9
Wyndham, John .... **CLC 19**
　　See also Harris, John (Wyndham Parkes Lucas)
　　　Beynon
Wyss, Johann David Von 1743-1818**NCLC 10**
　　See also JRDA; MAICYA; SATA 29; SATA-
　　　Brief 27
Xenophon c. 430B.C.-c. 354B.C. ... **CMLC 17**
　　See also DLB 176
Yakumo Koizumi
　　See Hearn, (Patricio) Lafcadio (Tessima Carlos)
Yanez, Jose Donoso
　　See Donoso (Yanez), Jose
Yanovsky, Basile S.
　　See Yanovsky, V(assily) S(emenovich)
Yanovsky, V(assily) S(emenovich) 1906-1989
　　CLC 2, 18
　　See also CA 97-100; 129
Yates, Richard 1926-1992 .... **CLC 7, 8, 23**
　　See also CA 5-8R; 139; CANR 10, 43; DLB 2;
　　　DLBY 81, 92; INT CANR-10
Yeats, W. B.
　　See Yeats, William Butler
Yeats, William Butler 1865-1939**TCLC 1, 11,**
　　18, 31; DA; DAB; DAC; DAM DRAM,
　　MST, POET; PC 20; WLC
　　See also CA 104; 127; CANR 45; CDBLB
　　　1890-1914; DLB 10, 19, 98, 156; MTCW
Yehoshua, A(braham) B. 1936- .. **CLC 13, 31**
　　See also CA 33-36R; CANR 43
Yep, Laurence Michael 1948-............ **CLC 35**
　　See also AAYA 5; CA 49-52; CANR 1, 46; CLR
　　　3, 17; DLB 52; JRDA; MAICYA; SATA 7,
　　　69
Yerby, Frank G(arvin) 1916-1991 .**CLC 1, 7,**
　　22; BLC; DAM MULT
　　See also BW 1; CA 9-12R; 136; CANR 16, 52;
　　　DLB 76; INT CANR-16; MTCW
Yesenin, Sergei Alexandrovich
　　See Esenin, Sergei (Alexandrovich)
Yevtushenko, Yevgeny (Alexandrovich) 1933-
　　CLC 1, 3, 13, 26, 51; DAM POET
　　See also CA 81-84; CANR 33, 54; MTCW
Yezierska, Anzia 1885(?)-1970 .... **CLC 46**
　　See also CA 126; 89-92; DLB 28; MTCW
Yglesias, Helen 1915- .... **CLC 7, 22**
　　See also CA 37-40R; CAAS 20; CANR 15; INT
　　　CANR-15; MTCW
Yokomitsu Riichi 1898-1947 .... **TCLC 47**
Yonge, Charlotte (Mary) 1823-1901**TCLC 48**
　　See also CA 109; DLB 18, 163; SATA 17
York, Jeremy
　　See Creasey, John
York, Simon
　　See Heinlein, Robert A(nson)
Yorke, Henry Vincent 1905-1974 ...... **CLC 13**
　　See also Green, Henry
　　See also CA 85-88; 49-52
Yosano Akiko 1878-1942 .... **TCLC 59; PC 11**
　　See also CA 161
Yoshimoto, Banana .... **CLC 84**
　　See also Yoshimoto, Mahoko
Yoshimoto, Mahoko 1964-
　　See Yoshimoto, Banana
　　See also CA 144
Young, Al(bert James) 1939- .**CLC 19; BLC;**
　　DAM MULT
　　See also BW 2; CA 29-32R; CANR 26; DLB
　　　33

Young, Andrew (John) 1885-1971 ...... **CLC 5**
　　See also CA 5-8R; CANR 7, 29
Young, Collier
　　See Bloch, Robert (Albert)
Young, Edward 1683-1765 .... **LC 3, 40**
　　See also DLB 95
Young, Marguerite (Vivian) 1909-1995 **C L C**
　　82
　　See also CA 13-16; 150; CAP 1
Young, Neil 1945- .... **CLC 17**
　　See also CA 110
Young Bear, Ray A. 1950- ...... **CLC 94; DAM**
　　MULT
　　See also CA 146; DLB 175; NNAL
Yourcenar, Marguerite 1903-1987**CLC 19, 38,**
　　50, 87; DAM NOV
　　See also CA 69-72; CANR 23, 60; DLB 72;
　　　DLBY 88; MTCW
Yurick, Sol 1925- .... **CLC 6**
　　See also CA 13-16R; CANR 25
Zabolotskii, Nikolai Alekseevich 1903-1958
　　TCLC 52
　　See also CA 116
Zamiatin, Yevgenii
　　See Zamyatin, Evgeny Ivanovich
Zamora, Bernice (B. Ortiz) 1938- .. **CLC 89;**
　　DAM MULT; HLC
　　See also CA 151; DLB 82; HW
Zamyatin, Evgeny Ivanovich 1884-1937
　　TCLC 8, 37
　　See also CA 105
Zangwill, Israel 1864-1926 .... **TCLC 16**
　　See also CA 109; DLB 10, 135
Zappa, Francis Vincent, Jr. 1940-1993
　　See Zappa, Frank
　　See also CA 108; 143; CANR 57
Zappa, Frank .... **CLC 17**
　　See also Zappa, Francis Vincent, Jr.
Zaturenska, Marya 1902-1982 ...... **CLC 6, 11**
　　See also CA 13-16R; 105; CANR 22
Zeami 1363-1443 .... **DC 7**
Zelazny, Roger (Joseph) 1937-1995 . **CLC 21**
　　See also AAYA 7; CA 21-24R; 148; CANR 26,
　　　60; DLB 8; MTCW; SATA 57; SATA-Brief
　　　39
Zhdanov, Andrei A(lexandrovich) 1896-1948
　　TCLC 18
　　See also CA 117
Zhukovsky, Vasily 1783-1852 .... **NCLC 35**
Ziegenhagen, Eric .... **CLC 55**
Zimmer, Jill Schary
　　See Robinson, Jill
Zimmerman, Robert
　　See Dylan, Bob
Zindel, Paul 1936-**CLC 6, 26; DA; DAB; DAC;**
　　DAM DRAM, MST, NOV; DC 5
　　See also AAYA 2; CA 73-76; CANR 31; CLR
　　　3, 45; DLB 7, 52; JRDA; MAICYA; MTCW;
　　　SATA 16, 58
Zinov'Ev, A. A.
　　See Zinoviev, Alexander (Aleksandrovich)
Zinoviev, Alexander (Aleksandrovich) 1922-
　　CLC 19
　　See also CA 116; 133; CAAS 10
Zoilus
　　See Lovecraft, H(oward) P(hillips)
Zola, Emile (Edouard Charles Antoine) 1840-
　　1902**TCLC 1, 6, 21, 41; DA; DAB; DAC;**
　　DAM MST, NOV; WLC
　　See also CA 104; 138; DLB 123
Zoline, Pamela 1941- .... **CLC 62**
　　See also CA 161
Zorrilla y Moral, Jose 1817-1893 .... **NCLC 6**

Zoshchenko, Mikhail (Mikhailovich) 1895-1958
　　TCLC 15; SSC 15
　　See also CA 115; 160
Zuckmayer, Carl 1896-1977 .... **CLC 18**
　　See also CA 69-72; DLB 56, 124
Zuk, Georges
　　See Skelton, Robin
Zukofsky, Louis 1904-1978**CLC 1, 2, 4, 7, 11,**
　　18; DAM POET; PC 11
　　See also CA 9-12R; 77-80; CANR 39; DLB 5,
　　　165; MTCW
Zweig, Paul 1935-1984 .... **CLC 34, 42**
　　See also CA 85-88; 113
Zweig, Stefan 1881-1942 .... **TCLC 17**
　　See also CA 112; DLB 81, 118
Zwingli, Huldreich 1484-1531 .... **LC 37**
　　See also DLB 179

Poetry Criticism
Cumulative Nationality Index

Pindar **19**
Sappho **5**

HUNGARIAN
Illyes, Gyula **16**

INDIAN
Tagore, Rabindranath **8**

IRISH
Day Lewis, C(ecil) **11**
Heaney, Seamus (Justin) **18**
Swift, Jonathan **9**
Yeats, William Butler **20**

ITALIAN
Dante Alighieri **21**
Gozzano, Guido **10**
Martial **10**
Montale, Eugenio **13**
Pasolini, Pier Paolo **17**
Pavese, Cesare **13**
Petrarch **8**

JAMAICAN
McKay, Claude **2**

JAPANESE
Hagiwara Sakutaro **18**
Ishikawa, Takuboku **10**
Matsuo Basho **3**
Nishiwaki, Junzaburo **15**
Yosano Akiko **11**

LEBANESE
Gibran, Kahlil **9**

MEXICAN
Paz, Octavio **1**

NICARAGUAN
Dario, Ruben **15**

NIGERIAN
Okigbo, Christopher (Ifenayichukwu) **7**

PERSIAN
Khayyam, Omar **8**

POLISH
Milosz, Czeslaw **8**

PORTUGUESE
Pessoa, Fernando (Antonio Nogueira) **20**

ROMAN
Ovid **2**
Vergil **12**

ROMANIAN
Cassian, Nina **17**
Celan, Paul **10**

RUSSIAN
Akhmatova, Anna **2**
Bely, Andrey **11**
Blok, Alexander (Alexandrovich) **21**
Brodsky, Joseph **9**
Lermontov, Mikhail Yuryevich **18**
Mandelstam, Osip (Emilievich) **14**
Pasternak, Boris (Leonidovich) **6**
Pushkin, Alexander (Sergeyevich) **10**
Tsvetaeva (Efron), Marina (Ivanovna) **14**

SCOTTISH
Burns, Robert **6**
MacDiarmid, Hugh **9**
Scott, Walter **13**

SPANISH
Aleixandre, Vicente **15**
Garcia Lorca, Federico **3**
Jimenez (Mantecon), Juan Ramon **7**

SYRIAN
Gibran, Kahlil **9**

WELSH
Thomas, Dylan (Marlais) **2**

Nationality Index

PC Cumulative Title Index

Title Index

Title Index

Title Index

"Psalm Concerning the Castle" (Levertov) **11**:177

"Psalm Praising the Hair of Man's Body" (Levertov) **11**:171

"Psalms" (Smart)
See *A Translation of the Psalms of David, Attempted in the Spirit of Christianity, and Adapted to the Divine Service*

Psalms of David (Smart)
See *A Translation of the Psalms of David, Attempted in the Spirit of Christianity, and Adapted to the Divine Service*

"The Psychiatrist's Song" (Bogan) **12**:101, 115

"Public Bar TV" (Hughes) **7**:120, 122

"Public Garden" (Lowell) **3**:199-200, 215

Published and Unpublished Poems (Pavese)
See *Poesie edite e inedite*

"Puck of Pook's Hill" (Kipling) **3**:192

"Puck's Song" (Kipling) **3**:183, 192

"Pueblo Pot" (Millay) **6**:215

"Puella Mea" (Cummings) **5**:104

"the pull" (Bissett) **14**:22

"The Pulley" (Herbert) **4**:102

Punascha (Tagore) **8**:417

"Punishment" (Heaney) **18**:196, 204, 210-11, 238

"The Puppets" (Page) **12**:184

Purabi (Tagore) **8**:415

"Pure Death" (Graves) **6**:137, 151

"The Pure Fury" (Roethke) **15**:258, 272, 277, 290

"Pure Love" (Tagore)
See "Pavitra prem"

"The Pure Ones" (Hass) **16**:198

"Purely Local" (Rich) **5**:352

Purgatorio (Dante) **21**:49, 52-4, 58, 62-3, 69-82, 84-6, 91, 95-6, 104-05, 107-09

"Purgatory" (Lowell) **3**:241

Purgatory (Dante)
See *Purgatorio*

"Purner abhav" (Tagore) **8**:414

"Purple Grackles" (Lowell) **13**:64, 67, 87, 98-9

"The Purse Seine" (Jeffers) **17**:117

"Pursuit" (H. D.) **5**:287-88

"Pushkinskomu domu" (Blok) **21**:44

"Pusti menia, Voronezh . . ." (Mandelstam) **14**:152

"La puttana contadina" (Pavese) **13**:210, 219

"Putting to Sea" (Bogan) **12**:123

"Pygmalion" (H. D.) **5**:270, 304

"Pygmies Are Pygmies Still, Though Percht on Alps" (Brooks) **7**:55

"Pyrotechnics" (Bogan) **12**:117

"Pyrotechnics" (Lowell) **13**:83

Pyth. III (Pindar)
See *Pythian 3*

Pyth. X (Pindar)
See *Pythian 10*

Pyth XI (Pindar)
See *Pythian 11*

Pythian 1 (Pindar) **19**:381, 389, 392-93, 400, 411-12, 424-25

Pythian 2 (Pindar) **19**:402, 410, 420

Pythian 3 (Pindar) **19**:390, 398, 402, 410, 412

Pythian 4 (Pindar) **19**:381, 390, 396, 398-99, 405, 413, 420, 425

Pythian 5 (Pindar) **19**:396, 408-11, 422-23, 425

Pythian 6 (Pindar) **19**:400, 406

Pythian 7 (Pindar) **19**:412

Pythian 8 (Pindar) **19**:381, 391, 400, 406-07, 413, 426

Pythian 9 (Pindar) **19**:391, 398, 400, 412-13

Pythian 10 (Pindar) **19**:411-12, 425-26

Pythian 11 (Pindar) **19**:413

Pythian Odes 10 (Pindar)
See *Pythian 10*

"La pythie" (Valery) **9**:353, 365-66, 369, 373, 379, 393

Quaderno de quattro anni (Montale) **13**:128, 153, 156, 160, 168

"Quai D'Orleans" (Bishop) **3**:37

"The Quaker Graveyard at Nantucket (for Warren Winslow, Dead at Sea)" (Lowell) **3**:200-02, 204, 212, 217, 223, 233, 235-38

"Quaker Hill" (Crane) **3**:86, 90, 106

"Quand vous serez bien vieille" (Ronsard) **11**:218-21

"Quando il soave mio fido conforto" (Petrarch) **8**:235

"The Quarrel" (Kunitz) **19**:175

"Quarrel in Old Age" (Yeats) **20**:328-31

"The Quarry" (Clampitt) **19**:82, 89

"Quarry Pigeon Cove" (Kumin) **15**:181

"Quashie to Buccra" (McKay) **2**:215, 223

"Quatrains" (Emerson) **18**:77

Quatre de P. de Ronsard aux injures et calomnies (Ronsard) **11**:291

Les quatre premiers livres de la Franciade (Ronsard) **11**:226, 234, 246, 271, 283, 286-87, 290

Les quatre vents de l'esprit (Hugo) **17**:65

"4e epoque" (Lamartine) **16**:264

"Que nous avons le doute en nous" (Hugo) **17**:92-93

"quebec bombers" (Bissett) **14**:21-2

"The Queen and the Young Princess" (Smith) **12**:326, 352

Queen Mab (Shelley) **14**:170, 173, 178, 185-86, 212-17, 219, 222

"The Queen of Hearts" (Rossetti) **7**:272, 274

"The Queen of the Night Walks Her Thin Dog" (Wakoski) **15**:363

"Queen Worship" (Browning) **2**:26

"Queen-Anne's Lace" (Williams) **7**:374

"Quelques Complaintes de la vie" (Laforgue) **14**:95

"The Quest of the Purple-Fringed" (Frost) **1**:218

"A Question" (Arnold) **5**:38

"The Question" (Rukeyser) **12**:225

"Question" (Swenson) **14**:250, 252, 282, 286

"Question and Answer" (Browning) **6**:5

"Question au clerc du quichet" (Villon) **13**:394

"A Question of Climate" (Lorde) **12**:136

"A Question of *Essence*" (Lorde) **12**:140

"Questions of Travel" (Bishop) **3**:55, 67

Questions of Travel (Bishop) **3**:48, 53, 59

"A questo punto" (Montale) **13**:158

"A qui la faute?" (Hugo) **17**:101

Quia pawper amavi (Pound) **4**:317

"Quick I the Death of Thing" (Cummings) **5**:108

"A Quickening: A Song for the Visitation" (Merton) **10**:339

"The Quickening of St. John Baptist" (Merton) **10**:339

"Quickly Delia" (Finch) **21**:178

"Quiero saber" (Aleixandre) **15**:31

"Quiero volver a sur" (Neruda) **4**:281

"Quiet Evening" (Gluck) **16**:172

"Quiet Work" (Arnold) **5**:12, 36, 38, 49

"Quietness" (Williams) **7**:382

"Quilted Spreads" (Ammons) **16**:44

Quilting: Poems 1987-1990 (Clifton) **17**:28-29, 36

"Quimérica" (Jimenez) **7**:197

"Quinnapoxet" (Kunitz) **19**:175, 178-79

"The Quip" (Herbert) **4**:100, 102, 108, 119, 130

"R. A. F." (H. D.) **5**:307

"The Rabbi" (Hayden) **6**:195, 198

"Rabbi Ben Ezra" (Browning) **2**:51, 75, 95

"The Rabbi's Song" (Kipling) **3**:183

"The Rabbit" (Millay) **6**:238

"Race" (Dario)
See "Raza"

"The Racer's Widow" (Gluck) **16**:139

"Rack" (Ammons) **16**:39

"Raft" (Ammons) **16**:20, 27

"The Rag Man" (Hayden) **6**:195

"Rages de césars" (Rimbaud) **3**:283

"The Ragged Schools of London" (Browning)
See "A Song for the Ragged Schools of London"

"The Ragged Stocking" (Harper) **21**:191

"Railroad Avenue" (Hughes) **1**:237

"Rain" (Giovanni) **19**:109

"The Rain" (Levertov) **11**:176

"Rain" (Williams) **7**:349

"Rain at Bellagio" (Clampitt) **19**:87

"Rain Charm for the Duchy, a Blessed, Devout Drench for the Christening of a Prince Harry" (Hughes) **7**:171

"Rain Festival" (Tagore)
See "Varsha-mangal"

"The Rain, It Streams on Stone and Hillock" (Housman) **2**:162

"Rain on a Grave" (Hardy) **8**:134

"Rain on the Borders" (Pasolini) **17**:287

"Rain or Hail" (Cummings) **5**:88

"Rain Outside of Everything" (Pasolini) **17**:287

"rainbow music" (Bissett) **14**:24

"Rainforest" (Wright) **14**:375, 377

"The Rainmaker" (Cassian) **17**:4

"Rain-Song" (Dunbar) **5**:125

"Raise the Shade" (Cummings) **5**:89

"Raleigh Was Right" (Williams) **7**:360

"La rameur" (Valery) **9**:367, 395-96

"Rano Raraku" (Breton) **15**:53-4

"Rap of a Fan..." (Apollinaire)
See "Coup d'evential..."

"Rape" (Rich) **5**:361

"Rape of the Leaf" (Kunitz) **19**:147

"The Raper from Passenack" (Williams) **7**:353, 368, 399

"Rapids" (Ammons) **16**:63

"Rapids by the Luan Trees" (Wang Wei) **18**:370

"Rapunzel" (Sexton) **2**:368

"Rapunzel, Rapunzel" (Smith) **12**:341

"Rasshchelina" (Tsvetaeva) **14**:306-08

"Ratbert" (Hugo) **17**:59

"The Ratcatcher" (Tsvetaeva)
See "Krysolov"

"Rational Man" (Rukeyser) **12**:220, 230

"rattle poem" (Bissett) **14**:21

"The Raven" (Poe) **1**:419-20, 424, 427, 429-34, 436, 439-40, 443-44, 447, 452-53

"The Raven: A Christmas Tale" (Coleridge) **11**:109-17

The Raven, and Other Poems (Poe) **1**:437, 449

"The Ravine" (Carruth) **10**:85, 90

Les rayons et les ombres (Hugo) **17**:45, 50-53,

Title Index

See "Epistle to a Young Friend"
"To a Young Girl" (Millay) **6**:217
"To a Young Girl" (Yeats) **20**:330
"To Adversity" (Gray)
  See "Ode to Adversity"
"To Alchymists" (Jonson) **17**:197
"To Alexander" (Pushkin)
  See "Aleksandru"
"To Alexis, in Answer to His Poem against Frui-
  tion" (Behn) **13**:26
"To All Brothers" (Sanchez) **9**:224, 232
"To All Brothers: From All Sisters" (Sanchez)
  9:221
"To All Gentleness" (Williams) **7**:354
"To All Sisters" (Sanchez) **9**:224, 231-32
"To Amintas, upon Reading the Lives of Some
  of the Romans" (Behn) **13**:32
"To an Ancient" (Frost) **1**:200
"To an Athlete Dying Young" (Housman)
  2:180, 183, 185, 191-94, 198, 201
"To an Old Philosopher in Rome" (Stevens)
  6:304, 324, 328
"To Another Housewife" (Wright) **14**:356
"To Anthea" (Herrick) **9**:145
"To Anthea Lying in Bed" (Herrick) **9**:137
"To Anthea, Who May Command Him Any
  Thing" (Herrick) **9**:102
"To Any Dead Officer Who Left School for
  the Army in 1914" (Sassoon) **12**:268,
  277
"To Autumn" (Gluck) **16**:142, 149
"To Autumn" (Keats) **1**:298-302, 314-15
"To Autumn" (Keats)
  See "Ode to Autumn"
"To Bargain Toboggan To-Woo!" (Nash)
  21:265
"To Be a Jew in the Twentieth Century"
  (Rukeyser) **12**:234
"To Be Carved on a Stone at Thoor Ballylee"
  (Yeats) **20**:346, 348
"To Be in Love" (Brooks) **7**:81-2
"To Be Liked by You Would Be a Calamity"
  (Moore) **4**:250
"To Be Quicker for Black Political Prisoners"
  (Madhubuti) **5**:330, 346
"To Be Sung on the Water" (Bogan) **12**:90,
  124
To Bedlam and Part Way Back (Sexton) **2**:345-
  47, 349-50, 353, 355, 357-58, 360, 363,
  367
"To Bennie" (McKay) **2**:221
"To Blk/Record/Buyers" (Sanchez) **9**:209, 217
"To Blossoms" (Herrick) **9**:145
"To Bring the Dead to Life" (Graves) **6**:143
"To Camden" (Jonson)
  See "To Camden"
"To Carl Sandburg" (Lowell) **13**:67
"To Carry the Child" (Smith) **12**:320
"To Cedars" (Herrick) **9**:91
"To Celia" (Jonson) **17**:170, 196
"To Certain Critics" (Cullen) **20**:66, 83
"To Chaadaev" (Pushkin)
  See "Chaadayevu"
"To Change in a Good Way" (Ortiz) **17**:234
"To Charis" (Jonson)
  See "To Charis"
To . . . Christopher Duke of Albemarle (Behn)
  13:8
"To Chuck" (Sanchez) **9**:224, 233
To Circumjack Cencrastus (MacDiarmid)
  9:151-53, 158, 171, 175-77, 197
"To Clarendon Hills and H.A.H." (McKay)
  2:222

"To Cole, the Painter, Departing For Europe"
  (Bryant) **20**:34, 44-5
"To Columbus" (Dario)
  See "A Colón"
"To Conclude" (Montale) **13**:146
"To Confirm a Thing" (Swenson) **14**:247,
  252, 278
"To Constantia Singing" (Shelley) **14**:177
"To Countess Rostopchina" (Lermontov)
  18:297
"To Daddy" (Lowell) **3**:226
"To Daffadills" (Herrick) **9**:101
"To Damon. To Inquire of Him If He Cou'd
  Tell Me by the Style, Who Writ Me a
  Copy of Verses That Came to Me in an
  Unknown Hand" (Behn) **13**:30-1
"To Daphnie and Virginia" (Williams) **7**:360,
  363, 392
"To Dean Swift" (Swift) **9**:295
"To Death" (Finch) **21**:179-80
"To Deism" (Wheatley) **3**:354
"To Delmore Schwartz" (Lowell) **3**:219, 222
"To Desire" (Behn) **13**:24
"To Dianeme" (Herrick) **9**:145
To Disembark (Brooks) **7**:84, 93
"To Dispel My Grief" (Tu Fu) **9**:326
"To *** Do not think I deserve regret"
  (Lermontov) **18**:301, 304
"To Doctor Alabaster" (Herrick) **9**:142
"To Don at Salaam" (Brooks) **7**:84, 92
To Dream of A Butterfly (Hagiwara Sakutaro)
  See *To Dream of A Butterfly*
"To Earthward" (Frost) **1**:197
"To Electra" (Herrick) **9**:94
"To Elizabeth Ward Perkins" (Lowell) **13**:90
"To Elsie" (Williams) **7**:382, 384, 411
"To E.M.E." (McKay) **2**:223
"To Endymion" (Cullen) **20**:67, 86
"To Enemies" (Bely) **11**:24
"To Enter That Rhythm Where the Self is
  Lost" (Rukeyser) **12**:227
"To Eros" (Owen) **19**:352
"To Ethelinda" (Smart) **13**:331, 347
"To Evoke Posterity" (Graves) **6**:143, 152
"To Fausta" (Arnold) **5**:49
"To Find God" (Herrick) **9**:109
"To Fine Lady Would-bee" (Jonson) **17**:197
"To Flowers" (Herrick) **9**:102
"To Flush My Dog" (Browning) **6**:6-7
"To Ford Madox Ford in Heaven" (Williams)
  7:370
"To France" (Cullen) **20**:66
"To Galich" (Pushkin) **10**:407
"To George Sand: A Recognition" (Browning)
  6:26
"To Gerhardt" (Olson) **19**:307
"To God" (Herrick) **9**:94-5, 109, 118
"To God, His Good Will" (Herrick) **9**:118
"To God, on His Sicknesse" (Herrick) **9**:144
"To Gurdjieff Dying" (Toomer) **7**:338
"To Hafiz of Shiraz" (Wright) **14**:356, 366
"To Have Done Nothing" (Williams) **7**:383,
  389, 410
"To Heaven" (Jonson)
  See "To Heaven"
"To Helen" (Poe) **1**:420, 424, 426, 428, 431,
  438-39, 441, 443-45, 447
"To Help" (Stein) **18**:313
"To Her" (Pushkin) **10**:408-09
"To Her Father with Some Verses" (Bradstreet)
  10:27, 35
"To Her Most Honoured Father Thomas
  Dudley" (Bradstreet) **10**:2

"To His Book" (Herrick) **9**:106, 109
"To His Closet-Gods" (Herrick) **9**:88
"To His Coy Mistress" (Marvell) **10**:259, 265,
  269, 271, 273-74, 277-79, 281-82, 290-
  94, 297, 304, 310-11, 313
"To His Excellency General George Washing-
  ton" (Wheatley) **3**:337, 341
"To His Father" (Jeffers) **17**:131
"To His Friend on the Untuneable Times"
  (Herrick) **9**:89
"To His Girles" (Herrick) **9**:107
"To His Girles Who Would Have Him Sportfull"
  (Herrick) **9**:107
"To His Honor the Lieutenant Governor on
  the Death of His Lady" (Wheatley) **3**:340
"To His Mistresses" (Herrick) **9**:128, 146
"To His Paternall Countrey" (Herrick) **9**:108
"To His Savior, a Child; a Present, by a Child"
  (Herrick) **9**:120, 143
"To His Saviour, the New Yeers Gift" (Herrick)
  9:95
"To His Saviours Sepulcher: His Devotion"
  (Herrick) **9**:122
"To His Watch" (Hopkins) **15**:167
"To Homer" (Keats) **1**:279, 314
"To Imagination" (Bronte) **8**:54
"To Imagination" (Wheatley)
  See "On Imagination"
"To Insure Survival" (Ortiz) **17**:225
"To Ireland in the Coming Times" (Yeats)
  20:324, 347, 353
"To Ivor Gurney" (Tomlinson) **17**:354-55
"to joan" (Clifton) **17**:18
"To John Goldie, August 1785" (Burns) **6**:70,
  78
"To John Keats, Poet: At Spring Time" (Cullen)
  20:62, 66, 86
"To Jos: Lo: Bishop of Exeter" (Herrick) **9**:146
"To Joseph Sadzik" (Milosz)
  See "Do Jozefa Sadzika"
"To Juan at the Winter Solstice" (Graves)
  6:137, 144, 146, 168, 171-72
"To Julia" (Herrick) **9**:128, 143
"To Julia, in Her Dawne, or Day-breake"
  (Herrick) **9**:143
"To Julia, the Flaminica Dialis, or Queen-Priest"
  (Herrick) **9**:143
"To . . . K. Charles" (Jonson)
  See "To . . . K. Charles"
"To K. Charles . . . 1629" (Jonson)
  See "To K. Charles . . . 1629"
"To Keorapetse Kgositsile (Willie)" (Brooks)
  7:83, 92, 105
"To Kevin O'Leary Wherever He Is"
  (Levertov) **11**:189
"To King James"
  See "To King James"
"To Lady Crew, upon the Death of Her Child"
  (Herrick)
  See "To the Lady Crew, upon the Death of
  Her Child"
"To Laurels" (Herrick) **9**:127
"To Licinius" (Pushkin)
  See "K Liciniju"
"To Live Merrily, and to Trust to Good Verses"
  (Herrick) **9**:96, 103-05, 107, 114
"To Lord Byron" (Keats) **1**:313
"To Lord Harley, on His Marriage" (Swift)
  9:254
"To Lose the Earth" (Sexton) **2**:363
"To Louise" (Dunbar) **5**:121
"To Love" (Aleixandre) **15**:19, 21
"To Lucia at Birth" (Graves) **6**:137

Title Index

ISBN 0-7876-2012-2

90000